FOREVER FINITE: The Case Against Infinity

INFINITY IS NOT WHAT IT SEEMS...

Infinity is commonly assumed to be a logical concept, reliable for conducting mathematics, describing the Universe, and understanding the divine. Most of us are educated to take for granted that there exist infinite sets of numbers, that lines contain an infinite number of points, that space is infinite in expanse, that time has an infinite succession of events, that possibilities are infinite in quantity, and over half of the world's population believes in a divine Creator infinite in knowledge, power, and benevolence.

According to this treatise, such assumptions are mistaken. In reality, to be is to be finite. The implications of this assessment are profound: the Universe and even God must necessarily be finite.

The author makes a compelling case against infinity, refuting its most prominent advocates. Any defense of the infinite will find it challenging to answer the arguments laid out in this book. But regardless of the reader's position, *Forever Finite* offers plenty of thought-provoking material for anyone interested in the subject of infinity from the perspectives of philosophy, mathematics, science, and theology.

Kip Sewell holds BA and MA degrees in Philosophy. His writings support the Rond Project, which aims to integrate ideas from science, philosophy, and spirituality into Rond, a novel worldview for understanding the nature of existence and coping with the human condition.

FOREVER FINITE
The Case Against Infinity

KIP K. SEWELL

ROND BOOKS
Alexandria, Virginia

Publisher's Cataloging-in-Publication
(Provided by Cassidy Cataloguing Services, Inc.)

Names: Sewell, Kip K., author.

Title: Forever finite : the case against infinity / Kip K. Sewell.

Description: First paperback edition. | Alexandria, Virginia : Rond Books, [2023] | Includes bibliographical references and glossary.

Identifiers: ISBN: 979-8-9881238-0-4 (paperback) | LCCN: 2023906343

Subjects: LCSH: Infinite. | Finite, The. | Meaning (Philosophy) | Mathematics. | Physics. | Cosmology. | Mortality. | Eternity. | Infinite--History. | Completeness theorem. | Logic, Symbolic and mathematical. | BISAC: PHILOSOPHY / Criticism.

Classification: LCC: BD411 .S49 2023 | DDC: 111/.6--dc23

---

10 9 8 7 6 5 4 3 2

There is a concept which corrupts and upsets all others. I refer not to Evil, whose limited realm is that of ethics; I refer to the infinite.

—Jorge Luis Borges

CONTENTS

PREFACE

Infinity is not what it appears to be. While most take for granted that infinity makes sense, it is actually a logically inconsistent concept that has caused a great deal of confusion for the past 2.5 millennia. My aim is to elucidate infinity, expose the many logical inconsistencies inherent in both the meaning of infinity and in its usage during discourse, explain why those inconsistencies result, and argue that we are better off to rid ourselves of infinity altogether in favor of more logically consistent concepts.

To be infinite is to be limitless—in quantity, in quality, or both. What the term 'infinity' refers to can imply any of these notions of limitlessness. Infinity as limitless quantity is the conception of infinity assumed in mathematics, but also throughout other academic fields of study such as physics and cosmology. Whereas infinity taken to be unlimited quality is a conception of infinity assumed in theology, as is infinity conceived to be a combination of both limitless quantity and unlimited quality.

I take the quantitative infinity of mathematics and the other two conceptions of infinity assumed in theology to be exhaustive of the relevant senses of what the term 'infinity' refers to. I will argue that all three ways of conceiving infinity are flawed because describing anything as limitless in terms of either its quantity or quality, let alone both together, results in logical inconsistencies. I make the case that infinity is a logically erroneous concept that does not accurately apply for descriptions of anything in existence. Consequently, all the objects of study in mathematics, physics, cosmology, and even theology should be reconceived in purely finite terms.

BACKGROUND

My critique of infinity began as a couple of chapters in a philosophical monograph published in the late 1990s on the subject of cosmology [1]. While my initial critique in that monograph was on the right track, I later assessed that I had not quite nailed the subject of infinity. Eventually, I decided the chapters on infinity needed to be amended. Around a decade later, I posted preprint versions of an article online to revise my earlier arguments. But when feedback from reviewers revealed some misunderstanding about my approach to the subject, it became clear to me that the page limitations of even a lengthy article would never suffice for my thesis. Ultimately, I opted to turn the article into this book—now a work of several hundred pages under a new title.

Although my skepticism toward infinity remains unchanged since my initial philosophical foray into cosmology, I have heavily revised my line of thought over the years, and so my prior writings on infinity are not entirely consistent with the content presented in this book [2]. Consequently, readers familiar with my prior writings on infinity should not take them as definitive of my position; rather, it is this book that represents my final conclusions on infinity.

INTENDED AUDIENCE

There are three categories of readers I aim to reach.

First, the primary focus of this book is on the quantitative conception of infinity—basically, infinity as conceived in mathematics and the philosophy of mathematics. However, this book is intended neither for mathematicians nor for philosophers of mathematics. Rather, I wrote this book primarily for philosophers (amateur and professional, students and instructors) who may specialize in other subjects—such as philosophy of science, philosophy of religion, metaphysics, epistemology, and so forth—but who have also developed an interest in the topic of infinity.

Second, I wrote this book with lay seekers in mind—those who have at least some familiarity with works written by professional philosophers but little or no familiarity with academic writings on the topic of infinity. Given such a wide audience, I will risk being pedant by explaining throughout the book certain terms and concepts frequently found in the literature on infinity. (However, those who are well-versed in academic philosophy will find that I do not always heed popular or traditional definitions of philosophical terms or positions.)

Third and finally, I suspect of readers with no formal education in academic philosophy that some are not as interested in the quantitative notion of infinity as they are in infinity as it relates to ideas about the divine—especially the divine conceived to be God. With that in mind, I address some of the main theological notions of infinity found in the academic literature. Although my treatment of the theological understanding of infinity is rather brief compared to the mathematical understanding, readers [3][4] interested in what my case against infinity entails for belief in the divine may find some content worthy of consideration.

RECOMMENDATIONS FOR READING THIS BOOK

Each chapter in this book either assumes or builds on the information in previous chapters. Those who intend to consume the entire book will therefore get more out of finishing earlier chapters prior to later chapters and covering the chapters in sequence.

However, I expect many readers will not be interested in reading the entire treatise, opting instead to skim the content for the main points. With that in mind, it is not crucial to read every chapter for a grasp of the book's thesis. If you prefer to cover only the crucial information, then the introductory chapter is the most important as it lays out the issues and provides an overview of later chapters. The final chapter is a summary of the main points over the entirety of the book. The chapters in between provide the details of the case against infinity. While those details are needed for a complete picture, a bulleted list of the main points is provided at the end of each chapter for those readers interested in merely skimming the content.

APPROACH

While the quantitative conception of infinity is the main topic of this book, I do not approach that conception of infinity as would a mathematician but rather as would a philosopher. That is to say, I subject the quantitative conception of infinity to logical analysis—logic being the tool of the philosopher. Although mathematics draws on logical reasoning for its practice, the discipline of logic owes its development, study, and instruction to the Department of Philosophy rather than the Department of Mathematics. It should therefore not be surprising if philosophers rather than mathematicians discover logical problems lurking in the quantitative conception of infinity—problems mathematicians either overlook or do not typically concern themselves with, given the specialized focus of their discipline.

Because my approach is philosophical rather than mathematical, an advanced degree in mathematics is not needed for the aspects of infinity I cover in this book. Readers should therefore not expect this book to be like a calculus or set theory textbook. I do not present long, formal proofs or rigorous calculations that would satisfy mathematicians or meet the requirements of academic journals in the philosophy of mathematics. While I do touch on some of the technical details regarding the quantitative conception of infinity, mathematicians would likely be disappointed that I stick primarily to prose rather than formal proofs. The non-mathematician, however, should appreciate that the mathematical content I provide requires no expertise to understand.

For any readers who do specialize in mathematics, you may find this book of some use for understanding the nuances between the concept of infinity as expressed in mathematics and the notion of infinity as expressed more broadly in natural language. The bulk of my thesis concerns not the formal language syntax of mathematical expressions of infinity but instead the underlying, natural language semantics (*meanings*) of infinity that are tacitly *assumed* behind those mathematical expressions. I intend to show how the underlying meaning of infinity, whether literal or taken figuratively, misleads both mathematics and mathematical disciplines such as theoretical physics and scientific cosmology into conceptual errors whenever infinity comes up.

As for the theological conceptions of infinity, here too I approach the subject of infinity as would a philosopher rather than a theologian, religious apologist, or mystic. I rely on conceptual analysis and logical argumentation to make the case that so-called 'divine infinity' (which includes both qualitative infinity and absolute infinity) is likewise a misleading notion, leading us astray from obtaining a proper understanding of the spiritual.

On Definitions

Like mathematicians, philosophers typically approach issues by first defining their terms. Words such as 'infinity' and 'infinite' can have several meanings. This book offers various definitions for infinity and for a variety of terms relating in some way to infinity (see also the glossary at the end of this book for a condensed list of definitions).

Some of the definitions I offer for terms will be technical in nature as found in the professional literature on infinity, some of the definitions will be colloquial, and some will be my own stipulated definitions. I endeavor to carefully distinguish between the ordinary language definitions of terms from their technical counterparts, such as the various theoretical and operational definitions used by professional mathematicians and logicians.

However, as I hope to show, the ordinary language definitions for the word 'infinity' and its cognates ('infinite', 'infinitely', etc.)—definitions that capture what we commonly mean by such words—are either assumed or implied in discourse of all kinds, even when the speaker intends to use such words as technical terms in a specialized field such as mathematics or theology.

On Sources and References

Throughout this book, I quote and cite various sources regarding views about infinity (and related subjects) in philosophy, science, mathematics, and theology [5]. While I will be citing contemporary professionals working in these fields, unlike some university-affiliated academics I feel no need to limit myself to such sources. Instead, I cite works from antiquity to the present day, from professionals to graduate students to freelance authors, from the primary literature of academia to secondary and even some tertiary sources for lay audiences. I cite scholarly forums, websites, blogs, specialized dictionary and encyclopedia entries, and even a few novels and poems. Most of my sources are those I believe make an impact, either directly or indirectly, on the wider culture and are not just influential in academia. Others are those I believe articulate a position particularly well, though the works may not be widely recognized.

On Intellectual Dissent

In arguing that infinity is a logically erroneous concept, I will unfortunately be attacking the positions of many well-known scholars. This is the part of analytic philosophy I do not particularly care for—in order for a philosopher to justify a highly unorthodox position or conclusion, the philosopher often cannot avoid arguing against the works of other scholars, including giants in their respective fields [6].

Nevertheless, as the late astronomer Carl Sagan remarked, "...intellectual capacity is no guarantee against being dead wrong" [7]. Even the brightest of us can be wrong [8]. Unfortunately, I think some of the most brilliant among us have been wrong about infinity and certain related topics. This book provides solid grounds that the current academic mainstream is mistaken in holding infinity to be a logically coherent concept able to be applied for accurate descriptions of real-world features.

That infinity is an erroneous concept is, as Sagan would have said, an extraordinary claim and as such requires extraordinary justification. This book is my attempt to provide that extraordinary justification (hence, the large page count). The reader should find the exposition and conceptual analysis provided in the chapters ahead to be more than sufficient in justifying a guilty verdict in the case against infinity.

INTRODUCTION

1: CHALLENGING INFINITY

Gazing into the sublime expanse of the starry night sky, pondering the awesome eons of the past and future, we naturally feel small and insignificant compared with such magnitudes. So vast and enduring is the Universe that it is commonly assumed to be spatially and temporally *infinite* [9].

On the contrary, I will make the case that the Universe is finite rather than infinite. Space is limited in dimension and scale, time is limited in succession and duration, and all things in space and time—all places and events, all objects and subjects, all states of motion—are limited as well.

In proclaiming the Universe is finite I do not mean to suggest it could ever be observed as a whole. It is far beyond our practical ability to experience the totalities of space and time. Even with the most powerful of telescopes, no one will ever survey all of space and its myriad worlds. Even with the greatest medical advances for longevity, no one will ever live through all of time with its cosmic series of events [10]. Certainly, space is vast and time enduring beyond any degree we can experience. Nevertheless, I take the position that neither space nor time is quantitatively limitless; the Universe is not infinite.

I realize this view of the Universe may not become popular. Infinity is an ancient and profound concept, holding a powerful emotional appeal across cultures and generations. The notion that the Universe is infinite in either space or time, or both, is deeply entrenched in customs around the world and has the momentum of history behind it. And yet, despite its popularity, the belief that the Universe is infinite is mistaken. The chapters that follow present the case for this conclusion.

In addition, my case against infinity carries implications for more than just our interpretation of the Universe. If my case is sound, even if there are metaphysical realities transcending the physical world, they too cannot be infinite. The very essence of *being* as such must be finite. The concept of infinity does not rationally apply to anything that exists—not to anything in the physical world, nor even to purported metaphysical realities such as God. I will make this case by analyzing and debunking the very concept of infinity itself.

My case will begin with some definitions. In this chapter I will clarify the definition of infinity and its related terms, then I will lay out the general nature of the case against infinity as a concept, and close with a brief overview of the content in the chapters ahead.

1.1 INFINITY DEFINED

Infinity can be a tricky concept to define in exact terms. Some prefer to say that infinity refers to "the incomprehensible" or "the inexpressible." However, while there certainly are aspects of infinity that cannot be comprehended or expressed, infinity cannot plausibly be defined as incomprehensibility or inexpressibility simply as such. After all, I may not be able to sufficiently comprehend or express what it feels like to be you, but that does not make the feeling of being you infinite. There are some things that are incomprehensible or inexpressible to which the word 'infinite' does not apply.

Others claim that infinity cannot be defined at all. They usually base this claim on the fact that scholars have never agreed about how to properly define infinity. Adrian William (A.W.) Moore, Professor of Philosophy at the University of Oxford, pointed out that "there have been many attempts throughout the history of thought about the infinite to define it...these attempts have revealed a striking lack of consensus" [11]. Although there is a lack of consensus among mathematicians, scientists, and philosophers as to the right *technical* definition for infinity, that lack of consensus does not necessarily mean infinity resists a common definition *per se*. As we will see, nearly all of the various technical definitions for infinity assume a more general conception of infinity, a conception of infinity as it is commonly used in ordinary language, handed down to us from ancient Greek philosophers and translated to English in the Middle Ages.

1.1.1 *Infinity as Commonly Known*

While mathematicians define infinity in several technical ways (which we'll explore later in this book), we should start with a more general notion of infinity that can be defined in ordinary, everyday colloquial language. Infinity and its related terms have a few such definitions, which I will number for convenient reference.

Here is our first definition for the noun 'infinity':

- infinity: (1) *the condition of being infinite*.

Sometimes the word 'infinity' is also used as a label for something that is not finite, as when something is referred to as "an infinity," such as an infinity of stars or an infinity of decimal places. The above definition of course raises the question of what the adjective 'infinite' means, which also has a few simple definitions, the first of which is as follows:

- infinite: (1) *not finite*.

Like the word 'infinity', the adjective 'infinite' is sometimes used as a noun to indicate something that is not finite. Philosophers, scientists, and mathematicians especially sometimes refer to a given group of things as 'an infinite' if the group is conceived to have no finite number of members. They may also occasionally make reference to 'infinites' or more generally use 'the infinite' as a substantive noun to indicate the concept of infinitude or the category of all that is infinite.

Since to be infinite is to be "not finite," this now brings up another question: what does it mean to be 'finite'? Mathematicians have various technical definitions for the term 'finite', narrow in meaning for their trade, but let's stick with a natural language definition for now.

The adjective 'finite' is a late Middle English word from around the 14th Century and stems from the Latin word *finītus*, which means "limited" [12]. Let's keep it simple and stick with "limited." We can now provide a preliminary, ordinary language definition for finite:

- finite: (1) *having a limit*.

Occasionally mathematicians and philosophers of mathematics will refer to 'the finite' (a substantive noun), which is sometimes used as a synonym for the property *finitude* (or *finiteness*), or they may at other times refer to the concept of finitude in order to indicate the category of all that is finite. The term 'finitude' is thus defined:

- finitude: (1) *the condition of being finite.*

Since to be finite is to have a limit, then finitude is the condition of having a limit.

Conversely, as the adjective 'infinite' is a negation of the adjective 'finite' and to be finite is to have a limit, then we logically have an alternative definition for 'infinite', a definition as accurate as the first:

- infinite: (2) *having no limit.*

In fact, the word 'infinite' is a Middle English word that also first appeared around 14th Century; it comes from the Latin word *infinitus*, composed from the Latin word *in*—"not" or "opposite of"—and the Latin word *finitus* which means "finite" [13]. Since to be finite is to have a limit, to be infinite is to have no limit, to be without limit. (For the definition of 'limit', see § 5.3.1.)

1.1.2 *'Infinite' is Not Synonymous with 'Endless' or 'Unbounded'*

When we say to be finite is to be limited, we should be careful to distinguish what kind of limit we have in mind because when we say something has a limit, we sometimes mean it has a limit of a particular type such as an *end* or *bound*. But not everything that is limited has an end or bound. Conversely, not everything that lacks an end or bound is without limit in a manner we would call "infinite."

For example, consider a circle.

A circle has a *circumference*. Easy enough, but there is a problem with the word 'circumference'—it means two different things.

The word 'circumference' can mean either (*a*) the perimeter of the circle—the continuous line that forms the boundary of a disk—or (*b*) the measure of distance around the circle—the extent of the circle's perimeter.

When necessary for clarity, instead of using 'circumference' according to the former meaning, *a*, I will simply refer to the *curve* of the circle and dub it a 'perimeter' when referencing the interior as a disk. I will primarily use 'circumference' according to the latter meaning, *b*, which is to say the distance around the circle—its measure—as opposed to the closed curve of the circle. However, I may occasionally need to use 'circumference' in the sense of the circle's closed curve. I'll endeavor to make it clear by context.

The curve of the circle has no end or bound; you will find no break or edge along the closed curve. The circle is in that sense without limit. The circumference (distance around) is another matter; a circle does indeed have a limit in the form of an end or bound with respect to circumference in this sense.

We see that the curve of the circle has no limit in the form of an end or bound when we notice how each of its directions (clockwise/counterclockwise) turns back to itself—there is no end or bound to either of the directions along the curve, no point at which they begin or stop. The left-hand image in **Figure 1.1** functions as an analogy to capture this concept.

The circumference of the circle, however, does have an end or bound because the circumference is the distance around the circle, and that distance has a beginning and end to its extent [14]. The limit of the circle's circumference can be shown in various ways.

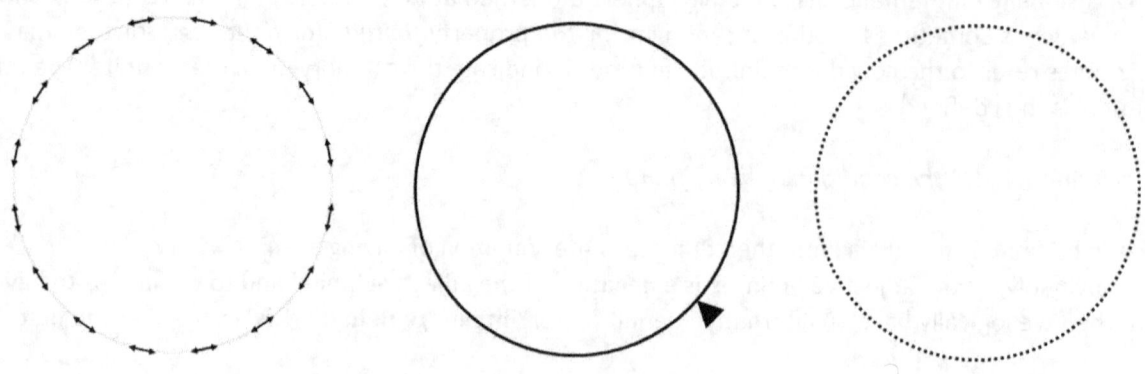

Figure 1.1: A set of arrows in a self-referencing pattern (left) provides an analogy for how the curve of a circle has no beginning and no end, yet clearly there are limits to a circle's circumference as revealed when placing a simple mark by the circle at any arbitrary point to measure the extent of the circle's circumference all the way around and back to the same point (center) or by dividing the circle's curve into a finite set of units (right).

One obvious way to show the limit of the circle's circumference is just to draw a circle. The circle is drawn by beginning its curve and forming that curve until it closes upon itself, and we make a complete stop upon closure of the curve. The stop to drawing the circle is indeed a limit in the form of an end. However, the end to the drawing process is not an end or bound to the curve of the circle. Rather, the end of the drawing process is simply what limits the circle's circumference—the distance around the circle as a closed curve. The curve of the circle itself still has no end or bound with respect to its two directions (as shown by the arrows in the leftmost image of **Figure 1.1**).

Another way to show the circumference of the circle is limited is to place a mark next to any arbitrary point along the closed curve of the circle and then trace the curve back to that mark, returning to the starting point. We can even place the mark next to the circle anywhere we like and achieve the same result, as shown in the center image of **Figure 1.1**. It is true that we return to a starting point and so the circle has an 'end' in that respect, but it is not the circle's curve that has the end, but rather the process of *circumnavigating* the curve of the circle that has an end. It is the end to the circumnavigation process that shows the circumference of the circle is limited even though the closed curve corresponding to that circumference has no end or bound.

The ability to return to the arbitrarily placed mark shows not only that there is a limit to the circle's circumference but also that the limit need not correspond to any specific location on the curve of the circle, such as an end or bound breaking the curve. The curve of the circle can be as smooth and seamless as we like, without any breaks or borders.

However, we can create breaks in the curve of the circle as one more way to demonstrate that the circle's circumference is limited. One way to do this is to divide the curve of the circle into a definite number of units, as shown in the right-hand image of **Figure 1.1**. If the extent of the circle's circumference were not limited at all, we would not be able to do so. Another way to show the limits of the circumference is to simply break the circle's curve at a single location and then stretch the broken circle flat, into a straight line from end to end. The fact that there are ends shows the extent of the circle's circumference is limited.

The limited nature of the circle's circumference reveals the limited nature of the circle itself, despite the fact that the circle has no end or bound to the directions along its curve. That is, the circle's curve has a limit with respect to its *extent* as shown by the circle's circumference, which is the measure of the curve's extent, even though the circle has no end or bound to the *directions* following that curve. In fact, it's precisely the circumference *as* a measure of the circle that makes the circle something measurable, even though the circle in either direction along its curve has no end or bound. We can obtain a limited measure of the circle as a closed curve because the circle's circumference is a limited measure and maps the extent of that curve.

Because a circle's circumference is limited despite the circle having no limit in the sense of an end or bound to the directions along its curve, the circle is itself still a *finite* figure. In fact, all objects of closed geometry like circles, spheres, and tori are finite even though unbounded—they are shapes that will be referred to as *finite-unbounded*.

What being finite-unbounded illustrates is that *to be finite cannot be simply to have a limit in the form of an end or bound*; if it were otherwise, the curve of the circle would be infinite, which is not the case. The circle's curve is finite *despite* the lack of end or bound to the two directions along the curve because the curve has a limit in its circumference, which is the *measure* of the curve's extent.

So, to be finite is to have the kind of limit that is able, at least in principle if not also in practice, to be demonstrated by making a *measurement*. And circles serve as a good example of what it is to be finite because circles are limited in the measure of their circumference, just as **Figure 1.1** illustrates. So even if there is no end or bound to a circle's curvature—even though the circle is not limited with respect to the two directions around its closed curve, being 'unbounded' with respect to its curve—a circle is still not something we would call 'infinite'.

This goes to show that to be finite is to have a limit, while the given 'limit' may in some circumstances be an end or bound while in other circumstances it need not be. But whatever kind of limit something has, it must have the kind of limit that is at least in principle measurable if that something is to be finite.

With respect to the example of the circle, I suppose I should caveat that some would argue there is such a thing as a circle composed of infinitely many points or facets (see § 17.3.2) or such a thing as an infinitely large circle (see § 18.4.2), but we'll worry about such matters later. Right now, I wish to show that just because something is endless or boundless in one respect, that doesn't make it infinite in the sense of being limitless altogether. It might still be limited, and therefore finite, by virtue of having an exact measurement.

1.1.3 *The Infinite is About Having No Limit in Measure*

Measurability, then, is the key indicator that something is finite. From this consideration, we can articulate a second, more precise definition for the adjective 'finite' as it is used in our colloquial speech:

- finite: (2) *having a limit to a given measure.*

And, of course, a second definition for its substantive noun:

- finitude: (2) *the condition of having a limit to a given measure.*

Still, the definition has a bit of vagueness to it. That vagueness has to do with *measurement*. We need to get a clearer idea of what is meant by 'measurement' and having a *measure*.

Measurement is simply the amount of what is measured or the activity of measuring. Definition:

- measure: *a comparison made according to a standard.*

To measure something is to assume a particular standard and then compare what's measured to the standard. For example, draw a standard for a given feature (e.g., for weight, beauty, etc.) that some things are said to have and then compare a given instance of that feature to the standard for sake of comparison.

We can now apply the concept of limit to the concept of measure for a better understanding of finitude. Having a *limit* to a given *measure* (that is, being finite) means having a limit by a standard of comparison—to have a limit to a given measure means that by the given standard defining the measurement, there is no more to compare. That is what it means for something to be finite.

With this understanding of measurement and the meaning of finitude, we can now derive a third, more precise, definition for the adjective 'infinite':

- infinite: (3) *having no limit to a given measure.*

It is not just lacking a limit per se that makes something infinite but lacking a limit to its measure—that is, lacking a limit by a given standard of comparison. A circle lacks a limit to its curvature in the sense of having no end or bound to the curvature, but the circle's curvature is still finite as shown by the limit to the extent to the curvature—the extent of curvature being a kind of standard of comparison (a measure). In contrast, what makes something infinite is not just that it lacks a limit of any kind to some feature, but rather that it lacks a limit to a particular, given *measure* for that feature.

We now arrive at a better understanding of infinity. Since "the condition of being infinite" is how infinity was previously defined, and the adjective 'infinite' means to have no limit to a given measure, then we can also add a second definition to the noun 'infinity':

- infinity: (2) *the condition of having no limit to a given measure.*

From ancient times to the present, this general notion of infinity—a condition of being infinite, of having no limit for a given measure—has predominated in colloquial discourse when the word 'infinity' is used. I take the second definition of infinity to be the general, underlying meaning of infinity when the word is used in discourse. Adding further content to that definition qualifies infinity according to particular contexts for the purpose of being more precise as to what exactly is being 'measured' and what kind of limit the measure lacks for that which is infinite.

1.2 THE MAIN TYPES OF INFINITY

So what kind of limit is lacking for that which is infinite? It depends on who you ask and what kind of thing you want to measure. Who you ask because many philosophers have proposed various classification schemes for infinity. What kind of thing you want to measure because, despite the various schemes that have been proposed for infinity, it seems to me that we can think of measures as coming in three broad types: quantitative measures, qualitative measures, and a combination of both. Because measures assume limits, then if something is infinite—if it lacks a limit in measure—it may either lack a limit to its quantity, or to its quality, or to both.

We can therefore regard infinity as falling into three general types:

- *quantitative infinity*
- *qualitative infinity*
- *absolute infinity*

To get a better idea of the similarities and differences of each type of infinity, we will need to define what it means to have measures that lack limits in all three respects. Let's take each type of infinity in order.

1.3 QUANTITATIVE INFINITY

To measure something by quantity is to compare that thing against a standard for quantity. For example, we may measure the size of a physical object by using a quantitative standard for size in numerical units of space (millimeters, meters, kilometers, etc.) and we may measure the duration of an event by using a quantitative standard for duration in units of time (seconds, minutes, hours, days, etc.). Such quantitative standards enable us to describe or designate the relative limits of what is being measured.

This assumes, of course, that what we are measuring has a limit. Something has a limit in measure if the feature or aspect that we are attempting to measure can be *exhaustively* quantified. We know it is exhaustively quantified if on measuring it we reach a final number that captures all the elements of what we are measuring at a given time. That final number, that measure, should tell us the relative amount we are looking to describe—such as how large or small something is compared to some scale of size or perhaps how brief or long an event is compared to a scale of time. The example of measuring the line segment was another instance of quantitative measure. Despite the issue of how many points are in the line segment, we can adopt a standard, such as the use of meters, to tell how long the segment is from end a to end b—a standard that provides a finite measure for the limits of the object.

In actual practice, even quantitative measurements themselves have a limit to both the scale used for measurement and the number of steps taken to measure something. Quantitative measurement captures limits and has limits of its own, at least in real-world situations.

The use of *quantitative* measurements to capture the limits of things entails that we have an alternate way of defining what it means to be finite. To define 'finite' as having a limit to measure while assuming quantitative measurement entails that to be finite is to have a limited quantity. Ergo, a third definition for 'finite':

- finite: (3) *having a limited quantity.*

This third definition of 'finite' has bearing for our definitions of 'infinite' and infinity. We previously defined 'infinite' as having no limit to a given measure. That means to be infinite is to lack a limit that can be compared to a given standard. So, if the standard of our measurement system is quantitative, then whatever quantity we attempt to assign as the measure of something infinite cannot be correct because any quantity we assign designates a limit, whereas if something is infinite, it has no limit—it cannot be quantitatively measured.

For example, if we say something is infinitely high when measuring it by, say, meters, and go on to assign a definite quantity like 50 meters to the full measure of height, then we have gone wrong somewhere: either what we are measuring is not infinitely high in meters or the assignment of 50 meters to its height cannot be correct. If you can assign an exact number to it, you are saying its measure is of a limited quantity—it is finite rather than infinite.

Hence, assuming a quantitative measurement is made, to say something is infinite is to say it *contains* quantities but cannot be exhaustively quantified as a whole. We may therefore provide a fourth definition for the adjective 'infinite' in terms of quantity:

- infinite: (4) *having a limitless quantity*.

The noun 'infinity' can also be given a third definition in terms of quantity:

- infinity: (3) *the condition of having a limitless quantity*.

Such a definition for infinity refines but does not contradict our first two definitions for infinity. It also reflects how most folks ordinarily think of infinity and have spoken of infinity since antiquity. In fact, the same can be said of the previous two definitions for infinity. Regarding the first two definitions of infinity and the quantitative definition that we have for infinity—

- infinity:
  (1) *the condition of being infinite*.
  (2) *the condition of having no limit to a given measure*.
  (3) *the condition of having a limitless quantity*.

—all of these definitions complement one another, and each definition expresses how most of us commonly think of infinity. We can even put them all together to form a still clearer idea of infinity in its quantitative sense:

- infinity: (4) *the condition of being infinite by lacking a quantitative limit to a given measure*.

We can think of definitions 3 and 4 for infinity as definitions of infinity in its quantitative sense—what I will call 'quantitative infinity'. It is quantitative infinity that I will be assuming when I refer to 'infinity' for the bulk of my case. Qualitative infinity and absolute infinity will both be of far less concern because infinity in its quantitative sense is what I take to be the most common use of the word 'infinity', and likewise for its cognates 'infinite', 'infinitely', and so forth.

1.3.1 *Making Quantitative Infinity Precise*

Even the previous quantitative definitions of infinity, while correct, are still not quite precise enough to fully explain how infinity is commonly referred to in ordinary, everyday discourse. When we use the word 'infinity' in everyday discourse, we typically have in mind an infinite amount or *quantity* of something— perhaps a magnitude that is infinitely great. But even when referring to infinity in the quantitative sense, we don't always mean it literally. Sometimes infinity, or talk of infinite quantities, is just a figure of speech. Hence, quantitative infinity can be articulated in two different but related senses. Both senses understand infinity to be a limitless quantity, but one of these senses takes infinity literally while the other regards it as only a figure of speech.

To be infinite in the literal sense is for a collection to have *no limit at all* to the amount of objects it contains, whereas to be 'infinite' in a figurative sense is for a collection to have no *definite* limit to its quantity of objects but, nonetheless, to still have a limit [15]. If we understand infinity in terms of quantity, more precise literal and figurative senses of infinity can be defined in natural language (i.e., ordinary language, everyday speech) like so:

- infinity: (5) literal – *the condition of being both complete and limitless in quantity.*
- infinity: (6) figurative – *the condition of indefinitely changing in quantity.*

The literal sense of infinity, or *literal infinity*, is consistent with definitions 1 and 2 of infinity in its general sense, but also with definitions 3 and 4 of infinity, which are the definitions of quantitative infinity in particular—that is, assuming all these definitions are also taken literally.

The figurative sense of infinity, or *figurative infinity*, on the other hand, while consistent with definitions 1 and 2 of infinity in its general sense, is only consistent with definitions 3 and 4 (quantitative infinity) if "having no limit" or being "limitless" likewise is to be taken in a figurative sense (i.e., to indicate that which *appears* to be without limit but really does have a limit).

In making these distinctions for two different senses of quantitative infinity, the definitions for literal infinity and figurative infinity articulate more precisely how we use the word 'infinity' in ordinary, everyday discourse. **Figure 1.2** captures these two senses of quantitative infinity as two 'types' of quantitative infinity. These two quantitative senses of infinity are the main focus of my case (especially literal infinity), so I will briefly elaborate on each of them before we move on.

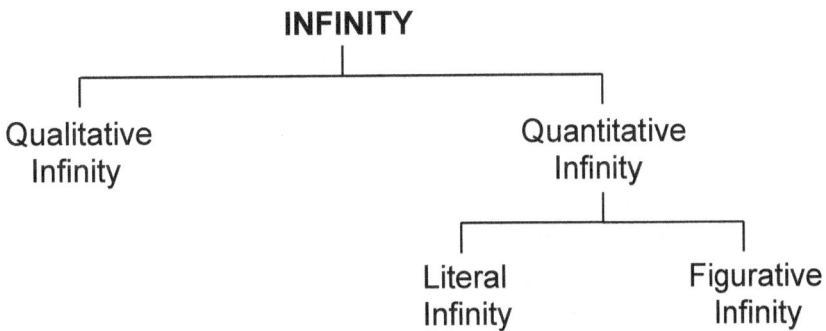

Figure 1.2: The two types of quantitative infinity as distinct from qualitative infinity.

1.3.2 *Literal Infinity*

Philosophers and mathematicians have given the literal sense of infinity various names—

- actual infinity
- proper infinity
- completed infinity
- determinate infinity

—and yet other names, but I will simply call it 'literal infinity' unless I need to refer to a specific scholar's interpretation of infinity for sake of clarity [16].

Regardless of what it is called, to say something is infinite in the literal sense of 'infinite' is to imply that which is infinite is a collection comprised of a *limitless* quantity of components existing together all at once and the collection is also *complete* as is, without further modification. If, for example, a bag contains an infinite quantity of marbles, then the quantity of marbles in the bag has no limit even while the collection of marbles in the bag is nevertheless complete [17]. To say there is no limit to the quantity of marbles means that no range of numbers (such as 1–10, 1–100, 1–1,000, etc.) can be specified for the size of the collection, even in principle [18]. For the collection of marbles to be complete is for the collection to be a whole, entire, full, and finished totality of members (see Chapter 3). For any collection to be complete and yet also limitless in its quantity of members is what it means for a collection to be infinite in the literal sense.

Literal infinity is not just a concept applied to collections of material objects. The concept of literal infinity is often applied for describing other features of the real world such as space and time. If space is literally infinite, then there is a complete collection of locations making up space and that quantity of locations is without limit. Likewise, if time is literally infinite, then it may be that the past or future (or both) are complete and limitless in their quantity of events. For example, if the past is literally infinite, then the collection of all events that have already occurred up to the present moment, m, is at m a complete collection of prior events and the events making up that collection are limitless in quantity. So too, if the future is literally infinite, then the collection of all events that will ever occur from m onward is a complete collection of events and those events are limitless in quantity.

In addition to matter, space, and time, the word 'infinity' in its literal sense has also been applied to mathematical objects. Dr. Peter Fletcher, a mathematician and philosopher of mathematics at Keele University, United Kingdom, provides mathematical examples of literal infinity. According to Fletcher, literal infinity includes "such things as lines of infinite length, infinitesimal numbers, sums of infinitely many terms, points at infinity, infinite sets, and infinite quantifiers" [19]. Mathematical 'objects' like lines, numbers, sums, points, sets, and quantifiers are often regarded as literally infinite: both complete and limitless in quantity.

Regardless of whether infinity, in the literal sense of the term, is said to be the condition of certain things in the physical world or of certain things in the conceptual world of mathematics, infinity means the same thing: it denotes a complete collection of something that is limitless in quantity or measure. For a collection to be 'limitless' means the process of measuring the infinite collection can never come to a definite end because there is a non-zero number of elements in the collection and yet there is no final number, no end or absolute bound to the collection's quantity of elements, and so no final measure to it; it cannot be fully measured *even as a matter of principle*. It is said to be, again speaking literally, *immeasurable*.

For these reasons, the meaning of literal infinity is often expressed in terms of synonyms such as the following:

- limitlessness
- endlessness
- boundlessness
- immeasurability

Although terms such as these are sometimes used as synonyms for infinity, that is not always the case. Such words as 'limitless', 'endless', 'boundless', and 'immeasurable' are sometimes used more narrowly or even figuratively, whereas to denote the literally infinite they must themselves be taken in a purely literal sense. Such words do not always imply the infinite in the literals sense of the term.

For example, the word 'immeasurable' is often (though not always) used to imply an infinite amount, but just because we cannot measure something does not mean it is infinite. Immeasurability and infinity are not quite the same thing.

The words 'endless' and 'boundless' are perhaps safer as synonyms for infinity. True, some finite things such as circles have no end or bound. However, while a circle has no end we tend to use the word 'closed' when talking about the curve of circles since 'endless' is a word most commonly applied to infinity. Likewise, a circle has no bound but we tend to use the word 'unbounded' rather than 'boundless' when describing a circle; 'boundless' being a word most often used for infinity. Perhaps 'endless' means a little more than simply to have no end, and perhaps 'boundless' means more than just having no bound. Then again, technically speaking, to be endless or boundless need not always be taken as implying infinity.

The word 'limitless' is perhaps the safest as a synonym for infinity, but literal infinity is more than just limitlessness. Literal infinity also denotes that which is literally *complete*, as is, *despite* having no limit.

On this last point I do admit there are some philosophers who might disagree and contend that infinity in its literal sense just is limitlessness, taken literally. In adopting that stance, they would deny literal infinity refers to that which is complete in quantity in addition to being limitless in quantity. They deny anything infinite in the literal sense of the term is ever a quantitatively complete collection, let alone that literal infinity can be the condition of a collection within bounds like a collection of marbles in a bag or points in a line segment [20].

However, I believe these philosophers are mistaken about what infinity, at least in its usual, literal meaning, implies. They are actually stipulating a new notion of infinity that is not the same as how infinity is usually thought of in its literal, quantitative sense. For that reason, I will stick to assuming infinity in its usual, literal, quantitative sense refers to that which is not just limitless but also complete in quantity. That said, I will address in § 12.7.3 and § 22.1.1 the conception of infinity as limitlessness without quantitative completeness and the reasons that such an alternative conception of literal infinity is flawed.

1.3.3 *Figurative Infinity*

While there is a common *literal* meaning of infinity, there are also many different *figurative* ways to use the word 'infinity' and its cognates ('infinite', 'infinitely', and so forth). Such words are often used in metaphorical, allegorical, or poetic senses and not always in a consistent manner. However, when I refer to the figurative sense of infinity or figurative infinity, it is the figurative sense of *quantitative infinity* that I most have in mind. I have already defined figurative infinity as "the condition of indefinitely changing in quantity." Unless otherwise noted then, that is what I will mean when I refer to figurative infinity or to the figurative sense of infinity.

As with the literal sense of infinity in its quantitative interpretation, so too the figurative sense of infinity goes by various names—

- potential infinity
- improper infinity
- incomplete infinity
- variable infinity

—and so forth, but I will refer to this sense of infinity simply as 'figurative infinity' unless referring to a specific scholar's conception of figurative infinity for clarity [21].

Whatever name we use, to say something is infinite, but only in its figurative sense, is to imply that it is really finite and so only *seems* to be literally infinite. To say something is infinite, but mean it only figuratively, is *not* to regard it as a completed collection of components, all of which exist together at once in a final totality that is also without limit. That way of being infinite is to be infinite in the literal sense. Rather, to say something is figuratively infinite is to regard it as a necessarily *incomplete* collection in which new members are added (or existing subsets of members divided) in such a manner that the collection continuously changes in the finite quantity of its members, yet never reaching a final quantity of members.

To illustrate the idea, let's continue with our marble analogy. Imagine that a marble-making company continues to manufacture new marbles. Each new marble they make is just one more added to the previous tally they made. At no time is the number of marbles produced ever limitless, no matter how long they go on making marbles. The series of marbles manufactured would not be *literally* infinite because at any given time only a finite number of marbles have been made, but the series of marbles could nevertheless be said to be 'infinite' in a *figurative* sense since there will always be more marbles made with no predefined end.

Now suppose you are continuously provided with new marbles from the marble-making company and suppose you continuously drop each new marble you receive into a bag for safekeeping. Unbeknownst to you, there is a device in the bag that annihilates every marble you drop in. Funny, the bag never seems to get full...But suppose you ignore that strange fact and just keep dropping new marbles into the same bag, ever dropping more in the bag, which never becomes full. Assuming you really enjoy this activity and didn't have to worry about dying, you could keep on dropping marbles into the bag without it ever becoming full.

In this scenario, there is the series of marbles that *have been* dropped into the bag and the series of marbles that *will be* dropped into the bag. The amount that has been dropped into the bag is never literally infinite, for each new marble dropped just adds one more to a growing finite number of marbles dropped into the bag. As for the amount of marbles to be dropped into the bag, it is not at all clear that amount must be literally infinite. If it is infinite at all, it could be only 'infinite' in a figurative sense. For, however large the quantity of marbles dropped into the bag ever becomes at any arbitrarily chosen future time, only a finite number of marbles at that time will have been dropped into the bag. Even if the dropping of marbles never ceases.

In other words, the marbles in the bag are never literally limitless in quantity because the series of marble drops into the bag at no time ever becomes limitless in amount—each drop is just one more than the previous amount of drops made. The process of dropping marbles in the bag is, at every step of the way, limited, even if the process never stops.

The process of dropping marbles has an *indefinitely* changing (in this scenario, indefinitely growing) quantity of steps. That is, the dropping of marbles can continue *without any predefined end* to the process—the dropping of marbles can continue "indefinitely" in that sense. But to say a process is indefinite is not synonymous with saying it is literally infinite. An indefinite process is always finite however long it continues. It may have an unknown end or it may never end, but even if it does keep going, at no time will it ever have accumulated a genuinely limitless—a literally infinite—quantity of steps along the way.

So if the process of dropping the marbles in the bag is indefinite rather than literally infinite, then it may *seem* infinite in the sense that it has no defined end. But actually, the process is finite in the sense that the quantity of steps composing the dropping process is not without limit at any given time. Hence, to call the process of ceaselessly dropping marbles into the bag "infinite" is a figure of speech; certainly, the process goes on at least *indefinitely*—maybe even in the sense of going on ceaselessly—but to say it goes on *infinitely* should not be taken literally because at any time the number of instances of placing a marble in the bag is *finite* and so at no time is the running total of instances without limit.

Now instead of the marbles being secretly annihilated in the bag, let's imagine the bag just keeps stretching to accommodate new marbles as they are dropped in. With each marble added, the set of marbles in the bag grows one marble larger.

Or, if you prefer, each additional marble makes a new set of marbles in the bag—a set with one more member than the previous set in the bag. In that case, the growing collection of marbles in the bag can be considered as an indefinitely growing *series* of marble sets. The amount of sets that have replaced sets can continue to increase with no defined end, but at each stage in the growth of the series of marble sets, the bag of marbles contains just one marble more than it had before.

The series of marble accumulations may even grow indefinitely, but there is never a literally infinite set of marbles in the bag—there is never a set that stands not just complete but also limitless. Some may say the growing series of marble sets is an infinite series, but that is just to use the term 'infinite' as a figure of speech.

For, if something is figuratively infinite, then it is a series or process, and the steps (actions) or members making up that process remain, at any given time, *limited and incomplete* no matter how long the series or process goes on successively adding new steps or new members. It might *seem* as though steps that lie ahead, yet to be taken, comprise a complete and yet limitless quantity, but that may be only an illusion; there need be no steps lying ahead, waiting to be taken. Rather, the process simply has the *potential* to be extended further, and it continuously changes its finite extent with no definite end to the process of change in sight. So, if one were to say something goes on infinitely in the figurative sense, one would be implying that it is part of an indefinitely changing series or process the exact measure of which is always limited no matter how much it changes.

The concept of figurative infinity can even be applied to examples of space and time. If space is infinite but only in a figurative sense, then no matter how long that dimension of space is made to extend, it will only reach a limited measure at any time. And if time is infinite in a figurative sense only, then no matter how many years it takes to produce such an extension of space, only a limited number of years would have passed. When we say that a collection grows "to infinity" and mean it figuratively speaking, we are merely indicating that the collection indefinitely changes in the quantity of its members, even though that quantity never reaches a literally infinite (complete and limitless) amount. Conversely, no matter how many times you divide something in only a figuratively infinite sense, you never divide it a literally infinite (complete and limitless) number of times.

Figurative infinity is not a condition of being literally limitless. However, just as synonyms are used for the literal sense of infinity, so too the very same synonyms are used for the word 'infinity' in its figurative usage:

- "limitlessness"
- "endlessness"
- "boundlessness"
- "immeasurability"

Hence, these are the same words used as synonyms for infinity in its literal sense; however, when these words are used as synonyms for figurative infinity, they too are intended to be understood only in a figurative sense as metaphors or hyperbole (which is why I put them in scare quotes as examples).

There are various figurative uses for the term 'infinity' and its metaphorical synonyms. For example, when we say the focus of a camera is set to infinity because the camera has a limitless zoom, that infinity is only figurative because the zoom on the camera is only "limitless" as a figure of speech. Infinity is also sometimes used to mean "endless" in a figurative sense as when a series of stories "continues endlessly" or "goes on infinitely." Sometimes the concept of infinity is used to denote that which is "boundless" in a figurative sense, as when a lover claims to have "boundless love" or "infinite love" for the beloved. Infinity is also used to denote something is immeasurable, but in a figurative or metaphorical way, as when a poet says humanity has an "immeasurable capacity for genius" or an "infinite capacity for genius" [22]. All of which illustrates that saying something is infinite in the sense of being "limitless", "endless", "boundless", or "immeasurable" can be construed as a way of saying the thing in question is infinite as a figure of speech: really, what we're talking about is finite, it's just indefinitely changing in quantity—growing ever larger or smaller, going on ever further to no predetermined point of rest [23].

Consider: a camera lens that is "set to infinity" does not have a limitless zoom in the literal sense of the word 'limitless' because the zoom only gets your focus to the horizon and no further. Likewise, saying that a series of stories goes on "endlessly" or has the potential to unfold "infinitely" is just to say the story-telling process has no predefined end, though the telling of stories itself remains always finite as there are only so many stories up to whatever is the latest story that has been told at any given time. To say one's love for another is infinite or "boundless" is simply to say one's love can be expressed in a quantity of ways that has no predetermined bound—the love is boundless only in the sense that the figurative 'bound' can always be expanded. So too, saying genius is infinite in the sense of being "immeasurable" merely implies that no matter how many measures of genius you continue to make, it will always be a finite number, but you won't find a final measure of genius.

All such colloquial expressions can be considered instances of using infinity in the figurative sense; they each imply finite amounts or processes that indefinitely change by growing ever vaster, shrinking ever smaller, or going ever onward. The progressions referred to as 'infinite' in the word's figurative sense always remain finite no matter how many iterations they have, but, because the quantity of iterations increases indefinitely, the quantity of iterations may suggest limitlessness in a literal sense and so may seem literally 'infinite' to those familiar with the concept of infinity, even when the iterations are not really without limit as they go but merely have a total that gets larger than before. To be infinite in a figurative sense is to always be finite (limited) though *indefinite* in quantity rather than literally limitless in quantity.

To be figuratively infinite is to be like a sand pile that grows ever larger or a length that is cut ever finer—there's always a finite amount to its quantity no matter how much it changes. In contrast, to be literally limitless requires the quantity to be without any limit but also complete as is; it has no limit but also does not grow or diminish in quantity.

It is quite common in colloquial discourse to use the term 'infinity' and its synonyms in the figurative sense. There are certain things that, when considered in quantitative terms, are commonly said to be infinite even when they are merely "infinite" in the figurative sense of undergoing indefinite quantitative change or when they are able to be ever further analyzed or refined [24]. As I'll argue, such language is misleading and it would be better to avoid such uses of the word 'infinity', even though that is in fact how people commonly speak.

Given that there are both literal and figurative uses of synonyms for infinity like the words 'endless', 'boundless', and so forth, I will set a rule of thumb for clarity: unless otherwise stated, or unless it is otherwise clear from context, for the pages to come assume the literal meaning for words such as limit/limitless, end/endless, bound/boundless, measurable/immeasurable, and so forth.

1.4 QUALITATIVE INFINITY

As quantitative infinity is about lack of limits to quantity, so *qualitative infinity* is about lack of limits to quality. In order to grasp what it means to have no limits to quality, in order to properly understand qualitative infinity, we first need to understand what is meant by *quality*.

With a little reflection, it's easy to see there are many uses of the word 'quality', but three in particular are philosophically relevant:

- quality:
  (1) *a property each instance of which has a particular appearance.*
  (2) *a distinctive property used to identify an object.*
  (3) *a property that sets a standard of value, importance, or performance.*

Each definition makes clear that a quality is a kind of *property*. A 'property' in this context means some aspect or feature shared among objects of the same kind. Some examples: wetness is a property of raindrops, mass is a property of atoms, mortality is a property of humans, and so forth. While it's not necessarily true that all properties are qualities, we do know that at least some properties are qualities— namely, those that fit one or more of the above definitions for the word 'quality'.

Let's take an example of a particular property and see how it fits all of the above definitions to be considered as not just a property but also as a quality. An example of such a property is intelligence.

Intelligence is a quality according to the first definition since intelligence is a property with a particular appearance for any of its instances. A given individual's intelligence is apparent from their manner of learning and ability to solve problems. One person may appear intelligent while another does not.

Intelligence is a quality according to the second definition since we can distinguish one person from another by their intelligence. Albert Einstein's intelligence is distinguishable from that of Salvador Dalí.

Intelligence is a quality according to the third definition because intelligence is a property that can set a standard of value, importance, or performance. The intelligence displayed by a particular professor may (for better or worse) set a standard for determining the value, importance, or performance of intelligence displayed by the rest of the faculty.

By any definition above, intelligence is not only a property but also a quality. It is not necessary, however, for every property to meet *all* of the above definitions in order for a given property to be a quality. Rather, if a property meets at least one of the above definitions, then the property is also a quality. For example, height is a property that may be used for distinguishing a person from various other people and so by the second definition of 'quality' height is not just a property but also a quality. But that does not mean an instance of height meets the third definition of 'quality', which entails setting a standard of value, importance, or performance. In some situations, a person's height may make no difference to the person's value, importance, or performance, and so in those situations the property would not count as a 'quality' by the third definition, though it may still be a quality according to the second definition.

Of the three definitions of 'quality' given above, it is the third definition of quality that is the most relevant for understanding qualitative infinity. Qualitative infinity is about being infinite (without limit) with respect to quality, where 'quality' means "a property that sets a standard of value, importance, or performance." That is, qualitative infinity is the condition in which a property, *as* a quality, sets a standard of value, importance, or performance that is in some manner not limited.

To get a clearer understanding of qualitative infinity, let's start by considering what it means to set standards, to be set by a standard (particularly, with respect to quality), and what it means for standards of quality to have limits. That will provide the needed contrast with qualitative infinity.

Standards enable comparisons to be drawn between things with the same or similar properties. We compare the intelligence of one person to that of another, the strength of one person to that of another, the beauty of one person to that of another, and so on. And we draw comparisons not just between properties shared by people; we draw comparisons between the properties of all manner of things. We compare the speed of one car to another, the fun of one celebration to another, and so on. However, setting a standard or having a standard to be set by is not *only* a matter of comparing one thing with another. A standard is set when a given instance of a property is used to judge the value, importance, or performance of something else with an instance of the same property. An instance of a property is a quality when it "sets the standard" for comparison with things purported to have the same property, in the same way—things purported to be of the same quality.

Recall that to compare things by a standard is to make a measurement. Setting a standard is a way of establishing a basis for measurement by comparison and being set to a standard is to be measured by (compared to) that basis. I bring this up because measurement is often assumed to be intrinsically quantitative, requiring the use of numbers. But that is not necessarily so. Measures can be qualitative. When the standards set for making comparisons are qualitative, we use those standards to make *qualitative measurements* of things having the same property or similar properties.

In making qualitative comparisons or taking qualitative measures, we use the manner in which one object or subject exemplifies a given property as the standard to judge the value, importance, or performance of how others manifest that property. That is, we can use a property of an object for comparing that object to something else having the same or similar property and in so doing we use the property of the former object as a way of *measuring* the relative value, importance, or performance of the latter object. For example, the beauty of one object might be used as a standard to measure the beauty of another object—we thereby judge the beauty of the latter object based on the standard of beauty set by the former object; the judgment of beauty establishes the latter object's relative value.

So in this example, the instance of beauty that sets the standard is not just a *property* but also a *quality* since that instance of beauty is used to determine how well something else meets, fails to meet, or exceeds that instance of beauty as the standard. Hence, a quality is a property that sets the standard for 'measuring' the value, importance, or performance of something else by how well it does or does not manifest or exemplify the same property and thereby also be or not be of the same quality.

The upshot of this explication of quality is that for a qualitative measure to take place—for a given instance of a property to be measured according to the standard of comparison set by a quality—the instance of the property measured must be *limited*. Otherwise, we would have no basis by which to compare the given instance of the property to the given quality. That is, without a *qualitative limit* we would have no way to make the qualitative measure.

The question then becomes the manner of limit for a qualitative measurement. That is, there are various ways something can be limited; so by what kind of limit are qualitative measures made?

It is true that in some circumstances properties are measured according to *quantitative* limits. For example, Olympic judges rate the properties of a figure skate according to how closely the skate matches a performance of quality as defined by a numeric score. But the maximum numeric score possible is a quantitative limit, not a qualitative limit. Consequently, that measure of a skate's properties is not a qualitive measure. Rather, it is a quantitative measure of the skate's quality—a number used to indicate how well the skate's given property meets the standard of a performance of quality. Properties and qualities are not always measured by quantitative limits, though. We don't always use numbers for measuring. In some cases, properties are measured by qualitative standards with *qualitative* limits.

So, a 'qualitative limit' is a condition by which we can specify how the given instance of a property can be improved to match the standard of value, importance, or performance set by the instance of the property we know as a quality. The 'qualitative measure' of something is thus the comparison of how well something's property meets a 'qualitative limit', where that limit is the standard of resemblance needed for a property to be a quality. The qualitative measure is thus defined not by a numerical, quantitative limit but by a conditional, qualitative limit.

For example, to qualitatively measure (vice quantitatively measure) an ice skating performance is to judge how well the ice skating performance's properties resemble or fail to resemble the properties of a given performance held to be a quality performance—a skate the properties of which are *quality*. The qualitative measure specifies the conditions for how the ice skating performance could be improved if it is not equivalent to the performance the quality of which sets the standard for other skates. Those conditions are the qualitative limits that the skate must be performed within in order to be a quality skate.

Essentially, the instance of a given property, insofar as that instance is also a quality, sets a standard for value, importance, or performance by establishing a qualitative limit for other instances of the property to match. Another way to put it is that an instance of a property, insofar as it is a quality, sets the standard for other instances of the property by establishing the specific conditions under which another instance of the same property could be improved to better match the quality to which it is compared.

As a further example, take the humor of a comedian's act as a property of the act. If we think of the act's humor as not just a property but a quality, then the humor of the act sets a standard for the humor of any following comedy acts to take the stage, such that some of the following acts may be judged as not performing to the qualitative limits of the standard of humor set by the first comedian's act. The other acts may therefore have specifiable ways they could be improved so that they would better match the standard of humor set by the act of the first comedian. Those improvements may lead the other acts to reach the qualitative limit of the first act.

That a particular property may set, or be set to, a standard of qualitative limits is what allows instances of the property shared between things to be compared—the qualitative limit is what allows a given instance of a property, as a quality, to set a standard for other instances of the property. A qualitative limit is thus a kind of limit that enables qualitative measurement; the qualitative limit is the means by which we can measure something's relative value, importance, or performance on the basis of how that thing exemplifies a given property (or if it fails to do so, how it could be improved to exemplify that property and so be of equal value, importance, or performance).

More generally, limits allow us to compare instances of a property and thereby measure quality between those instances. If we are able to make a qualitative measure between two things, at least one of the instances of the property shared between them must be able to be judged as having some qualitative limit, or no such qualitative measure can take place.

Now since to be limited is to be finite, then the notion of having a limit to quality implies another notion of what it means to be 'finite':

- finite: (4) *having limited quality*.

To be *qualitatively finite* is thus to have a quality that is in some way (quantitatively or categorically) limited; those limits then determine the quality or quality bearer's value, importance, or performance when compared to how something else expresses or exemplifies the same property with respect to the given limit. All finite things have qualities that are in some respect 'limited' according to comparisons of value, importance, or performance.

But what we want to know is what it is to be *qualitatively infinite*. Since to be infinite is to be not finite, and to be finite is to be limited in measure, then to be 'infinite' in a qualitative sense, or 'qualitatively infinite', is to be *unlimited* in measure of quality. We thus have a fifth definition for the adjective 'infinite', this time in terms of quality:

- infinite: (5) *having unlimited quality*.

Moreover, the noun 'infinity' can therefore also be given a seventh definition, this time in terms of quality:

- infinity: (7) *the condition of having unlimited quality*.

Since measures can be qualitative as well as quantitative, this way of defining infinity is consistent with, and even complementary to, our first two definitions for infinity:

- infinity:
  (1) *the condition of being infinite*.
  (2) *the condition of having no limit to a given measure*.
  (7) *the condition of having unlimited quality*.

We can combine the content of definitions 1, 2, and 7 together in order to provide yet a clearer idea of the noun 'infinity' it its qualitative sense:

- infinity: (8) *the condition of being infinite by lacking a limit to a qualitative measure*.

When philosophers speak of infinity in a purely qualitative sense, they typically have in mind infinity as articulated in definitions 7 and 8: the condition of having an unlimited quality or the condition of lacking a limit to a qualitative measure. We can thus think of definitions 7 and 8 as constituting the definitions for infinity in the qualitative sense—what I shall refer to as 'qualitative infinity'.

If infinity is "the condition of being infinite by lacking a limit to a qualitative measure," or of having an unlimited measure of *quality*, then to say something is infinite in this qualitative sense is to say that it is *without a specifiability condition for improvement in quality*. That is, there is no way even in principle to distinctly identify the conditions by which something of finite quality could be improved to become qualitatively infinite. Something is qualitatively infinite—something has no finite measure to its quality— if it has a property that sets a standard such that no finite property can compare in value, importance, or performance. In other words, the qualitatively infinite is that which is of such superior quality as to be 'immeasurable' or 'incomparable' to the qualitatively finite.

Typically, the superiority of the qualitatively infinite to the qualitatively finite is characterized in two different ways—one we might call 'negative' because it denies something and one that we might call 'positive' because it affirms something. There are thus two different types of qualitative infinity which I refer to respectively as *negative infinity* and *positive infinity*, and both stand in contrast to the two types of quantitative infinity: literal and figurative (see **Figure 1.3**).

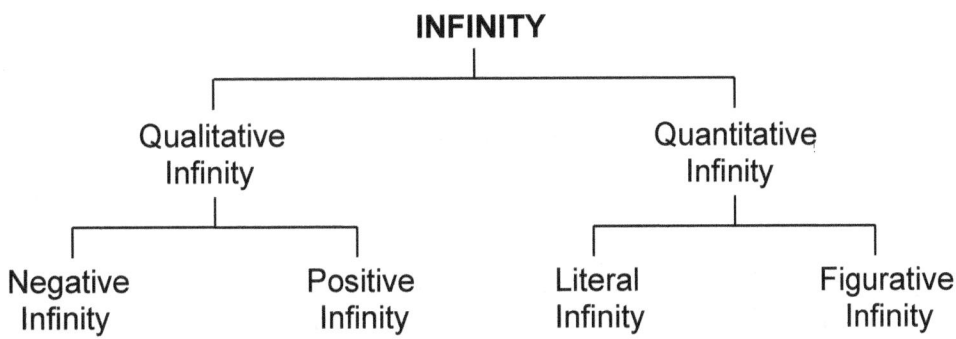

Figure 1.3: The two types of qualitative infinity in contrast with the two types of quantitative infinity.

The qualitative versions of infinity—negative infinity and positive infinity—are mainly concepts used in theology and philosophy of religion. Negative infinity and positive infinity are concepts used either to describe God as a being or to describe God's particular attributes (such as God's knowledge, power, presence, benevolence, etc.).

Insofar as an attribute of God or the being of God is regarded as qualitatively infinite in either the negative or positive sense, the qualitative infinity of God is known as *divine infinity*. Divine infinity is often conceived to be a qualitative infinity of either the positive or negative variety, depending on the views of the theologian making the given claim about God being infinite. However, there are also some theologians who think of God's divine infinity as an instance of, or identical with, yet another kind of infinity known as *absolute infinity* (see § 1.5).

With respect to God's divine infinity, theologians have had various ideas about what the terms 'negative infinity' and 'positive infinity' mean. Some theologians say that negative infinity is merely the denial that given attributes of God are qualitatively finite [25]. However, I find no consensus among theologians as to what the denial of qualitative finitude entails for God's attributes. As for positive infinity, theologian and philosopher of religion Denys A. Turner stated, "I confess to not being clear about what is meant by a 'positive' notion of the divine infinity" [26]. Likely that is because there is no universal theological understanding of it to be found. Even worse, the condition of divine nature that some theologians refer to as 'negative infinity' other theologians call 'positive infinity'.

Despite the lack of consensus among philosophers and theologians about the nature of qualitative infinity, and so about divine infinity as an instance thereof, some general themes are nevertheless present in the literature on the matter. After a review of the academic literature, I stipulate that in general the two types of qualitative infinity can be defined like so:

- infinity: (9) negative—*the condition in which unlimited qualities are indistinguishable.*
- infinity: (10) positive—*the condition in which distinguishable qualities are unlimited.*

These definitions may seem a little esoteric, but they are derived from the writings of what historical philosophers and theologians have had to say about infinity taken in the qualitative sense rather than the purely quantitative sense, particularly with respect to the qualities of God that are said to be infinite. The historical details of qualitative infinity I save for Chapter 25, but I will briefly elaborate on both qualitative infinity's negative and positive versions before we continue.

1.4.1 *Negative Infinity*

To describe something as infinite in a qualitative (or *non-quantitative*) sense may be taken in a negative way. I do not mean 'negative' in the mathematical sense or in the moral sense but rather in the sense that something is *negated* or denied. More specifically, the term 'infinite' means negative infinity whenever use of the term 'infinite' implies that a given quality is unlimited in such a way as to deny distinctions with other unlimited qualities—the quality's distinctions to other unlimited qualities is negated. That is, to be negatively infinite is to be categorically *indistinguishable* from other unlimited qualities, *including when those qualities are contrary to one another or even if they logically contradict one another*.

To see what this is supposed to mean, imagine a person who has some particular quality, like wisdom, beauty, or power. Take any one of those qualities and make it infinite such that the person is either 'infinitely wise' or 'infinitely beautiful' or 'infinitely powerful'. Whichever quality you pick—wisdom, beauty, or power—becomes *unlimited* when it is 'infinite'. But to say a quality is infinite is not a synonym for saying it is unlimited. There is more to qualitative infinity than that and so more to negative infinity than that. With respect to negative infinity, to be qualitatively 'infinite' is to be unlimited in a particular way: it is to be indistinguishable from other related qualities that are also unlimited.

In our example, a person is given a set of particular qualities that are infinite. The qualities when made negatively infinite *cannot be distinguished from each other*. Suppose a person is infinitely wise, infinitely beautiful, and infinitely powerful. If those qualities are negatively infinite, then it would be just as accurate to say the infinitely wise person's pronouncements are infinitely beautiful or infinitely powerful as it would be to call them infinitely wise. It would be just as accurate to say of the infinitely beautiful person's appearance that it is infinitely powerful or even infinitely wise as to call it infinitely beautiful. And it would be just as accurate to say of the infinitely powerful person's actions that they are infinitely wise actions or infinitely beautiful actions as to say they are infinitely powerful actions. In describing the person as having an infinite quality, such as to say the person is 'infinitely beautiful', one is, of course, *emphasizing* a particular quality as being infinite, such as beauty rather than some other quality, but one could just as well have cited a different infinite quality that the person has such as infinite wisdom or infinite power since all of the qualities become one and the same quality when they are made infinite in the qualitatively negative sense of the term. All distinctions between wisdom, beauty, and power break down when such qualities become 'infinite' in the negative sense.

If this example sounds to you like talk of God, you are not mistaken. This is how God's infinite qualities, or *divine attributes* as they are sometimes called, are described according to certain theologies. When God's attributes, such as omniscience and omnipotence, are conceived to be negatively infinite, then they are, as such, united together as a single attribute equivalent to God's very *essence*. God's essence is conceived of as a *divine simplicity* in which God's attributes, as infinite attributes, are all identical to God as such and therefore identical to each other [27]. According to philosopher of religion William F. Vallicella, "If each attribute is identical to God, then each attribute is identical to each other by the Transitivity of Identity. For example, if God = omniscience, and God = omnipotence, then omniscience = omnipotence...the perfections constitutive of the divine nature are identical with one another. For if each is identical to God, then each is identical to every other one" [28].

In theological circles, characterizing God's qualities as a negative infinity implies that God's attributes can also be *contrary* to one another, and yet still be identical in God's divine simplicity. Then too, some theologies go yet further by suggesting that God's attributes can *logically contradict one another* while still accurately portraying the essence of God [29]. Basically, some theologians suspend the logical principle of non-contradiction with respect to God's attributes, allowing for a conception of God as being "infinite" in the sense that God *does and does not* have given qualities or attributes. That is, when God's qualities or attributes (whether primary qualities like wisdom and power or secondary qualities like being or perfection) are described as infinite in the negative sense, those qualities or attributes are allowed to come into contradiction with another and so *negate* each other—hence, this qualitative form of infinity is, in that respect, "negative."

For example, in the theology of Ismailism, a sub-sect of Shia Islam, God's infinitude is such that God is "beyond being and nonbeing," implying that it would be "a radical error to seek to explain God in rational terms" [30]. Certain Jewish and Christian theologies also adopt this negative conception of God's qualitative infinity extending into the domain of conception where logic is suspended [31].

In Chapters 25 and 26 I will further elaborate on negative infinity and offer a critique of it and other paradoxical or logically *paraconsistent* conceptions of infinity [32]. In the meantime, I wish only to contrast the negative conception of qualitative infinity with the positive conception of such.

1.4.2 *Positive Infinity*

The term 'infinite' may be used in a qualitative sense that is positive rather than negative. Here too I do not mean 'positive' in the mathematical sense or in the moral sense but rather in the sense by which something is affirmed to have a given quality. Calling something 'infinite' in a qualitative sense that is positive implies that which is called 'infinite' has at least one unlimited quality, and the quality it has is unlimited in such a way that the quality is still categorically distinguishable from any other quality.

The qualities that are positively infinite are not 'negated' in comparison with other infinite qualities as they are in the concept of negative infinity. Moreover, those who believe qualities (e.g., divine attributes) can be infinite in the positive sense generally do not hold that those qualities may logically contradict one another, as is the case in a theology promoting the negative sense of qualitative infinity.

Not all theologians and philosophers of religion agree as to whether God's infinitude is of either the qualitatively negative or positive variety. However, what theologians mean by a "positive infinity" (or even a "negative infinity") varies widely. While I can't answer for theologians, I will use an analogy to indicate what I take positive infinity to usually mean in theology.

Suppose there is a pair of eyeglasses that has a quality such as optical functionality, by which I mean the eyeglasses work for their given purpose of helping the wearer to see better. Now suppose the optics of the eyeglasses are *infinitely functional*, but not in the quantitative sense of having infinitely many functions. Instead, suppose that to be 'infinitely functional' is understood in the sense of positive infinity. To be infinitely functional in this sense would mean to exceed any conceivable qualitative limit of the function. A pair of eyeglasses that is infinitely functional would allow the wearer to see anything the wearer desires to see, such that there is seemingly *no qualitative limit* to the vision afforded by the eyeglasses. Hence, we cannot specify the conditions by which regular eyeglasses would need to be improved in order to match the functionality of the infinitely functional eyeglasses—comparisons to regular eyeglass functionality break down. All we can say with regard to the functionality of the infinitely functional eyeglasses is that they allow the wearer to see whatever can *in principle* be seen, such as a single electron in a single atom, even though it is located on the opposite side of the Galaxy.

Unlike qualities that are negatively infinite, positively infinite qualities remain distinct from each other despite being unlimited. If the infinitely functional eyeglasses are also infinitely beautiful, the infinite functionality and infinite beauty of the eyeglasses each remain distinct qualities. Each quality is independently 'unlimited'.

A positively infinite quality is a quality that is 'unlimited' in the sense of being *incomparable*. It's not that something positively infinite is *absolutely* incomparable, such that we cannot know what it is that is incapable of being compared. It is also not that the positively infinite is that which is incomparable by losing distinction with other incomparable things. Rather, that which is positively infinite is that which is *relatively* incomparable, such that no finite instance of the same property can meet its standard. For example, incomparable beauty is still beauty; it is simply the kind of beauty that no (finitely) beautiful thing can match with regard to beauty. For something to be qualitatively 'infinite' in a positive sense is thus for it to be (relatively) 'incomparable' with respect to the limitations of finite instances of the same property. That is the idea behind qualitative infinity in the positive sense of the term.

As with negative infinity, positive infinity is a metaphysical concept chiefly claimed to characterize God. God's attributes (knowledge, power, benevolence, and so forth) are positively infinite in the sense of being incomparable—God has incomparable knowledge, incomparable presence, incomparable power, and so on. However, while God's attributes are positively infinite in the sense of being incomparable to their finite counterparts, God's attributes as positively infinite are not indistinguishable from one another, even though they are without qualitative limit [33].

We will take a closer look at positive infinity in Chapter 25, where we'll briefly review how it has been portrayed as a divine attribute of God by religious philosophers and theologians.

1.4.3 *Transcending Qualitative Limits*

Negative infinity and positive infinity are the two categories of qualitative infinity. Both of these qualitative versions of infinity have some things in common.

For one thing, they are each widely recognized as describing various attributes of a divine being, typically the God of the Western religions. The divine being is itself referred to as "infinite," as when it is said that "God is infinite," in either the negative or positive sense of the term 'infinite'. The divine being is infinite because the divine being has qualities (or 'attributes' such as knowledge, power, benevolence, etc.) that are 'infinite' in either the negative or positive sense.

Another thing negative and positive infinity have in common is that they tend to be associated, if not confused, with certain states or conditions. For example, that which is said to be 'infinite' in either the negative or positive sense is often regarded as being, by virtue of its infinitude, an *idealized* condition such as perfection or transcendence. Take the positive sense of infinity: according to professor of theology and science Robert John Russell, "Early Christian writers were informed by [Aristotle's] more 'positive' conception of infinity as they developed the doctrine of God...God's infinity is a mode of God's perfection..." [34]. As for the idealized conception of God's infinity as a *negative* infinity, which combines contrary or even contradictory properties into a single attribute, we find an example of such in the theology of Ismailism which holds that God "transcends unity and plurality, perfection and imperfection" [35].

Both negative and positive infinity also have in common that they are usually conceived of as *ineffable*—beyond words to accurately describe with literal language. Recall from § 1.1 above that some scholars have defined infinity as a condition of being incomprehensible or inexpressible. Such conditions are certainly true of negative and positive infinity since both versions of infinity have ineffable aspects, but neither version of infinity is *synonymous* with incomprehensibility or inexpressibility simply as such— precisely for the reasons given earlier.

Now let's consider the ineffability of these qualitative infinities.

Given negative infinity, we can know *that* God's attributes are infinite, but we cannot comprehend *how* they are each infinite [36]. According to one theologian holding this view of God's infinitude, the essence or nature of what it is to be God "is not of the nature of those things which can be comparatively greater and lesser, it is beyond all that we can conceive...Sacred ignorance has taught us that God is ineffable" [37]. Moreover, given the 'paraconsistent' nature of negative infinity, some ineffability of the divine nature is guaranteed.

Conversely, another theologian may contend that God's infinitude is positive rather than negative. Nevertheless, the theologian may hold that even positive infinity has an ineffable component. If God's infinity is said to be of the positive variety, the infinitude of God would still be ineffable in the sense that there cannot be a complete description of God's essence and attributes—there will always remain something more about God's qualities beyond any powers of articulation we will ever develop [38]. The positively infinite is, after all, a state of relative incomparability, and that incomparability implies at least some degree of ineffability.

Either the negative or positive nature of an infinite quality makes that quality ineffable. But there is yet another reason these forms of infinity are ineffable: they are each conceived to be intrinsically *mystical*. (That is not to say that which is ineffable is necessarily that which is mystical, but just that to be mystical implies ineffability.)

There are various conceptions of what words such as 'mystical', *mysticism*, and related terms mean [39]. Instead of attempting an overview of them all, I will simply stipulate definitions, starting with the following:

- mystical: *to be in an intrinsically mysterious state for which logical categories and rational descriptions cannot be consistently applied.*

For example, consider something described in terms that violate logic, such as a darkness that is described as luminous, something familiar described as "wholly other," or separate things described as being "one." Now suppose such contradictory descriptions are further presented as capturing some deeper, mysterious aspect of reality for which logic is claimed not to apply, not just in the manner of poetry and art but in the manner of metaphysics. That is the mystical—the appeal to a metaphysical mystery beyond reason.

Moreover, it is sometimes claimed one can have an experience of the mystical. Belief in, or the practice of obtaining experiences of the mystical is what 'mysticism' is about:

- mysticism: *belief in that which is mystical or the practice of obtaining experiences that are purportedly mystical.*

Those known as *mystics* are practitioners of mysticism; they engage in practices with the goal of obtaining a *mystical experience*:

- mystical experience: *an experience that purportedly provides knowledge or deep insight about a fundamental truth of existence that transcends all logical categories and rational descriptions.*

These definitions for 'mystical', 'mysticism', and 'mystical experience' are based on and adapted from the definition of 'mystical experience' provided by Dr. Jerome Gellman of Ben-Gurion University of the Negev, Israel [40]. You will notice in the definitions for 'mysticism' and 'mystical experience' the word 'purportedly', which I borrow from Gellman. Gellman states, "The inclusion of 'purportedly' is to allow the definition to be accepted without acknowledging that mystics ever really do experience realities or states of affairs in the way described" [41]. Not everyone agrees that mystics genuinely experience realities that are beyond logical categorization or rational description. Mystics may just be people who imagine they experience such.

Whether mystical experiences genuinely reveal some aspect(s) of reality or not, the point is that the mystical is about a state of being transcending logic and rational thought and, by virtue of that, mystical states are ineffable. So, to know a mystical truth about reality is to know a truth beyond logical categories and rational thought, a truth that is therefore inherently ineffable.

Whether the concept of a 'mystical truth' even makes sense is another issue. I simply offer that ineffability is implied by the very notion of mystical truth and, if there are mystical truths of reality, they are obtained via mystical experience.

Both the negative and positive versions of infinity have mysticism in common—that which is negatively or positively infinite is that which is infinite in the sense of *transcending all limits*, including the limits and limitations of human reason. Hence, negative infinity and positive infinity are mystical forms of infinity; they are states purportedly incomprehensible to reason and thus to logical conception [42]. Because these two types of qualitative infinity cannot be entirely understood with the use of logic, or more broadly, rational thought, both negative infinity and positive infinity denote conditions or states of qualities that are ineffable and so cannot be described in completely literal terms.

Positively infinite qualities may be described indirectly through metaphor or poetic language, including that which is paradoxical. Examples of paradoxical language used as descriptions for the divine nature include phrases like "dazzling darkness" [43]. The more mystical pronouncements of positive theology tend to use "both/and" expressions to describe divine attributes, sometimes in a paradoxical or logically 'paraconsistent' manner. For example, God is both x and not x—both light and not light (darkness)—hence, dazzling darkness.

Negative infinite qualities are described in even more intellectually confounding ways, delving into intentionally self-contradictory (i.e., paraconsistent) language to convey the ineffability of the divine, such as claiming that having and not having limits can be neither attributed to God nor denied of God who is "beyond being and nonbeing," a claim about God from the Persian poet Nasir Khusraw (1004–1088) [44]. The more mystical expressions of negative theology tend to use "beyond x and $\sim x$" or the equivalent "neither/nor" expressions to describe divine attributes, often in a paradoxical or paraconsistent manner. For example, God is neither x nor not x—neither being nor nonbeing; God is beyond both, as Khusraw had it.

Theologians are split over those who emphasize the positive and those who emphasize the negative versions of qualitative infinity claimed to be characteristic of the divine as revealed in either mystical experience or at least contemplation of the divine [45]. When God is said to be infinitely knowledgeable, powerful, present, benevolent, etc., such attributes are held to be known of God only by revelation or authority and understood only mystically as they are beyond words to describe in literal language [46].

1.4.4 *Qualitative Infinity: To Be Continued...*

We thus have two versions of qualitative infinity—negative and positive. Both are consistent with the broader definition of qualitative infinity ("the condition of having unlimited quality"); both negative infinity and positive infinity are refinements of qualitative infinity in general.

With that explication, we have most of what we need to know about qualitative infinity for now. Beyond this chapter, qualitative infinity will receive scant mention until Chapters 25 and 26, where it is covered in full. However, there is just a tad bit more to know about qualitative infinity until then, for qualitative infinity bears relation to our final category of infinity: absolute infinity.

1.5 ABSOLUTE INFINITY

Some philosophers and theologians combine elements of quantitative infinity and qualitative infinity together into a hybrid version of infinity. More specifically, they combine literal infinity (quantitative) and positive infinity (qualitative) into a version of infinity called 'absolute infinity' [47] [48].

Absolute infinity is infinity in the sense of negating the finite in both quality and quantity, which entails that to be finite has a fifth definition:

- finite: (5) *having limited quantity and quality*.

Absolute infinity is the denial of the finite in this fifth sense of the term—that is, to be absolutely infinite is to lack both quantitative and qualitative limits.

We can get a clearer conception of absolute infinity by comparing and contrasting it with the use of finite quantities to measure finite qualities. All qualities can be given quantitative measures, even if such measures are largely arbitrary. To use an amusing example, consider a quality such as sex appeal. In the 1979 American romantic comedy film entitled *10*, a man is asked to rate the physical attractiveness (sex appeal) of a particular woman on a scale from 1 to 10. The movie had quite an impact on culture: men and women have been using that scale to rate one another's physical attractiveness ever since. The scale of numbers used to rate attractiveness is, of course, arbitrary. We could just as well use a scale of 1 to 50 or 1 to 100, and so forth. But now suppose we say someone is *infinitely* attractive. If we reasonably take the word 'infinitely' to be a reference to quantitative infinity, we can interpret 'infinitely' in that context as expressing the measure of the quality in question: attractiveness. So, to say of someone that they are infinitely attractive is to say there is no finite scale of numbers that can measure just how attractive they are. You might think that is the sort of thing that is meant by absolute infinity—a quality that is "infinite" because its quality has no specifiable limit according to a quantitative measure. However, that is not correct. Just making a quality "infinite" according to a quantitative measure, as if put on a scale that goes to infinity, is *not* what is meant by absolute infinity. Absolute infinity is not the same as applying a quantitative standard for measuring a given quality. While quantitative infinity might be used as a way of expressing an excess in the measure of quality (e.g., attractiveness, beauty, knowledge, wisdom, power, etc.), that is not the case with absolute infinity.

To measure a quality, such as a divine attribute, with quantitative infinity is actually just another way of expressing that attribute's *qualitative* infinity, not its *absolute* infinity. Consider God's attributes such as God's knowledge, power, and benevolence. God could be said to know infinitely many truths, able to accomplish infinitely many goals, and prevent infinitely many evils. Those are ways of expressing God's qualitative (positive) infinity in quantitatively infinite terms—however, that in itself does not express God's infinitude as an absolute infinity.

Absolute infinity is a type of infinity that expresses the positive nature of a quality that *results from* or *emerges from* a limitless quantity. Suppose, for example, there is a sequence of numbers so quantitatively great that it is not only complete and limitless in quantity (literally infinite), but also of such quantity that the quantitative infinitude has *a quality of its own* that is positively infinite. And suppose that positive infinity, emerging as it does from such limitless quantity, has no finite analogies. The positive infinity of the sequence of numbers makes that sequence indescribable or ineffable. *That* would be an instance of absolute infinity—a positive infinity *from* a literal infinity. [49] [50].

Now let's again consider God's attributes, not just as positively infinite, but as *absolutely* infinite. For God's attributes to be absolutely infinite, they must be more than just brute quantities. It is not just that God knows infinitely many truths that would make God's omniscience an instance of absolute infinity, for example. It is something more than that.

Typically, theologians consider each 'divine attribute' of God to be so excellent or supreme in quality as to be a "perfection." God has perfect knowledge, perfect power, perfect benevolence, and so on. As a perfection, a given divine attribute is not just free of error but also qualitatively infinite. And, yes, that qualitative infinity may also have a quantitively infinite aspect (like knowing infinitely many truths in the case of God's omniscience). But in addition, each attribute is a whole *greater* than and *irreducible* to any quantitatively infinite degree of the attribute. That is, a divine attribute is "perfect" because it is positively infinite (a qualitative infinity) by virtue of being *greater than* the quantitatively infinite features that the infinite quality emerges from. God's attributes, as perfections, are 'absolutely infinite' in that sense.

For example, God has *absolutely infinite* knowledge because God's *positive infinitude* of knowledge is a result of God not only knowing *infinitely many* things but also because of the infinite quality—the perfection—with which God knows those infinitely many things. There is something about the infinitely many things God knows, all together, that makes God's knowledge a positive infinity greater and above the quantitatively infinite 'sum' of what God knows. It is the irreducibility of God's qualitative infinity to God's quantitatively infinite features that presents an instance of absolute infinity. The absolute infinity of God's knowledge, for example, is a positive infinity *emergent from and irreducible to* the quantitative infinity of what God knows.

Now suppose there are infinitely many—a complete and limitless quantity (a literal infinity)—of such "perfections" and suppose that as a quantitative infinitude of perfections they together comprise an additional, irreducible, positive infinity as a whole of infinitely many perfections—a perfect (positively infinite) whole of infinitely many perfections, each of which is also positively and quantitatively infinite. This perfect, infinite whole of infinitely many perfections may also be taken as *absolutely* infinite since it is a positive infinite that emerges from the quantitative infinity of each, individual, positively infinite attribute while also being irreducible to the collection of them. Thus, by both their individual and collective infinitude, in the sense of absolute infinity, the perfections (divine attributes) together create a further absolute infinity that is emergent from them as a whole: the absolute infinity of the divine is a mystical quality of being "all possible perfections" [51]. So that gives us yet another instance of absolute infinity.

Finally, suppose independent of each "perfection" (absolute infinite knowledge, absolute infinite goodness, etc.) and independent of them as an absolute infinitude of perfections together, that God can be absolutely infinite because God has some quantitative and qualitative "essence" beyond description. That absolute infinity would be independent of any of God's other perfections and so constitute God as such an instance of absolute infinity—God, in this view, just *is* Absolute Infinity.

The term 'absolute infinity' is thus a term for any notion of infinity that is an integration of literal infinity and positive infinity into a unique attribute of the divine, existing in addition to any other infinite feature, whether qualitative or quantitative, and interpreted to be a mystical condition of absolute perfection—either for God's individual attributes (knowledge, power, benevolence, etc.) or for God as a being.

Despite the ineffable aspects of absolute infinity, we can define some of its characteristics based on the expositions of quantitative and qualitative infinity. Here then is a very simple definition:

- infinite: (6) *having unlimited quality as a result of limitless quantity.*

The noun 'infinity' can therefore be redefined for this usage as well:

- infinity: (11) *the condition of having unlimited quality due to limitless quantity.*

This definition for infinity also refines the first two definitions for infinity, as we can compare

- infinity:
  (1) *the condition of being infinite.*
  (2) *the condition of having no limit to a given measure.*
  (11) *the condition of having unlimited quality due to limitless quantity.*

If we consider a given measure to be one of quality as well as quantity, then here again we find definitions for infinity that are complementary. Combining the content of both quantitative and qualitative infinity provides another, clearer, idea of the noun 'infinity' in its absolute sense when the term 'infinity' is used to refer to the property something has according to a standard of measurement:

- infinity: (12) *the condition of being infinite by having unlimited quality from a lack of quantitative limits in measure.*

Definitions 11 and 12 are only for the absolute sense of infinity, or 'absolute infinity' as I will refer to it.

As with the qualitative versions of infinity, absolute infinity will not be my primary concern. While it has its adherents, it is not the sense in which infinity is commonly used, which is my main focus.

1.6 A SURVEY OF INFINITY

The schema of infinity presented in **Figure 1.4** is my own way of categorizing various uses of infinity found in philosophy, mathematics, and theology. It is not my intent to suggest that all or even most philosophers would recognize this schema for the categories of infinity. There have been several different analyses of infinity over the centuries and various thinkers have had various schemas for classifying various types of infinity (some of the details are provided in Chapters 8, 23, and 25). Nevertheless, I think the schema of **Figure 1.4** captures the essence of the common uses of the term 'infinity' and its cognates.

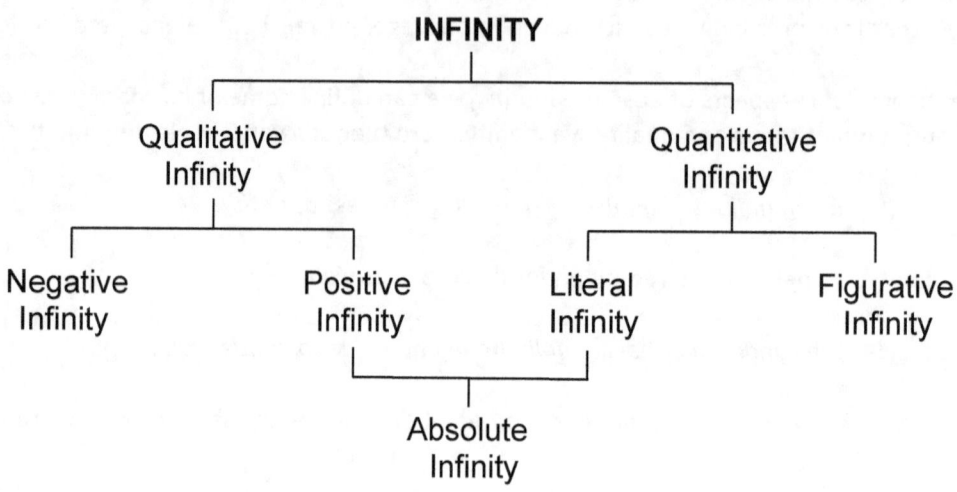

Figure 1.4: Absolute infinity combines the properties of positive infinity (a qualitative type of infinity) and literal infinity (a quantitative type of infinity).

We've seen so far that infinity, as "the condition of being infinite" or "the condition of having no limit to a given measure," can be taken in three common senses: quantitative, qualitative, and the so-called 'absolute' sense. The last two types—qualitative infinity and absolute infinity—are together the 'divine infinities' [52]. Hence,

- quantitative infinities: *literal infinity and figurative infinity.*
- divine infinities: *qualitative infinity (positive and negative) and absolute infinity.*

Of these various versions of infinity, the quantitative sense is the most common use of the term 'infinity' in colloquial speech and even in academic fields such as mathematics, physics, and cosmology. Typically, when folks say something is 'infinite', they are talking in a quantitative sense, implying that something is of an unlimited quantity—usually by magnitude or degree—and they mean it to be so in either a literal or figurative sense. Because of that, the literal and figurative senses of quantitative infinity will form the main focus of my case, with much less concern directed to the divine infinities.

1.7 MAKING THE CASE

The case I will make against infinity is that it is an erroneous concept, whether conceived in the sense of quantitative infinity (both literal and figurative) or divine infinity (either qualitative or absolute). Consequently, we should all avoid usage of infinity in favor of an alternative concept that is free of the logical errors characterizing infinity.

1.7.1 *The Charge Against Infinity and a Key Assumption of the Case*

Because infinity implies logical inconsistencies, it is an erroneous concept. However, in charging that infinity is an erroneous concept due to logical inconsistency, I am of course making an assumption—specifically, I am assuming concepts should be logical. I am therefore assuming infinity should be a logical concept if it is to be a concept that provides one with a reliable understanding of any subject to which the word 'infinite' is predicated.

As earlier indicated, there are philosophers who take the contrary point of view; they make exceptions to such a principle, asserting that some things are intrinsically paradoxical or logically 'paraconsistent' (able to violate certain logical principles) and that infinity is one of those paradoxical or paraconsistent things. I disagree. I will address appeals to mysticism in Chapters 25 and 26, and more narrowly analyze paraconsistent logic in § 25.4 and § 26.1. Until then, I will simply assume that any property claimed to be true of something must not be conceived in such a manner as to imply logical contradictions or other forms of logical inconsistency. If a property is claimed to be true of something but the property implies self contradictions or other logical inconsistencies, then the claim that something has that property is an erroneous claim and should be rejected.

Infinity is such a property—infinity is a property commonly claimed to be true of certain collections (for quantitative infinity) or certain attributes (for divine infinity), but the concept of infinity is erroneous for it implies unresolvable logical troubles. Infinity, as a logically problematic concept, is not reliable for understanding any given subject to which it is predicated (such when the term 'infinite' is used for describing space, time, motion, matter, possibilities, attributes, or even certain quantities or collections).

1.7.2 *The Trouble with Quantitative Infinities*

Let's start with a look at the quantitative types of infinity. On first inspection, both the literal and figurative senses of infinity appear to be logically consistent, each on its own terms. It is therefore not uncommon for infinity, in either the literal or figurative sense of the term, to be invoked for describing real-world features, such as measures of space, time, and matter. But suppose this appearance of consistency is only an illusion; suppose infinity, whether literal or figurative, turns out to be logically inconsistent [53]. That does not mean literal infinity and figurative infinity are both inconsistent in the same way, but they may both be inconsistent for reasons related to the concept of quantitative limitlessness.

1.7.3 *Literal Infinity as Self-contradictory*

One way to be inconsistent is to be self-contradictory. To be logically self-contradictory is either to hold two contradictory statements in conjunction or to make a statement from which two contradictory statements follow.

As an example of holding two contradictory statements in conjunction, consider a statement like, "The swan is completely white, and the swan is not completely white." To be both completely white and not completely white (in a literal sense, not in a metaphorical sense) is a self-contradiction.

As an example of having a belief from which two contradictory statements follow, consider a statement like, "Pat is both a bachelor and a wife." Saying that Pat is a bachelor implies that "Pat is a single man and not a married woman" and saying Pat is a wife implies that "Pat is a married woman and not a single man"—a single man and not a single man, a married woman and not a married woman; two contradictory statements implied from the original statement that Pat is "both a bachelor and a wife."

Now suppose the definition of literal infinity is self-contradictory. This would mean that to be "complete and limitless" is a self-contradiction—a logical absurdity—like being a square circle or a four-sided triangle [54]. A shape cannot be a "square circle" because a circle's points are all equidistant from its center while a square's points are not all equidistant from its center. Similarly, a triangle has three sides and not four, so being a "four-sided triangle" is both to have just three sides and not to have just three sides—another contradiction. The self-contradictions are *implied* by the very terms. If the definition of literal infinity is self-contradictory in this manner, then something can be complete but not limitless or it can be limitless and not complete, but it can't be both complete (which implies not limitless) and limitless (which implies not complete) simultaneously. Since literal infinity is a condition of being both complete and limitless, it would then have to be a self-contradictory concept. And since a self-contradiction cannot refer to anything that actually exists, then it would follow that there cannot be anything literally infinite. If this is true, then neither space nor time can be literally infinite; however vast the Universe is, it must nevertheless be finite (limited).

1.7.4 *Figurative Infinity as Inconsistent*

Suppose as well that use of the figurative sense of infinity is logically inconsistent, but not in the sense of being self-contradictory. Inconsistency is not synonymous with self-contradiction. If a concept is self-contradictory, it is inconsistent but not all inconsistent concepts are self-contradictory. Figurative infinity, I will argue, is an inherently inconsistent concept even though it is not self-contradictory.

As an example of an inconsistency that is not a self-contradiction, observe that people sometimes have inconsistent views because they hold two contradictory beliefs, *but not in conjunction*. For example, a person might believe at one time that no democratic country starts a war and believe at another time that a democratic country started a war. Or a person might hold two contradictory beliefs (like "New Year's Day is a religious holiday, not a secular holiday" and "New Year's Day is a secular holiday, not a religious holiday") while these two beliefs are not together implied by a single statement (such as, "New Year's Day is a holiday"). Perhaps a person holding the pair of contradictory beliefs only considered the beliefs separately in different contexts and so does not notice how they oppose one another, or maybe the person holds each belief at different times, vacillating between the two. Hence, a person is inconsistent by holding these contradictory beliefs, but because the beliefs are neither stated nor implied *in conjunction*, that individual's pair of beliefs contradict each other but are not *self-contradictory*. We simply say the person is 'inconsistent' because he or she holds two contradictory positions on different occasions or in different contexts; it is only when the person makes the contradictory claims on the same occasion or in the same context that we say a self-contradiction has been made rather than merely an inconsistent position adopted [55].

In a similar vein, there are some concepts that are not logically self-contradictory, but they are logically inconsistent—at least according to practical reasoning. Such concepts are prone to inconsistent use—at one time the concept is used to mean one thing, at another time it is used *quite unintentionally* to imply another thing or, worse, to imply the exact opposite.

It might be thought that such is the case with contranyms (words that function as their own antonyms) like the word 'oversight', which can mean either careful supervision or a failure to notice something. However, contranyms as such are not prone to result in confusion; context and phrasing usually make clear the intended meaning of the word (at least for native speakers of the language), such as when we say someone "has oversight" (careful supervision) vice something "was an oversight" (a failure to notice).

In contrast to contranyms, though, there are some concepts that, while not having self-contradictory definitions, are nevertheless prone to be used inconsistently even in the same context and so result either in confusion or with misleading implications. Such concepts may be intended to mean one thing but are all too often used in a way that unintentionally implies the opposite, even by the proponent of the concept. Consequently, such concepts are misleading and so as a matter of instrumental/pragmatic reasoning, such concepts should be avoided and replaced by less misleading ones.

This is the sense in which figurative infinity is inconsistent even though it is not self-contradictory; figurative infinity is an inconsistent concept in that it is inherently misleading, prone to being confused with the literal sense of infinity in certain contexts. The problem of figurative infinity's misleading nature is most noticeable in the field of mathematics.

For example, consider functions in mathematics with respect to infinity. A mathematician may say that a mathematical function maps or associates numerical values with the members of some other set; the function is said to "output" the values. Moreover, mathematicians sometimes refer to functions the outputs of which have infinity as a limit [56]. Some functions assume there are "infinitely many" values for the function to associate with members of another set. But what this means is less clear. It may mean that if, by analogy, the function is a machine that outputs mathematical values on softcopy or hardcopy, it would output the values persistently over time with no defined end (which implies a finite amount no matter how long it continues). This is in keeping with using infinity in a figurative sense. However, if the mathematician says there *are* infinitely many values for the function [57], then the mathematician implies a *literally* infinite quantity of values [58]. That is, the mathematician ends up implying that the function maps a literally infinite quantity of values—a complete and limitless quantity that exists all at once—to another literally infinite collection. The adverb "infinitely" slips from infinity as a figure of speech for what if carried out physically would be an ongoing (but actually finite) process over time to a literal descriptor of a complete and limitless collection that exists all at once.

It is in such contexts that figurative infinity may become confused with literal infinity. If this is so, then to describe something as "infinite" in a figurative sense is to employ a term prone to misleading implications. This is what I mean when I say figurative infinity is an inconsistent concept and should be rejected as such. (See Chapter 24 for more details.)

1.7.5 *The Trouble with Divine Infinities*

The quantitative types of infinity are logically problematic concepts because they refer to non-zero quantities that are supposed to be limitless. Literal infinity is logically self-contradictory if such limitlessness does not cohere with quantitative completeness, as I will argue it does not. Figurative infinity is logically inconsistent if the more metaphorical use of 'limitlessness' (taken as a condition of continuous change in quantity) has too strong of a tendency to be confused with the limitlessness of literal infinity, which I will argue is the case. Both quantitative forms of infinity may therefore have to be abandoned in order to have a precise and accurate view of reality.

Likewise, the 'divine infinities'—qualitative infinity and absolute infinity—when taken literally are also logically problematic in a manner that even appeals to paraconsistent reasoning and mysticism do not overcome. Moreover, I argue that insofar as the divine infinities are not to be taken as literally implying lack of limits per se, they become misnomers for finite qualities and are consequently prone to misleading implications in a manner similar to figurative infinity.

My case will therefore be that none of these notions of divine infinity are intellectually supportable. If there is a divine reality, it would be more accurate to describe it as finite. In Chapter 26 I will argue that any theology aiming to be rationally persuasive is thus better off without proposals of divine infinity.

1.7.6 *Debunking Infinity*

I will present a case that exposes the erroneousness of infinity—the condition of being limitless—both as quantitative infinity and as the divine infinities. Once again, my focus will primarily be on quantitative infinity as that is the usual sense in which the term 'infinity' or its cognates 'infinite' or 'infinitely' tend to be used. But in the interest of being thorough, I will close my case with a critique of the divine infinities (both the qualitative infinities and absolute infinity) since they too suffer from similar logical problems.

As to the quantitative infinities, I argue both versions are logically erroneous—the literal sense of infinity is self-contradictory while the figurative sense of infinity is misleading and prone to inconsistent use [59]. Infinity in its conventional, quantitative sense I will show has no logical consistency. Infinity, both in the literal sense of being complete and limitless in quantity and in the figurative sense of changing "limitlessly" in quantity, is not a logically consistent concept. In its literal sense infinity has no basis in reality and in its figurative sense 'infinity' is a misnomer that I will argue should be avoided, if for no other reason than for the sake of clarity and logical precision. Consequently, if we want to apply our quantitative notions to the real world, reason clearly about the Universe, and describe its nature accurately, we ought to reject the use of infinity altogether.

Of secondary importance to my case are the divine infinities—qualitative infinity and absolute infinity—the examination and critique of which I confine to Chapters 25 and 26. I will argue that, when divine infinities are taken literally, they are logically problematic and so cannot be accurate depictions of any purported divine being (paraconsistency or mysticism notwithstanding). When the divine infinities are not taken literally, they are misleading in what they refer to. Divine infinity I conclude is a concept that should be rejected due to its logical inconsistency.

What the quantitative and divine infinities share is the idea that something non-zero or non-empty can be limitless. Insofar as limitlessness is to be taken literally, I argue it turns out to be self-contradictory. Insofar as limitlessness is to be taken figuratively, I argue it is a misleading misnomer for finite properties. Either way, infinity is a flawed concept better left behind.

1.8 THE WAY AHEAD

In this introductory chapter, infinity was defined according to its general meaning in natural language and distinctions were made between various types of infinity: quantitative infinity, qualitative infinity, and absolute infinity with the latter two types of infinity categorized together under divine infinity. Until Chapter 25, you can assume my use of the term 'infinity', unless specifically called out otherwise, refers to one of the quantitative senses of infinity, and I'll try to be as precise as possible to avoid confusion.

Part I of this book examines quantitative infinity, elucidating the concepts we need to properly understand both of its forms: literal infinity and figurative infinity. Toward that end, we will begin by examining the nature of quantity and the way in which we typically speak of infinity in its literal and figurative senses. Since literal infinity and figurative infinity are both quantitative infinities, Chapter 2 will define the term 'quantity' so that we have a clearer understanding of what it means to be quantitatively infinite in these senses. Chapter 3 will then define the completeness that characterizes literal infinity and the incompleteness that characterizes figurative infinity. Chapters 4–6 follow with an exposition of the quantitative infinities, detailing how they compare and contrast both with each other and with concepts such as finitude—both definite and indefinite. Chapter 7 will then support the definitions I offered for both literal infinity and figurative infinity by showing how these conceptions of infinity are commonly assumed, even in the technical discourse of mathematics, whenever the term 'infinite' is used.

Part II will focus on literal infinity. Chapter 8 will provide further evidence that my proposed definition for literal infinity captures the common understanding of infinity, both by scholars throughout history, including mathematicians, and by the lay public. Chapter 9 will then show how infinity is mathematically coherent in its symbolism and grammatically coherent in its natural language expressions of axioms and theorems, but I will begin to make the case that literal infinity is not *logically* coherent, despite its grammatical and mathematical coherence. Chapters 10–16 then present the main arguments against literal infinity, proving it is a self-contradictory concept. In Chapter 16, I provide the reasons why mathematicians are not greatly concerned with the logical contradictions inherent in the concept of literal infinity and why they should be. Next, we examine the relationship between literal infinity and physical reality. Chapters 17–21 argue that literal infinity is a condition that does not apply to anything in the real world. Chapter 22 then presents some closing arguments against literal infinity by considering rebuttals to my charges and countering each of them. I conclude literal infinity does not exist in reality and should be replaced with the alternative concept of indefiniteness, which is a finite condition.

Part III addresses figurative infinity. Chapter 23 provides a brief history of infinity according to its figurative sense, adding more evidence that my proposed definition for figurative infinity correctly captures another of the common understandings of infinity. In Chapter 24, I argue that figurative infinity is a misnomer for serial indefiniteness and that it should be replaced by the use of various terms for indefiniteness, both for the sake of precision and to avoid confusion with literal infinity.

Part IV moves beyond concerns solely with the physical Universe to explore the details of divine infinity. Chapter 25 offers an exposition of how theologians talk about divine infinity, followed by a historical overview of the divine infinities. Chapter 26 then provides a critique of the divine infinities. I argue that insofar as qualitative infinity and absolute infinity can be conceived without contradiction, they both reduce to misnomers for more mundane qualities that are actually finite. I then provide counterarguments to apologetics for divine infinity, followed by a recommendation for theists to reconceive the divine, however superlative, in finite terms.

The Conclusion then wraps up the book with a summary of previous chapters and offers some final remarks on the implications of the case against infinity for common discourse as well as for fields such as philosophy, mathematics, physics, cosmology, and theology. I end by addressing concerns regarding prospects for immortality. As I aim to prove, all that is not void of properties—everything having properties, everything that exists—is finite.

CHAPTER 1 IN REVIEW

❖ Infinity (as defined in ordinary, natural language) is the condition of being infinite; that is, the condition of having no limit to a given measure.

❖ There are three main notions of what it is to lack a limit—something can lack a quantitative limit, or it can lack a qualitative limit, or both. These ways of lacking a limit correspond to the three main types of infinity:
  o quantitative infinity—limitlessness in quantity
  o qualitative infinity—limitlessness in quality
  o absolute infinity—limitlessness in quantity and quality

❖ The majority of my case concerns quantitative infinity, of which there are two types:
  o literal infinity—the condition of being both complete and limitless in quantity
  o figurative infinity—the condition of indefinitely changing in quantity

❖ Both qualitative infinity and absolute infinity are the two 'divine infinities', which are addressed toward the end of the case.

❖ In making a case against infinity, I argue for the following verdict:
  o Literal infinity is a self-contradictory concept and figurative infinity is used inconsistently as a misnomer for a kind of quantitative indefiniteness (a finite condition).
  o Insofar as the two divine infinities avoid self-contradiction, they are also misnomers for what are actually finite qualities and are thus misleading uses of the term 'infinite'.
  o Where the concept of infinity is not self-contradictory, it is misleading and so use of 'infinity' and its cognates should be rejected as logically inconsistent.
  o Quantitative infinity and the divine infinities should be replaced with more logical, finitistic concepts, such as 'the indefinite' and 'the superlative'.
  o The rejection of infinity entails all that is, is finite.

PART I:
QUANTITATIVE INFINITY

2: THE NATURE OF QUANTITY

The case against infinity is mainly a case against quantitative infinity in both its forms—'literal infinity' and 'figurative infinity'. Literal infinity is the condition of being both complete and limitless in quantity; figurative infinity is the condition of indefinitely changing in quantity.

To have a good understanding of these two forms of quantitative infinity, we should first ensure we have a good grasp of *quantity* as such. Although we have an intuitive sense of quantity, and it may seem an exercise in stating the obvious, it is worthwhile to lay bare some assumptions about quantity before proceeding further.

This chapter will define the term 'quantity' in terms that are simple on the surface, complex under the surface. Once we have ensured that we are making the same assumptions about quantity, we will have the background needed to understand what it means to be "complete and limitless" in quantity (literally infinite) or "indefinitely changing" in quantity (figuratively infinite). We will then be a step closer to a firm understanding of the literal and figurative senses of 'infinity' and so in a better position to examine where the logical inconsistencies are found in these notions of quantitative infinity.

2.1 DEFINING QUANTITY

I will define the term 'quantity' very simply:

- quantity: *an amount of objects*.

Just so there are no false assumptions, I will further explicate this definition. First, we'll take a look at the concept of *object* and some related concepts; next, we'll examine the meaning of *amount*; and, finally, we will see how these terms all work together in the concept of quantity.

2.2 OBJECTS AND COLLECTIONS

We should start by defining 'object':

- object: *that of which a subject can be aware*.

The term 'object' in this sense does not necessarily refer to a material thing. Rather, an 'object' may be substantial or insubstantial, material or immaterial, abstract or distinct, universal or particular. Objects may be spatial, temporal, perceptual, imaginary, conceptual, etc. Properties and qualities, relations and relationships, things, persons, places, events, ideas, concepts, and so forth, whether real or fictional, are all 'objects' in the sense that they can all be in the awareness of a *subject*.

In this context, the term 'subject' is defined quite simply as follows:

- subject: *that which may be aware of an object.*

A subject can be a person, animal, or anything else that is able to be aware. We won't worry about what the term 'aware' means; you can plug in your own intuitive understanding of that. The basic idea is that subjects are those things that are able to be aware of objects and objects are of what subjects can be aware of. That's not to say that to be an object requires a subject to be aware of it in order to exist; rather, it's just to say that if something is an object, it has the potential for a subject to be aware of it.

The above definition of 'object' also allows for self-reference. A 'subject' (that which can be aware of an object) can be regarded as an object—since we as subjects can be aware of other subjects, those subjects may become the objects of our awareness. Hence, to be aware of a subject, such as another person, is to make that subject into an object of awareness. I of course do not mean the person is an 'object' in some demoralized sense as if they are purely a material instrument; I simply mean they are an object in the sense that they are a being of which we can be aware. So too, when we as subjects become self-aware such as by thinking of ourselves, we become the objects of our own thoughts and therefore we become the objects of our own awareness.

According to the above definition of 'object', all subjects are also objects, though not all objects are subjects.

2.2.1 *An Amount as Equal to a Single Object or a Plurality of Objects*

The definition of quantity ("an amount of objects") refers to objects (plural). Does this definition imply a 'quantity' is necessarily *more* than a single object such that what we call a 'quantity' cannot be of just a single object? I don't believe the definition commits us to that position.

The concept of quantity—of having an "amount of objects"—is about drawing a kind of comparison to a plurality, even if only a hypothetical plurality. So, even where there is only a single object, we can still say that we have an "amount of objects" since, of the plurality of objects there *could* have been, what we do in fact have constitutes an *amount*, even if only of a single object. The quantity in such a case "amounts to" a single object. Hence an amount of objects can be either a plurality of objects or just a single object. If we have no object at all, though, then we have no quantity.

The subject of a hypothetical plurality brings up another point. Any plurality of objects, even a plurality of objects that is purely hypothetical or conceptual, is a *group* of some kind—that is, the objects are *grouped* together, even if only mentally. What constitutes a 'group' of objects I will leave rather vague. A group can be physical, imaginary, conceptual, or some combination thereof. To group together objects can mean to place them close together or to otherwise put them into mutual causal interaction, or simply associate them with one another as parts of a whole in symbolic representation. So, grouping objects together does not have to entail gathering objects into one physical location, but it can—it all depends on context and interest.

When objects are grouped in such a manner that the grouping allows for drawing comparisons with other groups of objects, such as for comparing the quantity of objects in each group, the objects of each group are then parts of a whole and the whole is called a *collection*. Another simple definition:

- collection: *a group of objects.*

Just categorizing objects as belonging to a group, whether the objects are near or far to one another, whether they are all of a kind or not, means the objects belong to a 'collection'—at least a conceptual one if not an actual, physical collection.

Some objects exist on their own, others exist only as a part of a collection, and some objects may or may not be part of a collection. But when establishing a quantity—an *amount of objects*—we are always attending to objects as grouped in a collection. This is so even if the collection in question is merely a mental conception of multiple objects of which we have in reality only a single object present on the occasion. The conceptual group of objects is the 'collection' from which the "amount of objects" (quantity) we have before us is but one real object, perhaps belonging to others that either do or could exist elsewhere. Hence, an "amount of objects" can be just one object and need not be multiple objects.

All of that is straightforward. But notice a similarity in the definitions for quantity and collection: quantity was defined as an *amount of objects* and collection was defined as a *group of objects*. But an amount of objects is not the same as a group of objects. The 'amount' is a way of denoting and distinguishing the objects (such as whether we discern a sole object or many objects) while the 'group' is the manner in which the objects are related to one another.

As for the objects themselves, each object (as a thing of which a subject can be aware) can be physical, imaginary, conceptual, etc. Regardless of the type or types of objects grouped together, objects have something in common with one another when they are grouped together: objects grouped together are the *components* or *members* of the collection to which they belong. Moreover, even an entire collection of objects can be regarded as an object in its own right.

2.2.2 *Objects as Elements of a Collection*

The most fundamental objects making up a collection are members called *elements*. However, there are two different ways to think about elements:

- element:
  (1) *an indivisible, distinct object.*
  (2) *a divisible, but undivided, distinct object.*

Unless otherwise specified, I will assume 'element' according to the second definition. According to the second definition, elements are treated *as if* they are fundamental. For an object to be an element, it cannot be divided up into further members or parts and still be regarded as an element. However, even as 'fundamental' members of a collection, elements need not be absolutely indivisible. Instead, an element is merely *considered* as a basic unit without regard to any parts it too may have. Elements, simply as such, are not divided (conceptually or physically), but they are divisible; they *can* be divided—at least in principle. Hence, elements do not have to be *absolutely* fundamental or irreducibly simple; they are merely treated as such for the purpose of considering their relationships to other objects and to the whole of the collection(s) to which they belong. At least, that is how we may think of an 'element' according to the second definition of the term, which is what we shall assume unless otherwise noted (see § 18.5.8 for use of the first definition with respect to space).

If an object that is regarded as an element at one time is later subjected to a process of division, the object is no longer considered an element. Only an object that is both undivided and considered fundamental is an element. Conversely, an object that has been conceptually divided by the discernment of various parts may later be treated as a conceptually undivided object and thereby regarded as an element.

While undivided, an element is regarded as 'fundamental' but is nevertheless an object that is possible to divide. Many objects can be regarded as elements if they are considered in the abstract as 'fundamental'. Some examples: the stars in a collection of stars may for some purposes be regarded as the elements of that particular collection, the years in a collection of years can be the elements of that collection, the ideas in a collection of ideas might be thought of as the elements of that collection, the digits in a collection of digits can be the elements of that collection, and so forth. Stars, years, ideas, digits, and all other objects can be further analyzed in terms of constituent parts or members; such objects are not fundamental in an absolute sense. However, they may be regarded as fundamental objects in a given collection if they are not subject to further conceptual distinction or physical dissection. So, in the abstract, they can be considered as elements.

It should be noted that although elements are whatever is regarded for practical purposes as fundamental, or basic, the terms 'fundamental' and 'basic' do not necessarily mean quantized, digital, or discrete. Not all collections are made up of elements that are discrete; some collections have elements that are continuous, such as vast expanses of space or time—as long as those expanses are each regarded as basic units for the purposes of consideration, they may be referred to as the 'elements' in a collection of expanses [60].

Moreover, what makes an object into an element of a collection is that the object is *distinct* from any other objects in that collection. To be considered an element, an object must be able to be distinguished as different from other objects in the given collection, and it must be regarded as one of the fundamental members of that collection, something for which parts or portions are not an issue.

Now that we have a grasp of the fundamental concepts of object and collection, we should ensure we understand the differences between the various kinds of collections which can be quantified, for some of them will play an important role in the sections to come.

2.2.3 *Collections as Aggregates, Multitudes, and Sets*

We will take a brief look at collections such as *aggregates*, *multitudes*, *sets*, *sequences*, and *series* in order to see both their similarities and their differences so as to make some distinctions that will become important when we examine infinity [61].

- aggregate: *a collection in which the members operate together as interactive parts forming a whole.*

A molecule is an aggregate of atoms, a cloud is an aggregate of chemical elements, a dune is an aggregate of sand grains, and so forth.

- multitude: *a collection the members of which are individuals of the same kind.*

A collection of people at a town hall is a multitude, a collection of animals at a zoo is a multitude, a collection of symbols arranged together in a string is yet another multitude, and so on.

Both aggregates and multitudes share some common traits and some differences, both with each other and with another kind of collection—sets. For instance, some aggregates and multitudes are *structured* collections while other aggregates and multitudes are *unstructured* collections. Structured aggregates like clouds, sand dunes, crowds, marching bands, and numerical strings, do not remain unchanged if the arrangements of their parts change; change the arrangement of the constituent objects and you change the form or structure of these aggregates. Or take a collection of celestial bodies such as the Earth, the Moon, and the Sun. Clearly, when we regard this collection as an aggregate of real bodies, the members of the collection cannot be rearranged in spatial position without physical consequence. We may also say the same of certain multitudes. Suppose we have a multitude of boats sailing in random directions at different speeds. They are not an aggregate as they do not *operate together* by *interacting* with one another to form a whole. However, it is not necessarily the case that we can swap one boat for another without changing the order in which they return to the harbor. Changing the order of the members may change the whole of the multitude over time. Order matters for structured collections. Unstructured multitudes and aggregates, however, can have their members altered in order without consequence. Such unstructured collections belong to the category of 'sets'.

A set, in the ordinary language use of the term, is a grouping together of objects of any kind (you can have sets of planets, people, chairs, trees, symbols, ideas, etc.) in which those objects are regarded as elements that may be arranged in any order without changing the properties that they have independent of membership in the set or the properties of the group to which they belong. We will define the term 'set' thus:

- set: *a collection of distinct elements for which order is irrelevant.*

A set may have its members placed in order or no order at all—order is irrelevant to set-hood.

This definition for a set is what some logicians and mathematicians refer to as a 'naïve'—read as '19th Century'—definition since it tells us what a set is without describing the process by which a set is formed [62]. Mathematicians known as *set theorists* prefer instead to define the term 'set' according to either a particular mathematical procedure for forming an abstract set or according to rules of 'membership' of what does and what does not 'belong' to a set (often merely taken for granted in the axioms of the mathematical theory) [63]. While the preliminary definition for 'set' that I have offered does not have the kind of utility that modern set theorists prefer, neither is it logically contradictory and it seems to still fit with what many professional set theorists assume to be the logical implications of set-hood [64]. Without delving too far into the esoterica of that system of logic and math called *set theory*, it will serve our purposes for the time being.

I therefore unapologetically adopt some modal words like "could" and "would" and "can" [65] and simply say I will assume sets are collections not merely that *could* be formed according to a rule, but that *if* formed *would* then have members that need have no particular order (and therefore no particular structure). That is not to say if a collection has order that it is not a set, because it *can* be. It's just to say that order is not important to identifying a collection as a set. (In fact, we'll later see in § 14.7.3 some instances in which assuming an order or sequence for members of a set can be highly misleading.)

Further, sets can be unordered in one of two ways—absolutely or relatively. Sets that are *relatively unordered*—unordered in a specific way—may either be sets of real objects in the real world or sets of abstract objects that are only grouped conceptually. As an added nuance, sets that are *absolutely unordered*—sets that have no relevant order of any kind—can only be sets of abstract objects in a purely conceptual world [66].

To see the difference, consider sets of real objects versus sets of abstract objects.

First, the real sets. Sets can be real wholes with real parts existing in the real world, regardless of a mind representing them. Of course, this can be true for other kinds of collections—it can be true of some multitudes and aggregates, like rain drops in a cloud, for instance—but it can even be true of some sets. Take a collection of elements that is a real grouping (like a chess collection) composed of real objects (the chess pieces). If we want to consider this collection to be a 'set', then we are unconcerned about any order the objects may or may not have in the real world; the pieces can be in any order on the chess board since a set is a collection for which order is irrelevant. So, to call a collection of real objects a 'set' is not to say that the collection does not have any order in the real world, but only that such order is not relevant for our considerations—it is 'relatively' unordered.

Now consider sets that are groupings of abstractions such as concepts, ideas, or representations such as signs and symbols. Some sets of things like these are unordered collections that may even, as sets, be represented by symbols. We may, for instance, have a set, S, as the set of symbols a, b, and c.

The symbols in a set of symbols may, of course, refer to real objects. As an example, start by recalling a collection of real objects, such the one mentioned earlier—the collection of celestial bodies consisting of the Earth, the Moon, and the Sun. They all have in common the property of being celestial bodies, so we can represent these celestial bodies in abstract terms by assigning a symbol, such as a letter, to each of them: a small "e" for the Earth, "m" for the Moon, "s" for the Sun, and a capital "C" for this whole set of celestial bodies.

Mathematicians often depict sets using curly braces { } with the members of sets represented by small case letters inside those braces. So, when the real collection is represented in symbolic terms as an abstract set, C, the celestial bodies as members of C can also be represented symbolically as abstract elements inside those curly braces: $C = \{e, m, s\}$.

Represented symbolically, the celestial bodies as members of an abstract set do not share the same relationship between one another as they did even when they were regarded as members of a real set. When we consider members of a real set, we simply disregard any order that may be there among the objects in the real world. Were the real objects to change position, the order we are not considering may suddenly become relevant, as with the gravitational organization of celestial bodies. But as members of an abstract set the elements do not necessarily have to be arranged in any particular order; their positions certainly do not need to correspond to the spatial locations of their physical counterparts in the real collection of bodies making up the Solar System. Instead, we are free to represent them in any order.

As the order of C's members is arbitrary, set C expressed as $\{e, m, s\}$ is the same as $\{s, m, e\}$, which is also the same set as $\{m, s, e\}$, and so on. The celestial bodies, considered as elements in an abstract set, may be represented in any combination of positions with regard to one another and the differences in their order do not change C's properties. The elements can be rearranged in any order without changing either their properties or that properties of the set to which they belong. This is what is meant by an abstract set being 'absolutely' unordered; order makes no difference at all.

Whether real or abstract, sets always remain in some sense (relatively or absolutely) *invariant* in terms of the properties of the collection we want to consider—that is, the properties that are relevant for our consideration are the same no matter what order their elements are in [67]. The term 'set', unless otherwise noted, will thus apply only to a collection having properties that remain invariant regardless of the order of its members; this definition holds whether the set is a collection of real objects, an abstract collection that merely represents real objects, or an abstract collection of purely conceptual objects.

Since some aggregates and multitudes are unstructured and also qualify as sets, while others do not, we see immediately that members of one kind of collection can also belong to collections of other kinds. As indicated in **Figure 2.1**, some aggregates and multitudes are also sets, and some are not. Where aggregates and multitudes overlap with sets, they are composed of members the order of which is irrelevant to consideration. You can also have sets of aggregates or sets of multitudes, and you can have aggregates of sets, as when subsets are parts of a greater set; then too, you can have multitudes of sets, as when you may consider many different sets of symbols.

Moreover, as shown in **Figure 2.1**, some multitudes are aggregates and some aggregates are multitudes. A hydrogen atom can belong to the aggregate of atoms making up a cloud of gas around a star, and the atoms in the hydrogen cloud together form a multitude of atoms as well since they are all atoms of the same kind. As these examples show, collections of different kinds are not exclusive; there is some overlap between them in terms of membership in elements.

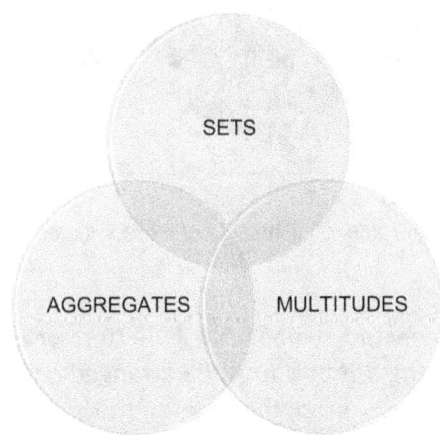

Figure 2.1: A collection of relationships between three kinds of collection. Some objects can belong to more than one kind of collection but not all members of one kind of collection are necessarily members of the others.

On the other hand, **Figure 2.1** also shows that different kinds of collections do not completely overlap. For example, not all multitudes are aggregates and vice versa. The people of New York City are a multitude and form an aggregate of people as members in the same city, but not all multitudes of people are aggregates of people; a thousand people isolated from one another are a multitude, but not an aggregate as they do not *operate together* or interact in any way to form a whole. Conversely, a rider and a horse may operate together as an aggregate, but do not form a multitude as they are different in kind—the horse carries and does not ride, and the rider does not carry a passenger. Hence, the different kinds of collections do have some distinctions and do not completely overlap in membership.

It is primarily sets rather than aggregates and multitudes per se that we will be concerned with, though some examples that we will consider may qualify as being more than one type of collection. Even so, we will need to attend to some differences between sets and other kinds of collections as well, such as 'sequences', 'successions', and 'series'.

To capture these differences, let's consider a real-world collection of objects, such as a collection of dominoes. Suppose the dominoes are thrown together in a loose pile, as shown in **Figure 2.2**. If we regard the collection as an aggregate, then of course the arrangement of dominoes can make a difference if altered. However, if we regard the collection of dominoes as constituting a 'set', then we regard the dominoes without concern as to what order they are arranged in. The dominoes can be arranged symmetrically in any combination or scattered randomly with no discernible order at all, just as they are in **Figure 2.2**, since a set is by definition an *unordered* collection.

Figure 2.2: A set of dominoes. As a set, the order of members—or the lack thereof—is unimportant.

When the dominoes are represented symbolically by letters or other characters—as in d for each domino and D for the whole set—the symbols must be arranged coherently in strings and formulas for mathematicians to make use of them. Even so, the order of the members in the set is unimportant since a set is an unordered collection. So, we may represent the dominoes falling into any order within a given string or equation. For example, a simple set of three dominoes might be represented mathematically as:

D = {$d\cdot$, $d\colon$, $d\vdots$}, or D = {$d\colon$, $d\vdots$, $d\cdot$}, or D = {$d\vdots$, $d\cdot$, $d\colon$}, etc.

This is primarily how mathematicians think of sets: as abstract collections of abstract symbols that need not represent real objects and groups (and, even when sets are used to represent real objects, the arrangement of their members is not important—insofar as the collections are *sets*—and so is given no consideration). Mathematicians Karel Hrbáček and Thomas Jech, offer the following position [68]:

> Sets are not objects of the real world, like tables or stars; they are created by our mind, not by our hands. A heap of potatoes is not a set of potatoes. The set of all molecules in a drop of water is not the same object as that drop of water. The human mind possesses the ability to abstract, to think of a variety of different objects as being bound together by some common property, and thus to form a set of objects having that property. The property in question may be nothing more than the ability to think of these objects (as being) together. Thus there is a set consisting of exactly the numbers 2, 7, 12, 13, 29, 34, and 11,000, although it is hard to see what binds exactly those numbers together, besides the fact that we collected them together in our mind.

When most set theorists think of 'sets', they consider them only as abstract objects that have no existence except in the mind; a set of potatoes or set of water molecules is just a mental representation of such objects as being together in a collection even if their physical counterparts are not. However, I will break with set theorists here to allow the term 'set' to refer in a more general sense to *any collection, whether real or purely conceptual, for which order is irrelevant to our consideration*. So, sets may be abstract objects merely defined as having members or they may be real-world collections of objects such as physical objects.

With regard to real-world sets, some such sets are collections that lack any *specific* order—yes, such as heaps of potatoes—while other sets are real-world collections that have no *relevant* order, at least with respect to the collection being regarded as a set. As an example of a collection with irrelevant order, consider a chess set, not as a game but *as a set*; the pieces can be placed on the game board in the order of their starting positions or arranged in any other order during play without changing the fact that the collection of game pieces constitutes a set. The collection of chess pieces, as a set of chess pieces, is the collection regarded without reference to the order of the pieces. The order of the pieces may be relevant to gameplay, but they are irrelevant to the fact that they also constitute a set. A set can therefore be a real-world collection, whether its members are ordered or not, so long as the order is either not specific or relevant to consider.

So, sets can either be real-world collections or they can be purely conceptual collections like unordered, abstract collections of symbols. However, I will endeavor to ensure that context makes clear what sort of 'set' is being discussed as we go forward.

2.2.4 *Set Theory and Notation for Sets*

The term 'set' as used in set theory can cause some philosophical confusion, so we should attend to that before proceeding.

You will notice that when we have less than two objects, we do not typically say we have a set in ordinary, colloquial language. The word 'set' colloquially implies *at least* one thing is grouped with at least one other thing; you ordinarily have to have at least two things to have a set. But set theorists and mathematicians seem to use the term 'set' in reference to only a single object or even no objects at all. They say that there are sets with only one member $\{x\}$ or even sets with no members $\{\ \}$. They frequently refer to a set having only one member as a *singleton* and a set with no members at all as the *empty set* or *null set*.

It seems odd to suggest that a set, even as a conceptual abstraction, can have only one member or no members and still be a set of something. After all, a real set—that is, a set of physical objects in the real world of everyday experience—is a *collection* of things. And that is precisely how 'set' was previously defined in § 2.2.3: "a collection of distinct elements for which order is irrelevant." In ordinary language, a 'set' refers to a collection of more than one thing, but mathematicians seem to suspend that requirement for collections that are sets. They instead distinguish sets from their members as if sets are entities that exist in addition to whatever may be in them. As Fletcher pointed out, "a collection is not usually distinguished from its members: for example, to fetch a pair of slippers it to fetch the slippers themselves, not to fetch a third object, the 'pair'" [69]. So too, a real set of something cannot be other than what makes up the set.

The odd use of the word 'set' has consequences for the idea of singletons and the empty set. Since a collection is nothing other than its members, then to have a collection with only one member or without members is not to have a collection. Fletcher states that "a stamp collection with no stamps is no collection" [70]. Therefore, concludes Fletcher, to have a set without members is not to have a set, so there can be no such thing as the 'empty set' [71]. Similarly, Fletcher argues, a set with only one member, a singleton, is not a set—it is not a genuine collection at all, but just a solitary object on its own.

Fletcher is right insofar as how words like 'set' are used in colloquial speech: a set is nothing other than its members and so a set with no members or just one member is not really a 'set' in the normal sense of the word or even a 'collection' of any kind. It is therefore a bit misleading for set theorists and mathematicians to adopt words like 'set' and 'collection' from ordinary language and use them to describe either a lack of elements or the presence of only one element.

Nevertheless, we can take a more charitable interpretation of what the term 'set' means in set theory and adapt it to our previous definition of 'set' so that the mathematical concept of a 'set' fits our earlier definition of a set as a collection. That way, a 'singleton' and the 'empty set' may each still be rightly considered as an instance of set according to the previous definition: a collection of distinct elements. We won't have to change that definition of 'set', but we can qualify what the definition refers to when dealing with sets represented in set theory and mathematics.

A 'set' as referred to in set theory and mathematics is indeed a collection of more than one thing alright: it is *a collection of braces* that can contain any number of objects or even no objects at all. A 'set' in set theory and mathematics is simply a set of braces in the form of a pair of curly braces, { }. The set of braces functions as a container for symbols.

Take the earlier example of dominoes symbolized with mathematical notation: $\{d\cdot, d\mathbin{:}, d\mathbin{\vdots}\}$. And consider that a 'set' is a collection of distinct objects. But now we may ask: don't we have *two* sets in this example—the pair of braces as one set and the symbols $d\cdot$, $d\mathbin{:}$, and $d\mathbin{\vdots}$ between them as another set? Strictly speaking, we do. However, set theorists usually refer to *the braces and everything within them* as all together constituting "the set" in question and for counting or comparing sets they ignore the braces to concentrate on what is inside them. So, it's the whole thing of $\{d\cdot, d\mathbin{:}, d\mathbin{\vdots}\}$ that constitutes "the set" in this example, though it is only the content between the braces that is used for comparison with other sets. The sets of set theory and mathematics are thus sets of braces that can contain collections of objects, typically symbols. Moreover, as a set, the pair of braces may contain multiple objects, only one object, or no objects at all. Hence, $\{x, y, z\}$ and $\{x\}$ and even { } are all examples of sets.

A set of braces that contains no other symbols is called the empty set: { }. If the braces contain only one other symbol, such as $\{x\}$ or $\{1\}$, then the set of braces and the symbol it contains is collectively called a 'singleton'. A set of braces containing the empty set—{{ }}—also counts as a singleton since the inner braces are a symbol.

Basically, since a pair of things is a collection, and a pair or 'set' of braces is a collection, then the 'sets' of set theory are still themselves collections—they are just collections in the form of pairs of braces used to contain other collections of symbols, like numbers and letters.

It is true, however, that we can more abstractly represent sets with other notation such as when we represent sets with letters like A, B, C, etc. as we did in the examples provided in § 2.2.3. Such notation is simply shorthand for representing sets as curly braces with object inside of them, such as $A = \{x, y, z\}$. The letter notations (such as A, B, C, etc.) are merely abstract symbols for sets, conceived as pairs of braces along with the symbols they contain. Then too, sets may also be represented with other notation. The empty set or null set, for example, is often denoted by a specialized symbol: $\emptyset$. The symbol $\emptyset$ is just a placeholder for { }. (Incidentally, a singleton containing the empty set can also be expressed as $\{\emptyset\}$.)

Such notation will be useful in representing not only sets as such but also sets that are sequences. In addition, this set-theoretic notation will come in handy for explaining the nature of numbers, which is at the heart of our analysis of quantity.

2.2.5 *Sets and Sequences*

There is a difference between sets (as well as aggregates and multitudes) on the one hand and other kinds of collections, like sequences and series, on the other. To capture these differences, suppose we give the dominoes a specific order. In that case, no longer do the dominoes comprise a 'set' pure and simple since sets do not have to have ordered members. The dominoes presented according to an order may be regarded as a set but need not be; they may just as easily be regarded as comprising an ordered aggregate and/or an ordered multitude. Further, depending on how we organize the dominoes, they may also constitute another kind of collection: a *sequence*, as shown in **Figure 2.3**.

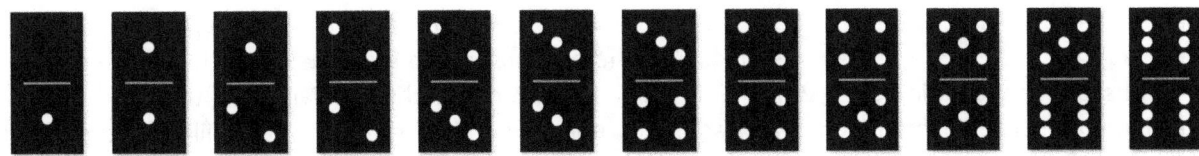

Figure 2.3: A sequence of dominoes.

The term 'sequence' is defined as follows:

- sequence: *a collection, the members of which are capable of being indexed as having either a successor or a predecessor, or both.*

In a sequence, a member with a successor but no predecessor is the *first* member, a member with a predecessor but no successor is the *last* member, and a member with both a predecessor and a successor is an *intermediate* member [72]. **Figure 2.3** depicts dominoes marked with symbols (in this case, representing numbers) indicating a first member, intermediate members, and a last member. Similarly, in mathematical expressions, a group of symbols can be represented according to a sequence, as in the example of $D = \{d\cdot, d\colon, d\vdots\}$.

Sequences differ from sets by necessarily having order to their members as an essential feature whereas sets may either have ordered members or unordered members. However, the category 'sequence' overlaps with that of 'set' in that sequences are a kind of set, and a set may have its members either in sequence or not.

Moreover, unlike a set, a sequence must be ordered so that change in the order alters the logical implications of the collection, especially in a connotative or semantic sense, but also in terms of syntax. For example, in terms of language, the order of the letters in SILENT carries different logical implications than does the order of the same letters in TINSEL. The differences in semantics (meaning) between these words ensure that they must have different syntax. The meaning of the word 'silent' identifies it in grammar as an adjective (and in logic as a 'predicate') and the meaning of the word 'tinsel' identifies it in grammar as a noun (and in logic as a subject) [73]. But even if the letters are treated mathematically rather than grammatically, their order will carry different mathematical implications, as when they are treated as variables in particular functions. Clearly, the order of the elements making up a string of elements like letters or numbers is crucial if we are to consider the collection as a sequence rather than as a set.

Sequences also need not be comprised merely of static arrangements. A sequence may be an order of events occurring over time rather than a collection of symbols or material objects arranged altogether at one time. So, any process, procedure, or progression of ordered events is also a sequence. Such sequences are referred to as *series*.

2.2.6 *Sequences and Series*

Mathematicians think of a 'sequence' as an ordered list of numbers and a 'series' as the addition of each number to produce a final sum. They define 'series' as *the sum of the terms of a sequence* [74]. However, I think it's a bit more accurate to say mathematicians regard a 'series' as a sequence of additions that results in a sum. Given a sequence of terms $\{a_1, a_2, a_3, ..., a_n\}$, a 'series' is the addition of those terms together. A series may be represented as $a_1 + a_2 + a_3 + ... + a_n$, for example [75]. So, if a *sequence* of numbers such as 1, 2, 3, 4, 5 is expressed as a mathematical *series* in this sense, then it is written in the form of sequential additions: $1 + 2 + 3 + 4 + 5 = 15$. When a mathematician hears the word 'series', the mathematician thinks of sequential additions equaling a final sum or of a similar function that produces a final mathematical result. (In mathematics, series depicted with indefinitely many terms, such as $\frac{1}{2} + \frac{1}{4} + \frac{1}{8} + \frac{1}{16} + ... = 1$ are regarded as 'infinite' series even though they result in a finite sum.)

Use of the term 'series' for a sequence of additions is a confusing technical appropriation of the word from ordinary language since the same word most often means something different:

- series: *a sequence formed by succession.*

That is an inherently temporal conception of series rather than an inherently mathematical conception. Let's examine the words in that definition—'formed' and 'succession'—starting with the latter:

- succession:
  (1) *the condition of succeeding.*
  (2) *the condition of having successors.*
  (3) *a sequence of elements that succeed other elements* ("a succession").
- succeed:
  (1) *to be placed or occur one after another in sequence.*
  (2) *to be subsequent or next in sequence.*
- successor: *an element that succeeds another element.*

The opposite of succession is, of course, *precession*:

- precession:
  (1) *the condition of preceding.*
  (2) *the condition of having predecessors.*
  (3) *a sequence of elements that precede other elements* ("a precession").
- precede:
  (1) *to be placed or occur one before another in sequence.*
  (2) *to be antecedent or previous in sequence.*
- predecessor: *an element that precedes another element*

The terms 'succeed' and 'precede' can be slippery in meaning because some of the words that define these terms (the words 'after' and 'before', respectively) have different, almost contrary, meanings depending on whether the succession or precession in question is spatial, temporal, or both. For instance, succeed means to occur after in sequence, but the word 'after' can mean either *behind* in spatial order or *later* in temporal order. Likewise, precede means to occur before in sequence, but the word 'before' can mean *ahead of* or *in front of* with respect to spatial order (as in, *I stand before you*) or it can mean *earlier* in temporal order (as when one event happens before another).

There are other definitions for 'succeed' and 'precede' given above, but these too can be slippery as they are also defined by words carrying multiple meanings. For example, 'succeed' may be defined with words like 'subsequent' and 'next' while 'precede' may be defined by words like 'antecedent' and 'previous'—all such words which may be construed as referring to either spatial order or temporal order.

Succession and precession, then, are concepts that can refer either to the spatial or the temporal (or both), which is why both the spatial ("place") and temporal ("occur") variations of their definitions are included above. It is succession, though, that defines series—a series is a sequence formed by succession; precession being the reverse order in which a series is formed.

Now notice the other word in the definition of the 'series'—the word 'formed'. The word 'formed' is a verb, *necessarily* implying time—the time it took for the succession to come to be. So with respect to 'series' as I use the term, to 'succeed' (or 'precede') indicates temporal rather than spatial sequence. Series are sequences that are formed by succession and forming something by succession necessarily happens over time. Series are inherently temporal; or, at least, they are products of time.

That the kind of succession defining a series is the temporal kind of succession fits with what it means for one thing to 'succeed' another according to the first definition of 'succeed'—"to be placed or occur one after another in sequence." To be *placed* (another verb) in spatial location is something that happens in time and to *occur* is a temporal concept as well:

- occur: *to happen as specified*.

For any series, the succession making the series involves a succession of 'occurrences':

- occurrence:
  (1) *the condition of occurring*.
  (2) *an instance of occurring* ("an occurrence")—i.e., an instance of happening as specified.

A series, being formed by succession (a sequence of occurrences during which the formation takes place), is intrinsically temporal in nature. However, while 'succession' in the context of a series is one thing occurring after another, the 'series' itself is the sequence that *results* from that temporal succession. That is, the series may itself be temporal or it may simply be what happens *in* time.

A temporal series, for example, is a "series of moments." On the other hand, we also refer to a 'series' as what "takes place" in time, such as a series of occurrences (e.g., actions or events), each occurrence of which takes place during a series of moments.

Consider a collection of dominoes arranged in a row (in a sequence), falling one after another (in succession) as shown in **Figure 2.4**. The successive falls, taken together as a sequence of falls, comprise a sequence of occurrences formed by succession—i.e., a series. In this example, the order of symbols on the dominoes is not what is in sequence; rather, it is the spacing of the dominoes that is in sequence as well as the succession of falls—each fall being an 'occurrence', each happening in sequence.

Figure 2.4: A row of dominoes in a sequence of falls that successively accumulate as a *series* of falls.

Figure 2.4 depicts a sequence of falls accumulating over time to comprise a series of falling dominoes. Had the sequence of symbols given in **Figure 2.3** accumulated one by one, that too would constitute a series—a succession of symbols appearing in sequence along with the sequence of their appearances; two overlapping series expressed by the same group of objects.

What I am referring to as a 'series', though formed temporally, need not have temporal intervals like moments or events, or even actions like falls, that define the elements of its sequence. Yes, a series is a sequence formed by a succession of occurrences that take place, but that does not mean what is called a 'series' must be the occurrences themselves.

Some series are not series of temporal occurrences like series of moments, nor need they be occurrences of activity like the falls of dominoes, even though series of actions were formed *by* another series—namely, the series of moments or events during which the actions took place. What is called a 'series' may instead refer to a sequence of objects that have been formed over a series of moments or events or intervals of time. A series of books written over a series of years, for example. (For further distinctions about time, see § 19.1.)

Now I should reiterate that mathematicians define terms like 'sequence', 'series', and related terms like 'succession' differently than I have here. (However, the mathematical definitions actually complement rather than contradict the more colloquial definitions I am using, as I will address further in § 3.11.1.)

Since I wish to stick with the more colloquial definition of series as a sequence formed over time by a succession of occurrences, I will need to offer substitute terms for what mathematicians typically call a 'series'. What mathematicians typically call a 'series' in their trade I will instead refer to as an *accession*:

- accession: *a sequence of additions resulting in a final sum—what mathematicians typically refer to as a 'series'.*

In mathematics, a sequence of subtractions can also be framed as a sequence in which negative numbers are added, but if we wanted to capture a sequence of subtractions as such, we could use the term *degression* to mean the opposite kind of arithmetical sequence of sums:

- degression: *a sequence of subtractions resulting in a final difference.*

The reason accessions and degressions are complementary to series (as I defined 'series') is because while accessions and degressions may be represented on the page all at once—

- example of accession: $1 + 2 + 3 + 4 + 5 = 15$
- example of degression: $15 - 5 - 4 - 3 - 2 - 1 = 0$

—nevertheless, their operations assume formation serially in the temporal sense. In practice, their arithmetical operations are made over time. I had to type each of those characters out, one by one, after all. Any mathematical function like addition or subtraction is a function that produces outputs in succession, over time, whether by human or machine; so, the objects resulting from functions such as addition or subtraction are themselves only constructed over time as well.

It is usually safe for mathematicians to ignore this fact in their practice. Nevertheless, at least some mathematical accessions and degressions seem to be instances of series in the usual temporal sense of the word.

Unless noted otherwise or clear from context, I will use the term 'series' in its usual temporal sense. I will also assume that mathematical accessions (and degressions) are typically instances of series because they form by succession over time, even if such a fact is ignored in mathematical practice.

2.3 AMOUNTS

Collections of any kind (aggregates, multitudes, sets, sequences, series, etc.) have a quantity. Quantity is defined as an *amount* of objects. Every collection therefore has an amount of objects; but what is meant by 'amount'? Definition:

- amount: *a value equal to a total*.

This is a simple enough definition, and we all have an intuitive understanding of amounts. But we need more than intuition; we need to be precise. To ensure we understand what it means for a collection to have an amount of objects, we need to have a good command of what the definition for the word 'amount' entails. To that end, we need to elucidate the definition's constituent terms—*value* and *total*.

The words 'value' and 'total' refer to numbers. We all know numbers when we see them and we have used them throughout our lives, but we should take a closer look at the concept of 'number' in order to avoid mistaken assumptions, for that is critical to a successful analysis of infinity.

So, let's take another step back by starting off with an examination of 'number' as a concept. Once we understand exactly what numbers are, and how numbers relate to one another, then we will have the conceptual tools to better understand totals and values, and therefore what it means for a collection to have an 'amount' of objects and therefore to have a quantity that might be "infinite."

2.3.1 *Numbers*

Consider the following symbols:

1   2   3   4   5

We can consider those symbols in a couple of ways: as *numerals* or as *numbers*.

Numerals and numbers are not quite the same thing, though the ideas of each are related to one another. A numeral is a kind of symbol, and 'number' is what a numeral represents. However, we sometimes refer to the numeral itself as a number since all numerals have the property of representing a number. For example, the numeral 1 is sometimes just referred to as the *number* 1.

Let's define 'numeral':

- numeral: *a symbol such as a word, a raised finger, a glyph, a token, etc. that represents a number.*

A numeral represents a number. So what is a number? A number is a certain kind of property that every numeral has. As a numeral is a symbol used to represent a number, and a number is a property of a numeral, we can say that a numeral is a symbol that represents, at least in part, a property of itself. The very symbols of mathematics are somewhat self-referential.

Number is a property of order and size that numerals have. We are all familiar with the Latin script versions of Arabic numerals—1, 2, 3, 4, 5, etc. (which were derived from numerals that originated in India). But the numerals in all *numeral systems*—whether a *unary system* or a *positional system*; whether Arabic, Hindu, Roman, Egyptian, Chinese, etc.—share a few of the same properties: each numeral is a symbol that has *ordinality* and *cardinality*. It is with these attributes that a numeral represents itself as a number.

Ordinality is the property that allows a numeral to represent itself in terms of order:

- ordinality: *the unique position of a numeral relative to the other numerals in a sequence of numerals.*

For example, consider the sequence of Arabic numerals where the numeral 2 falls in position between the numeral 1 and the numeral 3; the position of the numeral 2 relative to 1 and 3 (and all other numerals) is 2's 'ordinality'—its relative position in the sequence of numerals. The positions of the numerals in the sequence, from first to last, are the *ordinalities* of the numerals.

The ordinalities (positions of numerals in a sequence) are often expressed as first, second, third, fourth, fifth, etc. (or 1st, 2nd, 3rd, 4th, 5th...). In the list of numerals (1, 2, 3, 4, 5), the numeral 1 is in the first position, so '1st' is 1's ordinality, 2 is in the second position, so '2nd' is 2's ordinality, 3 is in the third position, so '3rd' is 3's ordinality, and so forth.

The numerals in those positions—in the first, second, third, etc. positions—are called *ordinals*. If I hold up my hand and label each finger with a numeral, I could say of the second finger that it will be called "finger 2"—in that case, the numeral 2 is the 'ordinal' of the second finger and 'second', or 2nd, is 2's ordinality. All the numerals in a sequence like 1, 2, 3, 4, 5, etc. denote *ordinal numbers* (or *ordinals*—see § 2.3.2).

However, it's also correct to say that numerals expressed *as* their ordinalities are also ordinals; so, when the ordinality of 2 is expressed as '2nd', it is also correct to say 2nd is an ordinal. What we call an 'ordinal' can thus be a numeral according to either expression: 1 or 1st, 2 or 2nd, 3 or 3rd, and so on.

All numeral systems have ordinals and ordinality. Consider a simple unary system of numerals:

I, II, III, IIII, IIIII, etc.

Although this simple system of numerals uses the same base numeral—I—as a digit to form the other numerals in sequence (like II, III, etc.), ordinality still applies: the numeral II falls between the numeral I and the numeral III, for example.

Convention has standardized the numerals and their ordinal sequence. For countries in which English is the primary language, the numerals are written by Latin script for the Arabic numeral system (which includes, for example, the sequence 1, 2, 3, 4, 5, etc.) that we all know so well.

Because the sequence of the notation has been made standard, the numerals in the system retain their same ordinality—their same positions in sequence—each time the system is represented, making the system, as a conceptual tool, consistent from one use to the next. If we begin to represent the system with the numeral 1, then 1 comes first (1st) and so 2 must follow second (2nd), 3 must follow third (3rd), and so on (unless you are indicating the opposite order of the system: ..., 3, 2, 1). The ordinalities of the numerals in the numeral system are hence conventionally ordered to be a common standard for mathematical application.

Since each numeral corresponds to a specific, unique position in the numeral system, we can say that each numeral has ordinality. But the ordinality of a numeral, as it falls in the numeral system, also determines something else: the cardinality of that which a numeral represents. Cardinality is defined in terms of size [76]:

- cardinality: *the size of set represented by a numeral.*

Each numeral represents the size of set. In the unary system of numerals, it is easy to see the size of the set each numeral represents. The numeral I represents a 'set' with a single member, the numeral II represents a set with a pair of members, and so forth.

However, while numerals represent the sizes of sets, the sizes of sets can be discerned independently from use of numerals. For example, take a set and attempt to match the members of the set to the members of another set in order to determine if there is equality in size between the sets. If a match can be made, the sets are equal in size. If a match cannot be made, then that is either because the former set is less than or greater than the latter set in size. Take, for instance, a pair of sets, each of which is a singleton. We can match each tit-for-tat, so they are equal in size. Now take another pair of sets in which one of the sets is a singleton and the other has a plurality of members. If we attempt to match tit-for-tat the singular member of the first set to the plurality of members in the second set, we will find the former is less than the latter because we will have a remainder for unmatched members left over in the second set. We don't even need to know how many members are in each set to determine if one has greater or fewer members than the other, or if they each have just as many members as the other.

Mathematician Dr. Judith Roitman uses the example of a collection of people matched to a collection of chairs: "We have a room with people and chairs. Suppose everyone in the room is sitting down. If there are some chairs left over, we know without counting that there are more chairs than people" [77]. Similarly, Roitman points out, if there are no empty chairs, we know without counting the collection of chairs and people are the exact same in size. On the other hand, if every chair is full and there are some people left standing, then we know without counting there are more people than chairs [78]. "The chairs can be in rows, a single line, in a circle, arranged as in a concert hall—it doesn't matter. We do not care about the arrangement, only whether every person has a chair or every chair a person" [79].

Attempting to match members between sets thus allows us to compare the 'relative sizes' of the sets in terms of establishing which set is 'bigger' or 'smaller' or the 'same size' as the other. If each set in a pair of sets has no more and no fewer members than the other, then the sets have the same cardinality—they have the same relative size that can be represented by a numeral. And of course, if a given set has more members than another set, then the set with more members has a greater cardinality (it's bigger); the set with fewer members has a lesser cardinality (it's smaller).

The same kind of matching can be done with sets of numerals. We can match any given set of numerals with another set of numerals and compare their relative sizes. To see how numerals enable this, we need to consider how numerals, as symbols, can represent sets—even sets of other numerals.

Numerals enable us to make this kind of representation via their ordinality and cardinality in the numeral system to which they belong. Take the numerals in the numeral system we've considered thus far. We can see that a particular numeral's ordinality (order) in the system also indicates that numeral's cardinality. That being so, the ordinality of a given numeral indicates the size of a set of numerals that the particular numeral in question is able to represent. Each numeral in the system can be used to symbolize a set of numerals consisting of the sequence of numerals in the very same system, up to and including the numeral doing the representing and thereby show us the size of numeral set the given numeral can represent.

For instance, consider the simplest numeral system—that starting with the numerals 1, 2, 3, 4, 5, ... The first numeral listed in the system's sequence (i.e., the numeral 1) can be used to represent a 'set' of numerals from the same numeral system it belongs to—the set that contains only itself since there are no previous numerals in the system. So, $1 = \{1\}$. In contrast, the second numeral in the numeral system (namely, 2) can be used to represent a set of numerals from the same system, where that set includes both the first numeral in the system (1) *and* itself (2). So, $2 = \{1, 2\}$. The second numeral (i.e., 2) thus refers to a *larger* set of numerals from the same numeral system than does the first numeral (i.e., 1) because the second numeral includes another member of the system. Similarly, the third numeral in the sequence can be used to represent a set of numerals from the same system that includes the first numeral in the system's sequence (1), the second numeral in the sequence (2), and itself (3). So, $3 = \{1, 2, 3\}$. The third numeral thus represents an even larger set of numerals than do the first and second numerals in the same numeral system. This pattern can be repeated for all successive numerals in the standard sequence comprising the numeral system:

$$1 = \{1\}$$
$$2 = \{1, 2\}$$
$$3 = \{1, 2, 3\}$$
$$4 = \{1, 2, 3, 4\}$$
$$5 = \{1, 2, 3, 4, 5\}$$
$$\vdots$$

As this sequence shows, each numeral's ordinality (1st position or 2nd position or 3rd position, etc. in the left-hand column's sequence) represents the numeral's relative position in the numeral system while at the same time each numeral in its ordinal place represents a unique cardinality (the size of a set—even if the set is a set of numerals from the same numeral system), as shown by the right-hand numeral set corresponding to each numeral listed at left.

From this we see that every numeral has both a unique ordinality and a unique cardinality just by being a member of the numeral system. A numeral can have ordinality by virtue of what position it has in the numeral system, and it can have cardinality by virtue of the relative size of set it is able to represent within that system. In fact, each numeral may not only be considered as an ordinal number but also a *cardinal number* (or *cardinal*—see § 2.3.2). For example, since the numeral 5 is an ordinal being by being in the place it has in the system (fifth), 5 is also a cardinal number by representing a set of objects with a size unique to its ordinal place in the system. Which is easily seen by the set of numerals that 5 matches from the very same system of numerals: $5 = \{1, 2, 3, 4, 5\}$. We can thus think of ordinality and cardinality as properties that are mutually related to comprise a single property that all numerals have simply because they are the members of a numeral system.

Taking this point of view, we now have a definition for number:

- number: *a numeral's unique ordinality-cardinality relationship in a numeral system.*

The preceding is a fairly formal definition of the term 'number'. To rephrase it even more formally:

- number: *numeral n has a property called 'number' if and only if n is a member of a numeral system and as a member of a numeral system n has a unique relation between ordinality and cardinality in the system.*

Or, if you prefer a pithier, informal definition:

- number: *a sequence-size relationship in a numeral system.*

Along with these literal definitions for the word 'number' we have a pair of figurative definitions. The figurative definitions fall into a *special figurative sense* and a *general figurative sense*:

- number: (special figurative sense) *a numeral in a numeral system.*
- number: (general figurative sense) *a numeral considered in terms of either its ordinality or its cardinality, regardless of appearing in or out of a numeral system.*

Since each numeral is recognized as having a unique ordinality and cardinality—a unique 'number' in the standardized sequence of a numeral system—the numerals themselves (e.g., the symbols 1, 2, 3, etc.) in a numeral system are often simply referred to as 'numbers' [80]. This is what I mean by the 'special figurative sense' for the term 'number'. It is figurative because the symbol is literally a numeral rather than a number, and it is 'special' in the sense of restricting its reference to numerals as they appear in a numeral system.

An even more colloquial use of the term 'number' is what I call the 'general figurative sense' of the term 'number', in which we identify or assign any numeral—whether it is depicted in its numeral system or not—as a 'number'. Although a numeral represents a number both according to the numeral's ordinality in a numeral system and according to the numeral's associated cardinality, we need not represent numerals only in a numeral system in order for numerals to be considered as numbers. Rather, we can appropriate numerals from a numeral system and use those numerals as numbers in various contexts. When we do, the numerals are 'numbers' in the general figurative sense of the term.

For example, numbers can be used solely with respect to their ordinality, as when we list an order of procedures; this comes first, that comes second, the other comes third, and so on. Numbers can also be used solely with respect to their cardinality, as when we compare the sizes of two collections—five apples to three oranges. Then too, we can use numbers with respect to their cardinality for other purposes, such as naming things or distinguishing them without regard for any necessary ordering. As one mathematician pointed out, "We use numbers for this purpose all the time, on license plates for example. You might guess a chronological order, but it's unimportant. The main thing is to have a 'primary key' distinguishing each item in inventory uniquely—a name, a code, a serial number" [81]. All of these examples are of numbers used according to the general figurative sense of the term 'number'.

Numbers, then, can be used for all sorts of purposes beyond their places in a numeral system; these are just a few such purposes. We can also use numbers in expressions of many sorts from formulas and equations to statements and even poems, as with the line from James Joyce's book, *Finnegans Wake*: "Three quarks for Muster Mark!" However, it will primarily be the use of numbers in terms of comparing sizes of collections—sets, series, and so forth—or the order of elements in sequences that will concern us, along with related uses in mathematics.

2.3.2 *Ordinals and Cardinals*

Mathematicians do not always want to express numbers in terms of both ordinality and cardinality. Sometimes, they want to consider numbers *only* in terms of either ordinality or cardinality, but not both. In such cases, mathematicians may make use of *ordinal numbers* (or "ordinals") and *cardinal numbers* (or "cardinals"). Of course, all numbers are really both ordinals and cardinals as previously pointed out. But in referring to a number specifically as an "ordinal" or a "cardinal", we are simply implying that, although every number represents a numeral's ordinality (unique position in a numeral system) and cardinality (size of the numeral system up to that numeral), it is not the case that both of these aspects are relevant to a particular mathematical operation being performed.

If expressing the size of a collection is not the issue but only the order in which the members in the collection are found, then mathematicians use an 'ordinal number' to represent the collection. If, on the other hand, the size of a given collection (relative to other collections) is the issue and not the order of the members comprising the collection, then mathematicians might use a 'cardinal number' to represent the collection.

Incidentally, the term 'cardinal number' or 'cardinal' is often used synonymously with 'counting number'. But all numbers have cardinality. Just consider the numbers other than counting numbers that depict relative sizes. For example, 1½ is larger than 1 and smaller than 2. If I have one and a half pieces of pie, and you only have one piece, I have more than you do—a bigger portion of the pie. So it seems to me that *rational numbers* also have cardinality, even if they are not typically called 'cardinals'. The same holds for irrational numbers such as 3.14159…, which represents not just a place in the number line but a quantity larger than 3 but smaller than 4. Hypothetically, one could have 3.14159… liters of water, for instance. So irrational numbers have cardinality as well, even if they are not typically called 'cardinals'.

The distinction between ordinal numbers and cardinal numbers becomes important when mathematicians use certain procedures to demonstrate sequences or sizes of collections, including infinite sets. We will return to the distinction between ordinal numbers and cardinal numbers when we deal with so-called 'infinite ordinals' and 'infinite cardinals' later on in Chapters 13 and 14. (Incidentally, we will even see examples of infinite ordinals with more than one cardinality and infinite cardinals with more than one ordinality. Even so, infinite ordinals and cardinals are part of a numerical scale of their own—one that also associates ordinality with cardinality, so the definition I stipulated for 'number' still applies even to the dubiously-named infinite ordinals and infinite cardinals.) Until we come back to the subject of infinite ordinals and cardinals, I will be referring to a numeral as a 'number' regardless of what its particular ordinality or cardinality is, unless I need to address a finite numeral in terms of its ordinality or cardinality alone.

2.3.3 *Number Scales and Systems of Numerals and Numbers*

Since the numerals of a numeral system represent themselves as numbers, we can consider a numeral system as filling the function of a *number system*—a system in which the numerals are used as numbers; that is, as symbols with ordinality and cardinality. The two terms—'numeral system' and 'number system'—are not quite synonymous since the former refers to the system of symbols and the latter refers to the system of what those symbols represent; even so, the two terms can sometimes be used interchangeably.

The numbers of a number system tend to be used for measuring and insofar as a number system is so used, it is a *scale* of measurement. However, for the sake of clarity, I wish to make a distinction between *number scale* and *scale of numbers*. A 'scale of numbers' can either refer to a number scale (a number system as a whole) or it can refer to a shorter sequence of numbers appropriated from a number system and used for making a measurement of some kind.

Let's consider an example. 1, 2, 3, 4, 5 is a sequence of numerals appropriated from our Latinized Arabic numeral system. The sequence can be regarded as a sequence of *numbers* appropriated from the same system regarded as a number system. The sequence so appropriated is a scale used for measuring; so we would say the sequence is "a scale from one to five." That's an example of a scale of numbers.

Scales of numbers can also be sequences of numbers fewer or greater than 5, of course, or even much greater. But when a scale of numbers has indefinitely many numbers, then the scale of numbers becomes identical to the number system from which it is derived—such a scale of numbers I will call a 'number scale':

- number scale: *a sequence of unique numbers represented by the sequence of unique numerals in a given numeral system (i.e., a number scale is an instance of a number system).*

Hopefully, I won't confuse matters too much when I refer to a 'number scale' as a 'scale of (particular) numbers' like the *natural numbers* or *whole numbers*. The natural number scale, for example, I will also refer to as the scale of natural numbers when appropriate.

To elaborate on the idea of a number system as a number scale, consider any numeral system. The further along the sequence of numerals, the larger the collection the numeral represents. Because each unique ordinality of a numeral in a numeral system is also associated with a unique cardinality, the cardinality must increase as ordinality progresses in the system and must decrease as ordinality regresses against the direction of the sequence. If we consider just the first five numerals from the Latinized Arabic numeral system, to proceed through the *numerals* from 1 to 5 is to progress in the sequence of *numbers* from 1 to 5 and so increase in size; to proceed through the *numbers* from 5 to 1 is to regress in sequence and so decrease in size. Since in each numeral system each numeral's ordinality (position in sequence) represents a unique cardinality (size of a set), and since numbers simply are the ordinality-cardinality associations that numerals have in a numeral system, we can regard each numeral system as a number system or number scale. I will refer to numeral systems as number systems or 'number scales' since that is the most basic function of a numeral system.

I should also point out that a 'number scale' is not quite the same thing as a *number line*. A number line is a graduated straight line serving as a graphical representation of numbers, whereas a number scale need not be so represented.

2.3.4 *Defining New Numbers*

The concept of 'number' has been defined and we have seen how each number is a property of a numeral. Each particular numeral (e.g., 3) represents a number that is defined according to the numeral's ordinality and cardinality—its place in a number scale. But this raises the issue of how new numerals are invented and thus what the process is for defining each new number.

There are various things we could mean by "defining a number"—that is, defining a particular number. I propose that to define a number means one or both of the following—

a. Proposing a new numeral to represent a new unique ordinality-cardinality association—a new number—in a number system.
b. Defining a procedure, operation, or function that outputs the number as a precise ordinality-cardinality association that is represented by a particular numeral or symbol.

An example of (a) is the invention of 5 (the numeral) to represent a unique number among the other numerals (1, 2, 3, and 4) each of which represents a unique number in a number system.

An example of (b) is an operation called the *successor function*. In non-technical terms, the successor function says for any number, add one more to get the next number in sequence and size. So, $4 + 1 = 5$.

Mathematicians can use operations like the successor function (and incredibly more powerful and complex functions than that) to define new numbers and extend the scale of a number system. If all we had were the first four counting numbers, the successor function would allow us to make a number equal to $4 + 1$, the output of which we can create a new numeral for (in this case, 5)—thus also defining a number according to (a) above. Mathematicians use various operations to invent new numerals with new ordinalities and cardinalities—hence to define, and thereby invent, new numbers—and in so doing extend the given number scale. As the new numerals are invented with new ordinalities and cardinalities, new numbers are defined, and the number scale is extended.

For now, the important point is that we have numerals and numeral systems, numbers and number systems (or number scales), and a way to define numbers for the number systems/scales. With that, we are ready to do something with numbers we have already listed 1, 2, 3, 4, 5. Such numbers can be used to *enumerate*.

2.3.5 *Enumeration*

Enumeration is a form of *quantification*:

- quantification: *the process of quantifying a collection*.
- quantify: *to ascribe quantity*.

Since to *quantify* is to ascribe quantity to something, and 'quantity' is an amount of objects, then to quantify means more precisely to ascribe an amount of objects, most often to a collection or 'set' of some kind, but series can also be quantified because quantification is a process. There are various forms of *quantification*, various ways to quantify. Enumeration, while not the only way to quantify, is a means of quantifying with precision.

Definition:

- enumeration: *the process of attempting to match numbers to objects.*

To match numbers to objects is to 'enumerate'. The word 'attempt' is included in the definition of 'enumeration' because not every collection of objects may be enumerable. Moreover, not every number can be matched to an object (zero, 0, matches to no objects at all).

There are various methods to enumerate and various reasons for doing so. One reason to enumerate a collection is to determine the size of a collection relative to some other collection. Another reason is simply to sort elements into different groups. There are yet other reasons for enumerating, but mostly we will be concerned with the size comparisons of collections.

The simplest form of enumerating is called *tallying*. Tallying can be used for sorting and/or for determining how much of something there is. Tallying a collection for size can be performed by using a series of identical marks (like straight lines) to represent the members of a collection, and thereby the size of the collection tallied. This is how tallying was performed in Neolithic times, when our ancestors represented the lowest numbers (1, 2, 3, etc.) as collections of simple lines, just as with the first three Roman numerals (I, II, III). Marks like these made it easy to represent the size of collections since each mark matched a single element in a given collection. Our Neolithic ancestors tallied collections with marks like these etched into bones, or 'tally sticks', in order to sort the collections by size, often for the purposes of trade.

But the invention of unique numerals in a number scale was far more useful. To see why, consider that we can also use a scale of numbers to enumerate what can be tallied. For instance, we can assign a number to a collection having the same size as the cardinality of the number itself. We know that the number 1 refers only to a single numeral (the symbol for 1 itself), so we can assign the *number* 1 to a single element in a collection; the element being the *numeral* 1 in the collection of numerals. Similarly, we know the number 2 refers to the numeral 1 and to its own numeral (2), so we can assign the number 2 to any collection with no less and no more than a pair of elements. We can repeat this process using the remaining numbers in sequence.

Take a sequence of fence posts. Each number in the scale of natural numbers can be matched to the set of numerals it represents, and the set of numerals can be matched tit-for-tat to the posts in a collection of posts that shares the same cardinality:

number	(time)	numeral sets	(space)	real sets
1	→	{1}	→	I
2	→	{1, 2}	→	⊨
3	→	{1, 2, 3}	→	⊨⊣
4	→	{1, 2, 3, 4}	→	⊨⊨
5	→	{1, 2, 3, 4, 5}	→	⊨⊨⊣
⋮				

In this example, each number in the sequence of the scale is equal to the size of a numeral set, whether the 'set' is a single numeral (e.g., 1 = {1}) or of multiple numerals (such as 2 = {1, 2}), and each numeral in the numeral set is matched in turn to a single fence post in the set of fence posts. By this procedure, a single number in the number scale can be used to represent the size of a set of objects like fence posts.

Because we know that each number in the scale matches to a set of numerals, with those numerals in the set listed in ordinal sequence to conclude with the same numeral matched to that of the number cited, we can skip this intermediate step of matching the numbers cited to their corresponding numeral sets before pairing the members of those numeral sets tit-for-tat with the object in a set of real objects (e.g., the fence posts).

To make such a match, we do not typically have all the numerals we need simultaneously available for the matching. Usually, we have to rely on time (which is often ignored in mathematics). For example, when we seek to directly match a set of numerals to the whole of a real world set for sake of determining the cardinality real set of objects, we use a method that relies on time. We use the procedure of citing the numbers themselves in the order of their scale—e.g., "One, two, three, four, five"—applying each one against a different object in the corresponding set, where the last number matched to an object is the size of the matching set. Essentially, what we do is *count*—another form of enumeration.

Definitions:

- count: (verb) *to successively assign numbers to members of sets according to the ordinalities of the numbers in a number scale.*
- count: (noun) *the process or procedure of successively listing members of sets by assigning numbers to them.*

A count is performed by assigning numbers from a number scale to objects or collections of objects (e.g., sets of objects) in such a way as to avoid representing the same object repeatedly, until every object is assigned a number and no unassigned objects remain. The procedure of counting ensures that each object's assigned number is unique in the count [82].

The standardization of the number scale makes the process of counting reliable: no matter what collection is counted the members are always counted with the same sequence of numbers. The ordinalities of the numbers do not vary from one instance of counting to another. In a count of objects, 2 always comes after 1, and 3 after 2, and 4 after 3, etc. (unless one is 'counting down'). So, counters cannot arrive at a different final number during a count of the same objects in the same collection.

Convention did not standardize the scale of numbers arbitrarily—the ordinalities of the numbers are ordered according to sequentially larger cardinalities. Each number used for listing an object during a count represents sequentially bigger collections of objects as the count progresses [83]. Counting is simply listing objects in a collection with numbers from a number scale until there are no more objects to list. When we count to determine how much of something there is, each number is used to indicate the cardinalities (corresponding sizes) of any collections counted up to the immediate number used. At the end of a counting process, the count indicates the size, or cardinality, of a given collection. And that is the essence of counting up a collection: the *ordinality* of the final number arrived at during a count of the elements in the collection is used to represent the *cardinality* of the collection counted.

Suppose we count the fence posts by labeling each post with a number in the sequence as we go: "one" for the first, "two" for the second, "three" for the third, and so forth. Since each post is matched to a number, each number indicates an increasingly larger collection of posts counted up to that point. Once the last post is counted, the final number we use is the number that represents the cardinality, or size, of the entire collection of posts counted.

Or take an even simpler example: counting all the fingers (to include the thumb) on a typical person's hand. 5 is the final numeral assigned in the count of fingers, so it is 5 that represents the size of the collection of fingers on the hand; in mathematical lingo, 5 is the 'cardinality' of that collection.

The size of a collection is represented by a number's cardinality, and that is in turn indicated by the final number's ordinality during a count of objects making up the collection. And it does not what the number is, if it is the same number that would be the final number assigned during a count, its ordinality represents the cardinality of the collection. In short, ordinality determines cardinality in a count.

Then too, cardinality also affects ordinality. Without differences in cardinality between collections counted, all ordinalities would be the same; they would all have the same count of elements. Cardinality (the size of a collection) can be used to determine the position (ordinality) that a numeral in a number scale falls into, and therefore cardinality can be used to fix ordinality for the number that ends the count of the objects in the collection—namely, the last position arrived at in the scale during the count. The bigger the collection counted, the greater the cardinality and therefore the higher the ordinality of the last number used from the number scale. So, these two concepts—cardinality and ordinality—are related. Just as ordinality (from a scale) determines cardinality, so too cardinality can be associated with ordinality (such as in a count).

Comparing the sizes of collections by count instead of by mapping or matching does not therefore change our definition of cardinality. If one collection has a longer count of objects than another, the collection with the longer count has more objects than the collection with the shorter count—this is merely confirmed by comparing collections and finding that the collection with the longer count will have objects left over when matched tit-for-tat with the objects in the collection of the shorter count [84]. The collection of fence posts counted up to 5 is larger than the collection of posts counted up to 4 because you can take each post in the 5-collection, pair it with a single post in the 4 collection, and still have one post left over. The number 5 assigned to a collection by count thus still represents a collection larger than does the number 4 when it is assigned to a collection by count.

Beyond using the simplest tally marks, enumerating anything depends on having a number scale. Even the earliest forms of tallying in Neolithic times seem to have involved a rudimentary number scale similar to the initial segment of the Roman numeral scale (I, II, III, etc.). Without a number scale, there might be tallying or counting for certain purposes, such as sorting collections, but there would be no enumeration in the form of counting up the members of a collection to determine its size. Number scales are essential for any form of enumeration we are interested in.

2.3.6 *Number Scales: Sets versus Series*

In standard set theory, double-struck capital letters ($\mathbb{N}$, $\mathbb{W}$, $\mathbb{Z}$, $\mathbb{Q}$, $\mathbb{R}$, etc.) are used to denote number systems as *sets* of numbers. Suppose we take $\mathbb{N}$ to be the set of only positive numbers used for counting, $\mathbb{W}$ to be the set both of the counting numbers and also zero (0), while $\mathbb{Z}$ is the set of both positive and negative numbers and zero, $\mathbb{Q}$ is the set of numbers that can be expressed as fractions, $\mathbb{R}$ is the set of those numbers that yield a positive result when multiplied by themselves, and so on. This isn't exactly spot-on for standard set theory, but close enough for our purposes.

The double-struck capital letters are not typically used in standard set theory to denote these various sets of numbers as number systems or 'number scales' *per se* because systems and scales imply ordinality (order) while sets are only about cardinality (size) regardless of ordinality. However, I disagree with the set theorists about the nature of such collections. Contrary to standard set theory, it is my position that number systems (number scales) do not form completed *sets* of numbers but instead are *series* of numbers that are always under further construction.

Assuming as much, we need to distinguish between two types of series: *closed series* and *open series*. Definitions:

- **closed series**: *a series formed by a succession that terminates.*
- **open series**: *a series formed by a succession without a determinate end.*

A closed series, once it terminates, can be considered a set. An 'open series', on the other hand, is not a set. Rather, an open series is a series that, if it depends on the action of some agent, may persist as long as the agent desires and if it does not depend on an actual agent, may even continue without ever ceasing—at least in principle (assuming there is no logical contradiction in the hypothetical scenario of continuing without ever ceasing). The open series has no 'determinate' end—that is, no quantitatively or mathematically specified end to the series, either in practice or also in principle.

An important distinction to keep in mind is that an open series is not a literally infinite series. An open series is simply a series with no pre-established end. This can mean one of two things.

On the one hand, an open series may be *provisionally* open—it eventually ends but its end is not preestablished or otherwise determined beforehand. Upon ending, the provisionally open series becomes a closed series (ergo, a set).

On the other hand, an open series may be *permanently* open—it continues without ever ceasing. The permanently open series is purely hypothetical: a series can, in principle, continue ceaselessly as long as there is no logical contradiction in doing so; whether it could also do so in practice as well as in principle depends on what properties the series possesses.

Regardless, an open series is not literally infinite because it is both never completed and it is never without limit per se to its quantity of elements. An open series is of a finite extension that continues to increase; it always has a "latest step" taken in the succession that stretches finitely back to the starting point of the series, rather than a succession that has no limit at all (including no limit that increases as the length of the series increases). So, an open series may be a series that continues to grow, but it is not literally *limitless*; at each step along the way, it is finite no matter how long it goes on.

So too, I propose each number scale is an open series in the sense that each is in practice provisionally open and, in principle, permanently open. There is in principle no end to the construction of a number scale, even if we cannot actually continue construction in practice.

It follows that being in principle permanently open does not necessarily entail number scales are literally infinite. Instead, number scales may just be open series in the sense that, even if the number of numbers in each scale continues to accumulate without ceasing, there will always be a finite number of numbers in each scale. The number scales are never both complete and limitless—never do they become literally infinite.

That is, at least, the view I support. However, I will try not to beg the question by offering further support for this view in § 2.3.7 below and as we investigate literal infinity in the chapters to come.

Regardless of whether the number scales are open series or infinite series, we do at least need some notation in order to express the distinction between the standard set-theoretic notation of number scales as infinite sets of numbers ($\mathbb{N}$, $\mathbb{W}$, $\mathbb{Z}$, $\mathbb{Q}$, $\mathbb{R}$, etc.) and the view I support that number scales are open series that always remain finite while under construction. With that in mind, I will borrow the double-struck capital letters from standard set theory but add a superscript 'clockwise gapped circle arrow' ($\circlearrowright$) next to each letter in order to represent each number system as an open series, an inherently incomplete number scale that is persistently under construction over time.

Thus, $\mathbb{N}^\circlearrowleft$, $\mathbb{W}^\circlearrowleft$, $\mathbb{Z}^\circlearrowleft$, $\mathbb{Q}^\circlearrowleft$, $\mathbb{R}^\circlearrowleft$, etc. denote number systems or number scales as incomplete, open series rather than as complete, closed sets. Each of these symbols will therefore be shorthand to denote series of numbers used as number systems or number scales, never complete, always being extended (at least in principle).

However, when I need to refer to these scales as they are regarded in standard set theory, I will revert to depicting them without the superscripted circle arrow ($\mathbb{N}$, $\mathbb{W}$, $\mathbb{Z}$, $\mathbb{Q}$, $\mathbb{R}$, etc.) and call them 'sets' instead of series, number systems or number scales.

2.3.7 *Constructing the Numbers Scales*

The numbers we have considered so far—those starting with 1 and proceeding on to 2, 3, 4, 5, etc. according to scale—are what we all know to be the same numbers used for counting objects. These numbers are, appropriately enough, the *counting numbers*. The symbol $\mathbb{N}^\circlearrowleft$ will denote the system of counting numbers, or *scale* of counting numbers, which most set theorists usually regard as a *set* of numbers. So, the collection of numbers used previously for counting the fence posts is the very same collection of counting numbers that defines $\mathbb{N}^\circlearrowleft$.

More accurately, the numbers depicted so far $(1, 2, 3, 4, 5)$ are numbers from an *initial segment* taken from the larger sequence of counting numbers, which is constructed over time as the ongoing *series* of natural numbers. Hence, the numbers 1–5 are just an initial segment in the extensible and growing sequence of $\mathbb{N}^\circlearrowleft$ since we all know there are more numbers to the scale of numbers that have already been commonly depicted and used for counting and conducting other mathematical operations. As a series, we N continues to grow as mathematicians define and depict larger numbers than have ever before been created and defined.

Numbers are both properties of numerals (ordinality-cardinality associations) and what we call numbers are numerals as symbols with ordinality and cardinality associations when in scale. But numerals are symbols, and symbols are inventions we create and define. So, the scale of $\mathbb{N}^\circlearrowleft$ only extends as far as anyone can (at least in principle) invent, or define, the numbers of $\mathbb{N}^\circlearrowleft$.

To understand the implications of this, suppose no one ever before used a number higher than 5; every quantity beyond that was just designated "many". In that case, $\mathbb{N}^\circlearrowleft$ would be defined only up to the number 5. The number 5 would be the highest counting number anyone would know. And in that situation, the last ordinal in $\mathbb{N}^\circlearrowleft$ would be the 5th position, corresponding to the last listed numeral, 5. Having the last ordinal of $\mathbb{N}^\circlearrowleft$, the numeral 5 would consequently indicate the cardinality of $\mathbb{N}^\circlearrowleft$ itself—five, and only five, counting numbers would exist in the scale of counting numbers.

To represent the cardinality of $\mathbb{N}^\circlearrowleft$—which is to say, the *series* $\mathbb{N}^\circlearrowleft$ at a given snapshot in time during its construction and so as an unfinished *set* at the time of consideration—I will use the vertical bars typically used for the 'absolute value' of a number and apply them to $\mathbb{N}^\circlearrowleft$ as a number system. Hence,

- Let $|\mathbb{N}^\circlearrowleft|$ represent the cardinality of $\mathbb{N}^\circlearrowleft$ as the set of existing natural numbers during a given moment in the ongoing construction of $\mathbb{N}^\circlearrowleft$ as a series.

A similar definition holds for any other number scale as an open series under construction. For example, the largest finite number for the number scale $\mathbb{W}^\circlearrowleft$ at any given time would also provide the cardinality for $\mathbb{W}^\circlearrowleft$ as such at that time, and which would be represented as $|\mathbb{W}^\circlearrowleft| = v$ where v is not just any whole number but instead is a placeholder for whatever the greatest whole number of $\mathbb{W}^C$ would be if we could determine it [85]. (As an aside, I would have used w for the variable whole number in $\mathbb{W}^C$, but w looks too much like ω, which the Greek small omega—a symbol for infinity to be discussed in § 5.4.8).

Since $|\mathbb{N}^C|$ represents $\mathbb{N}^C$ as having a cardinality, we can say $\mathbb{N}^C$, as a series of numbers under construction, has a "largest number" at any given time—namely, whatever is the largest number defined at the given time $|\mathbb{N}^C|$ is considered. Moreover, any collection of objects having no more elements than a number equal to $|\mathbb{N}^C|$ would share the same cardinality as $\mathbb{N}^C$ itself at that time. So, if at some time in the past 5 had been the largest number defined for $\mathbb{N}^C$, then it would have been the case that $|\mathbb{N}^C| = 5$ at that time (for no one would have yet defined a larger number than that). So, during that time any collection, X, that contained no more than 5 elements would at that time have had the same cardinality as $\mathbb{N}^C$. Thus, it would have been the case that $X = |\mathbb{N}^C| = 5$.

In the hypothetical fence post example, 5 was the last number used from $\mathbb{N}^C$ for counting and it matched the amount of fence posts, so there would then have been as many posts as counting numbers in existence. If, on the other hand, there are more objects, like fence posts or anything else, in a collection being counted than there are counting numbers, all we would need to do in order to count the left-over objects is extend the scale of counting numbers by defining new, larger numbers in the sequence of $\mathbb{N}^C$, making $\mathbb{N}^C$ longer in sequence in order to accommodate all the objects that need counting.

Now imagine the objects in a collection we wish to count are not fence posts, but rather are numerals in a collection of numerals (or perhaps they are numerals painted on fence posts, it doesn't really matter). Insofar as a numeral is a number, it may be used to enumerate. Insofar as a numeral is a numeral, it may be enumerated. In other words, we can use *numbers* to count *numerals*.

Now imagine also that the collection of *numerals* we wish to count is identical to the scale of counting *numbers* we have, but with an exception: someone has invented a new numeral with which to start off the sequence. The extra numeral that begins the sequence we wish to count is the numeral zero or 'naught' represented by a cipher: 0.

So, the collection of numerals we wish to count, when sequenced, would begin with 0 rather than with 1, and proceed through the sequence from there: 0, 1, 2, 3, 4, 5, etc. Let's denote this collection of numerals as the very same series of whole numbers: $\mathbb{W}^C$.

Now suppose we treat the numerals of $\mathbb{W}^C$ merely as objects to be counted. In that case, we would begin counting the numerals in $\mathbb{W}^C$ by listing each *numeral* in $\mathbb{W}^C$ with a *number* from the scale of numbers we typically use for counting, namely $\mathbb{N}^C$. Unlike $\mathbb{W}^C$, the sequence of $\mathbb{N}^C$ begins with 1 rather than 0, so we use 1 to begin counting the numerals of $\mathbb{W}^C$, starting with counting the first numeral in $\mathbb{W}^C$, which is the numeral 0. Using the numbers of $\mathbb{N}^C$ in sequence to count the objects of $\mathbb{W}^C$, we can continue to match each counting number in $\mathbb{N}^C$ to a single numeral in $\mathbb{W}^C$ as we count through the numerals:

numerals of $\mathbb{N}^C$ as *numbers* of $\mathbb{N}^C$		numerals of $\mathbb{W}^C$ as numerals of $\mathbb{W}^C$	
1	→	$\{0\}$	*One numeral counted.*
2	→	$\{0, 1\}$	*Two numerals counted.*
3	→	$\{0, 1, 2\}$	*Three numerals counted.*
4	→	$\{0, 1, 2, 3\}$	*Four numerals counted.*
5	→	$\{0, 1, 2, 3, 4\}$	*Five numerals counted.*
6	→	$\{0, 1, 2, 3, 4, 5\}$	*Six numerals counted.*

In using the numbers of $\mathbb{N}^C$ to count the numerals of $\mathbb{W}^C$, we find that we have to extend the scale of $\mathbb{N}^C$ by another number in order to count all the numerals we previously depicted for $\mathbb{W}^C$. So, we increased $\mathbb{N}^C$ from 5 to 6. The number 6 now occupies a new ordinality in $\mathbb{N}^C$—the 6th position—and because the 6th position is the last (latest) position of $\mathbb{N}^C$, 6 represents the new cardinality of $\mathbb{N}^C$ as a whole. Ergo, $|\mathbb{N}^C| = 6$. And as the last listed number of $\mathbb{N}^C$ was used for counting $\mathbb{W}^C$, which has no more numerals to count, 6 also exhausts the count of $\mathbb{W}^C$ at that time and so represents $|\mathbb{W}^C|$, the cardinality of $\mathbb{W}^C$. Hence, we can say that 6 represents the 'number of objects' in $\mathbb{W}^C$, with those objects being numerals themselves.

Here are the lessons of this hypothetical scenario:

- A sequence of numerals can be extended by creating new numerals and placing them in the sequence of numerals.

- The numerals placed in sequence each have an ordinality that can be associated with a unique cardinality, thus allowing the numerals to constitute *numbers* in a scale of numbers.

- We can therefore define new numbers in the scale(s) and use them for enumerating more objects when we run out of numbers with which to enumerate objects.

- Two scales do not have to have all the same numerals in order to share the same cardinality—the scales can be the same size in terms of the quantities of their constituent numerals if *all* the numerals can be paired tit-for-tat between the scales at a given time in which the scales are being constructed.

The foregoing also indicates that, like $\mathbb{N}^C$, the sequence of $\mathbb{W}^C$ constitutes not just a sequence of numerals but also a scale of *numbers*, since each numeral in $\mathbb{W}^C$ has the properties of both ordinality and cardinality associated together in their sequence.

The numerals in $\mathbb{W}^C$ obviously have ordinality. Given the scales *as represented above*, $\mathbb{W}^C$ has the same order of numerals as $\mathbb{N}^C$, aside from 0 in $\mathbb{W}^C$ and 6 in $\mathbb{N}^C$. The numerals in $\mathbb{W}^C$ are 6 as shown by a count using the numbers of $\mathbb{N}^C$. So, $|\mathbb{W}^C|$ and $|\mathbb{N}^C|$ have the same cardinality with respect to their numerals.

However, there are actually a couple of different cardinalities associated with $\mathbb{W}^C$ in terms of how it is represented in the comparison with $\mathbb{N}^C$ above. There is the cardinality of $\mathbb{W}^C$ as a *series of numerals* versus the cardinality of $\mathbb{W}^C$ as a *scale of numbers*. Cardinality is, after all, a property relative to the collections being compared.

As an open series of numerals, $\mathbb{W}^C$ has a cardinality of 6 at the time of measurement in the example given (hence, $|\mathbb{W}^C| = 6$ numerals), just as shown by matching the numerals of $\mathbb{W}^C$ to the counting numbers of $\mathbb{N}^C$. But as a scale of numbers, $\mathbb{W}^C$ has a cardinality representing the highest numerical value of *its own* scale, and that is 5; hence, $|\mathbb{W}^C| = 5$.

The reason $\mathbb{W}^C$ as a scale of numbers has a cardinality of 5 and not 6 is in terms of its own numbers is because of how the cardinalities of $\mathbb{W}^C$'s constituent numbers are defined. Notice that $\mathbb{W}^C$ starts with 0 rather than 1. The number 0 has a unique property not shared by any of the other numbers in either $\mathbb{W}^C$ or $\mathbb{N}^C$: 0 does not have the positive cardinality of an element, a cardinality of *at least* a single thing. Recall that cardinality is the relative size of a collection as given by matching the elements of that collection to the elements of another collection(s). We know that the cardinality of 1 represents a match of the numeral 1 to a single element, the cardinality of 2 represents a match of the numerals 1 *and* 2 to a pair of elements, and so on. So, what element does the cardinality of 0 match to? No elements at all; in fact, 0 *does not even match to* 0 *as a numeral*. The rest of the numbers in $\mathbb{W}^C$ point to actual elements; to at least a single if not multiple elements. Because 0 represents no element, or no collection containing an element, 0 adds nothing to the cardinality of $\mathbb{W}^C$ as a scale of numbers. That ensures the cardinality of $\mathbb{W}^C$ as a scale of numbers is one less than the cardinality of $\mathbb{N}^C$ as a scale of numbers. So, $\mathbb{W}^C$'s constituent non-zero numbers end up sharing the same cardinalities as the numbers comprising $\mathbb{N}^C$. And that means although there are six *numerals* in $\mathbb{W}^C$, the cardinality of $\mathbb{W}^C$ as a scale of *numbers* is still 5.

This is illustrated by defining each of the numbers of $\mathbb{W}^C$ by the earlier numbers in its own sequence. Since there are no numbers earlier in the sequence of $\mathbb{W}^C$ than 0, then 0 will be our only exception to the aggregation of cardinality from prior cardinalities for the scale of $\mathbb{W}^C$.

2.3.8 *Interlude About Nothing*

Before proceeding, we should clear up some things about zero (0).

Recall that numbers refer to sizes of sets. We know 1 corresponds to a singleton—a set of a single element. For example, $1 = \{1\}$, or $1 = \{0\}$, or $1 = \{x\}$, etc. Likewise, 2 corresponds to a pair of elements: $2 = \{1,2\}$, or $2 = \{0,1\}$, or $2 = \{x, y\}$, and so forth. So what does zero, 0, correspond to?

Nothing. Or you could say zero represents the empty set: $0 = \emptyset = \{\ \}$.

But now we seem to have a conceptual problem. If zero refers to a lack of something, such as to the emptiness of the empty set, then zero seems to correspond to a set without size. The empty set, after all, refers to a sizeless collection—at least where 'collection' or 'set' is the collection of that which acts as a container for other collections. The confusion settles in when we use zero to indicate a collection such as { } but { } indicates nothing with size and there is no such thing as a "sizeless collection" in the physical world. So, zero must refer to no collection at all, at least not in the physical world. And if it refers to no collection at all, a set of nothing, is zero even a number?

As pointed out by Dr. Michael Huemer, professor of philosophy at the University of Colorado, Boulder, "to have zero of something is simply to fail to have that thing...to have zero turtles is to have no turtles; to have zero liters of water is to have no water" [86]. From the fact that zero can correspond to no real-world, physical collection Huemer concludes zero must not be a number after all, at least not in the original sense of the term since number is a property only objects can have [87].

However, we need not go that far.

We can indeed consider zero to be a property of an object and even a number of sorts. A numeral is an object, and each numeral has 'number' as a property. Recall that a number is a numeral's unique ordinality-cardinality association in a numeral system. The numeral written in Arabic notation as *cipher* (0) also has the property of a unique ordinality-cardinality association in a numeral system. So, cipher has number as a property too. That number is zero. And since cipher is an object that has the number zero as its property, zero is indeed a number.

For zero to be a unique ordinality-cardinality association in a numeral system, we must be able to show what that association is. Zero as an ordinality does not present a problem since it designates cipher's first position in the system of whole numbers: 0, 1, 2, 3, ... That covers ordinality for zero. But what about cardinality?

It is true that cardinality is size, zero as a numeral symbolizes a condition in which there is no size to something, and so in that sense zero refers to no cardinality and so has no cardinality. That's why $\mathbb{N}^C$ and

$\mathbb{W}^C$ as scales of numbers can have the same cardinality for their *numbers* even though $\mathbb{W}^C$ has one more *numeral* (namely, cipher or 0) than $\mathbb{N}^C$ as a series of numerals under construction.

However, if we widen our conception of cardinality to denote *any outcome to a size measurement*, then in that loose sense zero does have a cardinality because zero refers to the outcome of a measure that is *less than* the size designated by the number 1. You can think of zero as having 'cardinality' as a measurement outcome held by an ordinal even when the ordinal is not positive: $0 < 1$.

So, we can still regard zero as a number in the respect of being the association of a unique ordinality (first whole number) with a unique cardinality (less than any positive whole number in the system of whole numbers). Zero can, with a charitable interpretation of cardinality, still fit our definition of a number.

Second, we can also regard zero as a property of another object—the empty set, { }. Zero is the property of something, such as the set of braces, being empty *instead of* containing an object or collection. If there is nothing between the pair of braces, there is nothing between the *set* of braces. That empty set has no collection of symbols between the braces that comprise the set and it is the presence of any symbols in the braces that non-zero numbers correspond to. Since the empty set contains no collection of symbols, that is why it is equal to zero. So, zero can indeed still be a number by being a property of an object—the object is the set of braces and zero is the property of the emptiness of that set as a container.

True, unlike other numbers, zero maps to nothing. Then again, we could say zero maps to the area that lacks the presence of something specific, like the area between braces lacking symbols or the emptiness of a box when we say the box contains zero objects. Unlike Huemer then, I do not see an inconsistency in saying that zero (0) is a number even though zero cannot be mapped to a physical object like a fence post or to a collection of objects like multiple fence posts.

Zero is still a property; it is the property of an object, such as a container, being empty. We simply regard zero as depicting the emptiness in the empty set—the emptiness between the pair of braces that contains no other symbols—or the emptiness of any physical container. And, of course, zero is the property of cipher as a number with a unique ordinality and as the indicator of a particular *measurement outcome* for size (cardinality, relative to other cardinalities). So, zero still qualifies as a number.

That covers zero as a number, but that still leaves zero as an index.

Huemer raises an interesting point: saying zero maps to a lack of something in the physical world might be taken as falsified when we say that "the Greenwich Observatory has a latitude of $0°$" because "this obviously does not indicate it fails to have latitude, nor that it lacks any other relative quality" [88]. Similarly, "a certain ice cube has a temperature of 0 °C. But this does not indicate that the ice cube lacks temperature, lacks heat, or lacks anything else relevant" [89]. Huemer also points out, however, that these are not uses of zero *as a number* but uses of zero *as a numeral* (e.g., cipher) for the purpose of indexing. This is a good distinction to keep in mind. We should avoid attempts to make zero *as a number* correspond to physical objects or collections of such; if zero, as a number, refers to any condition in the physical world, it refers to the condition of missing or lacking something as when a container lacks some relevant object.

With those caveats about zero attended to, we can return to the construction of number scales as extendible sets.

2.3.9 *Construction of Number Scales Continued...*

We now have zero representing no elements at all or representing the emptiness of the empty set if you prefer, as the base of $\mathbb{W}^C$. Further construction of $\mathbb{W}^C$ proceeds by defining the number 1 in $\mathbb{W}^C$ as representing only a single object, the sole element of the singleton. We had also defined the number 1 in $\mathbb{N}^C$ as representing only a single element, but let's define 1 in $\mathbb{W}^C$ as representing a single element in a different way than we defined 1 in $\mathbb{N}^C$. Rather than having the number 1 representing the numeral 1 as it does in $\mathbb{N}^C$, for $\mathbb{W}^C$ let's define 1 as still representing a single element, but it will represent the numeral (vice number) we already defined in $\mathbb{W}^C$: the numeral 0. So, for $\mathbb{W}^C$, we thus define $1 = \{0\}$ where the 0 in the brackets indicates 0 *as a symbol*. That is, in the scale of $\mathbb{W}^C$, the number 1 is equal to a set having only one element—the numeral known as cipher and denoted 0.

We can continue to define the higher *numbers* by reference to sets of the lower *numerals* using the same process [90]. So, we define the numbers in $\mathbb{W}^C$ as follows:

$$0 = \{\ \}$$
$$1 = \{0\}$$
$$2 = \{0, 1\}$$
$$3 = \{0, 1, 2\}$$
$$4 = \{0, 1, 2, 3\}$$
$$5 = \{0, 1, 2, 3, 4\}$$

Notice that each non-zero number in $\mathbb{W}^C$ still corresponds to a 'set' (pair of braces) the numeral contents of which have the same cardinality as the same number in $\mathbb{N}^C$. Now that we have our numbers in the scale of $\mathbb{W}^C$ defined, we see that, although there are more than five numerals in $\mathbb{W}^C$ due to the inclusion of 0, the cardinality of $\mathbb{W}^C$ as a scale of *numbers* is still equal to 5 since the number 5 is equal to the set of *numerals* 0–4 in the scale of $\mathbb{W}^C$. Moreover, just as with $\mathbb{N}^C$, we can match the numbers in $\mathbb{W}^C$ to corresponding sets of numerals or other elements, like our fence posts, with the only exception being 0 since it represents the empty set but not an element [91]:

Although the numbers shared by $\mathbb{N}^C$ and $\mathbb{W}^C$ are defined differently with respect to the *numerals* in their scales, the *numbers* in $\mathbb{N}^C$ and non-zero numbers in $\mathbb{W}^C$ refer to the same sizes of *numeral sets*. Hence, the shared numbers of $\mathbb{N}^C$ and $\mathbb{W}^C$ both have the same cardinality and so refer to the same sizes of collections measured in the physical world (real sets):

$\underline{\mathbb{N}^C \text{ defined}}$		$\underline{\mathbb{W}^C \text{ defined}}$		$\underline{\text{real sets}}$
		$0 = \{\ \}$		
$1 = \{1\}$	→	$1 = \{0\}$	→	
$2 = \{1, 2\}$	→	$2 = \{0, 1\}$	→	
$3 = \{1, 2, 3\}$	→	$3 = \{0, 1, 2\}$	→	
$4 = \{1, 2, 3, 4\}$	→	$4 = \{0, 1, 2, 3\}$	→	
$5 = \{1, 2, 3, 4, 5\}$	→	$5 = \{0, 1, 2, 3, 4\}$	→	
⋮				

Although $\mathbb{N}^{C}$ is the scale of counting numbers, we can likewise use $\mathbb{W}^{C}$ to count the numerals of $\mathbb{N}^{C}$ just as we used $\mathbb{N}^{C}$ to count the numerals of $\mathbb{W}^{C}$. But in so doing we find some key differences to counting with $\mathbb{N}^{C}$.

For example, remember that we had previously defined $\mathbb{N}^{C}$ up to 6, but $\mathbb{W}^{C}$ only up to 5. So, in using $\mathbb{W}^{C}$ to count $\mathbb{N}^{C}$, we would have a count only of $\mathbb{N}^{C}$'s first 5 numerals:

$\underline{\mathbb{W}^{C}}$		$\underline{\mathbb{N}^{C}}$
0		
1	→	1
2	→	2
3	→	3
4	→	4
5	→	5
		6

In order to count all of $\mathbb{N}^{C}$ with the numbers of $\mathbb{W}^{C}$, we would have to extend the scale of $\mathbb{W}^{C}$ to include the number 6 just as we extended $\mathbb{N}^{C}$ to include 6. In so doing, we could use $\mathbb{W}^{C}$ to count the entire collection of $\mathbb{N}^{C}$:

$\underline{\mathbb{W}^{C}}$		$\underline{\mathbb{N}^{C}}$
0		
1	→	1
2	→	2
3	→	3
4	→	4
5	→	5
6	→	6

We also see another difference between using $\mathbb{N}^{C}$ and using $\mathbb{W}^{C}$ to count a collection: all the defined numbers of $\mathbb{N}^{C}$ can be used to count the depicted numerals of $\mathbb{W}^{C}$, but not all the defined numbers of $\mathbb{W}^{C}$ are used to count the depicted numerals of $\mathbb{N}^{C}$.

When we used $\mathbb{N}^{C}$ to count $\mathbb{W}^{C}$, we used every number in $\mathbb{N}^{C}$ to count every numeral of $\mathbb{W}^{C}$. We found that $\mathbb{N}^{C}$ and $\mathbb{W}^{C}$ had the same cardinality for their collection of numerals (they both had 6 numerals at the hypothetical time upon which those numerals were the greatest invented: $|\mathbb{N}^{C}| = |\mathbb{W}^{C}| = 6$), despite that their respective numerals had different corresponding ordinalities: $\mathbb{N}^{C}$'s highest numeral was 6 in 6th place while $\mathbb{W}^{C}$'s highest numeral was 5 in 6th place (and then once we extended $\mathbb{W}^{C}$ by adding a 6 to it as $\mathbb{N}^{C}$ has, then $\mathbb{W}^{C}$'s highest numeral became 6 in the 7th place of $\mathbb{W}^{C}$).

But if we use $\mathbb{W}^{C}$ to count $\mathbb{N}^{C}$, we do not use every number in $\mathbb{W}^{C}$ for counting all the numerals of $\mathbb{N}^{C}$. This is because we do not use 0 to count anything—0 can only refer to the empty set, $\emptyset$, since 0 does not match to the element of a set. And because $\mathbb{N}^{C}$ does not have a representation of the empty set ($\emptyset$), then 0 has no reference to a numeral or set in $\mathbb{N}^{C}$.

The use of $\mathbb{W}^{C}$ for counting thus shows that, while cardinality is a relationship of *matching* members between sets in order to ascertain their relative size, *counting* only indicates cardinality where *non-zero* numbers are used. Consequently, using $\mathbb{W}^{C}$ instead of $\mathbb{N}^{C}$ to count does not really differ in process. A count of the number of fingers on a hand still comes up with 5; each number matches no more than one finger on the hand—0 is matched to no fingers at all. But as most counts don't start with 0, we will stick with regarding $\mathbb{N}^{C}$ as the scale of counting numbers.

As another aside, not all mathematicians use the same set of symbols for these scales of numbers. That is because, in part, there is more than one system of mathematics. There is *general mathematics* (which includes elementary arithmetic, algebra, calculus, geometry, etc.) and then there is *transfinite mathematics* (or the *transfinite theory of numbers*) which overlaps with set theory. (Transfinite mathematics and the transfinite version of set theory together comprise the *transfinite system*—see also § 13.1).

Most mathematicians in the tradition of set theory, and especially the transfinite system, refer to the system of counting numbers not as a series, $\mathbb{N}^C$, but as a set: $\mathbb{N}$. In the transfinite system, $\mathbb{N}$ is the set of natural numbers. Any quantity that is 'transfinite' is a quantity greater than any natural number in $\mathbb{N}$ (that is, $\geq \mathbb{N}$); ergo, the transfinite is that which is a literally infinite quantity, yet not a quantity so great as to be equal to absolute infinity (see §§ 1.5, 25.3).

In general mathematics, there is also the system of whole numbers, which I denote as the series $\mathbb{W}^C$, but that is not standard notation. If the mathematician practicing standard set theory were to refer to the system of whole numbers as being distinct from the natural numbers, the mathematician would not denote the system of whole numbers as I do (i.e., $\mathbb{W}^C$) but rather as the set $\mathbb{W}$.

However, that too would be atypical since standard set theory and transfinite mathematics have a contrary tradition: the 'whole numbers' of general mathematics are instead referred to as 'natural numbers'. So, set theorists and those practicing the transfinite system do not typically refer to the whole numbers as such. Consequently, transfinite mathematicians and, more broadly, set theorists typically use $\mathbb{N}$ to symbolize the set of counting numbers along with zero instead of using the symbol $\mathbb{W}$.

In fact, they don't make much use of the natural numbers as 'counting numbers' and so do not often refer to this number scale without zero. In standard set theory, you won't tend to find references to 'the whole numbers' at all and you probably won't see the symbol $\mathbb{W}$ for that reason.

But I prefer a more classical approach, and so I'll break with the tradition of transfinite mathematics and standard set theory by defining the natural numbers as *the scale of counting numbers*, which starts with the number 1 and proceeds incrementally in sequence. I will therefore use the symbol $\mathbb{N}^C$ for the scale of natural numbers as only the counting numbers, beginning with number 1. I will also keep the scale of whole numbers as beginning with zero, which is then succeeded by the sequence corresponding to that of the natural numbers. Hence, the whole numbers shall still be denoted by $\mathbb{W}^C$, just as we used previously.

Historically, $\mathbb{N}^C$ (the number scale, not the symbol) was invented first, followed much later by the invention of zero and its assignment in the same scale (i.e., $\mathbb{W}^C$). But set theorists have shown that a number system such as the system of natural numbers can be formed entirely from scratch by use of a mathematical technique known as the 'successor function'.

The word 'successor' is just what it sounds like, and in mathematics a 'function' is a rule-based relation between a set of inputs and a set of outputs with the property that each input is related to a single output. Numbers go into the function and new numbers come out expressing the size of the collection.

The successor function can be used to generate all the numbers starting with zero and proceeding to ever larger ordinality and cardinality.

To understand the successor function, start by considering a set, W, as containing a single element. We will denote the element as v (as consistent with § 2.3.7). We'll use the letter S for "successor of" and the symbol ∪ for the union of two sets. Set theorists might express the successor function this way: the *successor* of set W is the set $S(v) = v \cup \{v\}$.

From the application of this principle, we get a sequence of W sets. Considering numerals to be symbols for sets, we can apply the successor function as $S(v) = v + 1$ to numerals and thereby generate all the numbers—natural and whole—previously defined [92].

If we further consider W to be an initial instance of $|\mathbb{W}^C|$, then we can express the same thing this way:

a. Let v be a whole number in the sequence of the scale $\mathbb{W}^C$.
b. Let 0 (zero) be the first v in $\mathbb{W}^C$.
c. Let $0 = \{\,\} = \emptyset$ = all sets having no elements. There is only one such set: the empty set (or 'null set' in some systems).
d. If v is a whole number, then let its successor $(v + 1)$ equal the next whole in sequence.
e. $(v + 1) = n$.
f. Let n be a natural number in the sequence of the scale $\mathbb{N}^C$.
g. Now repeat steps d through f to the sequence begun with conditions a-c.

The procedure can be represented like so:

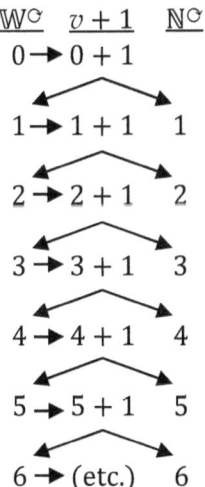

$$\begin{array}{ccc} \underline{\mathbb{W}^C} & v+1 & \underline{\mathbb{N}^C} \\ 0 \to & 0+1 & \\ 1 \to & 1+1 & 1 \\ 2 \to & 2+1 & 2 \\ 3 \to & 3+1 & 3 \\ 4 \to & 4+1 & 4 \\ 5 \to & 5+1 & 5 \\ 6 \to & (\text{etc.}) & 6 \end{array}$$

Or, just for short: 0, 0+1=1, 1+1=2, 2+1=3, 3+1=4, 4+1=5, 5+1=6, etc. Whatever number you leave off with, just add one to it and you can make the sequence of numbers one number bigger, whether for the whole numbers or the natural numbers.

As the process of using the successor function shows, our early ancestors could have started with the idea of the empty set, labeled it with 0 as the first whole number, and used the successor function to derive the scale of whole numbers, and therefore the scale of natural (or counting) numbers as a consequence. The ordinality of the highest natural number calculated (6) would still express not only the cardinality of the set of defined natural numbers {1–6} up to and including the latest natural number (6) derived but also the cardinality of the set of all the *numerals* {0–5} represented by the highest whole number (6) as well. So, the successor function preserves the logic of how numbers relate to one another in scale.

The use of the successor function to define the numbers from zero and up is not how numbers were originally invented. Our early ancestors in Central and Southern Africa started with the equivalent of natural or counting numbers, at first expressed as simple lines etched into tally sticks about 30–40,000 years ago, and no one fully developed the idea of zero as a number until around the 5th Century CE (Common Era) in India [93]. Even so, our early ancestors could have started with zero, had they the concept of an empty abstract set, and used some expression of the successor function to derive all the numbers from there based on sets of preceding numbers; only simple logic and a finitistic version of set theory are needed to provide us with the number scales. In fact, starting the scale at zero is the basis for how set theorists define 'sets' today. Alas, brilliant ideas always seem simple in hindsight.

Now, obviously, what I have so far labeled $\mathbb{N}^C$ and $\mathbb{W}^C$ are scales of numbers that do not actually end with the number 6. The portrayal of $\mathbb{N}^C$ as consisting only of the set {1–6} and $\mathbb{W}^C$ as consisting only of the set {0–6} was an example used to demonstrate a few points with respect to numerals in a number scale.

Namely, the following points:

- *A numeral's ordinality indicates its cardinality.* These properties of a numeral are purposively correlated with one another by virtue of a numeral's membership in a numeral system, and the interrelationship of a numeral's ordinality and cardinality in the system is precisely what makes the numeral constitute a *number* and the numeral system constitute a number system or, as I like to call it, a 'number scale'.

- *A numeral's cardinality represents sizes for sets that can be counted, at least in principle*—this includes mathematical sets of numerals or numbers.

- *New numerals, and thus new numbers, can be invented.* The number scales extend only so far as numerals and their numbers are, or can be, invented by following mathematical operations such as the successor function.

Having these points established, we can begin to consider the continued construction of $\mathbb{N}^C$ and $\mathbb{W}^C$. These scales can be extended as far as we like, even *indefinitely* (whether they can be extended *infinitely* is another issue). Consequently, each new extension of the scales makes $\mathbb{N}^C$ and $\mathbb{W}^C$ into new sequences of numbers that replace the previous, shorter versions of $\mathbb{N}^C$ and $\mathbb{W}^C$. As we all know, the scales of $\mathbb{N}^C$ and $\mathbb{W}^C$ have each been extended beyond 5 to include more numbers, like 6, 7, 8, 9, and so forth for $\mathbb{N}^C$ and 7, 8, 9, etc. for $\mathbb{W}^C$.

Let's suppose only numbers up to 9 have been invented so far. Let's also consider $\mathbb{N}^C$ and $\mathbb{W}^C$ not as series but instead as primitive *sets* of numbers ($\mathbb{N}$ and $\mathbb{W}$) with only the numbers depicted so far. At first, $\mathbb{N}$ was {1–6}, but it was extended to the sequence {1–9} with the invention of 7, 8, and 9 while the first instance of $\mathbb{W}$ was {0–6} but was then extended to the sequence {0–9}. In which case, we could say that $\mathbb{N}$ as {1–9} has replaced $\mathbb{N}$ as {1–6} while $\mathbb{W}$ as {0–9} has replaced $\mathbb{W}$ as {0–6}. With the scales of numbers becoming extended, we see the scales as larger sets of numbers replacing smaller sets of numbers. Hence, number systems, or number scales, need not be regarded as the complete sets ($\mathbb{N}$ and $\mathbb{W}$) after all. Rather, the systems of the naturals and wholes can instead be considered as extendable *series of sets* of numbers. It is this construction process of building new, larger sets of numbers from what were smaller sets of numbers that shows the number scales can be regarded as extensible, open series of numbers ($\mathbb{N}^C$ and $\mathbb{W}^C$).

As we continue to construct new numbers for these scales, we begin to see that the successor function alone is not sufficient for showing us how to invent and represent ever higher numbers on the number scale because, each time you need to depict a new higher number on the scale, you need a new symbol for doing so. And, clearly, creating a unique digit for every number that could be invented is not a very practical way to build a number scale and ever greater sets of numbers.

Instead, combining digits together from the Arabic base digits (0, 1, 2, 3, 4, 5, 6, 7, 8, 9) into different combinations is far more advantageous than concocting ever new symbols for numeral digits of greater scale. Ancient mathematicians learned to combine the base digits in a 'positional system' of numbers along with the successor function to represent ever higher numbers like 10, 11, 12, and so forth, up to higher numbers. When unique two-digit combinations run out, as when we reach 99, we can repeat the positional system of numbers and use the successor function to extend the two-digit combinations to three-digit combinations, moving from 99 to 100, 101, 102, etc. In short, just think of the highest number you can, and you can always use the positional system and successor function to make a new number with a value of one number bigger.

Hence, building the scales of $\mathbb{N}^C$ and $\mathbb{W}^C$ with the positional system and successor function applied to the Arabic base numerals shows that the single digits of the lower numerals can be combined into ever-larger sequences of digits to form ever-larger numbers (e.g., 1,001 and 1,002 and 1,003, ...). Once the scales of $\mathbb{N}^C$ and $\mathbb{W}^C$ are *under construction* using such techniques, ever higher numbers in the scale can be created by just this procedure.

Combining digits is useful for forming new numerals and thereby representing new numbers in a number scale; consequently, combining digits is also useful for enumeration, which is simply the assignment of numbers to collections. Ever-higher numbers on the scale, with ever more digits, represent ever-larger collections of numerals, and so can be used to represent ever-larger collections of objects to be measured.

2.3.10 *Calculation and Computation*

The simplest way to assign numbers to collections is to enumerate the members of the collections by tallying or counting. But tallying and counting are best used for collections that are relatively small. For large collections, there are easier ways to enumerate. In contrast to counting the objects of a collection by listing them one by one, we may instead *calculate* the size of the collection.

To *calculate* is to use a function for outputting a number that can be assigned to a collection. Use of the successor function is an example of calculation in which there is one input (a single digit) and one output (the next number higher). More complex calculations involving addition, multiplication, etc. make the job of enumeration much simpler for large collections.

We might also *compute* the size of the collection, where 'compute' simply means to use an effective procedure, such as an algorithm, for counting or calculating. Depending on the kind and size of collection, calculating and computing are often quicker and easier than counting the objects individually.

We all know the basic operations of elementary arithmetic which allow us to calculate or compute with numbers, so we don't need to explore that subject here. The important thing to note is that we build the scales of numbers to enumerate collections of objects in the world, collections of concepts and ideas, and even collections of numbers themselves—anything we can consider a collection or group of 'objects' can be enumerated. And as we construct higher numbers with which to enumerate objects and collections, numbers can be combined by various means of enumeration, from tallying to calculating to computing, in order to create a *total* that stands for the number of objects enumerated in a given collection.

2.3.11 *Total*

The term *total* can now be defined:

- total: *a number equal to an exact or approximate sum.*

A collection has a total if the elements in the collection can be numbered and the numbers are added together to give an exact sum. Other means of calculation can be used to yield a number equal to a total. For example, when numbers are multiplied together, the result is a *product* rather than a sum, but the product is equal to a sum that could be produced by addition. In that sense, multiplying numbers of members together to account for all the members in a collection still produces a total. And, of course, we can represent a collection as being diminished or split up into smaller collections by subtracting or dividing the numbers that represent subsets of the collection in order to arrive at new totals, which are still exact sums of yet smaller numbers. In the context of subtraction, a total is an exact *difference* and in the context of division, a total is an exact *quotient*. Products, differences, and quotients may all be considered as different kinds of totals which are all equivalent to sums of elements.

2.3.12 *Totals for the Number Scale*

We can use various methods of enumeration to yield totals for numbers on the number scale itself. After all, each number higher than 1 in the scale of natural numbers is equal to a sum of previous numbers [94]:

$\underline{N}^{\circ}$
$1 = 1$
$2 = 1 + 1$
$3 = 2 + 1$
$4 = 3 + 1$
$5 = 4 + 1$
$6 = 5 + 1$
$\vdots$

(And of course, for each number higher than 2 in the natural numbers there is more than one way to sum lower natural numbers into higher natural numbers.) The higher we develop the scale of natural numbers, the higher the sums of all numbers developed and the more combinations of sums equal the largest numbers.

Moreover, the higher the sums of the numbers in the scale, the higher the *total* number of numbers in the number scale. If 7 were the highest number ever invented, 7 would be the total of the number scale itself; if 8 were the highest number ever invented, then 8 would be the total of the number scale; if 9 were the highest number ever invented, then 9 would be the total of the number scale; and so on, up to the highest number invented to date. With, of course, each highest total reached to date exceedable tomorrow.

As each new, higher natural number is invented, the natural number scale gains a new, higher total of numbers. Number scales are not 'sets' of numbers that are finished once and for all. Rather, number scales are inherently temporal *series* of numbers with a total number of numbers that grows over time.

We need to therefore make a distinction between two different kinds of total: a *standing total* and a *running total*:

- standing total: *a total that is constant—a total that is the final total for a collection.*

- running total: *a total that is continually revised to take account of members added to or deducted from the collection for which a total is calculated—a total that continuously increases or decreases in value.*

Number scales, as inventions, are series of numbers, each of which has a running total equal to the highest number so far conceived at the given time for that series. Scales like $\mathbb{N}^C$ and $\mathbb{W}^C$ are ever under construction with new, running totals that increase in value with the continuous invention of numbers.

2.3.13 *Calculating Totals for a Number Scale*

We can, of course, use various mathematical means to extend the scale of natural numbers in order to have numbers that can be used to enumerate any collection we come across in the real world, provided we have a means of determining how much is in the collection. Since we started by defining 0–9 as the base numbers, we can extend the scale by repeated use of zero to create a scale by tens: 10, 20, 30, ... We can use operations like addition, multiplication, exponentiation, and so on to create yet higher numbers [95]. Take the use of exponents. To represent the number of times that 10 is multiplied by itself, we can use an exponent—a number represented in superscript next to the base number (in this case, 10) as in 10^2, which represents a 1 followed by two zeros (100): a hundred. Either through multiplying ten by itself repeatedly or through using exponents we can arrive at increasingly large numbers—thousand (10^3), million (10^6), billion (10^9), and so on. These and other techniques (see §§ 4.26–4.2.9) allow us to build the number scale with ever-higher numbers, unto the exhaustion of our resources.

2.3.14 *Values and Variables*

There must be some "highest number" invented to date, but whatever number we name, we can't be certain someone hasn't exceeded it. We can say that there must be such a number, but we do not necessarily know its mathematical *value*.

The concept of mathematical 'value' is key to understanding quantity, for quantity was defined as an amount of objects, and 'amount' was defined as a value equal to a total. We know what a total is. But what is a 'value'?

We often encounter situations in which we don't know how much is in a collection (like the number of trees in an orchard) but we do know how much is in some of the subsets in the collection (like the number of trees in one row and the number of rows). If we know how much is in each of the subsets of a collection, we can perform a calculation to capture the size of the entire collection with a number (like the number of trees multiplied by the number of rows for the total number of trees). When we seek to find a number for the total of the collection, we are using some known numbers for subsets to determine the mathematical value that will represent the collection as a total.

In mathematics the term 'value' has many meanings, especially when used in combination with other terms; there is *place value*, *absolute value*, etc. When I use the term 'value' in a mathematical context I mean a numerical value:

- value: *a constant number that can be specified*.

This definition for value has two terms that need elucidating: 'constant number' and 'specified'. Let's take a look at each. First, let's start with what it means to 'specify':

- specify: *to identify, refer to, or describe a distinct object*.

The term 'distinct' should also be defined:

- distinct: *able to be distinguished as different from other objects of reference*.

To specify is to refer to one thing in particular as opposed to something else in particular. In this sense, one way to specify a number is to identify or refer to a particular number, like 5, as opposed to any other particular number, like 2 or 3. I will begin by using the term 'specify' in this sense (which is similar but a bit different from how mathematicians use the term 'determine'.)

There are different senses of the term 'constant'—I will use the term here in its mathematical sense to mean a *constant number*, which is a numeral that has a *specific* ordinality and cardinality in a number scale. Any given number identified by a specific numeral in a number scale is a 'constant number'. Some examples: 0, 1, 2, 13, 502, or any others that do not increase or decrease in digits, or swap some digits for others, may all be considered constants.

A 'value', then, is simply a constant number that is specified, or distinctly referred to, from other numbers.

Suppose we know a collection has a cardinality larger than a second collection, but smaller than a third collection, but we don't know how many members make up the collection. In such cases, we sometimes speak in very general terms of 'large' or 'small' numbers without specifying exactly what number we mean; we don't use a particular numeral for designating the number of members in the collection. Sometimes we don't even know what general cardinality a number should have—whether large or small. When we refer to a number but cannot specify what constant it is, we refer to the number as a *variable*. Basically, *unspecified* numbers are called 'variables'. More precisely:

- variable: *a symbol representing an unspecified, but specifiable, number*.

The symbol for a variable represents only a number in an abstract, general sense rather than in the particular sense of a 'constant' number. The symbols used for variables are placeholders that represent these unspecified numbers. Mathematicians often use letters, upper or lower case, in distinct fonts for variables. For instance, a lower case 'x' can be used to represent a variable—an unspecified number. If we want to represent a different, but still unspecified number, we can use a different variable, like 'y'.

A variable represents an unspecified, perhaps unknown, number. However, a variable such as x or y could be given a value of 0 or 1 or 2 or 3 or any other constant number. To determine a constant number that can be used in place of a variable is to determine a 'value' for the variable.

Regardless of the particular numbers we plug into the equation for y and x, these same variables can also be used in a variety of expressions because the values assigned to those variables can *vary* from one mathematical expression to another—hence the term 'variable'.

This is an important distinction: a variable is not necessarily a number representing a value that changes over time like a bank account balance. Some variables can represent values that change over time but not all variables represent values that change with time. Rather, the term 'variable' only means a generic symbol that may have one value in one expression, a different value in another expression. So, variables may represent values that change in time, but need not—it is their use that changes.

We can use variables in a variety of circumstances. For instance, perhaps we have a collection of gemstones, but we don't know how many gemstones there are in the collection. We want to find out the *total* of the collection. But the total is an unknown, and therefore unspecified, number. Hence, we have no constant number to represent the total number of gemstones and so the collection's total can only be represented by a variable. In order to find out what the total must be, we need to remove uncertainty about what 'value' the collection needs to be given for an accurate measurement. That means we need to remove the variable that labels the collection in terms of its size and replace the variable with a constant number that accurately designates a total for the collection's members.

Variables are used throughout mathematics, such as in mathematical equations. In expressions like equations, variables are positioned where constant numbers are needed in order to complete the expression while no constant numbers are presented. For example, take the equation $y = 2x - 3$. We need to specify what the values for y and x must be to make the equation a complete and understandable expression. Not just any constant numbers will do for values; we need specific constants that make the expression consistent. In mathematical expressions like the equation $y = 2x - 3$, the variables are removed by identifying constant numbers that can replace the variables without losing consistency in the expression.

Mathematicians often make a distinction between 'free variables' and 'bound variables', but such a distinction will not be needed for our purposes.

The process of replacing variables with constants is what is meant by specifying values for variables. When the variable is replaced by a constant number, the constant number is identified or 'specified' for the variable. When we can specify constants to replace y and x, and those constants give us a consistent expression, we will have found 'values' for y and x—values that y and x should have in the equation to make the equation a consistent expression. If the replacement results in a consistent expression, the expression is 'solved'.

2.3.15 *Specifying Values for Variables*

Now I need to make a caveat: as I said, to specify a number is to identify or refer to a particular number as opposed to identifying some other number. This is true, but not the whole story because that kind of specifying is distinguishing between constant numbers *already known*; specifying a constant number for a *variable* is a bit different than merely drawing a distinction between known constants.

One way that values are specified for variables is by applying mathematical functions or operations on the variables that *replace* the variables with constant numbers in the mathematical equation. It is in this manner that the rules for mathematical operations, when properly implemented, allow the calculator—whether person or machine—to specify a value for a variable. 'Specifying' a value is, in this sense, *assigning* a value to a variable rather than discovering a value that is "already there" in disguise as the variable.

For example, in the equation $5 = 2x - 3$, the term x is the variable, the value for which we need to specify in order to solve the equation. Applying the rules of algebra, the variable x can be replaced by the constant number 4. As we identify x to be 4—more precisely, replace x with 4—we then solve the equation: $5 = 2(4) - 3$, which is correct. So in this case, we can 'specify' that 4 is the constant number to be identified in place of the variable x, and this is simply to show that 4 is the 'value' for x. Similarly, in an equation such as $3 \times 2 = x$, a value for x can be specified or 'solved for' by applying the operation of multiplication to 3 and 2. The operation identifies 6 as the correct value to assign for x. It is the operation's *assignment* of the constant numeral 6 to x, or again more precisely, the *replacement* of x with 6, that makes x 'identical' to 6 as when it is expressed, $x = 6$.

2.3.16 *Specifying with the Grammar of Mathematics*

When identifying values for variables, mathematicians sometimes describe the result with statements like, "The value of x is 6." We must be careful not to misunderstand this way of speaking; we don't specify the value of a variable the same way we specify the identity of a person.

When I ask for the name of a company's Chief Executive Officer (CEO), there really is someone specific in that role even though I do not know who the CEO is. When I seek the value of a variable, on the other hand, it is not necessarily true that the variable already has a value I don't know about. In the former case, the 'variable' (the CEO) is actually a particular individual (like, say, Alice) all along; in the latter case, the variable (x) is *assigned* a particular identity (6); that is, the variable is *replaced by* a numeral, such as 6, in the process of a mathematical operation. So, it was not that x was really 6 all along the way that the CEO was really Alice all along. Specifying 6 to be x is thus not like specifying that Alice is the CEO.

This would be more straightforward if our use of natural language were more precise. Part of the confusion is a consequence of grammar with respect to mathematics. Once we understand the grammar of mathematics, the confusion dissolves.

We can take an expression like "The value of x is 6" as short for a longer statement: "According to the mathematical rules, the value of x is 6." Expressing x's value this way implies that x gets its value of 6 upon execution of rules, which is correct, rather than x having been 6 all along, which is not correct.

Then too, consider that some sentences of declarative form are actually imperative sentences. For example, the sentence "We're finished" is declarative in form, but in function it can be imperative, as when "We're finished" means "Stop talking." So too, a sentence like, "According to the mathematical rules, the value of x is 6," or more briefly, "The value of x is 6," may be declarative in form but imperative in function. In fact, sometimes mathematicians use imperatives like, "Let the value of x be 6" (though imperatives like these are usually a part of mathematical proofs). So, "The value of x is 6" can be taken as an imperative expression with a meaning such as, "6 *shall be* the value *for x*," rather than implying 6 was really the value *of x* all along. The variable x shall be 6 because the variable x *must*, by the deductive constraints of mathematical rules, be assigned the value 6 in order to *create* a consistent mathematical expression and so to make an accurate claim about the number of elements in any collection x refers to.

The longer way of speaking ("According to the mathematical rules, the value of x is 6,") or the imperative way of speaking, "6 shall be the value for x," is much clearer in intent than the briefer way of speaking—"The value of x is 6." Part of the confusion is with our use of the English words like 'is' and 'of' in place of words like 'shall' and 'for'. The sentence "6 *shall* be the value *for x*" implies that we use a mathematical operation to assign a specific identity to a variable that has no identity of its own, while to say instead, "The value *of x is* 6," might be mistaken to imply that x was really 6 all along, we just didn't know it before we solved the equation, which isn't necessarily the case, especially if no one wrote the equation with the intention that x would be 6. However, saying 6 'is' the value 'of' the variable can mean instead that 6 is the only number x can be because the mathematical rules do not allow x to be replaced by any other number. And that is perfectly accurate to imply. Since using 'of' rather than 'for' can be misleading, however, saying 'for' is simply more precise.

We need not worry about correcting each other's grammar with regard to variable identity as long as we realize that specifying the value 'of' a variable does not necessarily mean the variable has an unknown value in the sense of having one, lying undiscovered before anyone assigns a value to it. We should just remember that are really specifying a value *for* the variable.

2.3.17 *Unspecified Isn't Always Unspecifiable*

Though a variable simply as such is an *unspecified*, abstract number—a mere x or y for instance—a variable is never absolutely *unspecifiable*. Every variable is at least in principle *able* to be specified, even if it is not in practice specified. That's not to say every variable is specifiable in practice; there may be some that we cannot actually assign a number to. But even if we cannot do so in practice, a variable is nevertheless a number able to be specified in principle.

So even if no one actually assigns, or due to lack of computing power can actually assign, a value to x, we can still give x a value if circumstances were different, and that possibility is what makes the variable x a 'number', albeit an unspecified number. In other words, if a given variable represents a total for a collection, it represents a (relatively) specifiable—though not necessarily a specified—number.

Hence if a variable, like x, is used for representing a total, then x must be specifiable as a constant number. We must be able, at least in principle, to solve for x even if we can't really do it in practice. If we can solve for x, if we can find a constant value for a total, then we have an 'amount' of something.

2.3.18 *'Finding' and 'Having' Amounts*

There are yet more ways natural language plays a role in expressing mathematics. Math isn't always a matter of speaking literally.

Sometimes we say we will "find the amount" of something when we enumerate, but we don't literally "find" an amount of something because things in the real world don't have amounts the way they have parts; collections don't have amounts you can find the way you would find objects.

As a mathematical value, an amount is an invention we use for the purposes of measurement, especially when we need to enumerate the size of a collection. When we say that we "find" an amount "of" something, that's really a figure of speech—a way of stating that the collection we measure is labeled with an amount as a result of the measurement; what we're actually doing is using numbers as descriptive tools to *assign* amounts *to* collections, rather than using numbers for discovering amounts as if they are features of nature.

To say, for instance, that Earth has x amount of sand is really to say that there is some specifiable number we can assign to the collection of all grains of sand on Earth. Or to say there is x amount of stars in a galaxy is to say that there is some specifiable constant number that we can accurately assign to the collection of stars in the galaxy as its current variable total. It is not really to say that the collection of sand grains or collection of stars as such has some property called an 'amount'. (In fact, no collection *literally* has this property unless we're talking about a collection of numbers.) Rather, we often speak *metaphorically* as if such collections "have" an amount as an intrinsic property we can "find."

The metaphor is useful because saying that there is an amount of something, like an amount of sand grains on Earth, or an amount of stars in the Milky Way Galaxy, is to imply that we could, in principle at least, calculate a constant number and assign that number for representing the size of the collection. Even if that number can't be specified—even if we can't know the "value of x" or, more precisely, assign an accurate "value for x" in practice—we could at least do so in principle.

If we could enumerate the sand grains or stars to come up with a total, we could then apply that number to the collection of stars for a match between the number's cardinality and the size of the collection; the value for x amount of stars would fit the collection. It doesn't really matter that for practical reasons we cannot actually count all the stars in a galaxy or all the grains of sand on every beach on Earth. If those stars or sand grains were not to move about, and if we had enough time and interest to do so, we could count them. These are examples of collections that are countable in principle even if they are not countable in practice, so such collections do "have" amounts in a figurative sense, albeit variable (unspecified) amounts that in practice we may only be able to estimate.

For a collection of something to have an 'amount' is for the collection to have a value representing the relative size of the group of objects making up the collection. The amount assigned to the collection is a value (a specified, constant number) equal to a total, which is a number equal to an exact sum of enumerated objects in the collection.

We now have an explication for the term 'amount,' defined as a "value equal to a total." An amount is a particular, constant number that we can specify as an *exact sum* of objects in a collection.

2.4 QUANTITY MADE CLEAR

From the foregoing analysis, we now have a better idea of what the word 'quantity' means when defined even so simply as "an amount of objects." A quantity is an amount (*a logically and mathematically possible value equal to a total*) of objects (*where 'object' denotes anything of which a subject can be aware*). Hence, in more precise terms, a quantity is a logically and mathematically possible value equal to a total of anything of which a subject can be aware.

2.4.1 *The Definition of Quantity and its Implied Self-Reference*

An 'object' is anything we can be aware of. But we can be aware of numbers. So, those too would qualify as 'objects'. Since a quantity is a logically and mathematically possible value equal to a total of objects, and numbers are objects, then there are quantities of numbers as well as quantities of other objects. To have a quantity of numbers shows the self-referential nature of mathematics, for quantities are expressed in numbers, the objects of mathematics. To have a quantity of numbers is to have a number of numbers.

But do not worry: this self-reference is not vicious. We saw earlier how we can consistently use numbers even for counting numbers, as in the example of the natural numbers used for counting other numbers such as those in the scale of whole numbers. The self-reference implied by the concept of quantity is quite consistent, and it can even be useful.

2.4.2 *Quantity has Plurality in its Definition*

And yet, we need to be careful with such self-referential implications of our definitions so as to avoid any question begging. For example, notice as well how the definition of quantity refers to the plural of the word 'object'—a quantity is an amount of *objects*. But suppose there is only one object. If quantity is defined as an amount of *objects* (plural), then how can only one object be a quantity? That is, if there is only one object, how can there be an "amount of objects" (objects, plural) and so a quantity equal only to one (1)?

As indicated in § 2.2.1, this may be more of a linguistic problem than a philosophical one. Consider how the term 'amount' was defined: "a value equal to a total." A total is a number equal to an exact sum. Take the sum of 0 and 1, which is 1. There you have a collection of objects—the numbers 0 and 1—which together constitute more than one object (ergo, a plurality), and the value of those numbers when summed is the total of 1. Hence, 1 qualifies as a logically and mathematically possible value equal to a total—i.e., an amount; namely, the amount which is the total of 0 and 1 as mathematical objects. Even one object is thus "an amount of objects"—a quantity.

Another way of putting it is this: when we think of quantity as an amount of objects (plural) then, we should not think 'amount' *is* the objects; rather, we should think 'amount' is *from* the objects. An amount is a value equal to a total, which may be of only one object or of even none at all, as when we say a given total is equal to zero. The "amount of objects" (the quantity) can be one, or even none, as the *result* or *implication* of considering many possible objects. That is to say, quantity is derived from some process of *quantification* from a plurality—the plurality of *possible* objects we *consider* in our process of quantifying. So when we quantify, we are considering many but the quantity that results from the consideration may be multiple, singular, or even none.

While the definition of quantity ("an amount of objects") may refer to 'object' in the plural, there is no question-begging problem. We can continue to regard quantity as "an amount of objects" even if the quantity in question is one (1), as in one object, or zero (0), as in no object or objects. For quantity is an amount, and the amount in question is the *result* (value equal to a total) of considering a plurality and is not necessarily identical to the plurality considered. That is to say, a quantity is simply the answer to the question: how many?

2.4.3 *The Moral from Defining Quantity: Nested Assumptions*

As the foregoing, lengthy explication of quantity shows, even a simple, self-consistent definition assumes quite a bit. The definition of 'quantity' assumes the definition of *amount*, which assumes the definitions for *total* and *value*, both of which assume the definition of *number*, which assumes the concept of *numeral*, which assumes the ability to *enumerate* (match numerals as symbols to) *objects* in *collections*—a form of quantifying. This nesting of assumptions with respect to what we call 'quantity' is good to keep in mind for, as we'll see, many of the logical problems involved with the main topic of this book—infinity—are found in the assumptions underlying its very conception.

2.5 IMPLICATIONS OF QUANTITY FOR INFINITY

The definition of quantity has direct bearing on the concept of infinity. To be quantitatively infinite is to have a limitless quantity—a limitless amount of objects that can be enumerated. Since quantity assumes the ability to enumerate the objects in a collection, an infinite collection must in some respect have no limit to the enumeration of its objects.

2.5.1 *Enumeration Without Limit*

To say a collection is somehow limitlessly enumerable may have more than one meaning. For there are two different notions of quantitative infinity—the literal sense and the figurative sense.

Literal infinity is the condition of being both complete and limitless in quantity. Figurative infinity is the condition of indefinitely changing in quantity, which implies inherent incompleteness.

So, if a collection is quantitatively infinite, it either has a completed enumeration that expresses a *complete* quantity of objects despite their limitlessness (literal infinity) or the collection must have its members indefinitely enumerated to ever-larger totals, the collection always being *incomplete* in quantity with the enumeration of its members never complete but instead continuing to grow through time "without limit" (figurative infinity).

2.5.2 *Limitless Quantity as a Problematic Concept—Trouble for Infinity*

The case against infinity is, in part, the case that a collection cannot be quantitatively limitless—either in the sense of lacking a quantitative limit while nevertheless being complete or in the sense of lacking a quantitative limit by virtue of being incomplete in quantity. As we'll see in the pages to come, the former implies logical self-contradictions; the latter is simply a misleading characterization of progressions that always remain finite. Either way, quantitative infinity will be shown to be an inconsistent concept.

CHAPTER 2 IN REVIEW

- ❖ The case against infinity is mainly a case that infinity, as a *quantitative* concept, is either inconsistent or logically incoherent.
- ❖ Since infinity concerns quantity, a definition of quantity is needed for conceptual clarity.
- ❖ Quantity is defined simply as "an amount of objects," which, if more than one, may exist together in a collection.
- ❖ If a given collection is conceived of as having, either figuratively or literally, a *limitless* amount of objects, then the collection is infinite.
- ❖ The case against infinity is therefore mainly an argument that a collection consisting of a limitless amount of objects is at best an inconsistent notion and at worst a logically incoherent concept.

3: QUANTITIES COMPLETE AND INCOMPLETE

A literally infinite collection is not just a collection that is limitless in quantity, it is also *complete* in quantity. Conversely, because a figuratively infinite collection is an indefinitely changing series, it is intrinsically *incomplete* in quantity because it never has a standing total of members no matter how much it grows.

But what are *completeness* and *incompleteness*, particularly with respect to collections having quantity? I will attempt an answer to this question with the aim of providing a clearer understanding of both literal infinity and figurative infinity.

3.1 ON DEFINING COMPLETENESS AND INCOMPLETENESS

How should completeness and incompleteness be defined? Dictionaries provide at least two types of definition: *lexical definition* and *technical definition*. Let's consider each for defining our terms.

These types of definition overlap somewhat, but there are differences. A lexical definition is a definition explicating the meaning of a word according to how it is commonly used. For example, the word 'power' in everyday discourse means *the ability or capacity to do something*. By contrast, a technical definition is a set of statements that explicates the specialized use of a word by an academic field or industry, or professional organization; the explication makes technical communication between subject matter experts succinct and unambiguous. For example, the word 'power' has one technical definition in physics and another in the study of law. A physics dictionary may define power as *the rate at which work is done or energy is transferred* [96]. Physicists may then use mathematical formulas to calculate 'power' according to their technical definition. Meanwhile, a legal dictionary may offer a different technical definition of power as *the right or authority to take an action or accomplish something* [97]. Lawyers might then specify a list of acts that constitute 'power' according to their technical use of the word (like executing documents, contracting, taking over title, transferring or exercising legal rights, etc.).

A word such as 'completeness', or its cognate 'complete', may also be defined either lexically or technically. The same goes for 'incompleteness' and its cognate 'incomplete'. Completeness and incompleteness may mean one thing in ordinary language and may mean something quite different when used technically by a particular field of study. I will draw upon both kinds of definition for defining completeness and incompleteness.

3.1.1 *Completeness and Incompleteness in Mathematics*

Our main topic in this section of the book is quantitative infinity, and quantitative infinity is a main concern of mathematics. Consequently, in defining completeness and incompleteness for a better grasp of quantitative infinity (both literal and figurative), we should proceed with the mathematical view of infinity in mind, being careful to distinguish it from nonmathematical views of the same.

Mathematicians have their own vocabulary, much of which consists of words borrowed from the ordinary, colloquial discourse of natural language, then redefined with technical meanings intended to narrow their scope of application for precision. The words 'complete' and 'incomplete' are such words. In mathematics, the words 'complete' and 'incomplete' are used in various technical senses within various systems and theories.

Take what it means for a mathematical object, such as an abstract collection or set of numbers, to be 'complete'. What mathematicians consider 'complete' in a technical sense according to a given mathematical system or theory may contradict what we would ordinarily call complete according to a lexical definition for completeness.

Moreover, the technical definitions for a term like 'complete' are so diverse among mathematical disciplines that what constitutes 'complete' in a given mathematical system or theory may even contradict what it is to be complete in a different mathematical system or theory. As Dr. Andre Kornell, professor of mathematics at the University of California, Davis points out, "Completeness is not a formal notion, and there are conceptual models for which the word 'complete' might sensibly be interpreted to opposite effect" [98]. In mathematics, there is no agreed-upon technical definition for 'completeness' or 'complete' that cuts across all mathematical disciplines.

Any definitions for completeness and incompleteness intended to apply in the various contexts of mathematics are therefore not going to please all mathematicians. With that in mind, I must point out that the definitions for completeness and incompleteness I will put forth are not meant to be particular to any given mathematical context—to any given system, procedure, function, technique, etc.

The definitions for completeness and incompleteness will cover the kinds of collections or quantities mathematicians would typically *assume* them to hold for, regardless of the particulars of a given mathematical context. The completeness or incompleteness so defined I take to be that which is typically assumed by mathematicians even while their mathematical formulas and procedures are based on more narrow, technical senses of such terms. So, the definitions for completeness and incompleteness will be as agnostic to context as possible, but without losing relevance.

This will ensure that the completeness of *literal infinity* is explicated according to its common meaning as assumed in any mathematical function or operation—the meaning it has beneath the formalism of mathematical expressions. Likewise, the incompleteness of *figurative infinity* must be explicated by its common meaning for any relevant mathematical function or operation, a meaning that holds regardless of how infinity is figuratively presented in the formalism of mathematics.

To help ensure the case I am building against infinity avoids bias, the definitions for completeness and incompleteness will be defined without assuming any particular application to infinity. The definitions will be general enough to apply to any kind of collection or quantity—whether finite or infinite.

I also wish to ensure the definitions for completeness and incompleteness do not mischaracterize how these words are used beyond mathematical contexts where quantitative infinity is referenced. So, the definitions will apply independently of how one might use the terms 'complete' or 'incomplete' with respect to any particular field of study. I intend the explications of completeness and incompleteness to be common among as many contexts as possible but without undue vagueness.

3.1.2 *A Common Conception of Completeness and Incompleteness*

We'll begin with a lexical definition of 'completeness' offered in ordinary, natural language. That definition, whether refined further or not, I will refer to as the literal definition of 'completeness' and the condition to which it refers as *literal completeness*. Its denial is *literal incompleteness*.

After lexically defining literal completeness, I will offer a more precise definition of 'complete' to reduce as much as possible any lingering vagueness in the notion of completeness. From there, we will also be able to discern why some collections are literally incomplete.

Despite the context-agnostic flavor of the definitions I pursue, the ultimate point to all of this is a better understanding of completeness and incompleteness as these properties apply to quantitative infinity—both literal infinity and figurative infinity. Since literal infinity implies the given collection is *literally complete* as well as literally limitless while figurative infinity implies a given series that is *literally incomplete* while being figuratively limitless, we need definitions for literal completeness and literal limitlessness that do these concepts justice.

The following sections will define completeness in detail prior to defining incompleteness as its denial.

3.2 COMPLETENESS DEFINED

Because we have to start somewhere in order to understand what it means for an infinite collection to be complete as well as limitless in quantity, I suggest we begin with a lexical definition for completeness, then refine what 'complete' means with a *precising definition* (a more precise version of a lexical definition), and then use that precising definition as a standard by which to judge various technical uses of the term 'complete' in mathematics in order to evaluate how straightforward or misleading they may be with respect to descriptions of collections, whether finite or infinite.

So, to kick things off here is a very simple lexical definition of the word 'completeness':

- completeness: *the condition of being complete.*

The definition refers to the adjective or logical predicate 'complete' which in ordinary, colloquial discourse has a variety of meanings and is often used as a synonym for other words (e.g., whole, entire, finished, full, total, etc.). However, we can be a bit more precise than offering synonyms.

The word 'complete' is a word that typically refers to a property of a collection of some kind (such as a group, aggregation, multitude, set, sequence, series, etc.) or an object of thought that can be analyzed as a collection. Assuming as much, we can propose a precising definition for 'complete' that fits how we ordinarily think of what it means for a collection to be complete:

- complete: (1) *having all members necessary to be representative of a given class.*

Though this definition for 'complete' may sound a bit technical, a little reflection will show this definition fits how we ordinarily think of collections called "complete" in everyday discourse.

3.2.1 *Completeness is About Membership*

If something is complete, then whatever else it may be, it is a collection. Every collection is made up of members. The human body, for example, is made up of members such as the body's organs. That's not to say a human body is nothing but a collection of members; only that it is a collection with respect to having members. If the body is complete, then it is complete as a collection. What we regard as 'complete' can only be so if it is a collection and, as such, is made up of more than one member.

3.2.2 *Completeness is About A Collection Representing a Class*

The members of a collection are objects related to one another in some fashion. For example, take a collection that is a group of objects in which the 'objects' are people. The people in one group may have a "works with" relation between them while the people of another group may have a "plays with" relation between them. Collections the members of which share the same type of relation with each other are called *classes*. We will define 'class' rather loosely:

- class: *a collection of objects sharing the same type of relation(s).*

For example, laborers, technicians, politicians, soldiers, etc. are all examples of collections of people sharing the same type of relation: they work with one another. Golfers, bowlers, gamblers, role players, etc. are all examples of collections of people that share a same-type relation: they play with one another. So, here we have two different 'classes' or people. We can also imagine a class of a more familiar variety: a collection of people sharing a "studies with" relation—a school class.

As another example, take collections of objects used to perform work. One collection of such objects is the class of objects known as 'tools' while another collection of such objects is the class of objects we call 'machines'. The difference between the two classes is the type of relations shared by the objects in the respective classes. There are collections of objects used to perform work via manual manipulation—objects with that type of relation belong to the class of objects known as tools. There are also collections of objects used to perform work automatically—objects with that type of relation belong to the class of objects known as machines.

We can then further categorize classes of objects into sub-classes of objects, such as machines into classes of various types—vehicles, appliances, etc. To do so, we must be able to define what type of relations among the objects of collections distinguish them from other objects among different collections under the same overall class. For example, of the class of numbers, consider the collection of numbers used for counting. Such numbers share the "counting with" relation. So, the counting numbers can be regarded as a class of its own—or, more precisely, a sub-class of the class of numbers.

Even counting numbers can be sub-classified. If we consider "has ordinality" to be the relevant relation between the objects of that collection, then the number 1 is of the same class as any other number in the counting numbers (which begins with the number 1). But if we consider only the relation of "follows next" to be the relevant relation for numbers in the scale of counting numbers, then we can say 1 is not in the same class as any other number in the scale of counting numbers because 1 does not follow next after a number in that scale.

Without getting into much further detail, the important point here is that a given collection must be representative of like collections—a collection must be an instance of a *class*—if it is to be regarded as a *complete* collection. Being an instance of a class is not a sufficient condition to be complete, but it is a necessary condition to be complete.

3.2.3 *Completeness Requires All the Necessary Members*

To be complete, a collection must have *all* the members necessary to be representative of its class. In this context, the word 'all' means *each and every*. For a collection to have 'each and every' necessary member implies the collection has those members that, *together as a group without exception*, are necessary for the collection to represent a class. If a collection has only *some* of the necessary members, then it does not have all the necessary members it needs to be representative of a class.

Let's consider an example. Take an object made up of smaller objects, each of which fit together in a particular way with one another. For example, a puzzle in which the puzzle pieces must all fit together in a particular way. The smaller objects (e.g., puzzle pieces) share the relation "fits together" with one another. In this example, we'll call the smaller objects sharing this relation the 'parts' that make up the larger object. Because the object is made up of parts, the object can be regarded as a collection in which the parts are members. In this example, of the parts comprising the object, the parts must have the "fits together" relation in order for the object that has the parts to be itself a member of a given 'class' of objects (for example, the class of objects known as puzzles).

Moreover, of the parts comprising a given object, at least some will be *necessary* for the object to be representative of a given class of objects, even if some of the parts are not. Of those parts that are necessary for the object to be representative of the given class, *all* of them (that is, each and every one of them) must be in the object for the object to be regarded as 'complete'. To make this less abstract, consider the example of a motor car. A car is an object, but it is also a collection of members. Some of the members are themselves objects sharing the "fits together" relation. Those members are the car's parts—e.g., its frame, seats, wheels, etc. If the parts share the "fits together" relation in a certain way, we can say the parts make up the object as a collection of parts and that the object is thus an instance of a 'class' of objects of a particular type—namely, the class of objects we know as 'car'.

Of the parts that are fit together, at least some of them are necessary for the object they comprise to be representative of a car—that particular class of objects. If *all* (each and every one of) the necessary parts are in the given car's collection of parts, then the car may be a *complete* car (though, there may be other 'members' that are not parts but are also necessary—see the next section below).

So, a given car (the object we can point to) as a collection of parts must have all (each and every one) of the parts necessary for that collection to be representative of the class 'car' in order to be considered complete. If not all the parts necessary for the object to be representative of the class of object known as 'car' are included in the collection making up the object, then the object (the car in this case) cannot be complete. The object can still be a car, but it won't be a *complete* car. If wheels are a necessary part, then without wheels the object we perceive can still be a collection of the class 'car' since it still has parts related in the particular "fits together" ways they need to be part of a car, but it is not a complete car—wheels would be necessary for the object to be a complete 'car' by that conception of car.

Moreover, we can apply this same stipulation for completeness to sub-classes as well. For example, if the given car (an object of the class 'car') is to be complete, it must have all (each and every one of) the wheels that are necessary for the car to be presentative of the class of car it is. Consider that if the car of a particular class of cars has four wheels, then for the car in question to be a complete car, it must have all four wheels. That is, each and every wheel that the car needs to be representative of a car of its class must be present as part of the collection of parts comprising the car or the car will not be complete. (As an obvious caveat, wheels alone are of course not sufficient to make a car complete; other parts are also necessary. And the same goes for particular parts of many other collective objects.)

3.2.4 *Members Can Be Relations As Well As Parts*

So far, we have only considered parts as examples of 'members' in a collection comprising a given object like a car. But when we consider an object as a collection, the parts are not the only 'members' of the collection because the parts have certain *relations* between them, like how the parts fit together. It is not just the parts that make the object a collection of a certain *class* but also how the parts combine and relate to one another. We can consider the relations between the parts to also be among the 'necessary members' of the collection that make that particular collection an instance of a given class.

Hence, to be complete, a collection requires 'all' the necessary members, including the relations among the parts. For the example of a car, it is not just the parts of the car alone that make the car 'complete' because, as a *collection*, the car is more than a collection of parts, it is also a collection of relations. The relations among the car parts, such as how all of them fit together, are also members of the car as a collection. And all the necessary relations of a given type must be included in the car if the car is to be representative of the class of object it is—that is, if the car is to be complete. The same holds for any type of collection or collective object: to be complete, it must be an instance of a class because it has the members (both the objects sharing particular types of relations and the relations themselves) necessary for representation of that class and all the members must be included.

3.2.5 *Necessary For Completeness—Membership Vice Condition*

It is true that what we call 'complete' depends on how we *define* the class to which a collection belongs. If we wish to change convention and define 'car' in a way that wheels are not necessary as parts, then the wheels also do not become necessary as members of a collection of parts making up a car (maybe a given model of car, but not a car in general), and so an object might still be a "complete car" even though it has no wheels or even if it has wheels that are unattached.

Even without such a change in conventional definition for a collection, some members we might find in a collection may not be necessary for the collection to be complete. A collection of the parts included in what we call a 'car' may not be necessary for the car to be complete as a car—for example, you can still have a complete car without having a bumper sticker. Including a bumper sticker would not violate the necessary conditions for the car to be complete, but any "extra" members (unnecessary members) are not part of the car as a *complete* car; rather, they are extraneous to the car that is complete without them. The same is true for anything we wish to regard as complete—when we construe it as some kind of collection, we can see if there are any extra or extraneous members; if there are, such members are not what would make that thing, as a collection, complete. Similarly, suppose we have an extra object to replace an object taken from the complete collection in order to make it complete again, like a spare tire for the car. The extra objects are not a part of the collection as a complete collection, even if they are of the same class as objects *in* the collection, like the other tires on the car.

Before continuing, I should make a distinction. Philosophers sometimes use the terms *necessary conditions* and *necessary members*. There is a difference between 'necessary conditions' on the one hand and 'necessary members' on the other hand. Having necessary *conditions* is not the same thing as having necessary *members*.

To have the necessary conditions does not in itself entail that something is complete. To be adult, male, and unmarried are necessary, and together sufficient, conditions to be a bachelor. But that does not mean a given unmarried, adult male is a complete bachelor unless we are saying something humous. Rather, to say something is complete is to imply it has necessary members, which in turn implies that the thing that is complete is being regarded as a collection of some kind, such as a group, set, sequence, or series.

The 'members' that together make a collection (simply as a collection) complete can be members of any sort, such as physical objects, relationships between objects, properties, conditions, ideas, etc. In the bachelor example, the collection to which we refer is a collection of conditions. If we are talking about the necessary conditions for being a bachelor, we might refer to those conditions as a *set* of conditions. And if they are a *complete* set of conditions, then each of those conditions is necessary as a member of the set of conditions needed for a person to be a bachelor. It isn't the bachelor we are referring to as complete; it is the set of conditions needed to be a bachelor—each of those conditions is a member of the set of conditions needed to be a bachelor and if all those conditions are present for a given man, then the set of conditions is complete for that instance.

So, what is necessary for completeness is a matter of membership to a collection: to be complete, a collection requires all the necessary members.

3.2.6 *Completeness in Overview*

From these considerations, we now have a definition of the word 'complete': "having all members necessary to be representative of a given class." That covers how the word 'complete' is used across a variety of contexts with respect to collections. This notion of completeness applies whether we are speaking of a physical collection like a set of chess pieces, or an abstract collection like a set or series of numbers, a collection of conditions, or even a collection of steps forming a process. When all the members—each *and* every one—for a collection are necessary to fit the collection's class and all those members are indeed together in the collection, then the collection can be accurately regarded as complete.

3.2.7 *Synonyms for 'Complete'*

In the definition of 'complete', the word 'all' is important to note: for a collection to be complete is for the collection to have *all* members necessary to be representative of a given class. If the members are all necessary for the collection to be representative of a given class, then it is "all" together that the members make the collection complete. Those members may be objects, properties, relations, conditions, etc., but regardless of what they are, they all together are needed to comprise a complete collection. The word 'all' (meaning each and every) in the definition of 'complete' thus carries certain implications. The word 'all' is a quantifier that in the definition of 'complete' implies the collection in question is—

- *whole*
- *entire*
- *finished*
- *full*
- *total*

In fact, these conditions are often used as synonyms for 'complete', just as you'll find in any dictionary of common language. However, a little analysis shows that these words, though often used as synonyms for 'complete', also have usage that is not strictly synonymous with being complete; the word 'complete' is often used differently than each of these other words.

To ensure we say exactly what we mean when we say a collection is infinite in the literal sense of being complete as well as limitless, we need to adopt the more precise way of defining 'complete' and avoid using other terms as synonyms unless we make ourselves clear that we are only speaking loosely. Instead of using 'whole', 'entire', 'finished', 'full', and 'total' as synonyms for 'complete', we can regard each of these alternative words as capturing distinctive features of completeness.

3.2.8 *Criteria for Completeness*

We can use the meanings of the synonyms for 'complete' as criteria for determining whether or not something is complete. *Wholeness, entirety, finish, fullness,* and *totality* are each a *condition* that by itself is not sufficient for something to be complete; rather, all of them together are necessary for something to be complete. If a given collection has all the necessary members to be representative of a given class, then the collection will be whole, entire, finished, full, and it will be a totality. Only if all such conditions obtain for a collection will that collection be a *complete* collection.

We can therefore create an even more formal definition for 'complete' like so:

- complete: (2) *a given collection is complete* [i.e., has all members necessary to be representative of a given class] *if and only if the collection is whole, entire, finished, full, and total.*

This second definition thus complements the previous precising definition. To say something is complete is to imply that if we consider it to be a collection made up of parts or members, it has all the members necessary to be representative of a particular class. That being so, we further imply its parts or members form a whole, entire, finished, full, and total collection.

We can begin to see the differences between these conditions for completeness by using some precising definitions for them, to which we will now turn.

3.3 WHOLENESS

Wholeness and entirety are often considered synonymous, but not always. I distinguish them so that we can consider each condition on its own. Definition:

- wholeness: *the condition of being whole or of being a whole.*

To say that something is 'a whole' (noun) is similar to saying it is 'whole' (adjective):

- whole: (noun) *a divisible, but undivided, collection of objects.*
- whole: (adjective) *to be divisible but undivided.*

For something to be whole (adjective), is for it to be divisible but undivided. This sounds similar to our definition for 'element'. However, whereas an element is a divisible, but undivided, distinct *object*, a whole (noun) is a divisible, but undivided, *collection of objects* [99].

3.3.1 *The Divisibility of Wholes*

Wholes are divisible but undivided; however, this needs some clarification because there are different senses of the term 'divide'. By 'divide' I do not necessarily mean the mathematical operation of division, although it can play a role. To divide a collection is to remove at least some of the logical relations among the members of the collection such that the collection is no longer representative of the given class.

A collection may be divided *analytically*, as when we *distinguish* parts (conceptually mark the whole into sections called 'parts') without mechanically changing the relationships between any parts that are in the whole. This is often done to reckon the number of times the collection contains subgroupings, as when the number of subsets within a set is calculated. (And, of course, there is mathematical division, which is another instance of dividing analytically.)

A collection may be divided *mechanically*, as when we *dissect* a whole into parts (physically split the whole into separate units). To mechanically 'divide' a collection is to separate members or groups of members in the collection from one another.

In the context of considering a collection to be a whole then, to 'divide' is either to distinguish parts analytically and attend only to those parts or to dissect into parts mechanically. If a collection can be divided in either sense but is not in fact divided, then it is considered as a whole or to be whole.

So, if something is literally whole, it may have parts, but the parts are together and you are not considering the parts as objects separate from the rest; the parts are divisible, in the sense of being distinguishable or dissectible, but actually undivided in either sense. To consider a person as a whole, for instance, is not to attend to any of the parts making up a person. That's what it means to be 'whole' in a (somewhat) more precise sense.

Wholeness cannot be applied to elements *as such*. As pointed out earlier, once an element is divided, it is no longer an element but considered to be a collection containing members. Suppose, however, that we don't actually divide the element either analytically by distinguishing parts within it or mechanically by dissecting it into parts, and yet we regard the element as something that *could* be so divided. In that case, the element still ceases to be an element and becomes instead a literal *whole*—a divisible, but undivided, *collection*. Something is an element only if it is regarded as a fundamental object rather than as a collection of objects.

3.3.2 *Wholeness as a Matter of Context*

There is no single type of relationship among parts that confers the property of wholeness upon the collection to which they belong. For example, take an object such as a circle. A circle may be divisible in the sense that the curve of its closed line can be divided such as by a break or gap, and so long as there is no such break or gap the circle is divisible but undivided—it is whole.

Now suppose we give the circle a property allowing it to split into 16 circles, each the same size as the original circle like a stack of coins spread around into a circle. In **Figure 3.1**, the first image (image A) depicts such an initial circle, which is a 'whole' circle because not only is its curve divisible, but there are no divisions along its curve. In addition, this circle has the property of being able to divide like a cell into further circles (images $B - F$) but is not divided in image A, which is why the circle at A is whole.

The interlocking circles of image B do not comprise a 'whole' in the sense of being consolidated into a single circle like in image A. However, the circles of image B do form a 'whole' ring comprised of interlocking circles; the ring of circles in image B is divisible into a collection of circles that do not interlock (as in images C–F). But since they are in fact still interlocked and so undivided as a collection of the interlocking type, they still comprise a ring of that type and therefore they still form a whole according to that standard.

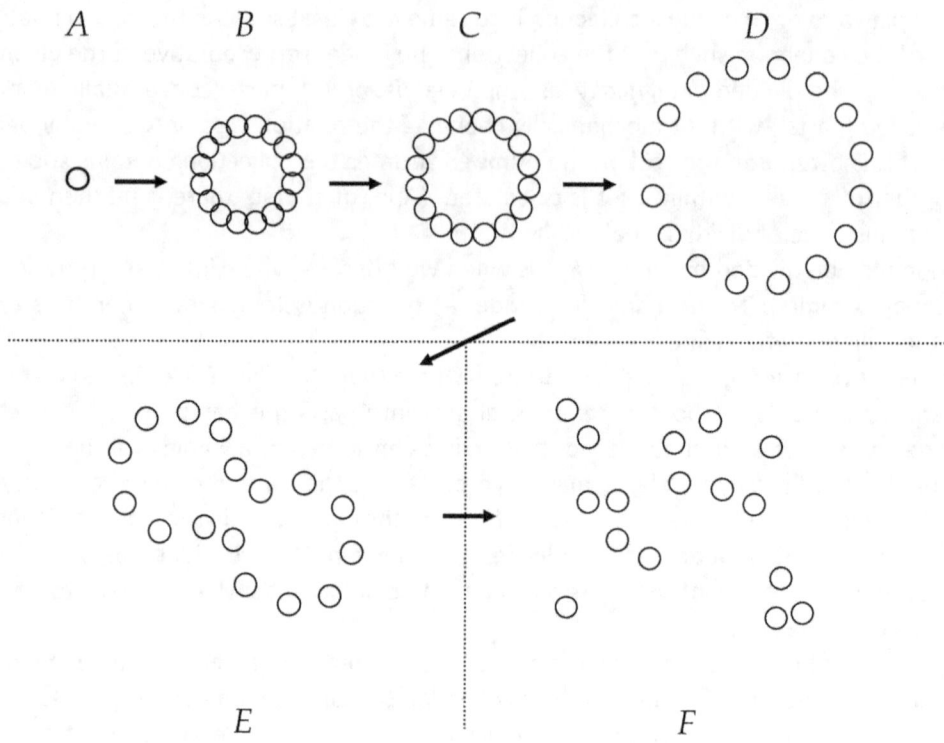

Figure 3.1: An example of wholeness as context relative. Collections of objects (A–F) can each be considered 'whole', or to constitute a 'whole', depending on what is considered 'divided' for the context of the collection in question.

Likewise, a ring of non-interlocking but touching circles (image C) can be considered 'whole' in the sense that while, as such, it is divisible into circles that do not touch each other (image D), they are in image C still in contact to form a solid ring of that type. However, the circles of image C also do not form a 'whole' in the sense of an interlocking ring, as in image B, let alone a set of circles consolidated into a single circle as in image A.

Moving on, the ring of non-touching circles in image D can be considered a 'whole' ring of circles because it too is divisible such as into halves (image E), but it is not so divided. And, of course, we can consider image E to be a 'whole' composed of two halves of the previous ring of circles divisible but not divided into separated parts as in image F. But even the collection of circles in image F can be considered a 'whole' collection of circles if all the circles are present, their relative positions unimportant, and yet they still form a single collection.

The examples from **Figure 3.1** illustrate that what constitutes a 'whole' is a matter of context because what is considered "divided" or "separated" depends on how you want to define those terms, which is likewise a matter of context. What kind of logical relations one has in mind among the parts determines if the collection in question is or is not a whole collection.

If, for example, the parts of a collection of spatially extended shapes or bodies must be touching one another but do not, then the collection is not 'whole'. But if only the presence of all the parts is important and not their mutual touch, then the collection can still be whole.

The same is true for the wholeness of a quantity. What constitutes a whole quantity of members in a collection depends on what quantity belongs to the same count and what quantity belongs to some other count.

When considering the wholeness of quantities, though, there is one nuance to keep in mind. It has to do with division. To be whole is to be "divisible but undivided," and yet there are different meanings of 'division' and so a whole can be divisible in various ways. For example, consider the following mathematical 'sentence', which contains a series of mathematical divisions:

$$3,125 \div 5 \div 5 \div 5 \div 5 \div 5 = 1$$

Though each dividend from left to right is divided by a divisor, it is the series of mathematical divisions ($\div 5 \div 5 \div 5 \div 5 \div 5$) that is itself undivided within a single mathematical 'sentence'. However, while the series of divisions may itself be undivided, it too is in a sense 'divisible'; for we could also divide (that is, separate) the series of mathematical divisions itself into two series of mathematical divisions, each in its own sentence placed in sequence—

$$(3,125 \div 5 \div 5 = 125), (125 \div 5 \div 5 \div 5 = 1)$$

—demonstrating that the original series of mathematical divisions was itself originally a *whole*—it was undivided, yet also divisible. After dividing (separating) the original series of (mathematical) divisions into two smaller series of divisions, and thereby making two resulting sentences, we can regard each series of divisions either as an independent series of divisions in its own sentence or as two *parts* of a sequence of divisions belonging as parts of a whole sentence that is equivalent to the original sentence.

Which goes to show that what constitutes a 'division' is in one context is not what does so in another context; so too, what is regarded as being whole ("divisible but undivided") in one context would not necessarily be called "whole" in another context. And because wholeness is context-dependent, and completeness implies wholeness, any collection we consider a complete collection must also be a 'whole' collection according to some criterion of wholeness, which remains purely relative to context.

3.3.3 *Wholeness and Completeness*

Despite the context relativity of wholeness, if a collection is complete, then it is whole according to *some* relevant criterion of what it means to be whole. Conversely, a collection is not complete if it is not whole. Moreover, a collection that is considered only in terms of some of its parts and not *all* of its parts (i.e., a divided collection) is either not considered complete or not considered with respect to completeness.

Then again, just because something is whole does not mean it is complete. Wholeness does not by itself imply completeness; a collection can be whole without being complete.

A beam of light issuing from a light source is an uninterrupted stream of photon particles (a kind of collection). At every location it travels through, the beam is 'whole' as it extends onward. But as the light source continues to shine, it causes the beam to lengthen its reach as the beam advances into space, thus adding more particles to the length of the beam. Since the beam can continuously add more particles (the elements of the collection), the beam is not 'complete' because as a collection of particles the beam continues to accumulate more particles (it is not finished forming) in the beam's length. Hence, the beam can be whole (it is undivided) without being complete.

3.3.4 *Wholeness and Completeness in Mathematics*

Mathematicians use the term 'complete' in various technical senses, some of which imply wholeness, some of which do not. And even when wholeness is implied by these specialized senses of the term 'complete', the word 'whole' is not necessarily used, nor is wholeness necessarily recognized as such.

For example, consider the mathematical concept of a *metric space*. A metric space is a set in which the *distances* between all members of the set are defined. Geometries can be considered metric spaces—there are fixed intervals in such spaces and the elements can be arbitrarily close to one another. To be 'complete' in the technical sense used by the mathematician is for the metric space to be 'entire' (see the next section) and for the metric space to be 'whole' (having no divisions, separations, breaks, or gaps in the sequence of the metric space).

However, mathematicians don't typically use the term 'whole' to capture the feature of metric spaces lacking gaps. Instead, mathematicians say a metric space is 'complete', although they use that term in technical senses as defined by the mathematical schemas of Augustin-Louis Cauchy (1789–1857) and Richard Dedekind (1831–1916). A *Cauchy complete* space and a *Dedekind complete* space are very similar: they both describe a metric space lacking measurable "gaps" between elements. Such metric spaces constitute whole spaces, but not necessarily complete spaces in the literal sense of completeness.

For Cauchy completeness, the metric space lacks gaps by virtue of having a sequence of elements that "converge"—that become arbitrarily close to one another according to mathematical operation [100] [101]. A Cauchy complete space would not be considered as complete according to the literal definition of completeness, which requires a collection (e.g., a sequence, series, set, etc.) to have the properties of being whole, entire, finished, full, and total.

A so-called 'Cauchy complete' metric space may be a space that is 'whole' and 'entire' as defined here, but the same metric space could lack the other properties such as 'finish' and 'fullness'. To be 'complete' in Cauchy's sense of the term may fit a narrow mathematical scheme, but that way of being 'complete' does not necessarily meet all the completeness criteria offered earlier. Moreover, Cauchy completeness does not generally apply across other mathematical schemes, nor does it always apply to collections considered infinite.

Literal infinity assumes a limitless collection is also a literally complete collection—that is, 'complete' in the sense defined earlier—to be whole, entire, finished, full, and total. And as mathematicians frequently claim certain collections are literally infinite, Cauchy completeness cannot be what even mathematicians tend to mean by something being "complete." At best, the 'completeness' of Cauchy may apply as a misnomer to a figuratively infinite (ergo, literally incomplete) function applied to a metric space, but Cauchy completeness cannot apply to a literal infinity and does not apply in a general sense across mathematics, let alone to other contexts.

A similar assessment can be made of Dedekind completeness (see § 3.6.2), which is also a form of wholeness for a metric space, and perhaps fullness, but does not meet all the completeness criteria.

Since 'Cauchy complete' and 'Dedekind complete' are rather misleading terms, I will stick to using terms like 'whole', 'entire', and 'full' as I define them in this chapter with regard to collections lacking gaps—such terms are less misleading. I will reserve 'complete' for that which has not just wholeness and perhaps entirety or fullness, but also finish and totality as well.

3.4 ENTIRETY

Entirety is often used synonymously with wholeness, but let's distinguish these two conditions for clarity. Definitions:

- entirety: *the condition of being entire*.
- entire: (1) *missing no elements*.

In order to make explicit what it is to be missing no elements, we can restate the definition of 'entire' with a criterion for determining whether a given collection is or is not entire. So here is the definition of 'entire' stated a bit more formally:

- entire: (2) *a given instance of a collection, C, is 'entire' if and only if it is logically possible to determine that no member is missing from the instance of C*.

3.4.1 *Entirety in Set Theory and Mathematics*

Now let's consider how we might use this definition of 'entire' in the context of set theory and mathematics. First, we need to add some more detail to the criterion for entirety by considering C as a set and its members as subsets of elements. To say collection C is entire, as in "the entire collection," is to imply the following conditions are met by C:

1. C can be represented as a set.
2. As a set, C is non-empty—C has at least one member within it. Example: $C = \{M\}$.
3. Every member, M, in C is itself either an element, e, or more than one element, or a subset of members (whether a subset of elements or a subset containing further subsets).
4. At least one member of C is not itself an empty set.
5. There are no missing members in C.
6. For any non-empty subsets [s] in C, the non-empty subsets in C are missing no members.

The notation is a bit nonstandard, but the point remains the same: any collection consistent with conditions 1–6 should be considered an 'entire' collection.

For example, suppose C is the set of the first five whole numbers and we are given C in the following form: $\{0, 1, 2, 3, 4, 5\}$. Clearly, if that is C, then C meets the first condition: we can represent it as a set.

C is also certainly not empty as it has six members. So, the second condition is met.

Each number in C is an element and they can be grouped into subsets, so the third condition is met. Furthermore, even if we consider 0 to be the empty set, then there are still non-empty members in C; namely, 1–5. That meets the fourth condition.

Now we need to know if C is missing members—either subsets or elements. Suppose we consider a single non-zero *element*, e, as one of C's members. Suppose as well that e is the number 4. According to the criteria, if 4 were missing from C, then C would not be the "entire" set of 0–5. But 4 is not missing from C as can be plainly seen: {0, 1, 2, 3, 4, 5}. In fact, C is missing no elements from 0 to 5. If instead we were to have considered *subsets*, the same conclusion would have been reached. For instance, if [s] is the subset [2, 3] and that subset were missing from C such that {0, 1, 4, 5}, then that too would have meant that C is not "entire." But no subsets are missing from {0, 1, 2, 3, 4, 5}. The fifth and sixth conditions are therefore met.

As you can see, if C is supposed to be the set of numbers from zero through five and we are given C as the set {0, 1, 2, 3, 4, 5}, then we can say we have the entire set—or the entire collection—of numbers that we are supposed to have according to the conditions given. That's an example of entirety.

3.4.2 *Entirety in the Real World*

We need not confine ourselves to set-theoretic or mathematical examples of entirety. The conditions a collection needs in order to be 'entire' can be met in real, physical collections as well as mathematical collections.

As an example of an entire collection of real objects, consider again a chess set with all its game pieces. We defined entirety as not missing any members. So, to be an entire chess set, it cannot contain any less than 32 game pieces. If the set is missing at least one piece, for example, it is not the entire set. And if the set is missing a piece, then it could include another piece and so must not be a *complete* set.

3.4.3 *Testing Entirety With Wholeness*

The terms 'entire' and 'whole' are often thought of as synonyms because the conditions are closely related. They are not the same, but we can test for the entirety of a collection by violating the wholeness of the collection. To be whole is to be undivided. By 'dividing' the collection in some sense, we might find whether or not the collection in question is an entire collection.

We might divide a collection in either a conceptual manner or in a physical manner. We divide in a physical manner when we *mechanically* separate the parts of the collection in an act of dissection, and in a conceptual manner by *analytically* distinguishing the parts from one another.

Once we distinguish parts in the collection, the collection may be 'whole' in the sense of being undissected but not whole in the sense of being unanalyzed since we did indeed divide the collection in a conceptual manner—we were not looking at the collection *as a whole*. Even so, we may go on to refer to the collection as 'whole' if, after having distinguished parts as individual members in the collection, we once again attend to the collection in a conceptually undivided manner—we once again look at it "as a whole."

Hence, we again conceive of it as unqualifiedly undivided—a literal whole. While analytically making the division of the collection, however, we can attend to the parts as distinguishable members, and in so attending see if all the parts are there or if some are missing—that is, see whether the collection is *entire* or not. If our test shows that a member of the collection is missing, then the collection is not entire.

3.4.4 *Gaps Indicate Lack of Wholeness and Possibly Lack of Entirety*

Returning again to mathematics for another example, consider a sequence of numbers. If there is a missing number somewhere between the first and last member in the sequence, then the sequence has a "gap." The gap divides the sequence into two, indicating it lacks wholeness in certain sense, but the gap also shows that a member is missing; so the given sequence is not the *entire* sequence.

And if the sequence is not entire, then it is not *complete*.

It is here again that mathematicians sometimes use the terms 'Cauchy complete'—a technical sense of completeness. To be Cauchy complete is for a sequence to be entire: no elements in the sequence are missing. Nevertheless, it would be less misleading to use the term 'entire' instead of 'complete' for describing a sequence as missing no elements since there is more to completeness than entirety, just as there is more to completeness than wholeness.

It would therefore be more accurate to say that if any collection (sequence or otherwise) is not entire, then it is not complete. Like wholeness, entirety is a condition that a collection must have for it to be complete, and like wholeness, entirety is not sufficient for completeness.

3.5 FINISH

To be complete, a collection must not only be whole and entire, but it must be finished as well. Here too we must be a little careful with our terms because 'finish' is sometimes considered synonymous with 'fullness', but I will draw a distinction between these conditions. First, we'll take a look at what it means to finish a collection and then in the next section we will see what it means for a collection to be full.

The finishing of a collection has to do with bringing the collection to a 'conclusion' with respect to the collection's quantity of members. A process may change a collection's magnitude by increasing or decreasing the plurality of members in the collection. A change to the collection's plurality changes what any count of the collection's members would yield. When some process that changes the plurality of objects in the collection ceases to change that plurality, the collection has a concluding number of members, or a 'finish', to any count of members comprising the collection. We can therefore define the term 'finish' with respect to the quantity of members in a collection:

- finish: *a concluding, non-zero number of members*.

We'll now proceed to take a closer look at what it means to finish a collection. In so doing, we'll first consider what it is to finish a finite collection before addressing the subject of what having a 'finish' means for an infinite collection.

3.5.1 *Two Kinds of 'Finish'*

When we say a collection of some kind is finished, we may have in mind two different kinds of collections and two different 'finishes'. In terms of collections, on the one hand we have C, a given collection being changed in quantity, and on the other hand we have S, a series (a collection of events or steps) that actively changes the quantity of members in C.

When a coin collector pours coins into a jar, there are two collections of relevance: the collection of steps (S) in the pouring process—such as a series of coins falling into the jar one after another—and the collection of coins (C) in the jar. So, we need to keep in mind that in addition to the two kinds of collections, there are two different finishes: there is the *finish to the process* that changes the quantity of coins collected and there is also *the finish of the collection's quantity of members*; for instance, there is the finish to the coin-pouring process (a collection of steps in sequence) and then there is the collection's finished amount of coins in the jar.

The two finishes are not the same; just because C is finished doesn't mean S is finished. Suppose the coin collector does not stop pouring coins into the jar until after the jar runs over with excess coins. The jar's collection of coins was finished (the jar had a concluding number of coins) before the series of steps in the pouring process was finished—the excess coins simply spilled over, adding nothing to the 'finished' amount of coins in the jar's collection.

Similarly, when a process diminishes or reduces a collection's size, we must again distinguish between the finish of the collection and the finish of the process that changes the quantity of the collection. When a collection is reduced to zero members—like when we take every coin from the coin jar—the collection cannot be called 'finished' because the concluding number of members must be some *non-zero* amount for the collection to be a 'finished' collection. A coin jar with no coins is hardly a finished coin collection. However, the *process* of removing the members from the collection, such as taking the coins from the jar is 'finished' (has a concluding number of steps) over whatever particular number of steps it took to remove the members. On the other hand, when the work (S) is finished, there is no more work to do, even if the product (C) is unfinished.

Not only must collection C have a non-zero number of members in order to be finished, but the process that changes C's quantity of members inherently has a non-zero amount of events in the series that changes C's size. This holds no matter what sort of process of change we consider—scheming up the collection, building it, removing parts, or otherwise altering its number of members. In terms of mathematically constructing collections, for example, it takes a number of steps for the mathematician to construct a given collection, whether it's conceiving of a set or writing down a series of variables.

The number of steps it takes to change the size of a collection need not be many; for some collections, a change in size can be concluded in just a single step. For example, stamping the first ten natural numbers on a sheet of paper will conclude the construction of that set in just one step (or just defining a set might do it: $C = 10$). For C to be 'finished' as a collection means only that whatever steps are needed to construct C must be finalized. It is even logically possible for there to be a collection, C, without any steps taken that yield its quantity of members. Such a scenario implies C has always existed for as long as there has been time to exist, and with that quantity of members. In which case, C was always 'finished' as a collection.

The notion of finish is related to the notion of being entire. Whether C is increased or decreased in size, C is 'finished' only when it has a concluding number of members. The collection has a "concluding number of members" when the process working to change the quantity of the collection has ceased to make the collection any larger or smaller, such as by including or removing further members to the collection, because the collection has achieved *entirety*—it has the quantity of members it needs to be representative of a given class. Similarly, the process of quantitatively changing a collection, C, is itself 'finished' only when no further steps are included in the process's series of steps, S.

In some cases, C and S are one and the same—a series, for instance, is itself a kind of collection and might grow or diminish in its constituent number of events or steps—but often C and S are considered as two different collections. In brief: whatever collection we have—an aggregate, multitude, set, sequence, or series—the collection in question is 'finished' when no more elements are included into it or taken from it because the collection becomes the entire collection.

If a collection is finished, it is not necessarily complete. If I have finished exercising while leaving out one of my usual exercises, my collection of exercises for the day may be finished but that collection is left incomplete because I left some exercises out (I did not perform the *entire* collection of exercises).

Conversely, if a collection is complete, it is necessarily finished. A tank that is a complete tank of fuel is a tank that is a finished tank of fuel; if a tank of fuel is a finished tank of fuel, then it has a concluding amount of fuel. However, if the tank is complete, that of course does not mean the driver is finished pouring fuel into the tank as the driver can attempt to fill the tank to excess, but it does mean that the tank *as such* is finished being filled—the tank is finished *as* a tank of fuel.

3.5.2 *Completeness Requires Finish*

If a collection is not finished, it cannot be complete. If it is complete, then it must be finished. A complete collection is 'finished' in at least two respects: it is finished in terms of the *process* by which it is formed (i.e., the series of steps by which the collection is formed), and it is finished with respect to having a *concluding quantity* of members making up the collection. The latter is determined by a mapping or counting of the elements that comprise the collection.

However, just because a complete collection is a finished collection, both in terms of concluding its formation and in terms of having a concluding element for an enumeration of its members, that does not mean the collection is 'finished' in *every* way its members relate to one another. For example, the notion of 'finish' need not apply with respect to the *arrangement* of members in a collection. There are some completed collections that have a non-zero number of members and yet these collections cannot be considered finished in terms of how their members are arranged because the arrangement of their members has no first member and no last member, no beginning and no ending member, no starting member and no member that finishes the collection.

For example, if the members of a collection are arranged in a circle or ring, the collection need not have both a first and a last member, need not have both beginning and ending members, need not have both starting and finishing members—at least, not in terms of the arrangement of members. Consider a ring of stones like the circle of dots portrayed in **Figure 1.1** of § 1.1.2. Go either way around the ring of stones, for example, and you never come to stone that is the first or last stone, a beginning or ending stone, a starting or finishing stone.

Even so, a circle or ring of elements can still be considered 'finished' in terms of how it was formed and the quantity of elements of which it is comprised. In terms of the ring of stones, the multitude of stones itself, by comprising a ring, has no first and last member with respect to the arrangement in which they were laid, and therefore no start or finish to that order, but the *process* of laying the stones did have a start and finish, a first and last step, even if accomplished all in one step by a party of workers. And we may *establish* another kind of order *for* the arrangement of stones, without moving a single stone, by *counting* the stones. The counting process will start with a first count of 1 and a finish at a last count, s, which totals the stones. In fact, as the middle circle of **Figure 1.1** in § 1.1.2 shows, a circle can be given a point that functions both as the start and finish to a sequencing of its members with the sequence extending all the way around the curve of the circle, finishing where it started. So, even a ring, though having no first or last member, no beginning and no end to its curve, no start or finish to its multitude of members, may as a collection of members still be matched to a description of the order that does have a first and a last member (its count), established by a process (the act of counting) that has a start and a finish.

In order to be complete then, collections must have the properties of being whole, entire, full, and total, but they must also be finished in formation and be enumerable, at least in principle, to a finished count or mapping of members making up the collection. In terms of being finished, the ring of stones in our example was finished with respect to being formed in a single step, and we can show the ring has a total number of members (another completeness criterion) with respect to a finished count of the members making up the ring. Finish is, therefore, still one of the properties that makes even a collection with a 'finite-unbounded' arrangement of members into a complete collection.

3.5.3 *A Completed Series is a Finished Series*

Every collection contains members. But the members in a collection do not necessarily have reciprocal relations between them, such as reciprocal logical implications. For example, consider the members making up a series or sequence. The order of those members, from *previous* to *next*, do not necessarily have reciprocal implications.

If any series or sequence has a *first* member, then it need not have a *last* member. For example, if a process has a first member, we can imagine without contradiction the process continuing without a last member (at least, without a "last" member in the sense of a final, concluding member that permanently finishes the process). Similarly, if series or sequence has a *beginning*, we can imagine it continuing without *ending* (again, in the permanent sense of finishing with a final, concluding member). So too, just because a series or sequence has a *start*, does not mean it will ever *finish*. A series or sequence without a first, beginning, or starting member but not last, ending, or finishing member is simply an *unfinished* series or sequence.

However, an unfinished series or sequence is not a complete series or sequence. To be complete, the series or sequence must *have* a finish and must *be* finished. The criterion of 'finish' must be met by any collection if it is to be 'complete'.

Recall that to be complete means a condition of having "all" members necessary to be representative of a class. To have "all" the members of a collection means there must be some last member to count or some last step in a collection of steps that finishes the collection and thereby establishes that *all* the necessary members are in the collection.

For example, suppose we wish to consider a collection of events or steps making up a process we desire to call 'complete', like a process of dividing a pie into pieces. Of course, the pie is no longer complete if it's divided, but the process of *dividing* the pie can still be completed. To complete the division of the pie into pie pieces requires all the needed divisions to take place. If there is no last operation in the series of divisions, then there is no such thing as *all* the divisions and therefore no completion of the dividing process because there must be more divisions to come that are not in the collection of divisions. To have *all* the steps of a series implies a last step in a series. And if the series is *finished*, it requires a last step to finish it.

Moreover, a reference to 'all' the members of a collection implies there is a 'last' member *to count* in a count of the collection's members, and a last member to count implies a finish to the counting process (even if the collection itself is not finished). A collection can only be considered 'finished' if its members can be counted to a non-zero, concluding member.

3.5.4 *Infinite Collections Must Be Finished to Be Complete*

I should note that some philosophers and mathematicians might concur with this analysis insofar as *finite* collections are concerned, but with respect to *infinite* collections many would disagree that 'finish' is a necessary criterion for a literally infinite collection to be 'complete'. However, the mathematician Georg Cantor (1845–1918) and set theorists following in his tradition disagree. Cantor, for example, referred to infinite collections as "finished" [102]. The concept of infinity in its literal sense is that it's a condition of a collection as somehow finished with a concluding quantity, a totality, *despite* having limitlessly many members, despite continuing "without end."

In Chapter 10 (see § 10.4) I will have more to say about how literally infinite collections are finished collections. For now, I will simply assert that, finite or infinite, if a collection is to be complete, it must be finished.

3.6 FULLNESS

A complete collection is also a full collection. Definitions:

- fullness: *the condition of being full.*
- full: (1) *unable to include additional members of the same class without changing the parameters of the collection.*

Something is *full* if it can appropriately be regarded as a collection and, as a collection, it is unable to include additional members that would have the same class (type of relation) as members already comprising the collection. A full collection is a collection that is "unable to include additional members of the same class" because including more of the same members would change the *parameters* of the collection. In other words, including more would change the conditions that determine how the members are related in the collection.

The 'parameters' of a collection may be a matter of logic or a matter of nature. Hence, a collection may be "unable to include additional members" for either logical or physical reasons.

Perhaps the members in the collection are related as a matter of logic and to include more such members would violate the logical relations defined by the parameters of the collection. For example, the collection of degrees comprising the latitude of a hemisphere cannot include more than 90 degrees without changing the logical relationship between the degrees and redefining the parameters of what 'latitude' means for a hemisphere. Recall the example of the chess set, which cannot include more than 32 game pieces without changing the parameters (which, in this case, are the rules) of the game. Or consider a passcode, which may be limited to a fixed number of characters. A user cannot create a passcode consisting of a string of characters longer than the character limit without changing the parameters of the passcode.

On the other hand, perhaps the collection is unable to include more members without changing parameters because the parameters are physical parameters, and the collection is in some way full of physical objects. In which case, the collection can have no more unless we change the physical parameters of the collection, like making the collection into part of a greater collection. A full pot of beans cannot include more beans unless we add volume to the container holding the bean, thereby changing its physical parameters.

Similarly, consider a tank of fuel and note how fullness is related to the notion of 'finish'. A tank that is a full tank of fuel can hold no more fuel. If you have filled the tank but find that it can indeed hold more fuel while you continue pouring fuel into the tank, as if the tank is a balloon being stretched as it is filled, that would mean the tank is not a full tank of fuel. In such a case, that would, in turn, imply what is considered the set of parameters for the tank (e.g., the size of the tank) is changing; if the parameters of the tank are changing to accommodate more fuel, then the tank does not have a full amount of fuel in it. Only if the tank is *finished* being filled in the sense that it can hold no more fuel is the tank a full tank of fuel. Of course, in the case of the tank of fuel, we are only considering the fuel to be a "collection" in the sense that the tank has its fuel portioned such as with a fuel gauge, but the principle is the same.

In all these examples, the given collection is a 'full' collection because the collection cannot include additional members of the same class without changing the parameters of the collection. When a collection is unable to include additional members in the same class as other objects in the collection, it is a full collection. If a collection can include more of the same members but does not, in fact, include those members that it could have included, then the collection is not full. This captures how we ordinarily think of something that is full.

Given the foregoing qualifications, we can stipulate a more formal definition for the term 'full' like so:

- full: (2) *a given collection, C, is full if and only if no additional element of the same class of elements in any non-empty subset of C can be included either as the member of any subset in C or to the entirety of elements in C without changing the parameters of C.*

We can now relate our conception of fullness to completeness by noting how something we wish to regard as 'complete' is something that is also full. Since we often use the word 'full' with respect to containers, this seems easy to do: a full pot of beans, a full tank of fuel, a full cup of coffee, and so forth are examples of full containers that might also qualify as complete if they meet the other completeness criteria. We also used examples of a full chess set, a full hemisphere, and a full passcode; these too, if full of their proper members (game pieces, degrees, characters, etc.), may also be considered complete—at least, provided they too meet the other completeness criteria.

But what about a single object we would ordinarily call 'complete' like a complete statue, or what about a succession of events? As to a single object, it can also be described as full if we analyze the object in terms of its parts and construe the parts as members of a collection. We may call a statue a "full statue" if the artist is finished carving the statue according to plan, but if the plan changed—if there is more to carve—then the parameters of the statue have changed and consequently we are not seeing the full statue. The statue was therefore not complete—there are more carvings to be included. A single object can thus be considered a collection of members and, as such, may be a full collection or a collection unfulfilled.

As to a succession of events, just think of a full race to the finish line—if the race continues on past the finish line, the parameters of the race have been changed; the race to the finish line was not the full race and the race was not complete at the finish line as more steps in the race must be included with the change of the race's parameters.

3.6.1 *Fullness and Completeness for Collections of Numbers*

Not all collections are full, of course. This is also true in mathematics where any collection of depicted values assumes a purpose of representation.

For example, consider the integers. An 'integer' is any number that can be written without a fractional component or decimal expression, which includes the positive natural numbers, their additive inverses (negative counterparts), and zero. Take two successive integers, such as 1 and 2. Next, consider a sequence of decimal numbers between 1 and 2, such as:

$$1, 1.4, 1.4137, 1.414201, 1.4142139, \sqrt{2}, 1.4142136, 1.41421, 1.41428, 1.46, 1.5, 2$$

If this sequence depicts only the numbers that we want to survey between 1 and 2, then we can say the sequence is the full sequence or a full collection of values. But this sequence of values depicts only a sample of some of the known decimal values between 1 and 2. Suppose we intended the list of numbers to include *all* known values between 1 and 2. In that case, the sequence as listed is not the full collection of values because there are plenty more known values between 1 and 2 that we can include and depict between 1 and 2. Let's suppose we can continue to list yet more such decimal numbers within the parameters of 1 and 2 until all known values are listed. Until if and when we list all the known numbers, the sequence as depicted would not be the full collection of known decimal numbers between 1 and 2.

Even supposing we can list all the *already-known* values between 1 and 2, consider what happens if our purpose is to represent the sequence as including not just those values between 1 and 2 known to date, but *all* decimal values between 1 and 2 *that anyone could ever list*. That would entail our listing for the sequence has the potential to include decimal values no one had previously written down before. In such a scenario, our list of values depicted in the sequence would *never* in practice become a full listing because at any time we could always expand the list yet further to include new values. So, in actual practice, there would never really be a full sequence of decimal values between 1 and 2—the sequence of depicted values will always remain inherently incomplete because we can always add to the list.

That covers prospects for having a full list of depicted values between 1 and 2, and a full list of in-practice depictable values between 1 and 2. But what about the full list of numbers that also includes numbers no one will ever depict, or be able to depict in actual practice, but nevertheless could depict at least *in principle*?

So let's consider those decimal values between 1 and 2 that include not just values depicted and values able to be practically depicted, but also values we are able only in principle to list. Such values are those we, counterfactually, would list if we not only had the interest but also the time and resources to do so—time and resources we do not and will not have in reality. If inclusion of in-principle values between 1 and 2 must also obtain in order to have a *full* list of values between 1 and 2, then the decimal values we can potentially list in practice between 1 and 2 would certainly not be the full list because it is still logically possible for the list to include values no one will ever, or could ever, know in actual practice. However, suppose we consider the purely logical possibility of a full list of decimal values between 1 and 2 in the sense that any list of decimal values we could potentially at some time depict between 1 and 2 (like the above example) has the logical possibility of being further expanded by including values no one will ever or could ever list in practice but could in principle. In that sense, the full listing is not the listing we have depicted in practice; rather, the "full listing" is the list we can only in principle depict.

3.6.2 *Fullness in Mathematics*

These distinctions for fullness have bearing on how some mathematicians use the term 'complete'. There is a technical use of the term 'complete' in mathematics for describing the set of decimal values between successive numbers. That technical form of completeness is 'Dedekind completeness', which we met earlier in § 3.3.4 [103].

Dedekind sought to define the completeness of a set of values as one in which no "gaps" are present in the sequence. In a 'Dedekind complete' set of values between any two numbers, there are so many intermediate decimal numbers that one could never list them all in practice. If the set of Dedekind complete numbers between any two integers can be *fully* listed at all, the full list can only be obtained in principle. However, a Dedekind complete sequence of decimal values between any two numbers includes not just all quantities of values able to be listed in principle, but it also includes too many values to be listed *even in principle*—in fact, a Dedekind complete sequence is conceived of as having "infinitely many" values [104].

It is not clear that a non-zero set of numbers the members of which are unable to be listed in principle is logically coherent. But assuming it is, there remains a problem with the term 'Dedekind complete' for describing it. The term is a misnomer since a Dedekind complete set does not satisfy all the completeness criteria. (A term such as *Dedekind continuous* would be more apt) [105].

Moreover, even if a Dedekind complete set is a *full* set of numbers, it is not a set that can be assigned a standing total. At the risk of grossly oversimplifying the concept of Dedekind completeness, consider again two successive integers such as 1 and 2. Because a Dedekind set of decimal numbers between any two numbers includes too many values to be listed even in principle, there is no such thing as a *total* number of decimal numbers between 1 and 2 or any other numbers you can name, no matter how close in value they are. So, even if we want to consider all the decimal numbers between 1 and 2 as constituting a 'full' set, it is a set without a total. For example, no matter how close to 2 a decimal number less than 2 is, there is always another decimal number (e.g., 1.999999...) just a bit closer to 2 in value—you can never arrive at a total number of decimal numbers between any two numbers.

As you can see, the implication of Dedekind's notion of a 'complete' set is rather like Cauchy's notion of 'complete'. Dedekind just had a different way of expressing his technical version of completeness using a mathematical technique of 'cuts' in a number line, which we won't worry about as the details are not important for our purposes.

Without a total to a Dedekind set, the full Dedekind set cannot be a complete set; its fullness is a necessary condition for its completeness, but not a sufficient condition. A Dedekind set of decimal numbers between any two numbers such as between 1 and 2 must have a total as well as fullness to count as 'complete' in the ordinary language sense defined earlier (see also the next section explicating totality). So, to say the numbers between 1 and 2 are 'Dedekind complete' is rather misleading. 'Dedekind full' might be a more appropriate term, but it is still not clear that it makes sense for a "full" collection to have too many values to list even in principle.

The Dedekind set example for use of the term 'complete' in mathematics shows that we must be careful to distinguish different uses of the word 'complete' in mathematics. Even while the use of the term 'complete' in mathematics may sometimes cohere with the usual lexical and precising definitions of completeness, there are times mathematicians say something is 'complete' that does not match completeness in the ordinary sense. They sometimes use 'complete' in specialized, technical senses and these senses can be misleading if they contradict what we normally take completeness to imply, such as the fullness of a collection.

As we saw earlier, Cauchy completeness is another example. 'Cauchy completeness' is a misnomer for 'complete' in our ordinary use of 'complete' because Cauchy completeness also does not satisfy all of the criteria for completeness in the precise sense of the term. 'Cauchy completeness' applies to collections that lack fullness. A 'Cauchy complete' sequence is not a full sequence; it is a sequence that only converges *near*, or *approximates*, another value and so can always include more values. So, this is yet another reason why a 'Cauchy complete' sequence is not a complete sequence in the precise sense of completeness, and it too is a misleading term. 'Cauchy whole and entire' would be more accurate since the kind of sequence it refers to is claimed to have no gaps and be missing no elements, even though it could always include more without changing parameters and so is never full.

For such reasons, I find all the mathematical definitions for 'complete' to be very misleading; it seems to me that mathematicians should have used a different term than 'complete' for describing orders of numeric series or elements since we usually take a complete collection to be a *finished* and *full* collection—neither of which apply to 'Cauchy complete' collections and both of which dubiously apply to 'Dedekind complete' collections.

3.7 TOTALITY

A complete collection is a collection with totality, but the word 'totality' can be a bit slippery. In contemporary set theory, totality has various technical meanings involving orders and relations between sets. For example, the term 'totality' may simply mean that for any two elements in a set, either one is greater or equal to the other, or vice versa. But that technical conception of totality is not the kind of totality that has bearing for quantitative completeness across multiple contexts, for there are contexts in which none of the members of a given collection have either $\geq$ or $\leq$ relations and yet we would say the collection is both quantitatively complete and a totality. So, instead of such a narrow, set-theoretic notion of totality, we need a more general, but still quantitative, concept of totality that is implied by what we usually think of as needed for a collection (ordered or not) to be complete.

Some possible definitions—

- totality:
    (1) *the state or condition of having a total (i.e., having an exact sum).*
    (2) *that which has a total (e.g., a collection that has a sum).*
    (3) *the state or condition of being total (i.e., being a whole and entire amount).*
    (4) *that which is total (e.g., a collection that is whole and entire in amount).*

Of these definitions, we need to know what kind of totality is implied by the completeness of a collection.

The third and fourth definitions of 'totality' reiterate the properties of wholeness and entirety, but with respect to having an *amount* (a value equal to a total). But completeness is more than wholeness and entirety with respect to the amount of members in a collection.

Completeness implies totality in the sense of the first two definitions of totality: a complete collection has totality (first sense) because it is a collection with a total. The collection can be accurately assigned a number equal to an exact sum of numbers. For a collection to be 'a totality' (second sense) is for a collection to have a total, a number equal to an exact sum of numbers.

Moreover, for a collection to be complete, it must have 'totality' in the first two senses but for a collection to have or be such a totality is not necessarily for the collection to be 'complete' because the collection may not be *whole*. A collection that is not whole may still have a total. A collection of books divided in half can still be totaled—two groups of books added back together will make one collection of books. The collection still has totality in the sense of having a total even if it is not the whole collection.

Then too, a collection may have totality and yet not be a 'complete' collection because it may be only a partial collection rather than an *entire* collection. That is, the elements that are in the collection can still be totaled even though the collection is not entire and therefore not complete. A collection is not 'entire' if it is missing elements. Despite missing elements, the collection can still have totality in the sense of having a total, but the collection cannot be complete. For example, a pearl necklace may be missing a pearl, but we can still count the pearls that are in the necklace and arrive at a total. The necklace has a totality of pearls, but not an entirety of pearls and therefore it is an incomplete necklace.

A collection can also have a total regardless of whether or not it is finished. A collection that is *unfinished* and therefore incomplete, may also still have a total as when the collection constitutes a series of changing values. For example, a bank account always has a total holding even if the total holding changes with each transaction; collections like the bank account have a variable total or a running total; a total that changes, showing that totality does not necessarily indicate finish.

A collection can therefore still have totality without being whole, entire, or finished.

But here we must make another distinction that has to do with our normative procedures for identifying collections as having a totality of members. We need to distinguish between the totality a collection *does* in fact have and the totality a collection *should* or *ought* to have [106]. If we define a collection in terms of having a value greater than zero—a positive value it should or ought to have—and yet the sum of elements in the collection we do have is equal to zero, then the collection lacks the total required. But that does not mean the collection lacks totality *per se*; rather, the collection is not complete by virtue of missing elements, being able to have more elements, and not being finished, but it still has a total number.

Having a total number brings up an important point. A total may be equal to an exact sum, but that sum need not be *specified*. That is, the total need not be in the form of a known, constant number you can write down. For finite collections, the total of a collection may be represented by a variable, and the variable would need to be assigned a value via calculation or computation in order to specify what number the total equals.

For example: $3{,}795 \times 5{,}286 = x$. Here x is the variable—the unknown total. So, having a total does not necessarily mean the value of the total is known prior to calculation; perhaps a constant number for the total is not specified and needs to be determined by a mathematical operation. However, an *unspecified* total is not an *unspecifiable* total. Having a total means that a constant number *can be* specified for the value of the variable representing the total, at least in principle.

The definition of totality also allows that even a collection with no members at all still has a total—an exact sum; namely a total equal to 0 (zero). As long as the collection can be given a constant value, even if that value is 0, it has totality. So, an empty or null set does have totality.

For now, let's stick to totals having non-zero values just to keep things simple. To have a total with a *non-zero* value means the collection is, at least in principle, *countable*. To be countable to have the ability to be counted to an exact sum. In order to be able to count all the members of a collection, a count of the collection requires a *first* member to count and a *last* member to count, even if the two are the same member. Without a first member to count, the count cannot occur for a count is always a count *from* a first number *to* a last number, and without a last member to count, the count cannot be *finished* at a last number. A count must be able to finish at a last number because the last number counted is equal to an exact sum, which is what a total is.

As mentioned previously, aside from collections with a 'standing total' representing a constant number of members in the collection, there are some collections that grow or diminish in size over time, with a 'running total' of members. When we enumerate the members of a series that is continuing to grow or diminish, the concluding, or 'last', member counted is not an absolutely last member in terms of representing a 'final' member after which no more members will ever be added to the collection. Instead, the series has a running total of members. Even so, the series, as a collection, still has a 'last' member in the sense of having a member that captures the size of the collection *at the time of the count*—a finish to the process of counting the members (rather than a finish to change in the number of members counted). And when a collection can be assigned a specific, constant value that captures its size at a given time, the collection has totality. Hence, even an unfolding series has a totality.

Any collection with a non-zero value of only one member is also a collection with a conclusion to its count of members. In the case of a collection having only one member, the first member and the last member are the same member—the count of members in the collection is over in one step.

All of this has bearing on completeness: if a collection is a complete collection, it is a collection that must have totality—a total that can, at least in principle, be reached by a count of the members, first to last. Moreover, to be complete, the collection's total must be a standing total rather than a running total—the collection's total must have a value in the form of a *constant number* assigned to it as a sum or product of its component members.

A collection with a running total of members is an unfinished and therefore incomplete collection. However, a collection with a running total may still be considered complete in a narrow sense. But a collection with a running total of members can be considered a complete collection when we consider the collection to be 'complete' *as it is at a given time* (something not often taken into consideration in the 'tenseless' formalism of mathematics). Taking time into consideration, we must consider the latest total in the running total to be our standing total *for that time*, defining the total for the collection. Without the ability to assign a definite time marking a finish to any possible count of the collection, a collection with a running total of members is not a complete collection.

There is one caveat I should point out with regard to a collection's completeness requiring a total count of members. In order to be complete, any collection must contain members able (in principle) to be countable to a total, but it is also true that a collection can be complete without having both a first member and a last member *with respect to the order in which its members are arranged*. A complete circle of stones has no first stone and no last stone in its closed curve of formation and yet the circle is complete (see **Figure 1.1** in § 1.1.2).

However, to be complete a collection *must* have both a first and last member *to a count of the members*, at least in principle. For example, as a complete collection, the circle of stones must, among other things, have members (stones) able to be counted to a total. We can perform such a count by arbitrarily selecting a stone from the circle by which to begin a count of the stones until the last stone is counted and we thereby arrive at a total. If a count of members in a collection cannot, even in principle, be given a standing total (as opposed to a running total) from a count of its members, then the collection is not a complete collection. It is an incomplete collection—perhaps an incomplete collection with a running total, but still not a complete collection.

Be that as it may, I can just hear protests that I have not considered collections that have too many elements to count, *even in principle*. In other words, *limitless* collections. Why can't limitless collections also be complete?

We will explore limitlessness in the next chapter. Until then, note that a limitless collection is a collection that cannot be given a total, even in principle. A limitless collection is, therefore, a collection *without a total* and, without a total, a collection does not have the property of totality. Without totality, a collection cannot be complete by our earlier definition of completeness.

That totality is required for completeness, if correct, does have implications for how terminology is used in mathematics. For example, a collection that is often said to be 'Dedekind complete', such as the set of *all* decimal numbers between any two integers, is rather misnamed because the number of numbers in the Dedekind set between any two integers, such as between 1 and 2, is said to be limitless [107]. But if there is *no limit* to the number of numbers between any two integers like 1 and 2, then such conflicts with the completeness of the same sequence of numbers because completeness requires totality. Even if we grant the number 2 is a quantity toward which all the numbers added from 1 on up through all the most incremental of the decimal numbers, that does not give us a *total* number of decimal numbers between 1 and 2 if such are *limitless*. And without such a total, the collection of decimal numbers cannot be complete. So here again, 'Dedekind complete' becomes a misnomer for what should be considered, at best, 'Dedekind full' or perhaps 'Dedekind continuous'.

In brief, totality is required for completeness. If a collection has no *totality*, it has no *total* and if it has no total, it cannot be complete. Conversely, completeness requires totality; no complete collection lacks a total.

3.8 APPLYING THE COMPLETENESS CRITERIA

We now have a much clearer idea of what it means for a collection to be complete: to be complete implies having the properties of being whole, entire, finished, full, and total. Now that completeness is sufficiently defined, we can use the definition's constituent terms (wholeness, entirety, finish, fullness, and totality) as criteria by which to assess whether a given collection is complete or incomplete.

The criteria help show the way in which a collection can be made complete over time, and the way in which collections complete in themselves can be added together to form a series, even a series that is not itself complete. The criteria for completeness also enable us to investigate the number scales, such as the scale of naturals and the scale of wholes ($\mathbb{N}^C$ and $\mathbb{W}^C$), to see what it is to have complete sets of numbers from those scales. That in turn will give us an indication of what it means for a collection to be 'infinite' in the literal sense of being complete in quantity as well as limitless in quantity.

First, let's apply the properties of wholeness, entirety, finish, fullness, and totality as criteria to a collection and see if the collection in question fits the definition of completeness. As an example, consider a 'complete' segment of whole numbers like the set of numbers we considered earlier—the first six whole numbers in $\mathbb{W}^C$; that is, $\{0, 1, 2, 3, 4, 5\}$.

Incidentally, despite their name, the whole numbers of $\mathbb{W}^C$ do not necessarily have to do with the property of wholeness as earlier defined. It is true that you can imagine a positive number from $\mathbb{W}^C$, such as 1, being divisible (for example, 1 can be divided into halves: 0.5 and 0.5) and yet not divided prior to the operation of division upon it. In that regard, I suppose 1 can be considered a number "divisible but undivided" and so aptly called a 'whole' number. On the other hand, 0 (zero) is a whole number too, but 0 is not divisible. So, the term 'whole number' is a bit misleading. Regardless, the name 'whole number' struck, so we'll roll with it—at least, for the positive numbers and zero as belonging to the same scale of numbers.

Anyway, applying the criteria of completeness to {0, 1, 2, 3, 4, 5}, a set of whole numbers from $\mathbb{W}^C$, we find that:

- The set is 'whole'. The set is not divided or separated into two or more sets such that the set no longer has the necessary members to represent a given class.

- The set is 'entire'. No subsets are missing. If a subset such as [2, 3] were missing, the set would not be entire, but no subsets are missing. And no elements are missing; if a single number, such as 3 or 4, were missing, the set would not be the entire set but all numerals representing numbers 0–5 are present.

- The set is 'finished'. The process of constructing the sequence of numbers (0–5) is all done, leaving a concluding number of numbers in the collection: 6.

- The set is 'full'. No more numbers, like 6, 7, 8, etc., can be added to the set without changing the parameters of the set as being a set of only the first six whole numbers.

- The set is a 'totality': 6 represents the total—the exact sum—of *numerals* in the collection and 5 represents the total with respect to the cardinality of *numbers* making up the collection.

Since the set is a whole collection that is also an entire, finished, full, and total collection, it is a *complete* set of the first six numbers in $\mathbb{W}^C$.

The criteria for completeness entail that any collection that would be called 'complete' must be a collection that is not separated into two or more subsets so as to lack members *necessary to represent a given class* (wholeness), the collection is not missing members *as subsets or elements* (entirety), the collection has necessarily reached a *concluding amount* at the close of any process that builds it up or reduces it in size (finish), the collection cannot contain any more members of the same class *without changing its parameters* (fullness), and the collection is able to be *assigned a constant number* for the number of members it contains (totality). That is what it means for a collection to be complete.

3.9 INCOMPLETENESS

Any collection that does not meet one or more of the completeness criteria is not a complete collection. To lack wholeness or entirety or finish or fullness or totality, or any combination of those properties, is to lack completeness. The following sub-sections provide some examples of how a collection may be incomplete.

3.9.1 *Total But Neither Whole, Nor Entire, Nor Finished, Nor Full*

Collections with non-zero totals lacking in wholeness, entirety, finish, and fullness are incomplete collections. Consider a puzzle for which all the puzzle pieces are not joined together. The puzzle is not *whole* because its pieces are 'divided' or separated from one another such that they lack the necessary relation of fitting together, the puzzle is not *entire* because there are pieces left out, the puzzle is not *finished* since there are more pieces to put in, and the puzzle is not *full* because more pieces are able to be put in without changing the puzzle's parameters. And while the puzzle may have a *total* number of pieces put together, lacking the other conditions makes the puzzle, as a collection of pieces, incomplete.

Even an empty set has a total—namely, a total of zero. In that sense, an empty set can be considered a 'totality' (defined as the state of condition of having a total) if we allow a "total of zero" to count as a totality.

But because an empty set has no members, it does not have 'finish' as a property at all—there is no concluding *non-zero* number of members. The empty set also lacks wholeness since it is not divisible and it lacks entirety because it is missing elements to enumerate. The empty set lacks fullness because, as a set, it could include at least one element but has none. Because of these conditions, the empty set is necessarily an incomplete set.

3.9.2 *Total and Finished But Neither Whole, Nor Entire, Nor Full*

A published book with pages ripped out is a good example of a collection (of pages) that is both a total collection (it has a number of pages) and a finished collection (it is published). But the book is not whole because it is divided from its pages, and it is not an entire book because it is missing pages. Moreover, the book is not full since the missing pages could be included without changing the parameters of the cover. Because the book lacks wholeness, entirety, and fullness, the book is therefore incomplete.

3.9.3 *Total and Whole But Neither Finished, Nor Entire, Nor Full*

Imagine a ring of beads. There is a total number of beads, satisfying the totality condition. When one bead is lost from the ring, the ring seals up. In one sense, the ring is still whole (undivided) since it is still a ring without gaps or divisions; in another sense, the ring is divided from the bead that was lost from the ring. Let's suppose the bead is not just removed but 'poof'—it no longer exists. In that case, the parameters for the collection allow us to consider the ring of beads, as a collection of beads, to be 'whole' despite the loss of the bead. Even so, the ring is not the entire collection of beads since it is missing the bead it lost and it is not the finished collection of beads since we must add a new bead back in for the collection to be entire and to be equal to its original total. Moreover, the ring of beads is not a full ring of beads in the sense that we could include another bead back in and not change the parameters of how we had defined the ring of beads. This goes to show that being 'whole' and having a total is not enough: without being finished, entire, and a full set of beads, the collection of beads forming the ring is incomplete.

3.10 ON BECOMING COMPLETE AND ON REMAINING INCOMPLETE

Some collections start life as complete and end life as complete; others begin life incomplete but end life complete, some start as complete but end as incomplete, and yet others start incomplete and end incomplete. In short, some collections are defined by completeness from the get-go, while others gain or lose members as they are formed or reduced. All of these ways in which the completeness of a collection either remains constant or undergoes changes have something in common: the completeness of a collection transpires over a series of events or steps.

The term 'series' was defined as a sequence formed by succession. The members of a sequence can be events over time, like the successive ticks of a clock, or the members of a sequence might instead be successive steps in a process, like the steps taken to follow a recipe or to play a song. Sequences of successive events or steps like these are examples of series.

Another example of a series is one in which the members of a sequence are events or steps in which there appears an object or collection of objects. For example, we might have a sequence of steps in which books are gathered, with each step in the sequence adding a new book to the sequence until the sequence ends. Then again, we might have a sequence of entire book collections that are formed over time (like the collection of Tolkien books followed by the collection of Tolstoy books); if so, we have another kind of series—a series of collections.

Whether we have a sequence of steps in which a new element is added to a collection or a sequence of steps in which a new collection is added to a sequence of collections, a series is formed. In the former instance, we have a series forming a collection; in the latter instance, we have a series of collections forming. To take the previous examples, as more books or book collections are added to the sequence collected, a series is formed and may come to completion.

These examples raise an important distinction in the way different kinds of series undergo change: One way is for a single collection of objects to undergo change over a series of events, while another way is for a sequence of new collections to appear over the successive events of the series.

Suppose we look at the members of a series with each member being a single step in a process. And suppose at each one of those steps there appears a collection of objects. In that case, each step in the series might correspond either to an event in which a change occurs in a single collection over the steps of the series or perhaps each step in the series corresponds to an event in which a new collection appears. In the former case, we have a single collection in which new members are added over a series of steps until the collection becomes (possibly, but not necessarily) completed. In the latter case, we have a series of new collections being born one after another.

As an example of a series in which a single collection becomes complete over a sequence of steps, consider a tin for baking muffins. The tin may potentially contain six muffins. It doesn't matter in which of the cups a particular muffin rests—the muffins may be in any order, so we can regard the collection of muffins as a *set* of muffins.

Of course, the collection of muffins is only loosely speaking a "set" in the mathematical sense since the cups in the tin are themselves physical rather than symbolic and are relatively ordered rather than unordered, but this caveat should not detract from the collection being regarded as a 'set' in a loose sense for the purposes of the example.

Suppose the tin only contains one muffin with five empty cups (as in **Figure 3.2**). If use the mathematical idea of a 'set', then we can regard the tin as either a complete 'set' of one muffin or an incomplete set of muffins in which six muffins would complete the set. Let's define a *complete set* of muffins as six muffins—a full tin. With that in mind, having only a single muffin in the tin makes an incomplete set, so we need to add more muffins to the tin until the tin is full and we have a complete set of muffins.

Figure 3.2: A muffin tin holding a set of muffins that has only one muffin as a member.

Next, let's suppose that we begin adding muffins, one by one in no particular order, to the muffin tin. Let's define a *complete series* in this example as a series of steps in which muffins are added to the tin until the tin can contain no more muffins. The series is complete when the muffin tin becomes full. In the last step the tin contains a complete set of muffins, while over the first five steps in the series the set of muffins is not complete (as in **Figure 3.3**).

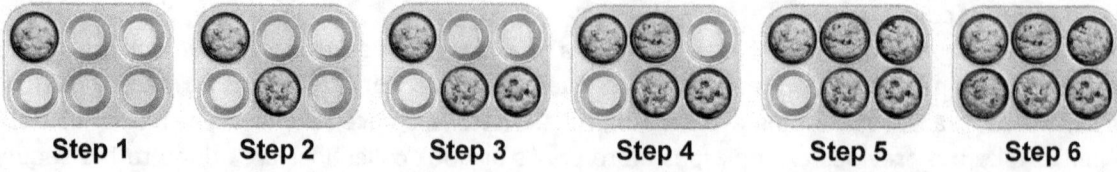

| Step 1 | Step 2 | Step 3 | Step 4 | Step 5 | Step 6 |

Figure 3.3: A complete series of steps in which an incomplete set in the first step of the series becomes a complete set in the last step of the series. In this example a 'set' is a real, physical set rather than the abstract set of the mathematician; however, abstract sets could likewise start as incomplete and become complete over a series of mental steps.

Sets are often thought of as complete, but the muffin tin example shows that we can consider a set as incomplete if it is missing members, and we can make that same set complete or incomplete over a series of steps. When there are no more steps for the series to take in completing the set, as when the muffin tin becomes full, the series of steps itself is also completed; a complete series in which an initially incomplete set is made complete in the last step of the series.

Now let's consider the contrary—an incomplete series of complete sets. Suppose, for example, we have a series of sets in which each set has a number of rabbits as members. We'll start with a set containing only one rabbit and then replace it with a set containing two clones of the first rabbit. The set of two rabbits is then replaced by a new set of three clones of the first rabbit, and so forth to create a series of increasingly larger sets (see **Figure 3.4**).

| Step 1 | Step 2 | Step 3 | Step 4 | Step 5 | Step 6 |

Figure 3.4: An incomplete series of steps in which each step is a set that is complete in itself. Once again, the example is meant to represent real, physical 'sets' rather than abstract sets, but abstract sets may also accumulate over a series of mental steps.

The rabbit example differs from the muffin example in certain respects. For one thing, we are not considering a single set changing over a series of steps as we did in the muffin example, but rather a series of individual sets with new sets replacing old sets as the series of sets progresses according to a sequence.

Also, unlike in the muffin example where a single set in the series was defined upfront as incomplete without a total number of members equal to six, the rabbit example defines a set as incomplete if it lacks a total equal to the sum produced by the successor function from the previous set in the sequence. Step 3 would be incomplete if it only contained two rabbits, for instance. As each new set is generated, the set in that step is complete *for that step* if it follows the pattern of the successor function. Hence, as the series begins with a set equal to only one rabbit $(0 + 1 = 1)$, that set is complete in itself. As the series goes on to form new versions of that original set, each new set in the series is also a complete set as is. We have a series of complete sets rather than a single incomplete set being made complete over a series of steps as in the muffin example.

There is also another significant difference between these examples: unlike the muffin example, in which the *series* of steps had a defined end (six steps to make a complete series and a competed set of muffins), the rabbit series has no defined end. The series in **Figure 3.4** is depicted with only six steps, but since there is no defined end for the series, the series of rabbit sets can continue to add new sets of rabbits. This entails that the series is incomplete because it is not finished and not full: there is not a concluding set of rabbits in the series and another new set can be included in the series according to the parameters of the series.

We therefore see at least two different ways in which to regard completeness with respect to sets within series:

1. A set may be incomplete but formed over a series of steps until it possibly becomes complete. Such a series—a series in which a set begins as incomplete but can be made complete over a succession of steps—is an example of what I call a 'closed series'.

2. A set may be complete as is, perhaps as just one complete set in a series of complete sets. Because the series as such has no defined end, the series is not finished; rather, the series remains incomplete as long as a succession of steps can continue to add new sets. Any incomplete series of sets is an 'open series'.

The foregoing examples are not the only ways a series can be 'open' or 'closed'. For example, a 'closed series' need not contain a set of objects brought to completion. If each step in the closed series corresponds to some change in the quantity of objects contained in a given set (like adding muffins to the set of muffins), then although that set can possibly be completed over a specifiable number of steps, the closed series can also end without completing a collection of objects. After all, we could have stopped adding muffins to the tin at Step 5, leaving the tin one member shy and the set of muffins unfinished. Further, a series could be closed by taking its steps in the opposite order—for example, by removing muffins from the tin one at a time until they are all gone. In that case also, the series closes with an incomplete set. We should also keep in mind that a closed series need not be a complete series in terms of the steps it takes. A closed series is simply a series that has a fixed and specifiable number of events or steps within it, regardless of whether or not it contains a complete sequence of steps.

A qualification about 'open series': an open series need not be a series of complete sets only. An open series could be an incomplete series of incomplete sets—as with one unfinished project after another—or an open series could be an incomplete series containing an incomplete set that changes in quantity over time. For example, we might have a set of rabbits continue to multiply into an ever-larger set of rabbits—an incomplete set growing over an inherently incomplete series of stages. What makes an open series 'open' is that it always remains incomplete as a series, without a defined end in terms of taking new steps or adding more events to its sequence; the sets of objects within such a series (like the rabbits) may themselves be either complete or incomplete. The rabbit example shows us the former—each set of rabbits in the series is complete, as is, while the series itself remains incomplete since it is open to new sets of rabbits being added to the series.

While there are other ways that collections can be complete within open and closed series, the two primary examples we have considered—the muffin example (a closed series that completes a set) and the rabbit example (an open series of complete sets)—will suffice for defining our terms.

3.11 SERIES

In § 2.2.6, I distinguished between 'series' and 'accessions' (the latter being a mathematical "series"—summed sequences of numbers). An example of an accession is $a_1 + a_2 + a_3 + ... + a_n$. The same accession may be expressed via an index of summation, like so:

$$\sum a_i \text{ or } \sum_{i=0}^{n} a_i$$

The term 'accession' is sometimes used in colloquial speech to refer to an increase that is temporal in nature, like a collection growing larger. However, I believe this is also true of mathematical accessions—the terms are written out in sequence or run with the command of a computer program, so they are instances of series in the temporal sense of the term.

Still, it is true that the mathematical notion of a 'series' (an accession) is atemporal in the sense that it makes no reference to the formation of a sequence by a succession of consecutive steps as does the ordinary use of the term 'series'. And in a sense, this is the strength of the mathematical approach. It is a strength in that it allows us to quantify the successive events or steps making up a series in order to accomplish tasks without attending to time. However, in another sense, it can also be a weakness of the mathematical approach in that it often misleads into thinking that what is represented as being added together is static when it is actually dynamic. All mathematical accessions are outputs that occur in time, whether the time such takes is taken notice of or not.

3.11.1 *Static or Dynamic?*

Because accessions—or 'series' in the mathematical sense of the term—are sequences of additions that equal sums and a sum corresponds to a set of mathematical objects, you might suppose an accession, or mathematical series, is a static object—an 'ordered set' of members all of which are contemporaneous with one another, grouped together into a total (a sum) that does not change. This common assumption is based on the notion that a sum indicates a final set of terms or mathematical objects, irrespective of the consecutive steps taken to produce the whole of the series. So, when mathematicians define the term 'series' in terms of a sum, that definition might seem to imply that a series must be a static object. However, this is not the case in the real world.

Every series—a series of baseball games, a series of television programs, a series of school years, etc.—is dynamically formed with a succession of events or steps and is merely *represented* in some static form. For example, in **Figure 3.4**, the rabbits at Step 6 appear consecutively after Steps 2 through 5 and so are not really contemporaneous with the rabbits at Step 2, though it can appear that way simply because the images of these steps have been represented on the page side-by-side for convenience.

Take a snapshot of a series in formation, such as the series of falling dominoes in § 2.2.6, **Figure 2.4**, and the series may appear "static" in terms of the frozen event captured. Even so, the series need not be considered as a static set in the sense of having its successive steps there "all at once," independent of a formation process.

If a series is "static" at all, it is only static in the sense of being represented at a particular event or step during its formation or having its steps all represented at once side by side. It's really the representation of the mathematical series that is static, not the series itself.

For this reason, in § 2.2.6 I distinguished a series as something temporally dynamic from the static representation of a sequence of elements added together (an accession), which mathematicians typically call a 'series'. An accession is "static" in the sense of being a representation of elements added together; after all, there they are on the page altogether:

$$a_1 + a_2 + a_3 + ... + a_n$$

Still, they were thought of and typed down, one after another in time. An accession is thus an example of a series in the usual sense: a sequence formed dynamically, over time.

This is certainly true of a mathematical object like $a_1 + a_2 + a_3 + ... + a_n$, the terms of which must have been invented or produced over consecutive moments of time. We can refer to $a_1 + a_2 + a_3 + ... + a_n$ as an 'accession' to express that it is a mathematical object, or we can refer to it as a 'series', which is to say each a_x represents a term appearing in temporal succession even if the series as a whole is represented as an accession with all the a_x next to each other on the page in static form.

The dynamic nature of even a mathematical accession becomes apparent in the fact that not only are new terms added as the accession is formed, but also the mathematical value of the accession changes successively as the new terms are added. The sum of members in the accession changes as the *succession* of steps forming accession proceeds. Thus, the accession as a *series* in the usual, temporal sense of the term has a running total—a succession of sums—until if and when the accession ends as a series, yielding a final sum.

The lexical definition of series thus applies regardless of mathematical context; a series is a sequence formed by succession regardless of how 'series' is defined or measured mathematically. An accession is simply an example of a series in that it is an object formed over time, and it may also represent a series in that its terms may symbolize objects or events that appear over time, like the members of the series in **Figures 3.3–3.4**.

3.11.2 *When a Sequence is a Series*

By using the term 'series' to indicate temporal succession and using other terms like 'accession' and 'degression' to represent sums and differences for mathematical sequences, it follows that any sequence formed over time is a series. So, what mathematicians usually call a 'sequence', a sting of terms separated by commas ($a_1, a_2, a_3, ..., a_n$), may itself be a series in the temporal sense because it is formed over time, the terms appearing one after another. (I suppose I could have typed the elements of the series in any order, inserting some prior to others, but that would just mean they appeared by a different order than in which they are represented—they still constitute a series with respect to time.) We may therefore refer to the sequence $a_1, a_2, a_3, ..., a_n$ or to the accession $a_1 + a_2 + a_3 + ... + a_n$ as a 'series' in that the elements or terms are created over time.

Unless otherwise noted or apparent from context, when I use the term 'series' I will mean the term in the lexical sense as implying temporal succession, but it will remain true that any of the events or steps in the sequence of a series can be totaled into a "static" sum or set of elements, at least as far as the series is formed up to the moment in time that it is measured.

3.12 SUMMING COMPLETE AND INCOMPLETE SERIES

A series can be summed *with or without being complete*. A closed series, for example, has a defined number, or definable number, of members—a number equal to a sum of members—that represents the total members of the series. That total may represent the closed series at some point during its formation or when the series is finished.

If the closed series has a new object that appears at each step in its sequence, then the closed series has at each moment in its formation a sum of terms representing the objects that have appeared so far. The series will also have a sum of terms representing all of the objects collected when the series as such ends. In the example of the muffin tin, we can label each muffin placed in the tin with a number and sum the muffins added to the tin along the way, and then draw a final sum of muffins when the tin is full.

Let's continue with a closed series formed by increasing membership. Not only may the sum of steps and the sum objects at each step increase during formation of the closed series, but also the closed series will have a mathematical sum of members comprising any collection that appears at any step along the way *regardless* of whether or not the series as such is complete or contains a complete collection of anything. Consider a closed series of steps in which the muffins are added to the tin, but with one cup left unfilled—the series ends without being finished and without a complete set of muffins. Here we have a sum (5 muffins in 5 steps) without a complete series (6 steps) and without a complete set of muffins (defined as 6 muffins). Here we have an example of a closed series with a sum—a sum of steps and a sum of the muffins, but without completeness when the series came to a close as a final, incomplete set.

An open series, on the other hand, is always *incomplete as a series* and so has only a variable sum of members. That is, the open series has a sum as a 'running total'—a sum that is updated as the series undergoes further change in the quantity of its members. Because the open series has no defined end, the open series has no *final* sum to its sequence of members; it only has a sum of members *so far*, at a particular time. The open series has no final sum of members either in terms of its events/steps or the collections of objects/terms composing its sequence. The "last" member of an open series is represented by a variable and, as such, it is always subject to change in value.

As an example, we have the series of rabbits; as a series that is 'open', it is necessarily incomplete in the respect of having a continuously changing sum. Another example of an open series is a series of issues published in a news periodical still going to press. The series of publications is not finished, and therefore not complete, but there is a sum of issues published so far.

So, a closed series has a *final sum* of events or steps regardless of whether or not it is complete while an open series also has a sum, despite being inherently incomplete, though in the form of a *running total*. These examples illustrate that, although open and closed series have sums, just having a sum does not entail completeness. The ability to be summed, at least in principle, is a necessary but not sufficient condition for the completeness of a series.

3.13 COMPLETENESS, INCOMPLETENESS, AND INFINITY

If to have a sum is necessary for a series to be complete, this would seem to have implications for what it means to be quantitatively infinite. Summation, as an implication of completeness, also has implications for both literal and figurative infinity.

3.13.1 *Literal Infinity as Complete*

Literal infinity is the condition of being *complete* as well as limitless. A literally infinite collection is not just limitless in its quantity of members, it is also a whole, entire, finished, and full *totality*—the latter property implying a total equal to a sum. Since to be complete implies having a sum, and to be literally infinite is to be complete as well as limitless, then a literally infinite collection must in some way have a 'sum' for the whole of the collection despite the limitlessness of the members in the collection. And if the literally infinite collection is a series brought to completion—which is to say, a complete set—then it would seem the collection as a completed infinite series must have a 'sum' of members that is limitless in mathematical value—an *infinite number*.

However, some mathematicians deny there is such a thing as an "infinite number" or an "infinite sum" and instead promote the notion that literal infinity can be a quantity alright, even a complete quantity, but not one equal to a sum. What it would mean for a quantity not to have a sum is difficult to comprehend (if it can be comprehended at all), and we will need to explore further what it means further in the chapters to follow.

3.13.2 *Figurative Infinity as Incomplete*

Figurative infinity, in contrast to literal infinity, is much easier to comprehend with respect to series and sums. To be 'infinite' in a figurative sense is simply to be an open series, a series that is inherently *incomplete* and continues to grow in quantity indefinitely but always remains finite at each step of the way no matter how long it goes on. A figurative infinity is a series that can be summed at any given time, but that sum is only one in a running total of increasing sums because a figurative infinity is never completed. It is best to think of figurative infinity as the condition of having a ceaseless series of sums with no final sum that halts the series.

3.13.3 *Enumerating Completely and Incompletely to Infinity*

Both kinds of infinity—the literal and the figurative—are quantitative conditions of collections. For a collection to have a quantity is for the collection to be *enumerable*. So, both literally infinite collections and figuratively infinite collections must be 'enumerable' collections, even if not in the same way.

The literally infinite collection is enumerable in the sense of the collection having a quantity of members that can be *completely* enumerated, despite the limitlessness of the collection. The figuratively infinite collection is enumerable in the sense of the collection having a continual series of new, finite sums for the collection—a running total that at any given time enumerates all the members of the collection for that time. Such a collection does not cease and so is, metaphorically speaking, 'limitless'. A figuratively infinite collection is thus a series that is always *incompletely* enumerated.

In the next chapter, we'll examine more closely what it means to use a scale of numbers to enumerate all the way to infinity, both for literal infinity and figurative infinity.

CHAPTER 3 IN REVIEW

❖ An infinite quantity is a limitless amount of objects comprising a collection. The collection may be either complete or incomplete but must be in some sense 'limitless' to be infinite.

❖ To be complete entails the given collection is whole, entire, finished, full, and total. Any collection that does not meet one or more of the completeness criteria is not a complete collection. For example, to lack wholeness or entirety or finish or fullness or totality, or any combination of those properties, is to not be complete.

❖ Literal infinity is the condition of being a collection that is *complete* as well as limitless in quantity. Since to be complete implies having a total, and to be literally infinite is to be complete as well as limitless, then a literally infinite collection must in some way have a 'total'—an infinite number—for the "sum" of the whole of the collection despite the limitlessness of the members in the collection.

❖ Figurative infinity is simply the condition of being an open series, a series that is inherently *incomplete* (never finished, full, or having a final sum). The open series continues to grow in quantity indefinitely but always remains finite at each step of the way no matter how long it goes on. An example is a figuratively 'infinite' series of finite numbers of which there is no "infinite number."

❖ An infinite quantity is therefore a quantity that is limitless either in the sense of being complete (literal infinity) or intrinsically incomplete (figurative infinity).

4: ON ENUMERATING TOWARD INFINITY

Mathematicians distinguish between two different kinds of infinite collections: those that are enumerable and those that are not. We'll save the notion of infinite collections that are not enumerable until § 13.10. In the meantime, this chapter will examine infinite collections that are enumerable and explore what it would mean for an infinite collection to be enumerable.

4.1 ENUMERATION TO INFINITY IS A MATTER OF SCALE

To enumerate is to assign numbers to objects, such as objects in a collection. However, to enumerate an *infinite* collection means different things depending on whether the collection is literally infinite or figuratively infinite.

If the collection to be enumerated is literally infinite, then it would take a number system that is itself literally infinite to enumerate it. And that enumeration can be brought to completion.

If, on the other hand, the collection to be enumerated is a figuratively infinite series, then it only takes a figuratively infinite number system to enumerate the members of the series as the series continues to grow. In that case, the enumeration will never be brought to completion because there will always be new members to count with ever newly invented numbers to count them.

How we would be able to, at least in principle, enumerate an infinite collection depends on what it means for a number system to be infinite. We have two options:

- A number system is a figuratively infinite series of numbers—the scale of numbers is indefinitely constructed over time (e.g., $\mathbb{N}^\circlearrowright$).

- A number system is a literally infinite set of numbers, the numbers being all there together in the set at once (e.g., $\mathbb{N}$).

If a number system is infinite, it must be one of these. It cannot be both.

4.1.1 *Interpreting Number Systems as Infinite*

So how do we interpret number systems—are they literally infinite sets or are they only 'infinite' in the figurative sense of series that grow indefinitely longer?

If number systems are literally infinite *sets* (e.g., $\mathbb{N}$ rather than $\mathbb{N}^\circlearrowright$) that mathematicians *discover* (as portrayed in standard set theory), then the number systems are complete sequences of numbers that we can, in principle, use to enumerate all the members of other infinite collections. Hypothetically, an infinite collection of fence posts may be completely numbered with an infinite set of unique numbers.

But there are two different ways that a literally infinite collection may be considered infinitely 'enumerable' and the choice between them depends on what it means to have a literal infinity of numbers to use in enumeration.

On the one hand, a literally infinite collection may be regarded as having members that are completely enumerable to an *infinite number* with no limit to the amount of digits expressing it as a sum; by that view, an infinite collection has a *limitless sum* or *infinite sum* of members.

On the other hand, some mathematicians say that even if the natural numbers are infinite, there is nevertheless no such thing as an 'infinite sum' or 'infinite number'—they see literally infinite quantities as quantities not equal to sums, and not totals in the finite sense of the word. They may say infinities are collections with *limitlessly many*, or *infinitely many*, members but they would not call such quantities infinite numbers or infinite sums. In that point of view, to be literally infinite is not to be 'enumerable' in the finite sense either.

If, to the contrary, number systems are not literally infinite sets of numbers but instead are only figuratively infinite *number scales* (e.g., $\mathbb{N}^{\circ}$ rather than $\mathbb{N}$) as in a nonstandard version of set theory, then the number systems always remain incomplete as finite, open series that can only be used to enumerate as many members in a given collection as there are numbers invented to date. And if we are enumerating a figurative infinity with those numbers, then we are enumerating the members or steps of an open series that may never complete no matter how high a finite number we invent. A figurative infinity is therefore a series that is 'enumerable' in the sense that the enumeration of the members comprising the series must remain *incomplete* as the series grows indefinitely. There is no infinite sum of the members in the series and there is not 'infinitely many' members of the series in the sense of a complete and limitless quantity; rather, there is just an 'infinite' (i.e., indefinite) series of sums.

We may attempt to enumerate a collection by a literally infinite set of natural numbers or by a figuratively infinite natural number scale. Mathematicians have regarded number systems according to both points of view: as inherently incomplete, open series (figurative infinities) and as completed sets (literal infinities).

4.1.2 *Enumerating with Figurative and Literal Infinities of Numbers*

First, we'll consider number systems as inherently incomplete number scales—open series of numbers that mathematicians continue to construct ever longer, with ever greater numbers invented. This interpretation of number systems will prove consistent with figurative infinity (though I believe that term is a misnomer as I will argue in Chapter 24).

After that, I will explicate how most mathematicians regard a number system to be not a figuratively infinite series of numbers but rather a literally infinite set of numbers; either a set with an infinite sum of numbers or simply an infinite "multiplicity" of numbers that is somehow not a sum at all. I'll briefly address each of these options for portraying a number system as literally infinite.

We will then be able to return to examining the notion of using those number systems to enumerate collections as infinite. I will elucidate the way in which mathematicians conceive of number systems as sets that, at least hypothetically, can be used to enumerate infinite collections (including infinite collections of other numbers) without any need for counting out, calculating, or computing the elements in the enumerated collections.

4.2 NUMBER SCALES AS FIGURATIVE INFINITIES

We'll start with number systems as figurative infinities. Figurative infinity is a property or condition that can plausibly be attributed to number systems as number scales, based on what we know of them and the numbers they contain.

§§ 2.3.1–2.3.9 offered an analysis of what a number is. A number is a numeral's unique ordinality-cardinality association in a number scale. Since a number is the property of a numeral—which is a kind of symbol—then to have a number, you must have a numeral. But as symbols, numerals are inventions. Scales as sequences of numerals—and therefore of numbers represented by the numerals—are therefore also inventions, making the numbers themselves inventions. If numbers and number scales are inventions that we make rather than objects that exist "out there" waiting to be discovered, the idea that number scales are only figuratively infinite rather than literally infinite begins to make sense...

4.2.1 *An Incomplete Process*

Each number scale, as an invention, must have as many numbers as there have been invented numerals with defined numbers. But the number of numbers that a number scale has could continue to grow as mathematicians invent new numbers. Numbers scales could, at least in principle, continue to be made longer indefinitely. Figurative infinity is the condition of indefinitely changing in quantity. As inventions that are able in principle to be indefinitely extended, number scales can indefinitely change in the quantity of their constituent numbers. That feature makes number scales at least figuratively infinite even if not literally infinite.

As a figurative infinity, each number scale would, metaphorically speaking, have "no limit" because there is no final number as a standing total for a number scale. In another sense though, number scales at any given time do have a limit in the form of a "largest number" invented to date, even though the scale can be further extended when new, larger numbers become invented. In either sense, number scales are intrinsically incomplete, open series ever under construction [108].

Recall that series (open or closed) can be summed, showing them to have a totality of members. It doesn't matter whether the members of the series are steps in a process or instead are objects, or collections of objects, successively appearing. The members can be summed up—given a total—and so they can be ascribed the property of totality however they are arranged to comprise a series. This is true for series of physical objects, like muffins or rabbits, but it is also true for series of mathematical objects. Even number scales, like $\mathbb{N}^C$ or $\mathbb{W}^C$, are series the members of which can be summed. We can at least in principle if not in practice, arrive at a total of members (numerals or numbers) for the series as a whole, and totality characterizes sets of members within these series as well.

But what kind of totality?

If a number scale were a closed series (like a muffin tin filled up with muffins), then it could be regarded as a complete series and given a *standing total*—a mathematical sum that ends the series and caps it off for good as a *final sum*, the number of all numbers period. This would make the scale not just a completed *series* of numbers but also a complete *set* of numbers since all the numbers could be represented side by side in a single collection.

However, if a number scale is an open series, then this is not possible—not even logically possible—because a number scale would have no absolutely last number that yields a final total for the scale in question. No number scale would be a completed set with a final sum; number scales would be finite at all times, but they would be an incomplete series of sums—or, you could say they would constitute a sum that changes over time.

This is because number scales would be *processes* in which the sum of steps taken (or in this case the quantity of numbers created for the number scale in question) always changes—even if the steps taken, or numbers invented, continue "to infinity" in a figurative sense. A figuratively infinite number scale is one that is never finished forming—it is inherently incomplete; as such, it is *limited* at each step of the way.

4.2.2 *Extremes*

One kind of limit is an *extreme*. Even number systems, or number scales, can have at least one extreme.

For example, if the system of natural (counting) numbers is literally infinite, then it has one extreme—the beginning of the scale, starting with 1. However, if the system of natural numbers is a figuratively infinite number scale, then it has two extremes—the beginning of the scale and, due to the incompleteness of the scale, whatever the "largest" number at any given time is (even if that number can be succeeded with the invention tomorrow of a new, bigger number).

Assuming all number systems are figuratively infinite number scales, it follows that every number scale has a limit in the form of a running total of numbers, and that totality means the number scale in question has a limit in the form of an 'extreme'. Given that assumption, we should be clear on what it means for a number scale, and indeed any collection said to be 'infinite', to have 'extremes' and what it does not mean.

First, what it does not mean: necessary constancy. Some extremes are constant, but not all extremes are constant in form; some extremes may change over time. This is the case with number scales, which continue to be constructed in the form of open series as mathematicians invent larger numbers. But because there is an, albeit temporary, largest number in a number scale at any given time, the scale in question does have an extreme, even if a temporally variant one.

Second, what it *does* mean: having an extreme means having some type of extreme, for there is more than one type. Definitions:

- extreme: (noun; plural—'extremes') *an extremity or extremum.*
  (adjective): *the quality of having or being an extremity or extremum.*
- extremity: (noun; plural—'extremities') *that which is either minimal or maximal.*
- extremum: (noun; plural—'extrema') *a minimum or maximum.*

To the casual reader, the definitions for the words 'extremity' and 'extremum' appear to say the same thing, but actually they don't. While all extremities and extrema are instances of extremes, it is also true that an extremity is not necessarily an extremum. The two are not synonymous; it's just that there is more than one way to be extreme.

We also have a few more distinctions: extremity is defined by the terms *minimal* and *maximal* while extremum is defined by the terms *minimum* and *maximum*. These are also similar sets of terms, but 'minimal' is not synonymous with 'minimum', and 'maximal' is not synonymous with 'maximum'. The relationship between these types of extremes is illustrated in **Figure 4.1** and their categorical overlap is illustrated in **Figure 4.2**.

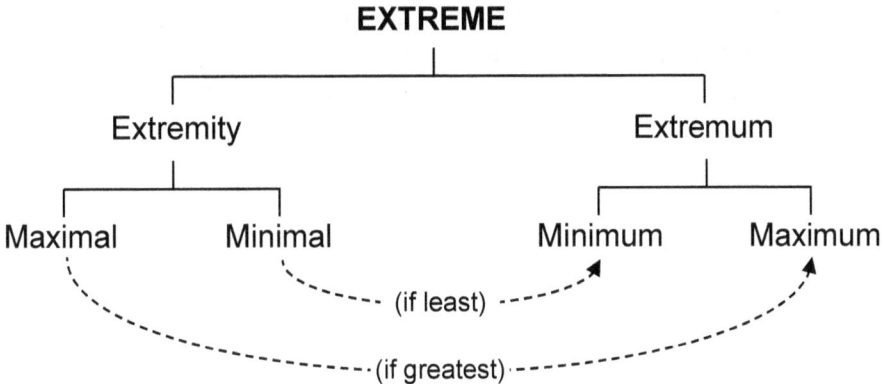

Figure 4.1: The types of extremes. A minimum is the least minimal element; a maximum is the greatest maximal element.

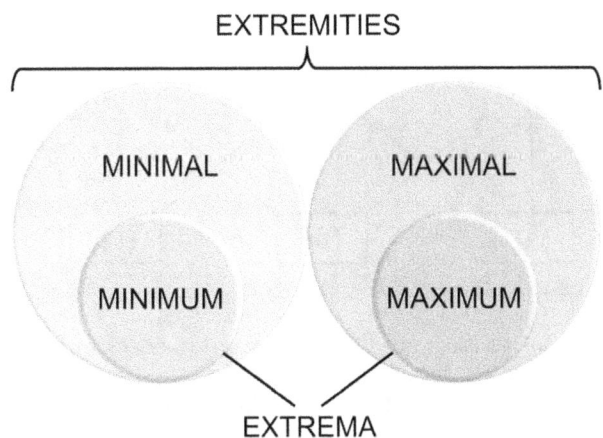

Figure 4.2: Overlap among the types of extremes. All extrema are extremities, but not all extremities are extrema.

4.2.3 *Extremities: Minimal and Maximal*

Mathematicians have particular definitions for these terms from which we can draw [109]. Consider extremities that are:

- minimal: (adjective) *the value for which nothing is less.*
- maximal: (adjective) *the value for which nothing is greater.*

We can state these definitions more formally when considering a collection, C, containing elements with different values. We'll use the variables x and y, which can be given specific values in C. Let's consider x as a minimal or maximal value, compared to another value, y, in the collection C:

- x is minimal if and only if, for all y in C, y cannot be less than x.
- x is maximal if and only if, for all y in C, y cannot be greater than x.

The best way to see what it means to have minimal and maximal elements is to consider sets from the perspective of *order theory*. Order theory is a branch of mathematics that investigates how members of collections precede or succeed one another in sequences. There are two basic kinds of sequences studied in order theory—*partially ordered sets*, or *posets* for short, and *totally ordered sets*, or *chains* for short. Both kinds of "sets" (which are actually sequences according to definition) have members that precede or succeed other members. Order theory studies the ways the members (especially, elements) are ordered in posets and chains [110].

Posets are sequences in which members of the sequences are paired and preceded by other pairs of members. Posets are only "partially ordered" in the sense that not every pair of members has to be related (see **Figure 4.3**).

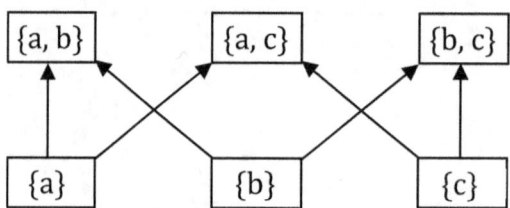

Figure 4.3: An example of a poset. The set is only "partially ordered" since subset {a, c} is related neither to {a, b} nor {b, c}, both of which are unrelated to each another. The subsets at top are maximal; the subsets at bottom are minimal. We can imagine repeating this pattern with more boxes on the top and bottom rows, perhaps indefinitely. The question remains if such can be done infinitely.

Posets each have at least one member that is an extremity—either minimal or maximal. **Figure 4.3** provides an example of a poset with multiple extremities, some in the form of minimal members and some in the form of maximal members. The top row of members in **Figure 4.3** is composed entirely of maximal members, and the members in the bottom row are all minimal elements.

Notice that none of the members in the figure is an extremum—a 'minimum' or 'maximum'—even though the members in the rows are extremities. Some posets, like that depicted in **Figure 4.3**, may in principle be constructed to have indefinitely many extremities. Whether they can in principle have *infinitely* many extremities in the literal sense of 'infinite' is another question (one I'm inclined to answer in the negative).

4.2.4 *Extrema: Minimum and Maximum*

We can define the kinds of extrema like this:

- minimum:
  (1) noun; plural—'minima': *an element or value less than any other.*
  (2) adjective: *less than any other; the least possible.*

- maximum:
  (1) noun; plural—'maxima': *an element or value greater than any other.*
  (2) adjective: *greater than any other; the greatest possible.*

Or, more formally:

- x is a minimum if and only if, for all y in C, y must be greater than x.
- x is a maximum if and only if, for all y in C, y must be less than x.

Basically, a minimum is *the least element or value in a totally ordered collection*—no element in the collection can be lesser in value. A maximum is *the greatest element or value in a totally ordered collection*—no element in the collection can be greater in value [111].

In **Figure 4.3**, neither {a} nor {b} nor {c} is less than the others on the bottom row, so none of them is a minimum. Likewise, neither {a, b} nor {a, c} nor {b, c} is greater than the others on the top row, so none of them are maximum. This shows that a set or sequence can have several minimal members without a minimum and several maximal members without a maximum.

On the other hand, minimal elements and minima are not entirely separate categories; *a minimum is a kind of minimal element* even though not all minimal elements are a minimum. So too, maximal elements and maxima are not entirely separate; we can say that *a maximum is a kind of maximal element* even though not all maximal elements are a maximum.

Minima and maxima can be found in some posets and in some totally ordered sets, or 'chains'. A chain is a set—actually a sequence by our earlier definition of 'sequence'—in which every pair of elements is related, or "totally ordered." Though mathematicians refer to chains as sets, chains can also be series (sequences formed by succession).

As an example of a chain, consider this set of elements:

$$\{a<b<c<d<e<f<g<h<i<j<k<l<m<n<o<p<q<r<s<t<u<v<w<x<y<z\}$$

This is an example of a 'chain' of elements in the form of an alphabet of values. In this chain, there is a minimum (a) since there is no relation before the first depicted element and a maximum (z) since there is no relation after the last depicted element.

A chain can have *at most* one minimal element and *at most* one maximal element. The minimal element will also be the *least element* and the maximal element will also be the *greatest element*. In other words, because a chain has no more than one minimal element, that element is the minimum and because the chain has no more than one maximal element, that element is the maximum. Any chain in the form of a definite, closed series or sequence is necessarily finite and always has a least element (minimum) and a greatest element (maximum).

The question for our purposes is whether a number system, such as the scale of natural numbers or the scale of whole numbers, is or is not a chain. If there is for the given number system either no such thing as either an absolutely last number or an absolutely first number, a number beyond which no further numbers can exist even in principle, then the answer is no—the number system is not a chain, for there is not both a minimum and maximum to the number system. If there is both a minimum and maximum number to a number system, then the answer is yes—the number system is a chain. The question as to whether or not number systems are chains, whether they have extrema (a minimum and a maximum), we can answer with respect to how numbers come to be in such systems.

4.2.5 *The Variant Extrema of Number Systems*

For a collection to be complete is for the collection to have a finish, fullness, and a totality, any of which implies the collection has 'extrema'—both a minimum and maximum value. So, if a number system begins its existence as a complete collection of numbers, then the number system would from the start have extrema as a consequence of being a finished, full, totality.

However, if number systems are continuously constructed 'number scales' that are only figuratively infinite, then they are necessarily incomplete. Any extreme(s) they may have at any given time must be only temporary in what is a running total of numbers for that instance of time in which the scale in question is considered. For example, if $\mathbb{N}^C$ is figuratively infinite, then $\mathbb{N}^C$ has a "highest number" at any given time, but that extremum must be a *variant maximum* rather than a *constant maximum*, the latter of which would be a standing total rather than a running total.

Once again time becomes an issue: a variant maximum for a collection at a time is also a *maximal* quantity with respect to the collection as a series that changes in quantity over time. A constant maximum, to the contrary, remains a maximum for the life of the collection.

Moreover, as incomplete, open series, some number scales need not have a minimum in the sense of a constant minimum. So when I say a number scale "has no maximum" or "has no minimum", it is only in the sense of a *constant* maximum or minimum I am referring to—not to lack of extremum per se, unless otherwise specified.

For example, consider a sequence that has a minimum but no (constant) maximum. Such is the scale of natural numbers— $\mathbb{N}^C$. In $\mathbb{N}^C$, the number 1 is the minimum and there is no maximum:

1, 2, 3, 4, 5, 6, 7, 8, 9, 10, ...

A maximum is "a value greater than any other;" if we take that definition as implying a constant value, a standing total, then $\mathbb{N}^C$ has no maximum because $\mathbb{N}^C$ is an open series with a running total, and a running total is not a constant value.

On the other hand, suppose we do not want to consider $\mathbb{N}^C$ as an open series but instead want to consider the phrase "all the natural numbers" to mean a *set*—a kind of snapshot of the state of $\mathbb{N}^C$ at any given time during the ongoing construction of $\mathbb{N}^C$. If that is the case, then we can consider $\mathbb{N}^C$ to have an, albeit temporary, 'maximum' in the form of the greatest number *yet defined* for $\mathbb{N}^C$ *at the present time*. In that sense, $\mathbb{N}^C$ does indeed have a maximum of sorts. As discussed in § 2.3.7, that 'variable maximum' can be denoted by a symbol such as $|\mathbb{N}^C|$.

Most mathematicians don't consider the system of natural numbers to have a maximum in this way because time usually does not figure into their view of sets [112]. We assuage such concerns to a degree by pointing out that the 'variant maximum' is simply a 'maximal' value with respect to the formation of

$\mathbb{N}^C$ over time. Nevertheless, that rests on a view of mathematics in which math is regarded as an invention, a construction carried out in time, which is not usually addressed in mathematics.

Regardless, let's keep going with this line of thought and consider the status of extrema for a similar sequence of the *smallest* numbers. An example of a sequence that has a maximum, but no minimum is the scale of negative numbers. We can think of the negative numbers as a number scale that is the counterpart to the scale of natural numbers and denoted it as $-\mathbb{N}^C$. In $-\mathbb{N}^C$, the number -1 is the maximum and there is no minimum since $-\mathbb{N}^C$ is also an open series:

$$..., -10, -9, -8, -7, -6, -5, -4, -3, -2, -1$$

A minimum is "a value less than any other;" if we take that definition as implying a constant value, a standing total, then $-\mathbb{N}^C$ has no minimum because $-\mathbb{N}^C$ is also an open series with a running total of negative numbers, and a running total is, again, not a constant value.

However, if we want to consider "all the negative natural numbers" as constituting a set at a given moment in construction, then we can consider $-\mathbb{N}^C$ to have a temporary 'minimum' in the form of the least number yet defined for $\mathbb{N}^C$ at the present time—a *variant minimum* (or 'minimal' for the series) rather than a *constant minimum*. Here again, time plays a role in our assumptions, while it is usually not given consideration in mathematics.

Now I should qualify that the negative numbers are not usually regarded as a scale of their own (i.e., $-\mathbb{N}^C$). Instead, mathematicians think of the negative numbers as belonging to the 'set' of *integers*, denoted as $\mathbb{Z}$, but which we can denote as the series of integers: $\mathbb{Z}^C$.

An 'integer' is *any positive number* (1, 2, 3, ...), *any negative number* (..., $-3, -2, -1$), *or zero* (0). The scale of integers, $\mathbb{Z}^C$, therefore includes natural numbers ($\mathbb{N}^C$), their negative counterparts ($-\mathbb{N}^C$), and whole numbers ($\mathbb{W}^C$) since 0 is included in $\mathbb{Z}^C$ as well.

Consider $\mathbb{Z}^C$ as a constructed sequence with no minimum (since $-\mathbb{N}^C$ has no minimum) and no maximum (since $\mathbb{N}^C$ has no maximum):

$$..., -10, -9, -8, -7, -6, -5, -4, -3, -2, -1, \ 0, \ 1, \ 2, \ 3, \ 4, \ 5, \ 6, \ 7, \ 8, \ 9, \ 10, ...,$$

$\mathbb{Z}^C$ has "no minimum" and "no maximum" only in the sense that $\mathbb{Z}^C$ is here considered as a growing scale. That is, $\mathbb{Z}^C$ has neither a minimum nor a maximum in the sense of constant numbers, standing totals. Only if we consider "all the integers" to mean $|\mathbb{Z}^C|$, which is to say all of $\mathbb{Z}^C$ at a snapshot in time—only then, considered as a set with a temporally variant cardinality having a specific value at a given point in time during its construction does $\mathbb{Z}^C$ have a minimum and a maximum (albeit still a variant minimum and a variant maximum). On the other hand, as a *series* rather than as a *set* at a moment in time, $\mathbb{Z}^C$ has *minimal* and *maximal* numbers but no minimum and no maximum.

These examples of extrema illustrate the two different ways to regard scales of numbers: (1) as a set in the form of a sequence that, at any given time, consists of definite, defined numbers—but only those numbers invented to date; and (2) as an open series with new numbers under construction over time.

As a *set*, a number scale will have only a variant minimum and/or a variant maximum; as a *series*, a number scale need not be considered with respect to having a minimum and/or maximum (though it does indeed have such in variable form) as it may not be considered relevant. And yet, as a series, a number scale without regard to such extrema will be indefinite (finite) rather than infinite because there is always a running total of defined numbers in the scale.

By lacking a constant extremum or extrema, a series of numbers comprising a number scale is finite with only a running total of members. Each scale of numbers can be considered to have extremities (minimal and maximal values) in the context of time: the running total of members indicates the scale in question has relevant extrema during any step of its construction, even if the scale, as a series, has only variant extrema. The scales are all indefinitely long, open series under construction.

4.2.6 *Number Scales are Under Construction*

If the numbers in number scales such as $\mathbb{N}^{C}$ (or $\mathbb{W}^{C}$), $\mathbb{Z}^{C}$, etc. are constructed serially, toward ever-larger numbers, it follows that whatever the highest number is, it will correspond to the largest numeral invented. But scales of numbers are never *finished* inventions. Number scales are always being increased as new, higher numbers are invented with the use of the various mathematical functions, operations, and procedures for outputting new numbers or otherwise defining them. Consequently, there is no *final* number that finishes a number scale. And since there is no final number that finishes a number scale, number scales are not closed series or complete sets.

However, while there may be no 'last number' in the sense of a number that even if only in principle halts the number scale, still the number scale has a "largest number" ever invented at any given time. That is, a kind of 'running total'—a total that is continuously replaced by a new, larger, finite total. With respect to the scale of natural numbers, $\mathbb{N}^{C}$ (and of course $\mathbb{W}^{C}$) has a new total every time someone exceeds the largest finite number ever invented. It is admittedly true that a number scale has a "last number" in the sense of having a number that is the *highest* number calculated *so far*, though such a number is not "last" in the sense of being a final number that *finishes* the scale *once and for all*. A number scale has no "last number" in the sense of a defined constant number that finishes the scale because the scale is always under construction, with new numbers being defined for it by mathematicians.

4.2.7 *A Variant Maximum—the Largest Number*

Somewhere in the world, someone must have mathematically defined the largest number to date. And, no, infinity is not that number (in fact, some mathematicians say infinity is not a number at all—see Chapter 5). By "largest number," I mean the largest *finite* number. And by such a number being "mathematically defined" I mean what some mathematicians refer to as a *well-defined number*.

Mathematicians have various ideas as to what "well-defined" means for a number, but in general a 'well-defined number' is an unambiguous, unique value able to be used consistently in mathematical expressions [113].

Well-defined numbers include all the numbers from the scales we have considered so far. For simplicity, we can consider those in the scale of whole numbers from 0 on up to the largest whole number a function is able to output as a growing series of digits that eventually end with a final digit. (That does not mean the function has to halt; it just means the outputted number has a final digit. Perhaps the function keeps indefinitely churning out larger numbers until killed.) So imagine an ideal computer able to output all the base digits in the sequence of a finite number, no matter how arbitrarily large the number. Of course, no such computer can really exist, for there are limits to the series of digits that any computer can output, and mathematicians already have well-defined (finite) numbers that dwarf those limits. However, *in principle* there could be such a computer—one easily able to output even the largest, well-defined finite number ever conceived.

I have no idea what that number is, but there is an online community of academics devoted to cataloging and inventing ever larger numbers. They call themselves *googologists* and their online encyclopedia is the *Googology Wiki*. Googologists define a variety of huge numbers, each larger than the last. However, even the googologists themselves are not in agreement as to which number is the largest finite number defined to date [114].

Regardless of whether there is a clear winner for largest finite number defined or not, let's suppose someone has invented a finite number with a value that, at least in principle, can be fully expressed only in a terminating series of base digits output by some function. Even though such a number may be too large to write out in actual practice, if it could in principle be written out, it would have a final digit and so constitute a finite number. But since we can't represent it that way, we need a variable or some kind of symbol or abbreviation for it.

With that in mind, I will refer to the largest *definite number* as d^*, pronounced "**dee**-star" [115]. The 'd' in d^* is for 'definite', as in definite number:

- definite number: *a logically coherent, mathematically well-defined number.*

A 'definite number' is a number that is not only mathematically well-defined but also logically coherent (i.e., the function able to output such a number is not based on any logically incoherent assumptions). The star symbol ($*$) in the superscript of d^* is to indicate that the value of the largest definite number at a particular time is subject to replacement by a different number of greater numerical value at a later time. Think of d^* as a placeholder for any definite number the value of which exceeds all definite numbers previously conceived—

- Let d^* be the variable representing the largest definite number ever conceived up to the present.

d^* is a temporal variable.—that is, d^* is the largest definite number *so far*. Of course, once someone has conceived the largest definite number to date, the value of that number can once again be exceeded tomorrow by the value of another definite number defined by some more powerful function. Hence, what *was* d^* yesterday may not be d^* today, and what *is* d^* today may not be d^* tomorrow.

Because d^*'s value is not constant, I am going to use d^* as a generic variable for whatever to date is a number equal to any *naïve extension* of the largest known number able to be defined using mathematical functions [116]. Hence, expressions such as $d^* + 1$ or $d^* \times d^*$ and similar naïve extensions simply reduce to a d^* since they do not change the definition for whatever is the largest number to date. Regardless of which function is used to define the latest value for d^*, the number for d^* is always finite: at any given time, d^* represents the largest definite number that, if it could be written out, would still be a *finite number*, no matter how large it is.

One implication of d^* being the largest definite number conceived up to the present is that we know numbers scales such as $\mathbb{N}^C$ and $\mathbb{W}^C$ must go up *at least* to d^* and, just to be clear, d^* is technically not an absolutely *final* number for the number scales, for there is always another new d^* as long as there are mathematicians proposing new, largest definite numbers. Hence, the number scales are openly extensible, at least in principle.

4.2.8 *Taking Leaps Toward* d^*

Mathematical operations with which you may be familiar (multiplication, exponentiation, etc.) make it much easier for mathematicians to extend a scale like $\mathbb{N}^{\circlearrowleft}$ further, increasing the latest value of d^*. But there are much more powerful functions than those that extend the number scale.

Consequently, the numbers leading up to d^* are too long to list in actual practice. In his book entitled *Billions and Billions*, the late astrophysicist Carl Sagan provided a comparison between the US names for large numbers, what each number looks like when written out, how each number is denoted according to its exponent notation, and how long it would take to count to each number, starting from 0, at a rate of one count per second, night and day [117]. Sagan's comparison includes the following:

- Thousand: 1,000 10^3 17 minutes
- Million: 1,000,000 10^6 12 days
- Billion: 1,000,000,000 10^9 32 years
- Trillion: 1,000,000,000,000 10^{12} 32,000 years
- Quadrillion: 1,000,000,000,000,000 10^{15} 32 million years

Fortunately, we have computers that can count much faster than the rate of one count per second, and processing speeds continue to improve. Currently, a moderately fast computer can count to a trillion in just under an hour—what might take you or me 32,000 years to achieve, provided we could live that long and really liked counting. Counting to a trillion, and thereby representing the whole scale of $\mathbb{N}^{\circlearrowleft}$ up to a trillion, is easily achievable for today's computers.

However, the hill gets steeper from there because there is a maximum computing power beyond which no further computations will be able to depict all the digits of a natural number that we can define by exponentiation. Some computer scientists believe that the limit to the number of digits able to be outputted by any computer capable of physically existing may be as small as just over 10^{15} (a quadrillion) digits [118]. I don't mean that a computer cannot produce a 1 followed by 15 zeros, because that is easy for it to do; rather, I mean a computer will never be able to produce a list of all the natural numbers, in sequence with all digits outputted, up to 10^{15} or, more precisely, up to 1,125,899,906,842,624 prior to exhaustion (breaking down). Needless to say, there will never be a *complete* listing of numbers up to d^*.

4.2.9 *Gaps in the Sequence of Calculated Numbers*

Not only is each number scale an incomplete, open series, but they are also each an unfinished sequence with many gaps. The sequence of any given number scale is riddled with gaps because we cannot in practice list out *all* the numbers up to a quadrillion, let alone beyond that. So, when we go on using exponents and other means to bypass counting for the purpose of creating new, higher natural numbers, not all the numbers in the sequence of the number scale have ever been explicitly depicted. Many numbers have never been actually calculated, computed, or otherwise represented by anyone. The sequence of all numbers that have ever been depicted to date has plenty of values left out between lower and higher values. True, all larger numbers are more inclusive of lower numbers, by definition, but that is only an implication rather than an explicit representation—it is an inference about the lower numbers not represented rather than an explicit representation of them. While such unused numbers fall under the umbrella definition of a number, they have never really been brought into actual existence at any time. If we were to have a list of all numbers ever counted, calculated, or computed, there would be plenty of gaps in our historical record.

That's not to say a number scale such as $\mathbb{N}^C$ does not have a running total, d^*, after all. Every number scale has a temporally variable d^*, but for a number scale to have any total at all, even a running total, does not necessarily mean *all* the lower numbers were counted or calculated.

There was a time in ancient history when one billion was the highest number anyone had ever calculated or defined; until then, no one had counted out numbers up to one billion. Such numbers as one billion were at least initially beyond what anyone had previously counted. By using techniques like exponentiation instead of counting to invent higher natural numbers, ancient mathematicians extended the scale of natural numbers, but the scale began to (historically speaking) have 'breaks' or 'gaps' in its sequence as new, higher numbers continued to be invented without all the lower numbers being counted out or otherwise invented first. Contrary to Dedekind, the *real* 'real number line' *does* have gaps—gaps of numbers uncalculated and merely implied. Number scales are only whole and entire in an idealized conception of them.

Our modern exponent notation was invented in the 17th Century. But at some time in ancient history an Indian mathematician used powers of ten to come up with the highest number at the time: a billion (10^9). Suppose before one billion was invented, no one had counted out or calculated any of the numbers between 10^6 and 10^9 (one million and one billion); suppose no one had ever counted out all the numbers one by one, and no set of people had represented all the numbers between 10^6 and 10^9 up to that time. Historically speaking, $\mathbb{N}^C$, as a human invention, would have had a break in its sequence at that point in time; a break between one million and one billion left by a gap in the sequence established in the count from 1 up to 1,000,000—break—1,000,000,000. Surely by now every number between one million and one billion has been represented many times over during the course of history by various people in various places and times, but since up to that time no one had ever counted them out or ever calculated anything in between a million and a billion, the number scale as an abstract historical artifact was missing numbers, so to speak, in the sequence of $\mathbb{N}^C$ as it was constructed over time. The missing numbers were never invented for the first time until others later came up with the numbers in their own calculations and $\mathbb{N}^C$, as a historical sequence of established numbers, began to be filled in for $\mathbb{N}^C$ as a social construction.

If the history of numeric invention (at least, here on Earth) is to have a whole, entire scale of numbers that have *all* been represented up to the highest number ever invented for $\mathbb{N}^C$, then those breaks need to be filled in by various people at various places and various times collectively coming up with the missing numbers until all the missing numbers are invented such that an ideal observer could survey them all. Until then, the missing numbers in the progression of $\mathbb{N}^C$'s construction are just *implied* to be in $\mathbb{N}^C$.

Of course, it's not as if the scale of $\mathbb{N}^C$ is written out in some ledger somewhere, with a scribe adding numbers to it whenever someone comes up with a new, higher number. Certainly, no one knows if all the numbers have in fact been expressed between any large numbers depicted in any public record. However, if we think of the scale of $\mathbb{N}^C$ as a social representation of all the natural numbers that anyone has ever come up with to date, surveyable by an ideal scribe, then $\mathbb{N}^C$ as a representation must still be incomplete. It is incomplete in part because all of the numbers that have ever been counted, calculated, or computed do not include among them the numbers that have yet to be calculated—such numbers would fall in the sequence between some of the larger numbers of $\mathbb{N}^C$ if or when they are ever invented. From the perspective of an ideal scribe, there would be gaps in $\mathbb{N}^C$ where no one has counted or calculated. $\mathbb{N}^C$ is an invention under construction—an invention that is always incomplete, with plenty of gaps, created and later "filled in" along the way. $\mathbb{N}^C$ is like a railroad track under construction, missing many rails along its length.

Given the limits of computing power, there must still be plenty of gaps in the depiction of numbers between a trillion and a quadrillion. And we haven't even touched on yet larger numbers that have been invented for $\mathbb{N}^C$: quintillion (10^{18}), sextillion (10^{21}), septillion (10^{24}), octillion (10^{27}), and nonillion (10^{30}), just to name a few of the lower ones. Even if we manage to break the computational barrier for counting out all the natural numbers up to a quadrillion, we will likely never create a computer with the capability of counting all the way up to a nonillion without the machine burning out first [119].

Just to press the point home, recall that I mentioned the googologists—the folks who come up with names for ever-larger finite numbers. The title 'googologist' comes from the name for one of the highest numbers that has ever been named: the *googol*, the name upon which the popular search engine, Google, is based. A googol is equal to 10^{100}—a one followed by 100 zeros which, when written out, looks like this:

10,000,000,000,000,000,000,000,000,000,000,000,000,000,000,000,000,000,000,000,000,000,000,000, 000,000,000,000,000,000,000,000,000,000,000,000

To get an idea of how large a googol is, consider that the observable portion of the Universe has about 10^{80} particles in it, which is orders of magnitude lower than a googol [120]. Needless to say, even if we represented each numeric digit using a single bit for storage and each bit was physically expressed using a single atom, listing all the numbers up to a googol would still far exceed the number of atoms in the observable part of the Universe—even a computer with a storage capacity of that size is not enough to count up to a googol.

Of course, we can conceive of yet higher numbers with use of repeated exponentiation and give large numbers generated by that method of calculation names too. For example, we can raise a googol in power to make the *googolplex*, which is $10^{10^{100}}$ or simply, 10^{Googol}. Just multiply ten by itself a googol number of times and you have a googolplex—a one followed by a googol of zeros. Such a number staggers the imagination, but it is actually quite puny compared to even larger numbers that mathematicians have calculated. Larger than a googolplex is a number called *Graham's number*, named after the late mathematician Ronald Graham (1935–2020). Graham's number is expressed as g_{64}, which looks small in notation but is actually much vaster than a googolplex.

The details of calculating large numbers like Graham's number will not concern us; the point is that we obviously cannot *in actual practice* define all the numbers for $\mathbb{N}^C$ up to a large number like Graham's number by writing out and representing each numeral successively since we'd need an impossibly powerful computer to assist us in doing so and there simply is no machine that can provide the necessary output. If we can't produce a googol of digits, we certainly can't produce a googolplex of digits let alone Graham's number.

Since no one has computed *all* the natural numbers up to Graham's number (let alone going to yet higher numbers defined by mathematicians), it is a truism that no one has depicted all the numbers there *could be* in $\mathbb{N}^C$ and so no one has ever or will ever exhaustively represent numbers for $\mathbb{N}^C$. Even so, we can use the rules of computation to create just about any number for $\mathbb{N}^C$ we need for most purposes, whether it's a number with 10^{66} digits, 10^{106} digits, 10^{Googol} digits, or whatever. And we could *in principle*, list all numbers in $\mathbb{N}^C$ up to the highest number invented, even if we can't in actual practice.

However, in there is at least a Graham's number of numbers in $\mathbb{N}^C$ and that we can never count that high can make it sound like the numbers are all "there" waiting to be counted. But that need not be so. The numbers never depicted, never represented, are only potentials of the mathematical rules governing the scale of numbers. We may say there are numbers far below Graham's number that have never been written out or calculated. But we should not think that implies such numbers exist "out there" waiting to be found. Rather, there "are" numbers never depicted and used below Graham's number in the sense that mathematical operations allow one to calculate lower numbers no one has calculated before. From that point of view, number scales like $\mathbb{N}^C$ do indeed have "gaps"—breaks in construction where no one has ever depicted numbers that are merely implied to be in the scale. Number scales like $\mathbb{N}^C$ are therefore always *incomplete* in the sense of having many gaps where no one had ever actually calculated and expressed a number between two known values—at least in an explicit manner.

4.2.10 *Numbers: Depicted and Implied*

All defined finite numbers fall into two categories:

- depicted numbers
- implied numbers

A number scale, such as $\mathbb{N}^C$, contains numbers that are defined and the numbers that have been defined can be depicted—expressed or written out. For example, $\mathbb{N}^C$ contains the following known subset of numbers: {1, 2, 3, 4, 5, 6}.

But when we want to show such numbers belonging to a larger sequence of numbers, such as the scale of natural numbers, we usually follow the *depicted numbers* (numbers represented and recognized in an expression) with an ellipsis, like so:

$$\mathbb{N}^C = 1, 2, 3, 4, 5, 6, ...$$

The ellipsis represents yet more numbers beyond those depicted. The numbers not depicted but to which the ellipsis (in part) refers I will call *implied numbers*—numbers that are logically implied by the progression of the numbers depicted.

In the above example, the ellipsis implies successive numbers like 7, 8, 9, 10—numbers we recognize as suggested from previous depictions even if they are not depicted in the given sequence—so, the numbers 7, 8, 9, and 10 are some of the 'implied numbers' for the given sequence above. The same is true for all the natural numbers that have ever been defined beyond those.

Then too, consider the following sequence:

$$10^1, 10^2, 10^3, 10^4, 10^5, 10^6, ..., 10^9, 10^{10}.$$

Even if no one ever counted out any numbers between 10^6 and 10^9, and even if no one had ever seen a depiction of numbers between those values, an understanding of the mathematical pattern of the depicted numbers would allow one infer 10^7 and 10^8 as the undepicted numbers. Hence, those two numbers are in the sequence implied numbers.

Suppose no one had ever written 10^7 but they had written 10^6, 10^8, and 10^9. Everyone would still be able to recognize 10^7 as 10 to the power of 7 when 10^7 is finally written, and ergo they would recognize that 10^7 means ten million (10,000,000), and so is a part of the scale of natural numbers. Therefore, everyone would also recognize where the value of 10^7 would fall in relation to the numbers already known. They would know this because the number is calculable from known mathematical operations.

10^7, prior to ever having ever been written before, was an implied number—it was a number implied by the numbers both smaller and larger than itself that have been depicted, because the definition of 10^7

was implicit in the definition of the operation to produce it. And so its place and size in the number scale would still be recognized if and when written.

Hence, the 'implied numbers' include the numbers that would lie in the "gaps" or "breaks" of the natural number scale—they are not explicitly represented, but they are implicitly represented and so easily producible. But if number scales are full of implied numbers—numbers only implicit and not explicit—number scales are like chains with missing links; links suggested to be there but not explicitly so. As an incomplete sequence of numbers, a number scale is like a railroad track with missing ties, or like a fragmented manuscript pieced together with missing passages. In both cases we may be able to infer what is missing, but the sequence is not explicitly defined all the way through. Once again, we have an interpretation of number scales as intrinsically incomplete constructions.

4.2.11 *Definite Numbers: Feasible and Unfeasible*

As we continue to leap past implied numbers on our way up the number scale toward d^*, we encounter some definite numbers along the way so large that, even though a value for them can be calculated (for example, g_{64}), the necessity of taking those leaps shows that there cannot in practice be a *complete* listing of *all* the numbers in the scale leading up to those large numbers. We can depict some numbers, but not all of them. So, both depicted and implied numbers can be categorized as either *feasible numbers* or *unfeasible numbers* [121]:

- depicted numbers
  - feasible depicted numbers
  - unfeasible depicted numbers
- implied numbers
  - feasible implied numbers
  - unfeasible implied numbers

Definitions:

- feasible number: *any number the value of which can, in practice, be reached by counting (whether performed by human or machine).*

- unfeasible number: *any number the value of which cannot, in practice, be reached by counting— not even by a machine.*

Every feasible number has already been defined by mathematicians, and all the digits of any feasible number can be written out, at least with any computer that is capable of being constructed and used for that purpose in real life. Even if not every feasible number has in fact been counted up to, every feasible number can be counted up to at some point in the future if the interest and computing resources are provided. For that reason, the feasible numbers are *computable in practice*; a computer can count all the way up to the largest feasible number.

Beyond the feasible numbers are yet larger numbers that have already been defined by mathematicians and that can be written out or represented in abbreviated notation, such as by use of exponents, but because they are so large no computer can count all the way up to them, listing out each number along the way with a string of digits. These large numbers are called the unfeasible numbers—even the most powerful computer that will ever be built would reach exhaustion before reaching the value of an unfeasible number by listing all the numbers up to it.

However, unfeasible numbers, while they cannot be counted up to in practice, are nonetheless countable or computable *in principle*—if only we had a powerful enough computer, we could have the computer 'count' (list numbers in consecutive order) all the way up to them; they are just 'unfeasible' because we cannot, in reality, do so in practice.

The following sequence contains samples of feasible numbers and some of the lesser unfeasible numbers:

$$10^3, 10^6, 10^9, ..., 10^{21}, 10^{24}, 10^{27}, 10^{30}.$$

The sequence of feasible and unfeasible numbers as listed in the above example using powers of 3 are categorized against depicted and implied numbers below in **Table 1**.

	Feasible Numbers	Unfeasible Numbers
Depicted Numbers	$10^3, 10^6, 10^9$	$10^{21}, 10^{24}, 10^{27}, 10^{30}$
Implied Numbers	10^{12}	$10^{15}, 10^{18}$

Table 1: A sample of categorized natural numbers from the sequence above. Whether depicted or implied, a quadrillion (10^{15}) is estimated to be the least unfeasible number.

The ellipsis used in representing the series of natural numbers (1, 2, 3, 4, 5, 6, ...) indicates a sequence of larger numbers that includes the category of implied numbers, both feasible implied numbers and unfeasible implied numbers. For example, the ellipsis at the end of the sequence 1, 2, 3, 4, 5, 6, ... implies feasible numbers from 7 on up to $n < 10^{15}$, which are all the defined numbers that a computer will ever be able to sequentially list before reaching exhaustion. But the ellipsis in the sequence 1, 2, 3, 4, 5, 6, ... also implies the known unfeasible numbers such as 10^{15} on up to 10^{Googol} and beyond even that, up to the largest-ever defined—d^*. The category of unfeasible numbers implied by an ellipsis includes all numbers larger than the feasible numbers that have been defined and depicted with notation, however abbreviated they may be (whether by exponents, tetration, or the like). Such unfeasible numbers have been defined by calculation, but they are not in practice 'computable' (able to be reached via counting, even by a computer). Still, they are *computable* in principle, despite the fact that in practice no machine will ever be able to count up to them.

Hence, the implied numbers, including both feasible and unfeasible numbers not depicted up to d^* as the largest number of $\mathbb{N}^C$ yet, are denoted by the ellipses:

$$\mathbb{N}^C = 1, 2, 3, ..., 10^{100}, ..., 10^{Googol}, ..., g_{64}, ..., d^*$$

Depending on what we wish the ellipsis to signify, the ellipsis may therefore imply all the natural numbers up to d^*, including the numbers only implicit in definition—for example, all the implied, unfeasible numbers that had never been explicitly represented between 10^{Googol} and d^*. But since we now recognize d^* as a genuine number (or hypothetical range of numbers), we can also regard d^* as implied by the ellipsis as when we write more simply 1, 2, 3, ...

Because mathematicians can always define new mathematical operations to generate yet higher numbers than any that can today be defined in practice, the scale $\mathbb{N}^C$ has the capability to include finite numbers even higher than any number that might currently be identified as equal to d^*. $\mathbb{N}^C$ can be made to include numbers higher than any number yet defined, even by the 'googologists' who compete to come up with the highest "infinity scraping" number to date [122]. So, the ellipsis used in the sequence of $\mathbb{N}^C$ may additionally imply more than just the feasible and unfeasible numbers already defined.

The ellipsis may also be used to represent a sequence of even higher implied numbers—namely, the unfeasible numbers *not yet defined*, including those beyond d^* (which is the highest finite number *up to present*, not the highest there ever will be):

$$\mathbb{N}^C = 1, 2, 3, ..., 10^{100}, ..., 10^{Googol}, ..., g_{64}, ..., d^*, ...$$

For that reason, we may consider number scales, such as $\mathbb{N}^C$, to be inherently incomplete. Each number scale holds plenty of potential for the construction of new, larger numbers never before calculated—numbers higher, much higher, than a googolplex. It seems that for the largest number anyone can define, another one higher can be defined even if not defined yet. A number scale, such as $\mathbb{N}^C$ or $\mathbb{W}^C$, seems like a tower being constructed ever higher, with no roof in the blueprint.

Then too, depending on the intent of the mathematician writing the ellipsis, the known feasible numbers along with whatever unfeasible numbers will *ever* be defined (and either depicted or implied) may not be all the numbers that the ellipsis is intended to represent. The ellipsis at the end of the sequence may also be intended to denote larger numbers that *will never be defined in practice* and are definable *only in principle*.

If that is so, then it would seem there is no greatest size for which a collection can in principle be enumerated. However, even if greater numbers could be defined, albeit only in principle, such entails that, at any given time, the number scale must ever remain unfinished in practice. The number scale is thus always incomplete, even if it is in principle extensible to ever greater finite lengths.

4.2.12 *Ellipses and Number Scales: An Admission of Incompleteness*

Numbers like the googolplex, and larger numbers still up to d^*, exceed any collection in the observable universe we could wish to enumerate. Nevertheless, suppose we did want to consider an even greater collection, one with a finite quantity of members so large that it surpasses any extension of d^* dreamed up so far. Unfortunately, surpassing d^* means exceeding our current ability to calculate greater finite numbers with any clarity. We do not and may not have operations to generate greater finite numbers with mathematical precision. This has implications for number scales themselves; the larger that a scale of numbers gets, the more it will fail us for quantifying increasingly large finite collections, let alone offer us any precision for quantifying something literally infinite in size.

Number scales necessarily become vague in symbolism because the larger the scale, the more we lose our ability to symbolize with precision. The best we can do is resort to symbols such as the ellipsis: .... We find such use of ellipses with the number scales we have considered so far: $\mathbb{N}^C$, $\mathbb{W}^C$, and $\mathbb{Z}^C$.

For example, the limitation of the defined sequence of natural numbers in $\mathbb{N}^\circ$ is represented by an ellipsis to the right of d^*, which indicates more numbers are possible to define beyond whatever value d^* has at any particular time. An ellipsis is required after d^* because there can be numbers defined beyond whatever value d^* presently has and mathematicians could in principle keep defining ever-larger numbers indefinitely:

$$1, 2, 3, 4, 5, 6, 7, 8, 9, 10, \ldots, 10^{100}, \ldots, 10^{Googol}, \ldots, d^*, \ldots$$

With respect to using the numbers of $\mathbb{N}^\circ$ to enumerate some large collection, X, of greater quantity than d^*, mathematicians could enumerate X if and when more powerful mathematical operations become available. Until then, we would have no precisely defined numbers to enumerate X; hence, the ellipsis after d^*.

The same is true if we wish to quantify a negative balance equivalent to a size greater than d^*. Like $\mathbb{N}^\circ$, the scale of $-\mathbb{N}^\circ$ also trails off with an ellipsis, but to the left:

$$\ldots, -d^*, \ldots, -10^{Googol}, \ldots, -10^{100}, \ldots, -10, -9, -8, -7, -6, -5, -4, -3, -2, -1$$

As with the positive naturals, we run into the same trouble; to the left of $-d^*$, no further negative quantity has been defined. So, quantifying X when $X < -d^*$ cannot be done in practice unless a more powerful mathematical means to do so becomes available.

$$\ldots, -d^*, \ldots, -10, -9, -8, -7, -6, -5, -4, -3, -2, -1, 0, 1, 2, 3, 4, 5, 6, 7, 8, 9, 10, \ldots, d^*, \ldots$$

As you can see, the ellipses go both ways, which means again we are limited in what we can express about collections less than $-d^*$ or greater than d^*.

It is true that $\mathbb{Z}^\circ$, like $\mathbb{W}^\circ$ and $\mathbb{N}^\circ$ which belong to it, is an open series. All of these scales are extensible. And that means we can invent new numbers for $\mathbb{Z}^\circ$ beyond those we already have in order to enumerate collections currently too large to quantify with our presently defined numbers. However, greater/lesser collections than $d^*/-d^*$ are *possible* to enumerate up to a point, beyond which we could enumerate only in principle. And if we can enumerate larger collections only in principle, then we certainly will not enumerate anything 'infinite' with precision.

4.2.13 *There are Many Number Scales, All Incomplete Constructions*

$\mathbb{N}^\circ$, $\mathbb{W}^\circ$, and $\mathbb{Z}^\circ$ are not the only number scales. Mostly it will be $\mathbb{N}^\circ$ and $\mathbb{W}^\circ$ that will concern us since the negatives are simply counterparts to the numbers we count with, but I will occasionally make some references to $\mathbb{Z}^\circ$ and to some other number scales, some of which I'll introduce to clarity, namely the following scales: $\mathbb{Q}^\circ$, $\mathbb{P}^\circ$, $\mathbb{A}^\circ$, $\mathbb{T}^\circ$, $\mathbb{R}^\circ$, $\mathbb{I}^\circ$, and $\mathbb{C}^\circ$. Let's take a brief look at these scales, starting with $\mathbb{R}^\circ$, the scale of *real numbers*:

- real number: *any number that, when multiplied by itself, gives a result that is necessarily non-negative.*

For example, 5 is a real number since $5 \times 5 = 25$ (a non-negative result), and so is -5 (because a negative multiplied by a negative is a positive: $-5 \times -5 = 25$), and so is the number 0 since $0 \times 0 = 0$, which is still non-negative. If any number multiplied by itself gives an answer that is not a negative number, then the number multiplied by itself is a real number.

The scale of $\mathbb{R}^{C}$ includes the scales of all natural numbers, whole numbers, integers, *rational numbers*, and *irrational numbers* (see **Figure 4.4**).

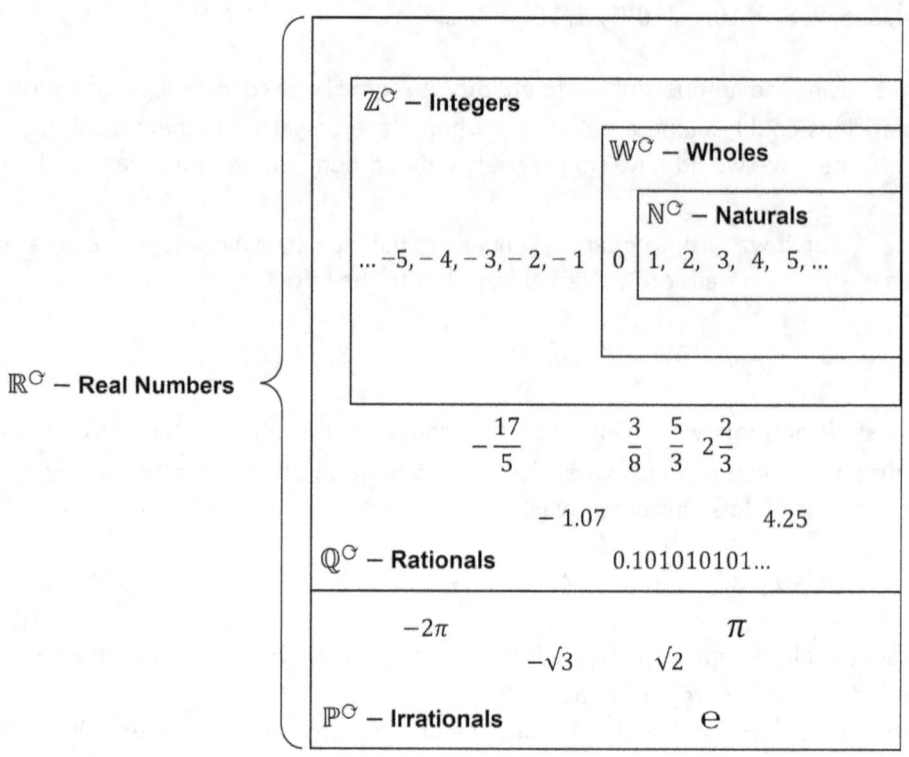

Figure 4.4: The category of real numbers includes the rational numbers and the irrational numbers. The rationals include the integers, which include the wholes, which include the naturals.

We can define rational numbers and irrational numbers thus:

- rational number: *any number that can be represented as a simple fraction where the denominator is not zero*. For example, $^{1}/_{2}$ (or 0.5) and other fractions with non-zero denominators are rational numbers. The rational numbers include all integers since a fraction with 1 as a denominator is equal to an integer ($^{2}/_{1} = 2$). The scale of rationals is denoted as $\mathbb{Q}^{C}$, for the 'quotient' series.

- Irrational number: *a number that cannot be expressed as an exact ratio of two integers*. One example is pi (π), which equals 3.14159..., where the ellipsis represents more values to be defined. Another example is the square root of three ($\sqrt{3}$), which like pi is also expressed with indefinite decimal places (1.73205...) and one more example is Euler's number (e or 2.71828...). There is no standard notation for irrational numbers, but we can follow the lead of set theorists and denote the scale of irrational numbers as $\mathbb{P}^{C}$.

'Real numbers' are used to solve real-world problems all the time, from adding up game scores and designing space vehicles to predicting the weather and reporting stock market trends. But real numbers have no more "reality" (and no less) in the colloquial sense of the term than any other kind of number. Their name is simply a convention that serves to contrast them with a different kind of number that was invented without any intention of being applied for solving real-world problems: the *imaginary number*.

Definition:

- imaginary number: *any number that, when multiplied by itself, gives a result that is necessarily non-positive.*

An example of an imaginary number is $\sqrt{-1}$ because $\sqrt{-1} \times \sqrt{-1} = -1$. Imaginary numbers also include numbers such as 3i and 0.01i, where "i" means "imaginary," since they result in negative numbers such as $3i \times 3i = -9$.

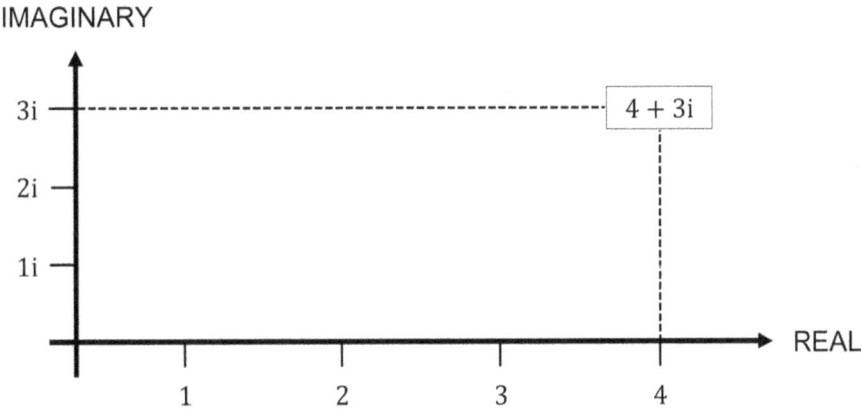

Figure 4.5: The imaginary number scale, as compared to the scale of real numbers. Both numbers can be combined (for example, 4+3i) to form 'complex numbers', for which yet another scale of numbers can be constructed.

Like 'real number', the term 'imaginary number' does not denote numbers any less or more imaginary than any other number—the name is just a convention. And despite that imaginary numbers were not invented to solve real-world problems, it turns out they do indeed have applications to the real world, such as quantifying alternating electrical currents and solving equations for signal processing in cellular communication.

A scale of imaginary numbers can be denoted as $\mathbb{I}^C$. The imaginary number scale can be represented as the y axis of a Cartesian coordinate system, with the scale of real numbers as the x axis (see **Figure 4.5**). Any point on the plane of both the x and y axes forms yet another kind of number: a *complex number*, which combines real and imaginary numbers. The scale of complex numbers can be denoted as $\mathbb{C}^C$.

There are yet other kinds of numbers for which scales can be constructed, such as the algebraic numbers ($\mathbb{A}^C$) and transcendental numbers ($\mathbb{T}^C$), but both are simply types of real or complex numbers, so their details will not concern us. All we need is a basic understanding of the various number scales in order to grasp what they have in common, especially with respect to their limits.

Each of the number systems or 'number scales'—$\mathbb{N}^C$, $\mathbb{W}^C$, $\mathbb{Z}^C$, $\mathbb{Q}^C$, $\mathbb{P}^C$, $\mathbb{A}^C$, $\mathbb{T}^C$, $\mathbb{R}^C$, $\mathbb{I}^C$, and $\mathbb{C}^C$ have some features in common.

For example, as inventions, each scale is an intrinsically incomplete construction. They are each incomplete in the sense that there are always new finite numbers being invented for them. They are also incomplete in another sense: if we could see every instance in which numbers from a particular scale have heretofore been used on the planet over the span of history and compose a list of all the numbers ever depicted from that scale according to the ordinality of the numbers in the scale, we would find many gaps in each scale where numbers are implied but have never been explicitly depicted, calculated, or defined. At any given moment in time, number scales are actually full of 'gaps' and hence incomplete in that sense.

Still, at any moment in time, the scale will be comprised of sequences of numbers explicitly represented in definition or depiction but also those that are implicit and merely implied—large numbers no one has ever depicted. During any given moment in which a number scale is used, the scale may be considered a set of numbers *for that moment*. Hence, scales such as $\mathbb{N}^C$, $\mathbb{W}^C$, $\mathbb{Z}^C$, $\mathbb{Q}^C$, $\mathbb{R}^C$, etc. are each series but can also be considered sets ($\mathbb{N}$, $\mathbb{W}$, $\mathbb{Z}$, $\mathbb{Q}$, $\mathbb{R}$, etc.) when time is abstracted out and we wish to consider the scales as they are for a given moment in their construction and use.

We can denote such with vertical bars to imply the scale, as a series, is depicted during a snapshot in time and so has a finite, variant maximum of numbers, a running total for all the numbers in it, and thus a temporary cardinality for that particular time—e.g., $|\mathbb{R}^C|$. However, take note of the superscript C, which indicates the scale is also a *series* ever under construction and is simply being denoted as a set during a snapshot in time. For example, $|\mathbb{R}^C| = R$ as a set for a given time, t.

Moreover, each number scale has either a constant minimum value in sequence and a variant maximum value in sequence, or a variant minimum and constant maximum, or both a variant minimum and variant maximum at any given time in the construction of the scale. For example, $\mathbb{N}^C$ has the constant minimum (namely, 1) but only a variant maximum as there is no final, largest number for the construction of $\mathbb{N}^C$. Conversely, the negative counterpart of $\mathbb{N}^C$ has a variant minimum (no final definition for a least negative number) but a constant maximum of -1. And then there is $\mathbb{Z}^C$, which has both a variant minimum number in sequence and a variant maximum in sequence. But no number scale—i.e., no number system— has both a constant minimum and a constant maximum of numbers.

The numbers of a given number scale at any moment in time during construction have no final number that halts their construction, at least not until human ingenuity is quelled for good. In fact, we cannot in practice define a constant number as a *final* total of numbers in a number scale—a total that would finish the given scale permanently.

So, none of the number scales are ever capable of having their numbers fully listed. The sequences of known numbers comprising these scales of numbers trail off into ellipses past d^* or its equivalent, indicating that greater numbers can at least in principle be defined in order to capture yet greater collections than d^* would allow.

All of these number scales as series are therefore *necessarily incomplete*; they are each ever incomplete, open series. We are again left with the ellipses...

4.2.14 *Number Scales as Open Series*

If mathematicians go extinct one day along with the rest of us, and if there are no computers around to compute, there would definitely be no one and no thing around to construct more numbers for $\mathbb{N}^C$, and so $\mathbb{N}^C$'s highest invented number would be "the last number" in the sense that there would be no higher numbers ever to be invented for $\mathbb{N}^C$. However, that still does not mean $\mathbb{N}^C$ would be *finished* because if to the contrary there were still mathematicians and machines still around to make yet higher numbers, $\mathbb{N}^C$ *could have* continued to grow. In such a situation, $\mathbb{N}^C$ may have a highest and last number made for it practice, but such a number would only be the highest ever invented, not the highest there could have been. In principle, higher numbers would still be possible for $\mathbb{N}^C$ even if no people are around to invent them in practice. So, $\mathbb{N}^C$ may cease growing, but $\mathbb{N}^C$ would still be unfinished as a series of numbers—and it would remain unfinished. Rather than say a number scale such as $\mathbb{N}^C$ has a "last number," which may be misleading, it is better to say that the number scale simply has a "provisionally highest number" or "provisionally largest number" for any time referenced.

On the other hand, just because a number scale is never finished being constructed does not mean that we should say the scale is at any time "endless" either, because that would also be misleading. Even though a number scale has no "last number" in the sense of an absolutely final number, this does not imply that a number scale has no end at all. Rather, a scale such as $\mathbb{N}^C$ always has an end, it is just that the "end" of the scale is always temporary, changing its total value when operations are employed to make the scale bigger or when someone calculates a number that can be included in the scale as the latest "end." Each number scale has a *series of ends*, and each end is an instance in which a new, higher number replaces the old end of the scale when the new number is invented. So, while it is not wrong to say a number scale is "endless" in the sense that it continues to be extended, it is clearer to say the number scale is 'extensible'.

In short, there is no absolute last number or absolute end to a number scale, and that means the scale is not a closed series or ever becomes a completed set in any final sense. We may speak of "the set of all whole numbers" or "the set of all natural numbers" to indicate the cardinality of all the numbers taken together *in* the given scale *at* a given point in time during the scale's construction, but we cannot speak of the scale *per se* as constituting a *complete* set. Number scales, as such, are open series—series that are always extensible.

If we wish to point out the sets of numbers that are already defined in number scales, we could say the number scales are open series *of* sets. The scales contain sets of defined numbers and a series of such sets. The scales may contain new, larger sets of numbers at a later time because the scales can be augmented with new numbers invented and added to them. The number scales are thus less like the muffin tin and more like the series of rabbits in our earlier example—number scales are always able to include more numbers and they are always being extended so long as there are people around to extend them.

4.2.15 *Number Scales as Incomplete Series*

Recall from § 3.2.8 the completeness criteria: wholeness, entirety, finish, fullness, and totality. We can now apply these criteria to assess number scales as either complete or incomplete.

Take the number scales such as $\mathbb{N}^C$ or $\mathbb{W}^C$. Neither are *whole* scales because there are "gaps" or "breaks" in the defined numbers of the counting numbers—portions between, for example, 10^{15} and 10^{30} that have never been counted out or calculated. That is not to say $\mathbb{N}^C$ and $\mathbb{W}^C$ cannot in principle be made whole; it is just to say they are not whole.

Moreover, because these scales are missing defined numbers, they cannot be considered *entire* scales.

We also know that $\mathbb{N}^C$ (and each of the other scales) has a total because every number scale, even as an open series, still has a total. At any time, the numbers that a number scale contains can, at least in principle, be summed and so given a total. In practice, this isn't possible, but in principle, a number scale's component numbers can be summed up to the largest number in the scale invented to date. Since that sum of numbers is only a sum of numbers invented to date, it is a sum in the sense of being a temporary total or running total of numbers.

So there are actually three different running totals that number scales have.

First, there is the total by which the scale is *in fact* defined—this is the highest number that someone has actually invented *so far* in the scale.

Second, there is the total number of numbers a number scale could *in practice* be defined as having—this is the total that could be arrived at using whatever mathematical technique that will eventually be invented to produce the largest, consistently defined number.

Third and finally, there is the total equal to the largest number able to be defined *in principle*—this is the total that it is logically possible to arrive at if we were to never run out of physical resources for defining new, larger numbers.

When we speak of a number scale's total, or the "number of numbers" in a number scale, such as "all" the numbers in $\mathbb{N}^{\circlearrowleft}$, we must realize that we are speaking either about the total of the number scale in fact, or the total of the scale that is possible in practice, or even the total of the scale that is possible only in principle.

What number, then, is the true total of $\mathbb{N}^{\circlearrowleft}$? There is no one answer. $\mathbb{N}^{\circlearrowleft}$ has a total according to each one of these distinctions.

There is a total for $\mathbb{N}^{\circlearrowleft}$ in fact (its largest number to date—whatever that is), a total for $\mathbb{N}^{\circlearrowleft}$ in practice (a number for which we now only have a variable because it is the number by which we may in the future extend $\mathbb{N}^{\circlearrowleft}$), and a total for $\mathbb{N}^{\circlearrowleft}$ in principle (the total that we could extend $\mathbb{N}^{\circlearrowleft}$ to at some logically possible time in a logically possible scenario, though it shall never be possible to do so in actual practice). Here is the really important part: all three types of totals for $\mathbb{N}^{\circlearrowleft}$ are finite, *running totals* since we are always extending $\mathbb{N}^{\circlearrowleft}$'s number of numbers.

However, because a number scale such as $\mathbb{N}^{\circlearrowleft}$ is an open series with only a running total of defined numbers, the scale in question is never *finished*, so the completeness criterion of 'finish' is a fail for number scales.

Then too, because a number scale such as $\mathbb{N}^{\circlearrowleft}$ has some numbers only implied but not depicted between any two large numbers like 10^{14} and 10^{15}, number scales can always include more numbers without changing the parameters defining the scale (say, 0 to d^*), and that means the scale will never be *full*.

Failure to meet the wholeness, entirety, finish, and fullness criteria implies that a number scale, as an open series, is never a complete set with constant extrema and a standing total. Instead, each number scale is an *incomplete* sequence with, at best, a variant extremum (or extrema) at each stage of construction [123].

Number scales are in this view open-ended series; that is, series that always remain incomplete because they grow indefinitely larger with construction. But because the number scales are open-ended in the sequence of numbers they contain, they are inherently extensible as finite constructions.

We can define new, larger numbers for the series, extending the scales of numbers as we need in order to enumerate collections currently too large to quantify with our presently defined numbers. However, this too has its limits; there will come a point beyond which further definitions of greater numbers to quantify greater collections will not be possible in practice as it would exceed our ability to calculate. After that point, we could continue enumerating only in principle, which means again we cannot approach quantifying an infinite collection with precision by enumeration.

4.3 NUMBER SCALES – FIGURATIVELY INFINITE OR LITERALLY INFINITE?

Because each number scale is inherently incomplete, because the number scales are always under construction, the so-called "last number" in a number scale, the "highest number" defined to date, has *no fixed value*. The "number of numbers" in a number scale is always increasing as the number scale is extended with the invention of new, larger numbers. Number scales, as incomplete *series*, have maximal quantities of numbers but not a maximum quantity of numbers—at least, not qua series.

This has implications for our main subject—infinity—because a scale that is inherently incomplete with only a running total of invented numbers is a scale that is only figuratively infinite rather than literally infinite. In view of this, I will argue in Chapter 24 that 'figurative infinity' is a misnomer for serial *indefiniteness*, so it would be best to say number scales are *indefinite* series rather than infinite series.

Most scholars would agree with me that figurative infinity is not the right term to use for characterizing number scales. However, not because they think number scales are inherently incomplete, open series as I contend them to be. Rather, they would instead say that number scales are not figuratively infinite series, or indefinite series, at all precisely because they are (literally) *infinite sets*. In their view, the ellipsis at the end of 1, 2, 3, 4, 5, 6, ... carries to a value well beyond d^* and beyond any number that can be calculated in practice; the ellipsis denotes not just an *indefinite* sequence but a literally *infinite* sequence.

4.4 TWO VIEWS OF ENUMERATING THE LITERALLY INFINITE

If we take number systems as literally infinite, then they are not just limitless, but complete as well—whole, entire, full, and finished totalities of numbers (see Chapter 3 for definitions and explications of these terms). But having a totality of numbers—a total number of numbers—would seem to imply having a quantity equal to a *sum* of numbers. Whereas to be limitless, in a literal sense, is to imply the inability to be summed since a sum is a limit. So how can the natural numbers, as a set, have a quantity equal to a complete sum of numbers and yet a limitless sequence of unique numbers, each of higher cardinality than the last?

In answer to this concern, most mathematicians regard a number system, such as the natural numbers, to be a literally infinite set according to one of two views. I'll call them Literal Infinity Option A (or LI-A) and Literal Infinity Option B (or LI-B):

LI-A: There is a complete set, the quantity of members for which is expressible, at least in principle, as a number with a limitless string of digits—an infinite sum of members.

LI-B: There is a complete set of *limitlessly many* members that together do not equal a sum, not even one with a limitless string of digits.

4.4.1 *Infinite Sums*

LI-A follows from the very concept of quantity. To quantify a collection is to identify its amount of members—a value equal to a total, which is a number equal to a sum. According to LI-A, a literally infinite collection has a quantity because it has a sum, albeit one that is equal to a number with a limitless string of digits (see **Figure 10.1** in § 10.5).

To express such a number would require some enumeration technique. There are various ways to enumerate as we well know, such as by tallying, counting, calculating, computing, etc. All of these techniques of enumeration are ways of *quantifying*—yielding a quantity, producing a total equal to a sum. If there is such a thing as an "infinite sum," then there must at least in principle be an enumeration technique that would produce such. And since a sum is produced by adding up numbers that could be counted out, then in order for a collection to have a sum and therefore a quantity, the objects making up the collection must be able to be enumerated by counting all (each and every one of) them.

That does not mean the collection to be enumerated is necessarily countable *in practice*. Maybe we don't have a computer with enough power to help us calculate the members of the collection using automated algorithms. But the members of the collection must be at least countable *in principle*—that is, in some logically and mathematically possible circumstance—if we are to accurately say the collection is enumerable and so is a whole with some *quantity* of objects.

The reasoning seems to be this: if a collection has a quantity, it is able to be enumerated, and if it is able to be enumerated, then it is able to be counted to a final sum, even if only in principle. Because literal infinity is a state of completeness as well as limitlessness, and completeness implies a quantity, then LI-A entails that one can at least in principle enumerate the collection by counting all the members of the infinite collection—*all the way up to infinity*. An infinite count, if it could be carried out, would be a final sum of members expressible as a number with no limit to its sequence of digits. Maybe we can't actually express such a number except with shorthand symbolism, but an infinite sum must be achievable in principle, *assuming* LI-A is correct.

4.4.2 *Limitless Totality Without Sum*

LI-B disagrees. According to LI-B, either infinity is not a number at all [124] or infinity may be expressed as an 'infinite number' that is not like a finite number [125]. Either way, there are no infinite sums. And yet, LI-B holds that collections can be complete as well as limitless.

According to LI-B, an infinite collection is not complete in quantity like a finite collection is complete in quantity. While a literally infinite collection does have a 'complete' quantity in the sense of having an *amount* of objects—a value equal to a *total*—the collection is not complete in the usual sense of completeness because the literally infinite collection has a 'total' in an unusual sense.

The infinite collection has a 'total' or 'totality' as a value equal to *a sequence of sums* but not equal to a *final* sum as a maximum quantity. To count every member of a literally infinite collection is to never stop counting; the counter never arrives at a final sum that is equal to a string of digits without limit. Instead, the sequence of sums itself is what an infinite 'totality' means, and it is the limitlessness of finite sums that must be captured in mathematical symbolism.

4.4.3 *Both Views Problematic*

Neither LI-A nor LI-B is obviously correct since there are conceptual difficulties facing both of these options.

LI-A affirms a literally infinite collection as complete because a limitless collection has an "infinite sum," but it is not clear that a 'sum' equal to a constant number with limitless digits is a logically coherent concept.

LI-B is also logically dubious. LI-B denies that a literally infinite set has a final, exact sum of members but that position also does not make clear how the literally infinite set is a genuinely *complete* set. Its 'totality', as a "sequence of sums" without an end to a count of members, is not clearly different from a *series* of sums—the running total of what we typically think of as an *incomplete* series and thus a case of figurative infinity rather than literal infinity.

We will next investigate how mathematicians respond to these problems, starting first with their response to the concerns over LI-B, then those over LI-A.

4.4.4 *Enumeration by Correspondence*

Mathematicians adhering to LI-B reject the idea that LI-B implies merely a running total and not a complete set of numbers. They retort that, while one cannot *count* up to infinity or produce an infinite *sum* to demonstrate the completeness of an infinite set, there is another way to 'enumerate' all the members of a collection that is literally infinite: by *correspondence*.

The term 'correspondence', in a mathematical sense, means the matching or mapping of elements between two sets where one element in one set is paired with at least one element in the other set.

Correspondence can show whether or not each of two given sets has just as many elements, no more and no less, than the other. If so, the members of one set (which we'll call A) are "evenly matched" with the members of a second set (we'll call it B). Mathematician J.R. Maddocks explains [126]:

> Evenly matched means that each member of A is paired with one and only one member of B, each member of B is paired with one and only one member of A, and none of the members from either set are left unpaired. The result is that every member of A is paired with exactly one member of B and every member of B is paired with exactly one member of A. In terms of ordered pairs (a, b), where a is a member of A and b is a member of B, no two ordered pairs created by this matching process have the same first element and no two have the same second element. When this type of matching can be shown to exist, mathematicians say that "a one-to-one correspondence exists between the sets A and B."

We saw a few examples of such one-to-one matching with the definition of cardinality back in § 2.3.1. As another simple example, consider matching all the 'digits' (fingers, including thumbs) between the two hands of a typical person. Imagine a person placing the thumb of their own left hand against their own right-hand thumb, the index finger of their left hand against the index finger of their right hand and doing the same for the remaining fingers. When there are no remaining digits, there is a one-to-one correspondence of the digits on the left hand to the digits on the right hand [127]. The individual doesn't even need to know how many fingers there are in order to see that the two collections of digits match evenly and are therefore the same (finite) size [128].

When two sets have their elements evenly matched in a one-to-one correspondence, mathematicians refer to the sets as 'bijected'; a *bijection* is a one-to-one correspondence of elements between sets. However, if one set has greater or fewer members than the other set, then the sets cannot be bijected because they are not evenly matched.

Between the disproportional sets, at least one element in one set will have to point to more than one element in the other or have more than one element in the other set pointing to it. For example, suppose set A has more elements than set B. In order to match all the elements in set A with those in set B, more than one element in A will have to be matched to the same element in set B. This kind of relation is not a bijection; rather, it is called a *surjection*.

On the other hand, if there are more elements in B than in A and each element in A is matched with only one element in B, with at least one element in B left over, then the sets are also not bijected; instead, they are *injected*. Injection is thus a correspondence of elements between sets in which no element of set A is paired with more than one element of set B but not every element of B is paired with an element of A.

Injection, bijection, and surjection are all forms of correspondence, as depicted in **Figure 4.6**.

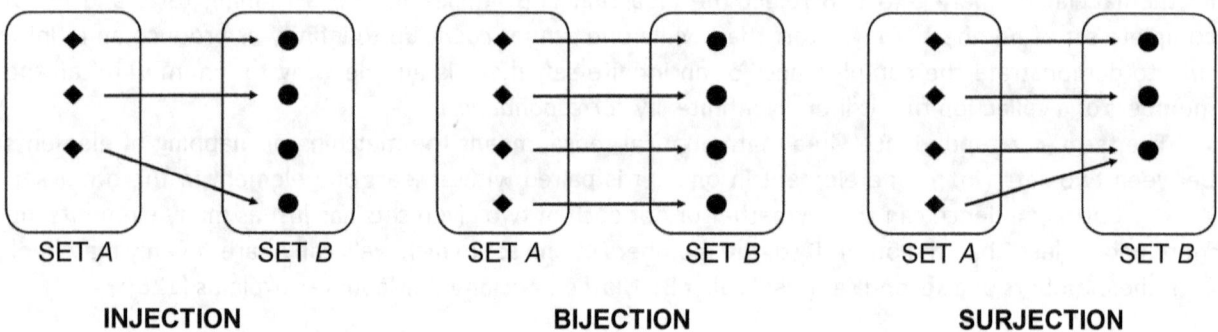

INJECTION   BIJECTION   SURJECTION

Figure 4.6: Three types of correspondence.

Mathematicians may not agree whether or not an infinite collection can be counted to an infinitely large number, but most agree that, at least in principle, a collection that is literally infinite can be shown to be such by the procedure of correspondence. A collection that is literally infinite can be *completely* enumerated by means of correspondence between that collection and the set of all natural numbers just as one would demonstrate two hands to have the same number of fingers by matching them up.

If a collection is literally infinite, then either all natural numbers must *biject* with the members of the collection or all the natural numbers must *inject* to the collection. Suppose in matching the members of a collection to a list of all the natural numbers we could determine that there are as many members of the collection as there are natural numbers or even more members of the given collection than natural numbers. Either way, the correspondence technique, just on its own, would say the collection is literally infinite because the natural numbers are infinite.

And yet, problems remain. There seems to be some question begging with LI-B's attempt to define a collection as infinite according to the correspondence procedure. Sure, a collection would be literally infinite if it has just as many members as a literally infinite set of natural numbers, but do the natural numbers themselves really constitute a literally infinite set? The foregoing exposition of building number scales would say otherwise. So, even if the correspondence technique is a necessary procedure in order to quantify a collection as literally infinite, it may not be sufficient since the assumption that number systems are themselves infinite may not be a safe assumption.

4.4.5 *Expression of Infinite Numbers by Symbolism*

Now let's return to the issue of LI-A. According to LI-A, infinite series are completable in principle and so some numbers can be *infinite numbers*, such as a natural number with infinitely many digits. For supporters of LI-A, an infinite natural number is not like a finite natural number. An infinite natural number, if it *could* be expressed, *would* in principle have a limitless string of digits. The idea of such a number is plausible, they hold, because we need not be able in practice to write out such a number. Rather than write out an infinitely long string of digits, we must instead rely on some other form of symbolism to express an infinite number. Consequently, the infinite number *of* all natural numbers is just expressed differently than any number *in* the set of natural numbers. The unique mathematical symbolism for an 'infinite number' is what expresses the complete quantity of any infinitely large collection. This goes for infinitely large collections of numbers as well, including the set of natural numbers. We will explore this symbolism toward the end of the next chapter.

4.4.6 *Infinite Collections are Enumerated Indirectly*

Both LI-A and LI-B for literally infinite quantities have something in common: mathematicians must employ different techniques of enumeration and expression of quantity in order to either express (a) an 'infinite number' or (b) enumeration of the infinite without counting to up to an infinite number.

Instead of enumerating by counting, calculating, or computing, they 'enumerate' hypothetically by correspondence, and instead of expressing an infinite quantity directly using digits, they express it indirectly with specialized mathematical symbols. That is how mathematicians conceive the enumeration of literally infinite collections.

CHAPTER 4 IN REVIEW

❖ Number systems may be interpreted as figuratively infinite scales of numbers built over time (e.g., the system of natural numbers as the scale $\mathbb{N}^\circlearrowright$). But number systems have been typically interpreted by mathematicians as literally infinite sets of numbers available all at once (e.g., the system of natural numbers represented as the set $\mathbb{N}$).

❖ Number systems, as *figurative* infinities, are inherently incomplete, open series that are always under construction. But many mathematicians contend that number systems are not at all figuratively infinite series, or indefinite series, precisely because they are (literally) *infinite sets*.

❖ If we take number systems as *literally* infinite, then they are not just limitless, but complete as well—whole, entire, full, and finished totalities of numbers.

❖ Completeness implies totality and totality means to have a total—an exact sum equal to a number able to be expressed, at least in principle.

❖ So, literal infinity implies the existence of an infinite total or "sum" in some respect.

❖ The notion of an infinite total may be interpreted in two different ways—
   o An infinite number—a number with infinitely many digits.
   o A quantity that is an infinite 'total' without an infinitely large number.

❖ Both options follow from the concept of literal infinity.

❖ Both options imply that some enumeration technique is needed to express infinite quantity, either as (a) an 'infinite number' or (b) enumeration of a given set as infinite by establishing a correspondence between the members of that set and the set of natural numbers, which is assumed to be literally infinite.

5: ON PREDICATING THE FINITE AND THE INFINITE

Some mathematicians say there are 'infinite numbers' [129] [130] [131]. Others say there is no such thing as an infinite number because infinity is not a number, even if it can be used as if it is a number [132].

But if infinity is not a number, then what sort of thing is it? The short answer: *infinity is a (purported) property*—a quantitative condition some collections allegedly have.

Such collections include, so it is often claimed, collections of numbers. Sometimes infinity is even said to be the property of certain kinds of numbers, for numbers themselves denote properties of collections, even if only collections of numerals or other symbols.

When the property called 'infinity' is ascribed to a collection, the collection is said to be 'infinite', thereby indicating that the cognate 'infinite' is not just an adjective as it is known to be in the study of grammar but also a 'predicate' as known in the study of logic. Even in the language of mathematics the term 'infinite' functions as a logical predicate.

Incidentally, when I say the term 'infinity' or one of its cognates like 'infinite' or 'infinitely' are predicates, I do not mean merely in the *grammatical* sense, but rather in the *logical* sense. In logic, any verb or adjective is a 'predicate'—a property or relation ascribed to a subject. The term 'infinite' is, more precisely, a logical predicate of a particular sort: it is a kind of *quantifier*—a predicate indicative of quantity. Just as saying 'all', 'some', 'many', 'few', and 'most' are quantifiers, saying a collection has 'finitely many' or 'infinitely many' members is to use a quantifier for the collection. Better still, the term 'infinity' and its various cognates are instances of a particular sort of quantifier—infinity (or any of its cognates) is a *quantifier for an unspecifiable quantity*.

In this chapter, we will very briefly examine the nature of logical predicates and quantifiers. We'll then see what it means to predicate a collection as finite or as infinite. Predication, and symbols for logical predicates, will be shown to be the means by which mathematicians *express* collections as 'infinite', regardless of whether the collection in question can be 'enumerated' to infinity by counting, by correspondence, or by some other technique. We'll then see how infinity, as a term in language and math, functions as a logical predicate—specifically, as a quantifier for unspecifiable quantity. But even though the term 'infinity' is a predicate of sorts, in symbolism it is used *as if* it is a kind of number, returning us to the question as to whether or not there really are 'infinite numbers'.

5.1 PREDICATION BY QUANTIFIERS

In grammar, a predicate is the part of a sentence or clause (usually an adjective) describing something about the subject of the sentence. For example, the noun 'cat' is the subject and the adjective 'black' is a predicate in the sentence, "The cat is black," because 'black' describes something about the subject of the sentence, which is the cat. In that example, the predicate is an adjective separated by a verb (such as the words 'is', 'are', 'was', etc.), which is what makes the adjective a predicate. But adjectives are not always separated from a subject by a verb. For example, there is no verb separating the adjective 'black' from the subject in the sentence, "The black cat purred." In that case, the field of grammar regards the adjective 'black' not as a predicate but instead as an *attribute* because the adjective precedes its noun. A predicate is distinguished from an 'attribute', even for the same word, because of where the word falls in the sentence.

In the academic study of logic, this grammatical distinction of place is unimportant to whether or not an adjective is regarded as a predicate. In logic, the word 'black' is a predicate both in the statement "the black cat purred" and in the statement "the cat is black." Hence, terms like 'predicate' and 'attribute' as used in the study of logic have different meanings than they do in the study of grammar.

Take 'predicate' as defined for the study of logic:

- predicate: *a word that attributes a property to an object.*

In the study of logic, the term 'attribute' is not used primarily in the grammatical sense but in a different sense. In the above definition, a predicate *attributes* a property by affirming the object has the property or denying the object has the opposite of the given property. For example, the word 'limited' affirms that something has limit as a property while the word 'limitless' denies something has limit as a property—limitlessness being the opposite of having a limit. Hence, the term 'attribute' in the study of logic is defined differently than it is in the study of grammar, as so indicated:

- attribute:
  (1) noun: *a property affirmed, or its opposite denied, as belonging to an object.*
  (2) verb: *to affirm a property or deny its opposite as belonging to an object.*

Moreover, to attribute a predicate to an object is to *predicate* (verb) the object. Definition:

- predication: *the attribution of a predicate to an object.*

Predication provides information about an object (e.g., the cat) such as what the object is, what the object(s) is doing, or what property the object has (e.g., black). When I use the terms 'predication' and 'predicate' I will use them according to the logical rather than the grammatical senses of these terms, so placement in a sentence or statement is unimportant to qualifying as a predicate.

There are many kinds of predicates and some of them can be used for quantities. Words such as 'all', 'some', 'none', 'both', 'either', 'each', 'every', 'any', 'many', 'few', 'less', 'lesser', 'least', 'more', 'most', 'equal', and so forth are all predicates that indicate quantity. As you can see from these examples, to predicate a quantity is not to express an exact number such as 0, 1, 50, 10^{12}, and so on. Predicates for quantity express instead what the quantity is like rather than provide an exact amount. (However, some predicates *imply* an exact amount. For example, 'none' implies zero and 'either' implies two.)

Even though predicates do not directly state exact quantities, we can nevertheless *quantify* a collection indirectly by using a predicate to indicate that the subject in question does have a quantity and to say something about what the quantity is, or should be, like. In fact, logicians refer to certain predicates for quantity as *quantifiers*. In particular, two of the words listed above—'all' and 'some'—are logical quantifiers; they are given letter-like symbols for use in formal logic: ∀ for 'all' and and ∃ 'some'. However, those are just two predicates that indicate quantity. In a looser sense, all predicates that indicate quantity—including predicates such as 'each', 'every', 'few', 'most', etc.—can be considered 'quantifiers'. Adopting this looser sense of the term 'quantifier', we can propose a definition:

- quantifier: *a predicate that indicates an unspecified quantity.*

A quantifier is a general indicator of quantity rather than a specifier of quantity.

Quantifiers can come in handy when an exact amount, the quantity per se, as not important. As long as we know a collection has an in-principle countable number of members, then we know the collection has a quantity, but it is not always necessary to actually count or calculate, or otherwise enumerate, a collection in order to inform about the quantity of its members. In some contexts, we may simply want to indicate that a given quantity is present or not, or that a quantity includes some members while excluding others. Or we may want to indicate that a given collection has a different quantity of members than another has *without performing an enumeration of any kind*. Instead of mathematically specifying a quantity by exact amounts in such cases, we may describe the quantity of members in a collection by use of 'quantifiers' according to the above definition [133].

There are at least two types of quantifier (which will be important in Chapters 13–14):

- membership quantifier: *a predicate that indicates a range of inclusion or exclusion from a given collection of unspecified quantity.*

- magnitude quantifier: *a predicate that indicates similarity or difference between collections of unspecified quantities.*

A 'membership quantifier' (sometimes called a 'determiner' in the study of grammar) depicts members included or excluded from a collection not in terms of exact amounts but in terms of unspecified quantity. Basically, a membership quantifier tells us how much or how little of something is being considered in a general sense without providing a quantity to the collection under consideration. Membership quantifiers include such words as 'all' and 'some' (the usual logical quantifiers), but also words such as 'none', 'both', 'either', 'some', 'each', 'every', and so forth. These words are used to express that a collection has some quantity of elements included or excluded from it. Examples of membership quantifiers can be found in sentences like the following:

- *Some* numbers have decimals.
- *All* humans are mortal.

Notice the statements do not tell us in any specific way how many numbers or humans there are; rather, the statements just tell us in a general way about the range of things included or excluded from those collections.

If we wish to consider the quantity of objects making up a collection relative to the quantity of objects in some other collection or collections, we can use 'magnitude quantifiers' to describe the similarity or difference in the sizes of the collections. Magnitude quantifiers are such words as 'equal', 'less', 'lesser', 'least', 'more', 'most', 'little', 'littlest', 'great', 'greater', 'greatest', etc. We use such magnitude quantifiers when we describe a collection's members as being 'equal to' or 'less than' or 'greater than' those of another collection.

Some examples of magnitude quantifiers:

- The amount of cars is *equal to* the amount of drivers.
- The multitude of sand grains on Earth is *less than* the multitude of planets in the Universe.
- The number of children is *greater than* the number of parents.

We might also use predicates like the adjectives 'small', 'smaller, 'smallest', 'large', 'larger', 'largest', etc. as magnitude quantifiers to indicate the differences in magnitude between various sizes of collections or quantities of objects in collections.

Membership quantifiers and magnitude quantifiers categorically overlap. There are some predicates that function both as a membership quantifier and as a magnitude quantifier because they tell us not only if something belongs to a given collection but also its magnitude relative to the collection. Such quantifiers include adjectives like 'single', 'couple', 'few', 'several', 'many', 'most', etc. Examples:

- *Many* people are called, but *few* people are chosen.
- A *single* member can influence *several* members.

In short, we may use *quantifiers* rather than *numbers* to express the quantity of members in a collection, or at least give an indication of quantity.

Such quantifiers are primarily used in symbolic logic, the field that studies the expression of quantity by quantifiers rather than numbers. However, as we'll later see, the disciplines of mathematics and set theory also use symbols for quantifiers—those symbols expressing sets or quantities as *finite* or *infinite*.

5.2 FINITE AND INFINITE AS PREDICATES

Since infinity is a denial of finitude, we'll first look at the term 'finite' as a predicate for quantity, and as a quantifier, before examining infinity as likewise.

5.3 PREDICATING AS FINITE

The word 'finite' as used in mathematics and set theory is given very precise, technical meanings. I will ignore these for now. The word 'finite', as a word, is a predicate. And as a predicate, 'finite' does not directly provide a number or quantity to a given collection predicated as finite. Rather, the word 'finite' tells us something *about* the number or quantity of the collection predicated as finite. The word 'finite', when predicated of a collection, tells us the collection has a *limit* to its quantity, or number, of members.

Chapter 1 defined 'finite' in five different ways, all having to do with limit. Here they are again:

- finite:
    - (1) *having a limit.*
    - (2) *having a limit to a given measure.*
    - (3) *having a limited quantity.*
    - (4) *having limited quality.*
    - (5) *having limited quantity and quality.*

These are complementary definitions, and they remain valid. But to fully grasp what it is that the predicate 'finite' describes of a collection, we need to have some clarity on what a 'limit' is.

5.3.1 *Limit*

Mathematicians have various definitions of the word 'limit', each pertaining to a branch of mathematics such as geometry and calculus. In calculus, for example, a limit is typically defined as a mathematical value toward which a sequence of elements or the output of a function converges. However, such is too narrow for our purposes, so I will stipulate a precising definition for the quantitative sense of 'limit' that captures how the term is used across several contexts in natural language, and even in mathematical contexts for which natural language has some use:

- limit: *a specifiability condition for a range.*

Let's unpack the constituent terms in this precising definition of 'limit'—we need to define 'specifiability', 'specifiability condition', and 'range'. Let's start with the first two:

- specifiability: *the property of being specifiable.*
- specifiable: *able to be specified.*

Recall from §2.3.14 that to 'specify' is to identify, refer to, or describe a distinct object. Specifiability is thus the ability to be identified, referred to, or described as a distinct object (where "distinct object" means a given, particular object as opposed to some other object). Ergo:

- specifiability condition: *a condition (feature or circumstance) that enables something to be specified (identified, referred to, or described as distinct from other things).*

Which leaves for our definition of limit the notion of 'range' [134]:

- range: *a collection's extent of elements.*

So, to have a limit is to have a condition—in particular, a range (extent of elements)—that enables whatever has the limit to be specified (distinctly identified, referred to, or described).

We are getting a clearer idea of 'limit', but it could be made still clearer. The term 'range' refers to an 'extent' of elements, so 'extent' must also be defined:

- extent: *the measure of difference between values assigned.*

A collection's extent is thus the difference between quantitative values assigned to the elements of the collection (for example, the mathematical difference between two points on a line, the difference between a pair of numbers in a sequence of numbers, the difference between smallest and largest volumes covering a cluster of elements, etc.). Any collection of some quantitative variety such as a domain, field, scope, scale, dimension, distance, spread, reach, region, breadth, depth, etc. has 'extent' as one of its features. Moreover, a collection has an 'extent' of elements for the *entirety* of the collection if the collection's elements are able to be assigned values in an act of measuring the collection without leaving out any elements. Extent is a collective property of elements together, whether the collection is a multitude, aggregate, set, sequence, or series. Even a series has an 'extent' of elements, at least in the sense of a succession of events or steps that comprise it at the time of measurement. We can therefore speak of the "range of a series" just as we can the range of any other kind of collection.

We might also speak of the 'range' of a purely conceptual collection that corresponds to nothing that actually exists in the physical world. For instance, in mathematics, the term 'range' often refers to the value of a set of variables such as a dispersion of statistics or an amount of values (like the difference between lowest and highest scores).

Regardless of what kind of collection we are considering, we can put the above definitions together for our concept of 'limit' by saying that a limit, as a "specifiability condition for a range," is a feature or circumstance of a collection that enables the extent (measurable difference between assigned values) of elements in the collection to be identified as distinct from the extent of elements in any other collection.

There is one last term in this explication of 'limit' that needs further clarity: *value*. Limit is defined in terms of range, range in terms of extent, and extent in terms of 'value'; so what is meant by 'value'?

That term has many uses (aesthetic, ethical, political, religious, etc.), but the kind of value that will concern us most is 'value' in the mathematical sense. Until Chapter 25, the term 'value' will mostly mean the mathematical sense of value since until then the kind of limits to be discussed will be mainly limits of quantity rather than limits of quality.

That is not to say that qualities cannot be assigned values and therefore limits, for they certainly can. But 'values' with respect to quality generally have a different meaning: a qualitative value is a specification of desirability or worth (see § 1.4), whereas a quantitative or mathematical value is a specifiable constant number (see § 2.3.14). So while something's qualitative limits are the conditions that specify its differences in desirability or worth (qualitative values) with respect to its properties, in contrast a collection's quantitative limits are the conditions that specify differences in the constant numbers (quantitative or mathematical values) assigned to its elements. Since we are considering the limits of collections, unless otherwise indicated we will be considering value, extent, range, and limit only in the quantitative senses of these terms rather than in their qualitative senses.

Quantitative limits include such examples as *ends*, *brinks*, *edges*, *borders*, *bounds*, *boundaries*, *extremes*, and *totals*. These are all examples of specifiability conditions for ranges (limits) that are quantitative descriptors because they can each determine the 'extent' of elements making up the collection in question via assigned numbers, which can be used to distinguish that collection's extent of elements from other extents. To elaborate on these examples, consider:

End. An 'end' is a condition that specifies the range of a sequence (such as the measure of a line or a list) or a series (like the succession of steps it takes to count the members of a list) by pointing to the first or last member in the sequence or series.

Brink. A 'brink' specifies the range of a sequence or series by pointing to the element or moment just before a marked change or event.

Edge. An 'edge' specifies the range of a geometrical shape or body because it is a brink that results in a change of angle.

Border. A 'border' specifies the range of an area by marking where the area is separated from another area.

Bound. A 'bound' specifies the range of a sequence beyond which extends more elements not in the sequence (for the set-theoretic understanding of a bound, see § 11.2.6).

Boundary. A 'boundary' specifies the range of a collection by marking where the collection meets its complement (elements not shared by another collection).

Extreme. An 'extreme' specifies a range either by the outermost mathematical value(s) of a collection's sequence or by the least/greatest amount of elements in the collection (see § 4.2.2).

Total. A 'total' specifies a range by providing the sum or product of all the elements in a collection, where that sum or product can, at least in principle, be expressed as a constant number.

All of these specifiability conditions enable us to tell one quantitative range from another in a collection, or the quantitative range of one collection from that of another collection. (There are other kinds of limits too, but these provide all the examples we will need for this book's examination of quantitative infinity.)

In some cases, conditions can specify different ranges in the same collection. For example, take a deck of playing cards. The deck is the collection of elements; each card is an element of the deck. Each suit in the deck—hearts, diamonds, spades, and clubs—is a different extent of the elements (the ranges of the elements). Each suit in the deck, as a range, has specifiability conditions: a card of least value and a card of greatest value with a quantitative scale of other cards between. So, here we have an example of one collection, the deck, with multiple limits in it.

In other cases, conditions can specify different ranges between collections, allowing us to distinguish one collection from another. A border specifies where the range of states forming the mainland of the United States leaves off and the range of Canadian provinces begins, and vice versa. The border is a specifiability condition for the ranges of these two collections—a kind of limit.

We therefore have several examples of features or circumstances that enable the extent of elements in (or the range of) a collection to be identified as distinct from any other extent of elements (or ranges of other collections)—that is, we have several examples of limits.

5.3.2 *On Being a Limit and Having a Limit*

Finitude was defined as "the quality or condition of being finite" and to be finite is "to have a limit." From the previous section, we now have 'limit' defined and examples of limits. From the definition of limit, we see that to be finite is to have a specifiability condition for a range (extent of elements) in a collection.

That is not the only way to define what it means to be finite. Mathematicians and set theorists also propose various technical definitions for what the word 'finite' means. However, their definitions tend to be narrowly focused on mathematical contexts. I prefer to keep the definition of the word 'finite' to a more general conception of being limited to fit a variety of contexts that may work across mathematical disciplines and in other contexts as well. I believe the words 'finite' and 'limit' have been precisely defined enough for that purpose.

But some questions remain. We sometimes say something *has* a limit and other times we say something *is* a limit. So how is to *have* a limit different from *being* a limit?

Since a limit is "a specifiability condition for a range," and since something can either have or be a limit, then something can either *have* a specifiability condition for a range or it can *be* a specifiability condition for a range.

For example, to say that X "is" the limit of a collection is to say that X specifies the collection's range by distinguishing its extent of elements from that of any other collection. By contrast, to say collection Y "has" a limit, such as a limit to the quantity of elements in Y, is to say that Y has a range of its own and that there is some specifiability condition for Y's range.

Let's take an example of the first case in which something *is* a limit. A circle can be considered a limit—it *is* a limit—because its shape specifies the range (extent of elements) that lies between the perimeter and the center.

Next, consider an example in which something *has* a limit. Again, the circle will suffice. It's also true that a circle *has* a limit because the circle's radius starts at a center point to the circle's interior, which is a disk, and ends at a point on the circle as the perimeter of the disk, with that end being the limit of the circle. And, as noted earlier, we can always mark a point on the curve of the circle and then trace around that closed curve back to the starting point—showing that the circle's circumference, the extent of the circle's closed curve, has a limit even if the circle is without bound with respect to the directions along its closed curve.

We are also not faced with a dichotomy of being or having a limit; something can not only *be* a limit but also *have* a limit. The curve of the circle both serves as a limit (the perimeter) to all that may be inside the circle and the curve of the circle has a limit in that its circumference has a limit to its measure.

But not everything serves as a limit while also having a limit; that is to say, something can *be* a limit but not *have* a limit, or vice versa.

As an example of something being a limit while not having a limit, take the number zero. Zero can *be* a limit to a collection of values but zero *has* no such limits of its own. As a constant number, zero is the lower limit of the whole numbers—so, zero *is* a limit. But as a mathematical value, zero cannot be divided; it has no condition within it to specify a range—it has no extent, or measurable difference, between values. That is, zero has no limit because it is not a collection of anything (see § 2.3.8). Hence if we take zero as referring to the emptiness of the empty set, zero refers to nothing with limit. And if we think of zero as simply being the empty set, the same pertains: there is nothing in the empty set at all and so nothing to specify a range (again, no limit) to the empty set simply as such. So, zero has no quantitative limits of its own. Zero, then, can *be* a limit without *having* a limit.

Conversely, something can have a limit but not be a limit. Consider the set of all numbers in the scale of natural numbers. As pointed out earlier, numbers are inventions. Where the *sequence* of natural numbers leaves off at the highest ordinality produced so far during construction of the scale as a sequence of numbers, the largest number is equal to the number of numbers making up the sequence taken as the *set* of all the numbers at the time the largest number is defined. So clearly the set of all numbers in a given number scale at a given time has a total—namely, the total that is the running total of the scale as an open series, and that total is kind of limit. And yet, while the set of all numbers in the scale at the given time has a limit (the running total), that series of numbers need not itself be a limit for something else.

There is, then, a difference between being a limit and having a limit. And yet, we also sometimes say that something "is limited," which is the same as saying it has a limit. These distinctions may sound like mere wordplay, but they are in fact useful distinctions for how we refer to limits and lack of limits, and they will become important as indicated in the next section.

5.3.3 *Endless and Unbounded, but Still Limited*

There are differences between the various kinds of limits—ends, edges, borders, boundaries, extremities, and any other specifiability conditions for ranges. If something is limited in one sense, it may not be limited in another sense. Something might have an end but no edge, an extremity but no border, etc. Moreover, there is a difference between being without a limit in any given respect (such as being endless) and being without any limit at all.

As pointed out in § 1.1.2, just because something has no limit in the sense of being "endless" does not mean it has no limit per se. For example, something can be without end or boundary and yet still be limited in terms of size. All bounded things may be limited, but not all unbounded things are without limit.

Though that might sound paradoxical at first, a simple example should clear it up: once again, consider a circle. Though a circle has no end or boundary to its curve, the circle's circumference is still limited in extent, and so the circle is still limited in size. The circle's diameter has a range, and the points at which that range intersects with the circle, as a perimeter to its interior disk, indicates the limit of the circle's size. The circle is thus "unbounded" or has "no end" (along its curve) and yet it is also limited (in terms of its diameter or in terms of tracing the extent of its circumference). And this simple example shows that just because something has no limits of one kind does not make it "limitless" per se.

5.3.4 *Defining the Finite by Enumeration*

If something can be without a limit of a particular type and yet still be finite, then what is it to be finite? While something finite can lack a limit of a particular type, to be finite is still to *have* a limit of some kind— it is still to have a "specifiability condition for a range," just as explicated above. If we can in some way specify the range of elements for a collection, we have a finite collection.

And we can specify the range of elements in a collection if the elements in the collection can be completely enumerated. A collection can be completely enumerated, at least in principle, if the enumeration would account for all the elements in the collection at a given time without elements remaining.

So in addition to the five definitions of 'finite' in Chapter 1, here is another complementary definition for the predicate 'finite', a definition that captures limit—a specifiability condition for a range—in terms of enumeration:

- finite: (6) *completely enumerable (at least, in principle) to a determinate amount*.

We can consider that to be a more technical version of the third definition of finite, which is "having a limited quantity."

Some mathematicians object that certain *infinite* collections are also enumerable (enumerability was explicated in § 2.3.5, § 2.5.1, § 3.13.3, and § 4.1.1). However, they are not using the term 'enumerable' in quite the same sense that I have thus far defined it. Instead, they are using the term 'enumerable' in a technical sense of the term (see § 13.10).

In reply, that's partly where the caveat "to a determinate amount" comes in for the above definition of 'finite'. A literally infinite collection may very well be in a technical sense 'enumerable', but the kind of technical 'enumerability' characterizing a literally infinite collection does not provide a determinate (quantitatively or mathematically specifiable) amount for the collection due to the collection's quantitative *limitlessness* (see § 5.4.2) [135]. In contrast, that which is finite is, in its own technical sense, that which is able—in principle if not also in practice—to be enumerated to a determinate amount.

Assuming a determinate amount must be specifiable for a given collection C is to be finite, if we *cannot* in principle completely enumerate C in this way, then C is not finite. I will therefore maintain that

C is finite if and only if *C* is able to be completely enumerated, at least in principle. (The following sections provide further qualifications to finitude as a condition of complete enumerability.)

5.3.5 *Mathematical Definitions for the Finite*

The five lexical and precising definitions for the term 'finite', and even the sixth—the above technical definition for 'finite'—are broader than various definitions used in mathematics. Mathematicians sometimes define the term 'finite' by particular procedures they can actually carry out to demonstrate the limit of a collection (especially sets, sequences, and series). Such definitions are consistent within the scope of particular mathematical disciplines, but they cannot capture what it means to be finite in a general sense as they are each far too narrow.

For instance, the finitude of a collection can be demonstrated with mathematical procedures for enumeration such as tallying, counting, calculation, and computation. Suppose while enumerating a collection of non-zero elements we run out of objects to enumerate; we would have reached the limit of the collection and so have shown that the collection to be finite.

It is a straightforward matter to demonstrate a collection is finite when the collection is small; just enumerate the members of the collection by tally, calculation, or computation. But what of collections too large to use such enumeration techniques? This is where enumeration becomes more a matter of theory than practice; set theorists propose the technique of correspondence for collections too large to count or compute in actual practice. A collection can, at least in principle, be shown as finite if it can be enumerated via correspondence with a segment of the sequence of natural numbers.

Suppose the elements of one set can be bijected with a *subset* of natural numbers (or we could say that the elements can be 'injected' with the set of all the natural numbers). And suppose we make *S* a finite set of boxes. In that case, *S* can be bijected with a subset of $\mathbb{N}^{\mathrm{C}}$, but only injected with $\mathbb{N}^{\mathrm{C}}$ as a scale that includes more numbers than the boxes:

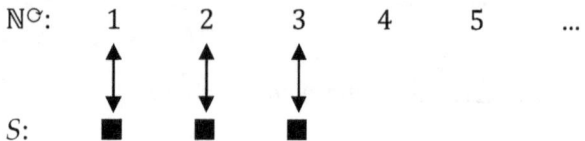

This situation jibes with the concept of finitude as presented in *transfinite set theory* (see § 13.1). Mathematicians and set theorists working with the transfinite system sometimes define 'finite' in a technical sense as having a number of elements (for example, objects) capable of being put into a one-to-one correspondence with a segment of the set of natural numbers, $\mathbb{N}$, through a process of correspondence [136].

Insofar as there are more defined numbers that we can use to enumerate the members of some collection smaller or equal in size, the definition of 'finite' in the transfinite system holds up. But does that definition necessarily hold as a matter of logic? Not necessarily.

There is no logical contradiction in supposing there can be more objects than defined numbers. If I am correct that number is a property of numerals and numerals are inventions made for establishing comparisons, then the scale of natural numbers only extends as far as anyone has ever depicted the largest finite number at any given time. If that is so for number scales in general, then every scale of numbers is an incomplete series with a running total of numbers, and that running total is finite because every number scale has only a finite number of numbers defined at any given time. And if *that* is so, then the question naturally arises: what if it is *not* the case that any finite collection must have fewer members than the scale of natural numbers? Suppose instead there is a finite number of numbers compared with a collection that has more elements than there are defined numbers. In that situation, it would not be true that any finite collection necessarily can be corresponded to a defined segment (subset) of natural numbers and only injected with the numbers of the whole number scale.

Suppose, then, that there is a collection with more objects than there are defined natural numbers to match [137]. In order to enumerate the additional objects under such conditions, the scale of natural numbers must be extended by defining new natural numbers—numbers not previously well-defined or calculable by known mathematical methods for precisely expressing such large finite numbers. Until then, we cannot say there is a one-to-one correspondence of natural numbers and objects in the observed collection—at most, we can only say there is *potentially* a bijection of natural numbers to objects, once new numbers are invented to match to the remaining objects.

Until we invent the new, higher numbers, there would be a collection greater in magnitude than any known scale of natural numbers, and therefore greater than any correspondence one could perform with the natural numbers. And yet, though the collection would have more members than any defined finite number in the scale of natural numbers, the collection we wish to enumerate need not be literally infinite after all. It could still be finite because it has the potential to be enumerated via a bijection with natural numbers. That is, the collection would be finite as long as the natural number scale can be extended, at least in principle, to capture the size of the collection.

This still holds true even if the collection being enumerated grows faster than the scale for enumerating the members of the collection. Such a collection would still be a finite series because there is a last member at each stage of growth to count even if that member is succeeded by yet new members generated and that need to be counted.

So, while the definition for 'finite' in the transfinite system is technically correct—while a collection is finite if it can be bijected with a *segment* of natural numbers—it is nevertheless misleading because it just assumes that the scale of natural numbers must already be as large as, or even larger than, the collection to be matched with a set of natural numbers. That is not necessarily a safe assumption if numbers are inventions.

Instead, a collection may be considered finite if *either* its members inject with a segment of natural numbers *or* if the sequence of natural numbers can, at least in principle, be defined so that all the numbers in the numerical sequence biject with the elements of the collection in question. Looking at finitude this way leaves open the possibility that we may need to invent new, larger numbers in order to make a *complete* bijection of natural numbers to elements in the collection we wish to measure. As long as by extending the scale of numbers we can enumerate all the elements of the collection, the collection is finite.

The moral is that we should not confine our definition of the term 'finite' or our conception of finitude to the technique of correspondence or the ability to establish a bijection between a collection and a sequence of numbers. Instead, we should define finitude only according to enumeration in a more general sense. That which is finite is that which can, *at least in principle*, be completely enumerated, whether by tallying, counting, computing, calculating, or corresponding with a scale of numbers.

5.3.6 *The Finite—Complete and Incomplete*

To be finite is to be *completely* enumerable to a determinate amount. But as with the example of the fast-growing collection, suppose the collection we wish to enumerate is not itself complete. Suppose it is a collection of replicating viruses, for instance—it grows as we quantify the collection. And suppose for any measurement we make, there will be further growth of the collection. Such a collection is not complete because it is not finished; it is an unfinished set or open series with a running total of members. As such, the collection being enumerated is not "completely enumerable" in the sense of having a definite, final, 'standing total' (i.e., a particular and stable total that remains constant) for all its members.

Having a standing total is not what being "completely enumerable to a specified amount" requires. To be completely enumerable is not necessarily to be enumerable with a standing total. Rather, to be completely enumerable means able to have an enumeration completely account for the elements in the collection *when enumeration takes place*.

Incomplete collections may still be regarded as finite if the collection's totality of elements can, at least in principle, be completely enumerated for a given moment in time. If the process of enumeration finishes measuring the whole, entire set of elements and the enumeration concludes with a defined total for the collection, then the collection is "completely enumerated" *just as it is at the time enumeration concludes*.

It is the enumeration of the collection that needs to be complete, not the collection so enumerated. Even if the collection continues to grow with a running total, we can consider enumeration "complete" *for that instance of enumeration* as long as the enumeration of members captures that running total. So, the collection being enumerated does not itself have to be complete in order for the collection to be completely enumerated.

Let's apply this distinction to another example. Imagine a cylindrical tower built of bricks. The base is circular, the height is linear. Once the top of the tower is capped by a rooftop (without construction of a taller extension such as a steeple or antenna and without inserting further layers of brick beneath the rooftop), we'll call the tower *complete*—it cannot be made any taller. Because the tower is capped, it has an end (and so a limit) to its height; it is finite. But suppose the tower has no roof and instead has merely an unfinished sequence of brickwork at the top. If construction has ceased, the tower stands as an *incomplete* set of bricks, but it is finite nonetheless since all the bricks can be enumerated. The set of bricks comprising the incomplete tower can be completely enumerated.

Now let's consider the tower as a series rather than as just a set. Removing all physical constraints, suppose that construction has not stopped and will never stop. For as long as there is time the tower will always be made ever taller. In that case, because it is continuously under construction, being made ever taller, the tower simply as such always remains incomplete—it is never finished. It is an ongoing process; a series of bricks being laid "without end." But even though the top of the tower is a sequence of brickwork that continually grows higher, the tower always remains finite because it always has a limited number of bricks from its base to its top at any time. No matter how many bricks are added to make the top higher, no matter how high the tower becomes, there is always a countable number of bricks to the top. The tower is ever incomplete but is always finite with a running total of bricks making it up. At any given time, a complete enumeration of the bricks would capture that running total, even though, as a running total, it will later be superseded.

But what about the number scales (for example, $\mathbb{N}^C$ or $\mathbb{W}^C$)—aren't they incomplete due to being open series with new numbers always being invented for them? And if that is so, how can anything with more numbers than those already invented be "completely enumerated" and so be finite?

Yes, the sequence of numbers in a scale of numbers such as $\mathbb{N}^C$ is an incomplete, open series. However, the numerical scales do not themselves need to be complete in order to be able to be useful for completely enumerating collections that are, at any given time, larger than the number scales themselves. That's precisely because the scales do have the potential to be extended with new numbers.

At one time, the largest number was no more than 10, but certainly larger collections could be counted when numbers became available for them to be counted. Likewise, consider the number scales used by our ancestors around 3,500 years ago, when there were no numbers invented as large as 10^{80}— the number of particles in the observable portion of the Universe. The set of particles comprising the observable portion of the Universe was, even then, in principle completely enumerable, despite that no invented scale of numbers went that high. The particles were completely enumerable because the scale of natural numbers always had the potential to be extended as far as our ancestors needed it to be in order for someone to put a definite number (10^{80}) on the set of particles. Given an extended scale of natural numbers, the of particles comprising the observable Universe could be completely enumerated with a definite quantity; consequently, the set of particles comprising the observable portion of the Universe must have been as finite for them as it is for us today. I am of course ignoring that the enumeration is hypothetical rather than experimental—the important point is what *would* be found if the enumeration by, say, counting all the particles *could* actually be carried out, and what would be found is the determinate amount of particles once the scale of numbers is extended to cover all the particles in the collection.

Any collection that, in principle, can be completely enumerated at a given time to a determinate, definite amount, is finite. And it can in principle be so enumerated if the scale of numbers is, also in principle, able to be extended that far. So, a number scale need not itself be complete in order for it to be used to completely enumerate a collection that has a limit. Either the limited collection is smaller than the set of defined numbers, or the set of defined numbers can be extended to match the collection's limits.

Then too, the collection so enumerated need not itself be complete in order to be completely enumerated and thus shown to be finite. Many collections are incomplete, some because they are not finished being constructed or formed, and yet what members they do have can be completely enumerated as the collection exists at the time of enumeration; ergo, incomplete collections, whatever their size, are finite collections.

5.3.7 *The Finite Can Be Endless or Unbounded*

Sometimes finitude is assumed to mean having an end or bound. But as previously pointed out (§ 1.1.2), a circle is finite and yet it has no end or bound to its curve. A circle is finite due to its measure. Therein lies finitude; the only "end" or "bound" there needs to be for something to be finite is the end or bound to the enumeration or measurement process of the elements in the given collection.

It's also sometimes thought that the scales of numbers like $\mathbb{N}^C$ must not be finite because they "have no end" or "no bound" to the numbers they may contain. However, as noted in § 4.2.14, this too is misleading. Number systems are "endless" or "boundless" not as sets but as processes. They are as constructed *number scales* still finite at any given time as we continue to invent new numbers for them, a process that is never finalized even unto the future extinction of the human species.

A number scale is like the increasing brickwork in the perpetually heightening tower. Since there is no "roof" to the scale of natural numbers, for example—no highest number beyond which we cannot continue to extrapolate—the scale of natural numbers is never complete. Instead, the scale of natural numbers is like that never-finished tower. There is always one more brick that could be laid, always one more number that could be calculated, but never a last one. Just as with the growing tower that is always incomplete, so too the natural number scale can be continually extended but will always be incomplete.

And because both the fictional tower and natural number scale are inherently incomplete, they both are "endless" or "boundless" as *processes* under construction.

Moreover, although the growing tower and the natural number scale are both "endless" as processes with a series of steps, the tower and the scale are always finite at any time—they each have an end in the sense of having a highest element at the time of measurement. There are a limited number of steps to the highest brick in the tower, and there are a limited number of values to the highest number in the scale of natural numbers at any given moment. Whatever the distance the highest brick is to the base of the tower, or the highest number in the scale of natural numbers is to the number 1, there are a finite number of steps to the top at any time. No matter how long we go on building the tower or inventing new numerical values, the steps are always countable and there is a highest definite number. Both are processes containing a series of steps "without end," but both are also limited as sets of elements since they would be bounded by their highest element at any given time; so, both are finite. As a perpetually constructing tower remains always unfinished but nevertheless finite, so the scale of natural numbers remains always incomplete but finite.

Put another way, the natural number scale could be construed as terminating or ending wherever the sequence of natural numbers currently leaves off—it would be finite in that regard since there is always a highest number in the set that has been or that can be calculated for it at a given moment of measurement. But the scale would also be "endless" as a series because its limit can always be *extended* as long as there is time to do so and no final values have been or will be calculated. Thus, having a limit that is "endlessly" extensible in this way merely means that the natural number scale is inherently and always *incomplete*, not that it is 'infinite' in a literal sense.

If this analysis is correct, then once again, contrary to the definition used by some mathematicians, the term 'finite' should not be defined as merely the ability to be put into a one-to-one correspondence with just a *segment* of natural numbers. No, finitude would also be a property of the scale of natural numbers taken either as a *set* at a given time in its construction (though, mathematicians usually don't consider the condition of time in relation to scales of numbers) or as an incomplete *series* (as categorized in **Figure 5.1**) that is able to be completely *enumerated* to a specified amount at a given time in its construction.

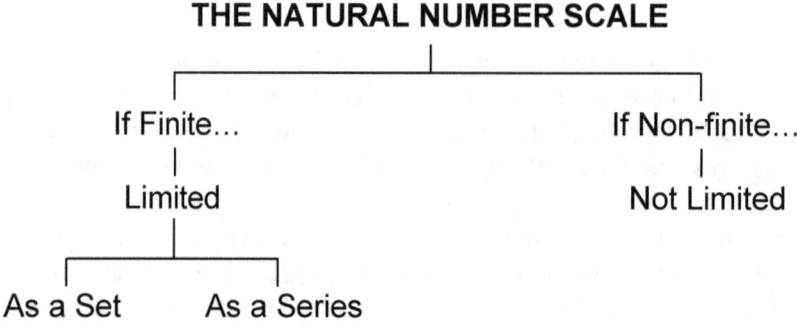

THE NATURAL NUMBER SCALE

Figure 5.1: The natural number scale, interpreted as either finite or non-finite.

This is not to say, of course, that segments of the natural number scale are not finite—far from it; any sequence of defined numbers is finite. It is merely to say that the term 'finite' should not be defined in too narrow of a sense as corresponding *only* to segments or sequences of natural numbers.

Rather, 'finite' also describes the scale of natural numbers as a series under construction if we take the scale as being enumerable to a highest number for the instance of time in which it is enumerated. While the number scale is an incomplete structure under construction, its numerals could in principle be listed to a finish *for that given time* in its construction. At time T_1 the numbers would range a to p, at T_2 the numbers would range a to q, at T_3 they would range a to r, and so forth. Hence, at any given time a number scale as a series is completely enumerable to a specifiable, determinate amount—the amount of its running total of numbers. So, even number scales can be finite, limited, as series under construction.

5.3.8 *'Finite' as Predicate and Quantifier*

Collections that have a limit, in the sense of a specifiability condition for a range, are those that can be completely enumerated. If we can specify the range of members for a collection via enumeration of the members in the collection to a determinate amount, then we have a finite collection. Basically, if you can enumerate the members of a collection completely, it's finite.

And to say of a collection that it is finite in this respect is to use the word 'finite' as a predicate. Anytime we say there is *a finite amount* of something or that there is only *finitely many* of something or simply that something is *finite*, we are using 'finite' as a predicate.

I suggest 'finite' is a particular kind of predicate: it is a quantifier of sorts. While there are membership quantifiers and magnitude quantifiers, we may wish to widen the category 'quantifier' to include other predicates indicating unspecified quantity. If so, we can consider a word like 'finite' to be a quantifier in the respect that it is a word indicating quantity as a property, but without directly specifying a particular quantity in the form of a number or mathematical formula.

While a sentence such as, "The number five is finite," specifies a number (5), the predicate 'finite' in the sentence is not indicating that something has that number; rather, it is ascribing a quantitative property to the specified number. To say of the number that it is finite does not speak to its mathematical value; rather, it tells us whatever is of that quantity is limited in the sense of being completely enumerable—we can bring a count of whatever is of that number to an end, with no members left to count. In that regard, the word 'finite' is a kind of quantifier—*a predicate that indicates a quantity has a given property*; in this case, the property of being limited.

The importance of identifying 'finite' as a predicate, and more narrowly as a quantifier, is that it tells us what *infinity* is. As 'finite' is a predicate, so is its negation—'infinite' is a predicate. And as 'finite' is a quantifier of sorts, so too is 'infinite'.

5.4 PREDICATING AS INFINITE

There is no number called 'infinity', at least not in the usual sense of 'number'. It would be more accurate to say infinity is a conjectured *state* or *condition*—a kind of property—that some collections are typically claimed to have with respect to the quantity of members in them. Including collections of numbers and even particular sorts of numbers (see § 5.4.7).

As infinity indicates a state or condition, to say there is "an infinity" of something is to imply the thing referred to is a collection the quantity of which is *infinite*, where the adjective 'infinite' functions as the predicate form of the noun 'infinity' for ascribing infinity as a quantitative property to the collection described.

Even in mathematics, 'infinite' is a predicate. It does not tell us a quantity. It tells us something *about* a quantity. To speak of "an infinite amount" is to make a statement about what kind of properties the amount has rather than specifying an exact total.

5.4.1 *Infinity as a Quantifier*

To use the adjective 'infinite' is to use a predicate denoting a collection the members of which are *so many* that the collection has 'infinity' as a property. Similarly, the adverb 'infinitely' is sometimes used to describe sequences, series, or sets as having the property of infinity with regard to the quantity of their members.

For instance, it is often claimed that the number of stars in the Universe is *infinite*, or that there are *infinitely* many stars in the Universe, where the words 'infinite' or 'infinitely' are quantifiers—predicates indicating quantity. With regard to the stars, to say they are infinite is to express something about the magnitude of the quantity of stars; namely, that their quantity is of a limitless magnitude. Similarly, it is sometimes claimed that the number of future days is infinite, or that the future is infinitely long—'infinite' and 'infinitely' are again quantifiers expressing something about the quantity of events in the sequence of events to come—that such a quantity is without limit. Hence use of 'infinite', or 'infinitely' in expressions like "infinitely many," is also just an instance of using a variant form of the word 'infinity' as a quantifier.

Infinity—whether in the form of the adjective 'infinite' or the adverb 'infinitely'—is therefore a kind of predicate for quantities and not really a number as such. The use of the adjective 'infinite' in expressions like "an infinite amount" and use of the adverb 'infinitely' in expressions like "infinitely many" are instances in which word variations for infinity work like other predicate terms, such as 'large' or 'great' or 'vast' in describing the quantity of a collection's members. And as with predicates such as 'large' or 'great' or 'vast', the adjective 'infinite' and adverb 'infinitely' do not designate a specific number, amount, or quantity as such, but rather a property that some collections are claimed to have with respect to their quantity of members.

To describe something with the adjective 'infinite' or to say it goes on 'infinitely' is to use 'infinity' as a predicate for saying something about our ability to count the elements, members, or parts of that thing. Such words describe the size or magnitude of a collection's quantity as greater than either an in-practice countable amount or even an in-principle countable amount. Once again this indicates that the terms 'infinite' and 'infinitely' work in a given expression as predicates for describing something about the quantity of a collection; so we can say infinity functions as a quantifier.

However, whereas a quantifier like "many" or "a lot" may in principle be specified with an exact, numeric quantity, infinity is a quantifier for a quantity that cannot be specified, not even in principle—infinity is a quantifier for an unspecifiable quantity.

When the amount of members in a collection is so large that the members become *limitless* in quantity, though still forming a *complete* set, then we have a literally infinite collection—a collection with infinitely many, or an infinity, of members.

But that is only the literal sense of infinity. There is also a figurative sense of infinity.

When the amount of events or steps in an *indefinitely changing* process is so large that the events or steps become *seemingly* limitless in quantity but are actually still finite, then we have a figuratively infinite series—a series said to have "infinitely many," or "an infinity" of, events or steps but in which the events or steps are really not limitless; they are actually limited but certainly greater than any scale we may construct in actual practice. But they *seem* truly limitless *as if* no quantity can be specified at all for them and so they are 'infinite' in a figurative sense.

Notice that the definitions for both literal infinity and figurative infinity (§ 1.3.1) contain words like 'limitless', 'complete', 'continuous', etc., which are also predicates. The very definitions of literal infinity as "the condition of being both complete and limitless in quantity" and figurative infinity as "the condition of indefinitely changing in quantity" contain their own predicates used to describe a quantity of members in a collection. Infinity is a predicate implying more predicates, and never stating an exact number. Further, the predicates of these definitions are like the word 'infinity' itself, negative—they are denials of something. After all, to be limitless is to be not limited and to be indefinite is to be not definite—both denials just as infinity is to be not finite. To understand infinity as such thus requires an understanding of the use of these predicates as well, along with an understanding of them as negations of their opposites.

5.4.2 *Infinity as Limitlessness of Quantity*

As noted in Chapter 1, infinity is most broadly defined as the condition of having *no limit* to measurement or quantity, either literally or just figuratively. For mathematicians, a condition of lacking a limit, a condition of 'limitlessness,' often means something more technical.

Terms like 'limitless' or 'unlimited' or 'without limit' are used according to various theoretical and operational senses, each of which is useful for certain mathematical procedures. However, we will primarily be concerned with examining the general *meaning* of limitlessness as a term used for defining infinity. We will again start with a lexical definition that captures how limitlessness is conceived independently of how one might use it in a particular mathematical procedure.

To put it simply:

- limitlessness: *the condition of being limitless.*
- limitless: *to be without limits or without a given type or instance of a limit.*

To be (literally) limitless or "without limit" is to have no specifiability condition for a range—no end, no brink, no edge, no border, no boundary, no extreme, no total, etc. If a more precise definition is needed, we can draw upon what I will refer to as *literal limitlessness* and the literal sense of the word 'limitless':

- limitlessness: *the condition in which a collection's range is unspecifiable, even in principle.*
- limitless: *to have a range that is unspecifiable, even in principle.*

The word 'unspecifiable' simply means *unable to be specified*. If a collection is limitless, then its range (its measure of extent) of elements cannot be specified (described, identified, or referenced with distinctness). Having an unspecifiable range of elements means the collection that is limitless is a collection without measure, even in principle.

But wait—the definition for limitlessness sounds like the description of infinity when portrayed as a quantifier for an unspecifiable quantity, which also implies immeasurability, even in principle. So is limitlessness synonymous with infinity?

Not quite. While collections called "limitless" may instead be called "infinite" or vice versa, infinity is not identical to limitlessness. Quantitative infinity comes in two varieties: literal infinity and figurative infinity. Literal infinity has the property of completeness *as well as* limitlessness, making limitlessness only part of literal infinity, even if it is the key part. Then too, figurative infinity is a condition ascribed only to successions—temporal series or processes—rather than to any collection that may be predicated as limitless, and figuratively infinite successions are those that are only figuratively "limitless" at any given time. Hence, limitlessness and infinity are not synonymous, though they are often used interchangeably in colloquial speech.

5.4.3 *Alternative Terms for 'Limitless'*

Most mathematical texts do not use terms like *limitless, unlimited, without limit,* and *having no limit,* etc. Instead, they refer to the conditions by which a collection has a limit or does not have a limit. But even when a collection does *not* have a limit in a particular sense, they usually do not use the term 'limitless' outright. Instead, and as if to confuse the lay audience (though that is not their intention), they use the term 'limit' in a specialized sense.

For example, in the transfinite system an infinite set of numbers is, despite being limitless in the literal sense, nevertheless said to have a kind of 'limit'. Specifically, infinite sets of numbers are said to have a *limit ordinal* or a *limit cardinal*. The idea is that no matter what finite number you select, no matter how far up the scale of numbers and no matter how great a size it denotes, it will always be prior to a limit ordinal and smaller than a limit cardinal [138]. A 'limit ordinal' and a 'limit cardinal' are each rather like an ideal limit toward which a process approaches but never meets, no longer how long it continues.

Still, we are also told number systems are complete sequences of numbers and they also have no last number or no greatest number to them, which implies they are limitless in the literal sense of the term. In which case, saying a number system such as $\mathbb{N}$ has a 'limit ordinal' or a 'limit cardinal' becomes logically confounding even if it is mathematically straightforward. After all, if there is no last or greatest to them, then they are limitless. And if they are limitless, then how can an ordinal or cardinal come after them?

This shows that mathematical definitions and logical implications do not always cohere. Perhaps one way around that problem would in this case be to suggest that number systems are not sets but incomplete scales under construction—e.g., not $\mathbb{N}$, but $\mathbb{N}^C$. If that is so, then there is no problem with the naturals, integers, or reals having some *ideal limit*—a limit ordinal or limit cardinal—toward which their values "approach" as we continue to construct the number scales. For, the ideal limits to which values approach would be merely finite numbers too large or too far along the given sequence to represent, and so they really would be limits, nonetheless.

There is much to recommend such a view, for mathematical operations are not carried out without limit anyway. It is only in theory that they continue indefinitely rather than in fact continuing without limit at all. See § 14.1.2 for examples of cases in which "limitless" operations are more accurately regarded as indefinitely continuous operations (and even then, only in theory).

However, interpreting number systems to be inherently incomplete number scales that are under construction would make them necessarily finite and so, at best, only figuratively infinite rather than literally infinite. Mathematicians holding to the contrary that number systems are literally infinite must interpret them as being both *complete* sets (e.g., $\mathbb{N}$, $\mathbb{Z}$, $\mathbb{Q}$, $\mathbb{P}$, $\mathbb{A}$, $\mathbb{T}$, $\mathbb{R}$, $\mathbb{I}$, $\mathbb{C}$, etc.) and collections that are *limitless* in their sequences of values ("no last number") while somehow extending *toward* further values that are indeed limits, such as 'limit ordinals' and 'limit cardinals', and yet without ever "reaching" them. We'll return to this dubious position again in § 13.5.4–5 and § 13.11. Until then, I only note that such is fine for mathematics, but whether it makes logical sense remains is questionable (see Chapter 14).

In the meantime, I'll stick to the use of the terms 'limitless' and 'limitlessness' as I've defined them for continuing this exposition of infinity. Unless otherwise specified, those interested in the math of infinity can interpret my use of these terms as consistent with the claim that number systems have no last or greatest number to them at all—an example of having a range that is unspecifiable, even in principle.

5.4.4 *Distinguishing Limitlessness from That Which is "Without Limit"—Consider Zero*

Because limitlessness is defined in opposition to having a limit, and it was pointed out in § 5.3.2 that zero (referring to a condition of being without quantity) *has* no limit of its own, then we are in the rather strange position of logically implying the adjective 'limitless' also applies to zero. As already pointed out, we can't specify a range for that which is designated as zero in quantity—not even in principle, because that which numbers zero has no range to be specified. Zero refers to a set of no size (see § 2.3.8) and therefore a set that has no end, brink, edge, boundary, extreme, or total of its own. So, according to our definition of the term 'limitless', that which is zero must be limitless. And yet, we can symbolize zero as 0 or as the empty set { } and we can use zero as a constant number such as a value for a variable. We can even say that zero is a total for some calculation. Isn't it inconsistent, then, to say that zero is limitless and yet say it is a total or a value for a variable?

The question rests on confusion of a variable's value (such as $x = 3$) with the representation of a constant number (such as 3) that is itself equal to a series of values (like $1+1+1$). Zero can be used as the constant numerical value for a variable (such as $x = 0$) without also being a set equal to a series of values. If you prefer, zero can *be* the value of a variable because zero *is* a limit to non-zero numbers; however, zero does not *have* a value in the sense of representing a set with a range of elements in it. While we cannot specify a range for zero because zero has no limits to specify, zero can nevertheless be a limit of other numbers, such as the lower limit of whole numbers. And this again merely means that according to the definition of 'limit' we are using, zero can be specified as the value for something else even if we cannot specify a range *within* zero, as if it corresponded to a set within which elements could be found.

Therefore, zero can be a total without having a total; zero can be a limit without having a limit. There is then, no inconsistency with saying that zero is a limit and yet is "limitless" in the sense of having no limit of its own. It is probably better, though, to say zero is "without limit" rather than call it "limitless." A good way to distinguish being limitless from being without limit is this:

- being limitless: to have a range that is unspecifiable.
- being without limit: to have no specifiable range.

5.4.5 *Distinguishing Infinity from Afinity*

There are different ways of being literally "without limit." There are actually two different ways something can be without limit: infinity and *afinity*.

Afinity (pronounced "ey-**fin**-i-tee," and not to be confused with the word 'affinity') is a term I am coining. Definition:

- afinity: *The condition of lacking limits due to lack of quantity or due to emptiness.*

Along with the word 'afinity' we can use related terms, such as 'the afinite' (a substantive noun, which is pronounced "**ey**-fin-it"). The afinite will function as either a synonym for afinity, a reference to the concept of afinity, or a reference to the category of all that is *afinite* (adjective) of which there is only one example: the empty set (∅).

I propose afinity as a condition to describe the lack of limits to a state of absolute emptiness, without regard to boundaries or borders of any kind. Although any set in set theory is really a set of brackets, { }, what those empty brackets are sometimes thought of as representing is emptiness *as such*. Absolute emptiness, as represented by the empty set, is also associated with the number zero in general mathematics [139]. In § 5.3.2 and § 5.4.4, we saw that zero can be a limit but does not have a limit of its own—it denotes a condition of being without content to be limited. So, zero represents, quite literally, a condition of being limitless (that is, without limit), even though zero functions *as* a limit to some finite quantity or magnitude. Both the empty set and zero, by virtue of the content-free state they represent, may be thought of as representing afinity—they each denote no limits by the very virtue of the emptiness they represent.

However, also as noted in § 5.4.4, neither the empty set nor zero are typically described as 'limitless'. We tend to use the word 'limitless' either in a literal sense to describe something assumed to have the property of literal infinity or in a metaphorical sense to describe a process or series assumed to have the property of figurative infinity or indefiniteness of process. We do not typically use 'limitless' to describe the nature of zero or the empty set, even though the emptiness of the empty set (as an abstraction) constitutes an instance of lacking limits. Think of it this way: if you have a condition in which there is no such thing as 'before', 'after', or 'next to', then how is that different from not having a limit? For that reason, the lack of limit to that which is merely a condition of emptiness should be termed 'afinite' to set it apart both from literal infinity (which is limitlessness in the sense of a complete, non-zero quantity beyond any limit) and from figurative infinity which is simply indefiniteness of series or processes.

Although both literal infinity and afinity are conditions of lacking a limit, literal infinity should not be confused with afinity. Literal infinity is not the afinite because to be afinite is to be *empty* whereas literal infinity is the condition in which a collection has non-zero elements and so is non-empty. Figurative infinity should also not be confused with the afinite—that which has an indefinitely changing limit is not that which is afinite. The afinite is thus without limit, but not like infinity is.

For that reason, it would be a good idea to keep with custom and not use the terms 'limitless' or 'unlimited' for the empty set or zero because such language would cause the empty set or zero to be confused with traditional notions of infinity (and even indefiniteness when we use "limitless" in a figurative sense). Instead, in response to questions as to the limits of zero or the empty set, we should point out that zero or the empty set is "without limit" and indicate such by use of the term 'afinite', which is another way of being *non-finite* (as depicted in **Figure 5.2**) rather than finite.

However, referring to zero as 'afinite' raises one curious issue: mathematicians often refer to zero as "finite," even though zero is in itself afinite because zero serves as a limit to finite quantities and magnitudes. Zero is a finite number in the respect that it is a bound to other finite numbers. Mathematicians also refer to the empty set as "finite" in the sense of being the foundational set and lowest bound upon which all other finite sets are built in set theory, even though the empty set is, in terms of its content, 'afinite' [140]. Nevertheless, zero, or the empty set, represents the afinite *in content* even though it functions as a limit for *other* quantities and magnitudes.

You could therefore say that zero is both a non-finite number in one sense (cardinality) and a finite, definite number in another (ordinality). Zero is non-finite in that it represents a set afinite in content—the empty set. However, zero is finite in that it serves as a bound for the scales of positive and negative numbers. In that respect, we can continue to regard zero as a part of general (finite) mathematics. Likewise, the empty set is non-finite in that it is afinite in content but finite as a bound to sets in set theory.

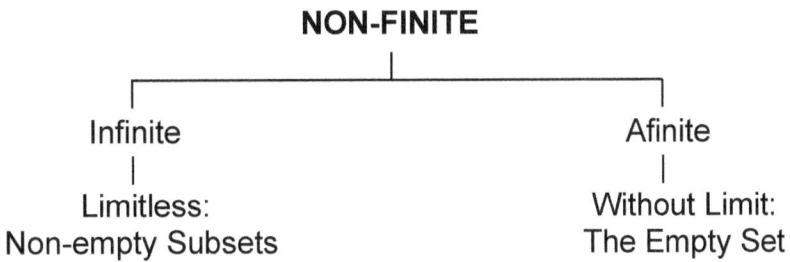

Figure 5.2: The non-finite categorized as either infinite or afinite with respect to subsets. A quantitatively infinite set may contain the empty set but need not; either way, a set that is quantitatively infinite is a set the limitlessness of which is expressed over non-empty subsets. In contrast, an afinite set is that which is "limitless" (more aptly said, without limit) by virtue of emptiness—the only afinite set is the empty set. It's not clear the empty set can have subsets at all, even empty ones, without the subsets themselves being quantities and thereby making the empty set not empty, resulting in contradiction. But if the empty set does have subsets, each empty subset must also be empty and so "without limit" or afinite by virtue of containing either no elements that are not empty sets or simply nothing at all.

5.4.6 *Limitlessness in Quantity*

As with zero, the lack of a limit to infinity is about quantity. While zero is without limit by virtue of its 'emptiness' of quantity, infinity is the condition of being *limitless* or *unlimited* in the sense of a *non*-zero range of elements that, nevertheless, cannot be specified. Limitlessness in the non-zero sense is a condition we often hear claimed of the Universe: limitless space, limitless time, limitless matter, and limitless energy (see Chapter 21 for further discussion of this topic). Such claims actually go back for millennia. The ancient Greek philosopher Epicurus (342–270 BCE) stated that "the totality of things" is "unlimited" both in the quantity of its atomic bodies and in its spatial magnitude [141]. Similarly, mathematicians sometimes refer to non-zero quantities of numbers that are 'limitless', such as number systems or decimal places in pi. But if we grant that something can both have no limit in quantity *and* be non-zero, then what exactly does it mean to have a limitless, but non-zero, quantity?

5.4.7 *Infinity as a Quantifier and as a 'Number'*

As pointed out previously, infinity is a condition or property, and it is predicated of things like collections when we use the term as the adjective 'infinite'. Though the word 'infinity' is a noun and not an adjective, I will still refer to infinity as a predicate in the sense that it is applied as a predicate in its adjectival form to certain collections. With regard to what kind of predicate infinity is, infinity is a quantifier for an unspecifiable quantity.

But is an unspecifiable quantity itself a number? If so, then infinity is not just a term used as a predicate to denote a property that some collections have; infinity also becomes the value for a kind of number and can even be treated as if it is a number itself. This is partly right and partly wrong. Yes, infinity refers to an unspecifiable quantity, but no—it is not itself a number. It can, however, be treated *as if* it is a number in mathematics since some numbers are said to be infinite.

Certainly, use of the term 'infinite number' is widespread, even among mathematicians and other academics in math-heavy disciplines like physics. Both have historically and recently referred to "an infinite number" of things, including an infinite number of numbers or an infinite number of mathematical objects.

As a historical example, the Italian polymath Galileo Galilei (1564–1642) wrote in his 1638 book, *Dialogues Concerning Two New Sciences*, that each mathematical line contains "an infinite number" of points [142].

For some contemporary examples, consider the following (italics mine for emphasis):

- A 2015 primer for math students provided by the Mathematics Department of the University of New Mexico states, "To write any irrational number in decimal notation would require an *infinite number* of decimal digits. .6, for instance, is not an irrational number. Even though it has an *infinite number of numbers* after the decimal place, it can be expressed as the ratio of two integers. Namely, 2 and 3, as $\frac{2}{3} = .6$" [143].

- A 2015 paper on the science publication website *arXiv* claims that "methods borrowed from physics can be used to 'count' an *infinite number* of points" [144].

- A 2017 paper by Japanese physicist Kazuhiko Minami solves for an *"infinite number* of spin chains"* [145].

Such examples show reference to an 'infinite number' is alive and well. Mathematicians and other academics frequently refer to an infinite number of things, whether those things are physical things such as an infinite number of atoms, stars, galaxies, universes, etc., or purely conceptual things like numbers or ideas [146] [147] [148].

But there are two ways to take such speech—literally or figuratively. On the one hand, to say a number is an "infinite number" is to say the number, if written out, would have no end of digits. On the other hand, some mathematicians hold that "infinite number" is a misnomer for "infinitely many" and does not mean a genuine number. So, do we mean there are literally an *infinite number* of stars in the Universe or decimal places in pi, or are there only figuratively an "infinite number" of stars or decimal places? If the former is the case, then infinity is not just a predicate but a category of numbers—an 'infinite number' would be a number with a limitless string of digits. If the latter is the case, then when we say there is "an infinite number" of something, all we mean is that there is infinitely many of it; infinity is a property predicated of things and not really a category of numbers at all.

To complicate things further, the literal and figurative ways of speaking about infinite numbers can both be applied to literal infinity. A literal infinity—a complete and limitless set—might be interpreted to either have an infinite number of elements in the literal sense of a number having limitless digits or in the figurative sense of a limitless string of finite numbers. However, a figurative infinity—a series that indefinitely changes in quantity—may only have an "infinite number" of elements figuratively, and even to say there are "infinitely many" elements in a series would be to use a figure of speech.

5.4.8 *An Infinite Number as a Number that is Literally Infinite*

According to the literal interpretation of infinite numbers, to say there is an infinite number of stars in the Universe or an infinite number of decimal places in pi or an infinite number of anything else really means that *if* you could write out a number that is infinitely large, *then* it would have a literally unlimited string of digits where all the necessary digits are present because there are no missing subsets of digits, no gaps in the string of digits, any process that composes the digits for the number is finished, no more digits can be included, and the string of digits does not loop back on itself in forming its sum. In other words, you have a *complete* string of *limitlessly many* digits.

Alternatively, an 'infinite number' could mean a natural number as big as the literally infinite collection to which the number refers. Hence, it would be a number that, *if* written out as a string of tally marks (as when 10 is written out like IIIIIIIIII), *would be* written with a limitless string of tally marks, with the tally marks corresponding one-for-one with the elements in the collection described. That is, if we were to express a number this way for infinitely many stars, we would have a limitless string of tally marks, with one tally mark per star, in which the complete tally corresponds to the complete collection of stars. That's not to say you couldn't use the successor function to keep on increasing the infinite number from there; rather it's that the number is already limitless, as is, and the infinite collection is already complete as a collection [149].

Infinitely large natural numbers are logically implied whenever a claim is made that a sequence or series of natural numbers progresses "to infinity" in a literal sense. When, for example, 1, 2, 3, … is implied to be literally infinite, the ellipsis is implied to show the progression continues the sequence of numbers to a complete and limitless amount of numbers. Since each successive number in the sequence 1, 2, 3, … is greater in cardinality than the prior number, the progression must reach a natural number, n, that is infinitely great in size.

Such a number would have *limitlessly many digits*, as would be the case with, say, a 1 followed by a limitless string of 0s:

$$1,000,000,000, …$$

If such a number were complete as well as limitless, then it would be an example of an infinitely large number [150]. However, an infinitely large number need not begin with 1 or be followed by limitlessly many 0s. An infinitely large number could also begin with any other base numeral, followed by a limitless string of any other combination of digits. For example:

$$9,536,190,023, …$$

In fact, according to the logical implications of continuing the progression 1, 2, 3, … up to infinity, where "infinity" is literal infinity and not merely figurative infinity, there would have to be *infinitely many combinations of infinitely large numbers* produced by a progression of numbers that becomes literally infinite.

But there is no way in practice to specify which base number would be the first digit in a sequence of *limitlessly* many digits (whether 1 as in a number like 1,000,000,000, … or a 9 as in a number such as 9,536,190,023, …, or any other base number). Moreover, we would be unable in practice to specify the digits in each succeeding place for a "first infinite number." So, we cannot say for sure which infinitely large number with a limitless combination of digits would be the first infinitely large number reached from the progression 1, 2, 3, … up to a literal infinity. There is no way to represent such a number in digits.

Or take the idea of a 'limitless quantity' of objects in a collection where the quantity is a number equal to a *limitless sum* of members. We might have a limitless accession $(1 + 1 + 1 + …)$ that is itself equal to a sum. And yet the sum of that series, precisely because it is limitless in quantity, would be equal to a number that has no possibility of being specified in digits. That is, the amount of elements in the collection would have to be represented by a constant number having a string of digits so large that its range, its extent of elements, cannot be specified, not even in principle.

This is different from a very large number, such as a googolplex, which we can simply specify either with shorthand ($10^{10^{100}}$) or, in principle, with longhand by writing it out (though, of course, not in actual practice since there isn't a big enough computer to do so). To the contrary, limitless quantity is unspecifiable with a constant number—it is uncountable and incalculable not just in practice, but also in principle. There is not even a logical possibility that an infinite number can be written out. We can't use iterated exponentials like $10^{10^{100}}$ to express an infinitely large number because an infinitely large number would be equal to a limitless iteration of higher powers upon powers.

Variables are also not adequate symbols for representing infinity as a specified number. Variables are used for representing coherently *specifiable* numbers such as reals and imaginaries up to d^*. A variable can, at least in principle, have a value specified for it by replacing the variable with a constant number. To be literally *limitless*, on the other hand, is to be *unspecifiable*, *even in principle*. No variable can be replaced with an exact number expressing a range without limit. Hence, the use of variables for representing infinitely large numbers does not seem appropriate, and mathematical systems do not typically use a variable, like n, just on its own to represent an infinite number.

That is not to say infinity is never denoted by use of letters just as variables are so denoted. Far from it. Mathematician Jailton C. Ferreira, for instance, proposes that there are indeed infinitely large natural numbers and he uses N to represent only the set of finite natural numbers while he uses M to represent the set of both finite *and* infinite natural numbers [151]. However, while mathematicians sometimes use Latin letters as notation for the infinite, the use of such notation is unlike the use of notation for variables, which denote *specifiable* numbers.

Most often, mathematicians use non-Latin letters to denote the *order* or *size* of the infinite quantities that characterize these sets. An example of such is the small Greek letter omega (denoted as ω), which stands for *infinite ordinality*—that is, a literally infinite *sequence* of elements. Another symbol for literal infinity is the Hebrew letter aleph (denoted as $\aleph$), which stands for *infinite cardinality*—a *set* that is literally infinite in size regardless of the order of its members. Both ω and $\aleph$ represent *literally* infinite sets, and so both symbols may represent an infinite number of elements, either in sequence or in size.

In addition to the use of Greek and Hebrew alphabetical letters to denote infinity, mathematicians typically represent an infinite number with a specialized symbol. The most famous symbol for infinity throughout mathematics is the *lemniscate*—the familiar "lazy eight" or "love knot" symbol denoted as ∞, first used in 1655 to symbolize infinity by mathematician John Wallis (1616–1703) [152]. The lemniscate represents an infinite quantity—sometimes an infinite number of members in a sequence or series while other times an infinite number of members in a set (a collection of members in no particular order).

The symbols for infinity (∞, ω, and $\aleph$) denote quantities not specified with digits. Still, it is important to note that such symbols should not be confused with the use of variables which also denote quantities not specified in digits. Variables indicate *specifiable* numbers—numbers able to be specified when they are "solved for." Infinity is not "solved for" like one would solve for a variable since the symbols for infinity represent quantities that cannot be coherently specified, not even in principle, with digits.

In saying a symbol for infinity is not like a variable, I do not mean that we cannot solve for a variable as being equal to infinity. We can specify that x is infinity such as with the expression $x = \infty$. I mean only that symbols for infinity (for example, ∞) are not themselves variables.

Symbols for infinity operate differently than variables. Unlike a variable, infinity as ∞ is not even in principle replaceable with a specified number expressed with a string of digits. Mathematically speaking, it may still be held that a symbol for infinity (e.g., ∞) *would* be replaced with a number having a limitless string of digits if the symbol *could* be coherently replaced with such, but since that is not so, we are simply reliant on specialized symbols like ∞ to represent numbers with unspecifiably long digits strings. For instance, the expression $\infty + \infty = \infty$ can be taken as denoting that some number of an unspecifiably large string of digits (∞) plus some other number of an unspecifiably large string of digits (∞) is equal to some number with an unspecifiably large string of digits (∞). Hence, ∞ would be replaced with digits if it could be, but it can't, so it won't; ∞ is thus not like a variable which can be, at least in principle if not in practice, replaced with a number having a definite expression in digits.

Similarly, the other symbols for infinity (e.g., ω and $\aleph$) are not like variables in that they do not just represent any value and they represent numbers unspecifiable with digits. But represent numbers they do. The ordinal (ω) and cardinal ($\aleph$) are held to represent a literally infinite number. Take the expressions $1, 2, 3, ..., \omega$ and $1, 2, 3, ..., \aleph$. Both expressions represent infinity as *following* other numbers in sequence as if infinity (ω or $\aleph$) is itself a number that is part of that same sequence—an 'infinite number'—and merely one that cannot be given in multiple digits like 100.

Hence, the use of infinity (∞) to make mathematical expressions like $\infty + \infty = \infty$ and the use of infinity (ω or $\aleph$) for similar operations thus speaks to infinity as being a kind of number, even if such cannot be written out with digits.

5.4.9 *An Infinite Number as Figurative for Infinitely Many Finite Numbers*

Another approach for dealing with our inability to write out or express infinitely large numbers is just to say there is no such thing. Instead, we take references to so-called "infinite numbers" as merely a figure of speech. The symbols like ∞, ω, and $\aleph$ are symbols for sets of "infinitely many" elements; that, and nothing more. The elements can even be numbers. For instance, $\mathbb{N}$ would be a set comprised of infinitely many (but all finite) natural numbers.

The distinction is between *infinitely many* on the one hand and *infinite numbers* on the other. Transfinite mathematicians in particular usually deny the existence of infinitely large natural numbers, but nevertheless say there are sets of infinitely many *finite* numbers (symbolized by ∞, ω, and $\aleph$) [153] [154] [155]. And while some mathematicians say it may be true that infinity is used in equations *as if* it is a number (e.g., $\infty + \infty = \infty$), they are careful to emphasize that infinity is not really a number at all.

5.4.10 *Figurative Infinity and Use of the Infinite Number Metaphor*

We've covered use of the term 'infinite number' in its literal sense and in a figurative sense:

- In its literal sense, an infinite number is a number that, if written out or tallied, would be infinitely large—that is, composed of a sequence of digits that is itself complete and yet limitlessly long.

- In its figurative sense, an 'infinite number' is a figurative term mathematicians use to mean "infinitely many" members while holding there is actually no natural number that is infinitely large.

But there is another sense in which the term 'infinite number' is figurative, and that is when it refers to the amount of members in a *series* that continues to grow while remaining finite no matter how long the series goes on.

The latter figurative sense of infinity is commonly used with respect to mathematical operations. For example, when some mathematicians refer to an "infinite number" of decimal places in pi, what they mean is that we could keep on *producing* more digits for the value of pi; not that pi already contains a literally infinite quantity of digits to find. There are even some scientists who also think of infinity in this figurative sense. In the figurative sense of infinity, to say there is "an infinite number" of stars would be to say the stars are actually finite in quantity at any given time but will keep populating the Universe without end. However, such figurative uses of "infinite number" too often slip into the literal usage of the term. (The topic of slippage will be further explored in Chapter 24.)

5.4.11 *Symbols for Figurative Infinity*

Just as the term 'infinite number' can be used in the sense of figurative infinity, so too can the mathematical symbols for infinity. For example, some mathematicians and philosophers, following in the footsteps of Cantor, believe the lemniscate (∞) is used *only* for sequences regarded as figuratively infinite rather than literally infinite [156]. However, this certainly has not been the case either historically or contemporarily.

It is true that many mathematicians today often associate the symbol ∞ with potential or figurative infinity, but Wallis himself used the symbol ∞ to denote a complete and limitless collection, or at least a progression that becomes literally infinite. We find literal infinity invoked in his 1656 book, *The Arithmetic of Infinitesimals*, describing the circumference (i.e., the closed curve) of a circle as composed of "an infinite number of infinitely short lines" and a cone as "composed of an infinite number of circles" [157]. Even today mathematicians still sometimes use ∞ to represent a literally infinite sequence, series, or set [158].

The lemniscate may either represent a collection as figuratively infinite or as literally infinite, *depending on the intent of the mathematician*. Regardless, if infinity as ∞ is used in a figurative sense, to say "an infinite number" or "an infinitely large number" means only that the value represented by ∞ is constantly changing and is, at any time, beyond our practical ability to calculate or represent (but could be produced in principle).

For example, we might take ∞ as representing an incomplete collection of objects that continues to grow or divide beyond our ability to compute. The collection of objects grows so large, or divides to small, that in actual practice we have no number to represent the value of all its members at a given time. Though it is not genuinely a variable, ∞ is like a special kind of variable—one with no constant value, such as a collection having a series of quantities produced by a function in calculus or an operation in algebra.

As a rule of thumb, ∞ is generally used to represent the figurative infinity of a function performed in mathematics. However, it is sometimes ambiguous whether ∞ is figurative or literal. There are cases where ∞ is used in a figurative sense to mean a continuously changing quantity such as in the increasing number of iterations that a mathematical function goes through to produce an ever-increasing series of decimal places for pi.

However, the symbol ∞ may simultaneously imply the literal infinity of any collection measured by the function—like there being all at once a literally infinite series of digits in pi for the function to uncover (as if the digits are "already there" awaiting discovery). Hence, ∞ is not always used consistently to refer only to figurative infinity; sometimes literal infinity is *implied* for the collection calculated while figurative infinity is intended for the steps or iterations taken in the calculating process itself.

I will attempt to make clear which sense of infinity—literal or figurative—is implied by mathematical representations of infinity as we proceed.

5.5 INFINITY AS PREDICATE: LITERAL AND FIGURATIVE

Infinity, as a linguistic term, is a predicate for indicating that something is considered a collection and, as such, is in some sense limitless. A collection is predicated as limitless either in the literal or the figurative sense. But even as a predicate of sorts, infinity can be symbolized and mathematically operate as if it is a number, whether infinity is taken as literal or figurative.

Literal infinity, for example, can be symbolized (∞, ω, $\aleph$, etc.) for use in mathematical expressions. Even though these symbols are for predicating a quantity as limitless, the symbols also mathematically operate in a number-like fashion. In that respect, literal infinity in symbolic form not only predicates quantities as limitless but can also be taken either as itself a kind of number—one of limitless size—or at least as an indicator for a limitless multitude of quantities.

We've explored the difference between 'infinite number' as referring to a number of limitless digits symbolized in shorthand (e.g., ω or $\aleph$), and as a figure of speech for a collection of "infinitely many" finite numbers that may be symbolized as if they are numbers—the so-called *transfinite numbers* (ω or $\aleph$). The symbols for infinity can be interpreted in either sense. I have so far left open the issue of which interpretation of literal infinity is correct—infinity as a predicate for a kind of number (as in 'infinite number') or as a predicate for a kind of multitude of elements ('infinitely many' finite numbers)—if indeed either one even makes sense. We will return to this issue in forthcoming chapters.

That leaves open the question of figurative infinity. Figurative infinity is also a predicate for a kind of quantity—a quantity that is a running total, a progression of totals that continues to accumulate. Figurative infinity can also be symbolized, typically as ∞, which is also used in a number-like manner.

However, ∞ can be taken either figuratively or literally in certain mathematical contexts, so the difference between figurative and literal infinity can be confused. This too is an issue that needs resolved.

CHAPTER 5 IN REVIEW

❖ As 'finite' is a predicate for quantity—a quantifier of sorts—so too is 'infinite'.

❖ Whereas the quantifier 'finite' indicates a given collection has a quantity that can be specified, the quantifier 'infinite' indicates a given collection has a quantity that cannot be specified.

❖ To be infinite is different from being 'afinite', which is to lack specification of range by virtue of being empty of members to specify. To be infinite, to the contrary, is not to be empty but to have a non-zero quantity of members that cannot be specified.

❖ As finite quantities can be expressed with exact numbers or variables for such, so too mathematicians propose the infinite can be represented according to various symbols such as ∞, ω, $\aleph$, etc. The lemniscate (∞) is often taken for figurative infinity, but it is also sometimes interpreted as indicating literal infinity. The small omega (ω) and capital aleph ($\aleph$) are always taken as symbols for literal infinity.

6: DISTINGUISHING FINITES AND INFINITES

Literal infinity and figurative infinity are sometimes confused with one another, even by professional philosophers and mathematicians. In fact, some philosophers try to destroy the distinction between the two [159]. I don't believe they are successful, but that is another issue. For now, I wish only to elucidate the distinction between literal infinity and figurative infinity. I will accomplish this by further distinguishing between two different forms of the finite—the *definite* and the *indefinite*—and then contrasting indefinite sets and series with those that are literally infinite. I will then address figurative infinity as the serial form of indefiniteness, thereby placing figurative infinity and literal infinity into stark contrast.

6.1 THE FINITE: DEFINITE AND INDEFINITE

So far, we've regarded finite sets and series and how they can each be either complete or incomplete. Since there are real, finite collections constructed over time such as towers finished while others are left unfinished or in ruins, the property of finitude characterizes collections such as sets (whether real or conceptual), some of which are complete and some of which remain incomplete. And since there are both closed series like alphabets and open series like number scales, we can also say finitude encompasses series both complete and incomplete.

Yet completeness and incompleteness also need to be distinguished from a couple of related categories—*definiteness* and *indefiniteness*. I have up to now mentioned numbers some of which are 'definite' and others that are 'indefinite', but the concepts of 'definiteness' and 'indefiniteness' were not defined. It's time to correct that:

- definiteness: *the state of having defined or specified limits.*
- indefiniteness: *the state of having undefined or unspecified limits.*

6.1.1 *Defined vs. Definable, Specified vs. Specifiable*

Both definitions make assumptions regarding definition and specification. That which is definite is that which has defined or specified limits because such limits are *definable* or *specifiable* to begin with. We have both the capability to define or specify the given limit and it is in fact defined or specified. For example, the distance from Earth to the Moon, or the speed of light in a vacuum. Conversely, that which is indefinite is that which has undefined or unspecified limits, but that does not mean such limits are also *undefinable* or *unspecifiable* per se.

Like definiteness, indefiniteness is a state of having definable or specifiable limits—limits able to be defined or specified—it's just that the limits happen to in fact be undefined or unspecified. For example, the entire Universe (vice the observable part of the Universe we see with telescopes) may be of indefinite size. Perhaps in practice we will never know what size it truly has, but in principle we could find out—if, for example, we had a spaceship that could travel far and fast enough. The size of the Universe is at least in principle definable or specifiable, even if in practice it is undefined or unspecified; until science can show otherwise, we can say the Universe is of indefinite size.

Of course, some might say the Universe is not just of indefinite size but of *infinite* size. That is a subject we will return to in Chapters 18 and 21; for now, the important distinction is this: indefiniteness, like definiteness, is a finite condition. Indefiniteness, like definiteness, is a species of finitude.

But wait: didn't I just say in § 5.3.4 that to be finite is to be "completely enumerable to a determinate amount," which is a specifiability condition? So how can something be indefinite (unspecified) and at the same time be finite?

This is precisely where the distinction between being *specified* and being *able* to be specified (*specifiability*) comes in. Indefiniteness is a finite state because it is the state in which the measure of something is specifi*able*—for example, *able* to be completely enumerated to a determinate amount— even if it is not so specif*ied* in actual practice. Ergo, indefiniteness is still a finite condition.

6.1.2 *The Indefinite as Finite*

Cognate nouns for definiteness and indefiniteness are 'the definite' and 'the indefinite'. 'The definite' is a substantive noun sometimes used as a synonym for definiteness and sometimes as the category of that which is definite; naturally, 'the indefinite' is also a substantive noun and at times it is a synonym for indefiniteness while other times it stands for the category of that which is indefinite. Both, I contend again, are species of the finite.

However, some philosophers disagree; they instead equate the definite with the finite and draw contrasts between the finite, the indefinite, and the infinite such that these three quantifiers are held to constitute non-overlapping categories [160]. But that is incorrect.

The term 'indefinite' designates not a separate category that stands alongside the finite and the infinite as something different and outside those two categories together. Instead, 'indefinite' refers to a subcategory of finitude alongside another subcategory of finitude known as 'definite'. Philosopher William Fleming (1791–1866) explained as follows [161]:

> The *definite* is that which the form and limits are determined and are apprehended by us. That of which we know not the limits, [fallaciously] comes to be regarded as having none; and hence *indefinite* has been confounded with the *infinite*, though these two must be carefully distinguished. The *infinite* is absolute; it is that which has and can have no limit; the *indefinite* is that of which the limits are not known to us. You can suppose it enlarged or diminished, but still it is finite.

The example of the Universe as indefinite in size, vice infinite in size, is a good example. And such an example raises another important distinction. Dr. Shaughan Lavine, a contemporary philosopher of mathematics, also writes of the indefinitely large; however, Lavine defines the 'indefinitely large' differently than I do [162]. So, we should be clear about what it means for something to be indefinitely large.

Whereas Lavine uses the term 'indefinitely large' for any collection we might judge as having too many members to count due to lack of effort or interest [163], I instead interpret such uses of 'indefinitely large' as mere hyperbole, an exaggeration. Lavine's idea of the indefinitely large is not what I would call indefinitely large; rather, what Lavine calls 'indefinitely large' I would simply call *inconveniently large*.

For example, in Lavine's sense of 'indefinitely large,' the number of grains in a pile of sand is indefinitely large, but the number can still be calculated with exponents already defined and even counted if one had the time and interest to do so. Whereas 'indefinitely large' quantities in the sense that I propose are those finite quantities so large that no one has invented (and perhaps never will) a technique to define or specify such quantities.

With respect to mathematical objects, there may be possible indefinitely large numbers in the sense that there could be invented numbers larger than anyone has heretofore invented—larger than any previously defined or specified. So, mathematical values for many of Lavine's 'indefinitely large' numbers would therefore be far smaller than the value for a quantity I propose as indefinitely large. In the world of mathematics, then, to be 'indefinitely large' in the sense I use the term is to be too large to specify with any definite number—that is, with any number heretofore defined. (Likewise, to be 'indefinitely small' would be too small to specify with any definite number in the form of a fraction or decimal place heretofore defined.)

With respect to measuring physical entities that might be indefinitely large, consider the Universe. The Universe may be 'indefinitely large'—so large no known quantity specifies the light-years of its magnitude. In that situation, it's not out of lack of effort or interest in measuring the Universe that it would be indefinitely large, but rather out of our inability to compute its (finite) magnitude.

On the other hand, maybe the Universe is not that big. Maybe instead of being 'indefinitely large' it is of unknown, but nevertheless finite size, because it is merely *indeterminately large*. In other words, too large to specify not because no one has invented finite numbers that go that high, but because we merely lack sufficient information to determine its exact size using any physical technique at our disposal. In principle we might be able to make a determination, but in practice we cannot. In that situation, it is also not out of lack of effort or interest that we would say the Universe is 'indeterminately large', but rather out of practical capability to find out just how big it is.

Whether the Universe is indefinitely large or just indeterminately large is not something I will pursue in this book. I will maintain in the chapters to come only that the Universe is not infinite in size owing to logical problems with the concept of infinity. (See §§ 18.2–4 and § 21.4 for more.)

6.2 THE INDEFINITE: COMPLETE AND INCOMPLETE

The distinction between the definite and the indefinite becomes important when we analyze how finite collections are to be quantified with respect to their completeness. Some finite collections are both complete and definite while some are complete but indefinite; then too, some finite collections are incomplete but definite while some are both incomplete and indefinite (see **Figure 6.1**).

Figure 6.1's categories illustrate two kinds of indefiniteness: (1) indefiniteness due to lacking a defined quantity for a complete collection, and (2) indefiniteness due to lacking a defined quantity for an incomplete collection.

The first kind of indefiniteness applies to any complete collection (aggregate, multitude, set, sequence, or series) in which there is a limit to the elements with some of the elements remaining undefined in quantity at any given time. This condition characterizes a finite collection that is a *complete collection*—complete because the collection in question is whole, entire, finished, full, and has, an albeit unknown, total. Because the total is unknown, perhaps even unable to be known in actual practice, the complete collection is in that respect indefinite. The total of an indefinitely large but complete collection is such that we can only assign a variable that in principle, but not in practice, is replaceable with a definite number. Though we do not know the total for the indefinitely large collection, the collection still has a total-in-principle, along with the other properties of completeness.

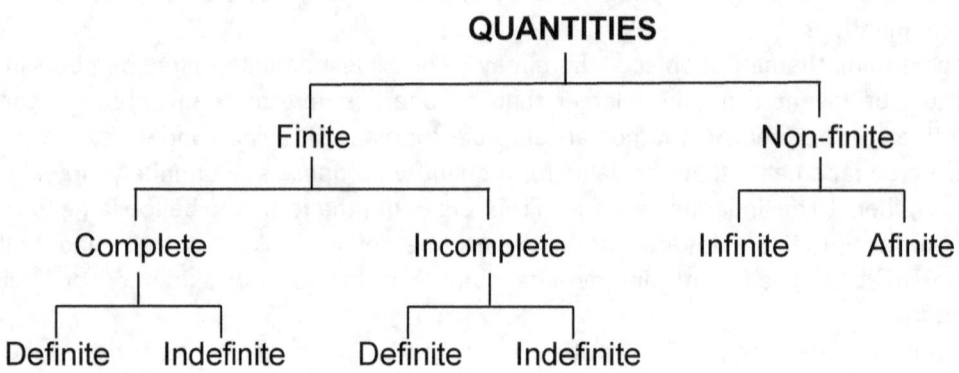

Figure 6.1: Quantities categorized by reference to the finite and the non-finite.

I said the first kind of indefiniteness applies to any complete collection, and that includes series. However, if the collection is a series that has *completed*, then the series is finished forming over time and, as such, it becomes thereupon and thereafter a static collection until if and when it ensues more change. As a static collection, the series is simply a set, 'multitude', 'aggregate', etc. that is done forming, as when a series is movies has completed production and the story ends.

The second kind of indefiniteness, that of an *incomplete collection*, can also apply to any kind of collection—set, series, etc. With respect to an incomplete set, imagine a set in which the number of members cannot be specified in practice, but that nevertheless could be specified in principle. And yet, suppose the set is incomplete—it lacks members required to qualify as 'complete'; it is an *unfinished* set. Such a set would be an indefinitely large set but also an incomplete set.

As an example of an incomplete set, consider a tower indefinitely tall—its height is finite because there are a finite number of bricks in it, but the height cannot in practice be specified because it is off the scale of all known numbers. Imagine as well that this tower has no roof—it is left unfinished in construction. Such a tower could be considered as an indefinitely large set of bricks, but an incomplete set because it is unfinished. Such a set is an example of an *incomplete-indefinite collection*.

On the other hand, because such a set is incomplete, we might also interpret it to be a *series* still under construction. That brings us to another way of expressing the second kind of indefiniteness— something can be indefinite because, as a collection, it is a series the members of which are ever changing in quantity, and so always incomplete. An *incomplete, indefinite series* is an open series in which not all of the elements in the series at any time are enumerable in actual practice and there are yet more elements adding to the series. The open series that is indefinite not only has so many elements we cannot count them in actual practice, but also the series is still getting new elements on top of those—the series is ever incomplete beyond what we can actually count and so always has indefinitely many members.

For example, take our fictional tower that is built ever higher, having only a running total of bricks at any time; but suppose the tower's running total of bricks is itself unknown at any time because there are too many bricks to count by any presently designed computer. The running total can only be expressed by a variable rather than by an exact amount. The tower would be an incomplete-indefinite collection because its quantity of bricks is off the known scale of numbers to count them, *and* the tower would also be an incomplete-indefinite series because, as a series of accumulating bricks, that unknown quantity of bricks (and the steps of laying them) is inherently incomplete as well as too large to specify in practice.

Now, if the tower, as an indefinitely growing collection of bricks, were to become complete, then the tower would not be an indefinite series, but rather an indefinitely large set. Either way, the tower is not infinite.

6.3 THE INDEFINITE: COLLECTIVE AND SERIAL

While indefiniteness is distinct from the infinite, another distinction that will be useful is the distinction between two different kinds of indefiniteness: one I will call a *collective indefinite* and the other a *serial indefinite*:

- collective indefinite: *a collection in which the members, at an assumed time, all together comprise an indefinite quantity.*
- serial indefinite: *a series that continues indefinitely.*

A series is a kind of collection, one in which entities become members in succession rather than all at once, but the term 'collective indefinite' refers more narrowly to collections such as multitudes, aggregates, and sets—collections in which the members exist all together at once and have too many members to compute in practice. The category 'collective indefinite' is therefore distinct from, rather than inclusive of, the category of a serial indefinite.

Notice that the above definitions do not distinguish a collection, whether set or series, as being either complete or incomplete. Hence to clarify, a collective indefinite can be either a complete collection or an incomplete collection; however, a series that is a *competed* series also constitutes a complete static collection, such as a set, and so is an instance of a collective indefinite, while an *incomplete* series is one that continues to indefinitely grow in quantity of instances (objects, events, etc.) and so it is the incomplete series that is the 'serial indefinite'. **Figure 6.2** represents these distinctions, which will come in handy particularly for contrast to collections that may be taken either as literal or figurative infinities.

6.4 THE VARIETIES OF INDEFINITENESS

To draw a sharper distinction between indefiniteness and infinity, we need some vocabulary to differentiate the different ways the collections can be quantitatively indefinite. These fall into two main types: indefiniteness of proportion and indefiniteness of series.

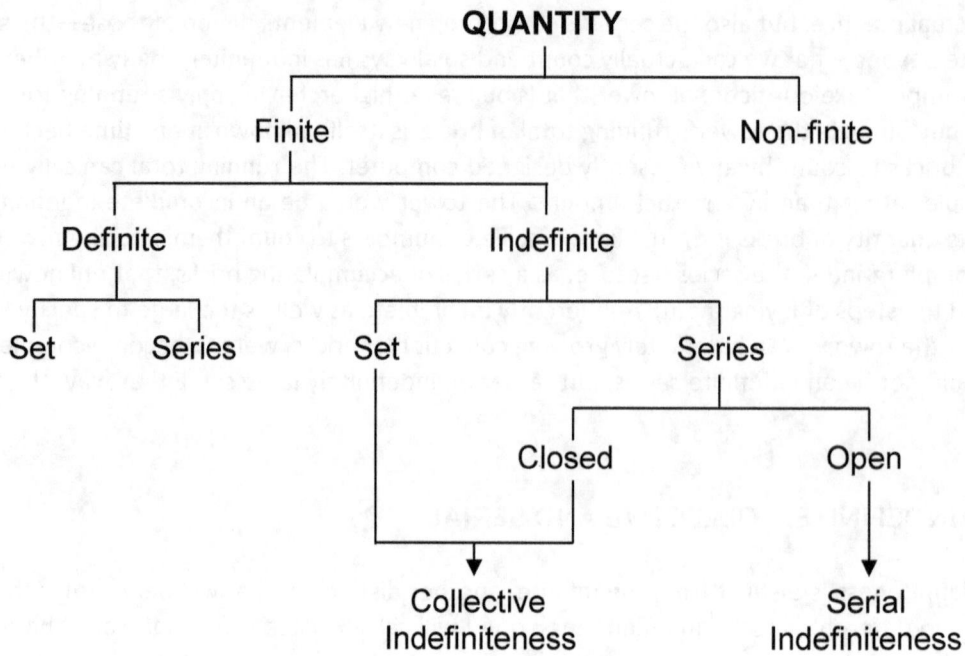

Figure 6.2: Collective indefiniteness and serial indefiniteness. (1) A 'collective indefinite' is a collection having indefiniteness as a property. As a set, the collective indefinite may be either complete or incomplete. As a series, if the collective indefinite is a closed series, then it is equivalent to an indefinitely large set and so may be either complete or incomplete. (2) A 'serial indefinite' is a series that has indefiniteness as a property of its succession of members. A series that has taken indefinitely many steps may eventually terminate, and in so doing become an indefinitely large collection (e.g., indefinitely large set), or 'collective indefinite', whether complete or incomplete. Such a series is protracted, but not a genuine 'serial indefinite'. A serial indefinite does not terminate; it is open—it never ceases to accumulate members or steps in its progression.

6.4.1 *Indefinite Proportions*

Definition:

- proportion: *a comparative measure*.

To describe the proportions of a collection is to describe how the collection compares to some other collection(s) with respect to given measurements. We may say, for instance, that a collection is smaller or larger than another, takes up so much or so little of another collection, or has elements that are closer or further apart than those of another collection, and so on. Alternatively, we may simply use adjectives to describe proportion like "huge" or "tiny."

There are many different proportions that might describe collections. For now, we will stick to descriptions of proportions that pertain to space. There are (at least) two different ways we might describe spatial proportions—by magnitude and by distance. As shown in **Figure 6.3**, some collections that are extended through space are indefinite in magnitude while others are indefinite in distance.

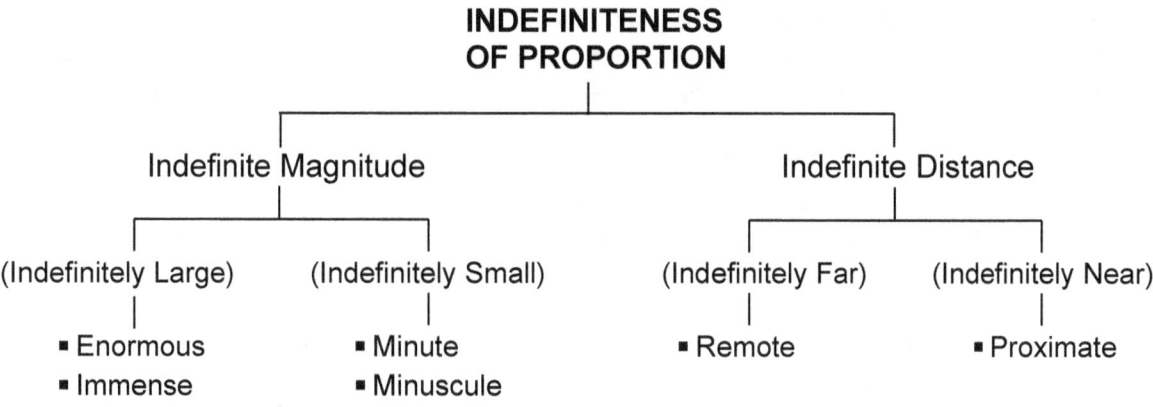

Figure 6.3: The varieties of indefiniteness in proportion that may describe spatially extended collections.

First, let's consider collections in terms of their magnitudes. We already know of finite numbers too big to count out—the unfeasible numbers. And we know of finite numbers too big to be represented in anything but shorthand notation, such as the googolplex. In addition, there are finite numbers verging on too big to be well-defined with any already-known mathematical function. Now think of numbers needed to quantify finite collections even bigger than that—indefinitely large collections, which are collections off any known finite scale of magnitude and yet they are not limitless in size.

Of course, since such collections are "off the scale," we would need to extend our scale of finite numbers in order to exactly quantify such collections. Fortunately, all the elements of such large collections can, at least in principle, be computed because, in principle if not also in practice, we can create well-defined functions for defining new definite numbers that would quantify what are for us currently indefinitely large, but nonetheless finite, collections. If such new functions are made to capture the quantity of such indefinitely large collections, we would also have in the process come up with a new definite number, one larger than any previous definite number ever invented. Of course, once quantified, the collection that was formerly thought of as indefinitely large would no longer be so. But there could be yet larger collections that are still indefinitely large, even given the new awesomely large number we just came up with. Once again, it would take an extension of the number scale to capture the size of such a collection—in principle, even if not in practice, we can come up with a function to create more new, even larger definite numbers, for such collections, to render them for us definite instead of indefinite.

All instances of collections for which we would need to extend the scale of defined natural numbers in order to fully quantify a collection's quantity of elements should be regarded as finite, but indefinitely large, collections. Assuming such collections exist, the size of any of these indefinitely large collections are such that they can be computed, albeit only in principle by an ideal computing machine.

However, for that ideal computing machine to represent how many members are in the collection once it's done computing, the machine would have to output a numeral of some kind that represents the definite number of members in the collection computed. Alas, if there is no robust function by which to define that definite number, then even the ideal computing machine could not represent the quantity in the collection it just computed. So, there must first exist a sufficiently robust mathematical function to well define a definite number for the ideal computing machine to use for identifying how many members are in the computed collection.

We can therefore assume that some indefinitely large collections can be quantified only given the future invention of a sufficiently robust algorithm or function—more powerful than we currently have—that will be used for defining a definite number that an ideal computing machine could represent for the size of the collection computed.

However, there would also be other indefinitely large collections, ones so big that we will never *in practice*—no matter how far in the future—be able to come up with a function for defining a definite number that large. Yet, *in principle* such a function and its definite number could be invented, and so we can still say that in principle the ideal computing machine could represent the size of the collection once its computation is completed.

In order to distinguish between these two different classes of the indefinitely large, I will draw on a couple of words from colloquial speech and stipulate new, technical definitions for them. The words I will use are *enormity* and *immensity* [164]. Both words are commonly used to simply mean "very big," but I offer definitions for these words that are narrower in meaning.

Stipulated definitions:

- enormity: *the condition of being enormous.*
- enormous: *too large to be quantified without defining a new definite number.*

- immensity: *the condition of being immense.*
- immense: *too large to be quantified without a definite number definable only in principle.*

A collection is 'enormous' if there are so many members in the collection that no definite number has yet been invented that can specify the exact size of the collection, but in the future such a number may be so defined. Once such a number is defined, the collection is no longer 'enormous'; instead, it has a definite size. Only collections of some indefinitely larger size (while still in practice computable) would then be considered enormous.

Of course, in everyday speech we call much smaller things "enormous," like my neighbor's cat. Given the definition for enormity I offered, the cat would of course not qualify as enormous. If we wanted the new definition for the term 'enormous' to be the word's colloquial meaning, then we would have to take use of the adjective 'enormous' in relation to anything we physically observe as mere hyperbole. Ironically, despite its vastness, even the observable universe is too small to qualify as enormous by this technical definition of the term. So, calling the observable universe "enormous" would also be hyperbole! That sounds odd, but we need a name for such an indefinitely large size and 'enormous' will have to do.

Now let's consider immensity. Although the word 'immense' comes from Latin for "unmeasured," to be immense is not to be infinite. In colloquial speech, to say something is immense is merely to say it is very large or very great but it is still implied to be of some finite size. That which is immense may be that which is large enough that it has not been measured, but that is not to say it is immeasurable even in principle, which is to be limitless in the sense of literal infinity. It is possible the entire Universe (beyond even the observable universe) may be, in the technical sense, enormous or even immense while still not being literally infinite.

Though 'immense' colloquially means to be very great in size, because the word comes from the Latin for "unmeasured," I believe we can safely use the word in a narrower, technical sense of being so large it is off of any established finite scale of numbers, not definable in practice and yet definable in principle. Like the term 'enormous', if we were to render the technical use of 'immense' as its literal usage in colloquial speech, then we would have to take the use of 'immense' for anything we observe as hyperbolic for inconveniently big to measure. I believe that sense fits how the term 'immense' is most often used in colloquial discourse, but I will instead use 'immense' in the technical sense I have stipulated for a class of the indefinitely large (unless otherwise noted or clear from context).

On the opposite end of the size scale, consider aggregates, multitudes, and sets that are finite but *indefinitely small*. Some such collections are too small to be expressed with definite numbers such as known decimals or fractions, but they could eventually be defined with definite numbers in practice at some point in the future. Other such collections are too small to ever be quantified by definite numbers in practice but nevertheless have a finite size since their size can be mathematically defined with definite numbers in principle. The former I term *minute* (pronounced my-**noot**) and the latter I term *minuscule* rather than 'infinitesimal' (infinitely small). Stipulated definitions:

- minuteness: *the condition of being minute.*
- minute: *too small to be quantified without defining a new definite number.*

- minuscularity: *the condition of being minuscule.*
- minuscule: *too small to be quantified without a definite number definable only in principle.*

'Minuscularity' is a word taken from William Faulkner's *The Town* [165]. I am using 'minuscularity' as a noun for designating that which can be regarded as minuscule. The adjective 'minuscule' comes from the French for "small letter" and in colloquial speech simply means "very small." However, I propose 'minuscule' to mean *indefinitely small*—so small as to be off of any finite scale of smallness, but still definable on a finite scale in principle. The more colloquial use of the word 'minuscule' to mean merely "very small" would be hyperbole by comparison.

Next, let's consider objects that have indefiniteness of distance between them—either an indefinitely large distance or an indefinitely short distance. Let's start with a distance that is indefinitely large. We will call such a distance *remote*. When something is remote, it has a definite relative position, just one that is indefinitely far away. Here too caution must be exercised: to say something is 'remote' often means something is "very far away," such as beyond the horizon, but not an immense distance as the word 'immense' is defined above. We will have to take such uses of 'remote' as a figure of speech in order for 'remote' to designate that which is at an immense (indefinitely large) distance.

In contrast with remoteness, some objects have a minuscule distance between them. The objects do not occupy the same space; they are not located at an identical position, so it is not that there is zero distance between them. They are, however, so close together that no fraction we can express in actual practice captures just how fine the distance of separation is between them. Let's refer to such a minuscule distance as a *proximate* distance.

This analysis, therefore, stipulates two more sets of definitions for common terms we can adopt to designate indefinite proportions of distance:

- remoteness: *the condition of being remote.*
- remote: *indefinitely removed or far away.*

- proximateness: *the condition of being proximate.*
- proximate: *indefinitely close or near.*

Immense, minuscule, remote, proximate: such terms demonstrate that there are plenty of terms for describing magnitudes and distances that are indefinite in proportion but not literally infinite.

6.4.2 *Indefinite Series*

To further distinguish indefiniteness from infinity, we may need yet more vocabulary to denote the various ways collections can be indefinite in temporal series rather than complete and limitless (infinite) over time. The categories of indefinite series are outlined in **Figure 6.4**.

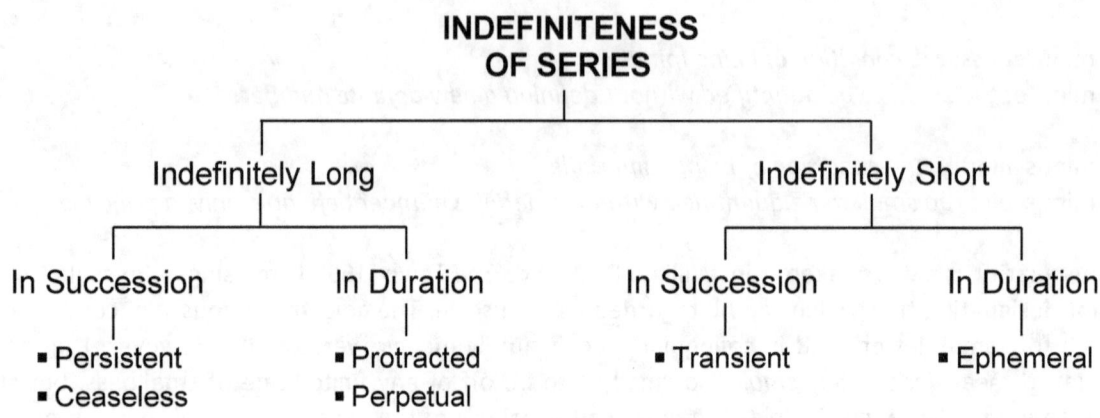

Figure 6.4: The varieties of indefinite series (in the temporal sense of the term 'series').

We will start by examining series as sequences formed by succession and then turn to series as sequences that have duration.

Consider series that are *indefinitely long*—that is, series that are indefinite in the number of successive steps or events they accrue. There are two ways a series can be indefinitely long; the series continues for an indefinitely large number of successive steps but eventually terminates (as when a computer continues calculating until exhaustion) or the series goes on without ever stopping (as with anything that is immortal) [166].

To easily reference these conditions, we need to introduce two more terms. I propose the former should be called *persistence* and the latter should be called *ceaselessness*:

- persistence: *the quality of continuing toward an indefinite end*.
- ceaselessness: *the quality of continuing indefinitely, without ceasing*.

With respect to persistence, we will need to distinguish the colloquial use of the term from the narrower, more technical use I am stipulating.

Colloquially, when we say something 'persists', we are merely saying it continues to some undefined end. One may persist with a hobby, persist with a career, persist with a relationship, etc. In all such cases, a series 'persists' if it continues *as long as desired* but they all cease at some step or event, albeit one that was not predefined at any earlier stage in the construction of the series. And in all such cases, when the series finally does end, it can be assigned a known, finite value (for example, a number of aggregates, steps, years, etc.).

However, there is another way a series can persist: a series may from some assumed beginning continue to an end that is an indefinitely large number of steps ahead of any step we denote. For example, the lifespan of certain subatomic units of matter may be 'persistent' in this sense. We can imagine the units of matter will 'persist' for a time indefinitely far in the future—a time so far in the future that we cannot presently calculate the number of years owing to the limits of our current mathematical ingenuity to define, yet at which the units of matter will finally decay or be destroyed. When they finally decay or are destroyed, they will have *persisted* for a duration off of any scale of years we *now* have finite numbers to express. If there are units of matter that will continue for such a length of time, they are units that 'persist' to an end indefinitely far in the future in the stronger sense of living for so long we currently have no math to define the number of years they will be around, but they will eventually come to an end.

Persistence differs from literal infinity and so from the condition of a limitless series considered as a complete set of steps, moments, or events, etc. Persistence has a limit in the form of an end—just an end that is not defined before the persistent series is underway and while the series continues. The more technical notion of persistence describes series that continue toward an end not only undefined during the process in which the series continues forming, but toward an end that can be defined in future practice only with some as yet unconceived mathematical operation. However, because the persistent succession of events will indeed end at some finite step from the beginning, the series is *not* absolutely limitless or equivalent to a literally infinite sequence.

Persistence is indefinite, but it also differs from ceaselessness.

That which is persistent has no *pre*-defined end, but it still eventually ends. That which is ceaseless, on the other hand, is indefinite in a stronger sense: to be ceaseless is to go on without ever coming to an end.

Persistence denotes the continuation of a series to an end that is not predefined but that becomes *definite* upon termination (and in its more technical sense, to 'persist' is to continue to an end that is too large to be expressed on any current scale of values, to an end indefinitely far in the future), but a ceaseless series is never terminated and so *cannot have a definite end* or even an end at all in terms of succession. A series is ceaseless if it continues 'indefinitely' in the stronger sense of going on without ever ceasing (stopping or terminating) at any time.

Moreover, persistence differs from ceaselessness looking backward through a series as well. For example, we can conceive of a series that has *persisted* for an indefinitely long time—from some time *indefinitely far in the past*, a time off of any known finite scale to express and yet a time at which the series began and so not infinitely far in the past. (It's not necessary that such a time existed; we can still conceive of such.) Since the series 'persisted' but no longer 'persists', such a series has come to an end. In contrast, a ceaseless series that has been around for an indefinitely long time is a series that does not stop—it is still going and will keep on going.

Just as persistence differs from sequential limitlessness and ergo the literally infinite, so too ceaselessness not only differs from persistence in that it has no end, but it also differs from the limitlessness of a literally infinite sequence of steps. Though a ceaseless series is one that lacks an end or bound to its process of growth, the ceaseless series still has (at least in principle) a limit by virtue of having a running total to its range of members at any given step in its growth, and so it is not a limitless sequence and therefore different from a literally infinite sequence.

Whereas literal infinity has no limit at all, ceaselessness has an ever-changing limit. Moreover, ceaselessness implies the series continues without stopping because it never becomes complete; one could say the series continues despite being always incomplete. Since ceaselessness is incomplete, yet limited, in succession, ceaselessness differs from literal infinity, which is a condition that would make a series complete as well as limitless in its number of events or steps.

We have thus far considered persistence and ceaselessness in terms of *successions* of steps or events in temporal series. Let's now turn to persistence and ceaselessness as notions that also apply to *durations* of time. More specifically, persistence and ceaselessness are notions that can be applied to *indefinite* durations of time.

An indefinitely long duration of time is either a duration that persists until an end that no established value on any number scale expresses or a duration that never ceases because it is never completed. The former we can call a *protraction*. The latter we may call *perpetuity*.

Stipulated definitions:

- protraction: *a duration that persists.*
- perpetuity: *an indefinitely long duration in which events ceaselessly occur by succession.*

A protraction is a finite period of time, just one so long that we can't express how long it is. A process or series that persists over a long time we sometimes call *lasting* or say that it 'has lasted' or 'will be lasting'; but a lasting time is not necessarily a protracted time. A lasting time may have some definite end; a protracted time has only an indefinite end. A protracted time is therefore a lasting period of time, but a lasting period of time is not necessarily a protracted period of time because a protracted period of time is indefinitely long in duration. However long a protracted period of time may be, it nevertheless has a total amount of events that either have passed or will reach a total amount of events when it ceases, and so a protracted period of time is a duration that always remains finite.

A perpetuity is a duration of time that continues into the future without ceasing because the future is never completed. To be *perpetual* usually implies a ceaseless recurrence, renewal, or regrowth. But if something lasts perpetually, then we call it *permanent*. (Although, sometimes the term 'permanent' is more a figure of speech than a literal claim. As a figure of speech, 'permanent' means protracted to an end that is not predefined.) Though unfolding ceaselessly, a perpetuity has a running total of events that have passed at any step of the way and so a perpetuity is finite despite its indefinitely long duration.

Both a protracted amount of time and a perpetuity are therefore not infinite amounts of time in a literal sense. A literally infinite amount of time has a complete series of events, not an incomplete series, and the infinite series of events is a quantity of events without limit rather than an indefinitely large number of events that has an end.

The opposite of protraction is *transience* (or of protracted is *transient*). Stipulated definitions:

- transience: *the condition of being transient.*
- transient: *occurring as a succession of ephemeral durations the total of which are less than any increment of time measurable in practice.*

An explosion may seem quick, but when watched in slow motion many successive events that took place during the explosion reveal themselves. If the succession of events—no matter how many there are—would add up to less than any measurable fraction of a second, that succession would be considered 'transient' by the above definition. In colloquial speech we of course refer to brief successions that take longer than that as 'transient'; but by the above definition, such use of the term 'transient' would be hyperbole.

In order for a series to be transient, each event in the series must be successive rather than simultaneous and each must be *ephemeral* in duration. Stipulated definitions:

- ephemerality: *the condition of being ephemeral.*
- ephemeral: *occurring with indefinite brevity.*

Suppose a sequence of successive events comprising a series of events is indefinitely brief—the sequence of events passes too quickly to be measured in practice, and yet can be measured in principle because the *duration* of the sequence of events can be quantified with a non-zero number of successive events. Such an indefinitely quick series of events is not *instantaneous* because it does not take place in no time at all (measure zero for their duration); instead, it has at least two events—a beginning and ending—that are not identical. And yet, the events in the series pass from start to finish so quickly that no scale can be created in actual practice that captures the quickness with which the events pass. Such indefinitely brief series of events will be called 'ephemeral'.

Ephemerality differs from an infinitesimally short duration because 'the ephemeral' can be measured in principle, whereas an infinitely short duration cannot be measured at all—an infinitely short duration would be a non-zero duration but *limitlessly* brief.

6.5 THE INDEFINITE IS NOT THE INFINITE

The varieties of indefiniteness are all distinct from literal infinity. To be *indefinite* is to be limited regardless of whether that which is indefinite is a set or series, and whether it is *either* complete (with an unknown limit) *or* incomplete (with a running total). In contrast, to be literally *infinite* is to necessarily be *both* complete *and* limitless. The post-Enlightenment mathematician and theologian Bernard Bolzano (1781–1848) stated that an "infinite plurality" (collection) has "absolutely *no last term*" in the sense of being *limitless* rather than merely indefinite [167].

He also went on to describe literal infinity as a condition of being complete (a "whole") in plurality as well as limitless [168]. He stated that infinity can be found, for example, in complete sets of infinitesimally brief moments in time and complete sets of infinitesimal 'points' in space, with those moments and points themselves being limitless in quantity [169]:

> ...the multitude of moments which lie between every two moments α and β, however close to one another, and in the same way the multitude of points which lie between every two points a and b however close to one another, is infinite.

Indefiniteness implies limits and either completeness or incompleteness; literal infinity implies limitlessness and completeness.

Literal infinity is also a state or condition that is either greater than any 'immensity' or smaller than any 'minuscularity' (if the infinitude is smaller, then it is infinitesimal). In terms of time or series, literal infinity must thus be either longer than the 'persistent' and 'protracted' (which eventually end) while being complete in succession (whereas 'ceaselessness' and 'perpetuity' never are) or shorter in succession than the merely 'transient' without being simultaneous (of zero difference in terms of succession), or 'ephemeral' without being instantaneous (zero in duration).

Literal infinity is also distinct from indefiniteness as a matter of scope. Bolzano pointed out that an infinite plurality is "a plurality which is greater than every finite one, i.e., a plurality which has the property that every finite multitude represents only a part of it" [170]. Literal infinity denotes a quantitative condition of a collection that, conceived as a set, contains non-empty subsets of finite quantity, some of which are definite in quantity, some of which are indefinitely large in quantity, and some of which are proposed to be beyond even these—quantities altogether unspecifiably great. Literal infinity is inclusive of indefinitely large quantity, just as indefinitely large quantity includes but goes beyond every definite finite quantity (**Figure 6.5**).

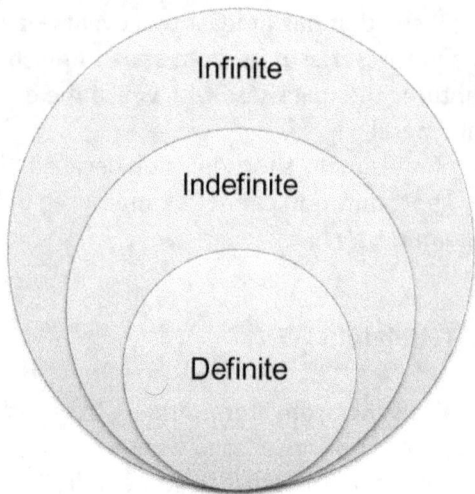

Figure 6.5: Literal infinity is typically conceived to include not only finitudes of definite quantity and those of indefinitely large quantity, but also even greater quantities not specifiable even in principle.

6.6 THE INDEFINITE IS NOT INDETERMINATELY INFINITE

There is another conceptual distinction that should be made between the indefinite and the literally infinite, though I bring this up particularly for philosophers familiar with Renaissance thought. To say something is 'indefinite' or goes on 'indefinitely' is not to be *uncertain* about whether or not it is either finite or infinite. Rather, to call something 'indefinite' or say it goes on 'indefinitely' is to imply that it is finite but too large or small to be measurable in practice.

This position is contrary to that of the Renaissance philosopher, scientist, and mathematician René Descartes (1596 – 1650). Although, I should first clarify that there are at least three different senses in which Descartes thought something could be 'indefinite':

- indefinite as serially indefinite.
- indefinite as the indefinitely large.
- indefinite as *indeterminately* finite or actually infinite.

While I agree with the first two, I do not agree with the third. Let's take them in order.

First, Descartes called 'indefinite' that which most of his contemporaries called 'infinite' in the sense of Aristotle's notion of 'potential infinity'. Descartes said that given a finite quantity, you can always divide it further [171]. However, he refused to call a process that continues without end "infinite". Descartes used the term 'indefinite' instead of 'potential infinity' to describe such a process because he wanted to avoid the use of infinity in mathematics and physics altogether. Descartes was hence using the word 'indefinite' in one of the ways I advocate as well: the serially indefinite.

Second, by 'indefinite' Descartes occasionally meant the indefinitely large. For example, Descartes said that the Universe "has no limits to its extension," but only in the sense that it has "indefinitely extended spaces" [172]. That is, the spatial expanse of the Universe lacks limits only with regard to any boundary we might *conceive* or *imagine*. I take Descartes to mean that this kind of indefiniteness is what I would call a 'collective indefinite' in quantity; applied to size, it is a reference to the indefinitely large. He seems to have believed the Universe is actually finite but likely large beyond any conceivable boundary.

Third and finally, Descartes used the term 'indefinite' in a way I *disagree* with. He said the 'indefinite' also refers to something "indeterminate"—that is, something we cannot determine to be finite or actually infinite. For Descartes, 'indefinite' refers to a collection that is *either* a finite collection of indefinitely large size (a collective indefinite) *or* a collection that is actually infinite; we simply cannot tell which is the case because our ability to measure is inadequate to the task of making the determination [173].

As an example, Descartes says the spatial expanse of the Universe fits the bill of being indefinitely large in another sense: it is *indeterminately* finite or actually (literally) infinite. The spatial expanse of the Universe *might* be limitless while having a complete set of places comprising its extent—it might be actually infinite—but we cannot know that for certain. Space also might just be a collective indefinite of places. Because we can't be sure which is the case—infinite space or finite space of some indefinitely large magnitude—Descartes recommends that we shouldn't *say* the Universe is actually infinite; we should only say it is 'indefinite'. He made the same recommendation for all other quantities in mathematics and the physical world that seem, or might be, limitless; they are all 'indefinite' [174] [175].

With that, we have covered the three uses of 'indefinite' Descartes offered. And what else do these three uses of the term 'indefinite' all have in common? They are epistemic; they denote our lack of knowledge about limits, or even if there are limits or not. That is quintessential Descartes—he was all about doubt versus certainty.

Descartes' notion of 'indefinite' stands in contrast to how the term 'indefinite' is used by other philosophers, such as Fleming, Lavine, and even me. While we each may scope the indefinite differently than one another, we might all agree that indefiniteness is a category of the *finite* and not a condition of being in a lack of determination as to whether a quantity is finite or infinite, as Descartes held 'indefinite' to be in certain contexts. Moreover, I believe Fleming would have agreed with me, as would Lavine, that 'indefinite' is *not* a term that should be used for collections implied to be literally (actually) infinite, whereas Descartes did just that.

Descartes' promotion of using the term 'indefinite' I fully sympathize with, at least with respect to replacing figurative uses of the term 'infinity' with 'indefiniteness' and denoting collections too large to count in practice, or that can go on ceaselessly. Where I would correct Descartes is on his use of 'indefinite' to denote uncertainty about whether or not a collection is literally infinite. We need have no such uncertainty, as I will show in debunking the concept of literal infinity in the chapters to follow.

6.7 THE INDEFINITE CONTRASTED WITH THE INFINITE IN MATHEMATICS

There is yet another common confusion of literal infinity with indefiniteness that must be resolved. Mathematicians have several technical definitions for infinity and infinite. In terms of performing mathematical operations, the definitions are clear enough. But with respect to what the terms 'infinity' and 'infinite' mean from a logical point of view, the mathematical definitions may not be distinguishable from other concepts that carry very different logical connotations.

For example, mathematicians sometimes define 'infinite' as a value that is "greater than any assignable quantity" [176]. Sometimes mathematicians use another definition for 'infinite' that refers to a quantity unable to be counted with a terminating sequence of natural numbers [177]. These technical definitions for infinity are consistent with mathematical use, but in more general academic use and colloquial discourse they are not semantically different from that which is indefinite, but still finite. Indefiniteness can also be interpreted as fitting these mathematical definitions of infinity and the term 'infinite'.

To be indefinite is to be *too small or too large to be assigned a definite number*, but still *either* (a) assignable a definite number in practice as well as in principle *or* (b) assignable a definite number, albeit only in principle.

Recall d^* as the variable for the largest number defined to date. A finite number higher than d^* would have a value in the known number scale if it could be computed with current mathematical operations, but because it cannot be computed with (at least current) mathematical operations, the value of such a number is "off the scale"—that is, off of any *known* sequence of numbers in the scale of numbers that is defined to date. A number with an indefinitely great value is therefore a number too big for anyone in current practice to define with conventional methods, though not necessarily in future practice, and certainly not in principle.

That is, some finite numbers that exceed the largest ever defined today (d^*) may yet one day be defined and so are only for now numbers of indefinitely large value. But there is also the possibility of another type of indefinite number—a type of finite number that includes those numbers exceeding the largest value of any number that will ever, or could ever, be defined *in practice* yet could still be defined *in principle*. Both types of indefinitely large numbers are $>d^*$, but both kinds of indefinitely large numbers are finite.

Notice that this description of an indefinite number entails it is at least in practice "greater than any [presently] assignable quantity," even though it is still finite. As such, indefinite numbers are therefore "unable to be counted with a terminating sequence of natural numbers"—at least with any natural numbers defined so far—but they are still finite numbers.

Moreover, consider the periodic rationals and irrational numbers. They too are "unable to be counted with a terminating sequence of natural numbers"—at least in the sense that they are *incomplete* numbers and so there may always be more to count. That is, they are numbers that have *series* of digits that in principle need not terminate growing, and so at any given time they have a countable quantity of digits, but their totals of digits keep running as their sequences grow, and so such sequences can even be construed as becoming indefinitely large (though still finite at any time) and in that sense unable to be counted, at least in practice. Yet, finite the incomplete numbers remain.

Hence, these descriptions of off-the-scale finite values are consistent with the technical definitions mathematicians gave to infinity. It is thus easy to confuse indefiniteness and infinity. And this confusion is a problem because our conception of literal infinity is not supposed to be the same thing as indefiniteness.

However, we can distinguish infinity from indefiniteness not by the uncountability of the numbers as such, but the way in which the numbers cannot be counted. Whereas an indefinite number is, among other things, a number that cannot be counted in present practice but could be in principle, an *infinite number* (in the literal sense of infinity) is a number that due to its *limitlessness* cannot be counted at all, not even with a running total of digits, and not even in principle [178].

Moreover, the inability to count an indefinitely large collection is a matter of practice but not a matter of principle; the inability to count an infinite collection is a matter of principle and not merely a matter of practice. To be indefinite is to have an in-principle *knowable*, but in practice *unknown*, limit (and in some cases, that unknown limit is variable in quantity); but to be literally infinite is to have a non-zero quantity with *no limit*. Infinity doesn't have a limit that is beyond calculation; rather, infinity is incalculable because it is *without* a limit at all [179].

That is the difference between the indefinite and the infinite—with respect to considerations of limits as such. However, if progressions of numbers are literally infinite sets, then they are also complete as well as limitless. For instance, if the natural numbers are taken as a literally infinite set, $\mathbb{N}$, then there is no limit to the numbers in $\mathbb{N}$, but they are also said to be 'countable' and 'enumerable' because $\mathbb{N}$ is also complete as a set. This is a logically problematic issue for limitlessness seems to imply incalculability while completeness seems to imply calculability, a problem we will return to in Chapters 10–14.

In contrast, progressions of numbers as indefinite series have no such problem. In the view that number systems are not infinite sets but instead are indefinite series, number systems are invented number scales comprised of the numbers that *have been* defined to date and under continual extension as new numbers are invented. In that view, the scale of naturals is not a paradoxically complete and limitless set ($\mathbb{N}$) but an inherently incomplete series ($\mathbb{N}^C$) with a running total. A series such as $\mathbb{N}^C$ is calculable only insofar as new numbers are invented for $\mathbb{N}^C$ and new numbers are always inevitable in principle. No paradox arises if the naturals are an open series, $\mathbb{N}^C$, rather than an infinite set, $\mathbb{N}$.

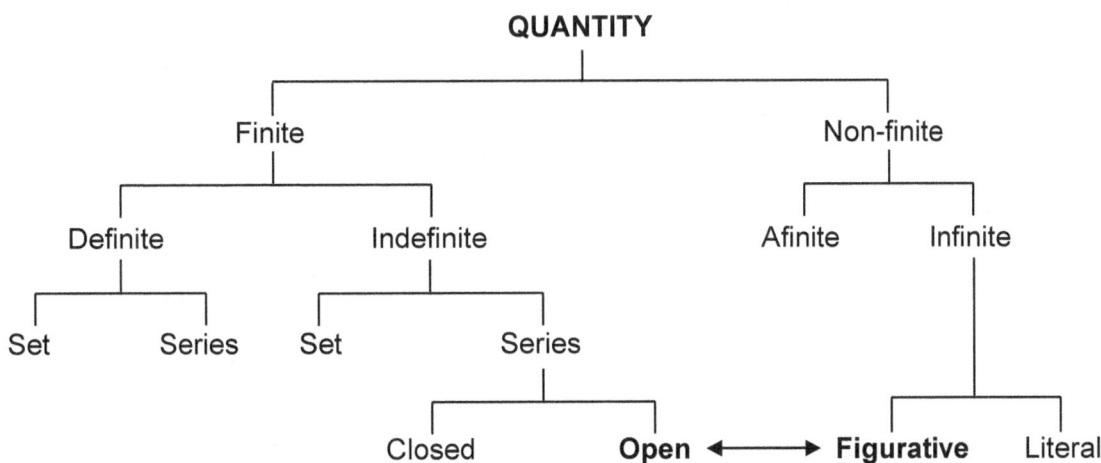

Figure 6.6: An open (intrinsically incomplete) series—a serial indefinite—is synonymous with a series that is 'infinite' in a figurative sense, whereas an indefinitely large set (or closed series, no matter how indefinitely protracted it was when it closed) is not a figurative infinite.

6.8 FIGURATIVE INFINITY AS SERIAL INDEFINITENESS

Quantitative infinity, in its figurative sense, is not a condition of being limitless per se but instead it is a condition of having a limit that is always changing in measure. The figurative sense of infinity refers not to a condition of being complete but rather of being forever incomplete, despite changing in quantity. Figurative infinity is best defined as *the condition of indefinitely changing in quantity*.

Figurative infinity is a condition that applies not to certain completed *sets* but rather to intrinsically incomplete *series*—series that are never completed because they never terminate in their progression. A figuratively infinite series is one composed of an *indefinitely* changing quantity of occurrences. Figurative infinity is thus the same as *serial indefiniteness*. A figurative infinity is the condition of being an indefinite series (**Figure 6.6**), a series with no definite end but a series that is nonetheless finite at all times.

As figurative infinity just is serial indefiniteness, the notion that a number system such as the naturals are indefinite series ($\mathbb{N}^{\circ}$) implies they can be considered as figuratively 'infinite' series. However, whether 'infinity' *should* be used as a synonym for that which is indefinite, even serially indefinite, is another matter. Because mathematical definitions of infinity can confuse the infinite with the indefinite, we find instances where the literally infinite can be confused with the figuratively infinite, a problem we were trying to avoid. And a problem which we will return to in Chapter 24, where I will promote the use of the term 'indefinite' over the figurative use of 'infinite' as a solution to avoid such confusion.

CHAPTER 6 IN REVIEW

❖ Finite quantities are either complete or incomplete.
❖ Either way, they are also either definite or indefinite:
  o definiteness: the state of having defined or specified limits.
  o indefiniteness: the state of having undefined or unspecified limits.
❖ The indefinite is different than the infinite: the infinite is that which has and can have no limit; the indefinite is that of which the limits are not known.
❖ There are two kinds of indefinite:
  o collective indefinite: a collection in which the members, at an assumed time, all together comprise an indefinite quantity.
  o serial indefinite: a series the quantitative limit of which changes indefinitely.
❖ Figurative infinity is serial indefiniteness.
❖ If number systems (such as the systems of natural numbers, integers, real numbers, etc.) are literally infinite sets, then they are complete as well as limitless.
❖ But if number systems are figuratively infinite series, then they are inherently incomplete and so always finite: they are not literally infinite sets but instead are serial indefinites.

7: SPEAKING OF INFINITE QUANTITIES

There are two different kinds of language we use to speak about quantitative infinity:

- *natural language*
- *formal language*

Natural language is what we speak in our everyday, colloquial discourse. It is also what we use in artistic discourse—such as poetry and the prose of literature—and what we use for some of the more academic discourse in specialized disciplines (such as linguistics, history, philosophy, and so on). In contrast to natural language, there is another broad area of discourse: formal language. Formal language is used for symbolically representing ideas and concepts in technically precise forms of communication like codes, formulas, proofs, axioms, theorems, and so on. Formal language is especially useful for making calculations and measurements. Infinity can be defined according to either natural language or formal language.

By contrast, there are two different kinds of language we use when speaking about qualitative infinity:

- *formal language*
- *informal language*

To make things even more confusing, the term 'formal language' has a different meaning when it is contrasted with informal language. In that context, formal language is not the language of mathematics and computer codes but instead the language of academic prose, journalism, political speeches, and the like. Which makes that version of formal language a subcategory of natural language.

We will return to the formal/informal language contrast in § 25.1 when we review qualitative infinity. Until then, I will stick to the natural/formal language contrast for the analysis of quantitative infinity.

7.1 INFINITY IN NATURAL LANGUAGE AND FORMAL LANGUAGE

The two definitions I supplied in § 1.3.1 for (quantitative) infinity—the definitions for both literal infinity and figurative infinity—were given in natural language. Literal infinity was defined as "the condition of being both complete and limitless in quantity," and figurative infinity was defined as "the condition of indefinitely changing in quantity." These definitions for infinity express the conventional understandings of infinity according to our ordinary, colloquial discourse in natural language.

When mathematicians define infinity, on the other hand, they sometimes do so in terms of the formal language of mathematics. They may use symbols for infinity ($\aleph$, ω, ∞), which serve as characters in the formal language of mathematics, and such symbols may be used to define infinity in terms of mathematical expressions, such as $\mathbb{N} \triangleq \aleph_0$, which means $\mathbb{N}$ is *by definition equal to* $\aleph_0$. Other expressions can be made from like formal language definitions; for example, $n \rightarrow \infty$ and $|2^\omega| = \aleph_1$.

However, mathematicians do not rely solely on formal language to express ideas and concepts about infinity. Mathematicians make assumptions and draw implications about infinity that can be expressed in natural language, and they also make explicit statements about infinity in natural language. With respect to discourse on infinity in the field of mathematics, the uses of formal and natural language are not mutually exclusive—you will find overlap in use of the two languages in mathematics.

For example, *MathWorld*, a mathematics website, defines infinity like so: "Infinity, most often denoted as ∞, is an unbounded quantity that is greater than every real number" [180]. Clearly, this is a natural language definition. However, the definition goes on to say, "Informally, $1/\infty = 0$, a statement that can be made rigorous using the limit concept" [181]. Although the definition says such an expression is "informal," the expression is still an equation in the formal language of mathematics. Moreover, the definition then continues with further formal language expressions about infinity, the details of which will not concern us. The point is that mathematicians do define infinity in natural language as well as formal language, and often there is overlapping use of the two kinds of language just as this definition entry shows.

Now you will notice the definition for infinity provided by a mathematics dictionary or by a resource like *MathWorld* does not necessarily define infinity as I did when I supplied the literal and figurative definitions for infinity. In fact, you will not find the definitions I provided for literal and figurative infinity in any dictionaries of mathematics composed to date. You won't even find them in common dictionaries which cover colloquial usage of words. There is a reason for this.

'Infinity' has technical definitions in mathematics that differ from its lexical definitions in colloquial speech. Any given dictionary will have several lexical definitions for the word 'infinity'. The definitions for 'infinity' I distinguished as literal infinity and figurative infinity are not articulated in common dictionaries, but I believe the definitions for those terms are lexical definitions insofar as they accurately articulate common uses of the word 'infinity'.

When in common discourse people say something is infinite and they mean it literally, they imply that what they speak of is a collection and that as such it is complete and limitless in its quantity of members. When people commonly say something is "infinite" in a figurative sense, they mean it just keeps going on without stopping, even if it's finite at each step of the way. So, the definitions for literal infinity and figurative infinity are lexical definitions in that they express how the world 'infinity' is commonly applied to collections.

However, the definitions for literal infinity and figurative infinity may also be considered 'precising definitions' (see §§ 3.1–3.2) insofar as the word 'infinity' is used for describing particular properties of a collection according to particular contexts (such as limitlessness and completeness in a literal context or merely ceaseless growth in a figurative context). Regardless, I will refer to the definitions provided for literal infinity and figurative infinity as lexical definitions for infinity since I believe those definitions capture what people assume the word 'infinity' means in ordinary, natural language.

In contrast to lexical definitions, especially as found in ordinary dictionaries, technical definitions for infinity—some of which are in natural language, some of which are in formal language, and most often a mix of both—are found in specialized dictionaries, such as dictionaries of mathematics and other mathematical resources. Regardless, I prefer to start with the more lexical-type definitions of infinity in order to show what assumptions are typically made about infinity before proceeding to more technical ground.

All the same, the two definitions for infinity I supplied in natural language characterize quite well how the word 'infinity' is used, not only in colloquial speech but even in the specialized discourse of mathematics. Mathematicians do indeed assume infinity is a condition of being complete and yet limitless in quantity (the literal sense of infinity) or a condition of indefinite change in quantity (the figurative sense of infinity). Notice the *MathWorld* definition of infinity as "an unbounded quantity that is greater than every real number" can be interpreted either literally or figuratively. Perhaps infinity is a quantity "greater than every real number" because real numbers are inventions of which we can always make more, in which case 'infinity' is just a figure of speech. Or perhaps infinity is a quantity "greater than every real number" because real numbers are already in a complete set that is itself "unbounded" in the sense of being limitless. Even the technical definitions found in mathematics assume one or the other precising definition for infinity I supplied: literal infinity or figurative infinity.

Let's take a closer look at how infinity is defined with precision in natural language and defined technically in the formal language of mathematics. From there we will see further evidence for how the technical definitions found in mathematics assume, or sometimes imply, the precising definitions for infinity I have already provided. As we'll see, the precising definitions for literal infinity and figurative infinity may therefore be understood as applying across any of the various contexts in which the term 'infinity' is used with respect to quantities, whether those contexts are of colloquial or academic discourse.

7.2 ON LEXICAL AND TECHNICAL DEFINITIONS FOR INFINITY

Infinity is not explicitly defined in mathematics by lexical definitions so much as it is by technical definitions. Moreover, there are also different kinds of technical definitions. Two common types in science and mathematics are *theoretical definitions* and *operational definitions*.

A 'theoretical definition' explicates the specialized use of word according to a particular hypothesis or theory. For instance, the word 'intelligence' may be defined according to a particular theory of mind proposed in the field of psychology. That definition may differ from another theoretical definition for intelligence proposed in psychology. And both of those definitions may differ from another theoretical definition proposed in the field of computer science (as found in the more specialized discipline of artificial intelligence). Likewise, there are various theoretical definitions for infinity found in both general mathematics and the transfinite system.

In general mathematics, infinity may be theoretically defined according to the aforementioned *MathWorld* definition or with a similar definition, like this one: "A 'number' which indicates a quantity, size, or magnitude that is larger than any real number" [182]. If we turn to the transfinite system, we find infinity according to different theoretical definitions. Transfinite mathematics and set theory also have various theoretical definitions of infinity. For example, infinity can be theoretically defined as the ordinality of a sequence of elements, or cardinality of a set of elements, greater than that of any natural number in $\mathbb{N}$. [183].

Moreover, mathematics and science often add precision to theoretical definitions with 'operational definitions'. An operational definition explicates the *operations* (independently repeatable procedures, such as empirical tests or mathematical functions) that determine the conditions under which the word applies.

For example, a chemist may operationally define a functional group of molecular compounds, such as the acyl group, as a compound group "formed by removing one or more hydroxy groups from oxoacids" [184]. Typically, this is followed by a chemical formula showing the formation of the compound. Hence, if the chemical operation is performed, the compound results according to the definition. So, we have an example of an operational definition in the field of chemistry.

Mathematics too relies heavily on operational definitions for the words and terms it uses. We already saw examples of this back in § 5.3.5 with respect to the word 'finite'. We also find operational definitions for 'infinite' and its cognates in set theory and transfinite mathematics. For example, Dedekind operationally defined the term 'infinite' according to how a mathematician might determine whether a collection is infinite or not: "a set is infinite if it can be placed in one-to-one correspondence with a proper subset of itself" [185]. (What this definition means, and whether or not it makes sense is explored further in § 14.1.4, §§ 15.2.9–15.2.12, and § 16.8.3).

The point is that in mathematics there are various theoretical definitions for the word 'infinity' and various *operational* definitions for the term 'infinite' as expressed in formal language. In contrast, the definitions for literal and figurative infinity I have provided are *precising* (but still lexical) definitions articulated in ordinary, natural language—definitions expressing how the word 'infinity' is used in a general, colloquial sense with respect to quantities, regardless of specific mathematical contexts or operations.

Be that as it may, precising definitions are not necessarily so different from technical definitions that none of them ever apply when the technical definitions are assumed. Indeed, despite their non-technical nature, the precising definitions I offered for literal infinity and figurative infinity are assumed or implied by most mathematicians, even as they refer to infinity according to its technical definitions in the midst of engaging in mathematical procedures. The precising definitions for infinity are also assumed or implied by most scientists and other scholars in their writings, as well as by much of the lay public. So much so, that if anything is claimed to be "infinite" in a *literal* sense (regardless of a particular mathematical operation involved) without assuming it to be both complete and limitless in quantity, then the claim that it is infinite is false: it is not really 'infinite', at least not according to how infinity is conventionally thought of in a literal sense. Similarly, if anything is claimed to be "infinite" in its *figurative* sense (again, regardless of a particular mathematical operation involved) without assuming it has a finite quantity that ceaselessly or persistently grows, then the claim that it is infinite is false according to how infinity is used in its figurative sense.

7.3 ANSWERING OBJECTIONS TO LEXICAL DEFINITIONS FOR INFINITY

Some mathematicians might dismiss the lexical definitions of infinity as too crudely pre-theoretic to be of practical use in their discipline. For mathematicians, terms like 'infinity' must be technically defined or expressed in a way that allows them to be operationally used in functions, formulas, equations, and the like. It is true that the literal and figurative definitions I offered for infinity do not (at least, not without further explication) describe how infinity can be used for mathematical functions or other procedures. However, the definitions were not intended for that. Rather, lexical definitions for infinity are intended to capture only the *tacitly assumed or implied* literal and figurative *meanings* for the term 'infinity' and its related forms ('infinite', 'infinitely', etc.), *regardless of how the term is operationally used* in particular formulas and equations.

This is similar to how the word 'heat' can be lexically defined according to its usage in natural language, while that understanding of heat is still assumed regardless of how heat is theoretically defined in physics, chemistry, or engineering and regardless of how heat is measured in those disciplines.

Consider a lexical definition for heat:

- heat: (lexical definition) *the state of having or generating a relatively high degree of warmth* [186].

This definition contains a subjective term, 'warmth', and a very imprecise description—"relatively high degree"—so it is not scientifically useful.

To make the concept of heat more useful for conducting science, the term heat has been given various technical definitions. For example:

- heat: (technical definition) *the process of energy transfer from one body or system to another as a result of a difference in temperature* [187].

Or even more technically, according to theory:

- heat: (theoretical definition) *the transfer of energy from one body or system (a transmitter) to another (a receiver) that reduces the chaotic motion in the transmitter and raises it in the receiver.*

Both definitions talk of 'energy' and 'temperature'—technical and theoretical terms.

A prime example of 'heat' according to these definitions is a set of molecules chaotically bouncing off one another but then calming down as their *energy* is transferred to another set of molecules, which become more agitated as they receive the energy. Just think of boiling water in a pot cooling down (losing chaotic motion) as the steam released from the pot (a form of energy) on a suspended tray of ice above the pot then causes the water molecules in the ice to agitate (the molecules in the ice becoming more chaotic), and the ice melts as a result of this transfer in energy. This is one of the ways heat can be exchanged and there are a number of others. Heat can be exchanged radiantly, electrically, chemically, mechanically, and so on.

In each case of heat transfer, heat is measured by changes in the *temperature*—the average kinetic energy—of the sender (lowering) and the receiver (rising). And the measure of temperature is expressed according to various scales: Fahrenheit, Celsius, Kelvin, and so forth. A chemist can then use such scales to calculate the specific heat capacity of a metal, as given by equations such as the following [188]:

$$(125 \, \text{J})/(2.40 \, \text{g})(182 \, \text{K}) = 0.287 \, \text{J K–1 g–1}.$$

However, the way that heat is represented in this equation is not important for our purposes, nor is the means of its measurement, nor is the scale of measurement used. The important point is that regardless of how heat is *technically* defined according to a theory or how it is measured in physics, chemistry, and engineering, those technical definitions of heat and its measurement assume the truth of heat as *lexically* defined—the perception of having or generating a relatively high degree of warmth.

Moreover, the lexical definition of heat does not contradict the theoretical definition of heat. In fact, the theoretical definition was designed to explain the phenomenon of heat as something understood according to this lexical definition. Why are some things perceived as having or generating a relatively high degree of warmth (heat by its lexical definition)? Because they reduce their own chaotic motion and raise it in the receiver by transferring energy (heat by its theoretical definition). The technical definitions of heat thus assume the relevance and applicability of heat's lexical definition.

All of this is a useful analogy for how the word 'infinity' is able to retain the relevance and applicability of its lexical definition and even of its precising definitions (the definitions for literal infinity and figurative infinity) regardless of how infinity is mathematically represented and used.

When mathematicians speak of a polygon of infinite sides, they are assuming literal infinity. Hence, infinity retains its precising meaning as a state of completeness and limitlessness in quantity despite how that condition might be represented and expressed in various theoretical and operational definitions in mathematics, and regardless of the mathematical formulas and equations used to express infinity (we'll take a closer look at these in later chapters).

Similarly, when mathematicians speak of iterations going "to infinity," they often assume figurative infinity. Hence, infinity retains its precising meaning as a state of continuous change in quantity despite how change is represented or expressed in mathematical theories and operations (calculus functions, transfinite progressions, etc.).

So regardless of how infinity might be technically defined and expressed in the formal language of mathematics, even those so expressing infinity assume the accuracy of infinity conceived as literal infinity or figurative infinity according to the precising definitions given.

And yet, some mathematicians might object to the use of a lexical definition for infinity altogether, no matter how precise it is made in natural language. For instance, mathematician Tobias Dantzig (1884 – 1956) had remarked that terms such as "finite and infinite, real and imaginary" have for mathematicians "a quite specific and unambiguous meaning" while "to the philosopher who uses these terms as his stock and trade they have also a very specific but an entirely different meaning" [189]. Dantzig went on to say [190]:

> No difficulty arises until the philosopher makes an attempt to present to the lay public his analysis of the fundamental concepts of mathematics. It is then that the different connotations attaching to such words as infinity or reality lead to hopeless confusion the mind of the layman.

While Dantzig had a legitimate concern, it is not too difficult to overcome. As long as the philosopher is aware of how mathematicians use terms like 'finite', 'infinite', 'real', etc., in the technical contexts of their field, and does not misrepresent the technical use of these terms in mathematics, then the philosopher not only can accurately present the mathematical meanings of these terms to the public but also logically assess and critique the mathematical use of such terms. As we proceed, I'll do my best to distinguish where mathematicians assume various theoretical and operational definitions for infinity of which there are many peculiar to their trade.

Dantzig also overlooked that the various theoretical and operational definitions for terms used by mathematicians do not always logically conflict with the lexical definitions for the same terms in lay discourse, nor with more technical definitions found in other disciplines such as philosophy. In fact, mathematicians may tacitly assume a term's lexical definition even while using the term in the technical contexts of mathematics. The philosopher merely points out that this is the situation for infinity.

While engaging in certain mathematical procedures involving use of infinity as a term, mathematicians typically assume infinity according to one of two conceptions:

- Infinity is a condition of completeness and limitlessness in quantity—the definition of literal infinity, assumed in the transfinite system of mathematics.

Versus:

- Infinity is a condition of indefinitely changing in quantity—the figurative definition of infinity, assumed in general mathematics fields such as calculus.

Either precising meaning for 'infinity' may be tacitly assumed by mathematicians or implied by them, even while performing mathematical operations and functions, just as such lexical meanings are assumed or implied by non-specialists in everyday, colloquial speech.

7.4 INFINITY IN NATURAL AND FORMAL LANGUAGES

Technical disciplines like mathematics, symbolic logic, computer programming, physics, cosmology, etc. are known for their use of formal language, but even they must use natural language to articulate the meaning of mathematical terms expressed formally.

For example, let's go back to one of our examples of an expression in the formal language of mathematics that contains a reference to infinity. $n \rightarrow \omega$. This expression can be restated in natural language as, "The sequence of numbers represented by the letter 'n' tends to infinity." The natural language translation of the formal language expression captures the meaning of the formal language expression as a whole, while the natural language meanings for the expression's individual characters or terms are unstated and simply assumed or implied. So, the phrase "tends to infinity" is a natural language translation of '$\rightarrow \infty$', in which the meaning of 'infinity' is simply assumed or implied.

When infinity as $\aleph$, ω, or ∞ is used in the formal language of mathematics, infinity is assumed to have the meaning of some technical definition, like the technical definitions shown in previous examples. In the expression $n \rightarrow \infty$, the symbol of infinity has a theoretical definition: *a quantity greater than any finite number*. However, formal language expressions involving infinity, while assuming theoretic or operational definitions, also tacitly imply one of the precising definitions for infinity. So the use of infinity in the expression $n \rightarrow \infty$ can be intended to imply either literal infinity (since to be "greater than any finite number" the sequence of elements in n may be taken as 'limitless' and 'complete' in quantity) or figurative infinity (if we take "greater than any finite number" to mean the ongoing construction of n as a *series* of values that will surpass the value of any finite number we think up at a given time, though the series as such is not really complete at any time and not literally limitless at any time). The theoretical or operational definitions assumed for infinity during its use in the formal language of mathematics thus still imply one of the precising definitions as well.

Nevertheless, some mathematicians resist any lexical definition for literal infinity by pointing out that there are many different kinds of infinity used in mathematics, each having a different definition. As noted earlier, the symbols for infinity ($\aleph$, ω, ∞) all represent infinity according to different technical definitions (infinity in terms of cardinality, ordinality, function, etc.) relative to their operational uses in the formal language of mathematics. But these "different kinds of infinity" are actually just different ways of *ascribing the property of infinity as the term is commonly used* to different mathematical operations, collections, or numbers. The different ways of ascribing infinity all imply infinity to be either a quantitatively complete-yet-limitless property (literal infinity) or an indefinitely changing process (figurative infinity). There are various symbols and technical definitions for infinity that are used for various mathematical operations and procedures, but their use all still assumes the same literal and figurative meanings according to infinity's precising definitions (again, similar to how the theoretical definition for heat has the same underlying meaning in physics despite the different ways to measure it).

Consider, for instance, the ongoing construction of a sequence of numbers as represented in the formal language of mathematics [191]:

$$f(0) = 1, f(1) = 2, f(2) = 4, \ldots$$

Here too mathematicians may represent the sequence with an expression such as $n \rightarrow \infty$. In more technical terms, the expression means that the nth member in the series is 2^n and is said to "tend to infinity" as n "tends to infinity." What the expression "tends to infinity" means is up to the mathematician: it can imply either the literal or figurative meaning of infinity regardless of the details of the mathematical operation the expression is used to describe.

If we take "tends to infinity" literally, then the expression basically means that if the entire sequence of numbers ever becomes *complete*, the numbers in the sequence become *limitless* in quantity; or, if the sequence *is* actually complete, then the numbers in the sequence *are* actually limitless in quantity. This is how the definition of literal infinity may be assumed or implied in the mathematical expression $n \rightarrow \infty$ and similar expressions [192].

On the other hand, if we take "tends to infinity" figuratively, then the expression means that the sequence of numbers represented by the letter 'n' *continuously changes in the quantity of its members, without a defined end*. This is only figuratively 'infinite' because the sequence always has a highest number generated at any time, and that highest number means the sequence is actually limited rather than limitless, even as new numbers are generated for the sequence.

Once again, we see that ∞ in the mathematical operation $n \rightarrow \infty$ refers to infinity but that "infinity" can be interpreted as either literal or figurative infinity, quite independently of how the operation works. The formal language expression of $n \rightarrow \infty$ can be translated into natural language as "the value of n tends to infinity," where infinity is either assumed or implied to be literal or figurative infinity, depending on the wishes of the mathematician.

There are other examples we can draw on as well. For instance, an equation in *projective geometry* such as this:

$$a\alpha + b\beta + c\gamma = 0$$

Wherein, $\alpha : \beta : \gamma$ are *trilinear* coordinates that represent the intersection of parallel lines on a *point at infinity* [193]. Here too the reference to 'infinity' in the expression "point at infinity" can be taken either literally or figuratively.

If we take the expression "point at infinity" literally, as it most often is in projective geometry, then it is implied that the parallel lines of the coordinates eventually meet at a point, the complete distance to which is *limitlessly far away*. The complete-though-limitless condition of these lines is an instance of infinity in its literal sense.

Some might object that in projective geometry the formal language does not really capture limitlessness, but only *indefiniteness* of extension. On the other hand, to say there is a point "at" infinity sounds like a particular distance toward which there is a completed progression. So, despite how infinity is technically represented in the formal language of geometrical expressions, the infinity of the formal language may still be assumed or implied to *mean* a quantitative condition of completeness and limitlessness—literal infinity.

Alternatively, because the formal language of geometry is really only indefiniteness in operation, we might instead take the notion of a "point at infinity" figuratively, as it is in ordinary geometry. In which case, extending the lines to a "point at infinity" simply means that no matter what value the coordinates are given, no matter how far we extend the lines, they never actually meet. To say the lines converge with a point at infinity would then be to use 'infinity' in its figurative sense as implying that we can continuously change the length of the lines, extending them ever further, and they are never brought to a point at which they meet—not even one limitlessly far away. Rather, the lines simply continue without intersecting. Again, this is only 'infinity' in a figurative sense because the extension of the lines is always limited no matter how far we make them reach or what values we give to the coordinates. The procedure of constructing the lines continues, but there is always a limit to the lines that have been constructed at each step of the way.

Therefore, the formal language expression $a\alpha + b\beta + c\gamma = 0$ for the convergence of parallel lines has a natural language translation as, "The three parallel lines with the distances a, b, and c converge to a point at infinity," and this translation in turn the mathematician either assumes or implies to be infinity according to either the literal or figurative sense. The figurative sense better fits the operations of geometry, which stresses the relative limitlessness of the lines but not their completeness. Arguably, the literal sense fits the operations of projective geometry, which at least partially seems to suggest the completeness of lines extended indefinitely in mathematical operation. But the choice as to which sense of infinity applies all depends on the intent of the mathematician making the expression or on the interpretation of the mathematician in construing the expression.

We can similarly translate other formal language expressions containing infinity into natural language and again find in each case that infinity can be meant either literally or figuratively according to the precising definitions. Some of these expressions include formal language representations for infinite sets like,

$$|2^\omega| = \aleph_1$$

and representations of infinite amounts summed,

$$\infty + \infty = \infty$$

and infinite products,

$$\prod_{i=1}^{\infty} a_i$$

and infinite accessions,

$$\sum_{i=0}^{\infty} a_i$$

and so on. In each formal language expression, use of the term 'infinity' can be assumed or implied to be infinity by either the literal or figurative definition (depending on the intent of the mathematician) when the natural language translation of the expression is made.

Regardless of how it is symbolically represented or used in calculation, infinity thus has the same underlying meaning. Even though different mathematical expressions may use different kinds of numbers that are manipulated by different rules, the expressions all have in common that representations of infinity, when translated into natural language, imply either infinity's literal meaning (complete and yet limitless in quantity) or its figurative meaning (continuously changing in quantity). Whichever of these meanings for infinity is implied depends only on the assumptions or intent of the individual mathematician making the given expression.

As to the various definitions of infinity stipulated in mathematics textbooks and dictionaries, these theoretical and operational definitions typically describe either how infinity is used in particular procedures (like extrapolating to a 'point at infinity') or what procedures can be used to determine whether something is infinite or not (like being able to pair off one-for-one all of a given set's elements with some proper subset of its elements). Such theoretic and operational definitions in the field of mathematics do not contradict my thesis that there can be articulated lexical definitions for infinity, the meanings of which most technical definitions and uses in formal language assume or imply by their natural language translations.

The precising definitions provided for literal and figurative infinity express what the concept of infinity itself is assumed or implied to mean, regardless of the details in any particular mathematical procedure referencing infinity. All of the usual mathematical expressions involving infinity, where presented either in symbolic notation or in verbal definition, fit infinity's literal and figurative senses as I have articulated them. Mathematicians who see the natural language definition of literal infinity as of no relevance are in fact *assuming it in the very way they speak of infinity*. To say there is a "point at infinity" or that something goes "to infinity" or that there is "infinitely many" of something are all verbal expressions that typically (though not always) mean literal infinity. On the other hand, if the mathematical operation said to be "infinite" is a process imagined to ceaselessly continue without reaching an end, then that idea of 'infinite' fits the definition of figurative infinity. In which case, the mathematician is still assuming an ordinary, natural language definition for infinity is as pertinent as any technical definition.

I shall therefore maintain that the precising definitions for literal infinity and figurative infinity represent well how the term infinity is conventionally used, even by mathematicians and scientists using formal language, because expressions in formal language can be translated into natural language, where a choice of infinity's precising definitions apply.

CHAPTER 7 IN REVIEW

❖ Infinity has lexical and precising definitions in natural language and technical definitions in the formal language of mathematics.

❖ The precising definitions for infinity capture the literal and figurative meanings of infinity in its quantitative sense, and these neither contradict nor imply the technical definitions and operational uses of infinity in mathematics.

❖ Just as the lexical definition of heat (as the state of having or generating a relatively high degree of warmth) may be assumed or implied regardless of how heat is technically defined and measured in the sciences, so too the lexical or precising definitions for infinity may be assumed or implied regardless of how infinity is technically defined or expressed in the formal language or mathematics.

❖ Use of the symbols for infinity ($\aleph$, ω, ∞) in equations all presuppose either the literal or figurative sense of quantitative infinity.

PART II:
ON LITERAL INFINITY

8: THE STORY OF LITERAL INFINITY

Infinity is "the condition of being complete and limitless in quantity." However, it should be emphasized that historical scholars never defined infinity with this exact phrasing. Even so, I do believe the definition correctly articulates the meaning of the word 'infinity' as the concept of infinity has been passed down through the ages, at least in its literal sense with respect to quantity. In Chapter 23 we will examine infinity according to its primary figurative sense, another version of quantitative infinity, and in Chapter 25 we will examine qualitative and absolute infinity, which are theological versions of infinity. But literal infinity I take to be the main sense of what infinity has been about from ancient to contemporary times.

8.1 INFINITY FROM PAST TO PRESENT

The earliest conception of infinity dates back to around 600 Before the Common Era (BCE). It's unclear who first proposed the idea of infinity. Depending on when the *Isa Upanishad* of the *Yajurveda* was written (which most scholars believe originated somewhere between 1,000 and 600 BCE), the concept of infinity may have originated in India. However, most scholars attribute the origin of the concept of infinity to the ancient Greeks of around the same time period.

The ancient Greeks used the term *apeiron* (ἄπειρον, pronounced in English as "ă-**peer**-on") for the condition of being endless, boundless, indefinite, or without quantitative limit. It was a term applied for quantities that had at least the *appearance* of no limit in measure, and so apeiron is usually translated as infinity. The variant *to apeiron* means 'the infinite', though the English adjective 'infinite' is usually the translation for the Greek cognate *apeiros*, which is also a Greek word sometimes used to indicate a condition of being quantitatively or qualitatively 'indefinite' [194].

Strictly speaking, apeiron applies to anything that has no end of a given kind even though it is limited in other respects. For example, the ancient Greeks described a circle as an instance of apeiron in terms of its curvature even though it is limited in diameter. The term 'apeiron' (more precisely, apeiros) was also used for what we would call 'indefinite' or 'indeterminate' since such things appear to be without limit to measurement even though they are really finite.

For example, apeiron was applied to what we would today refer to as a *fractal*, a term designating any shape comprised of self-similar patterns repeating across scales, like the spiral pattern of a seashell, or a shape made up of irregularities in structure, such as the boundary of a coastline or the surface of a crumpled cloth. Any instance of a fractal shape that we find in nature, like a seashell or a coastline, is limited in size but the shape will be hard to define with precision and, in principle, the fractal pattern can be constructed with no predefined end; fractals are in that sense 'indefinite' or, as the Greeks would have said, apeiros—without any apparent limit in measure.

The ancient Greeks thus regarded anything indeterminate—either due to being disorderly or due to being unmanageably complicated—as an instance of apeiron. They came to apply the concept of apeiron not only to closed curves or fractal objects but also to quantities that were so large as to be incapable of exact determination, quantities so large they can't be defined with known numbers—collective indefinites. Then too, in some contexts, the ancient Greeks used the term 'apeiron' to describe something finite as having unknown and changing limits that we cannot in practice measure—in other words, serial indefinites.

In other contexts, apeiron referred to that which is not just indefinite *in practice* but even *in principle*; that is, having absolutely no definable limit to the whole, entire, finished, and full amount. Which is to say, a quantity of members that cannot be defined because it is limitless even while being complete, as is. Hence, apeiron applied to what most English-speaking folks today call 'infinite' in the literal sense of the term.

8.1.1 *Infinity According to Anaximander*

The earliest known references to apeiron are from the philosopher Anaximander (610–546 BCE). In the philosophy of Anaximander, apeiron was the quantitatively complete and limitless state of the 'arche' (ἀρχή, pronounced "**ahr**-see"), the stuff out of which everything is made. Anaximander also held the arche to be the 'physis' (φύσις, pronounced "**fī**-seez")—the natural, prime cause of the Universe's existence [195] [196]. He further proposed the arche to be an instance of apeiron—that is, the arche is literally infinite, both as the fundamental element of reality and as the 'prime cause' of the Universe's existence [197]. Since the arche is the fundamental stuff of which everything is made, Anaximander also attributed apeiron, as the property of being literally infinite, to the Universe as a whole since the arche encompasses all (the complete quantity of) worlds that exist throughout space and time. And since Anaximander held the arche, and consequently the Universe, to be literally infinite, Anaximander named the arche *Infinity* (i.e., *the Infinite*—or in Greek, *the Apeiron* (τὸ ἄπειρον) [198].

That Anaximander knew about, and used, the concept of literal infinity would be considered controversial according to some modern scholars. It is sometimes claimed that ancient Greek thinkers sought to avoid the idea that some quantities might be literally infinite—both complete and limitless— since they did not have a mathematics of the infinite. But this is not entirely true since it confuses infinity as a quantitative concept *per se* with infinity as a quantitative concept *used in mathematical operation*.

It is true that early Greek mathematicians and philosophers like Anaximander proposed no mathematical operations using infinity in the literal sense of the term, and so did not apply literal infinity to geometrical measurements or add various infinite collections together. However, it is the opinion of some translators of ancient texts that many ancient Greeks, in using the Greek words ἄπειροι or ἄπειρον (apeiron as 'infinite' or 'infinity'), often implied a literally complete and limitless condition for multitudes of coexisting elements rather than simply a state of (finite) indefiniteness or indeterminateness.

Support for this interpretation of apeiron's meaning can be found in the work of a scholar of ancient Greek philosophy—John Burnet. He argued that what I have termed 'literal infinity' is implied by ἄπειροι or ἄπειρον, as used in the works not only of Anaximander but of other ancient philosophers such as Anaximenes (585–528 BCE). Burnet states that when Anaximander and Anaximenes described the magnitude of the primal substance from which all the worlds of the Universe appeared, their use of the term 'apeiron' meant literal infinity.

As Burnet explained [199]:

> We must picture, then, an endless mass…stretching out without limit on every side of the world we live in. This mass is a body, out of which our world once emerged, and into which it will one day be absorbed again…
>
> …I have assumed that the word ἄπειρον means *spatially infinite*, not *qualitatively indeterminate*, as maintained by Teichmüller and Tannery…the primary substance of Anaximander was ἄπειρον and contained all the worlds, and the word περιέχειν everywhere means "to encompass," not, as has been suggested, "to contain potentially."

If Burnet is correct, then even as far back as Anaximander, infinity was regarded in a literal sense as a condition of completeness and limitlessness that applied to multitudes (quantities) such as the multitude of worlds throughout the Universe. They may not have had the mathematical tools to calculate infinite sets, but they had a notion of what it would mean to be literally infinite.

8.1.2 *Zeno and Infinity*

It took another hundred years after Anaximander for philosophers to propose that infinity had logical implications for geometry and the measurement of collections in nature. The philosopher Zeno of Elea (490–430 BCE), for instance, applied the concept of (literal) infinity to finite portions of space and time.

Zeno was among the first to propose that any finite measure of distance (like the length of a stadium) contains a literally infinite quantity of points, that any finite measure of duration (like the time it takes to run the diameter of the stadium) contains a literally infinite quantity of *instants*, and that all finite measures are themselves part of a literally infinite magnitude [200]. Some scholars misinterpret Zeno as believing *only* in figurative infinity and not in literal infinity, but if Zeno had no conception of literal infinity, his famous paradoxes involving motion through infinite quantities of points in space and instants in time would have been much ado about nothing. (We will take a closer look at one of Zeno's paradoxes in Chapter 20.)

As with his contemporaries, Zeno did not propose calculations directly involving literal infinity, like adding infinite sets together. Mathematical operations involving literal infinity did not occur to the scholars of this day; they considered literal infinities to be beyond any direct calculation. At best, mathematics could only indirectly imply the literally infinite with figuratively infinite (indefinite) progressions. However, Zeno did make use of figuratively infinite progressions, like dividing a line in half, then dividing one of the half-lines in half again, and repeating this process indefinitely. He used such figuratively infinite progressions to imply the existence of literally infinite magnitudes. Literal infinity was assumed to be implied by our potential to carry out operations "without limit"—that is, implied by our potential to carry out operations either indefinitely ("without limit" in a figurative sense) or without any limit at all. If we could at least in principle ceaselessly carry out a mathematical operation like dividing a line into ever smaller units, this potential was thought to imply the existence of a literally infinite number of points making up the line. Zeno thus understood very well what infinity meant in its literal sense.

I therefore maintain with Burnet the interpretation that the ancients commonly regarded infinity as a literally complete and limitless condition of multitudes or collections. It may be that they simply had no conceptual tools to directly manipulate or calculate literally infinite collections with mathematical operations or functions; so instead, they relied on figuratively "infinite" progressions as a means to logically imply the literally infinite.

8.1.3 *Socrates and Plato Had a Different Take on Infinity*

However, the foregoing does not mean the ancients were unanimous in their convictions as to how infinity, or apeiron, should be regarded. Some ancient philosophers used apeiron to mean *only* a condition that is indefinite or indeterminate (figuratively infinite when applied to processes or sequences) rather than a condition that is complete and limitless in quantity (literally infinite). However, the writings of Plato (427–347 BCE) recorded that Socrates (~469–399 BCE) used the term 'apeiron' or 'infinity' to clearly mean literal infinity when he discussed multitudes and the diversity of things that we see in the world around us. In Plato's *Theaetetus*, Socrates speaks of an "infinite multitude" of motions and an "infinite number" of unnamed perceptions humans possess [201]. Socrates made many other references to literal infinity, such as those depicted in Plato's work *Philebus* [202]. Nevertheless, Plato, the star pupil of Socrates, believed literal infinity belongs only to the 'world of appearances' and not to the 'real world' of mathematical Forms beyond our sensory perceptions (see §§ 16.2.2–16.2.3 and § 16.2.6) [203] [204].

8.1.4 *Aristotle's Potential Infinity and Actual Infinity*

It was Aristotle (384–322 BCE) who explicitly distinguished between the two different senses of quantitative infinity. Aristotle coined the terms *actual infinity* and *potential infinity*. In Aristotle's view, the Universe was never created. So, the past contains, in some sense, an actually infinite collection of events that have already elapsed. All other infinities, including the "infinity" of future events, are *only* "potentials" [205]. In our terminology, Aristotle's position would seem to imply that the past is literally infinite while the future is only figuratively infinite (though he may have been using the term 'actual' in a slippery way—a subject we will return to in § 23.1).

Like his predecessors, Aristotle had no mathematical means of operating with literal infinity, such as adding two literally infinite sets together to produce totals of infinite sets, but his distinction between actual and potential infinity shows that he did conceive of actual infinity as a quantitative condition that is literally complete and limitless.

Aristotle did not really invent the concept of infinity in its literal sense as a complete but limitless quantity. Instead, Aristotle explicated one of the common uses of the term 'apeiron' or 'infinity' by giving it a more formal name—actual infinity—and explaining its use in contrast to another common usage of the term—which he called potential infinity—where no one had explicitly made this distinction before.

Likewise, it is also not the case that Aristotle invented use of the term 'apeiron' or 'infinity' in reference to processes that continue indefinitely while always remaining finite. Infinity was already commonly used according to these two senses—on the one hand, to mean that which is complete and limitless in quantity (literal infinity) and, on the other hand, to mean that which is indefinite but not literally complete and limitless (figurative infinity).

What Aristotle accomplished was to categorize and point out the differences between the two colloquial uses of infinity or 'apeiron' by distinguishing indefiniteness as a condition that could go on accumulating but is never complete at any given time (his 'potential infinity' and what we should call figurative infinity) from a condition of being complete but also limitless (literal infinity, or in his parlance 'actual infinity'). So, it's not that these concepts were invented with Aristotle; rather, they were simply not labeled or addressed until Aristotle formally named and attempted to explicate and define them [206]. (However, as I will argue in § 23.1, Aristotle's use of the terms 'actual' and 'potential' in application to infinity was misleading and led his analysis astray; he should have used 'literal' and 'figurative' instead.)

It's been commonly thought that, even after Aristotle, ancient mathematicians sought to avoid use of literal infinity (or actual infinity) in favor of a figurative notion of infinity (or potential infinity). However, that is rather misleading. While Aristotle's influence predominated among the intellectual elite writing on matters pertaining to infinity from ancient through medieval times, it's also true that we find examples of literal infinity referenced in the ancient world and on into later centuries.

8.1.5 *Euclid's Conception of Infinity*

A good example of another figure in the ancient world making use of literal infinity is the mathematician Euclid (325–265 BCE), who implied literal infinity to be a quantitatively complete and limitless condition for certain collections of objects and expanses of space. Some scholars, however, have argued that Euclid had no notion of literal infinity because he too had no mathematical operations—no algebra, calculus, or transfinite math—for dealing with literal infinity. Mathematician Samuel T. Sanders (1872–1970), for example, proposed that Euclid's concept of parallel lines as extending "to infinity" is simply a figurative way of saying lines are "indefinitely extensible" [207]. According to Sanders, Euclid was positing only figurative infinity. But contrary to those who believe that Euclid knew nothing of literal infinity or sought to avoid it, Euclid's writings do not state infinity to be only figurative [208]. The argument that Euclid regarded infinity to be only figurative is based more on what Euclid did not say—he did not claim to actually calculate the literally infinite—rather than anything he did say.

In some passages of his book *Elements*, Euclid talks of "producing" parallel lines to infinity where the production of the lines can only be carried "to infinity" in a figurative sense [209]. However, Euclid also says that "there exist an infinite multitude" of lines as if the infinitude of lines is already there waiting to be discovered [210]. I take it that Euclid thought the figurative infinity of lines we produce in mathematical operation implies a literal infinity of lines out there in a Platonic world waiting to be approximated by our constructions. To carry out a process of extending lines "infinitely" may be figurative, but the lines also go "to infinity" in the sense that there is a literal infinity that the lines are reaching for.

Euclid thus may have assumed literal infinity is logically implied by his figuratively infinite *method of exhaustion* [211]. This method could be used as a means of calculating the area of a shape, like the area of a circle, by exhaustively pursuing ever closer approximations to the shape [212]. For instance, one might keep adding sides to a polygon until the sides together become indistinguishable from the closed curve of a circle. According to Euclid's method of exhaustion, if we examine the area of the polygon closely, we will find it never quite matches the area of a circle, no matter how long we keep adding sides; we would become exhausted from trying to approximate a circle—hence the name of the method. Euclid realized his method of exhaustion was inadequate for producing a literally infinite multitude of sides. At best, his method of exhaustion shows only that geometrical figures can be ceaselessly constructed (figurative infinity). Nevertheless, Euclid seems to have regarded the circle as a polygon with a literally infinite number of sides and used his method of exhaustion as an analogy to demonstrate this, [213] an idea later supported by the ancient mathematician Archimedes (287–212 BCE). The idea was that if one could overcome exhaustion with godlike energy, one could create a polygon with infinitely many sides—a perfect circle; but alas we are not like the gods.

8.1.6 *Archimedes Reckons Infinity*

We find an even clearer example of literal infinity in *The Sand Reckoner* by Archimedes: "There are some, King Gelon, who think that the number of the sand is infinite in multitude" [214]. This statement is clearly a reference to the concept of literal infinity since "the sand" is a collection of components—individual grains of sand—existing together all at once. Archimedes does not use Aristotle's "actual infinity" and does not reference Aristotle at all in *The Sand Reckoner*. He simply takes it for granted that infinity is thought of as complete and limitless in quantity. In fact, Archimedes contrasts an infinite collection with one that is finite but indefinitely large in count. Archimedes states, "Again there are some who, without regarding [the quantity of grains of sand in the world] as infinite, yet think that no number has been named which is great enough to exceed its multitude" [215]. This is clearly a contrast of literal infinity with a condition of indefiniteness that characterizes figurative infinity. Scholars have even discovered that Archimedes not only knew of literal infinity but made some use of the concept in his mathematical writings (though nothing with the rigor of algebra, calculus, or transfinite mathematics) [216].

8.1.7 *Infinity Becomes Operational*

All of the foregoing examples illustrate that the notion of infinity as a complete and limitless quantity goes all the way back to Anaximander's time, maybe even earlier. Moreover, the use of literal infinity in quantitative thought experiments (from Zeno to Aristotle) and mathematics (Archimedes) even predates the invention of algebra and textbook calculus by over 1,800 years.

During the Medieval Period, or Middle Ages (5th to 15th Centuries), Aristotle's philosophy became popular among Christian theologians, and so his motto, *Infinitum actu non datur* (i.e., *There is no actual infinity*), held sway with the majority of mathematicians and philosophers in Europe in that time. You might recall, though, that Aristotle believed the past to be in some way an 'actual infinite', so his motto clearly shows an internal inconsistency on the subject (see § 23.1 for more). Regardless, the motto is how Aristotle was commonly understood in the Medieval Period, as shown in the writings of the theologian Thomas Aquinas (1225–1274), who acknowledged infinity according to Aristotle's distinctions of 'potential infinity' and 'actual infinity', denying that actual infinity exists and championing potential infinity as the infinities found in mathematics and physics [217].

Notice that in order for Aristotle's followers to *deny* that infinity can be literally complete and limitless just goes to show that the scholars of the time indeed knew what 'infinity' commonly means in its literal sense, according to its ordinary language usage. Moreover, despite that Aristotle's inconsistent motto was widely held among medieval scholars, there were nevertheless mathematicians and philosophers even in that period of time that championed the notion of literal infinity (for example, 13th Century scholar Robert Grosseteste and 14th Century scholars Gregory of Rimini and Gersonides) [218]. The work of those scholars did not catch on with respect to mathematical use, however, and so literal infinity remained regarded in European academia, through the Medieval Period until at least the 16th Century, as unusable in mathematical calculation, even though literal infinity is nevertheless a quantitative concept.

In the 16th Century, mathematicians then began using literal infinity not just as a quantitative concept but also as a 'mathematical concept' in the sense of working with infinity in numerical functions and operations the way it is in algebra and calculus today. Nevertheless, even during the 1700s, while mathematicians held that some collections (sequences, series, sets, etc.) have a condition of being complete and limitless in their quantity of elements, it was still the case that literally infinite collections could not be calculated in mathematics in a way that could give definite results without contradiction. At best, when literal infinity was dealt with in mathematics, it was treated only as the *implication* of "irrational" progressions (like 3.14159…); figuratively infinite operations were held to imply literally infinite conditions that could not be represented by a definite result. This much had not changed since Euclid's time.

In the 17th and 18th Centuries, the renowned scientist Isaac Newton (1642–1727) and the lesser renowned philosopher Gottfried Leibniz (1646–1716) independently reinvented calculus (it was first invented in medieval India) and further developed it into its modern form [219]. During this time, algebra was also further developed from its medieval Islamic roots. With the refinement of algebra and calculus, the situation changed somewhat, particularly in Europe: infinity became more widely recognized as usable in math to generate definite results [220]. For example, mathematicians created functions of calculus for using ∞ to produce numbers "converging" to 0 (figurative infinity) and most mathematicians assumed that ∞ implied a literal infinity of values between 0 and 1. But since the use of ∞ was, *operationally* speaking, 'infinity' only in the figurative sense, there was even by the 17th Century no method to calculate literal infinities in a direct and unambiguous manner.

This is not to say that literal infinity had no reference in mathematics. Even if literal infinity was not a concept used for making calculations in any direct manner, it was still something mathematicians thought was *implied* or connoted by operations carried out in a figuratively infinite fashion. Newton clearly assumed a geometrical line has a literally infinite number of *infinitesimals*, though he had no method for calculating them. Newton said such 'infinitesimals' could not be "distinguished" or "attended to." So, he instead posited 'fluents' (minuscule, yet finite, units of motion) that operated at a speed he called a 'fluxion' (an ephemeral, yet finite, rate) as the basis for constructing lines, planes, etc. for use in calculus [221]. Newton's fluents and fluxions did not catch on; instead, it was the calculus of Newton's rival Leibniz that would prove more influential. And yet, even Leibniz could not offer an entirely coherent calculus for dealing with literal infinity in a direct manner.

The functions of calculus only produced indefinite—figuratively 'infinite'—progressions that mathematicians regarded, at best, as pointing to literal infinity; there were still no mathematical operations to *directly* calculate literally infinite collections. It was not for lack of trying, however. Leibniz, for one, stated he was "totally in favor of actual infinity…" even if he had no idea how to calculate it [222]. (Though, as we will see in § 23.4.1, what he meant by 'actual infinity' may be misleading.) Mathematicians recognized their inability to directly use literal, or actual, infinity in mathematics until Bolzano proposed a system that attempted to directly calculate literal infinities [223].

This overview of infinity throughout history shows that, while it is true we have no evidence of mathematical treatments of literal infinity that allowed the concept to be (at least seemingly) used in calculations until a posthumous publication of Bolzano's work (1851), and certainly nothing rigorous until the work of Cantor (published in 1874), that does not mean literal infinity as a quantitative concept was not widely known prior to the 1800s. Philosophers, scientists, scholars, and the educated portions of the public throughout the centuries since Anaximander had the concept that 'infinity' referred to a condition of being limitless in quantity and yet also, in some sense, complete. It's simply that until the work of Bolzano and Cantor literal infinity had no technical definition as a counterpart that could be used in mathematical operations and functions. So even though mathematicians prior to the 17th and 18th Centuries did not have our current mathematical methods for manipulating 'infinities', this fact does not mean the literal meaning of infinity was not commonly assumed; it only means literal infinity was not regarded as calculable until the right methods were invented [224].

8.1.8 *False Claims to Orthodoxy on Infinity*

Literal infinity is a concept that has been around since Anaximander. And its logical coherence has been largely (but not entirely) unquestioned. Most of the skepticism regarding literal infinity came not from philosophers charging it with *logically* contradictory meaning, though there were a few who did (§ 23.2.3

and § 23.3.1 for details). Rather, most of the skepticism about the literally infinite came from those mathematicians, following in the tradition of Aristotle, who believed that literal infinity could not be used in *mathematical* operations without contradiction.

Due to the intractability of calculating literal infinities, mathematician Carl Friedrich Gauss (1777–1855), in a 12 July 1831 letter to astronomer Heinrich Christian Schumacher, stated his position that 'infinity' is only a figure of speech and not to be taken literally in mathematics [225]. Gauss did not say that, as a quantitative condition of completeness and limitlessness, literal infinity was illogical. Rather, he only indicated that 'infinity', taken literally, couldn't be used in mathematics with any precision and should therefore be regarded as only a figurative notion, like Aristotle's 'potential infinity'.

However, it seems many mathematicians understood the operations of algebra and functions of calculus as nevertheless implying literal infinity. This is seen some twenty years later when Bolzano in his *Paradoxes of the Infinite* stated that literal infinity is the commonly accepted implication of our ability to plot a figuratively infinite series of points along a line or index a figuratively infinite series of instants between any two moments of time [226]. Our ability to plot points or index instants only until exhaustion implies, in Bolzano's view, that there is already embedded in lines a literally infinite number of points to plot and there is already situated between any two moments a literally infinite number of instants to index. Bolzano assumed this was the common opinion among mathematicians [227]. He said that there is "scarcely any mathematician" who would deny literal infinities, like infinitely many points in a line segment, are mathematical realities and instead hold that infinities don't really exist but are instead only figuratively implied by mathematical calculations [228]. Bolzano claimed that being literally complete and limitless was implied by the concept of infinity and that this was the accepted norm among mathematicians, rejected only by "opponents of *all* infinity" (such as myself) whom in Bolzano's day proposed we should keep using the term 'infinite' as a figure of speech (like Gauss, but unlike myself) [229].

What Bolzano's contradiction of Gauss's view on the proper use of infinity shows is that literal infinity was indeed commonly understood to be a condition of completeness and limitlessness in quantity, as endless divisions or additions of numbers were often assumed to imply. It was simply due to the mathematical intractability of making literal infinity into anything more rigorous than an indirect implication that some scholars, such as Gauss, falsely claimed orthodoxy in their take on infinity as only a figurative notion while either implying or claiming that those not holding their view are the heretics. As the writings of Bolzano indicate, such claims to orthodoxy do not necessarily represent the common view. It appears then, there was an intellectual battle among mathematicians to establish an orthodoxy regarding how infinity *should* be considered—as literal or as figurative—a battle that had been quietly going on in academia for hundreds of years.

A little over twenty years after Bolzano's publications, Cantor took the side of Gauss insofar as agreeing that infinity is typically considered to be a figure of speech—at least, among mathematicians. And perhaps the majority opinion on the subject among mathematicians did vacillate from one decade or century to another. In any case, Cantor's view flew in direct contradiction to Bolzano's claim that scarcely any mathematician would make infinity solely figurative. But by the time of Cantor's career, perhaps opinion on the nature of infinity was beginning to favor Gauss's view, at least among academics practicing professional mathematics.

8.1.9 *Rise of the Transfinite System*

Despite the fluctuating consensus that infinity should only be thought of as a figurative notion, Cantor wanted to overthrow Gauss's popular position on the matter. Not only did Cantor believe literal infinity to be a logical concept, but he also sided with Bolzano in belief that the concept of literal infinity could be used in mathematical operations.

In the late 1800s, Cantor published his first work on the transfinite system [230], making direct use of literal infinities in calculations with the use of new symbols for literally infinite sets: ω and $\aleph$. Cantor distinguished his own procedures for calculating with literally infinite sets (what he called "proper infinities") from the operations used for infinite sequences and series in general mathematics, which Cantor claimed, like Gauss, are only for figurative (or "improper") infinities. In an 1871 paper, Cantor represented literal infinity by the symbol ∞ but by 1874 he was instead using ω for that purpose; the lemniscate (∞) and related symbols he began using more often as a representation for figurative infinity [231].

Essentially, Cantor's transfinite system interprets infinity to be literal while allowing infinity to be regarded as either figurative or literal in general mathematics. Mathematicians today largely side with Cantor on this interpretation, which is why they now often claim that ∞ should be taken as representing only figurative infinity while $\aleph$ and ω represent literal infinity. As shown previously, this dichotomy does not always hold in actual mathematical practice, however, as ∞ is sometimes taken quite literally even in algebra and calculus.

8.1.10 *Literal Infinity from Past to Present*

Table 2 depicts the views on infinity held by a sample of mathematicians, scientists, and philosophers from over the centuries [232]. Though the samples given in **Table 2** are, for the sake of brevity, far from comprehensive, they nevertheless represent what some of the major scholars have had to say about infinity up to the present. For convenience, I have paraphrased the statements of many scholars in the list to distill their positions on infinity, while all quotes are from their original works, or translations of them. As the table shows, each listed scholar has made statements that assume infinity to be a condition of both completeness and limitlessness in quantity.

That is not to say that all of the listed scholars believe that something quantitatively infinite in the literal sense of 'infinity' actually exists in the real, physical world (Thomas Aquinas, for example, did not). It's just to say that they all *recognize* what it *means* to be quantitatively infinite in the *literal* sense of the term.

It's also not to say that all the scholars listed in the table used *only* the concept of literal infinity. Some instead used the term 'infinity' or its cognates ('infinite', 'infinitely', etc.) in a variety of senses, including the figurative sense. And some—for example, Aquinas and Cantor—believed in types of infinity that were not purely quantitative. Aquinas believed not only in figurative ('potential') infinity but also a version of qualitative infinity. Cantor believed not only in literal ('actual' or 'proper') infinity and in the qualitative infinity of God's intellect, but he also went further, proposing that God has the attribute of *absolutely infinite totality* which Cantor referred to as "the absolute" [233] [234]. Chapter 23 will review what the major historical figures thought regarding figurative infinity; Chapter 25 will review the views of the major historical regarding divine (qualitative and absolute) infinity.

Scholar	Lifetime	Regards (Literal) Infinity as Complete and Limitless:
Zeno of Elea	490–430 BCE	**Complete:** Any finite distance (like the path from a runner's starting point to the finish line) is composed of a complete set of points. **Limitless:** The number of points in any finite distance is without limit.
Aristotle	384–322 BCE	**Complete:** There are "those who say that there is an infinite number of worlds…" **Limitless:** "…there cannot be a source of the [actual] infinite or limitless, for that would be a limit of it."
Euclid	325–265 BCE	**Complete:** In any geometrical shape, "it is proved that there exist" a "multitude of straight lines commensurable and incommensurable with an assigned straight line." **Limitless:** That same "multitude of straight lines" is "infinite" (without limit), as the method of exhaustion implies.
Archimedes	287–212 BCE	**Complete:** The number of triangles in a parabolic segment and the number of lines in the plane of a rectangle are "equal in magnitude." **Limitless:** A parabolic segment can be shown to contain a limitless number of triangles.
John Philoponus	~490–570	**Complete:** If the world had no beginning, an actual infinite number of things would already exist. **Limitless:** "…the infinite is by its nature untraversable…"
Robert Grosseteste	1175–1253	**Complete:** There are infinitely many points in part of a line. **Limitless:** To "subtract a number from an infinite sum" still yields "the infinite sum."
Galileo Galilei	1564–1642	**Complete:** A circle is a polygon with an infinite number of sides. **Limitless:** "To be infinite is to be without limit."
John Wallis	1616–1703	**Complete:** The circumference (i.e., closed curve) of a circle is composed of "an infinite number of infinitely short lines" and a cone is "composed of an infinite number of circles." **Limitless:** For a line and curve to converge "after an infinite distance" is for them never to meet.
Isaac Newton	1642–1727	**Complete:** Any complete line contains "infinite divisions and subdivisions" that one can neither distinguish nor attend to. **Limitless:** To be infinite is to be "interminate"—to have no termination or limit.
Bernard Bolzano	1781–1848	**Complete:** The single quantity $\sqrt{2}$ contains "a complete infinite series of decimal places." **Limitless:** "I shall call a plurality which is greater than every finite one, i.e., a plurality which has the property that every finite multitude represents only a part of it, an *infinite plurality*." Such a plurality has "absolutely *no last term*."
Georg Cantor	1845–1918	**Complete:** The actual infinite, or "transfinite," is a "finished" set in which all its elements "exist together" as a "compounded thing for itself;" that is, as a "totality." **Limitless:** The sequence of numbers in the transfinite set of all natural numbers is without limit.
George Gamow	1904–1968	**Complete:** "The number of all points on a plane is equal to the number of all points on a line," and "the infinity of all points within a cube is the same as the infinity of points within a square or on a line." **Limitless:** The universe is likely infinite in geometry, having a "limitless extension" of space in all directions.
Brian Greene	1963–	**Complete:** "There are infinitely many [places] in an infinite expanse of space." **Limitless:** There are "regions of space like the one we inhabit" that are "distributed through a limitless cosmos…"

Table 2: An incomplete sample of historical scholars describing infinity. Each scholar assumed the literal sense of infinity to denote a state of both completeness and limitlessness in quantity (See endnote 232).

8.1.11 *Literal Infinity in Contemporary Thought*

Even to the present day, most literal references to infinity assume it to be a quantitatively complete-yet-limitless condition or state. **Table 2** lists a couple of physicists from modern times: George Gamow, who died the year I was born, and Brian Greene, now prominent in the media. Their statements, referenced in **Table 2**, reflect the traditional view of literal infinity. And there are positions held by many other contemporary scholars that could have been included in the table as well.

A good example of a contemporary scholar taking the traditional understanding of infinity as a state of completeness and limitlessness is the late John D. Barrow (1952–2020), once Cambridge Professor of Applied Mathematics and Theoretical Physics, who wrote of the possibility of an "infinitely large universe"—a universe with a "limitless" magnitude of space that is "actually infinite" (completely so) [235]. Another contemporary theoretical physicist who assumes the traditional understanding of infinity is Roger Penrose; he believes the Universe has already gone through a complete set of limitless iterations and will continue to go through more without limit [236]. These are just a few examples of the views on infinity held by many contemporary scholars that can be cited in support of the definition I articulated as the conventional or traditional conception for literal infinity.

8.2 A HISTORY OF THE INFINITE AS COMPLETE

Throughout history, infinity in its literal sense has been regarded as a condition of being not just limitless, but also *complete* in quantity. What it means for a given collection, C, to be "complete in quantity" is that C has y amount (any variable amount that can be assigned a value equal to a total)—no more, no less—because C is a whole, entire, finished, and full collection. The writings of the scholars listed in **Table 2** all assume the completeness of collections to be a matter of wholeness, entirety, being finished, full, and having a total quantity. Even with respect to infinity.

For yet another historical example of literal infinity implying a state of quantitative completeness in this sense, consider infinity as portrayed in the work of the ancient poet and philosopher Titus Lucretius Carus (94–54 BCE), more often known simply as Lucretius. In his epic poem, *On the Nature of Things*, Lucretius wrote that "void" (space) is infinitely vast and contains an infinite amount of atoms [237]. Certainly, he would be surprised to hear that 'infinity' is only a figure of speech or merely a potential.

In the view of Lucretius, the two most fundamental things—infinitely vast void and an infinite amount of atomic matter—constitute everything that exists. It is clear from his descriptions of infinite amounts of matter and the infinitely vast void that Lucretius thought infinity to be a state or condition of being, literally, complete in quantity as well as limitless in quantity. He used various titles for the Universe to capture its completeness: the "All", the "All-that-Is", "the Whole" (or 'wholeness'), "the Sum of Being" and "the Sum of Things" (that is to say, a 'totality') [238].

Lucretius also implied that the whole, totality of matter in the Universe comprises a 'finished' collection in the sense that atoms form a fixed, unchanging amount—they were never created and will never be destroyed (implying an entirety)—and so he also gave the Universe another title: "the All" [239]. To be "the All" implies no more is being added—the collection of atoms in the Universe is a full collection just as it is. Since for Lucretius the amount of atoms in the Universe is infinite, it is clear that he regarded infinity as having the property of 'completeness' in a sense similar to the way I've portrayed it.

Jumping way ahead in history, we find the same old concept of literal infinity alive and well. The mathematician David Hilbert (1862–1943) stated [240],

> We meet the true infinite when we regard the totality of numbers 1, 2, 3, 4, ... itself as a completed unity, or when we regard the points of an interval as a totality of things which exist all at once. This kind of infinity is known as *actual infinity*.

Hilbert used Aristotle's label 'actual infinity' to denote literal infinity, noting that it is a "completed" unity.

Even today mathematicians refer to literal infinity or actual infinity as 'completed infinity' in order to emphasize that any set or sequence of members in a literally infinite collection are complete in quantity. For example, the contemporary mathematician Eric Schechter states [241],

> Completed infinity, or actual infinity, is an infinity that one actually reaches; the process is already done. For instance, let's put braces around the sequence mentioned earlier:
>
> {1, 2, 3, 4, ...}
>
> With this notation, we are indicating the set of all positive integers. This is just one object, a set. But that set has infinitely many members. By that I don't mean that it has a large finite number of members and it keeps getting more members. Rather, I mean that it already *has* infinitely many members.

Hilbert and Schechter both state that actual infinity—what I term 'literal infinity'—is a condition of being complete with members existing "all at once" in a "totality" that is "already done" forming—in other words, it refers to a whole, entire, full, and finished object with a total. Such examples again illustrate that mathematicians are assuming the *completeness* of infinite collections to be comprised of properties very similar to, if not identical with, those I've explicated in this chapter.

However, none of this is to say that scholars throughout history or today would necessarily use my precising definitions for the properties of completeness. Cantor, for instance, defined the term 'finished' with respect to infinite sets a bit differently [242]:

> I say of a set that it can be thought of as finished...if it is possible without contradiction...to think of *all its elements as existing together*, and to think of the set itself as *a compounded thing for itself*; or (in other words) if it is possible to imagine the set as *actually existing* with the totality of its elements.

Cantor's description of what he means by finished is different from my precising definition for 'finish'. His idea of finish sounds more like a combination of wholeness, entirety, fullness, and totality (most of the properties of completeness). However, his use of the term 'finish' does not necessarily contradict my analysis of what it commonly means for a set to be complete or what scholars have typically meant by the 'complete'; if "all" of a set's elements are "existing together" as a "totality" (which together constitutes Cantor's sense of 'finish'), then it follows that the process of constructing such a set is concluded or finished in the way I define the term 'finish'. So, I take my precising definition for 'finish' as complementary with how Cantor would construe completeness in a general sense.

Similarly, I believe the other scholars listed in **Table 2** (§ 8.1.10) would regard the lexical and precising definitions for 'completeness' as at least generally complementing their own sense of the term's meaning in ordinary language. The listed scholars may use other technical, theoretical, or operational definitions for 'complete' (or for 'whole', 'entire', 'finished', 'full', and 'total') when making mathematical calculations, but aside from use of the term 'complete' in relation to particular mathematical procedures or measurements, the lexical and precising sense remains the same.

In short, it's my contention that the lexical definition for completeness, and the precising definitions for its constituent properties, capture the essence of how various scholars throughout history have regarded completeness for collections, even with respect to infinity in its literal sense.

8.3 TROUBLE BETWEEN COMPLETENESS AND LIMITLESSNESS FOR LITERAL INFINITY

If I have correctly explicated the properties of completeness and limitlessness with respect to literal infinity, then problems begin to appear; we find the properties of completeness and the properties of limitlessness do not cohere with each other.

Take the completeness of an infinite collection, as exemplified by the infinite bag of marbles mentioned in § 1.3.2. In order for a bag to hold an infinitude of marbles, the bag would have to hold a limitless quantity of marbles. But the marbles are all in the bag and so the collection of marbles would also have to be complete. Drawing on our definition of 'complete', to say the collection of marbles in the bag is complete is just to say all the marbles necessary for the collection to be representative of a "bag of marbles" must actually be present in the collection. And drawing on the completeness criteria, to say the bag contains a complete collection of marbles implies the following:

- The process by which marbles are placed in the bag's collection, whether in a single step or over many steps, has ended.
- No subset of the marbles in the bag is quantitatively separated from the collection.
- No marbles required for the collection are missing from the collection.
- The collection of marbles can have no addition of further marbles without changing the parameters of the collection (like the size of the bag).
- The collection of marbles forms a totality—a quantitative 'total' of some kind.

This sounds reasonable enough until we investigate further what it means to for the quantity of marbles in the bag to be limitless. Recall that to be limitless means to be of unspecifiable range even in principle. So then, how can the collection have a quantitative total of *any* kind? The idea of a complete *and* limitless collection—a literal infinity—starts to exhibit internal contradictions.

In Chapters 10–12 I argue that literal infinity is a self-contradictory concept. I will make this argument by showing why a collection cannot be complete as well as limitless. If I am correct, no collection can be literally infinite. Even the number scales cannot be literally infinite and so must be inherently finite, existing only as open series that are always incomplete. Before proceeding, however, we need a little more background about what the charge of self-contradiction entails (and what it does not entail) for literal infinity, which is the subject of the next chapter.

CHAPTER 8 IN REVIEW

❖ The earliest conception we have of infinity as literal infinity dates to the ancient Greek philosophers. Aristotle used the term 'actual infinity' instead of literal infinity, which he contrasted with 'potential infinity' rather than figurative infinity.

❖ Most philosophers post-Aristotle were skeptical of there being anything literally (or "actually") infinite, though not always because they thought literal infinity is *logically* contradictory in meaning (there were only a few that went that far). Rather, most were skeptical that literal infinity could be used in *mathematical* operations without contradiction.

❖ However, in the 1800s, Bolzano pointed out that many mathematicians understood the operations of algebra and functions of calculus as nevertheless implying literal infinity. Still, calculating various kinds of infinite collections directly did not catch on until the late 1800s to early 1900s with the work of Cantor, who proposed a 'transfinite' system for calculating literal infinities, which he called 'proper' or 'genuine' infinites.

9: LOGIC VERSUS LITERAL INFINITY

The words 'infinity' and 'infinite' have been defined according to their literal usage in ordinary, natural language, irrespective of any particular mathematical procedure that might be used to ascribe such terms to a collection of some kind. By providing precising definitions for these words, we are able to have a deeper understanding of what literal infinity means as expressed in natural language. Only subsequently did the previous chapters address the common mathematical symbols for infinity, which are abstract representations for the natural language understanding of infinity. With that background established, we are now nearly ready to confront the logical self-contradictions inherent in the concept of literal infinity.

But before continuing there is something about the charge of self-contradiction that I'm leveling at literal infinity that must be cleared up so there is no misunderstanding. I want to make clear that in stating literal infinity is an illogical concept I am not claiming that any and all expressions of infinity are absurd or meaningless [243]. I am not claiming infinity is incoherent simply as a word used in natural language or as a term used in mathematical expressions. Instead, I only argue literal infinity is, with respect to logic, an incoherent concept regardless of how the term 'infinity' is used in mathematics.

To draw this distinction more clearly, I will start by defining, comparing, and contrasting these ways of expressing infinity. I will then show how (literal) infinity can be *coherent* as a natural language word or as a mathematical concept while being *incoherent* with respect to its logical implications.

9.1 EXPRESSION

We examined in § 7.1 how infinity is a term used in two different types of language: natural language and formal language. The distinction between these types of language will play an important role as we proceed.

Natural language and formal language each allow us to make *expressions*, where the term 'expression' is defined as follows:

- expression:
    (1) *a communicated idea or concept.*
    (2) *the form of a communicated idea or concept.*
    (3) *the act of communicating an idea or concept.*

Whenever we communicate an idea or concept, we are making an expression. When we speak in sentences, write down mathematical formulas, or compose proofs in symbolic logic, we are making expressions.

9.1.1 *Forms of Expression*

As implied by the second definition above, expressions come in various 'forms' (here the term 'form' is used rather loosely). Some examples of forms of expression for natural and formal language are as follows:

- *natural language forms of expression*: phrases, clauses, sentences, paragraphs, etc.

- *formal language forms of expression*: axioms, formulas, equations, statements, inferences, rationales (e.g., arguments and proofs), etc.

We thus have at least two types of language—natural language and formal language—each with its own forms of expression, and each type of language also has its own symbolism and notation.

9.1.2 *Fields of Expression*

Natural language comes in many flavors—English, French, Spanish, German, Italian, Chinese, Japanese, and so on. But there are also at least two formal languages: mathematics and logic.

As formal languages, logic and mathematics can be regarded as languages of their own alongside the natural languages. We can either make expressions in natural language *or* in the language of logic *or* in the language of math. However, there is also overlap among these languages.

For example, a form of expression in one language can be used to communicate an idea or concept native to one of the other languages. We can use natural language to make logical or mathematical expressions, we can use logic to make natural language and mathematical expressions, and we can use mathematics to make natural language and logical expressions.

Take an example of a form of expression: a sentence. While a 'sentence' is a form of expression in natural language, a sentence can also be made in a formal language. A natural language sentence can be symbolized as a logical 'statement'. A mathematical 'axiom' expressed in formal language can be re-expressed as a natural language 'sentence'.

Hence, both natural language and the formal languages of logic and mathematics all overlap with their various forms of expression.

Since mathematics and logic are the only two formal languages we will be considering, we can make the comparison across language types a bit simpler:

- natural language
- logic
- mathematics

I will refer to these as *fields of expression* since they are each a language in which expressions are made according to rules that are themselves 'fields' (topics of interest studied by the specialists of a profession). That's not to imply fields of expression are exclusive; it is only to say the principles governing expressions in these languages can each be studied on their own.

9.1.3 *Domains of Expression*

We know the fields of expression—natural language, logic, and mathematics—all share some common features. Expressions of one field's language can also be expressed by another field's language, and expressions can be translated from one field's language into another. But in order to coherently make expressions across language types of these fields, we need *rules* for making expressions and translating them from one language into another.

Fortunately, the fields of expression have such rules. The set of rules for natural language expression (rules for making phrases, clauses, sentences, paragraphs, etc.) is known as *grammar*. The set of rules for making axioms, formulas, equations, and so forth goes by the same name as its field: *mathematics*. Similarly, the set of rules for reasoning in general (in statements, rationales like arguments and proofs, and so forth) has the same name as its field: *logic*.

We can think of each set of rules for each field of expression as a 'domain' of its own. So, each 'field of expression' (natural language, mathematics, and logic) has an associated *domain of expression* consisting of the set of rules for making expressions in that field. The domains of expression are therefore as follows:

- grammar: rules for phrases, clauses, sentences, etc.
- mathematics: rules for axioms, formulas, equations, etc.
- logic: rules for statements, inferences, rationales, etc.

Insofar as the forms of expression in a given field are governed by rules, we can think of the forms of expression as falling into a 'domain of expression' studied and governed by the rules of the respective field.

Mathematicians use the term 'domain' in a particular way in their field but in this broader context, the term 'domain' will be defined as follows:

- domain: *the scope of a field's subject*.

Hence, while phrases, clauses, and sentences are forms of expression in the field of grammar, they can also be regarded as following rules in the *domain of grammar*. Likewise, while axioms, formulas, and equations are forms of expression in the field of mathematics, they must also follow the rules established in the *domain of mathematics*. And while statements, inferences, and rationales are forms of expression that fall into the field of logic, they are also forms of expression that must follow the rules defined in the *domain of logic* [244].

9.1.4 *What the Domains of Expression Have In Common*

Each domain of expression is the scope of how ideas and concepts are communicated with *signifiers* (signs, symbols, words, terms, etc. that represent the ideas and concepts to be communicated) particular to the domain's associated field. A domain of expression covers the rules for making and communicating expressions using those signifiers according to the forms of expression particular to the field. The fields of grammar, logic, and mathematics each study *signifiers* for expressing ideas and concepts, and all three of these fields have their own rules for expression. There are, however, overlap and similarities between the rules of expression among fields.

For instance, use of signifiers in natural language, mathematics, and logic are made according to rules of *syntax* and *semantics*:

- syntax: *the set of principles determining how signifiers are formed, structured, and organized in expressions.*

- semantics: *the set of principles that determine the meaning (the intended sense) of signifiers and their expressions.*

Syntax is all about form and structure; semantics, on the other hand, is all about meaning [245].

The meaning of a signifier or expression is its *usage* and its *intension*. Note the spelling of 'intension'—with an 's' rather than with a second 't' as has the word 'intention'. Intension and intention have very different meanings. An intention (with a 't') is a purpose, goal, aim or plan. An intension (with an 's'), on the other hand, is the 'sense'—the semantic content—of a signifier or expression. More narrowly, intension can be defined thus:

- intension: *the properties ascribed to (or implied as belonging to) members of a given collection or class.*

The properties ascribed by intension are made up of the necessary and sufficient conditions something needs in order to belong to the collection of things to which the signifier or expression refers. An oft-used example is the definition for bachelor: an unmarried male. Being male is a necessary condition for being a bachelor. Being unmarried is also a necessary condition for being a bachelor. But neither being male nor being unmarried alone is sufficient for being a bachelor; one must be both male and unmarried in order to be a bachelor—those properties together are sufficient conditions for bachelorhood. So, the intension of the word 'bachelor' is the set of properties—the necessary and sufficient conditions—one needs to be a bachelor (or to belong to the set of all bachelors): namely, the properties of being unmarried and male. So, we can say that being an unmarried male is the 'intension' of the word 'bachelor'. Basically, the set of properties ascribed to something comprises the primary meaning of a signifier or expression.

The intension of a signifier or expression can be used to make both 'denotations' and 'connotations'. The word 'denotation' has different senses. For example, sometimes 'denote' means "symbolized" as when a term with a specific meaning is given a particular symbolic representation (for example, infinity is denoted as ∞); other times denotation means the same thing as intension. Where I do not use the word 'denote' to refer to assigning a symbol, I will instead assume the following definition for denotation:

- denotation: *the reference to a particular, specified object or set of objects.*

A denotation is not what is referred to but rather the reference made to something, be it singular or plural. Reference is the act of referring, which is to direct one's attention to something. And the "something" denoted is a *referent*—something referred to. We can regard a referent as an object (as earlier defined—"that of which a subject can be aware") about which we are providing information. Denotation does not have to refer to concrete objects. Prepositions, conjunctions, disjunctions, determiners, etc. all denote conditions, properties, situations, etc. Denotation is about the specificity of reference, not concreteness.

The denotation of a signifier might be a designation for a single member in a set or it might be the list of all the members in a set, depending on the context. When a signifier, like a word or a term, "denotes" something, the signifier refers to it either by directing thought to a specific thing out of a list of things or by directing thought to a specific list of things as opposed to other lists. So, the word 'bachelor' may be used to denote a particular person, like John, as when we refer to John as 'the bachelor'. But the word 'bachelor' might also denote any bachelor, including John.

Denotation stands in contrast with connotation, which can also mean various things. I will define connotation as follows:

- connotation:
  (1) *an idea associated with what is signified or expressed.*
  (2) *a logical implication of what is signified or expressed.*

By its first definition, a connotation is an association that does not necessarily apply to all the members of the set of things signified. For example, if the word 'mouse' is used to denote a rodent, it might connote an agent of disease or the subject of a lab experiment or a snack for a cat, etc.—none of which will apply to all mice.

By its second definition, a connotation is a secondary, logical implication that follows from the intension or, more narrowly, the denotation of a signifier or expression. For example, if a male human being is a bachelor, then it logically follows that he is also an adult—a secondary, logical implication of what it means to be a bachelor.

Denotation and connotation are both aspects of intension. The intension of a signifier or expression is the set of properties defining membership in a collection. Those properties are used to denote members of a collection or denote the collection itself. And the intension also connotes secondary properties of the members of a collection.

Intension stands in contrast with *extension*. The term 'extension' sometimes means to expand in scope or lengthen in sequence, but here the word has a different meaning. While the 'denotation' of a signifier or expression is the reference itself to particular objects or sets of objects, the extension of a signifier or expression is what is referred to. (However, it should be noted that I am using the term 'extension' a bit differently than do many other philosophers [246]).

- extension: *the referent (object or class of objects) denoted by a signifier or expression.*

The denotation of 'bachelor' can be a reference to a particular man or a reference to the set of all unmarried men. The extension of 'bachelor', on the other hand, is a particular man referred to, or the extension can even be all the actual men—whether past, present, or future—to whom this term 'bachelor' applies. When a signifier 'denotes' something, it refers to it. When a signifier 'extends' to something, there is something (real or imagined) to which the signifier refers. So, when the word 'bachelor' denotes a particular unmarried man—for example, John—then John is the extension of 'bachelor'.

Examples of semantic properties (intension, connotation, and denotation) and the extension of what is signified by the semantics are provided in **Table 3**.

It's important to keep in mind with these examples that we need not hold mathematical symbols for infinity denote sets coherently or extend to anything real; **Table 3** merely portrays how symbols for infinity would extend if they were coherent.

PROPERTIES OF SIGNIFIERS				
SIGNIFIER (symbol)	**SEMANTICS**			**EXTENSION (referent)**
	INTENSION (primary meaning)	**CONNOTATION (secondary meaning)**	**DENOTATION (reference)**	
Bachelor	Man, unmarried.	Adult male able to marry.	"The bachelor" refers to a particular man who is not married.	The particular unmarried man referred to (e.g., John).
Wife	Woman, married.	A female who had been a bride.	"The wife" refers to a particular woman who is married.	The particular married woman referred to (e.g., Jane).
~	Logical operator, negation of a given statement, A.	A must be either affirmed or denied.	"Not," as in, "not A," written as $\sim A$.	The situation in which A is not the case.
∨	Logical operator, disjunction between two simple statements, A and B.	"Either A or B" is equivalent to "Either B or A."	"Or," as in, "A or B," written as $A \vee B$.	The situation in which at least one of the simple statements must be true for the complex statement to be true.
$\mathbb{Z}$	The set of numbers with the ability to be written without a fractional component.	The integers include the natural numbers.	$\{..., -2, -1, 0, 1, 2, ...\}$	All the numerals in or from the integer scale.
$\aleph$	Cardinality of any set equal to $\mathbb{N}$.	$\aleph$ is implies a set both complete and limitless in quantity.	$\aleph = \mathbb{N}$ or $\aleph = \mathbb{W}$ or $\aleph = \mathbb{Z}$ or $\aleph = \mathbb{Q}$ or etc.	The size of any collection having a literally infinite number of members.

Table 3: Examples of semantics and extensions for some given signifiers. The first two rows provide examples of natural language signifiers (in the case, words) which must be used according to the rules of natural language grammar. The next two rows provide examples of logic signifiers (in this case, operators) that must be used following the rules of logic. The last two rows provide examples of mathematical signifiers (in this case, notation) that must be used in accordance with the rules of mathematical operation.

The relationship between the intension/extension and the denotation/connotation of a signifier is depicted in **Figure 9.1**. The fields of expression we will consider—grammar, math, and logic—all study the expression of ideas and concepts according to the signifiers and rules of syntax for their respective languages, just as depicted in **Figure 9.1**.

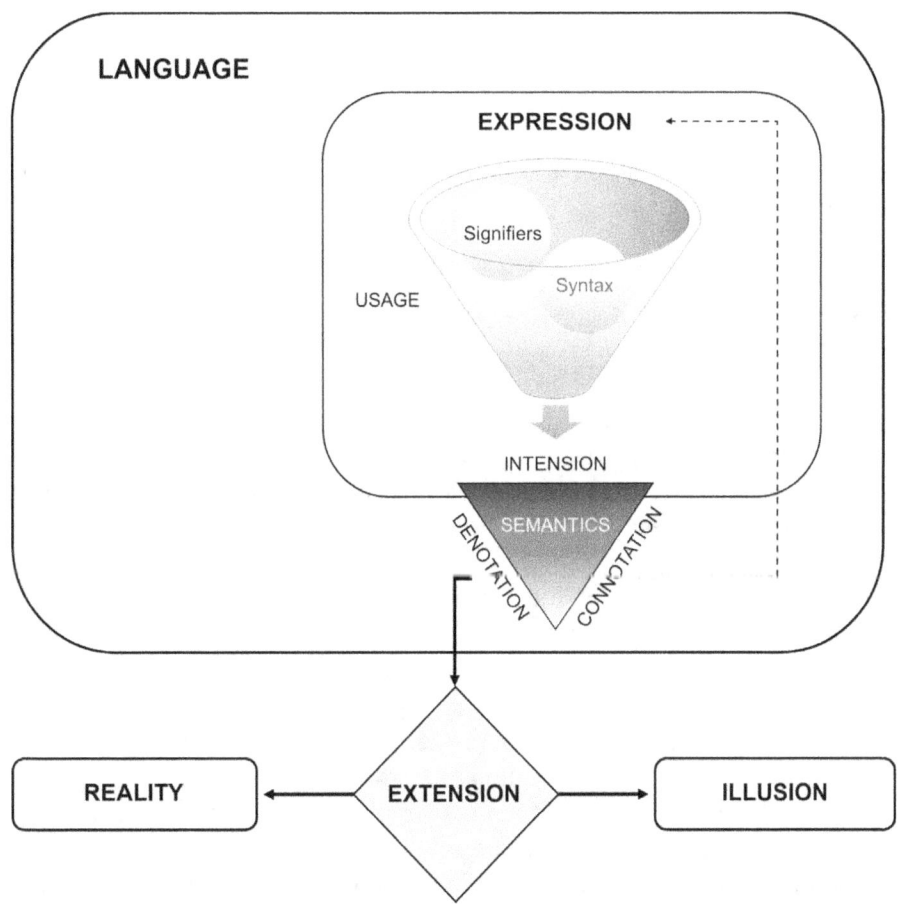

Figure 9.1: Each expression is composed of signifiers used with syntax. The manner of usage is what produces the expression's meaning—its semantics. The semantics of an expression is the expression's intension (primary meaning), its denotation (reference to something), and any connotation (secondary meaning) it may have. Denotation necessarily implies (solid arrow) extension; connotation only contingently implies (dashed arrow) further concepts and ideas that are expressed with other signifiers, and those other signifiers also have syntax of their own. However, the semantics of a connotation may also have further intension, denotation with extension, or even further connotations. A given expression may either denote something that extends to reality (that which exists) or denote something that extends merely to illusion (that which is fictional or purely imaginary). Some complex expressions may have extension as a mix of reality and illusion.

How expressions for a language relate to reality is also depicted in **Figure 9.1**. Just because an idea or concept is expressed consistently in the syntax of a language, that does not ensure such an idea corresponds to anything 'real'. The denotations of some expressions in a given language extend to things that are what they appear to be (realities) while others extend to things that are not what they appear to be (illusions). Alternatively, we could say some expressions denote things with extension (i.e., they denote realities—they refer to real things) while what some other expressions denote do not have extension (i.e., what they denote are illusions—they refer to nothing real). I would contend that this is true even in the languages of mathematics and logic. Some mathematically or logically consistent expressions have extension—they refer to real things; others do not have extension as they are merely ideas having the illusion of reality behind them.

The reality of infinity, or its lack thereof, will be addressed in later chapters. In this chapter, I wish only to address how infinity is expressed in natural and formal language according to the rules of grammar, mathematics, and logic. Each of these fields has its own rules for syntax and semantics that signifiers and expressions must follow to be included in the respective field but, as we shall see, there is much overlap between the ways in which the rules operate among these domains as well—rules that will become important to how we assess the coherence of infinity.

9.2 GRAMMAR

Natural language (or just 'language' for short), like logic and mathematics, is comprised of expressions. The forms of expression in language differ from those of mathematics, and in certain areas they differ from those forms of expression in logic, but expressions in language are nevertheless governed by rules. In the case of (natural) language, the signifiers are words, and the rules for making expressions in words are collectively called 'grammar'—which, quite broadly, is simply *the rules of expression for a natural language*.

Linguists have various ways of defining the domain of grammar. I prefer to take a bit of a nonstandard approach and define the domain of grammar according to three broad categories of rules that govern the use of words; the three categories of rules making up the domain of grammar are the same as for all the domains of expression: syntax, semantics, and morphology.

For grammar, which pertains to natural language, syntax includes the 'combinatorial system' of language, such as rules for consistency, predication, transformation of expressions, and phonology [247]. In fact, it is the syntax of natural language that is most often thought of when the word 'grammar' is used; however, philosophers widen 'grammar' to include semantics and morphology as well as syntax.

Semantics in natural language is the denotation and connotation of words, both of which are relative to their usage in various contexts. For example, if used as a noun, the word 'duck' might denote a member of the Anatidae family of birds; but if used as a verb, 'duck' might denote the action of stooping or bending suddenly to avoid an impact. This is an example of how denotation varies in usage according to context. Next, consider connotation and how the connotations of words vary with differences in word usage among changes in context. Connotations, in terms of natural language, include any associations a word may have, whether logical or analogical. Insofar as the word 'duck' denotes a bending or stooping action to avoid impact, it also connotes avoidance of unwanted physical contact—this is an example of a *logical* connotation. On the other hand, insofar as the word 'duck' denotes a kind of bird, it may also connote a target for hunters—this is an example of an *analogical* connotation; for hunters, the bird is likened to a target. These examples illustrate that the grammar of natural language includes semantic rules not only for the denotations of words but for their connotations as well.

The syntax and semantics of natural language grammar actually share a common subset of rules: *morphology*—the rules by which the signifiers used in expressions are structured so as to have particular meanings. In natural language, morphology is found in the use of words. For example, 'duck' and 'ducks' are variations of the same word, but their differences in structure indicate different meanings—the former is singular, the latter is plural. Morphology is the set of natural language rules relating word structure to word meaning. Morphology thus overlaps both syntax (structure) and semantics (meaning).

The grammar of natural language includes syntax, semantics, and morphology, but what about extension? Words that obey grammar also have extension, whether that extension is to something real (e.g., a president or prime minister) or illusory (e.g., something fictional or imaginary like pixies and unicorns). However, while extension is certainly a function of language—the way words "attach" to things in the world—extension is not a part of grammar proper (see **Figure 9.1**), so I will not assume that it is included in grammar. Instead, the denotation of a signifier such as a word—its reference to something—is included in grammar; the extension of the signifier—what is referred to—is not a part of language but is what language addresses.

Dividing grammar up into syntax, semantics, and morphology for natural language is not the only approach to categorizing the rules making up the domain of grammar, but it will suffice for our purposes. What I do want to make clear, though, is that syntax, semantics, and morphology only constitute 'grammar' insofar as they are types of rules for expressions made in *natural language*. These same rule types for expressions are not exclusive to natural language and so they are not exclusive to grammar—as we'll see, logic and mathematics also have their own forms of syntax, semantics, and morphology.

9.3 LOGIC

Our second domain of expression is logic. I don't intend this book to be a primer of logic, but it does help to make sure we all understand what is meant by 'logic' and its related terms for any readers who may not have majored in philosophy. So before proceeding further, I will lay out my basic assumptions on logic.

9.3.1 *Reason*

Logic concerns reason with a small 'r'—not Reason with a capital 'R' as a kind of epistemology. The word 'reason' can be defined both as a noun and as a verb:

- reason: (noun)
    (1) *a correct inference.*
    (2) *an inference intended or assumed to be correct.*
    (3) *a condition correctly inferred from another.*
    (4) *the ability to draw correct inferences.*

- reason: (verb) *to attempt a correct inference.*

Likewise, reason is also used as the adjective 'reasonable':

- reasonable: (adjective)
    (1) *able to draw correct inferences.*
    (2) *the property of being a correct inference.*

We use the adjective 'reasonable' in the first sense when we mean someone displays the ability to draw a correct inference ("She is being reasonable") or has a character of doing so ("She is a reasonable person"), and in the second when we indicate an inference is correct ("That is a reasonable position to take").

Clearly, all of these definitions regarding reason make much ado of *inference* and *correctness*.

9.3.2 *Inference*

As philosophers use the term, an 'inference' also has more than one use:

- inference:
  (1) *the act of recognizing an implication.*
  (2) *the implication that is recognized.*

Where *implication* can be defined as follows:

- implication: *any situation in which one particular condition either always or usually results in another particular condition.*

A classic example of an inference: we may infer from the fact that it is raining outside that the streets will be wet. The conditions implied or inferred (for example, the wetness of streets inferred from the condition of rain falling) need not be captured in language; the conditions need simply be recognized via observation, experience, imagination, or conception. In whatever manner the conditions are recognized, we say that one condition, B, is the 'implication' of another condition, A, when A *implies* B. To say that A 'implies' B means that A results in B unless prevented by a third set of conditions, C. Unless something is blocking the rain from hitting the streets, rain implies wet streets. So, when we recognize that B always, or at least usually, is the case as a result of A, then we 'infer' B from A. Hence, we infer wet streets (B) from falling rain (A). The recognition that one thing always or usually follows from another is what making an inference means [248].

9.3.3 *Correctness*

Definition:

- correctness: *the condition of being correct.*
- correct: *free of error.*

Some reasons are good, some bad. We have "good reasons" when we draw *correct* inferences—those free of error. We have "bad reasons" when we have *incorrect* inferences—those that contain at least one error. These are straightforward enough, but even simple definitions can be ambiguous. For instance, some might take 'correct inference' to be about truth and 'incorrect inference' to be about falsity, but that is not so. By 'correct inference' I do not mean a *true* statement; likewise, by 'incorrect inference' I do not mean a *false* statement—correctness and incorrectness are here a matter of whether or not an inference from one premise to another is valid or cogent, not whether the individual premises are true or false.

On those occasions when we don't draw correct inferences, when our reasons are bad, we may still have the *ability* to draw correct inferences—it's just that we do not *implement* that ability well on the occasion of bad reasoning. Clearly, we need some principles to distinguish good reasoning from bad reasoning—principles that help us recognize reasons that are, or are more likely to be, correct from those that are not correct or are unlikely to be correct. This is where logic enters the picture.

9.3.4 *Reasoning Effectively*

Reasoning is the *attempt* at drawing correct inferences, and the intended result of reasoning is having the correct inferences. If one uses principles that are effective for drawing correct inferences, one is reasoning *logically*. If one uses principles that are not effective for drawing correct inferences, one is not reasoning logically. We can thus define logic:

- logic: (1) *principles effective for reasoning.*

Where 'effective' means the following:

- effective: *producing or achieving the desired or intended result.*

While reasoning is the attempt to infer correctly, logic is the set of principles that are *effective* for inferring correctly, provided we use them and use them well.

9.3.5 *The Principles of Logic*

Logical reasoning may be expressed in natural language as a set of sentences or in the formal language of mathematics as a set of operations and equations, or in a hybrid of natural and formal language studied by philosophers and logicians. However, logic does not have to be expressed in these forms at all. A logical inference can be in any form of information. For instance, some animals display instances of demonstrative and instrumental reasoning, as when birds figure out how to use simple tools for retrieving food [249]. Regardless, logicians primarily study the principles for effective reasoning either in natural language or formal language, or a mix of the two. It is mainly that sort of logical inference that will concern us.

And this raises another distinction: there is 'logic' as a set of principles and then there is 'logic' as a domain of expression and a field of study. What I have referred to as the 'domain of logic' is the domain of all statements that are *logical*—statements that are effective for drawing correct inferences. Moreover, as a domain is the domain of a field of study, and 'logic' is an academic field of study, we may thus add another definition of logic:

- logic: (2) *the academic field that studies principles effective for reasoning.*

I don't intend for this to be a logic book in the sense of the second definition of 'logic'. A detailed examination of the principles of reason is beyond the scope of this book—entire textbooks are devoted to the study of logic, and I cannot cover all the same territory here.

However, I will need to refer to certain meta-logical principles of reason as we proceed, such as the *principle of sufficient reason*, and certain principles of logic such as the *principle of non-contradiction* and the *principle of excluded middle*, both of which will play an important role in the case against infinity and for the finitude of existence.

9.3.6 *What Logic Has in Common with Grammar*

All statements and rationales expressed in natural language are subject to the syntax, semantics, and morphology of natural language. The syntax, semantics, and morphology of natural language comprise what we call 'grammar'. So, logical statements and rationales, insofar as they are expressed in natural language, must follow the rules of grammar to be linguistically coherent.

However, there is another way of expressing statements and rationales: *symbolic* logic (sometimes called *formal logic*). As indicated above, logic expressed in formal language has syntax, semantics, and morphology just as grammar does.

Logical syntax. Symbolic or formal logic has its own syntax. A couple of examples of logical syntax were provided in **Table 3**. By having syntax, logic and grammar overlap in their respective domains. A statement in natural language can be translated into the syntax of symbolic logic. For example, the simple statement, "Philosophers attempt to express wisdom," may be signified as p, and the complex statement, "Either philosophers attempt to express wisdom, or they don't," might have syntax in symbolic logic like this:

$$p \lor \sim p.$$

Logical semantics. Forms of rationale called *arguments* and *proofs* can be constructed in formal logic with variables (e.g., p) that have unassigned meanings. For that reason, it might be assumed that formal logic is a syntax-only discipline. But that is not accurate; there are semantics involved even in formal logic.

Expressions in symbolic logic such as $p \lor \sim p$ can be used to represent particular states of affairs, so such expressions are not necessarily without *intension*. And not just intension but in particular the semantics of denotation and connotation. In the above example, the letter p denotes philosophers attempting to express wisdom. Ergo, what p denotes may also have further semantics—the semantics of logical connotation.

A connotation in logic is not just a psychological or cultural association as it can be in the grammar of natural language; instead, a connotation in logic is a (perhaps unstated) implication. For instance, if p denotes philosophers attempting to express wisdom, then a connotation is that there is at least one philosopher, possibly more than one.

Of course, the same variable, p, might mean something else in a different logical expression, but that is beside the point: the symbols can be given meaning; they can be used with semantics as well as syntax, and they can have connotations as well as denotations. Like grammar, logic is not just syntax alone—it also has semantics. In fact, is precisely in logical semantics that *informal* logical fallacies can arise—logical errors in *meaning*.

Logical morphology. Just as natural language grammar has its rules for word usage, so too does formal logic have rules for variations on the same variables. For instance, the letter 'T' may be a predicate as in Tx, but it may also represent the property of truth (T) vice falsity (F) in a truth table (see § 9.5.2, example in **Figure 9.3**).

All of the above goes to show that while syntax, semantics, and morphology comprise grammar (rules for natural language), they are also categories that pertain to expressions for logic. It's just that the formal language of logic has its *own* type of syntax, semantics, and morphology.

9.3.7 *Logic is not Math*

Logic can be compared and contrasted with grammar on the basis of different syntax, semantical connotations, and even morphology. But we can also draw some comparisons between logic and mathematics to show how logic and math overlap, and how they differ.

For instance, symbolic logic, with its use of variables and quantifiers (as in expressions like $p \vee \sim p$) is where logic appears very math-like. But logicians engage in a symbolic activity that mathematicians do not: translating natural language statements into symbolic syntax to check the validity of an argument's reasoning. Mathematicians do not engage in that kind of activity, but for logicians, it is the heart of the discipline of logic.

That is not to say there is no logic in math—far from it. But it is to say that *logic does not reduce to mathematics*. Logic is much broader than mathematics since logic concerns the use of *reason* per se, while math concerns a particular type and subject area of reasoning.

Conversely, some philosophers such as the German philosopher and mathematician Gottlob Frege (1848–1925) and the British philosopher Bertrand Russell (1872–1970) hoped to prove mathematics reduces to logic, but such projects have been likewise unsuccessful [250] [251] [252]. *Mathematics does not reduce to logic*, for mathematics is more than logic, just as logic is more than mathematics.

9.4 MATHEMATICS

Our third and final domain of expression is mathematics. There are various definitions of 'mathematics', but I propose the following definition:

- mathematics: *the study of numerical schemes and schemas.*

9.4.1 *Schemes and Schemas*

Mathematicians and philosophers of mathematics use terms like *scheme* and *schema* in various ways. I propose the following definitions:

- scheme: (pl., schemes) *a system of ideas or concepts used for organizing.*

- schema: (pl., schemas or schemata) *a category, pattern, or relation organized according to a scheme.*

A schema is not quite the same thing as a 'scheme', though the two words are related. Plans, operations, and programs are all examples of schemes, while schemes organize schemas.

Consider some examples of schemas, which are organized by schemes:

- Categories of collection such as 'aggregate', 'multitude', 'set', 'sequence', and 'series' are all examples of schemas organized in mathematics by schemes such as rule-based operations, functions, algorithms, and programs.

- Variables and operators are schemas, all organized by schemes like the rules of elementary arithmetic.

- Geometric shapes and points are schemas organized by the scheme of geometric rules.

- Axioms, theorems, scales, designs, and quantitative models are all schemas because they are patterns organized by rule-based schemes; one axiom may be proposed on the basis of a set-theoretic model, for example.

- Relations and relational properties expressed as quantifiers like 'finite', 'indefinite', and 'infinite' are schemas insofar as various schemes apply them as concepts for organizing other quantification schemas.

What do all these schemas and schemes have in common with respect to mathematics? Mathematics expresses them in terms of numbers and enumeration. Numbers (ordinality and cardinality relations) are also schemas; they are schemas for numerals, organized according to schemes such systems and rules for defining them and using them in enumeration schemes and other schemes that assume the ability to enumerate. In short, mathematics studies 'schemes' insofar as they are used for organizing numbers, organizing numerical schemas, and organizing schemas with the use of numbers. For that reason, I defined mathematics as "the study of numerical schemes and schemas".

My view on this matter is not too far from that of Dr. Stephen Simpson, a mathematician and logician at Pennsylvania State University and Vanderbilt University, who states [253]:

> Mathematics is a particular field of study. If you were to ask me to be more specific, I would follow Aristotle and define mathematics as "the science of quantity", with quantity interpreted broadly to include not only numbers but also higher quantities (matrices, etc.) and geometrical figures (triangles, manifolds, etc.)...
>
> This definition of mathematics may seem too old-fashioned, but I believe it can be stretched to cover not only ancient but also modern mathematics, and it has the additional advantage of being well-linked to applications and the rest of human knowledge.

My definition of mathematics, like Simpson's, is broad enough to include both the quantities and the figures he mentions. But my definition differs on a few technicalities.

First, Simpson refers to mathematics as a science, but I prefer to think of science as an activity that is more empirical in nature than mathematics. Second, I prefer to define mathematics in reference to the numerical rather than just to 'quantity' since the field of logic also addresses quantity indirectly with the use of predicate 'quantifiers'. Third and finally, the kind of things mathematicians study like 'matrices', 'fields', geometric figures, and so on are all studied by the use of numbers or variables for numbers.

So, I feel justified being narrower with reference to the numerical rather than broader with quantity. Even so, these differences are rather nitpicky; regarding the bottom line of what mathematics is about, I am in basic agreement with Simpson.

9.4.2 *The Categories of Mathematics*

I'll take a moment here to distinguish between some sub-disciplines in the field of mathematics. We can partition the field of mathematics into two broad categories of study:

- *pure mathematics*
- *applied mathematics*

Pure mathematics is the study of mathematical concepts without regard to practical application in other fields.

Applied mathematics is the study and use of mathematical concepts to solve problems in fields other than mathematics, such as in science, engineering, economics, business, and so forth.

There is no clear demarcation between these two categories of study [254].

Take the mathematical study of probability, for example. A mathematician may study the conceptual framework for probability theory as an instance of pure mathematics or may study the calculation of particular probabilities as an instance of applied mathematics [255].

Because there is no clear boundary between these categories of mathematical study, what is studied in pure mathematics may become part of applied mathematics and what is studied in applied mathematics may inspire novelty in pure mathematics. For example, some conclusions reached in the study of pure mathematics may find practical use in applied mathematics, as when the study of the factorization of whole numbers (pure math) became used for purposes of encryption (applied math) [256]. Conversely, some applications of mathematics inspire new theories pursued in pure mathematics, as when calculation of the speed of bodies in motion (applied math) inspired the invention of calculus (pure math) or when models of cartography (applied math) inspired the creation of differential geometry (pure math).

So, it's not always clear where pure mathematics ends and practical mathematics begins, and the two categories of study certainly influence one another.

Still, let's pause on this note a bit further to elucidate what pure mathematics and applied mathematics are each about before continuing with our distinctions between mathematics and other disciplines such as grammar and logic.

Pure Mathematics. As mathematics can be divided into the categories of pure and applied, so too pure mathematics, if very broadly conceived, can be subdivided into the following categories:

- *theoretical mathematics*
- *general mathematics*
- *experimental mathematics*

As with pure and applied mathematics, these categories also have no clear boundaries between them as they overlap in their various disciplines, but these categories will serve our purposes. We'll take each in turn.

Theoretical mathematics is the study of the logical justification of mathematics and the conceptual exploration of alternative mathematical schemes and schemas.

The alternative schemes studied by theoretical mathematics include new methods to calculate abstract schemas such as algebraic groups, higher dimensional geometries, and topologies that do not exist in physical space. One example of a schema in theoretical mathematics is an abstract object known as E8 (**Figure 9.2**) and another is the sphere eversion process discussed at the beginning of Chapter 18.

Figure 9.2: A two-dimensional, symbolic depiction of E8—an abstract object of 248 dimensions that does not exist in real, physical space.

In addition to generating novel quantitative theories about abstract objects, theoretical mathematics proposes logical justifications for all mathematical schemes and schemas. The justifications consist in part of what mathematicians refer to as the *foundation* of mathematics.

The 'foundation' is all of the most fundamental concepts assumed in mathematics (concepts such as set, function, number, figure, etc.) and how they can be used to logically justify the hierarchy of more complex mathematical schemes and schemas (the particular definitions, models, formulas, proofs, algorithms, etc.). Mathematicians typically hold all of the schemes and schemas of mathematics to be deducible from the foundational concepts.

The common assumption is that if mathematics rests on a 'solid foundation', it is rationally justified as a consistent and coherent part of human knowledge. The foundations of mathematics are usually framed according to axioms (allegedly "self-evident" truths) and theorems (proofs based on axioms and, in some cases, on other truths) such as those proposed in *set theory*, *number theory*, and what is often referred to as *first-order arithmetic* and *second-order arithmetic* (both of which concern the axioms that underly what most of us know as 'elementary arithmetic' in general mathematics). If the axioms are uncontroversial and the theorems are deducible from the axioms, then the theoretical mathematical system in question is considered a solid foundation for mathematics.

Theoretical mathematics includes several sub-disciplines such as transfinite set theory (see § 13.1), transfinite mathematics, and other speculative areas of mathematics. But theoretical mathematics also bleeds into general mathematics and experimental mathematics; there is no clear-cut distinction. For example, some universities consider theoretical mathematics to include some of the specialized areas of general mathematics, such as algebra and geometry [257].

General Mathematics covers number theory, arithmetic ('elementary arithmetic' or 'elementary calculation'), combinatorics, algebra, geometry, topology, analysis, trigonometry, calculus, statistics, and similar disciplines familiar to most folks. As theoretical mathematics has some overlap with general mathematics, so too does general mathematics have overlap with experimental mathematics. It is primarily the operations of general mathematics that are used in experimental mathematics [258].

Experimental Mathematics is the use of the schemes and schemas of theoretical mathematics and general mathematics to investigate mathematical objects and identify numeric properties and patterns. Some examples of experimental mathematics include:

- Consistency checks to support the search for analytical proofs of a conjecture.
- Searching for a counterexample to a conjecture.
- Inventing new mathematical objects with particular properties.
- Use of computer programs to complete a proof.

Since all these activities may be applied to solving problems outside the field of mathematics, experimental mathematics is not always distinguishable from applied mathematics [259].

Applied Mathematics. The professional study of mathematics to solve problems in other professional fields like cosmology, science, engineering, industry, economics, and business. The applications of mathematics in any of these fields may be the application of any of the disciplines of general mathematics [260]. Even theoretical mathematics may find some application as noted with the example of factorization having use for computer encryption. The application of mathematical schemes for analysis, asymptotic methods, variational methods, and probability theory have been key to the development of physics since the time of Newton.

9.4.3 *The Language of Mathematics*

Whether the mathematics is pure or applied, the numerical schemes of mathematics are expressed in terms of rules, which are not unlike the rules of a language. As with grammar and logic, the numerical schemes of math also have rules of syntax, semantics, and morphology—all of which play a big part in organizing the kinds of schemas mathematicians study.

However, I admit not all mathematicians would agree with this characterization of their field. Many mathematicians don't consider semantics and morphology as playing roles in the practice of mathematics. For instance, some mathematicians claim that mathematics is a 'first-order language' only [261]. First-order languages are languages that "have no meaning in themselves. There is syntax, but no semantics. At this level, sentences don't mean anything" [262].

By 'sentence' the mathematician means an expression composed of strings of symbols, but not necessarily words. Some examples [263]:

$$\forall x \exists y \forall z ((x \leq z \cdot x \neq z) \supset (x \leq y \cdot y \leq z \cdot x \neq y))$$

and

$$f\left(f^{-1}(x)\right) = x$$

and

$$8 \div 2 = 4$$

and

$$\infty + \infty = \infty$$

etc.

Mathematicians sometimes say such 'sentences' in first-order language "have no meaning" or that they have "no semantics." This view was proposed by the 20th Century philosopher Ludwig Wittgenstein (1889–1951). According to Wittgenstein, "An equation is a rule of syntax" [264]. He stated, "In mathematics *everything* is algorithm and *nothing* is meaning" [265]. This is what many mathematicians and philosophers claim of mathematics, but it is not accurate [266].

9.4.4 *Math is More Than Syntax*

It is certainly correct to say that equations and formulas in mathematics are expressed according to first-order language rules, as shown in the foregoing examples of mathematical 'sentences'. Mathematical definitions can also be made in the formalism of first-order language, as they sometimes are, so that too is correct. But from this it does not follow that math is *only* syntax and so without semantics. Mathematics involves more than syntax.

In support of this contention, let's start with a trivial observation: we will never find a textbook on mathematics the expositions in which are completely shorn of natural language. The reader needs at least some exposition of the terms and procedures in natural language in order to comprehend what the purely formal expressions are all about. And to the extent that a text on math does not contain natural language is the extent to which the author assumes the reader already has the necessary background information to understand the text, much of which was learned in natural language. Even journal articles on the transfinite system—pages dense with formulas and equations, written *by* mathematicians *for* mathematicians—nevertheless have to make at least some use of natural language in order for the content to be understood. And this holds true for general mathematics as well—all math makes use of the semantics of natural language.

More importantly, while formalized mathematical expressions (like, $x = a/b$) are indeed calculated according only to syntax, we find the terms (x, a, and b) in such expressions actually have meanings. In fact, all mathematical symbols (and formal logical symbols too) have meanings; they have semantics in the form of intension, including denotation and connotation.

Mathematics *denotes its own elements*—numerals, sets, and their orderly relationships. Math also *denotes operations* with these elements. We can say that the *extension* of mathematical symbols, relationships, and operations are those very symbols, sets, relationships, and operations—*math denotes itself and extends to itself*, as shown by the examples in **Table 3** above [267].

The intensions and denotations of math can even be translated into the grammar of natural language; in so doing, we see the semantic content. In fact, all mathematical expressions are *translatable* (though not in every case actually *translated*) into natural language. Mathematicians actually do this translating all the time without taking notice of the fact. For example, in speaking out loud $1 + 1 = 2$, we say, "One plus one equals two," or some variation thereof. We usually do not pay attention to the fact that we are using the grammar of natural language to translate mathematical expressions into natural language sentences. But that is exactly what we do all the time; the syntax of math is translated into the syntax of natural language while preserving the semantic content of the original mathematical form of the expression. Moreover, the implications of what "One plus one equals two" means can also be put into natural language: "If you have a single thing and another single thing of the same kind, then you have a pair of things of the same kind" (or a similar sentence that captures that meaning) [268].

We find further examples of the natural language translation of mathematical expressions when we examine definitions for mathematical terms. Though mathematical objects and their relations can be given formal, operational definitions in mathematics and written purely in syntactical symbolism (for example, $\emptyset = \{\ \}$), these terms and expressions are only comprehensible because they all assume meanings in ordinary, second-order, natural language. We have to be told what the symbol $\emptyset$ is, what the equals sign means, and what the curly braces are for. We have to be told what it means for a 'set' to be "empty."

The similarities between mathematics and natural language do not end there. It may surprise some mathematicians to think that metaphors and similes are assumed in set theory and mathematics, but they certainly are. We find that mathematical terms are based on analogies with words from natural language, and even assume the lexical meanings of corresponding words from ordinary, natural language. Consider Moore's point about how the first-order language of set theory and the transfinite system is not in itself sufficient to define sets and members of sets [269]:

> Suppose now that you had no idea what either 'Set' or 'member' meant, beyond knowing that they were mathematical terms. Think of them as two utterly alien terms, say 'zad' and 'nanpal'. How much could you determine about their meaning from being presented with true sentences from this language?
> You might be told, first,
> (1) No two zads have exactly the same nanpals,
>   then
> (2) There is one zad that has no nanpals.

Moore goes on to state that even if we can use transfinite axioms to make further deductions from the first and second statements about zads and nanpals, there is more to understanding what is meant by 'zad' and 'nanpal' than is presented in axioms about them. Likewise, there is more to the meaning of sets and members than can be said about them in the first-order language of set theory and the transfinite system [270]. What is needed in addition to deduction from the axioms, Moore states, is knowledge of how to use the terms correctly, which is an understanding acquired by learning the mathematical conventions through actual practice [271]. But I would go a bit further than Moore: even mathematical practice and rule-based demonstrations are not enough to capture the mathematical meanings of these terms. A familiarity with the semantic content (meaning) of concepts from ordinary, natural language is needed to comprehend the terms of mathematics in order to apply the terms in mathematical procedure. This holds for terms like 'set' and 'member', which are borrowed from natural language, as well as for predicates like 'infinite' which, as explicated in § 5.4, assume meanings of constituent concepts from natural language.

Using Moore's example, if math were just syntax without meaning, Cantor could have used terms like 'zad' and 'nanpal' instead of 'set' and 'member' when he formulated set theory and his transfinite system, but he didn't. And he didn't because mathematical conceptions of things like 'sets' and 'members' are only mathematically defined in the way they are because they are based on analogies with concepts that we are familiar with from our second-order language. The idea of a 'set' is based on collections we can see in the real world; the idea of 'member' is based on group membership of real things in the physical world we see [272]. Cantor drew upon words and their meanings in our second-order language to create abstract conceptions of sets and members and related them in formal, first-order schemas.

Mathematical and set-theoretic concepts are based on analogies drawn from ordinary, natural language. Mathematics assumes meanings for its terms that are drawn from natural language, and that is precisely why the language of mathematics is translatable into natural language.

9.4.5 *The Semantics of Mathematics*

The first-order language of mathematics assumes a second-order of natural language semantics, even if it doesn't explicitly reference the meanings of terms in operation. The first-order language of mathematics—its syntax-only formalism—is an *abstraction and simplification* from the first-order language (the syntax) of ordinary, natural language. The first-order language of math did not precede natural language and it is not more fundamental than natural language (which has both a first-order language of syntax and a second-order language containing the semantics of tense, predication, adverbs, prepositions, idioms, etc.). Rather, natural language and its grammar preceded math and it is natural language that is primary; the 'first-order' language of mathematics is the language that is not fundamental but rather is an abstraction derived from the syntax of natural language.

Because of this, terms like 'set', 'element', 'member', and 'infinite', while having formalized expressions in mathematics, also have natural language meanings assumed by mathematicians as they work. For example, mathematicians will often explain that sets, as calculated in set theory, are sets of anything, such as "the set of all students registered at the City University of New York in February 1998, the set of all even natural numbers, the set of all points in the plane π exactly 2 inches distant from a given point P, the set of all pink elephants" [273]. However, much of the semantic content assumed in terms like 'set', 'element' and so on is not made explicit in the formalism of mathematics.

The first-order language of math actually "abstracts out" (that is, ignores) the semantics and syntax of natural language in order to *simplify* and *systematize* the schemas it studies. But the ordinary, natural language meanings and semantics of terms adopted by, and used in, mathematics do not go away simply because they are not acknowledged or attended to. The semantics instead are *assumed*, or sometimes *implied*, by the mathematician and can even influence mathematical practice. In fact, those semantics influence the proposal of the formal, mathematical definitions of those terms (like the use of 'set' rather than a new word like 'zad', for sets are assumed to be sets *of* things).

As a caveat to this contention, it is true that when semantics are given any thought in math, it's only with regard to denotation rather than connotation. Mathematical definitions are used primarily for making denotations (which are numerical and ostensive in meaning) without interest in any secondary logical implications or connotations (which may have even metaphorical meanings). And when the first-order language 'sentences' in math are translated into second-order language concepts, the meaning of the terms is confined to denotation only for the sake of making calculations with little attention paid to connotation.

For example, '2', '3', and '5' denote the cardinalities of sets of different size, '+' denotes combining cardinalities, and '=' denotes identifying the cardinality of a set resulting from the cardinalities combined. Hence, $2 + 3 = 5$ denotes the cardinalities of sets added together to establish a combined cardinality of 5.

We notice the semantics of denotation more clearly when we translate the equation as a mathematical 'sentence' into an ordinary, second-order language sentence. (The syntax of any 'sentence' in a first-order language can be translated into the syntax of a second-order language sentence.) That is, a mathematical equation like $2 + 3 = 5$ can be translated into the second-order grammar of natural language like so: "A set of two elements added to a set of three elements is identical in size to a set of five elements," or in its commonly abbreviated form: "Two plus three equals five." When we express the equation $2 + 3 = 5$ in its mathematical syntax, we are assuming the second-order grammar of its natural language equivalent expression, which in turn denotes sets of various sizes.

So, the formalism of math assumes the semantics of second-order, natural language, though the semantics assumed in a mathematical expression are mainly meanings in the form of denotation. Connotations—secondary logical implications based on the meaning of terms—are not given much consideration in math. The operational procedures in math "abstract out" any further connotations.

Numbers and properties like infinity, considered only in the abstract, are said to denote sets or properties of sets, or even just the signifiers in the syntax of math itself. Any further connotations are not relevant to the mathematician.

And even when the issue of denotation is considered, denotation is often mistaken for extension and dismissed with the statement that mathematics is not about the extension of terms. However, it's not that mathematics has no denotations, for what is denoted in math are the properties of the mathematical schemas, or even the signifiers that refer to properties like ordinality, cardinality, and the like. Rather, such denotations of the terms are merely assumed in mathematical operation and taken for granted.

It's not hard to see why this confusion happens: numbers, after all, are properties of numerals and sets can be sets of numbers. So, mathematics, unapplied to measurement of the real world, references only properties of its own signifiers and so the properties of the signifiers become, even if not technically accurate, identified with the signifiers themselves and their syntax. Hence, even denotation can become ignored and only the syntax given notice in the practice of mathematics.

This appears to be the case at least insofar as pure mathematics is concerned, stripped of any concern for application to thought experiments or measurements that involve real-world entities. What is denoted (mathematical properties) can become mistaken for the signifiers as such so that only syntax is of concern, while any second-order logical connotations and natural language associations assumed in the use of mathematical terms, like infinity, simply aren't relevant with respect to mathematical operations which can be effectively considered solely with regard to first-language formalism. But this does not mean that mathematical 'sentences' carry no logical connotations at all, or that connotations cease to influence mathematical procedure.

9.4.6 *Connotations of Mathematical Expressions*

Not only do mathematical expressions carry meaning in terms of denotations, but the semantics of mathematical signifiers sometimes carry connotations that are tacitly assumed, even while habitually being "abstracted out" for convenience in making calculations. As an example of a connotation carried by a mathematical expression, consider the tense of mathematical expressions translated into natural language.

Some mathematicians point out that first-order languages have no past or future tense in their expression [274]. Instead, first-order languages are said to be *tenseless*. First-order languages are 'tenseless' in the sense that tense is not a relevant consideration in first-order languages. After all, notice that when the mathematical expression '$2+3=5$' is translated into second-order, natural language as, "Two plus three equals five," we never say that two plus three *equaled* five or *will equal* five; rather, we always say the sum *equals* five—present tense. What is regarded as "tenseless" in the syntax of math's first-order language only becomes tensed when translated into the syntax of natural language—though, the tense for mathematical expressions so translated is confined to the present tense.

Some mathematicians believe that the 'tenselessness' of expressions in first-order symbolism of math entails that mathematical expressions have no semantics and so are without meaning [275]. But this is not quite so.

Rather, the 'tenselessness' of the first-order syntax in math shows only that mathematicians can safely ignore tense when constructing their mathematical 'sentences' and performing operations. But when we translate the first-order 'sentence' into a second-order sentence in natural language (as "Two plus three *equals* five"), the resulting expression carries not only the denotations of the terms (the sets designated by the numbers) but also the logical connotation that the present-tensed operation implies *constancy* over time. The particular operation on sets of those sizes holds true or false *at all times and any time*; past, present, or future. It will always be true that two plus three equals five. This constancy is a logical connotation of what the mathematical expression means.

Even more significantly, connotations are found in the use of mathematical terms that function as predicates, or that are defined with predicates; such terms assume or imply concepts with lexical meanings. As pointed out earlier, the terms ω and ℵ mean 'infinite in order' and 'infinite in size' respectively; the term 'infinite' is a predicate. Hence, ω and ℵ represent concepts with the meaning of the natural language predicate 'infinite', the intension of which both denotes and connotes.

For example, ℵ may denote a set that has the same cardinality as the infinite set of naturals (ℕ) or the infinite set of wholes (𝕎), but it also implies that the set is both complete (whole, entire, finished, full, and total) and limitless (has no last member even in principle). Even if we want to define 'infinity' in the formalism of algebra, calculus or transfinite math, the concept of infinity, taken literally, still assumes the more lexical meanings of 'complete' and 'limitless' as commonly understood. Infinity is a great example of a term used in mathematics that has semantics as well as syntax, and the semantics of infinity carry lexical meanings even if they remain tacitly assumed. There is thus more to being infinite in the transfinite system than is stated in the formalism of its mathematical syntax. So once again we see that the mathematical symbols represent concepts with meanings, and the meanings of those concepts can even carry connotations.

9.4.7 *Math Expressed in Natural Language*

All of this so far shows that math is more than just syntax; its expressions both denote and even connote—they have semantics.

As further evidence of this contention consider that some mathematical postulates, axioms, and theorems are themselves written in natural language—whether English, French, Greek, Latin, Chinese, etc.—albeit with technical terminology. As a simple example, consider that *Euclid's First Postulate* of geometry is stated in natural language: "A straight line segment can be drawn joining any two points" [276]. As another example, consider *Goldbach's Conjecture (GC)*:

- GC: *Every even integer greater than 2 can be expressed as the sum of two primes.*

Clearly, at least some mathematical expressions, like certain axioms and theorems, are given in second-order natural language with natural language semantics. Hence, there is definitely some overlap between the domain of natural language grammar and that of math.

To get around this example and maintain math is just syntax, some philosophers like Wittgenstein protested that all mathematical 'sentences' must be testable, and testable by syntax alone. Wittgenstein maintained that we should confine our understanding of math to that which is written in the first-order language syntax of mathematical 'sentences' and test them only syntactically. He claimed that GC should therefore not be considered a genuine mathematical statement [277].

However, we can indeed translate axioms and theorems like GC into the first-order language of math. For instance, GC can, roughly speaking, be written as '$p + q = 2n$' (assuming p and q are primes, where $p \leq q$ and $n > 2$).

But such translation is only an instance of abstracting out meanings, like any logical connotations that we don't wish to attend to for the sake of calculation. Translate the syntax of the expression back into the syntax of natural language grammar and all the second-order language connotations return. For example, "every" in GC's natural language phrasing, "every even integer," implies that all even integers, no matter how much greater than 2, are available for scrutiny. In which case, we can at least in principle attend to them no matter how great they are. This is not stated, but it is implied—it's a logical connotation and therefore part of the semantics of the mathematical statement. Hence, once again we see that math does indeed entail semantics as well as syntax.

To rebut this point, Wittgenstein would claim that although GC can be translated into the first-order language of math, doing so still does not make GC syntactically testable—it does not give us a testable 'sentence'. However, this maneuver seems designed to avoid both the assumed and implied semantics that are indeed inherent in mathematics, and it turns out not to be true.

Clearly, GC is falsifiable (able to be shown false, if indeed it is false) by simple calculation. If, for example, we were to find that no two primes (like 3 and 5), when added together, equal an even integer (such as the number 8), then GC would be false. Of course, this isn't so, but that doesn't matter; the point is, we know what would prove GC false, so we can test GC to see if it's false, and the test can be performed only with syntax. Again: *at least in principle if not in practice*, for we can imagine some even integer too large for us to define today, but not at some point in the future and we can also imagine there could be even integers that are definable only in principle but not in practice. So, GC is certainly falsifiable in principle, arguably falsifiable in practice.

However, we can also ask if GC is verifiable (able to be shown true). That is harder to say. It depends on what "every even integer" means; does it mean every even integer invented so far, or every even integer that can be invented in practice, or every even integer that can be invented in principle, or does it mean every even integer from a literally infinite set of integers? If it means the latter condition, then it is difficult to see how GC can be verified without contradiction—a point in Wittgenstein's favor. If it means one of the former conditions, then we can see that GC can be verified.

Due to this ambiguity, GC may need a bit of refinement:

- GC: (revised) *For any even integer able in practice to be defined as greater than 2, the integer can be expressed as the sum of two primes.*

Logicians will notice in that version of GC some troublesome modal words (such as 'able' and 'can'), but let's assume this statement of GC is clear enough. If we state GC this way, then GC is verifiable as well as falsifiable.

It doesn't matter if we actually test GC to see what the outcome is. The only thing that matters is that we understand the *meaning* of GC enough to comprehend what testing it would be like. If upon exhausting our ability to define even integers, we find that all defined even integers greater than 2 are indeed expressible as the sum of two primes, then we have verified GC. If verifiability is to be the standard of meaningfulness, then GC can be a meaningful statement in mathematics—an instance of mathematical semantics.

Moreover, we could capture this modified version of GC in formal logic without much altering the first-order formulation. It is not necessarily true, then, that GC isn't syntactically testable even though its primary expression is in second-order, natural language.

This example illustrates again that math is more than syntax alone; semantics are either assumed or implied in axioms, theorems, and mathematical conjectures. And taking testability into account, the semantics may even imply which syntactical means should be used as a test for the consistency of the mathematical statement.

Some philosophers and mathematicians retort that, aside from natural language axioms, theorems, and such, mathematical *operations* performed on first-order language 'sentences' or 'statements' carry no meaning. Such expressions can only be assessed as 'true' or 'false' in the sense of being either syntactically consistent or inconsistent, not in the sense of *meaning* something that is representative of a state of affairs outside the mathematical system itself [278]. In math, a 'sentence' such as '$8 \div 2 = 4$' is true while '$8 \div 3 = 4$' is false because the former is consistent according to the syntactical rules of math while the latter is not. Since determining the truth of a mathematical 'sentence' is merely a matter of formal consistency, then comprehending a 'sentence' in the first-order language of mathematics does not require semantics, just syntax. Even a mindless computer can use formal, first-order language expressions (or at least voltage levels corresponding to them) to perform calculations on behalf of human users without any need for understanding the semantics of the concepts behind such expressions. So, any natural language expression is unnecessary or irrelevant.

But this is not entirely accurate. It is true that testing a mathematical expression for truth or falsity is a matter of simply testing it for syntactical consistency. But just because the truth or falsity of a mathematical expression is determined by syntactical test rather than semantic test against an observation does not mean that the mathematical expression in first-order language does not assume or imply meaning. An expression like '$8 \div 2 = 4$' carries a primary meaning—namely, that four (4) is the *solution* of the *division process*; the semantics of '$8 \div 2 = 4$' is thus directly implied by the denotation of the expression's terms. And '$8 \div 2 = 4$' also has a connotation: the expression can be applied to many situations as a *measure*, such as the division of a group of eight people into two parties of four people. Hence, mathematical operations are not shorn of all semantics, of all *meaning*. The meanings may be simply assumed or implied rather than attended to directly during procedure.

As for machines performing mathematical operations, the machines are programmed to output *meaningful* data. The machine may not understand the meaning of the output but the human user of the machine does indeed need to comprehend the semantic content of the concepts *assumed* by the formal syntax of the machine's outputted expressions in order to understand their significance.

Further, in order to be comprehensible and significant, mathematical expressions must be meaningful, not just organized strings of uninterpreted symbols. For example, the following expression will only be comprehensible to those who already know about derivatives in calculus:

$$y = \pm\sqrt{25 - x^2}$$

Such examples show yet again that mathematics is not just syntax alone and is not solely a first-order language and nothing more; mathematical expressions in first-order language translate into second-order language statements that have semantics, even if those semantics are considered in purely denotative terms and any further connotations are ignored for the sake of carrying out mathematical procedure, as demonstrated by first-order language calculations performed by machines but carrying significance only humans understand.

9.4.8 *Meaning Matters to Math*

Defining mathematical terms formally, using first-order language to make various mathematical expressions, testing the consistency of those expressions by using the formal syntax of math alone, and even the ability to program machines to output strings of symbols do not indicate that there is no semantic content in mathematics. Mathematics may be a formal, first-order language in terms of how its notation can be used without reference to semantic content. But it is a mistake to think mathematical terms have *no* semantics at all and that math does not make use of terms having assumed meanings and logical connotations.

As a further example, take $E = 7.76 \times 10^{18}$ J as an expression in formal, mathematical language. Certainly, it follows mathematical syntax. But it has more than just syntax; it's also an example of $E = mc^2$, which has meaning for physicists. That meaning becomes apparent to all of us when the expression is translated into the syntax of natural language grammar—"The quantity of energy in this body is equal to seven-point-seven-six times ten to the power of eighteen Joules." And if you know what a Joule is, not only are the primary semantics obvious, but the connotation in that mathematical expression also becomes apparent: an explosive force many thousands of times greater than an atom bomb.

But even more relevant to the case I am making in this book is the fact that semantics in mathematics definitely shows up when predicates are involved, such as 'finite' and 'infinite' and like terms—all such predicates, simply *as* predicates, have associated meanings. A 'sentence' in math like '$\infty + \infty = \infty$' thus carries semantic content because ∞ is a symbol for infinity, which is a predicate for a quantity—it *means* a collection having a size greater than that which is *finite* (another predicate).

Moreover, each use of infinity in '$\infty + \infty = \infty$' has a connotation—taken literally, each ∞ represents a set that is in quantity complete and limitless; taken figuratively, each ∞ represents a process that only seems limitless. Either way, more predicates are implied and they too have meanings. Further still, the expression as a whole has a connotation: to combine infinite collections or processes results in another collection or process that is also infinite. The connotation is readily seen when we consider the 'sentence' in its natural language syntax: "Infinity added to infinity is still infinity."

Hence, meaning of either a literal or figurative sense for infinity in '$\infty + \infty = \infty$' and the connotations thereof are still assumed or implied despite the abstractness of the expression's first-order syntax. Which just goes to show that mathematical expressions have *both* syntax *and* semantics. Consequently, even mathematical expressions—especially those involving infinity—must follow rules for syntax and semantics.

Moreover, even morphology plays a role in mathematics. A symbol such as Ω is used in various ways according to various mathematical systems, and mathematical variables and terms like 'infinite' also vary in usage among differing mathematical systems.

Hence, in order to be coherent in the domain of mathematics, any given mathematical expression must have consistent and comprehensible use according to rules not only for syntax but also for the semantics and morphology of the expressions.

9.5 OVERLAPPING MAGISTERIA

The domains of expression comprising grammar, logic, and mathematics overlap in various ways. Let's take a brief look at how these domains relate to one another.

9.5.1 *The Grammar of Mathematics*

The rules of syntax, semantics, and morphology must be followed so that our translation of a mathematical concept into natural language can be consistent and comprehensible. Whenever the formal use of a concept in math is translated into a natural language like English (such as when $n \to \infty$ is translated as, "The variable 'n' tends to infinity"), the translated expression must still follow the rules of grammar to make sense. Math and grammar thus overlap in their domains of expression.

However, the rules of syntax in most natural languages dictate that there is more than one way to use a word. This holds for words designating mathematical concepts as well as for words used in other fields. For instance, in the English language, there are rules of syntax and morphology that allow a mathematical concepts to be used according to various speech parts—noun, adjective, adverb, etc.—from natural language. The rules of grammar determine how a term is used according to its linguistic variants, as when 'infinity' is used as the adjective 'infinite', the adverb 'infinitely', and so on. This remains so even in technical domains of expression such as mathematics where mathematical expressions are translated or interpreted into natural language.

Consider how the rules of grammar apply to the cognates of the noun 'infinity' such as its related adjective 'infinite' and an adverb 'infinitely', both of which we have been using thus far. The semantics and morphology of natural language dictate that each cognate of a word still retains essentially *the same meaning*. If we mean infinity literally, then the cognates 'infinite' and 'infinitely' express that something is understood to be both complete and limitless in quantity.

So, when the word 'infinity' is used as a noun, it designates in its literal sense the *condition* of being both complete and limitless in quantity. When a sequence of numbers 'tends to infinity', the sequence is in the process of becoming complete and limitless, whereas to be 'infinite' (adjective) is *to have the property of* such a complete-limitless condition. Mathematicians often use the adjective 'infinite' in its literal sense to refer to a complete series of *prime numbers* (a natural number greater than 1 and divisible only by 1 and itself) that is also limitless in quantity—'an infinite number of primes'. Then too, there is the adverb 'infinitely', which designates a *complete-yet-limitless sequence between two elements*. Mathematics makes use of the cognates of infinity and all these cognates assume infinity, in its literal sense, to be that which has the properties of completeness and limitlessness in quantity.

By contrast, if we mean infinity figuratively, then the cognates 'infinite' and 'infinitely' express that a process continuously changes in quantity but is always limited. Even with the figurative sense of 'infinity', the grammar of the word's cognates is what allows the concept of infinity to retain a consistent meaning, just as the rules of mathematics ensure infinity is used consistently in formulas.

For another example of applying grammar to mathematics, consider how grammar allows the adjective 'infinite' to be used as a noun: 'the infinite'. In academia, when 'the infinite' is spoken of, the term either refers to something infinite or, more often, to the very concept of infinity [279]. Mathematicians often refer to 'the infinite' (that is, infinity as a concept) such as when they want to discuss how infinity can be calculated in certain ways, applied to certain areas of physics, and so on.

Then too, the adverb 'infinitely' is commonly used in mathematics and with the same meaning. For example, mathematicians often state that there are 'infinitely many' natural numbers, in which case there must be a natural number composed of a complete set of limitless digits, and that number is itself removed from any finite natural number by an intermediate (complete) set of limitless numbers.

Mathematicians also use the adverb 'infinitely' in reference to *infinitesimals*—points or portions of space that are claimed to be 'infinitely small' in size or instants of time claimed to be 'infinitely brief' in duration. Basically, any extent of space or span of time claimed to be subdivided into a complete set of units that are limitless in quantity. Scientists too make use of the adverb 'infinitely' as when astronomers claim that there exist galaxies that are *infinitely* far away from our own in space and, perhaps, in time; presumably, this means there is a complete collection of a limitless number of galaxies from here to there.

All of these examples illustrate how a mathematical term—in this case, infinity—is used according to the common speech parts (noun, adjective, and adverb) not only in colloquial discourse but also in the natural language expressions of mathematics itself. Math and grammar thus overlap in their domains of expression, with math relying heavily on natural language grammar for semantic content, perhaps especially with talk about infinity.

9.5.2 *The Logic of Math and the Mathematical Nature of Logic*

Math and logic also overlap in their domains of expression. Both math and logic, for instance, study schemas, though in different respects.

Mathematics studies schemas that are inherently numerical. Examples of numerical schemas include numerals, numbers, collections of numerals or numbers, scales or numbers, and numbers as values, variables, totals, amounts, quantities, ordinals, cardinals, etc. Numerical schemas are organized by schemes like axioms, theorems, operations, formulas, and so on.

Formal logic is like mathematics in that it too has schemas. For example, formal logic, as a sub-discipline of logic, studies schemas in terms of text templates, argument templates, and so on. Moreover, symbolic logic as a branch of formal logic studies schemas such as Venn diagrams, truth tables, etc. (See **Figure 9.3**.) The schemas of formal and symbolic logic are, like math, organized by schemes, but unlike math, they are not schemes for enumerating; rather, the schemes in logic include rules of inference, formal proofs, and other procedures.

But the schemas and schemes of formal logic are a bit different than those of mathematics. Although symbolic logic makes use of formal symbols (usually letters and operators) and diagrams, symbolic logic is based on statements rather than numeric expressions. The schemas of logic, as logic is studied academically, are thus linguistic and symbolic but not numerical or enumerative (concerned with a process of assigning numbers to the members of a collection) as they are in math.

1. P ⊃ Q
2. P
∴ Q

p	q	p • q	p ∨ q	(p • q) ⊃ (p ∨ q)
T	T	T	T	T
T	F	F	T	T
F	T	F	T	T
F	F	F	F	T

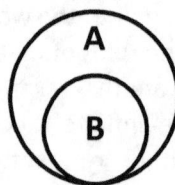

Figure 9.3: Examples of some logical schemas.

It is true that logic is also used to quantify, but formal logic quantifies with predicates like 'some', 'most', 'none', 'all', and so forth, whereas in mathematics more precise schemas like numbers and variables are used to quantify. So while some instances of logic involve quantification, logic (as formal or symbolic logic) quantifies differently from mathematics.

Logic is therefore not reducible to math. Logic, regarded narrowly as formal logic (and symbolic logic) is a set of principles for language-based reasoning; logic, regarded in a broader sense, may be taken as encompassing the principles of reasoning in any form of expression, whether in natural language or mathematical language. By contrast, the scope of mathematics is necessarily confined mainly to enumerative expressions, rather than more broadly as including statements in natural language or in symbols for such, as is the case with logic.

Logic and math should also not be considered mutually exclusive. Math makes use of logic as it is applied to numerical schemas, such as by deducing theorems from axioms and proposing rules that operations must follow in order to be mathematically coherent. And logic sometimes makes use of enumeration, numbers, or other mathematical concepts in composing linguistic arguments or accounts. For example, consider this argument:

If only five people are in the room and three are asleep, then two people are awake.
Only five people are in the room and three are asleep.
Therefore, two people are awake.

Here we have a valid argument involving constant numbers (five, three, and two)—a clear example that logic, expressed in natural language, can involve concepts used in mathematics.

For that matter, consider a statement that makes use of quantification by logical predicate as well as the concept of infinity (itself a predicate that is often applied to numerical sets):

All infinities are limitless collections.

In this statement, the predicate "all" in natural language translates into symbolic logic as the quantifier ∀. "Infinities"—multiple collections that are infinite—can be represented as Ix (x is a collection and the capital "I" means the collection is infinite); the rightwards horseshoe (⊃) represents an if/then conditional relation; and the limitless (L) collections (x) are represented by Lx.

So, in symbolic logic, the same statement "All infinities are limitless collections" reads like this:

$(\forall x)(Ix \supset Lx)$

Although, translating the symbols more precisely yields the statement, "If something is infinite, then it is a limitless collection." However, the logical implication is the same.

Or consider the following valid argument that makes use of quantification:

All infinities are limitless collections.
All limitless collections are complete.
Therefore, all infinities are complete.

Ignoring the fact that the truth value of the second premise is rather dubious, the important point is that the same argument can be restated in the formal notation of symbolic logic. The premises are numbered, a horizontal line separates the conclusion from the premises, and the symbol ∴ represents the conclusion indicator ("therefore", "thus", "hence", "so", etc.). The formal expression of the argument is given as:

1. $(\forall x)(Ix \supset Lx)$
2. $(\forall x)(Lx \supset Cx)$
∴ $(\forall x)(Ix \supset Cx)$

Once again, we have a formal, symbolic expression of a linguistic statement, this time in the form of an argument that quantifies, at least with the quantifier "all."

Although quantification characterizes the domain of mathematics, albeit with numbers, you can think of this type of symbolic logic (predicate calculus) as 'mathematical' in a loose sense. As the above examples show, logic and math thus overlap in subject matter (quantification) and one field can draw on the concepts (like infinity and inference) of the other field even while the domain of neither field reduces to that of the other. So, there is some overlap between math and logic, and neither field engulfs the other.

9.5.3 *On Mathematics as the Study of Possible Patterns and Abstract Structure*

Not all mathematicians would agree with defining mathematics in terms of numerical schemes. They would likely protest that math is not essentially about the study of the numerical but instead is about broader properties. For instance, Barrow defined mathematics as "the study of possible patterns" [280]. Many other mathematicians contend that mathematics is "the study of abstract structure" [281].

In and of themselves, these are not very useful definitions for distinguishing mathematics from other fields. Certain branches of logic can be said to study 'possible patterns,' but logic is not reducible to mathematics, nor vice versa. Similarly, fashion designers study possible patterns when they design prints for clothing, but this too is not mathematics. So, math cannot simply be the study of possible patterns. Then too, the same can be said for attempts to define mathematics as the study of abstract structure. Modern artists and art critics study 'abstract structure' in different respects and so do logicians, philosophers, and business model architects. There is also little consensus in the field of mathematics over what 'abstract structure' even means; the term 'abstract structure' is awfully vague for such a precise discipline.

To give such a definition more precision, Dr. Solomon Feferman, Professor of Mathematics and Philosophy at Stanford University, refers to a mathematical structure as a "coherently conceived group of objects interconnected by a few simple relations and operations" [282]. I'm sure this too is shorthand for a more technical definition, but as it stands it again cannot be quite right since the same definition would apply to structures studied in physics, chemistry, biology, computer science, and other fields rather than only mathematics (depending on how 'relation' and 'operation' are defined).

Dr. Daniel Isaacson, a philosopher of mathematics at Oxford University, attempted to justify the notion that mathematics is the study of abstract structure by noting that there are two sorts of structures studied in mathematics: *particular structures* and *general structures*. He gives examples of these [283]:

> We speak of *the* natural numbers and *a* group. Particular structures include the natural numbers, the Euclidean plane, the real numbers. General structures include groups, rings, fields, metric spaces, topologies. The particularity of a particular structure consists in the fact that all its exemplars are isomorphic to each other. The generality of a general structure consists in the fact that its various exemplars need not be, and in general are not, isomorphic to each other...
>
> For the first several thousand years of its development mathematics was all about using and studying particular structures (the natural numbers, later the integers, the Euclidean plane, Euclidean three-space, the rationals, later the reals, still later the complex numbers). The recognition and study of general structures began in the first half of the 19th century, with the work of Galois and others on the solution of polynomial equations, which led to the notion of a group. By the second half of the 20th century general structures were paramount in mathematics...

However, Isaacson's 'particular structures' (numbers, planes, etc.) and 'general structures' (fields, metric spaces, etc.) are just two categories of schemas, and you'll notice they are all schemas organized by schemes that *quantify*, not just with predicates, but with *numbers*. Even the structures of geometry (points, lines, planes, etc.) are studied in mathematics only insofar as they are numerical or can be enumerated—dealt with in terms of numbers, such as when we assign measures of length or degrees to angles. Therefore, I have to conclude my definition of mathematics as the study of numerical schemes and schemas does not need revision so far.

Of course, some mathematicians might retort that set theory—the study of sets—is a discipline of mathematics while set theory is not entirely about enumeration or numerical schemas. Isaacson states that set theory is not only a branch *of* mathematics, but it can also function as the foundation *for* mathematics because set theory "encompasses all of mathematics, in that all particular mathematical structures can be shown to exist within the cumulative hierarchy of pure sets" [284]. This is indeed the view held by many mathematicians.

However, it could be counterargued that when Georg Cantor invented modern set theory, he was acting as a *logician* and as a *philosopher* of mathematics, drawing on the concepts of formal logic to do so. We could therefore consider much of set theory to be in reality a sub-discipline of formal logic as well as mathematics.

Some mathematicians might respond by claiming that even if set theory is a sub-discipline of formal logic, formal logic itself is a mathematical discipline, and therefore so is set theory. But although math draws upon logical principles, and although formal logic contains inferences that "quantify" in the sense of predication, formal logic cannot be a sub-discipline of mathematics. Formal logic includes content beyond what mathematicians qua mathematicians study as part of their field. For example, non-quantitative forms of induction and practical reasoning. Formal logic, therefore, does not reduce to a mathematical discipline and neither does set theory.

At the same time, just as it is true that formal logic is not reducible to a mathematical discipline, so too mathematics is not just a special case of formal logic. Math includes content beyond formal logic (such as interpretations of numerical axioms, theorems, and quantity that have no justification according to the principles of formal logic, and mathematics even contains some logically dubious notions like, I argue, the concept of infinity).

Moreover, set-theoretical concepts are used in math for quantifying in a way not found in formal logic; set theory plays special roles both for mathematics in general and transfinite mathematics in particular. Set theory is therefore not exclusively a part of formal logic either.

Mathematics and formal logic overlap with common concepts and principles, but neither field can be reduced to the other, nor do either contain set theory exclusively. Set theory belongs to *both* mathematics and formal logic while *neither* field is a sub-discipline of the other. And in fact, some academics recognize set theory as a branch of *mathematical logic*.

Both the fields of mathematics and formal logic draw on set theory in different ways. Mathematics contains set theory insofar as set theory is used as the theoretical justification for constructing our concepts of number and enumeration, and formal logic contains set theory insofar as set theory is used as a basis for categorizing how sets relate to one another (which goes all the way back to Aristotelean logic and its later expression with the use of Venn diagrams) and as a basis for linguistic quantification (a form of predication rather than enumeration). The relationship of math and logic with respect to set theory is represented in **Figure 9.4**.

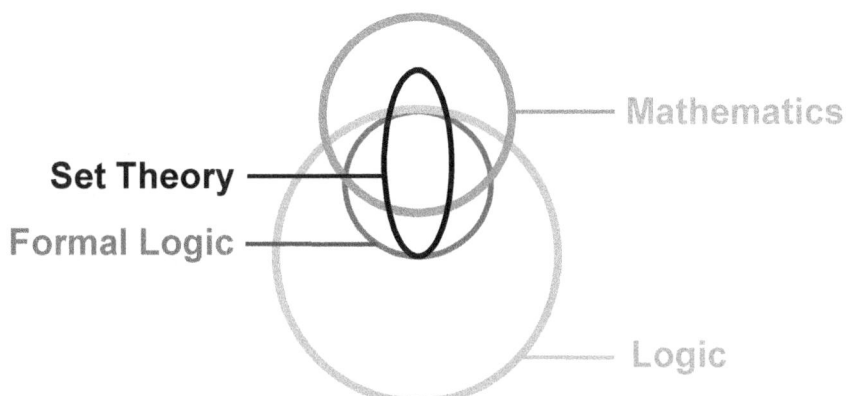

Figure 9.4: The domains of mathematics and logic not only overlap with each other but also share the sub-domains of formal logic and set theory. Note that some content in set theory (pertaining to infinity) is not in the domain of logic even if it is mathematical while some set theory content is logical but not mathematical. The relative sizes of the ellipse for set theory and circle of formal logic are not exact but made for compatibility with Figure 9.5, in which set theory overlaps with areas 2–4 and formal logic overlaps with areas 3 and 4; neither being outside the scope of grammar.

Set theory may be, in part, a branch of mathematics and it may be useful for studying the various schemas of mathematics. However, much of set theory rightly belongs as a branch of logic as well. What distinguishes whether we are dealing with set theory in terms of math or logic alone has to do with what place enumeration plays in set theory. It is enumeration rather than simply the study of categories or collections or sets as "abstract structures" that distinguishes mathematics from logic. When we study sets merely as abstract containers that relate to one another in terms of what elements and sets "belong" to one another, set theory belongs to logic. When we study sets of numbers in order to form axioms of enumeration, we are studying set theory as a mathematical discipline.

I therefore maintain that the subject of mathematics is the study of numerical schemas, to include number and quantity as such, while formal logic studies inference, some instances of which include quantification by predication (use of predicates rather than numbers to quantify) and use of categories such collections like sets, etc. Math and logic thus overlap, especially in terms of set theory, but each has distinct content the other does not.

The controversy over the relation between mathematics and formal logic will not be further addressed here since pursuing it would take us too far afield. Instead, I will simply propose that math is essentially about numerical schemas in general, while logic extends beyond these considerations, and both fields share set theory.

9.6 THE DOMAINS OF COHERENCE

Now that we have our domains of expression defined and distinguished, we can address the standards in these domains for what counts as a *coherent* expression and what counts as an incoherent expression. As depicted in **Figure 9.5**, the domains of expression contain somewhat narrower *domains of coherence*.

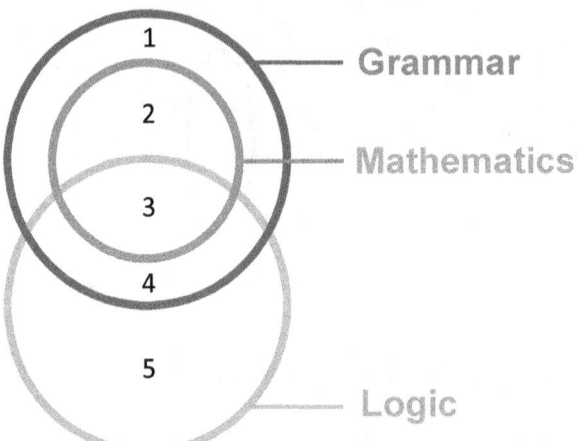

Figure 9.5: The domains of expression as domains of coherence. Where two domains overlap an expression is coherent according to the standards of both domains: the semantics remain constant while the syntax of one domain can be translated into the syntax of the other domain. (Various expressions of infinity are found in Areas 1–4.)

9.6.1 *Coherence*

Here is how I am using the term [285]:

- coherence: *the condition of having both consistency and comprehensibility.*

An expression is 'coherent' for a given domain if it is both *consistent* with the principles governing how expressions are structured in that domain (syntax) and *comprehensible* according to the standards of meaning in that domain (semantics). Incoherent expressions are those that violate the syntax and/or semantics of the given domain(s) [286].

9.6.2 *Standards of Coherence*

Each field's domain of expression has its own standards of coherence. Standards for coherence in grammar are not equivalent to standards of coherence in logic and math; and what counts as coherent in logic is not necessarily what would be considered coherent in math, and vice versa. Nevertheless, there is also overlap among the domains in terms of standards for coherent expression.

To better grasp where infinity loses coherence among these areas of discourse, and where it does not, we can make a Venn diagram of three circles: one circle representing the domain of grammar, another circle representing the domain of mathematics, and one more for the domain of logic, as portrayed in **Figure 9.5**. In **Figure 9.5**, the three domains (each domain denoted by a circle) represent all expressions that conform to the standards of coherence for their respective fields: The domain of grammar represents all grammatically coherent expressions in natural language, the domain of mathematics represents all mathematically coherent expressions, and the domain of logic represents all logically coherent expressions. Each domain has rules determining the conditions that expressions must satisfy to be considered coherent in that domain [287].

An expression is *incoherent* for a given domain if it violates that domain's rules (of either syntax or semantics, or both) [288]. Expressions that violate the syntactic rules of a domain may still be comprehensible in terms of semantics and yet not properly qualify as "coherent" due to their inconsistent syntax. "Ya ain't got no sense!" is an example of such an expression; it is *comprehensible* but nevertheless *grammatically incoherent* because it violates the rules of syntax for the domain of grammar, and so it cannot be included in the domain of grammar. Conversely, syntactically correct expressions that violate the semantic rules of a domain are *incomprehensible* for that domain and are, consequently, incoherent in terms of that domain. The following lines from Lewis Carroll's poem "Jabberwocky" provide a good example [289]:

> `Twas brillig, and the slithy toves
> Did gyre and gimble in the wabe;
> All mimsy were the borogoves,
> And the mome raths outgrabe.

Despite being syntactically correct for the style of poem, this expression is semantically incomprehensible. As such, it is grammatically incoherent and so does not belong in the domain of grammar [290]; rather, the poem belongs to categories of linguistic expression not illustrated in **Figure 9.5**. Expressions must follow *both* the syntactical *and* the semantic rules of a domain to be considered coherent in that domain;

any expression that is incoherent by the standards of a domain is not included in that domain. (However, if all the nonsensical words in the poem were given consistent definitions, then the poem would migrate at least into the domain of grammatical coherence.)

9.6.3 *Overlapping Domains*

While each domain has its own syntax and semantics, the semantics (and in some cases, the signifiers) do overlap among the domains as well; this is portrayed by the common areas of the circles in **Figure 9.5**. Where two domains overlap, a single expression meets the standards of coherence for both domains. Even if the expression has one form of syntax in one domain, it may have a different form of syntax in the other domain. As long as the expression's syntax can be translated from the form of syntax in the first domain to that of the second domain while sharing the same semantic, the expression can be coherent for both domains.

For example, the expression $1 + 1 = 2$ is not syntactically correct by the standards of grammar but, as we've seen, the expression can be translated into natural language when it is expressed as, "One plus one equals two." The syntax of the expression can be translated from math to proper grammar while the semantics of the expression remains the same in both domains. Hence the expression can be given proper syntax according to either domain without loss of semantic content; the expression therefore conforms to the standards of coherence for the domains of both math and grammar.

Suppose we then attempt to translate the expression into the syntax of formal logic. We may then give the expression as a conditional statement:

If one is added to one, then the sum is two.

This can also be restated as:

Twice the amount of one is the same as two.

In the notation of symbolic logic, the second form of the statement can be expressed:

$a \leftrightarrow s$

The variable a is used to represent $(1 + 1)$, the connective symbol $\leftrightarrow$ is the identity relation which means "is the same as" and s is a variable representing 2. Thus, $a \leftrightarrow s$ symbolizes the statement, "Twice the amount of one is the same as two."

As you can see, the logical syntax is just shorthand for a natural language expression. The logical syntax differs from that of grammar and math, but the semantic content is the same. The ability to translate an expression like $1 + 1 = 2$ into a natural language statement and from there into the symbolic form of a logical statement, $a \leftrightarrow s$, all while retaining consistent syntax and without loss of semantic content shows that the expression shares the same meaning in three different syntactical forms—math, grammar, and logic. So, the expression can be considered coherent according to all three domains—math, grammar, and logic—as long as the right syntax for the expression is used in the right context according to the rules of the respective domains.

On the other hand, notice that the domains in **Figure 9.5** do not entirely overlap. This is because some expressions, while coherent according to the rules of one domain may be incoherent by the rules of another domain and may not be either semantically or syntactically translatable into the other domain. In terms of the domains given in **Figure 9.5**, an expression that is grammatically coherent may be logically incoherent, or vice versa, as indicated by the non-overlap of Areas 1 and 5.

9.6.4 *Domain Areas*

We can use the domains of coherence to categorize different uses of terms—for our purposes, 'infinity' will serve as an example. Expressions containing infinity fall into various areas of **Figure 9.4**. Exactly which area a given expression of infinity falls into depends on what kind of expression is made; a given expression may be logical only, grammatical only, both logical and grammatical, etc.

Using these domains, we will see the ways in which talk of infinity is coherent and the ways in which (literal) infinity is an incoherent concept. To illustrate, let's take a brief look at some examples of expressions for each of the areas in **Figure 9.5**.

Area 1: Grammar Beyond Math and Logic

The area in **Figure 9.5** labeled with the numeral 1 contains expressions that are grammatically coherent according to the syntactic and semantic rules of natural language; however, the expressions in Area 1 also lie outside of the domains of mathematics and logic, making them mathematically and logically incoherent. Examples of Area 1 expressions include questions ("What do you think about infinity?") and exclamations ("Infinity—bah humbug!"); they fall outside of the rules of logic and math, but not of grammar [291].

Area 1 also contains some declarative sentences that are grammatically coherent, but make no sense in math or logic, like the sentence "Two plus two is infinity." Each of the words in this example, unlike those in the lines from "Jabberwocky," has an understood meaning, and the meaning of the sentence as a whole is understood, even if its claim is untrue and illogical—so it's grammatically coherent but not logically or mathematically coherent. All these examples show that a sentence need not be true or logical to be grammatically coherent, which is why even a declarative sentence like "Two plus two is infinity" still belongs in the domain of grammar.

Similarly, grammatically coherent expressions about infinity that make no mathematical or logical sense also fall into Area 1. An obvious example comes from William Blake's poem, "Auguries of Innocence," which contains the following lines:

> *To see a world in a grain of sand,*
> *And a heaven in a wildflower,*
> *Hold infinity in the palm of your hand,*
> *And eternity in an hour.*

Like the prior cited poem from Carroll, the lines are syntactically correct for the style of poem and, unlike Carroll's poem, all the individual words are semantically comprehensible. So, the poem can be considered grammatically coherent. Nevertheless, one cannot literally hold infinity in one's palm—the poem's line about infinity is a metaphorical sentence but not a statement (it's not a matter of accuracy) and it neither implies a rational conclusion nor is it a reasoned inference. It must therefore be included in Area 1, beyond the domain of logic; and as the line about infinity expresses no mathematical relations, it is also beyond the domain of mathematics.

I bring up these examples to illustrate that in constructing my case against infinity, I do not mean to say that infinity is, in terms of natural language, an incoherent word. Infinity is not *grammatically* nonsensical. The word 'infinity' is governed by the rules of grammar and so it can be used consistently in sentences with the usual literal and figurative meanings.

There is nothing grammatically wrong with the precising definition of literal infinity: "the condition of being both complete and limitless in quantity." In fact, the precising definition for literal infinity belongs here, in Area 1—outside of logic (since, as we'll later see, the definition implies logical contradictions) [292] and even outside of math (since there is no numerical scheme implied in this definition even though "quantity" is referenced).

Area 5: Logic Beyond Grammar and Math

Let's skip from Area 1 over to Area 5. This area is located in the domain of logic and so contains expressions that are logically coherent—logically consistent and comprehensible. However, since this area lies outside the domains of math and grammar, its logical expressions are also grammatically and mathematically incoherent.

Not all expressions of logic need to be grammatically or mathematically coherent. For example, the principles of logic do not themselves need to be articulated in order for an instance of reasoning to abide by them. Some logical reasoning is actually *non-linguistic*. Moreover, although all reasoning is expressed using signifiers of some kind, the signifiers do not necessarily need to be grammatical or mathematical in order for instances of reasoning with them to be logical. Area 5 contains logical expressions using non-linguistic and non-quantitative signifiers and syntax [293].

Statements are not a necessary component of logical reasoning, as scientists have shown with examples of non-linguistic and non-quantitative reasoning being carried out by animals. In such cases, inferences do not consist of reasoning from statements but, instead, reasoning from other forms of representation, such as mental images, memories, feelings, etc. Consider the analogical reasoning of a monkey. It's true—scientists have discovered that monkeys can reason by analogy. Analogical reasoning, when done *effectively*, is a form of logical reasoning by definition. Of course, monkeys don't use words to reason, nor in doing so are they forming equations; their mental signifiers are representational but non-symbolic. Though lacking symbols, monkeys do at times use mental signifiers to reason, as expressed by their behavior. And observation shows that animals such as monkeys can actually reason correctly according to logical principles [294].

So, non-linguistic and non-quantitative reasoning, though grammatically and mathematically incoherent, can still be logically coherent; not all coherent logical reasoning is necessarily expressed in accordance with the rules of grammar or math [295]. However, all reasoning about infinity is linguistic and so belongs within the grammatical domain, and insofar as infinity refers to quantity, the reasoning about infinity also falls in the domain of mathematics. Because of this, Area 5, which designates both non-linguistic and non-quantitative reasoning, contains no expressions of, or about, infinity. With respect to reasoning about infinity, we will therefore stick to logical inferences which fall in the domains of grammar and mathematics.

Area 2: Math Within Grammar and Beyond Logic

Coming back to the areas that overlap, let's turn to Area 2, which is made up of expressions that are grammatically and mathematically coherent, but logically incoherent. A good example of this is the technical redefinition of literal infinity.

We saw that the lexical, precising definition of literal infinity falls into Area 1 due to its logical incoherence. But any rearticulation of literal infinity with a technical definition for mathematics still does not constitute a *logical* definition due to the logically incoherent *connotations* the concept implies (see Chapters 14–16).

For example, take these definitions of infinity [296]:

- infinity: (an Area 1 precising definition) *the condition of being both complete and limitless in quantity.*

- infinity: (an Area 2 technical definition) *The ordinality of a sequence of elements, or cardinality of a set of elements, greater than that of any natural number in* $\mathbb{N}$.

The second, technical definition of infinity is infinity as defined in accordance with Cantor's transfinite system. Insofar as the technical definition assumes the accuracy of the precising definition of infinity, which is infinity in its literal sense (an Area 1 definition), the technical definition for infinity belongs in Area 2—within the domain of mathematics but not in Area 3 where mathematical expressions have logically coherent meanings and implications.

As another Area 2 example, take the fifth of Euclid's first five geometrical postulates [297]:

1. *A straight line segment can be drawn joining any two points.*
2. *Any straight line segment can be extended indefinitely in a straight line.*
3. *Given any straight line segment, a circle can be drawn having the segment as radius and one endpoint as center.*
4. *All right angles are congruent.*
5. *If two lines are drawn which intersect a third in such a way that the sum of the inner angles on one side is less than two right angles, then the two lines inevitably must intersect each other on that side if extended far enough.*

Euclid intended this collection of postulates to be a set of 'axioms'—a body of uncontroversial truths, easily demonstrable by observation and upon which all other geometrical theorems can be proposed. Geometrical theorems can be deduced using these axioms. The first four postulates fall in the domain of logic as well as grammar and math (Area 3) because they can be proven. But the fifth postulate, sometimes called the parallel postulate, cannot be logically proven or empirically demonstrated [298].

While the parallel postulate has intuitive appeal, it fails the requirement for logical consistency. Logic requires the postulate's consequent (that the two lines must eventually intersect) to either necessarily or generally follow from its antecedent (the drawing of two, less than parallel, lines). For Euclid's fifth postulate, the consequent is neither necessary nor generally true, so it's possible for contradictions to follow from the postulate. The parallel postulate may be a mathematical *theorem*, as some mathematicians propose that the lines "converge at infinity" (assuming that makes sense), but the parallel postulate is not logically supported as an *axiom*. In fact, some *non-Euclidean* geometries do not use the fifth postulate at all [299].

While Euclid's first four postulates belong to Area 3 (math within the domains of grammar and logic) as a body of axioms upon which to logically deduce geometrical theorems, the parallel postulate belongs to Area 2—it is grammatically and mathematically coherent (mathematicians do make use of it), but it is not necessarily a logical postulate as it is not logically supportable.

Similarly, there is another mathematical concept that falls into Area 2—the Axiom of Infinity. The axiom is stated in various ways, sometimes quite technically in the formal language of mathematics, other times very simply in natural language like so [300]:

- The Axiom of Infinity: (1) There exists an infinite set.

The Axiom of Infinity is proposed in the transfinite mathematics portion of set theory [301]. The axiom implies the existence of a set (where such a set is implied to be a complete set rather than an incomplete set) that contains every successor to any element in the set such that there is not, even in principle, a greatest element for the set at any time (the sequence is limitless).

Which is to say that, because the Axiom of Infinity is an application of the literal sense of infinity (the definition for which is in Area 1) to the domain of mathematics, such an application of infinity belongs to Area 2—still outside the domain of logical coherence. This is in turn because literal infinity, unlike the idea of indefinitely long parallel lines, is not just logically unsupported but is itself logically self-contradictory. It is a self-contradictory concept because being simultaneously "complete and limitless" implies logical contradictions (detailed in Chapter 14). Because the Axiom of Infinity assumes infinity in its literal sense, which is self-contradictory in definition, the Axiom of Infinity is therefore in worse logical shape than Euclid's parallel postulate, which is simply unproven.

Further, the inclusion of literal infinity (as defined in Area 1 of **Figure 9.5**) into the domain of mathematics is not simply found among the axioms of the transfinite system. Infinity, assumed in its literal sense, can be found in general mathematical disciplines like geometry, as when a circle is described as a polygon with infinite sides. It is also found in calculus where points are described as being infinitely small. All of these are applications of the literal sense of infinity, as defined in natural language, to the domain of mathematics. And none of these applications of the term 'infinity', *when assumed to be infinity in the literal sense*, fall into Area 3 but only Area 2. This is because literal infinity, by its lexical, *precising definition* (Area 1) does not become a logical concept simply because it is rearticulated according to a *technical definition* in mathematics, which is consequently an Area 2 expression of literal infinity.

Consider the way infinity may be technically defined in general mathematics: "A 'number' which indicates a quantity, size, or magnitude that is larger than any real number" [302]. This technical definition of infinity may also assume the Area 1 precising definition for literal infinity ("the condition of being both complete and limitless in quantity") because infinity as technically defined may assume a complete and limitless set of numbers. Since completeness and limitlessness are in logical contradiction, the quoted technical definition of infinity in general mathematics is also logically incoherent even though it is mathematically coherent. As such, the quoted technical definition falls into Area 2, just like the aforementioned technical definition for infinity from the transfinite system.

Then there is the symbolization of infinity to consider. If literal infinity is logically incoherent, then symbolizing it for use in mathematics is akin to symbolizing any other self-contradictory concept—like a square circle or four-side triangle—for use in mathematics. The symbolization of literal infinity (ω or $\aleph$ and sometimes ∞), or its denotation with such symbols, also belongs to Area 2 rather than Area 3.

However, insofar as formal rules of mathematical operation are proposed and can be logically applied to those symbols, the symbols for infinity then fall into Area 3.

Area 3: Math Within Grammar and Logic

Notice from **Figure 9.5** that the domain of mathematics falls entirely within the domain of grammar. This is because all coherent mathematical expressions can be translated into grammatically correct sentences. However, Area 3 of **Figure 9.5** designates the overlap of the domain of mathematics with both the domains of grammar and logic. In Area 3, expressions are grammatically, mathematically, and *logically* coherent. Some mathematical expressions of infinity fall into Area 3.

Whether certain expressions of infinity fall into Area 3 of **Figure 9.5** is, however, largely dependent on context.

Consider literal infinity: while the lexical, precising definition of literal infinity falls in Area 1 (grammar beyond the domains of math and logic), the technical definition for literal infinity falls into Area 2 (math within the domain of grammar but beyond logic). If my thesis is correct, the technical definitions of literal infinity do *not* fall into Area 3—at least, not directly—because technical definitions for literal infinity still connote self-contradictions. However, there are technical definitions for infinity that *do* fall into Area 3 (where grammar, math, and logic cohere together). In Area 3 are technical definitions for infinity that assume infinity to be either a collective indefinite or a serial indefinite--the latter being *figurative* infinity.

Now take these technical definitions for infinity given back in § 7.2:

- infinity: (general mathematics) A 'number' which indicates a quantity, size, or magnitude that is larger than any real number. [303]

- infinity: (transfinite mathematics) The ordinality of a sequence of elements, or cardinality of a set of elements, greater than that of any natural number in $\mathbb{N}$. [304]

The second definition I previously noted falls into Area 2, and that is true insofar as it assumes literal infinity. But simply as stated, neither of the above definitions are at first glance technical definitions of *literal* infinity. After all, neither definition is, at least on its surface, logically self-contradictory. Any logical contradictions would result only from assuming they are technical expressions of literal infinity, in which case, the contradictions would follow from the secondary implications, the connotations, of the technical definitions. Otherwise, we could take these technical definitions as expressing only a figurative infinity, in which case these technical definitions for infinity could be taken as falling into Area 3 of **Figure 9.5**.

Then too, $\mathbb{N}$ as a "set" could be interpreted as a collective indefinite rather than as a literal infinity, and "any natural number" may be interpreted to mean the naturals are constructed as a serial indefinite rather than a literal infinity. The same goes for the real numbers. Collective and serial indefinites are not logically self-contradictory, making the Area 3 designation of these definitions justified.

However, in systems such as the transfinite theory of numbers, these technical definitions of infinity would not be taken as technical expressions of figurative infinity, but rather as technical expressions of literal infinity. In fact, the second definition, which is from the transfinite system, was proposed under the assumption that $\mathbb{N}$ is literally infinite and it is intended to connote that $\mathbb{N}$ is a complete and limitless quantity of natural numbers. So, if interpreted as technical definitions of literal infinity, the two definitions are not so straightforwardly in Area 3, for the technical definitions of literal infinity imply completeness and limitlessness as lexically defined, and they contract each other as such (Area 1).

Here, then, is where context is important to mathematical definitions.

We can say that insofar as these technical definitions for infinity are technical definitions for *literal infinity*, they fall into Area 2 with respect to what they connote or assume infinity to be. That is, they fall in Area 2, which is outside of the domain of logical coherence, if they *connote* infinity to be a complete and limitless quantity—the lexical definition of literal infinity in Area 1. We could also say that insofar as a given technical definition for infinity is *assumed* to be the technical expression of literal infinity as so lexically defined (Area 1), that technical definition belongs to Area 2.

On the other hand, insofar as the given technical definitions for infinity *denote* or *imply* only a serial indefinite (figurative infinity) or a collective indefinite in terms of mathematical operation, the technical definitions for infinity as so defined imply no contradictions and so could be said to fall into Area 3. Hence, the second technical definition for infinity above, may be intended as an expression of literal infinity is in Area 2, but it may nevertheless be construed as logically coherent with respect to what it actually denotes in terms of mathematical operation—results that are only "infinite" in the figurative sense (Area 3).

This indicates that while mathematicians may propose technical definitions in order to be "more precise" about infinity, when they propose the technical definitions for literal infinity, they quit working with infinity as everyone thinks of infinity—infinity as a condition of the limitlessness of a complete set (Area 1)—and, instead, redefine literal infinity in technical terms (Area 2) that end up only denoting mathematical conditions that are figuratively infinite in terms of their actual operation (Area 3).

In other words, it's not that *technical* definitions for literal infinity are logically self-contradictory in *all* respects and therefore exclusively fall into Area 2. Rather, it's that technical definitions for literal infinity are necessarily *misleading* since, with respect to the mathematical operations based on them, they do not actually refer to what the term 'infinity', in its literal sense, is commonly assumed to imply: a state of literal completeness and literal limitlessness in quantity.

While the technical definition of literal infinity (Area 2) may assume the lexically precising definition of literal infinity (Area 1), the technical definition may only imply figurative infinities in terms of the mathematical operations based upon it. Hence, the 'infinity' of the technical definitions—though they falsely assume to be mathematically expressing literal infinity (Area 1)—may nevertheless be logically consistent insofar as they denote the condition of formal operations that produce only the figuratively infinite (Area 3).

This mismatch between the precising definition of literal infinity (Area 1) redefined technically in mathematics (Area 2) and used in mathematical operations (Area 3) reveals the inconsistency between how infinity is used (Area 3) and how it is interpreted (Area 1) even by the same mathematical discipline.

When infinity is abstracted into symbolism, the matter is much more straightforward. We may find infinity in the formalism of mathematics without loss of coherence in either its grammar or logic. Consider, for example, the mathematical equation $\infty + \infty = \infty$. This shares the same semantic meaning as the sentence "Infinity plus infinity equals infinity," even though the two forms of expression have quite different syntax. Once again, the syntax of one expression can be translated into the other by reference to their common semantics, without loss of meaning.

Then too, suppose we translate the expression into formal logic:

If infinity is added to infinity, then the sum is infinity.

The previous sentence can also be stated as:

Twice the amount of infinity is the same as infinity.

This statement in turn can be expressed with the notation of symbolic logic:

$t \leftrightarrow f$

The symbol t represents $(\infty + \infty)$, the connective symbol $\leftrightarrow$ is the identity relation which means "is the same as," and f is a symbol representing ∞ alone. Thus, $t \leftrightarrow f$ symbolizes "Twice the amount of infinity is infinity" or "If infinity is added to infinity, then the sum is infinity." Since we can translate $\infty + \infty = \infty$ into a natural language statement and from there into logical symbolism, $t \leftrightarrow f$, this too shows that the expression shares the same meaning in three different syntactical forms—math, grammar, and logic.

Again, we see that, if an expression can be properly translated from one form of syntax to another without contradiction or loss of meaning, then it can be regarded as coherent according to the standards of any of the three domains. Even in logic the expression, as an expression about infinity, can be considered coherent since adding infinity to infinity to yield infinity assumes a technical definition for infinity that treats the term 'infinity' as a figurative notion, which is no more problematic than saying, "A lot plus a lot is equal to a lot." The given expression of infinity thus belongs to Area 3 in **Figure 9.5**—it is mathematically, grammatically, and logically coherent.

All coherent grammatical sentences that are also coherent logical statements and coherent mathematical equations hence fall into Area 3, even those regarding infinity.

But now for another nuance.

Not all formalized, logical expressions are translations of natural language counterparts. This is because a statement in symbolic form might be an elaboration on a natural language statement; a statement that goes beyond the natural language meaning. This has implications for certain mathematical expressions about infinity.

For example, take the Axiom of Infinity: "There exists an infinite set." That is its simplest natural language expression in standard set theory. Now consider how its full logical formulation may appear [305]:

- $\exists x[\exists y[y \in x \wedge (\forall z \neg z \in y)] \wedge \forall z[z \in x \rightarrow \exists w[w \in x \wedge \forall v[v \in w \leftrightarrow (v = z \vee v \in z)]]]]$.

And a more elegant but perhaps less exact version is the following [306]:

- $\exists N : \emptyset \in N \wedge [\forall x : x \in N \supset [(x \cup \{x\}) \in N]]$.

Both formalized versions of the Axiom of Infinity say more than, "There exists an infinite set." The elegant version of the logical expression for the Axiom of Infinity, for instance, can be translated into natural language like so:

- Axiom of Infinity: (2) Let there be a collection N such that the empty set is a member of N and such that for any element, x, if x is a member of N, then the set formed by uniting x with its 'singleton' (a set with exactly one element) is also a member of N.

That is quite an elaboration on the axiom. And it has implications for where the Axiom of Infinity stands in **Figure 9.5**.

While the axiom as originally stated—"There exists an infinite set"—falls in Area 2, this version does not. If we take N as a collection formed from a sequence of ascending numbers (each element, x, being a whole number, n) starting with 0, then the Axiom of Infinity is just another way of stating that we need to apply the successor function to that sequence to formulate the scale of whole numbers ($\mathbb{W}$). However, the first-order formalism of set theory used for this axiom could just as well be applied to N as an incomplete series rather than a complete set, which would mean that N is not literally infinite after all since it's not really a set. The logical expression of the Axiom of Infinity, in the purely symbolic formalization of logical syntax, is revealed to be merely another instance of figurative infinity, which is not logically self-contradictory. Hence, this version of the Axiom of Infinity belongs to Area 3.

There is yet another way of thinking about what the Axiom of Infinity means that would place it back into Area 2. If we take N not as an incomplete series in formation but instead as a complete set with limitless members, then that makes N into a literally infinite set (Area 1), which is a non-logical concept.

What about the axiom as framed in the transfinite system? Putting the Axiom of Infinity into the symbolism of the transfinite system [307], the axiom can be restated as follows:

- Axiom of Infinity: (3) There is an infinite number, ω, such that if n is a natural number less than ω, then $n + 1$ is also less than ω.

The axiom, as so stated, assumes there can in mathematics be an infinite number (ω). Regardless of how ω is used operationally, the meaning of "infinite" for ω in the Axiom of Infinity is the lexical, precising definition of *literal infinity*.

However, because ω refers to literal infinity, which has the self-contradictory definition falling in Area 1, the Axiom of Infinity according to this third definition therefore falls outside the domain of logic, still back in Area 2.

What all of this shows is that whether infinity is found in Area 3 of logical coherence depends on how infinity is defined and how infinity is used in mathematics. Figurative infinity, as technically defined in mathematics, is found in Area 3. But literal infinity is only in Area 2 unless it is abstracted into symbols for use in mathematical operations that are, at best, figuratively infinite so that it can be in Area 3. But expressing infinity in this manner is to use a concept that is "infinity" in name only (see § 14.1.3).

Area 4: Logic Within Grammar and Beyond Math

Area 4 makes up all expressions that are grammatically and logically coherent, but not mathematically coherent. They are either mathematically incoherent or simply not a matter of mathematics at all. Even so, statements that quantify with predicates or that logically interpret mathematical concepts in natural language can be found in this area.

While the lexical or precising definitions for *literal* infinity fall into Area 1 and the technical definitions of literal infinity fall into Area 2, the situation is different for *figurative* infinity. A lexical or precising definition of figurative infinity falls in Area 4 while the technical definitions of figurative infinity are all in Area 3.

Take the precising definition of figurative infinity: "The condition of indefinitely changing in quantity." Calling the condition of indefinitely changing in quantity "infinity" is to use the term 'infinity' as a misnomer for indefiniteness, but that is not necessarily a violation of logic as such. Hence this precising definition for literal infinity is in Area 4.

However, as I will argue in Chapter 24, it is because figurative infinity is a misnomer for serial indefiniteness that it becomes used in logically inconsistent ways. While the *definition* for figurative infinity is in Area 4, logically inconsistent *usage* of figurative infinity easily slips into Areas 1 or 2—the areas beyond logic.

The same is true of the technical definitions for infinity that assume its figurative sense—the technical *definitions* of figurative infinity assumed in mathematics are Area 3 expressions, but technical *uses* of the term 'infinity' that assume its figurative sense slip into Area 2 when they are used in logically inconsistent ways, such as to imply literal infinity.

Now let's turn back to literal infinity according to its precising definition (Area 1): the condition of being complete and limitless in quantity. And let's assume this definition for infinity but consider expressions *about* infinity that are not mathematical—at least not in the sense of involving calculations.

Take our earlier example: "All infinities are limitless collections." This statement uses a quantifier, but the quantifier ("all") is a logical quantifier rather than a mathematical quantity. So, such an expression is not necessarily mathematical. Moreover, while expression can be formulated in the notation of symbolic logic—$(\forall x)(Ix \supset Lx)$—that symbolic version is also not a mathematical expression even though it uses a quantifier because the quantifier is not numerical. And even if we construe the expression as belonging to set theory, it still belongs to the logical side of set theory rather than the mathematical side of set theory that deals with enumeration (see **Figure 9.4**). The expression is thus logical, but non-mathematical.

The expression $(\forall x)(Ix \supset Lx)$ is also logically *coherent* (though, not necessarily *true* since an expression can be coherent without being true). While the definition of literal infinity may be from Area 1, the expression "All infinities are limitless collections," or $(\forall x)(Ix \supset Lx)$, is not beyond logical coherence since there is no contradiction in the expression as such. Hence, the expression $(\forall x)(Ix \supset Lx)$ belongs to Area 4.

Even though it may be true that the definition of literal infinity implies self-contradictions, that is a matter separate from what the expression "All infinities are limitless collections," or $(\forall x)(Ix \supset Lx)$ states. So, the expression still belongs to Area 4.

All logically coherent quantification that is not numerical falls into Area 4, as do all logically valid arguments that quantify, such as in our earlier example:

All infinities are limitless collections	1. $(\forall x)(Ix \supset Lx)$
All limitless collections are complete	2. $(\forall x)(Lx \supset Cx)$
Therefore, all infinities are complete.	$\therefore$ $(\forall x)(Ix \supset Cx)$

The argument is not mathematical even though it 'quantifies' with the logical quantifier "all." Because there is no numerical schema involved, this argument falls into Area 4, the domain of logical and grammatical coherence but not mathematical coherence.

Again, all of that is aside from *what* the statements refer to—literal infinities—which, as a concept, still falls back into Area 1 (or Area 2 if literal infinity is technically redefined for mathematical use, but then it is arguably not really literal infinity).

9.7 CAUGHT IN SELF-CONTRADICTION

So, what is all this talk of the domains of coherence worth? The domains of coherence provide a framework for showing in what ways expressions about infinity are consistent and in what ways they are not. Grammatically, there is no problem with literal infinity since we use the word 'infinity' in grammatically correct sentences all the time. Mathematically, literal infinity is also unproblematic insofar as its *technical redefinitions* are mathematically expressed only for operations that are merely figuratively infinite in consequence. That in itself remains problematic since literal infinity technically redefined for mathematics is arguably just figurative infinity in disguise, but at least the math referencing what is dubbed 'infinite' can be consistent. Where literal infinity certainly goes wrong is in its logic. While we can make logically valid, deductive arguments with references to infinity, the very concept of infinity carries secondary implications, or logical connotations, that are caught in self-contradiction. It is in the logical implications of infinity's literal meaning—a meaning assumed even in mathematical frameworks—that outright contradictions emerge. So, yes, you can make logical arguments referring to infinity and coherent mathematical expressions using symbols for infinity; but the irony is that infinity itself remains logically incoherent as a concept.

To be logically coherent is to have *the condition of being both logically consistent and comprehensible.* In order to be logically coherent, no statement can be inconsistent with itself by violating *the principle of non-contradiction.* (Ironically, this principle is also called the "principle of contradiction" in some logic texts! Unfortunately, cultural conventions are not always consistent.)

The principle of non-contradiction holds that *a statement cannot be both accepted and rejected in the same way simultaneously.* Quite simply, you can't have it both ways; you cannot affirm and deny something and still have your position be logically coherent. To violate the principle of non-contradiction is to contradict oneself. If any statement violates the principle of non-contradiction, then it is not comprehensible and so falls outside the domain of logic.

So, we cannot make statements like "all swans are white and not all swans are white" and "there is and isn't life in other galaxies" (in any literal sense) without violating the principle of non-contradiction. If a statement violates the principle of non-contradiction, then the statement *is self-refuting* (showing itself to be in error) because it is *self-contradictory* (opposed to itself). Academic philosophers also refer to a self-contradictory statement as *absurd* (necessarily false precisely because it is self-contradictory). As I'll show in the chapters to come, the very definition of literal infinity contains a self-contradiction—it is 'absurd'; necessarily false. Self-contradictory statements lie outside the domain of logic since they are logically incoherent; as the definition of literal infinity violates the principle of non-contradiction, it too cannot be considered logically coherent—it is outside the domain of logic and so falls as an illogical concept.

The self-contradiction in literal infinity is in the secondary logical implications (i.e., the logical connotations) of literal infinity's definition: "the condition of being both complete and limitless in quantity." I will show that completeness implies extremes, totality, and countability; limitlessness implies lack of extremes, no totality, and inability to be counted. Ergo, the completeness of being literally infinite is in direct contradiction to the limitlessness of being literally infinite. This makes literal infinity a self-contradictory concept, by definition. (I'll also argue that alternative definitions for literal infinity are either irrelevant or misleading.)

Literal infinity is as self-contradictory as any other term that is defined by an oxymoron. Suppose we propose a new word: *pseudo-eligible*. We define pseudo-eligible is a bachelor who is also a wife. This is clearly an oxymoronic definition. A bachelor is an unmarried male and a wife is a married woman. One person clearly cannot be both at the same time.

Yet, we can make grammatically coherent sentences: "Pat is a pseudo-eligible." We can even form logical arguments using the term:

If Pat is a pseudo-eligible, then Pat is both married and a bachelor.
Pat is a pseudo-eligible.
Therefore, Pat is both married and a bachelor.

The argument is logically valid in form. Still, just being able to use the term 'pseudo-eligible' in grammatically coherent sentences and logically valid arguments does not make pseudo-eligible a logically coherent concept. It still violates the principle of non-contradiction by its connotations (which is why the argument, though deductively valid, is not logically sound). The *definition* of pseudo-eligible is illogical and clearly belongs in Area 1 of **Figure 9.5** even if the word 'pseudo-eligible' can be used in valid arguments.

Similarly, suppose ancient philosophers had proposed a novel geometrical shape: a *non-angularity* (so named to emphasize that it has no angles) and defined the shape as having four sides of equal length (square—clearly having angles) and all its points nevertheless equidistant from its center (circular—without angles). Since the shape has sides, it cannot have all its points equidistant from its center; but it does and so it must have no sides but rather a closed curve—hence the term 'non-angularity'. And yet it does have angles because it has straight sides and corners. The non-angularity is defined as having both sets of properties at once. A non-angularity is a square circle or circular square. Hence, a non-angularity is a term with a self-contradictory definition—an oxymoronic definition that also belongs to Area 1.

Despite having a self-contradictory definition, non-angularity is a noun that can be used in grammatically correct sentences and, like the term 'pseudo-eligible', it can be used in logically valid arguments. But unlike pseudo-eligible, suppose that non-angularity can also be appropriated into the axioms of mathematics and assumed into its symbolism. In that capacity, non-angularity would belong to Area 2—a mathematical concept that is not logical. Suppose further that we could make consistent mathematical formulas involving non-angularities; such would then become part of Area 3—mathematical formalism that is logically coherent.

What would the mathematics of non-angularity look like? Perhaps it would involve the creation of a formula allowing us to calculate the area of its squareness and of its circularity independently of one another so that no contradiction is noticed. Suppose we could get such a formula to work consistently but we also have to stipulate that it only works under certain conditions and that certain other operations in algebra and transcendental math break down in attempts to use them with squares and circles. The result would be that non-angularities are not any less self-contradictory; all that we would end up proving in the construction of such a formula is that a coherent game of square-circle calculation can be made as long as the rules are limited in an ad hoc fashion so that the self-contradictory nature of the non-angularity can be safely ignored. The concept of a non-angularity would be used coherently in math so long as the logical implications—the connotations—of the definition for non-angularity are "abstracted out," swept under the rug for the sake of continuing the game.

Such is also the case with literal infinity. Like non-angularity, the precising definition of literal infinity is self-contradictory (Area 1). Nevertheless, the precising definition of literal infinity from Area 1 is tacitly *assumed* or *implied* when infinity is used in much of mathematics. In fact, it is just that conception of infinity that mathematicians following in the tradition of Cantor claim to have made technically rigorous.

However, that is just what they have not done at all. Instead, they have appropriated the concept of literal infinity and *redefined* it in technical terms (making a different version of it—part of Area 2), then expressed it in formal, operational terms (Area 3) that sidestep the underlying contradictions implied by the precising definition of literal infinity. Just as with non-angularity, the original concept of literal infinity, which falls in Area 1, is when applied in Area 3 so redefined and abstracted from the logical connotations of its meaning in natural language that the concept ceases to be logically problematic in the domain of mathematics. Consequently, like non-angularity, infinity in its technical form can be used in mathematically coherent equations. Nevertheless, also similar to non-angularity, literal infinity still has self-contradictory implications that go unaddressed in its formal language usage.

We will next see exactly where literal infinity becomes logically incoherent. The root of the problem lies in the idea of that which is limitless being also complete. The definition of infinity in the literal sense of the term—a quantity that is "complete and limitless"—turns out to be an oxymoron, a contradiction in terms. The chapters to come thus present the evidence that to be "complete and limitless" is not just a paradoxical state, but a genuine logical contradiction.

CHAPTER 9 IN REVIEW

❖ Natural language and formal language each have various forms of expression in the fields of grammar, logic, and mathematics.

❖ Each field has a *domain of expression*—the scope of how ideas and concepts are communicated with signifiers particular to the field. A domain of expression covers the rules for making and communicating expressions according to the forms of expression particular to the field.

❖ The fields of grammar, symbolic logic, and mathematics each have their own signifiers for expressing ideas and concepts, and all three fields have their rules for expressing the intension, denotation, and connotations of signifiers.

❖ These rules of syntax, semantics, and morphology for each domain of expression determine what counts as a *coherent* expression and what counts as an *incoherent* expression with respect to the given field's domain.

❖ The domains of expression therefore have corresponding *domains of coherence*—grammatical coherence, logical coherence, and mathematical coherence.

❖ Infinity, however precisely defined in the grammar of natural language, is a term used in grammatically coherent ways, but as conceived in natural language it is neither a logically nor mathematically coherent concept.

❖ However, infinity as *technically defined in mathematics* is both mathematically and grammatically coherent, and it is even logically coherent insofar as the 'infinity' so technically defined is merely figurative infinity (serial indefiniteness) and not literal infinity. Even so, while literal infinity may be technically redefined in a way that is mathematically consistent in syntax, semantically it falls outside the domain of logical coherence.

10: COMPLETENESS — IMPLICATIONS FOR INFINITY

Infinity has various technical definitions in mathematics. While some technical definitions for infinity may imply infinity to be a condition of continuing "without limit" in merely a figurative sense [308], other technical definitions for infinity assume infinity to be a condition of *completeness* as well as limitlessness in quantity—infinity in the literal sense [309].

As an example of literal infinity in mathematics, number systems are often portrayed as complete *sets* (e.g., $\mathbb{N}$, $\mathbb{W}$, $\mathbb{Z}$, $\mathbb{Q}$, $\mathbb{R}$, etc.), each containing limitlessly many numbers, instead of as intrinsically incomplete *series* ($\mathbb{N}^C$, $\mathbb{W}^C$, $\mathbb{Z}^C$, $\mathbb{Q}^C$, $\mathbb{R}^C$, etc.) that grow indefinitely larger in their finite quantities of numbers as new numbers are defined or invented [310]. We also typically find the literal sense of infinity assumed in how mathematicians speak and write about collections claimed to be infinite.

For instance, some mathematicians say the real numbers ($\mathbb{R}$) and the rational numbers ($\mathbb{Q}$) taken as sets "with their usual orderings are two familiar examples of ordered fields...every ordered field contains infinitely many members" [311]. Notice the quote does not say every ordered field *proceeds* infinitely, as if the members of the ordered field go on 'infinitely' in the figurative sense. Rather, the quote says that every ordered field "contains infinitely many members" as if the members are already there, complete as well as limitless in their quantity. It is clear some mathematicians take the ordered fields as literally infinite rather than figuratively infinite, or at least slip into literal usage of infinity.

So even in mathematics an infinite collection—such as an infinite set of numbers, an ordered field of numbers, an infinite series of operations, etc.—is a collection implied to be complete with members limitless in quantity, where 'complete' and 'limitless' fit the literal definitions of those terms as explicated in Chapter 3 and Chapter 5.

However, there are logical implications that follow from a collection, such as a collection of numbers, being infinite in the literal sense. There are implications of a collection being complete in quantity and implications of a collection being limitless in quantity. This chapter will examine the implications of the completeness for infinite collections, and you may notice how those implications do not necessarily cohere with limitlessness (as explored in the next chapter).

10.1 THE COMPLETENESS OF INFINITY

Chapter 3 elucidated the concept of a complete collection by defining 'complete' as containing *all* members necessary for a collection to be representative of a given class. In this context, the word 'all' means *each and every*. The word 'all' in the definition of a complete collection therefore implies that a complete collection is a collection having every necessary member needed for the collection to be representative of some given class. As elucidated in Chapter 3, a collection has every member necessary for the collection to be representative of its class when the collection has the following properties:

- wholeness
- entirety
- finish
- fullness
- totality

When a collection is comprised of the *whole, entire, finished, full, and total quantity of members*, then the collection is complete. Bottom line: a collection must have those properties to be complete.

Because literally infinite collections are complete collections, they too must have a whole, entire, finished, full, and total quantity of members [312]. Moreover, each of these completeness properties carries logical implications for literally infinite collections, as we will see over the proceeding sections.

10.2 THE IMPLICATIONS OF FULLNESS

Of the various properties that make a collection complete, fullness is one such property. Recall from § 3.6 that to be full is to be "unable to include additional members of the same class without changing the parameters of the collection." A full collection is a collection the parameters of which we cannot change without denying fullness.

If a collection is full and therefore unable to include additional members without changing its parameters, then we must assume the collection not only has parameters, but those parameters are the 'extremes' within which *all* members of the collection are found. For a collection to be complete, the collection must be full, which means the collection has parameters, which in turn implies the collection has extrema.

Having extrema is critical to the completeness of a collection, for it is the extrema of a collection that determines what counts as *all* the members of the collection and what counts as *not all* members of the collection. In fact, *without* such extremes, it would be vacuous to claim a collection contains *all* the necessary members for it to be complete.

So, if infinite collections are complete, they too must have extremes of some sort that determine what 'all' means when we speak of all the members of an infinite collection.

10.2.1 *Fullness Implies a Minimum and a Maximum*

Mathematicians recognized various kinds of extrema, like the minimal and maximal elements discussed in § 4.2. However, it is extrema in the forms of a minimum and a maximum that are relevant for this discussion.

If a collection is complete and thereby full, then the collection must have a minimum and a maximum not only for any range of values in the collection (as when a scale of 1 to 5 has a minimum of 1 and a maximum of 5) but also for qualifying the amounts necessary for the collection to be full. Hence, a complete collection will have a minimum amount ("at least x") of members to qualify as *full* and a maximum amount ("at most z") to qualify as full [313].

It is true that just having extrema does not imply completeness; even an incomplete collection will have extrema, such as a 'variant minimum'—a minimum for a single iteration of a collection, the value of which changes as the collection is divided into ever smaller amounts, or a 'variant maximum'—a maximum for a single iteration of a collection, the value of which changes as the members of the collection are multiplied with ever greater amounts. Even so, while having extrema does not imply completeness, completeness does imply having extrema; there are always least and greatest amounts (a minimum and maximum) of elements in any collection that is complete.

Insofar as a collection is complete, and therefore a *full* collection, it will have extrema in the form of a 'constant minimum' and a 'constant maximum' number of elements—the minimum and maximum do not change as long as the collection is complete because, as a complete collection, the collection does not grow or diminish over time. Only if the collection loses its completeness does the collection become larger or smaller with more or fewer members.

This is true even for infinite collections—because they are complete collections, they are full collections and so should have both a constant minimum and a constant maximum—I don't mean for the sequence but for the amount of members. However, the constant minimum and constant maximum are, for the amount of members in the infinite collection, not a finite minimum and maximum. For example, to be complete, even a literally infinite *series* must be a closed (finished) series—a series that has reached a finished and full amount of members. Being finished with a full amount of members, even a literally infinite series must have a maximum of members—the infinite quantity itself.

If we were to assume there is *no such thing as a maximum* for an infinitely large collection, then the collection could *never be full*, therefore could not be completed, and so the collection would not be *literally* infinite but perhaps only *figuratively* infinite—a ceaselessly growing finite collection (a serial indefinite) rather than a collection that is already infinite without further modification.

10.2.2 *Infinite Collections with Minima and Maxima*

A literally infinite collection is a complete collection. A complete collection is a full collection and therefore a collection that has a constant maximum for its amount of members. But how can an infinite collection have a maximum? After all, an infinite amount does not seem to grow larger with the addition of any finite number to it. If we can keep repeating such addition, does that not entail there is no maximum to the infinite collection? Not necessarily. It depends on how we represent an infinite collection.

If we represent an infinite collection with the use of an abstract symbol such as $\aleph$, then infinity does not qualify as having a maximum because $\aleph$ is not a definite amount—it is necessarily vague. The reason $\aleph + 1$ is still equal to $\aleph$ even though one more member is added is because the expression $\aleph + 1 = \aleph$ is like saying "a lot plus one more is still a lot." Mathematically, infinity ($\aleph$) is not a maximum size because adding a finite amount to it provides no further definiteness of reference.

However, suppose we represent an infinite collection as a particular set of real numbers (or 'reals'):

- Let R equal the infinite amount of reals ranging from 0 to 1.

The integers 0 and 1 are themselves real numbers. Real numbers between integers include rational numbers (like ¼, ½, and so forth) and irrational numbers (like $1/\sqrt{2}$). The reals are all expressible with decimal values, and that includes numbers such as 0 and 1 since the whole numbers are also real numbers [314]; hence, in the notation of real numbers as rationals, we can say $0 = 0.0$ and $1 = 1.0$.

Assuming there are infinitely many reals from 0 to 1, "already there" in the sequence, then the sequence of real numbers *from* 0 *to* 1 has parameters—namely, 0 and 1—between which is a constant quantity of real numbers. And since $0 = 0.0$ and $1 = 1.0$, both being real numbers themselves, then 0 and 1 are the real number parameters to a closed interval of reals between them. And that establishes that there must be a minimum and maximum amount of real numbers between the closed interval of the two real numbers for that particular collection of reals in order for the collection to be 'full' and 'complete'.

The *minimum* amount that the set of reals from 0 to 1 must have in order to be literally infinite corresponds to the quantity of reals between 0 and 1 that can be placed into bijection with the set of natural numbers ($\mathbb{N}$), which are themselves said to be infinite. Let's call that number $^{(min)}\aleph$. So, we can say $^{(min)}\aleph = \mathbb{N}$.

The *maximum* amount of reals for the set of reals from 0 to 1 must also be an infinite number, but that number must also be at least in principle a definite number because no matter how many reals there are between 0 and 1, the number 1 is the *last* number of the infinite *sequence* of reals and so there must be a *sequence* of numbers culminating in the last number *from* 0 *to* 1 if *all* the reals between 0 and 1 are present at once. (We'll see a counterargument to this deduction later on in § 10.5, but let's run with it for now.) We may not be able to define *in practice* what that next-to-the last real number is, but if "all" the reals are "there" between 0 and 1, and in a linear order, then such a real number would have to exist, even if we cannot in practice identify it. Let's designate the total number of *all* real numbers from 0 to 1 as $^{(max)}\aleph$ since it must be a constant maximum, neither growing nor diminishing in quantity. Since the infinite whole of $\mathbb{R}$ is supposed to be equal to the infinite part of $\mathbb{R}$—namely, the reals from 0 to 1, we can say $^{(max)}\aleph = \mathbb{R}$.

Assuming all of this is correct so far, R can be described by an infinite minimum ($^{(min)}\aleph$) and an infinite maximum ($^{(max)}\aleph$) of reals, which denote that between 0 and 1 there is an infinite set of numbers, a set that is full and complete [315]. Moreover, since fullness implies the reals must be of some definite number that could be expressed (albeit only in principle) for $\aleph$, then it must be that $^{(min)}\aleph \leq {}^{(max)}\aleph$.

Suppose we consider another example: at time t_1 there are infinitely many blue marbles in the Universe and all those blue marbles are in one infinitely large bag [316]. In order to be a collection of infinitely many blue marbles, not only must the quantity of marbles in the bag be without limit, but the collection of marbles in the bag must also be complete, as is, and therefore the bag must be 'full' in the sense of containing at t_1 all the blue marbles necessary to be representative of an infinite bag of blue marbles. As a *full* bag of marbles, the parameters of the bag cannot be made any larger to accommodate more marbles and still represent the "full" bag of t_1 blue marbles; otherwise, the bag is not the full bag of t_1 marbles. If we had another bag of red marbles and at time t_2 colored one of the red ones blue and then tried to drop it into the bag of infinitely many blue marbles, the additional blue marble should just spill off the top of the bag because the bag is already *full*.

But how can a bag of infinitely many marbles be a *full* bag? Anyone can see that a bag of $\aleph$ blue marbles in which another blue marble is added is just a bag of $\aleph$ marbles because the quantity does not change by adding one: $\aleph + 1 = \aleph$. The quantity of marbles in the bag, qua *infinite* quantity, is not changed.

However, the collection at t_1 is a particular collection of marbles and that collection is full *as is*. At t_2 if we add *another* marble, then we have made a *different* collection of marbles—a collection beyond the full t_1 bag of marbles. Now instead we have again a full bag of t_2 blue marbles, but a full bag which is more than the full bag of t_1 blue marbles by virtue of having another marble that the previous iteration of the bag did not. From a mathematical standpoint, to capture the difference in a full bag of limitlessly many marbles from another bag of limitlessly many plus another marble would require further elaboration in notation in order to capture the difference between the bag at t_1 and the bag at t_2.

Suppose, then, that we can compare two bags of infinitely many marbles. One has an infinite set of $\aleph$ blue marbles and the other also has $\aleph$ blue marbles. The members of the sets can be placed into bijection. So, $\aleph = \aleph$. However, suppose we add another blue marble to one of those sets. Nevertheless, we know both sets can still be in bijection due to their *limitlessness*. Once again, $\aleph = \aleph$. Despite that, suppose we could be more precise in capturing the *completeness* of both sets—the completeness of the base-blue marble set and the completeness of the added-blue marble set (i.e., the infinite set plus one additional marble). For simplicity, let's add a superscript in parentheses to predicate the quantitative difference between the two sets. We'll give them arbitrary labels: $^{(x)}\aleph$ and $^{(y)}\aleph$. Without this qualification, it remains true that $\aleph = \aleph$ but with qualification $^{(x)}\aleph \neq {}^{(y)}\aleph$ since one set has one more blue marble than the other—namely, the added blue one. If the base-blue set (x) were given another marble too, then the new set made from it would then be quantitatively equal to the added-blue marble set (y) with respect to quantitative completeness: $^{(x)}\aleph + 1 = {}^{(y)}\aleph$ marbles.

A complete set implies a full set. So, consider again a bag of infinitely many marbles—a complete as well as limitless quantity of marbles—at a given time, t_1. The t_1 bag of marbles was 'full' because it *already had* the infinitude of *all* blue marbles that existed at t_1. To attempt to add any further marbles to the bag would be an attempt to add a finite quantity to an infinite quantity that is already full and complete, as is. To make *more* blue marbles and put them in the bag at t_2 would be to expand the parameters of the original collection, even if only by a finite amount. Such would be to imply either that the original collection was not full and therefore not complete, or it would instead be to create a new infinite collection inclusive of the prior collection as a proper subset, which was already infinite as is. Hence, an infinite collection, as a *full* collection, must have a *maximum* amount of members (e.g., $^{(x)}\aleph$) any further addition to which ($^{(x)}\aleph + 1$) would be *extra* rather than part of the *completeness* of the collection's original quantity.

Then too, the number of marbles in the bag must be an amount *any less than which* the bag would *not* be 'full'—the 'minimum' for the bag to be infinite in contents must itself be an infinity. For example, to be full at t_1, perhaps the bag must have $^{(z)}\aleph$ marbles.

It may be true that, unqualified, $\aleph - 1 = \aleph$, but we can qualify the expression to capture completeness (and ergo, fullness). Were the bag to have any less than the full amount of $^{(z)}\aleph$ marbles, such as $^{(z)}\aleph - 1$, then the resulting set in the bag ($^{(y)}\aleph$) would not be equal to the full bag of the original infinite set ($^{(z)}\aleph$). In other words, $^{(z)}\aleph \neq {}^{(y)}\aleph$. To remove at t_2 a marble from the original set in the bag that *was* full at t_1 would be to create a new set ($^{(y)}\aleph$) in the bag at t_2 that can only be considered full as a *different* infinite set than the original set ($^{(z)}\aleph$), for it remains that $^{(z)}\aleph - 1 = {}^{(y)}\aleph$.

So, both a set of reals from 0 to 1 and a bag of infinitely many marbles are two examples of literally infinite collections (we will revisit these examples in the next chapter and see some very different implications regarding the limitlessness of members in a literally infinite collection). In terms of *completeness only*, each of these examples illustrates that a complete collection implies a *full* collection and therefore a collection with a minimum and *maximum* amount of members, *despite* the limitless quantity in the collections.

This has implications for number scales conceived to be sets, such as $\mathbb{N}$ or $\mathbb{R}$. As the foregoing implies, they too are frequently claimed to be infinite in the literal sense of the term, which implies them to be complete sets of numbers, ergo 'full' sets of numbers, and therefore sets of numbers that must have a maximum amount of numbers, most often symbolized as $\aleph$.

10.2.3 *A Maximum Amount Implies Totality*

The completeness of an infinite collection implies it has a full amount of members, and that fullness entails a minimum and maximum amount of members to the collection. Moreover, having a maximum amount of members, in turn, implies a collection has a *totality* of members.

This is true even of infinite collections. As Hrbáček and Jech state, "Mathematicians ordinarily consider infinite collections, such as the set of natural numbers or the set of real numbers, as finished, completed totalities" [317].

10.3 THE IMPLICATIONS OF TOTALITY

An infinite collection is a complete collection. To be complete implies having a full amount, where a full amount implies an extreme in the form of a maximum, and a maximum implies a totality of members. In § 3.7, totality was defined as the state or condition of having a total. To be complete thus implies a total. A literally infinite collection, as a complete collection, *must* therefore have a total for its quantity of members.

10.3.1 *The Abstraction of Infinite Total*

What having a total means for a finite collection is easy enough to understand. For finite collections, a total may be an exact amount, but just having a total does not mean that the exact amount can in practice be specified. Some totals even for finite collections are so large that in practice they can only be indirectly referred to with a variable. Such is the case with d^* (see § 4.2.7).

But what it means for an infinite collection to have a total is not easy to state. The total of an infinite collection may not be able to be specified with any more precision than an abstract symbol such as $\aleph$ or ω as a placeholder for a more exact value. Yet, even if the total of an infinite collection cannot be *in practice* further specified other than by some symbol such as $\aleph$ or ω, the completeness of the infinite collection implies it to have a *specifiable* total, at least *in principle*.

10.3.2 *Totality Implies Countability*

In order to have an in-principle specifiable total, a complete collection must be *countable* (in principle if not in practice). If it were *not* countable, not even in principle, then the total could not in principle be specifiable. To have a total that cannot be specified even in principle is simply not to have a total at all. Since a complete collection is a collection with a total that can at least in principle be specified, a complete collection must therefore be countable.

To be *countable* is to have the ability to be counted—to have *every* element in a given collection listed with a unique counting numeral for an exact sum. Infinite collections too, by having a totality and thereby being complete, must also be countable in this sense [318]. For example, mathematicians say the set of natural numbers ($\mathbb{N}$) is an infinite set—not just an indefinite, open series—and the naturals are countable, as is any set equal in size to $\mathbb{N}$.

In fact, the transfinite system refers to $\mathbb{N}$, and any infinite set equal in size to it (for example, $\mathbb{W}$), as a 'countable infinity' or a 'countably infinite set'. Stanley J. (Jerry) Farlow, professor of mathematics at the University of Main states [319]:

> The set of positive integers ($\mathbb{N}$) provides a baseline for infinite sets whose cardinality is represented by Cantor's aleph null, $\aleph_0$. The infinity is called countable infinity since in principle it can be 'counted' as when one says 1, and 2, and ..., and so on.

Cantor's aleph, $\aleph$, has various expressions. One of them is 'aleph null' or 'aleph-naught' ($\aleph_0$) which is a more precise way of referring to the literal infinitude of the natural numbers as a set ($\mathbb{N}$). Farlow points out that this infinity is a "countable infinity." So, a literally infinite collection is a collection that in principle can be counted. Mathematician Christina Grossman elaborates on this point [320]:

> By way of counting an infinite set, it does not mean that you can sit there and be able to give the total number of elements in one sitting. It just refers to the fact that in an infinite set, you can choose a first element, then a second element, and so on, and that you can eventually get to every element of the infinite set by counting.

Notice how Grossman states that you can eventually get to "every" element of the infinite set by counting—if *every* number in the infinite set can be counted, then *all* the numbers in the infinite set are countable—the totality of the infinite set itself is in principle countable.

Since completeness is part of the definition of literal infinity, if $\aleph_0$ is taken to represent the quantity of numbers in $\mathbb{N}$ as a *literally* infinite *set*, then $\mathbb{N}$ must be a complete set of numbers where that 'complete' set is defined as *all* the positive integers. Likewise, $\mathbb{W}$ is then a literally infinite set of all the positive integers *and* zero—i.e., the whole numbers. The completeness of $\mathbb{N}$ and $\mathbb{W}$ in turn means the elements within such sets are *all* there, having the full amount with a maximum number that stands as the total ready to be counted. And this entails, as Fowler and Grossman state, sets like $\mathbb{N}$ and $\mathbb{W}$ can be, at least *in principle*, counted despite their infinity.

10.4 THE IMPLICATIONS OF FINISH

When we speak of "all" the members of a complete collection, "all" implies that if we were to conduct a count of the members in the collection, the count can be *finished* and thereby without a remainder of members to count. If "all" the members of a collection can in principle be counted so that the count finishes, then the collection itself must also be *finished* with respect to the formation or aggregation of its members. Hence, there are two ways the collection must be finished:

- The collection must be finished forming.

- Any process of counting the collection's members must be able to be finished.

Recall that a 'finish' is a *concluding*, non-zero number of members. For a collection to be finished means whatever process it took to form the collection must have a concluding quantity of steps, and the collection itself must have a countable quantity of members in the sense that a count of 'all' the members of the collection produces a concluding quantity (a standing total) of members for the collection, not just a running total as if the collection continues to grow. That is not to say that the collection, by virtue of being countable, has to actually have been counted, only that *if* it were to be counted without leaving any members out, there must be such a thing as arriving at a concluding member that finishes the count.

Without a concluding member for a count of members, the collection is not countable—at least not in the sense of being able to be counted up to a standing total of members instead of a running total of members. Such a collection would therefore be *unfinished* and so incomplete rather than complete.

10.4.1 *'All' Means From First to Last*

For a collection to be finished and so countable is for the collection to have a member or set of members that can be the first in a sequence of members to be counted. Without selecting a member or set of members to begin a count there is no way for there to be a first member(s) in a count of the collection, and so the count could not proceed and certainly could not become finished. For a collection to be 'countable' thus logically implies the ability to assign a first numeral that would start the counting process.

To begin a count, we usually begin with 1, matching it to a single member of the collection in the count. Of course, we need not begin a count with the number 1; we can always use 'skip counting' to count by adding the same number repeatedly as when counting by twos, threes, fours, fives, or any other number. But if we do use skip counting, that implies we *could have* counted the usual way by starting with 1. Regardless of the number used for counting, a count of a collection implies a first iteration of the number for counting and a first member or set of members counted.

So too, a count of *all* the members of a collection implies a *finish* to the counting process, so that *every* element in the counted collection can be assigned a unique numeral. To finish a count therefore implies the collection must have a *concluding* count of members. In other words, the collection must have a *final* or *last* member to count—a final member in a count that finishes the count of the collection so that *all* the elements are counted, yielding a total.

But we must be careful by what we mean when we say a collection has a 'final' or 'last' member to count. Suppose a collection that is counted is not complete. In that case, the final count may be a count to a relative extremum rather than an absolute extremum.

That extremum of an incomplete collection would be 'relative' in the sense that it may not be the extremum for every count that may be made of the collection. For example, the quantity of members in a collection changes if more members are included or some members are taken from the collection. In such a situation the collection is countable up to the last member counted, but that 'last member' is the last member only in the sense of being a final count of members *for the count made at a given point in time*—for that iteration of counting. Hence, a count of the incomplete collection's members is a count up to a 'last member' or a 'final count' only in the sense that the count is made up to a relative extremum such as a variant maximum.

Any iteration of counting the incomplete collection would only constitute a final count in the sense of a count up to an absolute extremum, such as a constant maximum, only if the process of generating members for the collection came to an absolute end despite leaving the collection incomplete, as is. If the collection is further modified, then the "final count" is only final for that iteration of counting but not for future iterations that might be made.

Provided the collection is complete rather than incomplete, then the collection can have all its members—every member taken together without remainder—counted to an absolute extremum, a constant maximum in the form of a standing total for the complete collection. And that implies the complete collection is a collection that is countable from the first member to the last member, which concludes the count and so provides the standing total of the collection. Since to conclude the count is to finish the count, a complete collection is a 'finished' collection in the sense that a count of its members can be finished with a final number capturing all its members.

This has implications for literal infinity. Since the definition of literal infinity includes the condition of having *completeness* in quantity, where completeness implies countability, and countability implies the ability to finish the count of all members so that a standing total of members is produced, then a literally infinite collection must be a finished collection in that sense as well. That is, a literally infinite collection must be able to have a count of all its members finished—at least in principle if not in practice—with a final number representing the last member in the collection. That final number is equal to a standing total of members produced as a result of the count.

10.4.2 *Finishing the Count of an Infinite Collection*

It might be objected that while a *finite* collection may be 'complete' in the sense of completeness explicated in Chapter 3, an *infinite* collection cannot be 'complete' in that sense. For instance, while the completeness of a finite collection entails that the collection is *finished* in the sense of having a last member to count, an infinite collection may be 'complete' but cannot be so in the sense of being 'finished' and so having a last element to count. However, while this objection raises a pertinent concern about the implications of *infinitude*, the objection is mistaken about the implications of *completeness* for at least two reasons.

The objection confuses the implications of completeness with the implications of limitlessness, *both* of which characterize a literally infinite collection. That is, the condition of infinitude as such implies both completeness and limitlessness together for the same collection.

The implications of limitless differ from those of completeness, as we'll see in Chapter 11. Despite the logical implications of limitlessness, the implications of completeness are the same for both finite and infinite collections because completeness has the same meaning for both kinds of collections regardless of any other kind of property the collections may have, including limitlessness for infinite collections. So, it's not that the meaning of completeness is different for infinite collections than for finite collections. Completeness as defined in § 3.2 still applies to infinite collections just as well as for finite collections.

As detailed in § 3.5, the completeness of a collection implies the same collection is a finished collection. Since completeness is a condition of infinite collections as well as of some finite collections, and the definition of completeness does not change between finitude and infinitude, completeness thus implies the same property of finish for infinite collections as it does for finite collections.

As *complete* collections, literally infinite collections have the property of finish and therefore require a last element to any count of all the elements in the collection. If we were to *complete* a run through all the real numbers between 0 and 1, then 1 would be the *last* real number of the infinite sequence of reals we ran through.

It is true that if the collection in question is not finished forming, then there's no such thing as listing *all* the members of the series with a standing total of members. But in such a case, the collection *cannot* be complete—rather, it must be incomplete precisely because it is still in the process of forming. Such a collection cannot be a *literal* infinity; to be a literal infinity, it must have a finish to the operation forming the collection and so a finish to any count of its members.

10.5 THE IMPLICATIONS OF ENTIRETY

We know from § 3.4 that a complete collection is also an 'entire' collection—the collection is missing no elements needed to be representative of its class. A literally infinite collection is a complete collection. Therefore, a literally infinite collection is an entire collection; presumably, a literally infinite collection is a collection missing no elements for it to be representative of its class.

However, we may face a logical problem with defining a literally infinite collection as a complete and therefore an entire collection. Suppose there is an infinite collection of a particular class, such as an infinite collection of numbers. If we leave just one element out of the collection, then presumably it would not be an 'entire' collection and so not a complete collection. But we defined a literally infinite collection as a complete, and therefore entire, collection. Because leaving just one element out of the infinite collection would render the collection not entire and so not complete, then leaving out just one element would seem to imply the collection cannot be literally infinite after all. And yet, we know that removing a finite quantity from an infinite quantity does not make the remainder finite. Can we make sense of this?

This may not be too serious of a problem for how literal infinity is defined. The reason is that just because a collection is not 'entire' as one kind of collection does not mean it isn't 'entire' as another kind of collection.

For example, suppose we take $\mathbb{N}$ to be the literally infinite collection of all natural numbers, such that $\{1, 2, 3, ...\}$. Now consider a collection of all the natural numbers in which the numbers are ordered in sequence starting with the number 2 instead of the number 1, as in $\{2, 3, 4, ...\}$. Let's call that collection S. We know S is not all the natural numbers ($\mathbb{N}$) since S leaves out the number 1. So, S cannot be the 'entire' collection of natural numbers. Even so, that does not mean that S is not an entire collection, nor that S is not a complete collection, nor that S is not a literally infinite collection. S can still be an entire collection, a complete collection, and therefore a literally infinite collection of natural numbers despite not including 1 as one of its numbers. S may not be the 'entire' set of natural numbers, but S can still be entire as another kind of collection of natural numbers: an infinite subset of natural numbers.

It is true that if S were to be defined as *identical* to $\mathbb{N}$ but missing a natural number such as 2, then S would not be the 'entire' collection of natural numbers and therefore an incomplete collection. However, such is not the case; S is not identical to $\mathbb{N}$ because S is not supposed to be all the natural numbers. Rather, S is merely a *subset* of $\mathbb{N}$ equal to all natural numbers >1. And as long as S is missing no natural number >1 in its sequence, then S is the 'entire' collection of naturals that are greater than one.

Even so, perhaps there is another logical problem with assuming a literally infinite collection is an entire collection of some kind. Consider that a literally infinite sequence of numbers has *no last number* [321]. S, like $\mathbb{N}$, is supposed to be a literally infinite sequence. It therefore follows that S, like any collection of numbers equal to the infinitude of $\mathbb{N}$, also has no last number [322]. Hence $\{2, 3, 4, ...\}$ is just as literally infinite as $\{1, 2, 3, ...\}$. The question then arises as to whether or not *any* sequence of numbers without a last number is really an 'entire' sequence of numbers, thus a complete sequence of numbers, and so a literally infinite sequence of numbers.

If such sequences are merely serial indefinites under construction, then the answer is no—a sequence of numbers under construction is not an entire sequence of numbers, not a complete sequence of numbers, and so not a literally infinite sequence of numbers. Take the natural numbers. It is true that for any natural number, n, in the sequence of natural numbers there is another number that follows. But the successor of every n may just be an invention with the iteration of $n + 1$, so the sequence need not be an entirety of natural numbers, it need not be complete, and it need not be infinite. Perhaps the sequence lacks a "last number" to count because it is always an incomplete sequence with a running total of numbers.

Jean Paul Van Bendegem, a mathematician and philosopher of science at the Vrije Universiteit Brussel in Belgium, reports having at one time proposed it does not make sense to talk about a 'largest number' but nevertheless he later came to accept the existence of "a provisional largest number in full knowledge of the fact that larger finite numerals are imaginable" [323]. That position implies that so-called "sets" like $\mathbb{N}$ are in reality incomplete, open series (e.g., $\mathbb{N}^C$), always under construction and so are not 'entire', not complete, and therefore not literally infinite collections.

However, not all mathematicians agree with that. In fact, most mathematicians these days hold the natural numbers do not comprise just an incomplete, indefinite $\mathbb{N}^C$. Rather, they hold the natural numbers constitute $\mathbb{N}$ as the *entire* set of naturals, the complete set of naturals, and so the literally infinite set of all naturals.

In their view, the successor function is not the invention but the discovery of preexisting numbers. To say that for every n there is an $n + 1$ is to say a number equal to $n + 1$ is *already* in the sequence. A literally infinite sequence, such as $\mathbb{N}$, can be 'entire' while nevertheless having "no last number" in the sense of being without a *known* or *identified* last number. The infinite sequence of $\mathbb{N}$, as an *entire* sequence, must still have a last number for the entirety of the sequence—it's just that as a literally infinite sequence, $\mathbb{N}$ has a last number for its entirety in the form of an infinitely large number that can never be identified or depicted.

Such follows from how the numbers in $\mathbb{N}$ are related to one another. The cardinality of all the numbers in $\mathbb{N}$ grows larger as the sequence of numbers proceeds in $\mathbb{N}$. Carrying this progression to its logical conclusion implies that if $\mathbb{N}$ is literally infinite, then the numbers in $\mathbb{N}$ necessarily continue in cardinality up to a natural number that has a cardinality *infinitely greater* than that of 1. That logically implies there is a number in $\mathbb{N}$ that is an *infinitely large natural number* that captures the entirety and whole of all the numbers in $\mathbb{N}$.

If, to the contrary, there is no natural number in $\mathbb{N}$ that has an infinite cardinality, then every n in $\mathbb{N}$ is only finite. That would make the complete scale of natural numbers, from 1 on up, necessarily finite [324]. After all, if $\mathbb{N}$ contains *all* the natural numbers, *every one of which* has a cardinality based on predecessors *but none of which are infinite themselves*, then it is certainly not clear what, if anything, is supposed to be "infinite" about $\mathbb{N}$, which is *nothing but* reducible finite numbers. So, if $\mathbb{N}$ is infinite in the literal sense of the term, then $\mathbb{N}$ must contain a *complete* set of natural numbers with at least one infinitely large natural number.

Moreover, if $\mathbb{N}$ contains a *complete* set of numbers, then $\mathbb{N}$ contains a *full* and *finished* set of numbers. If $\mathbb{N}$ contains a full and finished set of numbers, then there must be a finishing number, n, in $\mathbb{N}$—a number that finishes $\mathbb{N}$ and as a complete set and that thereby establishes $\mathbb{N}$ as a literally infinite set of numbers.

So, what kind of number could finish $\mathbb{N}$ as an infinite set? In principle, there should be an infinitely large number expressing $\mathbb{N}$; that number may be limitlessly far in sequence from finite numbers such as the number 1, but there should be an infinitely large number where $\mathbb{N}$ 'finishes' at infinity. (Yes, it is a dubious idea to "finish" a limitless sequence is problematic, to say the least, but just ignore that for now.)

Suppose then that there is a finishing number for $\mathbb{N}$ and that it is the number for the cardinality of $\mathbb{N}$. Since $\mathbb{N}$ is comprised *only* of natural numbers, then the infinitely large number would itself have to be a natural number.

An infinitely large natural number would have to be a natural number that has *infinitely many digits*— a natural number that, if written as a tally, would not just have some collective or serial indefinite of tally marks expressing its value, but a literally *limitless* string of tally marks.

Figure 10.1 illustrates the point by analogy. Take the number 1 and multiply it by 10 exponentially. If the exponential progression were to be literally infinite and not just figuratively infinite, then there must be in this progression at least one number that is written with 1 followed by a literal infinity of zeros. That infinite number would be equal to the infinitely many natural numbers in $\mathbb{N}$.

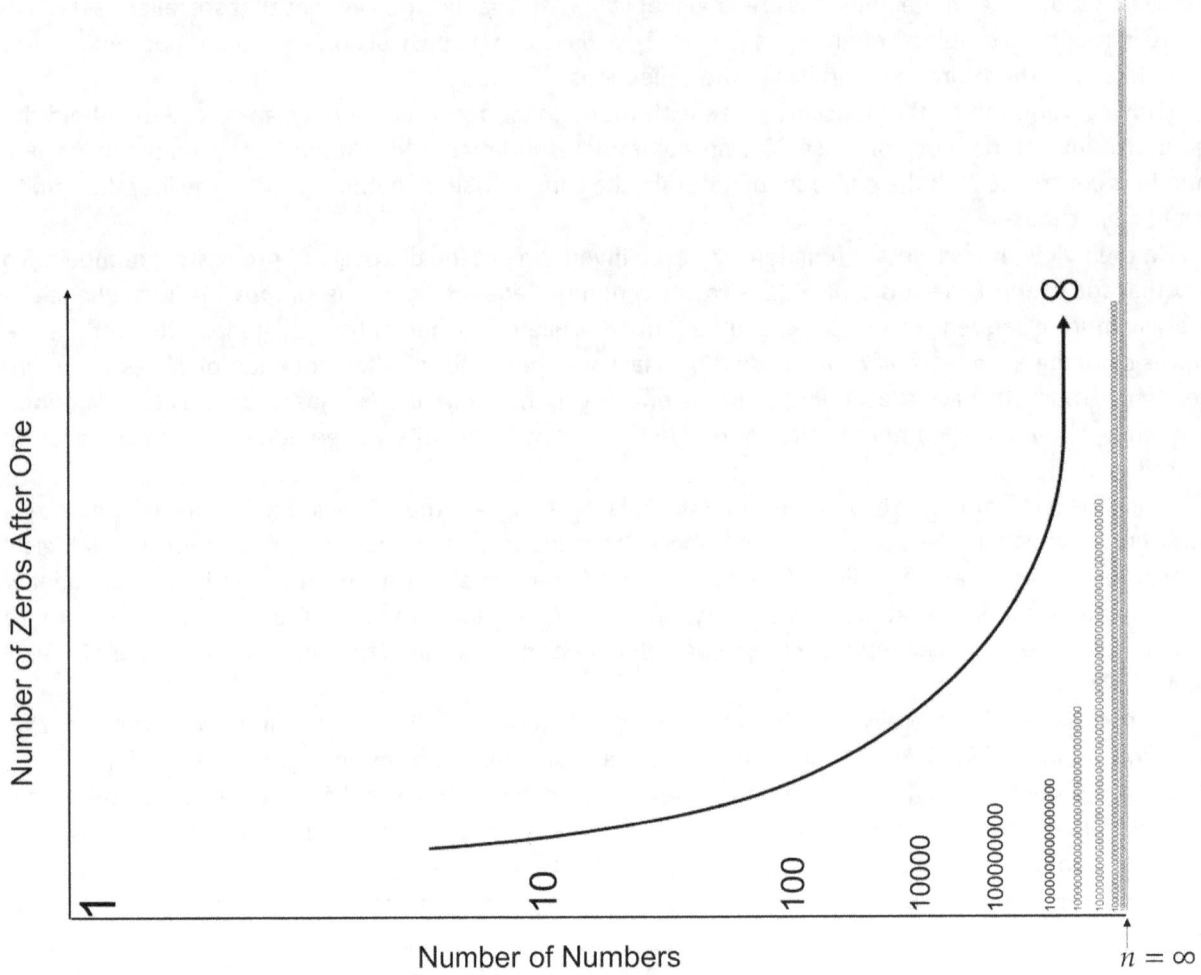

Figure 10.1: An exponential curve to illustrate a progression of natural numbers to an infinitely large natural number. Notice the use of a figurative infinity to represent how the number of zeros increases per iteration until they become (allegedly) literally infinite.

But there could be many different infinitely large numbers—perhaps an infinity of them as pointed out in § 5.4.8. We would thus have to assume that all infinitely large natural numbers might be in some sense 'equal' despite their differences in digits, but that they all would have to somehow be the equivalent total number of numbers in the sequence of $\mathbb{N}$.

Because of that, we may not be able to express the value of an infinitely large natural number; we may only be able to use a place-holder symbol such as ∞ (as shown in **Figure 10.1**) or perhaps $\aleph$ or ω borrowed from the transfinite system. Even so, if literal infinity is a coherent concept, then the completeness of a sequence of natural numbers that forms an infinite set must ensure that such symbols refer to an infinitely large natural number and that limitlessly long number must be considered the 'last' or 'final' number in the *complete* sequence, as portrayed in **Figure 10.1**. In other words, the number in $\mathbb{N}$ that finishes the sequence of numbers in $\mathbb{N}$ with infinity would itself be an infinitely large natural number with a literal infinity of digits, a number that we can perhaps only represent via mathematical *allusion*, as Cantor did with transfinite symbols like $\aleph$.

Whatever symbol we use for the infinitely large number, if $\mathbb{N}$ is to be complete as well as limitless, then that number must be regarded as denoting the *entirety* of $\mathbb{N}$. Recall that to be 'entire' means for a collection to be missing no elements. This applies as well to infinite collections. If a collection is literally infinite, it must not be missing any members needed for it to be infinite in quantity. That means every natural number there can be must already be in $\mathbb{N}$. Now since all numbers are in $\mathbb{N}$ because $\mathbb{N}$ is complete, then if we can, *at least in principle*, finish the count of members in a collection up to a concluding number, then we can count the *entirety* of the collection.

And yet, whatever number we count, it is also said of an infinite sequence of naturals that there must be an $n + 1$. True, but to say there is an infinitely large natural number for the cardinality expressing the 'entirety' of all natural numbers in $\mathbb{N}$ is not to say we cannot add 1 to that infinitely large number. It's just to say that if we add 1 to an infinitely large number in $\mathbb{N}$, then that does not change the number of numbers in $\mathbb{N}$; we know $\infty + 1 = \infty$ or $\aleph + 1 = \aleph$, as mathematicians already point out.

In which case, it is not clear that $\mathbb{N}$ would be made any "bigger" by adding 1 to the infinite value of $\mathbb{N}$ and thereby imply that $\mathbb{N}$ was not an 'entire' collection of numbers before we added 1 to $\aleph$. We could just as well argue that adding 1 to the infinitely large number in $\mathbb{N}$ is simply to re-express the value of the concluding, infinitely large cardinality of $\mathbb{N}$.

Hence, if the 'entirety' of $\mathbb{N}$ is such that $\mathbb{N}$ has an infinitely large natural number, that infinitely large natural number must have a special property ensuring that the addition of finite quantities to it does not yield a larger value. The infinite number would have to be rather like 0 in the sense that 0 has special properties no other whole number has in the sequence of whole numbers. And that may preserve the idea that there can be an 'entirety' of numbers in $\mathbb{N}$, despite the limitlessness of its sequence of numbers.

Still, as pointed out back in § 4.4, many mathematicians who believe infinity is a coherent concept nevertheless object that the concept of an infinitely large natural number itself leads to logical contradictions. Consequently, they object to the idea that there is a natural number that could have $\aleph$-many digits and thus equal $\aleph$ in value.

They stress that every natural number, n, is just one number larger than the previous natural number, so it's hard to see how *finite* naturals can be made to yield an *infinitely* large natural number. Besides, as Russell explained, while ω (which is equal to $\aleph$) follows all the naturals, ω has no immediate predecessor—there is no natural number right before it such that $n + 1 = \omega$, for that would make ω finite instead of infinite [325].

With that objection to the idea of an infinitely large natural number, we are already starting to see some logical, if not mathematical, inconsistencies with the idea that the naturals constitute a literally infinite set. Nevertheless, mathematicians have attempted to provide some rationales for why the idea of infinity might still be logically coherent.

For instance, due to concerns such as the fact that there is no such thing as $n + 1 = \omega$, some mathematicians and set theorists refuse to say literally infinite collections are those that have an "infinite number" of members [326]. As earlier discussed in § 4.4, they instead prefer to say that infinite collections just have "infinitely many members" but do not commit to the implication of an exact number of members that would be an infinitely large number.

Nevertheless, this does not seem to be universally agreed upon as an implication of what it means for a set to have an infinite sequence of numbers, as shown by how mathematicians speak when interpreting what infinity means. As historical precedent, I mentioned in § 5.4.7 that Galileo spoke of a mathematical line as having an "infinite number" of points, so the idea of an infinite number is not a new one [327]. Modern mathematicians also make occasional references to infinite numbers, as when they say irrational numbers such as pi have an infinite number of decimal places as if they are all there waiting to be discovered. Hence, even in modern mathematics the idea of infinitely large numbers is occasionally referred to, making such a connotation of infinite sets as complete sets.

So we now have two ways to interpret ℵ, ω, and ∞ as expressions of literal infinity—either they are placeholders for an infinitely large natural number, or they are symbols for the quantity of members in a collection equal to a set of "infinitely many" finite natural numbers. It seems to me, however, that the two interpretations are looking at different aspects of what it means for a collection to be infinite in the literal sense of the term.

The concept of literal infinity is that of a quantity both complete and limitless. While the mathematicians who maintain there is no infinite number of numbers in ℕ but rather only "infinitely many" finite numbers in ℕ are correct that such follows from the *limitlessness* of ℕ as a literally infinite set, it may also be the case that the *completeness* of ℕ as a literally infinite set implies that ℕ is 'entire', with the entirety of ℕ implying there is a total number—an infinite number—of numbers in ℕ, and thus an infinitely large natural number that is the value for *all* the natural numbers in ℕ.

Whether the implications of limitlessness ("infinitely many") and completeness (an "infinite number") make sense together, let alone individually, remains to be seen; we shall encounter this issue again in Chapters 12 and 14.

10.6 THE IMPLICATIONS OF WHOLENESS

To be complete implies a state of wholeness. To be whole is to be *divisible but undivided*. For example, a geometric figure 'divided' (in the sense of being separated) into parts is not a whole figure. Then too, consider a collection the members of which are arranged in a sequence; for the sequence to be whole implies there are no breaks or gaps in the sequence. If the sequence did have breaks or gaps, then the sequence would be missing necessary 'members', such as particular relations between other types of members in the sequence, needed for the sequence to be representative of a given class of sequence. Hence, by virtue of lacking wholeness, the sequence would not be a *complete* sequence.

To lack wholeness often violates one or more of the other completeness criteria. A break or gap in a sequence, for example, may violate entirety if that break or gap means a member is missing from the sequence. This relation of wholeness to the other completeness criteria holds for both finite and infinite collections, be those collections sets, series, etc.

So now consider a literally infinite collection. Because such a collection is complete, it is also whole—divisible but undivided. A literally infinite collection must also not have its members 'divided' in a relevant sense from one another such as to make the collection unfinished, lack fullness, be less than entire, or lose its totality. This holds not only for infinite sets but also for infinite *series*. As a *complete* series, a literally infinite series is a *whole* series, and so it too must have no 'divisions' (in the sense of breaks or gaps or separations) that would contradict other completeness criteria, such as having a totality of members.

10.6.1 *Infinity as Whole and Infinite Divisibility*

If to be literally infinite is to be complete and therefore a *whole*, then what about something that is infinitely *divisible*? How can it be infinitely divisible if infinitude is a state of wholeness? In reply, as long as that which is said to be "infinitely divisible" is divisible but *undivided*, then it can still be a whole collection of limitlessly many parts and so still infinite (provided, of course, that wholeness and limitlessness do not themselves conflict as I think they do, but more about that later).

Another objection to the notion that infinitude involves wholeness involves the concept of infinite division itself. A series of divisions certainly implies something divided. But isn't to be whole to be divisible and yet *undivided*? And if so, doesn't that mean there can be no infinite process of division? Possibly, but not for that reason.

What is under consideration as 'whole' in this case is the *series* of divisions, not what gets divided. An infinite series can be a *whole series of divisions*, as when a line would be divided infinitely many times. The series can still be a whole series even if each act in the series is an act of dividing something. So there is no logical problem between infinitely dividing something and the process of infinite division being a whole process that is itself "undivided."

There is, however, a more serious implication of an infinite collection being a whole collection: an infinite collection is a whole equal to the sum of its parts. That's right—the completeness of an infinite collection implies that the infinite collection has a *sum* of members, despite the limitlessness of the quantity of members comprising the collection.

We just saw that if $\mathbb{N}$ is a set of natural numbers, each of which is a cardinality based on the value of its predecessors, then in the entirety of $\mathbb{N}$ there would have to be at least one infinitely large natural number (ergo, an 'infinitieth' number). That number would be the *sum* of all the natural numbers below it. This complements the way in which the poet Lucretius referred to infinity: the Sum of all things (note the capital 'S' when translated in English). The infinite whole is equal to an infinite sum.

10.6.2 *A Variable for the Infinite Sum*

In keeping with § 10.2.2 above, the sum of infinitely many numbers in $\mathbb{N}$ should be, albeit only in principle, *specifiable* with a definite value. That would mean we should be able to use a variable, n, to represent some infinitely large number if any such number, or set of numbers, exists.

However, it is not clear that would even make mathematical sense because variables represent only numbers that have *definite* values and we can't, at least not in practice, replace a variable for an infinite quantity with a definite value. Mathematicians therefore do not typically use variables for infinity (as discussed in § 5.4.8). Instead of variables like n, mathematicians typically express infinite quantity with symbols such as ∞ or $\aleph$ or ω.

Nevertheless, *in principle*, if it makes sense to have an 'infinite number' of something, then we should be able to have a logically consistent mathematics in which a variable n can be given an exact, specifiable value that is equal to an infinitely large natural number. We can think of the variable as having the potential to be replaced with an infinitely large natural number.

We therefore seem to have a problem: On the one hand, infinity is not really a number and so a variable does not seem appropriate. On the other hand, if a collection has a literally infinite quantity for the whole of the collection, that implies a total and so a sum of members in the collection, and so an infinite number that could replace a variable for that infinite sum.

10.6.3 *Converging with Infinity*

To better see why an infinite collection, as a complete collection, has a whole equal to an infinitely large sum of its parts, take the operation of *convergence*. Suppose we have a collection we wish to divide a literally infinite number of times. The division process would make the collection ever incomplete with each division made but suppose we could finish an infinite number of divisions, dividing the collection an infinite number of times. It would be the collection of divisions (rather than the collection divided) that would be equal to an infinitely large number. However, if it could be carried out, the process would also show that the collection so divided may itself contain an infinite number of elements.

In calculus, dividing an interval down to a specified number is called 'convergence' because the operation can divide one specified number down over a number of times until the operation *converges* with another specified number. For example, suppose we divide the interval between 0 and 1 on the number line a particular quantity of times in order to make ever-smaller fractions that ultimately converge to the number 0.

To make such a convergence, start with elementary arithmetic and use a succession of subtractions from 1. Suppose we define 1 as equal to $^4/_4$ and then reduce the interval between 1 and 0 in the following manner:

$$\text{Step 1: } \frac{4}{4} - \frac{1}{4} = \frac{3}{4}$$

$$\text{Step 2: } \frac{3}{4} - \frac{1}{4} = \frac{2}{4}$$

$$\text{Step 3: } \frac{2}{4} - \frac{1}{4} = \frac{1}{4}$$

$$\text{Step 4: } \frac{1}{4} - \frac{1}{4} = 0$$

Now, suppose we could divide the interval between 0 and 1 an infinite number of times. Let's begin by repeating the above steps multiple times with successively greater fractions. Perhaps for our next iteration, we use $1 = {}^5/_5$ and then subtract $^1/_5$ from $^5/_5$ over a series of five times to arrive at 0 over five steps. After that, we use $1 = {}^6/_6$ and then subtract $^1/_6$ from $^6/_6$ over a series of six times in order to arrive at 0 over six steps. Next, we use $1 = {}^7/_7$ and then subtract $^1/_7$ from $^7/_7$ over a series of seven times in order to arrive at 0 over seven steps. We can continue this process indefinitely without contradiction. But suppose we could do this a literally infinite number of times until we can define 1 as an infinitely large numerator over an infinitely large denominator that is identical to the numerator. Mathematically, we *cannot* represent this as $^\infty/_\infty$ because dividing infinity by infinity without further qualification is mathematically *undefined*. But let's use this oversimplification as an analogy; suppose we could start with the logical equivalent of 1 equal to an infinite value over an identical infinite value and then reduce that infinite fraction over ∞ steps to arrive at 0. This last iteration is what convergence is like if it is truly infinite.

Mathematicians actually express the idea of convergence to 0 by using algebraic operations and calculus functions rather than subtraction, which makes it more complicated. Convergence of an infinite series of terms to 0 is expressed in various ways, such as:

$$\sum_{n=1}^{\infty} |a_n| = 0$$

In this example of an infinite sequence descending from 1 to 0, the operation producing the sequence is represented as being carried out infinitely (∞). In reality, the operation can only be iterated indefinitely; the ∞ in the equation functions merely as a placeholder to suggest indefiniteness of operation for a series of indefinitely many finite sums—a figurative infinity [328]. Nevertheless, if we interpret ∞ as an expression of literal infinity, then the operation would in principle be a *complete* series of steps that ends in 0.

Suppose we now reverse directions and use an operation to add a series of decimal reals to 0 until we produce 1 as a total. Mathematicians express this as an "infinite series that has a sum" [329].

For example, suppose we use an *indefinite* sequence of fractions between 0 and 1 to imply an *infinite* sequence of fractions between 0 and 1:

$$\left(\frac{1}{2}, \frac{1}{6}, \frac{1}{12}, \frac{1}{20}, \ ... \right)$$

We can add the elements of the sequence together as an accession. If we could carry out such an operation manually, we would in actuality be performing the operation an indefinite number of times, not a literally infinite number of times. The series never does land on 1; it just gets increasingly close to 1. In order to say the sequence ends up exactly equal to 1, mathematicians work backward: they posit 1 as a limit and allow the indefinite sequence to "converge" with 1 only in the loose sense of getting so arbitrarily close to 1 as a limit that, for practical purposes, they say the series sums to 1. Mathematicians express this in various ways, such as:

$$\sum_{k=1}^{\infty} \frac{1}{k(k+1)} = 1$$

Notice that the operation uses notation to suggest it iterates an 'infinite' (∞) number of times.

If the operation were carried out in reality, it could be iterated not a literal infinity of times but, at best, only indefinitely (persistently) toward 1 as an *asymptotic limit*. (An asymptotic limit is a limit with which a process cannot intersect no matter how indefinitely close it approaches the limit.) In which case, it is dubious the exact sum of 1 would be produced without 'rounding up', so to speak. We can carry out the operation indefinitely in the sense of persistently but not ceaselessly, let alone a literally infinite number of times. At best, we might say that the operation is carried out a figuratively infinite number of times.

However, if we interpret ∞ to be literal infinity and suppose the convergence operation were carried out infinitely in a literal sense, then logically the sum of 1 would be reached in an infinite number of steps. Literal infinity is, after all, a condition of *completeness*. So, use of infinity in the operation to arrive at the sum of 1 would thus assume the sequence from 0 to 1 is complete [330].

You would think that most mathematicians assume that if the operation were carried out, it could be carried out a literally infinite number of times to converge on an exact sum. However, as Fletcher points out, mathematicians these days admit the sum of 1 resulting from the convergence operation is "not viewed as the sum of infinitely many terms but as a limit of *finite* sums...the apparent reference to infinity (∞) is explained away in finite terms" [331]. Operationally, the reference to ∞ is a misnomer for indefiniteness and not at all a symbol of literal infinity.

Nevertheless, if ∞ in the operations were a reference to literal infinity, then whether the infinite series is produced from a descent of fractions from 1 to 0 or an ascent from 0 to 1, the convergence of the series with an exact value entails the series that produces that value must itself have a last step, however unspecifiable the quantity of steps in the series may be. Without such a step, the sequence would only be a figurative infinity.

Literal infinity implies completeness. So, that last step, if following a literally infinite number of steps, would have to be the iteration of an infinitely large number—namely, the infinitely large number of steps it took to complete the series. That would make the specified number (whether 0 or 1) the sum of a truly infinite series, the quantitative *whole* of the infinite collection.

10.7 COMPLETENESS IMPLICATIONS SUMMARIZED

Wholeness, entirety, finish, totality, and fullness—all are conditions of completeness that carry logical implications for literal infinity as a condition of quantitative completeness. **Figure 10.2** summarizes the implications of these conditions for literally infinite collections.

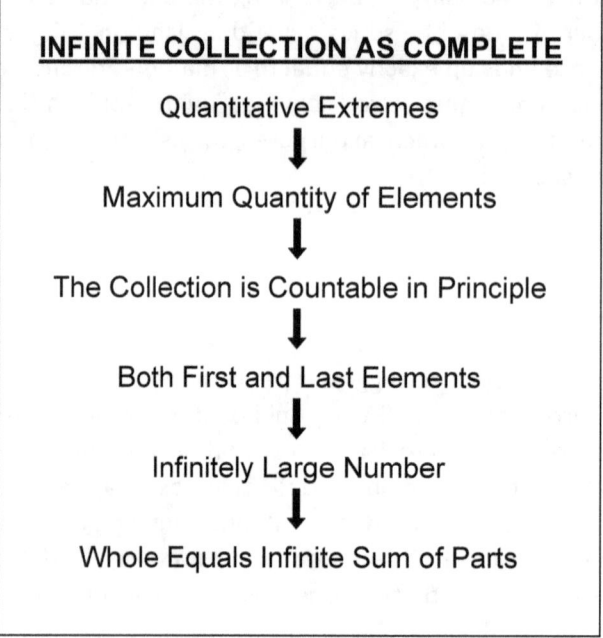

Figure 10.2: The implications of completeness for literally infinite collections.

CHAPTER 10 IN REVIEW

❖ Literal infinity is not just limitlessness but a state of completeness as well. A complete collection is a collection with a whole, entire, finished, full, and total quantity of members. A literally infinite collection must therefore have a whole, entire, finished, full, and total quantity of members.

❖ Each of the completeness properties carries logical implications for infinite collections. For example, since a complete collection is a full collection, and a literally infinite collection is a complete collection, it follows that a literally infinite collection is a full collection. To be 'full' implies parameters of minimum and maximum quantity, even if such cannot be numerically captured for an infinite collection due to the vagueness of mathematical notation for that which is infinite (without numerical limit).

❖ To have a maximum implies having a total. So as a complete collection, a literally infinite collection has a total quantity—one that is countable, albeit only in principle.

❖ To be countable, even if only in principle, further implies having both a first and last element to count.

❖ However, for an infinite collection in the literal sense of the term 'infinite', the "last" element to count (the total for the infinite collection) is itself a number with no end to its digits. An infinite total is a limitless total; it is a total equal to an infinitely large sum.

❖ The literally infinite collection, as a complete collection, is also a whole collection. The whole for a complete collection is equal to the sum of its parts. So, for a literally infinite collection, the whole of the collection is thus equal to the limitless sum of its parts.

11: LIMITLESSNESS — IMPLICATIONS FOR INFINITY

The root meaning of the word 'infinity' is "the condition of having no limit" [332]. Another word for having no limit is *limitless*, and infinity is hence the condition of *limitlessness*. In fact, limitlessness is often assumed to be a synonym for infinity in the literal sense of the term. In this chapter, we will explore the logical implications of what it means to be limitless, and you may notice right away conflict with the implications of completeness as given in the previous chapter.

11.1 INFINITY AS LIMITLESSNESS

With respect to infinity, being limitless is being an extent of elements that is "without limit" in the sense of having no feature or circumstance—such as an end, brink, edge, border, boundary, extreme, or total—that enables the extent (measurable difference) of elements to be distinctly identified from other extents. As indicated back in § 5.4.2, limitlessness is the condition in which an extent of elements (range) is unspecifiable, even in principle.

And yet, despite not being able to specify an extent of elements in a limitless collection, we can still make statements about *all* the elements in a limitless collection. We just need to keep in mind that whereas in the context of completeness 'all' means 'every', in the context of limitlessness 'all' means 'for any'.

To speak of "all" of the elements in a limitless collection is to say that *for any* element, e, in the given collection, it is the case that e has such and such a property. For example, if $\mathbb{N}$ is a limitless collection of natural numbers, then all the numbers in $\mathbb{N}$ have a successor—that is, for any n, n has a successor. We can therefore make statements about all the elements of a limitless collection and only with respect to the collection's limitlessness; we need not assume the limitless collection is complete in order to refer to 'all' of the collection's elements [333].

The reason this distinction becomes important is because referring to "all" members of a collection with respect to the collection's limitlessness as distinct from its completeness will enable us to see what follows from a collection being limitless irrespective of whether or not the collection can also be complete. In making such a distinction, we will find that the limitlessness of the collection makes the collection transcend any notion of fullness, without extreme or maximum, inherently lacking in a totality, such that it cannot therefore be counted to a final total, having no such thing as a 'finish' because it has no last member or term, and therefore such that it cannot be represented by a number because the whole of the collection is greater than any sum.

Whether a hard conceptual distinction between completeness and limitlessness can always be established for any non-zero set of members said to have both properties may not always be possible.

Even if don't *assume* a limitless collection is complete, we may end up *implying* as much—see § 22.1.1. Nevertheless, we should endeavor to see what follows from the one property (limitlessness) without confusing those implications with what follows from the other property (completeness) in order to ensure there is no confusion as to the implications of these properties as we analyze literal infinity, which implies both of them together.

11.2 TRANSCENDING FULLNESS

If to be full is to be unable to include more without changing parameters, a collection of *limitless* quantity is never full. Take a literally infinite collection, which is a limitless collection: add 1 to infinity and you still have infinity. You can add as much as you wish without the parameters of the collection changing a bit. Fullness does not apply to a collection that has no limit because to be without limit is to lack an *extremity* by which the collection would become full.

11.2.1 *Without Extreme*

An extreme (a minimal or maximal element, a minimum or maximum, etc.) is a kind of limit. To be limitless is to be *without extreme.* But we must be careful to qualify what it means to be "without extreme." To be limitless in terms of being without extreme means the collection in question has no extreme *relative to its subsets*.

A collection with some non-zero number of elements that is also non-circuitous (the elements don't form a circle or closed loop) but nevertheless limitless, can only be "without limit" in the sense of not having an extreme for the whole of the subsets within it. So, it's not that such a limitless collection has an extreme for the whole collection alright, just an extreme that is limitlessly removed from whatever count of the collection's elements is being performed. Rather, a limitless collection has no extreme at all for its whole extent, and so no extreme relative to any subset within it.

For a collection to be limitless is not necessarily for all the *sub*sets in the collection to have no extreme (subsets can have upper and lower bounds). Rather, for a collection to be limitless is for the *super*set to have no extreme with respect to any subsets it contains. Or another way we could put it is to say any non-zero, non-circuitous, yet limitless collection would have to have no extremes, but only in terms of the entire collection, not merely for some subset of the collection. It is therefore not that a limitless collection is without limit with respect to the properties of the subsets or elements within it per se. Rather, what we call a "limitless collection" can have many elements and subsets within it, each of which can have its own limits. Bottom line: to be limitless is *to have no extreme, therefore no quantitative parameter, and therefore no fullness.*

11.2.2 *A Limitless Sequence of Minimal and Maximal Elements*

Consider another example: limitlessness for a sequence of minimal and maximal elements. Suppose we could take a sequence of minimal and maximal elements and extend them indefinitely, as **Figure 11.1** indicates. Suppose further than we could extend this sequence, not just indefinitely, but *limitlessly* to obtain a subset of a limitless number of maximal elements and a subset of a limitless number of minimal elements [334].

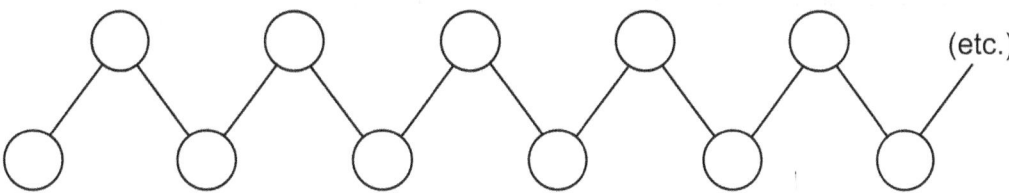

Figure 11.1: A "fence" Hasse-diagram of minimal elements (bottom row) and maximal elements (top row); such a fence can be indefinitely long as indicated by "etc." The question is, can it be *infinitely* long—a fence *without limit*?

To be limitless may be to have no extreme. Nevertheless, having subsets of minimal and maximal elements as such is in keeping with the definition of the sequence as being 'limitless' because when we refer to sequence as limitless, we are talking about the whole of it as not having a limit; the parts can still be limited. Still, because there is no final element in this sequence, the sequence is not a *full* sequence—there is no parameter by which to say the sequence is full. Limitless transcends fullness.

11.2.3 *A Limitless Sequence of Relative and Absolute Extrema*

Now consider extrema produced by mathematical functions in calculus such as *absolute (or global) extrema* and *relative (or local) extrema*. An 'absolute extremum' is *an absolute minimum or absolute maximum*; a 'relative extremum' is *a relative minimum or relative maximum*.

These terms are defined, somewhat non-technically, as follows:

- absolute minimum: *the lowest value a function produces in a domain.*
- relative minimum: *the lowest value around an interval within a domain's bounds.*

- absolute maximum: *the highest value a function produces in a domain.*
- relative maximum: *the highest value around an interval within a domain's bounds.*

The term 'domain' in this context means a given range of values (rather than "the scope of a field's subject," as I've been using the term with respect to grammatical, mathematical, and logical coherence). **Figure 11.2** shows both absolute and relative minima and maxima [335].

Values for relative extrema can be produced indefinitely, and the values themselves can be immense (indefinitely large) or minuscule (indefinitely small). As extrema, they are never individually limitless in magnitude, and there must be only one absolute minimum and one absolute maximum for the domain, however large we extend it.

Suppose, though, that we can have not just an indefinite quantity of minima and maxima, but a *limitless* quantity of them such that the domain is limitless. If we could multiply extrema limitlessly, it would mean that the domain (in the parlance of Bolzano) has "no last term" with respect to its quantity of extrema [336]. It's not that the minima and maxima can be themselves limitless (they can't be since they're limits); rather, it's that we would have a limitless supply of them along the x axis. Again, it is the whole that is supposed to be without limit, not the subsets.

The implications for fullness are straightforward: here too a limitless domain would have no upper parameter by which to say there is a *full* set of minima and maxima for the domain.

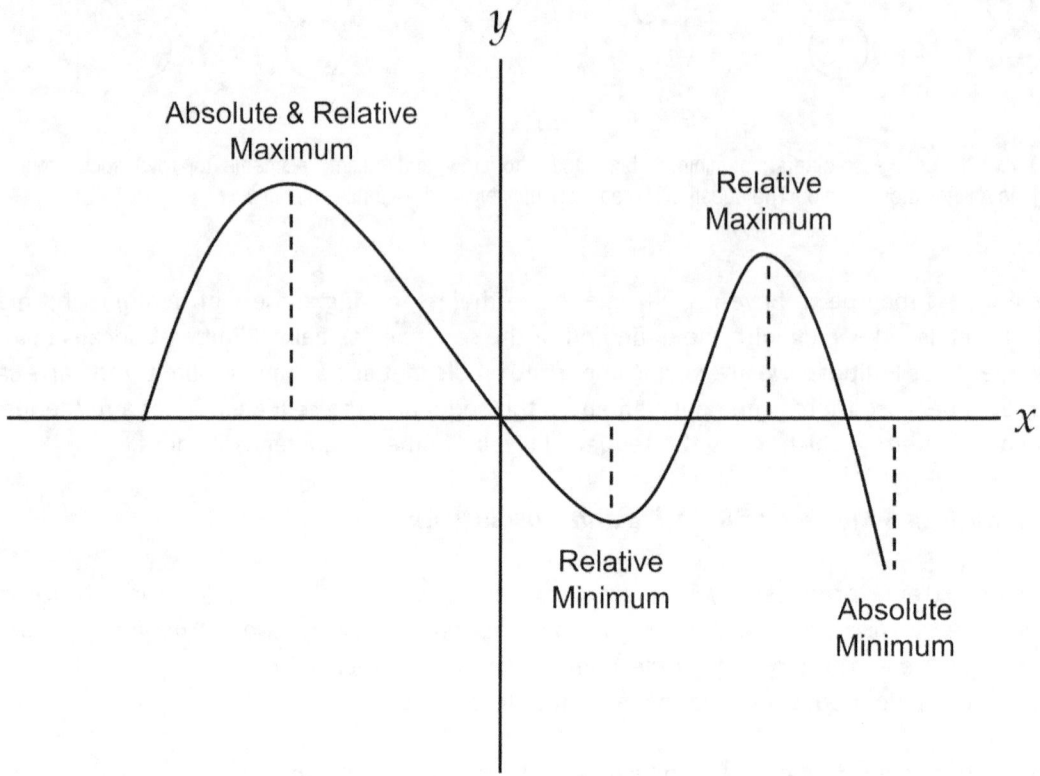

Figure 11.2: Examples of absolute and relative extrema in the domain marked by the x and y axes. Sometimes the absolute and relative extrema coincide; often they are different. Here too we can imagine many minima and maxima in a domain, but can there be a *limitless* quantity of them?

11.2.4 *Limitless Series*

So far, we have seen that to be limitless with respect to extremes is part of what it means to be literally infinite. Literally infinite collections are those which are non-zero, non-circuitous, and also limitless. Thus, any literally infinite collection is a collection without extreme to its quantity of elements. For, to be limitless is to be beyond extremes.

Now consider the limitlessness of a particular kind of collection—a *series*, a collection in which the members occur one after another in succession. We know that any *finite* series that has a beginning does not necessarily have an end; finite series without ends are either circuitous (looping back on themselves like a circle) or they are *indefinite* series, proceeding persistently or ceaselessly from an initial point. Either way, such series are still finite because, even though as series they have no end to their succession of steps or events, they still have an end (highest element) *to any count of their elements* at a snapshot in time, giving them running totals of elements. If, on the other hand, we are dealing with a literally *infinite* series that began at some starting point and increases in magnitude, then the series would have no higher end to its succession—not even a succession of ends that could be given running totals.

Generally, to be limitless is not to be circuitous (like a circle) in the sense of being able to come "full circle" back to a point. However, if we can make sense of the notion that a circle can have a limitless diameter, then the circle itself could have a limitless circumference. We'll put the issue of circles with limitless diameter aside for now and return to it in § 18.4.2. The important point for now is that a series is limitless when, again in the words of Bolzano, it is in a state of having "absolutely *no last term*" [337]. That means to be non-zero and limitless in succession is to have elements that are arranged in a linear, non-circuitous fashion with *no extreme* in the range of elements.

Take, for example, the natural numbers. Many mathematicians espouse the view that the natural numbers (and other number scales) are limitless *sets* rather than indefinite, open *series*. I argue that they are mistaken because numbers are properties of numerals, which are inventions, and no one has ever invented a literally limitless scale of numerals. At best, the natural number scale is only an indefinite (and ergo finite) series rather than a limitless set [338] [339]. Despite that, it is certainly the case that *if* the scale of natural numbers were without limit at all, *then* it would have no upper extremity, no matter how far the numbers extend—the scale of natural numbers would have "absolutely no last term," just as Bolzano stated. And consequently, it would be a sequence for which the predicate 'full' would not apply.

11.2.5 *Never Reaching a Limit*

In saying a collection such as a set, sequence, or series is limitless, we must exercise some caution to distinguish limitlessness from indefiniteness. This is important to keep in mind because mathematicians sometimes use the term 'limit' in a technical sense when engaging in certain kinds of mathematical operations. Though the various technical definitions of 'limit' proposed in mathematics do not contradict our precising definition for 'limit', the two different uses of the term can result in some confusion. So, we'll need a little more elaboration on the difference.

Recall from the previous chapter the examples in which an infinite series converged with an integer such as 0 or 1. Now consider another sequence: $0.19, 0.199, 0.1999, ...$ Mathematicians say this sequence "approaches" or "tends toward" or "relatively converges with" the value 0.2. Because of the way the function is defined (keep attaching more nines to the sequence), the sequence never "absolutely converges with" (arrives at) 0.2; basically, the idea is that the function can make the sequence as close to 0.2 as desired without actually reaching it.

It is here that talk of a 'limit' can be confusing because this type or 'relative convergence' has three different kinds of limit associated with it. The first kind of limit of which we may speak is *the limit of the sequence* generated by the function. The 'limit of the sequence' is *the fixed value which a varying quantity is regarded as approaching but never reaching*. In the provided example, 0.2 is the limit of the sequence that the decimal string can only approximate.

The limit of the sequence can itself create some confusion: if you can't reach the limit, doesn't that mean the limit is limitlessly far away? And if it is limitlessly far away, then is it really a "limit" at all that we're dealing with? And if it isn't limitlessly far away, then you should be able to reach it but the function in the example says you can't. So how do we resolve this apparent contradiction?

The contradiction is avoided by noting that in mathematics there are different kinds of limits to sequences—different kinds of specifiability conditions for ranges of elements in sequences. If we regard 0.2 as a 'limit' in the sense of an extremity (like a maximum) or a total (like a sum or product), then we have a contradiction because you can't have an extremity or total that is unable to be quantitatively reached—a limit that is limitlessly far removed. However, if we regard the number 0.2 in this example not as an extremity or total, but instead as a 'limit' in the sense of being a numerical *bound* for the sequence, then the contradiction dissolves: the sequence can be extended as far as we like, but only up to the bound established as 0.2, and that extension toward 0.2 is made by generating ever-smaller increments toward that bound. So, a 'limit' in this respect is not treated as a numerical extremity or total, but rather it serves as a numerical bound we work behind—a limit as a quantitative bound.

The second kind of limit is *the limit of the series* generated by the function—here you have a limit that is a running total—a limit that is persistently or ceaselessly extended but still a total at any given calculation. For example, in the above sequence 0.1999 would be the total for the latest calculation. If we decide to continue the calculation which results in another 9 to the sequence of nines, then 0.19999 would become the new total, and so the new limit of the series, and so on.

The third kind of limit is *the limit of the function* itself. The "limit of the function," is the limit of *the numerical generation process* as each value is refined closer towards a target. For example, starting with 0.19 and extending the sequence to 0.199 and so forth as the series of nines moves the sequence closer to 0.2, the function of generating nines approaches its own limit. That is, our *ability* to keep generating nines has a limit too. In this example, the function is a recursive process of generating new values to *approximate* 0.2 and, if the process persists without a defined end, the recursive process does not necessarily ever halt, no matter how many times the function is iterated (unless we simply become exhausted in our calculation efforts) because the function is incapable of creating a value equal to 0.2. This function is an example of an indefinite (nevertheless, finite) process both because the actual limit to our ability for adding on more nines is unknown (off any known scale) and because the process carried out by the function is always left incomplete no matter how long it continues; the function is one that carries on *indefinitely* (without a defined limit) but not necessarily *infinitely* (without any limit at all).

If, for example, computing power must eventually be exhausted, then the function cannot be carried on without limit. In that case, the approximation can only come so close and no closer; the function could then only "approximate" 0.2 up to the point where computability is exhausted. Of course, we may not be able to define exactly how much computing power we can have before we can compute no further, and therefore we may not be to tell how far the function can proceed, so it would have to be considered indefinite. And, as far as we can tell, the limit of the function can always be *extended* given more computing power and time to compute. Even so, the function is not necessarily "limitless" in capacity as there may be an inherent limit to computing power. To say, then, the limit of the function is "indefinite" rather than infinite would just be to say that the function's limit (such as the limit to the process of actually progressing closer to 0.2) is unknown and incomplete rather than necessarily nonexistent.

In this view, the sequence of nines is merely an *incomplete* series that generates a running total of values between the bounds of 0.1 and 0.2. The number 0.2 is a bound—a numerical bound—toward which we can extend the sequence *persistently* (for as long as we wish) or even *ceaselessly* but will never arrive at in practice because the number of nines we can generate is *indefinite* (in the sense of being an incomplete indefinite).

In contrast, most mathematicians say a function generating such a decimal sequence is not just indefinite but is "infinite" in the sense of having an "ideal limit" toward which the numbers extend. This is a poetic way of saying the function itself has *no limit at all*. When mathematicians say this, they imply there is also no limit to the sequence generated by the function (as when 0.1999... denotes a limitless sequence of nines).

11.2.6 *Suprema and Infima: Bounds for the Indefinite and the Infinite*

To put the preceding in mathematical lingo, a number in a sequence that serves as a numerical bound, like 0.2 in the foregoing example, is either an *infimum* or a *supremum*, depending on boundary conditions of the sequence or series.

The infimum can be defined in natural language as follows:

- infimum: (plural—'infima') *the greatest element less than or equal to all the elements of a given sequence, series, or interval of such.*

Not all sequences or series have an infimum, but if they do, the infimum is unique—there is only one infimum. The infimum is often referred to as the *greatest lower bound* [340]. Take a sequence of elements, such as the sequence of whole numbers. You can think of the infimum as a lower bound below which a given sequence has no members, so you can think of zero as the infimum to the whole numbers since there is no whole number less than zero.

Some sequences have a supremum, defined in natural language as follows:

- supremum: (plural—'suprema') *the least element greater than or equal to all the elements of a given sequence, series, or interval of such.*

Not all sequences or series have a supremum, but in those that do, the supremum is unique—there is only one supremum. The supremum is often referred to as the *least upper bound* [341]. Take a sequence of elements, such as the sequence of non-positive integers. You can think of the supremum as an upper bound above which a given sequence has no members, so you can think of zero as the supremum to the non-positive integers since there is no non-positive integer greater than zero.

With regard to the relation of infima to minima and suprema to maxima, the 'infimum' may be a minimum, but not always; and the 'supremum' is sometimes a maximum, but not always—it depends on the mathematical context and the collection in question. Suppose the collection is a number line of reals with a given interval in the sequence or series of numbers. Depending on the mathematical operation or function used for the numbers in the interval, the interval may or may not have a minimum or maximum. But if there is an infimum or supremum to a given sequence or series, it always acts as a boundary condition—a bound to the interval.

Figure 11.3 illustrates that for an *open* interval the infimum and supremum are bounds but not a minimum or maximum, whereas if the same interval is *closed*, then the infimum of that interval is its minimum and the supremum of that interval is its maximum.

If a sequence has a minimum (a least element), then that element is the infimum; but if the sequence has no minimum, then it either has no infimum at all or the infimum is outside of the sequence but still serves as a bound (the 'greatest lower bound') for the sequence. For example, consider again the positive real numbers; these do not have a least element (no minimum) since you can indefinitely create new positive values between zero and one. However, the positive real numbers do have an infimum: zero (0), which is not itself a positive real number. Zero simply serves as the lower bound for the positive reals (see **Figure 11.4**).

If a sequence has a maximum (a greatest element), then that element is the supremum; but if the sequence has no maximum, then it either has no supremum at all or the supremum is outside of the sequence but still serves as a bound (a 'least upper bound') for the sequence. For example, consider the negative real numbers. These do not have a greatest element (no maximum) since you can indefinitely create new negative values between negative one and zero. However, the negative real numbers do have a supremum: zero (0), which is not itself a negative real number. Zero simply serves as the least upper bound for the negative reals (see **Figure 11.5**).

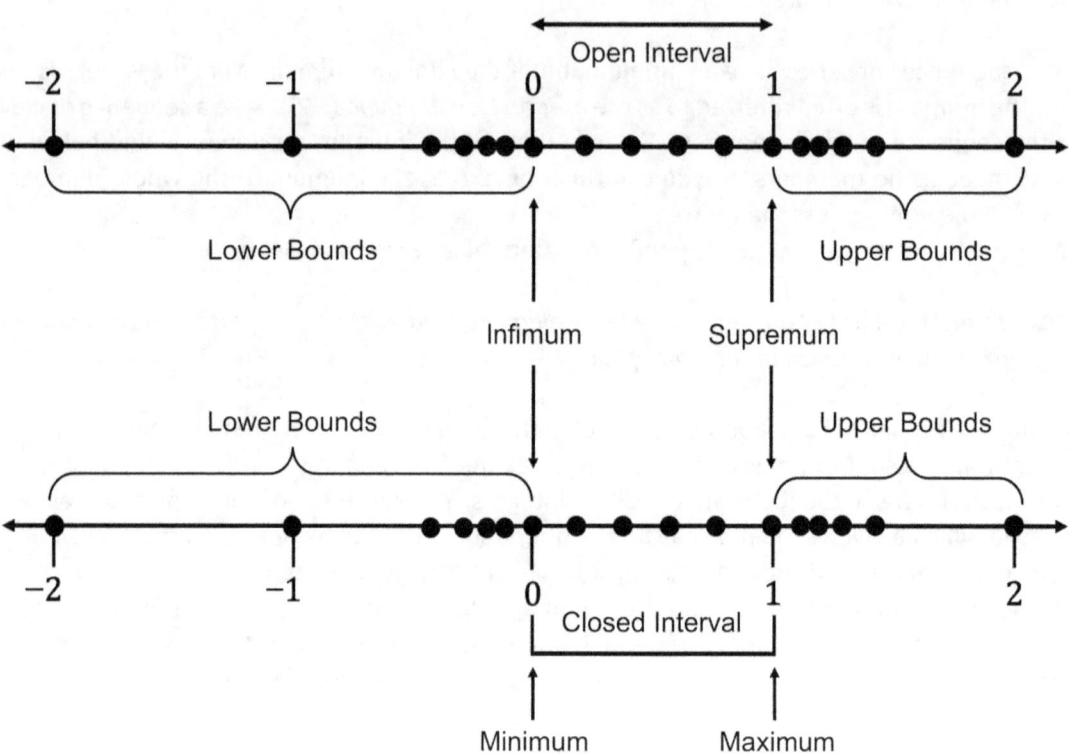

Figure 11.3: Examples of an infimum and supremum for a sequence of real numbers in interval 0, 1 on the real number line. *At top:* (0,1) is defined as an open interval; 0 is not a minimum and 1 is not a maximum for the reals in this interval. *At bottom:* For the same number line, {0, 1} is defined as a closed interval with 0 as the minimum and 1 as the maximum for the interval. Whether or not an infimum is a minimum and a supremum is a maximum is thus a matter of mathematical context.

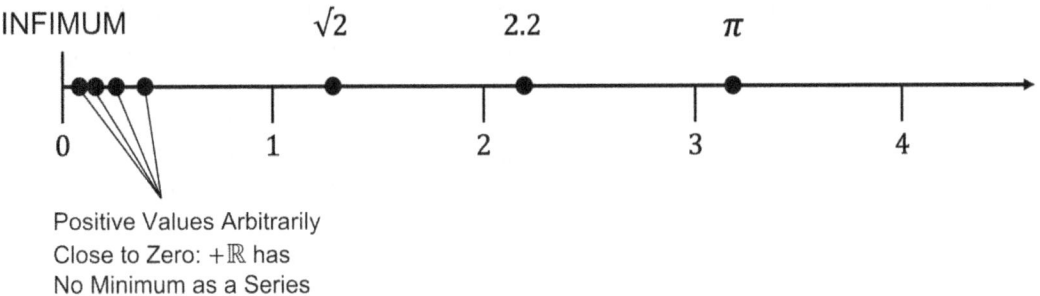

Figure 11.4: Examples of positive real numbers from what mathematicians usually conceive as the set (vice series) of positive reals (denoted $+\mathbb{R}$) with zero (0) as the infimum, but not as a minimum.

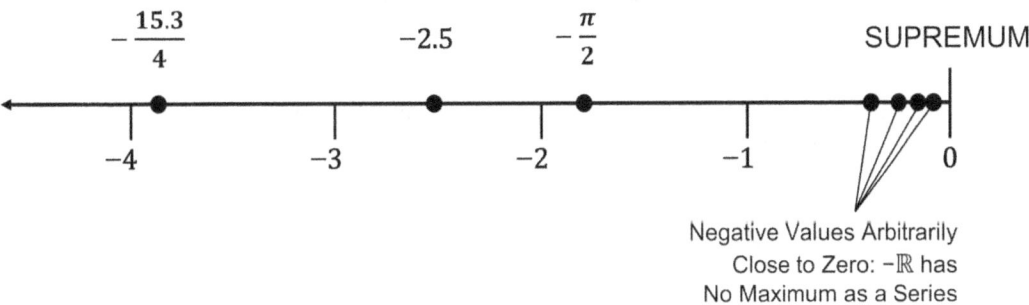

Figure 11.5: Examples of negative real numbers from what mathematicians usually conceive as the set (vice series) of negative reals (denoted $-\mathbb{R}$) with zero (0) as the supremum but not as a maximum.

These examples show that the status of being an infimum or supremum is a relative matter; zero is both the supremum of negative real numbers and the infimum of positive real numbers. In both cases, zero is the bound outside of the sequences (positive and negative) that are indefinitely being defined with new values ever closer to zero. As the infimum or supremum, zero functions as the bound toward which we may create new values for either the sequence of negative real numbers or the sequence of positive real numbers, respectively.

More importantly, these examples also show that new values can be invented *indefinitely* between any two real numbers such as between negative one and zero or between positive one and zero. But just having the ability to indefinitely invent new values toward an infimum or supremum does not indicate that there are *limitless* values there to find. That zero can function as either an infimum or a supremum could be taken as implying that $\mathbb{R}$, like all other number scales, is an incomplete series under indefinite construction.

However, most mathematicians hold that between any two real numbers, such as between two integers like 0 and 1, there are *limitlessly many* real numbers already there waiting for us to discover. Since the 19th Century, mathematicians have typically held that the real numbers between any pair of integers form a continuum that is *dense*, which means there are no gaps in the sequence of reals: between any two real numbers is another real number, with all the real numbers in the sequence already there in the number line waiting to be discovered by the mathematician [342] [343]. While I disagree that there exist *limitlessly* many numbers, let alone numbers that exist before anyone invents them, there is no *mathematical* problem with limitlessly many numbers falling within the bounds of suprema and infima of some other kind of number. But as we'll see in the next chapter, while there is no mathematical problem with this notion, it is the *logical* coherence of sets being limitless that is questionable.

11.2.7 *Variant Extremes and Constant Extremes*

If we think of sequences and series of numbers as collections under construction, the extremes of the sequences or series—such as infima and suprema—need not necessarily be static, or constant. Such extremes can change, such as when new numbers are added successively to a sequence of numbers. (It should be kept in mind, though, that changes in extremes are not usually attended to in the mathematical formalism, but rather are "behind" the formalism—you can think of them as meta-mathematical.)

Suppose we have a set of three integers: set $A = \{1, 2, 3\}$. Set A is complete, as is. But now suppose we want to add another member to this set. If we do add another integer, like 4, then either we are implying one of two things:

(1) set A was not, in fact, complete as we had formerly thought—something was missing, namely the number 4, which entails that we should have expressed $A = \{1, 2, 3, 4\}$,

or

(2) set A is complete as $\{1, 2, 3\}$ alright, but only as the set of the *first three* integers in the counting numbers.

If the second is what is meant, then when we add 4 to the A, we are actually creating a *new* set—we'll call it B. If that is so, then set A becomes a subset, to be designated as a in B. That is, set A becomes subset a, which is $[1, 2, 3]$ in set B, which equals $\{1, 2, 3, 4\}$ when 4 is added to the members of A.

In this example, if A is taken as a complete set, then in A we can find that 3 is the greatest element. But if the number 4 is added to the sequence of A to make the new set, B, then while 3 is still the greatest element of $\{1, 2, 3\}$ as set A, it is also the case that 3 then becomes only the supremum in the form of the *least upper bound* of the sequence $[1, 2, 3]$ which is also subset a within the supraset $\{1, 2, 3, 4\}$, in which 4 is the greatest element—the new maximum. At one moment, we had only set A, in which 3 was the greatest element. At a later moment, an element was added to the set such that what we call "the set" was no longer only set A but then became set B in which set A is only the subset a, with 3 having turned from being the greatest element in "the set" to being only the supremum for subset a, while the new element, 4, became the greatest element of "the set." In such a situation, sets A and B are two sets in what is actually a *series of sets*.

Moreover, as this situation illustrates, the extrema of the series (of sets) are not necessarily *constant extrema*, retaining the same mathematical values for the duration of the existence of the series, but may instead be *variant extrema*, changing their value over time. For example, while the value for the maximum of A may be constant for A as a set, and while the value for the maximum of B may be constant for B as a set, nevertheless A and B may be just two sets in an increasing series of sets and so what we would in that situation call "the extremum" for the *series* is not constant, but variant since the extremum for the whole changes with time.

Furthermore, a series of sets may continue to be constructed in this manner, with previous sets becoming subsets of new sets. The greatest element, the maximum, of the previous set becomes only a least upper bound, a supremum, in what becomes a subset to it as a new superset, which then has a new, different element as the maximum for the whole. If this is an open series, the maximum remains 'variant' in value. The variant maximum may continually change in value, with the series of sets perhaps growing indefinitely larger. However long the series continues to aggregate, though, the series remains limited and so finite with a variant maximum—at best, the series is only a figurative infinity.

When mathematicians consider sequences or series as continuing ever onward, though, most of them are not thinking of open, indefinite constructions with a variant maximum. Rather, most mathematicians regard sequences or series as *limitless* sets, the values of which 'converge' ever closer to an infimum or supremum along the extent of the sequence of values comprising the set. That is, the sequence of values extends toward an infimum or supremum, but it is unable to be absolutely convergent with the infimum or supremum toward which the sequence extends. The sequence is thus portrayed as a literal infinity of values.

To boil it down: a limitless sequence may contain subsequences having absolute and relative extrema along the orthogonal axis of the overall sequence to which they belong (as in **Figure 11.2**) but along the axis of progression the sequence can only be limitless if it makes sense for the sequence to increase *without limit* toward a supremum, or decrease *without limit* toward an infimum, as a constant extremum. If such limitless progressions are only figuratively 'limitless' (serially indefinite), then the sequence so progressing would only be figuratively infinite rather than literally infinite; but it is not figurative infinity that concerns us at this point. Rather, it is literal infinity that we need to explore with respect to the implications of limitlessness.

11.2.8 *No Maximum*

Consider any collection in which the elements can be arranged into a limitless sequence or series—no collection of that kind would have an extremum on both ends (both a minimum and a maximum) for the whole of it. Moreover, to have no extreme to the *order* of elements in a limitless collection also entails that the limitless collection would have no extreme to the cardinality of elements comprising the limitless collection; that is, the collection would have *no maximum size*. All non-zero, non-circuitous collections that are limitless are without a maximum to any count of their members.

Take once again our infinite marble bag analogy (from § 1.3.2, § 8.3, and § 10.2.2). The limitlessness of the set of marbles in the bag ensures that any finite number of marbles added to them does not increase the amount of marbles in the bag since the limitless quantity in the bag has no maximum and so the bag can never be full. That is, since there is no such thing as a maximum for an infinite quantity due to its limitlessness, a bag of $\aleph$ marbles plus one more marble is still a bag of $\aleph$ marbles. Drop another marble into the bag and the bag easily accommodates it without increasing in quantity: $\aleph + 1 = \aleph$. Distinguishing between the infinitude $(^{(x)}\aleph)$ in the bag at t_1 from the infinitude in the bag with just one more marble $(^{(y)}\aleph)$ at t_2 is irrelevant because, in terms of the *limitlessness* of the quantity in each iteration of the bag, it must be the case that $^{(x)}\aleph = {}^{(y)}\aleph = \aleph$. In other words, if we consider *only* the property of limitlessness for the set of marbles in the bag, then $^{(x)}\aleph$ and $^{(y)}\aleph$ are mathematically indistinguishable from the unqualified $\aleph$ [344]. (Notice this does not jibe with the conclusions we reached in the last chapter about the completeness of the infinite collection of marbles in the bag.)

Likewise, when we consider a collection of real numbers as having a limitless quantity of reals *between* any two real numbers (such as between 0.1 and 0.2, or between 0 and 1, or between −1 and 0, etc.), that limitlessness implies lack of a maximum. Even though one integer (e.g., 0) may be an infimum and the other (e.g., 1) may be a supremum, a limitless sequence of reals between them would imply there is no maximum amount of reals between them—not even a so-called variant maximum (a running total).

Now consider the concept of limitlessness applied to the number systems or 'number scales'. Suppose that the natural number scale as a set ($\mathbb{N}$) is limitless in the direction of its ascending values, rather than simply indefinite. If that were so, any finite subset of natural numbers could still have upper and lower bounds—an infimum and supremum, minimum and maximum values, etc. However, for $\mathbb{N}$ as a whole to be without limit would be for $\mathbb{N}$ as such to have no natural number as an ordinal maximum for $\mathbb{N}$, not even a variant maximum as an instance of a running total.

Moreover, just as the amount of naturals in $\mathbb{N}$ would have no maximum if $\mathbb{N}$ is a limitless set, so too the whole numbers of $\mathbb{W}$, the integers of $\mathbb{Z}$, the rationals of $\mathbb{Q}$, and reals or $\mathbb{R}$ would also have no maximum if these scales are also limitless sets. And again, this means not a variant maximum or a running total. After all, if these number systems are *literally infinite*, then we are supposed to be conceiving of these number systems as being literally *limitless*, not just figuratively 'limitless'.

11.2.9 *Beyond Fullness*

To sum up regarding the fullness of limitless collections: Because there is no relevant extremity—no maximum amount by which to judge a limitless collection as full—the notion of 'fullness' does not really apply to a limitless collection. This applies even if we define outer limits for an infinite collection, as when mathematicians define an infimum or supremum for an infinite sequence, for the limitlessness of the sequence of values *between* those limits—the values in descending order to the infimum or in ascending order up to the supremum—entails the sequence *never* converges with the infimum or supremum, no matter how many values we add to it. So, fullness does not apply to a limitless collection; insofar as $\mathbb{N}$, $\mathbb{W}$, $\mathbb{Z}$, $\mathbb{Q}$, $\mathbb{R}$, etc. are limitless collections of numbers, they too cannot be full collections of numbers.

11.3 MORE THAN A TOTAL

By lacking a maximum of elements, a collection that is limitless is a collection that cannot be numerically quantified (that is, it cannot be quantified with a number, as opposed to quantified with a predicate like "many" or "infinite"). The individual numbers in any sequence (like 1 or 42 or 10^{100}) are quantities and finite subsets to which they are applied can be numerically quantified, but if such finite subsets belong to an infinitely large superset, the whole of that limitless superset cannot be numerically quantified. Hence if it is the case that the sequence of numbers in $\mathbb{N}$ is limitless (and not just indefinitely large), then the numbers in $\mathbb{N}$, taken altogether as a set, cannot be numerically quantified (assigned a quantity), not even in principle. The same is true for any set that has a limitless sequence of members; if such a set is equal in quantity to $\mathbb{N}$ while $\mathbb{N}$ is infinite, then it too is absolutely unquantifiable as a whole due to its limitlessness.

If a collection as a whole is not quantifiable, that in itself does not mean there are no quantities *in* the collection. It just means the collection as a whole cannot be assigned a *total*. An infinite collection, as a limitless collection, is a collection that cannot be quantified in the sense of being given a total—such a collection cannot even have a running total. Limitlessness is consistent with wholeness and entirety, but limitlessness also implies *no totality*.

Moreover, because there is no total to an infinite collection as a limitless collection, the sequence of numbers in an infinite collection is *uncountable*. Due to the limitlessness of the collection, there is no such thing as counting *all* the numbers in an infinite collection. According to philosopher Cynthia MacDonald, a counting process for an infinite set "...cannot, even in principle, be completed..." [345]. Similarly, Lavine described a literally infinite collection (thus a collection that is limitless) as one that is "too large for anyone to count independent of context, abilities, or interest" [346]. This is essentially the same as saying that a literally infinite collection is uncountable *even in principle*. Then too, Dr. Gary Hardegree of the Department of Philosophy at the University of Massachusetts, states that "a set is *infinite* if and only if it is not finite, which means that it cannot be counted by a natural number" [347]. In principle, a counter may be able to count any arbitrarily-selected, finite subset of numbers in a sequence that is infinite, but one cannot—not even if principle—count all members (i.e., every member) in an infinite sequence. It is one thing to say that all the members of some *indefinitely* large subset of numbers in $\mathbb{N}$ can be counted in principle, for that still implies a limit, even if only in the form of a variable, or running total. It is quite another to say $\mathbb{N}$ constitutes a set that has a *limitless* quantity of numbers: such quantities cannot in principle, let alone in practice, be counted for there is no full number, no maximum number, no total number to count.

11.4 ABSENCE OF FINISH

A literally infinite collection, with respect to its being a limitless collection, is not a collection that is finished. That is, it is not a collection that has the property of 'finish'.

When number systems are portrayed not only as immense (and ergo, finite) *series* but instead as literally infinite *sets*—for example, when the naturals are given as $\mathbb{N}$ or the wholes as $\mathbb{W}$ in the transfinite system—then the number systems are portrayed as *limitless* sets and therefore as sets having no last element, no highest number, by which sequential invention or listing of their numbers is all done—finished. As Grossman put it [348]:

> In an *infinite* set, you still have the first element, second element, and so on. However there is no last element because the infinite set will contain a kth element and there will always be a $(k+1)^{th}$ element because there is no limit to the number of elements in an infinite set.

Grossman uses k for her example instead of n as I've been using, but the point is the same. An *indefinite series* of numbers has at any given moment a varying 'last' element (k) for which a new element ($k+1$) can then be created as its successor (which could then itself be displaced as the highest, 'last' element when yet another, higher element is created after it, and so on). For a literally *infinite set*, on the other hand, any 'last' k identified is never a 'last' member in an absolute sense.

Moreover, in a literally infinite set, k is never even a 'last' element in the sense of being the highest numbered element generated at any given time. Rather, the 'last' k is what has only been *identified* as the highest named element so far while the infinite set has at all times *no last element* in an absolute sense because there's always one more element ($k+1$) *already there* after it to find in the set.

For a literally infinite collection (such as $\mathbb{N}$ or $\mathbb{W}$ or any other number system taken to be a complete set) to have no last element means that such a collection cannot be *finished* because 'finish' means to have a *concluding* element. If there's no last element at all, there is no concluding element for the set to be finished.

It might be observed that the collection of non-positive reals (that is, the line of negative real numbers *and* zero), if assumed to comprise an infinite set, does have a finish—a concluding element to the sequence of the collection—in the form of a last number of sorts; namely, 0 (zero). **Figure 11.5** illustrates that although the negative reals have 0 as a supremum, the non-positive reals (which include 0) have 0 as a finish to the order of numbers in that sequence of numbers. However, while 0 is the 'conclusion' or 'last number' with respect to the *order* of non-positive reals of *least to greatest* magnitude, 0 is not the concluding element or last number with respect to either the process of *constructing* the sequence of the non-positive reals or to any process of sequentially *counting* them. It is such processes that the concept of 'finish' pertains to.

The non-positive reals 'descend' into the negative from a greatest element (0) to any least negative real you can name ($-k$). If the sequence of negative reals is constructed over time as an indefinite series, then any least $-k$ can always be supplanted by an even lesser $-k$ over what is a running total of negative reals constructed in the series. It is logically possible that such construction of the negative reals can continue indefinitely, so there is not necessarily a finish to the construction of the sequence of negative reals in that sense. There is a finish to a given instance of the negative reals as a set of all the negative reals for that particular time; thus, there is a finish for any $|-\mathbb{R}^C|$ but there is no finish for $-\mathbb{R}^C$ as a series.

If, to the contrary, the negative reals are a literally infinite set ($-\mathbb{R}$), then they could be construed as formed all at once. The same is true for the positive set of reals ($+\mathbb{R}$) and for the overset of all reals ($\mathbb{R}$). So, $\mathbb{R}$ may be considered to already be finished as the set of reals—negative, positive, and zero—all of which exist all in one step.

Yet, while $\mathbb{R}$ as a set may be formed in a timeless step and so $\mathbb{R}$ may be 'finished' with respect to its formation, such a finished state does not apply to the limitlessness of the *sequence* of $\mathbb{R}$, for to be of limitless sequence is to be without the property of finish in regard to any count of the members in that sequence. If a collection has a non-zero quantity of elements and the sequence of the elements in that collection is limitless, then the sequence of elements in that collection has no finish, period, as shown by any attempt to count it.

It's important to keep in mind that we should not think of the literal limitlessness of a given sequence as being 'unfinished' in the sense of a serial indefinite. A serial indefinite sequence is *provisionally unfinished*; by contrast, a limitless sequence is *irrelevant to finish*.

The conception of the system of reals as $\mathbb{R}^C$ portrays the reals as provisionally unfinished because $\mathbb{R}^C$ is an intrinsically incomplete series with a running total of reals under construction. If we conceive the system of reals as $\mathbb{R}^C$, then any count or listing of the reals can in principle be finished as far as the sequence in $\mathbb{R}^C$ has been extended at a given time—so, the count can be finished provided construction of $\mathbb{R}^C$ were to cease at that count. On the other hand, provided $\mathbb{R}^C$ continues to be extended with the invention of new reals, no count of $\mathbb{R}^C$ will ever be finished. So, $\mathbb{R}^C$ is "provisionally unfinished" in that sense.

In contrast, the conception of the system of reals as $\mathbb{R}$ portrays the reals as there all at once, not constructed serially over time. So, the concept of being finished or unfinished is irrelevant to any counting or listing of the numbers in $\mathbb{R}$ because there is no such thing as finish with respect to the limitlessness of the *sequence* of numbers in $\mathbb{R}$. That is, no count of the reals in $\mathbb{R}$ can ever finish, not even temporarily to capture a running total of reals in $\mathbb{R}$ at a given time, for no such running total of reals exists—not even provisionally. $\mathbb{R}$ has no finish at all because the sequence of $\mathbb{R}$ has no positive or negative limits that extend further over time as is the case with $\mathbb{R}^C$.

While the limitless sequence of $\mathbb{R}$ has no finish, we would not say the sequence of $\mathbb{R}$ is 'unfinished' in the sense that its sequence could be finished but happens not to be. Rather, $\mathbb{R}$ has no finish with respect to the sequence of its members because $\mathbb{R}$'s sequence is limitless and the concept of finish does not apply to limitlessness, just as the concept of dryness does not apply to size—it would be a category mistake to talk of being 'finished' or 'unfinished' for that which is without limit in the literal sense of the term. All we can say is that since there is *no first term* and *no last term* in $\mathbb{R}$, not even provisionally, the idea of finish is absent for $\mathbb{R}$. There is thus no such thing as a count of $\mathbb{R}$'s numbers being finished.

The same can be said, of course, for the other number systems: $\mathbb{N}$, $\mathbb{W}$, $\mathbb{Z}$, $\mathbb{Q}$, etc. As literally infinite sets, they are limitless in sequence and in the quantity of their numbers, and so they have no final terms by which a count of their numbers can be finished.

11.5 LIMITLESS ENTIRETY

A collection is an *entire* collection if the collection is missing no elements—all elements are in the collection. This applies even to collections said to be *limitless*.

For example, take the scale of natural numbers as the set $\mathbb{N}$. Mathematicians adopting set theory commonly say $\mathbb{N}$ is the set of *all* the natural numbers; there is no natural number that is not in $\mathbb{N}$. Assuming as much, $\mathbb{N}$ has the property of *entirety*—it is missing no natural number. But $\mathbb{N}$ is also typically claimed to be *limitless*, implying that there is no limit to the quantity of natural numbers in $\mathbb{N}$. In which case, $\mathbb{N}$ is both the limitless set of natural numbers as well as the entire set of natural numbers.

The *limitlessness* of $\mathbb{N}$ has implications for $\mathbb{N}$ as the *entirety* of natural numbers. Consider that each natural number has a cardinality. Since each number >1 in the sequence of $\mathbb{N}$ is just one $(+1)$ higher than the previous number, then *for any* number in $\mathbb{N}$ you could ever in principle name, that number must be a countable distance from 1 while the next number would also be just one higher (see § 11.1). Each number in $\mathbb{N}$ and its immediate successor *must* therefore have a finite cardinality. Now since $\mathbb{N}$ is the entirety of naturals, *all* naturals are in $\mathbb{N}$. So, you might think there must be a *highest* finite number in $\mathbb{N}$. But $\mathbb{N}$ is also limitless, which entails that there is no "highest natural number" quantifying the entirety of $\mathbb{N}$. Instead, the limitlessness of $\mathbb{N}$ as a set means that no matter how big any given natural number is in $\mathbb{N}$, that number is still finite—it has a finite string of digits. So, the limitlessness of $\mathbb{N}$ is said not to imply the existence of a natural number with a limitless string of digits—an *infinitely large natural number*.

With respect to the limitlessness of $\mathbb{N}$, mathematicians say that, while there are no natural numbers with limitlessly many digits, there is nevertheless no limit to the sequence of $\mathbb{N}$'s *finite* numbers [349]. In other words, because the *sequence* of natural numbers comprising $\mathbb{N}$ forms a limitless progression of finite numbers, there are said to be "infinitely many" finite natural numbers comprising the entirety of $\mathbb{N}$ while there is no such thing as an "infinite number" of numbers in $\mathbb{N}$ as if the natural numbers start at 1 and proceed up to infinitely large natural numbers. The entirety of $\mathbb{N}$ is infinite, but no number *in* $\mathbb{N}$ is infinite.

Although there is a subtle fallacy at play in the concept of limitless quantities of unique, finite, natural numbers, exploring the fallacy can wait until § 14.2. The important point for now is that mathematicians commonly hold $\mathbb{N}$ to be a set that has the *entire* sequence of natural numbers—infinitely many of them in the sense of a *progression* of numbers continuing *without limit*—but no number in $\mathbb{N}$ is infinitely large.

11.6 LIMITLESS IN WHOLE

Wholeness is a feature of a collection's completeness. For a collection to be 'whole' is for it to be 'undivided' in the sense of having no breaks or gaps or separation of members that would violate the completeness of the collection. But for literally infinite collections, the wholeness of the collection is also a feature of its limitlessness.

The wholeness of an infinite collection with respect to the collection's limitlessness is not of the same quality of wholeness the infinite collection has with respect to its completeness. Insofar as an infinite collection is a complete collection, the whole of that collection is *equal to* the sum of the collection's members; but insofar as the infinite collection is limitless, the whole of that collection is *greater than* the sum of its members.

11.6.1 *Greater Than Any Sum*

A literally infinite collection, as a limitless collection, cannot have a total—not even in principle—because a limitless collection has no last term to count. A limitless collection may have sums of subgroups of members but, as a whole, the collection *cannot be summed*.

Assuming $\mathbb{N}$ is a literally infinite collection that can exist in sequence (1, 2, 3, ...), if the sequence of numbers could extend to a natural number with infinitely many digits, then that would imply the numbers of $\mathbb{N}$ are equal to an infinite sum that is the cardinality of all the natural numbers. But there can be no sum that would exhaust all the numbers in $\mathbb{N}$ because, for any number in the series, there is a *next* number $(n + 1)$ and every next number in the sequence of $\mathbb{N}$ is only a finite number. Consequently, even though the whole of $\mathbb{N}$ is a *limitless* collection, $\mathbb{N}$ contains no single natural number that is an infinite sum of all natural numbers [350]. An infinite set of numbers has no number that constitutes a *sum* of all its numbers. The amount of numbers in $\mathbb{N}$ cannot be totaled or summed as there is no last number in $\mathbb{N}$ at all—not even a number that is infinite [351].

We must therefore think of a limitless set of numbers as a set that has quantity, or that contains quantities, but that does not have a total. The limitless quantity of $\mathbb{N}$ is a quantity such it that makes the *whole* of $\mathbb{N}$ greater than any sum of numbers $\mathbb{N}$ contains. For $\mathbb{N}$ to be *infinite* thus means $\mathbb{N}$ is greater than any number, any sum, in the sequence of numbers belonging to $\mathbb{N}$.

11.6.2 *There Can Be No Variable for Infinity*

As there is no "infinitely large" natural number in $\mathbb{N}$ and no so no infinite sum of numbers, then we can conclude that to be infinite is to be *greater than any natural number*. That means we cannot consistently use a variable, such as n or k or a, to represent some definite, yet infinite, value. No number, n, in $\mathbb{N}$ is an infinite number. Instead of a variable, we can use symbols like $\aleph$ to represent the limitless quantity of members in infinite collections. Mathematicians regard $\aleph$ as *by definition equal* ($\triangleq$) to the set of wholes numbers, $\mathbb{W}$, such that $\mathbb{W} \triangleq \{0, 1, 2, 3, ...\}$, as well as the set of natural numbers: $\mathbb{N} \triangleq \{1, 2, 3, ...\}$. Thus $\aleph$ represents the size of both $\mathbb{N}$ and $\mathbb{W}$ since each sequence shares the same cardinality, even though $\mathbb{W}$ has one more number than $\mathbb{N}$. The two scales have the same cardinality because the additional number in $\mathbb{W}$ is zero, which designates merely the empty set and so has no size (see §§ 2.3.7–2.3.9). So, both $\mathbb{W}$ and $\mathbb{N}$ are $\aleph$ in size, while each extends without limit. Rather than $\mathbb{N}$ being equal to some infinitely large natural number, n, the total of the sequence of $\mathbb{N}$ is equal to $\aleph$, a cardinal number which represents a quantity "greater than" ($>$) any n in the sequence of $\mathbb{N}$, where every n is finite; therefore, $\mathbb{N}$ is greater than any natural number, all of which are finite sums [352]. $\mathbb{N} \triangleq \aleph$, which is infinite (limitless), while no n in $\mathbb{N}$ has infinite digits.

11.6.3 *Converging Without Limit*

If there is no natural number that is infinitely large, no infinite sum, then there can be no such thing as an infinite sequence that *ends* at some exact, albeit unknowable, value. Take, for example, a series of reals extending from one integer to another, such as from 0 to 1 or from 1 down to 0. A mathematical operation may produce an *indefinite* descent toward a number such as 0 or an *indefinite* ascent toward a number such as 1. In either case, there is no last number in the sequence or series between 0 and 1 in the sense of a number that finishes the sequence with a standing total of numbers. That is what makes the sequence of numbers indefinite; it is produced by an open series of steps—a *figurative* infinity (indefinite process).

Consider a mathematical function that derives values between 0 and 1 in which the succession of generated values is said to "approach" or "draw near" to either of the numbers as a 'limit' (that is, as an infimum or a supremum). Let's suppose we are using a function that divides 1 by 10, then that quotient by 10, and so on into ever smaller decimal values, closer to 0:

$$0.1$$
$$0.01$$
$$0.001$$
$$0.0001$$
$$0.00001$$
$$0.000001$$
$$\vdots$$

In this case, 0 is the limit (infimum) that our function "tends to" as we continue to derive values ever smaller than 1 but still greater than 0. Ironically, the more times we iterate this function the larger the string of decimal places while we continue to get ever "nearer" to 0.

Above is depicted the output of the function iterated only six times. But, as the ellipsis indicates, we can continue this descent to 0 *indefinitely* without ever reaching 0. In fact, the actual mathematical procedure treats the function as an indefinite process. And if the function were to be carried out indefinitely, we could then take the ellipsis as indicating the series of values to have, at any time during the construction of these series, a running total of defined numbers. Hence, this function implies a total, even though it is only a running total of defined numbers.

While most contemporary mathematicians say such a function is carried out *infinitely*, in saying such they tend to mean "infinitely" only in the sense of figurative (or 'potential') infinity since they know in operation the function is a serial indefinite [353]. "However," says Fletcher, "underlying this use of potential infinity are two uses of actual infinity: the concept of an infinite set (primarily the set of all natural numbers, $\mathbb{N}$, and the set of all real numbers, $\mathbb{R}$) and the concept of infinite quantifiers ('for all x, ...', 'there exists a δ...'). Potential infinity and actual infinity are intertwined in modern mathematics" [354]. As Fletcher points out, ∞, taken in a figurative sense, indicates a direction rather than a destination [355]. In complement, ω is a literally infinite sequence that ∞ is the direction the sequence points along. So, for a function like the convergence with 0, it seems that most mathematicians assume that the function can be carried out a figuratively infinite number of times ("tending to infinity" as they say) precisely because there is a literally infinite sequence of numbers "already there" between 0 and 1 from which the function can uncover indefinitely long sequences. It's as if a muffin tin with a literal infinitude of empty cups is having those cups sequentially filled with muffins—a figuratively infinite process (see **Figure 3.3**).

Moreover, if figurative infinity (∞) is taken as implying a direction along a sequence that is literally infinite (ω), then a state of literal limitlessness is implied to exist. And if there is a limitless sequence or the potential for such, then there is *no end* in the steps the above function must take to actually converge with 0. There is no "infinitieth" place immediately prior to reaching 0 as infimum, and there is no such thing as a fraction that is an "infinitieth" the size of 1.

Carrying out a function infinitely in a literal sense (without limit) would therefore produce *no total at all* for the series of decimal values—*not even a running total*. And without such a total, there can be no infinite sum. The infinite series of numbers between 0 and 1 is limitless precisely because, no matter how close to the integer a real number is, there is always another one just a little closer and never a final real for which 0 would be the next number.

Infinite series never converge absolutely with a definite number due to their limitlessness, and so there is no infinitely large *number* even if a limitless *quantity* of finite numbers. The limitlessness of the natural number series makes its collection of numbers *greater than* any sum of numbers in the series.

11.7 LIMITLESSNESS IMPLICATIONS SUMMARIZED

Over the course of this chapter, we've seen the logical implications of limitlessness for literally infinite collections. **Figure 11.6** summarizes the implications.

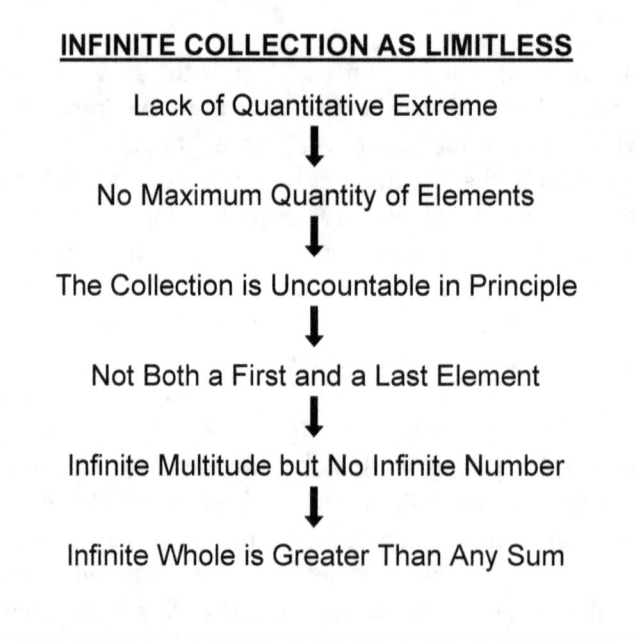

Figure 11.6: The implications of limitlessness for literally infinite collections.

CHAPTER 11 IN REVIEW

❖ Literal infinity is a condition of limitlessness, of being without limit in the sense of having an extent (range of elements) that is unspecifiable, even in principle.

❖ To have no specifiable range of elements in the context of being infinite implies a collection that does not meet completeness conditions. For example, a limitless collection is one that cannot be "full," that cannot have a maximum quantity.

❖ Since a limitless collection has no maximum, it does not even have a variable maximum as an instance of a running total. Rather, a limitless collection has no total at all.

❖ Having no total means the limitless collection is uncountable, even in principle, which implies there is not even an "infinitely large number" of members. Rather, a limitless collection is one in which the members cannot be summed at all.

❖ A literally infinite collection, as a limitless collection, is a collection *greater than* any sum of elements.

12: COMPLETE AND LIMITLESS: THE CONTRADICTIONS

Infinity in its literal sense is a condition of being both complete and limitless in quantity. There are logical implications to completeness, as there are to limitlessness. Chapter 10 explicated the implications of completeness for infinite collections. Chapter 11 explicated the implications of limitlessness for infinite collections. This chapter will contrast the implications, exposing them as contradicting each other.

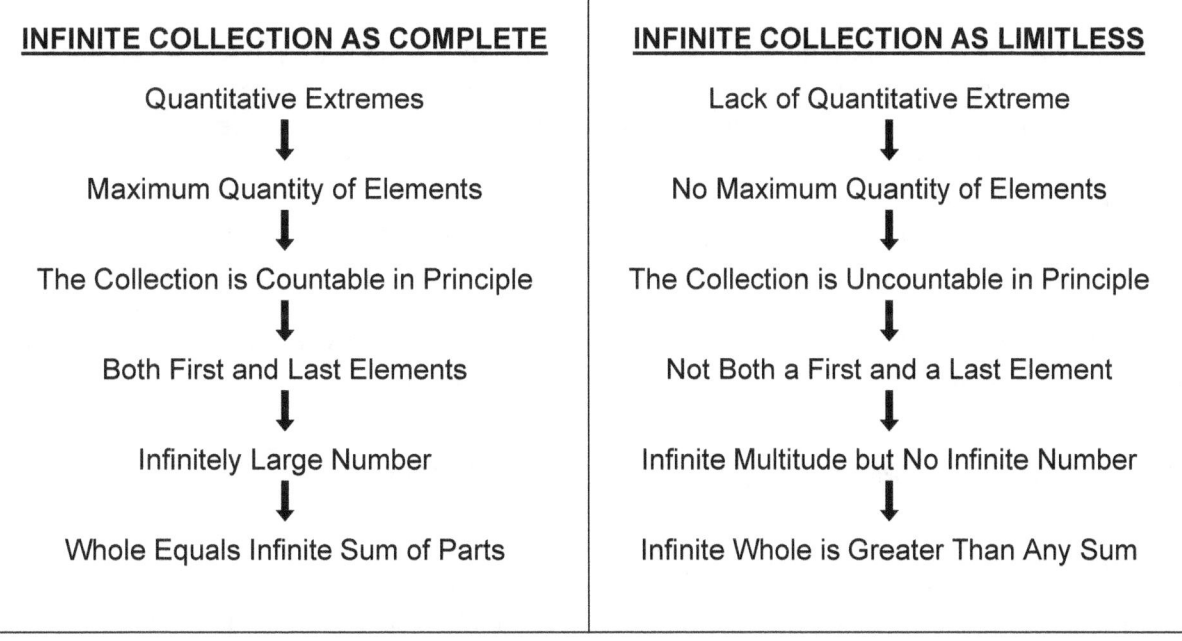

Figure 12.0: The implications (arrows) of completeness and limitlessness contrasted for infinite collections. There are at least six contradictions between completeness and limitlessness.

12.1 ON SPEAKING OF "ALL" THE MEMBERS IN INFINITE COLLECTIONS

As shown in **Figure 12.0**, the completeness and limitlessness of infinity entail contradictory implications. Consequently, we must be careful when we make a statement about "all" the members of a literally infinite collection because we may be considering "all" the members only with regard to the implications of one property (e.g., completeness) while ignoring the implications of the other property (e.g., limitlessness).

It is quite common for mathematicians, scientists, philosophers, and other scholars to state something about "all" the members of an infinite collection that actually applies only to the members of the collection insofar as they are limitless but not insofar as they form a complete collection or vice versa. As we'll see time and again over the pages to come, scholars continually make statements of infinite collections *per se* while their statements only apply to *either* the completeness *or* the limitlessness of the collection but cannot apply to both simultaneously.

Consequently, scholars writing about infinity are constantly getting into irresolvable disputes. As we'll see in § 19.3.7, one group of philosophers says an infinite series can be completed while another group says an infinite series cannot be completed. They are both wrong: an infinite series *can and cannot* be completed because an infinite series is a complete series—which has one set of implications—while the same infinite series is also a limitless series—which has an opposite set of implications. And this is precisely the problem with literal infinity, as illustrated in **Figure 12.0**.

The problem is revealed in the use of the word 'all' with respect to the members of a literally infinite collection. When we refer to *all* the members of a literally infinite collection, the meaning of 'all' with respect to the limitlessness of the collection differs from its meaning with respect to the completeness of the collection.

When we refer to 'all' the natural numbers in $\mathbb{N}$ as a *limitless* set of numbers, we merely mean that, *for any* natural number n, it is the case that n has such and such a property. With respect to *limitlessness*, the term 'all' does not mean *every* member of a collection as if the members are a totality. But with respect to *completeness*, the meaning of 'all' the numbers in $\mathbb{N}$ does indeed mean *every* natural number in $\mathbb{N}$ rather than merely *any* number in $\mathbb{N}$ as it does with respect to $\mathbb{N}$ as a limitless collection.

These two uses of 'all' ('every' and 'any') do not necessarily conflict across contexts, but we should be aware that just because we make a claim about 'all' the members in a literally infinite collection, that does not mean the claim holds true for the collection with respect to *both* the limitlessness of those members and the completeness of the collection. We'll see some examples of how this holds true as we take a closer look at each set of conflicting implications listed in **Figure 12.0**.

12.2 AFFIRMING EXTREMES AND MAXIMA WHILE DENYING THEM

Literal infinity is a condition of completeness, which entails being a full collection. Fullness in turn implies the collection has parameters, and so has extremities. Those extremities connote the collection has a constant maximum amount of elements. And yet, literal infinity is also the condition of being limitless, which entails the inability to become full—limitlessness implies not more than one extremity, such as both a minimum and a maximum amount of elements. Rather, limitlessness implies there is no maximum amount of elements. A literally infinite collection therefore has an extreme in the form of a greatest quantity—a maximum—and does not. A self-contradictory condition.

The infinite marble analogy (§ 1.3.2) provides a useful illustration of the contradiction. As presented in § 10.2.2, the literally infinite collection of marbles in the bag is a complete collection. Since completeness entails fullness, the bag of marbles must be a full collection of marbles. Which in turn entails a constant maximum ($^{(z)}\aleph$) of marbles, where any less ($^{(y)}\aleph$) would *not* be the full amount even if both amounts are infinite just as one less marble less in a finite amount is not the full amount; so, $^{(z)}\aleph \neq {}^{(y)}\aleph$.

In § 11.2.8, however, we saw that a bag containing an infinitude of marbles holds a limitless collection of marbles. One infinite is just as limitless as another. Hence, $\aleph = \aleph$.

But now we have a contradiction in logical implications. For it is not at all clear how to distinguish a collection of $\aleph$ members from $^{(z)}\aleph$ members or $\aleph$ from $^{(y)}\aleph$ members.

Worse still, to be complete is to have a maximum but to be without limit is to have no maximum. The infinite bag of marbles therefore cannot have a maximum (e.g., $^{(z)}\aleph$) amount of marbles because a maximum is a limit that the collection cannot have by virtue of its limitlessness (unqualified $\aleph$). Hence, the infinitude of marbles does and does not have a maximum—the infinitude of marbles can fit into an infinite bag by virtue of its completeness and yet cannot by virtue of its limitlessness. A maximum with no maximum, a full bag that can never be filled or that can never contain all the members of the collection—more contradictions.

So too, take the series of reals between 0 and 1. Recall from § 10.2.2 that the infinite sequence of reals *from* 0 *to* 1 is complete—the infinite series completely (absolutely) converges from one integer to another. The infinite series therefore has a maximum of steps to take. Now recall from § 11.2.8 that the infinite sequence of reals *between* 0 and 1 is limitless—the series is claimed to be not just *indefinite* with respect to mathematical operations that would converge toward one of the integers, but also the series of reals is said to be *limitless* and so to have no maximum at all between the integers. Again we have contradictions: there is and is not a maximum amount of steps for the infinite series to take; a maximum without a maximum, a completed sequence that is never complete.

I should hasten to add, however, that these contradictions are not *mathematical* because the operations for convergence are merely indefinite, producing a variant maximum or variant minimum in actual operation running totals of values. However, when they are expressed with infinity, the operations for convergence do represent a *logical* contradiction in *meaning*: one implies ∞ steps can be completed, the other implies ∞ steps cannot be completed.

12.3 COUNTABLE AND UNCOUNTABLE

To count the members of a collection is to undergo a series of tasks; each task in the series is the assignment of a number to a member in the collection—a count of the member. The larger the collection to be counted, the greater the number of tasks (counts) that must be performed. Presumably, to count a literally infinite collection would require a literally infinite series of such tasks; that is, the counting process must itself be literally infinite.

But it's not clear this is a sensible notion. Take a collection claimed to have infinitely many members. Assuming $\mathbb{N}$ is literally infinite, we should be able to use the numbers of $\mathbb{N}$ to count each member in the infinitely-many members of the collection in question. A collection the size of $\mathbb{N}$ constitutes a collection of $\aleph$ members that are *limitless* in extent and, on that basis, cannot be serially counted to a finished totality, not even in principle—there's no limit to the counting that must take place [356]. Yet, this goes against the implications of $\aleph$ and ω as representing collections that are *complete* and therefore countable, at least in principle [357].

We therefore have a problem: while a literally infinite collection is complete and so countable in principle, it is also limitless and so cannot be counted, not even in principle. Literal infinity thus must be uncountable but can't be—a contradiction yet again.

When faced with such contradictions, some mathematicians attempt to resolve them by bringing up technical forms of completeness like 'Dedekind completeness' or 'Cauchy completeness'. This is a bit of misdirection, however. Both technical forms of 'completeness' are misnomers, Cauchy completeness involves figuratively infinite convergence and Dedekind completeness involves purportedly limitless sets. And both lack the necessary properties like 'finish' and 'totality' to qualify as *complete* in anything but a highly misleading sense of the term. Besides, such technical senses of completeness do not resolve the contradictions that arise with claims of a set being limitless while also claiming the same set is 'complete' according to a different mathematical function, such as a function for demonstrating absolute convergence (which we'll return to toward the end of this chapter).

12.4 BOTH FIRST AND LAST...BUT NOT BOTH

We can finish counting a complete collection, but we can never finish counting a limitless collection. For a limitless collection, there may either be a first member but no last member (1, 2, 3, ...) or a last member without a first member (..., 3, 2, 1) or neither first nor last members (..., $-3, -2, -1, 0, 1, 2, 3, ...$). Whereas a complete collection has both a first member and a last member:

- $1, 2, 3, ..., n$
- $-n, ..., -3, -2, -1$
- $-n, ..., -3, -2, -1, 0, 1, 2, 3, ..., n$

The *finished* state of a complete collection, having both a first and last member to count, stands in contrast to the state of a limitless collection, for which a 'finish' is absent and for which there cannot be *both* a first and last member to count. However, a literally infinite collection is supposed to be both complete and limitless; hence there is a problem with the implications of both properties together.

12.4.1 *The 'Infinitieth Number'*

There is a problem with the kind of total, and lack thereof, implied by literal infinity. Literal infinity is a state of limitlessness. A limitless sequence of numbers can have no last number that is the "infinitieth" number in the sequence and that constitutes the total of the sequence. And yet, literal infinity is also a state of completeness. Because a literally infinite sequence of numbers is a complete sequence of numbers, there must then indeed be an "infinitieth" number in the sequence—the last member to count that completes the sequence and provides a total—an infinite total that is infinity itself. We thus have a pair of contradictory implications: no infinitieth number and yet an infinitieth number [358].

12.4.2 *Taking Infinity Seriously*

When analyzing infinite collections (sets, sequences, series, etc.), some scholars make one of two mistakes:

1. Confusion of the implications of infinity's limitlessness with those of its completeness, or vice versa.

2. Taking the limitlessness of infinity seriously while ignoring the implications of its completeness or taking the completeness of infinity seriously while ignoring the implications of its limitlessness.

And in some cases, scholars make both mistakes together. For example, philosopher Graham Oppy states that "there cannot be an infinite series with a first member and a last member, in which each member but the first is the unique successor of some other member, and in which each member but the last is the unique predecessor of some other member" [359]. Oppy is half right about that. In terms of the *limitlessness* of literal infinity, he is spot on. But in terms of the *completeness* of literal infinity, his position misses the mark.

Take again the sequence of real numbers from 0 to 1—such a sequence of reals is commonly claimed to be infinite even though there is a *first* real number (0) and a *last* real number (1) comprising the sequence. This seems to contradict Oppy's position.

To counter this point, Oppy holds that the real numbers form a 'dense continuum' that is not a *mathematical series* (in the sense of an accession in which the elements are related by the addition (+) operator). And because the reals aren't a mathematical 'series' (accession), then there is no immediate "successor" to 0 and no immediate "predecessor" to 1, so there cannot be both a first and last real to an infinite series from 0 to 1, or so the thinking goes [360].

However, such a retort does not take the completeness of an infinite sequence literally enough. Literally infinite sets are sets having literally complete collections and so collections that have both a first member with an immediate successor and a last member with an immediate predecessor in the collection. Such sets are, in the transfinite system, part of $\mathbb{R}$. So, even if between any two reals, a and c, there is another real, b, still there would have to be a literally complete *subset* of reals that falls *in sequence* between the first and last member of the collection.

For example, between 0 and 1 is a finite sequence: 0.2, 0.4, 0.6, and 0.8. Clearly, if we go by discrete even or odd decimals, then there is a sequence with a 'next' relation between each number; the even decimal 0.6 comes "next" after 0.4—it doesn't matter that we could identify another real like, say, 0.5 as falling between 0.4 and 0.6 because we aren't considering the odd decimals in this sequence. Now consider an infinite sequence of reals between 0 and 1. That there is a 'dense' continuum of reals between 0 and 1 is irrelevant to our concern, which is not the higher infinity of $\mathbb{R}$ but *any* sequence of numbers the members of which biject with those of the "least infinite" sequence for which the 'next' relation holds between members—the sequence equal to $\mathbb{N}$ in quantity. Regardless of any continuum, if the reals between 0 and 1 are literally infinite, then that set of reals *includes* an infinite *subset* of reals that can be placed in one-to-one correspondence with an infinite set of natural numbers ($\mathbb{N}$), which *do* form a sequence just as a sequence of square numbers or prime numbers forms a sequence.

Hence, the problem does not go away: we once again have an infinite subset of reals from 0 to 1 with a first real ($0 = 0.0$) and a last real ($1 = 1.0$) between which are *at least* $\mathbb{N}$-many reals and therefore the sequence from 0 to 1 must contain within it $\mathbb{N}$-many reals. So, the completeness of a literally infinite set of reals from 0 to 1—even if it is only an infinite *subset* equal to $\mathbb{N}$-many reals within the larger subset of $\mathbb{R}$—does indeed imply a first and last member. Namely, the real numbers 0 and 1. Which runs afoul of the limitlessness of the very same collection of $\mathbb{N}$-many numbers. And therefore, none of this talk of the real numbers ($\mathbb{R}$) addresses the problems that arise with the infinitude claimed for sets of numbers equal to the natural numbers ($\mathbb{N}$) when their completeness as well as their limitlessness is taken seriously.

Oppy might be able to make the rejoinder that completeness does not require a first and last member and so, as a dense continuum, $\mathbb{R}$ constitutes a counterexample to that completeness requirement. However, this would not be a convincing comeback. For if there is no last member or no first member, we would have to wonder how that would differ from a series under construction—a figurative rather than literal infinity.

Consider a *mathematical operation* listing numbers for any number system—$\mathbb{N}$, $\mathbb{R}$, etc. That there is no last number to list merely implies that the number system is an open series, under construction, and so for example $\mathbb{N}$ is actually $\mathbb{N}^C$ and thus has "no last number" because $\mathbb{N}^C$ has a running total of numbers. In other words, the number system or 'number scale' is an indefinite series with respect to how math works. There is no problem with having "no last number" in that sense of a series under construction.

We should, however, follow Oppy in taking limitlessness seriously with respect to claims about literal infinity. If we take the limitlessness of infinity seriously, then although a number system taken as a set, such as $\mathbb{N}$, can have a first number, there need be *no last number* just as Oppy pointed out with respect to infinite sequences. So, if we instead take "no last number" to mean there are a plurality of numbers in $\mathbb{N}$ alright, but there is still no last number anyway, *not even in principle*, then there can be neither a running total of numbers in $\mathbb{N}$ as a serial indefinite nor a standing total of numbers in $\mathbb{N}$ as a set. Now *that* is taking limitlessness seriously.

But such limitlessness is again a problem when we also take infinity's completeness seriously, because we can also deduce that if $\mathbb{N}$ is to be a *totality* of numbers that are "all" there at once, $\mathbb{N}$ must have a standing total of numbers. But that means $\mathbb{N}$ would have a 'last' number (or last set of numbers). The only way to make sense of $\mathbb{N}$ have a last number when $\mathbb{N}$ is infinite is to suggest that the 'last' number of $\mathbb{N}$ is infinite—a natural number with limitless digits. But having such a number contradicts the limitlessness of the *sequence* of numbers comprising $\mathbb{N}$ because the sequence can have no *greatest* value or set of values—not even a 'highest value' in the form of an infinite value.

The logical contradictions between the implications of completeness and limitlessness are therefore not so easy to dispense with. If we apply completeness to qualify limitlessness, we imply an infinitely large number as a total; if we apply limitlessness to qualify completeness, we imply a whole in which there is no total sum [361].

To be complete implies having a *total*, and a total can only be obtained by having a first and last member to a count of the members in a collection. In terms of its completeness, a literally infinite collection must be countable by having *both* a first *and* last member to any possible count of its members. And that is also the problem, for to be limitless is to have *no total* at all; and so, by virtue of limitlessness, a literally infinite collection cannot have both a first and last member to count. And yet, both connotations—a total and lack of a total—follow from the concept of infinity in its literal sense due to completeness and limitlessness being together affirmed; and so having both connotations together make literal infinity a self-contradictory concept.

12.4.3 *Word Play*

Philosophers and mathematicians have attempted to get around the contradiction of a total without a total or a countable-uncountable collection with various tricks of language. For example, some claim a collection can be *complete without having a last member* to a sequence of all the members comprising the collection. They say a literally infinite process of operations covering that sequence, like a count of the members in the sequence, constitutes a 'complete' series of operations in which *all* of the operations in the series are carried out but, even so, there is no *last* operation carried out in the series. For an infinite count, the series of counts is complete even though there's no last number to count [362].

But calling a collection without a last number to count a 'complete' collection stretches the use of the term 'complete' beyond its breaking point, just as it is too great a stretch to call an empty set a 'full' set. If there is no last member to count, what is it that makes such a collection 'complete' in a way that distinguishes it from a series that is ever under construction and ever incomplete? As far as I can tell, the answer is nothing at all.

Moreover, there is another reason it is mistaken to claim a literally infinite collection can be a complete collection without either a last or first member to count: it is the *limitlessness* rather than the completeness of the collection that implies either no first member or no last member (or neither) to count.

The *completeness and limitlessness of infinity are not one and the same property*, but two different properties that are each part of the complex condition called infinity (taken literally), and both properties are claimed to hold simultaneously for the same collection claimed to be infinite. This parallels how squareness and circularity are not one and the same property, but two different properties that are each a part of the complex condition called 'non-angularity' (see § 9.7).

Since literal infinity is a condition of being both complete *and* limitless, the scholars making the claim that complete collections need have no last member have confused the implications of completeness with limitlessness because the two properties are shared by the single condition of infinity. Consequently, they have been swayed by an illusion of semantical coherence between completeness and limitlessness where none exists [363].

A collection is complete only if *every* member necessary for the collection is present in the collection, which in turn implies a last member to count in any listing of necessary members for the collection, and that is what gives the term 'all' its meaning when we refer to *all* the members of a *complete* collection. We cannot sensibly refer to 'all' the members of a complete collection if there is no last member necessary for the collection.

The situation is different for a limitless collection, in which referring to a count of 'all' the members means, for *any* given member, that member can be counted. Just because you can count 'any' member that is a given does not mean you can count *every* member. All may mean all, but all means two different things for completeness and limitlessness.

Insofar as a collection is complete, to count all the members is to have a last member to count; insofar as a collection is limitless, to count all the members is to never stop counting members and so never to have a last member to count. So, it is not that a literally infinite collection is "complete without a last member" to count; rather, it's that a literally infinite collection is complete—therefore having a last member to count—and yet limitless—therefore having no last member to count.

12.4.D *Circular Reasoning*

Some attempts to dissolve the countable-uncountable contradiction end up committing a bit of circular reasoning. For example, philosopher Jim Holt argues that "…completing an infinite series of tasks is not impossible if you have an infinite amount of time in which to perform them all. In fact, it is mathematically possible to complete an infinite series of tasks in some finite amount of time, provided you perform them more and more quickly…" [364].

Holt is partially right. Yes, it is true that a literally infinite series of tasks is a complete series, and so a series that can be finished, provided there is an infinite amount of time to do so, or provided the series is finished at an infinitely fast pace over finite time. However, it's also true that an infinite series has *no last step* to take (it's limitless); so even if the tasks were to be performed infinitely fast, the series of tasks would still never be finished and so never completed—*not even over an infinite amount of time*—since a last step to take doesn't exist for an infinite series. The traveler at infinite speed would simply be traveling at infinite speed for the rest of time, without ever reaching completion. Holt is therefore not correct that infinite acceleration solves the problem of completing an infinite series. Holt did not take the limitlessness of literal infinity seriously enough. When it is taken seriously, we find an infinite series can be completed because such a series is a complete series by definition, but we also find the same infinite series can never be completed because there is no last member to finish it—the notion of a series being *infinite* is itself the problem.

Moreover, even if we posit going infinitely fast to cross an infinite sequence of steps in a finite time, we are still left with the same problem: infinite acceleration is acceleration *without limit* (there is no top speed to reach) and yet infinite acceleration is *complete* acceleration (you can't go any faster than infinitely fast). Infinite acceleration appears just as self-contradictory a notion as does the notion of going through an infinite sequence at any given speed.

Holt's argument has the same fallacy as that of Bertrand Russell's on this topic. Russell believed that a literally infinite set of numbers can, in principle, be counted out to completion in a finite amount of time if one were to accelerate the counting process infinitely [365]. Russell's argument, however, is flawed by begging the question: the literally infinite acceleration is a sequence of changes in speed that must itself reach completion just as much as the infinite sequence of counting steps that must be completed—both are literally infinite sequences and what was in question was how a literally infinite sequence can be completed at all when it is also limitless. Appealing to infinite acceleration in order to show that crossing an infinite sequence is coherent thus presupposes what it tries to prove [366]. To go infinitely fast we must suppose that traveling at ever faster speeds can proceed to infinity without contradiction, but the logical coherence of crossing a literal infinity of any kind was precisely what was in question.

All of this tells us that, at best, Holt and Russell are half right: the collection can be completely counted because a literally infinite collection is a complete collection and so has a total count to reach—be it in an infinite time or a finite time at infinite speed; a last number can be counted for a totality to the process. And they are both half wrong: the collection cannot be completely counted because a literally infinite collection is a limitless collection and so without a total count to reach—no matter how long or how fast the counter goes, there's no last number to form a totality. Holt and Russell's attempt to dissolve the contradiction involved in completing a limitless series therefore does not succeed. A literally infinite collection remains countable because it's complete and yet not countable because it's limitless.

12.5 INFINITELY LARGE NUMBERS VERSUS INFINITELY MANY NUMBERS

We therefore return to the problem we found over the previous chapters: the issue of "infinitely many" versus "infinite number."

Per § 10.5, to complete a count of an infinite collection of natural numbers ($\mathbb{N}$) would be to count up to an *infinitely large natural number* as the total number for the collection. If the natural numbers progress up to infinity in a literal sense, then there must be both a lowest number (in the case of $\mathbb{N}$ that number is 1) after which there follow *infinitely many other numbers*, until the progression of numbers arrives at a number that is an *infinitely great* number, n. If $\mathbb{N}$ is complete, then the whole of $\mathbb{N}$ must be equal in cardinality to its greatest number (or a greatest subset of numbers), n, that has limitlessly many digits.

Per § 11.5, we can also deduce the opposite: if $\mathbb{N}$ is infinite, and its numbers are in sequence, then it has a limitless sequence of natural numbers, each just 1 larger than its predecessor; however, a limitless sequence of numbers cannot be completely counted because there is *no infinitely large number* to arrive at for a total [367]. Therefore, $\mathbb{N}$ has an infinitely large number of numbers and yet also infinitely many finite numbers with none of the numbers infinitely large. We apparently have another contradiction on our hands.

To avoid this conclusion, mathematicians represent infinities with symbols (∞, ω, and $\aleph$) and treat those symbols in mathematical expressions *as if* they are numbers. Mathematically, there is no problem with the use of these symbols. But in terms of logic, it's not entirely clear what treating infinity like a number is supposed to mean.

On the one hand, the symbols ∞, ω, and $\aleph$ refer to infinite quantities that are *complete* quantities, and so should refer, at least in principle, to an infinitely large number. On the other hand, such symbols also refer to quantities are that *limitless* quantities and so none of them can refer to an exact number, not even in principle.

Consequently, mathematicians don't seem to agree on how to speak about infinite quantities like the infinite quantities of numbers claimed to comprise sets of numbers like $\mathbb{W}$ or $\mathbb{N}$ (or other number scales). Some mathematicians, for instance, say $\mathbb{N}$ has an infinite number of numbers in it, while other mathematicians instead claim that sets like $\mathbb{N}$ are infinite sets of finite numbers, but they deny that an infinite set of numbers is a set having an *infinite number* of numbers—instead, they simply say such sets have "infinitely many" finite numbers [368]. Which way of speaking about infinite sets and quantities the mathematician prefers—infinite numbers or infinitely many numbers—seems to depend on which feature of infinity the mathematician wishes to consider: its completeness or its limitlessness.

12.6 THE WHOLE AS EQUAL YET GREATER THAN THE SUM

As further evidence of the contradictory qualities of infinity, consider whether the whole of an infinite collection is either equal to or greater than the sum of its members. The completeness of infinity implies the former, the limitlessness of infinity implies the latter.

12.6.1 $\mathbb{N}$ *as Having an Infinite Sum and as Infinite Without a Sum*

From Chapter 10 we found that if $\mathbb{N}$ as an infinite collection is *complete*, then the quantity of all naturals in the whole of $\mathbb{N}$ is equal to an infinite sum of all naturals comprising $\mathbb{N}$. Let's start by examining what it would mean for $\mathbb{N}$, regarded as an infinite set, to have a *sum* of all its natural numbers.

In mathematics, every n is a cardinal equal to its predecessor $+ 1$. So, if the successor function were to form a literally infinite set, then it *must* produce a complete progression of finite numbers (1, 2, 3, ...) *up to* a number having *infinitely many digits*, a number that is a sum equal to the number of all previous numbers, and for which no value is greater—a 'last' and infinitely large number. If the progression 1, 2, 3, ... were *not* complete, there would be in $\mathbb{N}$ only a *running total* of finite numbers, which would make $\mathbb{N}$ into $\mathbb{N}^C$—an incomplete, finite *series* rather than an infinite *set*.

So, if $\mathbb{N}$ is literally infinite, then $\mathbb{N}$ should have an infinite sum of numbers, a sum produced by the progression of the entire sequence 1, 2, 3, ... up to $n = \infty$ as the sum of a complete collection of numbers. As Bolzano stated, "Now I must remind you that every assumption of an infinite series, as far as I can see, is the assumption of a sum of infinitely many quantities..." [369].

Next, let's consider from Chapter 11 the infinite collection $\mathbb{N}$ as a *limitless* collection of naturals. If $\mathbb{N}$ is limitless, then that would mean $\mathbb{N}$, again as an infinite set, is *greater than* any sum of natural numbers. If $\mathbb{N}$ is limitless, then $\mathbb{N}$ should have no sum of natural numbers at all, not even an "infinite sum" for its complete collection of numbers.

Because there can be no *highest* n in $\mathbb{N}$, then $\mathbb{N}$ contains no infinite number n that can give $\mathbb{N}$ its value. And so mathematics defines $\mathbb{N}$ as having ∞-many members while also stating that every n in $\mathbb{N}$ is finite.

The sequence of $\mathbb{N}$ is limitless but there is no natural number that has a limitless quantity of digits; ergo, the limitless whole must be greater than any sum (which must be finite in value) derived for the sequence.

We therefore have a logical contradiction between the 'infinite number' ($n = \infty$) implied by a *complete* sequence of numbers *up to* infinity and the 'infinitely many' finite numbers implied by a *limitless* sequence of numbers in which there is no highest number ($n < \infty$). This is not a mathematical contradiction but a logical one: the logical contradiction is between the implications of an operation that can carry a sequence of numbers up to infinity, thus producing a natural of infinitely many digits—an infinite sum for the whole—while simultaneously the infinitude of the same sequence, by virtue of its limitlessness, implies $\mathbb{N}$ is *greater than* any sum of numbers in it, all of which must be finite. Again, completeness and limitless do not play well together.

12.6.2 *A Variable for Infinity That Cannot Be*

Notice another contradiction: the completeness of $\mathbb{N}$ would suggest a variable, n, for an infinite number while the limitlessness of $\mathbb{N}$ demands there can be no such variable because there can be no infinitely large number as an 'infinitieth' number that would be reached by a count from 1 on up—if there were, that would imply a 'last' or 'highest' number to an infinite sequence, which is limitless. And yet, because infinity, in its literal sense, is complete, there should be an infinitely large number we can consistently represent with some variable in our equations, such as n. Hence, there should and should not be a last, highest n in $\mathbb{N}$ for any progression of natural numbers leading from finite quantities up to infinite quantities. There should be an infinite sum because $\mathbb{N}$ is complete but cannot be because $\mathbb{N}$ is limitless.

12.6.3 *Convergence Never Converging*

§ 10.6.3 illustrated how an infinite sum can be inferred from the calculus of absolute convergence:

$$\sum_{n=1}^{\infty} |a_n| = 0$$

and

$$\sum_{k=1}^{\infty} \frac{1}{k(k + 1)} = 1$$

The convergence implies an infinite series of steps, denoted by ∞, converging absolutely with a given number. However, if ∞ is interpreted as infinity in its literal sense, then the logic of what literal infinity means tells us the steps produced by the function form a complete and yet limitless series. The completeness of the operation ensures the exact result (0 or 1) is produced after an infinitely large number of steps, but the *limitlessness* implied by ∞ refutes that any infinite convergence can be completed by reaching an exact value—even by producing an infinitely large number ($x = \infty$) of steps— for there is no 'infinitieth' step to take.

These examples demonstrate two problems. First, there is an incongruity between how the functions actually *operate* and how the functions are *interpreted* to operate. No computer, no matter how large, carries out infinitely many operations. In reality, the convergence functions produce only indefinite, but limited, series of steps that are treated in abstraction as if they reach completion upon an exact number (e.g., 0 or 1). It is only in interpretation that the functions produce literal infinities of steps ending with exact numbers. The reality and the interpretation of reality don't meet in this case: indefiniteness is not infinity. Second, the interpretation of the functions as operating over an infinite series implies a complete series that is limitless—still a contradictory condition, as we've already seen.

With respect to the first problem, there is *no mathematical contradiction* involved with the convergence functions precisely because the functions produce only incomplete, indefinite series of values. An indefinitely large, but completed, series is not mathematically or logically problematic. But just because there is no mathematical contradiction with a series 'converging with' a finite number does not mean there is no *logical contradiction*, for there is: the series is *misinterpreted* as operating with the literally infinite when in operation it is merely completing an indefinitely large series of steps.

Then there is the second logical problem implied by the *meaning* of ∞, when interpreted as literal infinity in the equation: a function producing a literally infinite series of operations or steps would produce both a complete and limitless series, but completeness and limitlessness are in contradiction. While it is true the math behind the function works despite the logical contradiction between the completeness and limitlessness implied by the interpretation of the function as infinite, that is only because the function is indefinite and not infinite as so often supposed.

A similar function with similar logical difficulties was examined in § 11.6.3. The function descended values ever closer to 0 (zero) while implying no infinite sum of steps ($x = \infty$) can ever be reached because, while an infinite series may converge *toward* an exact number such as 0, the series can never achieve that number. But if the function is regarded as operating over a literal infinity of steps, then the infinite series resulting *must* be complete. Completeness implies totality—a total number. As the series is infinite, its totality must therefore have a sum of steps equal to an infinitely large number. And yet the series can't have an infinitely large number as a total because the infinite convergence is without limit—it never finishes.

Again, we have a logical contradiction between completeness and limitlessness of the convergence, and yet we know the mathematical function works. As before, the discrepancy between the math working consistently and logical contradictions implied by how the math is interpreted (complete and limitless in convergence) can be explained by noting the convergence toward a value is only carried out as an indefinite, open series and not as a completed, infinite series. So, the math never encounters the logical contradiction between completeness and limitlessness because those two mutually contradictory concepts are simply interpretations of the function and not a genuine portrayal of how the function actually works.

There is therefore no resolution for the logical contradiction resulting from the claim that such mathematical functions are carried out infinitely many times in a literal sense: the complete sequence (the infinitely large number of steps) is *equal* to an infinite sum and the sequence is without an infinite sum due to the limitlessness of the sequence. Because the functions are indefinite and not really infinite, they mathematically work in operational terms, but the interpretation of how they work—by literal infinity—remains logically contradictory on a semantic level.

12.7 CONTRADICTIONS IN REVIEW

From the foregoing analysis, we find several contradictions between the concept of completeness and the concept of limitlessness as applied to the same collection—an infinite collection such as a literally infinite sequence of numbers or an infinite series of operations. Among the contradictions:

- On countability:
  - Completeness implies the given collection must be countable with a first and last number to a count of its members—for an infinite collection that means the last number to count must be infinitely large.
  - Limitlessness demands that the sequence of members in an infinite collection cannot have both a first and last number in an infinite progression of numbers, and so there can be no natural number with infinitely many digits.

- On summation:
  - Completeness implies infinite collections must have infinite sums; for instance, every natural number in $\mathbb{N}$ has a cardinality such that $\mathbb{N}$ must be an infinite sum of its number of numbers.
  - Limitlessness demands infinite collections must be infinitely greater than any sum of its parts; so, there is no infinite sum of numbers comprising $\mathbb{N}$; the cardinality of $\mathbb{N}$ cannot be a number.

- On mathematical value:
  - Completeness implies that a variable, such as n or x, can, at least in principle, consistently have the value of an infinitely large number.
  - Limitlessness demands there can be no such variable, not even in principle.

These contradictions bring us back around to the logical problems in literal infinity's meaning. Literal infinity is a condition of completeness while its limitlessness implies that it cannot be complete.

For a given collection to be complete, it must be whole, entire, finished, full, and total (per § 3.2.8). In order to have a total, a collection needs to have a constant maximum number of elements. Without a constant maximum, the collection would be an incomplete series—either growing or shrinking in size.

If the collection were incomplete, to speak of all members in the collection would mean only "all" at any given time, but not all members, period—"all" in that context would mean "for any" member rather than "each and every" member (see § 3.2.3 and § 11.1). Conversely, to speak of all the members of the collection as a *complete* collection is to speak of them as an entirety; the term "all" for a complete collection means *every* member rather than just *any* member. Were that not so, claims about "all" the members for the completeness of a collection would become vacuous. We must be able to refer to all the members of a collection, as an entirety, in order to accurately describe the collection as complete.

And in order to be able to refer to all the members of a collection, the constant maximum of the collection must be a totality of members. If, to the contrary, a given collection *cannot* have a total, *not even in principle*, then there can be no concluding member that *completes* the collection. Completeness implies a maximum that specifies the total of all members in the collection.

Contrast these features of completeness with limitlessness: per Chapter 11, for a collection to be limitless is for it to have no extreme—that is, to be without an upper bound or maximum relative to the number of elements within it. A total is a kind of maximum, and to have no total is to have no maximum.

No maximum, then no standing total; no standing total, then no completeness. So, for a collection to be limitless is for the collection to lack completeness—either because it is always incomplete (as is the case with the null set—zero) or because it is beyond any application of the concepts of completeness and incompleteness. Whichever is the case, to be limitless is to lack completeness.

By definition, any collection that is literally infinite is a collection that is complete in the quantity of its members. But a literally infinite collection is also, by definition, a collection that is limitless and so cannot be complete. Ergo, literal infinity is and is not a condition of being complete in quantity: a contradiction.

That should be the end of the matter. But maybe I'm missing something, so let's do a quick check of the logical implications for what it means to have a quantity.

12.7.1 *Reexamining the Concept of Quantity for Complete and Incomplete Collections*

We know that to have a quantity is to have a limit—at least, that is true for *complete* collections.

Consider that for a collection to be complete, the collection must have a *quantity* of members. To have a quantity of members implies the collection is *quantifiable*. Quantifiability means one is in principle able to count *all* (every one of) the members in a collection and arrive at a *total* for the collection. A quantity is, after all, an amount equal to a total. But a total is a kind of limit. So, for a collection to be complete is for the collection to have a limit to the collection's quantity of members—a limit by which one could (at least in principle) arrive at a total of members for the collection.

But what of *incomplete* collections?

If an incomplete collection has a quantity of members, then it too has a limit in the form of a total of members. Suppose we have a collection of bricks comprising a building. Even if construction has ceased and the building is left unfinished, the collection of bricks in the building nevertheless does have a total. The building as a collection of bricks does not need to be a complete collection in order to have a total. The same can be said for the mathematical construction of any sequence of numbers—an unfinished sequence will still have a total and ergo a limit to its quantity.

This too is true even of an incomplete, *open series* that grows within an upper bound. At any step of the series' growth, its number of elements can be counted up to a running total and so one can still quantify the series—one can count up to the temporary limit of its running total of members.

The bottom line for both complete and incomplete collections: they are quantifiable, quantifiability entails having a total, and a total is a kind of limit; so quantifiability entails having a limit.

And this also works the other way around: limits imply quantifiability. For a collection to have a limit to the amount of elements it contains is for the collection to be quantifiable. Such is certainly the case for complete collections, and it is even so for an open series with an indefinite number of elements since it is limited by the amount of its unfinished elements, and that limit means the series is quantifiable with a running total at any step of its growth.

However, it might be objected: that is all fine for complete and incomplete *finite* collections, but what of *literally infinite* collections?

Recall that literal infinity is a condition in which a collection has a complete quantity of members. Since completeness of quantity entails a total of members and so a limit of members, even a literally infinite collection must have some limit to its members—even if it must be in the form of an infinitely large number to constitute its total quantity.

Then again, a literally infinite collection is a collection that is *limitless* in quantity—it is without limit to its quantity of members. While limits imply quantifiability, having no limits implies just the opposite: to be limitless is to have no total and thus to be unable to be quantified.

And therein lies the problem, for completeness entails a total, and if one is not able to quantify a collection—if the collection has no total at all—then the collection cannot be complete. Moreover, a complete collection, having a total, is a limited collection—it cannot be limitless. And a limitless collection, having no total, cannot be complete. Literal infinity is both limited, because it is complete, and yet by definition must also be limitless. Ergo, literal infinity is a self-contradictory concept.

One possible objection to the conclusion that literal infinity implies a condition of being both limited and also limitlessness as well might lie in what it means to be "limitless." Perhaps to be "limitless" does not mean what we think it means.

12.7.2 *Reexamining Limitlessness in Quantity*

Perhaps a collection may be limitless in quantity due to:

1. Having no elements to count.
2. Having so many elements, they cannot all be counted in actual practice, though they can be counted in principle.
3. Having a number of elements that is more than anyone can, even in principle, count.

We've encountered these possibilities earlier, so I'll only briefly treat them here.

The first option is what I called 'afinity'—which is not what most people mean by "limitless" and certainly not what is meant when we refer to something that is literally infinite.

The second option is the same as being indefinite. An indefinite amount is a finite amount and so can still be counted in principle (at least up to its running total if it's a series). But this is not what is meant by "limitless" with respect to literal infinity.

The third option affirms a literal sense of limitlessness as being inherently unable to be quantitatively specified. A limitless collection is a collection that cannot be quantitatively specified because it has no total—no sum or product—for its range of elements, *not even in principle*. To be limitless, in a literal sense, means that there is no way to produce a total at all for the whole of that which is limitless.

To lack even the logical possibility of numerically quantifying a collection is not the same as just saying that the collection cannot be numerically quantified in actual practice. To say that a collection is numerically unquantifiable in practice is simply to say the collection is finite with some unknown quantity—maybe because there are too many elements to count in practice, but not in principle. In other words, it's an indefinite (finite) collection. Whereas, to say a collection is not quantifiable even in principle is to state something much stronger: it is to say there is a non-zero amount of members in the collection and there are so many members in the collection that the multitude of members exceeds those of any finite collection, even those finite collections that are indefinitely large. There is *no such thing* as assigning a total amount to *all* the elements in the collection together, not even in principle.

We can say, more simply, that to be limitless is to be *too large to count even in principle*.

However, supposing limitlessness entails "too many" to count even in principle, the very fact that limitlessness is applied to the quantifier "many" means this notion of limitlessness is still regarded as a quantitative property. Suppose a collection contains only non-zero, finite quantities and that the collection as a whole is *without limit* to the finite quantities it contains.

However, go back to what a quantity is—it's specified by numbers and every number is equal to a sum of preceding numbers in the number scale. Even though we say the collection has no limit to its component finite quantities, the collection is nevertheless a collection of quantities—of elements that can be correlated with numbers. And that still implies the collection as a whole has a quantity and that quantity is a *limitless quantity* of all the finite quantities.

Moreover, a literally limitless quantity is the same as a literally infinite quantity. So, to say a collection is without limit is to say it has an infinite quantity. And that is a logically problematic notion because any quantity can be treated as a *complete* set and then we have a conflict again between the limitlessness of the quantity and the completeness of the same quantity.

Is there a way around this? What about an infinite collection that is limitless but not complete? Let's consider that.

12.7.3 *Limitlessness in Quantity Without Completeness in Quantity: Alternative Infinity*

Huemer is an advocate of infinity. He realizes that any quantity, simply as a quantity, can be regarded as a complete collection and that completeness and limitlessness do not play well together. But he wishes to save infinity from contradiction. His strategy is to affirm the limitlessness of infinity but deny there are such things as infinite quantities. He says that "there are no infinite quantities" but also affirms there are "infinitely many" numbers; in fact, he says there are "infinitely numerous numbers" [370]. I contend Huemer's conclusion that there are no infinite quantities is correct, but for the wrong reason.

He was wrong that there can be "infinitely many" of something—a collection of non-zero members that are so many they are limitlessness or "infinitely numerous"—while also holding there is no such thing as an infinite quantity. To say there are infinitely many of something while simultaneously denying there is an infinite quantity of something is not coherent. Just the opposite is the case: if there are "infinitely many" numbers, if they are "infinitely numerous," that implies an infinite quantity of numbers and ergo an infinite number of numbers. The word 'many' is a quantifier and implies the ability to be *quantified*—assigned a number—at least in principle.

Consider: if there are infinitely many numbers, if they are truly infinitely *numerous*, then there must be at least one number *infinitely greater* than 1 because, if there isn't, then *every* number in the collection of numbers is only some *finite* cardinality greater than 1. After all, every cardinal number is equal to a combination of its predecessors. If there is no infinitely great number, then there is no collection of "infinitely numerous" predecessors, no matter how many numbers there are. That means *every* number would have to be finite.

But as pointed out earlier in § 10.5, if *every* number is finite in the collection, and if a collection of numbers *just is* the numbers comprising the collection, then it is muddy as to what it is supposed to be about the collection that is infinite in the literal sense. What is it about the multitude of numbers that is without quantitative limit if not any of the numbers and not the number of numbers? If we end up affirming that every quantity comprising the collection is finite, we are left to wonder what it is that is supposed to be "limitless" about the collection if not its number of numbers, its quantity of quantities. I submit that as far as anyone can tell, nothing at all.

It does no good to say "the whole" is limitless if the collection referred to as a whole is composed only of parts that reduce to parts, as clearly the numbers of ℕ do since each natural number is defined as the successor of its predecessor. A collection of *only* finite numbers is a collection in which every number is finite. And a collection in which every number is finite is not a collection of infinitely numerous numbers in the literal sense; rather, it can only be a collection of finitely numerous numbers and so at best one that is merely 'infinite' in the figurative sense of the term.

Hence, if a collection of numbers is infinite, if there are "infinitely numerous numbers," then there must be at least one infinitely great number to confer infinity upon those numbers. There must be an 'infinite number' after all. In fact, if we assume collections can be infinite, including collections of "infinitely many" numbers, then it's hard to avoid infinite numbers.

As Fletcher noted, an infinite collection can be construed as an infinite conjunction of statements [371]. Huemer agrees: "Suppose that infinitely many numbers exist. Then there will be the fact that 1 exists, the fact that 2 exists, the fact that 3 exists, and so on" [372]. But, says Fletcher, we can substitute sums for the conjunctions of "1 and 2 and 3 and..." [373]. So, it's hard to see how an infinitely large *sum* is not implied. If we are to affirm infinite collections but deny they imply infinite sums, then in the words of Fletcher we need "a special argument, showing why the step from finite to infinite works for conjunctions but doesn't work for sums. As far as I know, no such argument has ever been proposed" [374].

If there are infinitely many objects in a collection, there must be infinite sums and therefore infinite numbers. Which is exactly the conclusion Huemer denied because he knew that to be a contradictory concept. But it is hard to affirm infinity is "quantitative" while avoiding logical double speak in denying an infinite quantity.

Huemer tries to address this problem by taking the position that "infinitely many" implies infinity is a quantitative property but not a "determinate quantity" in the sense that to be infinite is to *exceed* any named quantity [375]. But a quantity that is not determinate because it exceeds any named quantity is simply a quantity too large for us to 'determine'—that is, too large to in practice specify a quantitative limit. In other words, it's hard to see how Huemer's notion of "infinitely many" is any different than an *indefinitely large*, but nevertheless finite, quantity. In which case, then "infinitely many" would be a figurative use of 'infinity', not a literal use of the term. Hence, the 'limitlessness' of the collection in question would also be figurative, not literal. Huemer's "infinitely many" would just be a misnomer for indefinitely many, which was the second option we rejected for taking infinity literally.

In order for us to avoid this confusion of limitlessness with indefiniteness, we have to affirm the concept of a limitless quantity—a quantity too large to determine not only in practice, as is the case with indefinite quantities, but also in principle. And that is precisely the problematic concept we face with limitlessness.

Recall that a quantity is the amount of objects making up a collection. An amount is a value equal to a total. So, a quantity implies a total. But to have a collection *without limit* is to have a quantity without a total. A quantity without a total is not a quantity, and a quantity that is not a quantity is a contradiction. A collection without a limit to a non-zero quantity of members—a limitless quantity—is therefore a contradiction in terms.

It now appears the only coherent way there can be no such thing as assigning a total amount of elements to a collection, not even in principle, without implying contradiction is for the collection to have *no amount of elements at all*. And this brings us back to our first option: define infinity as we would afinity, which is to be 'limitless' in the sense of having no elements to be limited. In such a condition, the concept of limit does not apply to that collection—a collection with no elements is not quantifiable, except in a negative sense of admitting the set has no quantity—it is zero in size or amount. In that respect, it *has* no limit. But again, being 'limitless' in the sense of having no members at all by which to have a limit is not what is typically meant by the limitlessness of infinity and would only confuse matters.

It would appear, then, that of our three previous options given in § 12.7.2, the only relevant option for defining "limitless" with respect to literal infinity is the third option, but that one implies logical self-contradiction. To be literally infinite is to be limitless in the literal sense of having no limit to a non-zero quantity of members; yet to be literally infinite is to have a quantity of members in a collection and so to have a limit. Limited and yet not—a self-contradiction.

The only other possible way out seems to be to affirm limitlessness while somehow denying the usual understanding of completeness as implying a totality of members to a collection. That is, we would need to reinterpret literal infinity as a limitless condition that may be "complete" but not as a *quantity*. In other words, even if completeness applies to infinite collections, *quantitative* completeness does not apply to infinite collections.

Which means we would need to revise our earlier understanding of completeness since it implies a collection has a total of elements. Instead, we would need to hold that completeness does not in itself imply there is (at least in principle if not in practice) a particular, determinate quantity for the whole of that which is said to be complete. So, completeness for literal infinity yes, but as a quantity no.

This seems to be the position adopted by Huemer [376]. However, I find this approach for dissolving the problems with literal infinity highly dubious for three reasons.

First, it is not how completeness is normally understood and so it is not really a way of addressing the problems with literal infinities as complete collections in the usual, literal sense of the term 'complete'—instead, it is stipulating a new, nonstandard way of thinking about completeness and applying that nonstandard way of thinking about completeness to infinity. That is fine for technical definitions of completeness, but what we need to resolve the problems of literal infinity is to show how *quantitative* completeness does not contradict quantitative limitlessness. Huemer's approach does not provide such; instead, it attempts to redefine completeness in terms agnostic to quantity. In so doing, it does not really address literal infinity but rather substitutes a new, nonstandard version of infinity for the common understanding of infinity which is to be not just limitless in quantity but complete in quantity as well.

Second, Huemer's approach does not adequately answer the question of how is it that a collection of numbers, points, etc. can be "complete" and yet *not* have a quantity for the whole of the collection. If there's no total quantity to the members of a given collection, how is it that collection is not simply what we would usually think of as an *incomplete* collection under construction—that is, why is the collection not simply a serial indefinite and ergo a figurative infinity rather than a literal infinity? Huemer does not provide a clear answer. This is especially problematic since he claims certain processes are instances of "completed" infinities (as we will see later in § 20.2.1) but it is not at all clear such processes should be thought of as "completed" and also limitless.

Third, and on a related point to the previous two, it is not clear that interpreting the completeness of a collection as *not* implying a quantity—a total amount—is to use the term 'complete' in a *literal* sense. Such an interpretation of what it means to be complete would instead appear to turn 'complete' into a metaphor, and that again implies figurative infinity, which Huemer was trying to avoid.

We therefore have yet to find a solution to having both completeness and limitlessness, *each taken literally*, while also avoiding contradiction in the literal sense of infinity.

CHAPTER 12 IN REVIEW

- ❖ Literal infinity is a condition of being both complete and limitless in quantity.
- ❖ The properties of completeness and limitlessness have contradictory implications.
- ❖ The completeness of a literally infinite collection affirms extremes—a maximum and total number of elements—while the limitlessness of the same collection denies these extremes.
- ❖ Because a literally infinite collection is complete in the quantity of its members, the members of the collection are, in principle, countable. But because the literally infinite collection is limitless in the quantity of its members, the collection cannot be counted—not even in principle.
- ❖ Since a literally infinite collection is complete, with completeness implying a countable totality of elements (at least in principle), the collection *must have an infinite number* of elements. But as the literally infinite collection is limitless in the quantity of its members, with limitlessness implying there is no countable totality of elements (not even in principle), the collection may have "infinitely many" elements but *cannot have an infinite number* of elements.
- ❖ The completeness of a literally infinite collection implies the collection is a whole equal to an infinite number of elements comprising it. The limitlessness of the literally infinite collection implies the collection is greater than (not equal to) the infinitely many elements comprising it. "Equal to" and "greater than" are in contradiction.
- ❖ Even without completeness, however, a non-zero limitless collection is still a problematic notion if the collection is said to have a quantity encompassing "all" the members of the collection.
- ❖ The foregoing shows literal infinity to be an intrinsically self-contradictory concept.

13: HAS INFINITY BEEN TAMED?

Infinity is proving to be a logically incoherent concept, riddled as it is with contradictory connotations. Chapters 10–12 proved that to be complete and limitless in quantity is a self-contradictory concept, like a square circle or a married bachelor.

Chapter 10 illustrated that completeness implies a collection with a maximum quantity and a *totality* of elements. A totality of elements for a complete collection, even for a literally infinite collection, means a *standing total* in the form of an exact sum of elements (at least in principle). For an infinite collection, a standing total equals a sum as an infinitely large number—a natural number with infinitely many digits.

Chapter 11 pointed out that the limitlessness of a literally infinite collection implies exactly the opposite. Because the infinite collection is limitless, it has no maximum quantity of elements in it. So, the collection must have *no totality* and therefore *no standing total* of elements. That implies the infinite collection can have no sum at all, not even one in the form of an infinitely large natural number.

Chapter 12 then compared the implications of completeness in Chapter 10 to the implications of limitlessness in Chapter 11, and in so doing laid bare the contradictions inherent in the concept of literal infinity. (Although even the concept of a non-zero, quantitative state of limitlessness—quite aside from completeness—was found to be logically suspect as well.)

In order to believe in infinity according to its literal sense, one must be able to either accept or somehow avoid the cognitive dissonance induced by believing the contradictory implications of the same collection being both complete and limitless simultaneously. Those that accept the cognitive dissonance are those that propose infinity is a paraconsistent, mystical concept. But most academics prefer to somehow eliminate, rather than accept, the cognitive dissonance. To that end, some philosophers and mathematicians have attempted various analytic strategies designed to dissolve the contradictions between the completeness and limitlessness of infinite collections—strategies to "tame infinity" [377].

13.1 THE STRATEGY TO TAME INFINITY

Exactly what it means for a collection to be literally infinite, to be complete and limitless in quantity, has been elucidated in previous chapters via precising definitions for 'quantity', 'complete', and 'limitless'. The terms 'complete' and 'limitless' are so defined—

- complete: *having all members necessary to be representative of a given class; a given collection is complete if and only if the collection is whole, entire, finished, full, and total.*

- limitless: *to have a range (extent of elements) that is unspecifiable, even in principle.*

The concept of infinity, as expressed in ordinary, natural language and according to its literal usage, assumes both completeness and limitlessness for any collection said to be infinite.

However, while the above precising definitions for 'complete' and 'limitless' are accurate for portraying the properties of infinity according to its literal sense in natural language, they imply contradictions between each other as revealed in Chapters 10–12. Aristotle argued nothing can be literally infinite (or, in his vocabulary, 'actually infinite') because nothing can be both complete and limitless: "Nothing is complete which has no end, and the end is a limit" [378]. Consequently, for centuries mathematicians knew that literal infinity, however precisely defined in natural language, was logically problematic already; it certainly did not seem like a notion that could be made mathematically coherent.

Eventually, mathematicians concluded the contradictions between completeness and limitlessness may boil down to some vagueness with respect to the ordinary, natural language use of these terms. That is, mathematicians realized the lexical definitions for properties such as 'complete', 'limitless', and the like are too imprecise as stated in natural language to render infinity useful in mathematical functions and operations.

With regard to a literal understanding of infinity, some mathematicians during the 1800s and early 1900s wanted to remedy this. They wanted to be able to *redefine* infinity in a way that sidesteps the implications of the lexical definitions for infinity insofar as the term 'infinity' is used as a predicate in the framework of mathematics. This involved giving literal infinity a technical definition in the formal language of mathematics, a definition that makes literal infinity into a mathematically coherent and useful concept.

Bolzano and Cantor were the first mathematicians to take this approach. Bolzano's work was largely overlooked or ignored by most European mathematicians while Cantor's alternative solution eventually won the day and became influential [379]. Cantor's solution was the invention of set theory, transfinite mathematics, and the marriage of the two as a single system—what I refer to as 'the transfinite system'.

***

As an aside for clarity, I also distinguish between set theory, transfinite mathematics, and both together as the transfinite system. But mathematicians usually do not distinguish between these. Instead, they typically refer either more generally to 'set theory' or more narrowly to the 'transfinite theory of numbers' as a part of set theory. This is because modern set theory contains axioms such as the Axiom of Infinity, which is one of the axioms from which transfinite mathematics (or the transfinite theory of numbers) is constructed using set theory principles (see § 9.6.4).

There are alas two problems with this view.

First, no mathematics of any sort, either general mathematics or transfinite mathematics, is a subcategory of set theory by itself because much of set theory is based on formal logic, which does not fall entirely under mathematics. One can even imagine an Aristotelean version of set theory that is categorical but not mathematical at all. Mathematics is not subsumed under set theory, nor vice versa; rather, the disciplines overlap with each other and with symbolic logic (see **Figure 9.4** in Chapter 9).

Second, the axioms and theorems for infinity are not necessary for set theory to be consistent and comprehensive enough for use, as there are mathematical versions of set theory that do not make use of infinity [380]. Of the mathematical versions of set theory, I will distinguish between two versions. One version of set theory regards sets as generated by finite processes; this version can stand on its own without the use of infinities. The other version of set theory is based on the Axiom of Infinity. The latter version I'll call *transfinite set theory*, which provides the set-theoretic assumptions upon which transfinite mathematics is based.

I therefore consider transfinite mathematics to be a branch of mathematics based on transfinite set theory, which is itself a mathematical version of set theory that assumes infinity. But neither transfinite mathematics nor transfinite set theory is equivalent to set theory per se since there are finite versions of set theory. Assuming all that, I will stick with referring to transfinite set theory and transfinite mathematics together, along with their philosophical assumptions about infinity, as the 'transfinite system'.

Now, back to the main topic at hand.

***

Mathematicians [381] have widely credited Cantor's transfinite system as having resolved the logical and mathematical contradictions involved with infinity taken as literal rather than as a figure of speech (the latter view of infinity promoted by Gauss). Specifically, it is the transfinite system that is regarded as having resolved the logical contradictions between the implications of more colloquial notions of completeness and limitlessness, such as the contradiction arising between the implication that there exists an infinitely large number (due to the completeness of the system of natural numbers as a collection of numbers) and the implication that there are infinitely many finite numbers but no infinitely large number (due to the limitlessness of the sequence of naturals). Mathematicians are largely in agreement that Cantor's transfinite system has dissolved such problems and is able to treat literal infinity (which they usually call 'actual infinity' or 'proper infinity') in not just a mathematically coherent manner but also in a logically coherent manner.

When academics [382] [383] credit Cantor with "taming the infinite," they mean that Cantor has explicated the concept of infinity with enough analytic precision to dissolve the logical paradoxes associated with infinity, revealing infinity as not only a logical concept but also a mathematically coherent and systematically rigorous concept. Most mathematicians now take for granted that Cantor's transfinite system has succeeded in taming infinity in that sense.

Here is Cantor's strategy for taming infinity:

1. Propose technical definitions for the term 'infinite' and for the properties of infinite collections.
2. Propose consistent, finitistic mathematical operations according to the technical redefinitions of the term 'infinite'.
3. Proclaim 'the infinite' as technically defined and used in mathematical operations corresponds to what everyone refers to as infinity in the literal sense of the term.
4. Claim success in revealing infinity to be a logically coherent concept amenable to mathematical calculation.

13.2 REDEFINING INFINITY IN TECHNICAL TERMS

Cantor began constructing his solution for taming infinity by first distinguishing between the two kinds of infinities.

The first he called *improper infinity* or a *non-genuine infinite* [384]. That kind of infinity he also called a *variable finitude*, and it is the same as Aristotle's concept of potential infinity and what I prefer to call figurative infinity.

The second kind of infinity Cantor had in mind was Aristotle's actual infinity, which Cantor called *proper infinity* or a *genuine infinite* or a *determinate infinite* [385]. This is the kind of infinity I refer to as literal infinity—a condition that implies both completeness and limitlessness with respect to the quantity of elements in a collection, where the collection's completeness and limitlessness can be defined as precisely as we like in natural language.

The Aristotelian distinction between potential infinity and actual infinity—or figurative infinity and literal infinity as I prefer to call them—was alive and well in Cantor's day and Cantor aimed to further *refine* the Aristotelian concept of actual infinity with more mathematical precision so that it could be revealed to be what he thought it really to be: a genuine or determinate property able to be directly calculable in mathematics without contradiction [386].

In order to make actual infinity into a mathematically calculable concept, Cantor redefined what it means for infinity to be a condition of both completeness and limitlessness so that these concepts do not come into contradiction with one another. His approach was intended to ensure the concept of infinity could be defined in such a manner as to avoid operational contradictions in the formal syntax of mathematics. Subsequent mathematicians adopting Cantor's approach have further refined these concepts for mathematical use. We'll turn now to examine technical definitions for completeness and limitlessness in the transfinite system's conceptual framework and show they can be combined into a technical definition for infinity amenable to mathematics.

13.2.1 *Technical Completeness*

As analyzed in § 3.2.8, literal completeness—that is, completeness as lexically and precisely defined in the ordinary, natural language sense of the term—implies further properties like wholeness, entirety, etc. However, mathematicians and set theorists are always free to propose more technical definitions of the word 'complete'. And as long as a technical definition of 'complete' does not logically *contradict* what completeness means in its literal usage in ordinary, natural language, then that technical definition for 'complete' and the more literal definition for 'complete' can be considered complementary.

Assuming a transfinite set theorist's technical manner of defining a set or sequence as complete is complementary to the natural language sense of complete as precisely defined, when the theorist says a collection can be both complete and limitless, the theorist proposes a logically consistent claim (depending on how the term 'limitless' is also technically defined in the mathematical system). If so, then the theorist may accurately say a given collection can be literally infinite—both complete and limitless.

However, with regard to collections said to be an actual infinite (i.e., a literal infinite) in a set-theoretic context, it is not clear completeness is being technically used in a manner consistent with the literal completeness implied by a collection assumed to be infinite in the literal sense of the term. This is because mathematicians use many, narrow, technical conceptions for what counts as complete and those various technical conceptions possibly contradict what the term 'complete' implies according to its literal usage in natural language, even for infinite collections.

With that in mind, we need to identify the transfinite system's technical version of completeness that is most complementary to Chapter 3's precising definition of literal completeness as given in natural language. That way, we are not stacking the deck against the transfinite system plausibly claiming number systems are sets ($\mathbb{N}$, $\mathbb{W}$, $\mathbb{Q}$, $\mathbb{R}$, etc.) and that they are literal (or 'actual') infinities as Cantor claimed.

Here, are two technical definitions of completeness based on a conception of completeness in transfinite set theory that are most complementary to literal completeness [387]:

- complete: (first version) P *is 'complete' if* P *is a dense, linearly ordered set and every non-empty subset that is a member of* P *is bounded from above by a supremum.*

- complete: (second version) P is 'complete' if P is a set and every non-empty subset that is a member of P is bounded from above by a supremum.

These technical definitions for the term 'complete' are paraphrased versions of a set-theoretic definition for completeness in the transfinite system [388]. However, they will suffice for our purposes.

Take the first technical definition of completeness in which completeness is defined as being a set with a dense, linear order of elements between the elements. Being 'dense' (having an element between any two elements) fits the wholeness criterion of literal completeness. Moreover, the definition also does not *contradict* a set being entire, finished, full, and having a total (at least, not directly), and so the definition also appears on the surface to be complementary to literal completeness. Even so, this is a very narrow definition of 'complete' because it does not apply to all the sets of the transfinite system. Instead, it applies only to sets of a certain kind—those that are "densely ordered" such as the number systems $\mathbb{Q}$ and $\mathbb{R}$—but not to those that are not densely ordered such as $\mathbb{N}$, $\mathbb{W}$, and $\mathbb{Z}$.

Now take the second technical definition of 'complete' above. It has the advantage of mathematically applying to all sets that have non-empty subsets, for all such sets can be placed into a linear order with a supremum. Thus, this technical definition of 'complete' applies to finite sets such as {1, 2, 3, ..., 100} and also to infinite sets such as any of the number systems ($\mathbb{N}$, $\mathbb{W}$, $\mathbb{Q}$, $\mathbb{R}$, and so forth) since they too are all ordered sets below a supremum.

The supremum in the case of infinite sets is an infinite ordinal number such as ω [389]. For example:

$$\mathbb{N} \triangleq \{1, 2, 3, \dots\} \triangleq \omega$$

or

$$\mathbb{W} \triangleq \{0, 1, 2, 3, \dots\} \triangleq \omega$$

Both expressions just mean the number system denoted is by definition equal ($\triangleq$) to the unbounded (...) set of numbers and also equal by definition to ω since ω is the supremum having all the natural and whole numbers as its members.

Incidentally, the sequences of both $\mathbb{N}$ and $\mathbb{W}$ extend, so to speak, to ω since the sequences of $\mathbb{N}$ and $\mathbb{W}$ are "equally infinite" (for further details on infinite ordinals, see § 13.5.4 and § 13.11). Regardless, the second technical definition for 'complete' ensures that all sets with non-empty subsets can be said to be technically complete since for any of them it is true that every non-empty subset that is a member of the set in question is bounded from above by a supremum.

Moreover, the second technical definition for 'complete' also seems to be, at least upon first glance, complementary with the precising definition for literal completeness as defined in Chapter 3. If a collection has elements bounded from above by a supremum when placed in linear order, that technical way of being complete may be construed as consistent with literal completeness' criteria of wholeness and entirety—being undivided (gapless) and not missing elements. The second technical definition of 'complete' also does not directly contradict that a literally complete collection is one that is finished, full, and has a total (for an infinite set, the 'total' would have to be an infinite number such as ω or $\aleph$). The second technical definition for 'complete' as given above then, does not appear to violate the conditions of literal completeness, at least not in any direct manner.

As this analysis shows, the transfinite system has technical definitions for the word 'complete'. Neither technical definition for 'complete' as stated above directly contradicts what it means to be complete in the literal sense as defined in Chapter 3. However, we would need to see if there are any counterexamples to their application in order to determine whether these technical definitions are logically coherent, particularly with literal completeness—a matter to be explored in § 14.1.1.

13.2.2 *Transfinite Limitlessness*

With few exceptions, mathematicians typically do not use the term 'limitless' as they consider it rather vague. However, literal infinity is the condition of being both complete and *limitless* in quantity, so we need a technical definition of what it means to be 'limitless'. Fortunately, it is possible to ascertain how the term would be technically defined in the transfinite system, for there is a term mathematicians and set theorists do like: *unbounded*. They use the term 'unbounded' for a set (more specifically, a linearly-ordered set or sequence) that lacks at least one 'bound' as bounds are described in § 5.3.1 and § 11.2.6. In other words, to be 'unbounded' in the mathematical sense of the term is to lack *at least* one bound (the infimum or supremum) to a sequence of elements [390]. Instead of solely using the term 'unbounded', let's keep our emphasis on the word 'limitless' so as to ensure contrast with the limitlessness of literal infinity. We may then define 'limitless' in terms of being mathematically unbounded:

- limitless: (transfinite version) P *is 'limitless' if* P *lacks one or both bounds to a linear sequence of the elements within* P.

This technical definition of the term 'limitless' does not seem to contradict the precising definition given in § 5.4.2 for defining how literal infinity is limitless—"to have a range that is unspecifiable, even in principle." If P lacks one or both bounds to a linear sequencing of the elements within P, then certainly P's extent of elements can be unspecifiable.

That's not to say if a collection is literally limitless, then it is limitless in the above technical sense too. Nor does it mean that if a collection is technically limitless, it must be literally limitless. Rather, it's just to say the two definitions for the term 'limitless' don't seem to directly *contradict* each other. So, the technical and precising definitions for 'limitless' are complementary in that respect (though, with the caveats given in § 14.1.2).

13.2.3 *A Transfinite Definition of Infinity*

Now that we have technical versions of completeness (§ 13.2.1) and limitlessness (§ 13.2.2) as these are understood in the conceptual framework of the transfinite system, let's combine them to capture how Cantor conceived collections to be infinite. We can then see if that conception is consistent with literal (actual) infinity.

Let's start by combining the first of the technical definitions for 'complete' with the technical version of 'limitless' for a preliminary transfinite version of 'infinite':

- infinite: (as transfinite, version 1) P *is 'infinite' if* P *is a dense, linearly ordered set and every non-empty subset that is a member of* P *is bounded from above by a supremum such that the supremum of* P *is greater than the unbounded sequence of elements within* P.

Version 1 combines the first technical version of completeness (a dense, linearly ordered set under a supremum) with a technical version of limitlessness (an unbounded sequence) by identifying the supremum of the whole set as greater than the unbounded sequence within the set. The result is internally consistent, but unfortunately not consistent with the rest of the transfinite system.

This version of 'infinite' certainly fits the transfinite system's descriptions of the rationals ($\mathbb{Q}$) and the reals ($\mathbb{R}$) since they are each said to be infinite and densely ordered. However, there are other sets in the transfinite system said to be infinite, and not all of them are densely ordered (§§ 12.4.2, 13.2.1). For example, $\mathbb{N}$ is not. Therefore, the version 1 definition of 'infinite' does not fit all of the infinite sets in the transfinite system. Consequently, having a dense order cannot be a necessary property for infinity, even as the transfinite. The version 1 definition fails.

However, the failure of defining what it is to be infinite in terms of having completeness as denseness is not catastrophic to the transfinite system. We can instead simply distinguish between infinite sets that are "dense" in the sense of being mathematically *continuous* (e.g., $\mathbb{R}$) and those that are not continuous in this fashion (e.g., $\mathbb{N}$) while both are 'complete' in some other technical sense suitable to the operations of the transfinite system while also, keeping with Cantor's claim of taming infinity, consistent with completeness in the literal sense.

That brings us to version 2 for a technical definition of 'infinite'. To build the version 2 definition of 'infinite', we need a better definition of 'complete' to combine with the technical definition of 'limitless'. Fortunately, we have one on hand—the second technical definition of 'complete' offered in § 13.2.1, reiterated—

- complete: P is 'complete' if P is a set and every non-empty subset that is a member of P is bounded from above by a supremum.

Now take the technical definition for the term 'limitless' as given in § 13.2.2, reiterated—

- limitless: P is 'limitless' if P lacks one or both bounds to a linear sequence of the elements within P.

Next, combine the second definition of the term 'complete' with the salient features of the technical definition for 'limitless' to build version 2 of a technical definition for the term 'infinite'—

- infinite: (as transfinite, version 2) P is 'infinite' if P is a set and every non-empty subset that is a member of P is bounded from above by a supremum such that the supremum of P is greater than the unbounded sequence of elements within P.

The version 2 technical definition for the term 'infinite' [391] is much more promising for application in the transfinite system than was version 1. Version 2 applies to all sets usually said to be infinite in the transfinite system, not just some of them.

For example, P can be $\mathbb{N}$ as well as $\mathbb{R}$. Set P taken as $\mathbb{N}$ is infinite since $\mathbb{N}$ is bounded above by a supremum (namely, the limit ordinal ω) that is greater than any n that is in $\mathbb{N}$. You could say there are limitless (or "unbounded") n's below the bound of ω. More formally: $\mathbb{N} \triangleq \omega$, where $\omega > n$. Another example of P is $\mathbb{R}$ since it too a limitless, or 'unbounded', sequence reals below an infinite supremum. [392].

That said, a couple of caveats are now in order. First, despite being amenable to expression in formal notation, the above technical redefinition of 'infinite' isn't *quite* phrased with the operational rigor of the transfinite theory of numbers, but it's sufficient for capturing how the term 'infinite' is *used* in the transfinite system with respect to mathematical operations. Second, the above technical definition of 'infinite' is also not the only definition of 'infinite' provided by the transfinite system. We will see a couple more in § 14.1.4.

Those caveats aside, the technical definition of 'infinite' offered here serves to show how the transfinite system's conception of what it is to be infinite can at least be defined in a manner consistent with its more technical conceptions of completeness and limitlessness so as to avoid the kind of contradictions that arise between the non-technical definitions of 'complete' and 'limitless' as they define literal infinity.

Moreover, if $P = \mathbb{N}$, then version 2 of the technical definition for 'infinite' fits quite well the technical definition for 'infinity' as cited earlier in § 7.2:

- **infinity:** (in transfinite mathematics) *the ordinality of a sequence of elements, or cardinality of a set of elements, greater than that of any natural number in* $\mathbb{N}$.

That basically means infinity is the property of a set having ω or $\aleph$-many elements, which makes the set of greater quantity than the value of any natural number, and that applies to other number scales such as the real numbers as well (see § 13.9) [393]. Hence, both version 2 of the technical definition for 'infinite' and the above technical definition of 'infinity' complement each other with respect to how these terms are *mathematically* used with consistency in the transfinite system. Whether the technical definition of infinity is *logically* coherent and adequate to express literal infinity is a separate issue explored in § 14.1.3.

13.3 NO LAST, INFINITELY LARGE NUMBERS

What does it mean to have an ordinal or cardinal greater than any natural number in $\mathbb{N}$—that is, what is it to be infinite in the transfinite sense of the term? For one thing, it means while there are infinite numbers (ω and $\aleph$) greater than any natural number, there also can be no natural numbers infinitely large—there are no natural numbers that could even in principle be written out with infinitely many digits. This conception of 'infinity' is one of the ways the transfinite system is designed to prevent contradictions from being implied between the properties of completeness and limitlessness for infinite sets of numbers.

Recall from **Figure 12.0** that the precising definition of completeness derived from ordinary, natural language ('literal completeness') implies both a first and last element to a count of elements in a collection, while the precising definition of limitlessness from ordinary language ('literal limitlessness') implies the opposite: there cannot be both a first and last element to a count of elements in a collection. Moreover, if the collection in question is literally infinite, then the literal completeness of the collection implies an infinitely large natural number to the scale of numbers used for counting the collection. But the literal infinity of the same collection means the collection is literally limitless, and that limitlessness of the collection means the sequence of numbers used for counting the collection entails that there is never an infinitely large number but instead just infinitely many finite numbers [394].

With respect to these contradictory implications, the transfinite system sides with the limitlessness of the collection over the literal completeness of the collection. The transfinite system holds there is not both a first and last element to an infinite collection of elements [395] and maintains that there is no infinitely large natural number but rather there are "infinitely many" (finite) numbers [396]. As a result of this way of redefining 'infinity', if collection P is infinite and equal to $\mathbb{N}$, then it is impossible to count every element of P such that the count ends with a last number, even with one that is infinitely large. And the reason there is no way to count a last element of P with an infinitely large natural number is because $\mathbb{N}$ has no last natural number that is infinitely large.

In other words, because there is no natural number, n, that does not have another finite natural number as a successor, the sequence of $\mathbb{N}$ has no last, highest, greatest natural number in the sense of some infinitely large n with a *standing total* of all the natural numbers. In fact, transfinite mathematics rejects altogether the notion of infinitely great natural numbers [397]. Every n in $\mathbb{N}$ is only 1 bigger than the previous number in sequence while no subsequence of natural numbers—no matter how far it extends, no matter how much larger the numbers get further along in that sequence relative to the numbers prior in the sequence—has an infinitely large number, n, that represents the size of $\mathbb{N}$. Infinite collections are 'limitless' in this sense, which is contrary to the precising definition of 'complete' in ordinary language.

Nevertheless, the transfinite system does retain the use of the term 'complete' to *describe* infinite collections of elements like P. It's simply that, for the sake of consistent mathematical operation, the transfinite system brings in the technical version of completeness (§ 13.2.1) which allows for *indefinite* progression toward a supremum, thus sidestepping any logical implication of an infinitely large natural number of elements as falling counter to "infinitely many" finite numbers without an 'infinitieth' natural number.

The logical contradictions involved with the concept of infinitely large natural numbers are avoided by use of the technical definition of 'complete', which is nonetheless not really complete in the ordinary, natural language sense of the term. And because of that, it's certainly not clear that the transfinite system's technical definition for 'infinite', which is based in part on the technical version of completeness, is really a mathematical expression of literal infinity as Cantor claimed.

13.4 EXTREMITY WITHOUT MAXIMUM

Another way to see this same point is to think in terms of extremities.

For a collection to be infinite in a literal sense, Cantor needed to overcome the logically contradictory implications of what being 'complete' and 'limitless' usually mean. He found a loophole in the logic of mathematical progression that would allow for progressions without limit to nevertheless be complete, at least in a technical sense (he preferred the term "finished"). He hoped that would allow for a collection to be 'infinite' without merely being so in a figurative sense.

Redefining the meaning of 'complete' for infinity allows mathematicians to conceive of the natural numbers in $\mathbb{N}$ as extending limitlessly while nevertheless being 'complete' in a technical sense of the term. The natural numbers of $\mathbb{N}$ are said to extend without limit (or without bound) as they *tend to* the limit (the bound) that is the ordinal ω as their supremum. They keep going up in ever-higher values but are nevertheless bounded from above by that limit ordinal [398]. A sequence of numbers that is "bounded from above" by an ordinal is a sequence that is 'compete' in the technical sense of the term even if not complete by the precising definition of literal completeness offered in § 3.2.

In the ordinary sense of 'complete', a collection that is complete is a collection with *extrema*. In the technical sense of 'complete', a collection is complete if it can be sequenced up to a particular kind of *extremity*—a supremum, whether that supremum is a successor ordinal or a limit ordinal. For example, the limit ordinal ω is a supremum for the natural numbers, an extremity of sorts in that it represents *all* the natural numbers, which are lesser in value than it, but that is not a maximum of the numbers below it. While the limit ordinal of $\mathbb{N}$ is an extremity, the limit ordinal of $\mathbb{N}$ cannot be a maximum for the natural numbers because all the natural numbers have successors—there is no last natural number that can be the maximum for all the natural numbers. That makes the technical version of 'complete' different from the original sense of completeness, which requires a maximum. Even so, the limit ordinal of the natural numbers is an extremity that makes the natural numbers "bounded from above" despite not having a maximum—despite lacking a 'largest' natural number [399].

Transfinite set theory thus defines completeness for infinite sets in terms of a limit ordinal that is an extremity but not a maximum, allowing for limitless progression within bounds as if a continuous construction under a supremum. The technical completeness of the transfinite is thus not necessarily consistent with the literal completeness of a literal infinity.

13.5 MATHEMATICAL NOTATION FOR INFINITE SETS

In order to express the infinitude of a collection in coherent *mathematical* terms that would avoid the logical contradictions or "paradoxes" implied by the literal sense of infinity, Cantor needed to build on the notation put forth by previous generations and mathematicians and create a new notation for "infinite numbers." This involved reframing the use of notations such as ellipses, braces, and use of letter-like symbols.

13.5.1 *Ellipses*

Take once again the use of an ellipsis, as in the expression 1, 2, 3, … In mathematical operation, use of ellipses indicates a progression that keeps on going persistently or ceaselessly (indefinite, yet finite). However, mathematicians typically interpret the ellipsis as suggesting something more than what its operational use denotes: that the progression goes on not just indefinitely but limitlessly. That is, we can only construct indefinite progressions of symbols in actual practice, which is how ellipses work operationally, but mathematicians use an ellipsis to express *limitlessness* in the sense of infinite progression. Hence, the indefinite progression of natural numbers is used for suggesting the natural numbers go on limitlessly. Cantor's innovation was to take the limitless interpretation of the ellipsis and add to that interpretation a representation of completeness with the use of parentheses or braces around the list of symbols suggested to be limitless by use of the ellipsis that follows them [400].

13.5.2 *Braces and Letters*

Transfinite mathematics represents a limitless progression by an ellipsis and then places that representation in braces like so: $\{1, 2, 3, …\}$. Transfinite math then interprets the progression denoted by the ellipsis not as an indefinite, open series under construction but instead as a limitless progression bounded as a set—a single unit, already finished—which implies the limitless numbers are already "out there" beyond any depiction of them, waiting to be depicted in the braces.

Transfinite mathematics further abstracts this set with letters such as S for 'set', or with any other arbitrary letter like our earlier used P. Because the numbers in $\{1, 2, 3, …\}$ are natural numbers, we can replace the use of $\{1, 2, 3, …\}$ with the conventional $\mathbb{N}$ is its symbol. Therefore, $\mathbb{N} \triangleq \{1, 2, 3, …\}$. We can even extend the progression of depicted natural numbers as far as we like within the braces without changing the quantity of numbers that $\mathbb{N}$ represents; for instance, $\mathbb{N} \triangleq \{1, 2, 3, 4, 5, …, n, …\}$. After all, we know that $\{1, 2, 3, …\}$ is the same quantity as $\{1, 2, 3, 4, 5, …, n, …\}$.

The first brace functions similarly to an infimum and the second brace functions similarly to a supremum: the sequence of natural numbers between them, no matter how large, never exceeds the boundaries of the braces. The only reason the braces are further apart in the second example is because we extended the *depicted numbers*; but if all the natural numbers are allegedly already "out there" waiting to be depicted, we can imagine the braces as representing static boundaries within which all the numbers are found. The quantity of natural numbers making up the set of numbers in the braces is fixed, and by virtue of the ellipsis, the quantity of numbers inside the braces remains the same: ∞, interpreted as literal infinity rather than figurative infinity.

13.5.3 *A New Kind of Number: The Transfinite Numbers*

Transfinite mathematics takes the representation of sets one step further. First, Cantor assumed the progression 1, 2, 3, ... indicates a limitless sequence of elements with no greatest number—no standing total of numbers as elements. But he also thought there was no mathematical rule preventing a limitless sequence from being represented as a complete set. Simply place the progression in braces: $\{1, 2, 3, ...\}$. And, voila, we can then treat it as a complete unit despite the limitlessness suggested by the ellipsis.

Since the progression goes "to infinity" (∞), we can then treat ∞ *as if* it is a literal infinity rather than a figurative infinity, and as a determinate number expressing the size of the set: $\{1, 2, 3, ...\} = \infty$. Because $\mathbb{N} \triangleq \{1, 2, 3, ...\}$ and $\{1, 2, 3, ...\} = \infty$, then $\mathbb{N} \triangleq \infty$, as the transfinite system states [401].

Assuming as much, Cantor proposed [402] that although the infinite set of natural numbers, $\mathbb{N}$, has no greatest natural number in it, that does not prevent the set from falling into sequence prior to a new and different kind of number—a *non-natural* number—that would *follow after* the complete set of natural numbers in $\mathbb{N}$. Imagine the sequence of natural numbers inside the braces $\{1, 2, 3, ...\}$ is abbreviated with a single letter, P, so as to avoid writing out 1, 2, 3, ... repeatedly in the ensuing discussion. So, $\mathbb{N} \triangleq \{P\}$. We have then but to posit that another set of numbers in which the numbers are abbreviated as Q, could be placed in sequence after $\{P\}$, like so: $\{P\}$, $\{Q\}$. However, since P is *all* the natural numbers, then whatever the numbers Q are, they cannot be natural numbers. For there to be numbers "following after" a sequence of infinitely many natural numbers in $\mathbb{N}$, the new numbers represented by Q in the set $\{Q\}$ would have to themselves be both infinite and non-natural numbers.

Assuming further that there is more than one of such a number represented by Q, there must be a *least infinite* number that is somehow greater than any of the infinitely many natural numbers in sequence P preceding the least of Q. Now the logic of a "least infinite" number is dubious because it's one thing to place two infinite sets—$\{P\}$ and $\{Q\}$—into order, one after the other, but it's quite another to say $\{P\}$ contains infinitely many numbers, none of which can be the greatest number, and yet $\{Q\}$ is "greater than" the sequence which has no greatest number. However, let's ignore that conceptual problem for the time being. Instead, assuming we can make sense of a number that is greater than infinitely many natural numbers, we know that because the 'least' non-natural number of Q follows "after" all the infinitely many numbers of P, that Q must itself be an infinite number(s). That is not to say Q is an infinitely large natural number(s). Rather, there are "infinitely many" finite numbers in P while Q has truly infinite number(s).

Assuming further still that there is a 'least' Q-number, the least Q-number following after all the natural numbers as an infinite supremum to the natural numbers. No matter how many natural numbers $\{P\}$ represents, the numbers can only "tend to," or progress toward but never converge with, the least of the infinitely great numbers in $\{Q\}$.

Moreover, because a 'least' Q-number (somehow) comes in sequence *after* all the infinitely many natural numbers, it therefore represents the *order* of the infinite sequence of natural numbers prior to it and the least Q-number must also (somehow) represent a greater *size* of set than the P-set of infinitely many natural numbers. Hence, the least Q-number must itself have an *ordinality* somehow further than the natural numbers in sequence and a *cardinality* somehow greater than any natural number below it.

The least Q-number is an infinitely large number but not a natural number, whole number, or integer. Cantor referred to this kind of number as a *transfinite number* in order to distinguish it from the kind of infinity he called *the absolute* or *absolutely infinite totality* (which we'll return to in § 25.3). Hence, transfinite mathematics is the mathematics of transfinite numbers while 'the absolute' is a notion of infinity that cannot be mathematically calculated but which only alludes to an unfathomable quantity [403].

13.5.4 *Transfinite Ordinals*

This is where set theory and transfinite notation come in to represent the whole numbers and the natural numbers. The transfinite system has a rather confusing symbolism. As mentioned in § 2.3.6, transfinite set theorists and mathematicians today typically use $\mathbb{N}$ to represent the natural numbers, which they take to include zero. But at least in my country (the United States) mathematics instructors typically refer to the natural numbers as the counting numbers, the sequence of which starts with 1 rather than 0. In keeping both with Cantor's original writings and the convention of general mathematics in the U.S., I will stick with the whole numbers as the sequence of numbers starting with zero as a member instead of the natural numbers. So, I will use $\mathbb{N}$ for the set of natural numbers and $\mathbb{W}$ for the set of whole numbers.

Assuming both $\mathbb{N}$ and $\mathbb{W}$ are complete sets, their elements can have any order; however, the transfinite system usually regards the naturals in terms of its *sequence* of numbers, so we will do likewise with $\mathbb{N}$ and $\mathbb{W}$. The sequence of $\mathbb{W}$ starts with 0 (zero) and then proceeds through the counting numbers in order, while the sequence of $\mathbb{N}$ starts directly with the first counting number, 1, and continues with the counting numbers in order. After 0, both the sequence of $\mathbb{W}$ and the sequence of $\mathbb{N}$ share the same numbers.

Because both $\mathbb{W}$ and $\mathbb{N}$ have the same sequence after zero, it doesn't really matter for our topic which scale we use for examples—we can use the scales interchangeably even though $\mathbb{N}$ starts with 1 and $\mathbb{W}$ starts with 0. Either $\mathbb{W}$ or $\mathbb{N}$ could be used to illustrate the points I want to make, but since Cantor framed his transfinite system with reference to the whole numbers, which start with 0 instead of with 1, I will use $\mathbb{W}$ for many of my examples.

Let's assume $\mathbb{W}$ is an infinite set of whole numbers: $\{0, 1, 2, 3, ...\}$. Transfinite set theory posits that every whole number in $\mathbb{W}$ is finite even though the entirety of $\mathbb{W}$ has "infinitely many" whole numbers. The same of course goes for the naturals of $\mathbb{N}$.

Moreover, the transfinite system still holds the progression of whole or natural numbers to have infinitely many numbers as represented by ∞. (However, while in general mathematics "infinitely many" is represented as ∞ and may be interpreted either as referring to either figurative infinity or literal infinity, in the transfinite system, ∞ is rarely if ever used. That is because ∞ must in the transfinite system be interpreted as *literal* infinity, but that alone still is not precise enough—ω and $\aleph$ tend to be used more often.) Since there is no end to the ∞-many numbers in $\mathbb{W}$ and $\mathbb{N}$, the transfinite system represents $\mathbb{W}$ and $\mathbb{N}$ as having the same infinite, or 'transfinite', quantity of numbers—the same ∞-many members in each set. After all, $\mathbb{W}$ is just $\mathbb{N}$ starting with 0 instead of 1: $\mathbb{W} = \mathbb{N}$.

To get to an even more precise conception of infinity in the transfinite system, we can begin by abstractly representing the totality of whole numbers in the set $\{0, 1, 2, 3, ...\}$ as $\{P\}$, which means that $\{P\} \triangleq \mathbb{W}$. So, if we assume $\mathbb{W} \triangleq \infty$, where ∞ is literal infinity, then $\{P\} \triangleq \mathbb{W} \triangleq \infty$.

Now comes another conceptual leap. In the transfinite system, one infinite set can be represented *after* another as when we place the two sets in sequence.

Suppose $\{P\}$ is followed by $\{Q\}$. Since $\{P\}$ is infinitely many whole numbers so that $\{P\} \triangleq \mathbb{W}$, then that means $\mathbb{W}$ is a set of infinitely many finite whole numbers *followed* by $\{Q\}$, an infinite set of *infinite numbers* each of which is larger than any whole number in $\mathbb{W}$. Since Cantor proposed the set of whole numbers contains (literally) ∞-many numbers, he needed to propose the ∞-many whole numbers in $\mathbb{W}$ together comprise $\{P\}$ as the "least infinite" set of numbers that can be followed by an even "greater infinite" of numbers that comprise $\{Q\}$.

However, the set of all whole numbers, $\mathbb{W}$, is also said to have ∞-many whole numbers as members. For $\mathbb{W}$ as $\{P\}$ to have a successor that is $\{Q\}$ means $\{P\}$ and $\{Q\}$ must have corresponding numbers that work differently than ∞ typically does in general mathematics.

$\mathbb{W}$ as a set must somehow be represented by an 'infinite number' of sorts—a *transfinite* number—that is not itself a whole number. That transfinite number must be greater than every whole number [404]. In fact, such a number can be represented either as the number of the infinite sequence of wholes in $\mathbb{W}$ or as the infinite size of all the whole numbers in $\mathbb{W}$.

When Cantor wished to further represent the ∞-many whole numbers in terms of their infinitude of sequence, he represented the sequence of $\mathbb{W}$ not just as ∞ interpreted as literal infinity but by his new transfinite ordinal: ω. In a sense, he qualified ∞ by instead using ω.

Hence, if ∞ is taken as the literal infinity of the sequence of all the whole numbers in $\mathbb{W}$, then in that regard $\infty = \omega$. Therefore, while $\mathbb{W}$ has a sequence of ∞ members in a literal sense, the infinite ordinal that represents the infinite sequence of wholes in $\mathbb{W}$ is ω. Further, the transfinite ω is the quantity of all whole numbers together in $\mathbb{W}$, so it *exceeds* any particular whole number in $\mathbb{W}$, no matter how great that number [405].

The transfinite ordinal ω can be understood by comparison to finite ordinals. With respect to finite ordinals, to know a sequence of numbers that precedes a given ordinal is to know that ordinal. We should thus *identify* each ordinal with the sequence of its predecessors [406]. For example, 4, as an ordinal, just is the sequence 0, 1, 2, 3. Similarly, 5, as an ordinal, is the sequence 0, 1, 2, 3, 4. Now consider the sequence 0, 1, 2, 3, 4, 5, ... where the ellipsis represents a limitless progression; its ordinal is ω. The ordinal of the whole numbers in $\mathbb{W}$ is the transfinite ordinal ω. Just as a finite number like 5 follows after all the numbers prior to it, so too the transfinite ordinal ω "follows after" all of $\mathbb{W}$'s constituent whole numbers [407].

It is certainly odd to think of a limitless sequence of numbers having another number that "follows after" them. After all, if the whole numbers are infinite, they are without limit. And if they are without limit, then how can there be yet another infinite number that follows *after* all of them in sequence? Transfinite mathematics seeks to frame the "following after" of ω to $\mathbb{W}$ in four respects.

First, the sequence of the whole numbers is not unordered like $\{21, 5, 300, 0, 4, ...\}$. Instead, it is *ordered*; more specifically, it is *well-ordered* [408]. A 'well-ordered' set is a set in which every member equivalent to a non-empty subset with a predecessor has a least element. In Cantor's system, $\mathbb{W}$ is a set, so that description applies to the whole numbers: $\{0, 1, 2, 3, 4, ...\}$. Such an 'infinite' sequence is denoted ω, which thus represents $\mathbb{W}$ as a well-ordered sequence of whole numbers. In that respect, ω is a symbol for a *category* of numbers; mathematicians say ω is not the terminus of the sequence or series but instead represents how a sequence or series is ordered [409].

However, ω cannot be *solely* a category for the numbers of $\mathbb{W}$ as well-ordered rather than unordered. This is because Cantor tells us that ω *follows after* all the whole numbers, which is why ω is the *ordinal* of $\mathbb{W}$ and not just a symbol for *categorizing* the numbers in $\mathbb{W}$ as "well-ordered." Were ω just the category of ordered numbers, it would not function as an ordinal, nor would it be said to "follow after" the whole number or be "greater than" any whole number. The ordinal ω is said to be "greater" or "larger" than any whole number, v, in $\mathbb{W}$ because for any v we can find another whole number larger than it (for example, $v + 1$), but still less than a value we may give ω per se: $(v + 1) < ω$. What transfinite mathematicians mean by ω being "larger" than any whole number, v, is that no one can write out the complete set of whole numbers for $\mathbb{W}$ because, for any number cited for $\mathbb{W}$, we can a "discover" one whole number larger in $\mathbb{W}$. So, they regard ω as the ordinal number whose predecessors are the numbers comprising $\mathbb{W}$ [410].

Second, the transfinite system proposes ω "follows after" the whole numbers of $\mathbb{W}$ in terms of the *completeness* of $\mathbb{W}$. Just as set $\{Q\}$ follows after set $\{P\}$ in the expression $\{P\}, \{Q\}$, so too ω is the "least infinite" of the Q-numbers can follow after $\{P\}$ since $\{P\}$ represents all the whole numbers of $\mathbb{W}$ [411]. Therefore, $\{P\}, \{Q\}$ is the same as 0, 1, 2, 3, ..., ω. Set theorists say, "The idea is that we can imagine an infinite number ω that comes 'after' all natural numbers and then continue the counting process into the transfinite: ω, ω + 1, (ω + 1) + 1, and so on" [412].

Third, the above entails $\mathbb{W}$ has ω as the *limit* to the sequence of whole numbers while the transfinite ordinal ω is not itself a whole number—at least not in the usual sense. Because of that, although $\mathbb{W}$ may have "no limit" to the quantity of its whole numbers, $\mathbb{W}$ can still have a limit in the form of a number that is *not* a *whole* number but toward which all those whole numbers tend: namely, ω, which functions as the limit to the sequence of whole numbers [413]. As Cantor stated [414]:

> It is even permissible to think of the newly created number ω as the *limit* toward which the numbers v tend, if by that nothing else is understood than that ω is to be the first whole number which follows all the other numbers v, i.e., is to be called greater than every one of the numbers v.

Here Cantor calls ω a "whole number" but only in a loose sense. In his introduction to Cantor's work, mathematician Philip E.B. Jourdain expounded upon this point [415]:

> Cantor remarked that ω may, in a sense, be regarded as the limit to which the variable finite whole number v tends. Here "is the least transfinite ordinal number which is greater than all finite numbers; exactly in the same way that $\sqrt{2}$ is the limit of certain variable, increasing, rational numbers, with this difference: the difference between $\sqrt{2}$ and these approximating fractions becomes as small as we wish, whereas $ω-v$ is always equal to ω...I conceive the minimum of the transfinite as the limit of the increasing finite."

At first, this passage seems to imply the sequence of whole numbers in $\mathbb{W}$ are merely a figurative infinity that *approaches* ω as a kind of bound. It is true Cantor did indicate for any whole number, v, we can always increase the value of v, as with the successor function: $v + 1$. Cantor declared that the whole numbers we write down constitute merely an "increasing finite" [416].

However, Cantor did not think we *invent* whole numbers in an open series of constructions; he thought instead that we *discover* them. If the highest whole number ever written down was 11, then when someone calculated $11 + 1$ to get 12, the number 12 was "already there" in $\mathbb{W}$, waiting to be discovered by our use of the successor function.

His transfinite set theory holds a number scale such as $\mathbb{W}$ to be not just an incomplete, indefinite sequence of invented whole numbers but rather a literally infinite sequence of discovered whole numbers. Cantor thought the "potential infinity" of discovered number sequences implies there is an "actual infinity" of numbers already there in a set, waiting to be identified—waiting to be *discovered* [417]. Cantor thus believed there is "no highest whole number" not because $\mathbb{W}$ is an incomplete series, but rather because the scale $\mathbb{W}$ is itself already 'complete' while also having a *limitless* number of numbers in it waiting to be discovered.

In transfinite mathematics, this is expressed by saying that ω is the ordinal of *all* the whole numbers of $\mathbb{W}$. In other words, $\omega \triangleq \mathbb{W}$. And yet, $\omega \triangleq \mathbb{W}$, while no $v + 1$ can ever be equal to ω, or $\mathbb{W}$ itself. Hence, any "increasing finite" of numbers we identify ("discover") as belonging to $\mathbb{W}$, no matter how high those numbers extend, never approach the quantity ω any closer than does the least finite number [418]. In Cantor's view [419], ω does not just succeed the sequence of all *other* numbers in $\mathbb{W}$, or whatever is the highest v so far defined for $\mathbb{W}$; rather, ω succeeds *all* the whole numbers there can be in $\mathbb{W}$, *even in principle*, and so much so that no v, no matter how high in ordinality, is any closer to ω than is 1.

However, Cantor viewed the transfinite ω as itself complete and definite. He went on to say, "ω is to be regarded as definite and completed as $\sqrt{2}$, and in no way alters the fact that ω has no more trace of the numbers v which tend to it than $\sqrt{2}$ has of the approximating fractions. The transfinite numbers are in a sense *new irrationalities*..." [420].

The ordinal ω is definite and complete in itself, but also proposed to be *infinitely* far down the sequence of whole numbers in the sense that ω always represents a value larger than $v + 1$; you can keep adding numbers to any v in $\mathbb{W}$ and yet not reach ω. In that sense, the symbol ω functions as a kind of supremum to all numbers in $\mathbb{W}$ since there is no highest whole number in $\mathbb{W}$. In proposing ω follows all the whole numbers as a supremum to them, Cantor wanted us to think of ω as equal to a completed numerical scale of whole numbers ($\mathbb{W} \triangleq \omega$) which, simultaneously, can have no last whole number, v, even in principle.

So, on the one hand, ω is itself an ordinal number, and it is *identified* with the complete sequence of whole numbers. Formally, ω is *by definition equal to* $\mathbb{W}$; that is, $\omega \triangleq \mathbb{W}$ or $\omega \triangleq \{0, 1, 2, 3, ...\}$. On the other hand, as an ordinal, ω *succeeds* every number in $\mathbb{W}$ as if ω is a kind of supremum for the sequence of whole numbers in $\mathbb{W}$ such that $\omega + 1 = \{0, 1, 2, 3, ..., \omega\}$. As mathematician James Clark explains, "The ordinal ω is the supremum of all finite ordinals, and has as its member all finite ordinals..." [421].

And, of course, all of this applies to the natural numbers of $\mathbb{N}$ since $\mathbb{N}$ and $\mathbb{W}$ are equal to one another. Assuming as much, it must also be the case that $\{1, 2, 3, ...\} \triangleq \mathbb{N}$ or $\mathbb{W} \triangleq \omega$.

13.5.5 *Transfinite Cardinals*

The transfinite system distinguishes between collections having an infinite number of members arranged according to a particular sequence and collections with an infinite number of members arranged in *any* sequence or no particular order at all. Infinite collections having an order or sequence to their members are represented by the transfinite ordinals, denoted with ω; infinite collections considered only in terms of their relative size regardless of any sequence or order of their members are represented by the transfinite cardinal, denoted with $\aleph$.

The transfinite system considers $\mathbb{N}$ and $\mathbb{W}$ as prime examples of infinitely large sets of numbers for which $\aleph$ represents cardinality. For *finite* collections, a natural or whole number indicates cardinality and cardinality represents the size of a set corresponding to the number. For *infinite* collections, there is no natural or whole number that can indicate size. Take $\mathbb{N}$ for example. Ironically, since the scale of $\mathbb{N}$ is itself considered infinite in transfinite math, we cannot use a natural number from $\mathbb{N}$ to indicate the size of $\mathbb{N}$. But since $\mathbb{N}$ is 'complete', it must have a cardinality and therefore a size. So, in developing transfinite mathematics, Cantor proposed that to express the size of the set of all the natural numbers, "there is at least one size that is not a natural number" [422]. Transfinite math uses the 'transfinite cardinal', $\aleph$, to designate the literally infinite size of such a set as $\mathbb{N}$. Since $\mathbb{W}$ is the same as $\mathbb{N}$, but with 0 (zero) starting the sequence, $\mathbb{N}$ and $\mathbb{W}$ share the same cardinality: $\aleph$.

In representing the cardinality of a number system such as $\mathbb{N}$ or $\mathbb{W}$, it doesn't matter if the numbers are unordered like in the set {21, 300, 0, 3, 432, ...} or a well-ordered sequence such as {0, 1, 2, 3, ...}; just as long as "all" (the complete collection) of the numbers are included and those numbers are simultaneously limitless in quantity; in which case, the transfinite cardinal $\aleph$ can represent them. So, the ordinal ω represents an infinite, well-ordered sequence—like the well-ordering of the sequence of numbers in a number scale as a set of numbers (for example, $\mathbb{W}$) while the cardinal $\aleph$ represents the infinite magnitude of the number of numbers in the very same set, or any set of equivalent size [423].

Furthermore, the sequence 0, 1, 2, 3, ... is *succeeded by* ω, so that 0, 1, 2, 3, ..., ω. Likewise, the sequence 0, 1, 2, 3, ... is also succeeded by $\aleph$ in the expression 0, 1, 2, 3, ..., $\aleph$. Therefore, $\aleph$, as the cardinality of $\mathbb{W}$, must represent an infinite number equal to a size that is *greater than* the size of any v in $\mathbb{W}$.

And since in transfinite theory $\mathbb{W} \triangleq \aleph$, the implication of $\aleph$ succeeding every v in $\mathbb{W}$ is that $\mathbb{W}$ is *greater than* every v inside $\mathbb{W}$, no matter how high v's cardinality. Consequently, while there are 'infinitely many' *finite* numbers in $\mathbb{W}$, the transfinite system holds there need be no whole number, v, that is infinitely large [424]. Instead, just as ω functions as a supremum to the order of whole numbers in $\mathbb{W}$, so too $\aleph$ also functions as a least upper bound for finite cardinalities in $\mathbb{W}$. For that reason, we can express the following: {0, 1, 2, 3, ...} $\triangleq \mathbb{W} \triangleq \aleph$.

There are more similarities between ω and $\aleph$. Both ω and $\aleph$ are equal to $\mathbb{W}$ when $\mathbb{W}$ is intended to represent the whole numbers as a complete set; ω represents *both* $\mathbb{W}$ as a well-ordered sequence *and* $\mathbb{W}$'s supremum, while $\aleph$ is the size of $\mathbb{W}$ *as* a set. While Cantor's transfinite mathematics states infinity (ω or $\aleph$) both succeeds and is greater than every v in $\mathbb{W}$, it also states that $\mathbb{W}$ has "infinitely many" whole numbers in the sense that the transfinite cardinal $\aleph$ is equal in size to the entirety of the sequence of whole numbers with the transfinite ordinal ω. In notation: $\omega \triangleq \aleph$ (or, more precisely, $\omega_0 \triangleq \aleph_0$) [425].

13.6 GREATER THAN THE SUM

The (literal) completeness of literal infinity implies the existence of infinitely large natural and whole numbers while the (literal) limitlessness of literal infinity implies that there are infinitely many natural and whole numbers with none of them being infinitely large. The transfinite system attempts to dissolve this pair of contradictory implications by redefining completeness and limitlessness in technical terms.

For instance, in transfinite set theory the 'completeness' of a set is a matter of the set having members in an ordered sequence such that the sequence has an ordinal as an upper bound. If an infinite set is a 'complete' set by this technical conception of completeness, the ω expressing the infinite order of elements in the set operates as a supremum (specifically, a limit ordinal) such that ω marks a least upper bound to the sequences of infinitely many finite numbers in $\mathbb{N}$ and $\mathbb{W}$.

With respect to "infinitely many finite numbers," transfinite set theory also posits the infinite sets $\mathbb{N}$ and $\mathbb{W}$ are each 'limitless' in the respect that there is *no such thing* as a *largest* natural number or whole number—not even in principle—because any natural number or whole number that is a successor to a previous natural or whole number also has a successor [426]. That is, transfinite set theory [427] holds that the 'limitlessness' of a number system implies that every natural or whole number is just 1 larger than the previous number and hence there is no natural or whole number infinitely greater than 1.

When mathematicians regard $\mathbb{N}$ and $\mathbb{W}$ as sets having "infinitely many finite numbers," they do not think of these sets as temporal series—as each having a temporally limited quantity of numbers with a running total, generated as new numbers are invented. If $\mathbb{N}$ and $\mathbb{W}$ represent infinitely large sets—sets of $\aleph$ size—then the sequences of numbers in $\mathbb{N}$ and $\mathbb{W}$ do not *accumulate* in a series of iterations from their base numbers such that the scale comprises a series with infinitely large natural and whole numbers. Rather, most mathematicians think of $\mathbb{N}$ and $\mathbb{W}$ as sets of genuinely unlimited quantities of *finite* numbers, with all their numbers already there at once, waiting to be discovered.

So too ω and $\aleph$ are not regarded as symbols for an infinitely large natural number for $\mathbb{N}$ or whole number for $\mathbb{W}$ as if ω and $\aleph$ represent a maximum for $\mathbb{N}$ and $\mathbb{W}$. Rather, $\aleph$, which is equal to ω, is not a 'sum' of the natural or whole numbers in the finite sense of the term 'sum'. It is true that according to transfinite mathematics $\{1 + 2 + 3 + ...\} = \aleph$, but the 'equals' sign in the expression need not denote $\aleph$ as a 'sum' of members. Instead, the 'equals' sign can be taken as indicating the identity of the sequence. That is, the ellipsis represents limitless additions while the equals sign denotes not a conclusion with a sum but rather that the limitless additions are identical to the aleph ($\aleph$), which then only denotes the cardinality of the set as a whole. So while $\aleph$ and ω are infinite or 'transfinite' numbers, they are not considered genuine sums of finite sequences of numbers and so they are not themselves symbols for infinitely large natural or whole numbers.

The transfinite system therefore claims that due to the 'limitlessness' of infinity the infinite sets $\mathbb{N}$ and $\mathbb{W}$ are quantitatively *greater* (ω or $\aleph$) than any sum of their parts. Both ω and $\aleph$ represent wholes greater than any sum of members in $\mathbb{N}$ or $\mathbb{W}$. According to transfinite set theory, that's what having "infinitely many finite numbers" means for $\mathbb{N}$ and $\mathbb{W}$ [428].

That is the transfinite system's solution of the contradiction of literal completeness for an infinite set implying infinitely large natural/whole numbers while literal limitlessness implies that such numbers do not exist. The transfinite system's solution is to redefine what 'complete' and 'limitless' mean. The term 'complete' is redefined in such a way that no sum of members is implied, making it more consistent with limitlessness. With the redefinition of completeness, the transfinite approach sidesteps the problem of simultaneously implying and denying the existence of infinitely large natural or whole numbers as well as the problem of implying and denying infinite sums.

In short, the transfinite definition of 'infinite' implies there are no infinitely large natural or whole numbers that could be sums for infinite collections. Transfinite mathematics rejects infinitely large sums (natural and whole numbers) in favor of 'infinitely many' finite sums, making the whole of an infinite collection greater than any sum of its parts rather than equal to the sum of its parts.

13.7 REDEFINING COUNTABILITY

The transfinite redefinition of completeness has implications for the *countability* of infinite collections. A collection that is literally complete according to the precising definition of completeness given in ordinary language (see § 3.2) is a collection that is capable of having a sum of members and therefore a collection for which every member can be *counted*. To be 'countable' is to be able to be counted to a concluding number that is the total of the collection counted. Typically, when we say a collection is *uncountable*, we mean the collection is too large to count in practice, despite being finite. Such collections are those that cannot in practice be given a sum for all their members. However, in its ordinary language sense at least, limitlessness implies uncountability—not just in practice but also in principle. As we saw earlier, a literally infinite set is both complete and limitless and so in principle countable, yet also in principle uncountable:

a contradiction. The transfinite system attempts to get around this contradiction, however, by redefining not only completeness but also countability and uncountability.

Ordinarily, for a collection to be countable means that *every* member in the collection can be counted to arrive at an exact sum for the collection. In contrast, the transfinite approach redefines 'countable' to mean not that every element in the collection can be *counted* to arrive at an exact sum, but merely that *any* element in the collection is an element that can be matched with a counting number [429]. $\mathbb{N}$, as the set having infinitely many counting numbers, is a 'countable' set of numbers in the sense that any given number in $\mathbb{N}$ can at least in principle be counted with another number; for example, we saw in § 2.3.9 an illustration of how the whole numbers can be used to count the naturals. Contrast that with certain other scales of numbers like $\mathbb{R}$, the set of reals, which is not 'countable' in this sense because not all of $\mathbb{R}$'s numbers can be counted with all the numbers of $\mathbb{N}$ [430] (for reasons we'll explore in §§ 13.8–13.9).

Set theorists specializing in transfinite mathematics believe redefining what the terms 'countable' and 'uncountable' mean, thereby distinguishing between sets that are countable (e.g., $\mathbb{N}$) and sets that are uncountable (e.g., $\mathbb{R}$), is enough to overcome the problem of how infinity can be referred to as "countable" by virtue of its completeness and "uncountable" by virtue of its limitlessness according to the ordinary language use of these quoted terms. That is, they believe we just need to accurately attribute the properties of countability and uncountability to the right infinite sets ($\mathbb{N}$ for countable and $\mathbb{R}$ for uncountable) according to narrower definitions of what 'countable' and 'uncountable' mean [431].

13.8 THE RELATIVE SIZES OF INFINITE SETS

That $\mathbb{N}$ is 'countable' and $\mathbb{R}$ is an 'uncountable' raises another problem: why can't we just use all the numbers of $\mathbb{N}$ to count all the numbers of $\mathbb{R}$ so that $\mathbb{R}$ is also countable? In answer, transfinite mathematics proposes that while any set *equal* in size to $\mathbb{N}$ or to a subset of $\mathbb{N}$ is 'countable', any set *greater than* $\mathbb{N}$ is 'uncountable'. $\mathbb{R}$ is greater than $\mathbb{N}$, so $\mathbb{R}$ is 'uncountable'.

Anyone hearing this for the first time should become automatically confused: How can there be a set "greater" than $\mathbb{N}$, which is claimed to be infinitely large and, for that matter, how can any set be "equal" in size to $\mathbb{N}$ if $\mathbb{N}$ is infinite—do notions of equality or difference in size even apply to infinitudes? How can two limitless sets be of *different sizes*? This certainly sounds like double talk because infinity is, in part, limitlessness, and it's hard to imagine what's bigger than that which is limitless.

Set theorists answer this objection, in part, by pointing out that infinite collections are not just limitless; they are also complete. The transfinite conception of completeness proposes that infinite sets can be compared in size by virtue of their completeness despite that they are also limitless in size. By abstracting infinite progressions behind braces or simply representing them with letters, transfinite mathematics treats infinite sets as if they are single, distinct units that can be compared with other such sets according to different interpretations of "size." This allows infinite sets like $\mathbb{N}$ and $\mathbb{R}$ to become comparable and calculable relative to one another.

The means of mathematically distinguishing different sizes of infinity therefore rests on a conception of infinite sets being technically 'complete' in a way that allows us to redefine what "size" means for infinite sets [432]. Set theorists working with transfinite set theory propose that not all the rules which apply for expressing sizes of finite sets apply for expressing the sizes of infinite sets. So yes, transfinite mathematics holds that infinities can be compared and contrasted in size. Some infinities are "equal" in size (for example, $\mathbb{N}$ is equal to $\mathbb{W}$) while some are "bigger" or "smaller" than others ($\mathbb{N}$ and $\mathbb{W}$ are smaller than $\mathbb{R}$).

Transfinite set theorists claim that the 'countability' or 'uncountability' of an infinite set is a consequence of the relative size differences between infinite sets. We can't use $\mathbb{N}$ to count all of $\mathbb{R}$ because while sets equal in size to $\mathbb{N}$ may be countable, $\mathbb{R}$ and sets equal to it are larger than the countable numbers of $\mathbb{N}$, thereby making $\mathbb{R}$ and like sets uncountable. Infinity is thereby portrayed as 'countable' in one sense ($\mathbb{N}$ and any set equal in size to it) and 'uncountable' in another (e.g., $\mathbb{R}$ and any set equal or larger in size to it).

13.9 SIZING UP INFINITIES

The transfinite system's distinction between 'countable' infinities that are somehow "smaller" than 'uncountable' infinities which are somehow "larger" hinges on certain methods for comparing the relative sizes of infinite sets. One method is correspondence and the other is *formal quantification*.

13.9.1 *Correspondence*

In the method of 'correspondence', the elements of two collections are matched up so that each element in the first collection is paired with at least one element of the second collection. Correspondence is a kind of mapping process.

As seen earlier in § 5.3.5, the correspondence of elements between sets can result in surjection, injection, or bijection. So long as the collection in question has all of its elements matched to at least one element in the other collection (through injection or bijection), then the collection has all its members 'corresponding' to at least some of the elements of the other collection.

In the transfinite system, the method of correspondence can be applied between sets that are infinite. For example, in principle, all the members of an infinite set of objects can be placed bijected with all the members of the infinite set of natural numbers, $\mathbb{N}$. Let's make S a literally infinite set of objects. In that case, S can be 'bijected' (i.e., placed into bijection) with $\mathbb{N}$ as shown in **Figure 13.1**.

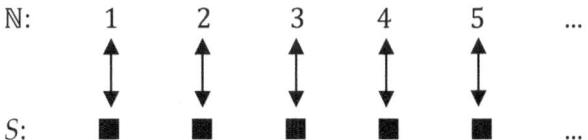

Figure 13.1: The bijection between $\mathbb{N}$, regarded as the set of natural numbers, and S, a set of objects.

13.9.2 *Formal Quantification*

Another method for comparing the relative sizes of infinite sets is formal quantification—not by use of numbers but rather by use of 'quantifiers' and *relational operators*.

As § 5.1 explained, there are two kinds of quantifiers: membership quantifiers and magnitude quantifiers. Transfinite set theory uses these two types of quantifiers to define the relative sizes of the number scales (assumed to be infinite sets) with the aid of 'relational operators' for each type of quantifier.

Consider these expressions made with membership quantifiers and operators for comparing sets:

- "No $\mathbb{I}$ are $\mathbb{R}$." ($\mathbb{I} \cap \mathbb{R} = \emptyset$)
- "Some $\mathbb{W}$ are $\mathbb{Z}$." $\neg(\mathbb{W} \cap \mathbb{Z} = \emptyset)$
- "All $\mathbb{Z}$ are $\mathbb{Q}$." ($\mathbb{Z} \subseteq \mathbb{Q}$)
- "All $\mathbb{N}$ are $\mathbb{Z}$ but not all $\mathbb{Z}$ are $\mathbb{N}$." ($\mathbb{N} \subset \mathbb{Z}$)

These examples show that membership quantifiers (no, some, all, etc.) each have their own set of operators ($\cap$, $=$, $\neg$, $\subseteq$, $\subset$, etc.) to designate membership relations [433].

Then again, we might use magnitude quantifiers and operators to form expressions such as the following:

- "$\mathbb{N}$ is equal to $\mathbb{W}$" or "$\mathbb{N}$ is the same size as $\mathbb{W}$." ($\mathbb{N} = \mathbb{W}$)
- "$\mathbb{W}$ is less than $\mathbb{R}$" or "$\mathbb{W}$ is smaller than $\mathbb{R}$." ($\mathbb{W} < \mathbb{R}$)
- "$\mathbb{R}$ is greater than $\mathbb{W}$" or "$\mathbb{R}$ is larger than $\mathbb{W}$." ($\mathbb{R} > \mathbb{W}$)

These examples show that magnitude quantifiers (equal, less than, greater than, etc.) also have their own associated operators ($=$, $<$, $>$, etc.).

We will see some examples of how transfinite set theory uses quantifiers and operators to define size differences between infinite sets established by the method of correspondence [434].

13.9.3 *On Comparing Infinite Sets by Relative Size*

A simple example of using correspondence for comparing two infinite sets is the use of such for comparing the set natural numbers ($\mathbb{N}$) with the set of whole numbers ($\mathbb{W}$). Since all naturals are wholes but not all wholes are naturals, we write $\mathbb{N} \subset \mathbb{W}$. However, while there are fewer numbers in $\mathbb{N}$ than in $\mathbb{W}$ since $\mathbb{W}$ also includes zero (0), we cannot say $\mathbb{N}$ is "less than" $\mathbb{W}$ since zero does not increase cardinality: $\mathbb{N} = \mathbb{W}$.

The situation is different, though, with respect to corresponding naturals to integers. True, all the natural numbers are integers while not all integers are natural numbers, so $\mathbb{N} \subset \mathbb{Z}$. And that denotes how these two sets relate to each other with correspondence because the integers include not only zero but negative numbers as well (see **Figure 13.2**). Nevertheless, the integers have more *non-zero* numbers than the naturals. Since $\mathbb{N} \subset \mathbb{Z}$ while there are more non-zero numbers in $\mathbb{Z}$ than $\mathbb{N}$, Bolzano would say the natural numbers are therefore *fewer than* the integers in what Moore called the *subset sense of size* [435]. It would thus follow that the naturals are *less than* the integers ($\mathbb{N} < \mathbb{Z}$). So, $\mathbb{N}$ is *smaller than* $\mathbb{Z}$, despite that both are infinite. Hence, while $\mathbb{N} \subset \mathbb{W}$ does *not* imply $\mathbb{N} < \mathbb{W}$, it would seem that $\mathbb{N} \subset \mathbb{Z}$ *does* imply $\mathbb{N} < \mathbb{Z}$, even though both sets are infinite. That would be Bolzano's point of view.

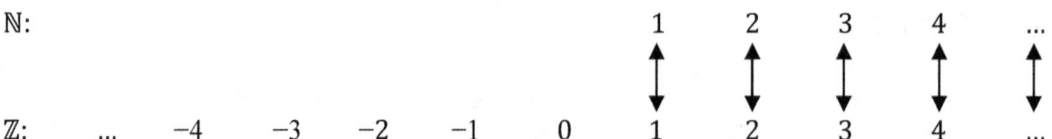

Figure 13.2: $\mathbb{N}$, the set of natural numbers, as a subset of $\mathbb{Z}$, the set of integers. The naturals are only part of the set of integers, which Bolzano would say by the above comparison implies there are fewer naturals than integers.

Cantor would counter that we can rearrange the sequence of integers, not leaving any out, to correspond the natural numbers to the integers in bijection as shown in **Figure 13.3**. So, there are *just as many* naturals as integers. Ergo, ℕ is *the same size* as ℤ. The two sets are quantitatively equal (ℕ = ℤ) in what Moore calls the *correlation sense of size* [436]—i.e., equal in cardinality, despite each being infinite.

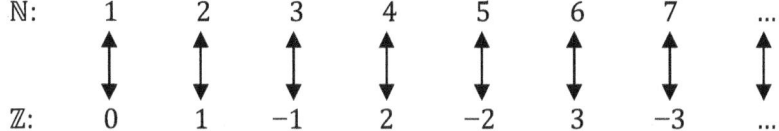

Figure 13.3: The bijection between ℕ, taken as the set of natural numbers, and ℤ, as the set of integers. Cantor would say this comparison implies there are just as many naturals as integers.

We now have two expressions: ℕ < ℤ and ℕ = ℤ, which are opposed to one another. We can say there are fewer naturals in ℕ than (non-zero) integers in ℤ by the 'subset sense' of size (so in that case we can say ℕ ⊂ ℤ implies ℕ < ℤ), but ℕ is also equal to ℤ in the 'correlation sense' of size (ℕ = ℤ).

This example shows three things.

First, the transfinite system can use both membership and magnitude quantifiers, and associated relational operators and functions, to express size in two different ways—the subset sense and the correlation sense.

Second, we can also conclude from this example that the use of membership quantifiers don't directly *express* sizes for sets. Instead, they may *imply* descriptions of size stated with the use of magnitude quantifiers. Given the (non-zero) numbers in ℤ, we can say ℕ ⊂ ℤ *implies* ℕ < ℤ. Insofar as a quantifier is a membership quantifier (e.g., ⊂), at best it only *indirectly* indicates size, which is more directly expressed in terms of magnitude quantifiers (e.g., <).

And as the example of comparing infinite sets shows, the relationship between the membership and magnitude quantifiers applies to descriptions of size between infinite sets just as it does to finite sets. Descriptions of size for infinite sets are also given indirectly with membership quantifiers and more directly with magnitude quantifiers. In fact, it is the magnitude quantifiers "equal to" (=) and "greater than" (>) or "less than" (<) *rather than* the membership quantifiers by which transfinite mathematics compares infinite sets like ℕ and ℤ.

Third, just using magnitude quantifiers, we can conclude ℕ < ℤ and ℕ = ℤ depending on how we wish to compare ℕ and ℤ—either with ℕ as a subset of ℤ or with a sequence matched between ℕ and ℤ.

However, despite that ℕ ⊂ ℤ logically *implies* ℕ < ℤ as Bolzano would have pointed out, transfinite mathematics states that ℕ < ℤ is not the correct way to express the relationship between ℕ and ℤ. The transfinite system overrules ℕ < ℤ based on the preference for bijection. That is, since a bijection between ℕ and ℤ is mathematically possible (**Figure 13.3**), that overrules any comparison that says otherwise (**Figure 13.2**). ℕ and ℤ can be placed into bijection; so that means they are to be held as the "same size" as one another in the correlation sense of size.

Hence, while in transfinite mathematics you will find it expressed that ℕ ⊂ ℤ, you will not find it expressed that ℕ < ℤ but only that ℕ = ℤ. That's because while Bolzano thought ℕ = ℤ is an illusion caused by a misleading use of bijection, with ℕ < ℤ being the true relationship, Cantor's transfinite system says the opposite: it is only an illusion that $\mathbb{N} \subset \mathbb{Z}$ implies $\mathbb{N} < \mathbb{Z}$ while bijection establishes the reality of $\mathbb{N} = \mathbb{Z}$. At least, that's according to Cantor's transfinite system.

13.9.4 *The Diagonal Argument*

Transfinite set theory defines the size of *countably infinite* sets (e.g., $\mathbb{N}$, $\mathbb{W}$, $\mathbb{Z}$, etc.) in terms of the correlation sense of size, contrasting the size of such sets with the *uncountably infinite* sets (e.g., $\mathbb{R}$) in the subset sense of size [437] [438]. While Cantor's transfinite set theory notes that there are *fewer* natural numbers in $\mathbb{N}$ than real numbers in $\mathbb{R}$ (by the subset sense of size), Bolzano would have pointed out the same can be said of natural numbers ($\mathbb{N}$) in comparison with the integers ($\mathbb{Z}$) as shown in **Figure 13.2**. Only if we change the pattern with which the numbers of $\mathbb{N}$ and those of $\mathbb{Z}$ are represented and let the ellipses trail off do $\mathbb{N}$ and $\mathbb{Z}$ *appear* to be the "same size" as shown in **Figure 13.3**. But Cantor objected that while $\mathbb{Z}$ can be placed into bijection with the countably infinite set $\mathbb{N}$, the same is not true for $\mathbb{R}$. Transfinite set theory holds that the set of reals ($\mathbb{R}$) is even "bigger" than either the set of natural numbers or the set of integers in the sense that the reals *cannot* be placed into bijection with either the naturals or integers in the way that the naturals can with the integers.

If we were to try corresponding the members of $\mathbb{N}$ with those of $\mathbb{R}$, so Cantor's claim goes, we would never find a one-to-one correspondence. There is no *bijection* of $\mathbb{N}$ with $\mathbb{R}$ but rather only an *injection* of $\mathbb{N}$ into $\mathbb{R}$. So, $\mathbb{N}$ is not only smaller than $\mathbb{R}$ in the subset sense of size (since, at best, $\mathbb{N} \subset \mathbb{R}$ may be taken to imply $\mathbb{N} < \mathbb{R}$) but $\mathbb{N}$ is also smaller than $\mathbb{R}$ in the correlation sense of size (since $\mathbb{N} < \mathbb{R}$ implies $\mathbb{N} \neq \mathbb{R}$).

As $\mathbb{N}$, and any set such as $\mathbb{W}$ and $\mathbb{Z}$ equal to $\mathbb{N}$, are 'countably infinite' by virtue of mutual bijection, any set larger than these sets by virtue of lacking bijection with any of them is 'uncountably infinite'—the prime example of that is $\mathbb{R}$.

One of Cantor's proofs for the claim that infinities come in different sizes (like $\mathbb{N} < \mathbb{R}$) is called the *diagonal argument* or 'diagonalization argument' [439]. The diagonal argument begins by stating that we should assume the list of numbers comprising $\mathbb{N}$ is 'complete' and 'limitless' according to the transfinite definitions provided earlier. We should also assume that $\mathbb{R}$ is equally complete and limitless in this sense.

If both $\mathbb{N}$ and $\mathbb{R}$ are literally infinite, then they are both complete sets. And if that is so, we should be able to form a bijection between $\mathbb{N}$ and $\mathbb{R}$. However, according to Cantor's system [440], this is not possible because after we "use up" all the natural numbers in $\mathbb{N}$, we still have numbers in $\mathbb{R}$ left over; so not all unique real numbers that one can identify in $\mathbb{R}$ will have a matching natural number in $\mathbb{N}$.

To see how this is so in the view of transfinite mathematics, start by composing a column of all the natural numbers. Of course, you can't write them all out, but you compose an initial list of numbers and use an ellipsis to imply the continuation of the numbers.

Next, take the scale of real numbers ($\mathbb{R}$), which includes all the rational and irrational numbers, and select any arbitrary list of numbers from the real number scale. The most often used example is to select real numbers between 0 and 1, such as 0.010101…. We'll use the reals between 0 and 1 as our example. Then, write the selection of real numbers out vertically in a second column, matching each real number to one and only one natural number, as shown in **Figure 13.4**.

After that, underscore or boldface the first digit of the first real number, the second digit of the second real number, the third digit of the third real number, and so forth (also as shown in **Figure 13.4**).

Now take the diagonal string of digits and write it out horizontally as a new real number (0.010001…), which we will label p. Next, use the numbers in p to create a new real number, q, by writing a '1' in place of any 0 after the decimal in p and a '0' in place of any '1' after the decimal in p (see **Figure 13.4**).

$\mathbb{N}$		$\mathbb{R}$ $(0-1)$
1	↔	0.**0**00000...
2	↔	0.1**1**1111...
3	↔	0.01**0**101...
4	↔	0.101**0**10...
5	↔	0.1101**0**1...
6	↔	0.00110**1**...
⋮	↔	⋮ ⋱

$$p = 0.010001...$$

$$q = 0.101110...$$

Figure 13.4: The diagonal argument. In the transfinite system, $\mathbb{R}$ must be "bigger" than $\mathbb{N}$ because the numbers of $\mathbb{N}$ are presumed to be all "used up" when matched against a simple segment of $\mathbb{R}$ that leaves out many real numbers that we could generate between 0 and 1, not to mention the rest of the scale of $\mathbb{R}$. For example, the numbers in boldface (establishing a diagonal string of digits) are used to make p, which is then used to generate q, a new real number that cannot appear in any list of values between 0 and 1 according to the sequence we made for the $\mathbb{R}$ segment.

Notice the resulting real number, q, is not in the list of reals we have already paired with $\mathbb{N}$. According to Cantor, the proof also indicates that q would *nowhere and never* appear in the sequence of reals we listed for the segment of $\mathbb{R}$ between 0 and 1, no matter how far it could be made to extend where the ellipsis leaves off [441].

Transfinite mathematics has us begin with the assumption that the selection of reals between 0 and 1 is a complete set in itself—no more reals between 0 and 1 is possible—even though the column made for this segment of $\mathbb{R}$ is also presumed to be limitless. If this is so, then this infinite subset, as a part of $\mathbb{R}$, must not be missing any numbers between 0 and 1.

But, says the diagonal argument, we just formed a new real number, q, that nowhere appears in the column of reals we listed for our segment of $\mathbb{R}$. **Figure 13.5** illustrates the point of the diagonal argument.

$\mathbb{R}$ $(0-1)$

$$\overline{0.101110... = q}$$

Figure 13.5: The new real number, q, written horizontally and falling straight down in the direction of the arrow, through the diagonal string of digits (equal to p from Figure 13.4), would produce a conflict at each row where a digit of q overlaps with a digit of the diagonal string. If the depicted sequence of digits for p and q each repeat, there would continue to be mismatches at each subsequent row as well, demonstrating that q nowhere can be found in the list we established for $\mathbb{R}$ as shown in Figure 13.4.

As **Figure 13.5** shows, in **Figure 13.4** you won't find q in the first row, nor in the second row, nor the third row, etc. that we made for the segment of $\mathbb{R}$. Not only that, but q can also *never* appear in the column of reals according to the pattern of sequencing we defined for the segment of $\mathbb{R}$.

Notice that q is a real number between 0 and 1, which appears nowhere in our original listing of real numbers (from **Figure 13.4**). This means that our original sequence of real numbers between 0 and 1 is *not* complete as we had initially assumed. However, the progression of numbers in $\mathbb{N}$ is missing no natural number. So, $\mathbb{N}$ is the complete set of all the natural numbers, each of which is matched to one real number, but there are yet more real numbers not matched to a natural number.

Science educator Michael Stevens, in presenting the transfinite system, describes the natural numbers as "used up" in comparison with the real numbers, the list for which was incomplete by comparison [442]. The list of natural numbers in relation to a list of real numbers are both regarded as limitless, but somehow the naturals can be used up, indicating there are more reals than naturals [443].

In other words, even though we "used up" all the numbers for $\mathbb{N}$ by matching them with our original list of reals between 0 and 1, there are still more reals we could have generated between 0 and 1 for $\mathbb{R}$—like the number q that was created from a diagonally produced real number (p); such missing reals would not match up one-for-one with the numbers in $\mathbb{N}$ as the complete set of all naturals [444].

According to transfinite mathematics, our inability to completely match all of the reals we sequenced for $\mathbb{R}$ with all the numbers of $\mathbb{N}$ means $\mathbb{R}$ cannot be placed into a bijection with $\mathbb{N}$ because there will always be numbers in $\mathbb{R}$ left over. So, as a set, $\mathbb{R}$ must be "bigger" than $\mathbb{N}$ in the correlation sense of size (even though both sets are limitless). Infinite sets must therefore come in different sizes.

The diagonal argument concludes that $\mathbb{N}$, composed of counting numbers, is the "smallest" infinite set and is itself 'countably infinite' in the sense that any number in $\mathbb{N}$ can be used for counting despite that there is no last natural number in $\mathbb{N}$ that sums all the counting numbers. $\mathbb{R}$, on the other hand, is 'uncountably infinite' because it cannot be completely counted even with the infinite set of $\mathbb{N}$.

13.10 ENUMERABLE AND INNUMERABLE INFINITIES

The use of correspondence to determine the relative size of a set *enumerates* the set. To 'enumerate' is to assign numbers to the members of a collection such that each member is assigned a particular number. *Enumeration* is the process of enumerating. You might think that enumerating is the same as counting, but that is not so; rather, counting is an example of enumeration and there are other methods of enumeration.

To count is to *successively* assign a number to each object in a collection according to each number's ordinality in a scale of numbers. Suppose, however, that we wish to enumerate is a finite set, S, that has too many members to count in actual practice. If we could, we would use the natural numbers of $\mathbb{N}$ to enumerate all the members of S by counting them out. Since the task of counting all the members of S is too great to accomplish in reality, we need another method of enumeration.

Rather than attempting to count the members of such large collections in order to establish their sizes relative to $\mathbb{N}$, transfinite set theory proposes the method of 'correspondence' to enumerate S. Unlike counting, correspondence does not necessarily list elements in a collection successively—by listing one subset of elements after another. Using correspondence for enumeration entails that we don't have to actually count the elements of set S in order to say that S is *enumerable* (able to be enumerated). A collection can be enumerable without being countable or enumerated without being counted. The members of $\mathbb{N}$, which are all the natural numbers, can be placed into correspondence with the members of S. From transfinite set theory, $\mathbb{N}$ is a complete set of natural (counting) numbers in which all of the set's numbers already exist, ready for counting the members of other sets. Since all the numbers of $\mathbb{N}$ are already there at once for us to use in determining the relative size of another set, the numbers of $\mathbb{N}$ can be mapped one for one with the members of S to 'enumerate' the members of S.

Suppose that in correspondence S has its members matched one to one with an initial segment of natural numbers, $\mathbb{N}$. We can say the elements of S are 'enumerable' because they can all be matched to natural numbers. In other words, if after correspondence is carried out every member in collection S is matched to one and only one member in an initial segment of $\mathbb{N}$ with no members of S left over, then the resulting injection of S-members to numbers of $\mathbb{N}$ enumerates all the members of S which are consequently shown to be enumerable.

It is easy to see how any finite collection can be enumerated using this method. If the collection is both finite and complete in the ordinary sense, then all its elements can be placed into bijection with a segment of natural numbers equal in size. Even if collection S is finite but incomplete, like an open series, it will still have extrema. The least element of S will match the least number of the $\mathbb{N}$ segment, and the greatest element of S will match the greatest number of the $\mathbb{N}$ segment. All the elements between the extrema of S will match up with natural numbers in the $\mathbb{N}$ segment.

As a caveat, in order for the enumeration of a finite collection to be 'complete' in the ordinary language sense of the term, the least and greatest elements cannot be merely lower and upper bounds like infima and suprema per se because these do not necessarily need to be a part of the collection to be enumerated—they are just the boundary conditions by which the collection is measured. Instead, to completely enumerate a finite collection, at least one extremum must be a minimum and at least one extremum in the same collection must be a maximum. Such extrema can be part of the bijection. At any point in time, the elements of a finite collection with these kinds of extrema can be, at least in principle, completely enumerated when correspondence establishes a bijection with an initial segment of $\mathbb{N}$.

In actual practice, correspondence of members between sets can be, and often is, established over a succession of steps, but it need not be. In principle, correspondence can be established in a single step for a finite number of elements in a pair of collections not sharing the same elements. As mentioned earlier (§ 4.4.4), a simple example of correspondence is matching all the 'digits' (fingers, including the thumb) of one hand to all the digits on the other hand. With a single clap of our hands, we can accomplish this bijection in one step. So too it is possible, in principle if not in practice, to biject in a single step all the elements of any finite set, S, no matter how immense, with the elements of another finite set of equal size—such as a finite and equal segment of $\mathbb{N}$.

Through a one-step bijection with a segment of $\mathbb{N}$, a set such as S can be shown to be enumerable. If every member of a collection can be bijected with a segment of $\mathbb{N}$, the bijected collection is able, at least in principle, to have all its members numbered; the collection is *enumerable* via correspondence, even if not actually *enumerated* by counting.

Now suppose S is infinite. Can we enumerate S? Maybe not. Infinite collections are limitless and so have *no last number* with which to enumerate. Ergo, they cannot be enumerated; they are *innumerable*. Being limitless, an infinite collection has no total number of elements, no ability to be enumerated.

However, this is only half the story. Literal infinity is not just limitlessness but also a state of completeness. For there to be an infinite collection is for there to be a complete collection in the ordinary language sense of the word 'complete'. A complete collection is a collection with a total number of elements that represents the size of the collection. A literally infinite collection, as a complete collection, must therefore have a total number of elements and so the ability to be enumerated. Because an infinite collection is enumerable by virtue of completeness, it must have a cardinality that constitutes the size of the collection.

So how can an infinite collection have a determinate size due to completeness while also having no last member and therefore no determinate size to capture? Transfinite set theory seeks to solve this problem by redefining what 'complete' means (having supremum such as a limit ordinal) and what cardinality means (ω and $\aleph$) for infinite collections, thereby redefining what "size" means for infinite collections and, consequently, redefining what it means for an infinite collection to be 'enumerable' in one sense while 'innumerable' in another.

Transfinite set theory proposes that because bijection can be established in a single step, as with matching the fingers of one hand to those of the other hand in a single clap, we can establish the bijection of two infinite sets in one step as well. We don't actually have to count the members of S in order to enumerate S—the bijection enumerates the infinite extent of S in one step. $\mathbb{N}$ can be used to enumerate S if there are no more members of S than there are of $\mathbb{N}$. For example, an instance of establishing a bijection between all the members of S with all the numbers in $\mathbb{N}$ through correspondence is an instance of enumerating S with the numbers of $\mathbb{N}$, even though both sets are infinite.

According to transfinite mathematicians, "An infinite set that is enumerable is said to be *enumerably infinite* or *denumerable*" [445]. In transfinite set theory and mathematics, the "infinite set of natural numbers ($\mathbb{N}$) is considered a denumerable set…" [446]. In the case in which $\mathbb{N}$ and S are in bijection, S would like $\mathbb{N}$ also be 'enumerably infinite' or 'denumerable'.

Moreover, since S is not only enumerable (or denumerable) but also equal to $\mathbb{N}$, then S and $\mathbb{N}$ are, in the jargon of transfinite mathematics, *equinumerous* (equal in number). Even though both sets have no limit by virtue of their infinitude, they are still said to be equinumerous.

Assuming the set of integers, $\mathbb{Z}$, is set S, then $\mathbb{Z}$ is equinumerous with $\mathbb{N}$ because $\mathbb{Z}$ can be placed into bijection with $\mathbb{N}$, showing $\mathbb{Z}$ to be enumerably infinite (or denumerable). On the other hand, if $\mathbb{N}$ can be shown to somehow run out of numbers to match with some set, S, then $\mathbb{N}$ would not be the same size as S, nor would $\mathbb{Z}$ be the same size as S since $\mathbb{N}$ and $\mathbb{Z}$ can be in bijection. Instead, $\mathbb{N}$ would only be 'injected' with S as there would not be a full one-to-one correspondence between the natural numbers of $\mathbb{N}$ and the members of S. In that case, S must be *innumerably infinite* or *non-denumerable*. In this context, 'innumerable' (or 'non-denumerable') means *non-equinumerous* (not equal in number) with $\mathbb{N}$ nor any of $\mathbb{N}$'s subsets.

Assuming $\mathbb{R}$ is an infinite S that is "greater than" $\mathbb{N}$, we can consider $\mathbb{R}$ to be an example of S that is 'innumerably infinite' or 'non-denumerable'. Moreover, if $\mathbb{N}$ is enumerably infinite, then $\mathbb{N}$ is countable in the sense that any number in $\mathbb{N}$ can be used for counting while $\mathbb{R}$ if innumerably infinite is uncountable in the sense that not all the numbers of $\mathbb{R}$ can be used for counting. $\mathbb{N}$ would thus be countable/enumerable while $\mathbb{R}$ is not because the numbers of $\mathbb{N}$ cannot all be placed into bijection (that is, into one-to-one correspondence) with all the numbers of $\mathbb{R}$.

In short, the transfinite system proposes that an infinite set like $\mathbb{Z}$ is enumerable, or 'denumerable', in the sense that it can be placed into bijection with $\mathbb{N}$ while $\mathbb{R}$, on the other hand, is innumerable, or 'non-denumerable', in the sense that $\mathbb{R}$ cannot be bijected with $\mathbb{N}$, and therefore not enumerated by $\mathbb{N}$.

13.11 REDEFINING INFINITY BY ORDINALITY AND CARDINALITY

A set with a supremum greater than the successor to any element in the set defines the transfinite system's conception of the natural numbers comprising $\mathbb{N}$. The sequence of natural numbers in $\mathbb{N}$ has such a 'supremum' that is the first transfinite ordinal, ω, which is not itself a natural number.

Although $\mathbb{N}$ is the set of natural numbers and all the natural numbers are succeeded by ω, which is not itself a natural number, it is also the case that $\mathbb{N} \triangleq \omega$ because, as an ordinal, ω is equal to the value of all the numbers below it—which are all the natural numbers. In transfinite mathematics, the relation of ω to the natural numbers is often visualized with use of 'matchstick' lines—one line per natural number, with each line a fraction smaller and closer than the last until the lines are infinitely small and close, succeeded only by a new line to represent ω (see **Figure 13.6**).

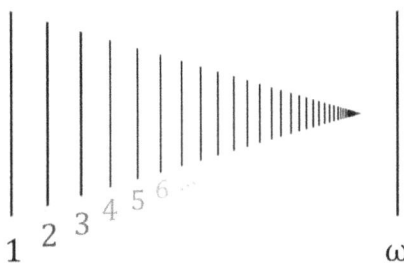

Figure 13.6: A matchstick visualization of the infinite (∞) sequence of all the natural numbers, which is succeeded by the transfinite ordinal ω.

To see what this means, we need to first contrast how infinity works in transfinite mathematics according to its representation as a transfinite ordinal (ω) and transfinite cardinal ($\aleph$) with how infinity (∞) works in the operations of general mathematics.

In general mathematics, adding a finite number (a) and infinity (b) is commutative: ($a + b = b + a$). So, $1 + \infty$ and $\infty + 1$ provide the same result: $1 + \infty = \infty$ and $\infty + 1 = \infty$. The reason the same result occurs either way is because these equations treat ∞ as a figurative infinity—an indefinite *process* that Cantor would have called a 'variable finite'. In contrast, Cantor's transfinite mathematics intends to treat infinity as a 'complete' *set* of 'limitlessly' many members.

Where transfinite mathematics treats an infinite set as *ordered* into a *sequence* of members, the infinite set (sequence) is represented by the transfinite ordinal, ω. According to Cantor's transfinite mathematics, the position of infinity (ω) in the mathematical expression is not commutative with a single finite value as it is above where $1 + \infty$ produces the same result as $\infty + 1$. Instead, $1 + \omega$ is different from $\omega + 1$.

Rather, the result is as follows: $1 + \omega = \omega$, while on the other hand, $\omega + 1 = (\omega + 1)$. Where one must keep in mind that $\omega + 1$ is "an entirely different number than ω" [447].

Cantor explains the difference, noting that "...everything depends upon the *position* of the finite vis-à-vis the infinite. If the former comes first, then it merges with the infinite and disappears in it; if, however, it *contents* itself and takes place behind the infinite, then it is preserved and joins with the former to become a new, because modified, infinite" [448]. (It is different for transfinite cardinals, where order does not matter: $\aleph + 1 = \aleph$ sums exactly the same as $1 + \aleph = \aleph$.)

However, even if $\omega + 1$ is "an entirely different number than ω," that does not mean that $\omega + 1$ is larger than ω in the correlation sense of size. Take, for instance, the following sequence:

$$\omega + 1, \omega + 2, \omega + 3, \dots$$

We can use a line to represent each of these numbers as we did for the natural numbers in **Figure 13.6**, and then add this infinite sequence to the first as shown in **Figure 13.7** so that one infinite sequence is succeeded by the other. Since we can match the lines from each sequence one to one, we know the two sequences are in bijection with one another and are therefore the same size. Two literally infinite sequences, both the same size: ω.

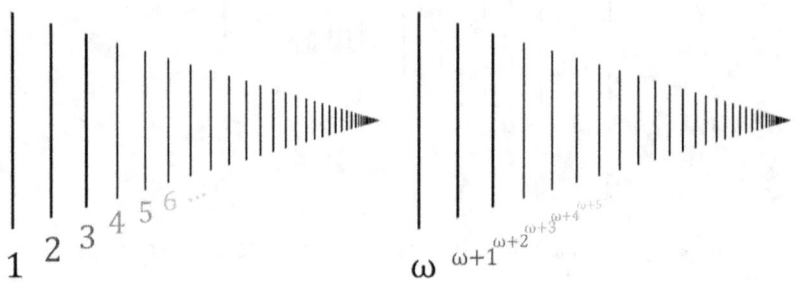

Figure 13.7: A matchstick visualization of the infinite sequence of natural numbers (= ω) continued with the infinite ω sequence, with the members of each sequence able to be matched one to one.

Each of the numbers in the ordinal progression $\omega + 1$, $\omega + 2$, etc. up to $\omega + \omega$ are all greater than ω in the subset sense of size, but in the correlation sense of size the sequence of numbers from $\omega + 1$ up to $\omega + \omega$ (i.e., $\omega 2$) can still be placed into bijection with the sequence of natural numbers:

$$
\begin{array}{ccccc}
1, & 2, & 3, & \dots, & \omega \\
\updownarrow & \updownarrow & \updownarrow & \updownarrow & \updownarrow \\
\omega + 1, & \omega + 2, & \omega + 3, & \dots, & \omega 2
\end{array}
$$

So, in that sense, a set of $\omega 2$ elements is no larger than a set of ω elements, and so $\omega 2$ is still equal to the smallest infinity, that of $\mathbb{N}$ [449].

Yet higher sequences of transfinite ordinals share the same result. After ω and the $\omega + 1$ sequence comes $\omega 2$, which is succeeded by $\omega 2 + 1$, $\omega 2 + 2$, $\omega 2 + 3$, and so on. Next comes $\omega 3$, then $\omega 4$, etc. Now the set of ordinals formed in this way leads to an ordinal multiplied by itself: $\omega \cdot \omega$, which is the same as

ω^2. Next, there will be ω^3, then ω^4, and so on up to ω^ω, then on to indefinitely higher tetrations of ω. Nevertheless, assuming transfinite set theory, all of these infinities can be placed into bijection with the sequence of numbers under ω, which is to say the natural numbers of $\mathbb{N}$. So, we cannot reach a "bigger" infinity than $\mathbb{N}$ in the correlation sense of size just by adding more of ω onto ω.

Calculating larger infinities than ω will require a new notation for transfinite numbers, most often represented with the aleph. The aleph ($\aleph$) just by itself just symbolizes that $\mathbb{N}$ is a 'complete' set of infinite size, as is any set with the same quantity of members as $\mathbb{N}$. To distinguish an infinite set of greater size than $\mathbb{N}$, such as $\mathbb{R}$, Cantor proposed a different cardinality for $\mathbb{R}$ even though like $\mathbb{N}$ it too is infinite. To better represent size differences between these infinite sets, Cantor proposed transfinite cardinals, symbolized by the aleph ($\aleph$) followed by subscript integers, to designate the apparent size, or power, of infinite sets.

For example, $\aleph$ is the cardinality of the *least infinite* set; more precisely, such is represented as $\aleph_0$ [450]. $\aleph$ or $\aleph_0$ represents a 'countably infinite' set, such as $\mathbb{N}$. However, we can also compare various sizes of infinite sets using the method of correspondence and express those comparisons with relational operators. Assuming the correlation sense of size, we know the infinite set of natural numbers ($\mathbb{N}$) is equal in size to other infinite sets (such as $\mathbb{W}$, $\mathbb{Z}$, and $\mathbb{Q}$), all of which are equal in size to each other—

$$\mathbb{N} = \mathbb{W} = \mathbb{Z} = \mathbb{Q}$$

—and so each of these sets has the cardinality of $\aleph_0$.

The next largest infinity is $\mathbb{R}$, an 'uncountable infinite' represented by aleph-one ($\aleph_1$).

Using the method of correspondence, we can also conclude from Cantor's diagonal argument that because $\mathbb{N} < \mathbb{R}$, it is also true that all of the other sets equal to $\mathbb{N}$ are likewise smaller than the set of real numbers:

$$(\mathbb{N} = \mathbb{W} = \mathbb{Z} = \mathbb{Q}) < \mathbb{R}.$$

We can then put magnitude operators together with notation for transfinite numbers to further express the size differences of the infinite sets with the transfinite cardinals. Since $\mathbb{N}$ and the sets equal to it are of size $\aleph_0$ and $\mathbb{R}$ is of size $\aleph_1$, then—

$$(\mathbb{N} < \mathbb{R}) = (\aleph_0 < \aleph_1).$$

After aleph-zero and aleph-one is aleph-two, $\aleph_2$, which represents the next largest infinity after aleph-one. $\aleph_2$ is equal to the 'power set' of any set with $\aleph_1$-many members. A power set is the number of all subsets in a set, such as every number combination possible using the set of natural numbers. So, $\aleph_2$ is equal to the set of all number combinations in $\aleph_1$.

Similarly, aleph-three ($\aleph_3$) is the power set of $\aleph_2$, and so on. We can keep proposing ever-larger infinite sets: $\aleph_4$, $\aleph_5$, $\aleph_6$, $\aleph_7$, $\aleph_8$, $\aleph_9$, ... And the series can keep going on, proceeding through ever-higher ω subscripts: $\aleph_0$, $\aleph_1$, $\aleph_2$, ..., $\aleph_{\omega, ...}$, $\aleph_{\omega^\omega}$, ... Each lower aleph cardinal is the size of an infinite set, the numbers of which can only be injected to, and not bijected with, an infinite set of elements denoted by the next higher aleph cardinal [451].

Moreover, each aleph cardinal represents an infinite set, the elements of which are in any order, while each omega (ω) ordinal represents the same infinite set but where the elements are arranged according to an established order in a completed series. For example, $\aleph_0$ is equal to all the natural numbers in $\mathbb{N}$ (or the whole numbers in $\mathbb{W}$ if we include zero) and it doesn't matter what order the numbers fall into; but the transfinite ordinal ω is equal to $\mathbb{N}$ or $\mathbb{W}$ as the elements fall into sequence: $\{0, 1, 2, 3, ...\}$. Basically, the elements of $\aleph_0$ and ω are the same, it's just a matter of whether we want to consider the order of the elements or not—whether we want to consider the numbers in sequence.

There is another parallel between $\aleph$ and ω: just as there are higher alephs as given in the sequence $\aleph_0, \aleph_1, \aleph_2, ...$, there are also further omegas. As the first $\aleph$ is $\aleph_0$, likewise we can label the first ω as ω_0. Hence, the sequence of omegas: $\omega_0, \omega_1, \omega_2, ...$. Each $\aleph$ also corresponds to the order of an ω. Hence:

$$\aleph_0 = \omega_0$$
$$\aleph_1 = \omega_1$$
$$\aleph_2 = \omega_2$$
$$\aleph_3 = \omega_3$$
$$\vdots$$

The elements of ω_1 are those of $\aleph_1$ arranged in order, the elements of ω_2 are those of $\aleph_2$ arranged in order, and so forth [452]. There is no highest transfinite number—they just keep going up, indefinitely. We can make a transfinite number as large as we wish.

Cantor also proposed a kind of higher transfinite arithmetic, but one which works a bit differently than ordinary arithmetic. As Moore explained, to add and multiply 'infinite' cardinals together is for the larger value to replace the smaller because the "smaller" infinite set becomes included in the "larger" infinite set [453]. Hence, $\aleph_3 + \aleph_4 = \aleph_4$ and $\aleph_3 \times \aleph_4 = \aleph_4$. Despite that the cardinals do not add or multiply together like finite numbers, the transfinite system still proposes a hierarchy of increasingly larger cardinal numbers that correspond to the transfinite ordinals as indicated above.

Consequently, the theoretical definition for 'infinity' cited in § 7.2, § 9.6.4, and above in § 13.2.3 is still appropriate [454]:

- infinity: (transfinite) the ordinality of a sequence of elements, or cardinality of a set of elements, greater than that of any natural number in $\mathbb{N}$.

This definition for 'infinity' covers any infinite sequence no matter its ordinality relative to other infinite sequences ($\omega_0, \omega_1, \omega_2, \omega_3, ...$) and any infinite set no matter its cardinality relative to other infinite sets ($\aleph_0, \aleph_1, \aleph_2, \aleph_3, ...$). The definition also identifies $\mathbb{N}$, which equals ω (or ω_0) and $\aleph$ (or, more precisely, $\aleph_0$), as the least of the infinite sets. Hence the theoretical definition for 'infinity' captures well how 'infinity' operates according to the assumptions of the transfinite system.

13.12 CLAIMS OF TRANSFINITE SUCCESS

So far, we've seen how infinity in its literal sense, when claimed to be a condition possessed by a particular collection, implies that collection to be complete and yet to have limitlessly many members. But the concepts of completeness and limitlessness, when defined precisely in natural language, imply contradictions with one another as summarized in **Figure 12.0**. The result is that the very definition of literal infinity is an oxymoron—a contradiction in terms—because a collection cannot be both complete and limitless at the same time, as Aristotle rightfully pointed out.

We then examined how, in order to overcome this contradiction and make literal infinity a mathematically coherent concept, the term 'infinity' or 'infinite' must be redefined in technical terms that do not contradict, but also do not assume, literal completeness and literal limitlessness as defined in ordinary, natural language. In transfinite set theory, completeness entails having an order of members below an upper bound while limitlessness is to have no upper bound with respect to successors greater than any element that can be included in a set. Completeness and limitlessness, as so redefined, are not contradictory because each refers to a different kind of "bound" or limit—completeness refers to the bound of a set as a whole, limitlessness to the lack of bound for the sequencing of members *in* the set. Hence, infinity can be technically redefined in such a way that a technical notion of completeness does not contradict a technical notion of limitlessness.

Moreover, infinity can even be further redefined in transfinite mathematics. For example, infinity is sometimes defined in transfinite mathematics as the ordinality or cardinality of a set of elements greater than that of any natural number in $\mathbb{N}$ [455]. When defined in such technical terms, infinity can be rendered operational in transfinite mathematics without worries of causing mathematical incoherence.

To this effect, Cantor and subsequent mathematicians proposed a number of abstract tools—

- letters like $\mathbb{N}$, $\mathbb{W}$, $\mathbb{Z}$, $\mathbb{R}$, etc. for sets of numbers;

- operators like $<$, $>$, $\subseteq$, $\subset$, etc. for use with infinite sets;

- ordinals (ω_0, ω_1, ω_2, ω_3, etc.) and cardinals ($\aleph_0$, $\aleph_1$, $\aleph_2$, $\aleph_3$, etc.) for infinite numbers

—allowing mathematicians to treat infinite sets *as if* they are finite, and further enable mathematicians to perform operations such as adding and multiplying transfinite numbers. Some mathematicians have even called these abstract tools and their rules of operation as "Cantor's finitism" (though Cantor would not have appreciated that label for his work) [456].

With the success of Cantor's system in rendering technically 'infinite' sets mathematically calculable (as finitudes), subsequent set theorists and transfinite mathematicians believe that infinity has been made into an intellectually rigorous notion, and thereby proven to be a logically coherent concept [457] [458]. Nevertheless, despite the mathematical consistency of modern versions of Cantor's work, I argue that transfinite set theory is not a successful solution for demonstrating infinity to be a logically coherent notion. Rather, the transfinite system provides only the *illusion of logical coherence* for infinity.

CHAPTER 13 IN REVIEW

❖ To resolve the contradictions inherent in the conception of literal infinity, mathematicians must resort to redefining infinity. Cantor redefined literal (or "actual") infinity in technical terms and proposed a formal syntax (mathematical symbols, operators, notation, functions, etc.) for a 'transfinite' version of literal infinity.

❖ Cantor's transfinite system redefines what it means for an infinite set to be complete, limitless, countable or enumerable, etc.

❖ In addition, Cantor's system states some infinite sets, such $\mathbb{R}$, is "larger" than other infinite sets, such as the set of naturals: $\mathbb{N} < \mathbb{R}$. So some infinities are larger than others.

❖ In saying some infinities are larger than others, Cantor also proposed some infinite progressions can follow "after" others. For example, the infinite ordinals ω, ω_1, ω_2, ω_3, etc. follow *after* the infinite progression of naturals $\{1, 2, 3, ...\}$.

❖ While most mathematicians believe Cantor's transfinite mathematics successfully "tames" infinity, I argue otherwise.

14: INFINITY UNTAMED

Cantor did not tame infinity. His transfinite system does not make infinity mathematically and logically coherent. It is true the transfinite system is *mathematically* coherent with respect to its formalism—there are no internal inconsistencies in its technical definitions for infinity as the transfinite, nor in its symbolism and use of mathematical syntax, nor in its operational rules for calculating the relative orderings and sizes of transfinite sets. Even so, mathematical coherence and logical coherence are two different things. In this chapter, I argue that, despite its mathematical coherence, the transfinite system is not *logically* coherent.

The transfinite system mistakes the 'transfinite' of its mathematical operations as expressions of literal infinity. Despite this misidentification, the transfinite system is still operationally consistent in terms of its mathematics, but because of the misidentification of the transfinite with literal infinity, the transfinite system offers erroneous claims as to the literal infinitude of 'transfinite sets'. The supposed transfinite sets turn out to be finite, indefinite series or collections with respect to actual mathematical operation. Moreover, I argue were it true that the transfinite is literal infinity, that would entail the transfinite still implies the same logical self-contradictions already implied from the meaning of literal infinity, as detailed in Chapters 10–12. The formalism of the transfinite system fails to either address or dissolve these contradictions. Reports that Cantor's transfinite system has tamed infinity are therefore mistaken.

14.1 TROUBLES WITH TECHNICAL REDEFINITIONS

Cantor's transfinite system refers to 'infinity' as 'the transfinite', and the condition of being 'infinite' as the condition of being 'transfinite'. The transfinite is further interpreted as the mathematical expression of literal infinity—the transfinite *just is* literal infinity, at least according to Cantor and his followers. This is evident in a letter Cantor sent to Hilbert wherein Cantor stated that "the 'transfinite' coincides with what has since antiquity been called the 'actual infinite', and is to be considered as [something determined]" [459]. By "something determined" Cantor means a finished totality of elements existing all together at once rather than a growing series of elements that remains finite no matter how big it gets. Cantor made clear that his conception of infinity has since antiquity been called the 'actual infinite', which is what I refer to as literal infinity. Cantor's notion of the transfinite is therefore intended to be the same as literal infinity.

Regardless of what we call it—literal infinity, the actual infinite, or the transfinite—the meaning is the same: a complete collection with a limitless quantity of elements.

If we are to consider a transfinite collection to be a literally infinite or actually infinite collection, then a transfinite collection must be a collection that is literally complete: a whole, entire, finished, and full totality. In fact, according to Cantor, a 'transfinite' or 'actually infinite' collection is a "finished" set in which all the elements "exist together" as a "compounded thing for itself;" that is, as a "totality" [460]. This is reiterated by set theorists today. According to Hrbáček and Jech, "Mathematicians ordinarily consider infinite collections, such as the set of natural numbers or the set of real numbers as finished, completed, totalities" [461].

Moreover, for a transfinite collection to be a literally infinite or actually infinite collection, the transfinite collection must also have a literally limitless quantity of members—no last element, no maximum as a limit. This is, in fact, what the transfinite system says of any infinite progression [462]. The transfinite is greater than any natural or real number.

It is clear then, that mathematicians think of a transfinite collection as what Aristotle would have called an actually infinite collection and what I prefer to call a literally infinite collection—a collection complete and limitless in quantity. However, I argue it is wrong to identify the transfinite of Cantor's set-theoretic and mathematical system with literal infinity, for the 'transfinite' is not nearly as literally infinite as it is purported to be. And even if Cantor's 'transfinite' were literal infinity, his expression of the transfinite is not framed to dissolve the logical contradictions that plague literal infinity's definition.

14.1.1 *Critique of the Transfinite Definition for Completeness*

The transfinite system redefines in technical terms what it means for infinity to be complete and limitless in quantity. Let's take a closer look at how the transfinite system technically defines the completeness side of infinity.

As mentioned in Chapter 3, there are various technical definitions for 'complete' in mathematics. For example, the transfinite system frames completeness based on Cauchy completeness and Dedekind completeness [463]. However, I believe the articulation of the technical definition for 'complete' as given in § 13.2.1 captures best how the transfinite system uses the term: "P is 'complete' if P is a set and every non-empty subset that is a member of P is bounded from above by a supremum" [464].

For the reasons already outlined in § 13.2.1, this technical definition of 'complete' is not, at least on its surface, inconsistent with literal completeness. Even so, this technical version of completeness may not prove to be complementary enough for consistency with literal completeness either.

Consistency with literal completeness is required for the transfinite conception of what it means to be 'complete' due to Cantor's claim that the transfinite version of 'infinity' *just is* literal infinity, which is itself literally complete as well as literally limitless. And yet, it is dubious that the technical version of completeness is consistent with literal completeness since the two conceptions do not necessarily carry the same implications.

As pointed out in Chapter 3, completeness as defined literally, and as precisely as possible, in natural language implies the complete collection in question to be *whole* (undivided), *entire* (nothing missing), *finished* (done forming), *full* (unable to include more of the same), and *total* (able to be summed). In contrast to Chapter 3's precising definition for literal completeness, the § 13.2.1 technical version of completeness only references boundary conditions for sets. As such, the technical definition of 'complete' does not necessarily ensure consistency with the literal completeness of a literally infinite collection.

It is even possible that a set considered complete in the transfinite system is not really complete in the literal sense of the term. For example, suppose P is a set of natural numbers between the infimum 0 and the supremum d^* (see § 4.2.7). This sequence can contain non-empty subsets bounded from above by a supremum. Likewise, P as a whole has the supremum d^*. However, d^* has no invariant value. Suppose we continue to invent new, larger natural numbers—they lie between 0 and whatever the new, largest value is for d^*. We can thus imagine continuing to calculate non-empty subsets within the bounds of P, in sequence below the supremum of d^*. Without completeness requiring a *standing total* of values generated below the supremum, P at best has only a *running total* of elements or subsets over time. That means P is an *unfinished* set—a series, actually—between bounds instead of a closed and *finished* set between those bounds. P in that situation is incomplete in the literal sense even while being always complete in the technical sense. The transfinite system's technical definition for 'complete' is thus not adequate for entailing all the properties characteristic of the literal understanding of completeness as used in natural language. Worse, the example shows that the technical conception of completeness can even be applied to collections we would otherwise regard as incomplete.

Without meeting the criteria for literal completeness, such as having the property of finish, any collection that is only technically 'complete' is not necessarily different than a collection we usually regard as literally *incomplete*. In fact, because the technical sense of completeness does not reflect all the connotations of literal completeness, it is also possible to apply the technical definition of 'complete' to collections that *violate* the conditions for being literally complete—collections *necessarily* lacking one of the properties of wholeness, entirety, finish, fullness, or totality and cannot be literally complete.

Picture of a row of black dominoes standing on end with the dominoes falling in succession. If P is a set (sequence) of dominoes in which each domino is fallen, falling, or about to fall (like in **Figure 2.4**), then every subset (subsequence) of dominoes in the row will have a supremum—namely, the next domino in sequence. Moreover, suppose the entire row of black dominoes in P is succeeded by a single white domino at the end of the row. Let Q be the white domino that succeeds all the black ones in sequence, but which itself never falls. We'll take Q to be the supremum for the whole of P. Now suppose that as dominoes keep falling, we keep adding more black dominoes to fall immediately prior to the last white one, Q. In that situation, domino 'set' P here too is not finished, for there is always another domino about to fall. Suppose this process is an open series. In that case, in the literal sense of completeness, at no time is P complete while dominoes continue to fall or are about to fall because finish is required for literal completeness. To be unfinished with a running total of elements or subsets is the opposite of what it means to be literally complete. However, by the transfinite system's technical definition of 'complete', P is at all times complete since P always has a sequence of elements (the fallen, falling, or about-to-fall dominoes) in non-empty subsets of such elements below a supremum (the next domino, including Q which is always about to fall but never actually does). P may be 'complete' in the technical sense, but the technical sense of being 'complete' thus seems to be a misnomer when normally we'd say such a sequence is never completed.

Since P could both fit the transfinite definition for being 'complete' while also being a literally incomplete series under ceaseless construction as an open series, P could very well constitute a *figurative* infinity rather than a *literal* infinity. Consequently, Cantor's broader claim [465] that the transfinite system mathematically defines literal (or actual) infinity in a rigorous manner is necessarily mistaken.

14.1.2 *Critique of the Transfinite Definition for Limitlessness*

Recall from § 13.2.2 what it means according to the transfinite system for a set to be 'limitless' in the technical sense of the term—"P is 'limitless' if P lacks one or both bounds to a linear sequence of the elements within P." Suppose P has a linear sequence of elements without a least upper bound. If so, there is no such thing as specifying the extent of elements in P. So, this technically defined sense of the term 'limitless' is certainly *consistent* with the literal definition of the word 'limitless', which is "to have a range that is unspecifiable, even in principle" (see § 5.4.2 and § 13.2.2).

However, it should be kept in mind that this technical version of being limitless cannot be *identical* to being limitless as literally defined.

Suppose there is at least one collection, P, that is technically limitless—P is a linear sequence lacking an upper bound.

Suppose there is at least one collection, X, that is literally limitless—X has a range (an extent of elements) that is unspecifiable, even in principle.

However, an extent of elements—a range—need be neither linear nor a sequence. So, suppose further the extent of elements in X is neither a linear sequence nor isomorphic to a linear sequence. It follows that X cannot be an instance of P, for P is defined as having a linear sequence.

The moral of the story: even supposing all *technically* limitless collections are *literally* infinite, it does not follow that all literally infinite collections are also limitless in the technical sense of the term. So, the two conceptions of what it means to be limitless are not identical. The transfinite system's concept of being limitless, of having an 'unbounded' sequence of elements, is not as Cantor proposed just a more precise expression of what it is to be literally limitless.

Moreover, there are some sets or sequences that the transfinite system defines as (technically) limitless, or unbounded, but which cannot be literally limitless. That entails the term 'limitless' as technically defined cannot always be taken literally. Accordingly, not all claims to literally limitless sets in the transfinite system are accurate claims.

As evidence of this, there is, at least apparently, one kind of collection the transfinite system holds is always technically limitless or unbounded. However, we cannot in fact ensure instances of that kind of collection are indeed limitless in the literal sense of the term. Instances of that same kind of collection may be technically 'limitless', but they certainly seem to be so only as a figure of speech rather than literally so. That kind of collection is the number system.

Suppose P is a set of numbers in linear order that lacks an upper bound. P is *technically* limitless or, as mathematicians would say, P is unbounded. However, there are some good reasons we cannot ensure that being technically limitless in this sense is identical to being literally limitless.

Suppose numbers are properties of numerals and numerals are inventions—things we invent to help us map the plurality of objects in the world or to concoct conceptual worlds of our own. From what we know of how numbers are invented, whatever number, n, that we invent, n will always have a finite value no matter how great the cardinality of n we can define. There cannot actually be a literally limitless sequence of numbers such that there are absolutely no bounds to the sequence of numbers at all. And numbers are only invented over time, so any number system is a series constructed over time, not a set that exists all at once.

Just take the precising definition of 'limitless' in its literal sense above and apply it to P. For P to be literally limitless would be for P to have an unspecifiable range to its sequence of numbers, *even in principle*. That cannot describe P as an invented construction. It is true that the range of P (the extent of numbers in P) need not necessarily be specifiable *in practice* since we cannot be sure of the value for the highest number in P at any given time (someone, somewhere, might have thought of one bigger). But as a series of invented numbers under continual construction, P's range is always specifiable *in principle*.

So, if we say that, as a set of numbers, P "lacks one or both bounds" according to the technical definition of 'limitless', then what we say must be only a figure of speech. What we would actually be implying is that P lacks permanent bounds, constant extremes, or a standing total of numbers. P is not really a 'set' so much as an open series. Consequently, there can be no number in P that at any time is *limitlessly* far in sequence from any given number n—at least not in a literal sense. P is limitless or unbounded only in the figurative sense that P is continually having its limits or bounds *extended* as we invent new, higher numbers for P. As a sequence of (invented) numbers, P can be an indefinite series and so *figuratively* limitless, but not literally limitless.

Supposing further that P is the system of natural numbers. Every natural number is an invention in an invented system of numbers. So again from an operational perspective, $\mathbb{N}$ is really just $\mathbb{N}^O$—an open series rather than a set. Ergo, even the system of natural numbers is not literally limitless.

In which case, just as the technical use of the term 'complete' is not identical to literal completeness, so too the technical use of the term 'limitless' (or 'unbounded') is not identical to literal limitlessness because in the transfinite system the technical conception of limitlessness is applied to systems of numbers, which can only be figuratively limitless as serial indefinites.

If this argument is to be successfully countered, it must be countered by evidence that numbers are not just inventions, but discoveries—entities that are all there waiting for us to find rather than invent. But there is no scientific evidence establishing such. The notion that numbers are discoveries rather than inventions is a philosophical belief, and a rather dubious one as further argued in Chapter 16.

So, we may take the technically limitless sequence of $P = \{a, b, c, ...\}$ to mean there is no *defined* upper bound to the sequence of P, but to say P is therefore absolutely boundless or literally limitless is a philosophical *interpretation* added on to the ellipsis and the operational rules for how P is constructed as an indefinitely large sequence or series. The syntax of the transfinite system's formal mathematics provides nothing limitless in the literal sense. To say P is "limitless" is a meta-operational proposal for what $\{a, b, c, ...\}$ *means*—limitlessness is in the semantics proposed for the lack of defined bounds for P rather than in the syntax for how P, as referenced in the technical definition of 'limitless', functions in mathematical practice.

For these reasons, the transfinite system's definition of the term 'limitless' (or, more commonly, 'unbounded') may be *mathematically* rigorous, but it is not sufficient to make *logically* rigorous the notion that so-called transfinite sets are genuinely limitless in the literal sense as Cantor intended.

14.1.3 *Critique of the Transfinite Definition for Infinity*

I have provided a critique of the technical definitions of 'complete' and 'limitless' (or 'unbounded'). Now it is time to critique how these work together in the transfinite system as parts of a technical version of infinity.

The transfinite system regards infinity as, quite generally, the ordinality of a sequence of elements, or cardinality of a set of elements, greater than that of any natural number in $\mathbb{N}$ (see § 13.2.3). To have an ordinality $>\mathbb{N}$ is to have an infinite limit ordinal, represented as ω. To have a cardinality $>\mathbb{N}$ is to have an infinite cardinal, represented as $\aleph$. Cantor identified these 'transfinite' numbers as the mathematical expressions of actual (literal) infinity [466].

Most mathematicians assume Cantor's transfinite system succeeded in demonstrating that literal infinity just is his 'transfinite' and that the transfinite, as infinity, is a logically airtight concept. The reason mathematicians tend to make that assumption is because they believe the transfinite system makes literal infinity mathematically precise through its technical definitions and formal syntax.

I do not disagree that Cantor's system is mathematically consistent. Rather, given the preceding two sections, I contend that Cantor did not succeed in making infinity—*literal infinity*—into a mathematically coherent concept, nor has he made a mathematics of the (literally) infinite at all.

I say Cantor's approach has not succeeded in making literal infinity mathematically precise because the transfinite is not a more precise version of infinity as we know it in its common, literal usage. Rather, Cantor's transfinite system *misidentifies* these two different conceptions of infinity with one another under the label 'transfinite'. So while there's nothing wrong with how the mathematics works for 'transfinite sets', Cantor's mathematical framework does not reveal anything about literal infinity because the 'transfinite' of Cantor's math is not really the literal infinity he claimed it to be. That is why Cantor has not succeeded in making infinity mathematically precise and coherent—his system rests on confusing two different conceptions of infinity.

To see more clearly why the infinity of mathematical operation (e.g., the transfinite) is not literal infinity, let's compare how these versions of infinity are defined.

On the one hand, there is the so-called "transfinite," which is the infinity of *mathematical operation* [467]. From § 13.2.3, to be 'infinite' in the transfinite sense is for every non-empty subset that is a member of a set, P, to be "bounded from above by a supremum such that the supremum of P is greater than the unbounded sequence of elements within P" [468]. Which is complementary to the transfinite system's technical definition for infinity as stated in § 13.2.3—"the ordinality of a sequence of elements, or cardinality of a set of elements, greater than that of any natural number in $\mathbb{N}$." We can simply take P to be $\mathbb{N}$ (or any set of at least as many elements), and $\mathbb{N}$ to have a supremum which is an ordinality (ω) or cardinality ($\aleph$) greater than any natural number in an unbounded sequence of finite numbers "below" that supremum. That is infinity according to the transfinite system. I will refer to this technical version of 'infinity' as an infinity of mathematical operation because its definition tells us how mathematicians determine if a set is or is not infinite according to the transfinite system.

On the other hand, there is literal infinity, which is the infinity of *philosophical interpretation* [469]. Literal infinity is, as we know, the condition of being (literally) complete and (literally) limitless in quantity. I refer to literal infinity as the infinity of philosophical interpretation since Cantor *interpreted* the infinity of mathematical operation—infinity as the "transfinite"—to be identical with literal (or 'actual') infinity [470].

Cantor's transfinite system confuses these conceptions of infinity by misidentifying the former as the latter. It is a case of misidentification in two respects:

- Transfinite sets in mathematical operation carry different logical implications from literally infinite collections.

- The transfinite is, with respect to mathematical operations, an expression of serial indefiniteness and so it is a philosophical misinterpretation of the transfinite to identify such with literal infinity.

As we will see, the transfinite and literal infinity are not synonymous since they each have some conceptual content not contained in the other, nor do instances of either of them necessarily imply the other. Let's take a brief look at each of these cases of misidentification between conceptions of infinity.

Implications of the Transfinite Versus the Implications of Literal Infinity. Cantor's transfinite system technically defines 'infinite' in formal notation as (ω or $\aleph$) $> \mathbb{N}$, where $\mathbb{N} \triangleq \{1, 2, 3, ...\}$. (Actually, he used whole numbers, which is how $\mathbb{N}$ is used in standard set theory, but it amounts to the same thing [471]. This way of defining 'infinite' aligns with the technical definitions for 'complete' (having a supremum) and 'limitless' (having unspecifiable range). The transfinite version of infinity works great for set theory. However, the transfinite system's technical conceptions of completeness and limitlessness carry different implications from their literal counterparts as shown in § 14.1.1–14.1.2. So much so, that the transfinite conception of infinity can be applied to collections that are not necessarily literally complete or literally limitless. It is thus not at all proven that the transfinite is identical to literal infinity as Cantor thought.

Operations of the Transfinite Versus their Interpretation as Literally Infinite. The technical definitions of 'infinite' and 'infinity' as provided above for the transfinite system, when applied in transfinite mathematics, can be taken as figures of speech and thereby construed as no different than a description of open series constructed between bounds. In fact, Cantor's 'transfinite' is, in actual operation, a mathematics not of the infinite but of the indefinite—specifically, the serial indefinite. (Though, arguably in some cases the collective indefinite as well.) For the most part, we can regard Cantor's transfinite as a guise of figurative infinity in mathematical operation rather than as literal infinity.

Again take set P as an example. Per § 14.1.1, P as a number system is possibly a construction over time rather than truly a set of members existing all at once. P in such a case would be literally *incomplete* rather than literally complete. And per § 14.1.2, P as a series constructed over time may be serially *indefinite* but would not necessarily be literally limitless. All we have to do is ask at any given time what the highest defined *finite* number is known to be at that time. If we can provisionally identify such a number (best to ask a googologist), then it is plausible that P is not *literally* limitless after all. Being neither literally complete nor literally limitless, P would not be literally infinite.

Assuming as much, if P is the system of natural numbers, then to say the supremum of $\mathbb{N}$ (symbolized as ω or ℵ) is "greater than" any successor to any term we might construct for $\mathbb{N}$ is just to say $\mathbb{N}$ is really the open series $\mathbb{N}^C$, constructed toward ω or ℵ as an *indefinitely large* upper bound rather than as a literally infinite upper bound. In mathematical operation an 'infinite set' like {1, 2, 3, ...} is just an incomplete-indefinite *series* ($\mathbb{N}^C$) treated *as if* it is an infinitely large *set* ($\mathbb{N}$) equal to some unspecified amount denoted as ω or ℵ. The transfinite system's 'infinite sets' are no different from indefinite series imagined as progressing between ideal bounds with the sequence further abstracted behind symbols. Just take an indefinite progression of numbers (1, 2, 3, ...) abstracted behind a symbol such as $\mathbb{N}$. It is only in the philosophical interpretation of such mathematical expressions, as opposed to the formalism of the expressions, that the 'infinite set' or 'transfinite set' is taken to be an expression of literal infinity rather than just a figurative infinity (a serial indefinite).

This is fatal to Cantor's system because Cantor did not want his mathematics to be just another expression of figurative infinity. His goal was to make the 'actual infinite' (i.e., literal infinity) both logically and mathematically coherent—to "tame infinity" [472] [473].

But the transfinite system's technical definitions and operational rules do not directly portray literal infinity. In order to make these indefinites into representations of literal infinities, the transfinite set theory also needed an *interpretation*—a semantic description—added to its formalism. The added interpretation allowed Cantor to propose the figurative 'infinite' of his technical definitions, formal syntax, and mathematical operations instead signify infinity in the literal sense of the term and not just the figurative sense. But from an operational perspective, Cantor's use of 'transfinite' is just indefiniteness of series or collection, and so is misidentified, or misportrayed, as literal infinity in philosophical interpretation.

It is when, for instance, the transfinite system is used to further interpret $\mathbb{N}$ to be a set with *no total*—not even in principle—rather than just a series with a running total, that $\mathbb{N}$ becomes conceived as a *limitless set* rather than the *indefinite series* it actually functions as in the formalism of the math. This added interpretation is necessary in order to affirm $\mathbb{N}$, or any other 'transfinite' set, is not just 'complete' and 'limitless' in the technical senses offered by transfinite mathematics for formal representation and calculation (which is equivalent to merely a figurative infinite), but also in the literal senses of these terms as defined in natural language. This extra interpretation is necessary if the 'infinite' or 'transfinite' sets of the transfinite system are to be taken as literal infinities. Otherwise, the sets are just figurative infinities, which would have defeated Cantor's purpose in proposing the transfinite system.

So we have two problems from these cases of misidentification between conceptions of infinity.

First, when we properly distinguish between the technical and literal versions of infinity that are both referred to as 'transfinite', then we begin to notice Cantor's technical conception of the 'infinite' as the 'transfinite' is different from literal infinity. The technical definition of 'infinity' as the transfinite *underdetermines* what Cantor purported the transfinite to be—namely, infinity in the literal sense of the term—what Aristotle called 'actual infinity'. Moreover, claiming the two infinities are the same creates problems in the internal logic of Cantor's transfinite system.

Second, there is a big difference between the mathematical *operations* for abstract collections represented in the transfinite system on the one hand and the philosophical interpretation of those collections as literally infinite sets on the other hand. The transfinite system does not adequately distinguish the difference between the operational formalism of its mathematics and its own philosophical interpretation of that formalism. Consequently, here too we find instances of how the expression of 'infinity' or 'the transfinite' is an underdetermination of literal infinity. We also see instances in which to interpret the formalism literally leads back to the same contradictory implications between completeness and limitlessness that we found in Chapter 12.

Going forward, we will see that for both of these cases of misidentification, there is a common denominator: a misrepresentation of the transfinite. The transfinite system misrepresents its technical definitions for 'infinity' as more precise definitions of literal infinity and it misrepresents its mathematical operations as operations on supposedly transfinite sets when really they are operations involving indefinite series and collective indefinites. The claim to be mathematically expressing literal infinity is thus underdetermined both by the transfinite system's definitions of the infinite and by its operational formalism for transfinite sets—Cantor claimed to be delivering more than he actually did.

14.1.4 *A Critique of Alternative Definitions for Infinity in the Transfinite System*

So far my critique has been toward specific conceptions of infinity in a technical sense as expressed in Cantor's transfinite system. But some might counter that the technical definition of infinity as provided in § 13.2.3 and critiqued in § 14.1.3 is not the only technical definition in the transfinite system. There are, after all, multiple definitions of infinity in the transfinite system.

For example, take the following theoretical definition:

- infinity: *the one-to-one correspondence of a set with a proper subset of itself*.

As noted in § 7.2, Dedekind operationally defined the cognate 'infinite' in alignment with this conception of infinity[474]:

- infinite: *a set is infinite if it can be placed in one-to-one correspondence with a proper subset of itself*.

These technical definitions are based on the operation of establishing a bijection [475]. A finite set of defined upper and lower bounds cannot be placed into a one-to-one correspondence with a proper subset of itself. But in the transfinite system, an infinite set can be placed in one-to-one correspondence with a proper subset of itself [476].

So, if a complete and limitless set of natural numbers can be placed into bijection with a complete and limitless subset of natural numbers, then it can be shown the literally infinite whole is no greater than the literally infinite part, supporting this alternate technical definition for infinity in the transfinite system.

To see if this is true, just take the set of all the natural numbers, $\mathbb{N}$, and match them one-to-one with the subset of all even natural numbers (E) or odd natural numbers or any other infinite subset of $\mathbb{N}$. As shown in **Figure 14.1**, the two sets are equinumerous. According to the transfinite system's 'correlation sense' of size (see § 13.9.3), there are just as many *even* natural numbers as there are *all* the natural numbers. The infinite whole is equal to the infinite part. Hence, $\mathbb{N}$ is infinite by the transfinite operational definition of 'infinite'.

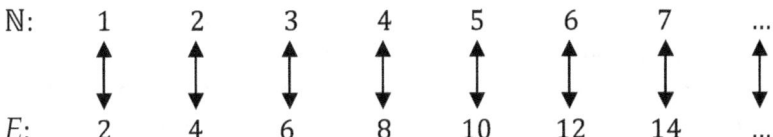

Figure 14.1: The bijection of $\mathbb{N}$, as an infinite set, with E as the infinite subset of even natural numbers.

As further support for this notion, recall that the naturals ($\mathbb{N}$) are just a subset of the integers ($\mathbb{Z}$). As shown in **Figure 13.3**, because the natural numbers can be placed in bijection with the integers, the two sets are the same size ($\mathbb{N} = \mathbb{Z}$). So again, the infinite whole is not greater than the infinite part.

However, the operational definition of 'infinite' as a set's ability to be in bijection with an infinite proper subset of itself may not be quite accurate, even by the standards of transfinite set theory or transfinite mathematics because:

- $\mathbb{N}$ and $\mathbb{R}$ are both infinite sets.
- $\mathbb{N} \subset \mathbb{R}$ (that is, $\mathbb{N}$ is a proper subset of $\mathbb{R}$).
- $\mathbb{N} < \mathbb{R}$ is implied by $\mathbb{N}$ being "smaller" than $\mathbb{R}$ both as a subset and as lacking a correlation of members with $\mathbb{R}$.

Hence, $\mathbb{R}$ cannot be placed into bijection with $\mathbb{N}$ as a proper subset of $\mathbb{R}$. Therefore, $\mathbb{R}$ cannot be placed into bijection with a proper subset of $\mathbb{R}$. Hence, $\mathbb{R}$ does not fit the operational definition of 'infinite' which states that "a set is infinite if it can be placed in one-to-one correspondence with a proper subset of itself." Ergo, we have a case of an infinite whole that does not correspond one-to-one with its infinite part.

Moreover, since $\mathbb{R} > \mathbb{N}$, we have a case in which the infinite whole is greater than an infinite part—a proper subset of itself. Hence, given the assumptions of the transfinite system, some infinite sets can be placed into bijection with every infinite part while others cannot. This means a set being in bijection with a proper subset of itself is not what defines a set as being infinite, even if it is a feature of some infinite sets. It may be something only an infinite set could do, but it cannot be the defining characteristic of infinite sets per se.

There is also something dubiously circular about the correspondence way of defining a set as infinite. Notice that the proper subset also has to be infinite. After all, the set $\{1, 2, 3\}$ is a proper subset of the naturals, yet infinite $\mathbb{N}$ cannot be placed into bijection with *that* proper subset of itself. Instead, that proper subset only injects into $\mathbb{N}$. Clearly, for Dedekind's definition of 'infinite' to work, the proper subset has to be infinite too. But wasn't that what we were trying to define?

That's just one logical problem with this correspondence approach to defining infinity. I will give you one more.

Consider correspondence between collections greater than any defined finite number of elements—collections that are at least indefinitely large (see **Figure 6.5**). Suppose establishing the bijection of a collection of *at least* indefinitely many members with a proper subset of that collection that also has at least indefinitely many members cannot be a single act but is necessarily a *process*. Suppose $\mathbb{N}$ is an indefinite collection of that kind. In that case, $\mathbb{N}$ is necessarily $\mathbb{N}^{\circ}$. So, the correspondence between the indefinitely large sequence of natural numbers and an indefinitely large proper subset of itself is not an act but a process.

As such, no correlation can exist between "all" the natural numbers and "all" the even natural numbers—that is, not if "all" means the exhaustion of the natural numbers. Rather, in actual practice, the bijection of both even and odd natural numbers in one row to only evens or only odds in the other row is just a bijection of "all" of them *so far*, at any given time. For bijection of such quantities is a process of depicting numbers in two lists that are constructed over time and so only extend as far as we choose to keep on constructing them. In that case, it is little wonder we can match elements tit-for-tat between indefinitely large collections. Keep on listing, or defining, numbers for each and you can always match the elements between them. That does not show the collections to be limitless, or that the whole and part are equal. It just shows you can engage in a matching process indefinitely as long as you can keep on extending the lists by a rule [477].

For these reasons, I do not believe Dedekind's way of theoretically defining 'infinity' and operationally defining its cognate 'infinite' is sound. But they are also not the only alternative technical definitions available for infinity as the transfinite. I won't go over many more; instead, I will just point out one more for flavor.

Some transfinite set theorists simply define the term 'infinity' as being infinite, define 'infinite' as the property of a non-empty set that is "not finite," and then define the term 'finite' as equal to a positive cardinal number (i.e., a counting number) assignable at least in principle [478] (recall the definition of 'infinite' from § 11.3). This is basically the same as saying $\omega > n$; that is, infinity is greater than any natural number.

While such a definition is consistent with the transfinite system, it is really just equivalent to the version 2 technical definition of 'infinite' and the transfinite definition of 'infinity' as given in § 13.2.3. As such it has the same troubles, for those definitions I contend are, in the context of mathematical operation, only expressions of figurative versions of infinity rather than of literal infinity. The remainder of this chapter presents the evidence for this conclusion.

14.2 ON LIMITLESSNESS WITHOUT LIMITLESSLY LARGE NUMBERS

A good example of the 'transfinite' operating as figurative infinity while misinterpreted to be literal infinity can be found in how Cantor framed the rules for infinitely large numbers. Cantor framed the rules to avoid the contradiction between proposing that there is an infinitely large natural number while also implying there are *instead* "infinitely many" unique natural numbers, each of which is finite—a contradiction implied by the properties of literal infinity as discussed in Chapters 10–12. Whether Cantor was successful in avoiding that contradiction entirely is another matter. The success of his framework with respect to *logical* consistency is something I dispute, regardless of its *mathematical* coherence.

14.2.1 *Limitlessly Large Natural Numbers Implied but Denied*

Cantor's transfinite system avoids reference to infinitely large natural numbers in favor of representing 'infinite' sequences of unique, finite natural numbers [479] [480]. That is not to say Cantor's transfinite system makes no use of infinitely large numbers at all because his framework does affirm the existence of infinitely large numbers in the sense of the infinite ordinals (ω) and infinite cardinals ($\aleph$). The transfinite system simply does not recognize infinitely large *natural* (counting) numbers as existing.

In order to adopt the position that there are infinite sets—sets of ω or $\aleph$ size—while rejecting the existence of infinitely large natural numbers, Cantor technically redefined the 'infinite' in a manner that is, with respect to mathematical operation, no different than the figuratively infinite even while mistakenly interpreting his technical conception of 'infinite' to be the same as literal infinity.

Take the properties of completeness and limitlessness that characterize literal infinity. The transfinite system proposes a technical definition of 'complete' and a technical definition of 'limitless'.

To be technically 'limitless' is to operationally lack an upper bound to how many elements in a sequence can be generated. For any natural number (n) in $\mathbb{N}$, there is an $n + 1$ (another finite amount). In other words, to say $\mathbb{N}$ is 'limitless' in the technical sense of mathematical operation is just to say, "For every n in $\mathbb{N}$, construct another number equal to $n + 1$." That makes $\mathbb{N}$ an indefinite series under construction—$\mathbb{N}$ (the 'set') is operationally just $\mathbb{N}^C$ (a series) in disguise. This kind of 'limitlessness' for $\mathbb{N}$ is metaphorical. If we were to attempt to show the numbers of $\mathbb{N}$, we have to resort to a process, to a series of iterations of numbers. Hence, $\mathbb{N}$ as a collection of numbers is in actual mathematical operation no different from figurative infinity—a growing finite.

Moreover, to be technically 'complete' in the transfinite sense implies an ordering up to a supremum. By that definition, the natural numbers are a 'complete' set because the transfinite system posits a non-natural number as an ordinal (ω) that *follows after* all the natural numbers, thus providing a kind of supremum to any given sequence of natural numbers—no matter great they become.

But now we have another problem: by that conception of what it is to be complete, a collection that is a growing finitude within bounds is also merely 'complete' in a figurative sense. So, putting these conceptions of 'limitless' and 'complete' together, the so-called "set" of natural numbers is just a growing finitude—a figurative infinity—getting ever larger under the bound labeled as ω or $\aleph_0$ in terms of order and size—both of which express no *definite* size. So, these technical conceptions of 'limitless' and 'complete' together make the 'transfinite' no different than a figurative infinite—a condition of indefiniteness, a type of finitude.

The transfinite system thereby swaps talk of infinitely large natural numbers for infinitely large non-natural numbers. But the notion that ω and $\aleph$ extend as literal infinities is just an interpretation—there is nothing in the technical definitions or operational rules necessitating such. As for the so-called "infinitely many" natural numbers in $\mathbb{N}$, the sequence of natural numbers does not in mathematical operation differ from figurative infinity—an incomplete, open series of indefinite length rather than a genuinely limitless sequence of numbers.

That is how Cantor's transfinite system *operationally* treats 'transfinite' sets as indefinite series and so mathematically avoids the problem of simultaneously claiming the existence of infinitely large natural numbers while also denying them. That is, Cantor avoided the contradiction of implying and denying infinitely large natural numbers in the mathematical formalism of the transfinite system only by technically defining the 'transfinite' in a manner that makes it a *figurative infinity* in operation. By making the 'transfinite' figuratively infinite in operation, Cantor could rightfully claim there are no 'infinitely large' natural numbers in his transfinite system.

But no sooner than avoiding the contradiction of both affirming and denying infinitely large natural numbers on a mathematical level, Cantor's transfinite system implies the contradiction all over again on a semantic level. It does so as soon as it *interprets* $\mathbb{N}$ and other 'transfinite sets' as actual infinities—literally infinite sets. Cantor interpreted the 'transfinite' in the formalism of the system as an expression of *literal infinity*. By interpreting that 'transfinite' to be literal infinity, Cantor confused his mathematical 'transfinite', a figurative infinity in operation, with the 'transfinite' as literal infinity—a misidentification that mistakes the figurative infinity for literal infinity. In so doing, the contradictions reappear.

14.2.2 *Interpretations have Logical Implications*

Since the technical infinity of the transfinite system is interpreted to be the actual infinity of antiquity (i.e., literal infinity), the technical conceptions of what it is to be complete and limitless become confused with their ordinary language counterparts. This confusion of reference once again results in the contradictory implications identified in Chapters 10–12, particularly with respect to there being implied infinitely large vs. infinitely many natural numbers.

For example, if $\mathbb{N}$ were literally infinite, then $\mathbb{N}$ would have to have at least one number, n, *infinitely* far down the sequence from the number 1 such that n has a cardinality *infinitely greater than* 1. In other words, the progression of numbers in a set said to be infinite must be a progression carried to a literally *limitless* degree, logically implying there to be an infinitely large natural number—a positive natural number with a literally limitless string of digits. But the transfinite system includes a philosophical interpretation that recognizes *no such thing as an infinitely large natural number*—so, there is no n that is "infinitely greater" than 1; each number is finitely larger than the previous ($n' = n + 1$). But the problem won't go away: as shown in **Figure 10.1**, there *must* be a natural number (n) infinitely greater than 1 because no sequence in which the members are all reducible to finite sums has members that can render the whole sequence anything other than finite, a serial indefinite at best. Which the transfinite system denies while simultaneously stating that $\mathbb{N}$ has infinitely many natural numbers. A contradiction—at least, one implied from the *semantic* content of the transfinite system in stating that there are *infinitely* many naturals in a set of only *finite* naturals.

Some mathematicians try to help Cantor get around this problem by reiterating the formalism, offering technical definitions for terms and supporting operations. They point out that, operationally, having a number such as $\aleph$ identified as greater than any number in a set of numbers isn't a problem: $\forall n(n + 1) < \aleph_0$. An expression that says for all the natural numbers, any natural number plus another that is 1 greater is still less than the least transfinite number. There is nothing mathematically inconsistent there, nor a logical problem since the symbol works operationally as if it is a collective indefinite. Neither is there any mathematical problem in the expression $\mathbb{N} \triangleq \{1, 2, 3, ...\} \triangleq \aleph_0$, which means the whole of $\mathbb{N}$ is by definition equal to $\aleph_0$—a symbol that operates as if representing a serial or collective indefinite.

Citing the formal expressions is an act of trying to dodge the issue. Again, it's not the *syntax* or *formal rules* of set theory and transfinite math that is the problem, but rather interpreting a 'transfinite' set as a literal infinite. The formalism of the transfinite system is not contradictory because it does not express literal completeness and literal limitlessness together for the same set at all. A set such as $\{1, 2, 3, ...\}$ is not from an operational point of view the literally complete and limitless set it's claimed to be according to Cantor's interpretation of 'transfinite' sets as literal infinities. Rather, a set like $\{1, 2, 3, ...\}$, symbolized as $\mathbb{N}$, is not really a set at all in the formalism; at best the sequence represented is just an incomplete, indefinite sequence interpreted and purported to be a literally complete and limitless set behind the symbol $\mathbb{N}$. So, the consistency of the mathematics is beside the point—it's the meaning of the math (its semantics) and not the formalism of the math (its syntax) that is problematic.

Mathematically, the sequence represented in the braces carries implications for the operations of the system that reveal the sequence to be, at best, an indefinitely large sequence formed over a series of steps rather than anything limitless. As for the completeness of the sequence of numbers, transfinite mathematics treats $\mathbb{N}$ as a technically 'complete' set only of some unspecified amount of numbers represented by the symbol $\aleph_0$ for the purposes of designating $\aleph_0$ as a number greater than any n we can in practice invent for $\mathbb{N}$—that is not functionally different than the incompleteness of a series under construction below an element designated to be an indefinitely large (but still finite) supremum. So an incomplete, indefinite series of numbers constructed under a hypothetical supremum of indefinitely large cardinality is not a literally complete and literally limitless sequence as it must be in order to be a literally infinite set, an 'actual infinite' as Cantor said corresponds to a transfinite set [481].

It is true that the transfinite system, insofar as it is technically defined for mathematical operation, avoids the problem of having an infinitely large natural number as a *last* or *highest* number for $\mathbb{N}$ when there cannot be such for a sequence that does not stop getting bigger over increasing increments of 1. However, the avoidance of this contradiction only holds with respect to the set-theoretic and mathematical formalism of the transfinite system. It does not hold true for the transfinite system's philosophical interpretation of what that formalism means—a literal infinity of natural numbers still has its internal contradictions.

For example, expressions like $\forall n (n + 1) < \aleph_0$ and $\mathbb{N} \triangleq \aleph_0$ are not mathematically problematic, but there are nevertheless logical problems with *interpreting* $\aleph_0$ as denoting a *literally infinite* quantity. The transfinite system's philosophical misidentification of the figurative 'infinity' expressed in transfinite formalism (series represented as $\aleph$ and ω) with literal infinity results in contradictory connotations whenever so-called 'infinite' or 'transfinite' sets of numbers—as $\mathbb{N}$ is claimed to be—are described.

Recall the definition of infinity cited back in § 14.1—"the ordinality of a sequence of elements, or cardinality of a set of elements, greater than that of any natural number in $\mathbb{N}$." It is contradictory to state that $\aleph_0$ is a "least number" *greater than* any and every natural number in $\mathbb{N}$ as a *set* (implying $\mathbb{N}$ to be complete) while simultaneously saying there is *no greatest* natural number in $\mathbb{N}$, even in principle (implying $\mathbb{N}$ to be limitless in its quantity of natural numbers) [482]. If there's no greatest natural number in $\mathbb{N}$ because $\mathbb{N}$ is a sequence of *limitlessly* many (finite) natural numbers—all of which already exist, at once, with each number in the sequence of $\mathbb{N}$ greater in cardinality than the last—then, it makes no sense to say there is a number ($\aleph_0$) *greater than* that which has *no limit* to its greatness. The sequence of naturals $(1, 2, 3, ...)$, when infinite, already has no limit to its greatness—there is nothing greater than that which has no greatest.

Perhaps mathematically the sequence $(1, 2, 3, ...)$ can lack an upper bound because we can always *create* new numbers to include in the set of numbers, but if we instead interpret the numbers as already being in the set and also having no upper bound, then how can another quantity in the sequence be even *greater* than all the naturals *and* an upper bound for a sequence with no upper bound? The answer would seem to be there cannot be such because there's no such thing as being "greater" in that context—a number cannot be greater than all the numbers in a completed sequence if the sequence has no greatest number. It's one thing to write abstractions like $\{P\}$, $\{Q\}$; it's quite another to say P has no limit but Q starts where P leaves off.

So, even though there are no mathematical contradictions in the syntactical formalism or operations, the philosophical *interpretation* of $\mathbb{N}$ as a literally infinite set and $\aleph_0$ as a symbol of literal infinity still implies logical contradictions in meaning. While avoiding a mathematical problem, the transfinite system simultaneously confuses the figurative infinities of its mathematical definitions and operations with the literal infinities of its philosophical interpretation of its technical 'infinity' as literal infinity. And as soon as that misidentification occurs, the logical implications of a set being literally complete while also literally limitless return with all their contradictions.

14.3 ON INFINITY WITHOUT AN INFINITE SUM

The 'transfinite' way of defining infinity (see § 13.2.3) may further be shown as equivalent to only the figuratively infinite in operation, and therefore a misinterpretation as being the same as literal infinity. This becomes abundantly clear in the transfinite's use of infinite sequences without *infinite sums*.

14.3.1 *Of Infinite Numbers as Infinite Sums*

The transfinite system tells us $\mathbb{N}$ has "infinitely many" natural numbers but all of them are finite—there is no natural number with infinitely many digits, so in reality there is no number that is an 'infinite sum' of infinitely many natural numbers [483] [484]. However, Cantor also said that $\mathbb{N}$ is a 'transfinite' set of numbers and that the transfinite is the same as literal (actual) infinity [485] [486]. As pointed out in Chapters 10–12, the claim that $\mathbb{N}$ is a literally infinite set implies both (a) there are no infinite sums by virtue of $\mathbb{N}$'s limitlessness and (b) there are infinite sums by virtue of $\mathbb{N}$'s completeness. So, as soon as the 'transfinite' is interpreted to be literal infinity, the logical contradictions between (a) and (b) are implied all over again. To avoid this problem, the transfinite system proposes an infinite set is only a technically 'complete' set (see § 13.2.1 and § 14.1.1), so as not to imply an infinite *sum* of members.

According to this position, a set can be limitless (or 'unbounded') in the quantity of its members without having a sum of members for two reasons:

1. The 'completeness' of an infinite collection is redefined without implying an infinite sum.
2. An infinite set, as a 'limitless' set, is redefined as *greater than* any sum of its members.

So, literal infinity's self-contradiction of implying an infinite sum by virtue of completeness while simultaneously denying any such sum exists by virtue of limitlessness is avoided in the technical definitions of Cantor's transfinite system.

However, in reconceiving completeness and limitlessness in technical terms, the technical redefinition of infinity and its properties support the conclusion that an 'infinite' (i.e., transfinite) set is, operationally, an *indefinite series* under construction and not a literally infinite set as Cantor claimed.

14.3.2 *Completeness with or without a Sum*

For a transfinite set to be a literally infinite set is for the transfinite set to be literally complete. But to be literally complete implies totality and so a total equal to a *sum* of members. The transfinite system, on the other hand, defines the term 'complete' in such a technical manner that any "totality" is not necessarily equal to a sum for the complete collection as a whole.

For example, in the technical sense, $\mathbb{N}$ is a 'complete' set of natural numbers because it is bounded from above by the non-natural ordinal ω as its supremum [487]. However, this way of defining 'complete' does not necessarily imply a sum, even an infinite one, and so does not necessarily imply $\mathbb{N}$ to be literally complete.

To see why, start by considering the following sequence of numbers:

1, 2, 3, 4, 5, **5.1, 5.2, 5.3, 5.4, 5.5, 5.6, 5.7, 5.8, 5.9,** 6, 7, 8, 9, 10

Although all the numbers are real numbers, the sequence contains two sub-sequences of natural numbers: 1–5 and 6–10. The real number 5.1 is the least upper bound to the first sub-sequence of naturals—the number sequence 1–5. The count of the first five numbers—all of which are natural numbers—is 5. So, there is a sum of natural numbers right below the real number 5.1, which is offered as the least upper bound for the natural numbers below it.

Now consider the sequence of natural numbers:

$\mathbb{N} \triangleq \{1, 2, 3, ...\}$

The natural number set is said to have ω as the least upper bound [488] to them all such that ω comes "after" the natural numbers:

1, 2, 3, ..., ω

So does ω make the sequence of all the natural numbers a *literally complete* set and so a set with a *sum* of *all* the natural numbers *below* ω?

As argued in § 14.1.1, just by the technical definition of 'complete', the answer is unclear as to whether we can consider the sequence to have a standing total equal to an infinite number of some kind. On the one hand, we could answer no, for the transfinite system says ω is not a *successor ordinal* but rather it is a *limit ordinal*, and so there is no natural number immediately below ω by which to say there is an infinite total of natural numbers under ω equal to an 'infinite sum' of natural numbers under ω. Alas, if there is no infinite sum of natural numbers under ω, and ergo no such thing as a natural number succeeded by ω, then one is left to wonder what the difference between such a sequence of natural numbers is and a sequence of natural numbers that is simply a *series* of numbers under construction.

In which case, we must suppose all the ellipsis in the expression $\{1, 2, 3, ...\}$ shows is that we can keep on generating or inventing more natural numbers to include in the sequence prior to topping off the sequence with the symbol ω. We must then further suppose that we cannot rely on "all" the numbers being "already out there" hiding behind the ellipsis. So, what we have is, operationally speaking, a series under construction that is indefinitely *incomplete* according to completeness as literally defined.

True, by the technical definition of 'complete', the sequence of $\{1, 2, 3, ...\}$ is completed as shown by 1, 2, 3, ..., ω because ω is the least upper bound to the sequence 1, 2, 3, ... But if by "complete" we mean *literally* complete per Chapter 3, then the sequence in $\{1, 2, 3, ...\}$ is not necessarily complete in that sense from a purely operational point of view. Operationally, we do not necessarily have a *sum* underneath that supremum as a *standing total* such that the set is a literally complete set. All we may have instead is the running total of an incomplete series—new sums generated as the series continues under construction.

On those grounds, it is fallacious to interpret the transfinite system's technical conception of being 'complete' as *equivalent* to the kind of completeness a collection must have in order for it to be literally infinite. Literal infinity *necessarily* implies a literally complete set, which connotes having a *standing* total that is equal to an infinite *sum* of numbers. Whereas 'infinity' as technically defined rests only on a technical conception of 'complete' that implies no particular kind of sum and so at best is complementary to literal completeness while also being operationally consistent with a running total without final sum.

The technical conception of what it is to be 'complete' therefore again falls short of what completeness needs to be if, as Cantor claimed, a so-called 'transfinite' set "coincides with what has since antiquity been called the 'actual infinite'"—that is, with literal infinity [489].

On the other hand, literal infinity implies an *infinite sum by virtue of literal completeness* and yet also the *lack of an infinite sum by virtue of literal limitlessness*—a contradictory state of affairs. So too, if the transfinite system's technical definition of 'complete' did imply a transfinite set has an infinitely large sum of members in the form of a standing total while its technical definition of 'limitless' implied the opposite, then the transfinite system would on an operational level be just as self-contradictory as literal infinity has been since antiquity. But the transfinite system adopts technical definitions for 'complete' and 'limitless' and 'infinite' that avoid such self-contradictions with respect to mathematical operations.

Even so, the transfinite system stumbles right back into the contradictions by *interpreting* so-called 'transfinite' sets to be literal infinities even while in operation a 'transfinite' set is merely an indefinitely large set or a figurative infinity. So, infinite sums are avoided operationally, but they end up being logically implied when collections, such as $\mathbb{N}$, are interpreted to be literally infinite sets and so literally complete "totalities" [490].

14.3.3 *An Infinite Whole without an Infinite Sum*

According to the transfinite system [491], for set P to be 'limitless' is for P to lack one or both bounds to a linear sequence of the elements within P. For example, is P is $\mathbb{N}$ and $\mathbb{N} \triangleq \{1, 2, 3, ...\}$, the P lacks an upper bound. In the formal expression, if we can always name a new, higher number, n, for the sequence of P, then this is consistent with interpreting P to be an indefinite series under continuous construction rather than an infinitely large set of elements having an infinitely large sum.

As another example, consider an indefinite accession with a running sum:

$$1 + 2 = 3$$
$$2 + 3 = 5$$
$$3 + 4 = 7$$
$$4 + 5 = 9$$
$$\vdots$$

We need never come to an *infinitely* large sum, no matter how many times we repeat this operation.

The same is true for real numbers, such as when we have an indefinite accession of fractions under the least upper bound of 1. For example: $1/2 + 3/4 + 7/8 + 15/16 + 31/32 + ...$ The sums can continue without ever arriving at 1 as the exact sum for the whole sequence, though we could call them "equal" to 1 for practical purposes since mathematicians say the sums get "arbitrarily close" to the bound [492].

With respect to the mathematical operations forming sequences, the ellipsis in each of the above examples implies an indefinite progression, which has a running sum of elements no matter how far we carry on the progression. The ellipsis just means "keep going." From an operational point of view, at no time is the progression ever literally *limitless* and so at no time does the progression ever reach a literally limitless sequence for the whole series.

All of this is consistent with the technical definition for 'limitless', which can be interpreted as implying that there is always another greater number that can be invented or added to the sequence. In a figurative sense, we can say the technically 'limitless' progression, as a process, is at any given time "greater" than its sum because the process can always supersede any sum for the sequence with a new, higher sum. But the sequence is not literally greater than its finite parts because it can always, at any time, be given a running total equal to a new sum.

This again means the technical definition of 'limitless' falls short of what it means to be *literally limitless* because to be 'limitless' in this technical sense need not be different than a serial indefinite—a figurative infinity in which new, larger values can always be invented to supersede the largest given before. Whereas to be literally limitless is to have no greatest value *at any time*, not even a largest value so far—not even in principle. That the technical definition of 'limitless' falls short of *necessarily* implying literal limitlessness is a problem because Cantor identified his idea of the 'transfinite' with the 'actual infinite' (with literal infinity) and not with 'potential' or figurative infinity.

For the transfinite system to identify numeric sequences as literally infinite sets, Cantor had to add a philosophical interpretation to the technical conception of what it is to be a 'limitless' progression. His added interpretation involved the notion that the whole can be, literally and not just figuratively, *greater than* any sum of parts such that the whole can be literally limitless even if additions are only figuratively limitless.

To that end, the transfinite system interprets sets to be not just technically limitless according to the math, but literally limitless in our precising sense of the term 'limitless': there is no infinitely large sum of natural numbers in $\mathbb{N}$ because finite subsets cannot aggregate into an infinite set. Instead, the whole of the infinite set is greater than any sum of finite subsets in the collection. That is, if $\mathbb{N}$ is infinite, then $\mathbb{N}$ is infinite precisely because the infinite whole is greater than all the finite parts combined. If the sequence of numbers in $\mathbb{N}$ is literally limitless, then there is *no sum at all* to the sequence of natural numbers comprising $\mathbb{N}$, even though the progression of numbers can clearly be summed with a finite total at each and every step of the way, *no matter how far*. The infinite whole is greater than the infinitely many finite sums that compose it; the whole is a limitless sequence of sums but is not itself a sum. So this interpretation of technical limitlessness is complementary with literal limitlessness, as acknowledged back in § 13.2.2.

And it also has the ring of plausibility because we are familiar with wholes that have properties not belonging to their parts and vice versa. A brick may be red, but that does not mean each atom in the brick is red. So too, an atom in a brick is bonded to another atom in the brick, but that does not mean a brick must be bonded to other bricks. Likewise, transfinite mathematics suggests that an infinite whole has properties not belonging to its finite parts and vice versa. The whole of $\mathbb{N}$ is limitless, but a part of that whole need not be limitless. Then too, while *finite* sequences of numbers in $\mathbb{N}$ may be equal to sums of numbers, such need not be true of the entire sequence of $\mathbb{N}$ as an *infinite* whole [493]. This position suggests that it is not the case that properties of finite subsets, such as the ability to be summed, scale up from finite subsets to the infinite superset.

The plausibility of this philosophical interpretation of the transfinite system's technically defined idea of limitlessness, however, rests on the logical consistency of the claim that $\mathbb{N}$ can be infinite as a whole while being composed *only* of finite numbers as its basic elements. I argue such a position does not hold up to scrutiny.

14.3.4 *When the Whole Must Equal the Number of Parts*

The transfinite system portrays the natural numbers as $\mathbb{N}$, a 'transfinite' set, which is 'infinite' in the sense of being *limitless* as a whole even though all the natural number parts in $\mathbb{N}$ are finite. According to the transfinite system, the limitlessness of $\mathbb{N}$ is what makes $\mathbb{N}$ quantitatively "greater" as a whole than any of the natural numbers it contains [494].

In the formal language of the system, $\mathbb{N} \triangleq \aleph_0$ where $\forall n[(n \in \mathbb{N}) \bullet [(n + 1) < \aleph_0]]$. Expressing the same point with an infinite ordinal (ω) instead of an infinite cardinal ($\aleph_0$), Cantor stated, "...my least transfinite ordinal number ω, and consequently all greater ordinal numbers, lie quite outside the endless series 1, 2, 3, and so on. Thus, ω is *not* a maximum of the finite numbers, for there is no such thing" [495]. So, if $\mathbb{N}$ is $\aleph_0$ or ω in size, while no natural number, n, can be equal to $\aleph_0$ or ω, then the whole of $\mathbb{N}$ is greater than its natural number parts.

I argue, contrary to the transfinite system, the cardinality relationships between each of the natural numbers precludes $\mathbb{N}$ from being either "greater" than its parts or a literally limitless whole. There are at least two reasons for this conclusion.

First, with the exception of the number 1, each natural (counting) number has the value it has *only because its ordinality and associated cardinality derive from the preceding natural numbers*, and so each natural number has its value precisely because it is equal to a sum made from prior numbers in the sequence (for example, $4 + 1 = 5$). A given sequence of natural numbers is therefore only as "great" or as "small" as a sum that is equal to a particular number. A property like the ability to have a sum cannot somehow become lost along the sequence from the scale of the finite part to the scale of the whole. If it could, then where along the sequence does finitude leave off such that all the numbers together become an infinitude, and such that sums cease to be made for the sequence? The answer is nowhere—nowhere do sums ever cease to exist as long as there is another natural number in the sequence. And since sums nowhere leave off, and neither does finitude, then the sequence never becomes non-finite, no matter how far along the sequence we progress.

Second, as pointed out before, $\mathbb{N}$ is *nothing but* the natural numbers and every natural number (except 1) *reduces* to other natural numbers. So, it is empty to claim that the whole of $\mathbb{N}$ can be quantitatively *limitless* while every number and every sequence of numbers inside the whole of $\mathbb{N}$ is only finite (ergo, limited). If every n in $\mathbb{N}$ is finite, and there is nothing beyond the finite numbers and finite sequences in $\mathbb{N}$, then there is nothing to give the whole of $\mathbb{N}$ the property of infinitude.

Cantor tried to get around these two problems for his theory by proposing that $\mathbb{N}$ as a whole is 'transfinite'—that is, equal to the value of a transfinite *limit ordinal* (ω) or cardinal ($\aleph$). Cantor stated, for instance, that ω is 'transfinite' in the sense that "any number v however great is quite as far off from ω as the least finite number" [496]. In other words, $\mathbb{N}$ as a whole is equal in quantitative value to the transfinite limit ordinal ω, which is itself as "far off" in value from the greatest natural number inside $\mathbb{N}$ as is the number 1.

But how is it that ω is "greater" or "far off" in value according to *numerical* value? The first transfinite ordinal cannot be "greater" or "far off" in the sense of having some *numeric* quantity greater than any natural number because there is *nothing but* the natural numbers comprising $\mathbb{N}$ to denote a quantitative value. Cantor stipulated that a transfinite number like ω is "greater" or "far off" than any natural number but only defines ω in operation as "greater" or "far off" in the sense of making ω a supremum *toward which* an "increasing finite" *tends* [497]. But that is just to make the natural numbers a figurative infinity inside a boundary denoted by a non-natural number. Which in terms of mathematical operation just makes a 'transfinite' number into an *indefinite* quantity, not the literally limitless yet literally complete quantity (literal infinity) Cantor claimed it to be.

It makes much more sense to conclude that, if the whole of $\mathbb{N}$ cannot have a sum, it is because $\mathbb{N}$ as a whole does not have a *final* sum in the form of a standing total. But such also follows if $\mathbb{N}$ is not a completed set after all, but rather an incomplete, open *series*: $\mathbb{N}^C$. Looking at the scale of naturals as a series instead of a set, it is precisely the sequence of the natural numbers in $\mathbb{N}^C$ as an open series, incomplete and indefinite, that allows the whole of $\mathbb{N}^C$ to have any quantitative value at all—the value of whatever the highest number is that anyone has invented for it at any given time. We can propose some greater, indefinite quantity as a "bound" that the definite natural numbers "tend to" if we like, but that alone would not make $\mathbb{N}^C$ into $\mathbb{N}$ —a set greater as a whole than the numbers or sequences of numbers it contains as parts, nor would it make the bound of $\mathbb{N}^C$ *limitless* as is supposedly the case for $\mathbb{N}$, and so it would not make $\mathbb{N}^C$ into $\mathbb{N}$, a literally infinite set. The natural number scale as the series $\mathbb{N}^C$ is thus not only distinguishable conceptually from $\mathbb{N}$ but also more logically supportable and more empirically grounded in mathematical experience.

14.3.5 *A Rhetorical Proposal: A 'Sum' In an Unusual Sense*

There is one last appeal that might be made to render $\mathbb{N}$ a complete "totality" with a "sum" while having no limit to its quantity of numbers. As pointed out in § 13.6, the transfinite system proposes a transfinite set has a 'sum' of infinitely many numbers only in the sense that the sum of numbers in the transfinite set *is the sequence of numbers itself*. Take a series of real numbers between any two successive integers. The real numbers of that series can be "summed," at least in the sense of an accession without a final addition. Rudy Rucker, professor of mathematics and computer science at San Jose State University, states, "Thus, the sum of the series $2/10 + 5/1{,}000 + 7/10{,}000 + 9/100{,}000 + \ldots$ is nothing other than the series itself, also known as .20579..." [498]. Perhaps if we say an infinite set is complete because it has a 'sum' in that sense, while still being limitless, we can save the concept of literal infinity from a contradiction between its completeness and limitlessness.

But the sum of a series is not a series of sums. Rather, the sum of a series is the final sum for the series as a whole. It is a total equaling the addition of all the members in a series. To say the sum of an infinite series "is nothing other than the series itself" is a misleading way of saying there is no sum for the series because the series has no total to calculate, other than perhaps a running total. On top of that, if the series of real numbers between the two successive integers does not sum at all, that is no different than saying the series is *incomplete* by the ordinary, natural language definition of 'complete' and so merely an open, indefinite (but nonetheless finite) series of sums.

Technical redefinitions for the term 'sum' do not help to *solve* the problem of literal infinity's internal contradiction between completeness and limitlessness. Rather, such redefinitions are an attempt to *dissolve* the problem, but it only does so at the cost of making what was supposed to be literal infinity into a figurative infinity, which is the opposite of what Cantor intended for his transfinite system.

14.3.6 *Infinity's Unresolved Problems with Sums*

In brief, the transfinite system tries to do away with infinite sums of natural numbers even though interpreting $\mathbb{N}$ to be literally infinite implies such sums insofar as $\mathbb{N}$'s literal completeness is concerned. To keep the completeness of $\mathbb{N}$ while rejecting the implication of infinite sums is to throw out the literal completeness of $\mathbb{N}$ in favor of describing $\mathbb{N}$ as only technically 'complete'. But that makes 'complete' a misnomer for what is described in ordinary language as an incomplete series, which undermines the notion that $\mathbb{N}$ is a literally infinite set instead of just a figurative infinite. And that runs contrary to the whole point of transfinite mathematics which was to make literal infinity calculable and logically coherent.

14.4 ABSTRACTING OUT INCONVENIENT CONNOTATIONS

By adopting technical definitions for the term 'infinite', mathematicians can sidestep the contradictory implications of literal infinity insofar as mathematical operation is concerned. In the transfinite system, for instance, the technical redefinition of 'infinite'—in reality, a figurative infinite dubbed the 'transfinite'—"abstracts out" the contradictory implications of interpreting the 'infinite' to be literal infinity, thereby hiding the contradictions from consideration.

Not only do technical definitions for 'infinite' hide the self-contradictions implied by literal infinity from view, so too the mathematical symbolism and operations of the transfinite system go even further in misdirection. Cantor inadvertently invented a means to avoid addressing the logical contradictions connoted by literally infinite sets being both literally complete and literally limitless. He accomplished this by framing the set-theoretic symbolism and rules of transfinite math in such a way that the contradictory connotations of literal infinity do not have to be faced in order to have coherent mathematical expressions when a figurative infinite is confused with literal infinity under the label of 'transfinite'.

A good example of the transfinite system abstracting out (i.e., safely ignoring) the logically contradictory connotations of the transfinite as a literal infinite can be found in the use of the symbolism of the transfinite system. The transfinite system uses an ellipsis (…), which depicts indefinite progression (a figurative infinite) like 1, 2, 3, … as 'transfinite'. The transfinite system also uses braces, { }, to depict indefinitely large sets as 'transfinite', and the transfinite system uses Latin letters (e.g., $\mathbb{N}$ and P) or Greek and Hebrew letters (ω and $\aleph$ respectively) to designate 'transfinite' sets. Since the mathematical operations involving such symbols are separate from any philosophical interpretation of the symbols as representations of literal infinity, the mathematician can practice the math while safely ignoring the secondary connotations of what the math, interpreted as calculations of literally infinite sets, would otherwise signify. The illogical connotations of literal infinity are therefore abstracted out of sight by the very formalism of the transfinite system.

14.4.1 *Ellipses as Symbols of Infinite Progressions in the Transfinite System*

The formal language of the transfinite system makes use of symbols such as the ellipsis. Use of an ellipsis after a progression of numbers inside braces functionally or operationally implies only running totals of numbers, which denotes incompleteness of progression. It is the separate, natural language interpretation of what the formal language means that states the progressions are *limitless* sequences of numbers and await discovery [499]. There is consequently a logical contradiction between the connotations of two languages in transfinite mathematics. The formal language of the transfinite system implies incomplete progressions of indefinite length; the natural language interpretation of the transfinite system claims complete progressions of limitless length. The two are in contradiction unless it is admitted that the formal language of transfinite mathematics is merely used as an *analogy* for limitless progressions like Euclid's method of exhaustion. But then, transfinite mathematics loses its claim to be calculating literally infinite sets in a direct way.

14.4.2 *Braces as Symbols for Sets in Transfinite Mathematics*

To depict a sequence of numbers as comprising a transfinite *set* of numbers, the transfinite system places the sequence into braces, like so: $\{1, 2, 3, ...\}$. However, what we actually have inside the braces is still an indefinite progression (only by technical definition is it a 'limitless' progression and, even then, it is at best only figuratively limitless since in principle one could indefinitely keep making the list longer); as such, it has a sum at any and all steps along the way. The symbolic representation of the progression in braces does not operationally imply a literally infinite progression.

But again, the transfinite system does not attend to this distinction. So, the claim that $\{1, 2, 3, ...\}$ is "transfinite"—i.e., literally infinite—is underdetermined by the formal language of the transfinite system. In the formal language of the transfinite system, what is really depicted inside the braces is an indefinite progression that is an incomplete progression, not a complete set.

It is only the natural language of the transfinite system that interprets the use of braces as representing such progressions to be "complete." Mathematician Norman Wildberger refers to this use of braces as a game of "let's pretend," as in let's pretend the progression in braces is complete [500].

14.4.3 *Letters as Symbols for Sets in Transfinite Mathematics*

As a further level of abstraction, the figurative infinite of numbers in braces, $\{1, 2, 3, ...\}$, can be symbolized by a letter such as $\mathbb{N}$ to depict the kind of numbers in the braces, such as the natural numbers. Or the 'set' of natural numbers can be depicted with a symbol to represent the ordinality of the number sequence (ω) or the cardinality ($\aleph_0$) of the collection as a whole. The use of the letters as symbols, like the use of braces, allows us to treat a sequence of numbers as a single, determinate unit in further set-theoretic expressions, even if the sequence of numbers referenced by such symbols is itself only an incomplete, indefinite sequence. Set theorists just symbolize such 'sets' as P (or as other symbols like $\mathbb{N}$, ω, $\aleph$, etc.) and treat the symbols as though they are finite units. The use of symbols therefore allows the set theorist to *interpret* the natural numbers as literally infinite during set-theoretic operation while simultaneously abstracting out literal infinity's connotations regarding sets as literally complete and yet literally limitless at the same time.

14.4.4 *The Contradictory Implications Remain*

The transfinite system's formal language, with its use of symbols and mathematical syntax, is intended to express literal infinity with mathematical precision while dissolving the self-contradictory implications and connotations inherent in its traditional meaning under the name 'actual infinity'. However, when literal infinity is reconceived as the 'transfinite' and redefined in technical terms, the result is instead the creation of a new, alternative conception of 'infinity' that in mathematical operation is no different than figurative infinity or indefiniteness. In the formal language of the transfinite system, braces surrounding a sequence of numbers followed an ellipsis—e.g., $\{1, 2, 3, ...\}$—is considered a 'transfinite set' but it mathematically operates as if it is a serial indefinite. Then too, 'transfinite sets' denoted by letter-like characters—e.g., P or even $\mathbb{N}$—mathematically operate as if they are collective indefinites. The transfinite system thus operates with what are, at best, figurative infinities dubbed 'transfinite' and mistaken for instances of literal infinity.

The transfinite system thus fails to capture literal infinity in its formal syntax; as a result, it never resolves the contradictions implied by the meaning of literal infinity. Instead, for operational purposes, it substitutes figurative infinities and misinterprets them as literal (or 'actual') infinities.

Take the logically contradictory implications of a set being both literally complete and literally limitless—such as implying infinitely large numbers while denying their existence or implying infinitely large sums while denying such sums result. These contradictory implications are simply ignored in the transfinite system because they never arise in the use of the formal syntax and set-theoretic symbolism. But the contradictory implications did not go away; they do not disappear just because they are "abstracted out" behind the formal symbolism and syntax for indefinite sets and series called 'infinite' or 'transfinite'. Rather, the contradictory implications remain in the transfinite system's philosophical *interpretation* of infinite sets even if not in the formalism used for their mathematical operation.

In *operation*, the 'transfinite' $\mathbb{N}$ is just the indefinite series of definite numbers (e.g.: 1, 2, 3, ...) given an indefinitely large supremum and represented in the transfinite system *as if* it is a finite set ($\mathbb{N}$) rather than an open series ($\mathbb{N}^C$). Meanwhile, in its philosophical *interpretation* of $\mathbb{N}$, the system of natural numbers is *interpreted* as being a literally infinite set. But as a literally infinite set, $\mathbb{N}$ is literally complete and literally limitless, each of which logical carries implications that come into conflict as detailed back in § 12.3: the set of naturals, $\mathbb{N}$, is both lexically 'countable' and yet 'uncountable'—both of these properties follow from a set being literally, or actually, infinite.

Because $\mathbb{N}$ is complete—a "finished totality" of elements as Cantor would say—$\mathbb{N}$ is countable. We can, at least in principle, count all its elements one by one [501].

But because $\mathbb{N}$ is limitless, with no maximum number of elements, $\mathbb{N}$ is uncountable even in principle; a count of its elements can never be finished [502].

Having technical definitions of 'complete', 'limitless', and 'infinite' along with formal syntax to express sets with these properties in mathematical operation avoids raising to awareness the contradictory logical implications of a transfinite being a literally infinite set. The formalism mathematically works precisely because it can avoid addressing such secondary implications. But the contradictions are still subtly implied when 'transfinite' sets are interpreted to be actually—literally—infinite and described as such.

§ 12.3 showed the countable-uncountable contradiction appears when mathematicians say the numbers of $\mathbb{N}$ can in principle be counted and yet they also say they cannot in principle be counted. Both statements must hold from the completeness and limitlessness of $\mathbb{N}$ and so be in contradiction with one another when $\mathbb{N}$ is interpreted to be literally infinite, despite the mathematical coherence of transfinite formalism.

14.5 ON REDEFINING COUNTABLE AND UNCOUNTABLE

The transfinite system seeks to resolve the countable-uncountable contradiction plaguing the notion of infinite sets by redefining what 'countable' and 'uncountable' mean. In the transfinite system, an infinite set is said to be 'countable' if its quantity of members is either equal to or less than that of the set of counting numbers, $\mathbb{N}$. In the transfinite system, an infinite set is instead 'uncountable' if its quantity of members is greater than that of $\mathbb{N}$.

But the transfinite system's solution to the countable-uncountable contradiction faces a few logical problems.

First, there is a logical problem with appealing to a distinction between correlation and subset senses of size, and use of quantifiers and operators, to distinguish sizes of infinite sets as 'countable' or 'uncountable'.

Second, there are a few logical problems with using the diagonal argument as proof that there are infinite sets of different sizes. And there is a related problem with appeals to relative sizes of infinite sets altogether. Redefining sets as 'countable' or 'uncountable' based on different "sizes" of infinite sets may not be as justified as often claimed.

Third, even if the first two sets of problems are handled, the transfinite system faces another problem with solving the countable-uncountable contradiction: the contradiction applies to *each* infinite set alone, not to comparisons between infinite sets as the transfinite system suggests.

We'll take a look at each of these problems.

14.6 A CRITIQUE OF SET-THEORETIC SIZE DISTINCTIONS

The transfinite system appeals to a distinction between a subset sense of size and a correlation sense of size (see § 13.9.3) in order to show that two infinite sets, A and B, can be different in size in terms of membership ($A \subset B$) while they can be the same size due to a correlation of their members ($A = B$). Whether or not one is smaller than the other or they are both equal in size thus depends on how we wish to compare sizes [503]. For example, according to the transfinite system, $\mathbb{N} \subset \mathbb{Z}$ because $\mathbb{Z}$ has numbers that $\mathbb{N}$ does not (namely, zero and the negative numbers). In that sense, we could say $\mathbb{N}$ is "smaller" than $\mathbb{Z}$. However, we can also say $\mathbb{N} = \mathbb{Z}$ because for any unique n in $\mathbb{N}$, we can match it to a unique z in $\mathbb{Z}$, so we could say $\mathbb{N}$ and $\mathbb{Z}$ are the "same size" (see **Figure 13.3**). On the other hand, $\mathbb{N} \subset \mathbb{R}$ because $\mathbb{R}$ has numbers $\mathbb{N}$ does not and so $\mathbb{N}$ is "smaller" than $\mathbb{R}$ in the subset sense of size; whereas, unlike how the naturals equal the integers, $\mathbb{N} \neq \mathbb{R}$ because not every n in $\mathbb{N}$ can be matched to a unique r in $\mathbb{R}$, and so the two sets are not "the same size" in the correlation sense of size (see § 13.9.4). Using this subset/correlation distinction for size, the transfinite system redefines what it means for sets to be 'countable' or 'uncountable'. A set like $\mathbb{Z}$ is 'countable' because every integer can be correlated to a natural while a set like $\mathbb{R}$ is 'uncountable' because not every natural can be correlated to a real.

But it does not appear to be true that there are two different meanings of size. Not making any assumptions from the transfinite system, when we would normally say one set belongs to another and not vice versa, we would be implying the former set is smaller (has fewer members) than the latter set. Hence, when expressing $A \subset B$, we are *implying* $A < B$. That is, because all members of A are members of B, but not vice versa, we're implying there is *more* of B than A. Which is to say $A < B$. Likewise, if we say $A = B$, we are implying $A \not\subset B$ *and* $B \not\subset A$ (i.e., A is not a proper subset of B and vice versa). In other words, because the two sets have an equal amount of members, there is not more in one than the other, so it cannot be that $A \subset B$, nor that $B \subset A$. So, if we don't assume the transfinite system to begin with, when we have $\mathbb{N} \subset \mathbb{Z}$, such naturally implies $\mathbb{N} < \mathbb{Z}$. That is, there are fewer natural numbers than integers. Likewise, not assuming the transfinite system, if we were to say $\mathbb{N} = \mathbb{Z}$, then we would be implying $\mathbb{N} \not\subset \mathbb{Z}$ and $\mathbb{Z} \not\subset \mathbb{N}$. In other words, in saying that there are just as many members in one set ($\mathbb{N}$) as in the other ($\mathbb{Z}$), we would be implying that the naturals are not a proper subset of the integers or vice versa.

The transfinite system denies that a difference of membership necessarily implies a difference of quantity between the sets under comparison and so it denies that proper subsets imply differences in quantity with their supersets—at least for infinite sets. But the plausibility of that position rests on first accepting the unproven assumptions of the transfinite system—both the assumption that number systems are infinite sets and the assumption that attempting correlations between the members of number systems as infinite sets is a good way to compare their relative sizes. We are not logically compelled to agree with the transfinite system on either of those assumptions.

If we instead assume that number systems are all incomplete series of indefinite size and not complete sets of limitless size, it follows that nonarbitrary size comparisons between number systems are not possible. As incomplete series of indefinite size, number systems have no non-arbitrary size comparisons between them. We cannot accurately say that $\mathbb{N}^C = \mathbb{Z}^C$, nor that $\mathbb{N}^C < \mathbb{Z}^C$, for we could just as well say $\mathbb{N}^C > \mathbb{Z}^C$. None of those expressions hold water. If all the number systems are incomplete series rather than completed sets, then the only size comparisons possible between collections of numbers are size comparisons between sets of numbers taken as selections from each incomplete, growing number system. So all we can say is that, for any set of numbers taken as a selection of known numbers from $\mathbb{W}^C$ or $\mathbb{Z}^C$ or $\mathbb{Q}^C$ or $\mathbb{R}^C$, etc., we can use the counting numbers of $\mathbb{N}^C$ to count the numbers in the selection.

To bolster this assessment, in the next sections we will see some fallacies of reasoning behind Cantor's diagonal argument. That exposition will support the conclusion of the erroneousness of the transfinite system's proposal—both for its subset/correlation size distinction between number systems and for its notion of what makes some sets 'countable' and others 'uncountable'.

14.7 FALLACIES IN THE DIAGONAL ARGUMENT

The transfinite system's solution to resolving the countable-uncountable contradiction in the concept of literal infinity faces further problems that have to do with Cantor's diagonal argument. Mathematicians are near-universally convinced that Cantor's diagonal argument is sound and the mathematics community no longer takes seriously challenges to it. However, Cantor's diagonal argument, contrary to popular opinion among mathematicians, also does not prove $\mathbb{R}$ is necessarily greater than $\mathbb{N}$ in terms of cardinality. This is so because the diagonal argument contains further logical fallacies:

- Specious analogy
- Erroneous premise
- Red herring
- Presumption

It is only based on these errors in reasoning that the diagonal argument concludes $\mathbb{N}$ must be of smaller cardinality than $\mathbb{R}$ in a correlation sense of size. Avoid these errors, and the conclusion of the diagonal argument has no support—the diagonal argument does not prove infinities come in different sizes. On the contrary, as illustrated in the following subsections, we are free to conclude that, if number systems are infinite *sets*, we can still consider them all—including the infinite set of natural numbers as compared to the infinite set of real numbers—to be "equally infinite" in the sense that they have no limit to their sequences. And yet, even the idea that there are infinite *sets* of numbers at all will be shown as doubtful.

14.7.1 *The Fallacy of Specious Analogy*

According to Cantor, the infinite size of one number system (e.g., $\mathbb{N}$) can be compared via correspondence techniques with the infinite sizes of other number systems, such as $\mathbb{Z}$ and $\mathbb{R}$. Size comparisons between infinite sets of numbers via correspondence techniques had already been considered by Bolzano who stated that one infinite set of numbers could be smaller in quantity than another infinite set of numbers [505]. Cantor had later claimed as much for the natural and real numbers: $\mathbb{N} < \mathbb{R}$.

However, whereas Cantor had said an infinite subset can be equal to the infinite superset of which it is a part, as when the natural numbers ($\mathbb{N}$) are placed into bijection with the integers ($\mathbb{Z}$), Bolzano would have called $\mathbb{N} = \mathbb{Z}$ preposterous. Instead, he would have said $\mathbb{N} < \mathbb{Z}$; there are fewer naturals than integers. Bolzano dismissed bijection for infinite sets, arguing that the attempt to match one-to-one all the members of an infinite subset with all members of an infinite superset does not establish that the two are equinumerous [506]. Instead, Bolzano argued the idea that an infinite subset is equal in quantity to an infinite superset is just a mathematical illusion [507]. Bolzano regarded it as an illusion resulting from inappropriately applying a comparison of incomplete, finite series (selections from the number systems) to literally infinite sets (the infinite number systems as wholes).

A series—as a sequence constructed by temporal succession—is not at all the same thing as a set, the members of which exist all at once.

Consider two sequences of numbers, like the odd natural numbers (1, 3, 5, ...) and the even natural numbers (2, 4, 6, ...). Note the use of ellipses: we have two sequences of numbers, each leaving off with higher numbers undepicted.

Now suppose we depict these series as in bijection by placing arrows not only between pairs of depicted numbers but also between the ellipses, as if to say, "For any further odd and even numbers depicted, keep on matching them up," like so:

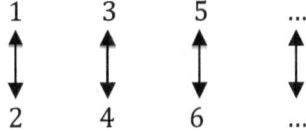

What we have is not really a bijection of a *complete set* of numbers, but rather a depiction of a *matching process* that results in a bijection for an arbitrarily large set of depicted pairs. There is no pair of final, finished sets placed into bijection in this example; there is instead just a depiction of two incomplete, *indefinite series* of numbers matched so long as numbers keep being generating tit-for-tat as the number generation process continues.

The so-called 'bijection' of odds and evens as finished sets is just an illusion; there is no comparison of two complete sets, just the ongoing comparison of two ever-incomplete series. Hence, Bolzano's objection would be that Cantor has used series to make a *specious analogy* to sets, creating the illusion of completed bijections where none exist.

Further illusions are generated due to similar specious analogies. For example, from one perspective, an infinite subset can appear to have a greater mathematical value than the superset it belongs to.

Consider the 'squares' of natural numbers. A 'square' is any number multiplied by itself. For example, the square of 2 is 2×2. Any number multiplied by itself is usually expressed as the number taken to the second power, or n^2. So, the square of 2 would be written as 2^2, which is equal to 4. The squares are said to be only a subset of the set of all the natural numbers.

Take a sequence of naturals such as the initial sequence of the first 16 natural numbers. This sequence contains the perfect squares of 1, 2, 3, and 4 which are, respectively, 1, 4, 9, and 16. We see fewer of the foregoing squares than all the natural numbers in that segment of the natural number scale [508]:

$\boxed{1}$ 2 3 $\boxed{4}$ 5 6 7 8 $\boxed{9}$ 10 11 12 13 14 15 $\boxed{16}$

However, something strange happens when we keep squaring ever-larger natural numbers. If we carry this to literal infinity, then we would expect the square of *all* the natural numbers to be greater in value than the sum of all the natural numbers:

$$1 + 2 + 3 + 4 + \ldots = n$$

$$1^2 + 2^2 + 3^2 + 4^2 + \ldots = n^2$$

Clearly, $n < n^2$. It therefore appears the squares are greater in total value than the set of numbers from which they derive their total value [509]. This certainly seems inconsistent—how can the squares have a value that goes higher than the scale of natural numbers to which they belong? And yet here we have the infinitely large value for an infinite subset being greater than the infinitely large value of the infinite superset to which it belongs.

Introductory books on set theory, transfinite mathematics, and infinity typically claim that "paradoxes" of infinite sets are based on common errors of reasoning about infinite sizes [510]. However, such confidence is misplaced. It's not that infinite sets are misunderstood because there are common errors of reasoning about infinite sizes; rather, it's that varying infinite sizes may be an indication there is something wrong with extrapolating to infinity. Bolzano, for one thinker, concluded squares and sums cannot be consistently carried to infinity, so the ability to extrapolate such squares and sums to infinity is just a mathematical illusion.

Bolzano thought the same could be true of carrying a bijection to infinity—a one-to-one correspondence of members in a subset to members of the superset produces an illusion that the two sets are equinumerous. As mathematician Guillermina Waldegg elucidated, Bolzano thought that "although two sets A and B are related in such a way that, by means of a rule, to each member of A corresponds a member of B and vice-versa, the conclusion that its members are equal when they are infinite is not justified" [511]. In other words, a bijection is a *process* that shows of two infinite sets that we can always continue matching up the elements between them, but such a matching process does not show the two infinite sets have an equal number of members; their equinumerosity is illusory [512].

To see why Bolzano might conclude this, take the following bijection in which we pair the infinite subset of odd natural numbers with the infinite subset of even natural numbers:

Notice that the numbers of each row are unique: there is no number in the top row that appears in the bottom row and vice versa. Now, let's pair the infinite subset of even natural numbers with the infinite superset of all natural numbers (both odd and even):

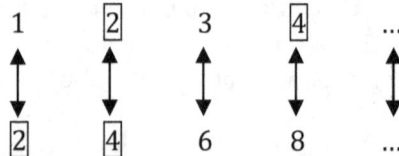

As you can see, the two rows of numbers do not *together* contain only unique numbers. The number 2 appears in both rows, as does the number 4, and if carried to infinity there would be an infinite amount of other repeated numbers between the rows. It is true that, vertically, the number 2 is paired with only a single, unique number in the opposite row—e.g., the number 1—but it is not true that between both rows 2 is a unique number. It is only by the unfinished series of number repetitions between the rows that the part (the evens) can be made to *appear* as great as the whole (both odds and evens).

This is not exactly Bolzano's argument, but it helps to show why he may have thought the technique of bijection between a subset and a superset produces only an illusion that the two are the same size when carried to infinity. So, he concluded, an infinite subset is not really equinumerous with its infinite superset [513] [514].

Although mathematicians have historically preferred Cantor's work, recent analysis suggests Bolzano's mathematical system can be regarded as equally consistent [515]. There is no logical necessity why we *must* prefer one to the other. In fact, for just the reasons given, Cantor's use of bijection to match a literally infinite subset, such as $\mathbb{N}$, to a literally infinite superset, such as $\mathbb{Z}$, may rest on a specious analogy between using bijection for sets that do not share members and using bijection for sets that do.

Now if that is so, then this spells trouble for Cantor's diagonal argument. Even though Bolzano would have agreed that $\mathbb{N} < \mathbb{R}$, he would not have agreed based on the diagonal argument. Rather, he would have simply stated that $\mathbb{R}$ includes all kinds of decimal numbers not found in $\mathbb{N}$ as a subset of $\mathbb{R}$, and that is why $\mathbb{N}$ must be less than $\mathbb{R}$, even though both are infinite. The lack of bijection between $\mathbb{N}$ and $\mathbb{R}$ would have simply been beside the point since bijection only produces mathematical illusions for infinite subset/superset relations.

Although I believe Bolzano and Cantor are both incorrect that literal infinity is a logically (vice mathematically) sensible concept, I do agree with Bolzano's charge of illusion against infinite enumeration via bijection and the specious analogy that produced it. Similarly, Bolzano would likely argue that Cantor's diagonal argument does not establish different sizes of infinity, and I think Bolzano would be right about that as well. However, contrary to Bolzano, neither does a sequence of $\mathbb{R}$ as containing numbers not found in $\mathbb{N}$ establish the reals as a differently sized infinite set, for that too is an illusion.

14.7.2 *The Fallacy of Erroneous Premise*

The erroneous premise assumed by the diagonal argument is this:

- The natural numbers of the literally infinite set $\mathbb{N}$ can be *all used up* when $\mathbb{N}$ is placed into bijection with another literally infinite set such as $\mathbb{R}$.

According to the diagonal argument, the numbers of $\mathbb{N}$ are "all used up" when they are placed into bijection with the numbers of only an incomplete segment of $\mathbb{R}$ [516]. But in saying the numbers of $\mathbb{N}$ can be "used up" in a bijection with another set, the diagonal argument supposes the system of natural numbers constitutes a complete set ($\mathbb{N}$). To say such, and leave it at that, is to "abstract out" (i.e., ignore) part of what it means to be a literally infinite set: having *limitlessly*-many members. It is the mistake of the diagonal argument to overlook its own claim that an infinitude has *no limit*—no maximum or last number.

By assuming the premise that the numbers of $\mathbb{N}$ can be used up, we ensure that we treat $\mathbb{N}$ as a *complete* set but not as a complete set that nevertheless contains a *limitless* number of numbers—in other words, as a literally infinite set. The diagonal argument "abstracts out" the limitlessness of $\mathbb{N}$ as a literally infinite set in favor of addressing only the issue of $\mathbb{N}$'s completeness, thus treating $\mathbb{N}$ as a complete *indefinite* set (i.e., a completed finite set of indefinitely large magnitude, a 'collective indefinite') rather than a set having a literally infinite amount of numbers. So, it is a misleading premise to say $\mathbb{N}$, as a literally *infinite* set, can be "all used up" in bijection because to be literally infinite is not just to be complete but also to have *limitlessly* many members. And that means the members of $\mathbb{N}$ can never be used up, not even in principle.

The premise that the numbers of $\mathbb{N}$ can all be used up is therefore ignoring, and only compounding, the contradiction that the completeness of $\mathbb{N}$ would imply totality (the numbers of $\mathbb{N}$ are used up) while the limitlessness of $\mathbb{N}$ would imply $\mathbb{N}$ has no total at all (the numbers of $\mathbb{N}$ can never be used up). This is a logical connotation caused by assuming number scales are literally infinite sets—a connotation that the diagonal argument not only doesn't address but obscures by abstracting out the limitlessness of what mathematicians assume to be a literally infinite set and instead focusing only on that allegedly infinite set as being a complete set [517].

Hence, the premise that $\mathbb{N}$, as a literally infinite set, can be used up is an erroneous premise in that it misleads from the truth: if $\mathbb{N}$ is literally infinite, then the numbers of $\mathbb{N}$ can *and* cannot be used up. The premise is misleading because it hides the inconsistency inherent in the conception of $\mathbb{N}$ as a literally infinite set. Moreover, if I am correct that $\mathbb{N}$ is not really literally infinite anyway because infinity in the literal sense of the term is self-contradictory, then the premise is not just misleading, it is also false.

14.7.3 *The Red Herring Fallacy*

There is a red herring in the diagonal argument:

- The infinite sequence of naturals in $\mathbb{N}$ cannot be placed into bijection with an infinite sequence of reals comprising a subset of $\mathbb{R}$.

To see why this is a red herring, begin by recalling again the diagonal argument assumes a bijection can be made between the infinite *set* of naturals and the infinite *set* of reals—or, more precisely, the set of naturals can be placed into bijection with an infinite subset (or "segment") of reals between 0 and 1. With respect to cardinality, sets are *groups for which order is irrelevant*. But notice the diagonal argument then switches topics to prove that the infinite *sequence* (ordered group) of naturals cannot be placed in bijection with a given infinite *sequence* (ordered group) of real numbers. Next, the diagonal argument switches back from the subject of comparing an infinite sequence of numbers comprising $\mathbb{N}$ with an infinite sequence of numbers in a segment of $\mathbb{R}$ to the subject of comparing two infinite sets (the complete set of $\mathbb{N}$ matched with an assumed complete set forming a segment of $\mathbb{R}$). It then concludes that the set of naturals ($\mathbb{N}$) cannot be bijected with the set of reals ($\mathbb{R}$) because there will always be reals left over.

The diagonal argument switched from an assertion about comparing the cardinalities of $\mathbb{N}$ and $\mathbb{R}$ as *sets* to demonstrating that the *sequence* of $\mathbb{N}$ as a scale cannot be matched to a certain *sequence* in $\mathbb{R}$ (established by designating the diagonal string of digits). This distinction between set and sequence is important because sequences are about ordinality rather than cardinality while sets are about cardinality rather than ordinality. The sequence of any subset of $\mathbb{R}$ is irrelevant to $\mathbb{R}$'s cardinality. What the diagonal argument proved is something about sequence, not size—something about ordinality rather than cardinality. Yet, the diagonal argument purports to prove something about size—about cardinality—and that's why the diagonal argument is a red herring argument.

If we are to compare the sizes of $\mathbb{N}$ and $\mathbb{R}$ correctly, we must compare the cardinality of $\mathbb{N}$ as a set to the cardinality of $\mathbb{R}$ as a set, or at least compare the cardinality of $\mathbb{N}$ as a set to the cardinality of a segment of $\mathbb{R}$, which is to deal with the segment as a set rather than as a sequence. What we cannot do without fallacy is attempt a bijection of $\mathbb{N}$ as a sequence to a segment of $\mathbb{R}$ as a sequence established by a given sequencing procedure, and then draw conclusions about the sizes of $\mathbb{N}$ and $\mathbb{R}$ as complete sets. But that's exactly what Cantor's diagonal argument does. Consequently, cardinality (set) and ordinality (sequence) become mistaken for one another.

The switch from the cardinalities of $\mathbb{N}$ and the $\mathbb{R}$ segment to their ordinalities was made as soon as we picked out a diagonal string of digits in $\mathbb{R}$'s listing by which to draw comparisons (see the boldface digits in **Figure 14.2**).

$\mathbb{N}$		$\mathbb{R}$ $(0-1)$
1	↔	0.**0**00000...
2	↔	0.1**1**1111...
3	↔	0.01**0**101...
4	↔	0.101**0**10...
5	↔	0.1101**0**1...
6	↔	0.00110**1**...
⋮	↔	⋮ ⋱

$$p = 0.010001...$$

$$q = 0.101110...$$

Figure 14.2: The diagonal argument (same as Figure 13.4, replicated here for convenience).

The diagonal argument has us begin by depicting the naturals in their usual order even though order is supposed to be irrelevant to $\mathbb{N}$ as a *set*, but we'll let that slide since "all" the naturals are assumed to be in the $\mathbb{N}$ column anyway; we can allow the numbers listed for $\mathbb{N}$ to be in sequence just as a matter of convenience. The diagonal argument then says we need to pick out an arbitrary sequence of real numbers written out horizontally in the column for $\mathbb{R}$. Any random listing would do because the randomness is meant to show that we are thinking of $\mathbb{R}$ purely in terms of cardinality rather than in terms of ordinality—even though that's not what we end up doing.

However, the selection of the diagonal string of digits cutting through the column of reals we listed for the segment of $\mathbb{R}$ does in fact establish a *sequence* for the column of real numbers, making the column into an ordinality and not just a cardinality as we had originally intended. Consequently, when we generate a real number guaranteed not to appear according to the column's diagonal sequence (q from p in **Figure 14.2**), just by the way the column's sequencing has been defined, we shouldn't be surprised that $\mathbb{N}$ can't match $\mathbb{R}$ under such conditions.

It's supposed to be the relative *size* of each set that matters, not their *sequences*. And yet, the diagonal argument relies on sequencing, as illustrated in **Figure 14.3**.

$\mathbb{N}$		$\mathbb{R}\ (0-1)$
1	$\leftrightarrow$	$0.\mathbf{d_{11}}d_{12}d_{13}d_{14}d_{15}d_{16}...$
2	$\leftrightarrow$	$0.d_{21}\mathbf{d_{22}}d_{23}d_{24}d_{25}d_{26}...$
3	$\leftrightarrow$	$0.d_{31}d_{32}\mathbf{d_{33}}d_{34}d_{35}d_{36}...$
4	$\leftrightarrow$	$0.d_{41}d_{42}d_{43}\mathbf{d_{44}}d_{45}d_{46}...$
5	$\leftrightarrow$	$0.d_{51}d_{52}d_{53}d_{54}\mathbf{d_{55}}d_{56}...$
6	$\leftrightarrow$	$0.d_{61}d_{62}d_{63}d_{64}d_{65}\mathbf{d_{66}}...$
$\vdots$	$\leftrightarrow$	$\vdots$
n	$\leftrightarrow$	$0.d_{n1}d_{n2}d_{n3}d_{n4}d_{n5}d_{n6}...$
$\vdots$		$\vdots$

Figure 14.3: An abstract formulation of the diagonal argument.

As shown in **Figure 14.3**, it is clear the next real number, a real number that will be matched with 7 in the natural number column, must be given the label $0.d_{71}d_{72}d_{73}d_{74}d_{75}d_{76}...$, which means the diagonal digit in that real number must then be d_{77}. So, the real numbers for $\mathbb{R}$ are indeed following a sequence.

Comparing **Figure 14.3** to **Figure 14.2**, it is clear that the diagonal argument says you cannot include q as falling somewhere *next* in the list of reals, nor anywhere between the first and last depicted rows of reals already established for $\mathbb{R}$. That means q can't be next in line—at least, that seems to be the reasoning.

But that reasoning ignores that we are supposed to be comparing cardinalities, not ordinalities. Sequence for real numbers in the $\mathbb{R}$ segment should be unimportant for establishing the list of horizontally written real numbers in the $\mathbb{R}$ column. The use of ordinality is the red herring of the diagonal argument for comparing the sizes of $\mathbb{N}$ and $\mathbb{R}$ rather than their orders.

To see the red herring in even starker terms, consider the following argument, which I will call the *non-ordinality argument*.

If the sequence of reals is truly unimportant and the size of the segment of reals is all that matters, then q can indeed follow *next* in the list of reals. The reason q can follow next in sequence is because q is formed from p and p is itself not a number that appears in the listing that we established for $\mathbb{R}$—not even diagonally.

That may sound surprising for me to say. After all, a mathematician might retort that in **Figure 14.2** the diagonal string of digits is the number p, or $0.010001....$ It just appears in the $\mathbb{R}$ segment diagonally instead of horizontally. So, as a diagonal number in $\mathbb{R}$, the value of p does have a sequence—a limitless sequence that determines what can follow next in the column of real numbers and q is not such a number. The mathematician might then conclude the use of a diagonal number to establish a sequence for the $\mathbb{R}$ segment is perfectly justified. Certainly, that is what Cantor claimed.

However, that retort contains a logical error: it falsely assumes the diagonal string of digits is the number p just because the diagonal string of digits and p have the same sequence of numerals prior to the ellipsis. We need not concede that the diagonal string is identical to the real number p.

Not just any string of digits is a *number* simply because it is a string of digits. To be a number, a string of digits must fit the definition of a number—it must be "a numeral's unique ordinality-cardinality association in a numeral system" (see § 2.3.1)—and it must be formed by the same rule as other numbers in the same system. So, whether a string of digits constitutes a number depends on its role in a system.

Suppose we have a string of digits such as 91224. Is this string of digits a number in the mathematical sense ($91{,}224$) as opposed to the colloquial sense (like a postal number)? Or is it just a string of numerals (9 and 1 and 2 and 2 and 4)? It depends on how the string of digits is formed and as a number defined.

So too, it's not at all clear that a diagonal string of digits plucked from rows of horizontally written numbers is itself a real number at all. Instead, the string of digits may just be a random string of *individual* numerals that do not together constitute a single number.

In support of this view, note that the diagonal digits selected after the decimal of the first real number in the column of **Figure 14.2** would be written horizontally as $010001...$, but this is not a real number. Perhaps it is just a 0 and 1 and 0 and 0, etc. If it is a number at all, it is equal to $10{,}001...$ or perhaps $100{,}01...$, neither of which are the same as $0.010001...$.

Furthermore, because the diagonal string leaves off with an ellipsis, and the horizontal numbers of the $\mathbb{R}$ segment do not necessarily belong to $\mathbb{R}$ as a set with a larger pattern of numbers, the next digit in the diagonal string need not be defined until we decide what real number should come next in the horizontal list or until we further define the value of p. We therefore need not concur that the underscored or boldfaced digits in the diagonal string of digits seen in **Figure 14.2** comprise a real number. We may instead simply assume any diagonal string of digits in the column of reals isn't a number at all—it's just an incomplete string of digits, the first digits of which will be used for creating a new real number, p.

The new real number, p, does not appear as a real number in our original sample of $\mathbb{R}$—not even diagonally. The diagonal sequence of digits selected has no decimal point ($010001...$); it is not an actual number. Rather, it is a selection of digits used to *create* the real number p which is nowhere listed horizontally in the column of reals. Only once we say that $010001...$ *means* $0.010001...$ does it then become the real number p and not just a random string of digits.

This is because all the numbers in our sample of $\mathbb{R}$ are written out *horizontally* and listed *vertically* in a column. If it's not written horizontally in the column, it's not a number—it's just a selection of digits. We can certainly *copy* the string of digits and write it out horizontally to *create* a new real number for inclusion in our column of reals, but the diagonal string is still just a string of digits and not really a number until we make it into the number p for creation of the real number q.

Here is the crux of the matter: because the diagonal string of digits is not actually the number p, where the diagonal string leaves off with the ellipsis is where the 'sequence' of the diagonal string ends our knowledge of what comes next. The next digit that appears in the diagonal string can be whatever we want it to be *if we are not using a preestablished sequence* for the reals. Which means the next horizontal real number can be whatever we like it to be as long as it is not a duplicate of a preceding number. So, the next number can indeed be q, but it can even be p because although p and the diagonal string have digits in common, it's only the horizontal number p with its decimal place that is a real number (0.010001) and not just the random diagonal string ($010001...$). So, nothing prevents either q or even p from appearing next in the list according to the non-ordinality argument. And that impales the diagonal argument.

After all, if the diagonal argument is about size alone and sequence does not matter, then the "d's" of **Figure 14.3** would be just variable labels for easy reference—they are not actually the real numbers of the $\mathbb{R}$ column, each of which can fall in *any* sequence, especially if we are not writing them down according to an ordinality. The horizontally-written real numbers can thus be any ol' set of real numbers we like (so long as the real numbers are unique to the list we depict) because we are not writing the real numbers according to ordinality—we only care about cardinality, which indicates the relative *size* of each set. So, q could very well be next in line; and that means d_{77} in **Figure 14.3** could very well be equal to whatever digit would correspond to that place in q, which means we could just put q next.

Now you can see the reason the non-ordinality argument contradicts the conclusion of Cantor's diagonal argument is that Cantor's argument is supposed to compare the *size* of $\mathbb{N}$ in its totality to the *size* of the $\mathbb{R}$ segment in its totality; but instead, the diagonal argument compares the *sequence* of depicted numbers from $\mathbb{N}$ to a *sequence* of depicted numbers from $\mathbb{R}$. Ordinality to ordinality instead of cardinality to cardinality as originally claimed. Showing that some reals were left out of a depicted sequence, therefore, does not show that bijection between $\mathbb{N}$ and $\mathbb{R}$ is impossible; it just shows that you must be careful with how you go about constructing your depicted lists of numbers. The same was true when we compared the naturals to the integers: present the sequences of $\mathbb{N}$ and $\mathbb{Z}$ one way and their members don't match up; present them a different way and they do (**Figure 13.2** and **Figure 13.3**).

Ignore listing the reals for the $\mathbb{R}$ segment according to sequence and instead allow each horizontal line of reals to be generated randomly, as unique naturals are generated for each real, and we find there's no problem "discovering" reals as we proceed in matching the $\mathbb{R}$ segment to $\mathbb{N}$. The naturals and reals will match tit for tat when the sequence of $\mathbb{R}$ is irrelevant. So, contrary to the diagonal argument, $\mathbb{N}$ and $\mathbb{R}$ can indeed maintain bijection after all if you (a) start with a different assumption about what the diagonal is—a string of arbitrary digits and not genuinely a real number—and (b) adopt a different procedure for generating a list of reals to biject with naturals as a matching process, even while assuming both $\mathbb{N}$ and $\mathbb{R}$ are themselves literally infinite sets that we "discover" as we list their members.

To adopt such an alternative starting point and means of correspondence between scales is to throw out the diagonal argument's comparison of $\mathbb{N}$ and $\mathbb{R}$ by ordinality in favor of comparing them by cardinality, which is more consistent with Cantor's claim that $\mathbb{N}$ and $\mathbb{R}$ can be compared by *size*. But to do that is to show we have no need to conclude that there are "different sizes" of literally infinite sets—$\mathbb{N}$ and $\mathbb{R}$ can instead be regarded as "equally infinite," if they are infinite at all. The diagonal argument thus does not succeed in necessitating the conclusion that there are different sizes of infinite sets. As the late mathematician Alexander A. Zenkin (1937–2006) noted, "the results of [Cantor's Diagonal Method] depend fatally upon the order of real numbers in the sequences to which it is applied" [518].

14.7.4 *The Fallacy of Presumption*

Systems of mathematics and symbolic logic are based on axioms, where an axiom is an assumption the truth of which is taken as "self-evident." There can be a problem, however, when the axiom is not self-evidently true (recall Euclid's fifth postulate in § 9.6.4). That problem surfaces in the diagonal argument of Cantor's transfinite system.

Specifically, there is a false axiom assumed in the diagonal argument: the Axiom of Infinity. The axiom is false *as* an axiom (a self-evidently true statement) because it constitutes an instance of *the fallacy of presumption*—the error of basing an argument on an unwarranted assumption.

This was Cantor's unwarranted assumption:

- The number systems are, by logical necessity, complete sets.

We find the origin of Cantor's presumption that number systems must be complete sets in his first article on set theory, where he states, "The real algebraic numbers constitute in their entirety a set of numbers..." [519] and in his later book on manifolds where he states that by the term 'set' he means "any multiplicity which can be thought of as one..." [520]. If this assumption were true, the Axiom of Infinity would indeed be a safe assumption. But the assumption is highly dubious for a few reasons.

For one thing, Cantor believed that mathematicians intellectually discover number systems when mathematicians are able to consistently define them, and such discoveries may in the future be able to be shown to be "realities" by the empirical sciences [521]. But there is no compelling *a priori* reason why number systems are necessarily complete sets that are *discovered*. We can just as well and without contradiction assume that number systems are intrinsically incomplete, open series *invented* according to hypothetical rules.

We will return to the distinction between inventing and discovering again in Chapter 16 where we will see further evidence that there is no compelling, a priori reason why we *must* believe that we are merely reproducing segments of preexisting real numbers when we write down real numbers, let alone that the real numbers are "out there" in some mental or metaphysical world of their own awaiting scientific confirmation [522]. We could of course *hypothesize* that number systems are complete sets the members of which we discover, and perhaps there are some good arguments to support such a view, but there are no arguments that logically *compel* us to take that view because such a view is not something that is true *by definition*. That number systems are complete sets is not a tautology; it is just a proposal. And since it is not a necessary truth that a number system is a complete set, the "Axiom of Infinity" (which assumes the completeness of number systems) is not really an axiom either.

Moreover, if we suppose real numbers are "out there" waiting for us to discover them, we have another problem: we "discover" them where? That is, where is this completed set of real algebraic numbers? As I will argue further in Chapter 16, there is no *a posteriori*, empirical evidence of such a metaphysical place "out there" where numbers reside, waiting to be discovered instead of invented.

So again, we could just as safely assume that real numbers are merely invented by applying a rule than assume they are discovered. Empirically speaking, we even have good reason to suppose the proposal that number scales are complete sets is not true—no one has ever, nor can one ever, witness such a thing as all the numbers of an absolutely complete number scale, at least not concerning the number scales we are considering ($\mathbb{N}$, $\mathbb{Z}$, $\mathbb{Q}$, $\mathbb{R}$, etc.).

We have historical evidence to the contrary: artifacts and documents from ancient times showing that numbers and number scales were invented, first from tallies, then from tokens, then from numeral symbols. We have no evidence that numbers exist outside of the inventions of mathematicians. What we do see is mathematicians inventing ever higher finite numbers, like googol, googolplex, etc.

It would thus appear that Cantor assumed, without any compelling evidence—and plenty of evidence to the contrary—that scales of numbers, such as the system of real numbers, are "discovered" as "entire" sets (i.e., complete sets). It is therefore neither an a priori truth that number scales are complete sets nor is it obviously an a posteriori, empirical truth they are such. Instead, all we have is conventional opinion in the mathematics community based on some dubious metaphysical conjectures about number systems. And conventions can be wrong.

Regardless, Cantor's assumption—seemingly shared by many mathematicians—that number systems are *necessarily* complete sets, is an unwarranted assumption. It just isn't so as a matter of necessity—not logically and not empirically—and there is no compelling evidence to support it; certainly not enough to make number systems as complete sets axiomatic. Ergo, we need not assume that scales of numbers must exist as already complete sets.

Cantor further assumed "all" the natural numbers of $\mathbb{N}$, as a complete set, are implied by the progression 1, 2, 3, ... Likewise, "all" the integers of $\mathbb{Z}$, as a complete set, are implied by the progression ..., $-3, -2, -1, 0, 1, 2, 3,$ .... The same holds for $\mathbb{R}$ and the other number systems. In saying "all," Cantor assumed that numbers are defined "out there," as if ready to be found. But Cantor's assumptions are big assumptions, and they are not necessarily an accurate way to regard number systems.

We need not assume that the progressions of numbers we depict somehow imply "all" numbers as if number systems were complete sets that we merely sample. Perhaps there is no such thing as "all" the natural numbers and no such thing as "all" the real numbers, or "all" the numbers for any other system of numbers—at least, not in the sense of having an absolutely completed set of predefined numbers. Instead, perhaps number systems are not sets (in the sense of completed collections) but are open series developed over time, as discussed in previous chapters. In which case, number systems are scales that can be made to go on indefinitely as new values are calculated or otherwise invented for them, but they always remain inherently incomplete and so finite. We may write down numbers that have already been defined, but that does not mean *all* possible numbers have already been defined in a complete set and that we can merely reproduce segments of number scales. Rather, at any given moment, a depicted sequence of numbers may constitute a finite, definite set, but such a set is just part of a scale of numbers that is an open, incomplete series. If that is so, when we refer to "all" the naturals or "all" the reals, we are only referring to all the numbers *that have so far been defined and that we are able, at least in principle, to depict*. This does not imply that number scales are in any way complete sets.

So, with respect to forming bijections between the sequences of numbers from two number systems such as $\mathbb{N}$ and $\mathbb{Z}$, it is true that if we match, one-to-one, the members between the sequences we find there are "just as many" members in one sequence as there are in the other, at any step along the way. But, operationally speaking, making the correspondence between increasingly larger amounts of members between sequences does not really demonstrate that the sequences are complete sets with limitless lengths. It could be that the sequences are simply *indefinite* series (e.g., $\mathbb{N}^C$ and $\mathbb{Z}^C$) rather than *infinite* sets ($\mathbb{N}$ and $\mathbb{Z}$), and they could therefore be incomplete series rather than complete sets—so, they stay matched as long as we keep inventing new numbers and matching them up.

Such is how the sequences we generate are treated operationally—as incomplete, finite sequences of indefinite length. After all, we never in actual practice biject all numbers capable of being defined. If we write out some initial segment, we just use an ellipsis in order to show the progression continuing according to the procedure we initiated. No one ever actually completes a bijection of "all" natural numbers with other sequences of numbers unless "all" just means *all we know*—and, actually, not even that many. To say, then, that the elements of $\mathbb{N}$ and $\mathbb{Z}$ are equinumerous (denoted, $\mathbb{N} = \mathbb{Z}$) is, from an operational point of view, just to say the numbers in two indefinite series can be evenly matched *as long as the activity of corresponding is continued* ($\mathbb{N}^C = \mathbb{Z}^C$), not that both are complete sets of limitless length.

Likewise, we could just as well assume that the naturals and reals are inherently incomplete, open series formed by processes of enumeration, and that they never were, nor could be, complete sets to begin with. In that case, when we construct a bijection intended to be a comprehensive matching of naturals and reals, all we can really attempt is a comprehensive matching of all natural and real numbers that have been *defined*, or invented, up to the present. We may continue such pairing with any new numbers we invent.

Then too, the ongoing invention of new numbers in $\mathbb{N}^C$ and $\mathbb{R}^C$ as open series brings us back to the red herring previously discussed: if we were to write the column of reals including any real number we desire (and *without sequence*, since we should be comparing subsets of $\mathbb{N}^C$ and subsets of $\mathbb{R}^C$ by cardinality and not by ordinality), then q can be included in the segment of $\mathbb{R}^C$ and matched with a single, unique natural number, just as any real in **Figure 14.2**. After all, the depicted numbers of $\mathbb{N}^C$ also do not comprise a complete set—rather, they are part of a series that it leaves off wherever we leave it off.

It's easiest to see the incompleteness of the "set" of naturals and the incompleteness of the sequence made for the reals with respect to the use of the ellipsis in the diagonal argument. Each row in the $\mathbb{R}$ column of in **Figure 14.2** ends in an ellipsis and the column of $\mathbb{R}$ itself ends in an ellipsis going down. So too, the diagonal string of digits in $\mathbb{R}$ ends in an ellipsis. An ellipsis does not necessarily indicate a complete set, the remainder of which has not been depicted. An ellipsis can also indicate an incomplete set or an incomplete, open series. So, the column of real numbers trailing off with an ellipsis as denoting a "segment" of $\mathbb{R}$ may just as well denote a continuing *construction* for $\mathbb{R}^C$ as itself an incomplete, open series of real numbers.

Notice as well that each real number listed in the "segment" of $\mathbb{R}$ is either a rational number of recurring digits or an irrational number; in either case, the value of the number trails off with an ellipsis. For example, $0.001101...$ Here too, the ellipsis need not be interpreted as an infinity but instead as an indefinite series.

Interpreted that way, not only are the reals in the $\mathbb{R}$ column actually part of an incomplete series, but also each listed rational with periodic sequences of digits (as well as any irrational numbers in that list of reals) may be thought of as an intrinsically *incomplete number*. [523]. If we hold numbers themselves to be either complete or incomplete, we can take numbers such as rationals with repeating decimals and irrational numbers with their non-repeating decimals as numbers with an intrinsically incomplete *series* of digits with a running total of base digits in their sequence rather than a literally infinite *set* of digits.

Moreover, the column of numbers in the $\mathbb{R}$ segment is not the only incomplete list. The column of $\mathbb{N}$ also ends in an ellipsis—it too can be taken as just an incomplete series of numbers ($\mathbb{N}^C$) [524]. If so, the list of numbers in the $\mathbb{N}$ and $\mathbb{R}$ columns do not make up literally infinite sets—they are actually just indefinite series that should have been denoted as such ($\mathbb{N}^C$ and $\mathbb{R}^C$). But then, that would have made Cantor's diagonal argument moot.

Some mathematicians might rebut this argument about the use of ellipses by pointing out that the diagonal argument can be made without making columns of numbers with ellipses. This has been the position of educator Charles Fisher ('Chip') Cooper [525]:

> Strangely, you'll find there are people who believe the diagonal argument is wrong because the proof uses dots when writing a series of numbers 1, 2, 3, ..., n, ..., etc. For some reason they triumphantly point out the dots—particularly at the end—mean you can always slip in as many counting numbers you need for any number of real numbers.
>
> Fortunately, that objection is totally erroneous because the dots are simply a simplification of more rigorous notation, an objection disposed of quite easily by *using* the more rigorous notation...

On the contrary: the critics are correct, and Cooper's rebuttal fails. The three dots, an ellipsis, need not mean the numbers are there to be found according to an established sequence. They can instead be taken to indicate *incompleteness of number generation*, and that is the key point of the criticism: the list of naturals, like the list of reals, *was never a complete set to begin with*. I'm not alone in this assessment: Fletcher too points out the ellipsis can be taken as indicating a growing finite list rather than the incomplete listing of a complete set [526].

Perhaps, then, Cantor was wrong to presume number scales are complete sets. Instead, perhaps the naturals *and* the reals in the depicted columns of numbers were both incomplete *series* of numbers (where 'series' means a collection formed by a succession of steps over time) to begin with, and so the diagonal argument is inadvertently just comparing two incomplete, open series, not comparing a complete set with an incomplete subset. The ellipses need not denote sets we haven't finished writing down, but series we may never finish inventing.

As for the more rigorous notation Cooper mentions, it is a formula that uses an ordered pair of numbers: (x, y_x), where x is a natural number and y_x is a randomly generated real number [527]. The formula starts by generating a unique real number, y_x, for any already-named natural number, x, and ends by generating a new real number not identical to any real number you have already matched to a natural number. The point of the formula is to show that for any match of a natural number to a real number already generated, you can use a formula to generate an extra real number not already matched. But again, this does not really show there are more reals in existence than naturals in existence.

What the formula shows is merely that you can *construct* more reals than appear in any already-constructed *partial* listing of reals and naturals, each of which is produced by a particular pairing method and remain ever *incomplete* as the list continues building. You can always use a formula to generate an extra real number—or invent another real number if no one ever invented that number before—from the reals already depicted so that there are more reals in your new list of reals than the naturals you have already *depicted* (written down) in the original list of naturals. Cooper just shows that, given *depicted* naturals bijected with *depicted* reals, there is a mathematical formula for constructing another real number that is not in the collection of depicted reals previously matched to depicted naturals [528]. That is all the formula shows, and nothing more.

What the formula does not and cannot show is that the natural numbers already listed comprise a *complete set* of naturals (both depicted and undepicted) existing "out there" waiting to be discovered—that is just metaphysical supposition. Instead, we could just as well assume that any generation of natural numbers is just an incomplete, open series. We could also just as well assume that any generated reals comprise an incomplete, open series.

Given these two alternative assumptions, Cooper's appeal to the formula is trivial because we could then simply add a few steps to the formula that says after you create your new y, you should extend your list of values for x by generating a new natural number value (equal to $x + 1$) and then insert your new y into the listing of reals to restore bijection with all the naturals generated so far, just as the non-ordinality argument does. Now, the tit-for-tat of bijection returns between two inherently incomplete series of depicted numbers. So, yes, for any natural I name in a depicted bijection of naturals to reals, you can think of a new real not in the established list, but for any real you dream up, I can add it to the list of reals and then generate another natural with the successor function to rematch the lists again since there is no final natural number either.

We now come to a fork in the road: which is it—are the scales of naturals and reals complete sets the parts of which we discover or are the number scales just incomplete series always under construction? For further evidence that both the naturals and reals are incomplete series ($\mathbb{N}^C$ and $\mathbb{R}^C$) rather than complete sets ($\mathbb{N}$ and $\mathbb{R}$), we have only to examine an indirect proof against Cantor's diagonal argument.

14.7.5 *Will the Next Number Please Stand Up?*

Let's examine an 'indirect proof' against the diagonal argument (**Figure 14.2**) by starting with a simple question regarding the listed numbers in the $\mathbb{R}$ column: what will the next horizontal number be in the column of the $\mathbb{R}$ segment, and what will the next diagonal digit be where the ellipses leave us in that column? The question cannot be answered based on the numbers already provided if the horizontal numbers listed for the segment of $\mathbb{R}$ are not listed according to ordinality. There would simply be no way to go through all the numbers to check. Looking at the sequence of q is no help because it also ends with the same number of spaces as the depicted numbers of the diagonal string—and we have no idea what the next number in that string will be either. The next number for $\mathbb{R}$ is therefore undefined until we decide what it will be, and it can be any irrational number we like because the next number for the diagonal string of digits is also undefined.

Nor would it do any good to appeal to probability here, as if the next real number must be randomly generated and it's just *unlikely* to be identical to your diagonally-generated real number. It does no good to appeal to probability because we are free to use whatever method we want to come up with whatever real number is next in line—including just inserting q as the next number.

Supposing we do just make q the next real number in the list and match it to the number 7 in the list of naturals. We could even use another diagonal string of digits to make another real number, r, by which to form yet another real number, s, that would nowhere appear in any of the depicted real numbers listed previously. We could then place the number s next in the list of the segment for $\mathbb{R}$ and match it to the number 8 in the list of naturals. And so on. (See **Figure 14.4**.)

$\mathbb{N}$		$\mathbb{R}$ $(0-1)$
1	$\leftrightarrow$	0.**0**00000...
2	$\leftrightarrow$	0.1**1**1111...
3	$\leftrightarrow$	0.01**0**101...
4	$\leftrightarrow$	0.101**0**10...
5	$\leftrightarrow$	0.1101**0**1...
6	$\leftrightarrow$	0.00110**1**...
7	$\leftrightarrow$	0.101110...
8	$\leftrightarrow$	0.000011...
$\vdots$	$\leftrightarrow$	$\vdots$ $\ddots$

$$p = 0.010001...$$
$$q = 0.101110...$$
$$r = 0.111100...$$
$$s = 0.000011...$$

Figure 14.4: The new real number, q, generated from p, which was derived from the diagonal string in bold, is matched to the number 7 in $\mathbb{N}$. Another diagonal string (underscored digits) is used to create the real number r, which in turn is used to make s. Then, s is placed next in the list and matched to 8 in $\mathbb{N}$. This process can be repeated as often as we wish, so long as any new real we make is unique given our previously depicted reals. This process casts doubt upon $\mathbb{N}$ and $\mathbb{R}$ as unequal in size.

Looking at it this way, there is no reason to assume that q cannot appear later in the list of $\mathbb{R}$—it just can't appear anywhere where the digits for the diagonal have *already* been depicted *if we wish to maintain that sequence of digits* (which is not necessary if we are comparing cardinalities as opposed to ordinalities). And since we can repeat this process as often as we wish, again $\mathbb{N}$ can be made to always equal $\mathbb{R}$ as long as we wish to keep extending our lists [529].

Even the requirement not to insert a new real number *inside* the bounds of the original sequence of depicted reals is not a necessary requirement for bijection of $\mathbb{N}$ and $\mathbb{R}$ because all we are required to do in order to maintain the bijection is ensure only unique (horizontally-written) numbers are matched. We ensure this if we do not use the same real number twice in the column of reals when we insert the new real, while also simply extending the naturals with the successor function to restore bijection. If we can manage that for each iteration, we ensure there is always a bijection of unique numbers no matter how long we go on listing new numbers for the column of naturals and the column of reals. The two series of numbers would always remain incomplete, but what numbers are ever depicted would always be uniquely matched, *no matter how far they are made to extend*.

And that means Cooper's claim that the diagonal argument shows "*any* [real] number that can be shown not to be in the original list shows us that the belief that natural and real numbers can be paired is incorrect," is not necessarily true. Rather, the diagonal argument must do more than that: it must show that we can *run out* of a *limitless number* of naturals to match with the reals—and that is what it has failed to do. Instead, it just *assumes* as much—not only without evidence but even contrary to mathematical experience.

What we now have is an indirect proof against the naturals and reals as literally infinite sets ($\mathbb{N}$ and $\mathbb{R}$) of different sizes. That is, we started by assuming $\mathbb{N}$ and $\mathbb{R}$ are each complete sets, but when measured by cardinality and not ordinality, we find there is no way to establish they are different in size.

14.7.6 *Number Scales Are Not Necessarily Infinite Sets*

I must therefore maintain that Cantor's assumption that number scales are *necessarily* complete sets, let alone literally infinite sets, is not warranted. His presumption that number systems can be complete sets is not certain to be true, and from an empirical standpoint looks to be dead wrong. It's just as possible, if not more likely, that number scales are incomplete, open series rather than complete sets. The view that number scales are incomplete, open series is not illogical and it is even an empirically supported view.

If we assume a number scale, simply as such, is not necessarily a complete set but may be an incomplete series under construction, we are free to conclude that the indirect proof of the diagonal argument is indirect evidence that the reals make up an incomplete series and not a complete set. Moreover, we may thus suppose the scale of natural numbers is, like the constructed sequence of reals, not a complete set of numbers but merely an incomplete, open series.

If we are not inconsistent to suppose the naturals and reals are incomplete series ($\mathbb{N}^C$ and $\mathbb{R}^C$) rather than complete sets ($\mathbb{N}$ and $\mathbb{R}$) as Cantor stipulated, then Cantor's diagonal argument for infinities of various sizes is not the only game in town. On the contrary, it becomes more plausible that Cantor's diagonal argument merely gives the illusion of two different sizes for the natural number system and real number system because the diagonal argument would really be comparing the sizes of two incomplete numeric series ($\mathbb{N}^C$ and $\mathbb{R}^C$) made with different sequencing techniques, not the size of a complete set of natural numbers ($\mathbb{N}$) to the size of an incomplete segment of real numbers ($\mathbb{R}$).

If that's so, then we can still always pair any set of reals we might compose one-for-one with any set of naturals we might compose, because neither 'set' will be anything other than a sample of an incomplete series of numbers under construction. Moreover, it is then not necessarily true that $\mathbb{N}$ is less than $\mathbb{R}$; neither scale is necessarily "bigger" than the other, contrary to Cantor's conclusion. Rather, we are rationally free to hold that both scales are open series, always under construction, and if we keep on constructing *incomplete* bijections between the number scales, we will find that $\mathbb{N}^C = \mathbb{R}^C$ as long as we continue the *process* of extending both number scales and forming a bijection between the members of the two scales as series.

Of course, if we can use some mathematical function to invent new real numbers at a faster pace than natural numbers to count them, then we can say $\mathbb{R}^C$ is in that regard "bigger" than $\mathbb{N}^C$. But then, suppose we use another function to invent at a fast pace new naturals than real numbers and so make $\mathbb{N}^C$ bigger than $\mathbb{R}^C$. Hence, $\mathbb{N}^C$ could have either fewer numbers than $\mathbb{R}^C$ or more numbers than $\mathbb{R}^C$, or even just the same amount, depending on how you want to invent new numbers for the two series and compare them. Basically, when you are comparing two inherently incomplete series, comparisons in size are arbitrary; so, contrary to Cantor's diagonal argument, it's not necessarily true we must hold there is a $\mathbb{N}$ and a $\mathbb{R}$ such that $\mathbb{N} < \mathbb{R}$. We could instead conclude there is a $\mathbb{N}^C$ and a $\mathbb{R}^C$ such that $\mathbb{N}^C$ and $\mathbb{R}^C$ can be compared in size only arbitrarily.

Cantor's diagonal argument, then, rests on his unwarranted assumption that number scales are complete sets rather than incomplete series under construction. Throw out that presupposition and you throw out Cantor's proof.

14.7.7 *The Contradiction Unresolved*

Now, in fairness to Cantor, he did propose arguments other than the diagonal argument for differing sizes of infinite sets. However, his proofs all rest on the same presumption that number scales are complete sets. Roitman stated that the only way to seriously deny the validity of Cantor's work is to deny even that the natural numbers are a set [530]. While I don't think that's the only way to poke holes in Cantor's work, she is correct that in denying the natural number system is a set, Cantor's work is undone. And that is the position I take: number scales—i.e., number systems like $\mathbb{N}^C$, $\mathbb{W}^C$, $\mathbb{Z}^C$, $\mathbb{R}^C$, etc.—are not complete sets. They are incomplete, open *series* (sequences formed by temporal succession) of indefinite length. Consequently, Cantor's "proofs" fail to prove either that number scales are sets or that they are infinite, or that they have relative infinite sizes.

14.7.8 *The Diagonal Argument Does Not Distinguish Countability and Uncountability*

There is one last point I'd like to emphasize about the diagonal argument: matching one-to-one a progression of elements to numbers does not necessarily show the elements to be 'countable' in the sense that a progression of elements can be correlated with a progression of natural (counting) numbers to *completion*. All that a 'bijection' of a progression of elements to an indefinite sequence of natural numbers (1, 2, 3, ...) shows is that no matter how long you go on making correlations, there's always a match. You could just be matching elements between two incomplete, open *series* rather than matching elements selected from completed *sets*. The same can be said for the inability to complete a bijection—it does not necessarily show the progression to be 'uncountable' in principle, it may just show two progressions are indefinite or that one is sequenced in a way the other is not, making them incompatible for pairing. The countable-uncountable contradiction inherent in the concept of a literally infinite set is therefore still not resolved by appeal to Cantor's diagonal argument.

14.8 MISDIRECTION

To use the transfinite system for dissolving the logical contradiction of a literally infinite set being both complete and therefore countable (able to have all elements counted to completion) while also being limitless and therefore uncountable (unable to have all the elements of a set counted to completion) does not succeed. And in Cantor's attempt to dissolve such contradictions in the concept of literal infinity this way, a third red herring fallacy was made. (Recall the first red herring was the use of the subset and correlation distinction for defining size, and the second red herring is the matching of sequences of naturals to sequences of reals instead of sets of naturals to sets of reals in the diagonal argument.)

The third red herring is as follows. Cantor's diagonal argument is often used to show that infinite sets of numbers can have different relative "sizes" when compared *with one another*. According to transfinite math, $\mathbb{N} = \mathbb{Z}$, so $\mathbb{Z}$ is 'countable', while $\mathbb{N} < \mathbb{R}$, so $\mathbb{R}$ is 'uncountable'. But it is just this way of redefining 'countable' and 'uncountable' that commits the third red herring argument for dissolving the countable-uncountable contradiction inherent in the conception of the transfinite as literal infinity.

The use of transfinite definitions for 'countable' and 'uncountable' is a red herring because the diagonal argument sidesteps the real issue pointed out earlier: the logical contradiction faced is of a *single* literally infinite set being both complete and therefore countable (able to be totally counted), yet also limitless and therefore uncountable (unable to be totally counted) at the same time. In other words, the contradiction is for a single infinite set, not between multiple infinite sets. How number systems like $\mathbb{N}$ and $\mathbb{Z}$ or $\mathbb{N}$ and $\mathbb{R}$ *compare to one another* in size is not the issue. $\mathbb{N}$, $\mathbb{Z}$, $\mathbb{R}$, and the other number systems, when assumed to be literally infinite sets, must *each* be countable (in the ordinary language sense) due to being literally complete and yet uncountable (in the ordinary language sense) due to being literally limitless. The operational definitions of 'countable' and 'uncountable' offered in the transfinite system are irrelevant to this point.

The same goes for infinite sets as compared with infinite subsets, like $\mathbb{N}$ as a proper subset of $\mathbb{R}$. The issue is not whether one infinite set can be "smaller" than another in terms of being a subset of the other while each can be "equal" in size in terms of being able to have a correlation of members between them. Rather, the issue is how a single infinite set can be complete with a totality (countable) and limitless with no total at all (uncountable) at the same time. A literally infinite set is supposed to be both, *all by itself*, regardless of how it compares to other sets.

The countable-uncountable contradiction stems not from comparing cardinalities *between* scales but from the properties of *each* scale, all on its own. If $\mathbb{N}$ is literally infinite, it is complete with a totality (ergo, countable) and limitless with no total at all (ergo, uncountable); the same goes for $\mathbb{R}$ and all other number systems if they are regarded as literally infinite sets instead of simply indefinite series. So, the countable-uncountable contradiction is not solved.

Appeals to showing how $\mathbb{N}$ and $\mathbb{R}$, when (unwarrantedly) assumed to be complete sets, cannot be bijected with another, and using this feature as a basis for calling $\mathbb{R}$ "uncountable" rather than "countable" evades the issue that each set, all on its own, is both countable and uncountable as a literally infinite set—a contradiction unresolved. The redefinition of terms and appeals to narrow operational procedures is, therefore, just a red herring.

14.9 REPRISE ON BEING COUNTABLE AND UNCOUNTABLE

The transfinite system swaps technical, operational definitions for 'countable' (to be shown as equal or less than any segment of $\mathbb{N}$) and 'uncountable' (to be shown as greater than $\mathbb{N}$) for more lexical meanings of countable (having the ability to be counted to an exact sum) and uncountable (not able to be counted to an exact sum) implied by the meaning of literal infinity. With these redefinitions of 'countable' and 'uncountable', Cantor intended to identify the transfinite as the literally infinite in such a way as to avoid the contradiction of an infinite set being countable in the ordinary sense as implied by the set's literal completeness while also being uncountable in the ordinary sense as implied by the set's literal limitlessness.

Mathematicians largely agree that the transfinite system's operational definitions for 'countable' and 'uncountable' avoid the contradictions raised by assuming the lexical definitions and also make such terms *mathematically* consistent. But I argue the technical and operational definitions do not solve the *logical* contradictions inherent in the concept of literal infinity.

In order to avoid the countable-uncountable contradiction implied by assuming transfinite sets are literally infinite sets, the mathematician must show (1) the lexical meanings of 'countable' and 'uncountable' are not assumed in mathematics with respect to infinity and (2) the lexical meanings were never implied by how infinity is conceived to be complete and limitless in the first place. If they can show both of those things, then they can show that the lexical meanings of 'countable' and 'uncountable' lead to contradiction only because they are the wrong meanings for these terms.

But such is not the case. True, collections said to have ω-many or $\aleph$-many members are formally defined in the transfinite system as either 'countable' ($=\mathbb{N}$) or 'uncountable' ($>\mathbb{N}$) in the technical sense. But when describing these 'transfinite' collections as literally (or actually) infinite, the lexical meanings for 'countable' and 'uncountable' are still logically implied because literal infinity is literally complete and literally limitless. The logical connotations do not go away simply because they are not used for mathematical operations. Instead, the connotations, contradictory though they may be, still appear in the *interpretations* of the transfinite—in how the transfinite is *described*.

The words mathematicians choose to describe 'transfinite' sets and operations reveal that they assume transfinite sets, taken as literally infinite sets, to be both countable in the lexical sense of being able to be completely counted and yet uncountable in the very same sense. For example, mathematicians say the infinitely many natural numbers of $\mathbb{N}$ are *all used up* prior to the first infinite ordinal, ω, which only appears in order *after* the naturals [531] [532]. The ability for the elements of $\mathbb{N}$ to be "used up" and to have an ordinal come "after" *all* the numbers in $\mathbb{N}$ shows that $\mathbb{N}$ is assumed to be literally complete. In fact, $\mathbb{N}$ is described as having an "amount" of numbers that constitutes a "quantity" in the form of a "total" [533]. On that basis, $\mathbb{N}$ is implied to be, at least in principle, *countable* in the lexical sense of the term [534]. However, $\mathbb{N}$ is also described as having "no maximum" because $\mathbb{N}$ is literally limitless in the ordinary sense of the term—it has no last number [535]. Ergo, $\mathbb{N}$ is also said to be "boundless," which implies $\mathbb{N}$ is *uncountable* in the ordinary, lexical sense as well [536]. Consequently, the terms 'countable' and 'uncountable' do not seem to be consistently used only in their technical senses, even by mathematicians adopting the transfinite system—the lexical sense of the terms slips through in assumption and implication when 'transfinite' sets are taken to be literally infinite.

It is therefore highly misleading to say $\mathbb{N}$ is operationally 'countable' and $\mathbb{R}$ is operationally 'uncountable' when the transfinite is simultaneously claimed to be actual, or literal, infinity. The meaning of literal infinity implies lexical meanings for terms like 'countable' and 'uncountable', which causes the contradiction of infinity being both countable in principle and not countable even in principle—whether we're considering the length of $\mathbb{N}$ or $\mathbb{R}$. The operational definitions for 'countable' and 'uncountable' avoid this contradiction, but only because they never address the issue of the underlying lexical meanings that are still assumed, even if left unstated in a direct manner.

What we have, then, is a situation in which theorists begin with the common conception of literal infinity, which implies the lexical meanings of countable and uncountable, and then sidestep the connotations of literal infinity being both of these simultaneously by positing different, technical definitions for 'countable' and 'uncountable'. These new, technical definitions are then claimed to denote properties of different kinds of infinite sets, like $\mathbb{N}$ and $\mathbb{R}$, and so we have created an argument that confuses the operational meanings of terms like 'countable' and 'uncountable' with their lexical counterparts. This provides the illusion that literal infinity implies no logical contradictions.

Such equivocations in meaning for 'countable' and 'uncountable' also commit the red herring fallacy. The differences in cardinality between $\mathbb{N}$ and $\mathbb{R}$ do not address the contradictory implications of completeness (ergo countability) and limitlessness (ergo uncountability) of each set *on its own*. Once again, how $\mathbb{N}$ and $\mathbb{R}$ *compare* to one another in size is not the issue. The contradiction of being both countable and yet uncountable stems not from comparing the cardinalities *between* scales but from the lexical definitions that apply to *each* scale on its own.

$\mathbb{N}$ and $\mathbb{R}$, as literally infinite sets, are each in principle (lexically) countable due to being complete and yet (lexically) uncountable, even in principle, due to being limitless. Any literally infinite set, whether $\mathbb{N}$ or $\mathbb{R}$ or any other, is both a complete and limitless set and that entails the logical contradiction between lexical countability and lexical uncountability. The contradiction applies to all literally infinite sets.

For that reason alone, the logical contradiction remains unaddressed by swapping the operational definitions for 'countable' and 'uncountable' for their lexical definitions. True, the redefinition "solution" avoids the contradictory connotations of a set being complete and limitless at the same time, but only because it never addresses that problem, and refusing to address a problem is different from solving it.

The logical implications of what it means to be simultaneously *complete and limitless* are what create the contradiction of being both *countable and uncountable* in the lexical sense of these terms. The contradictory implications are simply not addressed by changing the definitions of 'countable' and 'uncountable' to operational definitions because the lexical meanings of 'complete' and 'limitless' are still assumed of literally infinite sets and so the operational redefinitions of 'countable' and 'uncountable' are beside the point. It's their lexical counterparts that are still contradictory because they are still implied by the completeness and limitlessness of the same set in question.

Given that the lexical definitions of 'countable' and 'uncountable' are implied by our lexical understanding of what it is to be complete and limitless, and given that even mathematicians assume these lexical meanings when they speak of infinity in its literal sense, we can say the logical contradiction of an infinite set being countable-yet-uncountable has not gone away. The contradiction stands.

14.10 ENUMERABLE, ONLY NOT

As noted in § 13.10, sets can be numbered without counting. If the natural numbers form $\mathbb{N}$ as an infinite set, that set can in one step enumerate S as an infinite set of objects. There is not necessarily a need to count the elements of infinite sets in order to enumerate them. For that reason, set theorists and mathematicians working with the transfinite system often refer to an infinite set as 'enumerable' or 'denumerable' if its members can be placed into bijection with $\mathbb{N}$; an infinite set is said to be 'innumerable' or 'non-denumerable' if its members cannot be placed into bijection with either all the members of $\mathbb{N}$ or any subset of $\mathbb{N}$.

However, since $\mathbb{N}$ as an enumerable or denumerable set can have any of its numbers used for counting, $\mathbb{N}$ is called a 'countably infinite set' while any innumerable or non-denumerable set is an 'uncountably infinite set' because its members cannot all be used for counting.

Redefining the terms enumerable/denumerable and innumerable/non-denumerable makes the same errors we found in redefining what it means to be 'countable' or 'uncountable'. There are not two different meanings of size as commonly claimed, Cantor's diagonal argument is not successful in establishing different (literally) infinite sizes, and the redefinitions fail to address the contradiction that at each infinite set of elements on its own, by virtue of its completeness, is enumerable/denumerable in the sense that *all* its elements can be enumerated and yet, by virtue of its limitlessness, is innumerable/non-denumerable in the sense that its elements cannot be enumerated.

14.11 A CRITIQUE OF REDEFINING INFINITY BY ORDINALITY AND CARDINALITY

We've seen that infinity has various definitions in the transfinite system. Some of those definitions are framed in reference to the natural numbers: $\mathbb{N}$. For example, as pointed out in § 13.2.3 and § 14.1.3, infinity is sometimes said to be "the ordinality of a sequence of elements, or cardinality of a set of elements, greater than that of any natural number in $\mathbb{N}$" [537]. Though this theoretical definition of 'infinite' is better than the previous definitions we've examined from the transfinite system, it still suffers some logical problems. The definition is clearly based on the notion of different 'sizes' of infinite sets as portrayed from Cantor's diagonal argument, which we've seen implies (informal) logical errors. But there are additional problems as well, which have to do with the way in which transfinite ordinality and transfinite cardinality are expressed for $\mathbb{N}$ when $\mathbb{N}$ is assumed to represent a literally infinite set. We'll now take a closer look.

14.11.1 *A Critique of Infinite Ordinals*

The transfinite system represents the natural numbers as a set, $\mathbb{N}$, and the ordinality of the natural numbers as the infinite limit ordinal ω. So, $\mathbb{N} \triangleq \omega$, even though ω is not itself a natural number in $\mathbb{N}$. As the "least infinite" number, ω is the *limit* of the natural numbers which tend to but can never approximate ω [538] [539]. So, ω is an infinitely large number that "succeeds" or "follows after" the infinite sequence of all the natural numbers of $\mathbb{N}$ [540].

   Cantor also proposed one infinite numeric sequence ($\omega + 1, \omega + 2, \omega + 3, ...$) follows *after* another infinitely large sequence of numbers—in this case, the naturals which are equal to ω. But the infinite sequence of infinitely large numbers ($\omega + 1, ...$) could only follow after the infinite sequence of natural numbers if that infinite sequence (ω) is already *finished* in the ordinary sense of the term, and so already literally complete. Only thus could a sequence of ω length be *followed* by additional infinite sequences of transfinite ordinals.

   How any number (e.g., ω)—let alone an infinite sequence of numbers ($\omega + 1, \omega + 2, \omega + 3, ...$)—could *follow after* an infinite sequence of other numbers (e.g., that of $\mathbb{N}$) is certainly confusing. Science educator Michael Stevens used an analogy to articulate the concept: "If you got omegath [ωth] place in a race, that would mean an infinite number of people finished the race [1, 2, 3, ...] *and then* you did" [541]. Another way to express the concept is to picture it with a matchstick visualization as in **Figure 14.5**.

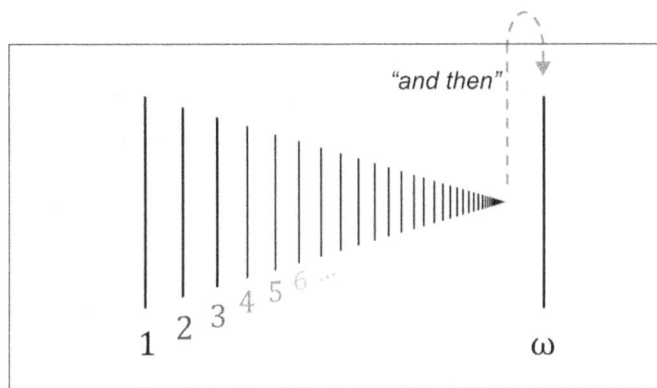

Figure 14.5: An infinite sequence of naturals comes first—only *after* all of them is the first transfinite ordinal, ω.

I submit the reason the idea of a particular number following *after* an infinite sequence of prior numbers seems confusing is that it *is* a confused idea. But I realize how that must sound to mathematicians who are used to working with one 'set' following another 'set', (e.g., P, Q) where they are each 'infinite'.

Bertrand Russell, for example, said that the series of transfinite ordinals (ω, $\omega + 1$, $\omega + 2$, $\omega + 3$, ...) can follow *after* a series of natural numbers (1, 2, 3, ..., ω, $\omega + 1$, $\omega + 2$, $\omega + 3$, ...) because an 'ordinal' to a series is a member for which prior terms in the series before the ordinal can be omitted (as the sequence "1, 2, 3, ..." omits "4, 5, 6," etc.) without changing the order of the remaining terms (for example, those after ω: $\omega + 1$, $\omega + 2$, $\omega + 3$, ...). So, Russell stated, "The usual objections to infinite numbers, and classes, and series, and the notion that the infinite as such is self-contradictory, may thus be dismissed as groundless" [542].

To which I say, not so fast, Russell—you begged the question. Russell assumed that between the largest natural number given—for example, the one I dub d^*—and the "least infinite" ω, there are "terms omitted" as in the second set of ellipses:

$$1, 2, 3, ..., d^*, ..., \omega.$$

But that is just an assumption, and not a safe one.

We could instead say it's not that the terms in the second set of ellipses before ω are "omitted" but that they have not been *invented* yet, supposing the system has the potential for their invention. In which case, ω is not a genuine quantity—it's just an ideal point that a process of construction tends toward but can never reach according to the rules of construction. In which case, the naturals after d^* that lead up to ω do not form a complete set of numbers—a literally infinite $\mathbb{N}$. Instead, they form an incomplete series—$\mathbb{N}^C$, that is only an indefinite process with a running total of naturals. And in that case, ω is not literally infinite after all, and so neither is $\aleph$.

In mathematical progression, ω and $\aleph$ are either like moving goalposts or just hypothetical, *indefinitely* (vice infinitely) large quantities toward which definite naturals tend. I favor the latter interpretation since any sequence that has a limit ordinal as a supremum (least upper bound) to that sequence must also double as a successor ordinal to any number that ever becomes the final definite number possible to define in actual practice for the sequence leading to that ordinal. That makes ω as the limit order of the naturals, and therefore $\aleph$ as its cardinality, indefinite but not infinite.

After all, if the ellipses before ω are just finite numbers "omitted" in the ellipses, then they would have to be natural numbers that are omitted for which ω is, eventually, "next." But Russell, like Cantor, said there is no natural before ω that would make ω "next." So, if no natural number precedes ω, then what does? It has to be a quantity of some kind, and it would have to be part of $\mathbb{N}$. But only naturals are in $\mathbb{N}$. Hence, no quantity can precede ω and thus no quantity can be "omitted" after the largest natural defined at any given time. In which case, it's hard to see how ω is really part of the "same series" as the naturals except in name only.

I thus maintain it's not that the concept of an infinite ordinal makes logical sense but is hard to understand; it's that the concept itself is not logical at all. It is just a concept in a mathematical game that follows a particular set of rules and that seems to make sense if you suspend disbelief.

Just consider Stevens' analogy. If you are the ωth runner in a race of infinitely many runners, your definite place in the race contradicts that there is *no last runner* to the *limitless* series counted by natural numbers: 1, 2, 3, ... There is no way to come "after" the last runner counted with a natural number because there is no last natural number to come after. So, as the ωth runner, you both finish the race because ω^{th} place in the race came *after* all the natural number placements occurred, and yet you also never finish the race because there is no such thing as a *last* natural number placing in the race—there will never be a time at which a natural number is followed by some other number (ω). Finishing the race and yet never finishing the race: a logical contradiction produced by the concept that an element can come in order "after" an infinite sequence of elements.

A mathematician might object that there is no mathematical contradiction in Cantor's idea of infinite ordinals. That is true: there may be no *mathematical* contradiction to ω following "after" a transfinite sequence of naturals and counting as a so-called "ordinal" to the naturals. But that is only because the 'transfinite' sequence of natural numbers is, operationally, just an indefinitely large sequence that leaves off at some undefined (finite) place prior to wherever we wish to instantiate the symbol ω.

Recall the sequence of transfinite ordinals following the naturals, which we'll call Pattern One:

$1, 2, 3, ...,$
$\omega, \omega + 1, \omega + 2, \omega + 3, ...,$
$\omega 2, \omega 2 + 1, \omega 2 + 2, \omega 2 + 3, ...,$
$\omega 3, \omega 3 + 1, \omega 3 + 2, \omega 3 + 3, ...,$
$\omega^2, ..., \omega^\omega, ..., \omega^{\omega^\omega}, ...$

Now consider how the above pattern is precisely the same as that of a mathematical sequence of natural number calculations following a finite sequence of natural numbers, which we'll call Pattern Two:

$1, 2, 3, ...,$
$10, 10 + 1, 10 + 2, 10 + 3, ...,$
$10 \times 2, (10 \times 2) + 1, (10 \times 2) + 2, (10 \times 2) + 3, ...,$
$10 \times 3, (10 \times 3) + 1, (10 \times 3) + 2, (10 \times 3) + 3, ...,$
$10^2, ..., 10^{10}, ..., 10^{10^{10}}, ...$

Next, let's increase the amount of implied numbers in the initial ellipsis in Pattern Two ($1, 2, 3, ...,$) by adding a zero to each of the tens in sequence, like so:

$1, 2, 3, ...,$
$100, 100 + 1, 100 + 2, 100 + 3, ...$
$100 \times 2, (100 \times 2) + 1, (100 \times 2) + 2, (100 \times 2) + 3, ...,$
$100 \times 3, (100 \times 3) + 1, (100 \times 3) + 2, (100 \times 3) + 3, ...,$
$10^3, ..., 10^{11}, ..., 10^{11^{11}}, ...$

After that, start over again but instead of adding an extra zero to each ten in Pattern Two, add two extra zeros:

$1, 2, 3, ...,$
$1,000; 1,000 + 1; 1,000 + 2; 1,000 + 3; ...$
$1,000 \times 2, (1,000 \times 2) + 1, (1,000 \times 2) + 2, (1,000 \times 2) + 3, ...,$
$1,000 \times 3, (1,000 \times 3) + 1, (1,000 \times 3) + 2, (1,000 \times 3) + 3, ...,$
$10^4, ..., 10^{12}, ..., 10^{12^{12}}, ...$

Keep repeating this operation until all the tens we started with in Pattern Two become natural numbers too large to depict: 1,000,000,000,000,000... When the numbers become indefinitely large, we can represent them by an arbitrary symbol like, say, ω. The result is that we have now replicated Pattern One.

It's therefore easy to see why Zenkin pointed out that Pattern One and Pattern Two are formally identical in terms of mathematical operation [543]. As Zenkin argued, Pattern One can be interpreted as just a symbolic model for Pattern Two as a 'potentially infinite' (i.e., figuratively infinite) series [544].

That is why from a purely *operational* perspective, I would argue the symbol ω functions as an *indefinitely large* natural number that is a supremum for an *indefinite*, yet always finite, *series* of definite numbers. The transfinite schema $1, 2, 3, ..., \omega, \omega + 1, \omega + 2, \omega + 3, ...$ works mathematically only because, operationally, the progression makes ω a finite supremum—a boundary condition within which the progression of the sequence continues to grow with a running total by which to compare a 'next' number, natural or otherwise, as following after the previous total. As for the 'transfinite' ordinals, they too comprise an indefinitely growing series of symbols for indefinitely large values, not a literally infinite sequence of literally infinite numbers. Because the transfinite system operationally treats ω as if it is merely an indefinitely large but nevertheless finite natural number, and there is no mathematical problem with an indefinite series of indefinitely large natural numbers, there is no mathematical contradiction in how the 'transfinite' ordinals operate, despite their *interpretation* to be representative of literally infinite sequences.

But while there may be no *mathematical* contradiction in the transfinite ordinal sequence, there is still an obvious *logical* contradiction in stating a sequence of numbers such as $1, 2, 3, ...$ is *infinite* in the sense of having, even in principle, no *limit* in the form of a *last* number to mark the end of the sequence while nevertheless claiming the sequence is *followed by* a limit in the form of some *other kind* of higher number (ω) as its supremum, at which point another sequence ($\omega, \omega + 1, \omega + 2, \omega + 3, ...$) of that other kind of numbers can begin. But that is exactly what the transfinite system is claiming and that is why it is logically contradictory despite its mathematical coherence.

Defenders of the transfinite system believe it is not incoherent to propose non-natural numbers can *follow* natural numbers, even though the natural numbers are without limit in their sequence, because non-natural numbers are a different kind of number [545]. But that claim is misleading. The transfinite ordinals are not different in kind *enough* to avoid logical contradiction in their infinitude precisely because they are claimed to fall *in sequence* with the natural numbers which are said to have no end (...) at all—not just in the sense of having no specified end but rather no last number after which something else can follow as part of the sequence.

The problem is that ω cannot be an *extension* of the sequence of numbers comprising $\mathbb{N}$—that is, ω cannot "follow after" every number in $\mathbb{N}$—if the numbers comprising $\mathbb{N}$ have, literally, *no limit*. For ω to be a number that *follows after* all the natural numbers in the sequence $1, 2, 3, ...$, there would have to be a quantitative limit to the sequence. But there isn't one according to transfinite mathematics—the natural numbers are themselves limitless. Cantor was very specific in stating that $\mathbb{N}$ is not just a figurative or "potential" infinite but a literally infinite (or an "actual infinite") set. Since a literally infinite sequence is a limitless sequence, then there can be no final number to it. By that very premise, the naturals cannot be "used up" [546]. If the sequence $1, 2, 3, ...$ really is *limitless*, then there is no quantitative limit to the natural numbers.

The only way around that logical contradiction is to ignore the limitlessness of numbers in $\mathbb{N}$ and instead treat $\mathbb{N}$ *as if* there is, at any given time, a 'greatest' natural number, n, in $\mathbb{N}$—a number that is merely a running total for natural numbers defined so far for $\mathbb{N}$. Only by doing so can ω be identified as the *ordinal* to $\mathbb{N}$ in the sense of a number that can *follow* every (in practice, definable) n comprising $\mathbb{N}$.

Cantor did not take that route, however, because he wanted it both ways: he wanted $\mathbb{N}$ to be actually infinite, and ergo limitless, while also having an ordinal for $\mathbb{N}$ follow after all the natural (or whole) numbers in $\mathbb{N}$. Logically, that won't work because you can't follow "after" something that has no limit to its sequence. The transfinite schema is logically fallacious because it confuses the literal infinity claimed for ω with a figurative infinity of numbers as they are sequenced.

But mathematically you can get away with it in operation by simply treating the series of numbers as an indefinite series instead of a limitless series or a completed set, then equivocate "no highest number" in the sense of an incomplete, open series with "no highest number" in the sense of being a limitless sequence of numbers. In fact, in one breath Cantor says ω is a supremum or "limit" to the sequence of whole numbers, while in the next he says that ω is "not a maximum" for any quantity of the whole numbers, which are all less than the quantity of ω, even though ω "follows after" all of them [547].

Some mathematicians might try to approach the relation of the finite naturals in $\mathbb{N}$ to the infinite ordinal ω from the other end, showing not how ω "follows after" every natural number, but how no natural number *immediately precedes* ω. For example, consider what mathematician James Clark, following Cantor and Bertrand Russell, says of set $\mathbb{N}$ insofar as it has the value ω [548]:

> Notice this set has no last element, and thus ω has no immediate predecessor, which is the definition of a limit ordinal. There is no ordinal a such that $a + 1 = \omega$. If there were, we would have a contradiction. As every element of ω is finite, if there were some element a that was an immediate predecessor of ω, a being a member of ω would imply that a is finite. This would then imply that ω, being the successor of a finite ordinal, would therefore be finite. There we have the desired contradiction.

Clark has correctly articulated Cantor's position and that position is only half right. The reason ω has "no immediate predecessor" with respect to mathematical *operation* is not because ω is infinite but simply because the mathematical formalism of the transfinite system treats ω as the supremum to a *growing* finitude of naturals having no *standing* total by which to say ω "follows next." In other words, because ω is the limit of the series of natural numbers and not itself a member of the series of natural numbers, we can keep growing the naturals toward ω as a bound being pushed ever outward without converging with ω.

And Cantor's position is also half wrong. As Clark points out, according to Cantor's system, because every element, a, of the sequence capped by ordinal ω is finite, ω cannot have an immediate predecessor. Otherwise, $a + 1 = \omega$ would entail a is finite and therefore ω is finite. However, this ignores the problem that each of the natural numbers prior to ω (except for 1) is larger than the previous number. So, to say there *infinitely many* (in a literal sense and not just in the figurative sense of a growing finitude of) natural numbers (ergo, *all the way* up to ω) implies the natural numbers progress to infinitely large size. So, not every a prior to ω can be finite after all [549]. Therefore, there must be at least one infinitely large a in ω. But Cantor's system says there is not because, if there were an infinitely large a, then ω would not be the "least infinite" number [550].

We therefore have a logical contradiction implied from the very idea of $\mathbb{N}$ containing a literal infinity of unique naturals in sequence while also proposing that prior to ω as $\mathbb{N}$'s supremum there are only finite naturals. Hence, what Clark has inadvertently pointed out is the reason ω, interpreted as a literally infinite number, must be logically contradictory—$\mathbb{N}$ must contain an infinitely large a as an immediate predecessor to ω while ω can have no such predecessor (which is another reason you can't be the ωth runner after an infinite sequence of runners).

A limitless sequence can have no supremum. Hence, from a logical standpoint, there is a logical contradiction here: ω cannot *follow* the sequence of numbers in $\mathbb{N}$ and yet must follow $\mathbb{N}$ to be the ordinal somehow "after" the numbers of $\mathbb{N}$; alternatively, ω can have no immediate predecessor that is finite, and yet must in order to be part of the quantitative sequence as its ordinal.

In retort, some advocates of the transfinite system say ω does not come "after" the sequence of naturals in the ordinary sense. Instead, "ω is not the terminus of the series, but stands outside of and above the whole series, informing us as to how it is ordered" [551]. But if this is so, then it's hard to see how $\{0, 1, 2, 3, ...\}$ is a literally infinite set and not just an incomplete, open series of numbers, indefinitely constructed within bounds while ω just designates the incomplete quantity under construction. And if the sequence is just an incomplete, indefinite construction of numbers, then the sequence $\{0, 1, 2, 3, ...\}$ denoted by ω is not literally infinite after all, contradicting what ω is proposed to represent. As an indefinite construction, ω would then represent an intrinsically *finite* series, even if it is persistently extensible.

Moreover, if ω is really "outside of and above the whole series," then it's hard to see how ω can be an *ordinal* to which we can add $+1$ as we can to any whole number, but that is what transfinite mathematics claims when it offers the progression: $\omega + 1, \omega + 2, \omega + 3, ...$ [552]. With respect to ω representing an infinite sequence, there seems to be a conflict between using ω as a *category* for numbers and ω as part of the *progression* of numbers.

We are therefore left with a dilemma: either we deny that $\{0, 1, 2, 3, ...\}$ is a complete sequence but affirm the sequence is equal to ω in which case ω does not represent a literal infinity in contradiction to transfinite mathematics, or affirm the completeness of $\{0, 1, 2, 3, ...\}$ but deny it is *equal* to ω as if ω is the ordinal *after* naturals in which case there is still no way to have a literally infinite sequence of whole numbers because $\{0, 1, 2, 3, ...\}$ must be equal to ω as the ordinal after the naturals for the transfinite system to be coherent. Either way, the transfinite system continues to imply logical contradictions even if its mathematical rules of operation for symbols and indefinite sets dubbed 'transfinite' are themselves consistent.

The lesson is clear: as long as you frame the mathematical rules properly for the 'transfinite', you can ignore the contradictory logical connotations and still make consistent calculations. That is what Cantor's transfinite mathematics does—it works with $\mathbb{N}$ as an incomplete, indefinite series while interpreting $\mathbb{N}$ as if it is a complete set, all the while ignoring the implications of what it would mean for the same collection of numbers to be truly *limitless* rather than just have an indefinitely running total of numbers in it.

14.11.2 *A Critique of Infinite Cardinality*

A similar logical problem besets Cantor's use of the infinite cardinal $\aleph$. If $\mathbb{N}$ is a literally infinite set, then $\mathbb{N}$ has a limitless amount of numbers in it. That means there is no greatest natural number in $\mathbb{N}$ at any time. But because $\aleph$ is supposed to be *greater* than any natural number, n, in $\mathbb{N}$, if there is no greatest n in $\mathbb{N}$, then there can be no number for $\mathbb{N}$ as a whole that is "greater than" the natural numbers of $\mathbb{N}$. There can therefore be no definite number $\aleph$ as the cardinality for $\mathbb{N}$ as a literally infinite set, or for any other set claimed to be literally infinite. This is the logical conclusion even if it can be ignored for the sake of mathematical operation.

Moreover, we run into another problem involving the use of alephs as infinite cardinals. Recall that Cantor proposed a hierarchy of ever-larger infinite sets, each denoted by a subscripted aleph cardinal in sequence ($\aleph_0, \aleph_1, \aleph_2, \aleph_3, ...$), and none of which can be placed into bijection with the next, higher set in the sequence. The problem is that this sequence of cardinals cannot be summed into a single set of all infinite sets without causing further logical problems. Cantor himself noted this problem in an 1897 letter to David Hilbert [553]:

> The totality of all Alephs is a totality which cannot be conceived as a distinct, well-defined set. If this was the case, it would entail another distinct Aleph following this totality, which would at the same time belong to this totality and not belong to it. This would be a contradiction.

To dissolve the contradiction, Cantor proposed that the sequence of transfinite sets (the "Alephs") cannot be collected into a set of all transfinite sets; instead, the sequence of transfinite sets must belong to what Cantor called an "inconsistent plurality," which set theorists now refer to as the *proper class* of all transfinite sets [554]. But as Moore pointed out, this 'proper class' is nothing but an indefinite series— a 'potential infinity' (i.e., a figurative infinity)—of transfinite sets that are iteratively built from each set they contain [555]:

> In order to safeguard his theory from various contradictions, Cantor operated with a certain conception of what a set is, often referred to as the iterative conception...
> ...But is it not strikingly Aristotelian? Notice the temporal metaphor that sustains it. Sets are depicted as coming into being "after" their members, in such a way that there are always more to come. Their collective infinitude, as opposed to the infinitude of any one of them, is potential, not actual...

The quantitative limitlessness that characterizes a literally infinite sequence is only coherently conceived by relying on the temporal metaphor of figurative infinity. It is only by escaping into figurative infinity that we can avoid the contradictions associated with the limitlessness of the transfinite hierarchy—the infinity of literal infinities.

For these reasons, Cantor's conception of transfinite sets, as denoted by transfinite aleph cardinals, may make mathematical sense by operationally treating the 'transfinite sets' as if they are indefinitely large collections or series invented over an indefinite series of iterations, but this makes the transfinite system into a system of figurative infinities, not literal infinities as Cantor claimed. Cantor's system thus reduces to the finite.

14.11.3 *Transfinite Ordinals and Cardinals as Providing the Illusion of Infinity*

As we've just seen, there are several logical contradictions connoted by interpreting 'transfinite' cardinals (the $\aleph$ series) and ordinals (the ω series) as representing literal infinites. Those problems resulted from the misinterpretation of *indefinite series* of numbers as "infinite sets" with "different sizes of infinity," some of which can be "all used up" in operations involving infinite sequences, and from the further misinterpretation of *serial and collective indefinites* following one another as being infinitely large numbers that "follow after" infinite sequences of numbers. In other words, the logical problems result from misconstruing what in the formal language and operations of the transfinite system amount to figurative infinities as if they are literal infinities.

Again, the logical contradictions connoted by interpreting the transfinite (ω or $\aleph$) as literal infinity are not a consequence of the formal *syntax* of the transfinite system. Transfinite mathematics contains no *mathematical* contradictions when it proposes the transfinite is a literally complete and limitless quantity because to regard ω and ℵ as denoting the literally infinite is not a part of the operation of either ω or ℵ in the syntax, or formal language, of transfinite mathematics. Rather, in operation ω and ℵ function as symbols for an indefinitely large sequence of indefinitely many members, stuck inside braces—a figurative infinity within boundaries. And there is nothing mathematically problematic or self-contradictory about that. It is only in the *semantics* (i.e., the meaning) of the transfinite as literal infinity, as articulated in natural language descriptions of the formalism, that the logical contradictions in the transfinite system emerge.

Because the formal operations of the transfinite system do not deal with literal infinity but only figurative infinities (serial indefinites, but arguably collective indefinites as well), the definition of 'infinity' in the transfinite system as given in §§ 13.2.3, 14.1.3, and 14.11 as "the ordinality of a sequence of elements, or cardinality of a set of elements, greater than that of any natural number in $\mathbb{N}$" also does not truly capture literal infinity as purported [556]. Rather, $\mathbb{N}$ is just a symbol that represents what is in the operations of Cantor's system just an indefinitely constructed series of numbers *misinterpreted* as being a literally infinite set of numbers that exist all at once. So, as earlier noted back in § 9.6.4, that theoretical definition for infinity fits figurative infinity just fine: we can tomorrow always invent or construct another natural number greater than the highest yet defined in $\mathbb{N}$ (that is, $\mathbb{N}$ as $\mathbb{N}^C$). We must conclude that the transfinite system merely misinterprets its own 'transfinite' version of infinity to be literal infinity when in fact it is only another guise of figurative infinity.

It would therefore appear the set-theoretic and mathematical formalism of the transfinite system provide only the illusion that literal infinity is a logically coherent concept. Cantor did not truly succeed in "taming infinity" [557].

CHAPTER 14 IN REVIEW

❖ Cantor's system identifies the transfinite with literal infinity. But that is a case of mistaken identity. The transfinite, as defined in Cantor's system, must be *interpreted* as literal infinity. In mathematical operation, the transfinite is just a version of figurative infinity in disguise.

❖ The transfinite system rejects the notion of infinitely large natural numbers for infinitely large non-natural numbers: ω and ℵ. But these "infinite numbers" are only literally infinite in philosophical interpretation rather than mathematical operation.

❖ According to the transfinite system, $\mathbb{N}$ is a set of "infinitely many" unique natural numbers, but it would be more accurate to interpret the so-called "set" of naturals ($\mathbb{N}$) as the series of naturals ($\mathbb{N}^C$).

❖ Cantor's diagonal argument, widely thought to have made the idea of "different sizes of infinity" coherent, accomplishes no such thing. In fact, the argument rests on a number of informal logical fallacies.

❖ As some mathematicians admit, the concept that number systems (for example, the natural numbers) are complete sets (e.g., $\mathbb{N}$) is just an assumption in Cantor's work for which there is no evidence—it is just taken as an axiom. But it is not "self-evident." To reject the axiom is to undo Cantor's transfinite system.

❖ Cantor's transfinite systems provides only the illusions that literal infinity is mathematically coherent and that literal infinity is expressed in calculations.

15: UNAVOIDABLE CONTRADICTIONS

Infinity in its literal sense and infinity in the formalism of the transfinite system are two different things. Literal infinity is a complete quantity—no more, no less—that is nevertheless a limitless quantity, and we've seen how literal completeness and literal limitlessness carry mutually contradictory implications. It is this conflict between completeness and limitlessness that underlies the self-contradictions inherent in the concept of literal infinity. As we saw in Chapter 13, Cantor's transfinite system sought to "tame" literal infinity by redefining it in formal terms that would avoid the contradictions [558]. In Chapter 14, we saw how the taming did not succeed—literal infinity is still untamed, at least as far as logic is concerned. In this chapter, we will see further how Cantor's system does not succeed in making literal infinity a logical notion or represented in mathematics as anything other than an illusion.

The transfinite system sought to tame infinity in part by establishing the number systems as sets (e.g., $\mathbb{N} = \{1, 2, 3, ...\}$) and proposing there is an infinite supremum (ω) to the sequences of numbers comprising such sets. The infinite supremum or 'transfinite' number, ω, was proposed as a kind of 'limit' toward which the sequence of naturals extends but never meets. This chapter explores logical problems with the notion of ω as a supremum to a sequence of numbers and ω as belonging to *the same progression* as the numbers in the sequence it "follows" $(1, 2, 3, ..., \omega)$.

15.1 PROGRESSIONS FROM THE FINITE TO THE INFINITE

Every ordinal number, except the first in sequence, is either a successor ordinal or a limit ordinal. Take any ordinal number, n. The successor to n is the smallest ordinal number greater than n. The successor to the ordinal number, n, is called the 'successor ordinal'. An ordinal, x, is a limit ordinal if there is an ordinal less than x, and whenever n is an ordinal less than x, there is another ordinal, y, such that $n < y < x$. In the transfinite system, ω is a limit ordinal because for any n it is the case that $n + 1 < \omega$, and there is no natural number for which ω is a successor ordinal. Some mathematicians like to say that ω is unreachable from any finite number—you only get to infinity from the finite in one big jump [559].

And yet, recall that Cantor proposed his transfinite numbers represent quantities that are equal to *extensions* of numerical progressions from general mathematics: $1, 2, 3, ..., \omega$. The logical problem is that if there is *no such thing* as a natural number for which ω is the successor ordinal such that $n + 1 = \omega$, then exactly what is it that lies *between* any natural number and ω such that ω can still be in the sequence of ordinals, *following* the naturals, and yet no natural number, no matter how big, finds ω next in sequence? In other words, if ω is a limit ordinal any natural number, n, then what is the y in $n < y < \omega$? And don't say $n + 1$ since that equals just another natural number. We cannot make y a natural number for that would mean a natural number would have ω as a successor ordinal, which we just denied. Nor can y be some infinite number, for Cantor's system takes ω to be equal to $\aleph$, which is the infinity of "least" size following all finite values of natural numbers. Worse still, ω follows *all* the naturals of $\mathbb{N}$ and there is *nothing but* naturals in $\mathbb{N}$. The only logical solution is that the ellipsis in 1, 2, 3, ..., ω is referring to a figuratively infinite progression of naturals. In other words, $y = \infty$ in $n < y < \omega$.

And yet, this answer too has its logical problems.

Consider that the sequence 1, 2, 3, ... as expressed in general mathematics is supposed to represent a progression that grows ceaselessly larger—a figurative infinity. This is what ∞ typically means in an expression such as the sequence 1, 2, 3, ... $= \infty$. But we cannot say $y = \infty$ where ∞ is taken as figurative infinity because a figurative infinity (indefinite series, which is always finite) can never become a literal infinity and, in the transfinite system, *the very same sequence* of numbers $(1, 2, 3, ... = \infty)$ is given in braces as a supposed literal infinity: $\{1, 2, 3, ...\} = \omega$ or $\aleph$.

Mathematically, ∞ and ω are not identical because mathematical operations involving them are different [560]. Though 1, 2, 3, ... has the same sequence as $\{1, 2, 3, ...\}$, there is no mathematical inconsistency in saying the former is figurative infinity (restricted to ∞) and the latter is literal infinity (ω or $\aleph$). Hence, if ∞ is figurative infinity while ω and $\aleph$ are literal infinity, it cannot be that $\infty = (\omega = \aleph)$. Yet, while all that might not be a mathematical problem, it is a logical problem since the natural numbers need to be followed by ω and yet they cannot if there are *only* naturals that are finite such that $y = \infty$. In other words, mathematically, it may "work" for the abstraction ω to abstractly follow $\{1, 2, 3, ...\}$, but because ω is interpreted to be literal infinity while the ellipsis in the brackets can at best just give us a figurative infinity (∞) and there is nothing in between the naturals and ω since ω is "least infinite" ordinal, we end up with logical nonsense. The mathematical formalism of the transfinite system "abstracts out" the semantic meaning of infinity, thus masking the logical implications of ω referring to a literal infinity.

As if in anticipation of this objection, though, there are two retorts that may be made, each based on proposals from Cantor for the understanding of the transfinite as literal infinity.

First, he said figurative infinity (∞) presupposes a literal infinity (ω or $\aleph$) [561]. This implies the listing of natural numbers progressively higher would be like the consecutive filling of the cups in a muffin tin (see **Figure 3.3**), but for which there are cups to fill is without limit. Filling the cups with muffins is like discovering numbers that are already there, waiting to be counted. Even if in practice there are too many cups to fill with muffins (too many numbers to list), the cups are there to fill (a complete list of numbers already exists). Cantor thought it's not that $\infty = (\omega = \aleph)$, but rather that ∞ as potential infinity (the ceaseless filling of cups) presupposes ω or $\aleph$ as actual infinity (the inexhaustible supply of cups waiting to be filled). So, it shouldn't be a logical problem that ∞ is different from the transfinite numbers.

Second, he proposed that $\omega - n = \omega$ and so we cannot therefore say the increasing progression of finite number toward ω comes even close to ω. Any finite number, no matter how large, "is quite as far off from ω as the least finite number. Here we see especially clearly the very important fact that my least transfinite ordinal number ω, and consequently all greater ordinal numbers, lie quite outside the endless series 1, 2, 3, and so on. Thus ω is not a maximum of the finite numbers, for there is no such thing" [562].

Neither of these answers is sufficient to resolve the logical muddle. I will address each in the order given over the following two sections.

15.2 ON RATIOS AND INFINITY

To say a figurative infinity (∞) of ordered numbers *presupposes* a literal infinity (ω or $\aleph$) of ordered numbers is to say there are always more numbers that can be consecutively listed because the numbers are already there waiting to be listed [563]. Any figuratively infinite (∞) sequence or order of elements that one could spend forever composing is already complete and limitless as a literally infinite (ω) set, waiting for its members to be listed. But if that is so, then logical (vice mathematical) contradictions are implied.

First, it is true that some wholes have properties not reducible to their parts. Just because a shape is circular does not mean the parts comprising the shape are circular. Each of the stones arranged in a circle need not itself be circular. However, in such cases the whole does not get its properties exclusively from its parts. That is not the case with number systems. In number systems, each number in the system's sequence derives its properties solely from those of its predecessors in the sequence and the whole only has the properties it does because of its parts. For any sequence of numbers, the numbers are defined by other numbers, the quantities by other quantities such that the whole sequence reduces to the sum of its parts. Hence, if the parts (numbers) are all finite, so too must be the whole (the system of numbers).

If, to the contrary, every number in $\{1, 2, 3, ...\}$ is finite while there are *infinitely many finite numbers* in the set, then for the whole sequence to be infinite there must be infinitely many finite numbers *infinitely far down the list of numbers from 1*. That is, there must be at least two finite numbers between which there are infinitely many others. If there were no such numbers—if every finite number is only a finite quantity away from every other—then the sequence as a whole *cannot* be infinite, for the sequence is nothing but numbers reducible to other numbers. But then, assuming the whole is infinite, we are left to ask: what is it about the sequence that makes it *limitless* if all the numbers are finite? The answer is nothing, even though there must be. A contradictory implication.

That brings us to the second point: for a sequence of numbers to extend from the finite (for example, $\{1, 2, 3\}$) all the way up to the infinite such that $\{1, 2, 3, ...\} = \omega$, where ω is interpreted to be literal infinity, such logically implies a sequence of increasingly larger natural numbers for which there must be an infinitely large natural number (for example, a 1 followed by an infinite sequence of zeros, as in 1,000,000, ...) that must be equal to ω. That must be the case if the sequence of ever-larger natural numbers in the set is to be *complete* as a literally infinite set and not just incomplete as a *figuratively* infinite series. The natural numbers, because they establish a complete sequence of increasing cardinality, must *scale up* to literal infinity if the sequence as a whole is to be infinite (ω). If the numbers are instead all finite with only figuratively infinite scaling among them, then the scale cannot be literally infinite and thus equal to ω. But, said Cantor, the whole sequence is infinite. So here again is another contradiction.

Third, and worst of all perhaps, Cantor seems to have violated his own principle with his use of the correspondence technique of determining the equal sizes of two infinite sets. If tit-for-tat bijection extends *infinitely* in the literal sense of the term, then the natural numbers in bijection with such an infinite order must get infinitely large. And that results in another contradiction—the existence of contrary ratios that become infinite. This too impales Cantor's system.

15.2.1 *Two Kinds of Ratios*

To understand how a sequence of numbers as the complete set $\{0, 1, 2, 3, ...\} = \omega$ logically implies a contradiction of ratios, we should first ensure we understand what a ratio is. In mathematics, a *ratio* is a relationship between two numbers indicating relative size. There are two kinds:

- subset-to-subset ratios
- subset-to-superset ratios

15.2.2 *Subset-to-Subset Ratios*

For a set that contains subsets, we can compare the number of members in one subset to the number of members in another subset. A ratio is typically written as "x to y" or $x{:}y$.

For example, suppose we have a set of children. The set contains two subsets—a subset of boys and a subset of girls. There are 2 boys making up the subset of boys and 3 girls making up the subset of girls. So, the set has 5 children total—2 boys and 3 girls. The subset-to-subset ratio of boys to girls, and girls to boys, can be expressed like this:

- The ratio of boys to girls is 2:3.
- The ratio of girls to boys is 3:2.

In general, a comparison of the quantities of a ratio can be expressed as a fraction derived from the ratio. For example, in a ratio of 2:3, the amount, size, volume, or quantity of the first subset is $2/3$ that of the second subset. So, the ratio of boys to girls is 2:3 or $2/3$, and the ratio of girls to boys is 3:2 or $3/2$.

15.2.3 *Subset-to-Superset Ratios*

A superset is a set containing more than one set as a member, each of which is a subset. We can compare the number of members in a subset to the total number of members in the superset. For example, the set of 5 children is a superset containing a subset of 2 boys and a subset of 3 girls. Therefore,

- The ratio of boys to *all* children is 2:5 or $2/5$.
- The ratio of girls to *all* children is 3:5 or $3/5$.

15.2.4 *Infinite Ratios as Indeterminate*

In mathematics, there are no 'infinite ratios' in the sense that there are no ratios directly denoting infinity. A ratio of $\infty{:}\infty$ has no syntactical coherence in mathematical operations because, while ratios can be expressed as fractions, the fraction ∞/∞ has no coherent rules of operation—its use is undefined in mathematics.

An infinite ratio is undefined in mathematics because ∞ is not a number and not even a definite quantity [564]. It's a symbol that represents a *quantifier* for a quantity—it functions as a kind of predicate that tells us *about* the condition of a quantity but does not *specify* a quantity as such. The symbol for infinity, ∞, just tells us there is some quantity that is "infinite," and perhaps literally so if we take ∞ to mean literal infinity—a complete and limitless quantity.

What that quantity is as an exact amount we have no mathematical rules to determine in practice; therefore, our mathematical practice cannot define $\infty{:}\infty$ or ∞/∞ in a way that would produce consistent results. An infinite amount divided by an infinite amount is about like saying "a lot divided by a lot." Not very precise. Mathematicians therefore say infinite ratios are "indeterminate," like the result of attempting to divide zero by zero, and they typically leave it at that.

15.2.5 *Infinite Ratios are Mathematically Denied but Logically Implied*

Mathematically, the conventional answer that infinite ratios are "indeterminate" makes sense, but logically, it is not the whole story.

Suppose we have two sets, B and A. Suppose B and A are both literally infinite sets, which means they are each not only limitless in terms of their quantities of membership but also complete with an exact quantity of members. Because of their completeness, we should be able to express a ratio between B and A, even though both sets are literally infinite. How to pull it off is another matter.

In transfinite mathematics, because a literally infinite set is complete, it has $\aleph$ members, the "smallest" of which is $\aleph_0$, equal to $\mathbb{N}$. However, even $\aleph_0$ is not a precise value in the way that a natural number is a precise value, so we cannot in practice pin a precise number on a set size of $\aleph_0$ the way we could substitute a finite value for some variable, n. Even so, there should be an exact, *albeit unknown and in practice unknowable*, quantity which, *were* it known, *would* specify a ratio between set B and set A, where both B $= \aleph_0$ and A $= \aleph_0$. Therefore, while saying $\aleph_0 : \aleph_0$ would not be precise enough in the formal language of transfinite mathematics to depict the ratio of one infinite set to another, in principle there should be some form of notation that would capture the notion of an infinite ratio with enough precision to allow such comparisons.

Moreover, the *meaning* of literal infinity is that of a collection complete as well as limitless in quantity. Set theorists say that some infinite sets can be shown to be the same size, at least in principle, with a bijection between them. However—and this would be controversial to say—a one-to-one correspondence that transfinite mathematicians propose between two infinite sets logically implies a ratio between them; namely, 1:1. Take a one-to-one correspondence, a bijection, established between the literally infinite subset of all even natural numbers and the literally infinite superset of all natural numbers:

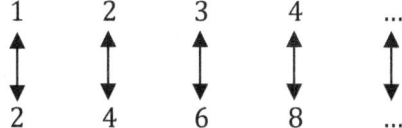

Now suppose we treat these two subsets of naturals not merely as segments of $\mathbb{N}$ but as constructions formed over time. If the naturals (1, 2, 3, 4, ...) and even naturals (2, 4, 6, 8, ...) were to both go on being constructed into ever-larger sequences, tit-for-tat, then the bijection between them would always be an incomplete progression of one-to-one matches, but a progression always maintained as the two sequences grow in synchrony. Despite their perpetual incompleteness, there would at any step of the way be a running total of elements in the progressions, with the elements of each evenly matched as long as both rows continue to be extended one to one. So, the one-to-one correspondence between those elements implies a 1:1 ratio between the sequences, no matter how big we allow the finite sequences to become.

But what about when we allow the sequences to become infinite—literally infinite? In § 14.7.1, we saw that Bolzano denied that a bijection between a subset and a superset carries to infinity [565]. In his view, such is just a mathematical illusion. However, for the sake of argument, let's grant to transfinite mathematicians that a literally infinite bijection is possible between a subset and a superset.

For that situation, mathematicians do not typically hold the one-to-one correspondence of elements between *infinite* sets implies a 1:1 ratio as it does for finite sets. Transfinite mathematicians say that for a bijection of infinite sets, the one-to-one correspondence between the sets does not imply a ratio between them at all.

Perhaps in terms of the *limitlessness* of the bijection, they are correct. But in terms of *completeness* of the bijection, such denial rings hollow.

If a one-to-one correspondence between ordered sets extends not only to the indefinitely large but to the literally infinite in size, then that means at no point along that extent does the bijection break down. Consequently, at no point should the 1:1 ratio break down between the sequences of the sets either. If there are "just as many" of one thing as another, and you can put them into bijection, then their ratio is, logically, 1:1—all the way up to literal infinity, at least as a matter of literal infinity's semantic logic even if such a ratio is not coherently expressible according to some conventions of mathematical syntax.

The convention of math may say there are no determinate ratios for infinite sets when we define ratios in terms of mathematical syntax and particular operations, but the logic of math says there must be, *at least in principle*, when we pay attention to the semantics of what "one to one" and 1:1 both *mean*: there are "just as many" of B as of A.

Therefore, if set B and set A are both literally infinite, and if each can be placed into bijection with the other unto *completion*, then in fact they do have a 1:1 ratio between their members, even if we cannot say $B:A = \aleph:\aleph = 1:1$ because $\aleph:\aleph$ is not syntactically precise enough to be coherent in the formal language of math. However, if literally infinite sets are indeed complete sets, then it should logically follow that B and A can both be infinite while $B:A = 1:1$.

15.2.6 *More than One Infinite Ratio*

So far, we've seen that a one-to-one correspondence between two finite sets logically implies a 1:1 ratio between the sets, even if such cannot be expressed in mathematical formalism consistently. We've also seen that when extrapolated to literal infinity, the 1:1 ratio must logically apply to infinite sets and so must be mathematically expressible in principle even if not in actual practice. But now we hit a logical snag, for 1:1 is not the only value possible for the B:A ratio when we allow B and A to grow from finitude to infinity.

15.2.7 *Half of Infinity*

Suppose we start with a finite subset B as part of a finite superset, A. Let B have 50 elements and let A have 100 elements. The value of the ratio B:A is 50:100 or 1:2, which is the same saying B is ½ (one half) of A.

Now, let's make subset B and superset A proportionally bigger in size by adding a zero onto the values of both: B = 500 and A = 1,000. The value of the ratio B:A becomes 500:1,000, which means a ratio of 1:2; in other words, B is still ½ of A.

Next, keep creating new iterations of this equation by adding one zero onto the value of A and the value of B with reach run:

$$B:A = 5,000:10,000 = \tfrac{1}{2} = 1:2$$
$$B:A = 50,000:100,000 = \tfrac{1}{2} = 1:2$$
$$B:A = 500,000:1,000,000 = \tfrac{1}{2} = 1:2$$
$$\vdots$$

Assume we can carry this process infinitely. As B 'approaches' infinity, A also 'approaches' infinity, but the ratio between B and A remains constant. Mathematicians might express it something like this:

$$lim[b \to \infty]\, b/(2b) = lim[b \to \infty]\, \tfrac{1}{2} = \tfrac{1}{2} = 1:2.$$

Now let's assume we can *complete* an infinite succession. In that case, B and A not only 'approach' infinity, they also both *become* literally infinite in size.

Because there is no standard notation for two infinite sets in ratio to one another such as $\infty{:}\infty$ or $\aleph{:}\aleph$, then once again we have no standard way to express B and A as literally infinite where a ratio such as B:A = 1:2 would hold. There are, however, some versions of transfinite mathematics that do indeed allow for one infinite set being half of another infinite set.

Such was proposed by mathematician John H. Conway (1937–2020) [566] [567]. Conway figured out a way to represent an abstract set of numbers, z, greater than any finite number that is half of a totally ordered infinite set ω:

$$z = \frac{\omega}{2}$$

At least in principle, then, we should be able to express the ratio of B:A as 1:2 even while B and A are both literally infinite sets.

That means in principle we should be able to qualify one infinite set as being half of another infinite set. For example, the even numbers as half of all the natural numbers, or the positive numbers as half of the integers. Two infinite sets, one as half of the other.

15.2.8 *The Infinite Ratios*

We therefore have two different situations. In one situation, B denoted the set of even natural numbers and A the set of all natural numbers. Because of the one-to-one correspondence of B to A, we concluded B:A = 1:1. In another situation, B denoted 50 elements out of A's 100 elements. We let B and A grow to literal infinity, which implied B:A = 1:2 because B is always half of A, even as the two sets are increased to infinity.

But now we have some apparent contradictions. Suppose we let B denote a finite selection of even natural numbers and A denote a finite selection of both odd and even natural numbers. Now let subset B and superset A exponentially double in size until they become literally infinite sets.

On the one hand, we know the elements of B can be placed into bijection with the elements of A as when we have ten elements of each set that grow to infinity:

B = {2, 4, 6, 8, 10, 12, 14, 16, 18, 20, ...}
A = {1, 2, 3, 4, 5, 6, 7, 8, 9, 10, ...}

We can therefore conclude B:A = 1:1.

On the other hand, take B as a finite proper subset of finite superset A:

B = {2, 4, 6, 8, 10}
A = {1, 2, 3, 4, 5, 6, 7, 8, 9, 10}

Now grow both sets to infinity:

$B = \{2, \ 4, \ 6, \ 8, \ 10, ...\}$
$A = \{1, \ 2, \ 3, \ 4, \ \ 5, \ 6, \ \ 7, \ 8, \ \ 9, \ 10, ...\}$

We know from Conway's math that one infinite set can be half of another infinite set. So, even though B and A are infinite sets, we can still conclude that $B:A = 1:2$.

But now notice that, as an infinite sequence, B has *the same progression in each case* when the ellipsis in either expression carries the progression 'infinitely' onward. B therefore has two ratios with respect to A; namely, 1:1 and 1:2. The first is on account of the bijection between B and A as infinite sets, the second is on account of one set having only half the members of the other *no matter how far* they are extrapolated—even infinitely. However, since $1:1 \neq 1:2$, then B cannot have both ratios to A. Therefore, B does and does not have both ratios with respect to A: a contradiction.

Mathematicians of course know that such would entail a contradiction. So, to avoid the need of addressing contradictions like this caused by extrapolations to infinity, mathematicians have defined the rules of mathematics in such a way as to retain use of infinity (∞) while dismissing infinite ratios as *indeterminate*.

But the extrapolation of numerical progressions all the way up to literal infinity, where ∞ becomes quantitatively identical to ω, which is equal to $\aleph$, which is interpreted to be a complete set, logically implies there *must* be ratios between infinite sets of numbers, at least in principle. Then again, if we allow there to be ratios with infinitely many members, we get logical contradictions.

It would seem that retaining infinity while calling infinite ratios "indeterminate" is more of a dodge to keep the math consistent than a solution to the logical problem of what progressions to infinity imply.

15.2.9 *Working Around the Problem*

To justify retaining infinity while dismissing infinite ratios as "indeterminate" instead of logically contradictory, mathematicians (especially those working with set theory) generally adopt two positions concerning infinite ratios.

The First Position: 'Size' Has Various Meanings. This position is about the relation of subsets to supersets and what a size comparison between them entails. It is true that there are fewer members in a finite subset when compared to the members of the whole finite set to which they belong, but that need not be true for infinite sets, so the position goes. For infinite sets, we have to take into consideration the difference between comparing a proper subset to a whole set per se versus comparing the subset to the whole set by correlating members between them.

Transfinite set theorists hold that it's true the subset of evens is a proper subset of the whole set of $\mathbb{N}$, but they also point out that the whole set of all the natural numbers of $\mathbb{N}$ can still be in one-to-one correspondence with all the evens (or odds) alone. Comparing the set of even natural numbers to the set of all the natural numbers by a subset-superset relation is *qualitatively* (not just quantitatively) different from comparing these sets by a one-to-one correspondence between their members. As noted in § 14.1.4, those adopting the transfinite system say there are "as many even natural numbers as natural numbers in the 'correlation' sense, but there are fewer of them in the 'subset' sense" [568].

Their position is that when we measure the size of two infinite sets according to the subset sense of 'size' and the correlation sense of 'size', we are not really talking about the same thing at all; the comparisons are using two different notions of size for infinite sets. Transfinite set theorists and mathematicians thus see the subset sense of size and the correlation sense of size as simply two different perspectives, each equally legitimate and producing no mathematical incoherence.

For that reason, introductory books on infinity now claim that the ratio problem is based on a false analogy between how finite subsets relate to their finite superset and how infinite subsets should relate to their infinite superset. It is a "common error," they say, to assume that "when things have similar properties, they can be equated" [569].

The Second Position: Correspondence is Not Ratio. This position asserts two additional things:

- An infinite superset can be larger than an infinite subset but *without* a ratio (e.g., 1:2) between them.
- A one-to-one correspondence between an infinite superset, like $\mathbb{N}$, and an infinite subset, like the set of all even positive integers, is not a 1:1 ratio.

From these two set-theoretic proposals, it follows that the ratio concept does not apply to literally infinite collections. Infinite collections do not have size *by ratio*. According to this view, at no time is there a ratio between all the elements of $\mathbb{N}$ and the elements of infinite subsets in $\mathbb{N}$. So, the ratio problem never arises because neither the 1:1 nor the 1:2 ratio applies to infinite sets. Therefore, because ratios don't apply to infinite collections, there is no infinite ratio problem.

Perhaps this two-pronged solution works for mathematicians because it allows them to keep doing math with infinite sets and progressions without having to worry about the logical implications of what it means for finite progressions to proceed to (literal) infinity. But, as I'll show, these positions do not dissolve the infinite ratio problem.

15.2.10 *Red Herrings*

Each of the above two positions for denying infinite ratios is based on the red herring fallacy, which seems to crop up often when set theorists and transfinite mathematicians try to make literal infinity into a logically rigorous concept. Recall that this fallacy is committed whenever an argument or explanation is irrelevant to the issue discussed. In this case, there are two related red herrings:

- First red herring: size has various meanings in set theory.
- Second red herring: correspondence is not the same thing as a ratio.

The first position is guilty of the first red herring, the second position is guilty of the second red herring. Let's take these in order.

15.2.11 *First Red Herring: Size Has Various Meanings in Set Theory*

The first red herring involves adopting an alternative meaning of 'size' according to contrasting criteria for size that are not pertinent to the infinite ratio problem. If it were true that there are two different senses of size (the subset sense and the correlation sense) when comparing the even natural numbers to all numbers in $\mathbb{N}$, then we would be comparing the set of even naturals to the set of all naturals in a fundamentally different manner when we compare these sets by subset criteria than when we compare them by correlation criteria. But the ratio problem is not based on using different criteria for determining the sizes of the two collections. Nor is the problem based on using different methods for establishing the sizes of the collections. So, the ratio problem is not the result of making an equivocation in the meaning of size as claimed by transfinite mathematicians.

If we say the set of natural numbers comprised of positive integers is "greater" than the set of even numbers within that segment, we are not making a statement about one set being greater than the other in the sense that "greater" means merely the *inclusiveness* of one set with respect to another. Rather, when we say the superset is "greater" than its subset, we are making a statement about the *quantity* of elements in each set, not the inclusiveness or exclusiveness of elements between the sets. To say a superset is "greater" than a subset is to say there are *more* elements in the superset than the subset, and so *fewer* elements in the subset than in the superset—therefore the quantity of elements in the subset is *less than* the quantity of elements in the superset, the superset being *greater than* the subset in terms of quantity; in other words, there are *not* just as many elements in each set.

Suppose we have two sets: A and B. Now some members of A were removed from A, resulting in a new set: C, which has a total of 24 members. Then, the members of B were counted, resulting in a total of 24. Hence, we find that B and C are of identical size owing to their identical quantities (24:24), and it is from their identical quantities that we conclude there is a one-to-one correspondence between the members of B and C. Not vice versa. That is, a correlation criterion need not be *assumed* at all for determining that B and C are the same sizes, but rather the correlation between the members of B and C is the *implication* of their quantitative equality in size.

The meaning of 'size' for the ratio $12:24 = 1:2$ and the meaning of 'size' for the ratio of $24:24 = 1:1$ is exactly the same meaning of 'size' between the two examples. Both sizes are about one quantity of elements being compared to another quantity of elements to demonstrate a ratio. The 1:2 ratio says nothing about inclusiveness or non-inclusiveness between the sets compared.

Suppose B is the even numbers {2, 4, 6, 8, 10, 12, 14, 16, 18, 20, 22, 24} and set C is the sequence of natural numbers (odd and even) 1–24. Clearly, the ratio of B:C is the ratio of 12 even numbers to 24 natural numbers (odd and even), a ratio of 1:2. Only if we extend our list of evens by multiplying the evens by two do we get a 1:1 ratio between the evens and naturals. True, the 1:2 ratio of 12 evens to 24 naturals supports the evens as a proper subset (inclusion) of the naturals. And true, the matching of evens extended up to the first 24 evens supports the set-to-set equality (correspondence) of 24 evens to 24 naturals. But this subset/correspondence distinction is the *outcome* of matching the sets when their sizes are first determined by quantity, which is what determines the size of the sets, not the matching process or the fact that one is a subset of the other. Hence, there is no equivocation of the meaning of size.

And this spells trouble for infinity. For if there is no logical necessity for a subset sense of size and a correlation sense of size—if size can just as well be about a comparison of quantity—then two sets with infinitely many members imply infinite ratios.

To see why this is so, start by supposing we grow the sizes of these sequences by using the first 100 positive integers—we first compare the list consisting of even naturals to the original list of 100 positive integers, finding 50 evens to 100 positive integers for a 1:2 ratio of even naturals to all the positive integers. Then, we extend the list of evens to match the 100 positive integers for a 1:1 ratio. After that, suppose we continue to repeat this process over a series of runs, adding zeros to the totals.

Each time, we exponentially increase the size of the set of positive integers (10^4, 10^8, 10^{16}, ...) and each time we let the sample of even numbers taken from the set of positive integers exponentially increase in size as well to maintain the 1:2 ratio, then extend to match the positive integers to maintain the 1:1 ratio. We allow the exponential curve to increase the number of even natural numbers (e) and the number of positive integers (n) "to infinity"—literal infinity—such that e becomes the value of the infinite set E and n becomes the value of the infinite set of all natural numbers: $\mathbb{N}$.

We find that the ratios hold no matter how high they are projected. Without some *quality* differentiating the finite and infinite to make the ratios break down somewhere along the progressions, the ratios must themselves become infinite just as the bijected sequence of two sets must become infinite since literal infinity is a *quantitative* condition. That expresses the outcome of the infinite ratio problem: the 1:2 ratio *never breaks down* as the collections grow to literal infinity, while the one-to-one correspondence (which is quantitatively equivalent to a 1:1 ratio) also never breaks down as the collections grow to infinity. Both are ratios for the size (quantity) of all even natural numbers (E) and the size (quantity) of all positive integers—all the odd and even natural numbers—combined ($\mathbb{N}$). Both establish that as the $e{:}n$ ratio continues to infinity, one comparison produces the 1:2 ratio and the second produces 1:1, while the meaning of 'size'—quantity in the form of sums or a ratio—is the same for both comparisons.

The conflict between the 1:2 and 1:1 ratios for the same infinite subset (E) compared to the same infinite superset ($\mathbb{N}$) comes about not because of an equivocation in the meaning of size for the subset and superset, but because increasing the sizes of the quantities for e and n to infinity ($e = E$ and $n = \mathbb{N}$) results in two different $e{:}n$ ratio values together (1:2 and 1:1) according to *the same* meaning of the terms 'size' and 'greater'.

The sizes of the sets were not established by *assuming* different meanings for size. Had the matching process produced only an injection of the evens to the naturals instead of a bijection as well, then the ratios may not have come into conflict. Instead, the sizes of the sets were established by using the same enumeration process—summing the number of numbers for values of both e and n—with determinate, constant values for the numbers representing the sum of elements in each set, just as the 1:2 and 1:1 ratios depict. So, according to the meaning of literal infinity, we can in principle compare the sizes of two infinite sets, demonstrating that as the evens (e) and the naturals (n) reach infinity "all" the evens to "all" the naturals have a 1:2 ratio while "all" the evens to "all" the naturals have a 1:1 ratio.

We therefore cannot evade the contradiction between ratios by appealing to two different sets of criteria—subset-to-superset and one-to-one correspondence—for providing two different senses of 'size', because there are not two different senses of size in the contradiction to begin with.

15.2.12 *Second Red Herring: Correspondence is Not the Same Thing as Ratio*

The second, and related, red herring is the misdirection of focusing on how correspondence comparisons are "not the same thing" as ratios (a matter of definition) when the real issue is that such comparisons logically *imply* ratios (a matter of quantifying), and so there seems to be no reason why ratios should not apply from finite to infinite collections as do correlations, such as a one-to-one correspondence of members between sets.

As framed today, mathematics holds that we cannot compare infinite quantities by ratio but only by correlation techniques. For comparison of infinite sets, we must label any one-to-one correspondence of size between them by quantifiers such as 'denumerable' or 'equinumerous' while a 1:1 ratio between their infinite sizes is not possible. Hence, transfinite mathematics would have us compare infinite subsets and supersets indirectly by quantifiers rather than directly by quantities in the form of ratios—safely ignoring that a one-to-one correspondence logically *implies* 1:1, despite dismissals that they are not the same thing.

Don't get me wrong: mathematically, such a position works. By refusing to address that a one-to-one correspondence *implies* a 1:1 ratio, modern mathematics can for the sake of operational consistency safely ignore any logical contradictions otherwise involved with one-to-one correspondence implying a literally infinite ratio, and therefore safely ignore the issue of contradictions implied by infinite ratios such as having both an infinite 1:1 ratio and infinite 1:2 ratio for the same infinite subset/superset. However, this practice sacrifices semantical logic to maintain mathematical coherence. That is, coherence in the syntactical rules of math is obtained by committing what is an informal logical fallacy in natural language— the red herring fallacy, which is a semantic fallacy.

In this case, the red herring is one of pointing out that correlations are not ratios, thus ignoring that a one-to-one correlation of members logically implies a ratio; namely, 1:1. Then, given the rejection of infinite ratios, infinities of the "same size" are instead described by quantifiers like 'denumerable' or 'equinumerous'. However, the same transfinite system insists there are infinite numbers (namely, ω and $\aleph$). And if there are infinite numbers, then there are infinite quantities, and if there are infinite quantities, then the issue is not that correspondence is not the same thing as a ratio but whether and how ratios can break down when sets are projected to infinity while correlations do not break down.

Recall that the sequence 1, 2, 3, ... is claimed in transfinite math to be the set {1, 2, 3, ...}, which is equal to ω, which has $\aleph$-many members. If any figuratively infinite 1, 2, 3, ... presupposes the literal infinity of {1, 2, 3, ...} as equal to ω, then the sequence of even naturals to odd-and-even naturals still implies the 1:1 and 1:2 ratios cannot break down and so must hold all the way to infinity (ω).

If it's mathematically valid to talk of a one-to-one correspondence between two finite sets projected to literally infinite sets, it should be just as mathematically valid to talk of 1:1 ratios between finite sets projected to literally infinite sets. Substituting quantifiers like 'denumerable' or 'equinumerous' to compare sets of equal infinite size for talk of the infinite ratios such comparisons seem to imply is merely a dodge.

So even if one set of mathematical rules do not allow for a 1:1 ratio between infinite sets while another set of mathematical rules allows for a one-to-one correspondence of members between infinite sets, the logic of the progressions to literal infinity in each case entails that a one-to-one correspondence between members of two infinite sets is not qualitatively different than a 1:1 ratio between two infinite sets. Hence, the logical contradictions of ratios carried to literal infinity hold precisely because the correlation procedure of transfinite mathematics is carried to literal infinity.

As a consequence, completeness and limitlessness together still imply a subset/superset ratio of both $1:(y>1)$ and yet also 1:1 between infinite subset and infinite superset as shown above. The same sets are being compared under projections that leave no natural number unaccounted for (via correlation techniques of comparison), and yet produce contradictory results: $(1:1) \neq (1:y>1)$.

Thus it is only by ignoring that bijection logically implies a 1:1 ratio, talking as if subset membership is a size claim rather than just an inclusiveness claim, and substituting talk of infinite sets in terms of quantifiers such as 'equinumerous' or 'denumerable' (e.g., $\mathbb{N} = \mathbb{Z}$) and 'non-equinumerous' or 'nondenumerable' (e.g., $\mathbb{N} \neq \mathbb{R}$) that the contradictions implied by infinite quantities are safely ignored in the mathematical rules for the sake of operational consistency. But the logical contradictions are still there in the logical implications. The infinite ratio problem is not dissolved by these red herrings.

15.2.13 *The Infinite Sequence Never Breaks Down, and that is the Problem*

There is perhaps one way that might be attempted to dissolve the ratio contradictions. The set theorist may simply deny B and A *become* infinite in the sense of growing "to infinity" by instead just insisting that

B and A are each infinite from the start. B and A have infinitely many numbers *all at once* so that any ratio we determine between B and A is just a finite comparison between finite *segments* of B and A. We therefore might use mathematical operations to *find* ratios between increasingly larger finite segments of B and A, but that does not mean B and A need to have ratios as infinite *wholes*.

This solution proposes two different uses of infinity: the use of *literal infinity* for correlation, in which the one-to-one correspondence is denied as being the ratio 1:1, and the use of *figurative infinity* as referring to the growth of identified segments of B and A, which is used for a ratio in any finite iteration. We may, for instance, begin by identifying the first 50 evens of B and the first 100 numbers of A to establish the 1:2 ratio before identifying the first 500 evens of B and the first 1,000 numbers of A, keeping the same 1:2 ratio, and repeating this process to maintain a constant 1:2 ratio, but the set theorist would say this 'infinite' process is merely the figurative infinity of identifying a series of finite segments of B and A for which ratios do not apply as a whole. The figurative infinity of ratio identification is different from the bijection of the two literally infinite wholes.

So, it may be that the series of identified ratios (like 1:2) never reach "infinity" as if ∞ is a quantity; instead, ∞ just means the value of the progression is "indeterminate." The growth of *identified segments* of B and A, though maintaining a constant 1:2 ratio, may be seen as "approaching" infinity or growing "to infinity" in the sense that the identified segments of B and A increase indefinitely—that is, in only a *figuratively* infinite manner—with the A-segments always staying double the value of the B-segments. Meanwhile, B and A as wholes are literally infinite, there are "just as many" of B as A. Hence, the process of growing B and A is really a process not of change between B and A but between what segments of B and A we have identified for comparison. The identified segments of B and A are always finite no matter how long we keep on identifying larger segments of B and A, but B as a whole and A as a whole are always literally infinite.

In this solution to the ratio contradictions, mathematics is said to work with two different infinities—one literal and one figurative. The one-to-one correspondence between B and A is interpreted as applying to a literally infinite subset B and a literally infinite superset A; but the growth of subset B and superset A up to infinity is really the growth of a series of increasingly larger identified segments of B and A—which is to say, a progression that is a figurative infinity.

Alas, this solution to the ratio contradictions may make for a convenient and workable convention, but its logic doesn't hold up.

First, many mathematicians and philosophers of mathematics believe a literally infinite series can be completed in a finite amount of time [570]. We only have to reinterpret B and A as identified subsets of $\mathbb{N}$ and then imagine that B begins as, say, the first identified 50 *even* numbers of the set $\mathbb{N}$—

$\{2, 4, 6, 8, 10, ..., 100\}$,

—while we imagine A begins as the first identified 100 numbers of $\mathbb{N}$, *both odd and even*:

$\{1, 2, 3, 4, 5, ..., 100\}$.

Now, if a series can start as finite and grow infinitely fast to become a literally infinite set in finite time, then we can allow B and A to grow from finitude to literal infinity, tit for tat, in finite time. That is, we propose that the process of generating larger B subsets and larger A supersets is itself not merely a *figuratively* infinite (never-ending) process of identifying even numbers but instead is a *literally* infinite (limitless but completed) process. The process of growing B and A to infinity is itself a literally infinite sequence of steps in which B members and A members grow from finitude to become literally infinite, both becoming identical to $\mathbb{N}$ as a literally infinite set.

In which case, whatever unspecifiable values B and A acquire when they become complete, A becomes identical to the entire set of $\mathbb{N}$, which is infinite, while B becomes identical to all the even numbers of $\mathbb{N}$, which is also infinite. The bijection between B and A at any given step in their growth implies there are always "just as many" of B and A, which is the same as a 1:1 ratio.

However, because A was always double B as the sets grew and B cannot catch up to A in quantitative value according to the progression, then there are still *twice as many* of A as there are of B when B and A become literally infinite. So, we arrive at an infinite value for A in which B is half of A, and yet B is infinite and so is A. Hence, the ratio of 1:2 *never breaks down* during the growth process; it always holds up, even to infinity if indeed infinity can be complete and limitless in quantity.

The two ratios, grown to infinity, still conflict. In short, the ratio problem is not so easily dissolved because it is not a problem of mathematical syntax or rules of operation, but rather of mathematical semantics as exposed by the logical connotations of what literal infinity means as a quantitative concept.

Second, the set $\{1, 2, 3, 4, 5, ...\}$ is *nothing but* natural numbers *and* equal to ω. In other words, there are just as many naturals in $\{1, 2, 3, 4, 5, ...\}$ as in the quantity ω, held to be an instance of literal infinity. Ergo, the sequence in that literally infinite set, must extend to the ordinal ω or the sequence in the set is not literally infinite and so the set cannot equal ω.

15.2.14 *Using Syntax to Avoid Semantics*

In § 15.1, I pointed out that when the ellipsis in the brackets $\{1, 2, 3, 4, 5, ...\}$ can at best just give us a figurative infinity (∞), and there is nothing *in between* the naturals and ω since ω is "least infinite" ordinal, we have logical nonsense, for a figurative infinity cannot give us a literally infinite set. Appealing to Cantor's proposal in § 15.1 that figurative infinity (∞) *presupposes* literal infinity (ω) does not help. It only reinforces the point that progressions carried to literal infinity result in contradictions, such as the logical contradiction of implying infinite ratios, which is not resolved by transfinite formalism.

15.3 INFINITELY GREATER THAN INFINITY

This brings us back to the second possible retort (§ 15.1) against the charge that ω cannot be a limit ordinal to a literally infinite sequence of naturals. Cantor stated that the greatest number one can name "is quite as far off from ω as the least finite number" and that "my least transfinite ordinal number ω, and consequently all greater ordinal numbers, lie quite outside the endless series 1, 2, 3, and so on." I submit this answer will not resolve the logical problems with the seeming gap between the naturals and ω , nor does it do anything to explain how a sequence of naturals can have no end and yet be followed by an ordinal.

We will not need to spend much time refuting Cantor on this point, for we have already covered much of this ground in Chapter 14 (see § 14.2, § 14.3, and § 14.11.1). I will only sum up the main point.

For any natural number, that number is only equal to a combination of its predecessors. So, what exactly is it about $\mathbb{N}$ as a set that makes its sequence of the natural numbers equal to ω if there is no infinitely great n equal to ω? Cantor just stipulates there are *infinitely many* naturals but none equal in size to ω, without offering any rationale for how only a sequence of nothing but increasing finite cardinalities can, in total, equal ω of $\aleph$ size while no natural number of that sequence is equal to ω.

I submit that for {1, 2, 3, 4, 5, ...} to equal ω requires that the sequence of natural numbers must not only "tend to" ω in a figuratively infinite sense but also the sequence of natural numbers must actually *be of infinite quantity* in a literal sense, which implies an infinitely great natural number. To deny that is to make vacuous any claim that ℕ has a literal infinity of naturals and that ω is an *ordinal*—a number in the *same sequence* of numbers as the naturals and the *least* number *after* the naturals.

As shown in Chapter 14, the only way to avoid such logically contradictory connotations is either to reject that {1, 2, 3, 4, 5, ...} is literally infinite or accept that ω, as a limit ordinal, functions in the formalism as merely the quantity of a collective indefinite toward which 1, 2, 3, 4, 5, ... as an indefinite series of definite numbers tends. But both of these ways out of the contradiction actually amount to the same thing: concluding that ω as a representation of literal infinity is an illusion and the transfinite formalism merely works with figurative infinity in disguise.

15.4 THE CONTRADICTIONS REMAIN

Once again Cantor's system has not tamed infinity. We've just seen that there are several logical self-contradictions inherent in the meaning of literal infinity, which the transfinite system fails to resolve even as it identifies the 'transfinite' with literal infinity. All of them follow from the fact that literal infinity's constituent properties—literal completeness and literal limitlessness—are contrary to one another and so simply cannot coexist for the same quantity of members in the same collection.

CHAPTER 15 IN REVIEW

❖ The transfinite system says ω is a kind of supremum—a limit ordinal—to the natural numbers. I argue the transfinite system's notion of a limit ordinal, while mathematically coherent, is not logically coherent with respect to being an instance of literal infinity.

❖ Cantor proposed that the figurative infinity of a numeric progression (∞) presupposes the literal infinity (ω) which follows all the naturals. He also proposed ω is just as far removed from the largest natural number one can calculate as the least natural number. Both claims have logical problems even if not mathematical ones.

❖ Cantor's first proposal results in the implication of ratios carried to infinity, which result in logical contradictions. However, this also seems to be the implication of Cantor's bijection thesis for equating the size of infinite sets. Mathematicians and set theorists have proposed solutions to dissolve such contradictions with the intent of saving infinity but to no avail. If the one-to-one correspondence between members of sequences does not break down extending to infinity, then neither should a ratio for the same sequences extended to infinity. Progressions of numbers carried to literal infinity therefore still imply logical contradictions.

❖ Cantor's second proposal is also problematic, resting on no clear explanation for how ω can follow after an infinite sequence which is composed of nothing but increasing numbers that somehow do not become infinite. His second proposal additionally suffers from the problems outlined in the previous chapter.

❖ Conclusion: Cantor's transfinite system does not resolve the logical contradictions in the very meaning of literal infinity as a condition of both completeness and limitlessness.

16: INVISIBLE CONTRADICTIONS

Occasionally, students of philosophy and members of the lay public notice the logical self-contradictions involving claims about infinite collections (like having a total and yet being uncountable) and suspect something is amiss with the notion of (quantitative) infinity. They then attempt to figure out why the self-contradictions occur with infinity. However, without explicitly defining all the terms involved, as we have done in preceding chapters, and without noting where the lexical meaning of (literal) infinity differs from the theoretical and operational meanings of infinity used in mathematics, it is hard for them to tease out where the problems with infinity are to be found. They intuitively sense something is wrong with infinity, but they are not quite sure where the problem lies. And when they think they understand where the problem is, they are most often mistaken.

The same can be said even of professional philosophers. From Aristotle to Wittgenstein, and on to some contemporary philosophers, there has been suspicion about literal infinity (most often referred to as 'actual infinity'). In recent decades that suspicion has increased among philosophers. Skeptical philosophers were all correct to be suspicious, and yet the exact nature of the problem with infinity eluded almost all of them. They knew there to be self-contradictions implied by the concept of infinity, but none of them had quite nailed down the right analysis of those contradictions.

And so, when anyone suspects that literal infinity might be a self-contradictory concept and then proceeds to question mathematicians or infinity-friendly philosophers of mathematics about the apparent absurdity of literal infinity, the usual response by such academics is to deny any contradictions exist and proceed to demonstrate how infinity makes mathematical sense. But it is precisely at this point that the two parties are speaking past one another. The breakdown in communication results from the two parties making mutually incompatible assumptions about the concept of infinity and its implications.

16.1 COMMON ASSUMPTIONS

There are three assumptions widespread in the practice of modern mathematics with respect to infinity:

- Infinity is a discovery.
- Infinity is expressed in mathematics via syntax alone.
- Infinity is directly used in mathematical operations.

It is because of this set of assumptions that the logical self-contradictions implied by the meaning of literal infinity go largely unnoticed and unattended by most mathematicians.

16.2 INFINITY AS A DISCOVERY

Mathematicians tend to hold one of two philosophies of mathematics. The first I will call *discoverism* and the second is called *inventionism* [571]. Each disagrees with the other about what it means for *mathematical objects*, including infinity when taken as such, to exist and how it is we can know about mathematical objects.

16.2.1 *Mathematical Objects*

In § 2.2 the term 'object' was defined as "that of which a subject can be aware." If you can be aware of it, it is an object. That's not to say that it isn't an object if you are unaware of it; it's just to say that it is an object if you *can* be aware of it. Since if you can think about something, you are aware of it, and if you are aware of it, it is an object, then if you can think about something, it is an object.

We can extend our definition of 'object' to mathematics. A mathematical object is anything mathematical of which we can be aware, including mathematical objects which are only conceptions. Mathematical objects include such things as sets, numerals, numbers, number scales (number systems), operators, functions, equations, diagrams, theorems, proofs, geometrical relations (points, partitions, boundaries), and shapes (lines, angles, planes, circles, polyhedra, hyperdimensional shapes, etc.), algebraic relations like groups, lattices, and so on. Even the collection of all mathematical objects is itself a mathematical object—it is something mathematical we can conceive or otherwise think about.

Mathematical objects exist, but what it means for a mathematical object to exist is a matter of debate. Certainly, mathematical objects need not be physical objects. Mathematical objects (for example, the number 2) may be associated with objects we see in the physical world (like a pair of apples) but mathematical objects need not be identical to the physical objects with which they are associated. On the other hand, what we see on the page when we write '2' is a numeral, which as a written symbol is a physical object. This would at first seem to suggest that mathematical objects are physical objects after all, like other physical objects we perceive. However, numerals can exist in the mind without being written down—they are still numerals as mere ideas unmanifested physically, save perhaps in the electrical patterns of our brain activity. Likewise, the *number* represented by a numeral is itself a mathematical object—an abstraction that need not have any particular physical manifestation. Numbers exist as abstract ideas that we contemplate with our intellect; the same is true for all mathematical objects.

So far, this is very straightforward and uncontroversial—mathematical objects are abstract ideas grasped by the mind. But now things begin to get less straightforward. For, in saying mathematical objects are objects of contemplation, we can ask further if mathematical objects are *invented* by the minds that conceive them or if they exist independently of the mind and are instead *discovered* by the minds conceiving them or otherwise thinking about them.

16.2.2 *Discoverism*

This is where one of the earliest, and certainly the most historically influential philosophy of mathematics comes in. The core idea of this ancient philosophy is that mathematical objects are things that mathematicians find or *discover* because mathematical objects preexist in an objective world of their own—a world not dependent on the thoughts or actions of human beings. Mathematical objects, including the mathematical treatment of properties like finitude and infinitude, are not just made-up inventions; they are *discoveries*.

Mathematicians have for centuries held this view of mathematical objects. We find reference to mathematical objects as discoveries in an eloquent (even if apocryphal) speech delivered by Cambridge mathematician G.H. Hardy (1877–1947) on behalf of his student Srinivasa Ramanujan (1887–1920) for fellowship in the Royal Society [572]:

> "...for is this not exactly our justification for pure mathematics? We are merely explorers of infinity in the pursuit of absolute perfection. We do not *invent* these formulae, they *already exist* and lie in wait for only the very brightest of minds, like Ramanujan, ever to divine and prove."

Many scientists also hold this view. For example, a recent article regarding a biologist's thesis on the evolution of human consciousness stated, "Humans didn't *invent* arithmetic, algebra, trigonometry, or even calculus. We *discovered* them" [573]. The claim is that mathematical objects (including mathematical systems) are, quite literally, discoveries in the sense of detected, pre-existing objects. In this view, mathematical objects are all "out there," waiting to be discovered, even if no human being is ever around to discover them.

This philosophy of mathematics I will refer to as 'discoverism'. The philosopher Plato was, perhaps, the first *discoverist* [574]. According to Plato, all the things we perceive with our senses are just imperfect copies of ideal things he called *Forms*. For example, if you see a chair, it's just an imperfect copy of a single, ideal chair—or, more accurately, an imperfect copy of the Form of the ideal chair. The Form of the ideal chair is just the property of 'chairness' that is inherent in the Universe. Brazilian physicist and astronomer Marcelo Gleiser simplified Plato's view like so [575]:

> Suffice it to think of Forms as some kind of blueprint of perfection, as the core ideas behind things or feelings. For example, the form of chairness contains in it the possibility of all chairs, which, once built, become mere shadows of the true Form. Forms are the universal essence of what is potentially existing, as they themselves are nonexistent in space and time. As limited beings, we can only dimly perceive what they comprise of, as we clumsily attempt to represent them within our perceived reality.

Hence, the idea of an ideal chair that we have in our minds is, ironically, the only real chair. All the other chairs—from those we draw or represent to those we see and sit on in the physical world—are not the real thing; they are just imperfect copies of the real thing: the Form of chairness. For Plato, the ideal world is the real world and what we think of as the "real" world is just an illusion, like a shadow. Only the ideal Forms are real, and collectively they comprise the metaphysical *World of Forms* [576].

Plato's concept of the Forms extends to mathematical objects. According to Plato, mathematical objects are all Forms in the World of Forms. For example, all the various shapes of things we see, real though they may seem, are but imperfect, distorted shadows cast as projections from the perfect geometrical Forms, which reside in the metaphysical World of Forms beyond the reach of our physical senses. So too numbers, as Forms, exist in the World of Forms. All numerals are but imperfect representations of numbers; they are shadows cast by numbers—the perfect Forms of the numerals. All depictions of the numeral 3 are mere shadows cast by the Form of 'three-ness' from the World of Forms. So in Plato's view, mathematical objects exist independently from our minds in the World of Forms and are not dependent on human thought. We don't invent mathematical objects with schemes; we discover mathematical objects in the World of Forms.

Apparently, most mathematicians today adhere to Plato's version of discoverism [577]. Plato's version of discoverism goes by various names: *Platonic realism*, *Platonic idealism*, *mathematical platonism*, or just *Platonism*; the same philosophy is also called *mathematical realism* or simply *realism* [578]. Some of these names are misleading because Plato's philosophy covers many more topics than only mathematics, and the term 'realism' is often used for philosophical positions independent of any of the positions held by Plato. Regardless of what we want to call it, most mathematicians these days adhere to some variation of the philosophical position that mathematical objects are discovered rather than invented; usually, it is Plato's version of this position that mathematicians hold.

In fact, in reviewing the primary and secondary literature I have found it affirmed that mathematicians prefer this position. Consider the following statement by mathematicians Winfried Just and Martin Weese, two members of the American Mathematical Society [579]:

> The underlying view is that THE UNIVERSE OF SETS exists independently of human intelligence, in much the same way as the physical universe exists independently of us. This philosophical standpoint is called *Platonism*. According to the Platonist view, mathematicians *discover* properties of THE UNIVERSE OF SETS. According to opposing views, mathematicians just *invent* models...
>
> ...we cannot ignore the observation that *when working on a mathematical problem*, all mathematicians are Platonists. A mathematician who is studying properties of the real line will think of this process as *discovering* truths about an object that exists independently of the human mind.

Just and Weese are going a bit far by stating "all" mathematicians are Platonists. However, it is true that most mathematicians are Platonists insofar as most of them adhere to Plato's version of discoverism.

In Plato's version of discoverism, the metaphysical world of mathematical Forms is an eternal world that exists independently of the physical world and, as such, it cannot be directly perceived through the senses [580]. But if we cannot perceive mathematical objects with the senses, then how do we know about them? Most mathematicians, in the tradition of Plato, answer that mathematical objects can be perceived in the World of Forms with a kind of perception that does not need physical senses. Mathematical objects are Forms perceived in some way by the mind alone.

16.2.3 *Mathematical Objects as Phenomena*

The discoverist believes that mathematical objects are phenomena. Scientists regard a *phenomenon* as what makes a given experience possible while most philosophers tend to regard a phenomenon to be the experience or appearance itself. In the former sense, what it feels like to see red is an experience caused by something (a phenomenon) that has redness as a property; in the latter sense, redness is itself an experience we have—the redness experience just is the phenomenon. Most mathematicians, being discoverists, regard mathematical objects as phenomena in the former sense. That is, mathematicians tend to regard mathematical objects as phenomena in the way that objects such as fossils are phenomena: they are entities that exist regardless of any mortal mind ever thinking about them and they are capable of being experienced—such as when we have the experience of discovering them.

In discoverism, the phenomenon is the mathematical form behind the experience. To the discoverist, we can imagine a circle only because there really is a circle phenomenon, namely the form of the circle. The form of a circle is its essence of 'circleness' and it is that form or essence that is the phenomenal cause of experiencing circles [581]. We experience the symmetrical, enclosed, round shape in our minds because there exists the form of a circle (the phenomenon of a circle) that causes the experience of what it is like to "see a circle" in our imagination.

That is far different from saying the experience of seeing a circle just is the phenomenon of a circle. In the discoverist view, the Form of the Circle is the phenomenon, it is what causes the experience of seeing any given circle; the perfect circle is not the experience itself. The discoverist considers all mathematical objects to be 'phenomena' in this sense: mathematical objects are phenomena in the sense that they are objects capable of being experienced.

Discoverism also holds that mathematical objects are ideal Forms we perceive mentally but they are not found in nature. For example, when we identify a given shape we see as a circle, we are not actually seeing a circle. According to Plato, when we say we "see a circle" on a written page (like **Figure 16.1**), we are not really seeing a *true circle*; rather, we are seeing an *approximate circle*.

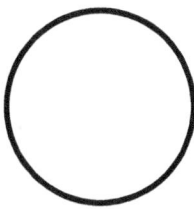

Figure 16.1: A circle—or, in Plato's philosophy, an approximate circle.

The true circle is in a metaphysical world of mathematical Forms—a world not perceived via the senses but rather perceived by our intellects. Plato would say we simply compare the Form of the circle, which we perceive mentally, to the shape we see with our eyes and call what we see "a circle" because it most closely resembles the abstract, ideal Form of a circle that we mentally perceive.

According to Platonism, all mathematical objects are phenomena in this sense—they are not experiences but rather the cause of them; mathematical objects are things that we can experience, but not by the senses. Instead, we perceive mathematical objects differently from how we perceive material things like the image of a tree or the sound of music. We experience mathematical objects with perception, but we do not perceive them with our senses. Rather, we perceive them with our minds, and especially with our consciousness. Our minds have access to a world of mathematical Forms that exists beyond the physical world; our minds are what perceive the mathematical objects in that eternal World of Forms while we use our senses to simply compare what we see in the physical world to the perfect mathematical shapes our minds perceive in the metaphysical World of Forms.

In this view, we literally discover mathematical objects—we obtain knowledge about them—through a kind of 'perception'; our conscious intellects 'perceive' mathematical objects as phenomena.

16.2.4 *Discoveries in the Mindscape*

Rucker modified Plato's version of discoverism. Whereas Plato believed the World of Forms exists independently of mind altogether, Rucker's philosophy contends that our minds inhabit a metaphysical world that he calls the *Mindscape*. Our bodies inhabit the physical world of the Universe; our minds inhabit the Mindscape.

Says Rucker [582],

> I think of consciousness as a point, an "eye," that moves about in a sort of mental space. All thoughts are already there in this multi-schematic space, which we might as well call the Mindscape. Our bodies move about in the physical space called the Universe; our consciousnesses move about in the mental space called the Mindscape.
>
> Just as we all share the same Universe, we all share the same Mindscape...
>
> Just as a rock is already in the Universe, whether or not someone is handling it, an idea is already in the Mindscape, whether or not someone is thinking it. A person who does mathematical research, writes stories, or meditates is an explorer of the Mindscape in much the same way that Armstrong, Livingstone, or Cousteau are explorers of the physical features of our Universe. The rocks on the Moon were there before the lunar module landed; and all the possible thoughts are already out there in the Mindscape.

Like Plato, Rucker believes mathematical objects are phenomena that can be perceived with the mind, via consciousness. Moreover, as we learn mathematics, we are actually perceiving the mathematical objects we learn about with our mind's "eye," our consciousness. And because mathematical objects are "already out there" in the Mindscape, Rucker regards mathematicians to be explorers of the Mindscape. In this view, mathematical objects are not really inventions that come to exist only as we invent them; rather, they are phenomena that already exist in the Mindscape and are waiting to be discovered.

The notion that mathematical objects are discoveries that exist in a world of their own seems to be the dominant view among mathematicians; most mathematicians, like Rucker, follow Plato on this view. For instance, in an interview with *The Economist*, University of California, Berkeley, mathematician Edward Frenkel stated, "I argue, as others have done before me, that mathematical concepts and ideas exist objectively, outside of the physical world and outside of the world of consciousness. We mathematicians discover them and are able to connect to this hidden reality through our consciousness" [583].

In the tradition of Plato, most mathematicians believe the conscious intellect discovers mathematical objects in the World of Forms, the Mindscape, or a similar metaphysical world. Consciousness provides awareness of what we discover while the intellect is the tool by which we make the discovery; when we become conscious of the fact that our intellect has uncovered a consistent mathematical idea, we have discovered (or rediscovered) that idea. Mathematicians, in exploring the Mindscape, use intellect to ensure the idea is precise and consistent; in so doing, they are using the intellect as their research tool to discover mathematical objects that lie waiting out there in the Mindscape.

16.2.5 *Set Theory: The Science of the Mindscape*

Rucker proposes that mathematicians, as explorers of the Mindscape, discover mathematical objects that are "already out there" in the Mindscape. Mathematical objects include mathematical sets. So, mathematical sets are already out there in the Mindscape waiting to be discovered.

Rucker's view has wide support among academics. Recall the statement of Just and Weese that the 'universe of sets' exists "independently of human intelligence" and that mathematicians "*discover*" the properties of the universe of sets [584].

Rucker expands on this view; he goes on to say a set is "the form of a possible thought" [585]. If sets are the forms of possible thoughts, then theories about sets are not just theories about mathematical objects, they are also theories about the forms of thoughts. Since these forms of thoughts form a "universe" of such forms, then theories about the forms of thoughts are theories about the Mindscape.

According to Rucker [586],

> Set theory is, indeed, the science of the Mindscape...Set theory enables us to put various facts about the Mindscape into one framework in the same way that the atomic theory of matter provides a framework in which the diverse physical and chemical qualities of matter can be simultaneously accommodated...
>
> The universe of set theory is closely bound up with the Mindscape—one can, perhaps, think of the former as a sort of blueprint for the latter.

Hence this version of discoverism implies a philosophy of mind in which all thoughts are part of the Mindscape that exists in one big mind—the mind of 'God' or 'The Absolute'—a mind Rucker believes is literally infinite.

16.2.6 *The Discovery of the Infinite*

Rucker's Mindscape and Plato's World of Forms both have implications for the mathematical concept of infinity. Both versions of discoverism consider infinity, as a mathematical object, to be a discovery. According to Rucker's version of discoverism, for instance, Cantor was the pioneer in mathematics who first "discovered" set theory and the theory of infinite (or transfinite) sets. Similarly, modern Platonists among mathematicians also hold that Cantor discovered literally infinite sets and even a (figuratively) infinite series of literally infinite sets. As Roitman put it, Cantor "discovered the variety of infinite cardinals" [587]. Notice how this is phrased: Cantor "discovered," rather than invented, these mathematical schemas. All of this is right in line with the idea that infinity is a mathematical object existing independently in a Platonic World of Forms, or in the Mindscape of God or the Absolute.

To this point, Rucker adds the caveat that Plato would not have approved of infinity as a mathematical discovery in his idea of the World of Forms because Plato did not believe in literal (or 'actual') infinity [588]. That may not be entirely true; it's not that Plato did not believe literal infinity exists at all, it's that he believed it is a condition only true of things that belong to the world of appearances with respect to the "diversity" of things we encounter [589]. Regardless of this nuance, Rucker notes that a modern Platonist "is someone who believes in the objective, external existence of [literally] infinite sets" [590]. And this includes the belief that "infinite sets of every size have a secure existence in the Mindscape" [591]. Rucker rhetorically asks if a mathematician in the tradition of Plato can be quite sure that the concept of (literal) infinity makes sense. Rucker answers that "yes, he is sure that there is no inconsistency in the theory of infinite sets. He is sure of this because the theory in question is a description of certain features of the Mindscape that 'anyone can see'" [592].

Taken at face value, this argument seems to beg the question as it suggests that the consistency of the theory of infinite sets is just self-evident to anyone who believes in the Mindscape. But I'll offer a more even-handed interpretation of what Rucker may be trying to express: discoverists believe literal infinity is "out there" in the Mindscape because Cantor's theory of infinite sets can be shown to be a mathematically and logically consistent system (mathematical and logical consistency being underlying features of the Mindscape), which Rucker believes anyone can see upon demonstration.

The notion that there are literally infinite sets waiting to be discovered in the Mindscape or in a Platonic World of Forms therefore rests on two more fundamental beliefs:

1. If literal infinity is mathematically consistent, then it's a logical concept.
2. If something is a logical concept, then it's a discovery.

From these beliefs, it follows that if literal infinity is mathematically consistent, then it is a discovery.

Generally, mathematicians and many physicists believe literally infinite sets are "out there" to be discovered because they assume literal infinity is not only mathematically consistent but makes logical sense, and this guarantees infinity must exist as a discovered property for some mathematical sets. Mathematical consistency and logical coherence thus work as the grounds by which mathematicians regard literal infinity as a discovered phenomenon.

Looked at in this way, it's not that claims of the logical coherence of literal infinity assume the discovery of infinity in the Mindscape. Rather, belief that infinity is a discovery in the Mindscape assumes infinity is both a mathematically consistent and logically coherent concept.

Mathematicians seek to prove literal infinity is a genuine discovery, and they believe they can do so by demonstrating the logic of literally infinite sets. They attempt to make the case that infinity is a logical concept by simply defining infinite sets in technical terms and providing mathematical proofs of the consistent results one gets when calculating infinite sets according to set theory's rules of syntax.

16.3 INFINITY AS EXPRESSIBLE WITH MATHEMATICAL SYNTAX ALONE

The lexical definition of infinity, in its literal sense, is a condition of being both complete and limitless in quantity. But mathematicians usually pay no mind to this. They only give consideration to technical definitions for mathematical objects, not to the lexical definitions associated with them. This is because lexical definitions include logical connotations that play no *obvious* or *direct* role in mathematical syntax, which is all mathematicians are concerned with. It's the consistent use of mathematical syntax that mathematicians pay attention to—not the semantics of the terms.

In the view of mathematicians, semantics is for lexically defined terms, not the technically defined terms found in mathematics. However, as we've seen, mathematical terms do indeed have associated semantics (meanings). So, the standard view of mathematicians that semantics plays no role in math is false. For instance, the 'intension' of a mathematical term is itself a part of the term's semantics. All the same, it is true that the technical nature of definitions for mathematical objects focuses primarily on the denotations for a term rather than the connotations of the term.

Because math pays no attention to infinity's natural language semantics—its lexical meaning, including its associated logical connotations—to the mathematician, such connotations are simply irrelevant. As Roitman points out, mathematicians deal solely with infinity's "extension" (though I would instead say denotation, unless by "extension" we mean the mathematical symbols) and so mathematicians don't care about the "intension" (actually, the logical *connotations*) of what it means for ∞ or ω or $\aleph$ to be literally infinite in the lexical sense [593]. By abstracting out the logical connotations of literal infinity's lexical meaning, the mathematician gains such precision with the language of math that reliance on syntax alone provides consistent systems of calculation, which is all that's important to the mathematician.

And it is in constructing a consistent, first-order language of formal syntax and systematic rules of calculation for a symbolized concept that the mathematician believes the logic of infinity has been proven, and therefore feels a "discovery" has been made. Ultimately, infinite sets—sets that are both complete and limitless—are held to be discoveries in the Mindscape because they are shown to be mathematically consistent when defined symbolically and used consistently according to the rules of mathematical syntax.

For example, in addition to technical definitions and axioms like the Axiom of Infinity, transfinite mathematics employs rules for representing infinity with abstract tools:

- Notation for limitlessness, such as an ellipsis: ...
- Notation for completeness, such as braces: { }.
- Symbols for literally infinite sets, such as P, or for number scales like $\mathbb{N}$, $\mathbb{W}$, $\mathbb{Q}$, etc. interpreted to be sets.
- Notation for transfinite numbers, such as ω and $\aleph$, where 'transfinite' means literally infinite.
- Quantifiers and operators ($\cap$, $\neg$, $\subseteq$, $\subset$, and $=$, $<$, $>$, etc.).

To the modern mathematician, the precise and consistent expression of the mathematical concept of literal infinity is enough to guarantee its existence as a discovery in the Mindscape or World of Forms. In fact, all mathematical concepts defined with technical definitions, and expressed in formal syntax, are held to be discoveries when they have enough precision to be used consistently in math.

16.4 INFINITY IN MATHEMATICAL OPERATION

When transfinite mathematicians make progressions of omega ordinals (ω, $\omega + 1$, $\omega + 2$, ...) or multiply alephs together ($\aleph_1 \times \aleph_1 = \aleph_1$), they believe they are operating with representations of literal infinity. Mathematicians in this tradition say that mathematical operations allow them to "manipulate infinities." As for infinity in general mathematics, while not all mathematicians hold that ∞ is an expression of literal infinity [594] [595], some mathematicians do indeed regard various functions to be carried out a literally infinite number of times. For example, take the following function in calculus:

$$\lim_{n \to \infty} f(x)$$

Some seem to regard it as an instance of literal infinity; after tall, there it is (∞) on the printed page [596]— so what could be more obvious than that (literal) infinity is being calculated? And because of the elegance and consistency of the operations involved, it is little wonder that the ability to obtain coherent mathematical outputs makes the math of literal infinity feel like a discovery.

16.5 THE INVISIBILITY OF THE CONTRADICTIONS

These days the majority of modern mathematicians assume infinity is a discovery because it can be defined precisely in formal syntax and used consistently in mathematical operations without regard to any further logical connotations of meaning. This assumption is based on yet a deeper assumption that mathematical rigor is logical rigor, and both are enough to prove the existence of infinity as a kind of intellectually beautiful 'discovery'. Cantor's conception of infinity, for instance, is so mathematically coherent and elegant in form that the mathematician finds transfinite math "beautiful," and the aesthetic experience of that math *feels* like a discovered phenomenon to the mathematician, who then assumes transfinite math is a discovery in a metaphysical World of Forms—or in a 'mindscape'.

Those whose specialties lie outside of mathematics, on the other hand, do not necessarily share either these aesthetic tastes or the same assumptions about mathematical objects, including infinity. Moreover, they may neither regard mathematical rigor as identical with logical rigor nor assume mathematical consistency alone is grounds for something being a discovery rather than simply an artifact of the imagination. They may even outright reject one or more of the three common assumptions mathematicians make about infinity and instead support the following positions in their place:

- Infinity is an invention and not a discovery.
- Infinity is an inherently semantic notion and not defined by syntax alone.
- Infinity is only figurative in mathematical operations.

16.6 INFINITY AS AN INVENTION

To the skeptic of infinity, mathematical objects—infinite or otherwise—are not so much discoveries as they are *inventions*.

16.6.1 *Inventing Versus Discovering*

To contrast inventing and discovering, we need to go back to what discovery means. There are two relevant definitions of 'discovery':

- discovery:
  (1) *something discovered.*
  (2) *the process of discovering.*

And the word 'discover' has at least three common meanings [597]:

- discover:
  (1) *to detect or find something that had either always or previously existed but had hitherto been unknown.*
  (2) *to ascertain or gain knowledge of for the first time.*
  (3) *to devise a new use or application for something already known.*

As an example of the first meaning of 'discover', one may discover evidence that a previously unknown species of dinosaur had roamed the Earth or that the Sun emits a form of radiation previously unknown. Discoverism is the belief that mathematical objects are discovered in this first sense of 'discover'—mathematical objects are *detected* or found because they are already there to find in the Platonic World of Forms or the Mindscape.

To invent something is not the same as discovering it according to the first sense of 'discover', which is to detect or find something already there. Rather, to invent is to *originate* something. Definitions [598]:

- invent: *to conceive, devise or create an original product from one's own ingenuity, experimentation, contrivance, or formulation.*

- invention:
  (1) *the product of inventing.*
  (2) *the act of inventing.*

We often use the first sense of the word 'invention' for a product such as a tool or a device that performs mechanical operations, but that sense of 'invention' is also used for products such as useful ideas, concepts, or methods [599]. So it's not just tools or machines that are inventions; so are ideas. One kind of idea is the idea of a rule. Rules are invented all the time, as when the rules for games are invented. So by this definition of 'invention', it is more than plausible that other kinds of rules are also invented, such as rules for grammar and even rules for mathematics.

To invent is not to detect but to *devise*. Devising is also the third sense of discovering. In the third sense of the word 'discover', to 'discover' something is to devise it—in other words, to invent a use for it. If one were to devise a new use for a household cleanser as a salad dressing, we could accurately say a new use for the cleanser has been invented—that, in a sense, someone has "discovered a new use" for the cleanser. But that kind of discovering is also, by definition, a way of inventing.

Invention also has a relation to the second sense of 'discover'. As an example of the second meaning of 'discover', one might discover what happens as the result of an experiment. So too, a musician "discovers" a catchy tune in the second sense of discovering: ascertaining whether or not an invention will be successful. The musician does not discover a new tune in the sense of finding the tune that was already there. Rather, the musician invents the tune and in so doing discovers (ascertains) whether or not the tune will be catchy.

I would argue that, like music, so too math. Mathematicians do not really discover mathematical objects in a sense of detecting them; rather, they invent mathematical objects and only discover them in the second sense of 'discover'—they ascertain whether or not the mathematical objects are consistent with the rules of math.

But when most mathematicians today say they 'discover' mathematical objects, such as axioms, or theorems, or new number systems, they do not mean the second or third sense of the term 'discover'. Instead, they mean it according to the first definition—mathematical objects are detected because they are out there to find. Rucker's Mindscape notion, for instance, takes the 'discovery' of ideas and concepts literally according to the first definition of 'discover'. Rucker believes, for example, that musicians discover new tunes and mathematicians discover new math in the sense of detecting what was already out there in the Mindscape awaiting detection [600].

In support of this notion, it might be argued that some musical and mathematical prodigies claim they just "hear the tune" in their heads or "see the formula" in their minds as if already complete—so, they literally discover (detect) these tunes and formulas. However, there are three problems with using evidence of prodigies as support for the notion that ideas are discoveries in a mindscape or a Platonic World of Forms.

The first problem is that the prodigy may "hear the tune" or "see the formula" in the way any artist does—as a product of imagination, not perception of something that already exists. Sans a physical

Forever Finite

stimulus from the environment, there is no way to distinguish mental detection of preexisting Forms from simply imagining them or otherwise mentally inventing them.

The second problem has to do with the completeness of the music or math upon first conception. I will concede that occasionally the first product is the final product. However, the prodigy may invent many musical tunes and mathematical formulas while only paying attention to the ideas they decide to keep, not their rejected ideas. The prodigy creates many alternative ideas, filters all the failed creations out, and selects only the mental creations recognized as worth something. It's not that the created idea that ends up being selected was "out there" all along; rather, the prodigy created it along with many others and just kept the one to their liking. The prodigy originated many thoughts and paid no attention to those the prodigy chose not to develop further. This may give the illusion that the prodigy literally 'discovered' the right musical tune or mathematical formula from the very start.

The third problem has to do with maturity. As prodigies mature, they begin to critique their own work; they begin to revise. And that shows that their unrevised ideas are not necessarily like discovered objects after all. The Mindscape notion does not adequately account for revision—quite simply, if we are discovering an idea, we shouldn't need to revise it. If it exists independently, our discovery should be like detecting something rather than originating something. But if we are originating or creating an idea that did not exist since the dawn of humanity, then it makes sense if we would need to revise or refine the idea. The Mindscape notion does not make sense of this difference.

Moreover, we don't need a mindscape to account for the objective nature of mathematics. All we need is to originate rules and the ability to teach others how to apply those rules consistently. That alone can account for the objectivity of mathematics. No extra mindscape or world of forms is needed.

The notions of the Mindscape and the Platonic World of Forms both take the term 'discovery', at least with respect to ideas and concepts, in the first sense of 'discover'. Whereas, when we say we have discovered an idea or concept, such as a mathematical object, we properly use the word 'discover' in the second or third senses—unless, of course, we are speaking like paleontologists, archeologists, historians, or detectives and mean we've literally discovered something that someone else created and that had become lost. But when we introduce a new idea or concept, something no one else came up with before, then we should not say we have discovered it as if in the first sense. If we do say we have discovered a new idea or concept, we should be using the word 'discover' in the third sense or even the second sense. Mathematicians may "discover" mathematical objects, but they only do so in the sense of devising and ascertaining them, not detecting or finding them.

Take the application of mathematical rules already established to new formulations and calculations, like adding numbers that have never before been added together; we are sometimes surprised by the mathematical outcome. Under such conditions, we may say we have "discovered" something new from our use of mathematics. This type of discovery—seeing what follows from the application of rules we already know—is simply an instance of the second literal sense of the word 'discover': this is discovering not in the sense of detecting what is already there, but in the sense of *ascertaining*—acquiring new knowledge for the first time. When we "see what follows" from rules, we are actually ascertaining what follows from rules with which we enforce consistent application. Perhaps we 'discover' rules in the sense of first devising or inventing them and then ascertaining the implications of those rules. These uses of the term 'discover' do not imply the rules or the outcomes were already out there in a World of Forms or a Mindscape awaiting detection.

It is not plausible that mathematics is something we detect "out there" in a metaphysical domain—a Platonic World of Forms or Mindscape. One reason for the implausibility of discoverism has to do with access to the metaphysical domain containing pre-existing mathematical forms or ideas.

Philosopher Victor Rodych explains [601],

> ...many of us who desire an acceptable philosophy of mathematics are troubled by the many problems with Platonism, most notably the problem of how we can *access* the objects of the mathematical realm. If, as it seems, most human beings cannot directly perceive the mathematical realm, it serves no explanatory purpose unless *some* mathematicians *can* access it in a way that enables them to do mathematics and discover some mathematical truths. But if, in fact, some mathematicians *can* access this realm, difficult questions arise. How, *exactly*, does a human being access the mathematical realm? Why cannot *any* person with sufficient mathematical training access the mathematical realm?...
>
> ...unless Platonism can offer some sort of description of our *access* to the mathematical realm, it serves (little or) no explanatory function.

Whether we consider Plato's World of Forms or Rucker's Mindscape, the result is the same—we need an adequate account of how and why such access is needed to explain mathematical ideas; without such an account, we have little reason to believe it's necessary to posit the existence of such abstract realms.

Furthermore, without such a description and a sufficient reason as to why we should suppose a special mathematical realm or metaphysical domain exists, both the World of Forms and the Mindscape notions share another problem: there is no way to distinguish perception of this metaphysical domain of forms or ideas from just plain old imagination or conception, and so again no compelling reason a metaphysical domain of pre-existing math should exist at all.

And so a minority of mathematicians and philosophers of mathematics confine the usage of 'discover' to the second and third meanings (to ascertain and devise) where mathematics and mathematical objects are concerned, and this is the correct approach in my opinion. As Jason Rosenhouse, professor of mathematics at James Madison University, points out [602],

> Of course, when you undertake mathematical research it certainly feels as though you are making discoveries about objects that exist independently of anyone's ideas about them...you're not so much making discoveries about the objects themselves, but about the logical relationships among the concepts you have chosen to define. It is like chess. The rules of chess are invented. But then you discover that a consequence of those rules is that a king, knight and bishop can force checkmate against a lone king while a king and two knights cannot. The rules of chess are so rich that even after centuries of analysis people continue to play the game and to make new discoveries about it. And so it is with the objects mathematicians choose to define and study.

Similarly, Robert Thomas, professor of mathematics and editor of the Oxford Journal *Philosophia Mathematica*, remarked that mathematics, like the game of chess, is invented, but the rules of both games and mathematics allow for discovery as well: "One occasionally hears the question, is mathematics invented or discovered?... both answers and the answer 'both' are appropriate. Once a game is invented, the consequences are discovered—genuinely discovered..." [603].

On the other hand, some scholars disagree that the term 'discover' should be applied at all with respect to mathematics. Wittgenstein, for example, rejected the view that, after we invent mathematical axioms and theorems, we discover the proofs and outcomes of calculations [604] [605]. Wittgenstein [606] suggested this is as ludicrous as saying "chess only had to be *discovered*, it was always there!"

However, Wittgenstein went too far on this point because he mistook two senses of 'discover'—to *detect* and to *ascertain*. Saying one has discovered a set of moves that are permitted by the rules of chess is different from saying one has discovered chess. So too, saying one discovers a new series of digits in a calculation of pi is not the same as saying one discovers pi like a paleontologist discovers a fossil. As Thomas and Rosenhouse rightly point out, we can indeed discover the consequences of rules once they are already invented; to do so is simply to "discover" what follows in the sense of *ascertaining* outcomes by a consistent application of rules.

Nevertheless, other scholars propose we should avoid using "discovery" or "invention" altogether for mathematical calculations. Theoretical physicist Lee Smolin holds that mathematical results are neither discovered nor invented. According to Smolin, "Discovered implies something already exists and it also implies we have no choice about what we find. Invented means that it did not exist before AND we have a choice about what we invent" [607]. Instead, Smolin says mathematical results are *evoked*. He likes the term 'evoked' because he (tentatively) believes it captures how we have no choice what mathematical results follow from the rules, which he holds is unlike inventing, but such results are also not preexistent objects as are things we discover [608]. Smolin too uses chess as an example [609]:

> When a game like chess is invented a whole bundle of facts become demonstrable, some of which indeed are theorems that become provable through straightforward mathematical reasoning. ...This is what the word evoked means to convey: the facts about chess are evoked into existence by the invention of the game.

Smolin, like Wittgenstein, took an unnecessary step; it's not necessary to coin a new term or a new definition for an old term, like 'evoke', to replace talk of mathematical discovery or invention. In fact, it makes sense to say we discover facts about chess, but it seems odd to say we "evoke" facts about chess. So too, it makes sense to say we invent new strategies in chess, while it seems odd to say we "evoke" new strategies in chess. And the same is the case for mathematical results.

To speak of "discovering" a mathematical result is only misleading if one misconstrues discovery to mean detecting rather than ascertaining or devising. So too, saying mathematics is an "invention" is only misleading if one misconstrues the nature of invention as intrinsically lacking logical necessity.

The word 'discovery' is not limited only to the sense of detecting something pre-existing. Once again, there are (at least) three different senses of the term 'discover'—to detect, to ascertain, and to devise. To say we discover results that deductively follow from rules is not to say we detect something that is already there. If the mathematical results or deductive consequences of game rules are "there" at all before we extrapolate or expand from the rules, they are only potentially "there," becoming actual when we apply the rules and ascertain their outcomes; the results are not things existing prior to the implementation of the rules. Even to say mathematical results are "potentials" in the rules can be misleading, though, as the results or outcomes have no concrete existence until the rules are applied—the only potential is in the rules themselves for having consequences. Such discovery is instead just a matter of inferential reasoning or performing calculations. And that kind of 'discovery' can be construed as a form of devising—devising calculations and proofs. When we 'discover' a new proof or outcome of an operation, we are merely 'discovering' in the sense of devising or ascertaining rather than detecting; and it is mainly in the sense of devising rather than detecting that mathematical discoveries are made. We can use an alternative term like "evoke" if we wish, but it isn't necessary.

We also need not avoid using the term 'invention' with mathematics just because math is characterized by a great deal of rule-based necessity rather than free choice. First, because we invent the rules anyway and we keep the ones we find reliable. Second, and contrary to Smolin's view, invention is not limited to social constructions free of constraints imposed by logical necessity, considerations of accuracy, or effectiveness of function. True, some inventions, like modern art and poetry, are characterized by far fewer constraints on creative output, but other inventions (for example, certain chess moves) are very much constrained by the game rules that are inventions themselves.

It's not that the choice to invent is constrained—we can invent or not invent as we wish. Rather, what is invented may be constrained either by the goal of the invention or by the rules for obtaining the goal.

For example, if the goal is creating a board game (e.g., chess), the rules we need to invent for the game will be limited to those that make sense for games played on boards (e.g., there is no tackling the other players in a game of chess). The rules of math, like the rules of a board game, can likewise be more constrained than rules for, say, art and literature in general.

Likewise, if the goal is to win the game, then the invented rules of the game, in turn, constrain the solutions that may be invented for winning the game (e.g., chess strategies)—not anything goes. Like game rules, we can hold mathematical rules are inventions constrained by the mathematical goal of producing consistent outputs and the solutions are also inventions constrained by the rules. Ergo, mathematical outcomes can still be inventions despite the rule-based necessity characterizing them. It is, after all, we who choose to do math at all, and the mathematical calculations only occur because of our choice to follow the rules we invent for math.

Furthermore, math is a little more like art and literature than many care to admit, for the outcomes of mathematics are not entirely forced anyway. There is some creative freedom even in generating mathematical results. For example, mathematicians have invented alternative geometries, like Riemannian Geometry, violating the axioms of other geometries, like Euclidian Geometry. There is also more than one version of calculus—the calculus of Leibniz did not make use of the fluxions and fluents of Newton's calculus, and neither of these versions of calculus is the same as medieval Indian calculus. The differences between the systems provide a fitting example of freedom of invention in mathematics. Then too, the ancient Babylonians, Egyptians, and Chinese never invented prime numbers despite inventing elaborate mathematical systems; their systems could do without prime numbers [610]. Not all mathematics and mathematical outputs are forced by logical necessity, and yet they can still be inventions. All such geometries, numerical schemes, and axioms are inventions just as are rules of games and rules of grammar.

So once again, we may therefore use a new term like "evoke" rather than "invent," but it isn't necessary. However, Smolin was after the right thing: clarity. I simply differ by thinking that, though we commit no intellectual faux pas by using the word 'discover' when we say a mathematician has discovered a new mathematical object (axiom, theorem, numeral system, formula, etc.), it would be clearer to say the mathematician *invented* a new mathematical object rather than discovered it or 'evoked' it. To say mathematical objects are discovered gives the misleading impression that we are assuming a Platonic World of Forms in which mathematical objects already exist for us to find. And to say mathematical objects are evoked makes them sound too much like magic spells. It would be better to say a mathematical object is invented than discovered or evoked.

In short, we invent new types of mathematical objects in the sense of creating them and establishing them as a practice. At best, we only 'discover' mathematical objects by first inventing them and then ascertaining their coherence or usefulness. It would therefore be clearer to simply say mathematical objects are invented or established rather than discovered.

Going forward, I will assume (unless otherwise stated) that 'discover' means *detect or find* rather than ascertain. Metaphorically 'discovering' something, in the sense of devising a new use for it, is a form of inventing and I will tend to refer to devising as inventing rather than 'discovering', just to be clear.

16.6.2 *Discoverism Versus Inventionism*

These days most mathematicians take the view that mathematical objects are discoveries. A notable defender of the discoverist position was the mathematician Martin Gardner (1914–2010). Gardner remarked that "almost all great mathematicians of the past and present" have been and are discoverists (though Gardner used the term 'realist') [611]. Gardner proclaimed that he himself "believes that mathematical objects and theorems are 'out there' with a peculiar kind of reality that is independent of minds and cultures..." [612]. Gardner defended what I call discoverism against the view that math is an invention. He likened the view that numbers are not "out there" before anyone invents them to the notion that physical objects like the Moon are not out there when nobody is around to see them. As the latter is patently absurd, so too the former [613].

However, Gardner's arguments for discoverism are not sound. The first argument is merely an appeal to the authority of "great mathematicians"—the strength of the argument unfortunately depends on who you have in mind as a great mathematician and opinions may vary. As for mathematical objects being real when nobody is looking because physical objects exist without sentient observers, we could just as well hold that fictional characters must somewhere be real because people who we know are independently real. The former cannot follow as a consequence of the latter.

Then too, once something is invented, of course it exists even if no one is there to see it. If all human beings perished, the Statue of Liberty might still be around, but the Statue of Liberty would not be around if no one had invented it. The same is true for math books. These considerations show that Gardner's argument from analogy does not hold up.

Discoverism may be a flawed philosophical position, but there are other options we can consider. In fact, there are several other philosophies of mathematics such as *intuitionism*, *formalism*, *predicativism*, *structuralism*, *constructibilism*, *fictionalism*, *figuralism*, *conventionalism*, *deductivism*, and yet others [614] [615] [616].

However, the many philosophies of mathematics are variations on either inventionism or discoverism because mathematical objects (where 'objects' are taken broadly to include ideas, concepts, structures, patterns, relations, etc.) are either invented or not, either discovered or not. The other philosophies of mathematics simply offer refinements on what it means to 'discover' or 'invent' mathematics. For that reason, I will stick to contrasting discoverism with inventionism in its broadest sense.

Throughout this book, I have been assuming the truth of inventionism. Inventionism is the antithesis of discoverism. Inventionism regards mathematics and mathematical objects as inventions rather than discoveries. Mathematical objects are devised rather than detected, created objects of intelligent origin rather than preexisting objects we find. Though Barrow leaned toward discoverism, it was he who coined the name 'inventionism' for a philosophy of mathematics that, in contrast to discoverism, holds mathematical objects to be inventions [617]. As Barrow put it [618],

> Inventionism is the belief that mathematics is simply what mathematicians do. We invent mathematics: We do not discover it. Mathematical entities like sets or triangles would not exist if there were no mathematicians.

Mathematicians who would fall into the inventionist camp, as I conceive it, would say that, yes, there are physical objects with straight edges and only three corners; some of them are in nature—in the petals of certain species of tulip, in the texture of a cauliflower, in a shard of ice or a facet of a crystal—and we can certainly draw artificial shapes with straight lines and only three corners to arbitrary precision. Such shapes in nature and cultural artifacts are commonly referred to as "triangles" when we apply the invented concept of an abstract set of three connected angles—the mathematical triangle—as a description of the similar shapes we find in nature. A triangle is an idealized shape from Euclidean mathematics that we use to describe objects in the physical world with straight (even if not *perfectly* straight) edges and three corners. The idea of a triangle is appropriate for describing the shape of a natural object insofar as the idea of a triangle resembles what we attempt to describe. But a triangle is an invention, nonetheless.

As further evidence that triangles are invented, take the fact that *angles* are themselves inventions of Euclidean geometry. Yes, there are objects in nature having three corners and approximately straight edges between them but the 'angles' of those edges are *measurements*. An angle is just the ratio of two lines along a circular arc centered at a vertex (where the edges or lines meet) with the arc being divided in some arbitrary number of increments for the purpose of establishing the ratio. Angles are not in nature as such but in the measurements of nature. Objects with straight edges and three corners need not be described with angles at all. In fact, Dr. Norman Wildberger, Associate Professor in Mathematics at the University of New South Wales in Sydney Australia, has devised a new system of trigonometry that does away with the use of angles to measure three-cornered objects. Instead of measuring three-cornered objects with angles, Wildberger's *rational trigonometry* measures three-cornered objects with *spreads* (straight separations of lines) [619]. Consequently, what we commonly call a 'triangle' may just as well be called a 'tricorner' or 'trispread'. However, spreads, like angles, are not really properties of nature either but are simply conceptual tools that rational trigonometry uses to measure three-cornered objects.

This is a beautiful example of why we must be careful not to confuse mathematical objects with what we discover in nature. Triangles, or trispreads, are useful conceptual tools for measuring objects with three corners but should not be taken as anything other than invented idealizations *applied to* the three-cornered objects we see in nature.

So too with the abstract sets of mathematics and set theory: an abstract 'set' as conceived in set theory is an invention, an idealization we can use to describe real-world sets—collections in the physical world that can be found in any order, such as a pile of rice dumped on a table. Abstract sets, ideal triangles, and other mathematical objects are inventions useful for describing real-world entities, but mathematical objects would not exist without someone to invent them. We discover physical objects in the world; we invent mathematical objects and apply their mathematical rules to describe the physical objects we see.

In further support of this point, the inventionist would say that it's evident mathematical objects are invented when they are named after words already used in ordinary language. Words like 'set' and 'circle' (or their counterparts in any ancient language) were in use before mathematicians ever conceived of sets or circles as abstract objects. Cantor appropriated 'set' from ordinary language to create the abstraction of ideal sets. So too, ancient mathematicians appropriated the label 'circle' as it was used in ordinary language for symmetrically closed shapes, whether those shapes were fabricated (as when we join hands while standing in a closed loop of people) or seen in nature (like the horizon, equally distant in every direction), and then abstracted the shape into a mathematical ideal.

Once mathematicians invent idealizations of ordinary concepts, those idealizations are then used to describe what we see in nature or create for use (see **Figure 16.2**). When we "see a circle" in nature, like one of the rings of Saturn, we are seeing a shape in nature that we compare to an idealization that mathematicians have invented: the idealized circle in which every point is equidistant from the center. The circle in nature is measured according to the ideal circle of conception. Hence, at least since Plato the term 'circle' has been used as an idealized conceptual invention, a standard tool that we apply to descriptions of similar shapes in nature and a tool we can use to draw something that we would call "a circle" even if it isn't so ideal. We don't 'discover' ideal circles in any literal sense; rather, we simply apply that mathematical invention to what we discover in nature—like the rings of Saturn [620].

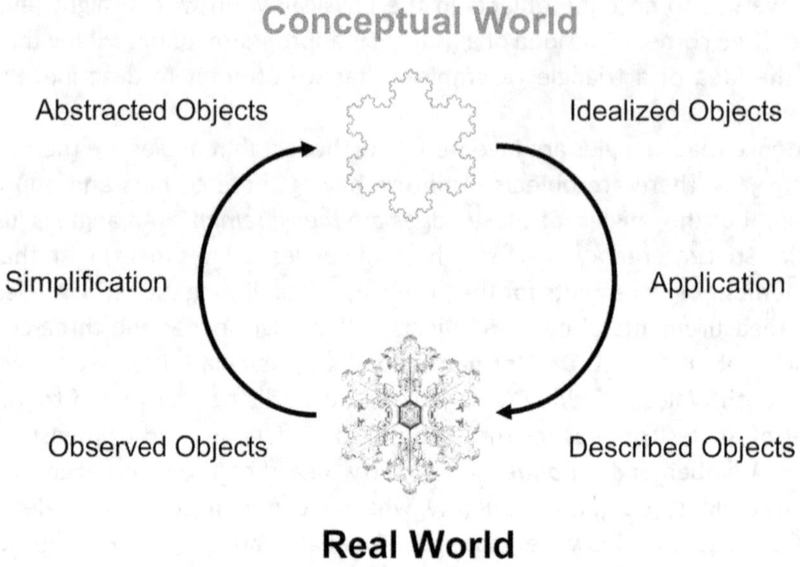

Conceptual World

Figure 16.2: Mathematical objects as idealized objects abstracted from real objects (for example, the Koch snowflake abstracted from real snowflakes), then applied as a description of reality (as when real-world features are described by fractal geometry). A caveat: not all of the ideas and concepts in mathematics are used to describe properties of the real world. Math also includes objects and relations made from abstractions that have no application at all to real-world entities—see the example of sphere eversion in Chapter 18.

Inventionism concedes that we sometimes use the word 'discover' for mathematical objects and results. However, the inventionist believes that if we say the mathematical objects are themselves "discoveries" at all, we usually mean it in only a figurative sense (it feels *as if* they are discoveries, as if we have detected objects that already exist). Incidentally, it is interesting that many mathematicians and physicists defend discoverism based on how it makes them feel. According to one physicist [621]:

> It feels as though one makes a discovery of something that was already there. It often feels that way. It's almost like the equations are trying to tell you a story. It's a little bit what I hear about when authors discuss how they work, that when you write a character, then the character at some point begins to take over and begins to...come to life, and then gets you to tell the story that the character wants to tell. This sense of finding the mathematics that was already there is very similar to that, I think.

If we follow this analogy to its logical conclusion, though, mathematics no more exists independently of mathematicians than do fictional characters of their authors. It may feel as if the character comes to life, but the character is still the product of the human mind. So too, it may feel as if we are discovering mathematics, but mathematics may still be an invention. If the latter is the case, as I believe it is, then we should think of the phrase "discovering math" as merely a figurative expression, not a literal description. And when we do mean it literally, we are only implying that the mathematical objects are results *devised* from known rules rather than things we *detect* in nature.

Though the name 'inventionism' is relatively recent for the view that mathematical objects, and mathematics itself, is an invention rather than a discovery (with respect to the first sense of 'discover'), this view of inventionism is not a new position. The view that mathematical objects are inventions has traces in the work of Aristotle, but in more recent times the philosopher Wittgenstein was the most prominent proponent of the view that math is an invention rather than a discovery.

According to Wittgenstein, we don't discover mathematics and mathematical objects because they are products of intelligence that do not exist independently of invention [622] [623]. We don't discover mathematical axioms or theorems, mathematical rules, numerals or numbers, functions or operations; they are all inventions that do not exist without someone to invent them. As Wittgenstein quipped, arithmetic is not the mineralogy of numbers [624].

In short, the 'inventionist' view of math rejects the discoverist view held by many modern mathematicians and physicists concerning the relationship of mathematics to the real world. According to inventionism, there is no World of Forms or Mindscape and so we do not discover mathematical objects or musical tunes in the sense of detecting them in some other world or "universe of sets," let alone the mind of a deity—we simply invent mathematical objects in this world with our mortal, human minds. If we literally "discover" mathematical objects at all, we do so in the sense of devising them, which is to invent them. Inventionism is the position mathematicians and physicists should take.

16.6.3 *In Defense of Inventionism*

So far, I have primarily supported that assumption with a critique of discoverism. Revealing the weaknesses of discoverism does not alone prove inventionism true. To rationally support inventionism also requires a refutation of attacks to its perspective and a positive demonstration of its merits.

One criticism of inventionism is offered by philosopher Roberto Mangabeira Unger. According to Unger, "The invention views fail to account for the applicability of mathematics in natural science by making its applicability appear to be either a happy accident or an abstract engineering" [625]. He believes mathematics cannot be invented because it's so useful for describing nature (not a happy accident), and it can't be an 'abstract engineering' because then we could make math say whatever we need it to say to justify any theory of nature we might have, which would be useless for doing science [626].

Unger's argument is, however, a false dichotomy for two reasons. First, let's again compare language and math for analogy. Language was invented and, if used correctly, it can be accurate for describing nature. Does that mean language is a 'happy accident'? Of course not. Language had to be refined over time to be useful for building concepts that accurately describe nature; the same is true of mathematics. Math did not spring forth, fully formed and useful for describing nature. The axioms and theorems that failed were left on the scrap heap of history, discarded and forgotten, while the successful axioms and theorems were retained and passed on. That is part of the reason why math is such a useful invention— like natural language, it could be, and has been, refined over time. And new mathematical systems are always being invented for new purposes, just as new philosophies are invented for new fields of thought.

As with new conceptual frameworks expressed in language, some systems of mathematics will be useful, others will prove trivial. But inventions they all remain.

Second, not all inventions of 'abstract engineering' are so flexible that they can be made to accomplish any end we want any more than any old abstract model invented for business engineering can be made to produce an effective business solution. Architectures used for business processes are instances of abstract engineering, but their abstraction does not make them so flexible as to be useless. Rather, such abstractions may be useful for manufacturing information systems to effectively support the business. If those abstractions are not engineered correctly, the technical solutions built on the abstract models might fail. So too, the axioms and theorems of mathematics may also be instances of abstract engineering that, if engineered correctly, will enable scientific theories to produce measurements with rigorous results. If engineered incorrectly, the theory may not be supported with rigorous measurements and will remain dubious. Hence, abstract engineering, simply as such, has various degrees of rigidity and flexibility, and so various degrees of relevance and irrelevance, accuracy and inaccuracy. Any instance of abstract engineering will have some degree of flexibility, but it need not be so arbitrarily flexible so as to be useless just because it is an invention.

Following on the previous point, if mathematics is an invention, it would indeed be an invention that contains abstractions, but that does not mean anything goes. It would not mean that mathematics would have such a degree of abstraction that it would have no empirical grounding at all and so could be made to justify any theory we desire about the natural world. If math is invented, then mathematics may be fashioned with a range of abstraction—from abstractions having more specific applications to the real world, like marks on a tally stick, to abstractions having a less direct bearing on the real world, like tesseracts (cubes of four spatial dimensions).

Regardless of its reference to the real world, a mathematical abstraction could still be invented in such a way as to be useful for producing consistent results. As previously pointed out, just because in this view a mathematical abstraction is an invention does not mean it would produce any output desired. Similarly, the rules of games are invented, and (depending on the game) not any move is permitted. Using our chess example, a pawn cannot jump like a knight. Not just anything goes in the game. So too with math—no matter how abstract, the rules we invent for it would not permit any arbitrary result. Instead, an abstraction in mathematics that produces inconsistent results would be judged as useless and jettisoned while the remaining abstractions that survive scrutiny can be retained.

Now consider mathematical abstractions that are used for describing the real world. Theorists are always inventing new mathematics for explaining how nature works—physicists have invented new mathematics behind *string theory* and *loop quantum gravity*, for example. One of these theories might be right while the others are wrong, or perhaps they are all wrong, but that does not mean they allow for just any possible result.

Moreover, intellectual competition can ensure mathematical inventions get better over time. To support a scientific theory, we may invent a mathematics with a set of rules providing consistent outputs *accurate enough* for describing the natural world. Or we may invent a mathematics that is inconsistent and doesn't have coherent results. In the competition of mathematical systems, the math that is more useful for obtaining accurate results is retained while the inaccurate math would be thrown out as a useless invention for doing science. Those that do produce inconsistencies or inaccuracies are thrown away; we never hear about them. Those that survive scrutiny are taken for granted as if "discovered". Once again, even if the math is invented, that doesn't mean all results are allowed. Invented abstractions are not necessarily arbitrary conventions just because they are invented; they can be inventions tested against reality; some succeed, others fail.

This bears on a similar point raised by Huemer who, like Unger, argued that, if math is invented, it would be merely an arbitrary game we were somehow lucky enough to come up with since its principles mirror relations in the physical world well enough to be useful [627]. The fact of competition between mathematical systems effectively handles the "just got lucky" critique.

Moreover, Huemer's argument attacks a straw figure with its reference to games. The inventionist need not hold that all of mathematics is *only* an invented game; the inventionist believes that much of mathematics is *also* a set of invented tools. We can invent mathematical games (for example, transfinite mathematics) and we can invent mathematical tools (like arithmetic), just like we invented languages that are used for both informing and entertaining. Hence, luck need have nothing to do with the usefulness of mathematics if indeed it is an invention.

For all of these reasons, the arguments of Unger and Huemer against inventionism are not sound. There may be other arguments against inventionism, but I will not belabor the point further. Instead, I will offer only that I have found no compelling case against inventionism and much to merit its consideration.

16.6.4 *The Merits of Inventionism*

Mathematician Keith Devlin remarks that mathematics is a process of experimentation [628]:

> ...take a look at the private notebooks of practically any of the mathematical greats and you will find page after page of trial-and-error experimentation (symbolic or numeric), exploratory calculations, guesses formulated, hypotheses examined, etc.
>
> The reason this view of mathematics is not common is that you have to look at the private, unpublished (during their career) work of the greats in order to find this stuff (by the bucketful).

Devlin emphasizes something important: mathematicians experiment in order to come up with correct formulations, equations, proofs, axioms, theorems, and the like. The process of such 'experimentation' is a kind of devising—a way of inventing rather than discovering. The trial-and-error aspect of thinking mathematically is in this respect like the trial-and-error process of inventing some new mechanical marvel.

Devlin still regards mathematics as "a process of discovery" and speaks of finding mathematical patterns underpinning nature [629]. This contrasts with inventionism, which sees mathematics as the application of idealizations (such as a mathematical sphere) to descriptions of nature (as when describing the shape of a planet)—see **Figure 16.2**. However, Devlin's emphasis on experimentation is more consistent with inventionism than discoverism.

Devlin contrasts the trial-and-error of mathematical experimentation with the final formulations of the mathematical greats, which are presented to the public as "precise statements of true facts, established by logical proofs..." [630]. To the inventionist way of thinking, the publication of the final product without mention of the failed attempts serves only to give the illusion that mathematicians have discovered their formulations, as if they were waiting to be found by a skillful detective, rather than having invented them via trial-and-error. But the trial-and-error approach, not the discovery of completed systems all at once, is what lies behind mathematical innovation. Inventionism thus fits the way mathematicians actually proceed more than does discoverism.

Inventionism also supports our experience of "doing math" better than does discoverism. Making a calculation to produce a mathematical result is not like digging up a fossil or seeing what flies out of an atomic collision—instances of discovering what was already there to be found. Rather, the result from a calculation is a product of the procedure itself. To calculate is to produce, not to detect. To calculate the number of stars in the galaxy is not to uncover the number of stars in the sense of finding a number already there, but to produce a number that can be matched tit-for-tat with the stars—it is the stars that are already there, not the number we use to describe them.

Inventionism fits how we speak of mathematical results better than does discoverism—when we say, "Two plus two equals four" we are not guessing the outcome, the way we might with a hypothesis about finding a fossil or a new particle. Instead, we are making a declaration predicated on assuming the rules of arithmetic. To say, "Two plus two equals four" is short for saying, "According to the rules of arithmetic, two plus two equals four."

Furthermore, mathematical sentences are not like statements of discovery. Sentences making a mathematical expression may be declarative sentences in form, but they are imperative in function. A parent may say to a disobedient child, "You are staying home." It's a declarative sentence in form, a statement that is true or false. But in function, it is actually an imperative sentence meaning, "Stay home." Saying "you are staying home" can be another way of commanding you to stay home. So too, a declarative sentence expressing a mathematical calculation like, "Two plus two equals four" is either true or false according to the rules of arithmetic, but the statement may also be taken as imperative in function— another way of saying, "Let two plus two be equal to four." This is because the product is a result of a rule-based procedure we create. Similarly, when a mathematician says, "Every number has a successor," this is a true or false statement for any number that is invented according to mathematical principles, but the statement may also be taken as an imperative: "Let every number have a successor." Mathematical sentences are therefore not just statements but also imperatives, unlike sentences declaring discovery which are not so. To say of a discovery, "The fossil is a Tyrannosaurus cranium" is to say something that cannot be restated in imperative form—"Let the fossil be a Tyrannosaurus cranium"—unless one is implying the 'discovery' is really a fabrication rather than a find.

In §§ 2.3.16–2.3.18, I mentioned that natural language grammar may make it seem that numbers are implied to be out there already, waiting to be discovered. Perhaps this is a point in discoverism's favor. However, we can explain this from an inventionist point of view as well.

I used an example of how saying, "The value of x is 6" is short for, and implies, "According to the mathematical rules, the value of x is 6," which can be put in imperative form as, "Let 6 be the value for x." Such declarative shorthand therefore becomes just a figurative way of saying that, *if* we are to apply mathematical rules consistently, *then* we must give the specific value 6 for the variable x. Hence, discoverism is not necessarily implied by such expressions after all.

Inventionism is therefore consistent with the way we conventionally speak with respect to mathematics and has the merit of better fitting mathematical experience than discoverism, which lacks logical and evidential support. I therefore maintain inventionism wins out over discoverism as the more accurate philosophy of mathematics. As we'll see, this has profound implications with respect to our main topic: infinity.

16.6.5 *Infinity as Invention and Inference*

If we start with the assumption that literal infinity is a logically consistent concept, then it's possible literal infinity is a property or condition of some collections. Most mathematicians these days certainly think so. They often claim that the number scales, interpreted as sets of numbers (such as $\mathbb{N}$, $\mathbb{W}$, $\mathbb{Z}$, $\mathbb{Q}$, $\mathbb{P}$, $\mathbb{R}$, and so on), are infinite in the literal sense of the term. Since no one can actually count *all* the numbers of such scales, the numbers are taken to be limitless in quantity. And if they are limitless in quantity, then literal infinity must be a discovery—a condition of number scales waiting to be found "out there" in a mindscape or World of Forms. But as we've seen, there are problems with this view.

For something to be literally infinite is for it to be a collection the members of which, all at once, are complete in quantity. Completeness means we should be able to list *all* the members of the complete collection. With respect to number scales being literally infinite, there must be such a thing as absolutely all the numbers of $\mathbb{N}$, absolutely all the numbers of $\mathbb{W}$, absolutely all the numbers of $\mathbb{Z}$, etc. and so we must, at least in principle, be able to generate all the numbers of such scales.

However, literal infinity is also limitless, and this too has its implications. Wildberger points out that the largest numbers we can generate in actual practice do not even come close to the largest finite numbers it's possible to generate in principle. And the largest finite numbers we can in principle generate would not even come close to approaching a literally infinite number. We cannot compose any number that would have a limitless amount of digits—not even in principle. That means there can be no such thing as having a set of "all" the numbers of $\mathbb{N}$ or any other numerical scale; to be limitless is to remain ever incomplete [631] [632].

Once again, we end up in logical contradiction: we can and cannot compose all the numbers of the infinite number scales because there is and isn't such a thing as "all numbers"—there is such a thing when we consider scales like $\mathbb{N}$ as complete, and there is not when we consider scales like $\mathbb{N}$ to be limitless. As literal infinity is completeness and limitlessness for the same set, this shows the conception of literal infinity cannot be logically coherent. And if it isn't logically coherent, then literal infinity can't be a property of anything, and so it certainly cannot be a discovery.

To the inventionist, this is not surprising. According to inventionism, numbers are inventions we use to describe collections. Back in Chapters 2, 4, and 5, I proposed that number scales are inventions; they are inventions that are inherently incomplete series rather than sets that exist "all at once" with numbers waiting to be discovered. (Though, this is not just my own position as there are many mathematicians and philosophers who hold it; rather, I was taking the inventionist position.) I also stated that considering numbers and number scales to be inventions has implications for infinity. And indeed, it does. As number scales are inventions, so too properties or conditions claimed to apply to number scales may also be inventions. Literal infinity is such an invented property. Infinity is not a discovered condition or state that number scales have in some metaphysical World of Forms or mindscape; literal infinity is not a phenomenon 'perceived'—it is not an a posteriori, empirical finding. Rather, literal infinity is an invented property applied as a schema to number scales and sets. And since not all schemas are logically consistent, it should not surprise us if literal infinity turns out to be a self-contradictory schema that can nowhere be discovered to obtain.

16.7 INFINITY AS A SEMANTIC CONCEPT

The concept of infinity is an invention not of mathematics but of ordinary language and it first appeared as the term 'apeiron' in ancient Greece (see § 8.1). Apeiron initially meant a state of indefiniteness or indeterminacy, but philosophers of a mystical bent narrowed its meaning to limitlessness. Anaximander further stipulated that a quantity that is apeiron is a complete and yet limitless quantity—a conflict of opposing qualities; in other words, apeiron is literal infinity. Mathematicians later appropriated the concept of infinity in its literal sense from popular philosophical speculation, seeking to make the concept mathematically rigorous.

But in so doing, mathematicians made a new conception of infinity, symbolized as ∞ in general mathematics or ω and $\aleph$ in the transfinite system, and that conception does not imply literal completeness and literal limitlessness as infinite collections are assumed to be when the word 'infinity' is used in ordinary language. The infinity of mathematical formalism is figurative infinity rather than literal infinity. Nevertheless, mathematicians have increasingly assumed the 'infinity' of their mathematics is what we all refer to as infinity in the literal sense of the term. Consequently, when they speak of infinity, such as describing what their equations involving infinity mean, they often use the term 'infinity' in the literal sense, even though that's not what the formalism demonstrates.

The understanding that infinity is a condition of literal completeness and literal limitlessness is therefore commonly assumed by mathematicians in their *interpretation* of mathematical calculations even though such properties do not appear in the actual equations or calculations. Infinity's meaning as completeness and limitlessness of quantity, as defined in the ordinary, literal sense is not abandoned by the mathematical expressions of infinity. Rather, such expressions are operationally indefinite but misinterpreted or erroneously assumed to refer to literal infinites. Infinity therefore remains a semantic concept even while applied in mathematics, and it therefore is not without logical connotations beyond its expression in mathematical syntax.

Infinity remains a semantic concept appropriated by mathematics and its ordinary language meaning is even assumed in mathematics despite formulas and equations not expressing anything beyond the merely finite indefinite. Infinity is not the purely syntactical concept it is often claimed to be.

Then too, we haven't really used first-order language syntax to 'discover' infinity in the world of mathematical forms when we use symbols like ∞, ω, and $\aleph$, or denote number scales, like $\mathbb{N}$, as equal to them. Rather, infinity is an invention of ordinary, natural language; it is replaced during mathematical operation with an alternate, figurative 'infinity' concept, and then it is brought back when infinite collections are described.

Nor has a mathematical infinity replaced the linguistic infinity of literal usage. Instead, the two have simply become mistaken for one another in mathematics, especially in the transfinite system.

16.8 INFINITY AS FIGURATIVE IN MATHEMATICAL OPERATION

What the foregoing analysis reveals is that the infinity technically defined in both transfinite math and general math is, from an operational point of view, only "infinity" in a figurative sense, not in a literal sense as is often claimed. Literal infinity is not represented in either the formal language of transfinite mathematics or the formal language of general mathematics, but rather only in the linguistic description of what the math purportedly demonstrates.

In terms of transfinite mathematics, the formal language treats the symbols ω and $\aleph$, and corresponding progressions in braces such as $\{1, 2, 3, ..., \omega, \omega + 1, \omega + 2, \omega + 3, ...\}$, not as representing literally infinite sets but as representing indefinitely large but incomplete series, each confined between bounds of infima and suprema, each a finite unit. But the natural language of transfinite math, in which mathematicians talk *about* what ω and $\aleph$ mean, refers to ω and $\aleph$ as the order and size of literally 'infinite sets' rather than merely the order and size of indefinite (finite) series considered as unitary wholes. Hence, the natural language semantics of transfinite math with its assumed lexical meaning for infinity is underdetermined by the syntax, the formal language, of transfinite math.

Both general mathematics and transfinite mathematics thereby allow the semantic contradictions of literal infinity to go unnoticed; the formalism of the math ensures that mathematicians need not attend to the incongruity between the operational use of infinity in mathematical syntax and the lexical meaning of infinity assumed in talk regarding transfinite sets.

16.8.1 *Literal Infinity Hidden from Operation*

In general mathematics, like algebra and calculus, mathematicians treat infinity as operationally distinct from its natural language connotations. Though, most mathematicians don't seem to realize this. And because they don't realize it, they believe there are no logical contradictions involving literal infinity when they find no mathematical trouble in the formal language of math that deals with 'infinity'. But they are looking in the wrong place; the trouble is not in the formal language of math but in the natural language of math, which reveals a lot more about what we assume infinity to be.

Recall convergence with infinity. In the first descending convergence (dividing 1 down *toward* 0), infinity was operationally treated as though it were lexically synonymous with an *incomplete*, indefinite series. In the second descending convergence (dividing 1 to *arrive at* 0), infinity is operationally treated as lexically synonymous with a *complete*, indefinite series. Similarly, in the ascending convergence (adding reals from 0 up to a total of 1), infinity was also operationally treated as lexically synonymous with a complete, indefinite series. There is no mathematical contradiction with any of this. And there is no logical contradiction insofar as the formalism of math is concerned because mathematicians mean two different things by 'infinity' in terms of its function in math: the series is either complete but indefinite or incomplete and indefinite. Basically, 'infinity' operationally means in the formal language of mathematics what indefiniteness lexically means the natural language of discourse. That is to say, infinity is used according to its figurative sense in general mathematics; the formal language of general mathematics operationally treats infinity as only figuratively "limitless"—that is, as indefinite—rather than literally infinite. So, considering only the technical definitions and operational uses of infinity as expressed in the formal language of general mathematics, no logical contradiction need occur. There is no self-contradiction involved if infinity is only figurative and refers to the indefinite. So far, so good.

Nevertheless, that only covers the formal use of 'infinity' in math. The natural language of mathematics is prone to misinterpreting the figurative infinity used in the formal language as being literally a state of completeness and limitlessness in quantity. For example, it's clear that when mathematicians say a function converges a sequence of decimals to 1, they are implying the function produces a sequence of "infinitely many" values in the literal sense of infinity. The same is true when mathematicians speak of an infinity of real numbers between 0 and 1, or between any two whole numbers; they mean infinity in a literal sense, just as lexically defined. Or when mathematicians speak of there being a division of 1 that absolutely converges to 0, they mean there is a complete and limitless quantity of divisions that produce that result.

Hence, in the formalism of mathematics "infinity" may indeed have an operational meaning synonymous with indefiniteness—that is to say, the figurative sense of infinity. But in the natural language of mathematics, the language even mathematicians use to talk about what the math means or what its functions signify, infinity has its usual literal meaning.

So there's a difference between, on the one hand, the *technical definitions* and *mathematical operations* that imply infinity to be no different than indefiniteness—and, on the other hand, the *lexical definition* and *common interpretation* for what those operations imply: literal infinity. Basically, there is an incongruity between what mathematicians actually do with these operations in general mathematics and how they interpret what they're doing. The mathematician ends up confusing indefiniteness with literal infinity.

To be indefinite (or figuratively infinite) according to mathematical operation is different from being literally infinite according to interpretation; a literally infinite set or series is complete, implying a total, and limitless, implying no total to find—an impossibility—while an indefinite set or series can be complete or incomplete but is always finite and no mathematical contradiction will be found. Because the formalism treats a so-called 'infinite' set or series as indefinite, the formalism contains no mathematical contradictions; the operational procedures of mathematics effectively mask the logical contradictions implied by misinterpreting figurative infinity as literal infinity. The contradictory implications of being limitless (e.g., having no total) and complete (e.g., having a total) in quantity go unnoticed in general mathematics because the very procedures of mathematics ensure that mathematicians need not attend to the incongruity between the operational use of infinity in the formal language of general mathematics and the meaning of infinity in the natural language of mathematics.

Yet even though there is no *mathematical* contradiction with 'infinity' in terms of its functional operation in the formal language of algebra and calculus, there are *logical* contradictions in the terms of the lexical meaning of infinity in the natural language used to describe what the math shows. Because mathematics assumes the natural language interpretation of what infinity means with respect to functions involving infinity, the mathematics of infinity implies the logical contradictions that are otherwise invisible from a purely formal standpoint.

16.8.2 *Transfinite Math Does Not Really Operate with Literal Infinity*

Like general mathematics, the formalism of transfinite math hides the contradictions of literal infinity from view because it uses technical definitions for infinity, which support only figuratively infinite operations. To put it another way, transfinite math can be operationally consistent with what it denotes in its formal language—figurative infinity, indefiniteness—while also being logically inconsistent by what its symbolism and operations purport to represent: literal infinity. We run into the logical contradictions only when we pursue the connotations of the infinite—to be not just immense but literally limitless and complete—rather than stick to the operational uses of 'infinity' that denote only figurative infinity (indefiniteness of progression). Because transfinite math simply doesn't attend to literal infinity in its formal rules of operation, such contradictions do not arise in the formal operations of transfinite math.

Even though transfinite math symbolizes what it purports to be literal infinity, its symbolism represents collections (such as sets or sequences or series) that are indefinitely large or immense—which still means finite and so having a total. As an example, consider the so-called 'transfinite numbers' like ω and $\aleph$. According to transfinite mathematics, infinite numbers like these can be calculated based on their relative sizes or powers, and they can also be added, multiplied, and raised in power [633]. But ω and $\aleph$ are just placeholders for indefinitely large, yet finite, collections—such as number scales or number systems like the natural numbers and real numbers, which are incomplete, open series. There is nothing really "infinite" about them.

The limitlessness of literal infinity that mathematicians intend to represent with ω and $\aleph$ is abstracted out while ω and $\aleph$ are operationally treated only as referring to sets or series of indeterminate size so that an expression such as $\aleph_0 < 2^{\aleph_0}$ (which means $\mathbb{W} < \mathbb{R}$) can make mathematical sense. And such expressions indeed do make mathematical sense, for we could assume that more real numbers have been *invented* than whole numbers. Hence, expressions like $\mathbb{W} < \mathbb{R}$ can also be logically coherent if conceived as finite, indefinite series ($\mathbb{W}^C$ and $\mathbb{R}^C$), incomplete and open-ended.

In fact, transfinite math always treats 'sets' like ω or $\aleph$ as finite in size even when they are used in transfinite arithmetic. Adding or multiplying alephs together ($\aleph_2 \times \aleph_3 = \aleph_3$) may not work like adding definite numbers together, but it is similar to adding indefinite but finite sets together. It's rather like saying, "A bunch of stuff added to a bigger bunch of stuff is equal to a bigger bunch of stuff." Adding or multiplying the subscripts of these cardinals is more like comparing numbers by $<$ and $>$ signs. We don't even have to know what the alephs mean to do this. From a purely operational standpoint, there is nothing literally infinite happening here.

Cantor claimed to be discovering a mathematics of literal or "proper" infinity, but his 'transfinite' operations treat infinite sets (sets claimed to be limitless—implying no maximum number of elements in the set) as though they are finite (limited by having a maximum number or a running total, of elements). Only with his 'finitism' was Cantor able to make consistent rules of operation for so-called 'infinite' sets.

16.8.3 *As the Transfinite System Defines Infinity*

Some might object that the transfinite system has other technical definitions for literal infinity that are supported by clearly infinite operations. One such technical definition for infinity was raised in § 14.1.4: "the one-to-one correspondence of a set with a proper subset of itself." This theoretical definition for infinity was rendered operational in the definition of its cognate 'infinite': "a set is infinite if it can be placed in one-to-one correspondence with a proper subset of itself" (see also § 7.2).

However, we've seen that there are some problems with this way of defining infinity. From §§ 15.2.9–15.2.12 we found that the correlation versus subset senses of size is not accurate, that Bolzano was justified in concluding infinite bijections to be illusory [635]. From § 14.1.4 we learned such definitions may be construed as too narrow, even in the transfinite system, let alone the scope of all that literal infinity is supposed to describe, such as collection in the physical world. And there are further problems with trying to describe sets of real, physical objects according to this definition of infinity, as will be shown in the thought experiment of §§ 17.3–17.4.

Then too, while these technical definitions provide a workaround for dealing with the contradictions inherent in literal infinity, they seem to be more of a dodge than a solution. The technical definitions of infinity are substituted for the lexical definition of infinity in its literal sense, which in turn allows the mathematician to use mathematical rules that are consistent because they avoid addressing literal completeness and literal limitlessness together for the same collection. The consequence of the switch from lexical to technical definition is therefore to treat what is supposed to be literally complete and limitless as if it is a collection of indefinite largeness—ergo, a finitude. This is simply a way of ignoring and working around the logical contradictions of literal infinity and provides only the illusion of success.

But the alleged literal limitlessness of ω and $\aleph$, while ignored in the technical definitions and formal operations of transfinite math, still tend to be implied in the philosophical interpretations of transfinite set theorists. Hence, the contradictions between completeness and limitlessness do not go away simply because they are not attended to in the mathematical operation for what is claimed to be infinity in its literal sense.

The upshot is that even though there is no *mathematical* contradiction in the formal rules of syntactical operation, there are still *logical* contradictions involving the semantic connotations of the system's underlying philosophical assumptions and interpretations regarding what the set-theoretic definitions and mathematical operations mean, as I've shown with the lexical definition of literal infinity that underlies the use of ω and $\aleph$. At the end of the day, the transfinite mathematician ends up erroneously claiming the "infinity" of their mathematical operations is literal infinity when it is indefiniteness (serial or collective)—a kind of finitude in disguise. And by claiming their technical version of infinity is literal infinity, they end up connoting the same contradictory implications as before while leaving them unresolved.

16.8.4 *The Operations Are Only Figuratively Infinite*

It is precisely in deviation from the lexical meaning, the natural language meaning, of literal infinity that the self-contradictions of literal infinity become invisible (that is to say, go unnoticed) to mathematicians. This is because the mathematical procedures and operations do not deal with the full, logical implications of infinity's underlying linguistic meaning.

When mathematicians engage in the operations of infinity, such as $1 + \omega = \omega$ in transfinite mathematics or $L + \infty = \infty$ in general mathematics, they are thinking solely in terms of the formal language of mathematics—applying mathematical operations and deducing the implications of mathematical theories. The math is consistent, but it is not in the formal language syntax of mathematical procedure per se that the logical self-contradictions of literal infinity are found. Rather, the self-contradictions are found in the natural language semantics of infinity, in literal infinity's lexical meaning—in the very meaning that the same mathematicians may assume this formalism implies.

Since the math itself does not address the logical connotations of literal infinity's semantics, you may hear many mathematicians deny that there is any contradiction in transfinite mathematics and keep reiterating that transfinite math "works." For example, Rucker put it this way [636]:

> If infinite sets do not behave like finite sets, this does not mean that infinity is an inconsistent notion. It means, rather, that infinite numbers obey a different "arithmetic" from finite numbers.

Rucker is, of course, assuming infinity as conceived in Cantor's transfinite mathematics. And in a sense, he is correct that the mathematical conception of infinity works: there is no mathematical inconsistency involving the operationally-defined "infinity" of transfinite math, nor is there a contradiction in what they most care about—the denotations and rules in the syntax of the system are all consistent.

However, that's only because the mathematical operations apply only to indefinite processes, like recursive functions to series, or denote indefinitely large sets that are assumed to be literally infinite but are not such at all. The mathematicians, in working the math with symbols for infinity, are actually dealing with indefinite, yet finite, sets and series, not the literally infinite ones they think they are dealing with.

And so most mathematicians do not attend to the logical implications of the lexical meaning of literal infinity that they routinely imply by the very way in which they use the word "infinity" even within the formal practice of their trade. In the formalism, the logical connotations of a quantity being literally infinite get "abstracted out;" chiefly because in the formal syntax of the math limitlessness gets treated as indefiniteness in progression—'infinite' in only a figurative sense—while sets and series can be incomplete in their braces while regarded as complete units. Then the operations that mathematicians apply to what are in reality indefinite progressions (like $\mathbb{W}$ and other number scales) allow the mathematician to just "abstract out" the contradictory logical connotations implied by regarding the denotations as literally infinite.

When the contradictory connotations of literal infinity's lexical meaning are abstracted out, they go unnoticed and unattended to by the mainstream mathematician even while they keep implying or stating their formalism is of infinity as understood in the literal sense. In reality, the operations on sets and series, whether dealing with those of general mathematics like convergences to 0 or those of transfinite mathematics like multiplying alephs together, are only figuratively 'infinite' in the formal language of the math involved. Consequently, the mathematical operations attend to only a narrow scope of denotation—indefinite sets and series; the figuratively infinite becomes misinterpreted as the literally infinite. And yet, most mathematicians today erroneously assume such operations are dealing with literally infinity sets and series. Only a minority of mathematicians today see behind this.

16.9 ASSUMPTIONS EXPOSED

Completeness and limitlessness by their lexical definitions never clash in mathematics because they are not addressed in the formalism of mathematics, which is all the mathematician, as a mathematician, really cares about. The rest is, for the mathematician, just so much semantics.

Unfortunately, in focusing on the formal language of math, the natural language assumptions get overlooked. The mathematician who believes in literal infinity is not dealing with literal infinity when operating according to the technical definitions for infinity because infinity is a semantic invention that is not addressed at all by mathematical operations. Instead, the 'infinity' of mathematical operation is indefiniteness given special symbolism and only purported to be literal infinity.

But it is literal infinity as lexically understood that mathematicians typically claim Cantor "tamed" and made rigorous, and it is literal infinity that the lay individual and the philosopher cares about. Because mathematics has provided only the illusion of addressing literal infinity, the formal proofs of mathematics turn out to be irrelevant to the concept of literal infinity, which is what non-mathematicians are concerned about. That's why dazzling the layperson with mathematics only gives the illusion that literal infinity makes sense.

But some mathematicians who believe in infinity, convinced that literal infinity is in the equations, may become incredulous at the skeptic's insistence that there is a contradiction lurking somewhere in the concept of infinity [637]. In turn, the skeptic remains baffled as to how infinity can seem so illogical and yet apparently make sense according to the math.

What the skeptic has not noticed is how the mathematician is operating according to the syntactical rules of math's formal language and no longer according to the semantics of the natural language in mathematics. The mathematician does not usually pay attention to the difference either, assuming incorrectly that there is only one 'infinity' and it is expressed only in the formal language of mathematics, though this is not so—the so-called "infinity" in the formal language is really indefiniteness, not literal infinity.

Consequently, the skeptic of infinity and the believer of infinity inadvertently confuse one another because they are not sharing the same assumptions about the language of mathematics and the nature of mathematical objects, particularly with respect to infinity. That is the root of this communication problem.

Ultimately, the communication problem has resulted because most mathematicians have been making the same three assumptions about literal infinity—that it's a discovery, that it's expressible with syntax alone, and that it's directly used in mathematical operations. Those assumptions lead to a technically-defined conception of infinity that, in terms of operation, is mathematically consistent but logically flawed because the operations represent only "infinity" in a figurative sense not in the literal sense as purported. The math created for infinity does not resolve the logically contradictory connotations we've examined for literal infinity, which therefore remains undiscovered in mathematics.

The correct interpretation of literal infinity is that it is an invention and not a discovery—at least, not in the sense of something detected. Literal infinity is an inherently semantic concept and not defined by syntax alone, and the 'infinity' of mathematical operation is only figurative and not literal infinity at all. Hence, literal infinity's logical connotations—unresolved self-contradictions and all—do not disappear but are still logically implied when mathematicians misconstrue the mathematical operations of their figurative version of 'infinity' as being about infinity in its literal sense.

Mathematics adopted the wrong assumptions about infinity because the main proponents of the discipline followed the wrong philosophers: Plato with respect to mathematical objects as discoveries and Zeno of Elea with respect to infinity as a logically coherent property of measurement. The mathematician Dantzig had warned that philosophers easily misconstrue mathematical concepts, but the reverse is also true: mathematicians can misconstrue philosophical concepts, and they can adopt the wrong philosophical assumptions. As Moore stated, "...it is not impossible for mathematicians themselves to mishandle their own apparatus and to import conceptual confusion into their own discipline" [638]. Such was the case when mathematicians appropriated the erroneous philosophical concept of infinity from ancient Greek philosophy [639]. The result has been confusion through the centuries.

CHAPTER 16 IN REVIEW

❖ The logical self-contradictions implied by the meaning of literal infinity go largely unnoticed and unattended by most mathematicians as a result of three widespread, and erroneous, assumptions:

  o Infinity is a discovery.
  o Infinity is expressible with syntax alone.
  o Infinity—literal infinity—is directly used in mathematical operations.

❖ A more accurate set of assumptions:

  o Infinity is an invention (an invented concept) and not a discovery.
  o Infinity is an inherently semantic concept and not defined by syntax alone.
  o Infinity is only figurative in mathematical operations.

❖ Mathematics adopted the wrong assumptions about infinity due to the influence of ancient philosophers such as Plato and Zeno of Elea.

17: INFINITY UNREAL

I take the position that literal infinity does not refer to a property that *necessarily* exists in the real world. In other words, the world could just as well exist without it. I also take the stronger position that because literal infinity is a self-contradictory idea, it *cannot possibly* exist in the real world at all. This and the subsequent chapters on literal infinity will reinforce this conclusion.

17.1 **INFINITY UNNECESSARY**

To say infinity is not 'necessary' is to speak either in the context of logic or in the context of *ontology*. To say infinity is not necessary is to say infinity is either not *logically* necessary or it is not *ontologically* necessary.

The term 'ontology' comes from the Greek *ontos* (being) and *logos* (which in this context means 'study of'); ontology's original meaning is *the study of being*. The study of being, the study of existence, the study of reality, the study of schemes categorizing being or reality, or simply a categorization of being or real things—I will be assuming use of the term 'ontology' in these philosophical senses.

From what I've read, it seems most mathematicians presently assume mathematical objects not only have an independent existence from our conception of them, but they also necessarily exist; that is, they are *ontological necessities*—they cannot fail to exist. Quantitative infinity in its literal sense they take to be one of those ontologically necessary 'objects' (more precisely, a property or condition of certain other mathematical objects). So, they assume infinity to be an ontological necessity—infinity cannot fail to exist. If they are right about that, then a statement such as, "Infinity exists," *must* be true because of the *extension* of the term 'infinity'. That is, infinity refers to a property of the real world that simply *must* be.

It seems the majority of mathematicians these days take the view that infinity is an ontological necessity because they already assume literal infinity not only makes logical sense, but they also believe mathematical operations of constructing number scales or multiplying aleph cardinals are evidence that literal infinity is a *logical necessity*—which is to say, the definition of infinity is true just by virtue of its consistent syntax. This view goes back at least to Cantor, who held that view that if the math is consistent, then the mathematical object in question must 'exist' [640].

Further still, it would appear mathematicians commonly hold literally infinite sets and operations necessarily exist "out there" in a metaphysical world waiting to be discovered [641]. Some academics, especially many theoretical physicists, believe literal infinity to be a property of the physical universe [642].

I argue that literal infinity is neither a logical necessity nor an ontological necessity; there is no such thing as a magnitude—either mathematical or physical—that *must* be literally infinite.

17.1.1 *Literal Infinity is not Logically Necessary*

If literal infinity were a logical necessity, it would be so in a couple of ways. One way would be for infinity to be a tautology. For example, take the Axiom of Infinity as expressed in formal notation [643]:

$$\exists I(\emptyset \in I \land \forall x \in I((x \cup \{x\}) \in I))$$

If this axiom were a tautology, then $\mathbb{N} = \aleph$ would also be a tautology, and so true by definition. Another way infinity might be logically necessary is if a statement that something is infinite must be true just by the form of the statement. For example, a statement like, "There is at least one x that is literally infinite" would have to be a statement that cannot fail to be true just by virtue of its syntax. But it is difficult to see how either of these examples makes a tautology.

We have already seen that the number systems are not necessarily complete sets but can be construed to be open series, inherently incomplete number scales. The system of natural numbers may then be an incomplete scale of numbers under construction and so it need not be literally infinite. It is therefore not a tautology that $\mathbb{N} \triangleq \aleph$ since $\mathbb{N}$ (the set) could really be $\mathbb{N}^\circ$ (the scale). Instead, the expression $\mathbb{N} \triangleq \aleph$ need not be at all *accurate* as a depiction of the nature of a number system even if the expression is *consistent* in the confines of transfinite mathematics.

Which in turn means the Axiom of Infinity may not be at all necessary to assume—at least not as an axiom of *literal infinity*. As we saw earlier, the formal language version of the Axiom of Infinity is merely an application of the successor function starting with zero (the empty set), and that again just gives us an incomplete, open series.

As for the statement that there is at least one x that is literally infinite, it is also not a tautology since the opposite statement, "No x is literally infinite," is not a statement that must lead to logical contradiction for every ontology and mathematical system we wish to consider.

Literal infinity is therefore not a *logically* necessary property. In fact, we can still do mathematics without any reference at all to literal infinity.

And there are such mathematical systems.

For example, mathematician Petr Vopěnka (1935–2015) offered an alternative to Cantorian set theory that in his words "by no means use any ideas of actually infinite sets," but instead represents infinite sets as "large, incomprehensible sets" [644]. In other words, while Vopěnka used the term 'infinity' for his Alternative Set Theory (AST), it seems to be a misnomer for a collective indefinite, which is still actually finite even though its quantity would be off any in-practice definable scale.

Similarly, Lavine also has proposed a system of *finite mathematics* for calculating collective indefinites (see § 6.1.2 and § 24.3) [645].

So, for magnitudes larger than any we can in practice calculate, we can draw upon the concept of *indefinitely* large magnitudes; and for those smaller than we can in practice calculate, we can use the concept of the indefinitely small in size. We need not refer to infinitudes or infinitesimals.

As for iterative processes that go on persistently or ceaselessly, we can always refer to these as indefinite processes, and they need not entail literal infinities. Moreover, we've already seen examples in both general mathematics and transfinite mathematics that, operationally speaking, mathematical functions really imply indefiniteness, which is figurative infinity and not literal infinity. Literal infinity is therefore not necessary to mathematics.

Moreover, consider the 'rational trigonometry' created by Wildberger, which also contains no use of literal infinities. As Wildberger explains, "This new theory unites the three core areas of mathematics—

geometry, number theory and algebra–and expels analysis and infinite processes from the foundations of the subject...the presentation given here avoids any mention of 'infinite sets'" [646].

Thus, as purely a matter of mathematics or logic, infinity is not necessary. However, that leaves open the question of literal infinity being *ontologically* necessary, to which we'll now turn.

17.1.2 *Literal Infinity is Not Ontologically Necessary*

It's popular to believe literal infinity is a reality and not just an abstract idea. From an informal review of the literature, it appears most academics believe the Universe has literally infinite features—infinite magnitudes of space, time, energy, and matter [647]. And a growing number of mathematicians and physicists go yet further, claiming there exists a collection of universes of which our physical universe is but one among many—perhaps *infinitely* many [648]. Most physicists are careful to suggest the Universe *may* be infinite, or even *probably* is infinite, but is not *proven* to be infinite in magnitude or one among infinitely many other universes [649]. But some physicists do go so far as to imply literal infinity is an ontological necessity, an inherent feature of the physical world that cannot be otherwise; in other words, infinity *must* exist as a feature of physical reality.

The position that the Universe is necessarily infinite is based on two other positions: that the nature of the Universe is essentially 'mathematical' and that literal infinity exists in the mathematical realm as a matter of logical necessity [650]. Given that the Universe is mathematical, and math assumes infinity, it is therefore easy to take the next step and conclude that literal infinity *must* exist as a real property of the physical Universe.

The Universe is not made of math. But even if it were a mathematical structure, that would not be a guarantee that the Universe is infinite. Systems of set theory and mathematics that contain no references to infinity provide all the evidence we need that, even if the Universe were mathematical, the Universe could just as well be a finite mathematical structure with only finite properties. Since it is *not necessarily* true that math requires infinity, even if the Universe does have some underlying mathematical structure as part of its essence, logic does not compel us to conclude the Universe *must* have literally infinite features as part of its mathematical structure.

There are in fact some cosmologists and physicists who have proposed models of the Universe in which the amount of space in the Universe is finite. Einstein had been a proponent of such a view [651] [652]. Some more recent cosmologists, such as the late Stephen Hawking (1942–2018), have also championed models of the Universe in which time—both past and future—is finite [653]. Cosmological models in accord with all the known facts while also assuming space and time are finite demonstrate that, from a strictly logical standpoint, we need not invoke literal infinity for explaining the Universe.

For all of these reasons, there is no rational obligation to believe literal infinity is an ontological necessity; there simply is no sound ontological argument that concludes the Universe *must* have literally infinite properties.

However, just because literal infinity is not an ontologically *necessary* feature either of some mathematical world or of the physical Universe, that in itself does not mean the Universe *cannot* be infinite. Literal infinity may be an invented property of an invented mathematics, but that in itself doesn't mean literal infinity cannot map to real space and time such as to accurately characterize properties of the Universe. It all depends on whether or not literal infinity is a logical concept even if not a necessary one.

If infinity is a logical concept, then it might map to some features of the Universe just as a number such as 10 can be mapped to a group of objects like a collection of apples or fence posts, or people. The

Universe could then still have literally infinite features even if the Universe does not reduce to mathematics alone. So even if the Universe does not *necessarily* have infinite properties, the Universe could still have infinite properties as a matter of *contingency*—the result of happenstance.

The question now becomes, is infinity an invention that we can map to features of the Universe, as when we describe magnitudes of space, durations of time, motion through space and time, or quantities of matter? The answer to that depends on whether it is even *possible* for the Universe to be literally infinite—whether it is possible for infinity to map onto properties or features of the Universe.

17.2 INFINITY IMPOSSIBLE

If infinity is a possible property for a collection, then infinity is either *ontologically possible* (which means it would not necessarily be false that infinity exists in the real world) or *logically possible* (which means it would not necessarily be false that infinity is a coherent idea), or both. If, on the other hand, infinity is a self-contradictory concept, then it is not possible—not logically and not ontologically—for anything in the Universe, or the Universe itself, to be infinite with respect to *any* property.

Figure 17.1 represents the domains of possibility—both that which is logically possible (possible to coherently conceive) and that which is ontologically possible (possible to exist).

According to the placement of the domains in **Figure 17.1**, ontological possibilities overlap with logical possibilities. If something is located inside the ontological circle, it is possible in reality and it is possible as a matter of reason; whereas if something is located outside the inner circle but still inside the outer circle, then it is possible as a matter of reason but not possible in reality. **Figure 17.1** does not represent *logical* impossibilities at all; if something is logically impossible, it is not found in the figure—such things can neither exist in reality nor even have a rational conception.

Ontological possibility is entirely within the domain of logical possibility; something can't exist in reality without being at least a logical possibility. Now I should qualify that I do *not* mean to imply "reality is logical" as if logic is baked into reality or as if reality is somehow designed according to a logical schema. Rather, to say a logical impossibility cannot be an ontological possibility is to say that if an idea or concept is not logical, it cannot make a rationally coherent reference to a reality. Basically, if you're going to claim something is ontologically possible and have any hope of your claim being accurate, then your claim cannot violate logic by, for example, assuming self-contradictory concepts—such do not map to reality. It's not that reality needs to be logical, it's that we need to make logical statements about reality if they are to be possibly accurate representations of reality.

Conversely, logical possibilities extend beyond the ontologically possible. Hence, whereas logical impossibilities are not represented in **Figure 17.1**, at least some *ontological* impossibilities are indeed allowed in the scope of the figure—they are all located outside of the ontological possibility circle but may still be within the bounds of logic. This is because some ontological impossibilities are logically possible even though they can't manifest in reality. For example, in physical reality it may be impossible to walk through a solid wall, but there is no logical contradiction in doing so—so, it's possible as a matter of reason even though it is not possible as a matter of reality. Just because something is ontologically impossible, that does not mean it's logically impossible. Logic is, so to speak, broader than reality—we can think up and talk about all kinds of things that don't stand a chance of existing.

On the other hand, there are also ontological impossibilities that are logical impossibilities as well. That is, some things are ontologically impossible precisely because they are logically impossible. For example, while $x = 6$ is a possible outcome for a roll of a six-sided die, the outcome $x = 7$ is not a possible outcome for a six-sided die, not logically and not ontologically. However, such impossibilities are not represented by **Figure 17.1**, except insofar as the boundary of the outer circle implies some things are logically (and, ergo, ontologically) impossible.

In short, if something is ontologically possible—that is, if it can exist in the real world—then it must be logically possible because the rules of logic allow us to articulate a statement that is able to map part of the nature of existence. However, logic is broader than ontology because the rules of logic allow us to express situations that are not ontologically possible. That is, just because something is logically possible, that does not mean it *must* exist in reality.

There are some thinkers who dispute this relation between logic and ontology; they want to allow for logical impossibilities to exist. They challenge logic itself, attempting to show how paradoxes exist in the real world (certain theologians in particular take this tack—see Chapters 25–26). On the contrary, I will simply assume the principles of logic accurately map to principles of reality—for example, the dispositions of nature. (That's not to say people reason logically all the time or always make logical decisions, it's just to say the dispositions of nature cohere with the principles of logic.)

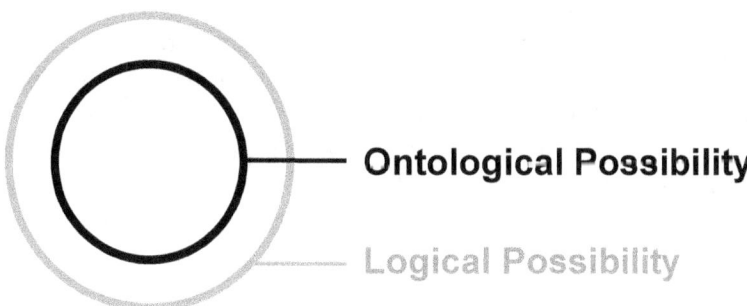

Figure 17.1: The domains of possibility. (The circle of logical possibility matches to the domain of logic in Figures 9.4 and 9.5, with ontological possibility overlapping areas 3, 4, and 5 in Figure 9.5.)

17.2.1 *Literal Infinity is not Logically Possible*

As detailed in Chapters 14–16, literal infinity is found only in mathematical *interpretation* while figurative infinity is found primarily in mathematical *operation*. In operational terms, the "infinity" of mathematics (∞, $\aleph$, or ω in syntax) works in only a figuratively infinite sense in that the mathematical operations produce, at best, only indefinite progressions and sets of indefinitely many objects. In general mathematics, ∞ refers to no exact quantity in operation and works rather like Euclid's method of exhaustion—just keep going as long as you can.

In transfinite mathematics, "sets" are represented only by abstractions denoted by letters like A and B or symbols such as $\aleph$ or ω. Such notations are, operationally speaking, representations of collective or serial indefinites. These notations are also often depicted with subscript numbers (such as $\aleph_0$, $\aleph_1$, etc.)

that can be 'added' and 'multiplied' without reference to the indefinites the sets correspond to. When the sets do reference their numeric contents, the sets reveal themselves to be only indefinite progressions of numbers in braces {1, 2, 3, …} or similar elements. In transfinite mathematics, "infinity" is operationally not infinity in the literal sense—rather, it is just philosophically interpreted to be such.

In general mathematics the "infinity" of mathematical operation is sometimes assumed, implied, or claimed to be literal infinity, as when a circle is described as a polygon with an infinite number of sides or an operation of increasingly smaller division converges not just near, but at zero. Such "operations," do not really carry out a literally infinite number of tasks, however—they are just indefinite extrapolations. In transfinite mathematics, the operations with "infinity" are also operationally indistinguishable from indefiniteness rather than genuinely a condition of completeness and limitlessness according to the lexical senses of these terms.

Figurative infinity, being only a misnomer for indefinite process, is a useful, hypothetical condition for some mathematical operations, but literal infinity is nowhere to be found in mathematical operation. Rather, literal infinity is merely a condition purported for some mathematical operations. As shown in Chapters 10–12, literal infinity contains self-contradictory connotations. Just as pseudo-eligible and non-angularity are terms that imply self-contradictions, so too the term 'infinity' in its literal sense implies self-contradictions from supposedly being both complete and limitless. Consequently, claims that literal infinity is a rigorous mathematical concept are not at all accurate.

Many philosophers and mathematicians push back on this charge, of course. Hardegree states, "To be sure, our minds are boggled when we consider the possibility of [literal infinities]…But boggling the human mind is not a reliable sign of impossibility, as history has repeatedly attested" [654]. That is true. But neither is boggling the human mind a reliable sign of possibility either. A non-angularity (square circle) can boggle the mind, but that does not mean it is logically possible. So too with literal infinity. It may boggle that mind, but that is because self-contradictions boggle the mind. And as a self-contradiction, literal infinity does not refer to a logical possibility.

17.2.2 *Literal Infinity is Not Ontologically Possible*

Because literal infinity is not a logically possible condition for quantities to have, it is not possible for literal infinity to be a property of collections in the real world. As portrayed in **Figure 17.1**, if a concept is not *logical*, it cannot refer to a reality. Such is the case with literal infinity—it is a condition that has no possibility of existing because literal infinity is logically self-contradictory; it cannot refer to anything that exists in the real world even if mathematicians have appropriated the term "infinity" from philosophers and continue to use it in mathematically consistent ways.

To see exactly what absurdities would characterize reality if it did contain collections that are literally infinite, I'll present the logical implications of applying the concept of literal infinity to:

- thought experiments
- measurements
- physical theories

In each category, literal infinity would result in absurdities if manifested in the real world. In this chapter, we'll explore the application of literal infinity in thought experiments involving hypothetical situations.

As an example of a 'hypothetical situation', try to imagine a hotel containing a literally infinite number of rooms. Another example would be a library containing a literally infinite number of books. These hypothetical scenarios are known respectively as Hilbert's Hotel and Craig's Library, each named after its inventor: mathematician David Hilbert (1862–1943) and philosopher William Lane Craig. Now imagine testing these hypothetical situations for consistency by making some inferences as to what conditions might logically follow from them. These tests, not carried out in reality but only in logical inference, are 'thought experiments' performed on hypothetical situations.

For instance, we might consider if it makes logical sense for a hotel containing an infinite number of guests to add yet more guests. On the one hand, the hotel has limitlessly many rooms, so we can just have each present guest move over to the next room so that Room 1 opens up for a new guest. And we should even be able to repeat this maneuver without limit, accommodating an infinite number of new guests to the infinite amount already occupying the hotel. On the other hand, the hotel's set of rooms is already completely full, so there should be no way to get the guests moving at all. We might also consider if it makes logical sense for an infinite number of books to be checked out from the infinite library. If an infinite number of books were checked out, would there still be infinitely many books on the shelves, or no books left at all?

These thought experiments suggest the hypothetical situations involving literal infinity imply paradoxes if not genuine contradictions. Paradoxes are only apparent self-contradictions. So, if we can make sense of the situations with further analysis of the thought experiments, then the application of literal infinity to the situations will turn out to be logically consistent and the paradoxes will be solved. But if we can't make sense of them, then we may find literal infinity cannot be applied to the given situations without contradiction, and so literal infinity would become a debunked concept. As I will show, when literal infinity is applied to hypothetical situations and thought experiments like these, the result is indeed self-contradiction and not just paradox.

Now it might be objected that such hypothetical situations and thought experiments are much ado about nothing because there really are no such things as infinite libraries and hotels. But this would miss the point. If literal infinity cannot be consistently applied to hypothetical situations and thought experiments, then it certainly cannot be consistently applied to descriptions of reality. As I will show, literal infinity has no coherent application to logical possibilities, let alone situations in the real world.

But Hilbert's Hotel and Craig's Library are only two hypothetical situations. There are many thought experiments involving the application of infinity to many other hypothetical situations, some of which date back to Zeno of Elea. We will not pursue them all. Instead, we will focus only on Hilbert's Hotel and Craig's Library for now, but we will address a paradox raised by Zeno in Chapter 20.

On that note, the following three chapters will reveal the absurdities of applying literal infinity to measures of space, time, and motion. These will be following by a chapter discussing the application of literal infinity to popular theories in physics and show why such a course of action should not be recommended. But first, it's onward to the thought experiments involving our infinite hotel and infinite library.

17.3 HILBERT'S HOTEL

During a January 1925 university lecture delivered in Göttingen, Germany, Hilbert explained how we can always continue listing new numbers for a set of numbers that is already infinite, like the set of natural numbers, $\mathbb{N}$, and yet not increase the size of that infinite set of numbers. As an analogy, Hilbert proposed a hypothetical situation involving a Grand Hotel that has a literally infinite quantity of rooms. Each and every room in the hotel is occupied. However, suppose a new guest arrives and wants a room. Can the guest be accommodated with a room or not? On the one hand, the hotel is completely full. On the other hand, it also has limitlessly many rooms—if there is no limit to the number of rooms, then we should be able to fit another finite quantity into a limitless quantity of rooms. In fact, Hilbert claimed that a hotel with infinitely many rooms, while fully occupied, can nevertheless accommodate additional guests—even infinitely many new guests [655]. This was originally just an analogy, an example, Hilbert used in his lecture to show how an infinite set of numbers can always have more numbers listed for it without increasing the size, or cardinality, of the set, but we can also regard the Grand Hotel as a kind of thought experiment to see what the logical outcome would be if it a real hotel could be infinitely large.

The Grand Hotel became popularized in works by other mathematicians and is now commonly known as Hilbert's Hotel. Dr. Helge Kragh of the Centre for Science Studies, Department of Physics and Astronomy, at Aarhus University in Denmark explains the reasoning behind Hilbert's Hotel: "If a hotel has only a finite number of rooms, all of them occupied, there is no way to accommodate new guests. For a finite set a part of the set is always smaller than the total set, but this is not the case for an infinite set" [656]. Recall that in transfinite mathematics the sequence of natural numbers comprises a literally infinite set of numbers that can be placed into a one-to-one correspondence with an infinite subset of itself. Hilbert's Hotel has a literally infinite set of rooms that can be placed in a one-to-one correspondence with the natural numbers. Since Hilbert's Hotel has just as many rooms as the set of natural numbers, its rooms can also be placed in bijection with any 'countably infinite' subset of rooms within it. As a consequence of the equality of infinite whole and any infinite part, that there is a guest to every room does not imply that no more guests can be accommodated in a hotel of infinitely many rooms [657]:

> *All rooms in the hotel are occupied.* Now suppose that a new guest arrives – will it be possible to find a free room for him or her? Surprisingly, the answer is yes. He (or she) may be accommodated in room 1, while the guest in this room is moved to room 2, the guest in room 2 moves to room 3, and so on. Since *there is no last room*, the newcomer can be accommodated without any of the guests having to leave the hotel. Hilbert's remarkable hotel can even accommodate a countable infinity of new guests without anyone leaving it. [Emphasis mine.]

Even if you try successively adding a 'countably infinite' number of guests to the hotel, you will still not have exceeded the total number of rooms in the hotel. Mathematicians conclude that, counterintuitive as Hilbert's Hotel might be, it is a logically consistent idea. You can keep moving guests over to accommodate new rooms because there is no last room.

Contrarily, I argue that the Hilbert Hotel thought experiment should not be taken too seriously as otherwise it is logically erroneous due to committing some informal logical fallacies.

17.3.1 *We'll Make Room for You*

As a hotel with a literally infinite number of rooms, Hilbert's Hotel has a *limitless* number of rooms, so there is no 'last room' in the hotel. To get a clearer picture of what that means, let's suppose the rooms are all sequentially numbered up to infinity.

To keep the hypothetical situation simple, suppose the door to the first room in the hotel is numbered as Room 1. Imagine each of the following rooms in the hotel is also numbered with a '1', but each successive room in sequence after the first room has a room number with double the amount of zeros following its 1 than does the room number for the immediately previous room.

Hence, the sequence:

Door to First Room:	1
Door to Second Room:	10
Door to Third Room:	100
Door to Fourth Room:	10,000
Door to Fifth Room:	100,000,000
$\vdots$	$\vdots$

Suppose there are so many doors in the hotel that the sequence of numbers follows an exponential curve of zeros, all the way to infinity. In such a situation, there would be doors further in the sequence labelled with too many zeros to distinguish. As for how we would represent such large numbers on the doors, we'll just have to imagine that as the numbers increase in size, each successive digit in each number is smaller than the previous digit such that the zeroes get increasingly smaller in font size until they become too small to measure as illustrated in **Figure 17.2**.

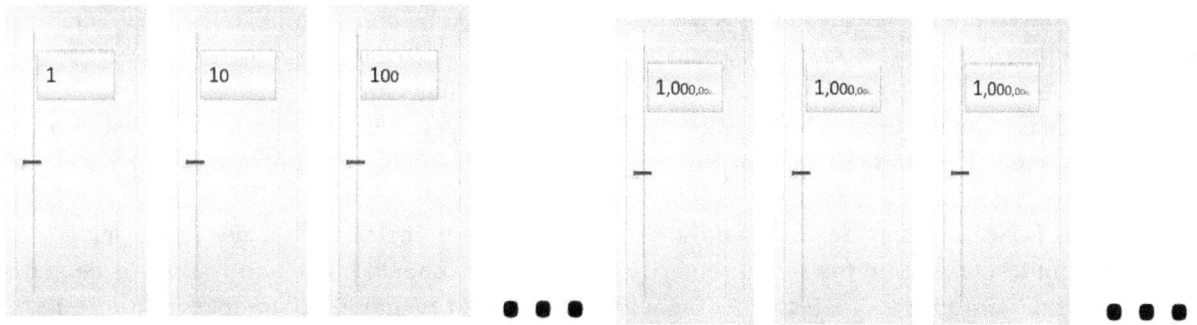

Figure 17.2: The hotel doors are shown very close together. Each hotel room door in Hilbert's Hotel is labeled with a 1, and each successive room has double the number of zeros than its predecessor. Because there are a limitless number of rooms in the hotel, the doors further along are labelled by ever higher sequences of zeros. The doors begin to look very much the same, with each successive door having an increasingly tiny zero as the last digit of the door number. And there is no 'last' room in the hotel.

From what the *completeness* of literal infinity would suggest (see Chapter 10), eventually in the sequence of doors there must be a single door labelled with a 1 followed by a limitless string of zeros—an infinitely large natural number. However, the *limitlessness* of a literally infinite sequence of doors tells us there is no such thing as an 'infinitieth' number—an infinitely large natural number—and therefore there is no single door with a *1* followed by a limitless string of zeros; there is no 'infinitieth' door in the sequence.

Instead, the limitlessness of the *sequence* of doors means that there is no limit to the number of doors with 1 followed by an increasing *finite* number of zeros. It is true the number represented on each door would increase the further along the sequence of doors; but no matter how large the number on any of the doors is, no matter no many zeros follow the 1, no matter how increasingly small the font size of the zeros must be in order to fit the number on the door, there is no door with infinitely many zeros following the 1, even though the sequence of doors is without limit (**Figure 17.2**).

There is, however, a problem. We saw back in Chapter 11 that limitlessness implies a literally infinite whole is greater than any sum of its parts. But it is actually worse than that, for it also implies the opposite—the same as completeness, that there must be a whole that is an infinite sum of the parts.

Consider: *if* there can be no such thing as an infinitely large natural number, *then* there can be no such thing as a literally limitless sequence of natural numbers either since each natural number is the sum of previous numbers in the list of numbers. But there *must* be a limitless sequence in order for the quantity of rooms in the hotel to be infinite. So, the limitlessness of the sequence of hotel rooms means there must be an infinitely large natural number on at least one door in the hotel—the infinite sum of all rooms in the hotel. The limitlessness of an infinite sequence of natural numbers therefore seems to imply the completeness of the quantity of hotel rooms—an Infinite Sum of all rooms.

However, we also cannot ignore the other implication of the limitlessness of the rooms: the limitlessness of the sequence of rooms in the hotel means that if were to number them according to the sequence of natural numbers, each room would have a finite number. We would therefore have a limitless quantity of finitely numbered rooms; so, the limitless quantity of hotel rooms also means that no matter how many rooms there are for the limitless whole, the whole must be *greater than*, rather than equal to, any sum of rooms.

So here we have a contradiction again: a sequence of rooms that sums and yet does not.

That alone is damning to the idea of Hilbert's Hotel. And yet, let's put that contradictory implication aside for a moment. Let's instead focus on just the implication of what it means for guests in a hotel that has *no limit* to its quantity of rooms.

One thing is clear: Hilbert claimed that if there is *no last room*, there is no barrier to moving guests over one room to make room for another guest. That means we should be able to transfer each guest over to the next room and repeat this task without limit, and so find ever more rooms for evermore guests. However, as we'll see, that too is problematic if the hotel is also supposed to be *complete*.

17.3.2 *No Vacancy*

While Hilbert claimed his hotel has a limitless quantity of rooms, Hilbert's Hotel also has a complete number of rooms. And as we've seen, completeness causes logical conflicts with limitlessness.

The completeness of Hilbert's Hotel implies that the hotel has a *total* number of rooms that is a *whole* and *entire* quantity of rooms—no subset of rooms is divided off from the hotel and no rooms are left out. Further, no more rooms are under construction—the hotel is *finished* being built. And the hotel, as Hilbert said, has an occupancy that is *full*. A full Hotel is a hotel that *cannot increase its number of members without changing the parameters of the hotel*—like building more rooms onto it. It is precisely the fullness of the occupancy of the room that entails *no new guests* can enter the hotel. To see why this is so, let's devise a picture of the hotel.

To grasp the significance of this, suppose we label the numbers on the door a bit differently. Each room after the first in Hilbert's Hotel is numbered just as before—a 1 followed by a string of zeros—but instead of marking the number on each door left to right, let's mark the number on each door right to left so that the final zero always stays on the right-hand margin of the number plate. In that case, the number 1 on each successive door recedes infinitely far away as the number of rooms approaches infinity:

Door to First Room:	1
Door to Second Room:	10
Door to Third Room:	100
Door to Fourth Room:	10,000
Door to Fifth Room:	100,000,000
⋮	⋮

And once again, we have a problem with how to represent increasingly large numbers on the surface of the doors. So, for the number on each door, we'll make each preceding digit smaller than its successor. (as shown in **Figure 17.3**).

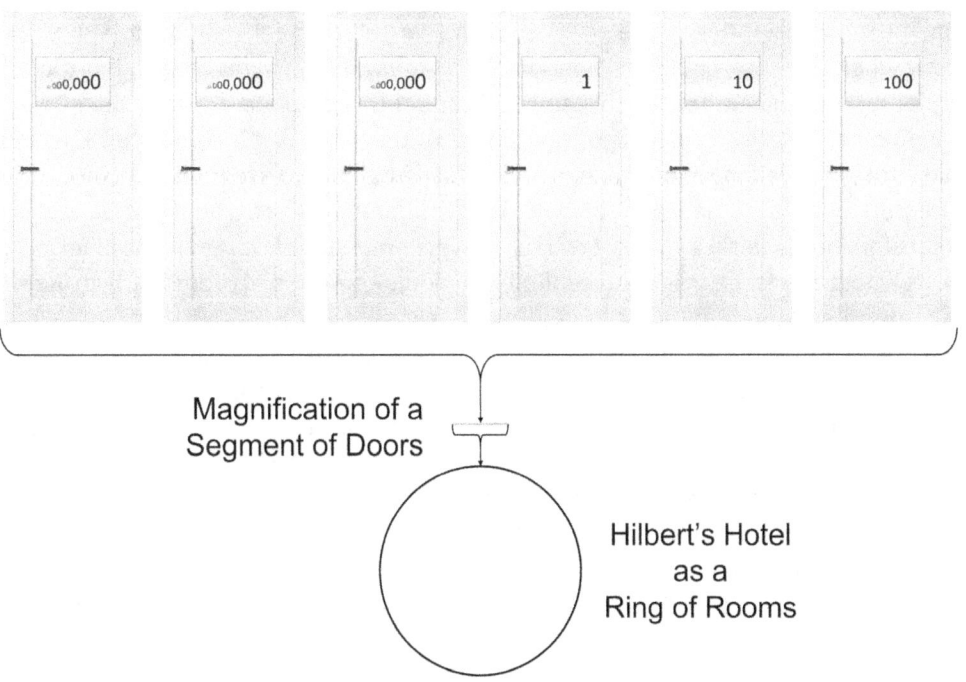

Figure 17.3: Hilbert's Hotel as a ring of infinitely many rooms. Each room after the first room is labelled by a number starting with 1 followed by double the amount of zeros as its predecessor (again the doors are shown close together for convenience). Because Hilbert's Hotel is literally infinite, it has a complete number of rooms. The final room, following an infinite number of rooms, is shown by the door immediately prior to the door of Room 1. At least the door immediately preceding Room 1, if not many others as well, must be labelled with a figure of infinitely many ($\aleph_0$) zeros *between* the infinitely small 1 on the door sign and the final zero on the door sign.

Next, let's change the configuration of the hotel. Instead of making the hotel linear, let's make it circular. After all, mathematicians sometimes say a circle is an *infinigon*—a polygon with an infinite number of sides. So, let's make Hilbert's Hotel circular—a hotel in the shape of an infinigon, with each side of the infinigon being a room of the hotel (also as shown in **Figure 17.3**).

And just to be clear, the number of rooms in the infinigon of Hilbert's Hotel need not be $\mathbb{R}$-many ($\aleph_1$) but could rather be $\mathbb{N}$-many ($\aleph_0$), the "least infinite" amount according to the transfinite system [658]. If Hilbert's Hotel were in the shape of a complete ring of rooms, the room numbers would progress infinitely around the ring-shaped architecture of the hotel. Because there is a room located before Room 1, there must be a final room somehow following *after* an infinite number of prior rooms.

A problem with Hilbert's Hotel now becomes obvious. Because the hotel has a *complete* quantity of rooms, it has a totality of rooms—there is indeed a final room next around the ring of rooms in the hotel, a room right next to Room 1 requiring a constant number on its door, a number that is a standing total of all the rooms in the hotel. This contradicts the *limitlessness* of literal infinity, which states there can be no such thing as a final room, just as there can be no such thing as a final zero for a number starting with a 1 followed by infinitely many zeros—that is, there must be ever-larger finite numbers *without limit* and for that reason no final room.

But now there is also another problem: limitlessness apparently denies completeness. If there were *no* final room in the hotel—if there were no room with a largest number right before Room 1 on the ring of hotel rooms—then the hotel could be "limitless" in its quantity of rooms alright, but then there would be no *totality* of rooms. And without such, the hotel cannot be *complete*. At best, the quantity of rooms in the hotel would be "limitless" in the figurative sense of the term—an *incomplete* series of multiplying rooms. Perhaps the ring of rooms would expand like a filling balloon to accommodate new rooms into the hotel's architecture, with each new room having its own number. That would not be a *complete* set of rooms and therefore not a literal infinity of rooms, however *indefinitely* large the number of rooms in the hotel may be. It would at best be a figurative infinity of rooms—a series of rooms with an indefinitely large running total, not a literal infinity.

A literally infinite set does not necessarily imply further construction isn't possible, as if no further rooms can be added; it's just to say that the hotel is *already* complete and is finished being built. If Hilbert's Hotel is a literally infinite hotel, there are no more rooms under construction because the hotel is complete, as is. If we were to add more rooms to it, we would be either denying the hotel was complete, or we would be modifying a hotel that was already complete. So, if the hotel is complete, and if its sequence of rooms loops back around on itself like a circle containing an infinitude of infinitely small edges along its circumference, then there must be a final room that comes right before Room 1. And that final room in a ring of rooms allows us to picture what it means for the hotel to be *full*, which is a trait of completeness.

The fullness of the hotel implies that, even if we allow Hilbert's Hotel to have infinitely many rooms arranged in a ring of rooms like a polygon with infinitely many sides, no more guests can be accommodated. If every guest moves to the next room, that just means the guest in the room to the right of Room 1 moves into Room 1, while the guest in the room immediately prior to that one moves into it, and so on all the way around the ring back to Room 1. A new guest cannot enter the hotel precisely because the hotel is full.

17.3.3 *A Complete and Limitless Number of Guests*

Notice that because the hotel is proposed to have a literal infinity of rooms, the hotel has a *complete and limitless* quantity of rooms, and those two properties stand in contradiction:

- "All rooms are completely occupied" implies the hotel is *full* and therefore no more guests can be added.

- "There is no last room" in the hotel implies the hotel has no limit to its rooms, so of course more guests can be added.

Even if a literally infinite set of hotel rooms has "counterintuitive" properties such as the ability to accommodate more guests despite there being a guest in every room, that only addresses the *limitlessness* of the rooms. It does not address the *completeness* of the rooms, which implies fullness— the inability to include more guests because there are no more rooms for guests to go to. Once we recall that the rooms are full and that implies no more guests can be added, we notice the contradiction right away.

By virtue of the fact that the hotel contains a complete number of rooms, no more guests can be added to the hotel; while by virtue of the fact that the hotel contains a limitless number of rooms, more guests can be added to the hotel. Therefore, more guests can and cannot be added to the hotel: a contradiction.

17.3.4 *Confusion of Categories*

If Hilbert's Hotel did not seem contradictory to Hilbert and subsequent mathematicians, that may be due to overlooking the difference between two properties of the hotel:

a) The fullness of rooms versus the 'totality' of rooms.
b) The quantitative limitlessness of rooms versus the indefiniteness in representing rooms.

Take fullness as compared to totality. Just having a 'totality' of guests in the sense of an infinite number of guests—symbolized as ω or $\aleph$ (or, more specifically, $\omega_0 = \aleph_0$)—does not mean the same thing as the hotel being 'full'. Hilbert implied that a hotel of $\omega = \aleph$ guests had a totality of guests and so is a full hotel, but just having $\aleph$ guests is different from being full since there is no *mathematical* problem with a hotel of $\aleph$ guests having 3 more people than another hotel that also has $\aleph$ guests. This is because $\aleph$ as an infinite 'number' is not an exact number. Symbols like ω and $\aleph$ are just placeholders for a condition that, if coherent, could apply to many different infinite sets of numbers.

If the hotel were expanding in size, with more rooms under construction, the hotel would still have a totality of $\aleph$ rooms and guests at any given time, but the hotel would not be "full" under such conditions. Fullness for the hotel would imply unchanging parameters for the hotel, such that quantity of rooms *cannot change to accommodate more guests without adding new rooms to the hotel*. A full hotel is not just a hotel with no empty rooms and a totality of guests to rooms, but also a hotel in which no new rooms are added. So, if the hotel is full, we must presume that whatever infinite natural number the symbol $\aleph$

would refer to for the amount of rooms in the hotel, the symbol corresponds to an exact total of guests and that number cannot change by adding more rooms for new guests.

Of course, Cantor would say there is no such thing as an "infinite natural number." Fair enough. But then, it's hard to see how the quantity of rooms can be 'infinite' in a sense that forms a *complete set* of rooms as opposed to just a growing indefinite quantity of rooms under some quantity labelled ω as an indefinitely removed supremum toward which newly constructed rooms continue to be built. In which case, the Hotel is not really "full" as stipulated and there is no complete set of rooms.

Hence, while Hilbert argued that the *limitlessness* of the hotel allows guests to always be moved over to make room for another guest, we could also counter that precisely because the hotel is *completely* filled, and by the definition of 'full', a guest in a room—no matter how far removed from the first room— still cannot move to the next room over because the guest already in that room cannot move to the next room over, because the guest already in the room after that cannot move to the next room over, and so on. By virtue of the literally infinite hotel being *full* as a condition of its completeness, it cannot change its parameters to accommodate more guests as if under construction with new rooms appearing somewhere off the horizon, hidden in an ellipsis of mathematical representation.

Now take limitlessness compared to indefiniteness with respect to the hotel rooms. Just because the hotel has a total of $\aleph$ guests and rooms, and $\aleph$ old guests plus $\aleph$ new guests still equals $\aleph$ guests, the use of $\aleph$ or ω is not necessarily more *semantically* precise than saying there are "a lot" of guests in the hotel, and "a lot" of old guests plus "a lot" of new guests is still "a lot" of guests. The operations of transfinite mathematics may be syntactically precise, but they are semantically imprecise enough to let us confuse limitlessness with an incomplete, indefinite collection.

Consider that moving a guest claimed to be limitlessly removed from the first room to a new room that is also claimed to be limitlessly far away is, *in mathematical operation*, no different from moving a guest from some *indefinite* amount of rooms away into a newly-constructed room for that guest also indefinitely far away. But an incomplete hotel perpetually under construction to accommodate new guests would be a finite hotel, not Hilbert's infinite hotel. So to be in keeping with Hilbert's thought experiment, the hotel should neither be imagined like a building ceaselessly under construction with newly appearing rooms to accommodate new guests, nor imagined as a wormhole into which the old guests disappear as new guests come in, while the hotel as a whole does not change its overall totality of rooms. For, if we do characterize the hotel with indefinitely many rooms and movements of guests, that is different from characterizing it with a limitless number of rooms and movements of guests, as it is most often characterized in the interpretation of the "transfinite" operations. But indefinite process is all the movement of guests from room to room accomplishes: an incomplete indefinite operation merely claimed to be 'limitless', giving us the illusion of limitless rooms with limitless guests shuffling from room to room.

We therefore have a confusion of totality with fullness and the illusion of limitlessness caused by a confusion with serial indefiniteness. The result is that a hotel complete and limitless in its quantity of rooms remains contradictory, even if that contradiction is obscured under the abstractions and rules of mathematical operation that allow us to confuse fullness with totality and limitlessness with serial indefiniteness.

17.4 CRAIG'S LIBRARY

Craig argues that if literal infinity (or actual infinity) were to exist, reality would manifest logical 'absurdities' (self-contradictions about a hypothetical or real-world situation). Since reality does not manifest logical absurdities, Craig proposes that literal infinity does not exist in the real world [659].

That is not to say Craig sees a logical problem with the concept of infinity as such. He believes literal infinity is *logically* possible; he just doesn't believe literal infinity is *ontologically* possible [660].

However, Craig confuses logical possibility with mathematical coherence [661]. The two are not the same. An expression, for example, can be mathematically coherent while that same expression represents a logical impossibility due to the expression's inconsistent semantic connotations—such is the case with expressions of literally infinite sets and progressions. Despite any mathematical coherence literal infinity may have with respect to syntactical operation, it is still a logical impossibility with respect to its semantic content. Therefore, contrary to Craig's point of view, I propose literal infinity is ontologically impossible precisely because it is logically impossible.

One piece of evidence in support of the position that literal infinity cannot represent actual states of affairs in the world was found in the contradictory implications of Hilbert's Hotel. We'll now take a look at another argument for the absurdity of literal infinity as a concept applied to collections of real objects—an argument proposed by Craig along similar lines as Hilbert's Hotel.

One of Craig's arguments against the possibility of literal infinity manifesting in physical reality is based on a hypothetical situation in which a library contains a literally infinite number of books [662]. Just as Hilbert's Hotel was named for Hilbert, so too Craig's Library is named for Craig. However, while Hilbert intended his hotel analogy to demonstrate the 'paradoxical' nature of literal infinity, Craig intends his library analogy to show the absurdity of assuming literal infinity could ever be a property of real-world collections.

Contrary to Hilbert's intent, I have argued that Hilbert's Hotel implies genuine logical contradictions involving literal infinity. However, in contrast to my disagreement with Hilbert over the implications of the hotel analogy, I am in agreement with Craig insofar as his hypothetical library does indeed show literal infinity to imply absurdities that cannot manifest in the real world [663].

There are several logical absurdities implied by a hypothetical library containing an infinite number of books. Here are three of them:

- *the checkout absurdity*
- *the available number absurdity*
- *the last page absurdity*

We'll address each of these in order.

17.4.1 *The Checkout Absurdity*

Suppose the library holds a literally infinite number of books. How we wish to mathematically represent the infinite number of books does not matter. We could say there are ∞ books in the library. Alternatively, we could say the size of the set of books in the library is $\aleph_0$. If the books are all numbered and placed on the shelf in order, we can say there are ω_0 books in the library. Whatever way you want to mathematically represent the collection of books, there is a literal infinity of books to choose from.

Craig argued that removing an infinite set of books from the library would result in contradictions [664]. For example, suppose we attempt to check out either *all* the books in the library or some infinite subset of books in the library. It does not matter for our purposes which option is chosen—all the books or an infinite subset—just so long as *infinitely many* books are checked out. Now if we check out a literally infinite quantity of books *all at once*, there is no logical problem. But we do find a logical problem if we try to check out infinitely many books *one after another* in succession until they are all checked out.

In such a case, two contradictory situations follow:

1. Because the set of library books we wish to check out is literally infinite, the set of books is a *complete* quantity of books. Because there is a complete quantity to check out, the initial set that was quantitatively complete when we started checking books out is left ever more incomplete with each removal of a book from the library. To speed things up, we check the books out infinitely fast. After an infinite number of books have been removed from the library, no books remain to be checked out. The complete quantity of infinitely many books has been checked out.

2. Because the quantity of library books is literally infinite, the collection of library books to be checked out is *limitless* in quantity—there is no 'last' library book that can be checked out in an infinite series of checkouts. That means even if we accelerate the check-out procedure infinitely, at no time does the library ever run out of library books for us to check out. We will never get to the end of checking out library books because there is no end to get to.

After checking out infinitely many books, no books remain in the library to be checked out and yet an infinite number of books remain in the library yet to be checked out: a quantitative contradiction.

This is not how Craig framed his argument [665], but his intent was to show that removing a literally infinite quantity from a literally infinite quantity results in logical contradictions that cannot manifest in the real world. He is right about that. Removing a literally infinite set of books from a library holding infinitely many books produces a logical absurdity in the hypothetical scenario. So too, operations with any literally infinite collection cannot occur in the real world.

I should hasten to add that it is not *mathematically* impossible to "remove" infinitely many objects from an infinite collection of objects, such as by subtraction or set difference, since some versions of transfinite mathematics and set theory allow such in the formal language of math (which operationally treats 'infinity' as only a *figurative infinity* anyway). However, it is indeed *logically* impossible to remove a literal infinity of objects from a literally infinite collection of objects. The reason it is logically impossible to do so is because of what literal infinity *means* as a natural language predicate—literal completeness of quantity and literal limitlessness of quantity—which together have contradictory implications.

The upshot is that sometimes mathematics can be just as misleading as natural language. Craig's Library is a perfect illustration of this. An infinite set of library books checked out from Craig's Library yields two different quantitative outcomes but can't, just as infinitely many new guests can and cannot check in to Hilbert's Hotel.

17.4.2 *The Available Number Absurdity*

Craig points out another absurdity that would result with the library, which I call the 'available number absurdity'. When we try to add additional books to the library's inventory of infinitely many books, we get logically absurd results.

Craig states [666],

> Suppose further that each book in the library has a number printed on its spine so as to create a one-to-one correspondence with the natural numbers. Because the collection is actually infinite, this means that *every possible* natural number is printed on some book. Therefore, it would be impossible to add another book to this library. For what would be the number of the new book? Clearly there is no number available to assign to it. Every possible number already has a counterpart to reality, for corresponding to every natural number is an already existent book. Therefore, there would be no number for the new book.

In other words, because a literally infinite collection of books is a *complete* collection, all the natural numbers are used up in that collection—there are no available, unique natural numbers to assign for new books.

But Craig merely pointed out half the trouble. The other half of the trouble is this: because the literally infinite collection of books is also a *limitless* collection, we can never run out of new, unique numbers to assign to books we wish to add to the library—if there is a limitless quantity of numbers, then there no such thing as "all" the possible numbers [667]. When we add a new book to the collection, the rest of the books just get relabelled with unique natural numbers like guests getting shifted in Hilbert's Hotel; the natural numbers can't be "used up." But that is the opposite conclusion we get from the completeness of the collection, which Craig correctly identified.

Conclusion: we cannot add any new, unique natural numbers for new books because the natural numbers are *already* complete for the collection, *as is*; and yet we can ceaselessly add new natural numbers for new books because there is no limit to the natural numbers we can use for new books. We therefore can *and* cannot add new natural numbers for new books. A clear contradiction, similar to that of Hilbert's Hotel, again shows the problem with having an infinite collection of anything in the real world.

17.4.3 *The Last Page Absurdity*

There is one last absurdity I wish to address related to Craig's Library. Suppose one of the books in Craig's Library is a very special book, as described by the late Syracuse philosopher José A. Benardete [668]:

> Open it. Look at the first page. Measure its thickness. It is very thick indeed for a single sheet of paper—$1/2$ inch thick. Now turn to the second page of the book. How thick is this second sheet of paper? $1/4$ inch thick. And the third page of the book, how thick is this third sheet of paper? $1/8$ inch thick, etc. *ad infinitum*. We are to posit not only that each page of the book is followed by an immediate successor the thickness of which is one-half that of the immediately preceding page...Close the book. Turn it over so that the front cover of the book is now lying face down upon the table. Now—slowly—lift the back cover of the book with the aim of exposing to view the stack of pages lying beneath it...

Benardete then proposed that, because a book with a literal infinity of pages has a limitless number of pages, we would have "nothing to see" upon opening the book since there is no last page [669].

Actually, the problem is much worse: we both can *and* cannot open the back cover of the book. Because the number of pages is complete, we can open the book to the last page, perhaps 'numbered' as page ω or at least with a number equivalent to a natural number with $\aleph_0$-many digits. However, because the number of pages is limitless, we cannot open the back cover of the book no matter how hard we try—there is no way to peel back the cover to get to a last page because there is no last page at all; in that respect, "there is nothing to see." So, we both can and cannot get to a last page—a contradiction. And as we know, logical contradictions cannot manifest in reality [670].

17.4.4 *Craig's Library Stands*

There are yet other contradictions and absurdities that would result from a literally infinite library or a book of infinite pages, but these examples should suffice to drive the point home: Craig's Library illustrates that literally infinite collections of real objects and literally infinite processes occurring in the real world are logical impossibilities and therefore ontological impossibilities.

17.5 CRITICS MISS THE POINT

As Reichenbach points out, critics fail to be convinced that Craig's Library, Hilbert's Hotel, and similar 'paradoxes' reveal genuine contradictions with the logic of literal infinity and/or a genuine inability to manifest as a property of the real world [671]. However, the critics often miss the point of the 'paradoxes' or fail to correctly interpret the problems raised by them.

For example, Oppy, a believer in the logical coherence of infinity [672], has criticized the Hilbert's Hotel thought experiment based on assumptions about the finite life span of the occupants of the hotel and whether the logistics of moving an infinite number of guests between rooms could be accomplished with infinite speeds of communication or transportation in a finite amount of time [673]. Oppy raised similar concerns about Craig's Library, pointing out that the books in Craig's Library need not be labelled with distinct natural numbers; instead, the books could be relabeled with a different system of numbers when new books are added to the library's inventory [674]. But such points, while interesting, are irrelevant because they have nothing to do with what the thought experiments are about.

The thought experiments of Hilbert's Hotel and Craig's Library do not pretend that a hotel or library of infinite magnitude could, as a practical matter, be built in the real world. So, the situations depicted in the thought experiments are not concerned with the necessary conditions for such structures to exist or what practical concerns such structures might raise. Rather, the point is whether it makes *logical* sense for there to be literally infinite quantities of real objects and literally infinite processes in the real world. The hotel and library are just meant as whimsical illustrations to show that there are logical problems in assuming so, and therefore it is problematic to suppose infinities exist in the real world.

Hence, the logical troubles with literal infinity do not go away even if we allow for infinite signal speeds between hotel guests. This is because an infinite speed can be fulfilled between all the guests (a literal infinity of guests is a complete amount, so the guests can all be reached by the signal) and yet cannot be fulfilled (there is no end of guests to contact, even with an infinitely speedy signal).

Likewise, relabeling the books to pin a new non-natural number on a new book to add to the infinite books already in the library does not address the problem: each book already in the library is in a one-to-one correspondence with the natural numbers, which means for a new book all the naturals are used up (the naturals are complete, so you've run out of them) and yet the naturals cannot be used up if a bijection is without limit (if the naturals are limitless, you can't run out of them). Such logical problems with having any quantity that is simultaneously complete and limitless completely go unaddressed in Oppy's critique.

One thing I will say in Oppy's defense, and the defense of other critics of Craig's Library: I have framed Craig's Library, and Hilbert's Hotel too, in terms that differ from their original portrayals, emphasizing the logical contradictions that follow from conceiving a collection of objects as being both complete and limitless in quantity, and which would therefore result in absurdities if such existed in reality. Oppy, on the other hand, was responding to Craig and others who feel there is nothing wrong with the logic of literal infinity, just its manifestation in reality. No wonder Oppy and other critics have missed the real issue—the trouble is not just with a real-world manifestation of literal infinities, as if the laws of physics are the only limitation; rather, the absurdities of real-world infinite collections would result from the logical implications of the very concept of literal infinity.

Critics of the paradoxes also tend to be concerned with whether the paradoxes have been analyzed correctly according to the formal language of infinity in transfinite mathematics rather than the *logical* coherence with respect to the implications or connotations that follow from the *meaning* of infinity in the natural language of mathematics. (You will notice this as soon as they start raising issues about the differences between infinite cardinal numbers and infinite ordinal numbers or begin writing down formulas.) As to proper use of the formal language of transfinite math, it's good to get such details right, but ultimately, it's not the issue; the problem is, again, the semantics of literal infinity assumed by what the formal language purports to show—not whether we stick to the proper form of the syntactical rules in the formal language itself, which only provides a figurative infinity in operation anyway.

For these reasons, neither the attacks by critics against Craig's Library nor the attempts to dismiss the contradictions of Hilbert's Hotel as a mere paradox succeed when we analyze the situations presented by the thought experiments correctly.

17.6 FURTHER EVIDENCE

There are plenty of other famous thought experiments involved with literal infinity that result in 'paradox' or contradiction. Oppy has categorized and summarized several paradoxes regarding infinity in his book *Philosophical Perspectives on Infinity* [675]. And Huemer also addresses many of them in his book *Approaching Infinity* [676]. Both Oppy and Huemer offer their own solutions to the paradoxes, aimed at defending infinity from refutation.

While it is tempting to address all the paradoxes and counter the apologetics for infinity, I will not run through the full list. It is not necessary. The treatment of Hilbert's Hotel and Craig's Library provided in this chapter already points out the general nature of the contradictions in the concept of literal infinity as it is applied to hypothetical situations and thought experiments. Nevertheless, I will address a few more logical problems with hypotheticals involving infinity, focusing specifically on only a few of them raised by scholars such as Oppy, Huemer, and others.

The 'paradoxes' we will look at have to do with proposals of infinite space, infinite time, and infinite motion. In the next three chapters, we will see why there cannot be a literally infinite number of places in space, a literally infinite number of moments in time, and a literally infinite number of motions through space and time. This will provide further evidence that literal infinity does not apply to the real world, and neither does Cantor's transfinite mathematics, which assumes sets are literally infinite.

CHAPTER 17 IN REVIEW

❖ If literal infinity is necessary, it is either logically necessary or ontologically necessary.

❖ Literal infinity is not logically necessary because it is not a tautology.

❖ A popular position in academia is to hold that literal infinity is an ontological necessity— a real, physical property of the Universe that cannot fail to be.

❖ Hypothetical scenarios and thought experiments show absurdities result by assuming literal infinities are real. Literal infinity is therefore not an ontological necessity because it is not even a genuine possibility: it cannot exist in the real world.

Infinity—in the literal sense of the word—is not, and cannot be, a property of space. Space does not contain infinitely many spaces, places, or portions in any literal sense.

However, I admit the arguments of the previous chapters are insufficient for establishing that conclusion. After all, infinity is often conceived to be a mathematical property and mathematical properties do not have to be real; they can be as fictional as we like.

A good example of a mathematical property that does not exist for objects in real, physical space is called *sphere eversion*. Whereas *inversion* is a process that reverses the position or order of an object (for instance, by turning an object upside down or downside up), *eversion* is the process of turning an object inside out or outside in. Sphere eversion is the process in which a sphere—a hollow ball with a two-dimensional (2D) surface—is turned inside out without creasing, pinching, puncturing, or tearing the surface in any way. Sphere eversion portrays a sphere as a flexible bubble in which the surface can be twisted and pushed through itself until the inside is on the outside and the outside is on the inside.

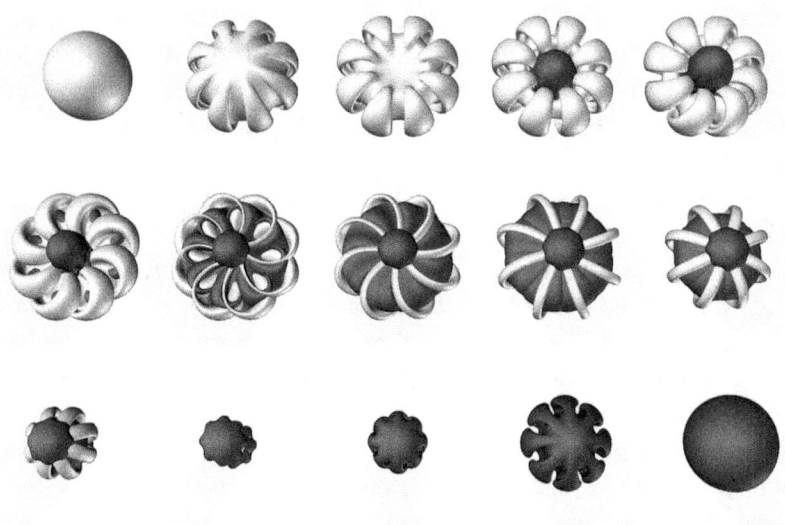

Figure 18.1: From left to right, top to bottom, a view from above of twelve stages of sphere eversion in Levy's *Making Waves*.

Mathematician William P. Thurston of the Mathematical Sciences Research Institute in Berkeley, California developed one successful technique of sphere eversion. Mathematicians Silvio Levy, Delle Maxwell, and Tamara Munzner of the Geometry Center at the University of Minnesota in Minneapolis have beautifully portrayed Thurston's technique in the 1994 award-winning, computer-animated movie *Outside In* [677]. Levy has also explained the sphere eversion process in his book, *Making Waves* [678]. **Figure 18.1** illustrates twelve arbitrarily divided stages of what is a smooth, seamless process of eversion that you can watch in the *Outside In* video [679].

The successful creation of the sphere eversion process is an excellent example of using mathematics not as a tool for measuring real-world features but rather just for the entertainment of overcoming an intellectual challenge. Like other entertaining ideas, sphere eversion is found nowhere in nature and does not exist outside of mathematical conception and visual representations in computer programs, animations, and artwork [680]. Sphere eversion is a form of mathematical entertainment, and its accomplishment is like the intellectual equivalent of an Olympic victory. As such, it is valuable for the same reason other works of art and forms of entertainment, like games, are valuable—it is an artifact that enriches the culture. Similarly, much of mathematics is valuable for cultural enrichment and so need not be useful for measuring the real world.

Just as mathematics has been applied for solving the puzzle of sphere eversion, so too mathematics has been used for taking on other intellectual challenges that have no bearing on reality, no application to describing real-world features or phenomena. Such challenges include the challenge of making infinity measurable or calculable. So, even if there is nothing infinite in the physical space separating empirical objects, that in itself does not entail there cannot be 'infinities' in a fictional, abstract space captured in mathematical formalism.

In fact, some mathematicians hold that infinity exists *only* in a fictional world of mathematical abstractions that has no bearing in reality. For instance, some mathematicians admit that transfinite mathematics, with its notion of measuring and calculating infinite sets, is not about the real world at all [681]. For instance, Harvard mathematician William Hugh Woodin says (literal) infinity, at least as it is portrayed in transfinite math and set theory, does not seem to correspond to anything we experience in the real world. Woodin states, "It might be we're just playing a game. Perhaps we are just doing some glorified sudoku puzzle" [682]. Transfinite mathematics is not a system that can be used to accurately describe features of the real world; like sphere eversion, it is simply a form of mathematical entertainment and intellectual accomplishment.

I admit not everyone would agree with me about that. Some mathematicians, philosophers of mathematics, and physicists have attempted to use the transfinite system as more than just intellectual entertainment. They have instead attempted to describe real-world features as actually being transfinite, where the transfinite is portrayed as literal infinity. Cantor, for one, thought his transfinite could in principle be applied to the real world and he thought it even had theological implications (see § 25.3). More recently, some quantum physicists have also attempted to apply the transfinite system to the physical world (see § 21.2.3).

I maintain they have been unsuccessful in doing so. While the transfinite (ω and $\aleph$), and even quantitative infinity as portrayed in portions of calculus and geometry (∞), can be (mis)interpreted as literal infinity for intellectual entertainment, the application of mathematical 'infinities' as literal infinities for descriptions of the real world is not accurate for that purpose. By analogy, just as sphere eversion is a form of mathematical entertainment that does not physically occur in any round object found in the real world, so too literal infinity—even in its mathematical forms—may present for some an interesting intellectual puzzle, but it does not accurately apply as a descriptor of features in the physical world.

If I am correct that literal infinity is not a feature of the real world, then it does not accurately apply as a descriptor for features such as space, time, and motion. This chapter will focus on literal infinity as applied to descriptions of space; I will show why space is not literally infinite in magnitude or extent and why space cannot be composed of portions literally infinite in quantity.

18.1 THE NATURE OF SPACE

I'll need to first make some distinctions about the nature of space itself. The term 'space' may mean different things, depending on context. These different meanings will become important as we analyze the infinitely great and small.

Without presenting a full philosophy of space, which would take a book in itself, I will briefly clarify the concept of 'space' [683]. One way to clarify the concept of space is to distinguish various kinds of space. Here is one schema I have found useful:

- *real space*: space as the separateness of objects for a single time. This is the space we experience as an empty medium between objects in the real world, the space without which there would be no distances to ascribe between objects.

- *apparent space*: space as the appearance of separateness between objects at a single time—i.e., the separateness between objects as it appears to a given observer's experience and/or measurement. This category of space includes both representations of real space that carry some degree of accuracy and representations of fictional spaces such as the space of make-believe places or of mathematical conceptions that are independent of reality. Representations of both real spaces and fictional spaces fall into three overlapping categories [684]:

  - *impressional space*: the separateness between objects as it appears according to an observer's experience. For example, there may appear to be a greater separation between any two objects according to one observer's perspective than according to another's; objects may appear closer for some observers than for others [685].

  - *indexical space*: the schema used for indexing the arrangement of objects relative to one another. For example, intervals of space we call distances, and they are divisible into locations, positions, and places (or 'spaces'). All of which are schema used for indexing the relationships between objects. Here/there, inside/outside, over/under, near/far are some other examples of space as indexes.

  - *schematic space*: the objective measurement schema for referencing the arrangement of objects relative to one another. Units of schematic space are based on the schemas of indexical space. For example, meters and yards are based on the concept of describing space with distance. Insofar as schematic space is applied for mapping real space, schematic space includes metric spaces, geometries, spatial dimensions, 'coordinate spaces' such as coordinates of longitude and latitude, 'vector spaces' such as mathematical plots of forces operating in real space, configuration space, state space, and so forth. Schematic space is 'space' as a type of measurement in mathematics and physics.

Insofar as an instance of apparent space (impressional, indexical, or schematic) is a representation of space as it is in the world, you can think of the apparent space as a map of real space. Real space and apparent space are therefore not mutually exclusive—real space and apparent space may in some circumstances be very different (a bad map) while in others they may be alike (a good map).

Apparent space does not accurately represent real space when distances between objects appear to be greater or lesser than they really are, which may in some circumstances be demonstrated if more accurate measurements are available. This is particularly true of impressional space.

The objective schemas of indexical and schematic space are meant to overcome the subjectivity of impressional space in order to better reveal space as it really is—the real space [686]. In some cases, the indexes and schemas are successful in differentiating reality from illusion, but not in all cases. The better our schemas, the more accurate our depiction of real space.

However, while some apparent spaces represent relationships between objects and properties in the real world, not all of the apparent spaces are literal depictions of space as it is in the real world. For example, some schematic spaces do not depict spatial relations between objects as we experience them with our senses. One example of a non-literal apparent space is *phase space*—a schematic space that is a graphical depiction of all the possible phases (states of motion) that a physical system may have. Phase space does not depict real space the way geometry describes a landscape.

Then too, mathematicians invent various multidimensional (ergo, schematic) spaces that may have no reference to reality. Some physicists regard eleven-dimensional 'string theories' of fundamental particles as mathematical fictions describing nothing that exists in reality; mere make-believe geometries [687]. Whether correct or not, the point is well taken: we are free to invent schematic spaces that do not actually exist.

Schematic spaces are examples of apparent spaces and, as such, they can be entirely illusory or they can depict the physical world accurately, or they can have some permutation in between.

Whenever I refer to 'lengths', 'magnitudes', 'portions', or other space-related terms, I will unless otherwise noted assume such to be schemas for describing relations between objects in real space—space as a real-world property independent of observation, but which can be measured in the apparent space units of mathematical schemas.

18.2 **ON INFINITE SPACE**

Many physicists and astronomers claim that space and time are infinite. For real space to be infinite in a literal sense, there would have to be a complete collection of locations that is limitless in quantity—an infinite number of locations that an object could occupy in any expanse of space.

But there is more than one way to measure space. We can measure an expanse of space as a line, as a plane, as a volume, etc. The use of geometry to measure space entails that if space is infinite, it may be:

- infinite in *extent* (for a line)
- infinite in *magnitude* (such as the size of a plane or volume)
- infinite in *portion* (for parts of a line, plane, or volume of space)

Let's take a look at each of these and examine the self-contradictions that ensue.

18.3 **INFINITE EXTENT**

If space is literally infinite, then in every direction there is a complete quantity of locations, and that quantity has no limit to the number of digits that would represent it. Take any point in space and imagine a set of straight lines intersecting at that point from all directions. If space is to be literally infinite, then for any one of those lines extending through space, the line must extend *limitlessly* outward from that point like the spoke of a wheel, and it must be a complete line, not an incomplete line that grows lengthier as it extends from the point of intersection. In terms of limitlessness, there must be no upper bound, no end, to the length of the straight line [688]. However, the limitlessness of the line contradicts its completeness. For if the line is to be a *complete* line, then it must have a measurable end; otherwise, it does not form a whole or total [689]. No end and yet an end: clearly, another contradiction.

To safely ignore the logical contradiction of an infinite line having no end and yet having an end for the sake of calculation, mathematicians treat infinite lines according to two different geometries. In ordinary Euclidean geometry, straight lines are just that—straight lines. They have no slope or gradient to them. If two lines are parallel with one another, they would therefore remain the same distance apart no matter how far they extend. To say that they are infinitely long is to say they are 'limitless' and so never meet. However, in projective geometry, lines can have a slope or gradient that, over vast distances, bends their extension. Any pair of lines may eventually intersect, including lines that are parallel in Euclidean geometry. In projective geometry, all lines eventually meet at what is called a 'point at infinity'.

Projective geometry therefore treats infinite lines as complete lines. This is unlike Euclidean geometry which sidesteps completeness in favor of treating lines as indefinite extensions that are never *completely* extended. That is, Euclidean geometry *operationally* treats 'limitlessness' in a figurative sense of always being able to be further extended—in other words, as simply an *incomplete indefinite*. So, whereas lines in projective geometry are complete, lines in Euclidean geometry are incomplete. In Euclidean geometry (operationally speaking anyway), if we deal with complete one-dimensional objects at all, we deal with them as only "segments" of longer, but incomplete, lines.

As an aside, there is a difference between how Euclid represented lines in his mathematics and what he thought those representations implied. As noted back in § 8.1.5, many mathematicians think the figurative infinity of Euclid's mathematical operations means Euclid thought infinity is only figurative (or "potential" in Aristotle's lingo). My take on Euclid is different. I interpret Euclid as regarding the figurative infinity of his mathematical operations as implying literal infinity. It's simply that the operations of his geometry did not deal *directly* with literal completeness and literal limitlessness together at once. Instead, he intended his geometry to *indirectly* suggest the existence of literally infinite extensions of space [690]. His mathematics treated infinity figuratively because he knew of no way to mathematically express literal infinity in a consistent manner. But that does not mean he didn't think figurative infinity pointed to literal infinity. Euclid's construction of incomplete indefinite lines was meant to suggest that literally infinite lines exist to be approximated by those constructions.

Like Euclidean geometry, projective geometry operationally treats 'limitlessness' in a figurative sense. In practice, we can only construct lines "infinitely long" in a figurative sense because they are only *indefinitely long* in reality. However, whereas Euclidean geometry operates with incomplete indefinite lines referred to as "infinite," projective geometry is based on *completed indefinite* lines also referred to as "infinite."

Projective geometry *must* treat the apparent limitlessness of parallel lines as only figuratively "limitless" because otherwise the limitlessness of the lines would mean the parallel lines both never end and *never meet*, as is the case with parallel lines in Euclidean geometry, rather than be completed extensions intersecting upon a point at infinity. So, when projective geometry makes reference to a point at infinity, the "infinity" it refers to is metaphorical for what is literally a completed indefinite in terms of mathematical operation.

It is therefore precisely because the operations of each geometry—Euclidean and projective—assume figurative notions either for both limitlessness and completeness (Euclidean geometry) or simply for limitlessness (projective geometry), and thereby abstract away half the logical implications of literal infinity, that the math for each geometry remains internally consistent in terms of syntactical rules. Now it may be true that projective geometry is often regarded as an "extension" of Euclidean geometry (i.e., a set of additional rules to Euclidean geometry), but in practice that means mathematicians are able to treat each geometry according to separate criteria for infinite lines, thus avoiding the inconvenient logical implications that a literally infinite line is limitless and so has no end at all (when limitlessness is interpreted literally in Euclidean geometry) while also being complete and therefore having an end (as implied by projective geometry).

And yet, despite the mathematical coherence of each geometry, the logic of infinity remains inconsistent because the intended *meaning* of infinity, when assumed according to its literal sense, still implies the contradictions between limitlessness and completeness. Needless to say, if use of these geometries cannot deal with literal infinity in its full meaning and in a logically consistent way, their uses of infinity cannot be applied to real space without contradiction.

18.4 INFINITE MAGNITUDE

There are two claims frequently made about infinite magnitudes: first, that it is possible for a geometrical object to be infinitely large; second, that the Universe is infinitely large. Of course, the Universe can be described geometrically and if the Universe is an object—and the Universe certainly fits our earlier definition of 'object'—then it follows that if a geometrical object can be infinitely large, so can the Universe be infinitely large.

18.4.1 *Spaces Don't Add Up to Infinity*

As to whether the Universe can be infinitely large, we must consider if there can be a coherent concept of infinite space. Albert Einstein once proposed an informal explication of infinite space [691]:

> What do we wish to express when we say that our space is infinite? Nothing more than that we might lay any number of bodies of equal sizes side by side without ever filling space. Suppose that we are provided with a great many cubic boxes all of the same size. In accordance with Euclidean geometry we can place them above, beside, and behind one another so as to fill an arbitrarily large part of space; but this construction would never be finished; we could go on adding more and more cubes without ever finding that there was no more room. That is what we wish to express when we say that space is infinite.

University of Warwick mathematician Ian Stewart has a similar, informal definition for infinity: "When something is infinite, there is always some spare room around to put things in" [692].

These characterizations of infinite magnitudes of space take the approach of Euclid's 'method of exhaustion' in that they use figurative infinity to illustrate literal infinity. Einstein spoke of a process of filling up space with cubes, starting with some finite amount (albeit, "a great many") and from there adding more. Einstein also said the process of filling space with cubes, even if continued without end, is never complete; he proposed we imagine ceaselessly "adding more and more cubes without ever finding that there was no more room." However, a ceaseless process, because it is never completed, is not a literally infinite process; no matter how many times we continue adding more cubes, we have only added a finite number of cubes to a finite number of cubes—an *indefinite* process, not a literally *infinite* process. At best, the process is only figuratively infinite. On the other hand, Einstein also stated that there is always more room to be filled. That implies he was thinking of empty space as literally infinite—a complete and limitless magnitude incessantly waiting to be filled with cubes from indefinite iterations of cube additions. This is also the implication of Stewart's remark that infinite space means "there is always some spare room around to put things in." Einstein and Stewart were attempting to illustrate a literally infinite magnitude of space as the implication of an incomplete, indefinite process (a figurative infinity) of filling space with objects.

While a process of indefinite construction is not problematic, the concept of a literally infinite space waiting to be filled like an infinite muffin tin waiting to be filled with an inexhaustible supply of muffins *is* problematic. A spatial magnitude that has a complete quantity of places to be filled implies a *totality* of places and therefore a *total* of places to be filled, while a spatial magnitude that is limitless implies *no totality* and so *no total* at all to the quantity of places needing filled. Such semantic contradictions therefore remain implied by the concept of literally infinite spatial magnitudes.

And yet, Einstein and Stewart proposed a concept of empty space that is certainly not gibberish. We understand what it means to keep adding cubes side by side and not run out of room. True enough, but being able to do so would not necessarily make space literally infinite. There is another way we can make the concept of ceaselessly filling space with cubes intelligible without space being literally infinite.

One option would be to propose that the Universe can grow larger so as to include more of Einstein's cubes, however many we wish to posit. And yet, however large space becomes, it would remain always finite at each step of the way, yet continuously able to accommodate the inclusion of ever more cubes.

So, if we interpret the claim "there is always some spare room around to put things in" (Stewart) or the claim "we could go on adding more and more cubes without ever finding that there was no more room" (Einstein) in terms of indefinitely growing more space to hold more things, then the idea of being able to ceaselessly construct ever-larger magnitudes of cubes loses the self-contradictory implications it would otherwise have by supposing empty space is literally infinite. Unlike literally infinite space, indefinitely expanding space is not logically problematic in terms of holding ever larger quantities.

This is not to say space does, in fact, grow larger on cosmic scales, though that is indeed the currently prevailing theory in the scientific community to account for certain astronomical observations. Rather, it is just to say there is no logical problem with the concept of increasing magnitudes of space holding ever larger quantities of objects. Whether space really is expanding, whether it does so ceaselessly, and whether space has an "edge" or "boundary", are separate issues I will return to in §§ 21.4.1–21.4.2. For now, I only wish to point out that there is nothing *logically* wrong with conceiving physical space to be an indefinitely growing expanse that makes the Universe larger over time.

However, space that remains finite while growing indefinitely larger is one thing, but literally infinite space, on the other hand, remains a logically problematic concept because completeness and limitlessness contradict one another. As further evidence of this claim, we also find logical problems with the concept of infinite space if we try to conceive of infinitely large shapes.

18.4.2 *On Infinitely Large Shapes*

Suppose we have a circle that is finite in size and then we balloon it up to infinite proportions. As we expand the circle to infinity, the curve of the circle becomes increasingly further away from the center until the radius of the circle is infinitely long, with the circumference of the circle becoming located "at infinity" from the center. The curvature of the circle thus drops to zero, becoming a straight line as in **Figure 18.2** [693].

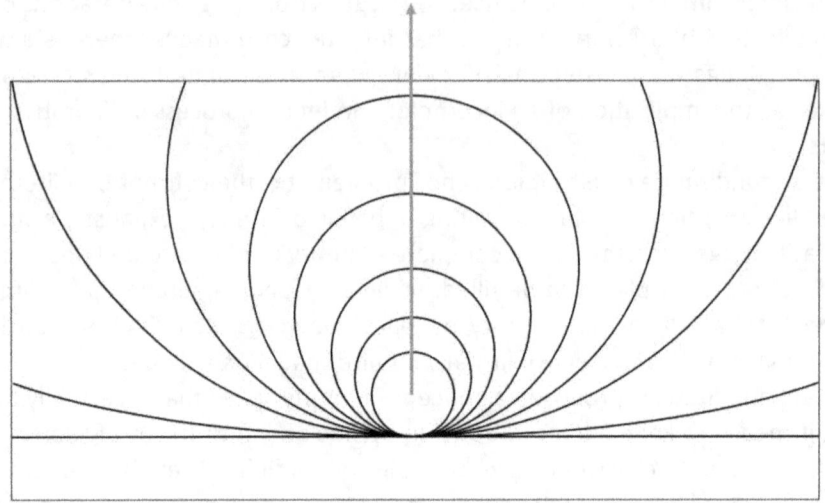

Figure 18.2: As the radius of the circle increases, the curvature of the circle straightens out from a given viewpoint on the circumference until the curve of the circle appears straight—a circle of "infinite radius."

But now we have a conceptual problem: it's one thing for a large, finite object like the Earth to appear flat for those standing on its surface—it can appear flat from the ground because the Earth is not a perfectly smooth sphere and any portion of it is not a flat surface that goes on without limit. It's quite another thing for a circle to be made infinite because the curve of the circle has become a straight, infinite line, which it cannot be since the circumference is a curve that loops back on itself. We have both an affirmation of the circle's curvature in a finite shape (it's a closed loop) and a denial of the curvature—the line forming the circle is straight and goes on without limit. An infinitely large object such as an infinitely large circle becomes a contradiction in terms. Its circumference becomes, relative to the center of the circle, a straight boundary that never ends in either direction along the curve; but that boundary cannot truly be straight and endless on the largest scale; otherwise, the shape would not be a circle.

With the use of differential geometry and projective geometry, mathematicians can avoid this logical contradiction by treating a circle as a flexible surface that can be made straight as it 'infinitely' grows, or by positing the curvature of the circle to be 'infinitely' small when the circle itself is 'infinitely' large. But neither of these geometric solutions addresses the concept of a literally infinite circle. Instead, the projective and differential geometries simply use 'infinity' in the figurative sense of *indefiniteness* to avoid the logical problems involved with a literally infinite circle. Once it is pointed out that the 'infinity' of the infinite circle in differential geometry and projective geometry is not really literal infinity as it is often assumed to be, the logical problems inherent in the concept of a shape of literally infinite magnitude reappear.

18.5 INFINITE PORTION

Any magnitude of space is mathematically divisible into smaller portions, which can also be divided into smaller portions, which can be divided into smaller portions, and so forth. The question arises: is there a smallest unit of space or is space divisible into ever smaller portions, and, if so, in what sense is it so divisible?

18.5.1 *Dimensions as Divisions of Space*

When we talk of dividing space into smaller units, we are making assumptions about space that have to do with concepts like 'dimension' and 'point'. Up to now, I have been using these terms as intuitively understood according to common parlance. Now it's time to be a little more exact.

Although the concept of dimension has also been applied as a mathematical tool to measure phenomena that are not space but are features of objects *in* space such as mass, temperature, luminosity, etc., we will be primarily concerned with dimension as a measure *of* space or the space that something occupies [694]. Definition:

- dimension: *extent in coordinates.*

Extent is a measure of difference in quantitative values. Coordinates are a set of unique numbers for measuring space. When we measure "a space," we are measuring only a portion *of* space per se with a set of unique numbers to specify an extent of space. Similarly, when we measure the space an object occupies, we use the set of unique numbers to specify the 'extent' of space so occupied—either the amount of space the object occupies (and doesn't occupy) or its location in space (where it is and where it is not according to the coordinates).

Because a dimension is an "extent in coordinates," and coordinates are measures for space, the concept of dimension is inherently spatial—dimension is about assigning a portion of space with a number of extents in coordinates. The number of dimensions a space has is determined by the minimal number of coordinates needed to specify spatial extent—either the extent(s) of space occupied by an object or the extent(s) of space at which an object is located.

For example, a *volume* is a portion of space in three dimensions (3D) since three coordinates (e.g., numbers assigning values of length, width, and height/depth) are needed to specify the three extents of space occupied by the object or the three extents of space at which the object is located (along x, y, and z axes). A *plane* is a space of two dimensions (2D) since only two coordinates (e.g., numbers assigning length and width) are needed to specify the two extents of space occupied by the object (e.g., length and width) or the two extents of space at which it is located (e.g., x degrees longitude and y degrees latitude). A *line* has only one dimension (1D) since only one coordinate is needed to specify the extent of space occupied by the object or the extent of space at which it is located.

This mathematical division of space into 'dimensions' for the purpose of measurement raises an interesting problem. A volume is 3D, a plane is 2D, a line is 1D, but how many dimensions does a point have? Mathematicians typically treat a point as having no dimensions (0D) and so no spatial extent of its own but having only the property of location in space. Or is a 'point' of space an infinitely small volume, an infinitely small surface, an infinitely small segment of space?

18.5.2 *The Infinitely Small*

Mathematicians commonly hold the "smallest" unit of space is *infinitely* small. However, there is a bit of disagreement among mathematicians over what that means. Some mathematicians say "infinitely small" just means we can keep dividing space into ever smaller portions toward some idealized limit. The word 'infinitely' in that sense is a reference to figurative infinity; the "infinitely small" is not genuinely without limit to its smallness, it just seems that way. Other mathematicians, however, believe that there are infinitely small units of space in the sense that such units of space are each in size equal to a finite portion of space that has been divided a complete and limitless quantity of times. Such units of space are called 'infinitesimal'—they are infinitely small in the sense that it takes a literal infinity of divisions to reach their size.

The English word 'infinitesimal' comes from the 17th-century Modern Latin words *infinitesimus* and *infinitesima* [695]. The word 'infinitesimus' referred to infinite ordinality: the 'infinitieth' item in a sequence [696]. The word 'infinitesima' was introduced in 1668 by Wallis [697] to indicate an infinitely small quantity: $1/\infty$. But the adjective 'infinitesimal' would also become a noun ("an infinitesimal" or "the infinitesimal") referring to an infinitely small size or an infinitely small portion of space. A mathematical line is sometimes described as composed of infinitesimals. In what is called the *standard analysis* version of calculus, the concept of convergence toward a 'limit' replaces use of infinitesimals, but in the version of calculus called *non-standard analysis* infinitesimals are still used [698].

There is some contention among mathematicians over what place talk of infinitesimals has and should have in modern mathematics. According to John Allen Paulos, professor of mathematics at Temple University [699],

> No one talks of infinitesimals anymore: The modern notion of limits accomplishes everything they did, but much more rigorously. One exception is a recent reconstruction of infinitesimals — positive "numbers" smaller than every real number — devised by the logician Abraham Robinson and developed further by H. Jerome Keisler, my adviser at the University of Wisconsin.

Perhaps talk of infinitesimals among mathematicians is uncommon these days, but it has not gone entirely out of style in the department of mathematics as Paulos suggests. There are mathematicians making use of infinitesimals, such as mathematicians Joel A. Tropp, James M. Henle, Eugene M. Kleinberg, John L. Bell, Thayer Watkins, Rebecca Vinsonhaler, and others [700]. So, the term 'infinitesimal' is still being used in mathematics.

In fact, mathematicians largely agree that Robinson's 1966 book *Non-standard Analysis* made infinitesimals into a syntactically consistent concept in the formal language of calculus [701]. Then too, the term 'infinitesimal' still appears in engineering, the sciences, and the philosophy of mathematics [702]. Regardless of its mathematical unpopularity in calculus, I can't agree with Paulos that talk of infinitesimals is dead, even if it is on life support. Particularly because 'infinitesimal' is still in common parlance and a subject of philosophical debate (at least, as of this writing).

18.5.3 *Infinitesimals and Points*

There is another topic of dispute among mathematicians: some mathematicians hold that infinitesimals are equivalent to spatial *points* in a mathematical line segment; other mathematicians hold that points in a line segment have no size whatsoever (zero dimensions) rather than a size that is infinitely small. Exactly what counts as an "infinitesimal" and what counts as a mathematical "point" are topics still in some dispute.

Points of space are sometimes described as 'infinitesimal', such as when a mathematical line segment is described as "a string of infinitesimals—of tiny, or infinitely small, points" [703]. However, spatial points in a line segment are not *necessarily* infinitesimal. Some mathematicians believe that points of space are infinitely small; others, however, disagree that points are infinitesimal [704]. On the one hand, spatial points, like infinitesimals, are immeasurable in their smallness; on the other hand, being infinitesimal need not be the same as being a point of space.

An infinitesimal, as its name suggests, is typically conceived as an entity *near*-zero in size (having a size smaller than any real number—immeasurably small) but not equal to zero in size [705]. Infinitesimals are *infinitely small*—so small that a fraction expressing their size would have a denominator of limitless digits if such could be expressed. In contrast, most mathematicians conceive of spatial points as immeasurably small only because points have zero size—they have no volume at all to measure [706]. In the standard view, points are not infinitely small but are instead what I term 'afinite' in size—they have no size by virtue of lacking any finite extent. If infinitesimals are near-zero in size while points are zero in size, then infinitesimals and points are not the same thing. Mathematicians holding this view therefore say infinitesimals are not point-like [707].

Moreover, some mathematicians also say points differ from infinitesimals in terms of being *indivisible*—points cannot be further divided [708]:

> The concept of an *indivisible* is closely allied to, but to be distinguished from, that of an infinitesimal. An indivisible is, by definition, something that cannot be divided, which is usually understood to mean that it has no proper parts. Now a partless, or indivisible entity does not necessarily have to be infinitesimal...

An indivisible is not necessarily an infinitesimal, and an infinitesimal is not necessarily an indivisible. Some mathematicians conceive of infinitesimals as infinitely divisible even though they are already themselves infinitely small. In which case, infinitesimals are composed of ever-smaller infinitesimals.

However, not all mathematicians conceive of infinitesimals this way; some instead hold that infinitesimals are themselves indivisible entities. So, one conception of infinitesimals is that they are *indivisible* while another is that they are ever *infinitely divisible*. Whereas for points, the situation is different: if we conceive of points not to be infinitesimal but instead to be of zero size, then points cannot be divided at all—they are necessarily indivisible.

Not all mathematicians distinguish infinitesimals from points of space; in fact, they sometimes refer to "infinitesimal points" [709]. For many of these scholars, points may have zero dimensions in the sense of having no directions by which something can move about *within* them but having zero dimensions is different from being zero in size. Instead, they assert points to be infinitesimal in size—infinitely small—rather than size-less.

According to this alternative position, space can be conceptually divided into a matrix like Einstein's stack of cubes; so too, each cube, or any number of them, can be divided into infinitely many planes like a stack of paper in which each sheet is infinitely thin. Each of those planes can also be divided into infinitely many parallel lines, and each line can be divided into infinitely many points—each point being infinitesimal in size. According to this view, space thus contains infinitely many *infinitesimal points* [710].

Whether or not the term 'infinitesimal' applies to spatial points (as in, "infinitesimal points") or instead to infinitely small portions of space distinct from zero-magnitude points, many mathematicians still suppose space to be divisible into a literal infinity of portions—whether infinitesimals, infinitesimal points, or just infinitely many points. However, even though this infinite divisibility may be mathematically coherent if the term 'infinite' is taken in the figurative sense, I argue the concept of infinite divisibility still leads to logical contradictions when taken in the literal sense.

18.5.4 *Indefinitely Divisible Space*

To best capture the nature of the contradictions involved with the conception of space as being *infinitely* divisible in the literal sense, we will need to draw more explicitly upon the 'real space' and 'apparent space' distinctions. We need to consider whether 'points', 'infinitesimals', and the like refer to portions of real space or simply to portions of apparent space—mathematical entities that may have no reference to reality. Let's start with real space and its mathematical division into *indefinitely* smaller units.

There are two different ways to conceive of space divided into indefinitely smaller units:

1. Real space could be an expanse composed of a substratum of preexisting, minuscule (indefinitely small) parts that are themselves indivisible.

2. Real space could instead be an expanse that is an undivided whole, not composed of any preexisting parts at all, but an expanse that nevertheless can be mathematically divided into indefinitely many minuscule parts that are themselves further indefinitely divisible.

18.5.5 *Minuscules as Indivisibles*

According to some physics theories, real space has properties that differ according to scale. On the macroscopic scale of mass objects, real space is a continuous, seamless, and fluid expanse—apparently without structure, breaks, or gaps. Zoom down in size and the microscopic scale appears no different. But on the *submicroscopic* scale (that is, on a scale well below what we can directly observe or detect with microscopes of any construction), real space is composed of discrete elements, as if space were made of fine-grained sand or perhaps a foam. Another way of putting it is that according to such theories, real space on the smallest of submicroscopic scales is composed of distinct, fundamental parts rather like atoms of space; with each fundamental part of real space as a distinct being [711]. Space, in this view, is structured emptiness—a void describable only by exotic geometries.

Some physicists refer to these "atoms of space" as *hodons* [712]. The theorists who believe real space is composed of hodons typically regard the hodons to be equal in size to the smallest scale of detectable energy exchange. Some quantum physicists propose the smallest extent of real space over which mass or energy could have any measurable physical effects on the motion of objects through real space would be no smaller than a *Planck length*, named after physicist Max Planck (1858–1947). The Planck length, denoted ℓ_P, is a unit of length approximately 10^{-35} meters (or about 10^{-20} the size of a proton) [713]. So, when theorists propose hodons to be units of real space, they tend to propose hodons to be units of space no larger in diameter than one Plank length [714].

The Planck scale is spectacularly small when compared to scales we are used to, but nevertheless large when compared to a 'minuscule' unit of real space, which, if such exists, would be *indefinitely* small. In which case, if space is comprised of hodons as "atoms of space," then hodons could be even smaller than the Planck length—they could be indefinitely small units of real space rather than units of space on the Planck scale. In which case, hodons would not be simply the smallest units of distance by which an in-practice *detectable* exchange of energy takes place, but rather the smallest distances over which motion occurs that is only detectible in principle rather than in scientific practice.

To avoid confusing hodons as Planck-length units of real space with the idea of hodons as units of space that are indefinitely small, I propose a change in vocabulary. I will sidestep references to hodons altogether and instead refer to an indefinitely small unit of space, *whether real or schematic*, as a 'minuscule' (noun).

A minuscule is not an ideal mathematical point, but it is point-like in the sense that it is so small we can only say a minuscule is off any scale of measurement we can practically devise (**Figure 18.3**). A minuscule is smaller even than that which is literally 'minute' (see § 6.4.1). Nevertheless, minuscules are neither infinitesimal (infinitely small) nor zero in size because we could in principle define its finite size exactly even if we cannot do so in practice.

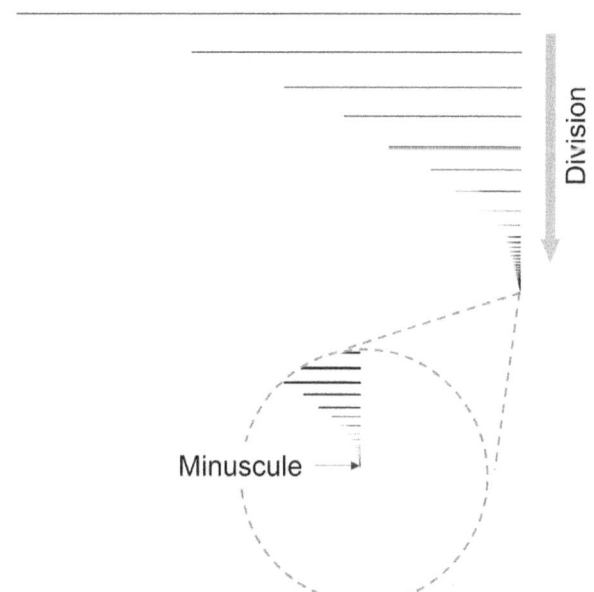

Figure 18.3: In one conception of 'indefinitely divisible' space, any portion of space, such as the line segment at top, is divisible down to the level of a *minuscule*—a fundamental unit of space that is indefinitely small (finite but off any known scale), symbolically represented by the smallest dot in this figure.

According to the first sense of the 'indefinite divisibility' of space then, space is 'indefinitely divisible' in the sense that it would take an immense (indefinitely large) number of divisions to reach the scale of minuscules, while each minuscule of space is indefinitely small *but not further divisible*. If this view of the structure of space were accurate, then minuscules of space would be *indivisibles*—fundamental spatial volumes, each of which is from our macro-scale perspective indefinitely small but not without volume.

What the first sense of 'indefinitely divisible space' implies is that space is divisible only down to the level of a minuscule—an indefinitely small unit that is itself indivisible, even in principle. What we would call 'minuscules' would therefore be both fundamental units of indexical or schematic space (there are no non-contradictory conceptions of units of measurement smaller than a minuscule) *and* fundamental elements of real space (nothing can physically be *smaller* than a minuscule, but there are minuscule units of real space). The concept of minuscules, if proposed as fundamental scale elements for indexical or schematic space, would therefore serve not only serve as ideal limits of smallness for all conceptual *measurements of* real space but also imply the existence of corresponding indivisibles, or "atomic units," of real space.

To put it another way, suppose it's not only the case that we can in principle mathematically divide an extent of space down to abstract minuscules but that there are also "atoms" of real space that are themselves minuscule in size. In that case, the minuscules of mathematical measurement would correspond to the physical minuscules comprising real space [715]. The upshot of proposing minuscules as indivisibles of measurement is that, if real space is divisible down to the level of minuscules as fundamental elements of real space, then minuscules of real space would have to preexist any measurements of them which describe real space in terms of corresponding mathematical units.

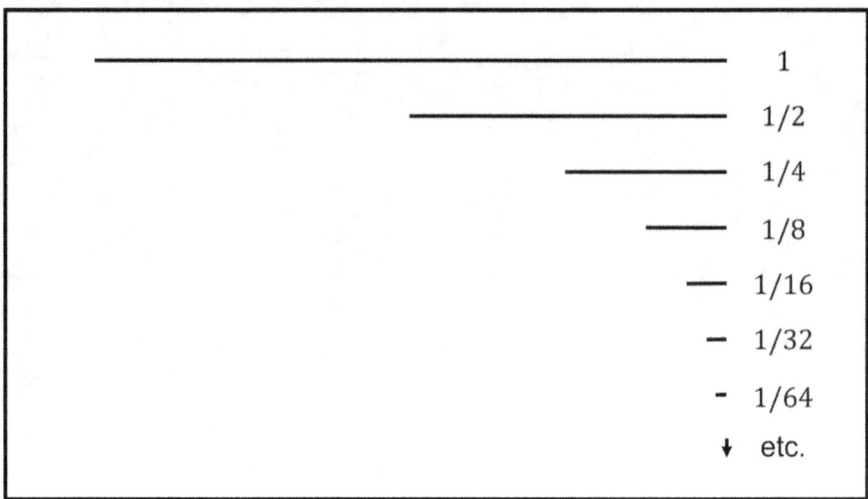

Figure 18.4: In another conception of 'indefinitely divisible' space, any portion of space, such as this line segment, is indefinitely divisible in the sense that there is no fundamental level. Moreover, no parts of space preexist division, and any parts made in the division process, however minuscule, are always further divisible. In this conception, even 'minuscules' are divisible into even more minuscule units.

18.5.6 *Minuscules as Indefinitely-divisibles*

In the second sense of the 'indefinite divisibility' of space, the term 'space' may also refer either to real space or to indexical/schematic space. It makes no difference since the process of measurement that is used for conceptually dividing space into units has the same implications. In this sense of indefinite divisibility, space does *not* have properties that differ according to scale. Instead, space is on *all* scales a seamless and fluid expanse—entirely without preexisting structure, parts, breaks, or gaps. Apart from any mathematical divisions we may conceive or imagine for space, space is instead between any two objects an unbroken separateness. But we can use objects to set standards by which we may measure space with 'distances' and we can divide those distances ever smaller. Space is thus only 'divided' into parts or portions in the sense of a mathematical description during a measurement or schematizing process. Space in this conception is an *undivided but divisible unity*.

Indefinitely divisible space, according to the second sense of the term, is space that no matter how often divided never ends with fundamental units—there are no indivisible minuscules that constitute either fundamental units of measurement or "atoms" of real space. Instead, any minuscule length can be further divided into smaller lengths that are also divisible into yet smaller lengths (see **Figure 18.4**). Indefinitely divisible space is space that is, at least in principle, capable of being ceaselessly divided, including indefinitely dividing minuscule units of space into ever smaller minuscule units.

18.5.7 *Minuscule Alternatives*

We therefore have two different senses of what it means for space to be 'indefinitely divisible'. On the one hand, 'indefinitely divisible space' could mean the ability to *completely* divide space down to fundamental, indivisible 'minuscules'. On the other hand, 'indefinitely divisible space' could mean the ability to, at least in principle, ceaselessly divide any length of space down toward no fundamental level—the division process is always *incomplete*, in which case minuscules would not be indivisible after all.

Whether or not space is indefinitely divisible, and in which of these two senses it would be so, is a topic I will save for another book [716]. For now, I bring up the conceptions of indefinitely divisible space only to draw a distinction between the *indefinite* divisibility of space and the *infinite* divisibility of space, the latter of which we will examine next.

18.5.8 *The Continuum of Infinitely Divisible Space*

Mathematicians commonly hold that schematic space is infinitely divisible because space is a *continuum*. And physicists sometimes claim the same about real space. However, we must be a little careful with the term 'continuum' because time is sometimes described as a continuum as well, and the word 'continuum' also applies to concepts that are not necessarily spatial or temporal. Here are two definitions of 'continuum', the first of which applies to measures of space or time, the second of which may be applied to measures of space or time, but not necessarily:

- continuum:
  (1) *a sequence of elements in which adjacent or immediate elements vary by indistinguishable amounts.*
  (2) *a set of self-similar elements such that an intermediate element separates any pairing of elements.*

When mathematicians say schematic space is a continuum, or physicists say real space is a continuum, they both mean that space is not only a continuum by the first definition but also by the second definition. Since it's the mathematical concept of a continuum (in either pure mathematics or physics) I wish to address, I will use the term 'continuum' according to the second definition—i.e., a 'dense' continuum—unless otherwise specified or obvious from context.

But once again, we must be careful with even the definition of a continuum because of another slippery term: element. Recall that an 'element' is defined as "a divisible, but undivided, distinct object," but also as noted in § 2.2.2 some scholars use 'element' in a different sense to mean instead "an indivisible, distinct object." A spatial point of zero size would be an example of an element by the latter definition, whereas infinitesimals are typically taken to be elements by the former definition.

In terms of a (dense) continuum, mathematicians commonly regard elements to be *divisible* but undivided. This has two meanings.

First, real numbers are elements in a continuum in the sense that the real numbers are undivided from one another in the number line while any adjacent real numbers we identify can be 'divided' (separated) by the inclusion of another real number of intermediate value between them. So too, any two infinitesimals in a geometric line initially regarded as adjacent to each other may be 'divided' (also in the sense of conceptually separated) when another infinitesimal is identified as the space between them.

Second, each real number other than zero, no matter how small in value, is itself mathematically divisible into real numbers of yet smaller value. Likewise, infinitesimals in a geometric line are sometimes conceived to be further divisible into yet more infinitesimal infinitesimals.

In contrast to infinitesimals, some philosophers of mathematics consider points to be indivisible. As philosopher John Bell notes [717]:

> ...a continuum entails that each of its (connected) parts is also a continuum, and, accordingly, divisible. Since points are indivisible, it follows that no point can be part of a continuum. Infinitesimal magnitudes, as parts of continua, cannot, of necessity, be points: they are, in a word, *nonpunctiform*.

This conception of a geometrical continuum rejects the idea that points are infinitesimal; instead, points have no volume at all, not an infinitely small volume. Regardless of whether we call such infinitesimals "points" or not, if space is a continuum of elements that are infinitesimals, and infinitesimals are divisible into further infinitely small infinitesimals, then the continuum of space is infinitely divisible into ever more infinitesimal elements.

However, we now have another distinction that needs to be made: in what sense is a continuum of space 'infinitely divisible'? Bell attempts to elaborate [718]:

> While it is the fundamental nature of a continuum to be *undivided*, it is nevertheless generally (although not invariably) held that any continuum admits of repeated or successive *division without limit*. This means that the process of dividing it into ever smaller parts will never terminate in an *indivisible* or an *atom*—that is, a part which, lacking proper parts itself, cannot be further divided. In a word, continua are *divisible without limit* or *infinitely divisible.*

Even this description needs further clarification: is the infinite divisibility only figuratively "without limit" or is it literally without limit and yet completely divisible? That is, is the divisibility of space only *figuratively infinite* or is it *literally infinite*?

If space is "infinitely divisible" in only a figurative sense, then that would be no different from space being a featureless separateness (between objects of a given kind), *indefinitely* divisible according to the second sense of 'indefinitely divisible', as illustrated in **Figure 18.4**. If that is so, then the mathematical division of real space is simply the creation or invention of further units of mathematical measurement (apparent space) applied to real space like lines of longitude and latitude are applied to measure a planet. In which case, when physicists speak of space as a "continuum," the space they speak of is apparent space as it is used to measure real space. That is, the continuum is itself an invention, not an independently existing feature of reality. Real space is only 'dense' with points in the sense that between any two points—mere invented divisions projected onto real space—we can always create another point by which to draw distinctions in space. So this concept of 'denseness' for the spatial continuum is actually an indefinite process of creating, or inventing, ever finer mathematical distinctions of what is ontologically simple and featureless—otherwise not comprised of any preexisting units. In which case, the so-called "infinite divisibility" of space is a misleading way of speaking because the 'infinity' referenced is merely figurative for an indefinite process of mathematical division carried out by the mathematician or physicist.

If on the other hand space is "infinitely divisible" in a literal sense, then the elements of the dense continuum of space would be "already there," waiting to be *discovered* as the mathematician or physicist uses a mathematical operation to map the continuum of real space. The process of mathematically dividing space into smaller units therefore would have the potential to reach a literal infinity of infinitely small units—infinitesimals—comprising any finite expanse of space we choose to divide without limit [719].

Note that infinite divisibility in the literal sense does not necessarily entail that we must reach a set of infinitesimals that are themselves indivisible. According to the common mathematical conception of (literally) infinite divisibility, there could be units of space infinitely smaller than other units of space that are already infinitely small—infinitesimals infinitely smaller than other infinitesimals. A sequence of increasingly smaller infinitesimals would be the counterpart in scale to Cantor's series of increasingly larger infinities. If we were to divide down to an infinitesimally small level, there would be achieved a literally infinite set of infinitesimals, but there could be infinitely many smaller levels of infinitesimals below those as well.

The idea of infinitesimals composed of smaller infinitesimals is consistent with the conception of space as a continuum (second definition). So, the idea that space is a continuum is not directly contradicted by the proposal that the divisibility of that continuum is literally infinite. Even so, there are still logical problems with the concept of infinitesimals.

For example, suppose we abstract from real space a one-dimensional line segment sequentially divided into sets of evenly divided line segments in which each segment is half the length of its predecessor. Suppose the sequence of divisions in this line mathematically progresses down to infinitesimal segments. The resulting line segment would then be composed of a literal infinity of units that are all the same infinitesimal size.

This is symbolized in **Figure 18.5**. The line segment at the top of **Figure 18.5** is diced into increasingly smaller line segments of equal size over a literally infinite sequence of divisions. A thickness (or height) is added to the line segment, and to the subsequent divisions of the line segment proceeding top to bottom, in order to make each set of divisions easily visible as the division process proceeds. Gaps between subsequent line segments are also added in the image as exaggerations to show where the successive divisions in prior segments take place.

In mathematical operation, line segments would have no thickness and the divisions of a line segment would not establish gaps in the line segment because the line segment is proposed to be a continuum (second definition)—anywhere you slice creates a separation between which there is always more to slice. For the line segment to be continuous when infinitely divided, the infinitesimals comprising the line segment must also be 'dense' and 'touch' one another (so, unlike the exaggeration shown in **Figure 18.5**, there must also be no gaps between infinitesimals).

All of this is seemingly straightforward but there is, nevertheless, a logical problem.

If the process of dividing the line into infinitesimals is completed, then there must have been preexisting in the line a literal infinitude of parts there to be found. The division process results in infinitesimals only because the infinitesimal parts we divided the line segment into are *already there* in the line segment waiting to be found, "embedded in the architecture of the whole: division merely separates or unveils them, it does not create them anew. The whole continuant is thus an aggregate: a composite of so many distinct parts, so many independent beings" [720]. The infinitesimal parts are aggregates composing the line segment as a compound whole, as symbolized in **Figure 18.5** [721].

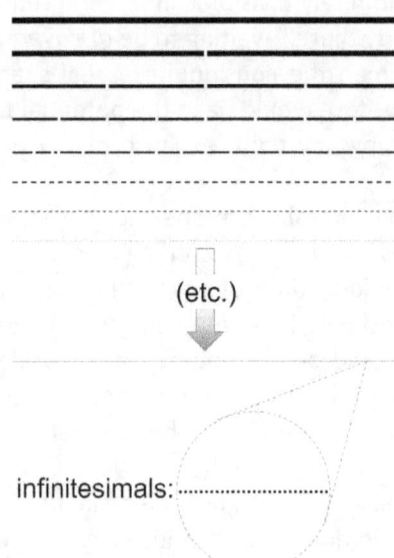

(etc.)

infinitesimals:

Figure 18.5: A line segment divided down into infinitesimals. Proportions of line segments (thickness of the lines and separations of line segments) are exaggerated for visibility.

This presents a logical problem because, supposing we have divided our line segment in **Figure 18.5** down to the level of infinitesimals, each infinitesimal part is the same size as all the other infinitesimals in the line and there are *limitlessly* many of them. The problem is that because the infinitesimals are arranged *next to* each other, comprising the line segment like pearls in a string, and each is the same size, the *limitlessness* of their number implies the line segment must actually not be finite at all as depicted in **Figure 18.5** but instead infinitely long.

As the philosopher David Hume (1711–1776) pointed out, an infinite number of same-sized parts, even if those parts are infinitely small, still logically entails an infinitely large collection due to the limitlessness of the quantity of parts [722]. However, the line segment we started with is not infinitely long; it is finite. We therefore have a contradiction: dividing a finite line segment a literally infinite number of times results should result in a finite line segment composed of infinitely many infinitesimals, and yet any line segment composed of infinitely many infinitesimals must be an infinite line and not a finite line by virtue of the limitlessness of the same-sized partitions.

One way around this contradiction is to propose that the infinitesimals, precisely because they are infinitely *small*, need not aggregate into an infinite length, but instead can compose a finite length. However, this does not take the *limitlessness* in the quantity of their aggregation seriously. Even if they are infinitely small, because they are all the same size the lack of *any* limit to their quantity means they must form an infinite length. Infinite smallness does not cancel out the limitlessness of the line formed by aggregation. Hume's refutation to infinitesimals still holds.

Another objection might be that the line segment is not actually composed of infinitesimals. Instead, perhaps the line segment begins as an undivided whole in which there are no preexisting parts just as there are no preexisting slices in a bowl of gelatin. The parts we divide the line into are created, or distinguished, in the division process. Infinitesimals are only ideal parts and not real parts—we never reach an infinitesimal in the division process. This objection was raised by the late philosopher Antony Flew (1923–2010) [723]. According to Flew, "[To] say that something may be divided *in infinitum* is not to say that it can be divided into an infinite number of parts. It is rather to say that it can be divided, and sub-divided, and sub-divided as often as anyone wishes: infinity, without limit" [724].

Flew's objection, however, is problematic because it confuses literal infinity with figurative infinity, which is the same as indefiniteness of process. That is, Flew's objection takes "infinite divisibility" to be a figure of speech for *indefinite divisibility* and "infinity, without limit" to be a figure of speech for *incomplete indefiniteness*, as explicated in **Figure 18.4**. Certainly, *indefinite* divisibility is not logically problematic because the division process and the lengths so divided remain finite at each step of the way, but that is beside the point—an incomplete indefinite is not literal infinity and so it is not correct to confuse it with literal infinity. To misidentify the indefinite as the infinite results in ignoring the real issue, which is whether the *infinite* division of space—that is, the process of dividing space down to infinitely small parts, or infinitesimals—is or is not a coherent concept. The issue is not whether space can be divided in only the figurative sense of 'infinity'. Flew's objection makes the false assumption that everyone uses the term 'infinity' in a figurative sense only and engages in the red herring of avoiding the issue about literal infinity's coherence. His objection therefore does not get around the apparent lack of logical coherence in the concept of infinitesimals when we take the notion of infinitely small portions literally instead of figuratively.

A final objection might be to propose that infinitesimals are variable in size instead of constant in size. As philosopher Thomas Holden remarked, "Certainly something that consists of an infinite number of *same-sized* parts will be infinitely large. But if those parts are of proportionally diminishing size, then the whole need not be infinite in size" [725]. The proposal of *diminishingly* small parts makes "infinitesimals" out to be a metaphor for minuscules that continue shrinking indefinitely. However, construing a set of "infinitesimals" in a portion of space to be nothing more than a set of ceaselessly shrinking minuscules is not equivalent to construing the set of infinitesimals to be a complete and limitless set of actual parts making up a portion of space. So, the proposal that "infinitesimals" may be conceived as diminishing minuscules is another red herring since the issue is whether or not the concept of infinitely small portions makes literal sense, not just figurative sense as a metaphor for indefinite smallness or indefinitely shrinking minuscules.

The bottom line is that none of these objections overcome Hume's criticism of the *infinitely small* when such is construed in a literal sense. So far, the concept that space is a continuum composed of (literal) infinitesimals is not holding up to scrutiny. And it gets worse, for there are at least four more logical problems with the concept of infinitesimals—each of which results from a conflict between the completeness and limitlessness of literal infinity.

18.5.9 *Infinitesimals Can and Cannot Be Totaled*

One of these problems has to do with the quantity of infinitesimals composing a geometrical line. Calculus and various forms of mathematical analysis typically claim there to be infinitely many infinitesimals in a line. Mathematically, such a claim poses no problem because, operationally, mathematics simply treats the infinitesimal elements composing a line as an incomplete, indefinite collection under construction (a figurative infinity only) or, at best, a collective indefinite. In terms of syntactical operation and technical definitions, the math does not actually treat a line as a literal infinity (i.e., as complete and limitless). Any claim as to the literal infinity of a line is not found in the technical definitions or operations but is only implied or assumed in the semantics of what infinity means. So, there are no mathematical problems with "infinitely many" infinitesimals per se. However, there is nevertheless a logical problem for a literal infinity of infinitesimals composing a line due to the implications of the meaning of infinity in its literal sense.

Because the infinitesimals composing a line are said to be "infinitely many" in a literal sense, the implication is that the line has a complete and limitless quantity of infinitesimals. Because the line has a complete quantity of infinitesimals, there is a totality of infinitesimals—a total of them, that nevertheless cannot be totaled because the quantity of infinitesimals in a line is also limitless, which implies there can be no totality of infinitesimals, and so no total of them, not even a running total. We therefore have a contradiction.

18.5.10 *Mapping the Continuum of Reals to the Continuum of Infinitesimals*

Another problem with infinitesimals comprising a spatial line is that that the infinitesimals are claimed to form a continuum, which produces logical absurdities of its own. Transfinite mathematics claims the sequence of reals in $\mathbb{R}$ comprise a continuum of numbers. The real numbers in $\mathbb{R}$ can be made to correspond one-to-one with the infinitesimals (or sometimes 'infinitesimal points') composing a geometric line. The implication is that there are at least as many infinitesimals in a line as there are real numbers in the sequence of real numbers, with the infinitesimals forming a continuum like the reals [726].

Moreover, if we consider $\mathbb{R}$ to be a literally infinite set of real numbers, then such a set must contain infinitely many rationals, irrationals, integers, wholes, and naturals. Now let's consider the sequence of integers within $\mathbb{R}$. Next, let's select two successive integers. Between any two successive integers, such as 0 and 1, are infinitely many reals (rationals and irrationals) that fill in the 'gap' between the two integers. For example, between 0 and 1 are values such as 3/8 and 0.6 and infinitely many other values. The interval of reals between any two integers is a continuum, and any continuum of reals is a set of reals packed so densely with numbers that there are no gaps between them—there are infinitely many reals between any two reals, which entails the continuum of reals is perfectly smooth.

Suppose a geometric line represents the sequence of all reals in $\mathbb{R}$. Each infinitesimal in the line is matched with a single real number. **Figure 18.6** illustrates a bijection of the literal infinity of reals between 0 and 1 with the literal infinity of reals for the entire line of real numbers.

The integers (..., -3, -2, -1, 0, 1, 2, 3, ...) within $\mathbb{R}$ can be matched to corresponding infinitesimals comprising a geometric line. The geometric line therefore has a sequence of segments or intervals, with the ends of each segment matching a pair of integers. Since all the reals have a one-to-one correspondence with the infinitesimals on the geometric line, then just as there must be a continuum of infinitely many reals in the interval between any two integers, so too any segment of the geometric line must be a continuum containing infinitely many infinitesimals.

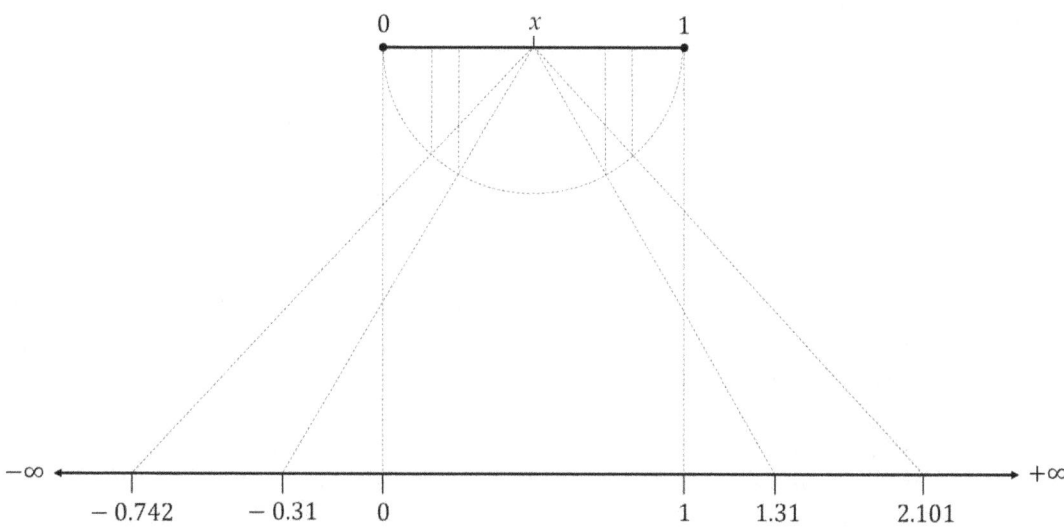

Figure 18.6: In the transfinite system there is said to be infinitely many more reals than integers or rationals. Using the midpoint of the 0–1 segment like the center of a protractor, it is presumed one can sweep rays outward from the midpoint along the number line of reals, pointing to infinitely many reals between each pair of integers or rationals on the line. If we assume each real number corresponds to an infinitesimal on the line, then this implies the 0–1 line segment has *just as many* infinitesimals corresponding to reals as does the whole number line.

As Rucker explained, Cantor used a figure like that in **Figure 18.6** to show there are many more reals than integers and rational numbers [727]. This idea is also said to apply to the set of infinitesimals, or 'infinitesimal points', comprising a geometrical line as each infinitesimal point corresponds to a real number plotted on that line. This means there must be infinitely many infinitesimals corresponding to those degrees of infinity—a continuum of infinitesimals.

However, the correspondence or reals with infinitesimals makes the infinitesimals subject to the same logical problem faced by assuming $\mathbb{R}$ is a complete and limitless (literally infinite) set. As $\mathbb{R}$ is an infinity larger than the literally infinite set of integers ($\mathbb{Z}$), so too the infinity of infinitesimals comprising a line must be larger than the literal infinity of infinitesimals corresponding to the integers associated with segments of that line. The idea of one infinity of infinitesimals larger than another takes us back around to the logical problem of one infinity of numbers (e.g., the reals) being larger than another (e.g., the integers, naturals, etc.)—neither infinity can be bigger or smaller than the other because both are not just complete but also *limitless* (i.e., without a last element, even in principle).

In order to dissolve the logical problem of different sized infinities which, by virtue of limitlessness cannot have different sizes, we have only to do some reinterpretation of what it means for a line to be partitioned and numbered:

- Reinterpret number scales like those of $\mathbb{R}$ and $\mathbb{Z}$ as incomplete, open series and for which new real numbers can be created between any two created real numbers,

- reinterpret geometric lines to be wholes without preexisting parts and for which parts are created in the division process (as in **Figure 18.4**); and then,

- reinterpret the correspondence of reals to places along a line as a process of *constructing* reals to associate with the divisions we *create* for the line as we continue the process of corresponding invented reals to invented places of division.

With this new interpretation, we replace the notion of a set of preexisting reals matched against a set of preexisting infinitesimals with a different notion: that of an indefinite process in which an incomplete, indefinite series of real numbers is generated and matched to an indefinite series of divisions that we create for the line as we continue the matching process. The process of making such reals, divisions, and their associations can perhaps persist indefinitely, but there is no preexisting, literally infinite set of reals, no literally infinite set of infinitesimals, and no bijection between complete and limitless sets of such entities.

Rejecting the infinitesimals and interpreting the geometric line as an invention rather than a discovery avoids the contradiction implied by one limitless set (reals or infinitesimals) larger than another limitless set (integers or integer-marked infinitesimals). Rejecting the assumption of literal infinity and conceptions of the infinitely small thus solves the logical problems raised by proposing there to be preexisting infinitesimals composing a line, such as the problem of how two limitless sets can have different sizes.

18.5.11 *Pairing Off Infinitesimal Points*

A third logical problem inherent in the concept of infinitesimals was identified by the Scottish Catholic priest and Franciscan friar John Duns (1266–1308), commonly known as Duns Scotus. According to Scotus, if we assume points are infinitely small rather than zero in size, then we end up with logical contradictions [728].

For example, suppose we have two concentric circles. As shown in **Figure 18.7**, we can use the radii of the two circles to pair off any point in the circumference of the inner circle with a point in the circumference of the outer circle. There is a one-to-one correspondence of points in the circumference of the inner circle with the points in the circumference of the outer circle. If we take points to be same-sized infinitesimals, then clearly each circle must have the same quantity, tit-for-tat, of 'infinitesimal points'. However, if each circle has the same quantity of infinitesimal points, then the two circumferences should be equal in size, which is not so since one circle is smaller than the other. We therefore must reject the concept that lines are composed of infinitesimal points [729].

However, followers of Cantor may object that there can be a different size of infinity for each of the circles [730]. However, that retort won't work because we just demonstrated a *one-to-one* correspondence between the circles.

Instead, a better solution is that lines are divisible, but undivided, wholes prior to any creation of 'points' in the lines for the measurement process. Points are merely conceptual in nature—inventions rather than discoveries—and so we can go on creating such 'points' *indefinitely* without any need to invoke the concept of infinity.

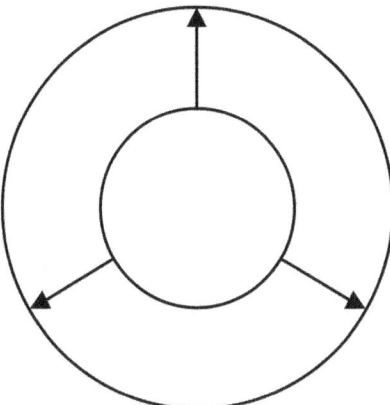

Figure 18.7: Concentric circles sharing a one-to-one correspondence of 'infinitesimal points' along their circumferences, and therefore sharing the same number of points, despite the circles being different sizes.

18.5.12 *Real Space without the Infinitesimal*

The logical problems implied by the concept of the infinitesimal, by something conceived to be infinitely small in a literal sense, show that the infinitesimal is not a logically coherent concept. The concept of something completely and limitlessly tiny turns out to imply self-contradictions and, in some cases, even mathematical contradictions [731]. Since logical contradictions cannot exist in the real world, real space cannot contain infinitesimals and mathematics is better off without their use as schemata.

Due to the logical incoherence of infinitesimals, we may consider space, if a continuum at all, to be so in one of two senses, depending on which type of space—real or apparent—we are considering:

- Apparent space may be a continuum in the sense that a continuum is an indexical schema constructed via a process: for any pair of elements, propose another element in between them. The elements don't all preexist as a completed set in this conception of a 'continuum' but are instead created as the continuum schema is constructed over a series of mappings. A continuum in this sense is 'indefinitely divisible' in the second sense of indefinite divisibility: there is no fundamental level of indivisibles.

- Real space may be a 'continuum' in the first sense of the term: "a sequence of elements in which adjacent elements vary by indistinguishable amounts" (§ 18.5.8). In this sense of continuum, real space may be indefinitely divisible in the first sense; that is, down to fundamental (finite) minuscules not further divisible. Or perhaps real space is a unity indefinitely divisible only in the second sense of indefinite divisibility—down to no fundamental entities at all.

Whichever space, real or apparent, we consider, space must be *indefinitely* divisible in one of the two senses of indefinite divisibility. What real space cannot be, is *infinitely* divisible—at least, not in the literal sense.

18.5.13 *Getting to the Point*

There is one last issue to consider concerning the infinitely small before we move on. It is sometimes said not that 'infinitesimals' make up a continuum of space, but instead that 'infinitesimal points' make up a continuum of space. On the contrary, infinitesimal points cannot make up a continuum of space for all the foregoing reasons I've argued concerning infinitesimals. In addition, points cannot be infinitesimal because points cannot aggregate to form an expanse or continuum.

To see why this must be so, consider that mathematicians propose 'infinitesimal points' to be indivisible (without parts). To grasp the implications of indivisibility, imagine that infinitesimal points are the fundamental constituents of space itself, like "partless atoms" that make up space [732].

As Westerhoff pointed out, this is not as straightforward a notion as it first appears [733]:

> Take a complex thing consisting of three atoms, one in the middle, one each on the left and right. Call the portion where the left-hand side atom touches the middle one A, that where the middle one touches the right-hand side one B. A and B can't be the same, otherwise the left-hand side and the right-hand side atom would touch directly, and there would be only two atoms, not three. But if they are not the same, the middle atom consists of at least two portions, A and B. But how can it do so if it has no parts? It seems that either (contrary to our assumption) atoms have to have parts, and thus are not really atoms, or a multitude of atoms cannot fill more space than a single one, in which case extended objects could not be made up of atoms.

To be indivisible, to be *partless*, entails an inability to aggregate and so if infinitesimal points are partless, they cannot aggregate to form a spatial extent. So much for points as indivisible elements, infinitely small.

Hume proposed that, instead of conceiving points as being of either zero or infinitesimal size, we should conceive of points as *extensionless indivisibles* of *finite* size so that points aggregate to comprise space [734].

It's important to keep in mind that Hume's conception of being 'extensionless' is not mathematical but empirical. Hume thought that, because even the most advanced technology can only peer down so far in scale, that limit to perceptibility is the limit to spatial extension itself. Indivisible units of space are, in Hume's view, indivisible units of sensory experience—'minima sensibilia'—that have "no extension" in the sense of being the limit to our capability of making further spatial distinctions between like units [735]. The limits of perception are where we find points.

However, Hume's attempt to solve the problem of how points comprise space merely substitutes impressional space for real space. His idea that points are extensionless indivisibles of finite size may be a good description of "points" as they are in impressional space but not points as they are in real space. His notion of points is a red herring if what we want to know about is points corresponding to the smallest units of real space rather than "points" as smallest noticeable units in some form of apparent space (assuming, as I do, that there is an ontological difference between the real and apparent space). Reject Hume's collapse of ontology into phenomenology and his notion of points falls with it [736]. For these reasons, Hume's notion of points is not adequate.

Suppose instead that points are simply "indivisible" because they have no size at all; they are of afinite size rather than infinitesimal size. As long as points so conceived are not also proposed to aggregate, there is no problem with their use in describing space. This conception of points only becomes problematic if points as so conceived are proposed to compose space by aggregating together; the picture we get when mathematicians say points "make up" a line or continuum.

A logical problem occurs for the aggregation of zero-size points because, in this conception, the points have zero volume—no size at all. They have no extension by which to form extension, no extension by which to form a continuum of space. As Bell noted, a continuum must be "nonpunctiform" because points cannot aggregate to form a continuum [737]. That is not to say that a continuum cannot *have* points (or be given points, such as in mathematical assignment); it just means that a continuum cannot, fundamentally, be made up from points as if points aggregate together to form the continuum. To have points of no size add up to something with size is like trying to add a sequence of zeros and get a result greater than zero or add nothing but empty sets to get a set that is not empty.

This is the exact opposite of the conclusion reached by some mathematicians like Rucker, who stated [738],

> Since a point has no length, no finite number of points could ever constitute a line segment, which *does* have length. So it seems evident that every line segment, or, for that matter, every continuous plane segment or region of space, must consist of an infinite number of points.

Rather, the opposite: we can use the mathematics of infinity to prove that if a point has a size of zero, infinitely many of those zeros do not add up to anything of non-zero size because an infinite number of zeros still adds to up to zero:

$$\sum_{i=0}^{\infty} 0 = \lim_{n\to\infty} \sum_{i=0}^{n} 0 = \lim_{n\to\infty} 0 = 0$$

The size of an infinite number of points would still be the size of only one point—no size at all. It doesn't matter how many points you have; even infinitely many of them still won't aggregate to form a space if none of them have spatial extension.

To this, philosophers such as Adolf Grünbaum and mathematicians like Henri Lebesgue claimed that points along the geometric line biject with the real numbers and so, on the basis of the non-denumerability of both the points in the line and a transfinite set of real numbers in $\mathbb{R}$, points can "add up" to a non-zero amount. Hence, sizeless points can form a line after all [739].

This answer, however, is not without problems. First, the difference between denumerable and non-denumerable infinites I have already attacked in § 14.10. Second, it's not clear that points would have relevant relations *between* them that make their individual lack of magnitudes together *aggregate* into magnitudes just because real numbers can be *assigned* to sets of points. That is, assigning real numbers to points may not be what makes points spatially different from one another. Hence, it's still not clear points "add up" to form a line just because they can be assigned real numbers.

Oppy counters that two 0-dimensional sets can be united into a 1-dimensional set because the 0-dimensional sets (points) do share a relation: *numerical dimensionality*. Oppy states that there are "non-empty sets" of "rational points" and "irrational points" that, united together, form the real number line, which has dimensionality [740]. Oppy's rejoinder assumes points correspond to numbers and the sequencing of numbers is what forms a spatial line.

This argument, like that of Grünbaum and Lebesgue, mistakes association for identity: just because numbers can be associated with points and just because we can associate a sequence of numbers with places along a line does not mean that points are identical to numbers or that a sequence of numbers is identical to a geometrical line. It could just as well be that 'rational points' and 'irrational points' are merely the associations of rational numbers to points and the associations of irrational numbers to points—associations that only exist so long as we bother to make them. In which case, points do not share identity with such numbers and a geometric line is not identical to a set of numbers. That is, just because we can use a geometrical line to *represent* a sequence of numbers (or vice versa), that does not mean lines *are* sequences of numbers.

In fact, take any line segment. What does the segment end on—a rational point or an irrational point? How would you know except by simply *defining* the points as you want to define them? In which case, it's not that there are rational points and irrational points to be discovered, but rather points are *designated* as corresponding to rational or irrational numbers according to schemas we *invent*. None of which shows that points, simply as such, have any intrinsic 'numerical dimensionality'.

So, the set-theoretic solutions for getting a positive number from a string of zeros or getting sizeless points to aggregate into an entity with size remain a logically conceptual problem despite enjoying mathematical consistency.

Still, some counter that a whole (space) can have a property (extension) that need not be shared by its parts (points), just as a song has the property of a melody not shared by any of its constituent notes. However, in order to realize why this appeal to the whole/part distinction won't work, we have only to ask what exactly this "relation" is between points as entities of no size at all that their "relations" can make up the extension of space among points.

The reason that musical notes can combine to make the melody of a song is because notes relate to one another with sound—each note is a sound and sound is a positive property that accumulates. As sizeless and partless entities more fundamental than none, however, points would have no such property among them by which to form spatial extension. That is, if points have *no size* and points are fundamental *rather than extension*, then there is nothing about points—no relational property—by which they can build up extension between them. Points all by themselves cannot make up a dimension of space as pearls can combine into a string of pearls.

Moreover, simply saying points have 'positions' next to each other is not enough. Without extension being just as fundamental, the position or location of one point would not differ from that of another—every point would be the same point [741]. If points have no size *and* they are more fundamental than extension, they cannot have different positions; *points only have different positions by virtue of something else more fundamental than points: the extension that defines their relative positions*. Points must thus be derivative, not fundamental.

All such conceptual problems with the indivisibility and sizelessness of points strongly indicate that space cannot be divided down to mathematical points—indivisible objects of either infinitesimal or zero size. No matter how far we successively divide down, we never reach entities either infinitely small or that have no size at all—we never get to points. At least, not as a matter of successive divisions of a spatial extent toward a limit [742].

It seems much more reasonable to assume that points do not preexist in space or compose space like bricks aggregating to form a wall, waiting for us to discover them via a successive division process. Instead, points are simply idealized units of measurement representing places in an abstract volume, plane, or line where we choose to mathematically punctuate an abstract space, as when we mathematically divide a line in a single act of mathematical division or where we choose to intersect two or more geometric lines.

However, just because points are not what discoverists think they are does not mean we have to jettison the concept of points altogether. We can still make sense of points; we just need to conceive of them correctly. Points are logically coherent if they are not conceived to be infinitesimal and if they cannot, as sizeless entities, *aggregate* together to form size.

Points are not entities in and of themselves, combined contiguously to form the whole of space. As philosopher P.O. Johnson put it [743],

> A line might be divisible at any arbitrarily chosen point, but this does not mean it is constituted by discrete points...The line is not a complex of which points are simple constituents. Moreover, if it was such a complex, and did contain or consist of points, then these could not be infinitely numerous, for this would imply that the series of points was unending, and therefore that they could not form a complex or constitute a whole.

Points of space do not make up the whole of space like a set of building blocks. Rather than supposing points aggregate to form space, we should instead suppose it is the expanse of space that is an undivided, but divisible, whole. In that case, space is a fundamental unity while it is the division of space into volumes, planes, lines, and—yes—sets of points that are artificial constructions. Space is a seamless, continuous entity without any course graining at all; we only conceptually divide space up into units that do not preexist; we *measure* space according to dimensions we invent as measurement devices, dimensions that we in turn subdivide into lengths and points.

In this view, points are of afinite size—they have zero volume and are 'extensionless indivisibles' in that sense. As such, they are not things that aggregate and so they exist only in mathematical idealization as invented ideas rather than the real world as discoverable entities. We do not reach points by a process of division; we merely *designate* or *assign* an artificial, idealized cut of space *as* a sizeless point, just as when we designate a point to be midway between two bounds or a point to be the intersection of two lines. Points are, in that sense, designations rather than discoveries. Looking at space this way dissolves the problem of how space can "have" points—space has points when we conceptually *make* points *for* space.

With respect to an infinite number of points, these conclusions imply that, because points do not exist as preexistent atoms of space, there are no literally infinite sets of points making up space. Points are merely sizeless *abstractions* invented for indexing space—schemas we create in our mathematical schemes. As finite beings, we can, at best, indefinitely keep on creating *indefinitely many* points by conception; what we cannot do is create a literally infinite set of points. And with that, the reasons to suppose space is composed of infinitudes of infinitesimals or points all fall apart.

18.6 INFINITE SPACE UNREAL

The foregoing shows there cannot be a length of infinitely many distances, nor infinitely many places comprising a magnitude or objects of infinite magnitude, nor infinitely many portions in space. Bottom line: space cannot be literally infinite or contain a literal infinity of objects.

CHAPTER 18 IN REVIEW

❖ Space is said to be infinite in three senses: in extent, in magnitude, and in portion. Infinite extents have "points at infinity," infinite magnitudes contain infinitely many places, and infinite portions are spaces that contain infinitely many "infinitesimals" or points.

❖ In operation, geometry calculates indefinite extents, magnitudes, and portions of space but not genuinely infinite ones.

❖ Insofar as geometrical features such as extents, magnitudes, and portions of space are philosophically interpreted as literally infinite, such features are interpreted in a logically incoherent manner due to the contradictions between the completeness and limitlessness of those features.

❖ As contradictions cannot manifest in reality, space cannot be literally infinite in the real world.

19: INFINITE TIME REFUTED

Time, like space, is in all respects finite. There is no infinite past, infinite future, or infinite quantity of instants embedded in durations of time. I offer several arguments in support of that conclusion.

But first, we must start by considering what time is, and without launching into a full philosophy of time, which would take a book in itself. To keep the topic manageable, I'll sidestep most of the issues that have to do with philosophical positions on the nature of time such as *presentism*, *eternalism*, *endurantism*, *perdurantism*, and so forth [744]. Instead, I will present a simplified conception of time and stick to addressing why it is that time cannot be infinite.

19.1 ON THE NATURE OF TIME

There are various schemas to distinguish different kinds of time. I find the following schema useful [745]:

- *real time*: time as it is, regardless of how it appears. Any object or subject, or group of either, has a *state*—a collection of attributes that describe its condition. Without real time, nothing would be observed to either change or stay the same since there would be no separation of states for which either change or constancy occurs from one state to another, or from one instance of a state to another instance of the same state. Clocks would not tick because there would be no change of motion. Stillness would not exist since there would be no time over which something could remain in the same inertial state. Without real time, nothing takes place.

- *apparent time*: time as it appears according to an observer's experience and/or measurement. This category of time includes both representations of real time that carry some degree of accuracy [746] as well as representations of times that are purely fictional—for example, the time of a make-believe era or of a mathematical process that does not play out in the real world. Representations of both real times and fictional times fall into three categories of apparent time: impressional time, indexical time, and schematic time.

  - *impressional time*: time as the subjective rate of succession according to an observer's experience (e.g., successive states may appear to transpire more quickly, more slowly, or in a different order for one observer than for another observer).

> – *indexical time*: time as the objective, categorical schema used for indexing the order of succession. For example, intervals of time—durations—such as moments, eras, and epochs (what we call 'times') are schema used for indexing real time [747]. *Past/present/future* is another schema of indexical time, as are their corresponding tenses (e.g., "has happened", "is happening", and "will happen"). So too, *before/during/after* is another schema as is *earlier-than/simultaneous with/later-than*, and so forth. Various geometrical depictions of time, such as worldlines and worldvolumes, are also examples of indexical time schemas.

> – *schematic time*: time as the objective, quantitative measurement schema for referencing the order of successions (e.g., "The time is now 12:00 am, January 1st"). Units of schematic time (years, days, hours, minutes, seconds, etc.) are based on the schemas of indexical time. A set of mathematical units applied to geometric depictions of time are another example of schematic time.

You may notice that the above categories mirror those used for space in Chapter 18. Just as some apparent spaces, such as indexical space and schematic space, are used for 'mapping' real space, so too some apparent times—namely, indexical time and schematic time—are representations that allow us to 'map' real time, as when we make chronologies, schedules, etc. As indexical and schematic space map real space by conceptually dividing real space up into intervals such as parsecs, kilometers, millimeters, nanometers, and so forth, so too indexical time and schematic time are used to conceptually divide real time into intervals such as millennia, decades, years, hours, seconds, nanoseconds, etc.

The shortest interval of indexical time we generically refer to as a *moment*. We need not worry about the exact duration of what is referred to as a 'moment' (the exact duration would be given as a schematic time measure). Instead, consider a moment to be the briefest interval of time according to the observer's use of indexical time. A moment shared between civilizations in history may be a thousand years while a moment shared by subatomic particles may be less than a femtosecond. Moreover, a moment of indexical time may correspond to a single time—the interval of time from one state to another—or to a whole series of such intervals, depending on the temporal index in use.

Intervals of indexical time, such as moments, are used to reference or even label intervals of real time. For example, although a 'moment' is an indexical unit for measuring real time, we also refer to intervals of real time as 'moments' since the indexical unit is used to refer to specific times—occurrences of real time. We may thus say moments have "taken place" or "will take place" even though no observer is around to experience their passage. In stating that such moments take place, we use an indexical time interval—the moment—to objectively describe real time.

In stating that no observer needs to experience a given moment for there to be a moment that occurs, I am denying that that apparent time and real time are the same thing. Real time is not an apparent time such as impressional time. Rather, an apparent time such as impressional time is simply how real time appears.

Assuming as much, then even if there were no humans around to experience particular moments, that does not mean moments did not take place before human beings were around or will not take place after human beings are all extinct. We simply index moments in the past and future relative to how they appear to us in the present. Moments of indexical time are therefore intended to depict real time.

We face the same situation with our use of measurement schemas for space, such as the equator. Although the equator as a concept was not around until someone thought it up, the Earth always had an equator in the sense of a physical area corresponding to the imaginary line used to map the planet. The same goes for moments of time. Though the concept of time and intervals of time were not around until human beings invented them, the reality of time and occurrences in time did take place before we were around, and those occurrences in prehistory are measurable from the perspective of the present via the application of units of indexical, schematic, or even impressional time.

With respect to indexing and measuring real time, we need not be too concerned with the many overlapping, indistinguishable moments in time during which nothing notable seems to happen. Unless otherwise specified, we will be mainly concerned with only the non-overlapping, distinct moments we would call *events*.

Moreover, I will be depicting some fictional events for the sake of thought experiment; however, the kind of time I will have in mind for the implication of such events (unless otherwise specified or obviously different due to context) will be real time, which I will refer to simply as time. And while I will be making use of time indexes like past/present/future or time schemas like years, days, etc., I will not make too much about calling out the distinctions between indexical, schematic, and real time as such, since it should be clear from context what is meant.

I will also put aside the issue of *absolute time* versus *relative time*. Instead, I will in this chapter simply refer to time as a cosmologist would with respect to the history of the Universe—the passage of events on a universal scale without respect to differences in how fast clocks tick for local states of motion or gravitation.

Adopting these assumptions about the nature of time, the question we need answered is whether time—real time—is finite or infinite in duration.

19.2 THE CONTRADICTIONS OF LITERALLY INFINITE TIME

To say time is literally infinite implies time can be accurately characterized as having a sequence of non-overlapping moments that is both complete as a collection but also limitless in the quantity of moments that occur over that sequence. For example, if the *future* is literally infinite, then the future contains a complete and limitless quantity of moments yet to happen; if the *past* is literally infinite, then the past contains a complete and limitless quantity of moments, each of which has already happened.

The concept of infinite time is common in science, philosophy, and religion. In all of these fields, it's most common to hear claims that the future is infinite, but there are also scientific theories, philosophical arguments, and religious narratives claiming the past is infinite. Of those asserting the past is infinite, most hold as well that the future is infinite with the present reduced to less than a blink in the eye of an eternity that stretches from infinite past to infinite future [748]. In contrast, of those who believe the future to be infinite, many do not necessarily believe the past is infinite as well. For example, many cosmologists, astrophysicists, and astronomers hold that time began between 13–14 billion years ago, but also that time might even continue to unfold through an infinite future [749].

Infinite future and infinite past aside, there is another sense in which time is commonly claimed to be infinite: some scientists, philosophers, and mathematicians believe that any finite period of time is a type of dense continuum that contains an infinite series of *instants* just as a finite expanse of space is a dense continuum containing an infinite set of points or infinitesimals [750].

To the contrary, I argue that all such conceptions of literally infinite time are inherently self-contradictory due to the conflict between what it means for a sequence of moments to be complete while also being quantitatively limitless. The logical problems generated by the complete/limitless conflict arise in the concept of infinite time, whether we consider time to be infinite with respect to the past or to the future; likewise, logical problems also appear in the concept of infinitely short instants making up a finite period of time. We'll consider each of these problems in turn.

19.3 A REFUTATION OF THE PAST AS INFINITE

If the past is infinite, then the past can be characterized as a series of moments in which there is no limit to the quantity of prior moments that occurred one after another in succession, and the series of moments now stands as completed in the present moment (after all, here we are). That is, an infinite past entails a *complete* collection of *all* prior moments that have ever occurred up to the present moment (where "all" implies a standing total of moments), and the moments making up that complete collection are *limitless* in quantity.

That's the concept of a literally infinite past and it is commonly claimed that such a concept makes logical sense even if it turns out not to be a true depiction of the way the past is in reality. As Holt remarked [751],

> There is nothing absurd about an infinite past. It is conceptually possible for there to have
> been an infinite succession of sunrises before the one this morning—provided there was
> an infinite span of time in which they could have occurred.

Gardner had the same position: "An endless regress is absurd only to someone who finds it ugly or disturbing. There is nothing logically absurd about an infinite regress" [752]. I, to the contrary, argue the concept of a completed but limitless past only has the illusion of making logical sense; the concept of a literally infinite quantity connotes logical contradictions and therefore cannot be applicable to the past.

In making my argument, I will first clarify what it means for the past to be literally infinite by contrasting a literally infinite past with a finite past. Next, I will provide a more precise description of what it means for the past to be complete and what it means for the past to be limitless. We'll then see how a limitless past contradicts a complete past and how a complete past contradicts a limitless past. This will force the conclusion that the past cannot be both complete and limitless in its quantity of moments.

19.3.1 *Back to the Beginning*

To clarify the concept of an infinite past, let's use a thought experiment. We'll start by first supposing the past is *finite* rather than infinite. A finite past is a past comprised of a series of moments—both moments that overlap with one another as well as non-overlapping, distinctive moments (events) which occur in succession. The quantity of all non-overlapping, distinct moments, or events, which occur in succession over an entire series is a standing total. Such a totality of events in a series comprises a finite amount of time. For the past to finite is for the past to be characterized by such a series.

The most common model of a finite past is that which assumes a temporal beginning—not just a beginning to a particular succession of events that takes place *in* time, as when a first domino is knocked over, beginning a succession of other falling dominos (**Figure 2.4** in Chapter 2), but rather a beginning *of* time as such. That is, a finite past is typically assumed to imply *time itself* must have a beginning.

The reason the concept of a finite past is commonly assumed to imply a beginning of time is that time tends to be portrayed with the spatial metaphor of a timeline. When we use a timeline, we are using a tool that depicts time as an *index* of change in order to represent real time as a succession of changes.

When time, as an index of change, is portrayed dimensionally in the form of a straight line representing a succession of events, one end marks the event of the present moment while the other end is either an arrowhead representing undepicted prior events—

past　　　　　　　　　present

—or a bound marking a specific event as an absolutely first event:

first event　　　　　　　present

It is the latter depiction—the linear, bounded model of a timeline of the past—that suggests a finite past must imply a beginning of time.

Assuming the linear model of time, there was some event in the past before which there were no prior events. If time had a beginning, then there would have to have been an *absolutely first event* to *all* succeeding events. It would thus be nonsensical to ask, "What happened before the beginning of time?" If time had a beginning, there would be no such thing as "before the beginning of time" because then whatever happened before the beginning of time would imply the beginning of time wasn't really the *beginning* of time—a contradiction. If there was a first event, absolutely nothing came before that; there was no time before the beginning of time for anything to happen.

Whether or not the idea of a beginning to time itself makes logical sense I will have to leave for another book [753]. For now, I only wish to posit a beginning of time for the sake of illustration. The concept that the past had a beginning will be useful for explaining the implications of an *infinite* past.

19.3.2 *Countdown to the Present*

Real time is a process comprised of a series of changes that can be indexed according to the undistinctive moments we usually ignore and the distinctive moments that stand out for the amount of change manifested in them; the latter are moments we call 'events'. Part of the indexical time we use to orient ourselves in real time is tense—past tense, present tense, and future tense [754]. We reference events in memory and history in the past tense ("has happened"), events unfolding now in the present tense ("happening now"), and events expected to come later in the future tense ("will happen").

But the present is rather elusive. What *will be* the present is now in the future, what *was* the present is now in the past, and what *is* now the present was in the future and will be in the past. What is referred to as "now" differs over time. Pick some date in the past; say, January 1st, 2001. In one sense, the past from that date to the present seems to grow because what we call the present is always changing, adding more events to the past. Tomorrow what we call the present will be one more day ahead of that date; so, our index of events is always getting larger as the date January 1st, 2001 "recedes" further away from the present into the past. Pick some date in the future, say, ten years hence. The future from now until that date seems to shrink as the date "approaches" the present from the future. The present is whatever real time we experience—whatever real time *presents* to us.

526 Forever Finite Kip K. Sewell

When I speak of "the present" in this chapter, I am not talking about the present as a generic present that ever-changes from one second to the next, one day to the next. Instead, I have in mind whatever the reader wishes to regard as the particular calendar date and clock reading—a single, arbitrarily selected moment on a single, arbitrarily selected date that can be indexed according to a clock and calendar.

With that in mind, we can say the present—a particular calendar date and clock reading given for the present moment is the result of all the events that led up to the present. All the events that have occurred over the past worked to construct whatever you now regard as the present moment—which we will label as m. To use a spatial metaphor, take any one event in the present and you can trace at least one causal chain of events leading from that present event back to through the entirety of the past.

Now, under those assumptions, suppose time is finite and that such a chain of events could be listed in a single book. Imagine a series of events that unfolded over the course of the entire past up to m, as being recorded in a book, *The Book of Time Past*. Imagine the book as an index of all the past events in that given chain of events, from the beginning of time to the present. We can therefore suppose the book lists a first event on the first page. The first event listed would be the record of the first moment of time, the event that began the entire chain of events that led to the present. So too the last event listed in the book is the last entry on the last page of the book; that last entry is an event in the present moment. All events in the chain of events that happened between the beginning of time and the event at the present are all recorded in *The Book of Time Past*.

Suppose as well that each event in the index of past events is listed by a unique natural number. *The Book of Time Past* could have the events of the past all numbered in sequence, from the absolutely first event numbered as the first entry on the first page of the book, all the way up to the last entry numbered on the last page of the book, marking the event of the present moment. Let's also imagine the first event, the beginning of time, as numbered with a large natural number, n. The last event in the book that corresponds m is listed in the book with the smallest natural number, 1; hence, $m = 1$. The intermediate events, between n and m, are listed with a descending order of numbers from the largest number that begins the series (n) on down to the present moment (m) listed as 1. Hence, the listing is like a countdown from the beginning of time to the present, a countdown that ends at 1.

Let's consider a hypothetical person; we'll call her Alice. Alice is immortal and has been around since the beginning of time. She lives in a bubble and never ages. Alice also holds *The Book of Time Past*. Alice can read the list of events in the book, from the very first event at which time began (listed as the first entry on the first page of the book) to the very last event that corresponds to the present moment (the last entry on the last page of the book).

Imagine Alice proceeds, from the first moment of time, to read off all the numbers listing all the events in the book from the first entry on the first page to the last entry on the last page at which the present event is listed. For her reading, Alice speaks aloud the numbers one after another, in sequence, over the entire sequence.

What events are listed in the book is not important; they could even be the events of Alice reading the list of numbers in the book. For example, the final three events in the book might be listed as:

- And then Alice said, "Three."
- And then Alice said, "Two."
- And then Alice said, "One—*Finished!*"

Alice would therefore be counting down from the beginning of time, from the first event listed in the book with a particular number (for which we will use the variable n), to the last event numbered as 1. Alice calls out the numbers at the rate of one number (a single count) per second. We won't worry about the number of syllables it would really take for Alice to say very large numbers—maybe she abbreviates or is just a fast talker; this is, after all, a fanciful analogy.

Let's suppose the first moment of time recorded in Alice's book is a number, n, equal to 10^9. As we saw back in § 4.2.8, at her rate of count it would have taken Alice a mere 32 years to finish the countdown to the present.

But Alice is reading from *The Book of Time Past*, which is comprised of a chain of events from the beginning to time itself to the present. So, if *The Book of Time Past* were numbered with only $n = 10^9$ events, then that would mean time began only 32 years ago. That's way too soon (some of us are a bit older than that). So, let's propose for this hypothetical scenario an even longer sequence of events in the past, and hence an even longer countdown of numbers.

For example, suppose $n = 10^{15}$ and Alice had been counting down at a rate of only one count per second. In that case, Alice started counting down 32 million years ago and has just finished. But our best science indicates that even 32 million years ago is too soon for time to have begun. We'll have to make n larger still: $n = 4.35 \times 10^{17}$, which would make Alice's reading of all the numbers last 13.8 billion years— the amount of time that has elapsed since the Universe began according to mainstream physical theory (according to some estimates) [755].

We'll have to allow Alice to pop into existence at the conclusion of the first second of time and start counting down from there; other than that, we won't worry about the physics about how Alice could be alive and counting down from 13.8 billion years ago.

Notice that as we made the number of numbers Alice needed to recite ever larger, it did not change the form of her countdown from n to 1 since the sequence remained n, ..., 3, 2, 1. But the larger the number n represents, the larger the number of events in the past, and so the further the beginning of time must have been from the present, and thus the longer it took for Alice to complete her countdown. Even so, that has no effect on the series insofar as it still ends with a count of 1 at m.

Next, suppose time did *not* begin ~13.8 billion years ago. Instead, suppose time began much longer ago than that. Let's continue to make n ever larger until n is, from our vantage, indefinitely large. In that situation, n would not be 'indefinite' for Alice, but it certainly would be indefinite for us. Whatever n is for Alice, we would judge n to be a 'zillion'—an indefinitely large number [756]. This is still not a problem because whatever a zillion is, it is finite and so still represents a *beginning* to the series of events, however long ago that beginning occurred. Hence, Alice's count still ends with a count of 1 at m.

Finally, we are ready to introduce infinity into this thought experiment. Suppose we wish the sequence of past events to be even longer than a zillion events. Let's suppose the past has an *infinitely* long sequence of events preceding the present.

In this thought experiment, *The Book of Time Past* is a *complete* index of a chain of events extending into the *limitless* past. From time without beginning, Alice has *always* been counting down the numbers of that index, and she has just completed her task of doing so right now, at moment m. In this thought experiment, the moment m is the present, and since Alice just completed her count, then m also corresponds to the calendar date and clock reading right now, at which Alice says, "One—*Finished!*" The past is a complete set of events at m. All the events from which Alice counted down are, at m, a complete set of events indexed in *The Book of Time Past*.

The past, at least relative to m, is therefore not characterized by a running total of events but a standing total of events because it will ever after m be true that, at m, Alice counted out a particular number of numbers, and lived through a particular number of events—namely, an infinite number of them.

Of course, life goes on—new events are added to Alice's past after her countdown is over. So, her past continues to "grow" in that sense. Thus, to be clear: *The Book of Time Past* only records the chain of events for Alice's past up to event m; the book does not record the past *per se* as would a journal with new entries being continuously added.

However, we don't need to worry about the past that accrues *after* the calendar date and clock reading of m. What we are concerned with is the past *up to m* because that past is said to have a complete sequence of events, which after Alice's reading recedes into the past like a set of train cars disappearing in the distance. Nevertheless, the entire set of those "train cars" is a limitless sequence of events—a limitless index of numbers Alice completely read all the way through.

The claim that Alice's countdown is a literally infinite series of tasks sounds profound, but I contend that is only because the scenario implies contradictions. The scenario implies contradictions between the completeness and limitlessness of a literally infinite past. First, we'll look at the implications of the past's limitlessness on the past's completeness, then we'll examine the implications of the past's completeness on the past's limitlessness. As we'll see, the contradictions obtaining between completeness and limitlessness entail the past cannot be both complete and limitless—the past cannot be literally infinite.

19.3.3 *Contradictory Implications of Limitlessness Upon a Complete Past*

A literally infinite past is a complete past—it is a series of past events that, as a series, meets the completeness criteria of § 3.2.8. The series of past events must be a *whole* series of events over the past and not just part of a series of past events; for example, the series cannot be only half the necessary occurrences leading up to the present. The series of events leading up to the present must also be *entire*—there can be no gaps or acausal jumps in the sequence of events leading up to the present. The series of past events must also be *finished*—the last event to occur in the series of events from the past is the present event at m. The series of events must be the *full* series of events—the series of events cannot include any more events that it already has at m or the series would have extra events from the future or from fictional claims. The series of events must also be a totality—that is, the past must at least in principle have a series of events that can be expressed as a *total number* of events. Hence, for the past of some present event to be complete is for the past to be a series of events that is whole, entire, finished, full, and total. In that respect, the *series* of events happening one after another constitute a complete *set* of events at m.

Because the completeness of the infinite past entails the past has a total number of events at m, the entire series of past events must be *countable*, at least in principle. If the past does not have a countable number of events, then there could be no sum of past events, and ergo no *total*. Without a sum—in the literal sense of the term 'sum'—the past would not be complete [757]. But the past is always complete at the present moment—after all, here we are.

This has implications for our thought experiment. If immortal Alice is to have made a *complete* countdown of numbered past events ("...Three, Two, One—*Finished!*"), then that implies the further into the past Alice had counted from, the larger the numbers she had previously counted. If Alice had started her countdown at 100 and reached 1, then she certainly would have to have counted the subseries of events numbered from 99 down to 1; if Alice had started her countdown at 1,000 and reached 1, she would have to have counted the subseries of events numbered from 999 down to 1; if Alice had started her countdown at 10,000 and reached 1, she would have to have counted the subseries of events numbered from 9,999 down to 1; and so forth. If Alice had therefore been counting down from infinity and reached 1, then she must have counted through *infinitely many* unique natural numbers in order to get to 1. That means there must be in *The Book of Time Past* at least one subseries of recorded events she would have had to have counted down from that starts with an infinitely large natural number and completes with the count of 1.

However, the infinite past is not just complete; it is also *limitless*. And the limitlessness of the past entails that there can be no such thing as an infinitely large number. Just as counting from 1 up to infinity (1, 2, 3, …) never finishes because the process is limitless—there is no 'infinitieth' number with infinitely many digits to reach by counting to infinity—so too a countdown from infinity to 1, as in …, 3, 2, 1, is a process that has no beginning at all, not even at an infinitely large natural number. The ellipses depicted in 1, 2, 3, … and …, 3, 2, 1 represent progressions without limit, *even in principle*. By virtue of the *limitlessness* of the series being counted, a count from 1 up to infinity would never finish; it is, therefore, the case that there is no infinitely large number *from* which to count down to 1. Our hypothetical immortal person, Alice, by counting down a series of numbers from infinity to 1, would have always been counting without ever having started the process from some 'infinitieth' number.

This implication, which follows from the limitlessness of literal infinity, therefore contradicts literal infinity's state of *completeness*. By virtue of its completeness, a count from 1 *up to* infinity does indeed have a finish at an infinity—either an infinitely large natural number or the first in a sequence of infinitely large numbers. So too, if Alice is to count *down from* infinity to 1, there must already be at least one infinitely large natural number from which Alice counted down. If there is no such thing as an infinitely large natural number that Alice had counted down from, then any large number Alice ever counted down from would have to have been only a *finite* number; consequently, the countdown would have taken her only a finite amount of natural numbers to reach 1 in the present, no matter how large the numbers were that she counted. And that would make the series of past events greatly protracted in time, but still finite rather than infinite as the scenario demands.

So, we already have a problem: for Alice to have finished counting down from infinity to 1, she must have counted down the complete sequence of numbers from an infinite set (ℕ) in which,

- there can be *no* infinitely large natural number because every number in ℕ is just one number higher than the previous number; however,

- there must be *at least one* natural number infinitely larger than 1 because otherwise ℕ would be only figuratively infinite (ergo, finite) rather than literally infinite.

We therefore again reach contradiction: There must be no infinitely large natural number for Alice to have counted—no natural number infinitely higher on the scale of ℕ than 1—and yet there must be such a number for Alice to count down "all" of an infinitude of natural numbers in order to get to 1. There must not be an infinitieth number because Alice's countdown is *limitless* (requiring ever-larger finite numbers only), but there must be an infinitieth number because otherwise Alice's countdown is either finite (due to having numbers of only finite cardinality) or simply cannot be *completed* at all and so cannot be a literally infinite countdown. That there "must not be" and yet "must be" an infinitely large natural number is a contradiction implied by the very concept of infinity in its literal sense. A contradiction entailing that neither ℕ nor the series of past events matched to natural numbers can be literally infinite.

If we try to avoid the contradictions by affirming the limitlessness of the past while denying the existence of infinitely large natural numbers, we also have an additional problem. Assuming the past is infinite, *The Book of Time Past* must have infinitely many pages indexing infinitely many events the numbers of which Alice has been calling out, one after another, from the infinite past. However, *The Book of Time Past* is similar to the special book pulled from Craig's Library (see § 17.4). As with *The Book of Time Past*, the book from Craig's Library has an infinite number of pages. In the book from Craig's Library, each page is thinner than the next until the pages become infinitely thin at the end of the book. Consequently, we both can and cannot open the last page of the book. We can open to the last page because the book has a complete number of pages but cannot because there is no last page—the pages are limitless. With *The Book of Time Past* we face the same problem, only it is the final page that is thickest and the preceding pages that become infinitely thin at the front of the book. Hence, *The Book of Time Past* cannot be opened in the front and yet can be, making it just as impossible as the book from Craig's Library.

Consequently, because the book has a complete number of pages, Alice could read from infinity past all the way through the indexed events to the last numbered event on the last page, read in the present moment; however, it is also the case that Alice never read a single numbered event on any page at the front of the book, nor did she read from subsequent pages because she could never in her reading come to a page with only a finite number of entries left to read. Hence, Alice both completes her countdown from infinity to the present and yet does not because the index of the book she reads from and the time over which she reads both are complete and yet can't be due to their limitlessness—a contradiction.

This alone shows the concept of an infinite past is logically contradictory, but let's not assume this argument is decisive. Instead, let's look further at what is entailed by the past being limitless and see how completeness contradicts that limitlessness. As we shall see, the implications only further justify the conclusion reached with the analogy of *The Book of Time Past* that the past must be finite.

19.3.4 *Contradictory Implications of Completeness for a Limitless Past*

A limitless past is a past without a beginning. It's not that there was a beginning infinitely far in the past; rather, there was never a beginning at all [758]. The past is a series of limitlessly many events, a series of events that occurred without any beginning but, since the past is comprised of all the events prior to the present, we can say the past ends at the present moment.

Suppose Alice, being immortal, has always been counting down from ever-higher numbers that are ever further back in time. Alice would have been counting "from infinity" down to 1. That would indeed entail a *limitless* past and a limitless countdown *without a first number*—without a beginning or a start to the counting process [759]. After a series of numbers from a limitless magnitude in the limitless past is read off, the count becomes *finished* when Alice reaches 1; she performs and ends a count despite the process never having had a beginning.

Superficially, this sounds plausible but upon further reflection it is not at all clear that the concept of ending without beginning is any less problematic than claiming there can be a top without a bottom or a front without a back. One way to know whether the concept of a series that terminates after having proceeded without beginning makes any kind of logical sense or not is to inquire if we can conceive of such a series *without fallacy* or *without contradiction*. I claim that such isn't possible. Rather, the notion of a limitless past only gives the illusion of making sense until it is sufficiently scrutinized.

Wes Morriston (formerly, Emeritus Professor of Philosophy at the University of Colorado—Boulder) argued that while counting from 0 or 1 up to infinity may have no infinite number to finish the count, it's nevertheless possible, at least in principle, to enumerate all numbers from infinity down to 1 or 0 over an infinite series of past events, finishing in the present [760]. But Morriston didn't take the limitlessness of a literally infinite past seriously enough.

The limitlessness of literal infinity means *any* infinite series—whether counting up or down the scale of numbers—simply by virtue of being literally infinite, is *uncountable*, even in principle. I do not mean an "uncountable infinity" in the transfinite sense of a sequence of reals as opposed to naturals, but in the sense that one can never count through all the members of a series for which there is no such thing as finishing the count of members, even in principle. Therefore, if the past were literally infinite, that would entail that the quantity of past events is absolutely uncountable; a count of those events would never become complete, not ever.

To see why the series must be uncountable in this manner, consider that even if there was no start to Alice's count, even if Alice had "always been" counting from the infinite past [761], she would still never make it down to any finite numbers we can name—not even to the largest one we can name let alone one smaller. Recall d^*, the largest finite number defined yet (see § 4.2.7). The lack of limit to the numbers she needs to count down through entails her counting never reaches even an *indefinitely* large natural number, let alone a smaller number such as d^*, so that she may proceed in counting all the way down to the number 1. Alice's countdown has *no limit* to the amount of numbers she must count through *before* reaching even the *zillionth* finite number from 1. An indefinitely large finite number, a zillionth number, would be for Alice's countdown like an infimum that her countdown can only "approach" but never meet. There are simply too many larger numbers for her to count down from—an amount of numbers *without any limit at all*; such a count *never* ends even if the *order* of numbers in the series does end at 1. The very limitlessness of Alice's countdown implies that Alice should never reach *any* finite number, no matter how high the finite number mere mortals can define for her to count down to; she'll never proceed in counting down to a finite subseries ending in 1. Alice may have "always been" counting down, but she will have to continue to count down *forever*, for a limitless count is a count that never ends: she will never reach the number 1.

So, it doesn't matter if Alice has limitless time in the past to do her counting. Even if Alice had been counting for an infinitely long time down an infinitely long list of natural numbers, the very *limitlessness* of the list Alice reads off implies no end to Alice's countdown. That Alice has been counting from an infinite past doesn't make a difference to the limitlessness of the numbers she must count through. The limitlessness of the past does not somehow cancel out the limitlessness of the list of numbers she must count through to reach a final number to count. Even proceeding down from infinity over infinite time is not enough to reach a finite number, for the finite can never be reached from an infinite condition—at least, not according to the *limitlessness* of infinity.

For these reasons, Morriston's belief that a literal infinite can be traversed therefore is not sound. And these same issues refute Holt's claim that an infinite past can be traversed without issue [762].

However, limitlessness is just part of what it means to be infinite in the literal sense. Literal infinity is also a state of *completeness*. Because the series of events listed in *The Book of Time Past* is literally infinite, the series of events is also a complete series. The completeness of the series of events entails that the quantity of past events is countable, at least in principle. Hence, infinitely far in the past, Alice could have read the entry for an event listed in *The Book of Time Past* with an infinitely large number and subsequently counted infinitely many numbers of events from there to reach the event in the present, labelled as 1. So, Morriston and Holt may also be half right that an individual like Alice can indeed complete an infinite count [763].

Even so, *they are only half right* about that because focusing on the completeness of the series abstracts out the limitlessness of infinity and it is the limitlessness of the series of past events that stands in contradiction to the completeness of the series of past events.

The completeness of the series entails the series is countable (able to be counted to a standing total) while the limitlessness of the series entails it is uncountable (not able to be counted to a standing total). Alice not only *does not* make it down to a count of 1 because of the limitlessness of the series of numbers she must count through, she also *does* make it through the series to complete her count to 1 because, as we've seen, a literally infinite series is a complete series and so a literally infinite count is a complete count.

19.3.5 *Reasoning in a Circle of Contradictions*

As we've repeatedly seen, the properties of limitlessness and completeness, when ascribed to the same thing, can produce contradictions. Such is the case when they are combined into the single property of (literal) infinity and applied to a sequence of past events. Alice both counts down to 1 because her literally infinite count is a complete count and yet she can never complete her count because she has limitlessly many numbers to count.

Some philosophers appeal to transfinite mathematics to dissolve the contradiction between a limitless past that is also a complete past, but transfinite math is really no help. Insofar as it can be applied to time, the transfinite system only abstracts out the contradictory implications of a complete and limitless past rather than resolving them. Insofar as it purports to represent literal infinity, it just makes the contradiction all the more apparent.

To see why, consider that the numbers Alice counts down through are natural numbers. According to the transfinite system, each natural number, n, is a finite number even though the entire set of natural numbers ($\mathbb{N}$) has infinitely many ($\aleph$-many) numbers in it. The transfinite system defines infinity ($\aleph$) as *greater* than *any* natural number ($\aleph > n$). For any quantity of numbers in a literally infinite set, sequence, or series of numbers, the infinite whole is greater than any of the sums of any of its finite parts [764]. Because the set of natural numbers is infinite ($\mathbb{N} \triangleq \aleph$), the set of natural numbers is greater than any sum of natural numbers within the set or any combination of such numbers. But it is precisely because the infinite whole of $\mathbb{N}$ is *limitlessly* greater than any of its finite parts (n) that a problem surfaces. Because $\mathbb{N}$ is infinite ($\aleph$), the infinite sequence of counts down through $\mathbb{N}$ to 1 implies a logical contradiction.

Consider that an infinite set of natural numbers has its numbers arranged in the ordinality $\{1, 2, 3, ...\}$, which is defined as the *order type* of ω. In the transfinite system [765], it is the case that $\omega = \aleph$; moreover, ω is not just a category of numbers but a quantity that follows *after* all natural numbers in sequence such that $1, 2, 3, ..., n, ..., \omega$. The infinite whole ($\omega = \aleph$) is infinitely greater than any of its parts ($\aleph > n$). According to Cantor [766], no matter how high the natural number, n, it is no closer to ω than is the number 1. And that is precisely the problem when counting down through infinitely many numbers.

No natural number, no matter how high (for example, $n = d^*$), can reduce an *infinite* quantity of natural numbers to a *finite* quantity of natural numbers. For any n that Alice has counted out, it will always and forevermore remain true that $\omega - n = \omega$; the infinite cannot be diminished by the finite [767]. Having infinite time to count down makes no difference because $\omega - n - n - n ... - n = \omega$.

Think of it this way: suppose at some time, t, Alice has counted in descending order the top ten numbers of 100 like so: "100. 99. 98. 97. 96. 95. 94. 93. 92. 91." At t she only has 90 numbers left to count because $100 - 10 = 90$. Suppose instead that at t Alice has counted in descending order the top 100 numbers of 1,000. So, at t she only has 900 numbers left to count. Suppose instead that at t Alice has counted in descending order the top 1,000 numbers of 10,000. She only has 9,000 numbers left to count. And so on. Thus, suppose instead that at t Alice has counted only some finite number (n) of numbers down from an infinitude (ω) of numbers. Remember: according to transfinite mathematics, Alice does not count infinite numbers; she only counts finite numbers in an infinite sequence. In which case, no matter what number n is equal to at t, it will still be so large that it is as far from the greatest finite number we can name as ω is from 1. In other words, Alice will *always* have *infinitely many more*, smaller, numbers left to count down from because $\omega - n = \omega$.

In short, if the sequence which Alice must count down through is infinite ($\omega = \aleph$-many), then she never gets down to a finite number of numbers left to count. Her countdown never ends.

Thus, if transfinite theorists are right that the infinite whole is "greater" than its finite parts by virtue of the limitlessness of that whole, then that just makes matters worse for poor Alice. It is precisely because the transfinite whole is greater than any finite part that sequentially counting down through an infinite sequence (ω) of numbers *to* 1 is impossible, *even assuming infinite time*. Alice can never count down to 1 even though she is immortal. For Alice to count down from infinity to 1 would for her be like trying to jump out of a bottomless pit [768].

But the problems don't end there for the application of transfinite mathematics to time. It is true that Alice can never count down to 1 because she always has infinitely many more numbers to count through ($\omega - n = \omega$). But it is *also* true that Alice *can* count down to 1 because her count down is a complete count in which she only ever counts a finite number of numbers.

"Wait a minute," you might be thinking, "I thought there were *infinitely* many numbers for her to count." True, but consider: for any natural number, n, that Alice has *ever* counted, that number belongs to the order type ω. But the ω order type has a curious property: "...a set with $\aleph_0$ members that is assigned the order type ω...is such that...no member is infinitely distant from any other member" [769].

That means for any n Alice ever counted, because n was itself a finite number in a sequence that belongs to order type ω, we know n was only *finitely* far down the sequence from 1. Thus, if a count of n, no matter how high n is in $\mathbb{N}$, took place, then it must have happened just a finite time ago from Alice's present count of the number 1.

In Morriston's view, the whole series of past events may be comprised of infinitely-many events, and yet *between* the present event, m, and any past event, e, in that series there is only a *finite* number of intermediate events [770]. Whatever number Alice ever counted, it was only a finite number away from the number 1 and so a finite time for her to count down to 1. Alice therefore can complete her infinite count down to 1.

Consequently, we end up with a contradiction. Because $\mathbb{N} \triangleq \omega$, and no n, no matter how high, can reduce the quantity of numbers in $\mathbb{N}$ left over ($\omega - n = \omega$), Alice never reaches any specific finite number that is only finitely away in sequence from 1. Her count never concludes. But because Alice only counts naturals and every n is finite ($n < \omega$), we know Alice completes her count down to 1; her count concludes. Alice does not and yet does conclude her count: a contradiction.

The contradiction occurs because of how $\mathbb{N}$ is defined in transfinite mathematics—both as a set containing limitlessly many numbers and so a set that is *greater* than any n in $\mathbb{N}$ (since $\mathbb{N} \triangleq \omega$) and yet as a set containing *only* finite numbers, each of which is an exact sum, which implies a reducible whole rather than a whole "greater" than a sum. Such a definition may be used in mathematically consistent ways, but only if you "abstract out" (ignore) the contradictory logical implications of such a definition by defining the operations in such a way that they never come up.

There is, of course, a way to resolve the contradiction but it comes at a cost too great for the transfinite system. Suppose the natural number scale is a whole "greater" than every n and every combination of naturals *but not as a set*. Suppose instead $\mathbb{N}$ is greater than any n and any combination of its own numbers because $\mathbb{N}$ is a (temporal) *series* rather than a set. Instead of $\mathbb{N}$, we have $\mathbb{N}^C$, and $\mathbb{N}^C$ is always finite. In that case, no contradiction occurs. Alice could count down from any natural number, no matter how indefinitely large from our point of view because however large that number is, it is only a finitely large number—the natural number scale is never a complete scale anyway. And so even if Alice had been counting for as long as the past has been, that would only entail the past is finite rather than infinite. But then, to resolve the contradiction caused by the transfinite definition of the natural number scale as a set is to deny the literal infinitude of $\mathbb{N}$ and so undermine the transfinite system.

Since that is the only way to make sense of $\mathbb{N}$ being greater than any number in $\mathbb{N}$ or any combination of such numbers, we are left to conclude the transfinite system is therefore not logically consistent even if its rules can be used in mathematically coherent ways. Because of that, the transfinite definition of literal infinity is of no help for resolving the contradiction faced by the concept of an infinite past.

Alice can complete her count because the literally infinite past is a complete sequence of events and Alice cannot compete her count because the literally infinite past is a limitless sequence of events. The infinite past cannot be traversed because it is limitless and yet it can be because it is complete. We are lost in a hopeless contradiction with the concept of an infinite past. Better to conclude that infinity simply does not apply to the past.

19.3.6 *The Past as Complete and Limitless*

In short, the completeness and limitlessness of the past, as illustrated in a countdown from infinity to 1, is problematic on two levels. First, while a countdown from infinity to 1 implies no first number by virtue of the limitlessness of the countdown, that implication does not consider that the completeness of the count requires an infinitely large number from which to count down. Second, because a countdown from infinity ends at 1, the countdown is complete, but this ignores that there would have to have been *limitlessly many* prior numbers to count and that contradicts that the count can *become* complete. So, an infinite past (a) has no beginning at all due to the limitlessness of the past but (b) must have an infinitely prior beginning due to completeness of the past, which gives us infinitely many intermediates. A contradiction that is irresolvable.

19.3.7 *An Infinite Past Is Sensible...But Only If You Ignore Half the Problem*

Philosophers, scientists, and mathematicians have debated for centuries whether the past is infinite. One set of authors (William Lane Craig, G. J. Whitrow, et al.) argues against an infinite past by stressing the limitlessness of literal infinity, and so the inability to cross an infinite series, while another set of authors (Wes Morriston, Graham Oppy, et al.) argues the past can be infinite by stressing the completeness of literal infinity and so the ability to cross an infinite series, at least in principle. Both sides get their reasoning wrong because both sides abstract out either the limitlessness or the completeness of literal infinity in various aspects of their analysis, not realizing the two imply inherent contradictions. Until the scholars on each side of the debate address *both* aspects of literal infinity together and admit the logical contradictions between the two properties of completeness and limitlessness, the opposing camps will each miss the point the other camp is making and debate themselves in circles.

Both camps will continue to believe an infinite series of past events cannot be completed (says Craig and Whitrow) or can be completed (says Morriston and Oppy) because both answers are implied by literal infinity. When both aspects of literal infinity—its completeness and limitlessness—are met head-on, we see that literal infinity is a self-contradiction. As we learn in the study of logic, you can get any answer you want from a contradiction.

Nevertheless, both camps of scholars are not equally wrong in their debate—one side does win the debate, but not in the way they expect. The philosophers arguing against an infinite past (Craig, Whitrow, et al.) are correct that the past cannot be infinite, but they have heretofore been correct in their conclusion for the wrong reasons—it's not that infinity is logical while the past cannot be infinite due to metaphysical constraints; rather, it's that the past cannot be infinite because infinity is a self-contradictory concept and self-contradictions cannot manifest in reality.

19.3.8 *Reductio Ad Absurdum*

The debate about an infinite past has gone on for centuries because an infinite past sounds like a plausible concept unless it is sufficiently scrutinized. Scholars have up to now assumed mathematics helps make the concept of infinity precise, but math actually obscures the incoherence of literal infinity instead of revealing it for what it is.

Our ability to form a mathematically indefinite sequence (such as ..., 3, 2, 1), like Euclid's method of exhaustion, gives the illusion of infinity. The illusion occurs when we confuse indefiniteness with limitlessness. When we use an indefinite sequence (..., 3, 2, 1) not only for an indefinitely long past but for a past without beginning, we create the illusion of logical consistency for an infinite past where none exists.

Exposing the contradictions implied by a literally infinite past was therefore never a matter of mathematical demonstration. The mathematics of infinity, as I pointed out earlier, is irrelevant since the mathematical operations only treat 'infinity' (whether denoted as ∞, ω, $\aleph$, etc.) in the expressions as either a serial indefinite or, at best, a collective indefinite sequence or set—either way, not as a genuinely *limitless* sequence or set. Consequently, the syntactical formalism of the mathematics of 'infinity' never addresses the logical contradictions inherent in the semantics of the literal infinity mathematicians often assume it to be.

19.4 ARGUMENTS AGAINST THE FUTURE AS INFINITE

If time has an infinite future, then the collection of all events that will ever occur from m onward is also a complete collection of future events and those events are limitless in quantity.

Just like the imaginary index of time past, listing all events that have ever happened from an infinite past, we can imagine an index of time future—a listing of "the things that have not happened, but will happen in the time before us," as Scrooge intoned to the Ghost of Christmas Yet To Come [771]. Suppose, then, we have an index listing a string of events that follow after m, going on into a literally infinite future. The index, being a listing of events that is literally infinite, would be a complete listing of all future events— the listing of events would be whole, entire, finished, full, and total. And yet, the index of time future would also be a listing of events without limit, so there would be a first page in which the first entry is m (perhaps the entry states, "You read this entry.") but there would be no last page and no last entry.

This should sound familiar. It's the same situation we found in § 17.4 with the book pulled from Craig's Library, in which there is and is not a last page to turn to. Once again, we find a contradiction: a complete index of future events that cannot be complete due to its limitlessness. The index, by virtue of limitlessness, has no last entry constituting a finished total. Nevertheless, it has a finished total by virtue of its completeness—there is a back cover of the index because it is an index of *all* events to come. The concept of a literally infinite future is therefore just as self-contradictory as the concept of a literally infinite past.

19.4.1 *A Literally Infinite Future Never Completed*

Morriston and Oppy are perhaps the two most prominent proponents of literal (or 'actual') infinity in academia. They both argue that carrying a literally infinite series of tasks is possible and therefore it is possible for the future to be infinite. I believe they are both mistaken. First, let's consider Morriston's view.

To explicate what an infinite future entails, Morriston offers a fanciful analogy in which two angels, Gabriel and Uriel, take turns praising God (for example, by saying, "Hallelujah") into an "endless"—that is, literally limitless—future [772]. According to Morriston, because God wills the two angels to keep praising and never stop, they will say a literally infinite quantity of praises [773] [774]:

> So as not to leave any opportunity for Gabriel or Uriel to mess things up, let's suppose that this is no mere instruction or recommendation, but that God has exercised His supreme power in such a way as to *make* it the case that *each* praise in the endless series of praises we have envisaged *will* occur. Each of them is discrete, wholly determinate, and certain to occur because God has determined that it *will* occur.
>
> It's true, of course, that Gabriel and Uriel will never *complete* the series of praises. They will never arrive at a time at which they have said all of them. Indeed, they will never arrive at a time at which they have said infinitely many praises. At every stage in the future series of events as I am imagining it, they will have said only finitely many. *But that makes not a particle of difference to the point I am about to make.* If you ask, "How many distinct praises *will be* said?" the only sensible answer is, *infinitely many.*

Morriston goes on to explain that in saying the angels will offer infinitely many praises, he does not mean the praises "are somehow 'there' in the future, waiting for their turn to become present" [775]. Rather, Morriston simply means that "God has *determined* that *each* member of the endless series of praises will occur" [776].

Moreover, says Morriston, the number of future praises is not "indefinite," which he says could only mean there's no fact of the matter whether or not the praises will actually occur. Instead, God has determined how many *must* occur: "Their number can only be infinite" [777]. In fact, Morriston says, the hallelujahs can be "placed in one-to-one correspondence with the series of natural numbers" [778]. So, we can be sure the number of praises is not indefinite but is instead infinite.

That, in a nutshell, is Morriston's view, and I argue it is erroneous because it logically confuses several properties, such as the following:

1. The difference between indefiniteness of quantity and indeterminism.
2. The difference between an ontologically determined future and an actual future.
3. The difference between actual (literal) infinity and potential (figurative) infinity.

Let's consider the first item. Suppose the number of future praises is 'infinite' in the figurative sense of the term and the number of praises in the future is therefore quantitatively *indefinite*. Morriston claims "indefinite" can only sensibly mean there's no fact of the matter as to whether the praises will occur. However, that is not true.

To say the number of future praises is indefinite is not to say we're unsure whether Gabriel and Uriel will say more praises. The term "indefinite" is a term used in reference to the *number* of praises that will be said. It is not an ontological property of whether or not the praises are said but rather an epistemic property about a statement regarding their *quantity*. Indefiniteness is not the same as quantum acausality or ontological indeterminism; it is not the happening of each praise that is indefinite, but the quantity of future praises that is epistemically indefinite relative to the present. To say the number of future praises is indefinite does not mean we are unsure whether they will be said at all but rather it is just to say we in the present cannot specify their quantity.

So, as to what indefiniteness of quantity means, to say the number of future praises—a quantity we claim them to have from our vantage point in the present—is 'indefinite' is just to say we can, from our vantage point, assign no definite value to the number of praises that will be said. Which is exactly what would be the case if the future is 'infinite' in only a figurative sense—perhaps the future contains too many events to quantify while nevertheless being finite at any step of the way. That is, perhaps the number of praises to take place is indefinite in the sense that any number we could attribute to a count of the praises that will be said shall be later exceeded. Moreover, perhaps the praises are also 'indefinite' in the sense that the praises will ceaselessly *continue to accrue* without any predefined quantity of praises taking place as a standing total of the praises to come. That kind of indefiniteness is just a figurative infinity of future praises and does not necessarily imply a literal infinity of praises exists to be said.

As if in retort, Morriston points out that the exact number of praises to happen in the future would be known by an omniscient God [779]. If there were a God to so determine, then Morriston's point is granted. But it is *we* who make the *claims* about *how many* praises God wills there to be. So, from *our* vantage point here and now, to claim God wills there to come "infinitely many" more praises may mean either a literal infinity of praises or a figurative infinity of praises.

If we claim God determines only a figuratively 'infinite' amount of praises is yet to come, then what we mean is this: Given the largest finite numbers invented up to now there always will be larger finite numbers of further praises to come. At any remote (indefinitely removed) time in the future that we could only in principle name, some indefinitely large quantity of praises will have been said at that time. To claim that "infinitely many" praises could be said by Gabriel and Uriel in the figurative (or "potential") sense of infinity is therefore to claim an indefinitely large running total of praises ceaselessly accrues *toward no defined end*. To say infinitely many praises will be said in the figurative sense of the term does not mean there is some quantity of praises to come that is a completed and yet limitless quantity of praises—a *literal* infinity of them.

Furthermore, to say there will be indefinitely many praises is not to imply indeterminism as to whether each future praise will be said. Gabriel and Uriel can continue with their praises, without ever stopping, and yet—as Morriston admitted—there will always be a finite number said [780]. So, the concept of a figuratively infinite future is consistent with the supposition that God causally determines the course of the future. What that leaves unaddressed is our main concern: does the concept of a literally infinite future make logical sense?

The issue of determinism brings us to the second item. Morriston proposes infinitely many praises *will be* said not because there will ever come a time that infinitely many *have been* said but rather because God will make sure praises never fail to be said [781]. In other words, God causally determines the future, so the future is actually infinite. So, there is no logical problem with the future being infinite. To which I say, Morriston's proposal makes no clear sense at all.

Just because God puts into place a provision to ensure a process will continue without ceasing does not mean the process, or the future over which it takes place, is literally infinite. The causal determinism for the sequence of future events taking place does not entail there is some specific, predetermined quantity of future time. A programmer may create a computer algorithm to run without stopping, but that doesn't mean the programmer determined how many iterations of the program would happen ahead of time. So too with God's determinism of future praises. Hence, there is no reason why that determinism must require a literally infinite quantity of praises to take place. All a causally determined future filled with praises entails is that, *for as long as there will be time*, there will be praises and, after each praise is said, another will be said. However, it need not be true that there is, right now, infinitely many—a complete and limitless quantity of—praises that will later be said.

In fact, according to Morriston, there cannot be a complete and limitless quantity of praises that will be said because he assures us that "Gabriel and Uriel will never *complete* the series of praises...Indeed, they will never arrive at a time at which they have said infinitely many praises... At every stage in the future series of events as I am imagining it, they will have said only finitely many" [782]. But that is exactly what figurative infinity is—not literal infinity. Completeness is a trait of what it means to be infinite in the literal sense. An incomplete series is not a literally infinite—or actually infinite—series; it can only be a figuratively infinite series. So, if Gabriel and Uriel will never complete a limitless quantity of praises, they will never have said infinitely many praises—at least, not in the literal sense. Unfortunately, this conflicts with Morriston's original claim to an actual, or literal, infinite series of future praises.

Of course, Morriston could point out that denying completion to a series of future events is certainly consistent with the *limitlessness* of that series. True enough, but denying completeness is also consistent with a figurative infinity rather than a literal infinity because a figurative infinity can also go on without ever completing and yet it is, in more literal terms, finite.

Further, to say the quantity of future praises is limitless means no range can be specified, even in principle, for the quantity of praises to be said. But Morriston then undercuts the limitlessness of infinity by pointing out that if God knows the future, then "the future hallelujahs in our example are also 'definite' and 'distinct' and can be 'numbered.' If not by us, then by God" [783]. If the infinite "number" of praises is not just loosely symbolized by a symbol such as $\aleph$ but instead by a more "definite and determinate" number, then not only does that conflict with what it means to be *without limit*, such would imply that the number must refer to a set we can take as a *complete* set, which contradicts his thesis that there is no such thing as completeness for an infinite quantity.

The problems don't end there. Morriston also refutes his own denial of the praises reaching a state of completeness by his own use of a past tense verb: "If you ask, 'How many distinct praises *will be* said?' the only sensible answer is, *infinitely many*" [784]. But that many cannot be *said* at all because the word "said" is the past tense of the verb "say," and Morriston just claimed that at any time only *finitely many* are ever *said* because the infinite future is never completed [785]. The only feasible way out of this is to admit "infinitely many" in the literal sense implies not just a limitless collection but also that the collection is a complete collection after all.

To see why this must be so, take the following sentences:

- It is true that Gabriel and Uriel *will say* infinitely many hallelujahs.
- It is true that infinitely many hallelujahs *will be said* by Gabriel and Uriel.

As to the first sentence, the phrase "infinitely many" may be taken either literally (a complete and limitless quantity) or figuratively (a continuously growing quantity). If figuratively, the sentence is merely claiming that Gabriel and Uriel never stop saying hallelujahs—what I have referred to as an incomplete, indefinite process or ceaseless process. That is not a literal infinity.

As to the second sentence, "infinitely many" here implies a literal infinity for exactly the reason Morriston claims it doesn't—the only reason infinitely many praises "will be said" is because at some time in the future infinitely many praises *have been* said. Infinitely many are "said" in the future because that many must be completed in the future for the past tense of "say" to be true.

Consider: if at *no time* in the future infinitely many praises *have been* said, then it is false that infinitely many *will be* said—on the contrary, infinitely many *will never be* said precisely *because* there will never be a time at which infinitely many have been said. If at no time will it ever be true that infinitely many *have been* said, then it is necessarily true infinitely many never *will be* said—only finitely many will ever be said. Hence, what "will be" said is a claim about what from the vantage of some later time "has been" said—the word 'said' is, after all, past tense.

The only other possible way to affirm the infinitude of the future while denying the completeness of that infinite future is to claim that the second sentence is just a restatement of the first—that to propose infinitely many hallelujahs *will be said* by Gabriel and Uriel is just another way of expressing that Gabriel and Uriel *will say* infinitely many. But even if we accept this, we now lose the use of tense for distinguishing literal infinity (a completed quantity of what is to be *said*—a 'definite' and 'distinct' number) from figurative infinity (an incomplete, running total of praises the angels *will say*). Since that distinction of tense is what Morriston rests his position on, his position is on conceptually shaky ground, for the difference between literal and figurative infinity is clear.

This brings us to the third and last item. Morriston asks rhetorically [786]: "How, exactly, are we supposed to distinguish between a true actual infinite and a mere potential one?" He then proceeds to claim there isn't a difference [787]. But of course, there is [788]. An 'actual infinite' (a literally infinite collection) is one in which the members all exist at once relative to a given time; a 'potential infinite' (a figuratively infinite series) is a process in which the members only come one after another in succession—not all at once relative to a given time—and there is never a literally limitless quantity of them relative to a given time.

With respect to future time, an actually infinite—or literally infinite—future is a future that is a complete collection of all events which from our vantage in the present "will be" in an ongoing succession without limit but are already "there" in the future as a complete sequence. The actually infinite future relative to the present is rather like having a prophetic book indexing everything that will happen...without end. It is a complete book with a limitless sequence of entries all provided at once. Whereas a 'potentially infinite'—that is, a figuratively infinite—future is a future without the possibility of such an index. If the future is only figuratively infinite, then all we can say about the quantity of praises that "will be" is that such a quantity *must* be ever greater than any number we can, in practice, name—an indefinitely large quantity that keeps growing larger without terminating.

In fact, Morriston, perhaps unintentionally, acknowledges the difference between the two senses of infinite future when he says, "This endless series of future hallelujahs can be placed in one-to-one correspondence to the series of natural numbers" [789]. By "series" of natural numbers, I take it he means $\mathbb{N}$ as a transfinite *set*. Hence, Morriston, in claiming a *series* of future events can be put into bijection with $\mathbb{N}$ as a transfinite *set*, is claiming the future is both complete and limitless in quantity after all. That is, unless he wants to deny $\mathbb{N}$ is a complete set, in which case the amount of numbers in $\mathbb{N}$ is always an incomplete series—a growing, finite succession and not a literally infinite collection.

The bottom line is that in attempting to justify the 'actual infinite' future by erasing the difference between actual and potential, literal and figurative, Morriston just ends up refuting the notion that the future can be an actual infinite in any coherent sense and reaffirming only a figuratively 'infinite' future.

19.4.2 *Another Argument for an Incomplete, yet Infinite, Future*

Morriston's thought experiment about angels saying infinitely many praises expresses the same principle as our thought experiment about Alice counting out infinitely many natural numbers. But we can make an even closer parity. Instead of Alice counting *down* an infinite sequence of natural numbers to finish at the present, suppose we imagine Alice starting a count from the present and proceeding *up* the sequence of natural numbers to infinity. Alice starts counting at 1 and proceeds to count *endlessly*. The count proceeds without end, not just in the sense of going on indefinitely, always having a larger finite amount in a running total, but rather without end in the sense of progressing through a *limitless* future. And yet, despite the limitlessness of Alice's count into the future, suppose the future count is a complete sequence as well. The numbers she will count are "all there" in the future waiting to be counted; they form a complete set despite their limitless quantity, and each number in the set will be counted.

Here is where Oppy's view of infinity comes in. Like Morriston, Oppy rejects the last premise—he initially proposes a literally infinite count can proceed from a first element even though the count does not have a subsequent element that *completes* the series [790]. In other words, a series can be infinite without being brought to completion.

Consider a sequence of days. Suppose Alice is counting days as they happen for her, crossing each day off her infinite calendar of days as each day passes. The days are all numbered, starting with 1 for Alice's first day and continuing up the series of natural numbers to enumerate each subsequent day. According to Oppy, an infinite collection with a first element has no subsequent element "*at which* the collection can be said to be completed or *by which* the collection can be said to be completed. If, for example, we are considering a possible world in which there is a first day, then there is no day in that world at which the collection of days forms a completed infinity" [791]. Supposing the first day is today, then Oppy's position suggests that there *will never be* a future day upon which an infinite sequence of future days has been completed.

The notion of having no last element or no last day is indeed consistent with the concept of limitlessness, which in turn is part of the concept of literal infinity—and by which infinity gets its name. However, while a literally infinite sequence of days has no limit in the sense of a last day, simply denying there is a day by which the collection of days ever becomes complete is not *sufficient* for the collection to be *literally* limitless.

A collection that has no final element is consistent with being a series that grows ceaselessly larger—a serial indefinite rather than a literally *infinite* series. As such, the series of days ahead would be only figuratively 'infinite' or 'limitless' rather than literally so. Thus far, the 'infinity' Oppy addresses is at best only a figurative 'infinity'—a sequence of elements (such as a sequence of future days) that is really finite after all by virtue of remaining ever incomplete by the common meaning of 'complete' explicated in Chapter 3.

But literal infinity is not just limitlessness, it is also a state of completeness. So, pointing out the lack of a final element does not address the completeness of literal infinity and that spells trouble for Oppy's view that the future is literally infinite.

However, Oppy seems to realize a collection can only be literally infinite if it is also a complete collection, so he proposes a way out of this problem by redefining what it means to be 'complete' for any sequence that is enumerated. After stating that there is no day at which the collection of days comes to completion, he goes on to say the sequence of days "nonetheless" forms a "completed infinity" because the sequence has "infinitely many days that are ordered by the 'is the next day after' relation" according to "a standpoint external" to this "possible world" of infinite days [792].

In other words, Oppy is implying that a literally infinite sequence can be considered 'complete' *despite* not having a last day that would otherwise complete the sequence in the ordinary sense of the term 'complete'. Basically, Oppy is proposing that there is more than one way for a collection to qualify as a 'complete' collection. Perhaps some collections are complete by virtue of being whole, entire, finished, full, and total collections while other collections do not have to be 'complete' in that sense to be 'complete' *per se*. So, he is instead proposing an alternative, technical definition for the term 'complete' and applying it specifically for infinite collections.

Oppy says an infinite sequence of days is a 'complete' sequence of days from the view of an observer in a frame of reference outside the sequence—at "a standpoint external" to the sequence of days—because, according to that outside observer, the days are ordered according to the "is the next day after" relation and such an order is *isomorphic* (i.e., matches one-to-one) with "a (perhaps improper) segment of the integers" [793]. In other words, the limitless future can be "complete" in the sense that it is a transfinite set of days, D, where $D = \mathbb{N}$, as seen from that external standpoint or frame of reference.

But in substituting this technical definition of completeness for the ordinary, lexical understanding of completeness, Oppy's argument mistakenly commits a red herring fallacy and a bit of circular reasoning. Let's take a look at each.

First, the red herring. If a sequence is 'complete' because it maps to $\mathbb{N}$ as an infinite set, then what is it about $\mathbb{N}$ as a set that confers completeness if $\mathbb{N}$ has no last number? Oppy's definition of completeness doesn't seem to apply to the set of numbers that he claims is infinite and that he therefore uses to demonstrate that some other collection regarded as infinite qualifies as complete. After all, we can't show $\mathbb{N}$ is "complete" by matching $\mathbb{N}$ to $\mathbb{N}$. So what is it about $\mathbb{N}$ that makes $\mathbb{N}$ complete? Oppy's technical use of complete never answers how it is that a set of numbers can be complete while having no highest number. It just evades the issue of what it means for any instance of literal infinity—including a set of numbers—to be "complete" as well as limitless.

Second, Oppy's argument is also somewhat circular. He assumes literal infinity is a property of a set of numbers ($\mathbb{N}$) that can be placed into bijection with a sequence of days ordered by the "is the next day after" relation, thereby demonstrating the sequence of days to be as literally infinite as the set of numbers in $\mathbb{N}$. From there he concludes a "completed infinity" of future days is demonstrated [794]. But the logical coherence of a literally infinite sequence of numbers rests on the assumption that literal infinity is itself a coherent concept and that $\mathbb{N}$ is itself an example of an infinite sequence. The problem is that this argument assumes what needs proving: that a literally infinite sequence of *any* kind makes logical sense. If it doesn't, then a sequence of days extending into a literally infinite future is not necessarily a coherent concept any more than is a literally infinite sequence of anything else, numbers included.

Hence, Oppy must first prove that literal infinity makes sense as a condition of being both limitless and *complete*—that is, 'complete' by independent criteria—before he can, in a non-question-begging manner, designate some ordered sequence, such as the numbers of $\mathbb{N}$, as 'complete' and therefore use $\mathbb{N}$ as the standard by which to designate other sets as literally infinite if they map to $\mathbb{N}$. Unfortunately, demonstrating that a collection can be both complete and limitless—and so literally infinite—Oppy has not done. Until such can be shown, particularly for a sequence of numbers, Oppy's technical use of the term 'complete' as an isomorphic ordering between days and numbers may make mathematical sense, but it does not make logical sense out of the meaning of literal infinity.

Oppy's reliance on mathematical isomorphism between a sequence and its enumeration may imply, at best, not a complete (literal) infinity but only a figurative infinity. § 2.3.9 proposed that number scales are invented rather than discovered and only go as high as anyone has defined numbers (or can, at least in principle, define them) at a given time. If that is correct, then even if we form a bijection between a sequence of days and a sequence of numbers, this simply implies the two sequences—days and numbers—are *growing* tit-for-tat in parallel; the bijection would not be a static structure formed all at once but instead a *process* of matching up elements between two inherently incomplete series. And that means there would be only a figurative infinity of days and numbers matched to them, not a literal infinity of days and numbers because even a bijection between days and numbers is itself a project under construction rather than a finished product. To counter such a proposal, Oppy needs a way to not only match days to the numbers of $\mathbb{N}$, but also a way to show $\mathbb{N}$ is complete without a highest number. That he has not done.

Finally, consider the "standpoint external" (outside frame of reference) to the "possible world" (infinite sequence of future days) that Oppy refers to. Oppy would counter that while Alice may be counting out each day, one at a time without end, the observer watching it from a standpoint external to the sequence of days—presumably, an observer in a frame of reference that can somehow 'timelessly' view the whole sequence at once—would see the sequence as complete because the days are all matched to the numbers of $\mathbb{N}$ [795]. But even if we suppose the numbers of $\mathbb{N}$ are infinite and waiting to be matched up with elements of another set, this still does not help Oppy's case for the days comprising an infinite future because an observer external to the sequence can only see the sequence as *complete* if in fact Alice has a last day to count out—as Stevens would have said, an "omegath" day [796]. If Alice can never count out such a day, then the observer at the standpoint external to Alice's world cannot see her sequence of days as complete because Alice never completes them. What we see from the external standpoint depends on what can possibly happen from Alice's internal standpoint. If she never marks off a last day, then there is no finish to the sequence, and without a finish, the sequence is never complete.

This conclusion also favors the natural numbers with which Alice counts out the days as being themselves an incomplete collection—$\mathbb{N}^{\circ}$ as an open series rather than $\mathbb{N}$ as a complete set. Which makes the bijection between the days and the naturals of $\mathbb{N}$ a matching-up of members during serial formation rather than a match-up of members in a complete set. At best, Oppy's argument simply provides us with grounds that a span of time can be a figurative infinity, not a literal infinity. His argument for a literally infinite future, as a 'complete' infinite span of time, is therefore not sound.

19.4.3 *Tristram Shandy's Autobiography*

We keep coming back to the conclusion that insofar as an infinite sequence of future days is mathematically coherent, such a sequence is figuratively infinite rather than literally infinite. This conclusion is reinforced by the solution to the well-known paradox of Tristram Shandy, introduced by Bertrand Russell in his book *The Principles of Mathematics* [797].

The immortal Tristram Shandy writes his autobiography at a rate of one day per year; in other words, it takes him a whole year to finish writing about a single day in his autobiography [798]. Though he falls further behind every year, he can still write about every day of his life if he lives for an infinite amount of time, thus catching up with his story and completing it at infinity. How can this be—how can he fall further and further behind and yet write about every day he will ever live?

The way to solve this conundrum is to reject that Shandy lives through a literal infinity of days to write about *all* of them to completion even though they are limitless in quantity. We simply reject the notion that Shandy must forever be falling behind in his task and yet at some point of time infinitely in the future will "catch up" to *complete* his autobiography. There is no such point of time in the future. Rather, Shandy will never complete his autobiography even though for any day of his life he will later write about that day [799]. This means only that, though the complete autobiography will never be written, no individual part of the autobiography will remain unwritten forever. For any day of Shandy's life, Shandy will eventually write about that day.

Contrary to Russell's analysis, Shandy does not live through a future that is complete or realized. His 'infinite' future is not *literally* infinite since his autobiography will never be completed—it is simply a process of writing carried out ceaselessly while always remaining finite. It is an indefinite future, a *figuratively* infinite future rather than a literally infinite future. This is yet another example of how mathematics provides us with figurative infinity while the interpretation of that infinity as literally infinite—complete and limitless—offers only contradictory implications.

19.4.4 *The Finite Future*

Like the concept of an infinite past, the concept of an infinite future is also plagued with contradictions—not just paradoxes, but outright contradictory implications. The only way to logically resolve them is to reject the notion of literally infinite successions of time and hold instead that time is finite.

However, that does not mean time will come to an end. Perhaps the future is an open-ended, indefinitely growing series of days to come—a future that is always a finite sequence of events no matter how large the sequence continues to grow. If so, the future would be ceaseless, but always remain finite—at best, this would be a *figuratively* infinite future rather than a *literally* infinite future. Alternatively, perhaps time is 'unbounded' in a different sense, with the future looping back to become the past in a closed circuit of moments—but that too makes time finite since a closed sequence is finite [800].

Regardless of which one is true, both of these temporal models present the future as finite rather than literally infinite because neither of these temporal models portrays a complete and limitless set of moments waiting to happen. So, whatever the situation may be, the future is finite rather than (literally) infinite.

19.5 ARGUMENTS AGAINST INFINITE BREVITY

Real time is objectively measured with durations of indexical and schematic time that can be further divided into smaller metrical durations—an hour can be divided into minutes, minutes into seconds, and seconds into orders of sub-seconds such as the decisecond, centisecond, millisecond, microsecond, nanosecond, etc. The question naturally arises: how brief can an interval of time be divided? I will argue that however brief an interval of time can be, it cannot be infinitely brief and real time contains no infinitely brief periods.

19.5.1 *Chronons, Planck Time, and Ephemerals*

Some quantum physicists hypothesize that any interval of real time—that is, 'real time' is the time during which physical processes occur—can only be indexed into a series of briefer intervals until we reach an interval too brief for physical effects to occur. Their hypothesized, smallest unit of real time during which a physical effect can take place is called a *chronon* [801]. A chronon is so brief it is equivalent to the duration a photon of light takes to travel the diameter of an electron, which makes a chronon about 10^{-24} seconds [802]. Take the number 1 followed by 24 zeros and divide a single second that many times; that's how brief a chronon is. Briefer than that, no measurable changes to physical states can take place.

However, other quantum physicists disagree, holding instead that there are intervals of time much briefer than a photon's traversal across the diameter of an electron, and yet during which physical changes can still take place. There is a wide range of values that physicists have suggested for a fundamental unit of time, but the most widely held view seems to be that energy and mass can still effect change during the passage of a photon over one Planck length, which you'll recall is near 10^{-35} meters. Such a brief interval of time, equal to nearly 10^{-44} seconds, is called a *Planck time*, again named after physicist Max Planck [803]. Hence, some quantum physicists hold it is Planck time that is the fundamental unit of time—an "atom of time," the briefest interval of time—an interval of time briefer than which no change can take place [804].

Because a chronon is held to be the briefest interval of real, physical time, briefer than which no physical change can take place [805], and the same has been claimed for Planck time [806], some physicists suggest the chronon just is Planck time [807] [808].

And yet, there are still many physicists who believe time is much more continuous than either 10^{-24} seconds or even 10^{-44} seconds allow. Some physicists specializing in Einstein's Theory of Relativity say that if there are chronons, they must be much briefer in duration than Planck time, and some quantum physicists would agree, suggesting the duration of a chronon can have just about any arbitrarily brief value [809].

It's hard enough to imagine just how brief Planck time is; but now suppose we divide Plank time into briefer intervals of time—intervals far less than that which would carry measurable, physical effects in the real world. Moreover, suppose we persist in dividing each of these sub-Planck time intervals into briefer intervals still. Rather than simply divide a Plank time into half its duration, suppose we instead divide that interval into half, then that one into half, and so on, indefinitely. That is, we divide an interval of Planck time into ever briefer intervals of time until an interval of time itself is indefinitely brief. Perhaps chronons are *indefinitely brief* measures of time—perhaps they are 'ephemeral' (see § 6.4.2).

We now have at least three different proposals for the duration of a chronon. We should avoid confusing chronons as intervals of photon flight time from chronons as intervals of Planck time, and either of those conceptions from chronons as indefinitely brief intervals of time. We also need to avoid confusing chronons as intervals of real time from chronons as solely schematic units of measurement for (real) time.

To make matters simpler for this discussion, I propose another change in vocabulary. I will refer to an indefinitely brief moment of time, *whether of purely indexical time or of real time*, as an 'ephemeral' (noun).

An ephemeral is not a chronon since a chronon has some definite duration according to a given theory (10^{-24}, 10^{-44} seconds, etc.) while an ephemeral is *indefinitely brief*. Which is to say, an ephemeral is a moment of time so small it is off of any scale of measurement we could ever devise in actual practice.

However, while to be indefinitely brief is to be *like* an instant of time because indefinite brevity is a brevity of which we can only say it's smaller than any defined length of time, it is also true that to be indefinitely brief is neither to be *instantaneous* nor to be *infinitely* brief. This means an 'ephemeral' is also not a timeless instant and an ephemeral is not an infinitely brief moment; indefinitely fleeting as it is, an ephemeral is a *finite* interval because we could in principle give it an exact mathematical value even if we cannot do so in practice.

With the proposal of ephemerals, we now have a new question to consider: is an ephemeral further divisible, or is an ephemeral the fundamental element of time—the briefest interval of time even in principle?

19.5.2 *On Times Briefer Than None*

Time may be indefinitely divisible in one of two ways.

One way is for time to be indefinitely divisible in the sense that it would take an indefinite number of divisions to reach the scale of ephemerals, and each ephemeral is indefinitely brief but not further divisible. Ephemerals would be fundamental moments of time, with each ephemeral approximately the same (albeit unspecified) duration.

Another way for time to be indefinitely divisible is for time to be continuously divisible. That is, no matter how many times we divide time into smaller units, the time so divided never ends with fundamental intervals—there are no indivisible ephemerals that constitute fundamental intervals of time, such as 'atoms' of real time.

We'll briefly explore each of these ways in turn.

19.5.3 *Ephemerals as Fundamental Units of Time*

There are three ways ephemerals might be conceived of as fundamental units of time:

1. Ephemerals are fundamental intervals of real time.
2. Ephemerals are fundamental intervals of schematic time.
3. Ephemerals are fundamental intervals of real *and* schematic time.

Given the first option, ephemerals would preexist any mathematical division of time into intervals. Ephemerals by this conception are indivisible intervals of real time, each of indefinite brevity.

The second option is to propose ephemerals are the briefest intervals of a measurement schema for time. When we propose ephemerals to be fundamental intervals of measurement schemas for time, we are simply claiming that our scale of temporal measurement goes down to the ephemeral—an indefinitely small fraction of a second in duration. The ephemeral is not a definite unit of time, but an indefinitely small unit of time. It is therefore a unit of time that could be used for measurement purposes only in principle rather than in practice. This would be an idealized unit of time that need not correspond to the real world. So if *real time* were composed of units equal to Planck time, our measurement schema for time could still propose ephemerals as fundamental units of *schematic time*, which would be therefore composed of units much smaller than the units of real time.

The third option is to claim both of the first two options hold true: our time schema has the ephemeral as its fundamental interval and that interval corresponds to the briefest interval of real time that can exist. As a unit of schematic time, the ephemeral points to a duration too small to measure in practice. As a unit of real time the ephemeral is therefore empirically indistinguishable from a non-quantized continuum of time.

All the above options hold ephemerals, whether intervals of real time or merely intervals of indexical/schematic time, to be fundamental intervals of time. That's one sense of indefinitely divisible time—to be in principle able to divide a duration of time down to a fundamental interval called an 'ephemeral'.

19.5.4 *Ephemerals as Increasingly Smaller Units of Time*

According to another sense of indefinitely divisible time, the term 'time' also refers either to real time or to indexical/schematic time; it makes no difference since the process of measurement used to divide time into intervals has the same implications. In the second sense of indefinite divisibility, time does not have properties that differ according to duration. Indefinitely divisible time, according to the second sense of indefinite divisibility, is time that no matter how often divided never ends with fundamental intervals—there are no indivisible ephemerals that constitute fundamental intervals of time, such as 'atoms' of real time.

Instead, time on *all* scales is a seamless and fluid process—entirely without preexisting pauses or stochastic jumps—and is only divided into parts or portions in mathematical description during a measurement or schematizing process. Any ephemeral duration is composed of even briefer durations that are also divisible into yet briefer durations, and so on. Indefinitely divisible time is time capable of being persistently or ceaselessly divided, including indefinitely dividing ephemerals into ever more ephemeral ephemerals.

19.5.5 *The Two Meanings of 'Ephemeral'*

We therefore have two different senses of what it means for time to be 'indefinitely divisible': on the one hand, the ability to completely divide down to fundamental 'ephemerals', and on the other hand the ability to, at least in principle, divide time down toward no fundamental level (i.e., divide time ceaselessly).

Whether or not real time is indefinitely divisible, and in which sense it would be so, is a topic that must wait for another book [810]. For now, the important point is that the two conceptions of indefinitely divisible time are both distinct from *infinitely* divisible time, to which we'll now turn.

19.5.6 *The Continuum of Infinitely Divisible Time*

While many physicists specializing in quantum physics believe there are briefest intervals of time (typically, held to be Planck-time intervals), other physicists disagree and hold that time is, like space, not just indefinitely divisible but infinitely divisible [811]. If time is infinitely divisible, then any 'instant' of time would not just be of Planck-time interval; rather, it would have to be an infinitely brief moment of time (assuming it is non-zero). This is how many physicists in the tradition of Einstein regard time—as infinitely divisible.

However, we must ask in what sense a continuum of time is 'infinitely divisible'. Is the infinite divisibility of time only figuratively "without limit" or is it literally without limit and yet completely divisible down to a fundamental size? That is, is the divisibility of time only *figuratively infinite* or is it *literally infinite*?

If time is "infinitely divisible" in only a figurative sense, then the divisibility of time is no different from indefinite divisibility—time could be divided toward no briefest interval of all, but each division of a time interval into briefer intervals would yield only more fleeting, yet still finite, durations of time. Since such fleeting durations of time would not be of *limitless brevity*, then for time to be "infinitely divisible" in this figurative sense is a misleading use of the word 'infinitely'.

If on the other hand time is infinitely divisible in a literal sense, then a process of mathematically dividing time into briefer intervals has the potential to produce in each second of time a literally infinite succession of infinitely brief durations. This conception of infinite divisibility implies the infinitely brief durations making up each second of time would be "already there" in a temporal *span*, waiting to be uncovered by our mathematical process of dividing a second into briefer intervals.

Some physicists and philosophers hold these *infinitely brief moments* in the temporal continuum to be *instants* of time that are *infinitesimally brief*, just as Cantor's real numbers ($\mathbb{R}$) correspond to infinitesimal points of space in a line [812]. So rather than instants being moments of zero temporal interval (moments of no duration at all) some academics define instants as infinitely brief moments—the temporal equivalent of infinitesimal points.

However, just as there are two different conceptions of what it means to be an *indefinitely* brief moment, so too there are two different conceptions of what an *infinitely* brief instant would entail in the literal sense of infinity. In one version of an infinitely brief instant, an instant is *indivisible*—like the concept of a fundamental ephemeral, only infinitely brief instead of just indefinitely brief. In this conception of an instant, an instant is a fundamental element of time that cannot be further divided.

In an alternative conception of infinitely brief instants, each instant need not be itself indivisible. Assuming the common mathematical conception of (literally) infinite divisibility, there could be intervals of time infinitely briefer than other intervals of time that are already infinitely brief—instants infinitely briefer than other instants. If we were to infinitely divide a second of time, we would find the second is comprised of a literally infinite set of instants. But there could be infinitely many, infinitely briefer instants within every infinitely brief instant. The idea of instants composed of instants is consistent with the conception of time as a continuum (second definition).

19.5.7 *Are Instants Infinitely Brief Moments or Moments of Zero Duration?*

While some philosophers and physicists [813] believe instants are best defined as having zero duration—instants as "durationless" moments of time—others [814] believe instants are infinitely brief intervals of time, which implies that instants are one of the following:

a) Infinitely brief moments that are not further divisible into briefer moments.

b) Infinitely brief moments (each being one $\aleph_0$-th of a moment) that can be divided into even briefer increments of time (perhaps each as one $\aleph_1$-th of a moment).

For example, biophysicists studying multiphoton fluorescence microscopy describe molecules stimulated with light as being in an "instantaneously excited" delta-pulse state, a state that is "an infinitely brief moment" [815]. So exactly what counts as an "instant"—a durationless moment or an infinitely brief moment of some stripe—depends on which philosopher or physicist you ask.

Regardless of whether instants are durationless or of infinitely brief duration, the common view in academia is that instants of time are arranged relative to one another in a continuum of time akin to the continuum of real numbers in the real number line or like the continuum of mathematical points along a geometric line. Philosopher Michael Dummett states that instants of time are "arranged in a dense linear ordering" such that "between any two instants another instant: there is, therefore, no such thing as the *next* instant after a given one. Moreover, time is *continuous*: there are therefore no gaps in the sequence of instants" [816].

This view is supported by philosopher Bradley Dowden of California State University [817]:

> In mathematical physics, the ordering of instants by the happens-before relation of temporal precedence is *complete* in the sense that there are no gaps in the sequence of instants. Any interval of time is smooth, so the points of time form *a linear continuum*. Unlike physical objects, physical time is believed to be infinitely divisible—that is, divisible in the sense of the actually infinite, not merely in Aristotle's sense of potentially infinite. Regarding the density of instants, the ordered instants are so densely packed that between any two there is a third so that no instant has a next instant. Regarding continuity, time's being a linear continuum implies that there is a nondenumerable infinity of instants between any two non-simultaneous instants.

However, while Dummett and Dowden agree time is a dense continuum of infinitely-many instants, they differ on the details. Dummett holds each instant to be a durationless moment embedded in that dense continuum [818]. Dowden, on the other hand, makes reference to infinitesimal units of space and has this to say about time: "Is time infinitely divisible? Yes, because general relativity theory and quantum theory require time to be a continuum" [819]. Dowden seems to imply that "points of time" are infinitesimal units of time and it is because they are infinitely small that they comprise a dense, temporal continuum. Hence, whether instants are durationless or instead are moments of infinitely brief duration, the standard view among academics today seems to be that instants are infinite in number and compose time as a dense continuum like the classical idea of the set of real numbers along a number line.

With that in mind, let's start by considering instants as infinitely brief moments that are fundamental units comprising a 'dense' continuum. This view is most common among scientists such as physicists and astronomers. Sten Odenwald at the United States National Aeronautics and Space Administration (NASA) Goddard Spaceflight Center states that space and time are believed to comprise a single, physical continuum because "so far as we know, there are no missing points in space or instants in time, and both can be subdivided without any apparent limit in size or duration" [820]. While not all theoretical physicists would agree, we can set this aside for our purposes. It remains common among physicists, astronomers, and other scientists to hold time is a dense continuum composed of infinitely brief instants just as space is commonly regarded to be a dense continuum of infinitely small points.

However, this view of time has a curious implication: it is not easy to see how one instant can follow *after* another if no instant of time can be "next" in line due to the density of the continuum. It's not that the idea of infinitely brief instants in a dense continuum of time is mathematically incoherent. The idea that time is a dense continuum seems consistent with the proposal that the divisibility of that continuum is mathematically infinite. Rather, the problem is that the conception of infinitely brief instants making up any finite duration entails a logical contradiction when infinity is taken in the literal sense.

The contradiction has to do with how instants are related to one another in a continuum. If instants are, in a literal sense, *infinitely* brief moments forming a dense continuum, then a finite span of time both *can and cannot* be comprised of instants due to the following conflict in implications.

On the one hand, the literally infinite continuum of infinitely brief instants is a *complete* linear order of instants, each of non-zero duration, within a finite span of time. So, there must be an infinite number of instants in any finite unit of time—an infinitely large number of instants comprising a completed, finite moment.

On the other hand, the *limitless* brevity of each instant means a succession of such instants cannot form a finite span of time—an infinitely brief space followed by an infinitely brief span yields only an infinitely brief span, not a finite span of time. A film strip in which each fame is infinitely narrow, and there is *no frame next* (that is, no adjacent frame) due to the 'denseness' of the continuum of change, means there can be no frame that 'runs' next. All successive frames, as all instants of time, are reduced to coincidence with a single instant. Everything that happens is collapsed into a single instant of infinite brevity: all the limitlessly-many instants in that sequence occur at once rather than in finite succession precisely because they are each infinitely brief. In other words, an infinite series of infinitely brief instants cannot comprise a finite span of time precisely because there is *no limit* to the brevity of each of those instants—each instant is so brief in its occurrence that no quantity of them can ever complete a single, finite moment of time.

So, we have a conflict:

- A finite span of time *can* be formed from infinitely many, infinitely brief instants because there is a *complete* set of non-zero instants.

- A finite span of time *cannot* be formed from infinitely many, infinitely brief instants because instants *limitlessly* brief do not combine to a finite span of time.

Both conclusions follow from the concept of infinitely brief instants when 'infinity' is taken in its literal sense, and so a contradiction occurs.

Suppose then that we instead regard instants as having zero duration rather than infinitely brief duration. Here too we must be careful because a similar problem to proposing instants with no limit to their brevity holds. Instants of zero duration cannot aggregate to form a finite span of time any more than points of zero size can aggregate to form a line like a string of pearls slung together. An extent of zero plus an extent of zero is still a zero extent; a duration of no time succeeded by a duration of no time is still no time at all.

However, this problem has a simple solution.

First, we can still suppose that instants are durationless, we just need to avoid assuming they are aggregates of time. That is, we can propose instants have zero duration but are not fundamental units of time which *accrete together* to form a span of time any more than there are fundamental points of zero size comprising a line like pearls along a string. As Dummett states, "Time is only notionally composed of instants, not actually so: instants are unattainable theoretical limits to the process of dissection" [821].

Don't get me wrong: I'm not saying time is not real. We should indeed consider time to be a real thing—events happened before anyone was around to conceive of time and will happen after no one is left to conceive of time. It's just that 'instants' are not actual properties of real time.

Consider any two events that stand in an earlier/later relation in time, then designate the time between the events as an 'interval' of time. That interval is itself purely a notional thing; not an attribute of real time in itself. After so designating an interval continue to notionally divide or "dissect" that interval into shorter intervals such as by halving each resulting interval. Undertake this process and you find that an 'instant' is the *ideal* limit to this notional dissection process.

This seems to me the correct way to conceive of instants. Hence, while I side with those who prefer to define an instant as having no duration at all rather than an infinitely brief duration, we need not conclude that instants are somehow things that exist "already there," pre-measurement, making up a dense continuum of instants to be discovered, let alone experienced. Instead, instants of time are *schemas*—they are purely *notional divisions* of time that we conceive the measuring process. Instants as divisions of time are not part of the world any more than are lines of longitude and latitude on a globe; they are merely mental creations useful for measuring successions of events.

Second, and on a related note, reject the idea that the continuum is an independently existing property of time. Instants do not comprise real time either like a line of train cars, frames in a film strip, or a string of pixels; nor are there real instants of time between every two instants of time in the sense of such a continuum being something that exists independently of conception, already there in some timeless Now. Instead, any 'dense continuum' of instants is also a measurement schema.

It is merely in the process of measuring—in conception or mathematical imagination—that between any two instants, as conceptual divisions of time, another instant can be *created* or *invented*. These divisions or "dissections" of temporal change are purely mathematical conceptions we place between other conceived divisions of time. We are the ones who make time into a 'continuum' by offering two more instants—one following the other—where a continuous duration of time can again be divided, and more instants defined. The temporal continuum is a measurement schema of time rather than a metaphysical feature of time. Time is thus neither an aggregate nor a continuum in itself—rather, the continuum of time is a map of real time. The continuum is a useful tool for measuring time, not a property of real time so measured; the continuum is an epistemic device, not an ontological feature of nature.

So instead of considering instants to be like successive film frames of zero duration that are somehow arranged in a 'dense' continuum of a temporal dimension, we could hold instants to be conceptual tools useful for indexing finite spans of time with each instant a notional dissection of a notional interval created in the act of measuring time. Just as points are arbitrary divisions of spatial extent, useful for indexing and measuring the separation between any two objects, so too are instants just arbitrary divisions of temporal change, useful for indexing and measuring the span between events.

Adopt this solution for conceiving of time and the problem of literal infinity applied to instants of time dissolves. No longer would we be attempting to conceive of infinitely many durationless instants or infinitely many infinitely brief instants. If we conceive of time as a divisible process of change in which any designation of intervals such as instants are merely conceptual devices to index and measure moments, then the logical problem of how to get finite time spans from infinitely brief moments dissolves—we do not aggregate or otherwise compose finite temporal spans from instants; we instead abstract instants from time, which we conceptually divide up into various spans [822].

And so we are free to *indefinitely* dissect time into durationless instants arranged over any intervals of time we decide to designate; intervals that can be indefinitely partitioned even further into ever more durationless instants between them. Because this notion of 'denseness' for the temporal 'continuum' is actually an indefinite process, it is at best only a figurative infinity. And it is, therefore, always a finite process.

19.6 AT NO TIME INFINITY

From the foregoing sections, we now have some conclusions. It is not clear the Universe has a technically 'immense' time scale—that is, an indefinitely long past and/or future—but even if it does, time as such is not infinite in the literal sense of 'infinite'. Nor is literal infinity found in any finite span of time as if time is an aggregate comprised of infinitely many, infinitely brief moments. Rather, for any (finite) span of time, we can index that span into indefinitely many instants of no duration at all—instants that are not atoms of time preexisting our conception of them, but instead are simply conceptual tools for indicating and measuring times during which change is fundamental.

CHAPTER 19 IN REVIEW

❖ A literally infinite amount of time is a sequence of moments that is both complete as a collection but also limitless in the quantity of those moments.

❖ For an infinite amount of time, there must be an infinite quantity of events between the present moment, m, and the infinitely removed event, e. If there is not, then the infinite sequence of moments is not infinite—a contradiction. But if there is, then between m and e there would have to be a complete and limitless quantity of moments or events—and completeness and limitlessness are in contradiction to one another.

❖ A literally infinite past and a literally infinite future implies contradictions. So, time cannot be literally infinite in succession.

❖ Neither can moments of time be infinitely brief instants. Infinitely brief instants would have to add up into complete and limitless sequences of time between any two moments, which again implies contradictions between completeness and limitlessness.

❖ Time must therefore be finite.

20: INFINITE MOTION REFUTED

Motion is illusion—nothing really moves. At least, that's what the ancient Greek philosopher Zeno of Elea thought [823]. But motion is not illusory, it's real. That is, motion *per se* is real; some instances of motion, of course, are illusions, but certainly not *all* motions or even most motions.

So why did Zeno think all motion is only apparent motion, just an illusion? Why did he think real motion is impossible? Zeno offered various arguments for the impossibility of real motion, but one of his arguments in particular is relevant for the thesis of this book because it has to do with infinity.

First, I'll present his argument as to why motion must be impossible, based as it is on the assumption that infinity is real. I'll then explain that Zeno's argument against the possibility of real motion fails because the concept of literal infinity cannot be consistently applied to collections in the real world.

20.1 THE DICHOTOMY PARADOX

Zeno had a few different arguments against the reality of motion, but I will not address each one. Instead, I'd like to focus on just one of his arguments in particular: the *dichotomy paradox* [824].

The argument is called the "dichotomy paradox" because it involves repeatedly cutting a distance into two parts (a dichotomy). The dichotomy paradox is often illustrated with a runner on a racetrack and so is also known as the *racetrack paradox* or *runner's paradox*. There are two different versions of the dichotomy paradox; we'll consider each in turn.

The first version. Suppose a runner is running along a racetrack. If the runner is to reach the finish line, then the runner must first pass through a point halfway between the starting point and the endpoint of the track. After the runner reaches the halfway point, the runner must again reach another point midway between the halfway point and the end of the track (one-fourth further along the track). After reaching that midpoint, the runner must again reach another point midway between the previous midpoint and the end of the track (one-eighth further still). Following that, the runner must again reach a point midway between the previous midpoint and the end of the track (one-sixteenth yet further still), and so on. If the runner must continue to reach another midway point after each midway point, then the runner must pass through an infinite number of midway points located ever closer together prior to reaching the finish line (see **Figure 20.1**).

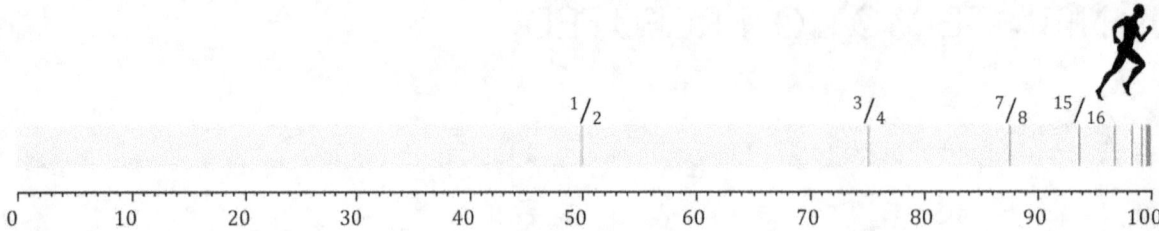

Figure 20.1: The runner cannot make it to the finish line before passing by an infinite number of points, each halfway between the previous point and the endpoint.

The second version. Now consider the sequence of midway points toward the beginning of the track instead of toward the end. Before the runner can get to the finish line, the runner must first make it to a point halfway there. But before the runner can get halfway there, the runner must get to a point one-fourth of the way. Before getting one-fourth of the way, the runner must get to a point one-eighth of the way; before that, the runner must make it one-sixteenth of the way, and so on. If the runner must reach a midway point before any midway point, then the runner must pass through an infinite number of midway points before even completing a single step (as depicted in **Figure 20.2**).

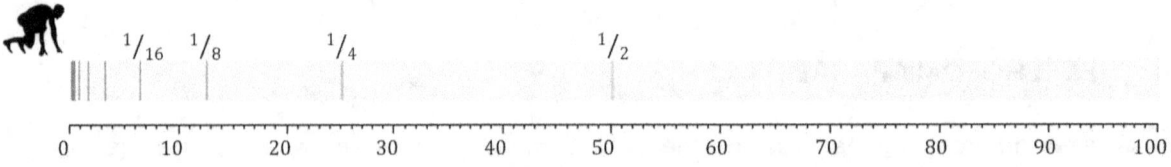

Figure 20.2: The runner cannot even complete a first step before passing through an infinite number of points, each halfway to the next point.

Both versions of the argument follow the same principle: *that which is in motion toward a given point must first arrive at another point midway* [825]. Assuming any finite length of space is comprised of a literal infinity of points, motion according to this principle implies movement through an infinite sequence. The dichotomy paradox results from that assumption.

As to the first version of the dichotomy (**Figure 20.1**), Zeno argued the runner cannot reach the endpoint of the track, the finish line, since an infinite number of prior points is a limitless quantity of points—there is no final point to reach before getting to the finish line. So, the runner cannot complete the run since there is no final point to cross prior to the finish line—it would take an infinite amount of time to go through infinitely many points [826]. It's as if the runner falls down a bottomless pit right before crossing the finish line.

As to the second version of the dichotomy (**Figure 20.2**), Zeno argued that prior to each point along the way to the finish line, the runner must first pass another point halfway. Because an infinite number of points is a limitless quantity of points, there is no first point to reach after the starting line. Once again, the runner cannot complete the run since there is an infinitude of points to go through even at the start of the track—it would take the runner an infinite amount of time to go through a sequence of points *without limit* prior to taking even the first step [827]. So, the runner can't even get started on the run; it's as if the runner is trying to jump out of a bottomless pit—an impossible task [828].

According to Zeno's assumption that any finite space contains an infinitude of points, it is irrelevant how long the track is. In modern units of measurement, the track could be a kilometer, a meter, or a millimeter. Zeno's argument is intended to prove that motion across the racetrack in a finite period of time is not possible—not only can motion not reach completion, but it also cannot even get started [829]. Even worse, since *any* object in motion anywhere must pass through infinitely many points over any finite extent of space in any finite amount of time, Zeno concluded that motion cannot begin, continue, or conclude: all motion is impossible.

If motion is thus impossible, why is it that we are always experiencing the motion of bodies? Zeno answered that, because motion is impossible and yet we experience what is impossible, all motion we experience must therefore be illusory.

20.2 DISSOLVING THE DICHOTOMY PARADOX

Ever since Aristotle, many philosophers have attempted to prove Zeno's dichotomy paradox is based on a misunderstanding of infinity. I agree. However, not for the usual reasons given. Most philosophers think Zeno did not interpret the nature of infinity correctly and that, if he had, he would have understood how there can be a literal infinity of points along a stretch of space and yet motion through all those points is still possible. I believe they are mistaken that that is where the problem with Zeno's dichotomy paradox lies.

20.2.1 *On Huemer's Solution to the Dichotomy Paradox*

Huemer attempts to dissolve the first version of Zeno's dichotomy paradox by proposing that Zeno misunderstood the nature of infinity by failing to distinguish between different senses of terms like 'endless' and 'completed' [830]. Huemer makes the following distinctions for some series S of events or actions ("members" of S) [831]:

- S is endless$_1$ = S has no last member.
- S is endless$_2$ = There is no time at which every member of S has occurred.
- S is completed$_1$ = The last member of S has occurred.
- S is completed$_2$ = Every member of S has occurred.

According to Huemer, it's true that if S is endless$_1$ then it cannot be complete$_1$ and if it is endless$_2$ then it cannot be complete$_2$, but "from the fact that an infinite series is endless$_1$, it does not follow that it cannot be completed$_2$" [832]. Huemer concludes that even if there is no last member (event) to S, one can still "complete" the series in the sense that every event of the series has occurred [833]. So, Huemer argues, Zeno's paradox is wrong: the runner can indeed complete the race in the sense that every instance of passing over a point along the track has occurred even though there is no such thing as a last instance of passing over a point along the track [834].

Though Huemer's distinctions are interesting, they are not successful in dissolving Zeno's paradox.

The first thing to note is that the completion of a series as such should not be confused with the completion of the series up to a particular total of events that have occurred by a given time in what is an open series of events that will continue from that time. In other words, we should not confuse a closed series that as a set is completed$_2$ (step 6 in **Figure 3.3**) with an incomplete, open series of completed$_2$ sets (**Figure 3.4**).

Take a series of events like the steps the runner takes along the track. For an open series (a serial indefinite) of "completed" events, it may be true that at any given time "every member" (that is, every event that has happened *so far*) "has occurred" while the series can still go on with ever more members (events) to come (endless$_1$). But for a closed series of events, which is the case for a literally infinite series as a completed$_2$ series, that is not so. Rather, completed$_2$ in the context of an infinite series, S, necessarily implies *all* the events of S have occurred such that there are *no more events yet to occur* that are not already in S (completed$_1$).

So, when Huemer says that every member—every event—of S can "have occurred" (completed$_2$) even if there is "no last member" of S to occur (endless$_1$), I maintain exactly the opposite is true with respect to a literally infinite, as opposed to indefinite, series. The fact of *every* event of S *having occurred* (completed$_2$) means *no events are left to occur in S*, which necessarily implies a *last* event for S *has occurred* (completed$_1$) that finishes S. The reason is quite simple: if no last event has occurred, there's no way for *every* member to have *occurred* because there are still more events yet to come—namely, more steps in the run left to complete. But that can't be true if the runner crossed the finish line. So, even for an infinite series, completed$_2$ implies completed$_1$. So, since for any series of events that is literally infinite, completed$_2$ implies completed$_1$, and endless$_1$ is not compatible with completed$_1$, then endless$_1$ cannot be compatible with completed$_2$ either, contrary to what Huemer claimed.

The second thing to note concerns Huemer's distinction between endless$_1$ (no last member) and endless$_2$ (no time at which every member has occurred). We must be careful with the word "last" because it can mean two different things: last in space or last in time.

If there is no member that is last in line, then it is not necessarily true there is no time at which every member has occurred because we just have to posit all members happen in one jump; so, they all occurred even though there is no last member in line. At least, that's the implication of a literally infinite set. In that context, endless$_1$ does not imply endless$_2$.

However, things are different if "no last member" means there is in a series no member that occurs last *with respect to time* such that there are always more to come later. In that case, "no last member" means there will never occur a final member, for there will be ever more in the future. In that context, it is necessarily true that "no last member" means there is no time at which every member has occurred. Endless$_1$ necessarily implies endless$_2$.

With respect to Zeno's runner, there are two sequences that have "no last member." Namely, the sequence of spatial points the runner must proceed through and the sequence of actions the runner must take to get through the points. The track is endless$_1$ with respect to space since there is no such thing as an immediately previous point to reach prior to the finish line (the line is a continuum in the mathematical sense) and so the run across the track is endless$_1$ with respect to time because the run through all the points never comes to a final point to run through.

With respect to running across the track, if there is no such thing as a "last member" (a final point to find immediately prior to the point marking the finish line), then there will never come a "last member" (a final point-crossing event) because there is no such thing as a time at which *every* event (i.e., the crossing of "every last one" of the points that need crossing) *has occurred*. In other words, the limitlessness as endless$_1$ of passing through points along the track necessarily implies the limitlessness as endless$_2$.

And because endless$_1$ implies endless$_2$, which Huemer admits is not compatible with completed$_2$, then endless$_1$ contradicts completed$_2$.

Think of it this way: if there is no such thing as a last event in S in the sense that S is literally infinite (endless$_1$), then that entails for any event you name that has occurred, there are more events in S *yet to occur*. Hence, contrary to Huemer's claim, *every* event that needs to happen in order for S to conclude with the runner at the finish line *cannot* "have occurred" (completed$_2$) if there is no such thing as a last event or action that concludes the series. Without a last event or action in the series, there is no event by which to say *all* the events of S *have occurred* such that none are still left to happen. If S is endless$_1$, then there are always more events or actions that have not yet occurred, which is the exact opposite of saying "every" event "has occurred" (completed$_2$).

So, contrary to Huemer's proposal, completed$_2$ denies endless$_1$ and endless$_1$ denies competed$_2$.

The problem with Huemer's proposal is that it is impossible for there to be a situation in which *every* member "has occurred" with respect to the limitlessness (endless$_1$) of the series. There are always more events—more members of S—to follow if you affirm S as an endless$_1$ string of events, but none left to follow if you affirm S as a completed$_2$ string of events since the events have all occurred. Given that there are always more events to come, the runner simply cannot get to the finish line to call the infinite series completed$_2$ as Huemer claims.

A second, and related, problem with Huemer's proposal is that it attempts to make the word "every" of "every member of S has occurred" (completed$_2$) cover only those events that have *already* happened up to some arbitrary named event examined at a particular time, rather than cover the *entire* sequence of events in S, each of which needs to happen for S to be *finished* and so become completed$_2$. In other words, "every" is confused with "each previous". To confuse "every" for "each previous" implies the misidentification of an *ongoing series* of completed sets as a *concluded set* of completed sets. The "every" member of completed$_2$ instead implies that S is finished rather than ongoing.

Huemer's attempt to dissolve Zeno's paradox therefore contradicts the conditions provided in the first version of Zeno's paradox (**Figure 20.1**). Namely, the condition of having an *end* to the racetrack and so a *last* point for the runner to pass over: the point that constitutes the intersection of the one-dimensional track with the one-dimensional finish line. For the race to be completed$_2$, the last point—the one at the finish line—must be passed. But if there's no such thing as passing over it (endless$_1$), then the race can never end; the finish line is forever away. With the run over the track being endless$_1$, there is no such thing as "every point has been passed" (completed$_2$) with respect to the finish line of the race, because with endless$_1$ the event of a finish is nonexistent or not obtainable.

Given Huemer's notion of endless$_1$ (that there is no last member), the phrase "every point *has been passed*" cannot refer to a last (final or concluding) point passed. Rather, it can only refer to *every point prior to now*, such that the point at "now" cannot be the point at the finish line because that would constitute a *last* point, which Huemer denied by acknowledging the lack of such a point to cross (endless$_1$). So, the "now" at which "every point has been passed" must instead be an arbitrary "now" somewhere along the track so long as the runner continues to run *without end* (endless$_1$).

Thus, in the scenario of the racetrack, completed$_2$ still implies completed$_1$: only when the last point of the track, the point at the finish line, is passed has *every* point in the race been passed. It's not enough that every *prior* point has been passed relative to a given point along the racetrack. Rather, to complete (completed$_2$) the race, the runner must pass every point *from start to finish* (completed$_1$).

Worse still, no arbitrary point along the way to the finish line, such as the halfway point, can be reached either, since crossing it would also constitute crossing a last member relative to the string of previous points along the track and we just said the quantity of points is, in Huemer's terms, endless$_1$.

That leads us directly back to the second version of Zeno's paradox (**Figure 20.2**) in which the runner can't even get started because there's no such thing as taking a first step if there is no such thing as a first point to pass over. And the same conditions apply: for a subseries of S to have been completed$_2$ implies the subseries has been completed$_1$. And since that subseries is endless$_1$, it is also endless$_2$ with respect to finishing that first step. Zeno's paradox holds.

Huemer's analysis therefore makes several mistakes:

1. It is incorrect that endless$_1$ does not imply endless$_2$ with respect to series, because it does.
2. It is incorrect that completed$_2$ does not imply completed$_1$ with respect to series, because that too is the case.
3. It is incorrect that endless$_1$ is compatible with completed$_2$; rather, their implications contradict each other.
4. His analysis abuses the notion of what "every" refers to with respect to the members of a series, making it refer to *some* instances of passing points—those prior to a given moment—rather than to *all* instances of passing points (the entire series without remainder).

Now at this point, Huemer has one last card up his sleeve. In an interview with freelance philosopher Steve Patterson on this topic, Huemer retreats to saying when the runner gets to the finish line, the runner is no longer "within" the infinite series and so has completed$_2$ the series while never reaching the end of the series because the finish line is outside the endless series [835]. However, there are two things wrong with such a response.

First, Huemer's reply is a bit of bait-and-switch because a *finite* series is completed$_2$ rather than the infinite series as claimed. The infinite series is not completed$_2$ at all according to Huemer's reply because he admits that if the runner is still in the (infinite) series, the runner cannot get to the end of the racetrack because the series of point-crossings is never over—"If you're within the series, you haven't arrived" [836]. Huemer indicates that at the finish line the runner is "outside" the infinite series, which means the runner "leaves" the infinite series. But since he just said the series has no end, that means the runner has left the infinite series prematurely to instead complete a purely finite series from the start of the track to its finish (**Figure 20.3**).

What the runner accomplished is rather like a player quitting a baseball game in the eighth inning and then proceeding to claim having completed the game by leaving the field. What becomes "completed" in Huemer's version of Zeno's racetrack is not the *infinite* series (because it never had an end by which to be finished and thus completed$_2$) but rather a different, finite series along the same track. The runner somehow left the infinite series without continuing through it to arrive at the finish line. That means, in one sense, that Zeno was right: an infinite sequence cannot be completed$_2$ because the runner really didn't leave the infinite series completed$_2$. Rather, the runner just left the infinite series period and completed$_2$ a finite series instead. Which is impossible according to the scenario anyway since the infinite series runs the course of the finite track.

The only plausible way the runner could complete (completed$_2$) the run across the track of "infinitely" many points is if the infinite series of point-crossings is only a *figuratively* infinite sequence after all, which is a rejection of the *literal* infinity of Zeno's paradox. Hence, Huemer's "solution" is not really a solution to Zeno's paradox since it does not show a genuine case of how a literally infinite series can be completed$_2$. Without telling us, Huemer's runner switched from one kind of infinity—literal infinity—to another kind of infinity—figurative infinity.

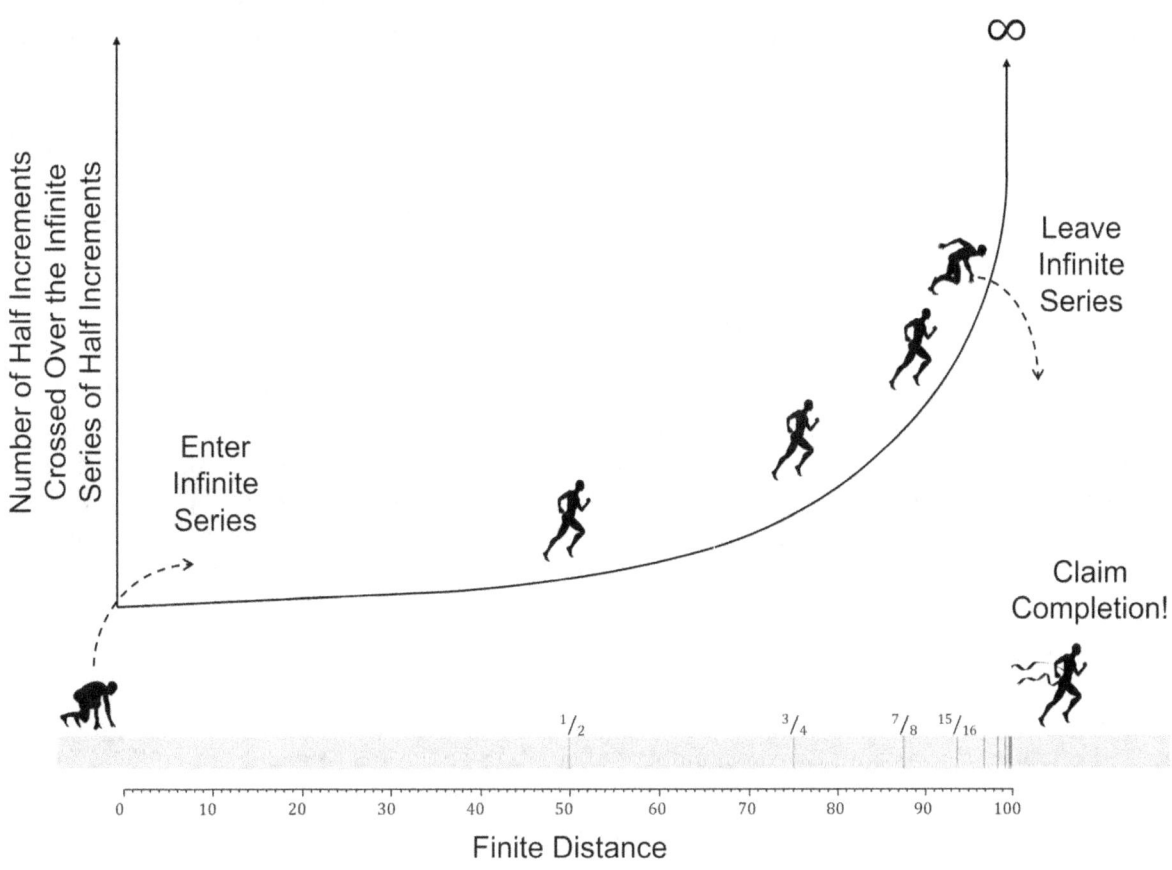

Figure 20.3: The implications of Huemer's solution to Zeno's paradox: the runner never really completes the infinite series of half increments; rather, the runner completes a finite series with the illusion of having completed an infinite series.

Second, as **Figure 20.2** shows, there are supposed to be infinitely many points at the beginning of the track too. But using Huemer's solution, the runner could just as well have "left" the infinite series right at the start of the run anyway, thus never running a distance that was infinite. In which case, this is definitely not a solution to Zeno's paradox; rather, it is just the avoidance of applying infinitely many points to the distance of the run since the runner would clearly not have completed₂ a run of "infinitely many" points across the track but instead would have only the completed₂ the finitely many increments as depicted in the measuring tape of the figure.

For all the above reasons, I have to conclude that Huemer's attempted dissolution of Zeno's dichotomy paradox is not successful.

20.2.2 *Mathematics Does not Solve the Dichotomy Paradox*

Most other philosophers attempting to refute Zeno cite Aristotle's original solutions to Zeno's paradoxes and then go on to explain why Aristotle's solutions were not sufficient and instead offer their own in a way they hope salvages the concept of literal infinity. Most of them try "modern solutions" that invoke calculus or transfinite mathematics to show how there can be a completed infinity [837]. I don't believe any of them work; philosophers are mistaken to attempt a refutation of Zeno's paradoxes on those grounds.

I do not take the approach of trying to dissolve Zeno's paradoxes with calculus or the transfinite framework because both of these approaches presuppose the logical coherence of literal infinity, which I have already refuted in Chapters 12 and 14. Moreover, Zeno's arguments assume that space is made up of a literal infinity of points and that time is comprised of a literal infinity of instants, both conceptions of which I debunked in the previous two chapters. If space has no infinitude of points and time no infinitude of instants, Zeno's dichotomy paradox disappears [838].

Refuting the dichotomy paradox is of course not sufficient for refuting Zeno's proposal that all motion is illusory since Zeno had other arguments against the reality of motion, but his other arguments are not relevant for my case as my scope concerns solely the application of literal infinity to motion [839]. Instead of addressing Zeno's arguments that motion is illusory, I wish to show why Zeno's paradox is mistaken by correcting his position on infinity. Zeno falsely assumed literal infinity is a sensible concept with which real motion does not cohere. That is not the case. Rather, literal infinity is not a sensible concept and so is irrelevant to real motion—that is the conclusion Zeno failed to reach.

20.2.3 *The Real Issue with the Dichotomy Paradox*

Zeno misidentified the problem. The problem is not that the runner appears to make it to the end of the track and yet never can because a limitless amount of points to go through would take a limitless amount of time. The problem is not one where experience contradicts logic with infinity being a logical concept. Rather, the problem is that literal infinity is not a logical concept and so cannot be applied to motion.

Literal infinity is illogical purely as a matter of conception: an infinite series of movements *both can and cannot* be completed according to the definition of infinity—a self-contradiction. The problem with the dichotomy paradox is that the runner both makes it to the end of the track after passing through an infinitude of points because the run through infinitely many points is complete (which is the conclusion of calculus and transfinite math) and yet the runner will never make it to the end of the track because the runner can never complete a series that is limitless (which the *operations* of calculus and transfinite math avoid addressing by making 'infinity' into an indefinite limit or indefinitely large set). So, the genuine contradiction involved with Zeno's dichotomy paradox is not between infinity and experience, but between infinity (the completeness of a quantity without limit) and infinity (the limitlessness of a completed quantity).

It's not that experience contradicts an infinite sum of movements. Rather, the problem is in the very notion of an "infinite sum of movements" or "the sum of infinitely many movements." That is, the 'infinite sum' (the completeness of infinity) contradicts that the movements to be summed are 'infinitely many' (the limitlessness of infinity). Stating that the run is carried out over an infinitude of points—or, alternatively, an infinitude of instants—thus implies a contradiction internal to infinity rather than between infinity and experience.

The proper conclusion for Zeno to have reached is that literal infinity cannot be applied coherently to real motion, but that would have undermined one of his main reasons for concluding motion is impossible.

20.2.4 *On the Mathematization of Space, Time, and Motion*

The conclusion that literal infinity does not coherently apply to real motion is supported by an additional observation of philosopher Raymond Tallis regarding Zeno's dichotomy paradox [840]:

> Zeno's error is to imagine that the mathematical description of motion (or indeed of anything else) trumps the experienced or lived reality of it...when I walk, I walk through *lived*, not mathematical space, taking steps, not fractions (1/2, 1/4, 1/8 of a step, etc.)...Zeno's paradoxes are the result of taking mathematics rather too literally as the actual material of the world (as if we walked in fractions rather than steps), or taking the space in which we live, move and have our being to be composed of points that somehow manage to have spatial locations without actually occupying space.

Tallis is not arguing that mathematics is ineffective as a tool for making measurements of space, time, and motion. Rather, he is simply pointing out that we should not reify our mathematical *measures* or *metric descriptions* of space, time, and motion; to do so is to confuse the map with what is mapped. So, the reification Tallis notes is yet another error in Zeno's dichotomy paradox. We move through real space, not schematic space, and we endure through real time, not schematic time. If the map tells us that something we see is impossible, better check to see where the map went wrong, not reality.

Tallis's conclusion (one which I share) entails that we should not think of space as composed of sizeless points, let alone infinitely many infinitesimals, and neither is time composed of durationless instants, let alone infinitely many infinitely brief moments. Consequently, Zeno's dichotomy paradox dissolves when we avoid entirely the reification of mathematical points and instants when describing real space and time, even apart from considerations about infinity.

CHAPTER 20 IN REVIEW

❖ Motion is impossible, said Zeno, because to move one would have to pass through an infinite number of points from here to there, which is impossible. Yet we see things move. This is the dichotomy paradox. From it Zeno concluded motion must be illusion.

❖ But Zeno's logic is flawed, and not because he didn't know calculus or transfinite mathematics. In fact, there are two flaws in Zeno's logic, and both have to do with assumptions about quantity, but neither is about mathematics.

❖ The first flaw is the assumption that literal infinity is a coherent concept. If that assumption is rejected, the dichotomy paradox dissolves.

❖ The second flaw is the reification of mathematical descriptions of space, time, and motion. We move over real time and space; we do not move through mathematical time and space.

❖ Both literal infinity and the reification of mathematical schemas are errors; identifying them as such debunks one of the main reasons Zeno had for arguing motion to be illusion and puts to rest an ancient philosophical problem.

21: PROBLEMS WITH INFINITY IN PHYSICS

Infinity is a fashionable nuisance in science, especially in physics. It's fashionable to explain the nature of the Universe with appeals to infinity, but it's also a nuisance when mathematical calculations produce infinities with nonsensical implications. Such is the case in several areas of physics including relativity theory, quantum physics, particle physics, and scientific cosmology just to name a few.

We'll examine some of the infinities appearing in each of these areas. With respect to each area, I will argue that there is no compelling evidence for the existence of the claimed infinities. I conclude that replacing references to infinity in physics with an alternative concept is necessary to improve the accuracy of our models of the physical world.

21.1 INFINITIES IN RELATIVITY

Every physical object has a *state of motion*—a set of variables that can be used to describe how the object moves relative to some other object(s). Relative to another object, a given object may be at rest, in uniform motion, or in accelerated motion (physicists refer to both increase and decrease of speed as 'acceleration' unlike in fields of study that refer to decrease of speed as 'deceleration').

The property physicists refer to as *inertia* is a physical object's resistance to change in motion—to get moving, stop moving, speed up or slow down. Inertia is related to, but different from, an object's *mass*, which is its *measure of inertia*. That is, mass is the *amount* of resistance to change in the state of motion an object has. The amount of resistance to change in motion is in turn the amount of *energy* that is needed to change that state of motion. So, basically, mass is the amount of energy needed to set an object at rest into motion, speed it up, slow it down, or stop it—to alter its inertial state.

Measures of mass and energy are therefore intimately related. For example, a train has a lot more mass than an automobile, so it takes much more energy to get a train moving than it does the automobile. Likewise, once an object is in motion, it takes energy to slow it down or stop it and the amount of energy it takes to do so depends on the amount of energy available and the amount of mass the object has. Suppose a piece of paper is caught by a breeze and blown into the front of a moving truck as it heads down the road. The paper that strikes the moving truck has too little mass and so too little energy to change the course of the truck while the speeding truck has more than enough mass and thus energy to change the course of the paper that runs into the front of the truck.

Incidentally, it might be tempting to think that size makes the difference for an object with mass, but size is not necessarily an indicator of mass. Consider that the Sun has about 333,000 times the mass of the Earth but a neutron star, which is only about the size of a small city (about 15 kilometers in radius), has a mass of about 1.4 times the mass of the Sun. Which just goes to show that some objects can be the same or even smaller in size than another object and yet have a lot more mass—the amount of an object's mass all depends on what kind of object it is, not just on how large or small it is. A small lead brick can have far more mass than a large Styrofoam brick—catching a lead brick tossed to you is much harder than catching a Styrofoam brick even though the lead brick is smaller in size.

Physicists distinguish between the mass an object has while unmoving relative to the observer from the mass an object has while in motion relative to the observer. The former is *intrinsic mass* [841] and the latter will be referred to as *extrinsic mass* [842].

Intrinsic mass (also known as *invariant mass, proper mass, inertial mass,* or *rest mass*) is the measure of mass an object has while the object is not in motion relative to an observer. Intrinsic mass is the amount of oomph it takes to get an object moving; that is, you can think of intrinsic mass as an object's resistance to not being at rest [843]. Pushing a car that ran out of fuel is a good example of setting an object with intrinsic mass in motion. But then, so is simply getting yourself up out of a chair.

Extrinsic mass (also called *variant mass, relativistic mass, dynamic mass,* or *moving mass*) [844] [845] is the measure of mass an object has while in motion relative to an observer. Extrinsic mass is the amount of oomph it takes to slow an object down or stop it. Consider extrinsic mass as an object's resistance to being stopped. Catching a ball thrown to you is a good example of bringing to rest an object with extrinsic mass.

These examples illustrate that objects with intrinsic mass also have extrinsic mass. For example, the car has intrinsic mass because it can be at rest relative to another object or observer, such as the driver sitting in the car. But the car also has extrinsic mass because while it may be at rest relative to one object or observer (the driver), it is also in motion relative to some other object or observer, like the pedestrian stepping in front of the oncoming car.

While all objects with intrinsic mass also have extrinsic mass, not all objects with extrinsic mass have intrinsic mass. Some objects *do not* have intrinsic mass, but they *do* have extrinsic mass. The prime example is a photon—a particle of light.

Photons start and end life in motion relative to objects that have intrinsic mass (like the objects we see or feel) but the photons themselves do not have any intrinsic mass of their own because there is no rest for a photon. In the vacuum of empty space, photons travel at a constant speed of approximately 300,000 kilometers (or 300 million meters or about 186,000 miles) per second—often referred to as "the speed of light" and mathematically denoted as c (an abbreviation for *celeritas*, a Latin word for "speed").

Relative to the emitting source, light starts travel at c: no photon is accelerated up to c. Relative to the receiving observer, light ends its journey traveling at c; no photon is slowed down below c if it travels only in the vacuum of space. However, light does not have to travel through a vacuum—in our everyday life we see light as it travels through various physical media such as atmosphere, water, glass, fiber optic cables, etc. Such material media slow the speed of light below c. Because a ray of light can be slowed down through a material medium and moves again at c when leaving the material medium for a vacuum, you can think of the photons in the light ray as having extrinsic mass even though they have no intrinsic mass.

As a further caveat on terminology, most physicists not specifically working with Einstein's Theory of Relativity refer to intrinsic mass as just plain old 'mass'; mass becomes shorthand for intrinsic mass [846] [847]. So, you'll sometimes hear physicists say light has "no mass", but what they really mean is that light has no intrinsic mass. Technically, light still has mass in the form of extrinsic mass, but many physicists don't address that nuanced difference anymore [848]; instead, they talk of the energy of light, or of a photon, because that's how they measure the extrinsic mass of light.

Still, the distinction between intrinsic mass and extrinsic mass is occasionally useful when physicists discuss speeds that approach c, the speed of light in a vacuum. So, although physicists often say light has "no mass" (i.e., no intrinsic mass), they also say an object "gains mass" as it is accelerated relative to an observer. What they mean is an object gains *extrinsic mass* as it speeds up while its *intrinsic mass* stays the same. To say an object gains mass as it is accelerated does not mean as the object speeds up it gets more "massive" in the sense of gaining a greater portion of intrinsic mass, and it certainly does not mean the object gets any larger in size; rather, it just means the object requires more oomph to slow it back down after getting it to go at an even faster pace—the object's extrinsic mass increases even though its intrinsic mass stays as invariant as always.

All observations and experimental evidence to date indicate that no object with intrinsic mass can be accelerated, relative to a given observer, up to c. Consequently, no object with intrinsic mass moves as fast as light through a vacuum [849].

No object with intrinsic mass can achieve c because, as the relative speed of an object is increased, the object's extrinsic mass also increases. And that gain in extrinsic mass entails that the faster the object goes, the harder it is to get it moving even faster, with c as the limit to how fast any object with intrinsic mass can move [850].

This is where Einstein's Theory of Relativity again makes an appearance [851]. The Theory of Relativity (or 'relativity theory') is actually two theories: the theory of Special Relativity (SR), or simply 'special relativity', and the General Theory of Relativity (GTR), also known more simply as 'general relativity' (see § 19.5.7 and § 21.4.3).

It was with SR that Einstein identified c as the speed limit for any object with *intrinsic* mass (which always remains the same) along with the deduction that the same object's *extrinsic* mass increases the closer to c the object gets. Assuming SR, physicists often say that as the object approaches c, the object's mass starts to "approach infinity." In other words, the object's extrinsic mass would become infinite if the object could be accelerated up to c.

However, because the object's extrinsic mass increases as the object approaches c, most physicists say it would also take an infinite amount of force to push that object up to c. Since that amount of force is impossible to achieve, it is impossible to accelerate an object with non-zero intrinsic mass up to c. As one physicist explained, "Another way of expressing the fact that a massive object cannot be accelerated to the speed of light is through the concept of energy. That is, an infinite amount of energy would have to be expended, via the accelerating force, to reach the speed of light" [852].

There are two things to be said about these references to infinity.

First, references to 'infinite' masses and energies are based on mathematical recursions or extrapolations toward asymptotic limits—limits that one can tend toward indefinitely. The speed of light is an asymptotic limit. No acceleration of a mass object reaches c, and so no mass ever becomes infinite in reality. Neither is there available an infinite amount of energy to accelerate a mass up to c.

Second, the approach to the asymptotic limit is itself not genuinely infinite in the literal sense; rather, the approach to light speed is just an indefinite process—a figurative infinity rather than a literal infinity. A massive object can, at least in principle, get *indefinitely* close to light speed, entailing that it will not reach light speed, but the object cannot actually get *infinitely* close to arrive at light speed. Even indefinitely approaching light speed is exaggerated, though, for in practice the best we can do is use an accelerator to propel a subatomic particle such as a proton up to a few decimal places over 99% the speed of light, while cosmic rays less than c can nevertheless travel at many decimal places closer to c than our artificial accelerators can manage [853]. Still, even cosmic rays do not come *indefinitely* close to light speed let alone "infinitely" close. There are still no genuine literal infinities found in the real world as described by the physics of SR.

So, when a physicist says an object's mass "becomes infinite" at c, what they mean is that an object with some amount of *intrinsic* mass increases its amount of *extrinsic* mass indefinitely as the object approaches c while no object with intrinsic mass ever reaches c, no matter how close to c its velocity gets. The increase of an accelerating object's extrinsic mass "toward infinity" is a good example of a misleading claim about infinity in physics.

21.2 INFINITIES IN QUANTUM PHYSICS

Various areas of physics study states of motion—inertia, acceleration, etc. One such area of physics is *mechanics*, the mathematical description of the motion and interaction of physical bodies through space and over time in which the masses of the types of bodies in motion are constants. Mechanics describes the operation of forces, the pushes and pulls on bodies, as well as states of inertia and acceleration. Like physics in general, mechanics too can be divided into various areas of study such as Newtonian mechanics and Relativistic mechanics, each of which has its mathematical formulas for describing the motion of bodies. But with respect to infinity, there is a particular subfield of mechanics that will concern us: *quantum mechanics*.

In physics, the term 'quantum' is not typically applied to physical bodies visible to the naked eye but rather to objects near or below the size of 10^{-9} meters such as (but not limited to) 'fundamental' particles: photons, electrons, protons, neutrons, atoms, and even some molecules. I will therefore refer to such particles as *quantum particles*. Quantum mechanics studies the motions of quantum particles and their effects on larger physical bodies and systems of physical bodies.

So what is it about such particles that makes them "quantum"? It is the way in which they are measured. The word 'quantum' (plural: *quanta*) is a Latin word meaning "how much." It was introduced into physics by Max Planck in December 1900 [854]. Planck used the word 'quantum' for a single, discrete amount of energy lost or gained by a particle of matter as it respectively emits or absorbs radiation; 'quanta' is the term for more than one quantum. A quantum is the opposite of a continuum (ergo, quanta the opposite of *continua*). While a quantum is a single, discrete unit of measurement, a continuum is a range of measurement units in which adjacent units vary by indistinguishable amounts. However, it is important to note that a quantum is discrete as a *unit of measurement* (e.g., a Planck scale unit) and not necessarily as the object or property so measured.

This is an important distinction since there are objects with *continuous* properties that nevertheless count as "quantum" objects because their *energy* is measured in discrete units. For example, an electron can be found just about anywhere in the continuum of space and a beam of light may have a continuum of frequencies. Certainly, particles have some continuous features. However, an electron is detected as a discrete particle at a particular location and even a continuum of light waves is emitted from an atom as a discrete pulse with a discrete energy value. As astronomer and physicist Arthur S. Eddington (1882–1944) explained [855],

> It turns out that the atom does emit light discontinuously. It sends out a long train of waves and then stops. It has to be restarted by some kind of stimulation before it emits again. We do not perceive this intermittence in an ordinary beam of light, because there are myriads of atoms engaged in the production.

Moreover, said Eddington, the amount of energy coming away from the atom during any one of these discontinuous emissions is found to be equal to the Planck constant [856], which is a discrete and precise quantity dubbed h (equal to $6.62607015 \times 10^{-34}$ joules per second in the International System of units). And the Planck constant, Eddington remarked, "applies to light absorbed by an atom as well as to light emitted, the absorption being discontinuous also. Evidently h is a kind of atom—something which coheres as one unit in the processes of radiation; it is not an atom of matter but an atom or, as we usually call it, a *quantum* of the more elusive entity action" [857].

The quantum is the minimum, discrete amount of energy involved in a physical interaction. For instance, photons show their quantum nature in having a minimal amount of energy they need to knock an electron out of an atom (the photoelectric effect) [858]. Moreover, notes physicist Chad Orzel [859],

> It's right there in the name—the word "quantum" comes from the Latin for "how much" and reflects the fact that quantum models always involve something coming in discrete amounts. The energy contained in a quantum field comes in integer multiples of some fundamental energy. For light, this is associated with the frequency and wavelength of the light—high-frequency, short-wavelength light has a large characteristic energy, which low-frequency, long-wavelength light has a small characteristic energy.
>
> In both cases, though, the total energy contained in a particular light field is an integer multiple of that energy—1, 2, 14, 137 times—never a weird fraction like one-and-a-half, π, or the square root of two. This property is also seen in the discrete energy levels of atoms, and the energy bands of solids—certain values of energy are allowed, others are not.

Then too, as physicist David Bohm (1917–1992) remarked, it is the discreteness of the measured values for energy exchange between particles of matter that makes quantum theory differ from classical theory: "...whereas classical theory always deals with *continuously varying quantities*, quantum theory must also deal with *discontinuous or indivisible processes*" as found in the photoelectric effect and in the "discrete values" measured from radiation oscillators [860]. Notice Bohm did *not* say material particles as studied by quantum physics have no physical properties or processes with continuous values. Rather, he pointed out that *in addition to* any continuous properties and processes a particle may have, there are also discrete (discontinuous or indivisible) properties and processes for which classical theories do not adequately account. Quantum theory describes the features of matter with discrete values classical theory does not address or cannot calculate—in particular, features involving certain discrete units of energy.

So, insofar as particles of matter exchange *quantized* energy—that is, insofar as they exchange energy measured in minimal, discrete quantities (the quanta) as opposed to continuously varying quantities of energy—they are regarded as *quantum particles* [861]. Imagine using a pool stick to hit a cue ball across a pool table and that there is a minimal amount of force it takes to get the cue ball rolling. The cue ball's energy would be quantized since it must take on a discrete, minimal value in order to be set in motion. On the macroscopic scale—that visible to the naked eye—the mechanical force moving an object like a cue ball is not really quantized but continuous because you can tap the cue ball as lightly as you like and get some reaction, at least on the ball's surface. But on the microscopic scale, forces operating between the fundamental particles comprising the pool stick, the particles comprising the cue ball, and the particles comprising the table are quantized. At that scale there are minimal, quantized units of energy, or 'quanta', exchanged between particles of matter. Hence, the appropriateness of the term 'quantum particle'.

It is the quanta of particles (and related physical phenomena) that are studied in quantum mechanics. Quantum mechanics is the mathematical description of quantized energy exchange exhibited by objects near or below the size of 10^{-9} meters—although, the physical effects of quantum behavior can, under some conditions, be observed at larger scales.

Quantum mechanics is sometimes used synonymously with *quantum theory* although, technically speaking, the two are not identical. Quantum theory is the theory that, *fundamentally*, all energy is exchanged and all forces are mediated by quanta. Quantum mechanics is the mathematical formalism used to describe and predict those exchanges and mediations of quanta.

Some physicists use the term 'quantum theory' to refer to the study of quanta during the early 1900s and distinguish that from what has become 'quantum mechanics', a qualification to the Newtonian mechanics characteristic of the macro-scale world [862]. However, other physicists still use the term 'quantum theory' to refer to the more theoretical, hypothetical, or even interpretative aspects of quantum mechanics [863] [864]. As I will use the terms, quantum theory has not been replaced by quantum mechanics; rather, quantum theory and quantum mechanics each have different scopes and roles to play in the broader area of *quantum physics*, which includes them both.

Quantum theory includes more than the mathematics and measurements of quantum mechanics; quantum theory also includes theories regarding the nature of quanta (including various interpretations of quantum phenomena such as the nature of wave/particle duality, quantum randomness or 'uncertainty', superposition, entanglement, quantum fluctuations, quantum tunneling, the 'measurement problem', etc.), predictions regarding previously undiscovered quantum phenomena, and possible practical applications for quantum physics. Quantum mechanics, on the other hand, is the mathematical description of such energy and force exchange and so is shared by all quantum theories and the various speculative interpretations of quantum phenomena.

Quantum mechanics is not wholly subsumed in quantum theory because much of the mathematics of quantum mechanics describes physical interactions that are no longer theoretical but established fact, providing knowledge rather than belief or opinion about observations of quantum phenomena and the outcomes of quantum experiments. So, quantum mechanics and quantum theory overlap in subject matter, but they are not identical. That said, many physicists still use the terms synonymously even if it is not entirely accurate to do so.

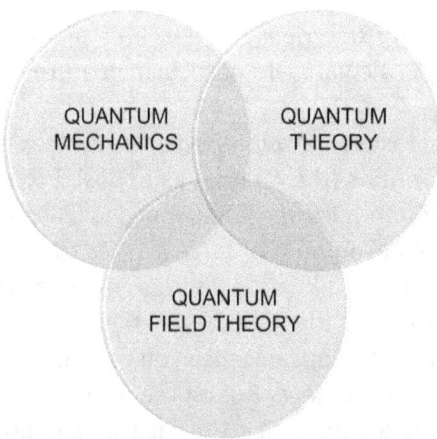

Figure 21.1: Areas of quantum physics overlap and diverge in scope.

Quantum mechanics and quantum theory are two areas of quantum physics. Another area of quantum physics is *quantum field theory* [865] [866] which contains elements of both quantum mechanics and quantum theory but goes beyond both by combining them with portions of SR and *classical field theory* (i.e., a set of theories about how particles interact with forces in a 'field' of space). **Figure 21.1** visualizes the relationship of the three areas of quantum physics.

We need not be concerned with the details of the many topics of study in these three areas of quantum physics. Rather, our concern will only be with the references to infinity that arise among them.

21.2.1 *On Infinitely Many Possible and Probable Particle Positions*

For objects in the macroworld visible to the naked eye, objects such as billiard balls rolling on a pool table, physicists can make very good predictions of where the objects will be at a given time if all they know is the speed and direction of the objects. If they know how fast and in which way a billiard ball is moving across the table at a given time, they can know where the ball will be prior to colliding with another object such as another ball on the side of the table (assuming nothing else interferes). The ability to make such determinations for objects in the macroworld stands in sharp contrast with the ability to make the same determinations for objects in the quantum world.

Physicists can measure the energy quanta exchanged by quantum particles such as photons, electrons, and so on, but they cannot observe both the *position* of a given particle (where it is) and the *momentum* of the same particle (how fast it's going and in what particular direction) at the same time. The physicist can either know where a quantum particle is now but cannot know exactly where it is going to end up, or the physicist can know how fast the particle is moving in a given direction but cannot know exactly where it is right now. This is referred to as the *uncertainty principle* or the *uncertainty relation* [867].

The uncertainty principle entails that when physicists measure the momentum of a quantum particle at a given time, they can only determine the *possible* locations of where the particle might be during that particular period of time and the *probability* of finding the particle there during that time. Physicists attempting to find a given quantum particle's location from measuring its momentum can only know where it's possible and where it's impossible to find the particle at a particular moment and the likelihood—the probability—that at that moment the particle can be found here as opposed to there. So too, if the physicist knows where the particle is, the physicist can only know the *probable* momentum the particle had in getting there, not the momentum the particle actually had.

To determine the set of possible and probable locations of a quantum particle (or, alternatively, the particle's possible and probable momentum), physicists use a mathematical function called a *wavefunction* [868] [869]. The wavefunction is, technically speaking, not itself a wave, nor is it a description of a substantive wave like a sound wave or a water wave. Rather, the wavefunction is a mathematical function denoted as psi (Ψ) multiplied by the particle's position (x) and the time (t) at which the particle is at a given location, like so: $\Psi(x,t)$. As such, the wavefunction is a quantitative tool that can be used to represent the abstract form of a wave moving in an abstract, dimensional representation of space (i.e., a schematic space physicists use to describe occurrences in real space).

The wavefunction is used to plot in the representation of space a statistical wave of likely events that may occur across real space and over real time, such as the likelihood of a particle's appearance at a specific location during a specified range of time in an experiment. The wavefunction allows physicists to determine the probability the event will occur here as opposed to there, at a particular time as opposed to some other time. The event is uncertain to take place at a given location during a given time—it could happen elsewhere or else-when instead—but the wavefunction tells the physicist how likely or unlikely it is to take place at a given place during a given time. You can think of the wavefunction as a tool for plotting the possibility and probability of a set of events, rather like plotting on a map the locations of a crime wave [870]. For that reason, physicists regard the wavefunction as simply a way of predicting the likely places a particle may be (or, alternatively, what its momentum is) at a given time [871].

Although the wavefunction of quantum particles is not itself a wave, it can be visually symbolized with curved lines along graphical axes (**Figure 21.2**), just as one might symbolize a water wave rippling down a stream. In quantum mechanics, the visual symbolism of the wave is a good example of something continuous that can be used as a tool to measure something discrete—namely, the quantum particle so measured.

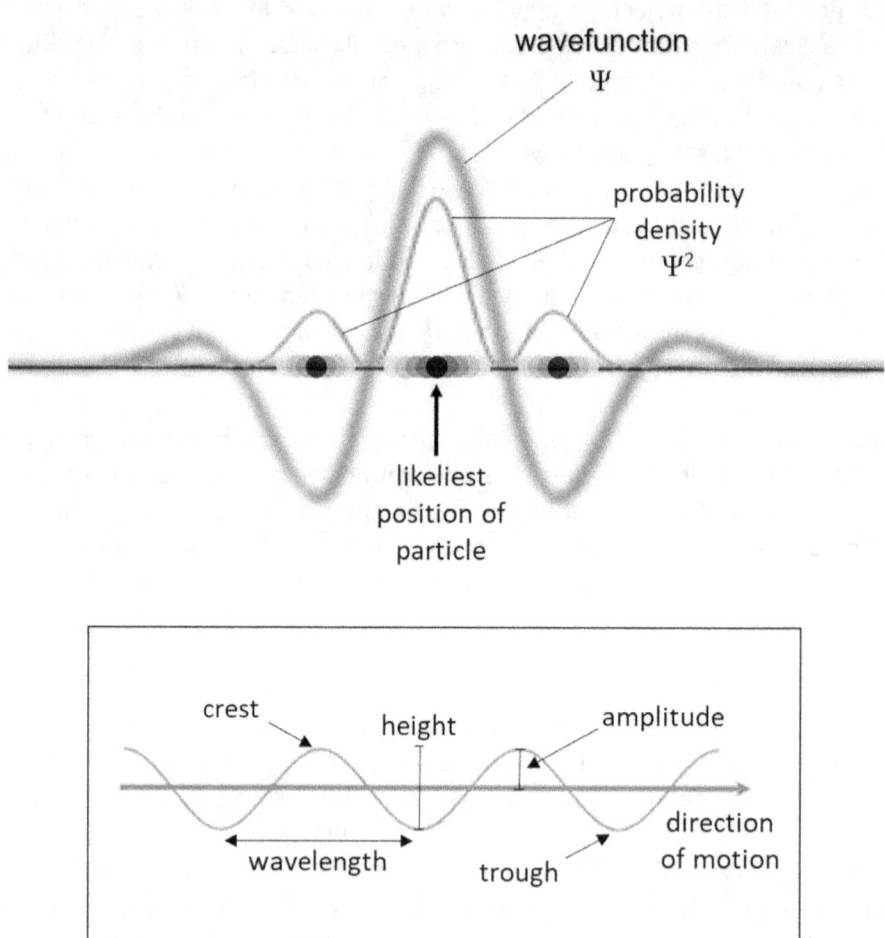

Figure 21.2: *Lower image*: the structure of a generic wave form. *Upper image*: a graphical depiction of a single particle's wavefunction—a wave of non-zero probability for positions a particle can possibly be during an interval of time—and the particle's probability density, which is the set of the most likely positions of where the particle might be during the given interval of time.

In **Figure 21.2**, the horizontal line is a dimension of space along which the particle moves. If we use the wavefunction to plot the location of a particle as it moves along that line during a given time interval, then the wavefunction's *wavelength* and *amplitude* together tell us both where it's *possible* for the particle to be and how *probable* it is to be there. The amplitude (either crest or trough for the wavefunction) indicates the likeliest locations for the particle—the greater the amplitude above or below the line, the more likely the particle is to be found there rather than elsewhere. The wavefunction also tells us where it is *impossible* (or, at least, close to it) for the particle to be and so has a zero chance of being found during a given time interval. The points where the wavefunction intersects the horizontal line—where there is no positive or negative amplitude—are places where the particle cannot possibly be along that line.

Since any two particles at a time will have different places where we might find them, they can each be described as having their own wavefunction. The wavefunction describing one particle may have a longer or shorter wavelength and higher or lower amplitude than that used for describing another particle, symbolizing that there are more possible places the particle can be and with a higher probability of being at a particular position in space during a given interval of time. **Figure 21.2** depicts dots representing the probable positions of a particle—a *single* particle—for which there are multiple positions that the wavefunction assigns a degree of non-zero probability for finding the particle during a given time interval.

The shape of the wavefunction in **Figure 21.2** is just an example of one particle's probable state at a snapshot of time. Different runs of the experiment may have different shaped wavefunctions. The calculation of the wavefunction depicts the shape of a given particle's wavefunction as changing over time, thus representing the change in the likely places of where the particle may be at during any given moment as it moves through space.

To narrow down the probable places of finding the particle at a given time, the value of the wavefunction, $\Psi(x,t)$, can be squared ($|\Psi(x,t)|^2$) to give us the *probability density* that a real particle *will be* found at a particular location in real space at a given time as opposed to some other likely location at that time. You can think of the probability density as the degree of *certainty* we can have in finding a particular particle at a particular location in space when a measurement is made. In **Figure 21.2**, the probability density of the wavefunction is represented as the smaller, narrower wave along with dots of varying transparency to indicate where the particle is likeliest to be (darker dots) or less likely to be (lighter dots); where the probability density's amplitude is greatest is the most likely place of all to find the particle at the time of measurement.

In order to calculate the exact numerical value for a particle's wavefunction, physicists use equations with complex numbers expressed in various ways, such as the following [872]:

$$\Psi(x,t) = A[\cos(kx - \omega t) + i\,\sin(kx - \omega t)]$$

Just so there is no misunderstanding, in this equation the italicized omega (ω) is not Cantor's infinite ordinal; rather, it is the scientific symbol for the rate of a waveform's change in time. Further details regarding the wavefunction's calculation will not be important for our purposes. The important point is that the wavefunction is calculated with complex numbers and it has a practical purpose for describing either the likeliest location or the likeliest momentum of a real particle in real space.

So what does all of this have to do with infinity? It is with such use of complex numbers in quantum mechanics that physicists bring in talk of infinity.

Recall that complex numbers are formed from real numbers and imaginary numbers. Physicists such as Penrose point out the number line of reals is a *mathematical continuum* [873]. Penrose assumes Dedekind's notion that a mathematical continuum is 'dense' in the sense of having *infinitely* many real numbers between any two real numbers. He further argues that because we cannot altogether eliminate the use of *complex* numbers in physics to make practical calculations (such as in calculating the 'Hilbert spaces' that describe wavefunctions), we cannot eliminate the use of *real* numbers and therefore cannot eliminate reliance on the mathematical continuum.

Penrose believes that because we cannot eliminate reliance on the mathematical continuum in quantum mechanics (such as for drawing on real and complex numbers for calculating the wavefunction), we therefore cannot eliminate the infinite in describing the physical world. Penrose concludes that the infinite must therefore exist in the real world, at least with respect to certain features of quantum particles such as their wavefunctions [874].

However, Penrose's argument assumes the number line of reals is a continuum comprised of a literal infinity (specifically, $2^{\aleph_0}$) of numbers, whereas I argue that is not so. If the reals comprise a 'dense continuum' at all, they do so only in the sense that the continuum of reals is simply a mathematical 'continuum' as an ever-incomplete and indefinite series of numbers for which new reals are always being invented or 'constructed' and inserted between the known reals as refinements to the established series. Because the series of numbers are under construction and so always incomplete, the quantity of reals in the 'continuum' cannot be infinite in the literal sense of the term. The reals of the so-called continuum are, at best, 'infinite' in only the figurative sense of the term. If that is so, then the reals used in calculations of wavefunctions are not a part of a literally infinite number line as Penrose assumes.

The wavefunction calculated from complex numbers may thus assume the use of real numbers, but if there is not a literal infinity of real numbers, then there is not a literally infinite number of complex numbers to draw on for calculating the wavefunction. Instead, like the reals, the complex numbers used to calculate the wavefunction may simply imply an indefinite series of numbers under construction. In which case, the quantum mechanical wavefunction is calculated in terms of indefinitely many complex numbers and not an infinite number of complex numbers.

At best then, the quantum mechanical wavefunction implies an *indefinite* number of probable and improbable positions a particle may occupy at a particular time. The number of positions is thus a number perhaps calculated with a *figurative infinity* but not a literal infinity as Penrose supposes.

In which case, the reliance on real and complex numbers in quantum mechanics does not, simply as such, imply the existence of literal infinities in the physical world. The use of real and complex numbers for calculating wavefunctions is not a discovery about the nature of space and time occupied by quantum particles but rather a useful technique for measuring our uncertainty about quantum states. Unger comes to a similar conclusion, stating, "It does not follow from the usefulness of real and complex numbers in science that the infinite must exist in nature" [875].

21.2.2 *On Infinitely Many Particle Paths*

Suppose we have a gun that fires electrons toward a target. If the electron were like a bullet from a rifle, we could determine the electron's initial velocity and the forces acting on it to calculate both the path the electron will take to the target and the time at which the electron will arrive at the target. Alas, the paths and flight times taken by quantum particles like electrons are much harder to calculate. When observers attempt to determine what path a quantum particle will take from source to target, all they can say is the outcome of an experiment with quantum particles is far less certain and far more statistical than the same experiment with bullets—hence the use of the quantum wavefunction.

Calculating a particle's wavefunction and its probability density can give us the particle's likeliest location at a given time *or* its likeliest momentum at a given time (not both its position and momentum simultaneously) between the particle's source and reaching its final destination. But suppose we want a more precise depiction of where the particle actually is at every step of its journey from start to finish. Quantum physics says we're out of luck—we can't know exactly where the particle is at all times unless we interact with it directly and thereby destroy its momentum. The wavefunction and probability density do not give us a picture of a particle as having a set of discrete, particular locations at each stage of its journey from source to destination. The wavefunction is, as its name implies, a mathematical tool representing a wave of the particle's *possibilities* and *probabilities*, not a picture of all the particle's definite, precise positions along the route from start to finish.

Because quantum physics, which is all about possibilities and probabilities for particles, says it's possible for particles to take many conceivable paths to the destination, and impossible to see the path a particle takes with certainty, some physicists prefer not to rely only on the wavefunction as a technique for representing a particle's motion. Rather than use a wave of probability stretched out over space to depict the uncertainty of the particle's trajectory from source to destination, some quantum physicists instead prefer to plot from start to finish the particle's *likeliest trajectories* during the entire length of its journey. So, rather than rely only on a wavy depiction of the particle's position or momentum at a moment in time between source and destination, we could instead depict all the mathematically possible paths a particle might take from source to destination, a few of which are shown in **Figure 21.3**.

Figure 21.3: An example of a finite subset of possible paths for a quantum particle from a source (e.g., an electron gun) to a destination (e.g., a target) according to path integral calculations, with the most likely path being the straight line.

Let's refer back to the electron as an example of a quantum particle for which we wish to define a trajectory. Because the momentum of a particle during its journey from source to destination cannot be known after the particle is found at a particular location, some quantum physicists believe the electron could have flown around the Earth or made a round trip to the Andromeda Galaxy and back before arriving at the destination, just so as long as the electron did so fast enough to appear as if it flew in a straight line from the electron gun to the target [876]. Aside from the fact that doing so would require the electron to violate the speed of light, the wavefunction of the electron may allow for the *possibility* of the electron's having done so, even if it is highly unlikely that it did [877]. It is doubtful such "possibilities" are genuine possibilities for states of affairs that could obtain in the real world. Just because something is logically or mathematically possible does not mean it is ontologically possible in general or physically possible in particular. Regardless of whether the more outlandish paths are genuine physical possibilities, quantum physicists treat them *as if* they are with respect to mathematical calculations.

While a particle has many possible and probable paths during its journey, actual measurements of particle momenta tell us the particle never seems to take the least likely of paths. Consequently, physicists needed some way of accounting for why quantum particles take some routes rather than others, and so typically end up taking more or less straight-line paths instead of all the weird, alternative paths. Enter the work of theoretical physicist Richard Feynman (1918–1988) [878]. Feynman devised a mathematical technique called the *path integral*, or *sum over paths* or *sum over histories*, to explain why the wildest paths never seem to happen and so predict the most likely paths of a particle and why those paths are so often taken [879].

The basic idea of 'sum over paths' is that each mathematically possible path a quantum particle can take from source to destination is assigned a number that captures the likelihood of the particle taking that path. The numbers associated with all the possible paths are then added up. Some of the numbers assigned to particular paths cancel out the numbers assigned to other particular paths while the numbers of yet other paths aggregate their sums together. The resulting sum of all these paths calculated together produces a final probability for the particle having taken that path during a specified time [880].

Aside from the fact that mathematically and physically possible paths are two different things, there is another conceptual problem with this approach: quantum physicists say the various wild paths shown in **Figure 21.3** are just a few of *infinitely many* possible paths a quantum particle can travel from source to destination [881]. But are there really "infinitely many" paths a particle can take—a complete and limitless number of them?

Not really. The number of paths would have to be complete and yet limitless—a situation resulting in contradiction as we've seen many times. If that is so, then there cannot be infinitely many paths for a particle to take in the real world—at least, not in the literal sense of infinity. In fact, the path integral calculation employs an (∞) of algebra and calculus to describe all possible paths, which is a figurative infinity—an indefinite finite—and not a literal infinity. Hence, the number of paths ontologically (ergo physically) possible for a particle to take in the real world would have to be, at best, immense (indefinitely large), but not infinite.

21.2.3 *Infinite Rooms in the Quantum Hilbert Hotel*

References to infinity continue to crop up in quantum physics. For example, in 2015 an international team of quantum physicists reported in *Physical Review Letters* that they had successfully created a real-world quantum mechanical version of Hilbert's Hotel (see § 17.3) [882]. Recall that Hilbert's Hotel has infinitely many rooms, but all the rooms are full. No vacancy. So, no further guests should be able to stay at the hotel. However, the Hilbert Hotel analogy states that by moving each guest over to another room, a previously occupied room is freed up to accommodate a new guest, and this procedure can be carried out an infinite number of times [883]:

> Each new visitor that arrives can be accommodated if every current guest in the hotel is asked to move up one room ($n \mapsto n + 1$). Even if a countably infinite number of new guests arrives at once, they can still be accommodated if each of the existing occupants moves to twice their current room number ($n \mapsto 2n$) leaving the odd-numbered rooms free.

Physicists claim to have replicated Hilbert's infinite guest accommodation process in the laboratory using a laser beam [884].

In the quantum version of Hilbert's Hotel, a laser beam is passed through an experimental apparatus of optical devices, refracting elements and reflectors, lenses, and cables until it arrives at its target—a photodetector—which records the attributes of the laser beam after the beam has been split apart, filtered, and recombined on its way across the experimental apparatus [885]. The team of physicists running the experiment refer to the accommodation of infinitely many new guests in Hilbert's Hotel as an analogy for the creation of infinitely many new positions along the laser beam where a photon might be found after the beam has been split, filtered, and recombined.

The laser beam is the hotel. The laser beam is associated with a mathematical continuum of all the possible positions with some degree of probability (the wavefunction) that a photon, construed to be a particle no larger than a mathematical point in space, may occupy in the laser beam. The infinitely-many possible positions correspond to the set of hotel rooms in Hilbert's Hotel [886]. Each possible position where a given photon might be found in the beam is one room in the hotel, and there are said to be infinitely many possible positions like infinitely many hotel rooms.

By passing the laser beam through various lenses, deflectors, and filters, to change the energy states of the photons in the beam, the physicists say they are able to increase the number of possible positions in the beam for which there is some non-zero amount (>0) of probability for finding a particular photon there, while the number of possible positions started with was already infinite to begin with. Suppose in a first run of the experiment, each point along a given stretch of the photon's path during a given time interval has infinitely many ($\aleph_0$) possible (Ψ) positions where there is at least some non-zero probability that the photon might be found. The wavefunction's amplitude (the height of the wave) has a peak at which the probability density (Ψ^2) of the particle's location is greatest. Suppose in the second run, the laser beam's attributes are altered such that we must divide and recombine the amplitudes of its wavefunction to create two separate, higher amplitudes for the wavefunction with two infinite sets (each $\aleph_0$) of probable positions where the photon might possibly (Ψ) be found. We thereby create two sets of infinitely many possible particle positions of non-zero probability in the beam where there was previously only one infinite set of such positions (**Figure 21.4**). The *most probable* position for the photon to be found in the time interval (the probability density Ψ^2) is denoted in **Figure 21.4** by the darkest dot in the center for the first run and the darkest dot on each side for the second run.

Notice the second run in **Figure 21.4** has two equally likely places where the photon is during a given moment in the experiment. When the calculations of a particle's quantum mechanical behavior indicate the particle is "equally likely" to be at two different places at the same time, physicists usually interpret the equally probable locations of the particle not to mean the particle is *either* here *or* there, but rather that it is somehow *both* here *and* there at once—violating our commonsense view of the world that no object can be in two different places at the same time. This state of a quantum particle being in apparently two different places at the same time is called a *superposition* [887].

The idea that a particle can be two places at once certainly sounds paradoxical. However, there are ways of interpreting superposition that do not violate logic even though matter in superposition does not behave like the objects we typically observe in the macroscopic world. Regardless, I won't pursue a further exposition of superposition here [888]. For the sake of keeping things simple in the analysis of this experiment, let's just roll with it and assume a particle can somehow be two different places at the same time—that 'superpositions' are real and not *only* probabilities about what we suppose particles might be up to.

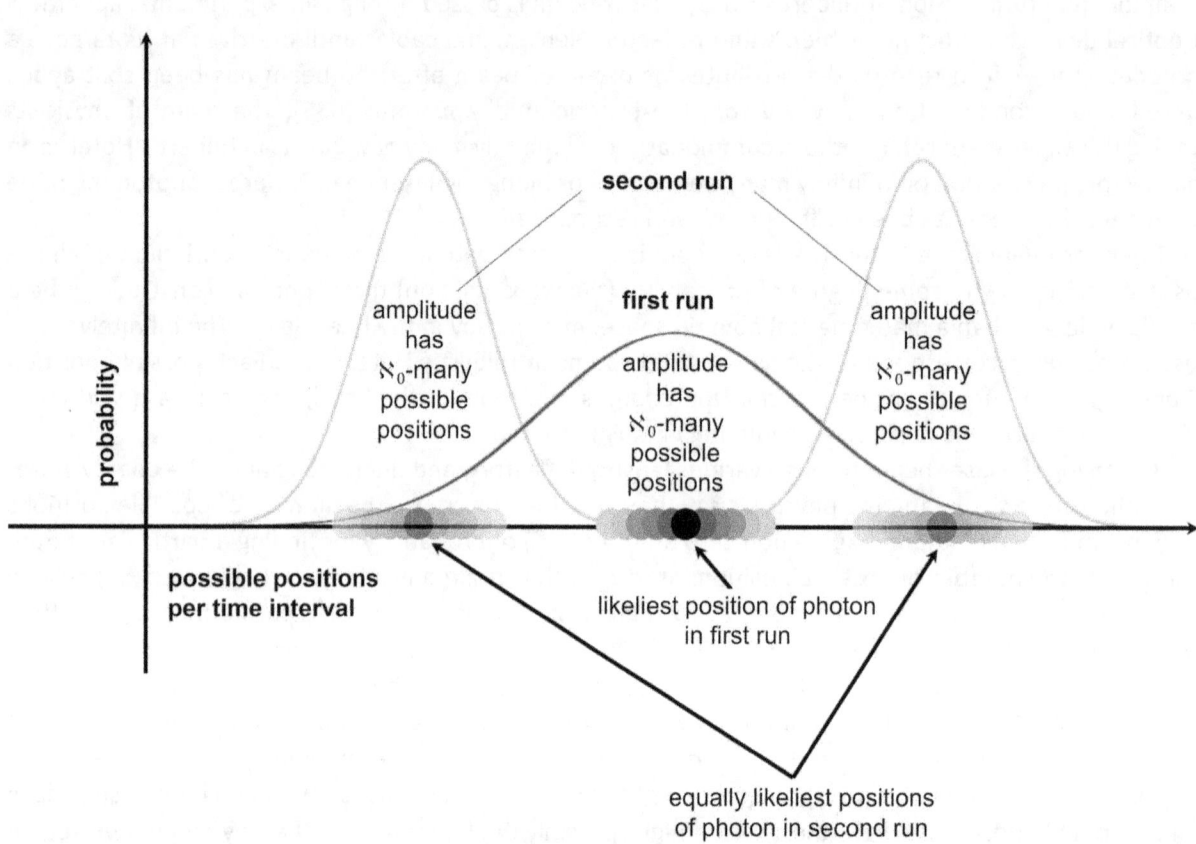

Figure 21.4: Two runs of the experiment shown overlapping for comparison. From the first to second run, an "infinite" set of possible and probable photon positions is multiplied by manipulating the wavefunction of photons in a laser beam.

According to most interpretations of quantum mechanics, when particles are not interacted with, they are in superposition—they are equally likely to be at two different places (or have other opposing properties) at the same time. But as soon as some physical body interacts with the particle, such as an experimenter performing a measurement to find the location of a quantum particle, the particle's wavefunction instantly "reduces" or "collapses"—that is, the wavefunction ceases to describe the particle as being in two places at once because the mathematics of quantum mechanics instead represents the particle as being in only one spot at the time of measurement [889] [890]. The mathematics of the particle's quantum mechanical description tells us that upon measurement we will only find the particle in one place at a time instead of two different places at the same time as it was before it was interacted with, such as it was before we attempted to measure where it is.

The quantum mechanical version of Hilbert's Hotel is an experiment dealing with particle superpositions; in this case, the superpositions of photons in a laser beam. However, even more technically, the 'superpositions' of the photons in the laser beam put certain features of the beam itself into superpositions. Specifically, the laser beam's *orbital angular momentum* (OAM) is placed into superposition.

The OAM of the laser beam is the way the beam 'twists' its way, so to speak, through space on the way to its target. For simplicity, picture the laser beam shaped like a drill bit or a corkscrew, the loops of which are multiplied as the beam extends from the point of emission to the target of the photomultiplier. The loops of a corkscrew can twist one way, or the opposite way, have more space between the loops or a tighter space between loops, and so forth. Likewise, for a laser beam. If the laser beam's OAM is in a superposition, the beam's OAM can have two different states simultaneously as if the length of the corkscrew of light is twisting in opposite directions at the same time, or as if a drill bit could spin in opposite directions simultaneously. (I should hasten to add these twisting analogies are just that—analogies. Don't take them too literally, since neither photons nor the laser beams they comprise actually rotate like a drill bit. This description is just meant to characterize the *effect* that photons or a beam of light has on a detector).

The physicists use their apparatus to multiply the superpositions of the laser beam's OAM from a supposed 'infinity' of such states to an even bigger infinity of such states. Hence, the physicists indicate they can (in principle) repeat multiplication of OAM superpositions infinitely many more times in a finite period of time to create even larger infinities of OAM from there, just as Hilbert's Hotel can accommodate infinitely many more guests [891].

This is an extremely simplified description of the experiment, but further details are not important. The important point regards the claims of instantiating infinity in this experiment. According to Filippo Miatto, one of the physicists behind the experiment [892],

> "Philosophically, after our findings, one could argue that the real world can accommodate
> for the mathematical notion of infinity in the sense of Hilbert's paradox," Miatto added
> in a press release. "Or at least, the formalism of quantum mechanics allows for that."

It is the last part of the quote that is telling: the mathematical formalism behind the experiment is what has the infinity (∞ or $\aleph$) rather than the real world that the formalism attempts to describe. In fact, run the experiment and the photodetector merely supplies an image of the wave-like interference fringes of the filtered laser beam, as shown in **Figure 21.5**. There are no infinities in the image, just petal-like areas of illumination where many photons have been detected.

The image in **Figure 21.5** illustrates the effects of OAM superpositions upon the photodetector. The only "infinities" in the superpositions to be uncontroversially found are in the *mathematics* of the experiment, corresponding to possible and probable positions photons can give the OAM of the laser beam when the photons are construed to be mere mathematical points.

Figure 21.5: 'Petals of light' left by the photons of the laser beam at the photodetector. As the energy states of the laser are increased, the number of petals triple from the lower energy states (top row) to the higher energy states (bottom row). Each petal of light is said to be like an infinite set of occupied rooms in Hilbert's Hotel. So, to triple petals of light is to triple the infinite sets of occupied rooms in Hilbert's Hotel, and therefore tripling the dark spaces between the petals also triples the infinite sets of rooms vacated in Hilbert's Hotel to make ready for new infinitudes of guests. But in no panel do we directly see an infinite quantity; all we see are light petals.

Not only does literal infinity ($\aleph$, or $\mathbb{H}$ for Hilbert in the mathematics of the experiment) never make an appearance outside of the mathematics, but also the math used for constructing the pattern of quantum energy states is only the figurative infinity of operations performed in calculus (denoted ∞). Moreover, even a figurative infinity is never actually produced, as the physicists themselves admit. Miatto says, "As far as there being an infinite amount of 'something,'...at the end of the day when you sum everything up the total energy is finite. The same can hold for all of the other quantum properties..." [893]. The infinities, whether expressed as ∞ or $\aleph$, may appear in the formalism of the mathematical description of the experiment, but they don't appear in reality.

Hence, while the experiment may be useful for certain areas of scientific study, such as new applications for information processing or creating communication channels, the analogy to Hilbert's Hotel is misleading. Entertaining, but misleading. Literal infinity still remains absent from the real world.

21.2.4 *Infinitely Many Quantum Speed Limits*

In 2016 news reports announced, "Physicists discover an infinite number of quantum speed limits" [894]. The notion of a *quantum speed limit* has to do with the speed at which a measurement can detect a change in the *quantum state* of a *quantum system*.

In classical physics, the *state* of a particle is a mathematical description of a particle's properties of motion (inertia, momentum, relativistic mass, etc.) consistent with the laws of physics that describe them either over time or at a particular time [895]. For quantum physics, the concept of 'state' is less definite with respect to a particle's properties. The 'quantum state' of a particle is a mathematical description of everything that can be provisionally known about the particle's properties of motion—the state of the particle is a description of the particle's *possible* and *probable* properties of motion as those properties are allowed by relevant physical laws either over a given time or at a particular time. [896] [898]. For example, in quantum physics, the state of a quantum particle is a mathematical description of where the particle can be (possible location) and where it is likely to be at a given time (probable location), how fast it is able to move in various directions (possible momentum) and how fast it is likely to be moving in those directions (probable momentum) over a given period of time, and so forth.

The 'state' of the quantum particle is its possible and probable properties of motion rather than its definite properties of motion because its behavior as a quantum particle cannot be known with the same kind of certainty as can the behavior of macro-scale physical bodies. These possible and probable properties of motion together, in a single mathematical description, is the quantum particle's 'state'.

This is where the wavefunction comes in. For quantum particles, one applicable law of physics describing the various properties of the particle—the particle's state—is captured in the mathematics of the particle's wavefunction (and thus the particle's probability density).

Consider the various properties of a particle such as its position (for example, at time t, the particle is between coordinates a-b-c and x-y-z), its momentum (for example, the particle is moving at speed A in direction B), or other measurable properties. The wavefunction is used for calculating the possibility and probability of the particle being measured with specific mathematical values for those properties rather than some other value. At time t, the particle is *most likely* between coordinates a-b-c and x-y-z whereas also at time t the particle is *most likely* moving at speed A in direction B. The various properties have various probabilities of appearing during any given instance of measuring the particle.

The square of the wavefunction gives us the particle's quantum state and the quantum state of a particle tells us *how probable* it is that the particle will be measured as having a particular set of mathematical values for the particle's various properties. Hence, the set of probabilities for the particle's various properties of motion gives us the 'quantum state' of the particle—a quantum state is thus a mathematical description of the particle's set of properties of motion according to the calculations for that particle's wavefunction.

In general, the term 'state' can also apply not just to a particle but to an entire *system*—a group of particles with specified properties (e.g., position, momentum, mass, charge, etc.) interacting according to specified physical laws [899]. More narrowly, the 'quantum state', for which the applicable law of physics is the operation of the wavefunction, can thus likewise apply to a 'quantum system', which is any collection of mutually-interacting physical objects that can be described with a wavefunction [900].

So, if a 'quantum state' is a mathematical description for an object's probable properties of motion according to its wavefunction, and the object in question is a whole system of particles, then the quantum state in that case refers to the mathematical description of the system's properties of motion as given by its wavefunction's values. In short, the quantum state for a quantum system is a description of the properties of the system by its wavefunction.

While I have referred to the wavefunction as the indicator of the state of a quantum system, that is only partly true because calculating the wavefunction is just one way to describe either the quantum state of the system as a whole or the quantum state of a particular particle(s) in the quantum system. But there are also other ways, such as with the use of Feynman's path integral for particle motions (**Figure 21.3**). And it is in determining the quantum state of a quantum system via a process similar to Feynman's path integral that the notion of a quantum speed limit comes in.

One property in a particle's quantum state is the particle's measure of energy or its 'level' of energy. The particle's level of energy is prone to change as the particle interacts with other particles, and therefore the particle's quantum state is prone to change during that interaction. Since the particle's energy can change, the particle's quantum state during the particle's energy exchange with another particle(s) changes, and because that change takes place with some speed, so does the quantum state of the entire quantum system to which the particle belongs. The 'quantum speed limits' have to do with how fast the quantum state of a quantum system, such as a quantum computer, can change [901] [902]:

> If an object in the quantum world travels from one location to another, researchers can't measure exactly when it has left nor when it will arrive. The limits of physics impose a tiny delay on detecting it. So no matter how quickly the movement actually happens, it won't be detected until slightly later. (The lengths of time here are incredibly tiny—quadrillionths of a second—but add up over trillions of computer calculations.) That delay effectively slows down the potential speed of a quantum computation—it imposes what we call the "quantum speed limit."

> Quantum speed limits impose limitations on how fast a quantum system can transition from one state to another, so that such a transition requires a minimum amount of time (typically on the order of nanoseconds).
> This means, for example, that a future quantum computer will not be able to perform computations faster than a certain time determined by these limits.

Physicists propose various metrics for distinguishing quantum states from one another, which in turn allows the physicists to determine the speed limit for how fast a quantum system, such as a quantum computer, can change states. One way to create metrics for the transformation of quantum states is to graph the transformation of one quantum state into another in a manner similar to Feynman's path integral, where the fastest quantum speed is a straight line between Quantum State X and Quantum State Y and all manner of other wavy paths from X to Y represent slower speeds—the wavier the path, the slower the speed of transition from X to Y. You can think of each of these possible paths as 'metrics' for measuring the transition of one quantum state to another. Just as there is claimed to be infinitely many Feynman paths a quantum particle can take across distance, so too researchers have proposed "an infinite number of corresponding metrics that can be used to measure the distinguishability of two quantum states...each of these metrics corresponds to a different quantum speed limit" [903] [904].

However, operationally speaking, the "infinity" referenced here is not really infinity in the literal sense of the term. Rather, the infinite set of quantum speed limits is only 'infinite' in the figurative sense: as long as we wish to keep on calculating more speed limits a quantum system *might* have, we can concoct another speed limit that it is mathematically possible for a quantum system to assume. Infinity (∞) merely makes its appearance in the formalism of mathematics, not in the real world. No system, quantum or classical, assumes infinitely many speed limits in the sense of a complete and limitless set of speed limits. At best, we have 'infinitely' many speed limits in the sense of an indefinite number of speed limits we can *assign* to a quantum system according to some family of measurement standards we wish to adopt—the physical world contains no set of infinite speeds.

21.3 INFINITIES IN THEORETICAL PARTICLE PHYSICS

Theoretical particle physics is the branch of physics that attempts to model fundamental particles and their interactions, especially as found in the high-energy collision events of particle colliders. Theoretical particle physics often draws upon quantum field theory (QFT) to explain particle interactions.

QFT is ambivalent about particles. Some models of QFT describe particles as small "ripples" or "disturbances" or "excitations" that travel through invisible and intangible energy 'fields' pervading space and time [905]. Other models of QFT regard fundamental particles *as if* they are mathematical points or 'point-like' entities that move each other about with their encompassing energy fields [906]. Some models of QFT estimate there are *infinitely many* of these point particles in the Universe [907] [908]. As we'll see, both the notion of point-like particles and their literal infinitude have been problematic in the related area of particle physics.

21.3.1 *Infinitesimal Particles*

In one sense, saying particles are points or point-like is simply a useful simplification to abstract out irrelevant details about particles when calculating their positions and trajectories. But the notion that a particle of matter *really is* a point in the sense of having zero size or, alternatively, infinitesimal size, is also a common view in physics. According to Dowden [909],

> All scientific experiments so far have been consistent with electrons and quarks having no internal structure (components), as our best scientific theories imply, so the "simple conclusion" is that electrons are infinitely small, or infinitesimal, and zero-dimensional.
>
> ...When probing an electron's particle nature it is found to have no limit to how small it can be...The more accurate theory of quantum electrodynamics (QED) that incorporates special relativity and improves on classical quantum theory for the smallest regions, also implies electrons are infinitesimal particles...When considering the electron's particle nature, QED's prediction of zero volume has been experimentally verified down to the limits of measurement technology.

Dowden's position is not unusual; many physicists hold fundamental particles to be infinitesimal or to have zero dimensions. However, the conclusion is not, strictly speaking, warranted by the empirical evidence.

To see why, start by considering the electron as a particle that carries an *electrical charge*—hence the name of the particle. As anyone familiar with electrical batteries knows, charge comes in two types: positive (+) and negative (−). The electron has a negative charge, while certain other particles, such as the proton, have a positive charge. Whether positive or negative, charges are influenced by magnetism. When running a magnet along an electrical wire, the electrons in the wire are influenced by the magnet. Likewise, with the right kind of equipment to generate a powerful magnetic grip on an electron, the electron can be trapped and held nearly still. Suppose, then, that we confine an electron in a magnetic trap and try to measure how big the electron is.

Even using the most sophisticated of magnetic traps, we must still measure the electron's position according to the electron's charge, and that approach offers only so much resolution. The limits of measurement technology only allow us to pin the electron's size down to less than 10^{-18} meters [910]. What the evidence shows is that, regardless of the electron's exact size, it is *no bigger than* approximately 10^{-18} meters in diameter. It may be substantially smaller, but even substantially smaller is not the same as zero size or infinitesimal.

QED, one of our best scientific theories, treats electrons like zero-dimensional points in its mathematical formalism, but that is just an abstraction for the sake of simplicity. Because the technology we have cannot directly detect a structure smaller than 10^{-18} meters, and because "our best scientific theories" treat electrons *as if* they are 'point particles', physicists find it useful, as Dowden says, to adopt the "simple conclusion" that a fundamental particle such as an electron has no size at all.

However, the simple conclusion is misleading. For one thing, the simple conclusion appears to have merit only depending on what you count as "our best scientific theories." Some quantum field theories hold that there is a smallest spatial size that anything can be. For example, theoretical physicist Carlo Rovelli states, "Quantum gravity is the discovery that no infinitely small point exists. There is a lower limit to the divisibility of space" [911]. According to Rovelli, "nothing exists that is smaller than the Planck scale" [912]. Not even supposedly fundamental particles like electrons. Recall the Planck scale is 10^{-34} meters. That's extremely small—much smaller than 10^{-18} meters—but not zero and certainly not infinitesimal.

Whether or not theories of quantum gravity are correct in portraying space as having a smallest size is a topic that will have to wait for another book [913]. For now, I would like to point out that some of the best scientific theories tell us fundamental particles need not be construed as points of either zero or infinitesimal size, and that treating them as such actually brings a host of mathematical troubles [914]. Moreover, the best empirical measurements we can make permit the electron to have a finite size, depending on which theory you choose to adopt. And there is no evidence that concludes they must necessarily have no size at all or be infinitesimally small.

21.3.2 *Infinitely Many Particles of Matter*

Taking particles to be finite in smallness may help with another problem—understanding how many particles of matter can exist in nature. Because it is precisely on this issue that once again QED brings as much conceptual trouble to particle physics as it solves.

The trouble begins with QED's explanation for positive and negative electrical charges. We know particles with opposite electrical charge attract each other (e.g., electrons and positrons, having opposite charges, move closer together) while particles with the same charge repel one another (e.g., two electrons will repel each other as will two positrons). But *how* do charges cause particles to attract and repel? QED explains this behavior by proposing that an electrical charge is the exchange of *virtual particles* between *real particles*. That is, a real particle can either emit a virtual particle which is absorbed by another real particle, or it can absorb a virtual particle emitted by some other real particle. This exchange of virtual particles is electrical charge [915] [916].

According to QED, 'real particles' such as electrons are entities point-like in size, which interact with one another by exchanging other point-like particles, the so-called 'virtual particles', between them. Just imagine two points separated in space with a third point between them zipping across space from the first point to the second point. The two outer points are the real particles, such as electrons, and the point transferred from one real particle to the other real particle is the virtual particle. QED explains electrical attraction and repulsion by this kind of exchange. One electron repels another electron by sending a virtual particle to knock the other electron away. Virtual particles are 'virtual' rather than 'real' in the sense that they are not directly observable as are real particles like electrons and protons, and yet virtual particles leave real effects on the matter we can measure. Electrons are repelled by exchanging virtual particles. All we see is the electrons repelling one another; we cannot detect the virtual particle they exchange. According to QED, an electrical charge *just is* an exchange of 'virtual photons' between electrons.

QED is a quantum field theory that recognizes the existence of virtual particles. In fact, QFT as such holds that what seems like empty space is actually filled with *vacuum fluctuations*—the activity of unseen virtual particles. Early versions of QFT, based on QED, even predicted that the quantity of virtual particles and their vacuum fluctuations across the Universe is infinite [917].

However, before we contemplate the existence of infinitely many virtual particles, we should consider that the notion of a virtual particle is itself rather slippery, even to some physicists specializing in QED or, more broadly, QFT. For instance, Michael de Podesta, a scientist at the United Kingdom's National Physical Laboratory, says, "Despite 35 years of exposure to [the concept of a virtual particle] – I haven't a clue what it means physically. I suspect strongly that its role is calculational rather than physical" [918]. Other theorists say virtual particles, while a reality, are nevertheless a misnomer for something else. According to Theoretical Physicist Matt Strassler, "The best way to approach this concept, I believe, is to forget you ever saw the word 'particle' in the term. A virtual particle is not a particle at all. It refers precisely to a disturbance in a field that is *not* a particle" [919]. Strassler believes the term 'virtual particle' is a misnomer for 'disturbance' in a quantum force field (a field of space carrying a force such as electrical attraction and repulsion between charges), a view now widely held in the physics community, a view which influences popular sources on the subject. Even so, many other physicists do not think of virtual particles as either just a bookkeeping device or as field disturbances, but as actual, material particles [920].

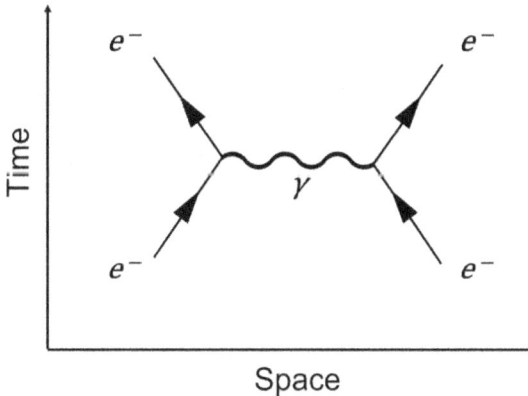

Figure 21.6: A Feynman diagram of two electrons (each labelled as e^-) repelling one another by exchanging of a virtual photon (denoted by the small Greek gamma, γ). Physicist David Kaiser describes the diagram: "One electron (solid line at bottom right) shoots out a force-carrying particle—a virtual photon (wavy line)—which then smacks into the second electron (solid line at bottom left). The first electron recoils backward, while the second electron gets pushed off its original course. The diagram thus sketches a quantum-mechanical view of how particles with the same charge repel each other." [Kaiser (March-April 2005), Figure 3, p. 158.]

Feynman, the one who first proposed the existence of virtual particles, was himself (for the most part) a particle guy [921]; he thought of virtual particles not as field disturbances but at least as particle-like entities, if not actual particles [922] [923] [924]. In Feynman's conception, virtual particles are particles that are emitted and absorbed by 'real particles' too quickly for instruments to detect or measure directly. To illustrate this process, Feynman created what came to be known as Feynman diagrams—pictorial representations of mathematical expressions describing the behavior of quantum particles [925]. A Feynman diagram is not a picture of what particle interaction looks like empirically, but rather a simplified, abstract visualization of what would otherwise be a complicated, mathematical formula. **Figure 21.6** is a Feynman diagram of two electrons repelling one another with a virtual photon.

According to QED, space is filled with *infinitely many* virtual particles exchanged among 'real particles' (particles that can be directly measured). Running with that idea, QFT further proposed that independent of matter emitting and absorbing virtual particles, there are infinitely many virtual particles materializing and dematerializing every second in the medium of physical space like bubbles in a boiling pot.

QED's notion of virtual particles is conceptually problematic because, if there really were infinitely many virtual particles materializing from the medium of physical space and vanishing back into it—even merely as "fluctuations" in quantum fields—QFT calculates that the Universe as we know it would not exist. Our galaxy with its stars, planets, and people would never have been able to get started.

This unsavory consequence of infinitely many virtual particles fizzing in the medium of space stems from two ideas in Einstein's GTR. One of those ideas is called *spacetime*, the other is called the *cosmological constant* [926] [927].

Spacetime. Einstein's GTR regards time to be a dimension like a spatial dimension of length, width, or height. Just as a dimension of space has locations all existing next to each other along a given axis, so too the dimension of time is pictured like a timeline in which past, present, and future events all exist side-by-side from the external viewpoint of some Eternal Now. Since each point of space has a corresponding timeline intersecting it, all of space is 'extended' through the temporal dimension. This temporal dimension is thus united with the three dimensions of space into a single multi-dimensional continuum called 'spacetime' (or space-time) [928] [930].

In GTR spacetime is said to be 'curved'. The dimensions of space and the temporal dimension are not as 'straight' as they appear to be on casual observation.

Take our view of space. Space appears to allow for straight-line paths no matter how far we look in any direction. But appearances can be deceiving. According to GTR, space is actually curved.

It's not that there is something *in* space that is curved. Rather, GTR says space itself is curved. The curvature of space is slight, however, and cannot be seen directly. Meter sticks look straight enough to the naked eye. Still, in GTR the curvature of space can be indirectly measured by gravitational effects.

GTR views gravity to be unlike the force Isaac Newton had proposed; instead, GTR posits that gravity just is spatial curvature [931] [932]. What Newton thought of as the "pull" of the Earth's gravity is in Einstein's view just falling down the curved slope of space around the Earth.

In the Newtonian picture, gravitational force is stronger for larger celestial bodies. The Sun's gravity is more powerful than the Earth's, which is more powerful than the Moon's, etc. In the Einsteinian picture, gravity as the curvature of space varies according to a body's mass. The more the body's mass, the greater space is curved around that mass object. So, space is more curved around the Earth than around the Moon, more around the Sun than around a planet such as the Earth, more around the Galaxy than around a star like the Sun, and so forth.

In Newton's theory of gravity as a force, one of the effects of gravity is that face clocks and atomic clocks tick more slowly at sea level where gravity is "stronger" than higher in elevation where gravity is "weaker," and clocks in outer space tick faster still. GTR interprets these effects differently. The rate at which a clock ticks depends on how much space is curved where the clock is located. The greater the curvature of space, the slower the ticking of the clock in that space; the fast a clock ticks, the less space is curved. Space is more curved at sea level and lessens with altitude from the Earth. So, clocks tick slower at sea level than higher up.

Experiments confirm that precision clocks tick slower at lower elevations and faster at higher elevations. [933] [934]. It's even been shown that astronauts age faster in space than do we down here on Earth [935]. The Newtonian theory of gravity interprets these differences in precision clock rates as caused by the decrease in gravitational force a body experiences the further it is from the center of the planet; Einstein's GTR interprets the rate differences not as the effect of a force but rather as the result of curved spacetime.

In Newton's view, gravity's effect on ticking clocks would be to distort our ability to measure real time correctly. In Einstein's view, time is just what the ticking clock reads—schematic time is real time. Since every volume of space is associated with a rate of temporal passage, GTR states that the curvature of space therefore has an associated 'curvature' in the dimension of time as well. Consequently, if clocks tick slower near the Earth than further away, GTR takes that as evidence the dimension of time is more "dilated" near a mass and less "dilated" further from that mass. So it seems to us that time "passes more slowly" in volumes of space that are more *curved* around larger masses than in volumes of space that are less 'curved' around smaller masses [936].

According to GTR, since space and time are part of a single spacetime continuum, it's not just that space is curved around masses, and not just that the dimension of time is curved (dilated) at those spaces, but that both space and time together are curved as parts of spacetime—it is spacetime as a single continuum that is curved. The greater the mass, the greater of spacetime curvature around that mass.

The Cosmological Constant. The problem faced by Einstein's GTR is that, at the scale of the Universe as a whole, the mass of all the galaxies combined should have increased the curvature of spacetime (gravitational attraction) so much that the Universe should have imploded long ago. The only reason that hasn't happened, Einstein thought, is that there must be some principle that cancels gravity out on the scale of the Universe. He proposed the 'cosmological constant', a kind of anti-gravity that keeps the Universe stable [937].

Einstein ultimately abandoned the idea of the cosmological constant, in part because he had to admit it was rather ad hoc, but mainly because of astronomical evidence gathered in support of a rival theory—the theory that would later become known as the *Big Bang theory* [938]. Einstein even came to regard his proposal of the cosmological constant as a scientific "blunder" but, ironically, astrophysicists have in recent decades found some use for the cosmological constant in explaining certain astrophysical phenomena [939]. The details of the cosmological constant will not concern us; the point is, physicists have a use for the cosmological constant that Einstein abandoned, despite the initial assumption that it would not be needed for the popular Big Bang theory.

But there is a snag: the cosmological constant does not jibe well with the notion of virtual particles and *vacuum energy*. Since virtual particles appear and disappear into the vacuum of space across the Universe, GTR implies the 'vacuum energy' from those *virtual reactions* must curve spacetime. According to calculations, the amount of virtual matter in the Universe predicted by QFT would give too large a mathematical value to Λ (the Greek capital letter lambda, used as a symbol for the cosmological constant) [940]. So large would be the *vacuum energy density* contribution of all the virtual reactions in the void of space that the value of Λ would have become infinite and the Universe would either have been torn apart or imploded before galaxies had a chance to form.

Physicist Sabine Hossenfelder explains that having an infinitely large vacuum energy density throughout space would cause spacetime to bend back on itself in such a way as to make the Universe inhospitable for human beings [941]:

> ...the infinite contribution becomes physically relevant because it would cause an infinite curvature of space-time. This clearly doesn't make sense. Further inspection luckily shows that the vacuum energy is unbounded only if one extrapolates the standard model up to

infinitely high energies. And since we expect this extrapolation to break down at the Planck energy (at the latest), the vacuum energy should instead be a power of the Planck energy. That's better—at least it's finite. But still it's much too large to be compatible with observation. A cosmological constant that large would have ripped us apart or would have recollapsed the universe long ago.

Well, which is it—would the Universe have been torn apart or would it have imploded? The calculations result in contradictory predictions. On the one hand, all the virtual matter would have increased the vacuum energy density, which implies an increased gravitational attraction between all the matter in the Universe to the point of imploding the Universe. On the other hand, all the virtual matter would have raised the repulsive effect of the cosmological constant so much that matter would never have been able to aggregate into galaxies, stars, and planets in the first place—the Universe would have torn itself apart. Two contrary predictions but with the same awful outcome: no Universe as we know it.

Science writer Jim Baggott also pointed out that physicists have refined their theories in an attempt to avoid an infinitude of vacuum energy, but noted there is still a problem with the gravitational contribution of virtual particles [942]:

> The vacuum energy density is no longer predicted to be infinite (yay!). Instead, it's predicted to have a value of the order of 100,000 googol (10^{105}) joules per cubic centimeter. In case you've forgotten already, the 'observed' value is 10^{-15} joules per cubic centimeter, so the theoretical prediction is out by a staggering hundred billion googol (10^{120}).
>
> That's got to be the worst theoretical prediction in the history of science.

The late science journalist John Boslough (1942–2010) summed up the implication of such a high value for the quantity of virtual particles [943]:

> Anybody can see that such a calculation is wildly wrong. Look outside. How far can you see? If the cosmological constant were as big as the equations indicated, the universe would at most be a mile or two across; space itself would be so curved that you literally couldn't see straight. Most likely, though, the universe never would have made it much beyond quantum dimensions. Almost immediately after the big bang the entire cosmos would have curled up on itself like a withered leaf.

On the other hand, Smolin pointed out that the sum of all the virtual particles in the Universe would have raised the repulsive effect of the cosmological constant to proportions too great for matter to aggregate at all [944]:

> ...quantum theory predicts a huge vacuum energy. In the context of Einstein's general theory of relativity, this implies a huge cosmological constant. We know this is wrong, because it implies that the universe would have expanded so fast that no structure at all could have formed. The fact that there are galaxies puts very strong limits on how big the cosmological constant can be. Those limits are 120 orders of magnitude smaller than the predictions given by quantum theory; it might just qualify as the worst prediction ever made by a scientific theory.

Either way you slice it, the notion that the vacuum of space is seething with virtual particles does not match observation—the Universe neither imploded nor tor itself apart; after all, here we are.

Physicists have proposed several wild, ad hoc theories to try to explain away the pair of contradictory predictions, each an application of the notion of virtual matter to GTR [945]. But we need not explore those theories here. Instead, the lesson is clear: even theories involving a *finite* amount of virtual particles for explaining forces acting between real particles is problematic, let alone having an *infinite* amount of virtual particles in the Universe. The most logical conclusion is that there is not an infinite number of point-sized particles popping in and out of existence across space.

Virtual matter might not even exist. Not all physicists are convinced that 'virtual particles' are actually physical particles in any true sense of the term. De Podesta states [946],

> Some people might argue that because 'virtual photons' are part of the way QED works, then the accuracy of QED is in itself evidence that virtual photons 'exist'. To these people I have a one word rebuttal: *'Epicycles'*: just because a calculational technique improves predictions does not mean that there is a physical counterpart to the 'calculational entities'.

Moreover, as the problem with applying virtual particles to the value of Λ shows, not all predictions are improved with the notion of virtual particles; some are made worse. Regardless, even if virtual particles do exist, we can be sure there are not infinitely many of them; if there were, the Universe as we know it would never have come to exist.

21.4 INFINITIES IN COSMOLOGY

Cosmology is the study of the Cosmos. The Cosmos is the Universe as an orderly system of interrelated objects, properties, and relations from the smallest portion of matter to the largest collection of galaxies. Cosmology studies the natural order of the Universe according to observable properties such as its structure, its fundamental processes, and the events influencing its development.

But there are different kinds of cosmology. Cosmology can be a branch of philosophy, a branch of theoretical physics, or both at the same time.

The kind of cosmology most popular in the media is scientific cosmology—more precisely, cosmology as portrayed by theoretical physics, astrophysics, and astronomy—and that is the kind of cosmology I will address with respect to infinity.

21.4.1 *Observable Magnitudes of Space are Finite*

In the academic field of scientific cosmology, it is widely assumed the Universe must be literally infinite in space or time or both. But we've already seen the logical problems involved with conceptions of infinite space (Chapter 18) and infinite time (Chapter 19). In addition, there is no empirical evidence for infinite magnitudes of space and time. All measurements for infinitely large magnitudes of space and time reveal only finitude.

Astronomy, for instance, provides no empirical evidence of either infinite space or infinite time. Astronomers rely mostly on the aid of electromagnetic radiation—light—to investigate the Universe. But electromagnetism has a speed limit which in turn places limits on how much of the Universe astronomers can empirically investigate.

Recall the speed of a photon of light is ~300,000 km per second in a vacuum. Assuming the speed of light always stays constant through a vacuum, astronomers interpret the one-way speed of light as approximately 9.4607×10^{12} km (nearly 6 trillion miles) per year through space—a distance commonly known as a light-year. Assuming a light-year is an accurate standard of measurement, astronomers can make reasonable estimates of distance in light-years to celestial bodies beyond the Solar System.

Figure 21.7: Each white pixel in the image is a galaxy; what looks like grey mist around the clusters of galaxies is a mixed gas of ordinary and 'dark' matter. According to astronomical distance measurements, galaxies are grouped together on the largest scales into vast 'filaments' of galaxy clusters that limn huge voids of mostly empty space. This image from the Millennium Simulation Project of the Max Planck Institute for Astrophysics represents how the Universe is structured on the scale of 2 billion cubic light-years containing over 20 million galaxies. [ESA/Hubble image credit: Volker Springel (Max Planck Institute for Astrophysics) et al.]

In measuring what can be seen of the Universe, astronomers have discovered our own galaxy, the Milky Way, to be approximately 105,700 light-years in diameter. It takes a particle of light approximately that long to travel the diameter of the entire galaxy. The Milky Way belongs to a cluster of galaxies called the *Local Group* of galaxies (a group of over 50 galaxies within a 5 million light-year radius from our own Milky Way galaxy). So, it takes light 5 million years to span that radius, and 10 million to cross the diameter of the Local Group [947]. These are vast distances and amounts of time, but they are not even close to being infinite.

However, the Local Group and other clusters of galaxies are not nearly the largest measurable structures in the Universe. They are arranged in increasingly larger structures—*sheets*, *walls*, and *filaments* of galaxy clusters limning vast voids in which next to no matter is found. The filaments comprise what's known as *the cosmic web* of galaxies (see **Figure 21.7**) [948] [949]. Of what astronomers are able to measure of the cosmic web, they find it contains trillions of galaxies in a volume extending billions of light-years in every direction. Great magnitudes of space and matter for sure, but still not infinite.

The most distant galaxy observed by telescopes is certainly a galaxy far, far away...but not infinitely far away. As of this writing, the most distant galaxy astronomers have detected was discovered in 2016 with the Hubble Space Telescope; the galaxy is labelled GN-z11 [950] [951]. Astronomers have estimated that GN-z11 is 32 billion light-years away [952]. That's a long way off, but hardly an infinite distance.

Astronomers cannot see galaxies or stars that are much further than 32 billion light-years in radius from Earth. Of course, that in itself doesn't mean no such galaxies and stars exist beyond that range of distance and so it doesn't mean the Universe is *not* infinite in size, for there may be more of the Universe to see beyond the furthest galaxy we have seen so far.

So why don't we see even more galaxies further out? Part of the reason we see no galaxies further away than GN-z11 is because of telescopic limits, but those will be overcome. However, no matter how powerful the telescope humanity creates, even the furthest galaxy we shall ever see will not be much more than several more billion light-years distant because of certain astrophysical features of the Cosmos. One of those features is an opaque fog that blocks astronomers' view of the Universe in every direction at a distance of just beyond 32 billion light-years away.

The "fog" preventing astronomers from seeing even further out into space is not fog in the usual sense. The fog is composed not of vapor but of radiation. It is as if the observable portion of the Universe is surrounded by a high-intensity but low-energy barrier of light beyond which nothing further can be seen. Astronomers refer to the radiation fog as the Cosmic Microwave Background (CMB) [953] [956].

The CMB permeates the Universe; its radiation is flying through your body right now from all directions. The CMB is transparent "close up" in astronomical terms; it's just opaque a bit beyond the furthest stars and galaxies we can telescopically detect. The CMB thus creates a kind of horizon beyond which we cannot see. This telescopic horizon is called *the particle horizon* since it marks the time during which the first atomic elements were formed in the Universe [957].

As astronomers explain, "The particle horizon at any particular time is a sphere around us whose radius equals the distance to the most distant object we can see" [958]. The particle horizon is about 46.5 billion light-years away and so that distance marks the radius of astronomical observability in all directions, which in turn means the portion of the Universe we can see has a diameter of roughly 93 billion light-years [959].

Figure 21.8 provides an artistic representation of the objects astronomers can observe from our solar system (at the center of the image) out to the particle horizon (the perimeter of the image). The particle horizon is therefore the edge of the *observable* portion of the Universe. Since all we will ever be able to see is the observable portion of the Universe that lies within the distance to the particle horizon, astronomers refer to the portion of the Universe we can physically observe as *the observable universe* [960].

However, it must be admitted that while the particle horizon is the edge of the observable universe, it is not an edge or boundary to the Universe itself. The Universe *as a whole* may extend well beyond the range of the diameter we can survey with telescopes; the particle horizon's CMB fog may be concealing a much larger Universe of which the billions of light-years we see are merely a small portion.

We can therefore assume the particle horizon differs not in the amount of distance from any given observer's galaxy but only in its location from the perspective of one observer's galaxy to the next. An observer in another galaxy would also see the CMB at the same distance from their own galaxy as do we from our galaxy, but each of us would have a different view of which celestial objects are within the horizon of observation and which are outside the horizon of observation, just as two observers in different boats afloat in the same sea may have different horizons and will not necessarily be able to see all of the same seafaring objects as one another.

Figure 21.8: The observable Universe according to logarithmic scale, as portrayed by musician and artist Pablo Carlos Budassi. At the center is our solar system. Moving outward, we first come to the Kuiper belt, then the Oort cloud, followed by the nearest stars, then the wispy arm of our galaxy stretching up to the Milky Way galaxy itself (topmost spiral) alongside nearby galaxies on the same general scale of size, and on to the cosmic web and finally to the CMB. This is not what the Universe actually looks like of course, but it is a useful image for symbolizing what can be seen from Earth to the edge of *observability*. Any observer in the Universe with an unobstructed view from their own solar system of the surrounding extragalactic space, no matter where they are, would see the Universe with the same general features.

Given that assumption, an observer viewing the Universe from a galaxy located 10 billion light-years beyond our surrounding particle horizon would not be able to see our galaxy any more than we can see theirs. To the other observer, our galaxy is beyond their particle horizon. Their view of our galaxy would be just as blocked by a CMB particle horizon as our view of their galaxy is blocked by the CMB horizon. Observers in different galaxies therefore have different 'observable universes' even though the galaxies of all observers belong to the same Universe as a whole (represented in **Figure 21.9**).

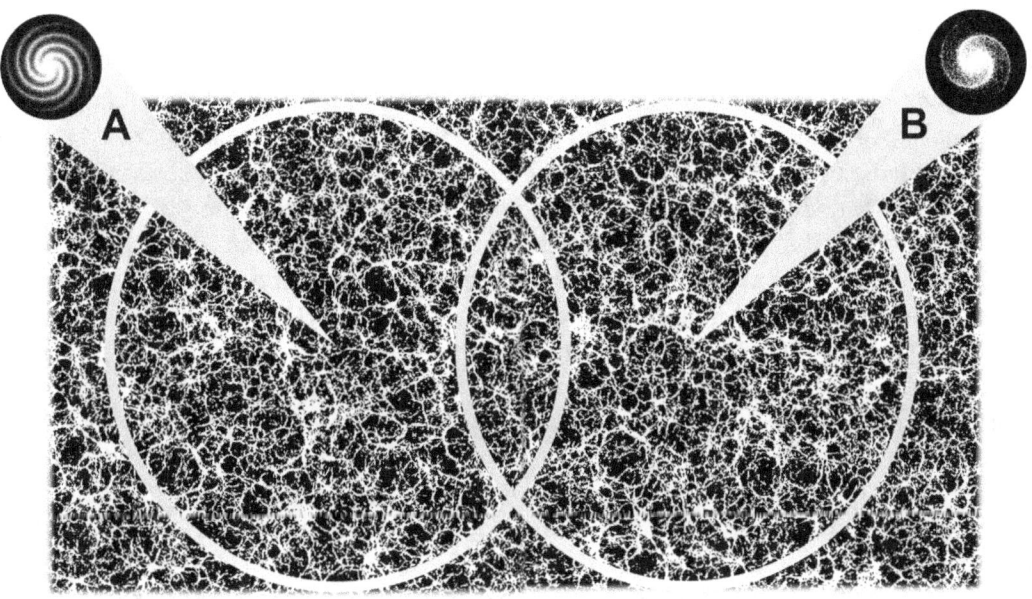

Figure 21.9: The cosmic web of galaxies in which two galaxies, labelled A and B, are beyond each other's particle horizon (marked by the overlapping circles). Observers in galaxy A cannot perceive galaxy B while observers in galaxy B cannot perceive galaxy A, both due to the CMB fog of their respective particle horizons blocking their views of each other. Notice that galaxies A and B can each see most of the same galaxies in the overlapping area shared between their respective observable universes.

Because observers in each galaxy of the Universe cannot see past their own particle horizon, all observers in all galaxies can see only so much of the larger Universe. The best astronomical measurements indicate the observable portion of the Universe within the particle horizon of the surrounding CMB fog has a diameter of about 93 billion light-years (which equals a radius of 46.5 billion light-years from the Earth in every direction) [961]. So, the observable universe from the vantage of any galaxy may be awe-inspiringly large, but it's still *finite*.

How big the whole Universe is beyond the range of our observable universe is not something that can be determined from physical evidence; nor is there any evidence that the Universe as a whole is infinite. All we can be sure of, *assuming* the theory-laden evidence [962] astronomers have so far gathered, is that the observable universe is a sphere with an internal volume equal to approximately 4×10^{32} cubic light-years [963] and the entire Universe must have a volume that is at a bare minimum equal to at least the size of a ball composed of 251 non-overlapping spheres, each with an inner volume equivalent to that of our observable universe [964]. Once again, that is certainly large, but it is not infinite.

None of this is to say the entire Universe must be *only* trillions of cubic light-years, though. It could be many more times larger than that. It could even be an 'immensity' (indefinitely large number) of light-years in volume. But if my arguments against the concept of infinity have held up, then however large the Universe is, we can be sure the Universe is finite in size.

The question remaining is in what manner the Universe is finite; for instance, does the Universe have an edge? After all, if the Universe is finite and it has a volume, then one is left to wonder what the "edge" or boundary of the Universe could be like. But the question of the Universe's edge can be answered in the negative: there is no edge of the Universe, not even if it is finite in size.

If the Universe is finite, that does not mean it has an edge or bound. Instead, the Universe may be *finite-unbounded*. That is to say, the Universe as a whole could still qualify as 'boundless' or 'unbounded' in any direction *despite* being finite in spatial volume [965] [966]. Just as a circle is unbounded along the one-dimensional curve of its circumference and yet is still finite in extent (recall **Figure 1.1**), and just as a sphere is unbounded along its two-dimensional surface and yet is still finite in surface area, so too the Universe may be unbounded in three-dimensions and yet still be finite in volume.

This is not something that can be pictured from a perspective *outside* the Universe as we can picture a circle or sphere from outside of it; we are not able to see the whole of the Universe's curvature at once. Instead, we can only imagine the finite-unbounded geometry of the Universe from the *inside*, picturing the Universe one part at a time. The best way to imagine the Universe's finite-unbounded curvature is by analogy. Imagine travelling along the spherical surface of the Earth: no matter which direction you travel, if you were to go far enough without making any turns, you would still end up back at your starting point. Likewise, you can imagine circumnavigating the closed and yet boundless extent of the Universe. The difference is that the Universe is unbounded in all three dimensions rather than just in the two dimensions of a spherical surface like a planet. Point in *any* direction you like—it bends back to the start [967].

This analogy does break down if we push it too far. Because the Earth's surface is only a (roughly) two-dimensional area curved around on itself, you can tunnel into the Earth or leave its surface for outer space; whereas, because the Universe is a three-dimensional volume curved around on itself, there is no such thing as travelling *beyond* the volume of the Universe. Nevertheless, the analogy holds up in the sense that we can imagine a spaceship able to return to its starting point without turning around if only it could travel far enough and fast enough in one direction *within* the volume of the Universe [968].

Given this 'non-Euclidean' geometry, the Universe may not have a boundary or edge to it just as the surface of a planet has no edge or boundary (only, for the Universe, the unbounded geometry applies in all three dimensions instead of just in the two dimensions of a globe's surface). Despite having no edge or boundary, the Universe could still be limited in spatial extent just as the curved planetary surface is limited in its measure. So, even if the Universe is "unbounded" in all three dimensions by virtue of its geometry curving back on itself, the Universe can still be finite rather than infinite. This is, incidentally, how Einstein originally imagined the shape of the Universe [969] [970].

At this point, I should mention that there are some philosophers who are skeptical of the finite-unbounded model of cosmic geometry [971]. Even so, their objections are not about empirical evidence. In fact, any such empirical concerns are already dispelled by the estimated size of the entire Universe as >251 'observable universes'. That size estimate is the minimum size that the Universe would have to be in order for a finite-unbounded model of the Universe to fit astrophysical measurements which otherwise make the Universe appear "flat" at our small scale just as the surface of the Earth appears "flat" to those standing on its surface. And there are no scientific problems with the whole Universe being at least 251 times the size of the observable universe.

Yet, it is not so much that lack of empirical evidence is behind the skepticism many philosophers feel toward the conjecture that the Universe is finite-unbounded. Rather, they object to the very concept of finite-unbounded geometry itself. Just as I challenge that the Universe cannot be infinite based on troubles with infinity as a concept, so too some rival philosophers would like to retain infinity and reject the idea of finite-unbounded geometry [972]. I believe their objections fall refuted but, alas, a more complete elucidation and defense of the finite-unbounded space proposal will have to wait for another book [973].

For now, the important point with respect to the quantity of space comprising the Universe is that astronomers only observe finitudes of space, however vast the Universe may be. While they do have evidence that the observable universe—the portion of the Universe we are able to see—can be accurately described with Euclidean geometry on the intergalactic scales telescopes can reach, that alone is not sufficient to prove the Universe is infinite in size [974].

21.4.2 *Observable Spans of Time are Finite*

So far, empirical evidence for infinite space comes up empty; we have only evidence for finite magnitudes of physical space. But what about evidence for infinite time?

Notice the word 'year' in the term 'light-year'. A light-year measures distance, but it also indicates time. Each light-year is just that—a year in time. The further out into space astronomers look, the further they are seeing back in time. An astronomical image detected 10 light-years away took 10 years to reach Earth's telescopes. The further away an object is in light-years, the further into the past it was when its light was emitted in our direction, and so the further into the past astronomers peer when they catch sight of it. Looking out into space is looking back in time, but there is only so far back in time we can see.

So how far back in time can we see? It all depends on what theoretical assumptions you want to make.

According to astronomical data as interpreted by the *standard model of cosmology* [975], the most distant galaxies astronomers were able to detect in 2021 are 32 billion light-years away (a figure currently being exceeded). But those distant galaxies weren't always that far away according to that model, which assumes the Big Bang theory. If we assume that theory, then at one point in the past the most distant galaxies (and all the matter between them and us) were a lot closer. At some time over 11 billion years ago, the observable Universe was itself a lot smaller than it is now. The theory states that the Universe emerged from a hot, dense state smaller than a single atom and "expanded" up to its present size, forming elements, stars, and galaxies along the way [976]. The CMB is often taken to be the light of the 'Big Bang' from which the Universe (as we know it, anyway) began [977]. Assuming as much, the best estimates from astronomical data as of this writing places the time of the Big Bang between 13.7 and 13.8 billion years ago [978]. A long time ago, but not infinitely long ago.

What happened before the Big Bang is sheer speculation however educated it may be. Some cosmologists and astrophysicists theorize there was a time before the Big Bang [979] while others believe that there was no time prior to the emergence of the Universe [980] [981]. If the latter is true, then the past is by definition finite. However, if the former is true, the past must still be finite for the reasons given in Chapter 19. Either way, we only have astrophysical evidence for a past that is, at most, on the order of billions of years rather than trillions of years or anything longer than that—certainly, we have no evidence for an infinite past [982].

Even if the CMB does not turn out to be the light of a 'Big Bang' but instead has some other source, and even if astronomical distance estimates are way off, we still know one thing: the further we look out into space, the further back in time we see owing to the finite speed of light and we can only see back in time so far. The CMB is opaque beyond the furthest galaxy we can detect (as of this publication, GN-z11) and provides the horizon beyond which we can detect no further celestial bodies. The CMB marks not just the limit of our sight out into space but also back in time as well. Even if we rejected the Big Bang theory for an alternative theory in which the observable universe is not expanding in size, yet while we retain our same distance estimate to the CMB's particle horizon, that would still place the most ancient event for which we have physical evidence at a time between 13.7 billion years ago and no more than ~46.5 billion years ago—still a far cry from infinitely long ago.

Whichever way you cut it we have no evidence for an infinite past.

As for the future, because we do not receive information travelling backward in time, we can't be sure from an empirical standpoint how much time the future holds. All we have to fall back on is theoretical estimates, given the astronomical measurements we can make in the present.

For example, drawing on the most recent astronomical measurements, astrophysicists have estimated that our Milky Way Galaxy and the Andromeda Galaxy will collide 3.85 billion years from now, throwing existing stars into new orbits while also triggering the formation of new stars in the galaxies [983] [984]. However, the distances between the stars in each of the galaxies are so vast and the time scales of the galactic merger so large that there will be virtually no collisions of the component stars in the galaxies [985]. Hence, although the merger of the Milky Way and the Andromeda Galaxy into a single Milkomeda Galaxy will rearrange the orbits of component stars, including our own Sun, nevertheless the structure of our Solar System will remain mostly unaffected by the merger of the two galaxies as such [986]. Despite the collision of galaxies then, our planet may still be around. It won't survive forever, though. Astrophysicists further estimate that, while the Solar System will survive for at least another few billion years after the galaxies merge, 7.5 billion years from now the Earth will most likely be engulfed by the Sun as it swells into a red giant star [987]. Beyond that time frame, cosmic events become increasingly speculative the further into the future they are predicted to occur.

Every plausible theory of the Universe's future promoted in the scientific community holds that the Universe will at the very least be around for tens of billions of years to come if not more [988], but will there *always* be a Universe? That is the question.

As of this writing, there are still plenty of cosmologists and astrophysicists who predict the Universe will end sometime in the future, that time itself will come to a halt in one fashion or another [989]. In their point of view, the future is not infinite in any sense.

However, most cosmologists and astrophysicists believe the future is at least figuratively infinite—the future goes on indefinitely in the sense of an open-ended series of future events and so will continue forever (which is to say, without ceasing). While some scientists go further in proposing the future is a spacetime structure stretching to literal infinity, none of the astrophysical scenarios for the future of the Universe necessitate such a thing. Of the open future predictions, any of them could fit a cosmology in which the past is finite and the future continues without invoking literal infinity.

The most popular prediction for the future of the Universe these days is the idea that the Universe will continue through a scenario called the *heat death* of the Universe [990]. In this scenario, the Universe starts with the Big Bang, space expands superclusters of galaxies away from one another at an accelerating pace with the cosmic web of galaxies growing more diffuse over time. Most cosmologists presently believe the accelerated expansion is not going to let up. After >100 trillion years, the Universe will have expanded to such vast proportions that gas clouds adrift in space will become too thin for stars to form. Eventually, all the stars burn out, leaving only black holes which evaporate away over billions of years as space itself gets colder and colder. Eventually, all that is left is a cold, massless diffusion of radiation which cannot form new matter [991]. And so the Universe becomes increasingly colder as matter breaks down into a sea of diffuse radiation—the so-called 'heat death' of the Universe.

Don't let the term 'heat death' fool you: time does not end in this scenario. Instead, as one cosmologist points out, "the universe would just keep expanding—forever" [992]. The Universe continues to expand without ceasing—an endless, cold night sometimes referred to as the Big Chill or Big Freeze [993].

Although time continues into the Big Freeze, this scenario does *not* imply the future is infinite in the literal sense of the term 'infinite'. There need be no "complete and limitless" quantity of years ahead. Instead, however long time continues on it is just one more year ahead of the finite number of years that have passed since the beginning of time. Time may continue to roll on without ceasing and, perhaps in a purely figurative sense, some might describe this as an "infinite" future. But the term 'indefinite' would be more appropriate for this scenario since even if time never ceases, it's only ever a finite number of years back to the Big Bang. In other words, it is more precise and accurate to say that, according to the Big Freeze scenario, time continues *indefinitely* rather than *infinitely*. Time in the Big Freeze scenario remains finite from the Big Bang on, no matter how long time continues to pass in the cold cosmic dark.

Assuming time continues in a linear ordering of events, there is no conceptual problem with the idea that time will continue indefinitely, as opposed to infinitely in the literal sense. So if there is a flaw in the Big Freeze scenario, it is not due to positing a literally infinite future.

Notwithstanding, an open future does not necessitate the Big Freeze scenario; the evidence for it, while scientifically plausible, is not rationally *compelling*. The scenario rests on too many untestable extrapolations beyond what the evidence warrants [994]. All we have physical evidence for with respect to the future is that time continues—for how long we cannot know; it's all a matter of educated opinion. The only thing we can know for sure, given the prior arguments in Chapter 19, is that the future will not be *infinite*—at least, not literally so.

21.4.3 *Infinite Density and Temperature*

In the field of scientific cosmology, infinite magnitudes other than those of space and time have been proposed. For example, take the Big Bang theory according to which the Universe as a whole is expanding. Cosmologists typically explain that if we trace the expansion of the Universe back in time, all galaxies were at one time closer together than they are now. If we keep tracing the expansion further into the past, the argument goes, then there must have been a time when all the matter that composes all the galaxies in the Universe was squashed down into a dense, hot ball of fundamental particles. Some versions of the Big Bang theory even propose that the initial ball of matter and energy was an infinitesimal point of *infinite density*, *infinite temperature*, and other infinite magnitudes such as infinitely strong gravitation or "spacetime curvature". Such an infinitesimal point is known as a *singularity* [995]. In some versions of the Big Bang theory, the "bang" was an event of rapid expansion of space out of this singularity, followed by a slower expansion of space that still continues [996].

Was there a cosmological singularity at the beginning of the Universe? Some philosophers and physicists think so. According to one philosopher of science, "there is good reason to believe that 13.8 billion years ago the entire universe was a singularity with infinite temperature, infinite density, infinitesimal volume, and infinite curvature of spacetime" [997].

But is there really "good reason" to believe in the cosmological singularity? Philosophers and theoretical physicists are becoming more skeptical. Writes Unger [998],

> In contemporary cosmology, the idea of an absolute beginning is suggested by the initial singularity that a long line of twentieth-century cosmologists argued to be implied by the field equations of general relativity. It was, however, widely recognized (even by Einstein himself) that this inference, rather than describing a physical state of affairs, revealed a breakdown of the theory when it was carried beyond its proper domain of application. More generally, as I argue throughout and as many have recognized in the history of both physics and mathematics, the infinite that is invoked in this view is a mathematical conception with no presence in nature.

In his book *Our Mathematical Universe*, Tegmark agrees [999]: "The question *Do we have evidence for a Big Bang singularity?* from the last chapter has a very simple answer: *No!*" The idea of a cosmological singularity was proposed by extrapolating the expansion of space back to a time at which it could have started as an infinitesimal point, but there is no physical evidence that such an extrapolation applies to physical reality. Just because a balloon blows up in size does not mean the balloon was infinitesimal when we started blowing air into it; so too, even if the Universe is expanding, that does not mean it started out as a singularity.

There is also a lack of evidence for singularities associated with so-called 'black holes'—gravitationally collapsed stars. Black holes are often claimed to have a core in which matter is crushed inward to an infinitesimal point of infinite heat, density, and gravitation—a singularity. However, since not even light can escape a black hole, we cannot see inside a black hole. And since we cannot see inside a black hole, we cannot gather any evidence to show if gravitation actually crushes the matter of a star into a singularity or if it just crushes matter down to some finite amount—after all, quantum theory posits that units of matter smaller than the Planck length cannot be measured [1,000]. Nor is there a compelling reason to posit that a singularity *must* exist inside a black hole; just because we can mathematically project gravitation as *indefinitely* collapsing an object into ever-smaller sizes does not mean the object ever becomes *infinitesimal*. As Unger argued, the infinitude of a singularity may be a mathematical ideal that has no presence in nature—even inside a black hole.

21.4.4 *The Question of Infinitely Many Parallel Universes*

Although astronomers have no evidence the universe in which our galaxy is located is anything other than finite in size and age, a popular idea in theoretical physics is that in addition to the universe we inhabit there exist *other* universes. By "other universes" theoretical physicists mean not simply that there are portions of *the* Universe we cannot in practice observe, portions of the Universe beyond the particle horizon. Rather, what they mean is that in addition to the three-dimensional universe we inhabit there are other universes (of three or more dimensions) that exist *separately* from our own—universes that exist with their own expanses of space and durations of time independent of those in our universe.

These other universes are often called *parallel universes* because they are thought to drift "in parallel" alongside our own universe in a higher-dimensional space, or *hyperspace*. However, the term 'parallel' is a bit misleading since universes are not stacked together like sheets of paper and the geometries of those other universes need not be Euclidean and equidistant from our own universe in hyperspace. Moreover, those other universes need have no temporal relation to the temporal succession of events in our universe. The so-called 'parallel universes', if they exist, would simply exist in hyperspace somewhere, somewhen, inaccessible to us—that is, barring some further theoretical connection between universes.

There are various notions of parallel universes, but only two will concern us: one proposal is typically called *the Multiverse*; the other is sometimes referred to as *the Omnium* (see § 21.4.7). There are also different versions of the Multiverse and the Omnium proposals, but I will not spend much time on their various distinctions. I will instead simply note that many adherents of these proposals (but not all) claim there are an infinite number of parallel universes of which ours is just one. We'll take a look at the claims of infinitude for each of these parallel universe proposals.

21.4.5 *The Multiverse*

The Big Bang theory was originally about how the Universe began, how it is structured, and how it evolves. Now that has changed. The Big Bang theory has in recent years become only about how the Universe began while the standard model of cosmology (or *standard cosmology* for short) is more about what the Universe is made of and how it changes over time rather than about how it began.

The standard cosmology holds that the Universe is composed of ordinary matter, *cold dark matter* (invisible, electrically neutral stuff), and *dark energy* (a kind of antigravity denoted by the Greek capital letter Lambda, or Λ). Consequently, the standard cosmology is also known as the Lambda Cold Dark Matter Model, Lambda-CDM, or ΛCDM [1,001][1,002]. Most scientists in the field now assume that any new theory must be "in concordance with" ΛCDM. Because of that standard, ΛCDM is also known as the *concordance model of cosmology* or simply the *concordance cosmology* [1,003] [1,004].

The standard, or 'concordance', cosmology assumes the Big Bang, which is an *expanding universe theory*. However, there is more than one version of the Big Bang theory. While they all agree the Universe is expanding, they do not all agree on what the term 'big bang' means.

In the original version of the theory, the Big Bang was an event—*bang!*—and the Universe expanded *from* that event [1,005] [1,006]. Specifically, the Big Bang event was the origin not just of all matter in the Universe, but also of space and time. Prior to the Big Bang, there was no space for anything to be in and no time passed because time did not exist—the very first moment of time just was the event of the Big Bang and the only place anything could be at during that event was inside the Big Bang singularity. At least, that would be true for *our* universe—some astrophysicists and cosmologists believe other universes exist in addition to the one we live in.

This brings us to another version of the theory, a version in which the Big Bang was not an event but a *process*, and that process is not what started the Universe. In this second version of the theory, what we call "the Big Bang" is *not* the event of space expanding out of a singularity some 13–14 billion years ago. Instead, in this new version of the Big Bang theory, the term 'Big Bang' is redefined as referring to the "slow" expansion of space that took place *after* our universe had already burst from the singularity (or some other small dense ball of energy). The Big Bang in this picture is actually a Big Bang Era, a time period in which our universe was a hot, dense ball of expanding space filled with radiation [1,007]. The Big Bang Era took place *between* the time our universe was ~1 second old and 380,000 years old, the latter age being the time at which matter across the Universe released the light we measure today as the CMB—the "flash" of the Bang. So in this second version of the Big Bang theory, there was an incredibly brief period of expansion *before* the Big Bang, which is to say a period of time before our universe was even one second old, in which the initial expansion of space was much more rapid. This initial burst of expanding space before the so-called Big Bang is known as *cosmic inflation* or *cosmological inflation* or just plain *inflation* for short [1,008].

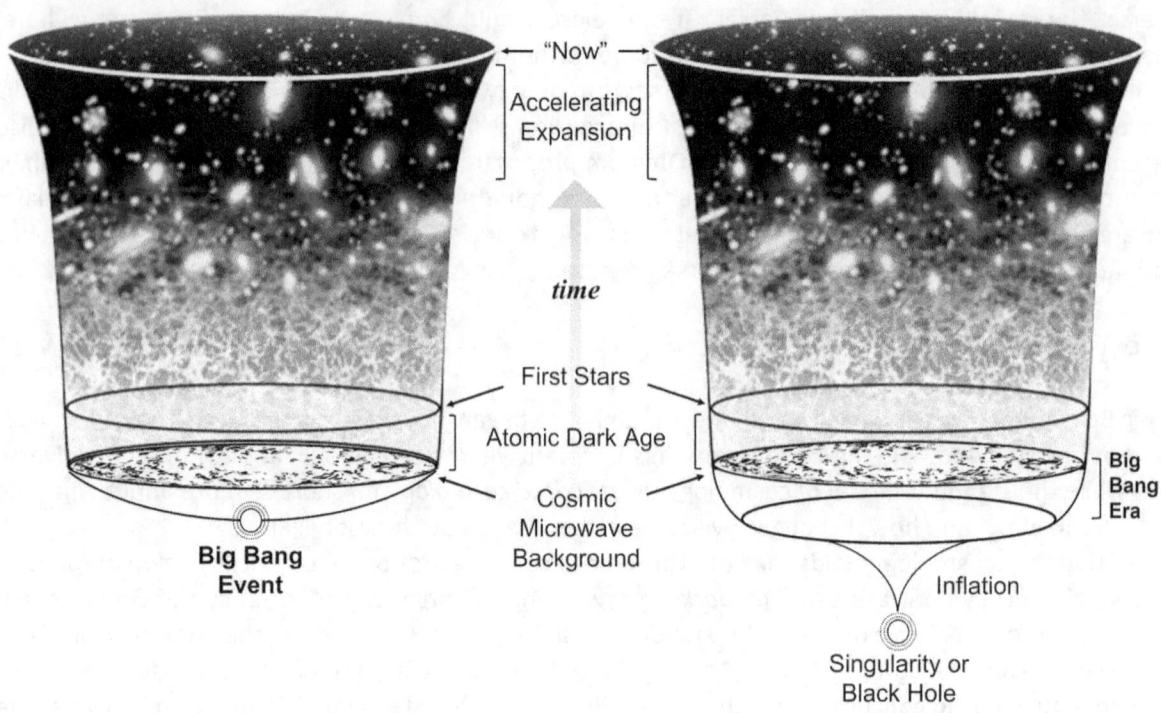

Figure 21.10: Two interpretations of the Big Bang theory. Both images depict abstractions of space, both in size and dimension, to give a view of space as it changes along the vertical time dimension. According to the original interpretation at the left, the Big Bang is the initial event of spacetime creation from a singularity or dense state of energy. In the more recent interpretation to the right, the Big Bang is the "slower" post-inflation era of expansion and particle formation. Magnitudes of time for both images are not to scale. In the image to the right, the epoch of inflation is said to have lasted only from between 10^{-36} to 10^{-34} of the first second of time while the Big Bang Era lasted for 380,000 years before culminating in the "flash" of the bang—release of the CMB radiation. In both interpretations, the first stars formed about 180 million years after the CMB was released and the observable universe is approximately 13.7–13.8 billion years old.

According to the inflation model of the Big Bang (the right hand image in **Figure 21.10**), our universe expanded exponentially in size from an initial singularity (or some kind of 'black hole' or other hot, dense state) until this universe reached almost its present size [1,009]. The exponential growth took place *in a fraction of a second*: the inflationary 'epoch' lasted from the time the Universe was only 10^{-36} seconds old and ended at around 10^{-34} seconds, at which time our universe was almost its present size [1,010]. Then, the epoch of rapid inflation stopped but our universe continued to expand at a much slower rate. That "slower" rate was the Big Bang era, which ended 380,000 years later with the flash of light that comes to us as the CMB. (Although, most astronomers believe the expansion of the universe later picked up speed again and could even now be accelerating—as also illustrated in **Figure 21.10**) [1,011].

The original ideas for cosmic inflation were proposed in 1979 by theoretical physicist Alexei Starobinsky at the L. D. Landau Institute for Theoretical Physics in Moscow, and independently by theoretical physicist and cosmologist Alan Guth in 1980 [1,012]. Since then, revisions to the cosmic inflation model of the Big Bang have been proposed. It is in certain versions of the inflation model that the existence of the Multiverse is implied, or "predicted" as Tegmark puts it [1,013].

According to the theory of inflation, our universe was not the only one that popped out of a singularity—what we commonly call "the Universe" is just *our* universe, and it's just one of many universes in the Multiverse [1,014]. The Multiverse is a set of independently existing universes of which ours is just one. Each universe originates from its own singularity and expands on its own, disconnected and independently of our universe. And more singularities are always occurring, generating ever more parallel universes outside of our universe. It is the group of all parallel universes generated by the increasing multitude of singularity events that is known as the Multiverse.

Although the idea of parallel universes was a science fiction staple long before inflationary theory came along, it's the theory of inflation that made the idea of the Multiverse popular in theoretical physics. Since its initial proposal, other versions of inflation have been proposed.

One of the revised versions of inflation is called *eternal inflation*, which was proposed in 1983 by theoretical physicists Paul Steinhardt and Alexander Vilenkin [1,015]. According to the idea of eternal inflation, our universe inflated out of singularity (or somehow popped out of a black hole, which is close enough to a singularity that I'll refer to it as such even if not technically correct). But in this model, our universe is itself just one universe that is part of a larger, multidimensional medium of hyperspace containing many other black holes, each of which also inflates into a universe external to all the others [1,016]. This conglomeration of universes had a beginning in time but will have no end as universes continue to multiply.

Another revised version of the inflation model, called *eternal self-reproducing chaotic inflation* (or *eternal chaotic inflation* or just plain *chaotic inflation*), was offered in 1986 by theoretical physicist Andre Linde [1,017]. According to the chaotic inflation model, a new universe can sprout either from a singularity in the hyperspace medium external to all universes or from a singularity in the spatial continuum of an existing universe, rather like a soap bubble ballooning up from the surface of another soap bubble. Many universes divide off from preexisting universes, with existence itself constituting a foam of universes in a never-ending fizz of popping singularities.

Whichever revised version of the inflation model one accepts, they agree there should be many universes, not just one. If any of these cosmic inflation models are true, then universes have been, are, and will continue to be generated by their own singularity events outside of our universe. Before our universe was around, other universes existed and if some of these universes—ours included—cease to exist, other universes will continue to be around and more will be generated to take their place in a series of independent big bangs.

Exactly how many parallel universes there *have been*, or how many there *are*, or how many there *will be* (if indeed it even makes any sense to speak of time *between* universes) is as speculative as the notion of the Multiverse itself. Most cosmologists adhering to the Multiverse theory believe the Multiverse contains *infinitely many* parallel universes. The late particle physicist Victor J. Stenger, for example, stated that there are infinitely many parallel universes: "...cosmologists have inferred that our universe is but one in an unbounded, eternal multiverse that contains an unlimited number of other universes" [1,018].

And yet, despite what has become widespread support for the Multiverse and an infinitude of universes within it, some cosmologists do not go so far as to say there are *infinitely* many parallel universes. Linde, writing with co-author Vitaly Vanchurin at Stanford University, calculates that there are at least $10^{10^{10^7}}$ universes comprising the Multiverse, which is a large but still finite number [1,019]. Although Linde believes the present set of universes were each preceded by an infinite past, that infinite past does not necessarily entail that an infinite number of other universes have come and gone; it just may mean a finite number have come and gone over infinite time.

However, according to Linde, the current set of universes may well be succeeded by an infinite quantity of future universes [1,020]:

> Eternal chaotic inflation answers the great unanswered question from the Big Bang: what came before? According to Linde's theory, there has always been a yesterday and there will always be a tomorrow. Our universe grew out of a quantum fluctuation in some preexisting region of the spacetime continuum. "Each particular part of the [multiverse] may stem from a singularity somewhere in the past and it may end up in a singularity somewhere in the future," Linde says. Some parts may stop their expansion and contract, but inflation ends at different times in different places. There are always parts of the multiverse that are still inflating, with universes like ours eternally being produced.

Some cosmologists are a bit more skeptical of an infinitude of universes. According to the final paper published by Stephen Hawking and co-authored by Thomas Hertog, the number of parallel universes *ever* in existence should be finite (even if it is a vast number like $10^{10^{10^7}}$) [1,021].

Hawking and Hertog are not the only ones who have expressed skepticism of infinitely many parallel universes. There are other cosmologists who have remained or have become even more skeptical of the Multiverse than Hawking and Hertog, rejecting not just the claim that there are infinitely many other universes, but that there is even one other universe parallel to our own. Smolin and Unger, for example, argue against even a finite Multiverse. They instead support the view that there is just one Universe—the one in which our own galaxy is located—and therefore parallel universes do not exist at all, let alone an infinite number of them. The whole Universe may extend far beyond the particle horizon, but there is only one Universe [1,022].

In their book, *The Singular Universe and the Reality of Time*, Smolin and Unger point out there is no empirical evidence for the Multiverse and argue that we have no need to posit its existence [1,023]. So too, mathematician and particle physicist Peter Woit writes, "Our current best understanding of science shows no evidence for a multiverse, so anyone who wants to posit one needs to come up with some significant evidence for one, experimental or theoretical, and I haven't seen that happening" [1,024].

Over a decade ago, Tegmark reassured us that the Multiverse is a testable, scientific proposal even if the evidence isn't in *yet* [1,025]. However, some cosmologists sympathetic to the idea of the Multiverse have since concluded there is probably no practical way to test it. As cosmologist and mathematician George Ellis recently stated, "I'm not against the multiverse...I'm just against saying it's established science" [1,026]. Without any indications of a forthcoming practical test that will obtain empirical evidence, the idea of the Multiverse not only hasn't been established as factual, it may not even be scientific in anything but the loose sense that it is *consistent* with the astronomical observations we already have. But then, certain rival cosmologies that deny the existence of parallel universes, such as the cosmology championed by Smolin and Unger, can also boast consistency with astronomical observations.

Without compelling empirical evidence or even a solid hope of obtaining any, believers in the Multiverse are instead forced to rely on indirect arguments for the existence of parallel universes. For example, the best argument Tegmark offers for parallel universes is that the Multiverse is a prediction necessitated by the mathematics behind inflationary theory [1,027]. However, inflation is not on the sure footing Tegmark seems to assume [1,028]. Astronomer Reza Tavakol and philosopher of science Fabio Gironi argue that the inflation proposal is "an incomplete theory under construction and without unambiguous empirical confirmation" [1,029]. According to Tavakol and Gironi, it is therefore dubious to say the Multiverse proposal, as an incomplete theory, can be truly called a 'prediction' of inflation [1,030].

Furthermore, suppose inflation theory is rejected, as it is by some cosmologists; if so, then there goes the best reason for believing in the Multiverse, and certainly for an infinite number of parallel universes comprising it. In fact, theoretical physicist Paul Steinhardt, who introduced one of the early versions of eternal inflation, eventually became a critic of the theory [1,031].

There is another problem with a mathematical defense of the Multiverse: while arguing that we must accept there are infinitely many parallel universes on the merits of inflationary theory, Tegmark undermined his own case by questioning the soundness of proposing infinite magnitudes of space and time [1,032]. He admits 'infinitely big' and 'infinitely small' are rather dubious notions; a skepticism I share [1,033]. He also argues there is no empirical evidence of infinity in nature, that physics can get along fine without infinity, and that we should probably abandon the concept of infinity [1,034]. All points I agree with. Nevertheless, because he can find no mathematically convenient alternative to infinity, Tegmark continues to describe the whole of space and time as a Multiverse containing infinitely many parallel universes [1,035]. This is the wrong approach to take. Lack of a mathematical alternative to infinity is not a good reason to retain the concept of infinity. Rather, it's a good reason to abstain from using infinity in conjectures about the nature of the Universe and to actively seek a replacement for infinity, revising all previous notions based on it—like inflation and the Multiverse. Tegmark therefore does not maintain a consistent position; he supports his infinite Multiverse in one breath and undermines it in another.

Without a better argument, we are faced with the conclusion that the Multiverse and inflation proposals, although consistent with observation, neither logically necessitate the existence of infinite magnitudes of space and time nor empirically necessitate the proposal of infinitely many parallel universes. Then too, theorists such as Smolin and Unger offer a rival picture of the Universe just as consistent with scientifically gathered observations as the Multiverse cosmology, while pointing out that their own cosmology is mathematically finite—or, at least, that it implies only figurative infinities rather than literal infinities [1,036]. I'm not saying I necessarily agree with all the details of Smolin and Unger's cosmology, just that they have successfully shown we need not posit the Universe to be infinite (or even that there is more than one universe) in order to be consistent with all the scientifically established observations.

For all these reasons, the Multiverse proposal and its supporting theory of inflation fail to establish that literal infinities are physically real.

21.4.6 *Infinite Duplicates and Infinite Repetition in the Multiverse*

Several theoretical physicists and cosmologists have claimed that there is an infinite amount of space in the Universe, and some say there are even infinitely many parallel universes comprising a Multiverse. However, they also point out that there are only a finite number of possible arrangements of material particles. The typical conclusion they draw from this is that there must then be infinitely many duplicates of everything we see somewhere else in existence, both in our own universe beyond the particle horizon and in parallel universes if they too exist.

Because humans are made of matter like everything else, there must therefore be infinitely many duplicates of each person. Just think, if space is infinite, there must be infinitely many copies of you out there somewhere. As Barrow put it [1,037],

> In a universe of infinite size, anything that has a non-zero probability of occurring must occur infinitely often. Thus at any instant of time—for example, the present moment—there must be an infinite number of identical copies of each of us doing

precisely what each of us is now doing. There are also infinite numbers of identical copies of each one of us doing something other than what we are doing at this moment. Indeed, an infinite number of copies of each of us could be found at this moment doing anything that it was possible for us to do with a non-zero probability at this moment.

And if the past and future are infinite, that would mean there have been and will be infinitely many copies of every finite configuration of matter—including infinitely many copies of each one of us throughout time.

This implication of infinite space and time is sometimes called the *doppelganger problem* (a 'doppelganger' being an unrelated duplicate of a person). It's a problem because it seems patently absurd to propose there are infinitely many copies of each one of us spread across infinite space, and perhaps infinitely many parallel universes. Nor does it help to think all of those copies of us differ from one another in some minute way, like a universe in which another copy of you exists with just one hair skewed a nanometer to the right [1,038].

It also seems too absurd to be true that there have been and will be an infinite number of universes, or infinitely many repetitions of this universe, in which infinitely many duplicates of our lives are repeated infinitely many times—an idea the philosopher Friedrich Nietzsche (1844 – 1900) called *the eternal recurrence* or *eternal return* [1,039] [1,040]. It seems just as absurd to suppose there are infinitely many variant repetitions of the universe in which we each live an infinite number of alternate lives, as Tegmark proposes [1,041]:

> ...everything that can happen according to the laws of physics does happen. And it happens an infinite number of times. This means that there are parallel universes where you never get a parking ticket, where you have a different name, where you've won a million-dollar lottery, where Germany won World War II, where dinosaurs still roam the Earth, and where Earth never formed in the first place.

Not everyone is convinced the doppelganger problem logically follows as an implication of infinite space and time. Karen Masters, Associate Professor of Astronomy and Astrophysics at the University of Portsmouth thinks not. Masters offers [1,042],

> If there is a finite probability of something happening (i.e., a planet forming around a star, or a galaxy forming), then in an infinite universe there will be an infinite number of that thing. So there would be an infinite number of galaxies and planets in an infinite universe. If however there is an infinitesimal probability of something happening, then in an infinite universe there would only be a finite number (for example 1) of those things. I would argue that the probability of creating a specific person with a specific genetic make-up and way of thinking may only be infinitesimal (it depends on how complex you think humans are)—therefore there is only one of you!

If Masters is correct, there need not be infinitely many copies of me and you even if space, time, and quantities of matter are themselves infinite rather than finite.

And there is some empirical evidence to back her argument. The *infinite monkey theorem* states that infinitely many monkeys randomly banging away on infinitely many typewriters would eventually reproduce a work of Shakespeare. Over the past two decades attempts have been made to prove the theorem, but none have been very convincing.

For instance, in 2011 computer programmer Jesse Anderson created a simulation consisting of millions of 'virtual monkeys', each typing nine-letter sequences randomly. If the nine-letter sequences matched any nine-letter sequences of any of Shakespeare's works, they were selected out of the clutter of other random outputs. When these nine-letter strings were compiled together, they yielded *A Lover's Compliant*, one of the Bard's poems [1,043]. This computer simulation is an argument by analogy to support the conclusion that an infinitude of real monkeys, which would be even more random in their behavior, could achieve the same success.

However, this argument from analogy is flawed in a number of respects. For one thing, it's not surprising that far less than an infinitude of these computer programs could output nine-letter strings able to be intelligently compiled into a match of an author's work; far more impressive would be a single monkey producing a whole work of Shakespeare *by itself*, as the original infinite monkey proposal seemed to suggest. For another thing, the virtual monkeys are nothing like real monkeys. While the virtual monkeys all output nine-letter strings according to a rule, real monkeys would not follow the rules and so may not produce intelligible results at all.

In fact, real monkeys would interact with a keyboard in a much more chaotic fashion, yielding absurdly random output. As noted by science correspondent Nick Collins [1,044],

> In 2003 the Arts Council for England paid £2,000 for a real-life test of the theorem involving six Sulawesi crested macaques, but the trial was abandoned after a month.
>
> The monkeys produced five pages of text, mainly composed of the letter S, but failed to type anything close to a word of English, broke the computer and used the keyboard as a lavatory.

There are a couple of morals to the real-life simulation. First, not all probable outputs need to be weighted the same, so even if finite patterns (for example, typing the letter 'S') are repeated an infinite number of times, that does not mean that complex patterns (typing out intelligible sentences) are just as likely as simple ones to repeat again, let alone infinitely. Second, this further entails that an infinite quantity of a particular behavior does not imply infinite repetitions of any and every possible behavior. In other words, infinite quantity does not imply infinite *variety*. An infinitude of real monkeys might just produce an infinite number of illegible pages and an infinite number of trashed keyboards...and little else. Not everything imaginable with "non-zero probability" must happen. So even if we assume infinity is an intelligible concept, then as Master argued, something with only an infinitesimal (ergo, non-zero) probability of happening may only happen once, if at all.

Applying these conclusions to the Universe, we can further conclude that some arrangements of matter may occur far more frequently than others. In an infinite universe, perhaps there would be infinitely many duplicates of relatively simple material objects like gas clouds, snowflakes, cyclones, or even rock formations, all strewn across infinitely many worlds. But that is not to say there must be infinitely many duplicates of more complex arrangements of matter such as of particular organisms, biospheres, or galaxies. It may even be that the more complex the arrangement of matter, the fewer duplicates there should be, such that, as organic life forms, each of us may just be unique after all [1,045].

It therefore remains open as to whether the notion of an infinite universe (or set of universes) implies infinitely many duplicates of the observable universe and/or infinitely many alternative versions of the observable universe, with ourselves included. The idea that such is the implication boils down to unverifiable assumptions about statistics for complex objects within magnitudes of infinite space, time, and matter. One might assume infinite quantities of matter, which can only take a finite number of forms, would entail infinite repetitions of the same forms and so there must be infinitely many copies of you out there in the Multiverse. On the other hand, it's just as consistent with the evidence we have to assume that infinite quantities of matter do not entail infinite variety in the forms that matter takes, in which case each of us, as a complex life form, can be unique even if space, time, and quantities of matter were infinite rather than finite. So here again we have a pair of contradictory conjectures following from the idea of infinity and neither is empirically testable.

21.4.7 *The Omnium*

Related to the idea of the Multiverse with its infinitude of doppelgangers is the Omnium. Penrose coined the term 'Omnium' for what Tegmark calls the set of "Level III parallel universes," which is to say a set of parallel universes generated not from separate big bang events but from a continuous series of instantaneous divisions of the Universe into multiple copies of itself [1,046] [1,047].

The notion of the Omnium comes from what quantum physicists call the Many-Worlds Interpretation (MWI) of quantum mechanics [1,048]. MWI has some renowned adherents. It was first proposed by physicist Hugh Everett III (1930–1982) [1,049] and is currently championed by Dr. Sean Carroll, a research professor in the Department of Physics at the California Institute of Technology [1,050] [1,051].

To grasp MWI, it's important to realize that no one knows for sure why quantum mechanics is so effective at describing certain behaviors of quantum particles. But there are several interpretations offered to explain the effectiveness of quantum mechanics. Each interpretation proposes a different speculation as to what the mathematical formalism of quantum mechanics implies about the nature of reality, and all of the interpretations contradict each other. Physicist Nick Herbert's 1987 book, *Quantum Reality*, is one of the best introductions to the various interpretations of quantum mechanics [1,052]. And even more interpretations have been proposed since Herbert's book was first published.

MWI is just one of over a dozen popular interpretations of quantum mechanics. As an interpretation, MWI is not a new theory, nor is it a testable theory. Rather, MWI is an untestable speculation of what the mathematics of quantum mechanics implies for physical reality. Hence, as an interpretation, MWI is more philosophical than scientific.

To grasp MWI, begin by recalling the quantum Hilbert Hotel experiment. In the second run of the experiment, a photon had two equally probable places it could be (**Figure 21.4**) and the experiment demonstrates a quantum particle can seemingly be in a 'superposition' of more than one location simultaneously (**Figure 21.5**). MWI, among various other interpretations of quantum mechanics, holds superpositions of particles to be a real, physical property of material particles—at least when nothing else interacts with the particles to disrupt such behavior. Where MWI differs from many other interpretations of quantum mechanics is in how it regards the nature of superposition and wavefunction collapse.

According to MWI, there really is no collapse of the wavefunction [1,053] [1,054]. Instead, we only find the particle in one location rather than both places at once because, when a particle is emitted, our universe splits into two versions of itself—in one universe, the particle goes one way and so manifests here when a measurement is made while in the other universe the particle went the other way and so instead manifests over there when a measurement is made. If you were to find the particle in one location, there's another universe created in which a copy of you finds the particle in the other, equally likely, location. The wavefunction (or *state vector*) never really "collapses" at all; it just tells us we will only see one of the two versions of the particle—the one in the universe we inhabit (at the moment) [1,055].

The act of emitting a particle, and thereby splitting the universe into copies of itself, need not be initiated by a conscious, intentional agent. Particles are emitted all the time when no one is around. Similarly, 'measurement' need not be made by a conscious, intentional agent. By 'measurement' or 'observation' physicists mean not just a case in which a physicist performs an experiment to obtain a result. Rather, they mean any interaction between quantum particles, whether a conscious/intentional agent is looking or not. When one object interacts with another, a 'measurement' or 'observation' has occurred. According to MWI, such interactions result in splitting our universe into multiple copies with different outcomes [1,056] [1,057].

In fact, MWI holds that each second, the universe you are in splits into multiple pairs of universes and those universes split into another pair of universes, and so on. Time becomes a branching tree of events in which all events that can occur do occur, rather than a linear progression of events in which only one of equally likely events occurs at a time [1,058].

So which universe are you in at any time? In one sense, after a universe splits into two versions of itself, you are in *both* universes. Which is to say, the prior *token* "you" ceases to exist when the parent universe divides in two, while the *type* "you" continues across both universes—two new tokens of you exist, one copy in each of the daughter universes.

According to MWI, all universes with alternative outcomes to quantum events are equally real, but we don't notice this splitting because any token instance of our consciousness inhabits only one universe at a time. Penrose, though no supporter of MWI, articulates the view quite well with respect to measurements of quantum particles [1,059]:

> ...there is effectively a 'different world' for each different possible result of the measurement, there being a separate 'copy' of the experimenter in each of these different worlds, all these worlds co-existing in quantum superposition. Each copy of the experimenter experiences a different outcome for the experiment, but since these 'copies' inhabit different worlds, there is no communication between them, and each thinks that only one result has occurred.

Gardner also elucidated a popular understanding of MWI [1,060]:

> Those holding what I call the realist view actually believe that the endlessly sprouting new universes are "out there," in some sort of vast super-space-time, just as "real" as the universe we know! Of course at every instant a split occurs each of us becomes one or more close duplicates, each travelling a new universe. We have no awareness of this happening because the many universes are not causally connected. We simply travel along the endless branches of time's monstrous tree in a series of universes, never aware that billions upon billions of our replicas are springing into existence somewhere out there.

Hence, we have the impression of being in only one world when worlds are actually multiplying exponentially every second that a quantum measurement is made—a vast and growing Omnium of parallel universes.

That, in a nutshell, is the MWI interpretation of quantum mechanics, a view criticized by both Penrose and Gardner alike. Gardner, for one, was deeply critical of MWI and its Omnium of parallel universes [1,061]:

> The stark truth is that there is not the slightest shred of reliable evidence that there is any universe other than the one we are in. No [Omnium or Multiverse] theory has so far provided a prediction that can be tested...As far as we can tell, universes are not as plentiful as even *two* blackberries.

Gardner's observation of the lack of evidence in support of the Omnium proposal has merit. MWI with its Omnium of parallel universes is an interesting speculation, but it's a speculation on par with any other in terms of the evidence, as most physicists will admit.

Moreover, there are plausible alternatives to the MWI interpretation of quantum mechanics that accurately describe all the observed behaviors of particles without even appealing to superposition. For example, Bohm offered a successful alternative to quantum mechanics that does not imply a token particle is in two different places at once when it is not observed (however, Bohmian Mechanics has other weird features of its own) [1,062] [1,063]. So, the MWI interpretation is not *necessarily* as compelling as some of its supporters regard it. And hence the Omnium lacks the evidence it needs to make its extraordinary claim of parallel universes credible to most researchers.

I must therefore agree with Gardner that the paucity of evidence in favor of even one parallel universe makes the Omnium, like the Multiverse, no more than speculation. And as far as speculations go, it's a rather extravagant one when compared with other interpretations of quantum mechanics that do not require entire universes to be duplicated at every moment, to say nothing of there being *infinitely many* parallel universes.

21.5 INFINITY AS BAD THEORY

So far, we've found not only a lack of evidence for infinities in the real world; we've also uncovered some reasons to suppose space, time, and quantities of matter should be finite rather than infinite. And those reasons seem to be persuading scientists as well as philosophers that something is amiss with infinity.

This shouldn't come as a great surprise to anyone familiar with the current state of affairs in theoretical physics. Physicists especially have always been ambivalent about infinity—on the one hand, speculating about infinite magnitudes of space, time, and matter while, on the other hand, admitting we don't actually see anything infinite in nature. In fact, theoretical physicist and cosmologist Raphael Bousso of the University of California, Berkeley says, "I don't think anyone likes infinity. It's not the outcome of any experiment" [1,064].

Not only is infinity not the outcome of any experiment; it can be downright problematic for making sensible calculations of physical quantities. A good example is the *self-energy problem* that infinity generates for calculating the amount of force exchanged between charged particles.

The self-energy problem stems from QFT—a theory that explains how quantum particles exchange force, repelling or attracting other particles. QFT proposes that particles attract or repel one another with *force fields* (more commonly referred to simply as 'fields') spread throughout the physical space between the particles [1,065]. For example, most physicists these days explain the electrical force between charged particles as the effect of a 'field' of force surrounding the particle. A field is simply a region of space in which other charged particles experience a force—a push or pull in a particular direction. Electrons, being negatively charged, push each other away with their electrical 'fields'.

Physicists do not usually attempt to explain what a field is or how it is generated with some kind of mechanical model; instead, they are typically content to mathematically describe how it behaves [1,066]. The idea of fields works well in many cases, but it does have a problem in the quantum world. If all electrical charges contribute to making a common electrical field, and if that common field acts on all electrical charges, then each charge must act back on itself in a feedback loop of self-energy. As a consequence, the equations describing this feedback loop predict the self-energy builds up infinitely (∞), giving the electron an infinite intrinsic mass, which obviously it does not have as experiments plainly show [1,067].

To make the field equations generate a sensible finite amount of energy and mass for electrons instead of infinities, physicists have to use an arcane mathematical maneuver called *renormalization* [1,068]. The mathematical technique of renormalization "works" in the sense that it produces finite results in agreement with observation, but it is also an ad hoc method for removing the pesky infinities. It works, but its addition to the equations seems arbitrary and no one is quite sure exactly why it works so well. While some physicists roll with renormalization, others find it unsatisfactory [1,069] and so some have looked for a better theory for electrical force (and quantum forces in general) in which the infinity of self-energy would not arise to begin with [1,070].

That was a big part of Feynman's motivation to develop QED and its use of virtual particles [1,071]—a theory that, as we've seen, still has its own problems with infinity [1,072]. The problem of needing to rely on the ad hoc mathematical technique of renormalization to avoid the infinities inherent in QED and QFT was also a motivator for physicists to develop an alternative model of matter and force: *string theory* [1,073].

String theory does not have the problem of infinities popping up in equations [1,074]. As far as this book is concerned, that is certainly a fine result. However, string theory will also not likely prove to be the theory physicists are looking for to avoid infinities since string theory also has several other conceptual and empirical troubles of its own [1,075].

I will not pursue here further discussion of the merits and problems of QED, QFT, and string theory. Instead, the point I wish to make is simply that the renormalization problem is a good illustration of why most physicists regard the appearance of infinity in an equation as a sign the theory has gone awry and that a finite alternative is needed. As Baggott explains [1,076],

> …it would obviously be much better if the infinities didn't arise in the first place. After all, infinity is a purely mathematical concept—*infinity does not exist in the real world*. When infinities start to jump out of the equations they're telling us that, in some essential respects, our mathematical description is not properly representing reality.

Similar sentiments are echoed by other scientists [1,077]. There seems to be increasing suspicion of infinity among scientists and theoretical physicists. Ellis, for one, remarked [1,078],

> If you hold your fingers 10cm apart and if you believe that there's a real line of points, like in mathematics, between your fingers, then there's an uncountable infinity of points between your fingers. That's completely unreasonable; I believe that's a mathematical idea which does not correspond to physics…

...I'll make a distinction; there are some times when people talk about infinity when all they really mean is a very large number, and they're just using infinity as a code word for a large number. In that case, I think it's more informative to make a guess what that large number is and to talk about that large number, not infinity. There are some cases where people use infinity in its deep sense; in the paradoxical sense. The paradoxical sense is, for instance, Hilbert's Hotel. In my opinion, if a physics argument or any other argument depends on those paradoxical arguments, then this is a false argument and it should be replaced by something else.

21.6 REPLACING INFINITY

Most physicists would love to replace infinity with an alternative concept because not only does infinity generate paradoxes and mathematical absurdities, but it also provides no definite quantities that can be compared to experimental outcomes. However, there is at present no consensus in the physics community regarding an alternative, and mathematically useful, concept to use in place of infinity [1,079].

And yet, from a purely conceptual standpoint, there is an alternative to infinity that can describe magnitudes of space, time, matter, and other physical properties without generating logical paradoxes. That concept is indefiniteness.

Indefiniteness avoids the logical paradoxes and self-contradictions of literal infinity because a quantity that is indefinitely large or indefinitely small is still a finite quantity the limits of which are simply not known, and a process that goes on indefinitely is at every step a finite process no matter how long it continues. So, for instance, while the laws of physics may break down within the singularity of a black hole conceived as an infinitesimal point, they would not break down if the core of the black hole implodes indefinitely without ever becoming infinitesimal. Similarly, were indefiniteness to replace infinity for describing quantities of virtual particles, quantum speed limits, parallel universes, or other physical properties usually claimed to be infinite, that alone would avoid the logical contradictions inherent in claims of such things being infinite. Which would in turn improve the accuracy of our models of the physical world.

Of course, while swapping indefiniteness for infinity may resolve *conceptual* problems, it would still not resolve *empirical* problems with claims of extreme quantities. For example, there is still an empirical problem with predicting an amount of virtual particles equal to the order of $100,000$ googol (10^{105}) joules per cubic centimeter of space—the amount that should have imploded the Universe. Saying there are indefinitely many virtual particles rather than infinitely many virtual particles would still yield too many virtual particles to match what we observe. Similarly, claiming there are indefinitely many parallel universes instead of infinitely many would still leave open the empirical problem that there is not a shred of credible evidence for the existence of parallel universes per se, even if there's not an infinite number of them. So, replacing infinity with indefiniteness gets us to only part of the solution that physicists are looking for.

What physicists would really like is a form of calculation that produces not indefinite results to their equations, but definite quantities—quantities for which we can plug in exact numbers. They want to be able to calculate the properties of the Universe with numbers that can be specified. I will, unfortunately, have to leave it to mathematicians and physicists to bridge that divide, but I will note there are already some efforts by theorists to build a system of finite mathematics as a new foundation for physics [1,080].

In taking the approach of academic philosophy to this topic, my only concern is to provide a conceptual solution for avoiding the *logical* problems generated by the concept of infinity, not to build a useful new form of mathematics that would allow physicists to calculate the Universe or its constituent phenomena with exact precision. To avoid the logical problems inherent in literal infinity requires only replacement of literal infinity with a logically coherent, alternative concept such as that of indefiniteness. Whereas, making the Universe calculable would require a new kind of finite mathematics that can produce definite results, rather than indefinite ones, and in a way that more accurately matches scientific observations.

To conclude, where scientists have heretofore attributed infinity to the Universe, they should instead attribute indefiniteness of quantity; and if equations under classical mathematics would provide us only with indefinitely large magnitudes that must instead have definite values to be consistent with observation, then scientists should look for a more accurate finite mathematics to use in place of classical mathematics. The bottom line is that indefiniteness may not be sufficient for what physicists are looking for in terms of building calculable models of the Universe's properties, but it does suffice for removing the self-contradictions inherent in relying on literal infinity. That alone guarantees us a more accurate view of the Universe than the currently popular use of infinities.

CHAPTER 21 IN REVIEW

- ❖ Physics is loaded with references to infinity. For example, infinity appears in equations of the Theory of Relativity, quantum physics, particle physics, and it appears in various theories proposed in the field of scientific cosmology.
- ❖ An examination of the empirical evidence, however, provides no support for assuming space, time, and quantities of matter should be infinite.
- ❖ Physicists are looking for an alternative to infinity, but none are well developed.
- ❖ One alternative, if properly developed, is the concept of indefiniteness. Allowing indefiniteness into physics may make physics into a field in which pursuit of more exact results would sometimes have to be sacrificed. However, indefiniteness has the conceptual advantage of avoiding the logical paradoxes and self-contradictions implied by proposing the physical reality of literal infinities.

22: CLOSING ARGUMENTS ON LITERAL INFINITY

The case against infinity, especially against literal infinity, in terms of impacting culture is a quixotic endeavor. I do realize that most scholars, at least in the foreseeable future, are likely to remain unconvinced that infinity needs to go. Most, after all, currently believe any self-contradictions implied by the concept of literal infinity merely indicate paradoxes—*apparent* contradictions, the illusion of self-contradictions where there are actually none. Convincing them of the opposite is quite a tall order.

Still, such a position is not universal. There is a minority in the academic community who are skeptical of infinity. To distinguish those who believe in the logical coherence of literal infinity (*infinitism*) from those skeptical of infinity (*finitism*—see § 22.1.4), I will refer to the believers as *infinitists* and the skeptics as *finitists*.

Some infinitists offer various arguments aimed to dissolve the paradoxes and thereby prove literal infinity to be logically coherent. If they are right and the finitists wrong—if literal infinity turns out to be a logically coherent concept—then it is indeed possible for infinite collections to exist in reality; the Universe could therefore be infinite after all. However, as I will show, the solutions that infinitists offer to dissolve the 'paradoxes' of infinity are not successful. Infinity remains as logically problematic as ever and there is no sound reason to suppose anything in the physical world is literally infinite.

22.1 CONSIDERING REBUTTALS

Infinitists offer several rebuttals to the charges of logical incoherence made against literal infinity. Each rebuttal is intended to show infinity is logically coherent—merely paradoxical and not self-contradictory as it appears to be. I will not attempt an exhaustive listing of such arguments or counter them all; rather, I will focus only on the arguments most frequently made:

1. Linguistic definitions do not adequately describe the properties of infinity.
2. Infinity works in counterintuitive ways.
3. Infinity is mathematically consistent—it mathematically "works"—and therefore must be logically consistent.
4. Infinity exists as a mathematical concept.
5. It is impossible to use natural numbers and deny that infinity makes logical sense.
6. Our ability to *imagine* infinite sets shows that infinity must be a logically coherent idea.
7. We have direct *experience* of infinity, proving infinity is not only a coherent concept but also a physical reality.

I will elucidate each of these rebuttals in sequence but, since they have each been touched upon in previous chapters, I will only make brief counterarguments against them.

22.1.1 *Use of Linguistic Definitions for Infinity*

Infinitists sometimes reply to the charge that infinity is an incoherent notion by stating that infinity is not logically problematic; rather, if there's a contradiction inherent in the meaning of infinity, then such simply proves infinity has not been correctly defined. Define infinity the right way and the logical problems disappear. They usually state that infinity has been properly defined in mathematics and set theory without contradiction and that it is only "pre-theoretic" definitions of infinity as stated in ordinary language that go awry.

We first encountered this line of argument back in § 7.3, but it's worth taking a second look now that all our terms have been defined and some (especially, completeness and limitlessness) have been shown to imply contradiction when used together. As I had pointed out, mathematicians prefer technical and operational definitions of infinity because the colloquial, or ordinary language, definitions for infinity are not precise enough for use in mathematical operation. So, the infinitist may argue that to charge inherent contradiction in the meaning of infinity is to attack a straw figure, for infinity is not properly conceived in terms of ordinary language.

But the infinitist's argument does not hold up because the literal sense of infinity as defined in ordinary language is *assumed* even according to its various technical uses in mathematics. As a caveat, it is true mathematicians sometimes use infinity in the figurative sense, especially where operations involve its expression as ∞. However, where mathematicians do *not* use the term 'infinity' in the figurative sense, they typically assume infinity in the literal sense as explicated over Chapters 5–8. Thus, the linguistic definition of infinity does not present a straw figure to attack after all. Infinity in the literal sense of the term is the tacit foundation for the various technical definitions of infinity in mathematics (even when their associated mathematical operations are themselves indefinite rather than literally limitless).

But the infinitist has another line of attack against the linguistic definition of literal infinity. The infinitist may now simply protest that while literal infinity is a condition of completeness and limitlessness of quantity, they may instead charge that I have explicated completeness and/or limitlessness inaccurately, and so I have misrepresented how infinity is regarded.

I maintain the accuracy of my conceptual analysis of both completeness and limitlessness. I do so while readily admitting words do not have an 'essence', just different uses [1,081]. So I do concede that there is no single and solely correct way for a word to be defined and used in all contexts, including words like 'complete' and 'limitless'. Various scholars will define the same words/terms in various ways. It's not surprising that some may define such terms as 'infinite', 'finite', 'complete', 'incomplete', 'limit', 'limitless', etc. differently than I have. Moreover, just as the meaning of words like 'proposition' and 'passion' have changed over the centuries, so too with various mathematical terms. And doubtless the same words will change in their nuances of meaning over the centuries to come. Assuming as much, the definitions I explicated for terms like 'complete', 'limitless', and so forth are not meant to exhaustively cover the usage of those terms in all contexts over all periods of history, nor are they intended to convey how those terms are technically defined relative to particular mathematical operations or procedures. Rather, my definitions for the various terms are meant to elucidate the usage of those terms in ordinary, natural language in reference to quantities and to expose how those definitions are commonly, or typically, *assumed* even when those same terms are given more technical definitions for use in mathematical and scientific contexts. I believe I have generally covered the common meanings of such terms, at least from a logical standpoint, and I believe I have adequately distinguished any relevant technical differences for the same terms as they are used by mathematicians relative to particular mathematical operations or procedures. So, I'm going to stick to my guns that I have the terms defined correctly and that I have not confused their ordinary language definitions with the technical definitions found in mathematics.

In order to show I am wrong about what it means to be 'complete' or 'limitless', the infinitist must do more than merely cite mathematical uses of these terms relative to various mathematical operations or procedures (e.g., completeness portrayed as calculations of Cauchy 'completeness' or limitlessness as the indefinite approach toward an ideal limit). Rather, the infinitist must give convincing examples of how such terms are commonly used in reference to infinite collections while contradicting the definitions I offered for those terms and yet ensuring infinity remains distinguished from the indefinite. That will be a tall order.

If the infinitist cannot do that, then one other option the infinitist has would be to show how it is that an infinite set or series can be, say, 'complete' according to the definition of that term I offered and yet *without* running into contradiction with the claim the set has members without limit in a literal (as opposed to merely figurative) sense. I don't believe the infinitist will succeed.

However, there is, perhaps, one last way to get around my charge of self-contradiction in the heart of infinity: reject the way I defined infinity to begin with, perhaps by proposing infinity is just a condition of having no limit but *not* also a condition of being quantitatively complete [1,082]. In other words, the infinitist could argue that infinity is simply *limitlessness*, period—not also a state of completeness, at least not in the literal, quantitative sense I elucidated back in Chapter 3.

Instead, they may contend that some things that are complete may be part of that which is infinite (limitless) but limitlessness is beyond that which is complete such that completeness is not part of the definition of infinity. Were this so, then there would be no *internal* contradiction in the concept of infinity. At best there might still be a problem between claiming something complete is infinite, but infinity as such would emerge unscathed and my thesis against literal infinity would fall.

Such a rebuttal, however, is not successful. We have only to ask, for any given collection said to be infinite, whether there is any member of the collection *limitlessly* far in sequence from, or greater in magnitude than, another member. That is to say, is there such a thing as a limitless quantity of members *between* at least two members in a limitless collection?

If no such pairing exists—if there is only a limited quantity of members between any two members— then all of the members of the collection are only *finitely* removed from one another and so the collection must not be limitless in its quantity of members after all; the collection itself would have to be finite.

It is sometimes claimed that this is no problem for an infinite collection because an infinite collection is greater than any sum of members comprising the collection such that the limitless whole can have nothing but finite quantities making it up. To which one only need ask what it is that makes the whole of a limitless collection limitless if not the relations between the members in the collection.

In reply, supporters of infinity may say the limitlessness (e.g., lack of an upper bound) to any sequence means only that the infinite whole of the sequence is greater than any sum of members in the sequence said to be infinite, all sums being finite. This is indeed the implication of limitlessness as stated in § 11.6.1. However, it is just that implication that is problematic.

Literal limitlessness, as applied to collections of any kind, implies a contradiction of its own. If a given collection, such as $\mathbb{N}$, is made of *nothing but* entities that can sum—and indeed all natural numbers >1 do sum from previous numbers in the sequence—then (as asked earlier in § 12.7.3) what is the feature of the whole collection that makes it limitless *as* a whole and therefore *greater than* any sum of members?

It is hard to see what such a property could be when applied to collections such as all naturals >1, which are collections of nothing but sums.

Lacking a clear explanation, we could be led to suppose the whole of a limitless collection is only limitless *as a collection* if there is at least one sub-collection that has no limit to its quantity of members. This would entail the whole of the collection is limitless only because when the collection is sequenced at least two members within the whole are limitlessly separated in the quantity of the members between them. In other words, we might suppose there is at least one member, A, *limitlessly far from or greater than* another member, B. But this solution too has a couple of problems.

First, this solution means there is between A and B a limitless *quantity* of other members in that sub-collection. Now if there is some quantity of members between A and B that does not increase while A and B are the 'bounds' of those other members, and if there are no further members that can be between A and B without changing the numerical values assigned to A and B as the bounds of that sub-collection, then A and B are the parameters the sub-collection as a *full* sub-collection. And if that intermediate, *full* sub-collection is itself a set that is also a *whole, entire,* and *finished* set, then it's hard to see how there cannot be (at least in principle) a *total* of all the members in the set between A and B. And to have a full, whole, entire, finished, and totality of members in the set between A and B would make a *complete* set of members between A and B. And since we know that the limitless sequence of members *from A to B* is also a totality of members comprising a complete set of members, we again find the infinite collection implies completeness as well as limitlessness in quantity. Unfortunately, that would lead us right back to the property we were trying to avoid: completeness for the whole that is supposed to be limitless only. And we were trying to avoid that because a complete and limitless collection is self-contradictory.

Second, the completeness of the collection of members from A to B is also at odds with the other implications of the A-B sequence as literally limitlessness: a limitless collection is supposed to have no totality at all, not even in principle.

We therefore have another dilemma: (a) affirm that the whole of the collection is limitless while denying its quantitative completeness without any clear explanation for how it can be that the collection can be limitless as a whole while no subset/sequence/series in that collection is limitless, or (b) make the limitlessness of the whole apply to at least one of the sub-collections as well, but consequently end up affirming the completeness of the whole which reintroduces the self-contradiction we sought to avoid.

Option (b) is a nonstarter, but option (a) also faces further problems.

For one thing, if option (a) is chosen, it's hard to see how Cantor's transfinite system survives. The transfinite system depends on sets being both complete and limitless. For example, a complete and limitless set of real numbers allegedly exists *between* any two real numbers (for example, between $A = 0$ and $B = 1$ on the real number line). Deny that there are limitlessly many members between any two members, and you destroy Cantor's system. If like some philosophers (Huemer [1,083], Patterson, [1,084] and myself) you are okay with rejecting transfinite mathematics, then that in itself is not problematic, but most mathematicians tend to resist that implication.

For another thing, there is still the problem pointed out in § 1.3.2 and in § 12.7.3: a literally limitless whole that is somehow "beyond" completeness is not literal infinity and, indeed, is not even a *quantitative* infinity which is what we are discussing in this section. Such a non-zero, literally limitless-but-not-complete collection would be an example of a *qualitative* infinity, which we will examine in Chapters 25–26. It would not be the kind of infinity we are discussing in this section.

So once again, literal infinity is defined as being quantitatively complete and limitless. But if all *literally* infinite sets are complete sets, then completeness can be regarded as part of what it means to be infinite in the literal sense of the term 'infinite'.

In fact, philosophers and mathematicians have long used the term 'completed infinity' in reference to the condition of being complete and yet also limitless in quantity. I am merely pointing out that the term is redundant since collections that are literally limitless in a non-zero, quantitative sense—that is, infinite in a literal sense—are only so by virtue of being complete in quantity. A collection that is an instance of an 'incomplete infinity' is merely 'infinite' in the figurative sense of the term, not literally so.

I'm going to have to maintain there is nothing misleading about the linguistic definition I provided and that the usual mathematical theories still assume it when they refer to sets, continua, or other quantities that are not finite. Unfortunately, that also means the logical contradictions inherent in the very concept of literal infinity have not been resolved by proposing more technical definitions of use in mathematical operations.

22.1.2 *Infinity as Counterintuitive*

Another possible objection to my thesis of infinity's logical incoherence is that our intuitions are often wrong when it comes to infinity; one hears this refrain quite a bit from infinitists who defend the logical coherence of infinity. This objection echoes the position of Galileo [1,085]:

> ...let us remember that we are dealing with infinites and indivisibles, both of which transcend our finite understanding, the former on account of their magnitude, the latter because of their smallness.

However, Galileo's way of framing the objection is the fallacy of *appeal to mystery* [1,086]. Such appeals are problematic with respect to their believability. Anyone can use the same argument to justify any idea, no matter how illogical. If you point to a contradiction in someone's idea, they can always say their idea "transcends understanding." It's hard to take such claims seriously.

A better version of the objection is to say any perceived incoherence in the concept of infinity results only from inappropriate application of finite properties to the infinite. That is, some properties of finite sets, such as quantification, apply to infinite sets while other properties of finite sets, like the whole of a set being necessarily greater than any subset in it, do not apply to infinite sets as one would normally expect. This was the view of Cantor, which Rucker articulated well [1,087]:

> If using the ordinary notions of "equal" and "less than" on infinite sets leads to contradictions, this is not a sign that infinite sets cannot exist, but, rather, that these notions do not apply without modification to infinite sets.

But back in Chapters 15–16 we found this position too is problematic.

One reason it's problematic is that, while Cantor's system says the infinite whole can be equal to the infinite part, Bolzano's mathematical system of the infinite says the contrary. And Bolzano's system is just as mathematically consistent as Cantor's [1,088]. So which finite notions apply to infinity and which do not? The answer appears to be relative to the system in question. Which suggests infinity is not something "out there" revealed in an absolute mathematical system but instead is a concept flexible enough to be used in relative ways across contrary mathematical systems as human inventions. If am right, that flexibility is due to the fact that infinity is a self-contradictory concept. As logicians know, you can derive whatever you like from a contradiction. Little wonder that contradictory mathematical systems for infinity can each be internally coherent in terms of rules governing the use of infinity. It's possible to create such contradictory systems because infinity is not an inherently logical concept.

However, the infinitist might further argue for the coherence of infinity by promoting one mathematical system for infinity over all rivals, like Cantor's over Bolzano's. But even if one accepts a particular mathematical system of the infinite over all rival systems, such does not affect my case, which thus far has not been about infinity's *mathematical* consistency.

As argued in Chapters 14–15, the sets and series commonly called 'infinite' in mathematics are actually *indefinite* sets and series erroneously called 'infinite'. The mathematical consistency of operations involving indefinite sets and series is not in question; what needs to be consistent is the *logic* of literal infinity's meaning.

And when it comes to the logic of infinity, however mathematically 'counterintuitive' infinity may be in any given mathematical system, it cannot be so counterintuitive that it contains logical contradictions between the implications of completeness and limitlessness; otherwise, infinity's very meaning is in self-contradiction and infinity would therefore need to be rejected on logical grounds. And this is precisely what I have argued over the preceding chapters.

22.1.3 *But the Mathematics 'Works'*

Related to the previous rebuttal, one often hears that the math of infinity "works" and therefore infinity must be a rational concept. Such an argument assumes, however, that mathematics cannot contain irrational concepts that nevertheless produce consistent mathematical results. On the contrary, I say mathematics can contain irrational concepts, the logical incoherence of which is irrelevant to the rules of mathematics.

To show how this could happen, in § 9.7 I offered the example of non-angularities (square circles). It's possible, at least in principle, to make non-angularities mathematically coherent even though the concept of a non-angularity is illogical. So too, I propose infinity is such a concept—it's logically incoherent but able to be manipulated in mathematically coherent ways.

As evidence of this contention, consider once again that transfinite mathematics is, from a mathematical standpoint, consistent, but need not be from a logical perspective. We find evidence of this with the *continuum problem*—a logical problem that results from what set theorists call the *continuum hypothesis*, which is a hypothesis based on Cantor's proposal of a bijection between infinite sets of numbers.

To grasp the continuum hypothesis (CH), start with a simple question: How many points on a straight line are there? In Cantor's transfinite system, the answer has to be greater than the number of numbers in $\mathbb{N}$, but his system doesn't say how much greater and so CH is an educated guess as to what the right answer to that question is.

If we assume that each point on a line could be labelled with a real number and that no points would remain without real numbers, then the answer should be that the number of points on a line are equal to the number of real numbers in $\mathbb{R}$. However, that is not necessarily the right answer even for the transfinite system.

Recall that number systems, such as $\mathbb{N}$ and $\mathbb{R}$, have cardinalities. Cantor proposed the cardinality of the natural numbers ($\mathbb{N}$) is less than that of the real numbers ($\mathbb{R}$); hence, $\mathbb{N} < \mathbb{R}$. However, this raises another question: Is there any infinite set of numbers larger than $\mathbb{N}$ (the "countable infinity") but smaller than $\mathbb{R}$? In other words, is $\mathbb{R}$ really the "least uncountable" infinity and so the infinity with the minimal infinite cardinality greater than $\mathbb{N}$?

CH says $\mathbb{R}$ has the minimal possible cardinality greater than $\mathbb{N}$ (and all infinite sets equal to $\mathbb{N}$). In other words, CH says there is no set S such that $\mathbb{N} < S < \mathbb{R}$.

Further, if we take the cardinality of $\mathbb{R}$ to be $2^{\aleph_0}$, then as stated in transfinite notation, there is no S such that $\aleph_0 < |S| < 2^{\aleph_0}$. Moreover, since $\aleph_1$ is the "least uncountable" of the uncountable infinite sets, then assuming $\aleph_1 = 2^{\aleph_0}$ means CH is the denial that $\aleph_0 < |S| < \aleph_1$. That's CH—the continuum hypothesis [1,089].

According to the CH, the real numbers of $\mathbb{R}$ biject with the points of a line. That is, if CH is correct, then the number of points in a straight line is equal to $\mathbb{R}$—in other words, equal to $2^{\aleph_0}$ which would be equal to $\aleph_1$.

So what is the 'continuum problem'? The continuum problem is that CH cannot be proven true or false [1,090].

That's a problem because transfinite mathematics, simply as a mathematical system, is supposed to be logically airtight and yield unambiguous results. But it doesn't.

And because of that, there does not seem to be a precise answer to the question as to how many points are on a line. The number of points could be either equal to $\mathbb{R}$ or equal to S (if there is an S), which is less than $\mathbb{R}$.

Moreover, if there is an S such that $\mathbb{N} < S < \mathbb{R}$, then $\aleph_1$ (the *least* uncountable infinity) would *not* be equal to $\mathbb{R}$. And since $\mathbb{R} = 2^{\aleph_0}$, the existence of S would mean that $\aleph_1$ is not equal to $2^{\aleph_0}$ after all. Instead, $\aleph_1$ would be equal to some intermediate cardinality (S) between $\aleph_0$ and $2^{\aleph_0}$ and so $\aleph_1$ would be less than $\mathbb{R}$ and so less than $2^{\aleph_0}$.

The number of points on a line could therefore still be $\aleph_1$, but so far we do not know if $\aleph_1$ is equal to $\mathbb{R}$ or if $\aleph_1$ is equal to some S that is less than $\mathbb{R}$. We therefore don't know the number of points on a line—it could be either $2^{\aleph_0}$ or a number less than $2^{\aleph_0}$. Mathematics requires a less vague answer than that in order to prove CH true.

Worse still, the continuum problem may even imply a logical inconsistency in the modern version of Cantor's set theory, called Zermelo–Fraenkel Set Theory, or ZF for short, named after the mathematicians Ernst Zermelo (1871–1953) and Abraham Fraenkel (1891–1965). However, most transfinite mathematicians simply believe ZF, as a mathematical system, is incomplete instead of inconsistent [1,091].

Insofar as the mathematical proofs of ZF are concerned, there is merit to that view since the *operations* of transfinite mathematics are really dealing with figurative infinities in disguise and so serial and collective indefinites rather than the literal infinities they purport to be about. On the other hand, *denying* $\aleph_0 < |S| < \aleph_1$ assumes the transfinite system is about the concept of literal infinity. We are therefore correct to be suspicious about the *logic* of ZF: it should not be surprising if there are logical inconsistencies in ZF because ZF assumes that infinite sets such as $\aleph_0$ and $\aleph_1$ are literal infinities, and it is literal infinity that over the last several chapters I've argued to be a self-contradictory concept.

We can thus assume mathematicians are correct that there is no genuine *mathematical* inconsistency in the transfinite system, but the continuum problem still indicates there is a *logical* inconsistency in the transfinite system. Which just goes to show that one can use 'infinity' (abstracted as ∞, $\aleph$, or ω) in mathematically coherent ways while ignoring logical problems like the continuum problem, even if it lies at the logical foundation of the discipline. Mathematical coherence is not logical coherence.

So again, the math of infinity may "work," but it can work *despite* infinity having unresolved logical problems. As Feferman notes, logical troubles in mathematics that involve infinity are "simply not relevant to everyday mathematics" [1,092].

22.1.4 *Infinity Exists as a Mathematical Concept*

Another rebuttal to my thesis involves the status of infinity as a mathematical concept and what it means for a mathematical concept to exist. Consider the following position offered by a physicist at the Perimeter Institute for Theoretical Physics in response to the question of whether or not there are any mathematical arguments against the existence of infinity [1,093]:

> Mathematical concepts do not "exist" in the same way that physical objects do. You do not need to "prove the existence" of the number 42, you do not need to "prove the existence" of the function $\sin x$, and in the same way, you do not need to "prove the existence" of any type of infinity used in mathematics (there are, in fact, infinite types of infinity, each "more infinite" than the other...
>
> So, in short: no, there are no mathematical arguments against the "existence" of infinity, or of any other mathematical concept for that matter...

This response to the question is a mix of logic and fallacy, truth and falsity. First, what the response gets right: there are no *mathematical* arguments against the existence of infinity. That is true simply because there are, technically speaking, no 'mathematical arguments' in the sense of logical arguments—where a logical argument is a series of premises establishing a conclusion.

Though the term 'argument' has a technical meaning in mathematics, it does not refer to argument as used in logical debate. Rather, mathematics is about enumerative schemas—the proofs of their consistency and their uses for calculation. Logic, on the other hand, is about argument in the debate sense—premises establishing a conclusion. It is in the logic *underlying* mathematical concepts that arguments regarding infinity are to be found. And there are indeed logical arguments against the existence of infinity even if there are no mathematical proofs against the existence of infinity.

On the other hand, if one wishes to include symbolic logic, 'predicate calculus', and modal logic in the domain of mathematics, then arguments formulated in these areas of logic can also be regarded as mathematical arguments. But then, it would not be true that there are no arguments against infinity that are mathematical arguments because there are indeed arguments that can be formulated in symbolic logic against the existence of infinity.

So, the issue of whether there are *mathematical* arguments against the existence of infinity should be rephrased in terms of *logical* arguments against the existence of infinity based on logical contradictions obtained from assuming sets or mathematical operations are literally infinite. But then, if the issue is framed that way, contrary to the physicist's thesis, there is indeed an argument against the existence of (literal) infinity.

The argument against the existence of literal infinity as articulated over the previous chapters establishes that literal infinity is a logically self-contradictory concept and can no more exist as a property of a collection, process, or mathematical operation than non-angularity (square circularity) can be a property of a geometrical object. Non-angularities do not exist, and neither does literal infinity.

Even if we grant that infinity exists "as a mathematical concept," that would only give us the existence of a mathematical concept that, *despite* its mathematical consistency, has proven to be logically self-contradictory. It would not give us the existence of a property that applies to a given collection, process, or operation. So, (literal) infinity is not at all like 42, $\sin x$, or other mathematical concepts that are not self-contradictory in meaning. 42 can exist as a logically coherent conceptual idea; literal infinity cannot.

At best, it is only 'infinity' in the *figurative* sense of the term that can exist as a mathematical concept that does not produce logical self-contradiction.

The physicist then goes on to argue against *finitism*, the philosophical position holding that all non-empty collections and non-zero quantities are finite and that literally infinite mathematical objects do not exist [1,094], and against the *finitist* (one advocating finitism):

> ...finitists do not actually present any mathematical arguments against the existence of infinity. They simply refuse to "accept" the notion of infinity for philosophical reasons. However, while they were busy "not accepting" the concept of infinity, other people have defined infinities of many types and forms in mathematically consistent ways, and we use these infinities all the time in mathematics itself as well as in physics and virtually all other fields of science."

There are a few false statements here. Once again, because there is in the philosophical sense of 'argument' no such thing as a mathematical argument regarding existence at all, then what the finitist needs in order to prove infinity does not exist is not a "mathematical argument." Rather, what the finitist needs to prove infinity nonexistent is a *logical argument* showing the *meaning* of infinity used in mathematics to be self-contradictory. Little wonder the physicist doesn't find any mathematical arguments from finitists; finitists don't offer any and are not required to for a sound position. Most finitists should know there are no mathematical 'arguments' of the sort needed—rather, there are logical arguments with implications for mathematical objects. And as we've seen with mathematical examples in previous chapters, there are indeed logical problems with claiming infinity exists as a property of mathematical objects such as quantitative values and numerical operations.

As for finitists simply refusing to "accept" the notion of infinity "for philosophical reasons," the physicist gets two things wrong with this charge: the motive of finitism and the nature of philosophy.

The physicist above holds that "philosophical reasons" are merely subjective points of view that are neither true nor false. While that position may be supported by some postmodernist schools of philosophy, it is hardly the consensus view among academic philosophers. Philosophers typically adopt or reject positions based on logical arguments, some quite formal and technical, and not simply because of subjective preferences. If all philosophers believed their viewpoints were only subjective, they wouldn't bother debating each other.

Moreover, the quoted physicist is certainly not well-versed in the philosophical literature if he thinks philosophical positions are neither true nor false. Certainly, some philosophical positions are not *known* to be true or *known* to be false, but that is different than their *being* neither true nor false. The physicist overlooked, among other things, that many philosophical positions rely on the accuracy of empirical claims, such as claims about the nature of matter or the nature of mind. Further still, he overlooked that some philosophical positions are even falsifiable. For example, if a particular philosophical position is shown by evidence or sound argument to contain, assume, or imply a logical contradiction, then the position is refuted as false. This is where the physicist has failed to notice where philosophical proposals are not so different from the thought experiments conducted in theoretical physics.

As to the motivation of finitists, they do not simply "refuse to 'accept' the notion of infinity" due to subjective preference. Rather, finitists hold their position for various reasons arrived at *through logical analysis*, which is what "philosophical reasons" properly are, after all.

In addition to misunderstanding the nature of philosophy and mischaracterizing finitism, the physicist stated that mathematicians have defined many types of infinities and "use these infinities all the time."

But I have already debunked that claim over the previous chapters: mathematicians have merely invented various schemes of figurative infinity (a misnomer for indefiniteness of process) and mistaken their various technical versions of figurative infinity to be 'infinities' in the literal sense of the term.

Lastly, as for finitism being a position confined only to academic philosophers, such is not the case. Simpson, himself a mathematician, argues that literal infinity (or 'actual infinity' in the lingo of Aristotle) does not exist and should not be assumed to exist in mathematics [1,095]. While such is a minority opinion in the mathematical community, just because an opinion is a minority view does not make it nonexistent, untrue, or irrelevant.

22.1.5 *Use of Natural Numbers and the Denial of Infinite Sets*

According to Cantor, mathematicians who deny $\mathbb{N}$ is a set contradict themselves by assuming $\mathbb{N}$ is a set from which to pull natural numbers. Here is how Cantor's argument was posed by Joseph Dauben, professor of History at the Graduate Center of the City University of New York:

> "...finitists, who only allowed arguments of the sort: 'For any arbitrarily large number N there exists a number $n > N$,' necessarily presupposed (said Cantor) the existence of *all* such numbers $n > N$, taken as an entire, completed collection which he called the *Transfinitum*" [1,096].

If finitists "only allowed arguments" in the manner that Cantor contended they do, then their position would indeed be self-contradictory. However, finitists need not resort to the position Cantor attributed to them. Instead, finitists could simply reject any claim that "For any arbitrarily large number $\mathbb{N}$ there exists a number $n > \mathbb{N}$" in favor of stating, "For the largest defined number N there can be invented a new number n such that $n > \mathbb{N}$." In which case, n only exists as an actual number after n is defined and thereby extends the scale of defined natural numbers as a *series* rather than n preexisting in the natural numbers as a set. Hence, use of natural numbers does not necessarily presuppose a set, $\mathbb{N}$, as Cantor argued; we could instead regard the scale of naturals to be a series: $\mathbb{N}^\circ$.

22.1.6 *Imagining Infinite Sets*

Logician H.C.M. (Harrie) de Swart of Tilburg University states, "Amazingly, although all sets we experience in the world are finite, we are still able to imagine infinite sets like $\mathbb{N}$ and to see amazing properties of them" [1,097]. But can we really *imagine* infinite sets?

Not all mathematicians agree that we can. Wildberger, for instance, retorts that, no, a person does not really imagine an infinite set; rather, one merely *imagines that one is imagining* an infinite set [1,098].

Wildberger has that right. What we hold in our imagination may be a large set or process, perhaps even an indefinitely large set or a process with indefinitely many steps, but those are still finite entities; we do not coherently imagine a set or process which is both complete in quantity and yet quantitatively limitless. Even saying we can "imagine" an indefinitely large set is not entirely accurate for who can imagine even a large list of say, one million members? I don't mean just conceive of them or refer to them or imply them; I mean *imagine* them—all of them together at once. It's doubtful anyone can. It's more than doubtful anyone truly imagines the infinite since it's very concept entails self-contradiction.

22.1.7 *Experiencing the Infinite*

Not everyone agrees with Wildberger or would agree with me on the previous point, however. Some argue that not only can we imagine the infinite, but we can also actually experience it.

For her doctoral dissertation, philosopher Lisa Ann Sereno argued that we can and do experience infinity [1,099]. Sereno made her case by presenting an illustration of rectangles. [1,100]. The rectangles all have the same dimensions, but they are arranged in a sequence of decreasing size, each one smaller than the next, with the whole sequence drawn so as to give the illusion that the rectangles are slabs standing on edge, one in front of the another, in a long, straight row like dominoes set up for a fall. There are so many duplicate rectangles of increasingly smaller size that the sequence gives the illusion of a row of rectangles receding from our perspective into the horizon. Sereno says there is nothing logically contradictory in this illusion—the picture is simply that of a sequence of self-similar rectangles on increasingly smaller scales until they become indiscernible. She argues that the illustration of duplicate rectangles arranged in diminishing size therefore gives one the illusion of an infinite sequence of rectangles: "...when we look at these pictures, we have a *perceptual illusion of an infinite sequence*" [1,101]. Sereno says further that because such an illusion of an infinite sequence does not violate logic, then the sequence could exist if physical nature allows [1,102]:

> ...if we can show that a picture depicts a certain object and if we form a non-contradictory profile of this picture, then we thereby obtain evidence that the depicted object could exist in three-dimensional space...

That is, the logical coherence of the illusion implies infinity *could* logically exist in the real world even if it turns out that it does not actually exist in the real world as a matter of physics. Whether or not anything literally infinite exists as a genuine physical phenomenon is irrelevant according to Sereno's argument; the conclusion remains the same: because the sequence could logically exist in the real world, we experience a logically coherent illusion of the infinite, and so we thereby experience the infinite.

There are at least four major problems with Sereno's case. First, it's not clear that Sereno's illusion is an illusion of the infinite. At best, the sequence we perceive can only offer the suggestion that there are more rectangles to find than we can see, not that there is an infinite quantity to find. To conclude that because the duplicates we perceive continue beyond the range of our perception that they are implied to proceed infinitely onward is a non sequitur. After all, just because we see a highway roll off into the horizon does not mean we experience an illusion of the highway as being infinite—we could expect it to end somewhere beyond our range of vision. In fact, the highway need not even be indefinitely long (in the sense of being longer than any length definable in practice). The notion that it could be indefinitely long, let alone infinitely long, is not necessitated merely by the highway's extension into the horizon. There is nothing in the repetition of a pattern to necessarily imply indefiniteness, let alone infinitude.

Second, even if we stipulate, as Sereno does, that the sequence of rectangles continues without a halting process, that in itself does not entail an *infinitely* long sequence, but only an *indefinitely* long series. Just because we might imagine following the highway without ever stopping still does not mean we have a coherent conception of the highway being infinite—all we have is a conception of a highway the end of which we never reach. Perhaps the highway does have an end that is always being extended, the highway ceaselessly under construction an indefinitely long distance ahead of us and built so quickly that we can never reach the end where the workers are building it, and yet that continuous construction implies the highway is at each step of the way a finite length away, however indefinitely long the highway is and continues to grow. So too, perhaps Sereno's rectangles are a sequence under construction rather than a set of rectangles already complete. Sereno's illusion of infinity is thus based on *assumptions* about what is seen—a set of rectangles that is already complete rather than a series of rectangles in progress. Make a different assumption and you have a different illusion to claim. Hence, to see Sereno's rectangles extend to the horizon provides just as much evidence supporting an illusion of the indefinite as it does an illusion of the infinite.

Third, it's not clear Sereno's "illusion of an infinite sequence" is an *experience* of the infinite, even merely as an illusion. Suppose the sequence of rectangles really were infinite. According to philosopher Peter Suber, even if there are infinite things, we would not experience them as infinite [1,103]:

> Do we ever experience something which is *literally* infinite? If time, space, or matter are infinitely divisible, then to experience a finite chunk of any one of them is to experience its infinity of parts...For even if time, space, and matter are infinitely divisible, we experience their infinite parts bundled into chunks most of whose parts are indiscernible to us. When a movie runs at 24 frames per second, it appears continuous, its separate frames indiscernible to us. We certainly experience 24 chunked frames, but not the 24-ness, or even the finitude, of the chunking. Once the eye is fooled into seeing continuity, the number of frames per second could increase to a billion, or to an infinite number, and we would not notice the difference. This is the sense in which we could experience something infinite without experiencing its infinitude. Similarly, if time, space, and matter were continuous and infinitely divisible, then the spectacle of life would be like a movie run at an (uncountably) infinite number of frames per second; but while we would experience expanses, durations, and objects with infinitely many parts, but we would not experience the infinitude of those parts.

From Suber's argument, we can conclude that to have a sequence of rectangles fade into the horizon may be *consistent* with the claim that there are infinitely many of them, but that is different from *experiencing* the sequence as infinite. Just because there are too many rectangles to discern does not mean we experience an infinitude of them, even if there are infinitely many of them. All we experience is a lot of rectangles, not the infinitude of them. And if we cannot—even in principle—experience a real infinite as infinite, then we do not have sufficient reason to suppose that an illusion we experience must be an illusion of the infinite. Instead, when we experience an illusion of a sequence proceeding beyond the bounds of perception, like Sereno's illustration of rectangles, what we have is an experience of an illusion that we might *assume* is an illusion of the infinite. But if infinity is an incoherent concept, that assumption is erroneous; what we really experience is an illusion of the merely indefinite.

This brings us to a fourth problem with Sereno's argument: the notion that the sequence of rectangles is an illusion of an *infinite* sequence is mistaken because Sereno's argument presupposes the logical coherence of literal infinity in order to make the case that a particular kind of illusion is an illusion of the infinite and thus an experience of the infinite. That is an incorrect presupposition. If, as I have argued over preceding chapters, the concept of the infinite is itself logically incoherent, then we have no experience of the infinite or of perceptual illusions of the infinite—all we can have experience of, with respect to literal infinity, is the *misconception that we experience* literal infinity or perceptual illusions of infinity.

Now, it is true that, although we experience nothing literally infinite, not even in perceptual illusion, there is a different sense in which there is an illusion of literal infinity. Literal infinity is an instance of a *conceptual* illusion rather than a *perceptual* illusion.

Perceptual illusions, like those in **Figure 22.0**, present objects or situations that are impossible in reality, but their impossibility is easily explainable by demonstrating the mistakes in visual perspective upon which the illusions are based.

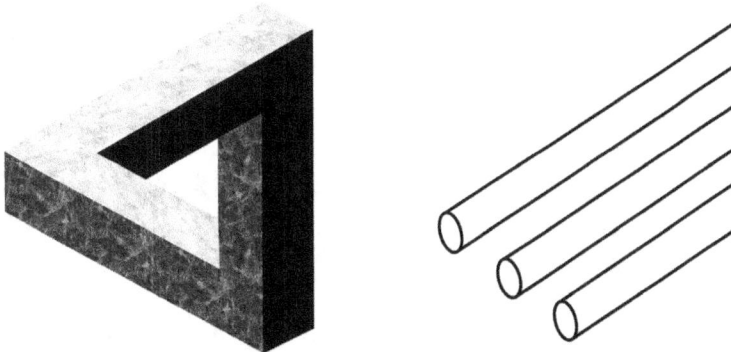

Figure 22.0: The impossible tribar and the impossible trident.

Infinity is "illusory" in the sense that a collection that is complete and limitless in quantity presents an impossibility that can readily be explained as a mistake of perspective, so to speak. However, infinity is not a perceptual illusion, and it is not based on a mistake of *visual* perspective; rather, infinity is a conceptual illusion based on a mistaken *interpretational* 'perspective'. That an infinite collection makes logical sense is a conceptual illusion caused by a mistaken interpretation about the properties of completeness and limitlessness and how they logically stand in relation to one another. The notion of literal infinity as logical is an illusion that is the outcome of misinterpreting completeness and limitlessness as properties that can apply to the same quantity of the same collection.

I have done my best in the preceding chapters to expose the conceptual illusion of literal infinity for what it is—the mistaken appearance of logic where there is none; the misunderstanding of literal infinity as merely 'paradoxical' rather than self-contradictory. An illusion merely rationalized with Cantorian set theory. Now that the inherent conflicts of meaning between completeness and limitlessness have been laid bare and infinity's supposed logical coherence has been exposed as an illusion, we have no support for the notion that we experience infinity in any form—real or otherwise.

22.2 INFINITY IN SUM

There are undoubtedly more rebuttals and counterarguments that could be made. It sometimes seems like debate about infinity will never end (pun intended), and that, if such debate did continue without ceasing, that would in itself prove literal infinity to be a coherent idea after all. However, not even debating without ceasing would prove the idea of literal infinity to be coherent or real in any strict sense either. A process can continue without end and not be infinite in the literal sense of the term—the process simply goes on *indefinitely*, remaining finite no matter how many new steps get added along the way. Construing the word 'forever' to mean not "for infinite time" but rather "for all time to come," however *indefinitely* long the future may be, I concede that it is at least logically possible to debate infinity forever in that sense. Realistically, though, we can be sure the debate about infinity will most likely *not* last forever—not even when 'forever' is construed as an ever-growing finitude, an open series or *figurative* 'infinity'. The idea of (literal) infinity has enjoyed a long life on planet Earth, but even the Earth must come to an end. And even if humanity manages to survive by colonizing distant worlds, eventually infinity may very well be replaced by some other concept.

And given the arguments of this and foregoing chapters, infinity *should* be replaced. Mathematics and science are better off without infinity. Mathematicians should replace infinity with an alternative concept since the logical self-contradictions implied by the meaning of literal infinity ensure it does not accurately apply to mathematical objects. Physicists are also right to be suspicious of infinity (at least, in its literal sense) because, once its meaning is articulated, it is revealed to imply logical self-contradictions and so it cannot be a property of physical reality. Consequently, space, time, motion, and matter are all finite, however large and enduring the Universe may be. Literal infinity should therefore be replaced with an alternative concept that both avoids the logical contradictions and paradoxes that have plagued literal infinity and provides a more accurate predicate for describing quantities in the real world that may be beyond practical calculation.

The concept that needs to replace infinity is indefiniteness. The concept of indefiniteness does not suffer the logical maladies afflicting infinity. That alone makes it more suitable for descriptions of the real world. If there are features of the world that no numerical scale can calculate, it is indefiniteness that better describes them. Mathematics and science are better off embracing the indefinite as an alternative concept. All the mathematicians and scientists need to do is take the plunge and replace infinity with an alternative concept that avoids self-contradictions and paradoxes with respect to that which is incalculable in any practical sense. Over the next two chapters, I will argue that indefiniteness is the best candidate to replace infinity—even in the figurative sense of the word.

CHAPTER 22 IN REVIEW

❖ Mathematicians and philosophers of mathematics have offered several rebuttals to arguments against the incoherence of literal infinity, but none of them hold up to scrutiny. Literal infinity is a conceptual illusion.
❖ Literal infinity should therefore be replaced with a more logically coherent concept for creating mathematical schemas and descriptions of the real world.
❖ Indefiniteness is at present the best alternative to literal infinity.
❖ Both mathematics and science should therefore embrace the indefinite over the literally infinite, revising the content of their fields accordingly.

PART III:
ON FIGURATIVE INFINITY

23: THE STORY OF FIGURATIVE INFINITY

Infinity is sometimes described as the condition of "never ending" or of "going on forever." Such phrases describe infinity in terms of a temporal component that does not necessarily imply a condition of being without limit in an absolute sense (constant over space and time); instead, such descriptions may only be implying a state of relative limitlessness (one that changes in space or time). That is, the description of a series as proceeding "without limit" may be referring to a series that never stops once having started while at each step of the way the series may only be finitely removed from its start. So, to "never end" or "go on forever" may capture what it is to be 'infinite' in a figurative sense of the word, rather than in its literal sense as addressed in previous chapters. This is figurative infinity: the condition of *indefinitely changing in quantity*.

In § 1.3.3, an example of figurative infinity was provided in which one ceaselessly drops ever more marbles into a bag that never gets full [1,104]. Though the process of dropping marbles into the bag never ends, the number of drops and number of corresponding marbles dropped always remains limited, no matter how long the dropping of marbles goes on. The example portrays a collection of steps or actions that exist *in succession* rather than a collection in which the members exist alongside one another, together all at once. Hence, the collection is a series rather than a set (or, if you prefer, you can think of it as a series of sets). And the series in the example is of an *indefinitely changing quantity* of occurrences (actions, iterations, etc.)—each new marble dropped in the bag adds to a running total of dropped marbles that never reaches completion and never becomes limitless in quantity. A series that never becomes limitless and is never completed is not an *infinite* series in the literal sense of the term; rather, it is an *indefinite* series that may be called 'infinite' as merely a figure of speech. Hence a more accurate term for a ceaselessly growing finitude is *serial indefiniteness*.

We find examples in mathematics of serial indefinites referred to as 'infinity' in the figurative sense. While in transfinite mathematics the scale of natural numbers is considered as a literally infinite *set*, labelled $\mathbb{N}$, in general mathematics the same scale is sometimes regarded as only a figuratively 'infinite' *series* (1, 2, 3, ...) in which the numbers are formed successively with the scale always remaining incomplete, under construction.

Similarly, in transfinite set theory a geometric line is conceived as being comprised of points, each of which corresponds to a number in a literally infinite 'continuum' of numbers; whereas, in general mathematics a line is sometimes regarded as a unity which, though undivided, is 'infinitely divisible' in a figurative sense—we may continue dividing the line into ever smaller segments as long as we wish.

So too, in analytic geometry a curve on a graph is sometimes regarded as converging with a straight asymptote "at infinity" (a literally infinite distance) but it is also sometimes regarded as a process that extends ever closer to an asymptote, approximating it 'infinitely' in a figurative sense, without ever intersecting with it.

These examples from mathematics indicate that the same 'objects' which followers of Cantor regard as instances of literal infinity can also be considered as instances of figurative infinity—serial indefiniteness [1,105].

Other examples of figurative infinity can be found in the sciences, such as for descriptions of time. Some cosmologists conjecture the Universe expands and never stops expanding. However, there will only ever be a finite number of days back to the Big Bang. If this is so, then time is 'infinite' but merely in a figurative sense. On the other end of the temporal scale, consider ever briefer periods of time such as hours, minutes, seconds, etc. The briefest known unit of time is sometimes said to be infinitely divisible, though only in the figurative sense that it can be divided into ever briefer increments of duration, measured to ever greater precision, while nevertheless remaining finite.

Even space can be considered 'infinite' in a figurative sense, given certain interpretations of physical theory. For example, if space is infinitely vast in only a *figurative* sense, then that means the number of places making up all of space at any time is actually limited, even though that amount changes without ceasing. This is often portrayed as a perpetual growth of space in some versions of the Big Bang theory in which the entire Universe is believed to be finite as a whole at any given moment but continues to expand in size. In the figurative sense of 'infinite space', no final amount of places comprising all of space can ever be generated—the growth of space is never completed, yet always limited in volume. On the other hand, consider ever shorter lengths of space such as meters, centimeters, millimeters, etc. The shortest known unit of length is sometimes said to be divisible into ever smaller lengths, seemingly without coming to a final level of smallness—space infinitely divisible, at least in a figurative sense. So, space too might be regarded as figuratively infinite either in the vastness of ever-expanding space or in the minuteness being achieved with ever smaller divisions. In the view that space is figuratively infinite, there are always only a *finite* number of places from here to anywhere at any given time, no matter how far apart here and there becomes, or no matter how long you go on dividing a given length.

Those are just a few examples, but they illustrate well how figurative infinity differs from literal infinity, and how figurative infinity is but a metaphor for serial indefiniteness.

This chapter will review use of the term 'infinity' in its figurative sense from ancient to contemporary times. We'll see instances in which infinity has been regarded merely as a metaphor for an indefinite series rather than as a predicate referring to a set that is both complete and limitless in quantity, but we'll also see how some philosophers and mathematicians interpreted the term 'infinite' more literally even while not differing from a condition of indefiniteness.

23.1 FIGURATIVE INFINITY FROM ANCIENT TIMES

As mentioned in § 8.1, use of the term 'infinity' (or 'apeiron' to the ancient Greeks) in its quantitative sense goes back at least to Anaximander and has always been used in both literal and figurative senses back at least as far as Socrates and Plato, both of whom rejected the idea that infinity in its literal sense applies to anything in *reality*. They instead held that 'infinity', whether taken literally or figuratively, is a term that applies only to magnitudes in the illusory world of *appearances* [1,106].

However, Socrates and Plato did not analyze the difference between literal and figurative uses of infinity as such. That would have to wait until Aristotle, who was the first to attempt a formal distinction of the two different meanings of infinity.

Alas, Aristotle did not quite have the correct interpretation of the two different uses of infinity. Instead of distinguishing between infinity as literal and infinity as figurative, he thought the two different uses of 'infinity' were both literal. He referred to what I call 'literal infinity' as 'actual infinity' (*apeiron hōs aphorismenon*) and he referred to what I call 'figurative infinity' as 'potential infinity' (*apeiron dunamei*) [1,107]. For Aristotle, both actual infinity and potential infinity are literal uses of the word 'infinity'. However, I propose his 'potential infinity' is not really infinity in a literal sense of the term; it is rather just 'infinity' in a figurative sense since Aristotle's idea of 'potentiality' is itself used in a metaphorical way with respect to infinity.

23.1.1 *Potential Infinity*

After Aristotle distinguished these two different senses of 'infinity', he contradicted Socrates and Plato, stating there to be no multitudes that are literally, or actually, infinite. There are no collections the members of which exist together all at once in a complete and limitless quantity, not even in the world of appearances. "Nothing is complete which has no end, and the end is a limit," he said [1,108]. Since nothing that is limitless is complete, then nothing can be actually infinite—there is nothing infinite in the literal sense of the term 'infinite'.

Even though he recognized there are no collections of things that are both complete *and* limitless in quantity, Aristotle still believed that some things in the real world can accurately be referred to as 'infinite'. To maintain use of the term 'infinite', Aristotle proposed that there is a sense in which certain things can be thought of as infinite even though they are not entirely without limit.

Specifically, Aristotle thought series rather than sets could be regarded as in some sense infinite even if there are no infinite collections of things existing all together at once. Series of occurrences (such as events or iterations or 'steps' in a process) always remain finite no matter how long they go on; they are never literally infinite. So, Aristotle proposed that despite series not being infinite in *actuality*, they can nevertheless be infinite in *potentiality* [1,109]. All series are in some way 'potentially infinite' but not 'actually infinite'. The earlier example of the ceaseless but ever incomplete process of dropping marbles into a bag is the kind of process Aristotle would have referred to as a 'potential infinity'.

23.1.2 *On Two Different Senses of 'Potential'*

There is an important caveat to Aristotle's view on potential infinity, one that will reveal why his 'potential infinity' I instead refer to as 'figurative infinity'. Normally, when we say something is potential that implies it can become actual. A block of marble is *potentially* a statue but then, after completion of the sculptor's work, it is *actually* a statue [1,110]. The block of marble has the potential to become a statue only if it can really be made into a statue. If the block of marble cannot be sculpted into a statue, then it is not a potential statue at all. Similarly, one might reasonably assume that by saying something is potentially infinite Aristotle meant it is able to become actually infinite (complete and without limit). But when Aristotle said that which is infinite is so potentially, he did not mean it can become actually infinite. He was very clear about this [1,111]:

> When we speak of the potential existence of a statue, we mean that there will be an actual statue. It is not so with the infinite. There will not be an actual infinite.

In saying the infinite is never actual but only potential, Aristotle used an ambiguity in the application of the word 'potential'. He distinguished between two different senses of 'potential'.

One sense of 'potential' is the sense we are familiar with: something is potential if can become actual. The other sense of 'potential', at least according to Aristotle, simply means the ability to become something else, to change in form. The Olympic Games, he pointed out, are subject to change over time because each game is planned, then occurs, and then is over. The Olympic Games therefore have a kind of 'potential' existence because they are not a single thing that exists over time as a constant but instead as a series of things, each instance of which changes in time from not being actual to being actual and then to again not being actual [1,112]. According to Aristotle, potentiality is the condition of that in which members come to be and then cease to be, rather than continue to exist together, all at once.

Likewise, Aristotle proposed, an *infinite* series has 'potential' existence because it is composed of things that are not, that come to be, and that then pass away...without end. Aristotle thus concluded the infinite is potential not in the first sense, which is how we talk about the potentiality of a block of marble to become a statue; rather, the infinite is potential in the second sense—it applies to series of elements, each of which come into and out of existence, while the series as such continues indefinitely. It is the transitory nature of the members comprising the series that makes an indefinite series a 'potential infinity'.

It is with this distinction of two different senses of what it means for something to be potential that Aristotle undoubtedly regarded himself as describing infinity in a literal sense when he referred to potential infinity. He thought that infinity is, literally, 'potential' in the sense of bringing things into and out of existence in a series and 'limitless' in the sense that if the series goes on without ceasing, it nevertheless will not produce an actually limitless amount of anything all at once.

23.1.3 *Are There Really Two Different Senses of 'Potential' in Colloquial Discourse?*

While Aristotle proposed there are two different senses of the word 'potential' and that the usual sense in which potential denotes something that can become actual does not apply to infinity, I counter that there is no alternative sense of 'potential' outside of Aristotle's proclamation that there is such. The reason is simply that he does not make use of this alternative sense of 'potential'—denoting merely the transitoriness of events—to anything else except a series that goes on indefinitely (which he calls 'infinite' even though it is not even *limitless* in a literal sense). His secondary sense of potentiality denotes a use of the term 'potential' that applies to nothing else but the 'infinite' in the sense of an indefinite series, and he admitted as much [1,113]. And no one used 'potential' with respect to series, including infinite ones, except Aristotle himself at the time he proposed this secondary use of 'potential'.

Of course, Aristotle was free to *stipulate* a new use of the word 'potential', but that was not what he was attempting. Rather, he was attempting to *explicate* what he thought was a common use of the term 'potential' and show how we all take for granted that it applies to the concept of infinity with respect to series that go on without end. But it's precisely on that point that Aristotle was really reaching. No one uses the term 'potential' in that manner with respect to series, even for series that have no end. His stipulation of a new sense of 'potential' did not elucidate how the term 'infinity' is commonly used.

Hence, there is no secondary sense of 'potential' as Aristotle stated, unless we simply accept his proposal that we *should* use the word 'potential' in this new way as well as the usual way, even if only about infinity and nothing else. To which I say, let's stick to using the term 'potential' as it is commonly used rather than propose some nonstandard use that applies to only one concept and nothing else.

23.1.4 *Why both the Potentiality and Infinitude of 'Potential Infinity' are Misleading*

Proposing this alternative use of the word 'potential' is not helpful in elucidating infinity as the word 'infinity' is used in common language. Instead, this alternative sense of 'potential' just sowed confusion because the word 'potential' is not used in that specialized, secondary sense for anything else. The word 'potential' has always commonly referred to that which can become actual. That which *cannot* become actual certainly has no potential in the usual, literal sense of the word 'potential'—there is really nothing 'potential' about something if it cannot be actual, even in principle.

Moreover, this confusion occurred because Aristotle exploited an ambiguity in the order of terms 'potential' and 'infinity' when used together. When the term 'potential infinity' is used, does it mean the infinitude of something is what is potential, or does it mean there is something potential that is also infinite? Aristotle seems to have meant the latter rather than the former (at least most of the time—he doesn't seem to have been entirely consistent), whereas the term 'potential infinity' would normally indicate the former rather than the latter. Hence why his term 'potential infinity' confused so many of his readers.

Aristotle's term 'potential infinity' is rather like the term 'theoretical physicist', by which it is meant not that the physicist is theoretical but rather that a particular physicist is the kind of physicist who theorizes. So too, by 'potential infinity' Aristotle primarily meant not that it is something's infinitude that is potential, but rather that something with potentiality can also be an infinite thing. Or at least, that seems to be what he (inconsistently) meant.

Notice, though, that when we tease out this meaning of 'potential infinity', any and every series would be 'potential' in Aristotle's stipulated sense of being transitory—of having members come into and go out of existence—whether the given series is infinite or simply finite. The potentiality of a series has nothing to do with whether it is infinite. So, the so-called 'potentiality' of 'potential infinity' is really irrelevant. All that calling a series that never ends a 'potential infinity' accomplishes is pointing out that an infinite series, like any other series formed over time, has transitory members. So, the word 'potential' in the term 'potential infinity' does no work other than to denote it is a series we're talking about as something infinite rather than a set. Besides, according to Aristotle, no series is literally without limit per se [1,114].

Given Aristotle's stipulated, technical sense of 'potential', I maintain his application of that predicate to infinity was ill conceived; it rendered his elucidation of infinity hollow. An elucidation is only worth something if it really does shine a light on how a concept is normally regarded, or at least clarifies rather than confuses how it should be regarded. And Aristotle's conception of 'potential' did not elucidate but rather clouded the issue because it is not potentiality as such that makes a series infinite or not infinite. What makes a series "infinite" is that it continues to go on without ceasing. In other words, an infinite series is one that has only a running total of occurrences comprising it instead of a literally limitless quantity of occurrences at any given time. It is that feature that makes Aristotle's series 'infinite', not its so-called "potentiality" of members. And it is precisely the feature of indefiniteness of progression that makes Aristotle's use of the term 'infinity' with respect to series not a literal use of the term 'infinity' at all, but merely a figure of speech.

The bottom line is that Aristotle's 'potential infinity' does not differ from an indefinite, but always finite, series. If we could potentially keep adding or dividing something (that is, if we were able to actually never stop adding or dividing something), that would not make the series of additions or divisions into a series that is *infinite*—without quantitative limit—in a literal sense. There is and always will be a limited number of occurrences in a series and so always a running total of occurrences rather than no total at all; hence, there is always a limit to series in that regard, even if it just "keeps on going." So, to say something is infinite because it 'exists potentially' is just another way of saying it is infinite because it is an *indefinite*, but always finite, *series*—in other words, a serial indefinite.

I therefore maintain Aristotle's 'potential infinity' is more accurately regarded as just 'infinity' in a figurative sense of the term. If my analysis is correct, when Aristotle said there is nothing actually infinite but only potentially infinite, he should instead have stated that there is nothing *literally* infinite but instead only *figuratively* infinite. That would have been much clearer. He simply mislabeled figurative infinity as potential infinity due to a mistaken attempt at elucidating a figurative use of 'infinite' in terms of his specialized sense of potentiality, which was in turn just a way of identifying ongoing series rather than completed collections as what should be called 'infinite' [1,115].

23.1.5 *Confusing Actuality and Potentiality with Respect to Infinite Time*

While Aristotle said there is nothing actually infinite, he did believe there is something potentially infinite: the future. Aristotle held the future is "potentially" (more precisely, figuratively) infinite because the future rolls on as a serial indefinite—always finite at any step of the way but continuing without end.

Since there is nothing actually infinite, you would think Aristotle would have claimed the past is finite, but he instead held the past is infinite. And with this proposal, a problem crops up: how can the past be infinite if all the events of the past have already *actually* happened and yet with nothing being actually infinite?

Think of it this way: imagine a timeline of sequential events stretching off in either direction to the horizon. In one direction is the timeline of the future, in the other is the timeline of the past. Aristotle held that the past is infinite, that there never was a "first moment" of time [1,116]. So, the timeline of the past cannot have a first moment in its sequence of moments. But if the past has, literally, no limit to its sequence of previous moments, then it would seem Aristotle would have to have held the past to be actually infinite in the usual, literal sense. There would be a one-to-one correspondence between the points on the timeline, which exist together all at once, and the past events that those points represent. So, you would think Aristotle would say the past, as the collection of events that *have happened*, must be actually infinite. And yet, Aristotle denied there is anything actually infinite.

The contradiction is obvious—if the past can stretch back in a linear sequence of events with no first event to start the sequence, then it would not be true that "nothing is actually infinite," which is in direct opposition to his doctrine that there is nothing actually infinite. So how could he claim the past has no limit at all and yet simultaneously claim nothing is actually infinite?

Worse yet, Aristotle could not avoid the contradiction by claiming the past is only a *potential* infinite and not an actual infinite because he implied that potentiality is not a property of the past. The past cannot have a potential form because it actually happened; only the present and future can be potentials—the present is potential in the sense that events now happening (events *actually* happening) nevertheless can become past events, and the future is potential in the sense that events that *will happen* actuality are, right now, *potentially present*. As Aristotle summed it up, "No capacity relates to being in the past, but always to being in the present or future" [1,117]. In which case, the past cannot be potentially infinite; if it is infinite in any sense, it must be an actual infinite, which it cannot be because he denied anything is infinite in actuality.

To get himself out of this contradiction, Aristotle seemed to occasionally imply a distinction between two different senses of 'actual infinity'. One sense of 'actual infinity' applies to nothing at all in the real world (including time) while a second sense of 'actual infinity' could be said to apply to the *past* but not to the *future* and not to anything else in the real world.

The first sense of actual infinity is what we've been referring to as literal infinity—the condition in which a collection has members existing together, *all at once*, in a complete and limitless quantity. Aristotle held that sense of 'actual infinity' does not exist anywhere or any-when.

The second sense of 'actual infinity' is the sense of infinity that Aristotle thought does indeed apply to the whole of the past, even if not to the future or to anything else. As the late philosopher Jaako Hintikka explained [1,118],

> When Aristotle says that the infinite 'will not exist actually', what he has primarily in mind is therefore merely the fact that there will not be any moment of time at which it can be said to be actualized. This does not go to show, however, that the infinite is not actualized in some other sense.

The secondary sense of 'actual infinity'—the infinity denoting the whole of the past as without beginning—regards infinity not as the condition of being a complete and limitless quantity of members existing all together at a single time but instead as an incomplete series of events growing "without limit" over time. The actual infinite in this sense is an infinite in which the members of a series—events or steps in a process—do not exist all at once but instead simply *one after another* [1,119]. As Moore elucidates, Aristotle had "no objection to something's being infinite *provided that its infinitude is not there 'all at once'*" [1,120]. Aristotle held that the past is not there all at once; it is purely consecutive. So, the past is not an 'actual infinite' in the sense of being a complete and limitless quantity of events, for that would say the events are "all there at once" in some timeless Now. Instead, Aristotle implied the past is an 'actual infinite' only in the sense of being a series of events that ceaselessly come into and fall out of existence.

Unfortunately, this does not dissolve the problem because the *quantity* of events that *has happened* for a linear, beginningless past would still be an actual infinite in the sense of a complete and limitless quantity that *did* take place; it would not just be a ceaselessly changing quantity that is always finite. It's hard to see how the past can be infinite as a linear, beginningless series without implying the past is, relative to a particular date, comprised of a complete and limitless accumulation of changes—a *set* of all events that have ever occurred prior to that date [1,121]. The past in this conception certainly seems to be more than an 'actual infinite' in merely a loose sense of a *series* of events that continuously pass away.

Then too, if the past is a linear series without beginning and yet does *not* comprise a complete and limitless quantity of events relative to the present, then Aristotle's distinction between actual and potential becomes far less clear. As Hintikka pointed out, "In the *precise* sense...in which the infinite was found to exist potentially for Aristotle, it also exists actually" [1,122]. In other words, the second sense of 'actual infinity' is not clearly different from potential infinity.

Hintikka pointed out that Aristotle's distinction between 'actual' and 'potential' infinity became muddled, particularly with respect to applying the concept of infinity to the past [1,123]. Hence, Aristotle still doesn't get out of a contradiction, for now he has just confused the meanings of 'actual' and 'potential' which he worked so hard to keep distinct.

Aristotle could of course have avoided all these contradictions simply by positing the past to be finite, but Aristotle did not take that route as he assumed that would imply a beginning to time and he consequently recognized the concept of a beginning to time may also face some logical problems of its own [1,124].

Another option Aristotle could have taken to avoid the contradictions would have been to drop reliance on the actuality/potentiality distinction with respect to infinity and instead distinguish literal from figurative uses of the term 'infinity' (apeiron). He could then have said the past is figuratively 'infinite' in some sense [1,125]. This too would have helped, but Aristotle either did not consider it or decided against it.

23.1.6 *The Enduring Influence of Potential Infinity*

Despite all its problems, Aristotle's distinction between actual infinity and potential infinity remained influential for thousands of years—philosophers across the world still write about infinity according to his terminology. I propose 'literal infinity' and 'figurative infinity' as alternative terms because they are less prone to confusion with one another and the terminology I offer has fewer (if any) misleading implications than Aristotle's terminology.

23.2 FIGURATIVE INFINITY IN MEDIEVAL TIMES

From the 5th to 15th Centuries of the Common Era, Aristotle's distinction between actual and potential infinity was among scholastics the most popular way to interpret infinity. Following Aristotle, most scholastics believed that the physical world is either finite or only 'potentially' (figuratively) infinite with regard to measures of space, time, and motion. However, a competing interest in the actual (literal) infinite and the qualitative infinite also grew steadily during this time as well, as revealed in some theologically-oriented writings of religious philosophers during the Medieval Period (see §§ 25.2.5–25.2.6 for details). Nevertheless, the trending interest in actual infinity and qualitative versions of infinity did not replace potential infinity, which remained as prominent in mathematics as actual infinity.

23.2.1 *Aquinas*

A good example of a medieval theologian with an interest in infinity is Thomas Aquinas. In his *Summa Theologica* (or *Summa Theologiae*) Aquinas says that "it is impossible for an actually infinite multitude to exist…But a potentially infinite multitude is possible" [1,126]. Here Aquinas has taken the position of Aristotle and made it even stricter; Aristotle at least allowed the past to in some way be actually infinite, but Aquinas denies even this manifestation of actual infinity. Yet, as a theologian he did uphold the doctrine that God is qualitatively infinite (see § 25.2.5).

Although Aquinas' position on quantitative infinity was influential, not all medieval philosophers and theologians were happy with Aquinas's separation of infinity into potential infinity for the physical world and qualitative infinity for the divine. In reaction to Aquinas, some medieval scholars revised the original potential/actual distinctions proposed by Aristotle, while others simply limited talk of infinity to Aristotle's potential infinity.

23.2.2 *Peter of Spain*

Another medieval theologian was Peter of Spain (1220–1277), whom some scholars believe became Pope John XXI. Though a theologian, Peter did have an interest in the philosophy of mathematics and he drew a distinction about quantitative infinity worth noting.

Peter distinguished between the *categorematic* use of infinity and the *syncategorematic* use of infinity. In Latin, it's not always clear if a word is categorematic (denoting a noun or adjective) or syncategorematic (denoting an adverb, preposition, or conjunction). For example, the Latin phrase "infinita diebus" can be translated into English as "infinite days" (the categorematic use of infinity) or "infinitely many days" (the syncategorematic use of infinity). Because the same Latin word, 'infinita', can have two different uses—adjective or adverb—in the same phrase ("infinita diebus"), such shows that the same Latin phrase involving infinity might be understood in two opposing ways, causing an ambiguity in meaning that may be more easily avoided with alternative phrasing or by expression in a more descriptive language such as English. However, if the intent of the phrase can be properly distinguished, then the meaning of infinity can be made clear. The distinction in meaning between the two uses of 'infinita' can be put like so [1,127]:

- categorematic infinite: *surpassing every finite quantity*.
- syncategorematic infinite: *surpassing any given finite quantity*.

The categorematic/syncategorematic distinction looks like Aristotle's distinction between actual infinity and potential infinity. If something is categorematically infinite, it is beyond *every* finite quantity and so is a quantity that is literally limitless (actually infinite). If something is syncategorematically infinite, then it can still be a finite quantity so long as it is larger than any quantity someone might name (in other words, it is an indefinitely large quantity). It is little wonder that some scholars wanted to say the categorematic infinite just is actual infinity and the syncategorematic infinite just is potential infinity; there does seem to be a resemblance. But such a simplification would not be quite correct [1,128].

The syncategorematic infinite *can* refer to a series that is potentially infinite in the Aristotelian sense. A 'potentially infinite' series is just an indefinite series, and an indefinite series can meet the definition of the syncategorematic infinite. For example, an indefinitely long process in which the furthest step surpasses any finite step one might name in practice would, by definition, count as an instance of the syncategorematic infinite. We can therefore take an indefinite series, which is the same as a figurative or 'potential' infinity, to be an instance of the syncategorematic infinite.

Incidentally, invoking the category 'syncategorematic' instead of 'potential' for describing an indefinitely long series as 'infinite' does solve an old problem: to say of a series that it has 'infinitely many' occurrences or events that comprise it is to use infinity in the syncategorematic sense, but in a way that has an advantage over Aristotle's 'potential infinity'. To categorize an instance of infinity as 'syncategorematic' instead of 'potential' avoids abuse of the word 'potential' such that there is no longer a misleading implication that a series called 'potentially infinite' can become an actually infinite set.

However, the syncategorematic infinite need not refer to a series. That's not to say a series cannot be an instance of the syncategorematic infinite, because it can. It's just to say the syncategorematic infinite does not *reduce* to Aristotle's potential infinity because the syncategorematic infinite is a category that includes more than indefinite *series*; it can also refer to indefinitely large *sets*.

The syncategorematic infinite can refer to a 'collective indefinite' as a completed set that is larger than any defined finite quantity, but nonetheless still finite. After all, an indefinitely large set can also be taken as a set in which the quantity of members in principle "surpasses any given finite quantity" but the collective indefinite is not synonymous with the literally infinite. And an indefinitely large set is not the same as Aristotle's potential infinity because a set is not a series.

But simply escaping Aristotle's unfortunate use of 'potential' for 'potential infinity' does not solve all the troubles with denoting the indefinite as 'infinite'. Because, when one says of a *set* that it has 'infinitely many' members, one may be using infinity in the syncategorematic sense, but then one is also using infinity as a *misnomer* for the indefinitely large. And that is just as misleading as Aristotle's use of 'potential' in potential infinity. Avoiding misleading talk about infinity was part of the whole point that

Peter of Spain proposed the categorematic/ syncategorematic categories of infinity over Aristotle's actual/potential categories of infinity. One problem was solved only to introduce another.

23.2.3 *Richard of Middleton*

One more figure of note during the Medieval Period was Richard of Middleton (1249 - 1308), who believed actual (literal) infinity is a contradiction in terms [1,129] [1,130]. In Richard's opinion, 'actual infinity' is an oxymoron, a contradiction in terms, because a magnitude of elements all existing together at once is a magnitude with the property of 'actuality', which implies a determinate quantity, while to be infinite is to be indeterminate in quantity and so not actual.

Just a few years ago a similar point was made by Patterson in an online article [1,131]. Patterson believes a set of all the natural numbers cannot exist "out there" as an infinite set because 'infinite set' is an oxymoron—a contradiction in terms. He states that 'infinite set' is an oxymoron because 'infinite' refers to a condition of being 'limitless' (however, Patterson takes that to mean indefinite in progression), a condition that is inherently incomplete, while a set is assumed to be defined as complete [1,132].

Both Richard's and Patterson's reasoning on actual infinity sounds superficially similar to my own analysis, but there are significant differences between our views.

My disagreement with Richard of Middleton's position is simply a matter of where the contradiction in terms lies. It's not that anything actual must be finite and so there cannot be an actual infinity; rather, the real contradiction is that infinity, in its literal sense, is a state of being complete (and so only actual insofar as 'actual' is taken as a synonym for 'complete') as well as limitless (which contradicts completeness). So, Richard had the right conclusion—when the word 'infinite' refers to an unchanging multitude of limitless quantity, it is a contradictory notion. He simply had the wrong analysis of why that is so; it has nothing to do with the property of actuality belonging only to finitude and not infinitude, but rather with infinity implying a state of both completeness and limitlessness in conjunction for the same quantity. It is infinity, taken in the literal sense, that is a contradiction and not just infinity conjoined with a separate notion of actuality.

With respect to Patterson's more contemporary take, I have the same contention—there's a contradiction involving infinity, but we would disagree as to where the contradiction in terms lies. Patterson is correct that in set theory the term 'set' typically refers to a collection that is complete. He is also correct to note that the word 'infinity' etymologically means 'not finite' or 'not limited'. However, I disagree that 'infinite set' is an oxymoron.

First, even if sets are *typically* assumed to have the property of completeness, that need not always be the case in every mathematical operation. A set per se can be either complete or incomplete; there is no a priori requirement that sets must be complete, *by definition*.

An incomplete set we may understand as a set that fails one of the completeness criteria: wholeness, entirety, finish, fullness, or totality. For instance, a set that is missing at least one element is not the entire set and therefore not the complete set. A set of ten members from which one member is missing results in an incomplete set of nine members, for example. It is true that we are also free to interpret that incomplete set of ten as also being a complete set of nine, but it remains that the notion of 'incomplete set' is not simply as such self-contradictory. And if lack of completeness does not contradict the notion of set-hood, then it is not set-hood per se that contradicts infinity. If x is a set and x has a property contradicting attribution of infinity to x, then it is something else about x to which attribution of (literal) infinity is in contradiction. So, if there is no necessary contradiction between 'infinite' and 'set' per se, then 'infinite set' is not in itself an oxymoron.

Second, to be literally infinite is not for a collection to lack a limit by virtue of being incomplete as if in continuous construction with only a running total of members as it goes—that is *figurative* infinity. To be infinite in a *literal* sense is to be genuinely limitless—to have no quantitative limit at all—but nevertheless complete as well. It is only in the figurative sense that 'infinity' refers to an *incomplete process*, which is merely to be an extensible finitude, a process that always has a running total, a variable finite quantity. What we are concerned with is the *literal* sense of the word 'infinity' and that must refer to a condition of being limitless in a particular way—namely, by being something complete, as is, while having no limit in quantity.

So, the problem is not that the terms 'infinite' and 'complete' are at odds as if infinity in the literal sense of the term implies incompleteness, nor is it that 'infinite' and 'set' are at odds as if sets must be complete while infinity is the incompleteness of an open series. Rather, the problem is with the underlying meaning of infinity in its literal sense; infinity is defined by the oxymoron of *completeness* and *limitlessness* together in the same quantitative concept, whether applied to sets or anything else. It is the completeness and limitlessness combination inherent in the concept of literal infinity that is the contradiction in terms.

Such nuances aside, the main point which distinguishes my view from Richard's, and now Patterson's, is that their shared position is to retain use of the word 'infinity' and its cognates ('infinite', 'infinitely', etc.) in the form of Aristotle's potential infinity—or what Richard called *the infinite in fieri* as opposed to *the infinite in facto esse*—whereas I believe the 'potential' form of infinity is merely a figure of speech for the *serially indefinite* and it would thus be more accurate to refer to a series that continues ceaselessly as being such, or at least as an indefinite series, rather than an 'infinite' series [1,133].

23.3 FIGURATIVE INFINITY IN THE RENAISSANCE

At the beginning of the Renaissance (1300 to the late 1600s), skepticism toward actual or literal infinity was still predominant in European intellectual circles, with some of that skepticism inspired by Richard of Middleton. Philosophers even began to argue that actual infinity might be a self-contradictory idea. Potential infinity, on the other hand, still retained broad (though not universal) support from academics during the Renaissance.

23.3.1 *Peter Aureol*

One scholar building on Richard's work was Peter Aureol (or Peter Auriol, Peter Oriole, Petrus Aureolus, Petrus Aureoli, and similar variations on his name)—the French Franciscan philosopher and theologian known as "Doctor Facundus" (c. 1280–1322) [1,134]. Like Richard, Aureol also thought of actual infinity as a self-contradictory concept, though for slightly different reasons.

Aureol thought the term 'infinite' in its literal sense implies a ceaseless *series*, which is never a complete quantity. Because multitudes and magnitudes are complete quantities, to talk of an "infinite multitude" or an "infinite magnitude" is to make use of an oxymoron—a contradiction in terms [1,135].

Once again, I agree with the conclusion that (literal) infinity is self-contradictory, but not on the reason why it is so. Aureol's analysis was not correct because the term 'infinite' does not necessarily imply a series rather than a set. In fact, in its literal sense, to say something is without limit is to say just the opposite—it is to imply a collection the members of which exist all together at once rather than serially. So, the problem with referring to something as infinite is not that the term 'infinite' denotes a series and is simply misapplied to that which has an unchanging quantity (a collection of some type such as a multitude or magnitude), but rather that 'infinite', taken literally, denotes both completeness and limitlessness for the same quantity.

Setting that issue aside, Aureol also had a different view on the figuratively infinite than did Richard of Middleton. Whereas Richard accepted figurative infinity in the form of Aristotle's 'potential infinity' reinterpreted as the infinite in fieri, Aureol instead argued that even potential infinity is impossible. According to Aureol, the impossibility of an infinite multitude or magnitude (actual infinity) entails the impossibility of potential infinity because, in order to be *potentially* infinite, a series must be capable of becoming actually infinite [1,136].

As theoretical physicist and historian of science Pierre Duhem (1861–1916) pointed out, Aureol's argument does not jibe with Aristotle's conception of 'potential infinity' because Aristotle defined 'potentiality' for infinity as different from the potentiality for finite things—a marble block is potentially a statue because it can become an actual statue but, in Aristotle's view, a series that is potentially infinite is not a series that can become actually infinite [1,137]. However, Duhem was incorrect that simply pointing this out would send Aureol's argument up in smoke [1,138]. All Aureol would have had to say in reply is that Aristotle's conception of potentiality with respect to 'potential infinity' is an empty misnomer because if there is no real potency for becoming limitless in a literal sense, then a series that is a 'potential infinity' is not genuinely infinite in any literal sense. Had he made such an argument, Aureol's critics would have been disarmed on that point.

However, Aureol did not correct Aristotle's technical conception of potentiality with respect to potential infinity, and so without a clear refutation of Aristotle on that point, Aureol's view did not become widely adopted. Aureol also missed the mark regarding potential infinity on another point: he did not object that processes could be carried out indefinitely, even if not to an actual infinity. So, the conclusion he should have come to is that Aristotle's conception of potential infinity makes 'infinity' itself into a mere figure of speech, a misnomer for the serially indefinite, which is just another form of finitude.

23.3.2 *William of Ockham*

Yet another Renaissance scholar with similar views to Richard of Middleton was theologian and philosopher William of Ockham (or Occam, 1280–1349). Ockham is now widely known for his *principle of simplicity* (or *principle of parsimony*) which later became referred to as *Ockham's Razor* because to follow the principle is to "cut away" unnecessary hypotheses—all other things being equal, the simplest hypothesis is the one most likely to be true [1,139]. Epistemology aside, Ockham offered views on several other topics, including infinity, and his views on infinity were very much like those of Richard [1,140].

As with Richard and Aristotle before him, Ockham rejected literal (actual) infinity, which was often referred to as *extensive infinity* in medieval writings. So too, Ockham embraced figurative ('potential') infinity, commonly known as *intensive infinity* in those times. Philosopher Sharon Kaye of John Carroll University explains Ockham's views [1,141]:

> An extensive infinity is an uncountable quantity of actually existing things. Mathematical Platonists conceive of the set of whole numbers as an extensive infinity. Ockham, however, deems the idea of an uncountable quantity contradictory: if the objects exist, then God can count them, and if God can count them, then they are not uncountable. An intensive infinity, on the other hand, is just a lack of limitation. As a nominalist, Ockham understands the set of whole numbers to be an intensive infinity in the sense that there

is no upward limit on how far someone can count. This does not mean that the set of whole numbers are an uncountable quantity of actually existing things.

I would simply add that so described the word 'set' is not appropriate; the lack of upper limit, in this case, means the scale of whole numbers is an incomplete series, never forming an uncountable quantity. That means the scale of whole numbers is not infinite in any literal sense but only infinite in a figurative sense. Which makes 'intensive infinity' a misnomer for serial indefiniteness. (Though, Aquinas used the term 'intensive infinity' in a qualitative sense as well—see § 25.2.5.) That caveat aside, Ockham's views on infinity can be seen as strongly in the Aristotelian tradition.

23.3.3 *Renaissance Trends for Infinity*

During the Renaissance, most philosophers believed a series called 'infinite' to be an instance of potential infinity, the (serial version of) syncategorematic infinite, the infinite in fieri, or intensive infinity. All these versions of infinity refer not to a condition in which a series has no limit at all but instead to the condition of being an *indefinite* series that remains at all times finite, even if it goes on ceaselessly. For that reason, infinity according to these various conceptions is only 'infinity' in a figurative sense; the various terms used for infinite series are, therefore, guises of figurative infinity, whether intended as such or not. As I have already pointed out, a figurative infinite is the same as a serial indefinite. And this would not be an entirely new conclusion for a philosopher to reach. The Renaissance philosopher René Descartes even preferred to use the term "indefinite" to "infinite" for use in mathematics and physics (see § 6.6) [1,142].

None of this is to say figurative infinity, even when rightfully termed indefiniteness, won the day. It is true that as the Renaissance wore on, there was increasing interest in literal infinity (see § 8.1.7) as well as qualitative infinity (see §§ 25.2.5–25.2.10). However, these types of infinity were primarily of interest because of their theological implications, whereas figurative infinity in its various guises remained dominant among mathematicians and physicists, even well into the Enlightenment.

23.4 FIGURATIVE INFINITY IN THE ENLIGHTENMENT

Despite references by Galileo and Wallis to actual infinity in mathematical measures, many mathematicians during the Age of Enlightenment (1685–1815) still preferred to keep the Aristotelian view that infinity, even in mathematical notation as ∞, refers to a figurative condition of progressions (serial indefiniteness) or at least is a misnomer for indefinitely large collections (collective indefiniteness) rather than a literal reference to a complete and limitless quantity.

23.4.1 *Leibniz*

According to Leibniz, infinity as it is known in mathematics is the syncategorematic infinite because that is the kind of 'infinite' established by mathematical generation rules for series [1,143]. However, if Leibniz is right and the syncategorematical infinite designates a series that goes on indefinitely without ever establishing a completed set, then it is no different than figurative infinity.

As for the categorematic infinite, Leibniz was skeptical. He rejected the existence of the categorematic infinite [1,144].

But with a qualification.

Some philosophers have regarded the categorematic infinite to be basically the same thing as Aristotle's actual infinity since both notions of infinity typically refer to a limitless quantity of objects grouped together all at once in a complete multitude or set—in other words, literal infinity. Leibniz, on the contrary, believed the difference between categorematic infinity and actual (literal) infinity was significant enough to reject the former and embrace the latter. While denying the categorematic infinite exists, Leibniz nevertheless said, "I am so much in favor of actual infinity that instead of admitting that nature abhors it, as is commonly said, I hold that it assumes it everywhere" [1,145]. Then again, while Leibniz claimed belief in 'actual infinity', what he meant by that term does not seem to be what everyone else since Aristotle meant by it [1,146].

In disagreement with Wallis and Galileo, Leibniz denied the existence of an actual infinity as a totality which one could express with an infinite number. For Leibniz there is no such thing as an 'infinite number'; instead, there is only an 'actual infinite' that can be compared to any finite number and judged as greater [1,147].

Leibniz proposed his own version of actual infinity in which elements can be "actually" infinite even if they do not form a totality or find expression as an infinite number. In Leibniz's view, something can be actually infinite only if it comprises a "distributive whole" *rather than* a collective whole, totality, or set [1,148].

But there are still some conceptual problems in Leibniz's view of infinity. For example, if elements *cannot* be grouped together into a set, even in principle, then there would appear to be no clear difference between being 'distributive' in that sense and simply existing in succession as a series. In which case, Leibniz's so-called "actual infinity" reduces to the syncategorematic infinite, which, given his use of the term for the so-called 'infinity' in mathematics, is no different than figurative infinity.

Then too, Leibniz may not have been entirely consistent on what he regarded as actually infinite. Some of his writings seem to indicate his 'actual infinity' is a misnomer for syncategorematic infinity, which refers either to a serial indefinite or a collective indefinite. Recall that a collective indefinite may be a collection having a quantity larger than any which can in practice be specified with a number. But that is not the same as a literally *limitless* collection. If Leibniz's actual infinity is just syncategorematic infinity in the form of a collective indefinite, then Leibniz's use of 'actual infinity' in his mathematical writings was still only 'infinity' in some figurative sense, not to be taken literally. If that is so, then it would further explain his attitude toward infinitesimals; he held that, while there is *no smallest* amount a finite line can be divided into, infinitesimals are mere "fictions of the mind" [1,149].

Aside from those nuances, Leibniz's views on infinity in mathematics and physics were not unlike those of his contemporaries. If anything, he was a bit old fashioned in his use of Peter of Spain's 'syncategorematic infinity'. And though he did not reject actual infinity outright as had many medieval and Renaissance philosophers before him, he did instead support keeping to a more metaphorical use of 'actual infinity' rather than support its literal usage.

23.4.2 *Kant*

One of the Enlightenment's most famous philosophers is Immanuel Kant (1724–1804), who also had a few things to say about infinity. Like most philosophers of his day, Kant drew on Aristotle's nomenclature to distinguish the two different senses of infinity—potential infinity and actual infinity. Although, Kant made this distinction a bit differently than did Aristotle.

Kant believed potential infinity to be a condition of incessant change in quantity. For example, he stated that a process that continues *without ever ceasing* is an infinite process [1,150]. He identified this as the 'potential infinity' of the mathematicians because such processes go "to infinity" [1,151].

Now you might think Kant meant going "to infinity" like Fletcher does: "The phrase 'going to ∞' refers to a direction, whereas 'going to 100' refers to a destination" [1,152]. However, that would not be correct. Rather, Kant believed that because we say of an infinite series or process that it goes "to infinity," the concept of potential infinity presupposes (in his own sense of) 'actual infinity', even if potential infinity does not imply an actual infinity can be achieved as a construction (or that an actually infinite whole can be completely divided or filled to completion) [1,153]. So, Kant held that to go "to infinity" is to go *toward* infinity, as if in the direction of that which is actually infinite.

However, while Kant held potential infinity presupposes actual infinity, Kant believed actual infinity to be a condition unlike Aristotle's conception of actual infinity. Whereas Aristotle held actual infinity to be the quantitative limitlessness of a multitude of objects existing together, all at once, Kant held 'actual infinity' not to be the condition of an actualized multitude at all. Rather than actual infinity being literally complete and limitless, Kant seems to have regarded 'actual infinity' to be "complete" only in the sense of constituting an irreducible whole, a unity *within* which multiplicity is found. In Kant's view, actual infinity cannot—even in principle—ever be a set comprised of members that exist together all at once in *limitless quantity*. While Kant did refer to his holistic version of infinity as actual infinity, it is thus clear he did not have in mind Aristotle's sense of actual infinity (or, in my parlance, literal infinity), which assumes a preexisting multitude of members *completely* comprising a collection.

Moreover, Kant thought of the 'actual infinite' not in the sense of a collection of limitless members (Aristotle's conception of actual infinity) but in the sense of an irreducible unity that *can* be ceaselessly divided, though never to completion, or that can be ceaselessly filled without ever becoming full [1,154].

Kant's version of actual infinity consequently relates to Aristotle's conception of 'potential' in potential infinity; for Kant, the 'potential' in potential infinity does not mean the potential for a series to *become* actually infinite, but rather the potential for the series to keep approximating the actual infinite, which can never be achieved by successive iteration of any kind [1,155]. A process or series can proceed "to infinity" in the sense of having the potential to ceaselessly progress toward the actual infinite as if to a horizon, but the process or series in question can never reach the horizon—it can never achieve the actual infinite. This is because, in Kant's opinion, actual infinity is an *ideal* state of wholeness that 'potentially' infinite processes approximate, not a *real* state of wholeness comprised of a limitless quantity of preexisting parts waiting to be uncovered [1,156].

Kant's nonstandard conception of actual infinity is certainly clever; it successfully avoids defining infinity in a logically self-contradictory way. An undivided whole is not infinite just because it can ceaselessly be divided or ceaselessly filled up without becoming full. However, there is no need to call an undivided or empty whole 'infinite' even if a process can continue to divide or fill it without ceasing. In fact, such a non-standard use of the term 'infinity' does not capture how infinity is commonly regarded with respect to mathematical use as a multiplicity rather than a unity, and so it just confuses matters.

In any case, Kant seemed to regard potential infinity as not different in kind from serial indefiniteness, but different merely by degree [1,157]:

> We may, with propriety, say of a straight line, that it may be produced to infinity. In this case the distinction between a *progressus in infinitum* and a *progressus indefinitum* is a mere piece of subtlety. For, although when we say, 'Produce a straight line,' it is more correct to say *in indefinitum* than *in infinitum*; because the former means, 'Produce it as

far as you please,' the second, 'You must not cease to produce it'; the expression *in infinitum* is, when we are speaking of the *power* to do it, perfectly correct, for we can always make it longer if we please—on to infinity...For in such a case reason does not demand absolute totality in the series...

Kant claimed the difference between serial indefiniteness and infinity (in the sense of 'potential infinity' or figurative infinity) is "a mere piece of subtlety" because serial indefiniteness means to go on as long as you please while potential infinity is to go on without ceasing at all.

Kant was only partly correct about the distinction between indefiniteness and infinity. He was right that there is a difference, at least when the term 'infinity' is used in a figurative or metaphorical fashion. But he was wrong that the two categories are distinct from one another, as if they do not overlap.

Indefiniteness means merely having no defined end or no end to define. So to say a process goes on indefinitely may imply *either* "produce as far as you please" (to an end not yet defined) *or* "you must not cease producing" (to no end ever to be defined) depending on the context in which the term is used. If you say a process *can* go on indefinitely, you imply it goes on as far as you please; if you say a process *must* go on indefinitely, then you imply it must not cease to be produced. If you simply say that a process "goes on" indefinitely, then you might be implying either one, and so you may need to clarify what you mean.

As for use of the term 'infinity', Kant was perhaps in his day correct to say a process that goes on "to infinity" is a figurative expression that implies it never ceases, but that is not necessarily different than a serial indefinite. Rather, to use a phrase like "to infinity" may be to use the term 'infinity' as a figure of speech, in which case saying a process goes to infinity simply delineates what *kind* of serial indefinite one has in mind—namely, the kind of indefinite series that never ceases, that goes on with an ever-running total, rather than the kind that goes on to an end yet to be defined and so will eventually cease at some point in time indefinitely in the future, as a collective indefinite (whether complete or incomplete).

I say Kant was "perhaps in his day correct" rather than correct more generally because at least these days some mathematicians indicate that ∞, taken as Aristotle's potential infinity with respect to functions or operations, means *either* to go on as far as you like *or* to go on without ceasing [1,158]. With respect to using infinity (∞) in this figurative sense, mathematicians do not draw a distinction between the two cases of what is really a serial indefinite.

However, we can afford to grant that "to infinity" may technically mean not to cease, even if we correct Kant that for a series or process to go on *indefinitely* is to imply the series or process goes on either as far as you please or goes on ceaselessly, whichever may be the case. So, contra Kant, indefiniteness and infinity in the figurative sense need not be wholly distinct, just as indicated in **Figure 6.6**.

I'll return to Kant again in § 24.1.1 where I expose the pitfalls of using phrases like "to infinity" when assuming a merely figurative sense of infinity.

23.5 FIGURATIVE INFINITY POST-ENLIGHTENMENT AND INTO THE VICTORIAN ERA

In § 8.1.8, I mentioned the mathematician Gauss, who in his 1831 letter to Schumacher, stated, "The infinite is only a façon de parler [figure of speech]; where one is really speaking of limits to which certain ratios come as close as one likes while others are allowed to grow without restriction" [1,159]. In other words, infinity is just figurative infinity—basically the same as Aristotle's 'potential infinity'—a metaphor for serial indefiniteness and not to be taken literally in mathematics. As pointed out by the late William C.

Waterhouse, a professor emeritus of mathematics at Pennsylvania State University, Gauss's opinion on the subject of infinity in mathematics was quite common for his day. Waterhouse noted, "Not everyone saw the point as clearly as Gauss, but it was hardly a new idea in his time. Careful students of the calculus had been saying similar things for many years, about infinity as well as about infinitesimals" [1,160].

During the Victorian Era (1837–1901) while Dedekind, Bolzano, and Cantor developed mathematical systems that were intended to portray literal infinity (for Dedekind and Bolzano, actual infinity; for Cantor, actual infinity as the transfinite), figurative infinity remained alive and well in mathematics. Victorian mathematicians such as Cauchy and Karl Weierstrass (1815–1897) made use of figurative infinity with respect to convergent series in calculus [1,161]. Like Gauss, they too held infinity to be just a figure of speech or convenient fiction. As did other Victorian mathematicians such as Cantor's arch nemesis Leopold Kronecker (1823–1891) and influential scientists such as the French physicist Jules Henri Poincaré (1854–1912), a colleague of Einstein's. [1,162] [1,163].

Despite the influence of such notable figures, however, the view that infinity is *only* figurative, or "potential," and never literal ("actual") did not prevail in the mathematics community.

23.6 FIGURATIVE INFINITY IN CONTEMPORARY THOUGHT

There is currently only a minority of mathematicians, scientists, and philosophers who are skeptical of infinity—both of its physical reality and its logical validity in mathematics. Most of these skeptics do not go as far as I do in rejecting infinity altogether. Instead, of those who are skeptical of literal infinity, the majority of them tend to support some version of figurative infinity, usually Aristotle's conception of potential infinity.

A good example was Dutch mathematician Luitzen Egbertus Jan Brouwer (1881–1966), who attempted to base all of mathematics on potential infinity [1,164]. But there are more recent advocates of this approach as well, both in and outside of academia.

An advocate outside of academia is Patterson, mentioned previously [1,165]. However, Patterson seems to take 'infinity' as a condition of being limitless while also defining limitlessness as apparently no different than the indefiniteness of a ceaselessly growing, and always finite, series. For that reason, his conception of 'infinity' seems to reduce to figurative or 'potential' infinity.

One of the most prominent contemporary advocates of potential infinity within academia has been Jan Mycielski, professor emeritus of mathematics at the University of Colorado at Boulder [1,166]. Mycielski promotes a mathematical schema he calls FIN, an axiomatic foundation for developing all mathematics applicable to natural science [1,167]. In FIN there is no actual infinity. Instead, Mycielski states that in creating FIN he was "surprised to find that potential infinity permits one to recover to some extent the efficiency of actual infinity," at least enough to conduct science [1,168].

Another recent supporter of potential infinity was the late Polish philosopher and logician Marcin Mostowski (1955–2017). Mostowski believed "the set of natural numbers used in computing technology is only potentially infinite" and that such is sufficient for mapping the real, physical world [1,169]. Though he used the term 'potential infinity', Mostowski seems not to have understood potential infinity in a strictly Aristotelean sense, which corresponds to what I call figurative infinity, a metaphorical term for a serial indefinite.

Mostowski instead regarded potential infinity as a term that denotes either a set that is so large it can be considered an approximation of the actually infinite or a series that is so large it is already indefinitely large and is in the process of becoming an ever-closer approximation to actual infinity [1,170]. Mostowski did not necessarily see potential infinity as a figurative sense of 'infinity', as I do, nor as corresponding *solely* to what I would call a 'serial indefinite'.

For Mostowski, a 'potential infinite' can be a collective indefinite. According to Mostowski, "The same thing considered as only potentially infinite is a finite collection which can be arbitrarily enlarged according to a given rule" [1,171]. Notice that he said something potentially infinite is a finite collection (such as a set) that "can be" arbitrarily enlarged, not that it "is" a *series* that is already arbitrarily large and *in the process of enlarging further*. If the potential infinite is a collection that can be (but is not necessarily becoming) arbitrarily enlarged, then that suggests it is a collective indefinite, albeit one that can also be a set in a series of indefinitely large sets.

Mostowski thus seems to include both the serially indefinite and the collectively indefinite in his conception of 'potential infinity'. The serially indefinite is the same as figurative infinity. And the collectively indefinite, when referred to as 'infinite' by Mostowski, is just another figurative use of infinity.

Other scholars making use of figurative or potential infinity include mathematician Matthias Eberl, formerly of Ludwig-Maximilians-University (LMU) in Munich, Germany. Eberl has delivered presentations on the use of potential infinity in mathematics, though he does point out that 'potential infinity' is a less precise term for what Dummett more precisely called the *indefinitely extensible* [1,172] [1,174]. The indefinitely extensible, says Eberl, has certain advantages, such as making it possible to define 'indefinitely large' but finite states [1,175].

The identification of at least one type of infinity with the indefinite brings us to the heart of the matter. As pointed out earlier, potential infinity, the (serial) syncategorematic infinite, the infinite in fieri, intensive infinity, etc. all function as guises for figurative infinity, and 'infinity' used in its figurative sense is a misnomer for indefiniteness. Eberl was certainly on the right track when he said that 'indefinite extensibility' is a better term to use than 'potential infinity' [1,176]. More on target yet would be denoting that which proceeds without predefined end with simpler adjectives such as indefinite, persistent, ceaseless, etc. Words such as these are not nearly as prone to logical problems as is the use of 'infinite'.

CHAPTER 23 IN REVIEW

❖ Figurative infinity is the condition of indefinitely changing in quantity. The figuratively infinite is always finite but ceaselessly accumulates changes to quantity.

❖ References to infinity in the figurative sense of the term are found throughout mathematics and science. Such references extend back to antiquity.

❖ Aristotle used the term 'potential infinity' instead of figurative infinity, which he contrasted with 'actual infinity' rather than literal infinity.

❖ Most philosophers post-Aristotle embraced figurative infinity in one guise or another and there are several. In addition to potential infinity there is the syncategorematic infinite, the infinite in fieri, intensive infinity, and yet others. Of them all, Aristotle's potential infinity is still the most widely used among the figurative infinities. However, 'figurative infinity' remains the more accurate term for labelling serial indefiniteness as 'infinite'.

❖ A better practice still is to reject the term 'infinite' altogether in favor of adjectives such as 'indefinite' and related words like 'persistent' and 'ceaseless'—none of which have the logical problems of infinity in its figurative sense.

24: INCONSISTENCIES IN FIGURATIVE INFINITY

When infinity (∞) is represented in mathematical formulas and calculations, it is, in operational terms, a serial indefinite. For that reason, Gauss regarded ∞ as denoting 'infinity' in only the figurative sense, a figure of speech for an ideal limit that can be indefinitely approximated or a series that continues to indefinitely grow [1,177]. However, there is a pernicious problem with *slippage* in use of the term 'infinity' and its cognates when infinity is intended to be taken figuratively. By 'slippage' I mean the term 'infinite' is often intended in its figurative sense but instead is inadvertently used in such a way as to imply a condition of being complete and limitless in quantity—an instance of literal infinity. The term 'infinite' unintentionally slips in meaning from figurative to literal. Infinity, according to its figurative sense, is thereby used inconsistently in practice, with the literal sense of infinity often erroneously implied. Because infinity in its figurative sense is not a consistently used term, prone to too much slippage, I argue there are more accurate terms that could and should be used in place of 'infinity' in its figurative sense, and in place of the very concept of infinity altogether.

24.1 INCONSISTENT USE OF COGNATES FOR INFINITY

As precise as mathematics tends to be, it nevertheless contains instances of misleading language. When the predicate 'infinite' and its cognates are only intended in a figurative sense, their use often unintentionally slips into a literal sense, giving us misleading impressions about series and quantities. Let's take a look at a few examples.

24.1.1 *The Figurative "To Infinity" Becomes the Literal "Infinitely"*

In § 23.4.2 we saw that Kant held actual infinity to be an ideal state which can only be approximated by a potentially infinite series. For Kant, a process that goes on "to infinity" is a potential infinity that proceeds ever closer toward an actual infinity [1,178]. Kant therefore uses two different meanings for the word 'infinity' and its cognates. One meaning of 'infinity' is (relative) limitlessness of process, a succession that is ceaseless, one that never completes [1,179]. The other meaning of 'infinity' refers to a "multiplicity...greater than any number" [1,180]. The former is Kant's version of potential infinity; the latter he says is "the mathematical concept of the infinite," [1,181] which is actual infinity.

The problem with this dual way of using the word 'infinity' and its cognates, is that it is prone to slippage and confusion.

For a process to be called 'infinite' in Kant's conception of potential infinity is for it to be a 'limitless' process in the sense of being a ceaseless process. But then to say the same process goes on "to infinity" implies the process is not itself infinite but rather tends toward a state called 'infinity'—a state the process itself is never in. A process can't go "to" something it's already in. It would therefore be a mistake to say a process is itself infinite—a mistake to use the term 'infinite process'—because no process is ever infinite if it proceeds *to* a state that is infinite. To avoid that implication, we could conclude that Kant regarded a ceaseless process to be one that proceeds *as if* to an actual state of infinity, a state in which the process's successive iterations *would* become a multiplicity greater than any finite number *if* it actually could. In other words, Kant's use of potential infinity and his references to processes or series as being themselves 'infinite' would have to be merely figures of speech.

Yet, Kant contradicted this when he said material bodies are in totality infinitely divisible [1,182], thereby implying it is logically possible for a division process not only to proceed figuratively "to infinity" but for there to be a literally infinite multitude. Hence, even Kant's use of infinity's cognates can sometimes slip from infinity as potential (figurative) to actual (literal), without his usually careful notice. Worse still, this use of language is not consistent with his notion of actual infinity as a more holistic state of ideal unity rather than multiplicity. He went from speaking of a potentially infinite series as a succession that proceeds "to infinity" as if to an ideal, holistic unity or state of wholeness never to be achieved, to speaking of proceeding "to infinity" as if toward a "multiplicity...greater than any number" rather than merely toward a unity or whole that is greater than any number [1,183]. And so he ends up implying once again good old-fashioned literal infinity—a complete and limitless totality.

Now it is true that he also denied a literally infinite series must exist as an empirical reality beyond our ideas of such. And it may also be objected that Kant thought the categories 'finite' and 'infinite' are merely ideas we have *about* the world—categories we erroneously use in a futile attempt to understand the world as it is in itself—while they are not really properties of the world as it is apart from our perceptions [1,184]. I readily grant that such was Kant's position, but it is also irrelevant.

At issue is the meaning he assumes for the word 'infinity' and its cognates, not the object to which he affirmed or denied their application. And that use shows slippage. My point is not to pick on Kant for his inconsistent use of infinity, but rather to show that even a careful thinker like he is prone to slippage with use of infinity's cognates because infinity is an inherently slippery notion.

24.1.2 *"Infinitely Many" from Figurative to Literal*

Sometimes when a process is said to continue for 'infinitely many' steps, saying such is meant to convey that the process continues as a figurative infinity (i.e., it continues indefinitely), but often this intended meaning is lost when the 'infinitely many' steps are subsequently spoken of in a way that implies a literally infinite number of steps instead. For example, recall from § 18.5 the discussion of dividing a line 'infinitely'. If one means such only figuratively, care must be taken not to confuse a figuratively infinite division process with a literal infinity. For example, some philosophers say that division of a line segment "is potentially infinite because there are infinitely many places where it *can be* divided" [1,185]. But as soon as one refers to infinitely many *places* of division, even if only places where divisions "can" occur, instead of infinitely many *occurrences* of division, one has just confused potential, or figurative, infinity with actual, or literal, infinity. Figurative/potential infinity is about series or processes such as successions of steps to take; literal/actual infinity is about sets or multiplicities such as places where a step can be taken. Alas, such confusion is all too common.

24.1.3 *"An Infinite Number of"*

Figurative infinity also becomes confused with literal infinity in references to an "infinite number" of something. This sometimes occurs in calculus when mathematicians take ∞ in a function as infinity in its figurative sense (e.g., Aristotle's 'potential infinity') but then refer to an "infinite number" as a given output of the function, which is a use of infinity in the literal sense of the term.

For example, an online mathematics text explains infinite sequences and series by first defining a series and then providing an example of an infinite series, at first assumed to be figuratively infinite, but then the text slips into referencing infinity in its literal sense. The text first defines a series: "A series is, informally speaking, the sum of the terms of a sequence. Finite sequences and series have defined first and last terms, whereas infinite sequences and series continue indefinitely" [1,186]. Then, after describing a function that indefinitely generates increasingly smaller terms—

$$(\tfrac{1}{2} + \tfrac{1}{4} + \tfrac{1}{8} + \cdots)$$

—the text goes on to state, "As there are an infinite number of terms, this notion is often called an infinite series" [1,187]. Notice the text changes from talk of the terms continuing "indefinitely" (without a defined end, as an incomplete series with a running total of terms) to saying that "there are an infinite number of terms," and even says such is a 'series' (which in mathematics is a sum of terms). Indefiniteness of continuation is 'infinity' in the figurative sense, while having an infinite number (or series as a sum) of terms is a reference to infinity in the literal sense. The text slips from figurative infinity to literal infinity in the same paragraph.

24.1.4 *A Slippery Concept*

Even in mathematics there is a persistent problem with use of the term 'infinity' for the functional role of ∞ in equations; references to ∞, even when intended as figurative for merely 'persistent' processes, lapses back into implying a condition of being literally complete and limitless in quantity. There seem to be two general reasons for the slippage.

First, slippage occurs because there tends to be a confusion of how the term 'infinite' is to be used with respect to the continuation of a serially indefinite process and how it is to be used with respect to the output or outcome of the same processes. For example, in mathematics a function is a combination of mathematical inputs/outputs producing relations between sets or a succession of relations between sets; when using the term 'infinite' to describe a function as executing 'infinitely', there is a tendency to then refer to the total output of the function as 'infinite'. In which case we have slipped from referring to a function as figuratively infinite in process to referring to the output of the function as a literally infinite collection. Consequently, what was supposed to be only figuratively infinite (the function in action) is inadvertently implied to be literally infinite. This happens, for instance, when the successor function, regarded as figuratively infinite, is said to produce an infinite number of numbers, a literal infinity, which thereby implies the function is not merely figuratively infinite after all but is itself literally infinite. A clear case of slippage.

Second, slippage occurs when a figuratively 'infinite' series or process is construed to be 'potentially' infinite not in the Aristotelian sense but in the Kantian sense. The series or process that is potentially infinite in Kant's sense of potentiality is thought to presuppose an actual, literal infinity [1,188]. Potential infinity in Kant's view is a latent actual infinity—the condition of a series or process that ceaselessly approximates, or at least progresses toward, actual infinity. Aristotle rejected this implication of potentiality, but Kant and Cantor embraced it. Regardless, the position that potential infinity is latent actual infinity also causes slippage to occur. Recall the slippage even in Kant's own use of infinity.

Reasons for the slippage from figurative to literal infinity (or Kantian-potential to actual infinity) aside, the fact is that such slippage is quite common, even among mathematicians. But you need not take my word for it. Here is what Cantor had to say [1,189]:

> Despite the essential difference between the concepts of the *potential* [figurative] and *actual* [literal] infinite, in that the former signifies a *changeable* finite magnitude, *growing* beyond all finite boundaries, the latter a *fixed in itself, constant* quantum, situated however beyond all finite magnitudes, it happens to be the case, unfortunately only too often, that the one is confused with the other. Thus for example, the not-seldom occurring conception of the *differentials,* as if they were *specific* infinitely small magnitudes (while they are, after all, only *changeable* auxiliary magnitudes, assumed to be as small as you please, which completely disappear from the end results of the calculations and therefore are characterized already by Leibniz as mere *fictions,* for example in Erdmann's edition, p. 436) is based on a confusion of these concepts.

The confusion of the two quantitative infinities is indeed common. The question is what to do about it.

24.2 WAYS TO AVOID SLIPPAGE

Because figurative infinity is easily and all too often confused with literal infinity, a concept with self-contradictory implications, we need a course of action to avoid such conceptual slippage. Two options come to mind. The first is to take extra care with how we speak of infinity and infinite series. The second is to simply reject the use of infinity altogether in favor of an alternative concept.

24.2.1 *First Option: Watch Your Language!*

This was the position of Wittgenstein, as elucidated by Rodych (quoting from Wittgenstein's own works) [1,190]:

> We mistakenly believe in the actual infinite, according to Wittgenstein, because...we are not careful to distinguish between the grammar of the words that we use to apply to each. When we are careful, we see that "the words 'finite' and 'infinite'...are not adjectives" which "signify a supplementary determination regarding 'class'." "'Infinite' is not a quantity," Wittgenstein states, "the word 'infinite' has a different syntax from a number word." "We mistakenly treat the word 'infinite' as if it were a number word, because in everyday speech both are given as answers to the question 'how many?'."

Wittgenstein concludes that if we just watch our language, if we are careful with our grammar, we can use the word 'infinity' and its cognates in a manner that avoids misconstruing infinity as actual infinity, and we will use the word 'infinity' properly (i.e., only in the Aristotelean sense of potential infinity).

More recently, Patterson proposed something similar. Patterson, also a critic of actual infinity and Cantor's work, proposed a "concept rescue" for infinity: "Is there any way, then, to rescue the concept of 'infinity'? Certainly. We simply have to abandon the contradictory concept of 'completed infinities'. Instead, 'infinite' *must be a statement about inherent limitations...*Infinity must strictly be understood as *shorthand*. It is never an adjective for a concrete noun." He emphasizes, "Whenever we want to use the term 'infinite', we must understand it as a concept. A statement about limitations. A never-ending process. It isn't an adjective to describe concrete objects," and states further, "What is 'infinite' is never fully realized, by its definition. What is 'actual' is fully realized, by its definition" [1,191] [1,192]. Patterson, like Wittgenstein, denies 'infinite' is an adjective for a noun, recommends that we take care to use speak of infinity in the proper way to avoid implying actual infinity, and essentially endorses the Aristotelean conception of potential infinity, or what I refer to as figurative infinity.

Contrary to Wittgenstein and Patterson, my own position is that the word 'infinite' is indeed an adjective just as every dictionary of the English language indicates and, yes, it is an adjective for the noun 'infinity'. As soon as you say something is infinite, you are using the word 'infinite' as an adjective, predicating something as having the condition known as infinity—i.e., as being an instance of infinity.

The word 'infinity' is, strictly speaking, a noun and it can be used in a literal sense or in a figurative sense. When it is used in its literal sense, it is a noun denoting a condition of being *limitless* and yet also complete in quantity; when used in its figurative sense, 'infinity' is a noun that typically refers to the condition of *indefinitely* changing in quantity.

The problem with 'infinite' is not that folks mistakenly take it to be an adjective for the noun 'infinity', because an adjective is indeed grammatically what it is when used to describe something. Rather, the problem with 'infinite' is that it is a term that is prone to slippage when it is used in the figurative sense as referring to the condition of being serially indefinite. This figurative use tends to slip into a reference of being literally infinite too easily, causing much confusion.

Although I believe Wittgenstein, Patterson, et al. are incorrect to say 'infinite' is not an adjective, that alone does not mean their strategy for avoiding slippage with use of the term is wrong. Perhaps we could avoid slipping from the figurative to literal usage of the 'infinite' simply by watching our language so as to be careful with the word and its cognates.

In support of this strategy, those taking this position have suggested construing infinity as *limitlessness, endlessness, boundlessness, immeasurability,* and so forth in the literal sense of these terms, but without associating such properties with collections that are also complete. Instead, they want 'limitlessness', 'endlessness', etc. in their literal senses to apply only to incomplete processes rather than to complete collections. That would reconstrue 'infinity' and its cognates as references to indefinites.

While that strategy to save infinity would help avoid self-contradiction, I am nevertheless skeptical that it would be successful. And there is more than one reason to be skeptical.

First, to refer to a serial indefinite as a series that continues limitlessly, endlessly, boundlessly, etc. is not to use the terms 'limitlessly', 'endlessly', 'boundlessly', etc. in their literal senses, as it seems those sharing Wittgenstein's position assume. Instead, 'limitless', 'endless', 'boundless', and related terms also become mere metaphors, or even hyperbole, for the indefiniteness of a linear, open series or process. Such terms as 'limitless', 'endless', and 'boundless' when used to express a serial indefinite indicate the series to have "no limit," but not in a literal sense of having no limit at all. It is true that an indefinite series or process has no limit relative to a particular kind and a particular situation, but it is not absolutely without limit, for it always has a limit—it always has an end or bound, just one that changes over time. It is one thing to say a circle is endless or boundless with respect to its finite geometry for that is literally true; it is quite another to call a linear, open series 'endless' or 'boundless', not to mention 'limitless', without qualification for that would be purely metaphorical. To refer to a serial indefinite as 'infinite' is still to use the term 'infinite' as a figure of speech.

Moreover, use of words like 'limitless', 'endless', 'boundless', and 'infinite' as figures of speech too often function as *misnomers* because they do not illuminate what they refer to—open series and processes with running totals of instances. Instead, such terms when used as a synonym for 'indefinite' are prone to mislead one into confusing the indefinite series with a literally infinite collection. For example, terms like 'limitless' or 'endless' when used for a serial indefinite may inadvertently suggest ceaselessly going through a preexisting collection that is complete and limitless. Like ever filling an empty muffin tin (see **Figure 3.3**) that has no quantitative limit to its cups and which themselves do not multiply. Or like travelling a stretch of road that is already complete and limitless, waiting to be travelled. To call a serial indefinite 'limitless', 'endless', 'boundless', or 'infinite' is thus to use such terms as figures of speech but, even as such, they too often convey a misleading picture.

Which brings me to the second point: the word 'infinity' and its cognates are much more pernicious than other misuses of language we find in mathematics and much harder to correct than other terms and phrases that can be misleading. Recall from §§ 2.3.14–18 that how we speak about variables can sometimes be misleading. When we refer to the value *of* a variable, for example, we should really be referring to the value *for* a variable since the variable has no value until one is assigned. Referring to the value "of" a variable is a misleading use of language in mathematics. It is, however, rather a minor case of misleading language, and it is relatively easy to correct any misunderstandings resulting from using "of" instead of "for" with respect to variables. Infinity, on the other hand, seems to be a special animal; it is much more difficult to prescribe a more proper use of the term that avoids misleading implications.

Part of this difficulty has to do with how infinity has been construed because of Aristotle's influence. If we assume Aristotle's distinction between actual infinity and potential infinity, then to reject 'actual infinity' is to reject literal infinity—use of the term 'infinity' and its cognates in their literal sense—in favor of retaining *only* a potential infinity as a figurative sense of infinity. But to prescribe use of infinity as *only* a figure of speech, a 'façon de parler', is to prescribe that we quit using infinity with respect to collections of things that exist *at a time*—such as the set of all points in space, particles of matter, stars in the Universe, or even universes—and instead use infinity only with respect to serial indefinites which exist *over time*. That is, the practice of using 'infinity' and its cognates in the figurative sense alone would require not only a shift from using the term 'infinite' from literal to purely figurative, but also a shift from the customary practice of using 'infinite' with respect to all kinds of collections to use of the term for only to one kind of thing—series or processes. Confining 'infinity', 'infinite', and 'infinitely' only to processes would only be successful in technical contexts if at all. It is highly dubious that the practice of using 'infinity' and its cognates only for descriptions of processes and not for collections will ever catch on.

Of course, just because something is difficult does not mean it shouldn't be attempted. But recommending that we all cease to use the word 'infinity' and its cognates in the literal sense and instead use them in the purely figurative sense seems unlikely to succeed. First, because we still need a term to describe collections too large to count in practice, and second because there is just too much cultural baggage with the concept of infinity to overhaul it.

Instead, there seems to me a much better strategy for avoiding inconsistent use of the concept of infinity, for reducing the slippage of infinity from figurative to literal. That strategy is to first recognize that infinity as a literal term does not apply to reality, reject literal infinity as misconceived, and drop figurative 'infinity' as a misleading misnomer for serial indefiniteness. Next, we need to adopt a less misleading alternative to infinity that lacks all the historical and cultural baggage. From there, philosophers would have to prescribe the alternative for use in mathematics. If the concept catches fire in the mathematics community, it will then become part of the common parlance in the culture.

24.2.2 *Second Option: Replace the Concept of Infinity with an Alternative*

From the preceding considerations, the course of action I would recommend for addressing the logical inconsistencies that have plagued infinity is simply to reject the concept of infinity altogether as erroneous. Rejecting infinity entails avoiding use of the noun 'infinity', the adjective 'infinite', and the adverb 'infinitely' for use in mathematics, science, cosmology, and philosophy (insofar as such terms are not needed for historical commentary or context). Rejecting infinity therefore entails ceasing its use as a concept for descriptions of real-world collections and series; it also entails ceasing use of its corresponding mathematical symbols (such as ∞, $\aleph$, and ω) to ensure mathematical expressions are not mistaken as denoting infinity.

In place of infinity, a new concept is needed. The concept that replaces infinity should be one that is clearer and more accurate both for describing (1) collections comprised of members so numerous they are beyond what we will ever be able to quantify in practice and (2) series that are both too great to quantify in practice and those that continue to grow without predefined end. The alternative concept, and the term we are looking for, is *indefiniteness*.

24.3 WHENCE INDEFINITENESS?

Kant recognized that most philosophers in his day preferred indefiniteness to infinity [1,193]:

> Mathematicians speak solely of a *progressus in infinitum*. But those who study concepts (philosophers) want, in place of this, to make the expression *progressus in indefinitum* the only valid one.

So why didn't indefiniteness replace infinity back in the 1800s? There may be at least three reasons.

First, because of the influence of philosophers such as Kant. Kant dismissed the distinction between infinity and indefiniteness in most cases as "an empty subtlety" and he thought it was just as correct to say something goes on infinitely as to say it goes on indefinitely [1,194]. If Kant's influence left the impression of a dead issue, philosophers may have moved on, and mathematicians never incorporated the distinction into their discipline.

Since I don't agree with Kant that the difference is too subtle to be concerned about, I must contend that it is not only more correct to say a process goes on indefinitely rather than "infinitely," it is better to just drop all talk of going on "infinitely" or "to infinity" in the figurative sense when going on *indefinitely* is what is really meant. For the sake of clarity and consistency, the term 'indefinite' should be used over infinity for that which has no defined end but remains at all times limited. With indefiniteness, there's no more need for figurative infinity, which is a misnomer for the serially indefinite. And if we need to refer to something as being without a particular limit, such as the closed curve of a circle, then we can just identify what relative limit is lacking, which does not in itself imply infinity. That would certainly seem to be a superior course of action than trying to rescue infinity by keeping it only for its figurative usage.

Be that as it may, the influence of Kant and like thinkers won out and few philosophers wanted to pursue leaving infinity entirely to the dust bin of history. So, indefiniteness was never promoted as a candidate to replace infinity in mathematics (a missed opportunity in my opinion).

A second reason indefiniteness did not catch on is related to the "subtlety" of distinction Kant mentioned. Since many mathematicians in Kant's time were already accustomed to using 'infinite' as a misnomer or a façon de parler for indefinite series, they saw no need to replace infinity with indefiniteness. When 'infinity' is used figuratively, like indefiniteness it refers to quantities too large to compute or values greater than any quantity assignable in practice. So, mathematicians saw no reason to treat indefiniteness as distinct from infinity.

Nevertheless, I believe they were mistaken about that. For one thing, indefiniteness is broader than figurative infinity. Indefiniteness includes not just the *serial indefinite* (figuratively infinite) but also the *collective indefinite*. There are now philosophers and mathematicians who are making use of this distinction between the indefinite and the infinite—whether literal or figurative. One of the most notable proponents of the indefinite is Lavine, who created a finite mathematics of the collective indefinite as an alternative to transfinite set theory [1,195]. The existence of alternative mathematics of the indefinite is enough to show that indefiniteness is distinct enough from infinity that it need not be taken as a mere synonym for figurative infinity, and indefiniteness can even be useful for mathematical theory more generally. I admit, though, that none of that theorizing was in place back in Kant's day and so that is one more reason the indefinite did not catch on as its own concept until recently.

Third and lastly, a reason as to why indefiniteness did not heretofore replace, or at least rival, infinity for use in mathematics is that mathematicians had always been more inclined to make infinity precise than incorporate indefiniteness into their schemas. Mathematics was the discipline of the definite; the indefinite was anathema. The thinking seemed to be that it is better to make infinity more precise (the project of Bolzano and Cantor) than let mathematics become even more indefinite.

But that attitude is changing in certain respects. Witness over the last century the rise of statistics, incompleteness theorems, fuzzy logic, chaos theory, mathematical 'vagueness', and even 'uncertainty' in quantum physics. The time seems promising for indefiniteness to bloom as a replacement for the antiquated concept of infinity. Whether it comes to fruit is another question.

24.4 FROM INFINITY TO INDEFINITENESS

Because infinity, as a figure of speech, is a misnomer for indefiniteness prone to slippage, I recommend avoiding use of the word 'infinity' in its figurative sense in favor of using the term 'indefiniteness' or its various cognates ('indefinite', 'indefinitely', etc.) or related terms (immense, minuscule, ephemeral, protracted, etc.). Such are far more accurate than figurative references to infinity and they have the additional advantage of avoiding implications that are misleading.

CHAPTER 24 IN REVIEW

- ❖ Figurative infinity is too often used in such a manner as to unintentionally imply the literal sense of infinity—cases of 'slippage' in terminology.
- ❖ For instance, saying something goes "to infinity" or that it proceeds "infinitely" may be intended as a figure of speech for serial indefiniteness, but often ends up implying literal infinity. The same is the case when we refer to "infinitely many" or an "infinite number" of something.
- ❖ Figurative infinity is perniciously prone to slippage. There are various ways to avoid such slippage, but the best way is to reject talk of infinity altogether and instead refer to that which goes on indefinitely simply as such or, alternatively, use one of the adjectives for serial indefiniteness like 'persistent' and 'ceaseless'. To take this course would avoid the slippage problem without losing any pertinent information.

PART IV:
DIVINE INFINITY

25: AN ACCOUNT OF DIVINE INFINITY

Infinity means various things to different theologians and philosophers of religion. However, despite the multiple meanings infinity may have in these fields, we can make some generalizations. For one thing, in a theological context the meaning of infinity and its cognates depends on *how* such words are used. Theologians sometimes use the word 'infinity' quite informally and other times much more formally.

You will recall a distinction I made at the beginning of Chapter 7 about language. A natural/formal language distinction was drawn and contrasted to a formal/informal language distinction. It is now time to shift from the former distinctions to the latter distinctions.

The 'formal language' that is distinguished from 'informal language' regards the *formality* (observance of proper rules and customs) with which we use words in writing and speech. The formality of a word's use, or lack thereof, determines how technical the meaning of that word can be or how colloquially the word can be used. The distinction between formal and informal language in this context has relevance for use of the word 'infinity' and its cognates in the context of theology.

When used informally in a theological context, the word 'infinity' often works as a figure of speech, but it does not have the same meaning as what I have heretofore referred to as 'figurative infinity', which is one of the quantitative versions of infinity. Instead, infinity used as a non-quantitative notion is sometimes applied informally to describe properties or relations for which concerns about limits are not at all obvious, as when infinity is used to predicate the existence of something as having 'infinite being' or the purity of something as having 'infinite purity'. Typically, that "something" is God, and such informal usage of infinity for the deity makes infinity into a term of metaphysical poetry about the divine.

In contrast, there is the formal use of infinity in a theological context. Generally speaking, when infinity is used more formally in theological writings and speech, infinity also refers to a qualitative, rather than a purely quantitative, property but is more literal in meaning. The specifics as to the nature of a qualitative property denoted 'infinite' depends on the particular views of the theology in question, but all the formal uses of infinity assume it refers to ineffable divine features or attributes of one kind or another.

I will start by making some distinctions between the informal uses and formal uses of infinity in theology. After further elaborating on the difference between the informal and formal uses of infinity, I will then draw yet further distinctions amongst the formal uses of infinity according to the categories of *divine infinity* overviewed in §§ 1.4–5 (see **Figure 25.0**). Next, I will provide a brief account of the development of divine infinity as it is conceived in the formal terms of theological thought over the centuries.

25.1 THEOLOGICAL USE OF INFINITY: INFORMAL AND FORMAL

Theology is not a science, even though some might wish it to be so. However, theology can be a systematic discipline that aims for clarity in its description of the divine. As such, theology makes use of specialized words and terms for describing the divine. One of those specialized words is 'infinity' (or its cognates) as the word is used in the formal language of philosophers. (Again, by 'formal language' I mean natural language used with grammatical formality of prose, though some theologians do use 'formal language' in the other sense of the term to draw logical proofs about theological concepts. We will not worry about that kind of formal language; our focus in this chapter will be on the formal *grammatical* use of specialized words in natural language.) So theologians, like philosophers, seek to make specialized words such as infinity as clear and precise in meaning as possible for their descriptions of divine nature.

We find instances of infinity used formally in the works of historical theologians and philosophers of religion, such as when they draw technical distinctions between various qualitative types of infinity in contrast to infinity's quantitative meanings (as shown in **Figure 25.0**).

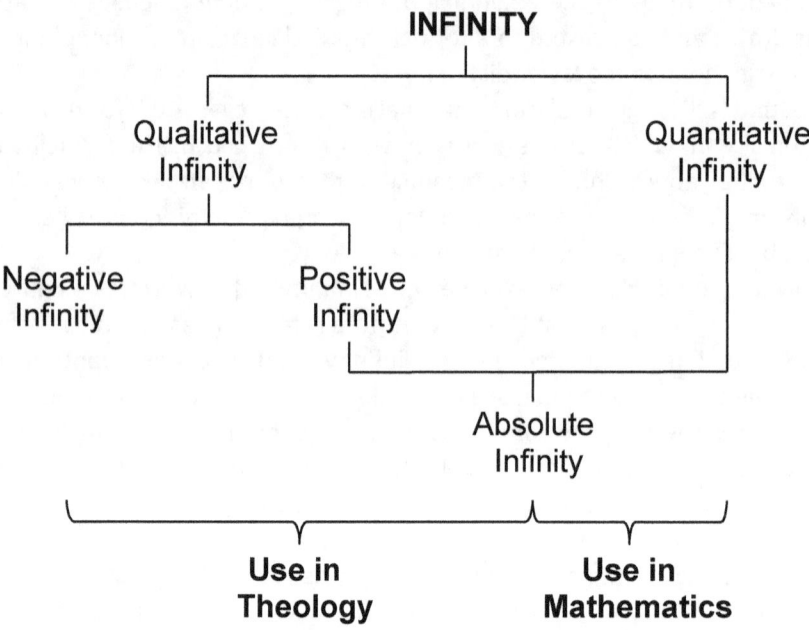

Figure 25.0: Versions of infinity in the formal language of theology compared and contrasted with infinity as a quantitative concept in mathematics. Absolute infinity, a hybrid of quantitative infinity (more precisely, literal infinity) and positive infinity, has some reference in Cantorian set theory and transfinite mathematics but is primarily a theological concept.

But not all theologies are logically rigorous and precise with terminology. Theology is often expressed with metaphor and poetic language. Unfortunately, this can make for inconsistent use of language in theology which can cause confusion, especially when slippery terms like infinity come into play.

To have a good understanding of infinity in the context of theology, we need to first clarify what it means for a divinity such as God to be infinite according to formal and informal ways of speaking.

25.1.1 *Informal Language for Infinity*

You have heard it said, "God is infinite," but what that means is rarely made clear. Fortunately, philosopher-theologians Benedikt Paul Göcke and Christian Tapp offer three possible interpretations of the expression [1,196]:

1. That God is infinite is just an abbreviated way of referring to God's features.
2. That God is infinite means God has a unique feature referred to as "infinity" in addition to God's other features.
3. That God is infinite means at least one of God's divine attributes is itself infinite.

We can consider each of these possible interpretations as an option for a theology concerning God's infinity.

Craig takes the first option. He suggests that to say God is infinite is *neither* to say a particular attribute(s) of God is infinite *nor* to ascribe an extra feature to God called infinity. Rather, that God is infinite means God possesses what Craig calls "superlative attributes" such as "moral perfection, omnipotence, omniscience, omnipresence, eternity, necessity, aseity, and so on and so forth" [1,197]. Craig explains that infinity in this context is simply "a collective term for all of these superlative attributes of God" [1,198]. So to say God is infinite is just a way of saying God's features are superlative attributes.

Moreover, Craig's exposition indicates that to take Göcke and Tapp's first option for understanding theological references to 'infinity' is to engage in informal language for speaking about God's nature. Infinity becomes an informal term used merely to indicate that God has the qualitatively greatest forms of certain attributes.

We find other examples of the first option for interpreting God's infinity provided by academics in fields outside theology. For example, professor of astronomy and astrophysics Marco Bersanelli at the University of Milan, Italy writes that the infinity of the divine is "the object of human longing for what is ultimately true, beautiful, just..." [1,199]. The infinity that the human heart longs for, says Bersanelli, is that which alone can provide fulfillment; infinity, unlike anything else, provides "ultimate meaning" [1,200]. So far, that description of infinity is sounding semantically formal since the term 'infinity' is given a specific meaning. But then Bersanelli begins to change his tone to a less formal way of talking about infinity. He goes on to identify infinity as "the Infinite" (i.e., God), reminiscent of Anaximander's use of "the Apeiron" for the arche [1,201]. In so doing, infinity becomes a term for the superlative nature of God as something supremely valuable, just as Craig suspected, which justifies Bersanelli's use of "the Infinite" as a name for God.

Moreover, we find in Bersanelli's writing another way infinity can be used in an informal manner. The same writer or speaker may use 'infinity' or 'infinite' in more than one way in a theological or philosophical context. In this example, Bersanelli goes on to use the adjective 'infinite' to qualify specific properties as when he writes of "the infinite gap between being and nothingness" and "the infinite faithfulness and eternity of God" [1,202]. Here Bersanelli mixes different types of infinity. He goes from using the word 'infinity' to denote God's superlative nature in general (Göcke and Tapp's first option) along with his use of 'the Infinite' as a name for God to then using infinity as a synonym for properties such as *immensity* or *inexhaustibility* when predicating a property like distance or faithfulness. This mixed usage of the term 'infinity' and its cognates shows another kind of informal usage of terms in relation to the divine—an informality that allows the writer or speaker to move from one way of using the word 'infinity' and its cognates to another, sometimes obscuring the meaning of the term.

The vagueness involved with informally using infinity more than one way may not end there. Bersanelli then adopts (or at least *seems* to) yet another use of 'infinity', making God's infinity a feature of its own—Göcke and Tapp's second option. Bersanelli refers to "God's transcendent and yet caring infinity," stating that it takes on various manifestations such as power and forgiveness [1,203]. However, unless Bersanelli means to anthropomorphize infinity as something that cares or provides forgiveness, we may take him to be using natural language for infinity in an informal manner; in other words, he may simply be writing metaphorically of God's superlative nature as a powerful but forgiving being.

All of these mixed uses of infinity with regard to describing God or features of God are good examples of *informal* use of infinity in a theological context, in contrast to the more technically *formal* ways of discussing infinity also found in the academic literature.

25.1.2 *Formal Language for Infinity: the Divine Infinities*

The more formal way of describing divine infinity we find with Göcke and Tapp's second and third options for understanding what it is for God to be infinite.

Historically, theologians have thought of God's infinity as being either a feature of its own (Göcke and Tapp's second option) or as a distinct property of God's superlative attributes (Göcke and Tapp's third option) such as omnipotence as infinite power, omniscience as infinite knowledge, omnipresence as infinite presence, etc. To take Göcke and Tapp's second option is to conceive of divine infinity as 'absolute infinity'—an attribute of its own. To take Göcke and Tapp's third option is to conceive of divine infinity as a 'qualitative infinity'—a feature of God's superlative attributes.

Theologians and philosophers of religion taking either the second or third option have tended to use more formal language in describing divine infinity than would be found in the poetry of homily and transcendentalist essay. As shown in **Figure 25.0**, we can simplify their formal, theological approach by dividing the concept of divine infinity into the following categories:

- qualitative infinity (positive infinity and negative infinity)
- absolute infinity

(An overview of these versions of divine infinity was provided in §§ 1.4–1.5; further elaboration is provided in the sections below.)

From classical antiquity to today, divine infinity has been almost exclusively regarded as a qualitative infinity (either negative or positive flavor), but there has been expressed a few alternative ways of thinking about divine infinity, 'absolute infinity' being one of them. To get further clarification on the similarities and differences between these main versions of divine infinity, we will next take a brief look at each and then review how each has been championed by various proponents over history.

25.1.3 *Divine Infinity as Qualitative Infinity—Negative and Positive*

Recall from § 1.4 that negative infinity is the condition in which a quality is unlimited in such a way as to be categorically indistinguishable from other qualities. Distinctions between attributes such as wisdom, beauty, power, etc. break down when they become 'infinite' in the qualitatively negative sense. Infinite beauty is indistinguishable from infinite wisdom, infinite wisdom indistinguishable from infinite power, and so forth. The result is that infinite wisdom, infinite beauty, infinite power, etc. become mystical attributes that can only be spoken of in metaphors and similes [1,204]. There are even versions of negative infinity in which God's attributes can be in logical contradiction with one another while still being claimed by the theologian to hold in a metaphysical unity they refer to as "divine simplicity."

Also discussed back in § 1.4 is positive infinity. In contrast to negative infinity which breaks down distinctions between unlimited qualities, positive infinity is the condition in which distinguishable qualities or features are unlimited. The given features that are positively infinite are always recognizable for what they are, but their seeming lack of qualitative limits is what makes them incomparable to finite instances of the same features with their known limitations. Thus infinite wisdom is still recognizable as wisdom even though it is of incomparable quality to the wisdom of mortals, infinite power is still recognizable as power even though it is also of incomparable quality to finite power, and so on. That is the idea behind qualitative infinity in the positive sense of the term [1,205].

Both forms of qualitative infinity—negative and positive—are not always used separately from a quantitative sense of infinity. In certain theologies, God's superlative attributes are spoken of as if they have quantitatively infinite implications. For example, one may take God's infinite knowledge as implying that God knows *infinitely many* distinct, true statements [1,206]. As further examples, one might take God's infinite presence as implying God must be at *infinitely many* places while God's infinite power means God can do *infinitely many* things at once. All these examples of God's attributes are examples of positive infinity. However, they can also be framed in terms of negative infinity. For example, if God's attributes are negatively infinite, then God's power and presence are indistinguishable in their infinitude. In which case, God can be infinitely many places because God is infinitely powerful, and God can do infinitely many things because God is infinitely present; omnipotence and omnipresence (and all of God's other 'omni' attributes) become equivalent if they are negatively infinite.

We thus have multiple examples showing that a qualitative infinity, whether positive or negative, may have quantitatively infinite implications. Not all theologies conceive the qualitative infinities of God in this way, of course. The conception of divine infinity varies according to the theology in question, which in turn determines whether divine infinity is spoken of only in qualitative terms or in quantitative terms as well.

25.1.4 *Divine Infinity as Absolute Infinity*

We now circle back around to Göcke and Tapp's second option for interpreting God's infinity—that God's infinity is a feature of its own apart from God's other features or attributes—for this too has a relation to quantitative infinity. There is a form of divine infinity that is a hybrid of both quantitative infinity and qualitative infinity (positive infinity in particular). That hybrid form is absolute infinity.

As explicated in § 1.5, absolute infinity is the condition of having unlimited quality due to properties with limitless quantity. Absolute infinity is the version of infinity that integrates literal infinity and positive infinity into a single concept of divine infinity. It is the idea that a literally infinite *quantity* of something has a positive, unlimited qualitative property of its own.

This conception of absolute infinity is applied to the divine. God has a complete and limitless quantity (a literal infinity) of superlative attributes—moral perfection, omnipotence, omniscience, omnipresence, eternity, necessity, aseity, etc.—referred to collectively as God's 'perfections'. Moreover, infinitely many of those perfections are each themselves literally infinite by degree. For example, God is omniscient because God knows infinitely many things, God is omnipotent because God can do infinitely many things, etc. And the infinitude of God does not stop there. Those perfections, by virtue of their collective infinity, constitute as a whole an instance of a qualitative infinity all its own. That is, absolute infinity is a qualitative infinity emerging from the quantitatively infinite collection of God's literally infinite perfections. Absolute infinity is the mystical quality of being "all possible perfections"—a unique feature of the divine [1,207].

Absolute infinity is thus an instance of Göcke and Tapp's second option for divine infinitude—God has a unique feature referred to as "infinity."

25.1.5 *Qualitative and Absolute Infinity over History*

As we'll see, both Göcke and Tapp's second and third options for conceiving of divine infinity have had their proponents. Unfortunately, I will not be able to cover all of them. I will have to leave out some prominent voices since to include them all would take a book in itself. However, those I leave out do not differ greatly from the ones I cover. So, despite leaving some gaps in the record, you will be able to see that divine infinity repeatedly appears as a qualitative (either negative or positive) concept, with absolute infinity making a more recent appearance in the history of theology.

25.2 QUALITATIVE INFINITY FROM ANCIENT TO MODERN TIMES

As discussed in § 8.1.1, the ancient Greek concept of apeiron was at first a more qualitative notion but then in the works of early philosophers such as Anaximander became applied as a quantitative concept—the first known references to infinity. As widespread as the quantitative interpretation of infinity became, it never completely replaced the qualitative interpretation. That qualitative interpretation of infinity became prominent in theology through the centuries since, and it survives in theology to this day.

25.2.1 *Philo of Alexandria*

Some scholars argue the first attribution of infinity to God can be found in the works of Philo of Alexandria (20 BCE – 50 CE), also known as Philo Judaeus. He was a Hellenistic Jewish philosopher who lived in Alexandria, a city in the Roman province of ancient Egypt.

Philo is known as the originator of *negative theology*—what is also called the *via negativa* approach or *apophatic way*—to understand God [1,208]. The idea of negative theology is that one can only understand God in negative terms: by what God is not rather than by what God is. "God is immortal" would be an example of a statement about God in negative theology since immortality is the denial of mortality.

Negative theology is of course opposed to *positive theology*—what is also called the *via positiva* approach or *cataphatic way* to understand God [1,209]. The idea of positive theology is that it is possible to make true affirmations about God; that is, to describe God by what God is rather than by what God is not. "God is good" would be an example of a statement about God in a positive theology.

Though Philo originated negative theology as a general approach for describing God's attributes, he did not limit himself to speaking about God solely in negative terms. Philo did indeed make use of positive theology. For instance, Philo refers to God the Creator, which is an affirmation rather than a denial about what God is [1,210]. Even so, Philo is renowned for his emphasis on negative theology.

Divine infinity plays a part in both negative and positive theology. To say God is infinite is to deny that God is finite, it is to say God lacks finitude; so, saying God is infinite is generally considered a statement from via negativa. However, to say God has attributes, such as power, is to make a positive statement about God—an expression of via positiva. This complicates matters, for the infinity of God applies to God's positive attributes. For example, saying God is infinitely powerful tells us something both positive about God (that God has power) as well as negative (but not limited power). It would seem then that divine infinity is not a purely negative attribute. So to predicate God as "infinite" with respect to individual attributes belongs to both positive and negative theology.

Despite Philo's emphasis on negative theology and that infinity is usually taken as a denial of finitude, we find no clear indication that Philo thought of God's attributes as infinite, not even in a negative sense. He did say that God is "uncircumscribed," which is suggestive of the kind of "boundlessness" associated with quantitative infinity, but Philo never explicitly said God is infinite, and Philo's writings require strained interpretation to read divine infinity into his theology [1,211].

Nevertheless, Philo's via negativa was influential—even more so on early Christian theology than on Jewish theology. Perhaps due to that influence, early Christians began to interpret God's attributes as a negative infinity.

25.2.2 *Clement of Alexandria*

One of the earliest fathers of the Catholic Church was Titus Flavius Clemens, or Clement of Alexandria (150–215 CE), not to be confused with the earlier Roman consul also named Clement (50–95 CE). Clement of Alexandria—or just Clement for short—noticed that everything made of parts depends on parts preexisting the whole, which ultimately decays, losing the parts it came from. But God is the Creator and so not something created. Therefore, Clement concluded, God must not be made of parts and that is why God is eternal. Since God has no parts, then God must be the ultimately *simple* being, having a single unitary essence unable to be divided into parts—God is an *indivisible unity*, lacking all form [1,212].

Since he believed God is an irreducibly simple, indivisible unity, Clement proposed God's essence is a state of 'oneness'. Like perhaps most folks at the time, Clement thought of 1 as a number but not as a 'quantity', for quantities were thought of as *more than one*. Since God has no multiplicity or plurality of parts, God has no quantity. Therefore, God is one but not a quantity. Clement even referred to God as "the One" [1,213].

However, like Philo, Clement believed God is ultimately beyond description. So, Clement regarded even the oneness of God as only an approximate description of God's mystical unity and simplicity: "God, in his simplicity, transcends the realm of numbers, which he created" [1,214].

But now a problem appears: if God is simple, then how can God have multiple attributes like knowledge, presence, power, benevolence, etc.? All those things are said to characterize God and so could be taken as "composing" the nature of God. In answer to this, Clement had to propose that such attributes are not what they seem. As philosophers Jeff Steele and Thomas Williams elucidate [1,215],

> "So what do we mean when we say things such as 'God is good' and 'God is powerful'? These things seem like distinct things: God's power is a matter of what God can do—what God can actualize...But if God is simple these attributes can't be distinct things in God, the way that they are in us. Perhaps, then, when we distinguish various divine attributes, it is our minds that make the distinction. Let's call this the "conceptualize solution": the distinction is on our part, not on God's part. The distinction between God's various attributes is mind-dependent: we distinguish these various attributes in our mind, but they are not distinct things in God.

According to Steele and Williams, philosophers such as Clement believed that "God lacks all metaphysical complexity or composition. God does not have attributes of which he is composed. God is identical with his attributes. God does not have goodness, he *is* goodness. God does not have power, he *is* power" [1,216]. Philosopher of religion William F. Vallicella elucidates further [1,217]:

> God is thus in some sense *identical* to each of his attributes, which implies that each attribute is identical to every other one. God is omniscient, then, not in virtue of instantiating or exemplifying omniscience—which would imply a real distinction between God and the property of omniscience—but by *being* omniscience. And the same holds for each of the divine omni-attributes: God *is* what he *has* as Augustine puts it in *The City of God*, XI, 10.

Vallicella states that this is called the *doctrine of divine simplicity* [1,218], which I touched on in § 1.4.1 in the overview of negative infinity.

Clement associated the One's divine simplicity—God's state of indivisible unity—with the concept of infinity; indeed, he may have been the first to genuinely propose God, as the One, is infinite [1,219]. Clement stated, "For the One is indivisible; wherefore also it is infinite, not considered with reference to inscrutability, but with reference to its being without dimensions, and not having a limit" [1,220].

It's not that Clement attributed a *quantitative* infinity to God's essence such that the divinely simple God, as the One, is infinite in the sense of $\infty = 1$. That is the wrong understanding of how Clement was thinking about God's infinitude. In Clement's view, saying God is "infinite," or without limit, with respect to God's essence is not to attribute a quantitative infinity to God at all. The limitlessness which Clement attributes to God is a *qualitative* limitlessness rather than a quantitative limitlessness. Clement conceived God's infinity to be the quality of God's indivisibility or unity rather than a quantity of those attributes or a measure of their degree.

That God can be "infinite" (without limit) with respect to a quality like indivisibility, rather than with respect to a quantity, makes Clement's idea of God's infinity an instance of attributing a *qualitative infinity* to God—God is qualitatively "infinite" by virtue of God's indivisibility rather than by some quantitative measure.

But that raises a question: Is Clement's qualitative infinity a case of positive infinity or negative infinity? This is where the doctrine of divine simplicity makes theology, ironically, quite complicated.

On the one hand, divine simplicity entails that God's 'essence' is a negative attribute—a *lack* of complexity—which would apply to God's qualitative infinity [1,221]. That is, because God is an indivisible unity, the infinitude of each of God's attributes are all *indistinct from one another*—there is but a single attribute that is identical to God and God just *is* that attribute. If God appears to *have* attributes—*multiple* attributes—then that's only because we misinterpret the activity of God as to be the expression of various attributes when they are in fact only one kind of act. So too, if God appears to have multiple infinite attributes, that is only our misapprehension of what is really a negative infinity—a single infinite attribute in which all our misapprehended positive infinities lose their distinction.

Clement's concept of divine simplicity therefore entails that all of God's multiple attributes are, in a sense, illusory distinctions we make for what is in just a single divine attribute that is itself identical to God as such. Since in that view all of God's attributes lose distinction with one another, that would make Clement's idea of divine infinity, as the essence of what God is, a negative infinity.

Clement recognized that there are a variety of attributes—power, presence, knowledge, goodness, etc.—all attributes *predicated* of God. God is said to be all-powerful, all-present, all-knowing, etc. and each of these attributes could be taken as qualitatively infinite. However, Clement sees these positive infinities as merely different expressions of what is a single, divine infinity: "For predicates are expressed either from what belongs to things themselves, or from their mutual relation. But none of these are admissible in reference to God" [1,222]. That is, we cannot predicate of God too literally. If we say God is infinite, we must mean it only allegorically or by analogy [1,223]. In Clement's view, the positive infinities of God's various attributes should not be taken literally. It would be more accurate to say God's essence is negative infinity and God's acts only make God *appear* to have positively infinite attributes.

25.2.3 *Plotinus*

Other philosophers and theologians of antiquity adopted similar views on God as an infinite being. The ancient philosopher Plotinus (205–270 CE), like Clement, regarded God in nonanthropomorphic terms as "the One" [1,224]. Though Plotinus described the One in mystical terms, stating that the One is beyond our full understanding, Plotinus nevertheless does describe some things about the One. Most importantly, he claimed in his work *The Six Enneads* that the One is infinite, but not in the sense of number or magnitude [1,225]:

> It is infinite also by right of being a pure unity with nothing towards which to direct any partial content. Absolutely One, it has never known measure and stands outside of number, and so is under no limit either in regard to any extern or within itself; for any such determination would bring something of the dual into it. And having no constituent parts it accepts no pattern, no forms, no shape.

So, infinity is a state of indivisible unity or 'oneness'.

However, Plotinus also said the infinitude of the One is a "Magnitude-Absolute" [1,226] that characterizes the power of the One [1,227]. To say the One is infinitely powerful (powerful in magnitude) and that the infinity of the One is its indivisible unity implies the One is just limitless magnitude of power itself. So far, this seems to say that there is but one divine infinity and that it is limitless power.

But then Plotinus says the One also has infinite presence [1,228]:

> Again, if we think of the divine nature as infinite—and certainly it is confined by no bounds—this must mean that it nowhere fails; its presence must reach to everything; at the point to which it does not reach, there it has failed; something exists in which it is not.

Plotinus describes that infinite presence by reference to space in the quantitatively infinite sense, suggesting there are infinitely many things that exist over infinitely many places the divine can reach [1,229]. In saying the divine infinity (a qualitative version of infinity) reaches an infinite number of spaces (a quantitative version of infinity), Plotinus implies the divine infinity also has a quantitively infinite trait of the literally infinite variety. Moreover, since the One is infinite in both power and presence, Plotinus seems to be proposing a positive infinity in which the One's infinite attributes of power and presence are distinct.

However, Plotinus in other passages seems to deny the distinction between individual divine attributes with respect to their infinitude. In some instances, he identifies infinite power with infinite presence and vice versa. For example, Plotinus [1,230] goes on to say that "the divine is one all-power, reaching out to infinity, powerful to infinity; and so great is God that his very members are infinites. What place can be named to which He does not reach?" In saying the One's power extends to infinitely many places, Plotinus may be uniting infinite power with infinite presence into one, indistinguishable infinitude: a negative infinity. As for God's "members," Plotinus describes them more like the emanations proposed by Philo—like rays from the Sun. Thus God (like the Sun) remains a part-less being—"the One"—despite having a literally infinite number of attributes of power (like the Sun emitting many rays).

In short, Plotinus uses both quantitative and qualitative infinity in his writings and he is not always clear whether the qualitative infinity he ascribes to God is a positive infinity of distinguishably infinite attributes or if it is a negative infinity with respect to God as such and only positive with respect to how God's attributes are exhibited toward Creation in a quantitatively infinite respect. Either way, for Plotinus the divine infinite is at least qualitative if not purely so.

25.2.4 *Gregory of Nyssa*

Another early Church father and theologian, Gregory of Nyssa (335–395 CE), also wrote of divine infinity. Gregory said that God is "unlimited in goodness," that "the unlimited is the same as the infinite," so God is infinite in goodness, though "it is not possible that that which is by nature infinite should be comprehended in any conception expressed by words" [1,231]. However, this kind of mysticism could be said of either positive or negative infinity—both are qualitative infinities that are beyond comprehension, albeit in different ways. The question is: for Gregory, are God's various infinite attributes all a single, indistinguishable attribute (a negative infinity) or are God's various infinite attributes distinguishable parts of God's essence or nature (a positive infinity)? I have to say Gregory does not make it clear, for his writings do not appear consistent on either what infinity is or whether infinity is a negative or positive quality.

At certain points in Gregory's writings, he says some apparently contradictory things about God's infinity. For example, he writes of God's infinity with respect to space and time as if God is a magnitude greater than any finite magnitude of space and finite stretch of time, then denies infinity is spatial or temporal at all.

With respect to space, Gregory writes as if divine infinity is a kind of container that is somehow *greater* than the space of the Universe. Of God's omnipresence, Gregory said that "it belongs to the Godhead to be in all places, and to pervade all things, and not to be limited by anything…" [1,232]. This certainly sounds like our usual idea of infinite space—God is so big that God is spatially unlimited.

But then Gregory turns around and says God has no spatial extension: "The Divine nature is a stranger to…the ideas of space…" [1,233]. God has no dimensions, "no size, no proportions," says Gregory [1,234]. Gregory adds that "the Divine Nature is without extension, and, being without extension, it has no limit; and that which is limitless is infinite" [1,235]. This statement makes it sound as if God's omnipresence has been shrunk to a spaceless point, the exact opposite of being everywhere.

On the subject of time, Gregory says God is eternal because God is "always the same, neither growing nor being consumed…He alone exists always in the same manner and abides forever…" [1,236]. Gregory believed God has been around for an infinite amount of time and exists infinitely into the future. God, says Gregory, "places no limit to His eternity in either direction, so that neither if we look to the beginning do we find any point marked *since* which He is and beyond which He was not, nor if we turn our thought to the future can we cut short by any boundary the eternal progress of Him Who is" [1,237]. Compared to the everlasting life of God, Gregory pointed out, our own lives are "so exceedingly brief" that they are "next to nothing at all" [1,238]. Gregory emphasized that God is "everlasting," across time without beginning [1,239] and the "infinite ages" of the Universe bear witness to God's power [1,240]. Hence, God's existence spans all of time, through an infinite past and through an infinite future.

Gregory also says we can spend forever getting to know God better. He stressed that "the infinity of God exceeds all the significance and comprehension that names can furnish" [1,241]. That is, God can never be *fully* comprehended precisely because of God's divine infinity. In other words, there is no such thing as comprehensive knowledge of God that can be articulated in words because no matter how *much* one figures out about God, there is always *more* to figure out [1,242]. Gregory proposed that there are always more truths for souls to learn about God—God's greatness is in *excess* of the finite, and so we can keep on affirming new things about God [1,243]. That would suggest God's divine infinity has a quantitative aspect: there are infinitely many things to know of God (literal infinity) because we will never learn them all despite continuous progress through eternity (figurative infinity) [1,244]. This portrays eternity as unending time, distinct from how Gregory portrayed space.

But then there are times Gregory says the opposite: God is atemporal, outside of time altogether. The life of God "is not in time, but time flows from it," and that it is "within that transcendent and blessed Power all things are equally present as in an instant: past and future are within its all-encircling grasp and its comprehensive view" [1,245].

Perhaps we can make sense of these seeming contradictions by positing that Gregory held infinity to be a seamless, featureless unity while space and time are distinguished by measurable differences in places and events. Imagine a white sheet of paper so large it stretches beyond the horizon. Upon the paper, a short series of marks are placed. Suppose the marks are then erased, leaving no trace behind. The paper would for Gregory be like God's spaceless, atemporality. As the sheet of paper is larger than the marks on it, so too God is greater than any *in-practice* measurable extension (space). As the paper is around before and after the marks on the page, so too God is both "everlasting" (present during all of the marks of time, even if they continue without ceasing) and yet also "eternal" (somehow *before* any beginning to the material universe and also "beyond all ages"—somehow *after* the end of the material universe) [1,246]. So, although God is spaceless and atemporal, this does not necessarily make God into a point-instant, or afinity. Instead, God is somehow "greater" than space while also being inclusive of, but also "beyond," time. Being somehow greater than space and beyond time is what Gregory is calling God's "infinity."

Whether this makes sense is another matter, for being "greater" than space and "beyond" time does not seem a coherent concept unless we confine our use of the words 'space' and 'time' to what is *in practice* measurable rather than including what is also *in principle* measurable. Aside from that concern, the question remains: in Gregory's view, is God's infinite being (omnipresence) and infinite life (eternity) indistinguishable from one another and from God's other infinite attributes as part of the same infinity, or are God's various infinite attributes distinguishable? Gregory seems to want it both ways.

On the one hand, while Gregory says that the divine nature is "in all respects" infinite, [1,247] he also stated that God's essence is so superior that it has "no distinctive attribute" [1,248]. So, God is in all respects infinite but with no distinctive attribute. That would suggest infinity is not a distinctive attribute, nor are God's other attributes distinctive attributes, which would imply that all of God's attributes are merely our subjective interpretations of what is a single, indistinguishable, unlimited essence. That would certainly suggest Gregory sees God's infinite attributes as not distinctive attributes but as a negative infinity.

Then again, Gregory also denies that certain attributes of God are synonymous with one another. For example, Gregory held that because God is infinite, we may *ascribe* to God the attributes of being ungenerate and indestructible, but we do not *bestow* these upon God by faculty of conception as if they are our inventions [1,249]. Rather, says Gregory, if God didn't have these attributes already, we would not be able to ascribe them [1,250]. This makes God's attributes, with respect to God's infinity, distinguishable from one another, and so a positive infinity after all.

It may just be that Gregory was not entirely consistent on the nature of God's infinity. If there is an escape hatch from this contradiction, I suppose it would be Gregory's thesis of divine infinity's mysticism: Even the angels, Gregory said, are "incapable of taking in and comprehending [God's divine] nature which is infinite" [1,251].

25.2.5 *Aquinas*

Moving from antiquity into the Medieval Period (5th to 15th Centuries of the Common Era) and the Renaissance (1300 to the late 1600s), we find qualitative infinity still promoted among religious philosophers and theologians. One such philosopher and theologian was Thomas Aquinas, writing around 1265–1274.

Aquinas used the word 'infinity' in both the quantitative and qualitative senses of the term, though he referred to these as 'extensive infinity' and 'intensive infinity', respectively [1,252] (see § 23.3.2 for a different use of these terms).

As to the quantitative (his 'extensive') sense of infinity, Aquinas followed Aristotle's distinction between actual infinity and potential infinity. However, Aquinas denied actual (literal) infinities exist in mathematics and physics and insisted that only potential (figurative) infinities describe mathematical and physical realities.

As to the qualitative (his 'intensive') sense of infinity, Aquinas held God's *being* to be infinite in two respects. First, Aquinas said that "in God the infinite is understood only in a negative way, because there is no terminus or limit to His perfection: He is supremely perfect. It is thus that the infinite ought to be attributed to God" [1,253].

Though Aquinas described God's infinity using a (mostly) *negative theology*, it is not always clear in Aquinas' writings that his idea of divine infinity is what I call *negative infinity*. For divine infinity to be a negative infinity as I've defined it, God's infinite attributes must not simply lack limits individually, but also they must be *indistinguishable* from one another. So, we must ask if Aquinas characterizes divine infinity in this manner.

However negative (apophatic) he considered his theology, Aquinas nevertheless provided positive descriptions for some of God's attributes—aseity, omnipotence, intellect, goodness, etc.—and argued why each one must individually be infinite, thus implying they are all distinct, which in turn suggests Aquinas regarded God's infinity as a positive infinity [1,254] [1,255]. On the other hand, Aquinas also affirmed the doctrine of divine simplicity, arguing that "there is only one God and that no composition of parts or accidents is found in Him" [1,256] [1,257]. Which would mean the distinctions between God's various infinite attributes are just our own impressions of what is really a single infinite attribute—an attribute in which all the positive infinitudes lose distinction. In that respect, Aquinas supports a view of divine infinity as negative infinity.

Aquinas seems to have wanted it both ways between positive and negative infinity. It may just be that Aquinas' views on God's divine infinity were not entirely consistent [1,258]. However, Aquinas was in good company holding the view that God's apparently positive attributes are just the outward effects God may have of what is in fact a single attribute expressed in many forms—an attribute that is the very essence of God. Such a view was held by several of his predecessors, such as Clement, and was typical of mid-to-late 13th Century theological views concerning God's divine infinity, which was by that time considered a perfection in itself [1,259].

25.2.6 *Duns Scotus*

Scotus, like Aquinas, also acknowledged infinity according to Aristotle's distinctions of 'potential infinity' and 'actual infinity'. Like Aquinas, Scotus also believed figurative infinity (or "potential infinity") is the only kind of infinity to be found in mathematics and the physical universe. But unlike Aquinas, Scotus believed God's attributes, such as God's intellect, are infinite both in the sense of being qualitatively infinite *and* literally infinite.

In fact, God has qualitatively infinite attributes precisely because they are attributes that admit of quantitative infinity in the literal sense. For example, Scotus says, "The infinite is that which exceeds the finite, not exactly by reason of any finite measure, but in excess of any measure that could be assigned" [1,260]. He further states that God's intellect is "infinitely perfect" because God knows a literal (or "actual") infinity of truths, all at once [1,261]. Scotus says the same of God's power: God has enough power to cause infinitely many things at once, even if God causes these things only in succession. Because God can cause infinitely many things at once, God's omnipotence is, like his omniscience, an "infinite perfection" [1,262].

Scotus described God's qualitatively infinite attributes (God's perfections) in terms of literal infinity, a quantitative concept. However, it would seem Scotus viewed God's divine infinity in even more positive terms.

25.2.7 *Cusanus*

The Renaissance theologian Nicolaus Cusanus—also known as Nicholas of Cusa (1401–1464)—proposed that God's qualitative infinity is the breakdown of distinctions between God's attributes just as numeric distinctions between mathematical objects break down when made quantitatively infinite.

Take an example from geometry. Consider an infinitely long line and an infinitely large circle. The line is straight and the circle is curved. But the curvature of an infinitely large circle appears at our finite scale to be a straight line, and the straightness of an infinitely long line could thus be the curve of an infinitely large circle. Though straightness implies no curvature and curvature implies no straightness, Cusanus pointed out that these "contradictories"—straightness versus curvature—lose all distinction when rendered infinite [1,263]. In certain contexts, even a maximum and minimum can appear identical when a quantity is projected to infinity [1,264].

Cusanus used the loss of distinctiveness between *quantitatively* infinite properties applied to the same object as an analogy for the lack of distinction between *qualitatively* infinite properties among God's divine attributes as they are united in one being. Just as the distinctiveness between straightness and circularity breaks down when those properties are made literally infinite, so too qualitatively infinite attributes lose their distinction when they are united in a non-quantitative state of 'oneness' which Cusanus called "infinite oneness"—a negative infinity. "Now, according to the theology of negation, there is not found in God anything other than infinity" [1,265].

Any positive quality you might affirm about God such as saying that God is truthful, virtuous, etc. is at best metaphorical because all opposite qualities—truth and falsehood, virtue and vice—are dissolved in God whose essence is mystically beyond all opposing qualities. Cusanus acknowledged that affirming desirable qualities of God like truth, virtue, knowledge, power, beauty, etc. is more accurate than affirming undesirable qualities like falsehood, vice, ignorance, impotence, ugliness, etc., but he insisted that the desirable qualities affirmed of God can only be "infinitesimally" accurate things to say of God because God is most genuinely beyond all affirmations which have a contrast with opposite ("contradictory") properties. In God everything is one thing: infinite light is darkness, infinite time is timelessness ("eternity"), and so forth. The distinctions between opposite properties or contrary properties become indistinguishable from one another, melding them into a single, coherent attribute of the divine which Cusanus said is "negatively infinite" [1,266].

Moreover, Cusanus drew another parallel between literal infinity and God's negative infinity. Cusanus stated that "the infinite, qua infinite, is unknown; for it escapes all comparative relation" [1,267]. Just as contrary properties (e.g., straightness and curvature) are contradictory when united in a literally infinite object (e.g., a literally infinite circle), a state that is incomprehensible, so too God's negative infinity as a union of contradictories is a condition beyond human comprehension: "Therefore, according to this theology [God] is not knowable either in this world or in the world to come (for in this respect every created thing is darkness, which cannot comprehend Infinite Light), but is known only to Himself" [1,268].

Although he acknowledged that God has some positive relations to the world (e.g., God is a Creator), Cusanus had one of the most consistent of via negativa theologies. With Cusanus we find the qualitative infinitude of God is a decisively negative infinity rather than a positive infinity.

25.2.8 *Bruno*

The philosopher Giordano Bruno (1548 – 1600) drew much from Cusanus but he took the idea of negative infinity in a different direction. On the one hand, Bruno thought of infinity in terms similar to Cusanus' idea of 'oneness' for describing God's qualitative infinity. Like Cusanus, Bruno interpreted infinity to be a non-quantitative unity or state of mystical wholeness entirely beyond quantitative comparisons. According to Bruno, "in the infinite there are no parts, however particularized the things of the universe are" [1,269].

Bruno thus went further than Cusanus or any of the other Christian theologians of his day in the application of this negative infinity not just to God but to the physical universe. Moreover, in a pantheistic vein, Bruno identified the negative infinity of the physical universe as the very same negative infinity of God, thereby making the Universe either the same as or at least part of God—a heresy to Catholic thought and one of the many reasons Bruno got himself into trouble with the Inquisition [1,270].

25.2.9 *Galileo*

The Renaissance scientist Galileo proposed his own version of quantitative infinity which has implications for his views on divine infinity. He argued that the quantifiers *less than*, *equal to*, and *greater than* apply for comparing finite quantities to each other but not for comparing infinite quantities to each other. In his book *Dialogues Concerning Two New Sciences*, Galileo presented a fictional dialog on the subject of infinity. A character named Salviati (who represents Galileo himself) says to his friend Sagredo [1,271],

> "...the attributes "equal," "greater," and "less," are not applicable to infinite, but only to finite, quantities. When therefore Simplicio introduces several lines of different lengths and asks me how it is possible that the longer ones do not contain more points than the shorter, I answer him that one line does not contain more or less or just as many points as another, but that each line contains an infinite number."

Not only cannot two infinite quantities be compared, but Galileo also went further, saying that "we are led to conclude that the attributes 'larger', 'smaller', and 'equal' have no place either in comparing infinite quantities with each other or in comparing infinite with finite quantities" [1,272].

But wait, the finite and infinite do have something in common: they are both about numbers and quantities. Throughout *Two New Sciences* Galileo uses these terms for both the finite and the infinite. He refers to both finite and infinite numbers, both finite and infinite quantities.

However, Galileo later clarified what he meant by "infinite quantity" and "infinite number." In Galileo's view, because finite numbers can be compared but infinite numbers cannot be, 'infinity' must be *quantitative incomparability*. An "infinite number" or "infinite quantity" is an incomparable number, an incomparable quantity.

Since numbers and quantities are only such because they can be compared, the idea of an incomparable number or quantity would seem to be an oxymoron. But perhaps not entirely so, for there is something that Galileo calls an infinite quantity or infinite number: a property he calls *unity* [1,273].

To help us understand, Galileo asks us to consider a continuum. By his conception of a continuum, the parts are such that together they form a 'unity', which in this context means *a collection of indeterminate quantity*. In other words, the continuum appears featureless to us and we can't tell *by any process* how many parts it really has. Because the continuum is a unity of this kind, the continuum—

1. Allows for indefinite division into smaller finite units or indefinite filling with finite units.
2. May be made to contain infinitely many, infinitely small points or infinitely many, finite or infinite magnitudes (read "infinitely" as "incomparably" in each case).

Either way, a continuum may have any arbitrary quantity within it—finite or infinite—precisely because it is a unity [1,274]. Hence, in this account of infinity, Galileo implies there is something the finite and infinite do have in common: they are related via 'unity'.

Since it is the property of unity that allows the continuum to be predicated with either finite numbers (comparable numbers) or infinite numbers (incomparable numbers) of any quantity, Galileo concludes that the unity of the continuum implies the infinite (incomparable quantity) must be present—either potentially or actually—within the continuum [1,275]. Moreover, Galileo says that, by virtue of its infinitude (lack of quantitative comparability), the property of unity implies the inclusion of all numbers—both finite and infinite—either actually or potentially [1,276].

Galileo thus holds this kind of 'unity' does not mean "one" so much as it means *any, every, and beyond* in a state of indistinctiveness. "Therefore we conclude that unity is the only infinite number," said Galileo [1,277]. And for that reason, infinity is quantitatively vexing [1,278]:

> These are some of the marvels which our imagination cannot grasp and which should warn us against the serious error of those who attempt to discuss the infinite by assigning to it the same properties which we employ for the finite, the natures of the two having nothing in common.

To which Galileo warns us about "the difficulties which arise when we attempt, with our finite minds, to discuss the infinite..." [1,279].

That latter quote echoes the position of past theologians who wrote of infinity as being incomprehensible, but it also reveals something else: his use of the phrase "our finite minds" implies a contrast to the mind of God which Galileo takes to be of a quality that has no trouble comprehending the quantitatively infinite. Galileo thus implies that infinite mind is a divine attribute, which would have been in keeping with the position of the Catholic Church at that time (yes, even after the Roman Inquisition put him under house arrest, Galileo remained devout) [1,280].

So, we can draw three conclusions about Galileo's infinity.

First, Galileo's conception of the infinite was quantitative. Some scholars believe Galileo agreed with Cusanus that infinity is not a quantitative concept at all [1,281] [1,282]. However, that interpretation is mistaken—both in terms of what Cusanus taught as well as with regard to what Galileo believed.

Cusanus referred to progressions that constitute infinities in the figurative sense: Aristotle's potential infinity [1,283]. Cusanus also believed the physical world could be actually infinite [1,284]. In addition to those quantitative versions of infinity, Cusanus believed God's infinity to be qualitative, which Cusanus identified as a "negative infinity"; he was simply using the apparently contradictory nature of literal infinity as an analogy for God's negative infinity [1,285].

The infinity Galileo refers to is his own version of literal infinity. He wrote of a circle as an infinitely-sided polygon [1,286] which implies an object that is both complete and limitless at the same time. He wrote of infinite quantity (e.g., infinitely many points in a line) [1,287] and an "infinite number" of various geometrical objects. In his fictional dialog, Galileo goes on to refer to "an infinite number of indivisible quantities," an "infinite number of points," parts that are "infinite in number," and so on [1,288]. Moreover, his *Two New Sciences* reveals that he believed entire sequences of numbers can themselves be "infinite" [1,289]. He wrote of the "totality of all numbers" being infinite [1,290]. All of this suggests that for Galileo infinity had a quantitative property or a relation to quantity, and so was not completely *non*-quantitative, despite its qualitative features. So even though he did say that "no assigned number is infinite," he did not reject infinity as a quantity per se. Rather, he went on to state that there is an infinite number, but it is not the kind of number that can be assigned to a collection as can a finite number; instead, the infinite number is 'unity' [1,291]. That suggests Galileo did support literal infinity but had a nuanced way of conceiving it, not just as limitlessness of a given multitude but limitlessness of that multitude by virtue of a "unity" among its members.

Second, Galileo held that the term 'infinity' refers to incomparability of quantity and so to a *qualitative category of quantity*, a conception of quantity that is qualitatively different from finite quantity. Galileo seems to have thought that while infinity is quantitative in that we can speak of an 'infinite number' of things, the word 'infinite' in the term 'infinite number' is a predicate that denotes something qualitative *about* a different category of number.

Infinity, as a quantitative condition of a number, refers to a condition of being incomparable to any finite number of things, such that the infinite cannot be calculated as finite amounts can. Infinity is the condition in which quantities become a 'unity', losing their distinctions with one another. In that sense, his idea of quantitative infinity is equivalent to the negative theological infinity, which is a version of qualitative infinity.

Moreover, because for Galileo the term 'infinite number' denotes a quantitative condition in which finite quantities dissolve into an enveloping 'unity', he regarded infinity as a condition beyond human comprehension altogether. In that respect, Galileo's view of literal infinity was similar to the conception held by Cusanus in that infinity is a condition that is opaque to reason—it cannot be further analyzed without engendering irresolvable paradoxes.

Third, Galileo also believed in the qualitative infinity of the divine. As a Catholic of his time, he would have held God to be infinite. The phrase "our finite minds" gives away that he believed in a version of infinity that is qualitative rather than simply quantitative. He seems to have implied that a (qualitatively) infinite mind, such as the mind of God, would be able to comprehend the quantitatively infinite [1,292].

The question then arises as to whether Galileo thought literal infinity and divine infinity were *one and the same* infinity. On the one hand, his description of literal infinity does sound similar to the theological idea of negative infinity. Both are described as a 'unity' beyond comprehension. On the other hand, Galileo never says his idea of literal infinity is a unity purely in the sense of the doctrine of divine simplicity—that is to say, a negative infinity.

Instead, Galileo's literal infinity is only described as a condition of *quantitative* incomparability while negative infinity is a *qualitative* state of indistinguishability between contrary or even contradictory attributes. His *Two New Sciences* never describes the infinitude of God in more negative terms other than by references to its mystical incomprehensibility, which could apply just as well to positively infinite attributes (the sense of "positive" I have adopted). Moreover, from his phraseology, I take Galileo as not necessarily implying literal infinity just is divine infinity. Instead, he believed that God's mind is qualitatively infinite and therefore powerful enough to grasp literal infinity while we with our (qualitatively) finite minds cannot fully grasp either literal infinity or divine infinity.

At best, all we can say is that Galileo seems to have believed in divine infinity of a qualitative variety (perhaps a positive infinity, but not certainly so) in addition to an inscrutable, quantitative infinity that is literal or 'actual'. Whether he thought divine infinity and quantitative infinity were one and the same infinity is not clear from his writings.

25.2.10 *Descartes*

Descartes was uncertain that anything in the physical world is quantitatively infinite (he preferred to use the word "indefinite" for that which in the real world lacks a relative limit of some kind), but he was certain that God is 'infinite' in the sense that God's being is an instance of qualitative infinity. Precisely because he could be sure of God's qualitative infinity but not of the infinity of anything else, Descartes recommended we reserve the word 'infinite' *only* for descriptions of God's divine essence [1,293] [1,295]. "The term 'infinite' strictly applies only to something in which no limits of any kind could be found; and in this sense God alone is infinite" [1,296].

Descartes was a bit more nuanced than some philosophers of religion as to whether divine infinity is a negative infinity or a positive infinity. Despite that the word 'infinite' means "not finite" and so is a denial of the finite, Descartes turned the concepts around: he believed to say something is finite is to qualify that it is not infinite. In that respect, Descartes held God's divine infinity to be a positive plenum while our apprehension of it could only be incomplete and therefore negative in the sense of revealing our ignorance. According to Descartes (paraphrased) [1,297]:

> Even if we understand infinity to be utterly positive, our way of understanding infinity is negative, because it depends on our not finding any limitation in the thing. Whereas our way of understanding the infinite thing itself is positive, but it isn't adequate, i.e., we don't have a complete grasp of everything in it that could be understood.

Descartes did not mean that if we don't understand all about something infinite, we don't understand it at all; he meant only that our understanding of something infinite must be incomplete such that we never *completely comprehend* (or as he says, "grasp") it. He expounds [1,298]:

> When we look at the ocean, our vision doesn't take it all in, and we get no sense of its vastness, but we are still said to 'see the ocean'. And this very partial view of the ocean may be the best we can have…But if we stare at some part of the ocean from close up, then our view can be vivid and clear…

So too, Descartes offered, the human mind can't grasp anything infinite in its entirety. Since God alone is truly infinite, we cannot intellectually grasp God—we must be content with only a partial understanding.

However, Descartes did think we could use our understanding of indefinite processes and of vast or indefinitely large spaces as analogies to get a rudimentary understanding of God's qualitative infinity [1,299]:

> Further, although my knowledge increase more and more, nevertheless I am not, therefore, induced to think that it will ever be actually infinite, since it can never reach that point beyond which it shall be incapable of further increase. But I conceive God as actually infinite, so that nothing can be added to his perfection.

Descartes' idea of divine infinity was more positive than the conception held by Bruno, and certainly more so than the purely negative infinity of Cusanus. But Descartes' conception of divine infinity was still the same as negative infinity in another sense: although God has many divine attributes like omniscience, omnipotence, and so on, these distinctions are only arbitrary distinctions on our part; they are merely different appearances of a single infinite attribute. Descartes (again paraphrased), stated as follows [1,300]:

> …we understand God as having an absolute immensity = simplicity = unity, a single great attribute which includes all his other attributes. There are no analogues of that in us or anything else; it is God's alone; and so any evidence of this uniquely divine attribute is, as I once said, "like the mark of the craftsman stamped on his work." We have certain attributes which (because of our limited intellects) we attribute to God separately, one by one, because that is how we perceive them in ourselves…

Hence, all such divine attributes—infinite knowledge, infinite power, etc.—lose distinction in the way God is beyond our limited perception and understanding. Divine infinity as negative infinity once again.

25.2.11 *Leibniz*

Insofar as philosophers and theologians (and devout scientists) from Philo to Galileo agreed that the divine infinity of God is a qualitative infinity beyond any full logical analysis and rational comprehension, their various versions of qualitative infinity were all deeply mystical. In academia, this mystical view of divine infinity continued from the Renaissance to the Enlightenment in the publications of various philosophers such as Leibniz.

Leibniz proposed some philosophical distinctions regarding infinity in his philosophical and theological works. Like the medieval philosophers, Leibniz referred to figurative infinity as the 'syncategorematic infinite' and literal infinity as the 'categorematic infinite' (see § 23.2.2 and § 23.4.1). In addition to these quantitative conceptions of infinity, Leibniz also proposed a version of qualitative infinity he called the *hypercategorematic infinite*, which does not belong to the category of things that can be quantitatively measured [1,301].

Infinity as the 'hypercategorematic infinite' is infinity *not* as a condition of sets or 'multitudes' but instead as a condition of irreducible *unity*—a condition of wholeness "without parts," which Leibniz believed to be a quality of perfection [1,302]. And there exists only one such unity, Leibniz thought, and that is God because God alone is perfect. So, the hypercategorematic infinite is the infinity of God [1,303].

Leibniz regarded this hypercategorematic infinite as a "positive" infinity since it affirms the unity and perfection to God [1,304]. However, going instead by my nomenclature of what constitutes a positive or negative infinity, Leibniz's hypercategorematic infinite is not clearly positive. To be a positive infinity, the infinite attributes of God must be able to be distinguished from one another. It is not clear this is so in Leibniz's conception of divine infinity.

On the one hand, Leibniz calls out three divine attributes—power, wisdom, and goodwill—the relationship between which he describes as follows [1,305]:

> "In God exists *power*, which is the source of all *knowledge*,—which comprehends the realm of ideas, down to its minutest detail,—and *will*, which directs all creations and changes according to the principle of the best." Or as he expands it at another time: …"Power has its end in being; wisdom, or understanding, in truth; and will in good. Thus the cause must be absolutely perfect in power, wisdom, and goodness. His understanding is the source of essences, and his will the origin of existences."

God's power, wisdom, and goodwill would seem to be distinct attributes, each infinite in itself.

On the other hand, Leibniz did say that divine infinity is a state of absolute, part-less *unity*. This could be interpreted as suggesting these three attributes, by virtue of being qualitatively infinite, must be a single attribute in accordance with the doctrine of divine simplicity handed down in Catholic theology. If so, then God's infinite attributes like omniscience and omnipotence are all once again collapsed into a single attribute of "unity" or "perfection" in which the individual attributes cannot be distinguished from one another. In which case, Leibniz's idea of God's divine, qualitative infinity is not a positive infinity but a negative infinity after all.

25.2.12 *Bolzano*

Earlier we saw how Cusanus used mathematical analogies to elucidate God's negative infinity. Bolzano was another theologian who took a mathematical approach to God's infinity, but unlike Cusanus, Bolzano did not just use mathematical to make analogies of divine infinity. Rather, Bolzano claimed divine infinity has mathematical properties. Moreover, while Cusanus' conception of divine infinity was negative, Bolzano's was positive—he regarded God's attributes as each distinct and infinite in itself.

Part of Bolzano's conception of God's positive infinity is that it is not purely qualitative but also quantitative; in fact, Bolzano thought there's no such thing as infinite that is purely non-quantitative. Tapp coined a slogan to capture Bolzano's attitude about qualitative infinity [1,306]: "No infinity without quantitative infinity!" In other words, if God is qualitatively infinite, that qualitative infinity must also be inclusive of quantitative infinity—literal infinity—because "all meaningful discourse about infinity presupposes quantitative infinity" [1,307].

According to Bolzano, even though God is "that being which we consider as the most perfect unity," nevertheless, "viewpoints can be identified from which we see in him an infinite plurality…" [1,308]. At first, that statement makes Bolzano sound like he's promoting negative infinity. However, he says that there is an infinite plurality *in* God which would suggest God is a complex being, contrary to the traditional doctrine of divine simplicity. If this is what Bolzano meant, then he saw God's infinite attributes as a case of positive infinity. However, the passage also sounds like Bolzano considers the "infinite plurality" as merely relative to our point of view of God rather than an objective feature of God. That would again suggest a negative infinity.

To reconcile these statements, perhaps Bolzano was holding the view of Scotus on divine simplicity, considering God as a complex being with a plurality of attributes "united" only in their complex integration with one another, not in some state of composite indistinctiveness (thus rejecting the doctrine of divine simplicity in all but name) [1,309]. In support of that interpretation, Bolzano said further that "we call God infinite because we concede to him powers of more than one kind that have an infinite magnitude. Thus, we attribute to him a power of knowledge that is true omniscience, that therefore comprehends an infinite multitude of truths..." [1,310]. Bolzano thus identifies more than one infinity in God—"powers of more than one kind," presumably omniscience, omnipotence, omnipresence, etc.—and Bolzano indicates each one is of infinite magnitude, a quantitative infinity.

So, Bolzano believed God's infinity is not just qualitative, but also quantitative. That too would suggest he believed God's divine infinity is a positive infinity rather than a purely negative infinity. This would have been a minority view among Catholic theologians of his day.

25.3 THE APPEARANCE OF ABSOLUTE INFINITY

Up to this point we have considered divine infinity as qualitative infinity—either positive or negative. But with Cantor, we find a new conception of divine infinity.

That is not to say Cantor completely broke with the past. Like those before him, he assumed God has many attributes such as freedom, goodness, omnipotence, and wisdom [1,311]. And he thought that at least some of those attributes are infinite. Like Bolzano, who identified in God "powers of more than one kind" that are infinite, [1,312] Cantor also seemed to assume God has a "multiplicity" of attributes, either some or all of which are infinite. For example, like Bolzano, Cantor assumed God has an infinite intellect in the sense that it holds infinitely many truths [1,313]. And in Cantor's view, one of those truths is the truth of Cantor's transfinite system of mathematics. As philosopher Kateřina Trlifajová explains [1,314]:

> Georg Cantor introduced actual infinity in mathematics in the form of infinite sets. He gave a theological justification for their existence, placing them in the mind of God. A characteristic excerpt from Cantor's letter to Jeiler from 1895...says "in particular, there are transfinite cardinal numbers and transfinite ordinal types which, just as much as the finite numbers and forms, possess a definite mathematical uniformity, discoverable by men. All these particular modes of the transfinite have existed from eternity as ideas in the Divine intellect."

In saying God's divine intellect holds truths, I interpret Cantor as assuming a distinction from God's other infinite attributes like omnipresence or omnipotence. Each attribute of God is assumed to be infinite but not identical to God's other attributes or with God's being as such. If this is correct, then Cantor's conception of divine infinity is qualitatively positive rather than negative. Moreover, since each qualitatively infinite attribute of God can hold a quantitative infinitude within it (e.g., infinitely many truths in the intellect of God), then that implies Cantor saw divine infinity as a positive infinity with quantitatively infinite aspects in the literal sense of the term.

However, Cantor's idea of God's infinity does not reduce to a positive infinity like that of Bolzano, for Cantor blended mathematics with theology to propose a different kind of infinity. So far in this historical overview, we have seen only instances of divine infinity as a *qualitative infinity*, either negative or positive in flavor. But while many theologians have portrayed divine infinity as qualitative infinity, Cantor portrayed divine infinity as *absolute infinity*—a qualitative infinity that is so by virtue of a quantitative infinity taken even beyond the transfinite [1,315].

Absolute infinity should not be confused with the metaphysical concept of *the Absolute*. What philosophers, and some theologians, refer to as 'the Absolute' is a perfect metaphysical reality of some sort. As pointed out by Rucker, "...all theologians and metaphysicians from Plotinus on have supposed the Absolute to be infinite. What is meant by 'the Absolute' depends, of course, on the philosopher in question: it might be taken to mean God, an overarching universal mind, or simply the class of all possible thought" [1,316]. Typically, the Absolute is identified as God and so I will here allow the idea of God to stand in for the Absolute.

Though God may be taken as the Absolute, God's identity as the Absolute is not necessarily synonymous with absolute infinity. The term 'absolute infinity' is used by Catholic theologians for God's possession of "all possible perfections" [1,317]. That conception of "absolute infinity" was until Cantor a negative infinity or positive infinity with respect to quality. Where Cantor differed theologically from his predecessors was to combine the mathematical concept of a quantitative, literal infinity with the theological concept of a qualitative, positive infinity into a new idea of absolute infinity characterizing the essence of God (**Figures 1.4** and **25.0**).

Cantor thus made use of absolute infinity in two senses—one mathematical and one theological. With respect to his mathematics, Cantor referred to this new infinity both as an *inconsistent multiplicity* and as an *absolutely infinite multiplicity* or *absolute infinite totality* [1,318] and he symbolized it by the capital omega (Ω). But Cantor's mathematics overlapped with his theology, for he also referred to the mathematical absolute infinity as "the Absolute"—the essence, or even the very identity, of God [1,319]. Cantor thus identified absolute infinite multiplicity with God as the Absolute.

To be clear, Cantor did not invent the idea of the Absolute, nor the idea that the Absolute is infinite, but he did invent the idea of 'absolute infinity' insofar as it is a hybrid of positive (qualitative) and literal (quantitative) infinity. Cantor's absolute infinity is quantitative in the sense that it is an ideal limit to quantity but that is exactly what in Cantor's view makes it a qualitative infinity with respect to God's being.

For simplicity, I will refer to Cantor's mathematical version of the concept as lower case 'absolute infinity' and his theological conception of the same as upper case 'Absolute Infinity'. Though, some authors mix the two contexts because both the mathematical absolute infinity and the divine Absolute Infinity are for Cantor one and the same [1,320]:

> What lies beyond even the transfinite numbers? According to Cantor, lying beyond the transfinites is "Absolute Infinity," symbolized as Ω...the transfinite numbers lead endlessly toward Absolute Infinity Ω but never begin to reach it, since Ω lies, absolute and unapproachable...

The transfinite cardinals and ordinals do not constitute a completed set within absolute infinity (Ω) but they are within absolute infinity in another sense. Cantor said absolute infinity is "to be understood a quantum which on the one hand is not variable, but rather is fixed and determined in all its parts—a genuine constant" [1,321] which "cannot in any way be added to or diminished, and it is therefore to be looked upon quantitatively as an absolute maximum" [1,322]. In one respect Ω represents a maximum quantity that is like a set in that it contains all finite numbers and all transfinite numbers below it, but Ω is nevertheless not itself a set: "In a certain sense it transcends the human power of comprehension, and in particular is beyond mathematical determination" [1,323]. In this respect, Cantor's idea of absolute infinity sounds a lot like Galileo's idea of infinity—a kind of unity that is an ideal limit of quantity itself.

Because Cantor's absolute infinity is beyond quantification or even human comprehension, he says it "can only be acknowledged but never be known, not even approximately" [1,324]. Philosophers Dionysis Mentzeniotis and Giannis Stamatellos elaborate on the mystical implications; they state that Cantor's absolute infinity is "inconceivable, unattainable, inexpressible, and unthinkable, hence confirming a link between the infinite and the ineffable" [1,325].

Philosophers Joanna Van der Veen and Leon Horsten add even more explicitly, "The Cantorian picture seems to be one of the cardinal numbers converging to a limit that lies beyond themselves, with that limit conceived of as 'God'" [1,326]. They quote Cantor himself spelling out the theological implications of his philosophical position on absolute infinity [1,327]:

> What lies beyond all that is finite and transfinite is not a 'Genus'; it is the unique, completely individual unity...[Absolute Infinity is], for human intelligence unfathomable, also that not subject to mathematics, unmeasurable...which is by many called 'God'.

Cantor did not just identify God's individual attributes as each absolutely infinite, nor even stop at saying there is an absolute infinity of them as a collective. Rather, Cantor went further by identifying God *as such* to be Absolute Infinity. Occasionally, Cantor even referred to God as Absolute Infinity or the Absolute for short [1,328].

Cantor thus mathematized divine infinity even beyond the positive infinity of Bolzano. For Bolzano, God *has* infinite attributes, but for Cantor God *is* Absolute Infinity—or at least Cantor believed Absolute Infinity to be the very nature and thus identity of God.

However, despite that Absolute Infinity is an "individual unity," Cantor's Absolute Infinity is not just a version of negative infinity like that of Cusanus or perhaps Galileo. While both used mathematics to illuminate infinity as the unity of God, unlike them Cantor did not reduce the divine attributes into a unity that makes them *indistinguishable* with each other and with God as such.

The indications that Cantor does not make absolute infinity into negative infinity are twofold. First, Cantor spoke of God's intellect in more positive terms as did Bolzano; God knows infinitely many truths [1,329]. This makes the infinitude of God's intellect distinct from another attribute like, say, power or presence. Second, evidence that Cantor did not think of God as identical to the various divine attributes is found in an 1886 letter to Cardinal Johann Baptiste Franzelin. In the letter, Cantor had also stated that "Infinitum aeternum sive Absolutum"—in other words, Absolute Infinity—"refers to God and His attributes" [1,330]. I take it that by saying God *and* God's attributes are Absolute Infinity that Cantor was thereby implying a distinction between the absolute infinitude of God as such and the absolute infinitude of the divine attributes God has.

That is, each of God's attributes are absolutely infinite in themselves, but if God had no attributes of intelligence, presence, power, etc., God would still be absolutely infinite. Despite the mystical unity of Cantor's Absolute Infinity then, it is not a negative infinity, for God as Absolute Infinity is distinct from God's various attributes that are each absolutely infinite in themselves. The divine attributes may each be absolutely infinite, and they may be absolutely infinite as a collective, but they are nevertheless distinct from God's divine infinity per se and so God's attributes do not lose their distinctiveness from one another as a result of being absolutely infinite as parts of God. In this conception, God is not *identical* to each of God's various attributes. Hence, Cantor's divine infinity is not negative infinity.

On the other hand, Cantor must have thought the attributes of God are each absolutely infinite precisely *because* God is, in essence, Absolute Infinity [1,331]. In this view, to be omniscient is to know an absolute infinity of truths, to be omnipotent is to be capable of an absolute infinity of actions, to be omnipresent is to be at an absolute infinity of places and time, and so on. Despite the fact that all these attributes are expressions of absolute infinity, each attribute is only absolutely infinite because Absolute Infinity is itself an attribute of its own. God's distinct attributes of knowledge, power, presence, benevolence, etc. are all absolutely infinite (Ω) because God has Absolute Infinity as its own attribute—an attribute that is the very qualitative and quantitative essence or nature of God [1,332].

So again, that divine attributes are each absolutely infinite does not make them indistinguishable from each other. Cantor's belief that God is a "unity" of absolutely infinite attributes seems to have been in agreement with Bolzano's conception of the divine unity, which in turn may be the same as that proposed by Scotus—an uncomposed complexity, a unity that is not absolute simplicity [1,333]. Cantor did, after all, describe "the Absolute" *not* as a unity where distinctions break down but instead as a "multiplicity" or "totality" of many [1,334]. That would also imply that the absolute infinite nature of God is so because there is in God multiplicity rather than the indistinct, purely non-quantitative unity of negative infinity.

The takeaway is that Cantor's absolute infinity is an integration of both positive infinity and literal infinity rather than of negative infinity and literal infinity. In that respect, Cantor's view of divine infinity did agree with that of Bolzano's—both held divine infinity to be qualitatively *positive* rather than negative. Cantor simply went further in implying that Absolute Infinity, as the divine infinity of God as such, is *its own attribute* in addition to and alongside God's other absolutely infinite attributes such as infinite intellect or knowledge, infinite power, infinite presence, infinite goodwill, and so forth.

Cantor's conception of absolute infinity is thus an instance of a theology that ran with Göcke and Tapp's second option for conceiving of divine infinity: that "God is infinite" means God has a unique feature referred to as "infinity" (i.e., absolute Infinity) in addition to God's other features [1,335].

25.4 CONTEMPORARY VIEWS OF DIVINE INFINITY

Some philosophers have taken up the torch of Cantor, identifying divine infinity as the mathematically absolute infinity (Ω). One such philosopher is Eric Steinhart, professor of philosophy at William Paterson University. Though Steinhart has not stated absolute infinity to be a divine attribute of its own—the Absolute Infinity proposed by Cantor—he has applied Cantor's absolute infinity to each of God's attributes or "perfections" individually [1,336]:

> The degree to which God has any perfection is absolutely infinite. We use contemporary mathematics to precisely define that absolute infinity. For any perfection, we use transfinite recursion to define an endlessly ascending series of degrees of that perfection. That series rises to an absolutely infinite degree of that perfection. God has that absolutely infinite degree…
>
> …To be God is to be maximally perfect. Maximal perfection is absolutely infinite. So, for any divine perfection **P**, the degree to which God has **P** is absolutely infinite. For example, the knowledge, power, and benevolence of God are all absolutely infinite. We

will provide a mathematical model of what it means to say that, for certain perfections, the degree to which God has those perfections is absolutely infinite. We will focus on the three main classical perfections of knowledge, power, and benevolence.

Since offering that view of divine infinity Steinhart has stated he does not believe in a monotheistic God [1,337]. Even so, his approach to mathematizing the attributes of God does serve as a contemporary example of applying Cantorian absolute infinity to the divine.

Most contemporary philosophers of religion and theologians do not mathematize divine infinity like Cantor and Steinhart. That is not to say philosophers and theologians avoid quantitative infinity altogether with regard to conceptions of God's divine infinity. Some of them may add a quantitative feature to their conception of God's infinity, such as proposing that God knows infinitely many true statements or can be at infinitely many places or times. However, they do not typically adopt mathematical models to explicate the divine infinity of God.

But theologians do continue to interpret and analyze conceptions of divine infinity. And they do so with philosophically formal language, most often in the scholastic tradition upholding negative infinity but there are some that portray God as having a positive infinity.

As an example of a theologian backing positive infinity, consider the theological views of philosopher Richard Swinburne, whose definition of God has been summed up like so [1,338]:

> Swinburne says that (1) "God is a personal being—that is, in some sense a person. By a person I mean an individual with basic powers (to act intentionally), purposes, and beliefs." Further, says Swinburne, God is a unique individual, because he is (2) omnipotent—"he can bring about as a basic action any event he chooses." (3) He is omniscient: "whatever is true, God knows that it is true." And (4) he is *perfectly free*, in that desires never exert causal influence on him at all." And (5) eternal: "he exists at each moment of unending time." In addition, God is (6) bodiless, and (7) omnipresent. Finally, (8) God is perfectly good. This, in brief, is Swinburne's concept of God.

Swinburne presents God's attributes as qualitatively infinite, but he regards them as distinct attributes that never violate logic [1,339]. His conception of divine infinity is not that of negative infinity.

Negative infinity is typically framed in terms of the doctrine of divine simplicity and Swinburne does say God is a "simple" being. However, I take it that Swinburne does not mean God is simple in the sense of the doctrine of divine simplicity [1,340]. For example, he does not state or imply that all of God's attributes are really the same attribute merely seen as different attributes from our human point of view, nor does he imply that God does and does not have various attributes because God's being is only "paraconsistently logical." Rather, by saying that God is "simple" Swinburne just means that his description of God's infinite attributes is as simple a description of a personal Creator as one can have. Swinburne posited the minimum number of infinite attributes he could (perfect freedom, omniscience, and omnipotence) in order to deduce God's secondary infinite attributes (omnipresence, omnibenevolence, etc.) [1,341]. None of that means God really has only one attribute that is infinite— that all of God's infinite attributes are really just different expressions of a single infinite attribute. Instead, Swinburne implies that God has multiple infinite attributes. Hence Swinburne's idea of divine infinity is what I would call a positive infinity.

While many contemporary theologians would agree with Swinburne that God's infinity is a positive infinity, there is hardly a consensus. Some theologians, like Craig, simply view talk of God's infinity as informal expressions of superlative qualities which (if I'm following Craig's thought correctly) means that if God's attributes could be measured, they would be considered by any appropriately quantitative scale *immense* but still finite. However, most contemporary theologians—Craig included—still use the term "infinite" to describe God's attributes, even if not in a quantitatively literal sense.

Other theologians, especially Catholic and Islamic theologians, continue to see God's divine infinity as a negative infinity of ontologically indistinguishable attributes. However, these theologians do largely concede that God's attributes are *expressed* or *experienced* from our point of view as if they are distinct from one another (power does not appear as knowledge and knowledge does not appear as benevolence). In that regard, even a theology that proclaims negative infinity still ends up portraying God as having a positive infinity.

Then there are the contemporary theologians who, while portraying God's infinity as a negative infinity, nevertheless refer to it as a positive infinity. They hold that God's infinite attributes lose distinction together as a single "irreducible unity" of the divine essence, but they nevertheless say that, because the attributes are a singular perfection, God has as "positive" infinity. Their use of the term "positive infinity" therefore conflicts with the nomenclature I offer.

Any view of God's infinity that unites his infinite attributes into a single attribute is, in my parlance, a negative infinity. The reason it is a negative infinity is for the same reason the divine infinity proposed by Cusanus is negative: the attributes of God—knowledge, power, etc.—have contrary if not contradictory implications to one another and so *deny* that each can be the same attribute. In a proposal of negative infinity, the infinities are united only in their mutual negation. In the nomenclature I propose, the mutual negation of contradictory statements about God's attributes found within a mystical conception of infinity would make that infinity a negative infinity, not a positive one.

We find an instance of proposing a negative infinity as a "positive infinity" most explicitly in the theology of Göcke, who states that God is "a qualitatively positive infinite entity which is beyond discursive understanding and which, in its being, unites opposites that are contradictory, in the ontology of qualitatively finite entities" [1,342].

Göcke implies his view of God's infinity is the orthodox theology. However, while the bit about uniting opposites that are *contradictory* may echo Cusanus' idea of God's infinity, such a view of divine infinity is certainly not found in the writings of all or even most theologians. Some theologians, for example, might admit that *contraries* (like benevolence and wrath) are expressed by God's infinite power, but not *contradictories* (such as God's power being and not being the same as presence or knowledge).

As for Göcke referring to his conception of divine infinity as a "positive infinite," Turner refers to Göcke's theology of divine infinity as negative or perhaps "double negative," but not positive [1,343]. I agree with Turner insofar as characterizing Göcke's idea of divine infinity as negative rather than positive. Any conception of divine infinity in which two or more infinite attributes share the same identity while contradicting each other's qualities is what I call a negative conception of infinity. From that point of view, Göcke's idea of divine infinity is a negative one since it embraces contradictions between attributes or qualities that thereby lose distinction from one another—it's an infinity of which no logically coherent statements can be made; at best, one can only say things about God's infinitude that are "paraconsistent," as Göcke would have it [1,344].

Quibbles over terminology aside, the examples from Swinburne and Göcke show that qualitative forms of infinity are alive and well in theology today.

25.4.1 *A Lack of Consensus on Divine Infinity...*

The examples I provided are just a few of the many instances of qualitative infinity attributed to God both over the long history of theological thought and in contemporary works of religious philosophy. As shown in the examples (Clement and Aquinas, in particular, come to mind), many theologians and philosophers have made mixed claims as to God's qualitative infinity, sometimes portraying God's infinity as negative infinity and sometimes as positive infinity. So, while I have presented qualitative infinity in the mutually exclusive categories of positive and negative, it's important to keep in mind that theologies are not always consistent in maintaining these distinctions and occasionally even slip back into less formal ways of talking about God's divine infinity.

25.4.2 *...And Yet A Common Theme Emerges in the History of Divine Infinities*

Theology has for centuries debated the best approach and interpretation of divine infinity. Some theologians have adopted the informal approach (Craig) while others have taken a more formal, even mathematical, approach (Steinhart). Some have interpreted divine infinity as being a positive infinity (Swinburn), some as a negative infinity (Cusanus), and some as an absolute infinity (Cantor). Despite the plurality in approaches and interpretations, what they all have in common is belief in the mystical nature of divine infinity—they see it as conferring upon God that property of being beyond human comprehension.

I do not mean theologians and religious philosophers expounding on divine infinity all claim to have had mystical experiences, for that is not the case. Rather, many if not most of them have had what I would call mystical *conceptions* of divine infinity. Whether or not divine attributes are taken as distinguishable from one another, whether God is held to be a simple unity or complex unity of attributes, theologians and religious philosophers generally agree that the attributes of God or "the Absolute" or "the One" are at least individually if not collectively intrinsically mysterious in a way that transcends logical categories and rational descriptions. As we'll see, this is precisely what makes the idea of divine infinity uncompelling to those who are not already believers.

CHAPTER 25 IN REVIEW

❖ Infinity is the concept of lacking limits, whether in quantity, in quality, or both.
❖ Absolute infinity is the combination of qualitative infinity and quantitative infinity.
❖ Qualitative infinity and absolute infinity are together the divine infinities.
❖ Divine infinity is infinity as a property of a divine being—typically, God.
❖ Some theologians hold that to say "God is infinite" is an informal way of saying God has superlative attributes: omniscience, omnipresence, omnipotence, omnibenevolence, etc.
❖ Other theologians believe "God is infinite" means either that those superlative attributes are themselves infinite (in a qualitatively positive or negative sense) or that in addition to any superlative attributes, God has infinity as its own attribute (i.e., absolute infinity).

26: A CRITIQUE OF DIVINE INFINITY

Divine infinity shares some conceptual problems with the quantitative infinities. Just as literal infinity implies contradictions, so too does divine infinity. Just as figurative infinity is a misleading misnomer for certain finite qualities, so it is with divine infinity.

As to self-contradictions, we find them in two versions of divine infinity: negative infinity and positive infinity.

In the via negativa, God is described as negatively infinite such that the laws of logic do not apply to the divine. Recall Khusraw's description of God as "beyond being and nonbeing" [1,345]. A clear violation of the logical principle of excluded middle, which further entails the self-contradiction that we both can and cannot make true statements about God's existence.

In the via positiva, God's various attributes are portrayed as positively infinite, but also in such a manner as to imply logical contradictions, primarily when infinite qualities are thought to imply infinite quantities. For example, take Bolzano's proposal, echoing those of some previous theologians, that God knows a literal infinity of truths [1,346]. This proposal is marred by the fact that literal infinity turns out to be self-contradictory as detailed in previous chapters. The same problem afflicts Cantor's conception of Absolute Infinity, for it too assumes a literal infinity of truths in the divine intellect [1,347].

Theologians and religious philosophers supporting divine infinity offer various arguments designed to make intellectually acceptable these self-contradictions inherent in the notion of divine infinity. I will offer a brief counter to these arguments, concluding that their attempts to intellectually justify divine infinity are not persuasive.

I will first address the problem of resolving self-contradictions in divine infinity. Next, I will offer some criticisms of divine infinity as a property of God taken metaphorically.

26.1 IS GOD LOGICAL?

Some theologians aim for a rational theology. They attempt to describe God's attributes in a manner that makes logical sense. For example, Aquinas argued that there are some things even God's omnipotence cannot accomplish: "He cannot make contradictories to exist simultaneously," such as by making a square circle [1,348]. Aquinas's theology was an attempt to make God's attributes comprehensible.

Insofar as Aquinas attempted a theology that would avoid contradiction, his approach had merit. Still, Aquinas' own conception of divine infinity does have some logical troubles.

Aquinas inconsistently attempted to describe God's attribute of omniscience in a comprehensible manner while also holding the omniscience of God is beyond human comprehension [1,349]. If God's attributes are beyond comprehension, then what is the point in trying to comprehend God's attributes?

For a being whose attributes are beyond comprehension, Aquinas sure had a lot to say about God's attributes.

As for the particulars of God's omniscience, Aquinas held that God is able to know a literal infinitude of things "simultaneously, and not successively" [1,350]—that is, all at once—and we have already seen that literal infinity violates logic due to the conflict between its completeness and limitlessness. Violation of logic tends to be the implication of divine infinity, no matter how otherwise well-reasoned the theology.

Some theologians, to the contrary, just admit that the attributes of God make no logical sense but still affirm them anyway. As we've seen, this is the approach most often taken in the via negativa tradition of theology, and even to some extent in the via positiva. But in admitting that God's attributes are not logically sound, theologians still needed a rationale for why we should believe in a divinity that is beyond rational description.

And so in retort to arguments that divine infinity is not a logical notion, the theologians setting reason aside assert that God, being divinely infinite, need not have a logical description. I have even come across writings by theologians proposing that, as the Creator, God made not only the laws of physics but also the laws of logic and yet need not follow either for that would make God "subordinate" to something else, which would never be true of God as the Supreme Being.

This retort, alas, commits two fallacies in one statement.

The first fallacy is an equivocation of two different meanings of "law"—law as a rule of conduct and law as, for example, a principle for making coherent expressions. The two kinds of law are not at all the same.

A person is not "subordinate" to logic by making statements according to laws of logic the way one is subordinate to the Nation when following the Nation's laws. Following laws of logic just means one is reasoning properly, not that one is lower in social status to logic as if logic is a social agent. The fallacy was to mistake a legal metaphor about logic—that it has "laws"—for a literal description of logic. The same would hold for grammar or math—they both have "rules" by which some expressions are "permitted" while others are "forbidden," but not in a legal sense. The rules are simply needed *if* one wants to make coherent expressions.

To say that God's nature need not be logical because that would make God subordinate to logic is no more accurate than saying if you "follow" the rules of grammar then you have made grammar an authority over you. Not at all. You *use* the convention of grammatical rules in order to be properly understood. So too, God need not be "subject" to logic merely by having a logical description.

The second fallacy is the fallacy of the straw figure. To accuse of an attempt to "subordinate" God to logic is a straw figure argument. In holding that a conception of God must be logical in order to be intellectually acceptable, no one is subordinating God to anything.

Rather, the charge that a given attribute of God violates logic is not an accusation against God but rather an accusation against a claim made *about* God. For example, to charge "God is infinite" as an illogical claim about God owing to the inconsistencies implied by the concept of infinity is not to accuse God of being illogical but rather it is to accuse a theology of holding an illogical doctrine about God.

For theologians and religious philosophers who stick to their guns about divine infinity, this is typically where they appeal to mysticism or mystery. As we've seen, the common claim is that, as a divinely infinite being, God's essence is "paraconsistent" (negative theology) or at least "humanly incomprehensible" (positive theology), so logic does not apply to descriptions of God, who is "ineffable." Göcke, for example, says that "as the ultimate ground of empirical reality, God is considered to be a positive qualitatively infinite entity that is not subject to the law of contradiction and in its essence unites what is contradictory in the realm of finitude" [1,351]. The implication is that God's nature is intrinsically mystical.

26.1.1 *Paraconsistent Troubles and Appeals to Mystery*

Claiming God is mystical—proposing that in God opposite attributes unite into a single, ineffable attribute—does not intellectually excuse theology for abiding contradictions in descriptions of God. There are at least four problems with appeals to mysticism.

First, they do not notice the irony of their own position. Göcke asserted that God is not subject to the "law of contradiction" (ironically, also called in philosophy the law or principle of non-contradiction). But then Göcke goes on to say, "Since nothing is excluded from God, it follows that God is not distinguishable from qualitatively finite entities—as such he is not-other; precisely because of this he is distinguished from finite entities and is found in a different category of ontological determinacy from qualitatively finite entities" [1,352]. What Göcke overlooked is that he just threw out the principle of non-contradiction. Hence what Göcke just claimed both does and does not apply to God. It must therefore also be true, contra Göcke's statement, that everything is *excluded* from God as well as not, and it follows God is *distinguishable* from qualitatively finite entities as well as not, and precisely because of that he is not distinguished from qualitatively finite entities and so is *not* in a different category. You get the idea: once it is said the principle of non-contradiction does not apply, any statement can only be half true at best and the theology dissolves into absurdity because anything follows from a contradiction.

As one reviewer of Göcke's theology noted [1,353],

> ...God possesses every property and its denial. Of course, this has a rather odd entailment that Göcke does not consider. If the paraconsistent God has every property and its denial, that means that the following statements are both true of God. It is true that "God is paraconsistent". It is also true that "God is not paraconsistent". Since the law of non-contradiction does not apply to the paraconsistent God, this may not be a problem for the view, but it certainly sounds odd to the say in the least.

Second, mystics are not consistent in what they claim of God's mystical nature. Consider God's infinite goodness expressed as the contraries of justice and mercy. As Steele and Williams pointed out, a problem appears when we consider that God's justice punishes some sinners while God's mercy spares others because "on the understanding of divine simplicity...Divine justice and divine mercy are one and the same, and both identical with the divine essence, so they can't be available to serve distinct roles in the economy of salvation" [1,354]. To get around this problem, theologies must make selective use of mysticism, thus inconsistently applying their claims of God's mystical nature. They start by saying God is not subject to logical laws and human reason and then go on to make qualifications about God's nature based on logic and human reason when the contradictions become too inconvenient to ignore. A similar problem arises when mystics say God is unknowable and then go on to write whole treatises about God.

Third, appeals to mysticism become self-defeating. If God's infinite nature is so mystical that it is beyond reason altogether—if divine infinity is beyond our ability to analyze with the aid of logical thought—then there wouldn't be any point in discussing divine infinity at all since anything anyone says about divine infinity would not be able to be shown either true or false, credible or dubious. For any claim that a mystic makes, I can make the opposite claim and be just as correct, justifying my position by pointing out that divine infinity is "beyond comprehension."

Fourth, and on a related note, the theologian's appeal to mysticism is an example of what some philosophers call the logical fallacy of appeal to mystery, which we first encountered back in § 22.1.2. The fallacy is to provide a non-explanation as if it is an explanation. To explain something mysterious by calling it mysterious is an obvious example. Another example is to explain a paradox that results from a theory about some natural phenomenon by claiming the phenomenon is paradoxical. For example, time travel theories often have the superficial appearance of being coherent until you ponder them and notice impossible situations implied by the theories. A time travel theory cannot be made more plausible simply by saying time travel is paradoxical. The same holds for divine infinity. Is it paraconsistent or is it simply illogical and claimed to be paraconsistent? Is divine infinity ineffable, or is the idea of divine infinity an illogical notion and the claim of its ineffability merely an excuse to cover up that fact?

The problem with using appeals to mystery is that anyone could use the same appeal to get just about any logically fallacious notion off the hook for its incoherence. Caught in a contradiction? Just reply some things are beyond the protestor's understanding.

It's one thing when challenged to just admit, "I don't know. I need more data." It's quite another to claim something is "beyond rationality" while offering no evidence for the claim that it is so, other than to say it is so. The former is honesty, the latter is a dodge.

Similarly, appeals to mysticism for explaining away the logical self-contradictions implied by divine infinity are rationalizations offered to lend divine infinity an air of intellectual legitimacy it would not otherwise have. The appeal to mysticism is a rhetorical strategy designed to make a theology appear intellectually plausible even while offering a logically bogus conception of God based on false assumptions. This is a harsh assessment, but I have heretofore found no counterargument compelling.

For all these reasons, there is no need to concede that divine infinity is a condition beyond the intellect. We could just as well conclude that mystical notions of divine infinity are illusions brought on by theologians trying to outdo one another with ever-loftier neoplatonic conceptions of the divine.

26.1.2 *Divine Infinity Shorn of Mysticism*

Were the discipline of theology to cease appeals to mysticism, that in itself would improve the plausibility of divine infinity. However, it would not be sufficient to save divine infinity from refutation.

Without mystical conceptions to fall back on, the logical contradictions implied by negative, positive, and absolute infinity would then stick, and the only way to remove them would be to affirm that the divine does have limitations. And that would entail the end of any literal interpretation of divine infinity. Gone would be the negative infinity of Clement, Cusanus, and Göcke. Gone would be the positive infinity of Scotus, Bolzano, and Swinburne. Gone would be the absolute infinity of Cantor (and perhaps Steinhart).

What would then become of divine infinity? At best it would continue to be used as a figure of speech—to say God's attributes are "infinite" would not be a literal description of God's attributes but simply a metaphor for their unfathomably great (albeit finite) quality.

26.2 DIVINE INFINITY AS MISNOMER

This brings us back to where we started, with Craig's take on the meaning of God's infinity. Craig believes claims as to the infinitude of God's attributes are merely hyperbolic references to the superlative quality of God's collective attributes [1,355]. His view cannot be historically accurate since theologians have emphasized that divine infinity is a condition of *lacking qualitative limits* per se, in a manner that suggests the divine is beyond comprehension. However, suppose in order to resolve the illogical implications of divine infinity according to its mystical conception theologians decide to break with the past, reject the former mystical views of God's attributes, and take Craig's position. In so doing, they reconceive divine infinity as a condition denoting the superlative (but not literally unlimited) condition of God's various attributes such as perfection, purity, aseity, power, etc.

In ceasing appeals to mysticism, theologians would solve at least one long-standing problem—they would avoid many of the logical contradictions plaguing their traditional descriptions of God's divine attributes. Any further use of 'infinity' for describing God or God's attributes would then be proposed as a metaphor for the superlative nature of God's attributes. To say, "God is infinite" would just mean "God has superlative attributes." To say some attribute of God is infinite, like "God has infinite knowledge," would be just to say that attribute is superlative. This I take to be the upshot of Craig's position on divine infinity.

However, some questions remain. In what sense are God's attributes superlative—are they superlative because they are indistinguishable as one attribute of the divine nature (negatively 'infinite') or are they superlative because they are each on their own superlative (positively 'infinite')?

If the former is the case, then the phrase "God is infinite" is just a figure of speech to indicate that God's attributes are indistinguishable from one another when we move beyond their appearances to the reality behind them, as if removing the prism through which we typically filter the attribute of God into many attributes. It's not that God's attributes are without limit in a literal sense. It's simply that all of God's various attributes are just different *appearances* of what is in reality a single, simple attribute where all distinctions between power, presence, knowledge, goodness, etc. break down—negative infinity. This negative conception of divine infinity makes infinity into a metaphor for *indistinguishability*.

While this is a sophisticated take on negative infinity for the divine, even this position does not rescue divine infinity from conceptual troubles. In abandoning talk of infinity as a state of being literally *limitless*, we still have the problem that various attributes of God would contradict each other if they were essentially, and not just apparently, indistinguishable from one another. God cannot be of infinite wrath and infinite grace if the word 'infinite' means to be *of indistinguishable quality*, for then wrath would be grace and grace would be wrath, which would be absurd. Contraries would become contradictories if they became indistinguishable, and then we are right back at the mystical theology we tried to overcome. Hence the intellectual bankruptcy of the apophatic tradition—the via negativa makes God not just different by kind, but *too different* by kind to be meaningful.

Perhaps things would fare better with a more positive theology that promotes positive infinity taken as a metaphor for being *of incomparable quality*. To say "God is infinite" in the sense of positive infinity, used metaphorically, in this way would simply mean God is a being of incomparable qualities. That is, each of God's attributes is qualitatively incomparable to other instances of the same attribute held by finite beings. So, to say God is infinitely pure would mean God is incomparably pure, to say God is infinitely powerful would mean God is incomparably powerful, etc.

According to this metaphorical version of positive infinity, it is not that God's divine attributes are *absolutely* incomparable such as to be unlike anything we know, for if that were so we wouldn't be able to meaningfully say God is "pure" or "powerful" or anything else since then each attribute would be unidentifiable or confused with others as in the negative theology. Rather, to say God's divine attributes are "incomparable" means that God is *relatively* incomparable with regard to various attributes such as purity, power, and so forth. And that relative incomparability is a matter of degree rather than kind: to say God is infinite would in this interpretation mean that God has attributes such that no other instances of the same attributes held by anything else are of comparable quality, but the divine attributes are still distinguishable for what they are.

This is a far superior position to take on positive infinity. But even here there is a lingering problem with positive infinity. The problem is that using the term 'infinite' at all is not only not needed, but also it too can be misleading. Why use the word 'infinite' when you can simply say 'incomparable' and be better understood?

Divine infinity, when taken as a positive infinity in only a metaphorical sense, suffers the same problem of pragmatic logic as does figurative infinity. Recall that figurative infinity turned out to be a misnomer for serial indefiniteness. Figurative use of the term 'infinite' for any series that is not truly limitless but is instead variable in limits is prone to mislead one into conflating the figurative with the literal usage. The same problem of practical reasoning would afflict divine infinity as a metaphorical 'infinite' in the positive sense.

We normally take 'infinite' to mean a lack of limitations. But saying that divine attributes are 'infinite' because they are incomparable with the attributes of anything else can be perniciously misleading. Something can be magnified in quality to the point of being 'incomparable' without lacking, or even seeming to lack, limits altogether—that is, without seeming to be *infinite*. In which case use of the term 'infinite' in the sense of positive infinity becomes a misleading bit of poetry and can even be an abuse of the term 'infinity'. To retain infinity as a metaphor would become a case of intellectual misdirection on the part of the theology using the term.

In short, divine infinity taken as *negative* infinity or *positive* infinity, even if only in a metaphorical sense, is still a problematic notion.

Then too, divine infinity as *absolute* infinity also has its troubles. Absolute infinity combines the concept of positive infinity with the concept of literal infinity without resolving the logical problems of either concept. Again, putting its mystical aspect to the side, the features of literal infinity and positive infinity that are combined into absolute infinity are both problematic for the aforementioned reasons of both. Literal infinity turns out to be self-contradictory and to say something is figuratively infinite in the positive sense of the term is to use a misnomer for incomparability and so becomes misleading since that which is incomparable need not lack limits and limitations are typically conceived to imply quantitative limits. As an amalgam of both literal and positive infinity, absolute infinity has the conceptual weaknesses of both.

We could instead metaphorize absolute infinity (Ω), making it into a metaphor for God's superlative nature in alignment with Craig's thesis. But that would still be as misleading as it is for negative or positive infinity. Indeed, perhaps more so since Cantor's transfinite system would be a case of using logically dubious 'numbers' for descriptions of God's attributes. Moreover, reducing absolute infinity to a metaphor for qualities that are not infinite in the sense of lacking limits per se seems to defeat the whole point of bringing in Cantor's mathematical schema.

The bottom line is that if there is nothing *literally* infinite—limitless, unlimited—about divine qualities however awesome they may be, then 'infinite' is a misleading characterization of divine qualities. If all "God is infinite" means is "God is superlative" or "God has superlative attributes" or "God is really awesome," then why not just say God's attributes are superlative or awesome or supreme or whatever, and leave it at that—why use "infinite" at all? Bringing up infinity when what is described is not genuinely without limit, or even quantitative at all, only spreads more confusion about what God is supposed to be. It would again seem better to drop the use of infinity altogether, even in theology.

Of course, I do not own language. No one does. Everyone is free to keep using terms like 'infinite' in any metaphorical sense they so choose, whether with respect to quantities (figurative infinity) or God (divine infinity). But just as it would be more precise and less misleading to replace figurative infinity with alternative terms for quantitative indefiniteness, so too would be the replacement of divine infinity with divine supremacy. God is, after all, said to be the Supreme Being, and that should be good enough.

26.3 ON APOLOGETICS FOR DIVINE INFINITY

Theologians have offered several philosophical arguments intended to prove God infinite [1,356]. I cannot address all their reasons and arguments, but I will address those that seem to hold the most sway. The following are three recorded by Otto Zimmerman (1873–1932), a priest and editor for the 1913 *Catholic Encyclopedia* [1,357], a resource now online.

26.3.1 *The Argument from Experience*

For any essential craving human beings experience, that which is craved must be real. Human beings essentially crave infinite knowledge and eternal happiness. Hence, infinite knowledge and eternal happiness must be real. But infinite knowledge and eternal happiness are attributes of God. Ergo, God must really have infinite knowledge and eternal happiness, and so God must be infinite.

26.3.2 *The Argument from Perfection*

If God's attributes (unity, simplicity, immutability, wisdom, power, etc.) are qualitatively limited, then there is a chance that God could have had those attributes to a better degree of quality, which would mean God is not necessarily perfect. But God is necessarily perfect. So, God's attributes cannot be qualitatively limited—God must be infinite.

26.3.3 *The Argument from Aseity*

If God were limited, then God would be dependent on external causes and conditions for existence. But God is the self-existing, uncreated Being, who is independent of external causes and conditions. Hence, God cannot be so limited. Therefore, God is infinite in being [1,358].

26.4 REPLIES TO THE ARGUMENTS FOR DIVINE INFINITY

None of these arguments for divine infinity are convincing. At best, they only prove that to ascribe infinity to God is consistent with ascribing other divine attributes to God such as eternal happiness, perfection, and aseity. The arguments do not establish that infinity is a necessary feature of God. Replies to each argument are as follows.

26.4.1 *Reply to the Argument from Experience*

Is it really true that infinite knowledge and eternal happiness are "essential cravings?" Zimmerman thought so, but the evidence does not support it.

There have been societies around the globe that have had neither a conception of infinite knowledge nor belief in an afterlife of eternal happiness [1,359]. Had human beings really craved those things "essentially," then you would expect belief in them to be universal across cultures and millennia. Zimmerman may have craved those things, but there is no anthropological or sociological evidence that such desires are *universal* and *necessary* features of being human.

And even if infinite knowledge and eternal happiness were universally craved, that would not necessarily mean they are real. People can crave all kinds of things that they will never have, such as being universally loved by all and having an ideal sex life—that doesn't mean those things are real. Further, even if infinite knowledge and eternal happiness were real, that does not entail a singular being would have both of those attributes or that such a being would be God.

So, the argument from experience fails to establish that God must have qualitatively (or quantitatively) infinite attributes.

26.4.2 *Reply to the Argument from Perfection*

The argument from perfection fairs no better. It too makes some assumptions that are not necessarily true.

First, the argument seems to assume chance is an *ontological* feature of existence such that if something is one way, it could as well have been another, and without any cause to make it so. That is not a necessary assumption to make. We could just as well assume chance is only an *epistemic* feature of claims made *about* things. It may be true that, *for all we know*, things could be different—but what do we know? In which case, though one person may assess there is a chance attribute x could have been better, another person may assess the chance of x being better is zero, given a different base of knowledge. So maybe the attribute in question, though limited, could *not* have been any better—no matter what conditions were different. In which case, maybe God's attributes could be limited without any chance of being better.

Second, the argument assumes anything with a finite degree of quality could have been of better quality. But that need not be true of just anything that has qualities. Take God's attributes; perhaps they are limited, and perhaps their limits are not a matter of contingency but a matter of logical necessity. If we know the limits of God's attributes, we could always stipulate they could have been better, but perhaps in doing so we would be speaking from ignorance, not realizing the reason(s) that the attributes are not as we say they could have been, and for quite logical reasons. For example, consider God's attribute of omnipotence. Assuming my case against infinity is correct and the amount of energy in the Universe cannot be literally infinite, then to say God is omnipotent would be to say God can accomplish anything it takes power to do in the Universe, which we know is necessarily finite. Hence, God's omnipotence would not be infinite power but rather a monopoly on power that is necessarily finite. If power is necessarily finite, then having all power, despite its finitude, would be as "perfect" as one can get with respect to power.

Third, and on a related note, the argument from perfection assumes that to be perfect requires a lack of qualitative limit. Not so. All perfection would require is that the quality cannot be better than it is. Even if we can *imagine* something better, maybe there is a good reason why in reality it cannot be better in the way we imagined it "could" be. So perhaps perfection does not require the infinite; perhaps perfection just implies nothing can be better than whatever finite degree it already has.

By way of counterargument, it might be asked, as Oppy does [1,360], that if divine attributes are finite, "what reason could there be for God to possess a given magnitude to degree N rather than to degree N + 1?" However, Oppy's question is based on a couple of incorrect assumptions.

Oppy assumes any proposal of God as finite must answer why a particular divine attribute is of "a given magnitude." Such a demand is hardly reasonable. The theologian proposing a finite God need not be held to providing a particular value N as a magnitude of some attribute that God has any more than the scientist proposing the existence of extraterrestrials needs to provide an exact number of them in the galaxy to have a plausible hypothesis. Certainly, if someone says there are 10^{99} life forms in the galaxy, we could always ask why that number and not another, such as $10^{99} + 1$. But just as proposing that extraterrestrial biological life exists does not require the proposal of a specific number of extraterrestrial organisms to be plausible, so too speculations about God's attributes, even if proposed to be finite, do not require the assignment of specific measures of those attributes.

And anyway, Oppy also assumes for any N degree of magnitude, $N + 1$ is just as possible. But that's a big assumption and not necessarily true.

Suppose at any given time, N is finite. And suppose N is a degree of knowledge; namely, N is equal to all that it is logically possible for *anyone* to know at the given time. Suppose God always knows N. Since N represents the most that it is logically possible for anyone to know at a given time, if God knew one more thing than N at that time, then N would not be *all* that is logically possible to know at that time—a contradiction. So, there is no such thing as $N + 1$ for God to know at any given time. God knows all there is to know, which is the finite quantity N. Notice that none of that entails N is infinite.

Fourth and finally, the argument from perfection assumes God is perfect. That is not a surprising assumption given that orthodox Judaism, Christianity, and Islam all hold that God is perfect. However, it is not an axiom universally shared about a supreme deity (and as we'll see in a bit, the perfection of God is not a doctrine consistently supported in the Scriptures of any of these religions) and we are not forced by logic to agree with any particular conception of perfection.

26.4.3 *Reply to the Argument from Aseity*

It is not necessarily true that if God were limited, then God would be dependent on external causes and conditions for existence. There is no a priori reason why a limited God could not have aseity as an attribute. If, for example, time had a beginning, God could still have been the first being to exist. God does not require limitlessness of any kind to be self-sufficient.

26.5 ON OBJECTIONS TO CONCEPTIONS OF THE DIVINE AS FINITE

Theologians have not only argued *for* divine infinity, but they have argued as well *against* conceptions of God as finite. The reasons theologians have for rejecting depictions of God as finite have less to do with logic and evidence, however, as they have to do with aesthetic tastes and long-standing religious doctrine.

26.5.1 *A Finite God and Polytheism*

One concern theologians and philosophers of the Abrahamic religions have expressed concerning conceptions of God as finite is that finitude makes God too much like the gods of the polytheistic religions. "To associate with God the attributes of his creatures entails polytheism," says one religious philosopher [1,361]. Zimmerman had a similar concern, stating a finite God would entail that "the existence of other gods, His equals or even His superiors in perfection would be possible, and it would be mere chance if they did not exist" [1,362].

There are a couple of logical problems with the above quotes.

Notice the first quote refers to God by a male pronoun, thus violating its own principle not to associate God with creaturely attributes. And yet in so doing, polytheism is not being endorsed. So why would proposing God to be finite be an endorsement of belief in more than one god? It does not logically follow that if God is finite that God cannot be unique.

As for the second quote, there are two problems with it. For one thing, Zimmerman once again confused the epistemic category of chance with the ontological category of contingency. If God were finite, that would not entail reality allows for the "chance" of more than one god to exist. Reality may not be capable of more than one finite god. All that a "chance" of more than one finite god would imply is that some folks—the ones calculating the odds—may be uncertain as to how many finite gods there can actually be; it would not imply reality is uncertain about the matter. Given different assumptions, others might calculate the odds of more than a single finite deity existing to be zero.

In short, the claim that a conception of deity as finite implies polytheism is not justified.

26.5.2 *Is a Finite God a Diminished God?*

Another concern theologians and religious philosophers have is that a finite God would be less worthy of ultimate reverence or worship than an infinite God. But there are at least four reasons why that is a fallacious inference.

First, infinity in a quantitative sense is either self-contradictory (literal infinity) or a misnomer for the indefinite (figurative infinity) which is finite anyway. A finite God is hardly a diminished deity on account of not have a description that includes the self-contradictions of literal infinity and a more honest description than a figurative use of the term 'infinite'. Given the logical problems with infinity, I have to maintain that proposing God to be finite rather than infinite would be of benefit to any conception of God worthy of serious consideration as a candidate for belief.

Second, a conception of God as finite can still be portrayed in such a manner as to inspire reverence for those who believe in the existence of a deity. For example, God's attributes of omnipotence, omnipresence, etc. can be carefully conceived in finite terms with no relevant diminishment in their impressiveness. Take Oppy's description of divine attributes [1,363]:

> To say that God is omnipotent is, at least roughly, to say that it is within God's power to do anything that it is logically possible for God to do. To say that God is omniscient is, at least roughly, to say that God knows the truth status of every proposition for which it is logically possible that God know the truth status of that proposition. To say that God is omnipresent is to say that every spatiotemporal location is present ("available") to God. To say that God is eternal is to say that every time is present ("available") to God. (Some say, rather, that God is sempiternal, i.e., that God exists at every time. My formulation is neutral on the question of whether God is *in* time.) To say that God is perfectly good is to say, inter alia, that there is no moral obligation, moral duty, or moral good to which God fails to pay due accord.

As Oppy describes God's attributes, none of them imply the attributes are necessarily infinite, and they would still be more than awesome enough if God by such description were to exist.

Third, if the worry theologians have is that God would not be worthy of worship without being dubbed by a lofty predicate like "infinite," one could instead substitute in the description of God's attributes more appropriate terms such as *supremacy* or *ultimacy*. Instead of saying God is "infinitely powerful," for example, one would say God is "supremely powerful" or "ultimately powerful" to establish that God has power superior to all others. Even a term like 'omnipotent' can be used to imply that all power, rather than infinite power, belongs to God. Those are not the only options, of course, as there are similar designations such as *most powerful*. And we could just as well apply these less-paradoxical predicates to God's other attributes: God is *supremely* knowing, *most* present, *ultimately* benevolent, etc. All such terms could do the same emotive job of inspiring reverence as the older use of cognates for infinity and without conjuring up any logical problems.

Fourth, people have worshipped far less lofty figures. People have worshipped pharaohs, kings, dictators, and even ghosts of ancestors who had no social status in life. Conceptions of even a finite God are far and away more impressive than any of those, so it's hard to take seriously that a finite God with the attributes described by Oppy above would somehow be unworthy of worship merely on the basis of being finite rather than infinite.

For God to be finite, then, would not on its own make God unworthy of reverence and worship.

26.5.3 *A Finite God and the Problem of Anthropomorphism*

God is a supernatural being and as such must have many attributes unlike those of human beings. It would therefore be an error to ascribe to God attributes that are too *anthropomorphic*—that is, characteristic of human beings as biological organisms instead of metaphysically different in kind from anything in the created order. As part of the natural created order, human beings are finite and have finite attributes. Some theologians conclude that finitude is an attribute of human beings but not an attribute of God as Creator. They therefore charge portrayals of God with finite attributes as committing the error of *anthropomorphism* [1,364].

But claiming that being finite is an anthropomorphic trait goes way too far. There are many non-human things that are finite. The number 3 is finite. Does that make it "anthropomorphic"?

Another problem with the anthropomorphism charge is that it is leveled inconsistently. Theologians seem to engage in the very anthropomorphism they reject. They have no trouble, for instance, claiming God to have a mind, an intellect, a will, personhood (God goes by gendered pronouns like "He", "His", etc.), virtues like wisdom, the power of speech, a language, status (Lord, King, etc.), and so forth—all qualities typical of humans and so which should likewise count as anthropomorphic. Especially given the broad brush in which the charge of anthropomorphism was leveled merely on the basis of attributing finitude to God—a feature even the most non-human of things can have.

Last but not least, worries of anthropomorphism seem to contradict some of the founding scriptures of the Abrahamic religions, all of which portray God as having created humanity in *imago dei*—the "image" of God [1,365]. It's hard to see how finite beings like human beings can be in the "image" of an *infinite* being—one would really have to strain the meaning of the word 'image' to make it even metaphorically accurate as something infinite. A far less strained interpretation of the image of God—a feature humans are said to share with the divine—is that the 'image' is something finite even if not completely literal in meaning. In which case, the notion that the divine is finite would be consistent with scripture and would not constitute an error of anthropomorphism. It would not be that attributing to God finitude is anthropomorphism, but rather that human finitude is part of what it is to be in the image of God.

26.5.4 *The Infinite God of Scripture*

The scriptures of the Abrahamic religions all attribute superlative attributes to God which theologians have termed omniscience, omnipotence, omnipresence, etc. However, as argued in the previous chapter, any of these attributes can be interpreted as *finitely* superlative, especially relative to the Universe as a finite reality. As it turns out, there is only one unambiguous reference in scripture to any of God's attributes as *infinite*, and that is a reference to God's omniscience.

The reference is found in Psalms 147:5, which states, "Great is our Lord and mighty in power; his understanding has no limit" [1,366]. That is a clear reference to the concept of infinity—at least, to qualitative infinity [1,367]. To say there is no limit to what God understands, especially in reference to power, is not necessarily to say God understands a literal infinity of things; it may just mean that God has the power to understand anything capable of being understood. In which case, even Psalms 147:5 is not a reference to quantitative infinity; at best, it is just a figurative usage of positive infinity.

There are also other scriptural passages that may be interpreted as references to infinity—quantitative infinity in particular. For example, the scriptures contain references to eternity and life everlasting. However, it is not clear such references are really to quantitative infinity, at least in the literal sense of the term. The scriptural references to eternity can also be interpreted as referring to time passing ceaselessly from the beginning of creation—a figuratively infinite future, which is serially indefinite time rather than literally infinite time.

Moreover, some theologians interpret scriptural references to eternity (and related terms like "forever" and "everlasting") as references to a state of *timelessness*—the state of being completely outside of time itself. For example, the theologian and philosopher Aurelius Augustine (354–430 CE) referenced Psalms 101:28 (God's "years do not fail") and Romans 11:36 ("all these things have their being in [God]") as evidence for eternity as timelessness [1,368]. But neither of these scriptures clearly state such, and the idea of eternity as timelessness even appears to be a later, post-biblical invention of early Christian theologians such as Gregory of Nyssa [1,369]. And anyway, timelessness is not the same as infinity, so reinterpreting eternity as timelessness still does not imply that temporal infinity—either in some sense qualitative or literally quantitative—is referenced in scripture.

So, as far as scriptural references to eternity are concerned, the scriptures neither make clear that eternity is timelessness nor that eternity is the same as a literally infinite amount of time. Literally infinite time appears more convincingly to have originated with ancient Greek philosophers such as Anaximander (see § 8.1.1). Likely, the scriptural references to eternity are much more plausibly references to serial indefiniteness ('infinity' in the figurative sense)—unceasing time but not literally infinite time [1,370].

The most that can be said for sure is that, aside from God's omniscience as possibly an instance of divine infinity, the scriptures are ambiguous about divine infinity and make no clear references to literal (quantitative) infinity either. Regardless, one clear reference is all we need to establish that God is depicted in scripture as having an infinite attribute of either a figurative or literal variety, and Psalms 147:5 provides that reference.

So does that mean God is infinite? Only if scripture *accurately* describes a real God. If God is real, that alone does not necessarily mean scriptures about God are accurate with respect to whether or not God has infinite attributes. The scriptures could be incorrect accounts of a real God the way a fake news story offers a false or misleading account about a real person. If scriptures do not offer accurate depictions of God, then scriptural depictions of God as infinite only reveal what some authors over the course of history have thought *about* God, not that God is both a real being and an infinite one at that.

For sake of argument, let's start by assuming the scriptures are accurate depictions of a real God. Assuming as much, we should find no logical errors in the canonical scriptures concerning the way God is depicted. Unfortunately, we find the opposite: the scriptures do not offer logically consistent depictions of God as infinite—either literally or figuratively. Because of that, the scriptures cannot be entirely accurate depictions of a real God.

For example, while Psalm 147:5 says the power of God's understanding "has no limit," other biblical passages imply the opposite—that there are indeed very obvious limits to the power of God's understanding and, more narrowly, to God's foreknowledge. For example, Genesis 6:6 states, "The Lord regretted that he had made human beings on the earth, and his heart was deeply troubled" [1,371]. As Swinburne pointed out, God could not have regretted (or "repented" of) creating humanity if God already knew in advance what they would become [1,372]. If God's understanding were unlimited, and understanding implies knowledge, then God's knowledge would be unlimited. So, God would have foreknowledge, which would also be unlimited. Even if we take God's understanding to be "unlimited" in a figurative sense, that means God understood what would result from creating humanity to begin with. Surely God would have at least that much 'foreknowledge'. But then, there would have been no need for God to regret or repent of anything because God would not have made humanity in such a way that God would later come to regret it. Ergo, either it is not true that there is no limit to the power of God's understanding as Psalm 147:5 states, or Genesis 6:6 is incorrect—both cannot be true.

One way to dodge such contradictions is by stating that not only are scriptural descriptions of God metaphorical, but also scriptural metaphors do not have to be consistent with one another. However, we then have to wonder how it is that the scriptures "reveal" God at all if they only speak to us via inconsistent metaphors. Revelation by confounding figures of speech is not much of a revelation. Moreover, which metaphor is to be taken more seriously than the other—is it that God's knowledge is only "without limit" but not *that* unlimited, or is it that God was "deeply troubled" about making humanity, but not *that* troubled? Either way is problematic for claims of biblical revelation and scriptural inerrancy.

It seems to me that if we are not trying to force scripture to read in a logically consistent manner out of a preestablished bias that scripture *must* be inerrant, then we cannot honestly interpret scriptural passages as metaphorical that on their own would have been taken literally. Without comparing the two scriptures, we would normally take Psalms 147:5 as a statement that God can understand anything able to be understood, including human nature and tendencies, and we would normally take Genesis 6:6 to mean what it says—God regretted creating humanity and God was genuinely troubled. Assuming the principle that scriptures should not have to be given strained interpretations to make them logically consistent with one another, I submit that the scriptures genuinely contradict each other as to God's nature—one of the scriptures (Psalms 147:5) implies God has qualitatively infinite power of understanding and other scripture (Genesis 6:6) implies God's power of understanding, while qualitatively greater than anyone's, is not in *any* sense "without limit."

Due to the logical contradictions in how scripture portrays the nature of God, the assumption of scriptural inerrancy must be wrong: the scriptures, simply *qua* scriptures, cannot be entirely accurate depictions of a real God. While the Abrahamic religions have accorded them holy status, the scriptures must not be genuine revelations from a divine source but instead an anthology of religious opinions by all-too-human writers. That alone explains why some scriptures cohere and some conflict [1,373].

Because contradictory scriptural claims cannot both be true, and we have the foregoing logical reasons for believing infinity is conceptually erroneous, we are left with the conclusion that only those scriptural passages depicting or implying God to be finite have any chance at all of being true—assuming, of course, that the God those scriptures attempt to describe is real.

26.6 DIVINITY WITHOUT INFINITY

Conservative theologians defend divine infinity because they believe its refutation would undermine orthodox belief in the inerrancy of scripture. Assuming scripture cannot both be inerrant and self-contradictory, the inerrancy issue is settled, and not in its favor. That does not mean all scripture is false, it just means not all scripture can be true. I will leave the reader to further assess the accuracy of scriptures.

26.6.1 *This is Highly Unorthodox*

Said theologians may worry about maintaining scriptural inerrancy out of fear that if one doctrine of God should fall, they all might topple. But such concerns are overblown. It would be a case of the slippery slope fallacy to suggest that just because one doctrine of orthodox belief changes, they must all change. Even if divine infinity goes, that does not mean theism itself goes with it. Consequently, if critical atheists wish to make a case against theism, arguments against divine infinity like those I have presented in this book would not be sufficient for that purpose.

   Moreover, anyone who looks will find it hard to come up with an example of someone who quit being a theist altogether over losing belief in infinity. For those persuaded by my thesis that any real God would have to have finite attributes rather than infinite attributes, I am positive it would make little if any difference to their belief in God's reality. It is true that a theist who does not hold God to be infinite is unorthodox, but they would still be a theist, nonetheless.

   There have always been unorthodox theists, [1,374] including some who have thrown out belief in divine infinity or at least concluded that some of God's attributes must be finite. A good example is Rabbi Harold Kushner, who wrote the bestseller *When Bad Things Happen to Good People* [1,375]. In his book, Kushner argued that God would like to do something about all the evil in the world, but lacks the power necessary to prevent it [1,376]:

> I believe in God. But I do not believe the same things about Him that I did years ago, when I was growing up or when I was a theological student. I recognize His limitations. He is limited in what He can do by laws of nature and by the evolution of human nature and human moral freedom.
>
> I no longer hold God responsible for illnesses, accidents, and natural disasters, because I realize that I gain little and I lose so much when I blame God for those things. I can worship a God who hates suffering but cannot eliminate it, more easily than I can worship a God who chooses to make children suffer and die, for whatever exalted reason.

Kushner did not give up his belief in God, just his belief that God has infinite or otherwise unrestricted power. Which goes to show that rejection of divine infinity does not entail rejection of theism per se. From this we may conclude that losing belief in divine infinity would not undermine belief in God as such, nor belief in anything else held to be divine. The need to give up the preestablished orthodoxy on divine infinity is not the need to give up on theism.

26.6.2 *Recommendations for Future Theology*

Given the conceptual problems with divine infinity, the proper conclusion to reach is that any deity that truly exists must be finite. Committed theists should therefore hold the most plausible conception of God's attributes is that they are finite, however superlative they may be.

   That said, theologians are loath to give up on the idea of divine infinity. They tend to justify infinity as a divine attribute by appealing to the mystical, adopting the position that God is not describable in rational terms [1,377]. In response, I maintain that any theology that would be worthy of adherence must, as a theoretical minimum, portray God as both quantitatively and qualitatively finite, for only a rational conception of deity would require no rationalizations on the part of the believer [1,378].

Still, there can certainly be aspects of God that are ineffable. As pointed out back in § 1.1, there are some aspects even about other people we cannot put into words—at least, not without use of metaphors that, however apt they may be, nevertheless do not adequately express the subjective qualities of the person in question. Likewise, we will never know, to borrow an example from philosopher Thomas Nagel, what it is like to be a bat [1,379]. But that does not make being a bat, or being any other animal, or even being a person "infinite." Nor does it mean they have attributes beyond logic. It just means some things need to be experienced to be adequately understood.

To which a believer might say that what I need is an experience of the divine. But I do not have such. And as the psychologist William James (1842–1910) pointed out, the mystic cannot expect the non-mystic to be moved by private experiences only the mystic has [1,380]. Then too, we non-mystics have to wonder if the mystics aren't just fooling themselves—their imaginations having run wild with paradoxical thoughts. Until the non-mystic receives a mystical experience, only a rational account of the divine would appear to have any plausibility to the non-mystic.

Since most people, myself included, are not mystics, if I had a recommendation for theologians and theists in general, it would be to drop the proposals of divine infinity altogether in favor of a more logically consistent, alternative concept. Such would avoid many intellectual rabbit holes from the start and certainly be far more persuasive than rationalizations for the mystical.

However, I do recognize that such a recommendation would likely have little if any influence for three reasons. First, because the recommendation comes from an outsider both to theology and to theism—and one without the prominent platform of a media giant. Second, there would be no point to replacing divine infinity with a logically consistent account of divine attributes if the theology in question already embraces a "paraconsistent," mystical, or generally apophatic approach to understanding the divine—all of which throw out logic with respect to the divine anyway. Third, and most importantly, most theologians aim to avoid contradicting the founding scriptures and revered religious leaders who have already endorsed divine infinity as the official position.

Nevertheless, I maintain that theologians have offered neither persuasive reasons for belief in an infinite God nor persuasive arguments against conceptions of God as finite. Even so, I conclude that the refutation of infinity—including divine infinity—does not undermine theism as such. A finite conception of divinity remains the right approach for any theology that would hope to be intellectually credible.

CHAPTER 26 IN REVIEW

❖ Both versions of divine infinity—qualitative infinity and absolute infinity—are riddled with contradictions. To remove those contradictions makes divine infinity into merely a misnomer for some finite property such as being indistinguishable, incomparable, superlative, supreme, ultimate, etc.

❖ Since in order to exist God cannot have self-contradictory attributes, and even the notion of divine infinity contains self-contradictions, then for God to exist would mean God must have only finite attributes for which it would be misleading to call any of them "infinite."

❖ Bottom line: if God exists, then God must be finite.

CONCLUSION

27: WRAPPING UP THE CASE AGAINST INFINITY

We have come to the end. It is now time to review the main points of the case against infinity, read the verdict, and consider the implications.

27.1 KEY ASSUMPTIONS OF THE CASE

As indicated in § 1.7, the case against infinity rests on certain assumptions. Chief among them:

- Infinity can be defined.
- There are various kinds of infinity.
- Infinity of any kind must at least be logically coherent in order to be a reality.

27.1.1 *Infinity Can Be Defined*

While there has never been a scholarly consensus on a definition for infinity, there has never been much of a consensus on definitions for a variety of other philosophical concepts either. Lack of consensus does not mean a word or term cannot be accurately defined. Put another way, just because there is no consensus regarding the proper technical definition for a particular word does not mean the word lacks definition per se. One thing all can agree on is that etymologically infinity is the condition of being infinite; that is, the condition of having no limit with respect to some form of measurement.

27.1.2 *There are Various Kinds of Infinity*

There are different ways of measuring—we can measure according to quantity, according to quality, or both. Assuming something can lack a limit according to one or more of these kinds of measurement, I proposed infinity can be categorized accordingly:

- quantitative infinity
- qualitative infinity
- absolute infinity

I also proposed that quantitative infinity can be divided into two categories:

- literal infinity
- figurative infinity

Both of which have been given technical definitions in philosophy, set theory, and mathematics under various other names.

I then proposed qualitative infinity can be likewise divided into two categories:

- negative infinity
- positive infinity

Both forms of qualitative infinity have had various expressions in theology.

Another version of infinity found in theology and philosophy of religion is 'absolute infinity', which I defined as a hybrid of literal infinity and positive infinity. Along with both of the qualitative infinities, absolute infinity is also a version of 'divine infinity'—the infinity commonly claimed as a feature of God.

27.1.3 *Infinity of Any Kind Must at Least be Logically Coherent In Order to be a Reality*

Concepts that violate the principles of logic are logically incoherent concepts. Logically incoherent concepts are unreliable for accurately predicating their subjects and thus unreliable for describing real states of affairs.

Take concepts that violate the logical principle of non-contradiction. Suppose a predicate is applied to something, such as when a physical object is predicated as having a given shape. And suppose the predicate, as conceived, is by definition self-contradictory. For example, suppose you are sitting in a room and someone claims the floor is not square, not rectangular, not oval, not circular, etc. but rather is a non-angularity (a square circle). But the floor cannot have the shape of a non-angularity if the property of non-angularity is self-contradictory by definition. Which, of course, it is—nothing can be both entirely a square and entirely a circle simultaneously. To attempt to describe a room's floor as being in the shape of a non-angularity is to offer a description of the floor that cannot be accurate due to the predicate's self-contradictory definition.

Likewise, infinity, as a property claimed to be possessed by certain collections or attributes, must also not have a meaning that implies self-contradictions if infinity is to be a logically coherent concept. If infinity, as a concept, does imply self-contradictions, then it cannot be a logically coherent concept and so is unreliable for an accurate description of the subject said to be infinite. And, in fact, infinity in the literal sense of the term is self-contradictory and so cannot be accurately applied to anything in the real world.

However, not everyone agrees with that assessment. There are some philosophers who throw out the principle of non-contradiction, at least with respect to divine infinity, by appealing either to 'paraconsistent logic' [1,381] or to mysticism (or to both).

I argued in § 26.1 that such appeals are intellectual flimflam. Paraconsistent logic can always be invoked, like argumentative smoke and mirrors, to get a philosopher out of a conceptual jam. And the same holds for appeals to mysticism and concepts that are said to "transcend human understanding." I therefore contend concepts must be logical in order to be coherent.

The assumption that claims should not be based on logical fallacies such as equivocations in meaning, specious analogies, red herring arguments, and the like is also a justified assumption if the claims are to be considered reliable. Hence, I assumed claims to infinity should be free of such fallacies if we are to hold infinity is reliable for rationally describing relevant subjects, let alone conditions of the real world.

27.1.4 *Additional Assumptions*

The foregoing assumptions (about infinity's ability to be defined, about there being various kinds of infinity, and about the requirement that infinity must be a logical concept to be both coherent and reliable for accurate predication of subjects) were all philosophically conservative enough to serve as a reasonable starting point for analysis. However, over the course of this book I have made certain other assumptions relevant to the analysis of infinity.

For example, I made additional assumptions that impact any assessment of quantitative infinity. As early as Chapter 2 I assumed that abstract mathematical objects, such as numbers, are invented rather than discovered (that is, they are not detected, as if preexisting conception). That assumption brings into question whether quantitative infinity, as a property often ascribed to certain mathematical objects, is either an invention or a discovery. Many mathematicians, following in the tradition of Plato, assume infinity and mathematical objects, in general, are discoveries. I assumed otherwise—infinity is an invented condition like a game score, applied to invented mathematical objects.

So as not to beg the question about infinity's invention, in Chapter 16 I provided some justification for my earlier assumption about the invention of mathematical objects and about infinity itself being a conceptual invention rather than a discovered property. Moreover, I conceded that regarding infinity to be an invented concept would not in itself entail that infinity cannot be applied to reality. Lines of longitude and latitude are also mathematical inventions and yet they can be used to accurately describe the geography of the planet. I contend, though, that there are also some mathematical inventions that do not apply to real objects, such as sphere eversion (see Chapter 17). Likewise for concepts such as literal infinity.

Which brings up another assumption: The case I built against infinity assumed that the reification of mathematical objects is fallacious. That assumption is well supported. Explorers did not travel to the North Pole expecting to find a real, physical pole or travel to South America in search of a line running around the Earth where the equator is indicated on a map. So too, as argued in Chapters 18–20, there are other mathematical objects that should not be reified. I provided the example of points and instants; one shouldn't expect there to be points and instants making up reality like atoms. Nor should one expect there to be, literally, infinitely many such objects in the real world either—infinitely many points and instants. However, to avoid again the charge of begging the question about reifying infinity, I provided some justification for this position over Chapters 18–20.

Both assumptions—about the invention of mathematical objects and about the fallaciousness of reifying them—are examples of some assumptions that were at least addressed and argued for in the course of the case. There are surely other assumptions I've made throughout the case against infinity that remain to be brought to light and examined. However, until any fallacious assumptions can be found, I maintain the case against infinity rests on firm grounds.

27.2 THE SUPPORTING ARGUMENTS

The case began by elucidating the various concepts needed for a proper understanding of quantitative infinity in both of its forms: literal infinity and figurative infinity. I wrapped up the first part of the book by arguing that even as infinity is used in the technical discourse of mathematics, it is assumed to mean either literal infinity or figurative infinity (along with some occasional confusion between the two in mathematical discourse). I then provided examples to support the claim that infinity in these senses is in the common understanding of quantitative infinity among scholars and the lay public alike. Further, I argued that despite how use of infinity can be coherent with respect to grammar and the formal language of mathematics, infinity is not necessarily a logically coherent concept. All of this set up the main arguments against both the logical coherence of literal infinity and logical consistency of figurative infinity.

27.2.1 *Despite Mathematical Coherence, Infinity Remains Logically Problematic*

Of the quantitative infinities, it is literal infinity that my thesis exposes as the most logically problematic. The problem lies in what it means for something to be literally infinite—to be literally infinite is to be complete and limitless in quantity.

For there to be infinitely many of something in the literal sense of 'infinity', the collection that is infinite in quantity must be such that sequencing all the members of that collection would make at least one member *infinitely* (limitlessly) far in sequence from at least one other member. If to the contrary there is no member of the collection that is infinitely removed from another in the sequence of the collection, then the collection would be finite as a whole rather than infinite—perhaps a serial indefinite, but still finite.

But this notion of two members *infinitely* removed from one another is in itself problematic, for to have some sequence of members *between* two members is to set bounds. The concept of betweenness itself establishes bounds and therefore limits, and ergo quantitative limits. Hence, to say there is a sequence at all between two members, however far removed they are from one another, is therefore to inadvertently imply the denial that there are limitlessly many members in the sequence—in contradiction to them being "infinitely," or limitlessly, removed from one another.

On the other hand, such bounds confirm the *completeness* of the collection, which is required for the collection to be literally infinite. For the betweenness of the sequence between two members establishes that there is a last member to any count of the members that may in principle be conducted. If to the contrary there were, even in principle, no such thing as a last term to the sequence of members in the collection, then there could not be a totality of members in the collection and therefore the collection would not be complete as it must be for the collection to be literally infinite.

So, while the limitlessness of the collection denies there can be any totality of members to the collection, the completeness of the collection affirms there is. Both implications must hold for a limitless collection that is also complete, as is, and yet they cannot both hold. It is thus these properties of literal infinity—completeness and limitlessness—that contradict one another.

Mathematicians such as Cantor sought to dissolve these contradictions with new technical definitions for infinity and its abstraction as transfinite sets and numbers. Although Cantor claimed his transfinite system made literal infinities calculable, his transfinite system did not actually address the logical self-contradictions still implied by literal infinity because his identification of the transfinite with literal infinity is a case of mistaken identity.

Cantor's attempted redefinition of the literal (or "actual") infinity as the transfinite does not represent what literal infinity implies. Cantor erroneously interpreted his transfinite as literal infinity while his mathematical operations for the transfinite imply only figurative infinity. In other words, Cantor's so-called 'transfinite sets' are really just figurative infinities masquerading as instances of literal infinity, leaving the logical implications of the literal infinities they are claimed to be still unaddressed.

Furthermore, despite the *mathematical* coherence of Cantor's transfinite system, it is nevertheless plagued with *logical* problems of its own. For instance, his diagonal argument, which is commonly assumed to have made the idea of "different sizes of infinity" coherent, commits several logical fallacies, such as the fallacy of presumption. As some mathematicians admit, number systems such as the natural numbers ($\mathbb{N}$) need not be complete sets; that is just an assumption for which there is no evidence—it is just taken as an axiom. But the alleged axiom is hardly "self-evident." Deny the Axiom of Infinity, and Cantor's transfinite system is undone. The transfinite system's mathematical coherence provides only the illusion of logical coherence, which unravels upon further scrutiny.

Then too, such is the case even for references to literal infinity in general mathematics. The idea of progressions of numbers being carried "to infinity," where infinity is interpreted to be a state in which the progression has achieved a complete collection of limitlessly many members, still implies logical contradictions between completeness and limitlessness.

Mathematicians tend not to be concerned by these logical implications of literal infinity's definition because their discipline is not concerned with semantical implications expressed in natural language but instead the syntactical operations supported by narrow, technical definitions of infinity. Most of the semantic connotations of infinity are not necessarily relevant for being able to use the syntax of infinity correctly in equations. So, symbols for infinity such as ∞ can be used according to the formalism of mathematical functions and operations without any need to address the logical contradictions between completeness and limitlessness that appear when infinity is conceived and expressed in natural language. Consequently, mathematicians are able to safely ignore the contradictory connotations for their practice.

And yet, the connotations (the self-contradictory implications of a complete yet limitless collection) are still logically implied, still connoted, even if they cause no mathematical mischief. Just because symbols for infinity (e.g.: ∞, $\aleph$, and ω) can be made to operate with well-defined mathematical rules, that does not mean the concept such symbols are supposed to represent are not logically flawed. Non-angularities can be symbolized. They can also be made to work consistently in mathematics while the implications of squareness and circularity contradict each other. So too, infinity can be made to work in a mathematically consistent manner while implying logical contradictions between the properties of completeness and limitlessness.

27.2.2 *Literal Infinity Lacks Physical Reality*

If infinity were a discovery—an inherent feature of reality rather than an invented concept—then it is hard to explain how such a "paradoxical" condition could exist. But if infinity is an *invented* schema rather than a *discovered* property of real-world things, then it is not surprising that infinity can be given a symbol and that a consistent set of mathematical rules can be created for use of that symbol even while as a concept each of infinity's sub-properties (completeness and limitlessness) may imply logical contradictions with one another. As an invention, any secondary logical implications, or connotations, can be "abstracted out" during operation according to mathematical rules so that the contradictions can simply be ignored.

Because ignored contradictions are still contradictions and cannot apply to the real world, over the course of Chapters 17–21 I argued that literal infinity, as a self-contradictory condition, cannot apply to anything in the real world. In support of this contention, I assessed thought experiments involving hypothetical scenarios about infinities such as Hilbert's Hotel of infinitely many rooms and Craig's Library of infinitely many books. I showed how each thought experiment results in irresolvable contradictions. This too casts into doubt that infinity describes anything real.

Literal infinity's constituent properties of completeness and limitlessness were then further argued to produce irresolvable contradictions when ascribed to quantities of real space, time, motion, and matter. I argued against the possibility of both infinite spatial magnitudes and infinitesimals. I also argued against the coherence of an infinite past, infinite future, and infinitely brief increments of time. The problem with all these infinities of space and time is once again the contradictory implications of between a state of completeness and a state of limitlessness. I then used Zeno's so-called 'dichotomy paradox' as an example to argue that some applications of infinity to the real world are fallacious reifications of the mathematical.

Physics, being an inherently mathematical discipline, all too often engages in mathematical reification, especially reification of mathematical infinities. We find such in various theories such as the Theory of Relativity and certain theories of quantum physics, particle physics, and scientific cosmology. I argued to the contrary that there is no empirical evidence for infinity as a property of any physical collection or phenomenon. Proposals for infinitely many quantum states of matter, particle masses, Feynman paths, or parallel universes in the Omnium or Multiverse remain speculative at best and at worst imply logical self-contradictions that cannot manifest in reality.

Also pointed out was that many physicists have been troubled by expressions of infinity cropping up in equations; they take it as a sign that something has gone awry with corresponding physical theories. That is a further reason to distrust the concept of infinity and instead look for an alternative.

I proposed that if properly developed, the concept of indefiniteness could serve as an alternative to infinity in physical theory. Allowing indefiniteness into physics may make physics into a field in which pursuit of more exact results would sometimes have to be sacrificed. However, indefiniteness has the conceptual advantage of avoiding the logical paradoxes and self-contradictions implied by proposing the physical reality of literal infinities. Indefiniteness would not be a cure for troubles in physical theory, but it would be a start on the road to recovery. Besides, science is already allowing in some indefiniteness with probabilities, the uncertainty principle, fuzzy logic, chaos theory, and so forth.

27.2.3 *The Case Against Literal Infinity Holds Up Against Objections*

Various rebuttals could be made to the case against infinity. There have already appeared in the literature many counterarguments to the charge that literal infinity is a logically incoherent concept. In Chapter 22, seven such rebuttals were considered but none of them held up to scrutiny. In closing the case against literal infinity, I concluded that literal infinity is a conceptual illusion and maintained that it should be replaced with the alternative concept of indefiniteness.

27.2.4 *Figurative Infinity as a Misleading Misnomer*

After an overview of the history of infinity according to its figurative sense, I argued that figurative infinity is perniciously prone to slippage into the literal sense of infinity. To say a progression goes on "infinitely" may slip into assuming there is a literal infinity that can be reached by the progression. This slippage seems to be common in mathematics, where the formal language used (e.g., $n \rightarrow \infty$) is abstract enough that what is at first intended to express a figuratively infinite progression is described in a way that may imply a literal infinity for the progression to reach.

I argued that because figurative infinity is overly prone to slippage into the literal sense of infinity, and is more accurately a misnomer for serial indefiniteness, figurative infinity should be dropped as a term in favor of the various expressions for serial indefiniteness. We should instead refer to that which goes on indefinitely simply as such or, alternatively, use one of the adjectives for serial indefiniteness like 'persistent' and 'ceaseless'. This avoids the slippage problem, has more precision, and ensures greater conceptual accuracy.

27.2.5 *Divine Infinities Logically Inconsistent*

Aside from quantitative infinity is divine infinity, of which there are two varieties: qualitative infinity and absolute infinity. Following an exposition of theological discourse about divine infinity and a brief historical overview of the divine infinities, I proposed a critique of the divine infinities. I argued that, insofar as the divine infinities—both qualitative infinity and absolute infinity—can be conceived without contradiction, they reduce to misnomers for some finite property such as being indistinguishable, incomparable, superlative, supreme, ultimate, etc. In that respect, divine infinity has the same logical problem as figurative infinity, often implying something it is not. A few apologetics for divine infinity were considered and refuted. I then recommended theists reconceive the divine in finite terms.

27.2.6 *Bottom Line for The Case Against Infinity*

We have examined the most relevant sense of infinity: quantitative infinity and divine infinity. Quantitative infinity has proven self-contradictory. Ideas of infinite quantities of space, time, and degrees of motion have been debunked (Chapters 18–20). Even if we broaden our metaphysical scope to divine infinity (Chapter 25), we find both versions of such—qualitative infinity and absolute infinity—still violate logic wherever use of the term 'infinite' is not simply a misnomer for certain finite properties such as indistinguishability, incomparability, supremacy, ultimacy, etc. (per Chapter 26). If I had to make a statement that captures the essence of the case against infinity, it is this:

- *The degree to which infinity is not a self-contradictory concept is the degree to which it remains a misnomer for certain finite properties, and thus a misleading term prone to inconsistent usage.*

27.3 THE VERDICT

Ultimately, the verdict rests with the consensus of readers, but in philosophically 'prosecuting' this case, I maintain that infinity has lost the case. We have exhausted the most relevant conceptions of infinity and are left with little choice but to conclude infinity is guilty of being a logically erroneous concept that refers to no existing state of affairs. If we wish to say there *is* (i.e., exists) something non-finite at all, we can reference only the afinite—emptiness, zero. Otherwise, finitude is the nature of *being* as such—the nature of existence itself. Distilling this conclusion down to a slogan, *esse est finitus*—to be is to be finite.

27.4 IMPLICATIONS OF THE CASE AGAINST INFINITY

The case against infinity carries implications—some serious, some trivial. The implications concern the language we use in colloquial discourse and the concepts we use in scholarly fields of inquiry—especially philosophy, mathematics, physics, cosmology, and theology. There are even some implications for the perennial hope of personal immortality. We'll close with a brief look at the implications that rejection of infinity has in all of these areas.

27.4.1 *Implications for Common Discourse*

There are some implications of the case against infinity for common discourse, but those implications are not too dramatic. Although infinity stands refuted, there is still such a thing as being without a *particular kind* of limit—for example, some things lack an end or bound, though they are not typically called 'infinite'. Consequently, even if use of the term 'infinite' were to go out of vogue altogether due to infinity's refutation, references to certain things as being without a particular kind of limit would certainly continue.

For example, consider again a simple circle. Its closed curve is quite literally without end and without bound, but because its circumference (distance around) is limited, a circle is not infinite. So too, there are some things that are without limit and without measure but are also not infinite. As pointed out back in §§ 5.4.4–5, zero (or the 'null set') is quite literally without limit and without measure, but it does not qualify as infinite. In rejecting infinity we may still accept the concept of lacking limits, ends, bounds, or measurability and continue referring to certain things as so lacking. It's just that such things do not, and should not be said to, lack limits out of being "infinite" and so should not be referred to as infinite.

Moreover, the way in which we say a property, such as a limit, is lacking is what carries implications for what we mean. The examples of the circle and of zero show that to be "without limit" should not always be taken as synonymous with what we usually mean by being 'limitless', to be "without end" should not always be taken as synonymous with what is typically referred to as 'endless', to be "without bound" should not always be taken as synonymous with what we commonly understand as being 'boundless', and to be "without measure" should not always be taken as synonymous with what is colloquially termed 'immeasurable'.

A circle is literally without end and without bound, but we would not say it is "endless" or "boundless" except in a figurative sense because endlessness and boundlessness, when meant literally, are terms normally reserved for infinity [1,382]. (However, a circle can be referred to as a 'finite-unbounded' figure without causing confusion since 'unbounded' is qualified by the word 'finite'.) So too, zero, or the null set, is without limit and without measure, but we would not say zero is "limitless" or "immeasurable" except in a figurative sense since these terms, when used literally, are also commonly reserved for infinity. Lacking limits, ends, bounds, or measurability may refer to concepts that either are finite (as with a circle's circumference) or do not fit the category of the infinite (as with zero, the null set), but such is different from being literally limitless, endless, boundless, or immeasurable—those conditions, at least in their non-hyperbolic *literal* senses, are ways of saying something is infinite.

So, rejecting infinity does not mean that the concepts of being without limit, without end, without bound, without measure would no longer play any role at all in our discourse. It just means there are correct and incorrect ways to make use of these concepts, and so there are more and less precise and accurate ways to speak of such conditions in literal and figurative language so as not to be misleading. To reject infinity and its use for descriptions is an invitation to use more precise concepts and language with respect to limits. It is to invite a change of habits in referring to the immense, the minuscule, the protracted, the ephemeral, the ceaseless, the persistent, the inexhaustible, the unrestricted for what they are—finite but indefinite rather than infinite.

As I've admitted before, whether such recommendations for conceptual clarity and precision in terminology will ever catch on in common discourse is another matter. I have my doubts. I don't own the language and there's no such thing as enforcing its colloquial usage.

Even so, that does not mean there is no right or wrong about the matter. Words have meaning. Words matter. Just look at how the words of presidents can move supporters. Talk of infinity is usually not that consequential, but there are more or less precise, and more or less accurate, ways to describe things without (relative) limit, without (min/max) bound, without (predefined) end, or without (definite) measure.

27.4.2 *Implications for Philosophy*

The implications of the case against infinity are more serious for philosophy. Because the literal sense of infinity implies logical contradictions, philosophers should not expect logical outcomes from applications of infinity to hypothetical situations and thought experiments such as Hilbert's Hotel, Craig's Library, Zeno's dichotomy paradox, and the like. Alas, many philosophers have to date accepted the notion of literal infinity and subsequently wasted a great deal of time and energy seeking to unravel its "paradoxical" implications (this conclusion comes from hard experience, by the way). What the case against infinity implies for philosophy is that, as a field that makes use of hypothetical situations and thought experiments for understanding the possibilities of reality, it is better off avoiding reliance on literal infinity.

As for figurative infinity, if philosophers wish their concepts to have some application to hypothetical situations and thought experiments, and especially to descriptions of the real world, then it's better that usage of infinity is dropped altogether in favor of a more logically sound and precise concept. Figurative infinity remains a misnomer that is highly misleading. Philosophers, precise as they are, too often slip from using infinity as a figure of speech to using it in its literal sense without realizing the slip. Since philosophers pride themselves on being logically precise, they should replace any use of figurative infinity with a more precise alternative to avoid misleading implications.

27.4.3 *Implications for Mathematics*

As far as the practice of mathematics is concerned, the implications of the case against infinity are important but would not cause a crisis for mathematicians. This is because realizing that quantitative infinity is a logically erroneous concept would not impact the bulk of mathematical operation. In fact, some mathematicians already believe nearly all mathematics can be framed in finite terms [1,383].

If quantitative infinity is an illogical concept as I contend, then all we have to do is replace the term 'infinity' and its associated notation with alternatives that accomplish the same operations while avoiding the logical self-contradictions and inconsistent implications of infinity. Toward that end, I proposed 'indefiniteness' as an alternative concept to infinity, along with associated terminology for its various manifestations (as introduced in Chapter 6, **Figures 6.3–6.4**). With respect to notation for indefiniteness, **Table 4** illustrates that an alternative (and somewhat arbitrary) notation for the varieties of indefiniteness could be used in mathematics for distinguishing indefiniteness of quantity from both literal infinity and figurative infinity [1,384]. With indefiniteness in place of infinity, the operations in general mathematics that previously relied on infinity can go on as usual even if their interpretations have changed.

INDEFINITENESS TYPE	SYMBOL
Indefiniteness of Size	
▪ Indefinitely Large	
▫ Enormity	ə
▫ Immensity	ɣ
▪ Indefinitely Small	
▫ Minuteness	⊙
▫ Minuscularity	⊖
Indefiniteness of Distance	
▪ Indefinitely Far: Remoteness	<>
▪ Indefinitely Near: Proximateness	⟩⟨
Indefinitely Long Series	
▪ Indefinitely Long Succession	
▫ Persistence	⊢
▫ Ceaselessness	↻
▪ Indefinitely Long Duration	
▫ Protraction	X̅
▫ Perpetuity	◔
Indefinitely Short Series	
▪ Indefinitely Short Succession: Transience	ǂ
▪ Indefinitely Short Duration: Ephemerality	∓
Indefinite Iteration Toward A Limit	
▪ Indefinite Increase Toward A Limit	↑
▪ Indefinite Decrease Toward A Limit	↓
Indefinite Limit	
▪ Indefinite Limit To Definite Numbers Definable In Practice	☐

Table 4: Examples of possible mathematical notation (admittedly arbitrary) for the varieties of indefiniteness.

I expect some may dismiss the proposal that 'indefiniteness' should replace 'infinity' on the grounds that this is all "just a matter of semantics," or wordplay. After all, isn't the replacement of 'infinity' with 'indefiniteness' nothing more than just a change of terminology? Isn't it like calling a rose by another name? And doesn't replacement of one notation with another yield nothing of mathematical significance?

I grant that aside from a change in terminology and symbolic notation for mathematical operations (such as the notation used in adding sets of incalculably many members together or dividing a quantity ever closer to zero) there would not be much impact by replacing infinity with indefiniteness. The operations in general mathematics would remain largely if not entirely the same; it would simply be more accurate to say the operations apply to 'indefinite' sequences rather than 'infinite' sets. With respect to how mathematical operations work then, the critics would be correct that it is mainly (but not entirely) labels that are changed by my proposal. So, I am more than willing to concede that, even if mathematicians were to cease use of infinity, much of pure mathematics and most of applied mathematics would remain intact with only slight modification required and, even then, such modifications would mostly pertain to a change in terminology and symbolism. I also readily admit that, aside from the transfinite system, most of the remaining content in set theory would remain as is.

However, even if with respect to mathematical operation most of what would change with a shift from infinity to indefiniteness is little more than symbolic notation, I nevertheless contend that the shift has importance and is not just a word game. First, because semantics is, after all, a matter of *meaning* and the meanings of terms carry degrees of clarity about their subjects. Replacement of infinity with indefiniteness would provide greater precision and clarity of meaning in mathematics by preventing slippage between the figurative and literal meanings of infinity along with the attendant, misleading, logical implications. Second, the shift would not only help the field of mathematics; it would also help science propose more accurate applications of mathematics for theories and measurements of the real world because replacing infinity with indefiniteness would reframe investigation along new lines—in finite terms with finite solutions. Third and finally, there are versions of finite mathematics that do in fact operate differently than mathematics with infinity (see § 16.6.2, § 17.1.1, and § 24.3); so, it is conceivable to create new operations involving indefiniteness—although, such is beyond the scope of this book.

27.4.4 *Implications for Physics and Cosmology*

If my case is solid, and quantitative infinity is in fact logically erroneous, then continued use of the term 'infinity' in fields like physics and cosmology can distort the way we interpret the Universe, sending us down a blind alley. If quantitative infinity is a self-contradictory or inconsistent concept, then physics and cosmology must reject all theories of infinite physical magnitudes such as infinite expanses of space; infinite durations of time; infinite amounts of energy, matter, density, and temperature; and infinite quantities of universes. Since the models of the Universe currently favored by cosmologists are based on such ideas—everything from certain versions of the Big Bang theory to various speculations about infinitely many universes making up 'the Multiverse'—those models will require either revision or replacement.

Replacing infinity is thus necessary for physics and cosmology to improve the accuracy of scientific models of the Universe. More than this, replacing infinity with indefiniteness would also suggest that alternative models of the Universe based on the assumption of finitude are far more likely to be accurate since such models from initial conception avoid the logical inconsistencies inherent in infinity.

27.4.5 *Implications for Theology*

The implications of the case against infinity as described so far have had to do with the impact of rejecting quantitative infinity—both in its literal and figurative senses—in favor of the varieties of indefiniteness. But the case against infinity also argued against the notion of divine infinity, both in the forms of qualitative infinity and absolute infinity. My thesis on the erroneousness of divine infinity carries with it some implications for theology and theism in general.

More than two-thirds of the world's population believes in the existence of an infinite God [1,385]. But divine infinity turns out to be at best a misnomer for finite qualities and at worst a viciously self-contradictory notion. So what does the refutation of infinity entail for belief in God?

In terms of the number of people who believe in the existence of an infinite God, the answer is not much. The population that believes in some version of a personal God with infinite attributes will continue to climb for the foreseeable future as new children are born into families carrying on the religious traditions of their parents [1,386]. Nevertheless, in terms of the accuracy of beliefs about God, the world's religions are badly in need of reform.

For if my thesis is correct, there can be nothing literally limitless, or unlimited, about divine qualities, however awesome they would be if they were real. Some theologians might roll with this by reconstruing the term 'infinite' as a metaphor for awesome, but purely finite, qualities of the divine. However, to do so makes the term 'infinite' a misleading characterization when applied to descriptions of the divine. Basically, to call God "infinite" is to say something misleading about God—and that is so regardless of whether or not God is real.

Since portrayals of divine infinity are logically inconsistent, theologians would lose nothing important in rejecting notions of divine infinity in favor of alternative, finite conceptions of God's various attributes. Indeed, to take such a course would even benefit theology by removing intellectually objectionable content from the scope of discussion regarding divine nature.

27.4.6 *Implications for Hopes of Immortality*

Though the case against infinity is intellectually solid, I expect there to be resistance to the conclusion that infinity is bunk. I suspect many will not be willing to accept the case against infinity out of concern that, if the future is not literally infinite, we are left to face the apparent grimness of a common fate, adeptly captured by Greene [1,387]:

> For more than three billion years, as species simple and complex found their place in earth's hierarchy, the scythe of death has cast a persistent shadow over the flowering of life...it's a foreboding that quietly lives within us, one we learn to tamp down, to accept, to make light of. But underneath the obscuring layers is the ever-present, unsettling fact of what lies in store...

And not just for ourselves. In addition to the concerns of our own mortality, we carry the burden of knowing a time will come when our loved ones shall be deprived of future days as we shall be deprived of their company—that is, if we are not already grieving their passing.

The awful truth just gets worse, for we know the extinction of our species waits somewhere on the horizon. Bergström states, "Just as a single life can appear to be a preparation for nothing, so the whole history of humanity can seem to be futile since it plays such a small role from the point of view of the universe as a whole. In the words of Bertrand Russell [1,388],

> Man is the product of causes which had no prevision of the end they were achieving [... and] all the labors of the ages, all the devotion, all the inspiration, all the noonday brightness of human genius, are destined to extinction in the vast death of the solar system, and [...] the whole temple of Man's achievement must inevitably be buried beneath the debris of a universe in ruins...."

Given such a bleak picture, it's little wonder infinity has always been an idea passionately held: it is often taken as the rationale for the idea that death is not the end it appears to be. The concept of infinity— the literal infinity of the future in particular—is widely valued for making plausible the possibility of immortality.

Over half the world's population believes in some form of personal immortality—particularly, in the form of a life lived through an infinite future [1,389]. But since the preceding chapters have proven literal infinity to be self-contradictory, figurative infinity to be a misnomer for indefiniteness, and that even the divine must be finite, what becomes of prospects for personal immortality?

For those who have rested their hope for personal immortality on the concept of an infinite future, I offer a bit of good news—even though infinity lies impaled on its own logic, immortality as such remains untouched. The refutation of infinity does not in itself undermine the concept of immortality.

This is because immortality may be conceived of in more than one way, each having to do with the concept of *eternity*. Definitions:

- eternity: *the condition of being eternal.*
- eternal: *always existing; unsubject to deterioration, decay, or destruction.*

There are three main versions of eternity: infinite time, immutable time, and timelessness.

The first version of eternity, that of infinite time, may be subdivided according to the categories of literal infinity and figurative infinity. We have already addressed infinite time in the literal sense and found it violates logic. However, some conceive of eternity as 'infinite' time in the figurative sense, which is the same as an *indefinite* future in the strong sense: an open, or ceaseless, future that proceeds with an ever-growing finitude of days to come. If we were to reject the misnomer of 'infinite' for a ceaseless future of linear time and instead use a more appropriate label for such, we could simply refer to it as *open time* [1,390]. In which case, eternity would just mean open time, a concept not critiqued in this book.

And there are also the other senses of eternity to consider. The second version of eternity is a state of *immutable time* in which past, present, and future all co-exist in a static, spacetime dimension—a temporally tenseless "Now" relative to which the change we experience from birth to death is only an illusion. [1,391] [1,392]. And then there is the third version of eternity, which is also popular: eternity as *timelessness*—a state that is somehow "outside" of time altogether [1,393].

Eternity as open time, as immutable time, and as timelessness are not impugned by the case against infinity. And so, the possibility of *eternal life*—that is, the possibility of personal immortality as either 'open-ended life' or 'immutable life' or 'timeless life'—also remains free of refutation by the case I have presented. That does not mean, however, that the concept of eternity should not face similar scrutiny, for it too needs to be tried in the court of logic.

NOTES

PREFACE

[1] I am referring to my previous book on cosmology (Sewell 1999). My views on cosmology have changed over the past couple of decades since that book was written. I have abandoned the cosmology presented in my 1999 book, which is no longer in print. My new (post-2022) monograph on cosmology will be a correction to my previous work on the topic, but it will also be consistent with the views on infinity presented in this book.

[2] For example, I have thrown out several flawed arguments presented in my previous writings on infinity. In this book, I have improved the technical vocabulary, refined definitions, expounded on some points with much more detail, and updated the content with new references.

The changes come as a result of further reflection. Sometimes, a philosopher intuits that there is something wrong with an idea everyone takes for granted, but the philosopher doesn't know exactly what the problem is. It's as if the philosopher has smelled a rat but doesn't know where the rat is or what to do about it. The philosopher may consequently make unsound arguments against the idea, and having made those arguments may come to admit the arguments are flawed. If the philosopher finds that some of his or her own arguments are mistaken, yet not enough to warrant recanting the conclusion, then the persistent philosopher may reason out new arguments that are sound. That is how it has been with my analysis of infinity. The arguments I formerly marshaled against infinity were not all sound, but they weren't completely off course either. After further study, I believe I have found where the "rat" (set of fallacies) is hiding in the idea of infinity, and how to successfully deal with it. This book is the result of my findings.

[3] You may notice that I do not refer to readers, or generic individuals, in the text as 'he' or 'she'. Since readers may be either male or female, I will be using plural pronouns as singular for individuals of indeterminate sex.

[4] My use of plural pronouns as singular for generic individuals is a break with academic convention. Starting in the 18th and 19th Centuries, grammarians cracked down on use of the singular 'they' (also 'their', 'theirself' or 'themself', and 'theirs') in favor of using 'he', 'him', 'himself' and 'his' for referring to a generic individual—see Miller and Swift 1988, pp. 44–50. But in an attempt to correct centuries of male chauvinism, many academics are now using 'she', 'her', 'herself', and 'hers' for a generic individual of indeterminate sex. For example, I recently read in a book by a prominent philosopher the following line: "I would like to invite the reader to spend a few minutes reflecting on the thesis and deciding for herself whether it seems evident enough to be taken as bedrock." (Goff 2017, p. 108.) I can't do that for "herself" because I'm male. In my opinion, the outcome of using she/her/herself/hers for a generic individual is just as awkward as the convention of using he/him/himself/his for the same. As for the mandate by grammarians to avoid using plural pronouns as singulars to indicate individuals of indeterminate sex, I believe it is not justified since use of plural pronouns as singular for generic individuals already has widespread precedent in both contemporary speech and historical literature. The bias on the part of grammarians against the singular 'they' has unfortunately persisted even into this century. To avoid sexism, we simply need to return to the practice of using plural pronouns for generic (as opposed to specific) individuals. And that is exactly what I intend to do in my own works unless directly quoting from another author who does not follow the practice.

[5] Since I am not affiliated with a university and I am not publishing through an academic press, I need not stringently follow any particular academic style of citation such as that of the Modern Language Association (MLA), the American Psychological Association (APA), or the Chicago Style Manual, but I will endeavor to be as clear, consistent, and comprehensive as I can be with regard to citing sources.

[6] Alas, in my prior works I was not always successful at avoiding rhetorical flourishes; I aspire to take a more objective and professional tone going forward. If at any time I lapse in this work, I will make an effort to correct the text in a later edition.

[7] Sagan 1980, p. 11.

[8] Ohanian 2008.

CHAPTER 1: CHALLENGING INFINITY

[9]   Incidentally, I write 'universe' with a small 'u' when referring to any kind of universe, while I write 'Universe' with a capital 'U' when referring to the physical universe we inhabit—just as I would write 'sun' with a small 's' when referring to any star that is the center of a solar system while I write 'Sun' with a capital 'S' when referring to our own sun. Moreover, I take the position that the universe we live in is the one and only Universe with real, physical existence, while other physical universes disconnected from ours are fictions. Hence, you can think of 'Universe' with a capital 'U' as referring to the single, unique entity comprised not only of the 'observable universe'—i.e., everything physically observable from our planet—but also the greater whole of all space and time in which the observable universe belongs as just one portion.

[10]   This claim does not necessarily apply to all observers that *might* exist, but it certainly applies to human beings.

[11]   Moore 2019, p.1.

[12]   See entry for 'finite' in *Collins English Dictionary* (Collins 2021).

[13]   See entry for 'infinite' in *Collins English Dictionary* (Collins 2021).

[14]   A circle has a radius and diameter, which might also be used to illustrate the finitude of a circle. However, I wish to emphasize how the circumference of the circle can be limited without reference to radius and diameter.

[15]   I have already presented online two previous versions of this work (the first in 2008 and the second in 2010). This book vastly revises and expands on the previous versions: some arguments I have since abandoned as they were more polemical than logical, while other points have been extended for clarity.

I have also altered some of the terminology previously used, such as 'the infinite' for what in this edition I call 'literal infinity' or just plain 'infinity'. Conversely, in the previous editions I used the word 'infinity' for what I now refer to as 'figurative infinity'. To avoid confusion, the reader should disregard the 2008 and 2010 versions of my case against infinity as well as the content about infinity presented in my previous book on cosmology (Sewell 1999).

[16]   There are some hair-splitting distinctions philosophers sometimes make between infinity under various labels; for example, 'actual infinity' is sometimes distinguished from 'extensive infinity' when the term is used in a particular sense, but we need not worry about such distinctions. The upshot is the same for all of them: they denote a complete and limitless quantity of members in a collection.

[17]   This example is based on that offered by Dr. William Lane Craig presented in Strobel 2004, p. 103.

[18]   By 'range' I mean not the set of *possible* outputs to a function, as is a common use of the term in mathematics, but rather the extent of elements in a collection as expressed by a measurement of the collection.

[19]   Fletcher 1998, p. vii.

[20]   Huemer 2016, pp. 185–186, 249, 251.

Huemer accepts that infinite sequences can be "completed" but his conception of completeness does not seem to capture all that the word 'complete' typically implies with respect to collections. For instance, Huemer's notion of completeness does not imply a total of elements, and so he denies there are infinite numbers, including transfinite numbers. Huemer's notion of 'complete' is more like what it means to become 'finished' in the course of time, but it is a curious form of finish for a sequence that has non-zero elements and yet no total once it's done. In my view, that is a dubious proposition.

[21]   As with literal infinity, there are some hair-splitting distinctions made by some philosophers with respect to these various labels for infinity. For example, the term 'potential infinity' is sometimes distinguished from 'intensive infinity' when the term is used in a particular sense, but we need not worry about these distinctions. In Chapter 23, we'll see that the upshot is the same for all of them: they denote a quantity of occurrences in a series that accumulates a running total, but which is always finite at every step of the way. For that reason, I say these conceptions of infinity merely use the term 'infinity' in a figurative sense.

[22]   To paraphrase the writer William Saroyan.

[23]   I pointed out in my previous book on cosmology (Sewell 1999, p. 32) that the lexical or lay definitions for infinity have non-literal meanings such as "boundless" and "vast beyond comprehension." Though most of

that earlier work I now consider erroneous and in need of correction with a new, forthcoming book on cosmology, the point I had made in the 1999 book is correct—there are many figurative uses of infinity. However, the *primary* (most common) figurative sense of 'infinity' implies a process that is always finite but goes on without a defined end, while there are also many *secondary* (less common) figurative senses for 'infinity'.

[24] While much of my previous book on cosmology (Sewell 1999) is incorrect on the analysis of infinity, on this point my position remains unchanged: I will continue to maintain that infinity is often used metaphorically— it is often used in a figurative sense for what is more literally called *serial indefiniteness*.

[25] Russell (Robert John) 2011, p. 277.

[26] Turner 2011, p. 293.

[27] Vallicella 2019.

[28] Vallicella 2019.

[29] Göcke 2016, Chapter in Schärtl, Tapp, and Wegener 2016, pp. 177–199.

[30] Khusraw ~1060 CE (1949 translation), p. 31.
      The quote is referenced in Ahmad 2017.

[31] Göcke 2016 in Schärtl, Tapp, and Wegener 2016.

[32] Göcke 2016 in Schärtl, Tapp, and Wegener 2016.

[33] Oppy 2011 in Heller and Woodin 2011, pp. 241–242.

[34] Russell (Robert John) 2011, pp. 278–279.

[35] Ahmad 2017.

[36] Robert John Russell states this of God's perfection, pointing out that God's attributes of perfection are positive infinites. See Russell (Robert John) 2011, pp. 278–279.

[37] Cusanus 1440 (1985 edition), Book I, Chapter Four, Section 11, p. 8; Book I, Chapter Twenty-six, Section 87, p. 45.

[38] See § 25.2.4.

[39] Zarrabizadeh 2008.

[40] Gellman 2019.

[41] Gellman 2019.

[42] For example, take the claim, "God's infinity is incomprehensible. We cannot imagine or conceive it." Quoted from Owen 1967.

[43] The quoted phrase seems to have originated in a poem (see Vaughan 1650).
      The idea of a darkness that is also light goes back at least to a 6th Century mystic monk ghostwriting as the 1st Century Dionysius the Areopagite, a judge at the Athenian judicial council (known as 'the Areopagus') and a convert to Christianity. The 6th Century ghostwriter is sometimes called Pseudo-Dionysius or more simply Dionysius. The darkness-as-light of Pseudo-Dionysius, translated as Vaughan's "dazzling darkness," can be found in Chapter 2 of the work by Pseudo-Dionysius entitled *Mystical Teaching*. See Pseudo-Dionysius ~6th Century CE (1978 translation).
      Clifton Wolters, a translator of the works of Pseudo-Dionysius, states the "dazzling darkness" as presented in the so-called 'via negativa' of Dionysius is "negative in name only. It is because the truths about God are so overwhelmingly positive and real that we cannot describe them." Quote from Wolters' Introduction to Pseudo-Dionysius ~6th Century CE (1978 translation), pp. 17, 212.

[44] Khusraw ~1060 CE (1949 translation), p. 31. Referenced in Ahmad 2017.

[45] See Chapter 25 for further examples of divine infinity as negative and positive in quality.

[46] The Renaissance theologian Nicolaus Cusanus (a.k.a., Nicholas of Cusa) stated that "the infinite, qua infinite, is unknown; for it escapes all comparative relation." Quote from Cusanus 1440 (1985 edition), Book I, Chapter 1, paragraph 3.

[47] Cantor 1883 (1976 translation), p. 78.

[48] Cantor 1908, letter to Chisholm-Young in Van der Veen and Horsten 2013, p. 125.

[49] Cantor 1883 (1976 translation), pp. 70, 75–76, 94.

[50] Cantor 1897 letter to Hilbert in Ewald 2005, p. 927.

[51]   "The different kinds of infinity must be carefully distinguished. The two principal divisions are...the infinite in only one respect (*secundum quid*) or the partially infinite, and the infinite in every respect (*simpliciter*) or the absolutely infinite...[the] infinite in every respect is that being alone, which contains in itself all possible perfections and which is above every species and genus and order." Quoted from Zimmerman 1910.

[52]   The term 'divine infinity' is found in academic writings pertaining to theology: Sweeney 1992.

[53]   In Sewell 1999, I criticized the traditional, most common understanding of infinity—which is to say, literal infinity—as "meaningless" and "unintelligible." This is *technically* correct when by "meaning" and "intelligible" we imply logical consistency and scrutinize the *logic* behind the definition of literal infinity. However, I now think using terms like "meaningless" and "unintelligible" in that way is a misleading way of speaking.

It's not that infinity has no meaning at all or that its meaning cannot be understood. Rather, it is just that while the term 'infinity' can have multiple meanings, the most common meaning of infinity—which is for a complete set of stuff to be quantitatively limitless—is nevertheless self-contradictory, and this comes out when we truly do understand infinity in its literal sense.

Hence, the most common notion of infinity, taken in its literal sense, can give the impression of being intelligible as long as the self-contradictions in its literal meaning are not noticed or examined. Once the self-contradictions are brought to light, the traditional way of conceiving (literal) infinity is found to be logically incoherent and ergo "unintelligible" in that sense.

My forthcoming, second monograph on cosmology will avoid the misleading critique of infinity presented in my earlier works and will instead assume the skeptical position as articulated in this book. Regardless, many if not most scholars would likely still take issue with my position that literal infinity is *logically* incoherent.

For example, Fletcher asserts that "if you believe that all talk of actual infinity is meaningless then you cannot even pose the question of whether actual infinity exists; if you believe that no actual infinities exist then you evidently believe the question is meaningful and answerable." (Quoted from Fletcher 2007, p. 548.) Fletcher's statement is true enough, but it does not apply to my argument (see Chapter 9 of this book).

I am not asserting that "all talk" of infinity is meaningless. I am simply asserting that the common, traditional understanding of infinity—that is to say, the meaning of infinity according to its literal usage—is logically incoherent, just as the idea of a four-sided triangle is incoherent. And just as one logical absurdity, a four-sided triangle, cannot exist, so too another logical absurdity, literal infinity, cannot refer to something that exists.

As we'll see in later chapters of this book, literal infinity provides the illusion of logical coherence because the mathematical operations that purportedly demonstrate literal infinity in fact do no such thing. The operations are only "infinite" in a figurative sense. Infinity in the figurative sense, I will argue, is an inconsistent concept, but not a self-contradictory concept as is literal infinity. When the figuratively infinite operations are claimed to be literally infinite, that gives literal infinity the illusion of logical coherence.

[54]   I made this square circle analogy in my previous book on cosmology (Sewell 1999) and in earlier editions of this work (2008 and 2010). But I was not the first to do so. See, for instance, Johnson 1994, p. 369.

Independently, other philosophers have since come to the same conclusion about literal infinity and have even used a similar square circle analogy. For example, freelance philosopher Steve Patterson has made similar arguments in his more recent articles and webcasts—see Patterson 2015. However, Patterson and many other philosophers champion figurative (or "potential") infinity over literal (or "actual") infinity, whereas I argue even against use of the term 'infinity' according to its figurative sense.

[55]   Williams 1981, pp. 600–602.

[56]   Dawkins 2018.

[57]   For example, in discussing the limits of a graph, mathematician Paul Dawkins states, "Notice that there are actually an infinite number of possible δ's that we can choose." See Dawkins 2021.

[58]   Recently, I found Patterson made essentially the same point in an interview with Dr. Daniel Isaacson, a philosopher of mathematics at Oxford University. See Patterson 11 September 2016.

[59]   Dr. Rafael E. Núñez of the Department of Cognitive Science, University of California in San Diego argues that literal infinity is actually understood by means of 'conceptual metaphors' that are "blended" together. My position is that Núñez gives too much credit to literal infinity being a logically coherent concept in need of

scientific explanation. One might as well argue that a round triangle or any other self-contradictory idea is understood by a conceptually blended metaphor, but that doesn't make the idea any less self-contradictory. Moreover, even if we use conceptual metaphors to understand something, whether atoms or formulas, it may nevertheless be true that the aspects of the idea we are trying to understand is meant to be taken literally. See Núñez 2003, pp. 68–69.

CHAPTER 2: THE NATURE OF QUANTITY

[60]   By 'continuous' I do *not* mean including another element between any two elements but rather having adjacent elements that vary by indistinguishable amounts.

[61]   My definitions for aggregates, multitudes, and sets are similar to those of the post-Enlightenment mathematician Bernard Bolzano, but not entirely the same. For Bolzano, a 'set' is a kind of 'aggregate' and a 'multitude' is a kind of set. (See Waldegg 2005, p. 565.) My proposal is that, while these three kinds of collection overlap, one kind of collection cannot be defined as only a subcategory of the other.

[62]   Just and Weese 1996, pp. 5–6.

[63]   Hrbáček and Jech 1999, pp. 4, 7–11.

[64]   For an example in which set theorists refer to sets as "finished" constructions with a "completed totality" of members, see Hrbáček and Jech 1999, pp. 1, 260, 279.

[65]   Mathematicians cannot stand such modal terms since they are too vague for their discipline. See Hrbáček and Jech 1999, p. 4.

[66]   Absolutely unordered sets are merely abstractions defined according to a rule; they have 'members, but such members are themselves abstractions and are included only in principle.

[67]   Rusnock 2000, p. 190.

[68]   Hrbáček and Jech 1999, p. 1.

[69]   Fletcher 1998, p. 16.

[70]   Fletcher 1998, p. 16.

[71]   Fletcher 1998, p. 16.

[72]   This way of describing a sequence is based on the work of Bolzano. See Rusnock 2000, p. 191.

[73]   With respect to the study of English grammar, the adjective 'silent' is a predicate if it falls in the 'predicative position' (e.g., "The night is silent.") while it is an attribute if it falls in the 'attributive position' (e.g., "silent night"). However, in the study of predicate logic, we treat adjectives as predicates regardless of where they fall in a sentence.

[74]   Gullberg 1997, p. 264.

[75]   Gullberg 1997, p. 264.

[76]   For more on how set theorists define cardinality, see Just and Weese 1996, p. 30.

[77]   Roitman 2011, pp. 63–64.

[78]   Roitman 2011, p. 64.

[79]   Roitman 2011, p. 64.

[80]   Some mathematicians argue that the integers cannot be ordinals because the integers include negative numbers, and there is no 'lowest' negative number to be the 'first' number by which to define ordinals. However, this overlooks that the natural numbers are the primary system of numbers from which all other number systems, including the integers, are derived. As such, the negative integers do not comprise a *complete set* but rather an *incomplete series*. As an incomplete series that is always under construction, the 'lowest' or 'first' integer is whatever has been defined as lowest for the system of integers at any given time. So, it's not that the integers can't be assigned a first ordinal; it's that they are always being assigned a new "first" ordinal relative to all the other integers as the system of negative integers is increased.

[81]   Urner 1999.

[82]   Butterworth 1999, p. 11. Butterworth seems to use the term 'numerosity' for what most would call a 'number' and 'number' for what most would call a 'numeral'.

[83]   This is a variation of the view expressed by Butterworth 1999, p. 10.

[84]   This is described in a similar manner by Butterworth 1999, p. 10.

[85]   This notation is inspired by the following: Mueckenheim 2006, p. 6.

[86]   Huemer 2016, p. 164.

[87]   Huemer 2016, p. 125.

[88]   Huemer 2016, p. 165.

[89]   Huemer 2016, p. 166.

[90]   Hrbáček and Jech 1999, pp. 39–40.

[91]   Hrbáček and Jech 1999, pp. 39–40.

[92]   See a similar explication by Hrbáček and Jech 1999, p. 40.

[93]   Kaplan 2000.

[94]   Butterworth 1999, p. 10.

[95]   And beyond the use of exponents, even larger numbers can be created by use of iterated exponentials.

CHAPTER 3: QUANTITIES COMPLETE AND INCOMPLETE

[96]   See entry for 'power' in *A Dictionary of Physics*: Daintith 2014.

[97]   See entry for 'power' in *The People's Law Dictionary*: Hill and Hill 2002.

[98]   Kornell 2018.

[99]   A continuum is also sometimes defined with respect to divisibility, but a whole is not the same as a continuum. There are several definitions of the term 'continuum' in scientific and mathematical literature. For example, a continuum can be defined as *a set that can be divided only into subsets of which none are decomposable into elements*. By this definition, a continuum can be a whole because it is divisible ("can be divided") but is not in fact divided. However, not all wholes are continuums because the property of wholeness does not require subsets or a group of elements to be instantiated.

[100]   Lang 1993, p. 45.

[101]   Kreyszig 1989, p. 28.

[102]   Cantor 1897 letter to Hilbert in Ewald 2005, p. 927.

[103]   Dedekind 1872 (1991 translation).

[104]   Dedekind 1872 (1991 translation), pp. 6–9.

[105]   Dedekind 1872 (1991 translation), p. 9.

[106]   I do not mean "should" or "ought" in a moral sense, but in a rational sense.

[107]   Or in Dedekind's own words, "infinite." See Dedekind 1872 (1991 translation), pp. 6, 9.

CHAPTER 4: ON ENUMERATING TO INFINITY

[108]   By 'construction' I mean purposely made with mathematical operations; I am not assuming the philosophy known as *constructivism*.

[109]   For example, see Sylvestre 2020.

[110]   André 2014, pp. 54–56, 252.

[111]   For similar definitions, see Sylvestre 2020.

[112]   Barr 1964, pp. 150–151, 156.

[113]   A well-defined number is not necessarily the same as what mathematicians refer to as a *computable number*—a number that is the output of a computable function. A *computable function* is a function (such as an algorithm) that eventually halts (self-terminates) outputting digits for a number. An *uncomputable function* is a function that does not halt but rather proceeds indefinitely unless terminated by interruption. An *uncomputable number* is the number output by an uncomputable function. Computable numbers and uncomputable numbers both can be either mathematically well-defined numbers or ill-defined numbers.

[114]   See "List of googolisms/Higher computable level" entry in Wikia.org 2021.

[115]   This notation is inspired by a number proposed by philosopher Michael Huemer to be the largest known finite number. See Huemer 2016, pp. 127–129.

[116]   See "Naïve extension" definition in Wikia.org 2021.

[117]   Sagan 1997, p. 9.

[118]   Sazonov 1995, Slide 1.

[119]   Sazonov 1995.

[120]   Sagan 1980, p. 181.

[121]   The concepts of 'feasible numbers' and 'non-feasible numbers' are from mathematician Vladimir Sazonov of the Russian Academy of Sciences (see Sazonov 1995). My definitions for the terms 'feasible number' and 'unfeasible number' are inspired by, but differ significantly from, Sazonov's conceptions.

[122]   See "Infinity Scrapers" entry in Bowers 2016.

[123]   One interesting implication of this view is that the extensibility of number scales shows there to be a temporal element to mathematics that is often ignored by mathematicians in their practice.

[124]   Mathematicians who say this have the infinity of calculus in mind: ∞.

[125]   This is typically the view of mathematicians who are set theorists; they have transfinite numbers in mind such as ω and $\aleph$.

[126]   Maddocks 2010.

[127]   Example from Farlow 2008, Section 2.4, p. 217.

[128]   Farlow 2008, Section 2.4, p. 217.

CHAPTER 5: ON PREDICATING THE FINITE AND THE INFINITE

[129]   Examples would include both transfinite numbers and real numbers with infinitely many digits.

[130]   Cantor 1883 (1976 translation), p. 71.

[131]   Ferreira 2002.

[132]   Donaldson and Pantano 2020, pp. 63–64.

[133]   Here I am widening the term 'quantifier' from how it is more narrowly used in predicate logic.

[134]   Once again, the term 'range' is *not* being used to mean the set of possible outputs of a function, as it is so used in some areas of mathematics.

[135]   However, as we'll see, a literally infinite collection's property of *completeness* does not jibe well with the *limitlessness* of literal infinity, for its completeness does imply a specifiable amount is possible in principle for the literally infinite collection.

[136]   By "natural numbers" set theorists mean the whole numbers. See entry for 'finite' in Borowski and Borwein 1991, p. 221.

[137]   The use of words such as 'more' or 'less', like the words 'some' and 'all', can be taken as instances of quantification (in terms of predicate quantifiers) without implying the collections under comparisons already have been assigned definite numbers to account for their members. It is rather like saying $X > Y$ without being told how many are in X or how many are in Y. To say of a given collection that it has 'more' or 'less' of something than another collection without having assigned numbers to go by is *either* to imply both collections can be accurately assigned defined numbers for their quantities *or* to imply that at least one of the collections being compared has an undefined, indefinite number of members.

[138]   Roitman 2011, pp. 49, 69.

[139]   Technically speaking, zero and the empty set are not synonymous, but the empty set can be taken as the set zero denotes.

[140]   Hrbáček and Jech 1999, p. 41.

[141]   Epicurus 270 BCE (2012 translation), pp. 94–95.

[142]   However, an infinite number is a peculiar kind of number for Galileo: an "infinite number" is *not* an extension of finite numbers and that is why relations such as "equal," "greater," and "less" are not

applicable to an infinite number. See Galilei 1638 (1914 translation). By contrast, Cantor proposed relations such as "equal," "greater," and "less" are indeed applicable to infinities.

[143]   University of New Mexico 2015.

[144]   Guo, Paycha, and Zhang 2015.

[145]   Minami 2017.

[146]   Leitzell 2016.

[147]   Zyga 2016.

[148]   Sharaf 2017.

[149]   Or course, the notion of adding to a limitless quantity is itself problematic, but we'll ignore this until later in this book.

[150]   See Ferreira 2001 and Ferreira 2002. Ferreira 2002 states, "In [the article, 'On the Set of Natural Numbers'] we showed that there are natural numbers with an endless number of digits; we considered that the limit of a sequence n of zeros, when n tends to infinite, is an infinite sequence of zeros." Ferreira's phrasing sounds more like a reference to figurative infinity than literal infinity, but since he proposes there is a *set* of infinite natural numbers, I take him to mean that the numbers themselves are infinitely large in the literal sense of the term.

[151]   Ferreira 2002.

[152]   Wallis 1655, *Tract on Conic Sections*, presented in Scott 1938.

[153]   Yarnelle 1964, pp. 8–9.

[154]   Hardegree 2002, p. 2.

[155]   Cook 2007, p. 151.

[156]   For example, take the following quote about figurative infinity (called 'potential infinity') and literal infinity (called 'an actual infinite'): "A potential infinity may be symbolized by a lemniscate: ∞. An actual infinite can be depicted by the aleph-null or aleph-naught: $\aleph_0$ (The Hebrew letter aleph with a subscript zero)." Quote from Andrews 2011.

[157]   Wallis 1656 (2004 translation), pp. 2, 71.

[158]   For an example see Schechter 2009. For claims of "infinitely many" numbers and an "infinite number" of terms, see McKee 2013.

CHAPTER 6: DISTINGUISHING FINITES AND INFINITES

[159]   Morriston 2010, pp. 439–440, 444–449.

[160]   Craig and Sinclair 2009, pp. 104–105.

[161]   Fleming 1857 (1887 edition), p. 211.

[162]   See Lavine 1994 in which Lavine introduced his "Theory of Zillions." Lavine proposed 'zillion' as the term designating the quantity of members in an 'indefinitely large' set, and he proposed indefinitely large sets account for our "intuition" about the infinite. While I agree with him that there are indefinitely large sets, I argue to the contrary that an accurate intuition about the infinite is that the infinite is illusion. Moreover, Lavine holds the "indefinitely large" to be a matter of too large to count for lack of convenience, whereas I hold the indefinitely large to be too large to count in present practice (but not in principle).

In my previous monograph on cosmology (Sewell 1999, pp. 32–33) I used the terms 'immeasurable' and 'immeasurability' instead of the terms 'indefinite' and 'indefiniteness' for finite magnitudes that are either so vast or so small they are off any given scale. I now believe the terms 'immeasurable' and 'immeasurability' are misleading: the indefinite is that which is measurable at least in principle even if not in actual practice, while values that cannot be measured even in principle are traditionally referred to as "infinite." So, the terms 'indefinite' and 'indefiniteness' I now consider more proper to use.

[163]   See Lavine 1994, p. 248, and Lavine 1995, p. 391.

[164]   I am aware 'enormity' may be a controversial choice of vocabulary. (See Merriam-Webster 2021.)

[165]   Faulkner 1957 (2012 collection), p. 571.

[166]   Immortality does not necessarily imply a literally infinite amount of time for two reasons: first, an immortal may have a finite past; second, an immortal's future may have a running total of years, no matter how long it continues, without having a future that is both complete and limitless in duration. (This is touched upon at the close of Chapter 27).

[167]   Bolzano 1847 (in Russ 2004), §§ 9, 12, 15: pp. 603, 606, 611.

[168]   Bolzano 1847 (in Russ 2004), § 18: p. 613.

[169]   Bolzano 1847 (in Russ 2004), § 17: p. 612.

[170]   Bolzano 1847 (in Russ 2004), § 9: p. 603.

[171]   Descartes 1642 in Bennett 2017a, First Objections, Reply 3, p. 12.

[172]   Descartes 1644, Part Two (in Bennett 2017b), p. 28.

[173]   Descartes 1644, Part One (in Cottingham, Stoothoff, and Murdoch 1985), Article 27, p. 202.

[174]   Descartes 1644, Part One (in Cottingham, Stoothoff, and Murdoch 1985), Article 27, p. 202.

[175]   Descartes 1642 (in Bennett 2017a), First Objections, Reply 3, p. 12.

[176]   Weisstein 2021, entry for 'infinite'.

[177]   See entry for 'infinite', definitions 1 and 2 in Borowski and Borwein 1991, p. 292. Similar definitions are found in a variety of mathematics dictionaries.

[178]   More precisely, an infinite number is one that cannot be computed or counted even in principle due to limitlessness but can be computed or counted in principle due to completeness—a contradiction addressed further in § 12.3.

[179]   Here again it is more precise to say infinity is incalculable due to limitlessness but also calculable due to completeness, a contradiction addressed further in § 12.3.

CHAPTER 7: SPEAKING OF INFINITE QUANTITIES

[180]   Weisstein 2021, entry for 'infinity'.

[181]   Weisstein 2021, entry for 'infinity'.

[182]   Simmons 2017, entry for 'infinity'.

[183]   "Definition: *A set S is finite if and only if its cardinal number is a positive integer. A non-empty set which is not finite is called infinite*." (Quote from Yarnelle 1964, p. 6.) The set of positive integers is equal to the set of natural numbers (counting numbers). Hence, to be greater than any positive integer is to be greater than any natural number. Other number systems are sets equal to, or even greater than, the set of naturals (see §§ 13.8–13.10).

[184]   IUPAC 1997, entry for "acyl groups."

[185]   Simmons 2017, entry for 'infinite'.

[186]   Based on entry for 'heat' in *Random House Dictionary*: Random House 2020.

[187]   Entry for 'heat' in *A Concise Dictionary of Physics*: Isaacs 1990.

[188]   Lower 2017.

[189]   Dantzig 1930 (2005 edition), p. 243.

[190]   Dantzig 1930 (2005 edition), p. 243.

[191]   Bogomolny 1996.

[192]   Kreyszig 1989, p. 25.

[193]   Weisstein 2021, entry for 'point at infinity'.

CHAPTER 8: THE STORY OF LITERAL INFINITY

[194]   See entry for 'apeiros' (ἄπειρος (B)) in Liddell and Scott 1940. See also Rucker 2005 (2019 edition), pp. 2–3.

[195]   Physis is also sometimes spelled 'phusis' and pronounced fū-seez.

[196]   Anaximander believed the arche, the fundamental stuff, was an irrational union of opposites, a chaos from which all dualities in the Universe arose according to the nature of the arche as the physis, the prime cause of everything.

[197]   Sweeney 1992, pp.544–546.

[198]   Some scholars translate 'Apeiron' variously as 'Ultimate', 'Boundless', or 'Unlimited'. I take Anaximander to emphasize that the arche of the Universe is literally infinite and not just indefinite (a finitude of undefined size). I am not alone in that assessment; see Sweeney 1992, pp. 554–546.

[199]   Burnet 1920, § 16 and endnote 68.

[200]   Some sources reference the Hindu *Isha Upanishad* (*Shukla Yajur Veda*) as one of the first sources of the concept of literal infinity, which in Sanskrit is called *purnam*, a word that means 'whole' in a special sense when used for that which is both limitless and complete. There is, however, some disagreement over the time in which the *Yajur Veda* was written. Most sources hold that Zeno of Elea's writings on infinity were earlier than the *Yajur Veda*, and so Zeno's writings may have indirectly influenced the authors of the *Yajur Veda* as ideas were shared along trade routes in the ancient world.

[201]   See *Theaetetus*: Plato 369 BCE, cited in Cooper (John M.) 1997, pp. 173–174.

[202]   For example, see *Philebus*: Plato 360 BCE (1888 translation).

[203]   See *The Republic*: Plato 375 BCE (1888 translation), Book VI.

[204]   Moore 2019, pp. 25–26.

[205]   See *Physics*: Aristotle ~350 BCE (1930 translation), *Physics*, Book III and Book VIII.

[206]   My view of Aristotle's potential infinity is therefore contrary to that offered by some philosophers. For example, mathematician Rudy Rucker states that Aristotle "invented the notion of the *potentially infinite* as opposed to the *actually infinite*." (Quote from Rucker 2005, p. 3.) This can be considered technically true, since Aristotle conceived of figurative infinity and literal infinity as potential and actual respectively, which was unique to his philosophy. However, it is also misleading because what Aristotle really accomplished was drawing a distinction between two different uses of 'infinity'—one for what I call serial indefinites and one for complete-yet-limitless collections.

[207]   Sanders (Samuel) 1930, p. 15.

[208]   There are areas in Euclid's writing where infinity seems to be taken as literal. For example, see *The Elements*: Euclid 3rd Century BCE (2008 translation), Book 10, Definition 3, p. 282.

[209]   Euclid 3rd Century BCE (2008 translation), Book 1, Definition 23, p. 7 and Book 10, Proposition 115, p. 422.

[210]   Euclid 3rd Century BCE (2008 translation), Book 10, Definition 3, p. 282.

[211]   Euclid 3rd Century BCE (2008 translation), Book 10, Proposition 1, pp. 282–283.

[212]   Euclid 3rd Century BCE (2008 translation), Book 12, Propositions 2, 16, and 17: pp. 472–475, 498–499, 499–502.

    Euclid's method was used by Archimedes more explicitly to show how an indefinitely-many-sided polygon approximates a circle.

[213]   This may also be what Euclid meant by lines extending "to infinity" as being approximated by creating an "infinite series" of lines. The "infinite series" (figurative infinity) goes "to infinity" (literal infinity) in the sense of proceeding ceaselessly toward it as an ideal. See Euclid 3rd Century BCE (2008 translation), Book 10, Proposition 115, p. 422.

[214]   See *The Sand Reckoner*: Archimedes ~216 BCE (1897 translation).

[215]   Archimedes ~216 BCE (1897 translation).

[216]   Netz 2009.

[217]   Aquinas 1273 (1947 translation), *The Summa Theologica*, First Part, Question 7: The Infinity of God (Four Articles), Article 4.

[218]   Hylwa 2013, pp. 6–9.

[219]   Manuel 2018.

[220]   Joseph 2011.

[221]   Smestad 1995.

[222]   Quote from Waldegg 2005, p. 564.

[223]   Bolzano 1847 (in Russ 2004).

[224]   As I will later show, literal infinity is actually not calculated in any mathematical system. This is because mathematical systems treat literal infinity as merely an indefinite (finite) quantity in terms of actual operation. Moreover, some of the operations—even in transfinite mathematics—treat sets that are supposedly literally infinite as incomplete rather than complete, thus violating the definition of literal infinity. My point here is simply that the concept of literal infinity has been around since antiquity and that mathematical systems were only later developed to make rigorous *mathematical* use of the concept, even if such systems fail to represent literal infinity in a *logically* consistent manner.

[225]   Waterhouse 1979, p. 432.

[226]   Bolzano 1847 (in Russ 2004), § 17: p. 612.

[227]   Bolzano 1847 (in Russ 2004), § 17: p. 612.

[228]   Bolzano 1847 (in Russ 2004), § 17: p. 612.

[229]   Bolzano 1847 (in Russ 2004), § 17: p. 612.

[230]   Cantor 1895/1897 (1915 translation), Article I, Section 6, pp. 103–104 and Article I, Section 7, p. 115.

[231]   Jourdain's Introduction to Cantor 1895/1897 (1915 translation), pp. 32, 36, and 38.

[232]   Sources for the positions of the scholars in Table 1 are listed in chronological order:
   - Zeno of Elea. 5th Century BCE. Reported in Aristotle ~350 BCE (1999 translation), *Physics*, Book VI: Chapters 1–2 and 9, 239b9.
   - Aristotle ~350 BCE (1930 translation), *Physics*, Book VIII (Part 1) and Book III (Part 4).
   - Euclid 3rd Century BCE (2008 translation), Book 10, Definition 3, p. 282.
   - Archimedes ~216 BCE (1897 translation), Proposition 14.
   - Philoponus 529 CE (2005 translation), Chapter 1, Section 3, pp. 23–24.
   - Grosseteste 1225 (1942 translation), pp. 10–17.
   - Galilei 1638 (1914 translation), p. 57.
   - Wallis 1656, pp. 2, 71.
   - Newton 1736, pp. 251–252, 277–278.
   - Bolzano 1847 (in Russ 2004), §§ 9, 12: pp. 603, 606.
   - Cantor 1897 letter to Hilbert in Ewald 2005, p. 927.
   - Gamow 1947 (1988 edition), p. 21.
   - Greene 2011, pp. 33, 38.

[233]   Cantor 1883 (1976 translation), pp. 76 and 94.

[234]   Cantor 1899 letter to Dedekind in Van Heijenoort 1967, pp. 114–115.

[235]   Barrow 2006.

[236]   Penrose 2011.

[237]   Lucretius 54 BCE (2011 translation), Book I: verses 950–1050; 300–307; 522–531; 1084–1095, pp. 23–25, 36, 41, 53–54.

[238]   See endnote 237.

[239]   Lucretius 54 BCE (2011 translation), Book I: verses 965–967, p. 23.

[240]   Hilbert 1925 (1983 edition), pp. 183–201.

[241]   Schechter 2009, "Potential versus Completed Infinity."

[242]   Cantor 1897 letter to Hilbert in Ewald 2005, p. 927.

CHAPTER 9: LOGIC VERSUS LITERAL INFINITY

[243]   This is to clarify a charge I made against infinity in the first edition of my prior work on cosmology (Sewell 1999), which I believe was misleading on this point. See endnote 53 for further details.

[244]   This is a bit of an oversimplification since 'grammar' is also used in the sense of 'formal grammar' of which mathematical rules would be an example; here I use 'grammar' only in a broader linguistic sense.

[245]   Roitman 2011, p. 22.

[246]   For example, philosopher William J. Rapaport of State University of New York uses 'extension' more like I would use 'denotation' or in some contexts 'implication' or even 'connotation'. See Rapaport 2012.

[247]   Evolutionary psychologist Steven Pinker has written an excellent overview of the structure of grammar and its evolution. However, I am here taking a bit of a different approach than the one he and many linguists take on categorizing the building blocks of grammar. See Pinker 2003.

[248]   To say that condition A "always" or "usually" results in B indicates that there is more than one kind of implication and so more than one kind of inference. Implications fall into two broad categories: *necessary implications* and *general implications* from which we may respectively draw either necessary inferences or general inferences.

When condition B cannot fail to result from condition A, we say that A *necessarily implies* B; that is, B always results from A. For example, A necessarily implies B when B follows from A as a matter of definition. If we know that a particular man, John, is a bachelor, then we know John is an unmarried male because being a bachelor necessarily implies being an unmarried male by definition. So, we can *infer* that since John is a bachelor (condition A), John is an unmarried male (condition B). In this example, A necessarily implies B, which means B cannot be false if A is true. More stringently, A necessarily implies B if and only if it would be *self-contradictory* to state A while denying B.

In contrast, it is said that A *generally implies* B when B usually results from A, but not always. An implication generally holds when the implied condition, B, is recognized as being *contingent* upon, *caused* by, or at least *strongly correlated* with, the implying condition, A.

Suppose we have rain falling over a city, and we label this condition as A. Suppose we also have another condition, that of the city streets being wet, and we label this condition as B. We know from experience that, generally speaking, when rain falls in the city (condition denoted by A), the streets get wet (condition denoted by B). If we are in the city and are told it is raining outside, we know the implication: the streets are getting wet. So, we are able to *infer* (recognize the implication) from news of condition A that condition B follows.

Incidentally, the opposite is not true: just because the streets are wet doesn't mean it is raining (maybe a dam broke, causing a river to flood the city streets, or maybe a water truck is hosing down the streets after a parade, or any number of other things that might make the streets wet). So, A generally implies B, but B does not imply A.

Even though for this example we can safely assume A implies B in most circumstances, we can only say A *generally* implies B and not that A *necessarily* implies B. That is because some third set of conditions, C, might interfere with A resulting in B. For example, it is physically possible that the falling rain (condition A) is being blown by a strong wind (condition C) past the city, preventing the streets from getting wet (no condition B). If that were so, it could be raining without the streets getting wet. It would therefore not be *self-contradictory* to affirm A, the rain, and deny B, the wet streets. Unlikely as condition C is, it is logically and physically possible, so we can only say that A (rain) "generally implies" B (wet streets), not that A "necessarily implies" B.

And yet, because C is unlikely, the implication *generally*, or usually, holds up under tests against reality. So, inferring B from A is still considered a 'correct' inference to make—it would be correct to assume that no unusual circumstances are in play, even if it accidentally turns out not to be true.

[249]   Auersperg, von Bayern, et al. 2014.

[250]   Frege 1893/1903 (2013 edition).

[251]   Russell (Bertrand) 1903 (2010 edition).

[252]   Some philosophers continue the project of attempting to reduce mathematics to something non-mathematical. See Linsky and Zalta 2006, pp. 60–99.

[253]   Simpson 2006.

[254]   Just and Weese 1996, p. 2.

[255]   Just and Weese 1996, p. 2.

[256]   Giblin 2011.

[257] See the scope of theoretical mathematics at Arizona State University's School of Mathematical and Statistical Sciences:
<https://math.asu.edu/research/theoretical-mathematics>

[258] Devlin 2009.

[259] Devlin 2009.

[260] Goriely 2018.

[261] Roitman 2011, p. 22.

[262] Roitman 2011, p. 22.

[263] Examples based on the following:
(a) Roitman 2011, p. 22.
(b) Kleitman 2021, Chapter 8.

[264] Wittgenstein 1930 (1975), § 121: p. 24.

[265] Wittgenstein 1932 (1974), p. 468.

[266] For a defense of the thesis that math is nothing but syntax, see Rodych 2001, pp. 527–555. My thesis is in partial agreement with that of Rodych: yes, math is an invention, but no, it is not "nothing but syntax."

[267] Though, in my view, while ℵ operationally refers to indefinite sets of numbers, the *intended* meaning of the symbol—the size of a literally infinite set—refers to nothing logically coherent.

[268] Huemer 2016, pp. 121–122.

[269] Moore 2019, p. 160.

[270] Moore 2019, pp. 160–161.

[271] Moore 2019, pp. 167–168.

[272] For further support that much of mathematics is based on analogies with concepts used in natural language descriptions of the empirical world, see Hofstadter and Sander 2013. See Lakoff and Johnson 2008.

[273] Hrbáček and Jech 1999, p. 1.

[274] Roitman 2011, p. 22.

[275] Roitman 2011, p. 22.

[276] Weisstein 2021, entry for 'Euclid's Postulates'.

[277] Plebani 2011, p. 100.

[278] This is a position taken by adopting the so-called *coherence theory of truth*. I don't subscribe to that theory as a general theory of what the word 'truth' means since the theory is too limited. Consistency checks are sufficient for testing the truth of mathematical expressions but not for the truth of statements about the real world.

[279] Examples cited in the present work include, but are certainly not limited to, the following: Barrow 2006, Cantor 1883, Hilbert 1925, Lavine 1994, Moore 2019, and Rucker 2005. (Additionally, endnote 15 provides some background on my own use of 'the infinite' as a term in my previous writings.)

[280] Bragg 2001.

[281] Kneebone 1963 (2001 edition), p. 4.

[282] Feferman 2009, p. 3.

[283] Isaacson 2011, pp 1–76.

[284] Isaacson 2011.

[285] Definition adapted from Sparkes 1991, p. 70.

[286] I am not here endorsing the 'coherence theory of truth'; rather, I am simply pointing out that in order to understand an expression, it must be coherent. I'm not suggesting that just because an expression is coherent that it is therefore true. The test of an expression's truth is entirely dependent on context. Testing a mathematical expression may be a matter of coherence but testing a statement for truth about the real world is not just a matter of its being coherent.

[287] **Figure 9.4** can be made to overlap with **Figure 9.5**, as formal logic and set theory overlap with mathematics while set-theoretic expressions can be stated to conform with the rules of grammar.

[288] I am here using the terms 'coherent' and 'incoherent' a bit differently than how they are used by academic philosophers. As I will be using the term, *coherence* characterizes expressions that follow both the syntactic

and the semantic rules of the pertinent domain(s). Therefore, an expression is incoherent if it violates *either* rules of syntax *or* conventions for semantics, or both. However, just because an expression is incoherent for a given domain does not mean it is *incomprehensible*—we can still get the gist of an expression even if it isn't syntactically coherent for the domain in question.

[289]   Carroll (Lewis) 1871 (2015 edition), p. 130.

[290]   I am using the term "grammar" a bit more widely than do linguists. Taking the example of Wittgenstein, I am using the term "grammar" to include principles of semantics in natural language as well as syntax and other rules of proper structure.

[291]   There is another kind of expression, the *imperative*, which has a less clear place in the domains. Most imperatives fall in Area 1—outside of math and logic—but some may actually belong to Area 2, which is in the scope of mathematics. For example, mathematicians offer imperatives in their practice, such as "Let x be equal to 5." Also consider statements *about* imperatives, such as those made in practical reasoning about duties and obligations; these must conform to the principles of *deontic logic* in Area 4 in order to be regarded as logically coherent. Outside of drawing inferences about obligations, however, most imperatives fall into Area 1 of non-logical grammar.

[292]   See Endnote 53. In Sewell 1999, I claimed that infinity is "meaningless"—but this is *only* true in the technical sense of formal logic; it is not true in either a grammatical sense or a mathematical sense. Even in the logical sense, to say literal infinity is "meaningless" is actually a bit of hyperbole—it is more precise to say it has a self-contradictory meaning than to say it is meaningless since that might be taken to imply it is without meaning. This more nuanced view will be assumed in any forthcoming works I publish on cosmology.

[293]   "Syntax" is a term I am using to cover principles determining how the signifiers are organized in expressions. Non-linguistic and non-quantitative signifiers are not symbolic but can be representative. Examples include memories and behaviors. Syntax for signifiers of these kinds is not found in symbolic form, but an observer may infer the use of this sort of syntax by interpreting its expression in order to represent it formally for analysis.

[294]   Not all logical reasoning is done formally with symbols or with quantification. I must therefore disagree with those mathematicians who claim that "logic has no existence independent of mathematics"—as an example of this incorrect claim, see Dantzig 1930 (2005 edition), p. 254. Quantification aside, most reasoning in natural language also does not necessarily need formalization to be logical. Consider reasoning via enthymemes; such can be made formally valid by supplying the assumed premises, so it's not clear that informal reasoning in natural language is intrinsically non-logical. Then too, not all reasoning occurs with language at all; some animals display evidence of forming reliable inferences without any linguistic ability (see CNRS 2011). Since not all reliable forms of inference occur with the use of language, logic (at least as I have defined it) is not dependent on language.

[295]   That's not to say that animals cannot reason mathematically; evidence shows that some animals can understand quantity and can even count or make rudimentary calculations. See the following:
(a)   Duke University Medical Center 2007.
(b)   Brandeis University 2005.
That would suggest that animals have a kind of mental grammar by which to reason about quantity. Yet, this shouldn't be too surprising as many animals also seem to have a very rudimentary grammar for communicating with vocal signals, gestures, or even scents (though, some might say that's pushing the term 'grammar' a bit far).

[296]   Derived from Yarnelle 1964, p. 6. See also endnote 183.

[297]   See endnote 276. And notice again these postulates are stated in second-order, natural language—the postulates are not just syntax alone.

[298]   See endnote 276.

[299]   Berger 2003.

[300]   Vaught 2001, p. 41.

[301]   In the opinion of most set theorists, there is no sharp distinction between set theory and transfinite mathematics, so they take the Axiom of Infinity as the basis of set theory. However, that's a disputable notion since there are finite versions of set theory.

[302]   Simmons 2017, entry for 'infinity'.

[303]   Simmons 2017, entry for 'infinity'.

[304]   Derived from Yarnelle 1964, p. 6. (See endnote 183.)

[305]   Based on the expression by Oxford professor of mathematics Dr. Robin W. Knight. See Knight 2018b, p. 2.

[306]   Based on Chu-Carroll 2007.

[307]   Compare with Holmes, Forster, and Libert 2012, p. 564.

CHAPTER 10: COMPLETENESS—IMPLICATIONS FOR INFINITY

[308]   Such definitions belong to Area 3 of **Figure 9.5**.

[309]   These technical definitions are in Area 2 of **Figure 9.5** while the literal infinity they are intended to convey is in Area 1 of the same figure.

[310]   By 'series' I mean a sequence formed by temporal succession rather than more narrowly a mathematical 'series' (an accession) in which the members are related by addition.

[311]   Schechter 2009b.

[312]   In Cantor's transfinite system, the members of the sequence {2, 3, 4, …} can be placed into bijection with the members of the sequence {1, 2, 3, …}, making them "equally infinite."

[313]   In use of the terms 'minimum' and 'maximum', I do not mean the relative minima and maxima of indefinite magnitudes as produced in a calculus domain marked by x/y coordinates but rather minimum and maximum quantities that a given collection must have in order to be considered 'full'.

[314]   Similarly, mathematician Stephen Barr wrote, "If we define a set of all fractional numbers from 1 to 2 inclusive, then 1 is the minimum and 2 is the maximum." Barr 1964, p. 150.

[315]   In Chapter 13, we'll see how transfinite mathematics defines the infinitude of the natural (counting) numbers ($\aleph_0$) as "less than" the infinitude of the real numbers ($\aleph_1$). The maximum quantity of reals for the set of reals from 0 to 1 is thus equal to at least $\aleph_0$ but less than $\aleph_1$. The mathematics of the transfinite system does not allow for more specificity than that, although the transfinite system holds that the reals do extend *from* 0 *to* 1. So, if literal infinity is a state of completeness, we can be sure completeness implies a *maximum quantity* of reals from 0 to 1. That maximum quantity is $< \aleph_2$, which is not very definite, but there must be a definite number in principle since there must be a next number right before 1 in the sequence from 0 to 1 or there would be no such thing as reals *from* 0 *to* 1. The limitlessness of the same collection of numbers implies otherwise, as we'll see in Chapter 11.

[316]   This example is based on an analogy by Craig. See endnote 17.

[317]   Hrbáček and Jech 1999, p.279.

[318]   At least, this is the claim for some infinite sets, like $\mathbb{N}$ or $\mathbb{W}$. Transfinite math holds that other infinite sets, like $\mathbb{R}$, are not countable. We will return to this distinction in § 13.7 and § 13.9.

[319]   Farlow 2008, Section 2.4, pp. 217–218.

[320]   Grossman 2010, p. 6.

[321]   Mathematicians say, for instance, that the set {1, 2, 3, …} "has no largest element." See Yarnelle 1964, p. 7.

[322]   Grossman 2010, p.6.

[323]   Van Bendegem 1994, p. 34. Van Bendegem has also considered 'paradoxical' last numbers in 'paraconsistent mathematics', which is beyond my present scope.

[324]   As we'll see, this conclusion, while following from the completeness of a literally infinite sequence of numbers in $\mathbb{N}$, is contradicted by the limitlessness of the same literally infinite sequence of numbers in $\mathbb{N}$.

[325]   Russell (Bertrand) 1903 (2010 edition), Section 343, p. 366.

[326]   See also Chapters 4, 5, and 11.

[327]   Galilei 1638 (1914 translation). His idea of an infinite number is not without qualification, as he seems to have thought any scale of numbers ends with the same infinite number—see § 25.2.9.

[328]   For a similar example, see Fletcher 2007, p. 524.

[329]   mathcentre 2009, pp. 2–4.

[330]   For further discussion of infinity as a complete sequence, and an example of the lemniscate's use to illustrate a "completed infinity," see Schechter 2009, "Potential versus Completed Infinity."

[331]   Fletcher 2007, p. 524.

CHAPTER 11: LIMITLESSNESS—IMPLICATIONS FOR INFINITY

[332]   See the definitions of infinity in Chapter 1.

[333]   Still, I should make two qualifications to this analysis. First, speaking of "all" the elements of a collection as meaning "for any" characterizes not just how the term 'all' works with limitlessness but also with serial indefinites—serial indefiniteness being the property of finite progression with a running total—see § 14.1.2. Second, while I take it that "all" for limitlessness has a different *assumed* meaning than it does for completeness, limitlessness may at times inadvertently *imply* completeness and its meaning of "all." The limitlessness of a collection may thus *ironically* entail a limit and even completeness for a collection when we apply the predicate 'limitless' as a measure to a particular member of a collection—see § 22.1.1.

[334]   Mathematicians more often use the term 'countably infinite' rather than 'limitless' for a fence of minimal and maximal elements. See Dimitrova, Koppitz, and Lohapan 2017, p. 281.

[335]   Dawkins 2019.

[336]   Bolzano 1847 (in Russ 2004), § 9: p. 603.

[337]   Bolzano 1847 (in Russ 2004), § 9: p. 603.

[338]   Wittgenstein defended this view. See Wittgenstein 1930 (1975 edition).

[339]   Waismann 1979.

[340]   Rudin 1976, p. 4.

[341]   Rudin 1976, p. 4.

[342]   Ackerman 2009.

[343]   Trench 2000, p. 6.

[344]   Compare this conclusion to its opposite ($^{(x)}\aleph \neq {}^{(y)}\aleph$), which in the previous chapter was presented as following from the *completeness* of two literally infinite collections.

[345]   MacDonald 2005, p. 243.

[346]   Lavine 1994, p. 248.

[347]   Hardegree 2002, p. 3.

[348]   Grossman 2010, p. 6.

[349]   Hardegree 2002, p. 2.

[350]   Rucker states that the "sum" of an infinite series is the series itself. See Rudy Rucker's discussion of infinite series in Rucker 2005, p. 62.

[351]   This is how mathematician Norman Wildberger explains the set theorist's take on infinite numbers. See Patterson 12 March 2017.

[352]   Cantor 1895/1897 (1915 translation), p. 104.

[353]   Fletcher 2007, p. 524.

[354]   Fletcher 2007, p. 524.

[355]   Fletcher 2007, p. 524.

CHAPTER 12: COMPLETE AND LIMITLESS: THE CONTRADICTIONS

[356]   Hardegree 2002, p. 2.

[357]   Grossman 2010, p. 6.

[358]   This is contrary to the position of Craig, who asserts that there is no infinitieth member of an infinite sequence as a matter of logic but that there would have to be in the real world if it were a matter of causality (see Craig 1979a, pp. 75, 178–179, 181–183). I say that's incorrect: it is a matter of logic that the completeness of a literally infinite sequence requires it to have an infinitieth member, while the limitlessness of the same sequence implies that it has no such member. Hence the self-contradictory nature of literal infinity.

[359]   Oppy 2006, p. 116.

[360]   Oppy 2006, pp. 116, 139–140.

[361]   And even if we do allow for an infinitely large number (e.g., 1,000,000,000,000...) we have only to ask how that number can be complete and yet also limitless.

[362]   Oppy 2006, p. 105.

[363]   I am countering claims made by various other philosophers such as Graham Oppy, Richard Taylor, J. Watling, Paul Benacerraf, and William Lane Craig that a literally infinite series can be complete without a last element or member. See the following:
(a)   Oppy 2006, p. 105.
(b)   Taylor 1951.
(c)   Watling 1952.
(d)   Benacerraf 1962.
(e)   Craig 1979a.

[364]   Holt 2012, p. 82.

[365]   See Bertrand Russell's proposals of the ability to cross a literal infinite provided *infinite acceleration* is assumed. Russell's illustration is mentioned in Thomson 1967, pp. 183–190.

Rucker proposes a different solution: slow down time infinitely via relativistic time dilation and you can cross an infinite amount of space in finite time. Rucker's illustration is in *Infinity and the Mind* (Rucker 2005, p. 87).

However, both Russell and Rucker's illustrations propose crossing a literally (or 'actually') infinite set with what amounts to a figurative, or 'potential', infinite acceleration or time dilation. A figurative infinite is never complete. Hence, even the examples of Russell and Rucker do not show that literal infinites can be crossed. And even if we allow their acceleration or time dilation to be literally infinite, the argument becomes circular since completing a literal infinity of any kind is what is in question.

[366]   Ambrose 1993, p. 137.

[367]   Hardegree 2002, p. 3.

[368]   Hardegree 2002, p. 2.

[369]   Bolzano 1816, p. 157.

[370]   Huemer 2016, pp. 65, 249.

[371]   Fletcher 1998, p. 24.

[372]   Huemer 2016, p. 67.

[373]   Fletcher 1998, p. 24.

[374]   Fletcher 1998, p. 25.

[375]   Huemer 2016, pp. 65, 69, 147.

[376]   Huemer 2016, pp. 185–186, 248–251.

CHAPTER 13: HAS INFINITY BEEN TAMED?

[377]   Moore 1997, p. 53–56.

[378]   Aristotle ~350 BCE (1984 edition), *Physics*, § 207^{a}7–15, as cited in Bowin 2007, p. 241.

[379]   Cantor 1883 (1976 translation), p. 78.

[380]   For example, consider Lavine's mathematics of indefinitely large—but still finite—sets. (Lavine 1994 and 1995).

[381]   Hrbáček and Jech 1999, p. 41.

[382]   Moore 1997, pp. 53–56.

[383]   Schechter 2002.

[384]   Cantor 1883 (1976 translation), p. 70.

[385]   Cantor 1883 (1976 translation), pp. 70, 75. See also Jourdain's Introduction to Cantor 1895/1897 (1915 translation), pp. 55–56, 79.

[386]   This is, perhaps, a bit of an oversimplification since Cantor divided 'actual infinity' into two types: *the transfinite* (a calculable infinity which his ordinal and cardinal numbers refer to) and *the Absolute*—the absolute infinity which he thought characterizes the nature of God—see § 25.3 of this book. See also Cantor 1883 (1976 translation), pp. 75–76, 78.

[387]   Both versions paraphrased from a single definition in Hrbáček and Jech 1999, p. 87.

[388]   "Let $(P, <)$ be a dense linearly ordered set. P is *complete* if every non-empty $S \subseteq P$ bounded from above has a supremum. Note that $(P, <)$ is complete if and only if it does not have any gaps." Quote from Hrbáček and Jech 1999, p. 87.

[389]   Clark 2017, p. 7.

[390]   Costin 2006.

[391]   This definition is further refined in transfinite mathematics with reference to the ordinality and cardinality of the set of natural numbers. For example, another way of expressing 'infinite' according to this definition is by reference to a limit ordinal: there is a supremum (symbolized by ω) which is a limit ordinal toward which a limitless (or "unbounded") sequence of natural numbers in $\mathbb{N}$ extends. See Roitman 2011, p. 49; see also Hrbáček and Jech 1999, pp. 35, 72, 87, 107, 109, 110, 129.

[392]   Hrbáček and Jech 1999, pp. 41, 87, 89.

[393]   Derived from Yarnelle 1964, p. 6 (See endnote 183 for § 7.2.), and Moore 2019, Figure 10.1 on p. 157.

[394]   For some examples, see the following:

      (a)   Yarnelle 1964, pp. 8–9.

      (b)   Hardegree 2002, p. 2.

      (c)   Cook 2007, p. 151.

[395]   Oppy 2006, p. 77.

[396]   Hardegree 2002, p. 2.

[397]   Jourdain's Introduction to Cantor 1895/1897 (1915 translation), pp. 53–54.

[398]   Clark 2017, p. 8.

[399]   Cantor 1886 letter in Jourdain's Introduction to Cantor 1895/1897 (1915 translation), p. 78.

[400]   Cantor 1895/1897 (1915 translation), p. 85.

[401]   I am here allowing ∞ to represent a literal infinity, as Cantor originally did, and some mathematicians still do. Other mathematicians and philosophers of mathematics insist ∞ refers only to a potential infinity (i.e., figurative infinity).

[402]   Jourdain's Introduction to Cantor's 1895/1897 (1915 translation), pp. 53–54.

[403]   Cantor 1883 (1976 translation), pp. 76, 94.

[404]   Cantor 1883 (1976 translation), p. 87.

[405]   Cantor 1883 (1976 translation), p. 87.

[406]   Moore 2019, p. 151.

[407]   According to Cantor, the transfinite "follows after" the finite. See Cantor 1883 (1976 translation), pp. 72, 76, 87.

[408]   Notice each 'set' is presented as an incomplete listing of numbers and so is, operationally speaking, only an incomplete listing of numbers continuing on indefinitely but not necessarily 'infinitely' as supposed in transfinite mathematics.

[409]   Craig 1979a, p. 181.

[410]   Again, transfinite mathematicians tend to use $\mathbb{N}$ as the natural numbers instead of $\mathbb{W}$ for the whole numbers, even though they are referring to the same sequence as the whole numbers. For discussion on the meaning of ω, see Moore 2019, p. 151.

[411]   Machover 1996, p. 65.

[412] Hrbáček and Jech 1999, p. 103.

[413] Cantor 1883 (1976 translation), p. 87.

[414] Cantor 1883 (1976 translation), p. 87. This is also how Cantor, in an 1886 letter, described ω. See Jourdain's Introduction to Cantor 1895/1897 (1915 translation), p. 78.

[415] Jourdain's Introduction to Cantor 1895/1897 (1915 translation), pp. 77–78.

[416] Jourdain's Introduction to Cantor 1895/1897 (1915 translation), p. 78.

[417] Jourdain's Introduction to Cantor 1895/1897 (1915 translation), p. 79.

[418] Jourdain's Introduction to Cantor 1895/1897 (1915 translation), pp. 77–78.

[419] More precisely, transfinite mathematics today says that ω follows the sequence of numbers comprising $\mathbb{N}$ because these days transfinite mathematicians prefer to take $\mathbb{N}$ as including 0.

[420] Jourdain's Introduction to Cantor 1895/1897 (1915 translation), pp. 77.

[421] Clark 2017, p. 7.

[422] Hardegree 2002, p. 2.

[423] Cantor 1895/1897 (1915 translation), pp. 103–104.

[424] Cantor 1895/1897 (1915 translation), pp. 103–104.

[425] See the following:
    (a) André 2014, pp. 219, 303, 308–309.
    (b) Jourdain 1910, pp. 94–95, 97–98.
    (c) Moore 2019, Figure 10.1 on p. 157.
    (d) Bain 2006, p. 5.

[426] For some examples of this position, see the following:
    (a) Yarnelle 1964, pp. 8–9.
    (b) Hardegree 2002, p. 2.
    (c) Cook 2007, p. 151.

[427] Jourdain's Introduction to Cantor 1895/1897 (1915 translation), pp. 53–56.

[428] As philosopher Christian Tapp states, "...the actually infinite magnitude is larger than every finite magnitude, independently of any kind of process or function." See Tapp 2005, p. 160.

[429] Yarnelle 1964, p. 10.

[430] Yarnelle 1964, p. 35.

[431] Hardegree 2002, pp. 6, 8, 14, 16.

[432] Moore 2019, pp. 110, 151.

[433] The leftwards horseshoe (⊂) of set theory is different than the rightwards horseshoe (⊃) of predicate calculus. But the symbols are arbitrary and may be used inconsistently between systems.

[434] Caveat: Not all texts on transfinite set theory or transfinite mathematics use the same notation.

[435] Moore 2019, p. 110.

[436] Moore 2019, p. 110.

[437] Hardegree 2002, pp. 8, 10.

[438] Farlow 2008, Section 2.5, p. 235.

[439] Farlow 2008, Section 2.5, p. 235–237.

[440] Stevens 2016.

[441] This version of the diagonal argument is based on Gray 1994, p. 826.

[442] Stevens 2016, at 6.30–40 minutes into 23.45-minute video.

[443] Knight 2018a, p. 5.

[444] Stevens 2016, at 6.30–40 minutes into 23.45-minute video.

[445] Boolos, Burgess, and Jeffrey 2007, p. 4.

[446] Grossman 2010, p. 7.

[447] Cantor 1883 (1976 translation), p. 77.

[448] Cantor 1883 (1976 translation), p. 77.

[449] Clark 2017, p. 29.

[450] Stoll 1979, p. 119.

[451]　Jourdain's Introduction to Cantor 1895/1897 (1915 translation), pp. 51–52.

[452]　Stevens 2016, at 17.48 minutes into 23.45-minute video.

[453]　Moore 2019, p. 153.

[454]　Derived from Yarnelle 1964, p. 6.

[455]　Derived from Yarnelle 1964, p. 6.

[456]　Hallett 1996, p. 32.

[457]　Roitman 2011, p. 63

[458]　Hrbáček and Jech 1999, p. 41.

CHAPTER 14: INFINITY UNTAMED

[459]　Cantor 1897 letter to Hilbert in Ewald 2005, p. 927.

[460]　Cantor 1897 letter to Hilbert in Ewald 2005, p. 927.

[461]　Hrbáček and Jech 1999, p. 279.

[462]　Cantor 1886; see Jourdain's Introduction to Cantor 1895/1897 (1915 translation), pp. 77–78.

[463]　See §§ 3.3.4, 3.4.4, 3.6.2.

[464]　Paraphrased from Hrbáček and Jech 1999, p. 87.

[465]　Cantor 1895/1897 (1915 translation), pp. 97–98. See also Cantor 1897 letter to Hilbert in Ewald 2005, p. 927.

[466]　Cantor 1883 (1976 translation), pp. 75–77. See also Cantor 1895/1897 (1915 translation), pp. 97–98.

[467]　Infinity defined as the transfinite falls either into Area 2 of **Figure 9.5** or Area 3 of the same figure, depending on whether or not it implies either a figurative infinity or a collective indefinite only. If not, then Area 2; if so, then Area 3.

[468]　Definition from § 13.2.3 derived from the implications of limit ordinals in transfinite set theory and transfinite mathematics. See endnote 391.

[469]　This is the literal infinity of Area 1 in **Figure 9.5**.

[470]　See endnotes 465–466.

[471]　Cantor 1886 letter in Jourdain's Introduction to Cantor 1895/1897 (1915 translation), p. 78.

[472]　Cantor 1883 (1976 translation), pp. 70–71, 74–77.

[473]　Moore 1997, p. 53–56.

[474]　Based on Simmons 2017, entry for 'infinite'.

[475]　See § 4.4.4.

[476]　Simmons 2017, entry for 'infinite'.

[477]　We will encounter this again in § 14.7.

[478]　Yarnelle 1964, p. 6, including footnote.

[479]　Cantor 1883 (1976 translation), p. 71.

[480]　Cantor 1895/1897 (1915 translation), p. 99.

[481]　Cantor 1897 letter to Hilbert in Ewald 2005, p. 927.

[482]　Jourdain's Introduction to Cantor 1895/1897 (1915 translation), p. 57.

[483]　Cantor 1895/1897 (1915 translation), p. 99.

[484]　Cantor 1883 (1976 translation), p. 71.

[485]　Cantor 1897 letter to Hilbert in Ewald 2005, p. 927.

[486]　Cantor 1895/1897 (1915 translation), pp. 97–98.

[487]　This way of defining 'complete' aligns with Hrbáček and Jech 1999, p. 89 and Clark 2017, p. 7.

[488]　Hilbert 1925 (1983 edition), p. 7.

[489]　Cantor 1897 letter to Hilbert in Ewald 2005, p. 927.

[490]　Hrbáček and Jech 1999, p. 279.

[491]　See 'Transfinite Limitlessness' section of § 13.2.2.

[492]　See also § 14.3.5 for an example from Rucker (endnote 498) involving an indefinite accession of reals.

[493]　Yarnelle 1964, pp. 6, 9.

[494]   Cantor 1886 letter in Jourdain's Introduction to Cantor 1895/1897 (1915 translation), p. 78.

[495]   Cantor 1886 letter in Jourdain's Introduction to Cantor 1895/1897 (1915 translation), p. 78.

[496]   Jourdain's Introduction to Cantor 1895/1897 (1915 translation), p. 78.

[497]   Jourdain's Introduction to Cantor 1895/1897 (1915 translation), p. 77–78.

[498]   Rucker 2005, p. 62. (See also endnotes 350.)

[499]   I found a similar argument has been presented by Patterson, who derides the assumption that ellipses represent literally limitless progressions as "magic ellipses": Patterson 20 July 2016.

[500]   Wildberger 2016.

[501]   Farlow 2008, Section 2.4, pp. 217–218.

[502]   MacDonald 2005, p. 243.

[503]   Moore 2019, p. 110.

[504]   Moore 2019, p. 110.

[505]   Bolzano 1847 (in Russ 2004), § 28: p. 624.

[506]   Trlifajová 2017, p. 10.

[507]   Bolzano 1847 (in Russ 2004), § 33: pp. 630–631.

[508]   Farlow 2008, Section 2.4, p. 215.

[509]   Bolzano 1847 (in Russ 2004), §§ 21, 33: pp. 617, 631.

[510]   Clegg 2012, p. 59.

[511]   Waldegg 2005, p. 569.

[512]   Waldegg 2005, p. 570.

[513]   Parker 2008, p. 25.

[514]   Keele 2008, p. 58.

[515]   Trlifajová 2017.

[516]   Stevens 2016, at 6.30–40 minutes into 23.45-minute video.

[517]   We find the converse is the problem with the 'paradox' of Hilbert's Hotel, addressed in § 17.3. Hilbert's Hotel abstracts out the completeness of the quantity of hotel rooms in favor of their limitlessness, while Cantor's diagonal argument abstracts out the limitlessness of $\mathbb{N}$ in favor of its completeness. Both maneuvers are fallacious because they avoid addressing half the implications of literal infinity while purporting to demonstrate the concept of literal infinity as a whole is sound.

[518]   Zenkin 2003–2004, pp. 28, 43–44.

[519]   Cantor 1874, pp. 258–262.

[520]   Cantor 1883 (1976 translation).

[521]   It is not clear that Cantor had a Platonic notion of numbers, but he did speak of them as having a "transient reality" that is able to be uncovered by "the sciences" (other than mathematics). See Tate 2001, pp. 11–14.

[522]   Not long ago, I found a similar argument had been made by other thinkers. For example, see Patterson 20 July 2016. Patterson is correct to argue there is no "set of all natural numbers" that exists "out there" as an actually infinite set.

[523]   Wittgenstein called irrational numbers "rules" for developing strings of digits and did not consider them to be genuine numbers at all. See the following:
(a)   Wittgenstein 1930 (1975 edition), § 174.
(b)   Wittgenstein 1937–44 (1978 edition), § 10 and §§ 21–22.
   I don't go as far as Wittgenstein does with respect to irrational numbers. Irrational numbers are not rules; they are numbers because they can each be placed into order on a number line with unique ordinality correlated to a cardinality between other cardinalities. So, an irrational number is still a number. However, an irrational number the sequence of digits for which is does not in principle terminate may be regarded as an *incomplete number* constructed as it is of an incomplete sequence of digits formed according to a rule.

[524]   A similar point was made by Patterson in his online article about Cantor's set theory: Patterson 20 July 2016.

[525]   Cooper (Charles Fisher) 2015. (Caveat: Cooper occasionally updates his webpage; the quote is from his webpage as it appeared on 26 November 2016.)

[526]   Fletcher 1998, p. 24.

[527]   Cooper 2015. (See also endnote 525.)

[528]   This was the position L. E. J. Brouwer held toward the diagonal argument. See Moore 2019, p. 132.

[529]   The only retort to this is that the diagonal string must be contingent upon any horizontal value that would come next. But again, there is nothing stopping this next horizontal number from being q if the list of numbers for the 0–1 segment of $\mathbb{R}$ is not formed by ordinality—that is, according to a pre-established sequence.

[530]   Roitman 2011, pp. 63.

Roitman admitted that the notion of $\mathbb{N}$ as a set is just an assumption in Cantor's work and yet she did not investigate whether the assumption was sound. Instead, she pointed out that Cantor's academic nemesis, Leopold Kronecker, failed in his attempt to convince the mathematics community not to follow Cantor, also noting that in 1925 David Hilbert acknowledged the general acceptance of Cantor's transfinite mathematics. However, this is just an appeal to convention, not a good reason to assume Cantor's work is *logically* sound.

[531]   Knight 2018a, p. 5.

[532]   Stevens 2016, at 6.30–40 minutes into 23.45-minute video.

[533]   Stevens 2016, at 3.40–6.20 minutes into 23.45-minute video.

[534]   Farlow 2008, Sections 2.4–2.5, pp. 217–218, 235–237.

[535]   Cantor 1886 letter in Jourdain's Introduction to Cantor 1895/1897 (1915 translation), p. 78.

[536]   MacDonald 2005, p. 243.

[537]   Derived from Yarnelle 1964, p. 6.

[538]   Machover 1996, p. 65.

[539]   Clark 2017.

[540]   Cantor 1883 (1976 translation), pp. 72, 76, 87.

[541]   Stevens 2016, at 6.40–50 minutes into 23.45-minute video.

[542]   Russell (Bertrand) 1903 (2010 edition), Sections 343–344, pp. 366–367.

[543]   Zenkin 2003–2004, pp. 65–66.

[544]   However, Zenkin used Aristotle's term 'potentially infinite series'. See Zenkin 2003–2004, p. 66.

[545]   Jourdain's Introduction to Cantor 1895/1897 (1915 translation), pp. 53–54.

[546]   Knight 2018a, p. 5.

[547]   Jourdain's Introduction to Cantor 1895/1897 (1915 translation), p. 78.

[548]   Clark 2017, p. 8.

[549]   Ferreira 2002.

[550]   Machover 1996, p. 65.

[551]   Craig 1979a, p. 181.

[552]   Cantor 1883 (1976 translation), p. 87.

[553]   Cantor 1897 letter to Hilbert cited in Achtner 2011, Footnote 109 on p. 41.

[554]   Achtner 2011, p. 41.

[555]   Moore 1997, p. 55.

[556]   Derived from Yarnelle 1964, p. 6.

[557]   Moore 1997, p. 56.

CHAPTER 15: UNAVOIDABLE CONTRADICTIONS

[558]   Moore 1997, 53–56.

[559]   As one googologist says "There is no 'gradual' journey towards infinity. A journey to infinity MUST always be a finite one, otherwise we never actually reach it. The only way to infinity is to instantly 'jump' to it." Quote from Saibian 2021, Appendix A.4: "Infinite Numbers."

[560]   Donaldson and Pantano 2020, p. 171.

[561]   Tapp 2005, p. 161.

[562]   Jourdain's Introduction to Cantor 1895/1897 (1915), p. 78–79

[563]   See endnotes 561 and 562.

[564]   Donaldson and Pantano 2020, pp. 63–64.

[565]   Bolzano 1847 (in Russ 2004), § 21, § 33: pp. 617, 630–631.

[566]   Conway 1976.

[567]   Grim 2012.

[568]   Moore 2019, p. 110.

[569]   Clegg 2012, p. 59.

[570]   As earlier noted in § 12.4.4 with reference to the positions of Jim Holt and Bertrand Russell.

CHAPTER 16: INVISIBLE CONTRADICTIONS

[571]   The term 'inventionism' was coined by Dr. John D. Barrow. See Barrow 2008, p. 212.

[572]   The speech is a dramatization delivered by an actor (Jeremy Irons) playing the part of Hardy in *The Man Who Knew Infinity*, Dir. Matthew Brown. Pressman Film, Xeitgeist Entertainment Group, and Cayenne Pepper Productions, 2015. Film.

[573]   Lents 2018, p. 59.

[574]   Plato attributed many of his beliefs to his teacher Socrates, but it's not clear that these attributions were accurate; in Plato's narrative accounts, Socrates is a character whose function is to serve as a mouthpiece for Plato's own philosophy.

[575]   Gleiser 2014, p. 27.

[576]   Plato 375 BCE (1888 translation), Book VI.

[577]   Mumford 2008.

[578]   For an overview of mathematical platonism, see Linnebo 2018.

[579]   Just and Weese 1996, p. 121.

[580]   Plato 375 BCE (1888 translation), Book VI.

[581]   Jannotta 2010, Article 28. p. 155.

[582]   Rucker 2005, pp. 35–36.

[583]   Anonymous: A. B. 2013.

[584]   Just and Weese 1996, p. 121.

[585]   Rucker 2005, p. 41.

[586]   Rucker, 2005, p. 41–42.

[587]   Roitman 2011 p. 63.

[588]   Rucker 2005, p. 42.

[589]   Moore 2019, p. 26.

[590]   Rucker 2005, p. 207.

[591]   Rucker 2005, p. 42.

[592]   Rucker 2005, p. 43.

[593]   Roitman 2011, p. 25.

[594]   See Gauss's statement in Waterhouse 1979, p. 432.

[595]   See also Fraenkel 1961, pp. 5–6, as quoted in Craig 1979a, Endnote 13, p. 155.

[596]   Berlinski 2008, p. 138.

[597]   Based on entries for 'discover' in *The Random House Unabridged Dictionary*: Random House 2020.

[598]   Based on the first entry for 'invent' in *The Random House Unabridged Dictionary*: Random House 2020.

[599]   See endnote 598.

[600]   Rucker 2005, pp. 35–36.

[601]   Rodych 2001, pp. 529, 532.

[602]   Rosenhouse 2013.

[603]   Thomas 2010, p. 85.

[604]   Wittgenstein 1939 (1976 edition), p. 144.

[605]   Wittgenstein 1937–44 (1956 translation, 1978 edition), Section I, § 21; IV, § 48.

[606]   Wittgenstein 1932 (1974 edition), p. 374.

[607]   Unger and Smolin 2015, p. 422.

[608]   Unger and Smolin 2015, pp. 422–423, 529.

[609]   Unger and Smolin 2015, p. 424.

[610]   Livio 2009, p. 238.

[611]   Gardner 2008, p. 93.

[612]   Gardner 2008, p. 94.

[613]   Gardner 2008, p. 93.

[614]   Horsten 2016.

[615]   Craig and Sinclair 2009, Figure 3.1, p. 107.

[616]   Unger and Smolin 2015, p. 529.

[617]   Barrow 2008, p. 212.

[618]   Barrow 2008, p. 212.

[619]   Wildberger 2005.

[620]   This model of abstraction and idealization differs somewhat from the model proposed by Peter Fletcher. See Fletcher 1998, p. 48.

[621]   Quote from Dr. S. James Gates Jr., Toll Professor of Physics and Director of the Center for String and Particle Theory at the University of Maryland in College Park. Quote from Tippett 2012.

[622]   Wittgenstein 1937–44 (1956 translation, 1978 edition), Sections: I, § 168; II, § 38; V, § 5, 9 and 11.

[623]   Wittgenstein 1932 (1974 edition), pp. 468–470, 481.

[624]   Wittgenstein 1937–44 (1956 translation, 1978 edition). Section IV, § 11.

[625]   Unger and Smolin 2015, p. 304.

[626]   Unger and Smolin 2015, pp. 304–305.

[627]   Huemer 2016, p. 107.

[628]   Devlin 2009.

[629]   Devlin 2009.

[630]   Devlin 2009.

[631]   Wildberger 2009a.

[632]   Wildberger 2009b.

[633]   Cantor 1895/1897 (1915 translation).

[634]   Weisstein 2021, entry for 'Infinite Set'.

[635]   Bolzano 1847 (in Russ 2004), §§ 21, 33: pp. 617, 630–631.

[636]   Rucker 2005, p. 6

[637]   I've noticed a lot of commentary like this from mathematicians and physicists online. The following is an example:

       <http://www.quora.com/Are-there-mathematical-arguments-against-the-existence-of-infinity>

[638]   Moore 2019, p. 139.

[639]   The time of this occurrence is hard to pin down, but it dates at least as far back as Zeno of Elea, who referred to infinities in measures of space and time. (See endnote 200).

CHAPTER 17: INFINITY UNREAL

[640]   Jourdain's Introduction to Cantor 1895/1897 (1915 translation), pp. 67–68.

[641]   For one example among many: Rucker 2005, pp. 35–36.

[642]   An example: Greene 2011, pp. 33, 38.

[643]   Based on Chu-Carroll 2007.

[644]   Vopěnka 1979, p. 11.

[645]   Lavine 1994 and Lavine 1995.

[646]   Wildberger 2005, pp. xv, xvii.

[647]   Aguirre 2011.

[648]   Stenger 2014, p. 372.

[649]   For example, this position is taken by theoretical physicist Sean Carroll. See Berman 2012.

[650]   Theoretical physicist and cosmologist Max Tegmark argues that mathematics underlies the nature of the Universe—that the Universe *is* math. He also describes the mathematical Universe as infinite. See the following:

   (a)   Tegmark 2014, pp. 5, 123, 316–317.

   (b)   Tegmark 2021.

      However, Tegmark is also ambivalent about the Universe being infinite. It seems that he reluctantly keeps references to infinity as part of his cosmology for what he feels is the lack of a better concept. See Tegmark 2015.

[651]   Einstein initially proposed the Universe to be a finite but 'unbounded' hypersphere of four spatial dimensions. See Einstein 1917, § 3, p. 427.

[652]   Einstein 1954 (1982 edition), pp. 242–243.

[653]   Stephen Hawking initially proposed a model of finite time. See Hawking 1988, pp. 133–141. (A diagram of Hawking's no-boundary proposal of time can be found in Figure 8.1 on p. 138 of his 1988 book.)

[654]   Hardegree 2002, Footnote, p. 2.

[655]   Hilbert 1925 in Ewald and Sieg 2013.

[656]   Kragh 2014. p. 8.

[657]   Kragh 2014, p. 2.

[658]   In fact, if there were $\mathbb{R}$-many rooms, then we'd have another problem: no one would be able to change rooms because $\mathbb{R}$ is "dense"—between any two doors is another door, so no one in the hotel would ever be able to change rooms to allow for a new guest!

[659]   There may be people with absurd ideas or who do "absurd" (i.e., silly) things, but *logical* absurdities—such as self-contradictions (e.g., all-white swans that are not all white)—do not and cannot exist in the real world.

[660]   Craig 1979b (2017 excerpt).

[661]   Craig 1979b (2017 excerpt).

[662]   Craig 1979a, pp. 82–83.

[663]   However, there are some problems with Craig's original exposition of the problem, so I'll present a different analysis than Craig as to why exactly the absurdities would occur.

[664]   Craig 1979a, p. 86.

[665]   In the first and second versions of this work (2008 and 2010 respectively), I attempted to lend support to Craig's original analysis of the contradiction involved with removing one infinite set from another via "inverse operations" in transfinite mathematics. Craig stated that subtracting infinity from infinity produces a contradiction and that the contradiction "lies in the fact that one can subtract equal quantities from equal quantities and arrive at different answers." See Craig and Sinclair 2009, p. 112.

      I had initially followed Craig in regarding the contradictions involved with removing an infinite set of books from the library to be contradictions resulting from subtracting infinities—a mathematical problem. Graham Oppy had already issued a rejoinder to Craig's charge regarding inverse operations involving infinite sets. See Oppy 1995, pp. 219–221.

      Subsequent to my 2008 and 2010 versions of this work, I have concluded that Craig did not correctly identify a problem with inverse operations involving transfinite sets. However, that does not mean Craig wasn't on to something. It just means he misidentified the details of the contradiction that would result.

      I now believe the contradictions involving calculations of infinite sets are logical contradictions of semantic meaning rather than mathematical contradictions of syntactical formalism. In this present revision of my case against infinity, I therefore, wish to correct the source of the logical contradictions involved with applying a transfinite inverse operation to remove one infinite set of from another.

It's not a mathematical contradiction to subtract equal quantities from equal quantities and get different results if those quantities are themselves not enumerated but instead labeled only by a predicate or a symbol for a predicate (like ∞, ω, ℵ, etc.), and that predicate (infinity) is itself no more precise than saying "a lot." A lot minus a lot can equal a lot, or it can equal zero, or it can equal 1, or any other amount because "a lot" is a vague notion. In mathematical terms, such a situation is no more mathematically problematic than dividing by zero—it's simply too vague to be a part of the rules of mathematics.

So, Craig is wrong that there is a mathematical contradiction. However, Craig is correct that there is a contradiction involved; but it's a logical contradiction in the implications of what infinity *means* as a concept rather than a mathematical contradiction in the arithmetical rules involving symbols for infinity.

[666]　　Craig 1979a, p. 83.

[667]　　Where "all" means "every" and not merely "each" or "any".

[668]　　Benardete 1964, pp. 236, 237. Quoted in Craig and Sinclair 2009.

[669]　　Benardete 1964, pp. 236, 237.

[670]　　Benardete did not come to this conclusion because he did not believe literal infinity is logically problematic, just ontologically problematic. I hold the contrary view—it is both.

[671]　　Reichenbach 2017.

[672]　　Oppy does not use the term 'literal infinity'. He draws distinctions between actual infinity and a sub-category of completed infinities. See Oppy 2006, p. 236.

[673]　　Oppy 2006, pp. 51–53.

[674]　　Oppy 2006, pp. 53–56.

[675]　　Oppy 2006, Chapter 1.

[676]　　Huemer 2016.

CHAPTER 18: INFINITE SPACE REFUTED

[677]　　Levy, Maxwell, and Munzner 1994.

[678]　　Levy 1995.

[679]　　Levy, Maxwell, and Munzner 1994.

[680]　　In my earlier book on cosmology (Sewell 1999), I proposed that sphere eversion might be applied as a model for certain behaviors of fundamental physical particles, but I no longer hold this view. I now see sphere eversion as an interesting mathematical game with no direct bearing on how anything in nature works. Sphere eversion as a physical model of particle topology will not be assumed in any of my forthcoming works on cosmology.

[681]　　Clegg 2012, p. 103.

[682]　　Woodin quote from Webb 2017, p. 43.

[683]　　What follows is a modification of the views on space that were presented in my earlier book on cosmology (1999), which I no longer stand by. My forthcoming publications on cosmology will assume the views presented in this book and elaborate by addressing philosophies of space such as *relationism* versus *substantivalism*.

[684]　　I am assuming that some appearances can be objective—how they appear to an observer regardless of how one might feel emotionally about it—while others are only subjective, contingent on how the observer may feel at the time.

[685]　　Even 'personal space' can count as a kind of impressional space.

[686]　　We won't worry about Einstein's relative space versus Newton's absolute space—that's a separate issue for another discussion.

[687]　　Baggott 2013.

[688]　　Oppy 2006, p. 90.

[689]   Caveat: It is true that the closed curve forming a circle has no end, but the circle does have an end to its measure (circumference) because any mark on the closed curve of a circle ends in measure back at its starting point.

[690]   In taking this position, I am contradicting the interpretation of many mathematicians that Euclid had *only* a figurative conception of infinity and did not intend to imply infinity in a literal sense. For an interpretation of Euclid as assuming only figurative infinity, see Sanders (Samuel) 1930, p. 15.

[691]   Einstein 1954 (1982 edition), p. 241.

[692]   Stewart quote from Webb 2017, p. 43.

[693]   O'Leary 2010, Section 12.2: Horocycles, p. 405.

[694]   McMullen 2008, pp. 11–12.

[695]   See entry for 'infinitesimal' in *Random House Unabridged Dictionary*: Random House 2020.

[696]   See also Alexander 2014, p. 218.

[697]   Probst 2018, pp. 200–202.

[698]   Colyvan 2010.

[699]   Paulos 2014, Section D, p. 5. Paulos references Keisler 1976.

[700]   Examples:
         (a) Tropp 1999.
         (b) Henle and Kleinberg 2003.
         (c) Bell 2008.
         (d) Watkins 2015.
         (e) Vinsonhaler 2016, pp. 249–276.

[701]   Robinson 1966 (Reprinted 1996).

[702]   See, for example, Katz and Tall 2011.

[703]   Alexander 1 April 2014.

[704]   Bell 2017.

[705]   Examples include (1) Bell 2008 and (2) Henle and Kleinberg 2003.

[706]   In 1964, mathematician Stephen Barr noted geometry textbooks used to say points have "position but no magnitude"—in other words, they have no size at all. See Barr 1964, p. 150.

[707]   Bell 2017.

[708]   Bell 2017.

[709]   Goze 1995 in Diener and Diener 1995, pp. 95–96.

[710]   Author Peter F. Erickson, in disagreement with Barr, states that, "a point does take up space" because, according to Erickson, points are infinitesimals. See Erickson 2006, pp. 32, 33.

[711]   Theories in which space is composed of real, discrete units are known in theoretical physics as *quantum field theories*, of which there are many varieties (I touch on this topic again in §§ 21.2–3). However, even in most quantum field theories, discrete units of space are not necessarily fundamentally minimal volumes of space.

[712]   Dainton 2010, p. 295.

[713]   NIST 2018.

[714]   Gudder 2017.

[715]   Based on the 'early modern' writing of philosophers regarding spatial divisibility. See Holden 2002, p. 9.

[716]   I will address the divisibility of space in my forthcoming monograph on cosmology, which will be a complete revision of my earlier book on the subject (i.e., Sewell 1999).

[717]   Bell 2017.

[718]   Bell 2017.

[719]   As Vinsonhaler stated, the mathematical definition of an infinitesimal "goes directly there" to the infinitely small level rather than "tending to" some ideal limit. See Vinsonhaler 2016, p. 264.

[720]   Holden 2002, p. 7.

[721]   Holden 2002, p. 12.

[722]   Hume 1739 (1888 edition), Book I, Part II, Section II, pp. 29–30.

[723]   Holden 2002, p. 5.

[723]   Holden 2002, p. 17.

[724]   Flew quoted in Holden 2002, p. 5. Notice Flew's position contradicts Kant's. According to Kant, 'in infinitum' means to continue without ceasing while 'in definitum' means to continue as often as anyone wishes; see Kant 1781 (1990 edition), p. 289.

[725]   Holden 2002, p. 6.

[726]   Rucker 2005, pp. 81–83, 109.

[727]   Rucker 2005, pp. 108–109. Online source: <http://abyss.uoregon.edu/~js/cosmo/lectures/lec18.html>

[728]   Moore 2019, p. 49.

[729]   Moore 2019, p. 48.

[730]   This was argued by Robert Grosseteste as noted by Jean-Luc Solère. See Solère 2013, p. 12 (online).

[731]   *Smooth infinitesimal analysis* (SIA) proposes throwing out a principle of logic known as the *law of excluded middle* in order to ensure infinitesimals are mathematically coherent. In my view, the problem is not with logic, but with infinitesimals. If a theory has to throw out a law of logic to be made 'coherent' in its own domain, there's something wrong with the theory.

[732]   Westerhoff, Jan. 2011. *Reality: A Very Short Introduction*. Oxford: Oxford University Press. p. 36.

[733]   Westerhoff 2011, pp. 36–38.

[734]   The finitude of such 'extensible indivisibles' follows from Hume's position that points must be 'sensible' entities. See Hume 1739 (1888 edition), Book I, Part II, Section IV, pp. 39–40.

[735]   Jacquette 2001, pp. 45–56, 116–117, 201.

[736]   At best, we find in Hume's position a justification for the view that points are constructs for dividing space that, within or between material objects, preexists as a simple, partless unity. (Jacquette 2001, p. 203.) But then, why posit points as empirical at all? The mathematical notion that points have no size at all would do just as well if space is a conceptually divisible unity.

[737]   Bell 2017.

[738]   Rucker 2005, p. 24.

[739]   Dainton 2010, pp. 280–283.

[740]   Oppy 2006, p. 102.

[741]   Barr noted this problem plagued earlier works of geometry (Barr 1964, p. 150). Barr's solution is to treat sizeless points as arbitrary divisions of a spatial continuum that can be as near one another as we please to designate them (Barr 1964, p. 155). This seems to me to be the right solution.

[742]   In my previous book on cosmology (Sewell 1999, pp. 18–20), I proposed mathematical points as units corresponding to fundamental units of real space and that points could be posited to be finite in size like pixels that correspond to units of real space. What we refer to as "points" of space would still be immeasurably small—minuscule but nonetheless finite—and they would have an inherently curved structure. That proposal was meant to be a solution to the 'Equals Two' paradox as applied to real space.

         The Equals Two paradox states that a semicircle with a half circumference equal to pi (π) can be infinitely subdivided to be made equal to a row of infinitely small semicircles and so equal to the diameter of the original semicircle, which is 2. Therefore, $\pi = 2$, which is nonsense. My solution to this paradox was to propose that points, even if they are arbitrary selections of space, nevertheless are necessarily finite. In addition, I proposed to have a consistent conception of space required points to themselves have structure, a curvature equivalent to the half circles that together are necessarily unequal in sum to the original, idealized, 1D diameter equal to 2. So, the Equals Two paradox cannot arise. (Sewell 1999, pp. 81–87.)

         However, I need to change the position I offered in Sewell 1999 to the Equals Two paradox because I now believe that solution to be incorrect. Instead, there is a much simpler solution, which is as follows.

         First, it is still true that points do not preexist but are simply conceptual, idealized partitions of geometrical length. Also as I held before, points as such partitions can be used as a mathematical tool for measuring space and setting asymptotic limits.

However, I do need to revise my previous position which held points to be selections of space as an expanse with a hidden, foamlike structure. Instead, we should regard points as selections of space as an otherwise featureless, undivided expanse. I am ergo rejecting the idea that space requires conception as a quantized field in order to be coherent.

Second, I no longer hold points to be like minuscule pixels, nor do points have a kind of structure of their own. Instead, as purely conceptual, *idealized* divisions of space, points can be sizeless and without structure at all. So, there is no such thing as a sphere or semicircle equal to the size of a point.

Now, applying this revised way of regarding points to the Equals Two paradox, some of the analysis stays the same, and some changes.

What stays the same: the diameter of the original semicircle is still seen as a line segment that is *not* composed of points as preexisting parts. The diameter is an undivided, but divisible, extent that may be merely conceptually divided into two or more partitions of space ('equals two').

What changes: Because I now hold points to be themselves idealized, sizeless divisions of geometric lengths that may function as asymptotic limits, already the paradox is solved. Divide a mathematical length as much as you like, and you'll never get down to the size of a point since it is just a schematic ideal for indexical space and only as an ideal is it without size. Semicircles, no matter how small, can never become sizeless and still be semicircles. Hence, there can be no row of semicircles equal to the diameter of 2 in this example.

We can go even further in avoiding the paradox if we also reject the existence of infinitesimals—infinitely small units. Do this and the semicircles can be bisected *indefinitely* but not a literally *infinite* number of times. Once again, the semicircles in the 'paradox' do not become infinitesimals or infinitesimal points and so still never become equal to the diameter of 2.

In short, no matter how far down we divide the semicircles, the half-circumferences of the semicircles never do correspond in their combined length to that of the straight line of the original diameter. A row of minuscule (indefinitely small) semicircles formed by the process of bisection still has half-circumferences totaling π when added together and not 2. The row of semicircles is therefore never equal in length to the diameter of the original circle no matter how small we make the semicircles, because the diameter is an extent not composed of infinitesimals at all. The paradox is thus dissolved.

This is my final proposal for a solution to the Equals Two paradox, though neither the paradox nor this solution to it will be further presented in the forthcoming rewrite of my book on cosmology.

[743]   Johnson 1992, p. 373.

CHAPTER 19: INFINITE TIME REFUTED

[744]   Dainton 2010.
[745]   What follows is a modification of the views on time that were presented in my earlier book on cosmology (Sewell 1999). My forthcoming publication(s) on cosmology will assume the modified positions regarding time as given in this book.
[746]   I am assuming that some appearances can be objective—how they appear to an observer regardless of how one might feel emotionally about it—while others are only subjective, contingent on how the observer may feel at the time.
[747]   What we call 'instants' are moments of either zero duration or infinitely brief duration. I argue they should be conceived as moments of zero duration.
[748]   Veneziano 2006, pp. 72–81.
[749]   Most astronomers assume the Big Bang Theory, according to which the observable universe was much smaller in the past but has been expanding in size. According to some astronomers, "it is possible that even if the universe just has a very large volume now, it will reach infinite volume in the infinite future." Quote from Temming 2014.
[750]   Bolzano 1847 (in Russ 2004), § 17 p. 612.

[751]   Holt 2012, p. 82.

[752]   Gardner 1999, p. 194.

[753]   I will address this issue in a forthcoming monograph on the subject of cosmology.

[754]   Dainton 2010.

[755]   Every few years, new estimates emerge in the scientific community for the exact amount of time the Universe has been around. A couple of examples:

      (a)   Redd 2017.

      (b)   Gohd 2021.

[756]   Lavine uses 'zillion' as a term for any number that is *countable in practice* but *uncountable in practicality*. In other words, in Lavine's view a zillion is any large number which we are capable of counting up to, but which we don't bother to simply from lack of interest. (See Lavine 1994, p. 248; and Lavine 1995, p. 391–393). In other words, what he calls a zillion is any number that is 'indefinitely large' in the sense that it is "much larger than any with which we were immediately concerned." (Lavine 1995, p. 391). Such a number may be called "too large to count," but only as a practical matter. It is purely for practical reasons that we don't make the count or calculation of some quantity called a 'zillion' even though we could do so in actual practice if we were to make the time and effort. Lavine's use of zillion is hyperbole for some big but unknown number.

      In contrast, I propose restricting use of the term 'zillion' for much larger quantities. What I propose is that the term 'zillion' should denote any quantity *uncountable in practice* though still *countable in principle*. That is, 'zillion' should denote any number we cannot count up to given present-day resources in mathematical ability and/or computational power; nevertheless, any number called a 'zillion' is a finite number that *could* be reached by counting or calculating if only we had the resources to do so. Hence, such an indefinitely large number is a number countable in principle (as a matter of logical possibility) but not countable in actual practice (as a matter of present-day capability).

      So, just as our hypothetical scenario presents a situation in which a person such as Alice could only exist in principle, so too we can propose Alice can in principle count down from a zillion. Hence, even if what I call a 'zillion' does not exist in actuality, we can still let Alice count up to a zillion or down from a zillion in our thought experiment.

[757]   It might be objected that the total of a complete series need not be a *sum*. True, but at least in principle it must be equal to a sum, or the series is not a *complete* series (see Chapters 12 and 14). Moreover, it does no good to hold that a complete series just has a "sum" in a metaphorical sense of a supremum—a limit of a sequence—as portrayed in the transfinite system. (See Jourdain's 1915 Introduction to Cantor 1895/1897 (1915 translation), pp. 17–21.) A supremum is simply a limit to a continuously incomplete series of invented values, not a sum in the sense of a completed, standing total.

[758]   See the following:

      (a)   Morriston 1999, pp. 8, 11, 18.

      (b)   Oppy 1991, pp. 194–195.

      (c)   Mackie 1982, pp. 93–94.

[759]   Morriston 1999, p. 11.

[760]   Morriston 1999, pp. 8, 11.

[761]   Morriston 2003, p. 290.

[762]   Holt 2012, p. 82.

[763]   Morriston 2003, pp. 290–291. See also Holt 2012, p. 82.

[764]   Morriston 1999, p. 17–18.

[765]   Cantor 1883 (1976 translation), p. 87. See also Hilbert 1925 (1983 edition), pp. 183–201.

[766]   Jourdain's Introduction to Cantor 1895/1897 (1915 translation), pp. 77–78. See also Cantor 1895/1897 (1915 translation), p. 104.

[767]   Jourdain's 1915 Introduction to Cantor 1895/1897 (1915 translation), p. 78.

[768]   Moreland 1993, p. 37.

[769]   Exapologist 2006.

[770]   Morriston 1999, pp. 17–18. Morriston responds to the argument against an infinite past by philosopher Gerald James Whitrow (1912–2000). See Whitrow 1978, p. 43.

[771]   Dickens 1858, p. 73.

[772]   Morriston 2010, pp. 443–445.

[773]   Morriston 2010, pp. 443–445.

[774]   Morriston 2010, p. 443.

[775]   Morriston 2010, p. 445, footnote 6.

[776]   Morriston 2010, p. 446.

[777]   Morriston 2010, pp. 447.

[778]   Morriston 2003, p. 301.

[779]   Morriston 2010, p. 446.

[780]   Morriston 2010, p. 443.

[781]   Morriston 2010, pp. 443, 448.

[782]   Morriston 2010, p. 443.

[783]   Morriston 2003, p. 302.

[784]   Morriston 2010, p. 443.

[785]   Morriston 2010, p. 443.

[786]   Morriston 2010, p. 444.

[787]   Morriston 2010, pp. 440, 445–446.

[788]   Some philosophers even try to claim there is no difference between an *actually infinite series* and a *potentially infinite series* with regard to the past as well as the future. But this too is fallacious since there is a difference between the past as actually infinite vice potentially infinite.

The past leaves traces on the present (forward causation) while the future does not leave traces on the present (which would be backward causation). An accident in the past is why the dent on the car fender is now apparent, but no one sees the dent on the car fender now as a result of an accident that has yet to happen. So in that sense, the past is not *potential* but actual—or more precisely, the record of the past is actual because all past events have been *actualized*. (Conversely, the future is potential and not actual since such events either may or will occur, but do not leave traces now as occurring or as having occurred.)

So, if the past is infinite in the sense of 'actual infinity', then the past must have a complete and limitless number of actualized events—events that *have occurred*. In order for that to be so, the *series* of past events would have to collectively comprise a complete *set* of events that "have occurred" as of some specific date (any date we can name will do).

In contrast, if we regard the past as 'potentially infinite', then we are not considering the past to be a complete set of events all of which have occurred by x time. What we call "the past" in that case would not be a complete and limitless set of actualized events—i.e., events that have occurred. Rather, for the past to be only potentially infinite, the past would have to have a first event that recedes further from the present with each new event that occurs so that at any timestamp we name, what we call "the past" is only a series with a running total of actualized events (i.e., events that have occurred), albeit a total that is indefinitely large from the vantage point in the present. Potentially, the past can ceaselessly continue to grow in the number of actualized events while always being finite—that would be a potentially infinite past.

Philosophers such as Craig typically contrast the actuality of the past with the potentiality of the future, holding the past to be 'actually' finite and only 'potentially' infinite (i.e., a figurative infinity) like the future (see Craig 1979b).

[789]   Morriston 2003, p. 301.

[790]   Oppy 2006, p. 237.

[791]   Oppy 2006, p. 237.

[792]   Oppy 2006, p. 237.

[793]   Oppy 2006, p. 237.

[794]   Oppy 2006, p. 237.

[795]   Oppy 2006, p. 237.

[796]   Stevens 2016, at 6.40–50 minutes into 23.45-minute video.

[797]   Russell (Bertrand) 1903 (2010 edition), Sections 340–341, pp. 363–365.

[798]   Oppy 2006, p. 9.

[799]   Johnson 1992, pp. 370–372. Johnson cites the Tristram Shandy example from Russell (Bertrand) 1903 (2010 edition), Sections 340–341, pp. 363–365. Be sure to also see Johnson's rebuttals to Raymond Godfrey's remarks in Johnson 1994, pp. 369–370.

[800]   I will explore this notion further in a forthcoming monograph on cosmology that will revise my previous publication on the topic (Sewell 1999). In the meantime, I recommend reading Weir 1988, pp. 203–209.

[801]   Lévi 1927, pp. 182–198.

[802]   Margenau 1950.

[803]   NIST 2018.

[804]   Some physicists argue that the upper limit to a fundamental unit of time is 10^{-33} seconds. See the following:
        (a) Yirka 2020.
        (b) Mann 2020.
        (c) Wendel, Martínez, and Bojowald 2020.

[805]   Dainton 2010, p. 295.

[806]   See the following:
        (a) Swinburne University 2021, "Planck Time."
        (b) NIST 2018.

[807]   Kozlowski and Marciak-Kozlowska 2008, p. 15.

[808]   Identification of the chronon with Planck time is also noted in some pop science sources. As an example: Holzer 2006, p. 350.

[809]   Farias and Erasmo 2010.

[810]   I will pursue this topic further in a forthcoming monograph on cosmology that will revise the views offered in Sewell 1999.

[811]   Penrose, Roger. 2004. *The Road to Reality: A Complete Guide to the Laws of the Universe*. London: Jonathan Cape. pp. 61–62, 363, 378.

[812]   Penrose 2004, pp. 61–62, 363, 378.

[813]   Dummett 2000, p. 499.

[814]   Penrose 2004, pp. 61–62, 363, 378.

[815]   Zamai, Malengo, and Caiolfa 2008, p. 188.

[816]   Dummett 2000, p. 499.

[817]   Dowden 2021.

[818]   Dummett 2000, p. 499.

[819]   Dowden 2021. (However, Dowden does caveat the infinite divisibility of space and time by pointing out that some quantum theories posit finite granularity of space and time.)

[820]   Odenwald 2021b.

[821]   Dummett 2000, p. 515.
        In agreement with Dummett on this matter, I should also clarify another matter: In my previous book on cosmology (Sewell 1999, p. 15), while I stated that instants are arbitrary divisions of time (which is correct), I also proposed that instants of time can be considered "immeasurably small" (indefinite but finite) durations of time. I now believe the latter assertion is incorrect: as arbitrary divisions of the continuum of time, instants have no duration at all, not an indefinitely or "immeasurably" small finite duration.

[822]   This conclusion of course leaves open the question of what a "temporal span" really is. A more complete investigation of the nature of time is beyond the scope of this book, so I will confine myself to saying that we should not be seduced by spatial metaphors for time. Time is a species of change, not a species of space.

CHAPTER 20: INFINITE MOTION REFUTED

[823]   Aristotle ~350 BCE (1930 translation), *Physics*, Book VI (Part 2 and Part 9).

[824]   I discussed a couple of Zeno's paradoxes of motion in the earlier book on cosmology (Sewell 1999). However, my analysis of Zeno's paradoxes and their solutions has changed since then, so the reader will have to disregard the analysis I offered in my earlier publication. The present work is my final position regarding Zeno's paradoxes of motion.

[825]   Paraphrased from Aristotle. See Aristotle ~350 BCE (1930 translation), *Physics*, Book VI (Part 9).

[826]   Aristotle ~350 BCE (1930 translation), *Physics*, Book VI (Part 2).

[827]   Aristotle ~350 BCE (1930 translation), *Physics*, Book VI (Part 2).

[828]   For a similar analogy see Moreland 1993, p. 37.

[829]   See endnote 828.

[830]   Actually, Huemer used the scenario of a ball falling to the ground, but the principle is the same as Zeno's racetrack paradox. See Huemer 2016, p. 185.

[831]   Huemer 2016, p. 185.

[832]   Huemer 2016, p. 185.

[833]   Huemer 2016, p. 186.

[834]   Huemer 2016, p. 186.

[835]   Patterson 28 May 2017, 22:30–23:15 minutes into video (1:20:10 full length).

[836]   Patterson 28 May 2017, 20:35–20:45 minutes into video (1:20:10 full length).

[837]   Some examples:
(a) Dainton 2010, pp. 267–312.
(b) Dowden 2019.

[838]   This, by the way, was also a point Aristotle made. Contrary to many contemporary philosophers, I believe Aristotle was correct that space is not an aggregate of points, nor time an accretion of instants.

[839]   Another argument Zeno offered against the possibility of motion is the arrow paradox. The arrow paradox is sometimes interpreted as assuming motion is comprised of moments of infinite brevity, but that is not so. Instead, the arrow paradox assumes motion is impossible based on instants of zero duration—no duration at all rather than infinitely brief duration. Hence, the arrow paradox is not about infinite magnitudes or quantities.

This is an amendment to my previous position on the arrow paradox offered in my earlier book on cosmology (Sewell 1999), in which I assumed infinity was part of the problem with the arrow paradox. I now believe that infinite brevity and infinite accumulations of infinitely brief moments are not relevant to the arrow paradox.

Regardless, as Aristotle pointed out, if you throw out the assumption that durationless instants aggregate into intervals of finite time (an assumption rejected in § 19.5.7), then you dissolve the arrow paradox.

[840]   Tallis 2011, p. 49 of pp. 48–49.

CHAPTER 21: PROBLEMS WITH INFINITY IN PHYSICS

[841]   Wilczek 2012.

[842]   Three caveats: First, 'extrinsic mass' is not a formal term in the physics community, though it is used by a minority of physicists. Second, when the term is used, it sometimes refers to the property usually identified as the 'intrinsic mass' or 'invariant mass' of a particle (which is confusing and not how I am using the term 'extrinsic mass'). Third, even as an invariant form of mass, extrinsic mass is a property that is only contextual; see Bauer 2011.

[843]   It is intrinsic mass that is also identified as equal to the potential energy of a particle or the amount of energy a particle has to produce radiation.

[844]   Cramer, John G. 2016. *The Quantum Handshake: Entanglement, Nonlocality and Transactions*. New York: Springer. Footnote 1, p. 58.

[845]   Chang 2016, p. 5.

[846]   Strassler 2013.

[847]   Strassler 2012.

[848]   Koks, Gibbs, and Carr 2012.

[849]   It is true that some pop theories on the physics fringe propose faster-than-light travel may be possible in principle through manipulation of hypothesized wormholes or by "warping" space in some way, but there is no evidence that such capability is achievable in actual practice.

[850]   Einstein 1922 (1970 edition), p. 26.

[851]   Einstein 1922 (1970 edition).

[852]   Davis 2019.

[853]   Johnson-Groh 2019.

[854]   Kragh 2000.

[855]   Eddington 1929, p. 183.

[856]   Eddington 1929, p. 183.

[857]   Eddington 1929, p. 184.

[858]   Bohm 1951, p. 23.

[859]   Orzel 2015.

[860]   Bohm 1951, pp. 26–27.

[861]   It is true that continuous waves are also described in quantum theory, however, they refer to aspects of particle motion while the particles themselves are discrete, as are their energy states. Moreover, the waves are issued and absorbed discontinuously between particles. See the next section's description of the wavefunction.

[862]   Al-Khalili 2003, p. 20.

[863]   Ananthaswamy 2018.

[864]   Ball 2017.

[865]   Strassler 2012.

[866]   Brooks 2010.

[867]   Sen 2014, pp. 203–218.

[868]   Nave 2016, "Wavefunction."

[869]   Herbert 1987, pp. 96, 105–107.

[870]   Herbert 1987, p. 107.

[871]   The wavefunction can also be used to calculate the probability that a given particle will display other properties as well, such as having a certain 'spin' as opposed to a different 'spin', but we can ignore that distinction for the purposes of this chapter.

[872]   Nave 2016, "Free Particle Waves."

[873]   Penrose 2004, pp. 61–62, 363–364.

[874]   Or, more precisely, the 'Hilbert space' of the wavefunction. See Penrose 2004, pp. 363–364, 378–380.

[875]   Unger and Smolin 2015, p. 517.

[876]   Pössel 2006.

[877]   Pössel 2006.

[878]   Feynman and Hibbs 1965.

[879]   Pössel 2006.

[880]   Feynman and Hibbs 1965, pp. 28–39, 42–47, 59.

[881]   Perepelitsa 2007.

[882]   Potoček, Miatto, et al. 2015.

[883]   Potoček, Miatto, et al. 2015.

[884]   Potoček, Miatto, et al. 2015.

[885]   Potoček, Miatto, et al. 2015.

[886]   More technically, the hotel rooms correspond to *excitation modes* or *quantum energy levels*, but the energy levels are associated with *quantum states*, which are described in terms of the wavefunction, which in turn is used to calculate the probability that a given photon is at a given location. So, these quantum hotel rooms really boil down to being possible locations of where the photon can be. See Potoček, Miatto, et al. 2015.

[887]   Having two different locations simultaneously is not the only form of superposition a particle may have. There are other forms taken by superposition as well. For example, a particle is often described in the formalism of quantum mechanics as being in both an "excited" and "unexcited" state at the same time, or as having a spin in the "up" direction while simultaneously having a spin in the "down" direction. There are many other such opposing properties described as obtaining for the same particle in 'superposition'.

   The following are some good reference sources about quantum superposition (even if they don't all agree with one another):
   (a) Physics Reimagined 2021.
   (b) Hossenfelder 2020.
   (c) Ball 2018, pp. 60–62.
   (d) Haroche 1998, pp. 36–42.
   (e) Yam 1997, pp. 124–129.
   (f) Dirac 1958, pp. 10–14.

[888]   I will provide an interpretation of quantum mechanics in a forthcoming monograph on cosmology, a complete revision of Sewell 1999—my previous book on the subject.

[889]   Bohm 1951, pp. 120–121.

[890]   Steiner and Rendell 2018.

[891]   Oberhaus 2015.

[892]   Oberhaus 2015.

[893]   Zyga 2015.

[894]   Zyga 2016.

[895]   Dirac, 1958, pp. 11–12.

[896]   Ball 2018, pp. 60–61.

[897]   Smolin 2019, p. 15.

[898]   Dirac 1958, pp. 11–12.

[899]   Dirac 1958, pp. 11–12.

[900]   Cramer 2016, Appendix A, p. 173.

[901]   Deffner 2018.

[902]   Zyga 2016.

[903]   Zyga 2016.

[904]   Pires, Cianciaruso, et al. 2016.

[905]   For a few examples of sources providing such descriptions of particles, see the following:
   (a) Wolchover 2020.
   (b) Berghofer 2018, p. 180.
   (c) Lancaster and Blundell 2014, pp. 1–2
   (d) Hobson 2013, pp. 211–223.

[906]   Lincoln 2013.

[907]   Freiberger 22 July 2013.

[908]   Kaiser 2005, pp. 157–158.

[909]   Dowden 2020.

[910]   Gabrielse and Hanneke 2006.

[911]   Rovelli 2017, p. 230.

[912]   Rovelli 2017, p. 230.

[913]   This is another topic to be explored in my forthcoming monograph on cosmology.

[914]   Baggott 2018, p. 142.

[915]   Penrose 2004, p. 673

[916]   Kaiser 2005.
[917]   Greiner 2001, p. 11.
[918]   de Podesta 2014.
[919]   Strassler 2011.
[920]   Kane 2006.
[921]   Feynman 1985 (2006 edition), pp. 14–15.
[922]   Feynman 1985 (2006 edition), pp. 95–96, 120.
[923]   Kaiser 2005, Figure 3 on p. 158.
[924]   Wilczek 2008, p. 84.
[925]   Kaiser 2005, p. 157.
[926]   Einstein 1917 (1952 translation), pp. 430–432.
[927]   Einstein 1922 (1970 edition), p. 65
[928]   Einstein 1922 (1970 edition), pp. 16–17.
[929]   For a less technical exposition, see Norton 2015.
[930]   For a more in-depth exposition, see Taylor and Wheeler 1992.
[931]   Einstein 1922 (1970 edition), pp. 46, 54.
[932]   Beiser 1992, pp. 755–756.
[933]   Pound and Rebka 1960.
[934]   Chou, et al. 2010.
[935]   Odenwald 2021a.
[936]   Ohanian 1989, pp. IX-7 to IX-10.
[937]   Einstein 1917, pp. 430–432.
[938]   Associated Press 1931.
[939]   Moskowitz 2010.
[940]   Einstein 1917, pp. 430–432.
[941]   Hossenfelder 2018, p. 210.
[942]   Baggott 2013, p. 145.
[943]   Boslough 1993, pp. 205–206.
[944]   Smolin 2006, pp. 152–153.
[945]   Boslough 1993, pp. 206–209.
[946]   de Podesta 2014.
[947]   Eicher 2015, p. 165.
[948]   University of California-Riverside 2014.
[949]   Darvish, et al. 2014.
[950]   Morrow 2016.
[951]   Oesch, et al. 2016.
[952]   See Powell 2006: Astronomers use four different distance estimates for galaxies far, far away: luminosity distance (D_L), angular diameter distance (D_A), comoving distance (D_C), and light travel time distance (D_T). Each of these distance estimates can vary widely for the same galaxy. For example, the same galaxy may appear at D_L = 560 Billion Lyr, D_A = 2.2 Billion Lyr, D_C = 35 Billion Lyr, D_T = 13.6 Billion Lyr.

    Galaxy GN-z11 is just over redshift 11, which puts it at 32 billion light-years away according to its 'comoving distance' (D_C) estimate. It differs from the same galaxy's theoretical light travel time distance (D_T) which is "only" about 13.4 billion light-years away. (I say "theoretical" since that time estimate assumes space is expanding in accordance with the Big Bang theory.)
[953]   Swinburne University 2021, "Cosmic Microwave Background."
[954]   Dodelson and Schmidt 2021, p. 4.
[955]   Castelvecchi 2018.
[956]   Penzias and Wilson 1965.
[957]   Davis and Lineweaver 2004, pp. 97–109.
[958]   Davis and Lineweaver 2004, preprint p. 9.

[959]   Baraniuk 2016.

[960]   Even some well-known astronomers and cosmologists mistakenly refer to the observable universe as a Hubble volume, but that is not correct. See: Davis and Lineweaver 2004, preprint pp. 1–4.

[961]   Baraniuk 2016.

[962]   All distance measures of the observable universe are based on the assumption that the cosmological redshift is caused by the expansion of space in accordance with Einstein's General Theory of Relativity. Not all cosmologists agree, but they are in the minority.

[963]   Wolfram|Alpha. Input: volume of the universe.

[964]   Vardanyan, Trotta, and Silk 2011, preprint p. 5.

         The paper actually says the entire Universe must have a volume >251 *Hubble Spheres*, implying that 251 Hubble Spheres is the smallest size the Universe can be. Unfortunately, that is very misleading. The abstract of the paper makes it clear the authors take 'Hubble Sphere' to be synonymous with 'observable universe', but the two are not the same as pointed out in Davis and Lineweaver 2004.

         The Hubble Sphere is neither the ball-shaped volume of the *visible universe* nor the ball-shaped volume of the *observable universe* (the interior to the particle horizon). Rather, the Hubble Sphere is the spherical boundary in space within which galaxies are observed as having a *recession velocity* less than c. The galaxies we observe beyond the distance of the Hubble Sphere are galaxies that have larger recession velocities according to the interpretation of redshift as the expansion of space. So, a single "Hubble Sphere" is smaller than both the visible and observable universe: a Hubble Sphere is a sphere that surrounds a Hubble Volume of 3×10^{30} cubic light-years—only about 0.007 the volume of the entire observable universe which is 4×10^{32} cubic light-years. See Wolfram|Alpha. Input: Hubble Volume.

         We are located at the center of the Hubble Sphere as if in the middle of a bubble, and that sphere is itself a region centered *within* the observable universe like the pit in a peach (See Davis and Lineweaver 2004, preprint pp. 2, 9).

         Ergo, if we were to say the Universe is equal in size to 251 Hubble Volumes, then the whole Universe surrounding our Hubble Volume would have to be equal in size to a ball comprised of no less than 250 more Hubble Volumes or "Hubble Spheres" (in addition to ours at the center of it all), and each one of those Hubble Volumes would be only 3×10^{30} cubic light-years in size rather than 4×10^{32} cubic light-years. That would be too small to fit the astrophysical data based on mainstream cosmological theory.

[965]   Rucker 2014, p. 93.

[966]   McMullen 2008, pp. 46, 58, 113–116.

[967]   Rucker 2014, p. 97, 101–102.

[968]   Rucker 2014, p. 97, 101–102.

[969]   Einstein 1917, pp. 431–432.

[970]   Einstein 1922 (1970 edition), pp. 65–77.

[971]   Huemer, for example, is skeptical that the Universe is finite-unbounded. In this book *Approaching Infinity*, he refers to the sphere analogy for the higher dimensional shape of the Universe as talk of "round space." (See Huemer 2016, p. 58.) Says Huemer, "Many people take this analogy quite seriously, and many students when first introduced to it seem to find it quite clever. Yet it always struck me as the silliest sophistry." (Huemer 2016, p. 59.)

[972]   Huemer 2016.

[973]   I will provide further details refuting objections raised to the finite-unbounded geometry of the Universe in my forthcoming monograph on cosmology.

[974]   An article in *Symmetry Magazine*, a joint publication of Fermi National Accelerator Laboratory and SLAC National Accelerator Laboratory funded by the US Department of Energy states, "On the largest of all scales, it is still possible that the universe is curved, beyond the edge of our perception. Much like standing in the middle of the Great Plains might lead you to believe the Earth is flat, our understanding of the universe might be limited by our vantage point and the horizon of our visible universe. There's a chance that the universe is a sphere, or a donut, or a saddle, or a dodecahedron, or some kind of twisted manifold. But if it

is, [David Spergel, a theoretical astrophysicist at Princeton University who worked on WMAP] says, it's several times larger than our observable universe." See Biron 2015.

[975]   Scott (Douglas) 2018.

[976]   Pasachoff and Filippenko 2014, pp. 479–502, 522–528.

[977]   Eicher 2015, p. 146–149.

[978]   Eicher 2015, p. 146.

[979]   Shackelford 2007.

[980]   Di Tucci and Lehners 2019.

[981]   Zyga 2019.

[982]   What astronomers call *the surface of last scattering*, beyond which nothing is visible, is only a finite distance away and therefore it marks an event that occurred a finite time ago, prior to which we have no evidence of any events having taken place. At best, astronomers *hope* to investigate events prior to last scattering "indirectly." See Carroll and Ostlie 2017, p. 1181.

[983]   NASA 2012.

[984]   Byrd and Wiegert 2020.

[985]   NASA 2012. See also Byrd and Wiegert 2020.

[986]   Cox and Loeb 2008.

[987]   Byrd and Wiegert 2020.

[988]   Zolfagharifard 2015.

[989]   For an overview of different *scientific eschatologies*, see Mack 2020.

[990]   Eicher 2015, p. 196.

[991]   Pasachoff and Filippenko 2014, pp. 503, 505.

[992]   Cendes 2019.

[993]   Cendes 2019.

[994]   Hands 2016, pp. 141–151.

[995]   "This singularity is termed the *Big Bang*." Quote from Roos 2008, p. 18.

[996]   Roos 2008, p. 18.

[997]   Dowden 2020.

[998]   Unger, p. 112.

[999]   Tegmark 2014, p. 65.

[1,000]   Hossenfelder 2015.

[1,001]   Swinburne University 2020.

[1,002]   Dodelson and Schmidt 2021, p. 15.

[1,003]   Sanders (Robert) 2016, Chapter 5: pp. 49–65.

[1,004]   Dodelson and Schmidt 2021, pp. 1–19.

[1,005]   Hawking 1996.

[1,006]   Roos 2008, p. 18.

[1,007]   Veneziano 2006.

[1,008]   In Siegel 2018, astrophysicist Ethan Siegel states that the idea of a Big Bang singularity is out of date. But he goes on to say the Big Bang happened, it's just not a single event. Instead, the Big Bang is a period of time that succeeded cosmic inflation. It is cosmic inflation that may have started from an initial singularity, taking place in less than a single second of time, and subsequently decayed into a post-inflation period of time that culminated in a flash of light throughout the cosmos (the flash of the Big Bang)—that period of time starting after cosmic inflation and ending with the cosmic flash of light is the Big Bang Era.

    Referring to the Big Bang as something that happened *after* the origin of space and time is a departure from the term's original meaning. During a 1949 radio broadcast, English astronomer Fred Hoyle coined the term 'big bang' to characterize the *event* that some scientists claimed started the Universe, not an *era* of time that followed some earlier time of expansion. Hoyle's original notion of what the term 'big bang' referred to had been in play from 1949 until at least 1966. From that point, some physicists thought of the 'Big Bang' as the moment of initial element creation while others, such as Hawking, regarded it as the initial spacetime singularity, more in line with Hoyle's coinage. (See Kragh 2013.)

From 1966 until around 1980, the term 'big bang' continued to refer to an initial spacetime creation event in both academic literature and the popular press. In fact, Alan Guth, who proposed the idea of cosmic inflation, referred to inflation as the "bang" in the Big Bang. (See Guth 1997.)

So even with the proposal of inflation, the Big Bang more often than not meant the time prior to the flash of light that created the CMB. And that remained the mainstream view until about 2012 when the theory of cosmic inflation began to dominate academic publications of the Big Bang theory and the situation changed (Kragh 2013, Figure 3). Since then, the overwhelming majority of theorists have adopted the new meaning of the term 'big bang' as referring to the hot, dense soup of particles spreading apart as the Universe continues to expand *after* inflation.

I'm not so sure this change of definition for 'Big Bang' is an improvement. It strikes me as more like an attempt by inflation backers to promote their own cosmogony by putting the emphasis on the mechanism of inflation for cosmic origins.

[1,009]   Siegel 2018.
[1,010]   Carroll and Ostlie 2017, pp. 1242–1243.
[1,011]   Pasachoff and Filippenko 2014, pp. 498–502.
[1,012]   Guth 1981, pp. 347–356.
[1,013]   Tegmark 2014, pp. 124–125.
[1,014]   Tegmark 2014, pp. 321–323.
[1,015]   Vilenkin 1983.
[1,016]   Vilenkin 1983.
[1,017]   Linde 1986.
[1,018]   Stenger 2014, p. 372.
[1,019]   Linde and Vanchurin 2010, preprint p. 10.
[1,020]   Shackelford 2007.
[1,021]   Hawking and Hertog 2018.
[1,022]   Unger and Smolin 2015.
[1,023]   Unger and Smolin 2015.
[1,024]   Woit 2015.
[1,025]   Tegmark 2003, p. 44.
[1,026]   Ellis quoted in Hossenfelder 2018, p. 216.
[1,027]   Tegmark 2014, pp. 123–125.

I should point out that Tegmark actually proposes the existence of four different types of multiverse, all of which he labels according to "levels" as in Level I Multiverse, Level II Multiverse, and so on. We won't be concerned with these distinctions since he claims each one may be spatially infinite, and he also claims there are an infinite number of universes for each type of multiverse anyway. Consequently, all those types of multiverse suffer the same logical problems implied by the notion of taking infinity literally.

[1,028]   Curiously, Tegmark expresses skepticism toward inflation where it comes to the mathematical use of infinities to describe it; but he is otherwise supportive of inflation.
[1,029]   Tavakol and Gironi 2017, p. 792.
[1,030]   Tavakol and Gironi 2017, p. 792.
[1,031]   Ijjas, Steinhardt, and Loeb 2017.
[1,032]   Tegmark 2015.
[1,033]   Tegmark 2014, p. 316.
[1,034]   Tegmark 2015.
[1,035]   Tegmark 2014, pp. 5, 123, 316–317.
[1,036]   Unger and Smolin 2015.
[1,037]   Barrow 2006, p. 156.
[1,038]   Kuhn 2015.

[1,039]   Nietzsche 1882 (2001 edition), Section 341.

[1,040]   Nietzsche 1883 (2006 edition), Third Part: "On Old and New Tablets."

[1,041]   Tegmark 2014, p. 123.

[1,042]   Masters 2019.

[1,043]   Collins (Nick) 2011.

[1,044]   Collins (Nick) 2011.

[1,045]   After all, even identical twins here on Earth, similar though they may be, differ in many of their details despite having grown from the same source. So too, how unlikely it would be to have a twin in some other galaxy far, far away.

[1,046]   Penrose 2004, p. 784.

[1,047]   Tegmark 2003, p. 46.

[1,048]   Penrose 2004, p. 784.

[1,049]   Everett 1973.

[1,050]   Carroll (Sean) 2010.

[1,051]   Carroll (Sean) 2014.

[1,052]   Herbert 1987.

[1,053]   Everett 1973, p. v.

[1,054]   Carroll (Sean) 2010.

[1,055]   See endnotes 1,053 and 1,054.

[1,056]   Barrett 2018.

[1,057]   Vaidman 2018.

[1,058]   Barrett 2018.

[1,059]   Penrose 2004, p. 784.

[1,060]   Gardner 2001, p. 14.

[1,061]   Gardner 2001, p. 16.

[1,062]   Bohm and Hiley 1995.

[1,063]   For a technical overview of Bohmian Mechanics, see Tumulka 2018.

[1,064]   Bousso quoted in Gefter 2017, p. 46.

[1,065]   Hobson 2013, pp. 211–223.

[1,066]   Lancaster and Blundell 2014, p. 2.

[1,067]   Feynman 1965 (1972 publication), Lecture.

[1,068]   Penrose 2004, pp. 675–679.

[1,069]   Penrose 2004, p. 678.

[1,070]   Feynman 1965 (1972 publication), Lecture.

[1,071]   Kaiser 2005, pp. 156–165.

[1,072]   See the following:
          (a) Hossenfelder 2018, p. 210.
          (b) Baggott 2013, p. 145.
          (c) Smolin 2006, pp. 152–153.
          (d) Boslough 1993, pp. 205–206.

[1,073]   Greene 2000.

[1,074]   Barrow 2012.

[1,075]   Smolin 2006.

[1,076]   Baggott 2018, p. 224.

[1,077]   See, for example, the chapter entitled "The End of Infinity" in Rovelli 2017.

[1,078]   Ellis quoted in Freiberger 26 September 2013.

[1,079]   Tegmark 2014, p. 316.

[1,080]   Lev 2017.

CHAPTER 22: CLOSING ARGUMENTS ON LITERAL INFINITY

[1,081]   Wittgenstein 1936–1949 (2009 edition), § 371 and § 373 on p. 123.

[1,082]   I contend Huemer takes this approach since his idea of completeness seems to me to be a misnomer for being finished while lacking a total. See Huemer 2016, pp. 185, 248–251.

[1,083]   Huemer 2016, Chapter Six.

[1,084]   Patterson 20 July 2016.

[1,085]   Galilei 1638 (1914 translation), p. 26. Quoted from Rucker 2005, p. 5.

[1,086]   See the definition for 'appeal to mystery' as an informal logical fallacy listed in Thompson 2020. This fallacy makes an appearance in some arguments against skepticism toward infinity. For example, a couple decades ago in an online article philosopher Thomas Ash had leveled a charge of fallacy against skepticism of infinity (Ash 2001), but in so doing I believe his own charge of fallacy itself committed the appeal to mystery fallacy.

Ash had stated that skepticism of (literal) infinity constitutes the fallacy known as the *argument from personal incredulity*. He made that charge of fallacy since allegedly those arguing against infinity assert that the infinite must not make sense merely because they have a hard time imagining infinite sets and series. He went on to say that "our limited human imaginations are poor guides to what properties the universe can have." (Ash 2001.)

Since Ash's article is now offline, I don't know if he still holds that view, but it's worth noting there are at least two problems with making a charge of fallacy by personal incredulity.

First, the charge of committing the argument from personal incredulity may apply to some arguments that have been made against the infinite, but it does not apply to arguments such as mine. My arguments make the case that there are inherent *logical contradictions* in the concept of literal infinity. That issue has nothing to do with the limits of human imagination. If something is self-contradictory, it isn't a rational concept—in which case it is little wonder one can't imagine it.

Second, to dismiss skepticism of infinity or the infinite by claiming that it only looks contradictory because of "our limited human imaginations" is not really evidence; rather, such a claim is an instance of the fallacy of the appeal to mystery (Thompson 2020).

So, to disprove my case against infinity, one would need more than dismissive charges or appeals to mystery: it would have to be shown where my reasoning is inconsistent and why the contradictions I attribute to infinity are not really contradictions after all. If such can be shown, I will, of course, recant.

[1,087]   Rucker 2005, p. 6

[1,088]   Trlifajová 2017, p. 27–28.

[1,089]   For a good exposition, see McGough 2020.

[1,090]   Moore 2019, p. 154.

In recent years there have been mathematicians who have proven certain cardinalities—let's call them P and T—are equal to each other while being greater than $\mathbb{N}$ and *either* less than *or* equal to $\mathbb{R}$. Therefore, $\mathbb{N} < (P = T) \leq \mathbb{R}$. But because P and T *may* be equal to $\mathbb{R}$, and we do not know if P and T are less than $\mathbb{R}$, this mathematical proof is not proof that the continuum hypothesis is false, and so the proof does not solve the continuum problem. For a good overview, see Soukup 2018.

[1,091]   Gödel 1947, p. 520.

[1,092]   Solomon Feferman quoted in Wolchover 2013.

[1,093]   Shoshany 2014.

[1,094]   Shoshany, 2014.

[1,095]   Wolchover, Natalie, 2013.

[1,096]   Dauben 1979, p. 127. Quoted in Carey 2005, p. 46.

[1,097]   de Swart 2018, p. 129.

[1,098]   Wildberger 2016.

[1,099]   Sereno 1999.

[1,100]　　Sereno 1999, p. 124.

[1,101]　　Sereno 1999, p. 141.

[1,102]　　Sereno 1999, p. 139.

[1,103]　　Suber 1998.

CHAPTER 23: THE STORY OF FIGURATIVE INFINITY

[1,104]　　The bag need not be bottomless—in our fanciful scenario, we could imagine a small gravitational 'black hole' in the bag that crushes the marbles into ever finer particles while at no time ever crushing them so small as to become 'infinitesimal' or of no size at all.

[1,105]　　Similar examples for literal infinity as actual infinity and figurative infinity as potential infinity can be found in McAllister 2011, p. 105.

[1,106]　　Moore 2019, pp. 25–26.

[1,107]　　Fenves 2001, p. 331.

[1,108]　　Aristotle ~350 BCE (1984 edition), *Physics*, Section 207^{a}7–15.

[1,109]　　Aristotle ~350 BCE (1930 translation), *Physics*, Book III (Part 6).

[1,110]　　Aristotle used a bronze statue in his analogy. See Aristotle ~350 BCE (1930 translation), *Physics*, Book III.

[1,111]　　Aristotle ~350 BCE (1930 translation), *Physics*, Book III.

[1,112]　　Aristotle ~350 BCE (1930 translation), *Physics*, Book III.

[1,113]　　Aristotle ~350 BCE (1930 translation), *Physics*, Book III.

[1,114]　　Aristotle ~350 BCE (1930 translation), *Physics*, Book III.

[1,115]　　I should note that I am apparently not the only one who arrived at this conclusion. This take on Aristotle's view of potential infinity seems to be held by many mathematicians as well. Fletcher, for instance, states, "According to the idea of potential infinity, infinity is merely a figure of speech…" See Fletcher 2007, p. 1.

[1,116]　　Aristotle ~350 BCE (1930 translation), *Physics*, Book VIII.

[1,117]　　Aristotle ~350 BCE (2015 translation), *On the Heavens*, Book I, Section 12.

[1,118]　　Hintikka 1973, p. 123.

[1,119]　　Hintikka 1973, pp. 116–117.

[1,120]　　Moore 2019, p. 37.

[1,121]　　Moore 2019, p. 42.

[1,122]　　Hintikka 1973, p. 117.

[1,123]　　Hintikka 1973, p. 116.

[1,124]　　Aristotle raised some problems involved with the concept of a beginning of time. See Aristotle ~350 BCE (1930 translation), *Physics*, Book VIII.

[1,125]　　That move in itself would not have been sufficient to resolve his logical dilemma because he would have needed to avoid a beginning to time for his philosophy to be consistent. He would have needed to take the next step and propose a circular model of time, a topic I will address in my forthcoming monograph on cosmology.

[1,126]　　Aquinas 1273 (1947 translation), *The Summa Theologica*, First Part, Question 7: The Infinity of God (Four Articles), Article 4.

[1,127]　　Moore 2019, p. 49–50.

[1,128]　　Moore 2019, p. 50.

[1,129]　　Duhem 1985, pp. 81–83.

[1,130]　　Moore 2019, p. 50.

[1,131]　　Patterson 10 January 2016 and 20 July 2016.

[1,132]　　Patterson 10 January 2016 and 20 July 2016.

[1,133]　　Duhem 1985, p. 78.

[1,134]　　Duhem 1985, pp. 81–83.

[1,135]　　Duhem 1985, p. 82.

[1,136]   Duhem 1985, pp. 83–85.
[1,137]   Duhem 1985, p. 84.
[1,138]   Duhem 1985, p. 84.
[1,139]   Kaye 2019.
[1,140]   Duhem 1985, p. 87.
[1,141]   Kaye 2019.
[1,142]   Descartes 6 June 1647 letter to Chanut in Ariew 2000, pp. 277–288.
[1,143]   Arthur 2018, p. 172.
[1,144]   Leibniz in a 1 September 1706 draft letter to the Jesuit Father, Bartholomew Des Bosses. See Arthur 2018, p. 172.
[1,145]   Leibniz 1693 letter to Simon Foucher cited in the German Academy of Sciences at Berlin, pp. 712–713.
[1,146]   Arthur 2018, pp. 155–179.
[1,147]   Leibniz wrote to De Bosses, "Instead of 'infinite number' it should be said that there are more than can be expressed by any number." See Arthur 2018, p. 175.
[1,148]   Leibniz in the 1 September 1706 draft letter to Des Bosses; see Arthur 2018, p. 172.
[1,149]   Arthur 2018, p. 176.
[1,150]   Kant 1781/1787 (1998 edition), p. 522 (Section A512/B540).
[1,151]   Kant 1781/1787 (1998 edition), p. 465 (Section A418); pp. 472–473 (Section A432/B460).
[1,152]   Fletcher 2007, p. 2.
[1,153]   As indicated in Kant's notes and fragments. See Guyer 2018 in Nachtomy and Winegar 2018, p. 186.
[1,154]   Kant 1781/1787 (1998 edition), pp. 472–473 (Section A432/B460), p. 523 (Section A515/B543), and pp. 528–530 (Sections A525/B552 and A527/B555).
[1,155]   Kant 1781/1787 (1998 edition), pp. 528–530 (Sections A525/B552 and A527/B555).
[1,156]   Kant 1781 (1990 edition), pp. 295–296.
[1,157]   Kant 1781 (1990 edition), p. 289.
[1,158]   Recall that philosopher Antony Flew refers to a process of 'infinite' division as a process that goes on "as often as anyone wishes: infinity, without limit." See Flew quoted in Holden 2002, p. 5.
[1,159]   Waterhouse 1979, p. 432.
[1,160]   Waterhouse 1979, p. 433.
[1,161]   Moore 2019, page 64–65.
[1,162]   On Kronecker: All of Kronecker's mathematical definitions "extend to some indeterminate finite number n, and never continue to infinity." Quote from Carey 2005, p. 40.
[1,163]   On Poincaré see Mauro 2019.
[1,164]   Brouwer 1907.
[1,165]   Patterson 2015.
[1,166]   Mycielski 1981.
[1,167]   Mycielski 1981.
[1,168]   Mycielski 1981, p. 632.
[1,169]   Mostowski 2007, pp. 243–244.
[1,170]   Mostowski 2016, p. 78.
[1,171]   Mostowski 2012.
[1,172]   Eberl 2017, slide 2 of 11.
[1,173]   Eberl 2019, slide 4 of 14.
[1,174]   Dummett 1991, p. 317.
[1,175]   Eberl 2019, slide 4 of 14.
[1,176]   Eberl 2019, slide 4 of 14.

CHAPTER 24: INCONSISTENCIES IN FIGURATIVE INFINITY

[1,177]   Waterhouse 1979, p. 432.

[1,178]   Kant 1781/1787 (1998 edition), pp. 465 (Section A418) and pp. 472–473 (Section A432/B460).

[1,179]   Kant 1781/1787 (1998 edition), pp. 472 (Section A432/B460).

[1,180]   Kant 1781/1787 (1998 edition), pp. 473–474 (Section A432/B460).

[1,181]   See endnote 1,180.

[1,182]   Kant 1781/1787 (1998 edition), p. 479 (Section A439/B467).

[1,183]   Compare endnote 1,180 reference to Kant 1781/1787 (1998 edition), pp. 518–519 (Sections A506/B534).

[1,184]   Kant 1781/1787 (1998 edition), pp. 517–519 (Sections A504–A507/B532–B535).

[1,185]   Linnebo and Shapiro 2019, p. 163.

[1,186]   Lumen 2019.

[1,187]   Lumen 2019.

[1,188]   Moore 2011, p. 117.

[1,189]   Cantor 1885 letter to Gustav Eneström presented in The Schiller Institute 1994, p. 100.

[1,190]   Rodych 1997, p. 208. Rodych quotes the following sources:
           (a) Waismann 1979.
           (b) Wittgenstein, Ludwig:
                • 1939 (1976 edition) – *Lectures on the Foundations of Mathematics*.
                • 1932 (1974 edition) – *Philosophical Grammar*.
                • 1930 (1975 edition) – *Philosophical Remarks*.
                • 1937–44 (1956 translation) – *Remarks on the Foundations of Mathematics*.

[1,191]   Patterson 10 January 2016

[1,192]   Patterson 2015.

[1,193]   Kant 1781/1787 (1998 edition), p. 521 (Section A511/B539).

[1,194]   Kant 1781/1787 (1998 edition), p. 522 (Section A511/B539).

[1,195]   Lavine 1994 and 1995.

In my previous book on cosmology (Sewell 1999, p. 33), I remarked that transfinite mathematics might be revised in the form of a mathematics of the indefinite, thus saving its basic operations. However, I now believe this to be incorrect for two reasons.

First, there is a difference between the infinite as defined in transfinite mathematics and the concept of the indefinite. Transfinite mathematics is based on the idea that an infinite set is equal to an infinite subset (producing contradictions as I've pointed out in this work); but it is not at all clear that an *indefinite* set can be "equal" to an indefinite subset.

Second, there is no need to attempt such a revision of transfinite mathematics; Dr. Shaughan Lavine's (1995) system of "finite mathematics" makes a revision of transfinite mathematics superfluous for revealing the genuine nature of indefinite sets.

CHAPTER 25: AN ACCOUNT OF DIVINE INFINITY

[1,196]   Göcke and Tapp 2018, p. 2.

[1,197]   Craig 2013.

[1,198]   Craig 2013.

[1,199]   Bersanelli 2011, p. 193.

[1,200]   Bersanelli 2011, p. 206.

[1,201]   Bersanelli 2011, p. 212.

[1,202]   Bersanelli 2011, pp. 211, 213.

[1,203]   Bersanelli 2011, pp. 211–212.

[1,204]   Negative infinity should not be confused with negative theology, or the via negative—see § 25.2.1. Negative infinity can be a concept in a negative theology, but it can also be part of a positive theology since one can affirm *that* God is infinite in a negative sense.

[1,205]   Positive infinity should not be confused with positive theology, or the via positive—see § 25.2.1. Positive infinity can be part of a positive theology, but it is not necessary for a positive theology to affirm that God is infinite in order to have a positive theology.

[1,206]   Oppy 2011 in Heller and Woodin 2011, p. 243.

[1,207]   Zimmerman 1910. Qualitative infinity may also be associated with the Absolute. For a description of the Absolute, see the section on absolute infinity.

[1,208]   Urbańczyk 2018, p. 150.

[1,209]   Urbańczyk 2018, p. 151.

[1,210]   Philo. 30–40 CE (1929 edition), Section X (36), p. 27.

[1,211]   Geljon 2005, p. 172, 176 pp. 152–177.

[1,212]   Clemens ~215 (1885 translation), Book V, Chapter 12.

[1,213]   Clemens ~215 (1885 translation), Book V, Chapter 12.

[2,214]   Kalvesmaki 2013.

[2,215]   Steele and Williams 2019, p. 612.

[2,216]   Steele and Williams 2019, p. 611.

[1,217]   Vallicella 2019.

[1,218]   Vallicella 2019.

[1,219]   Clemens ~215 (1885 edition), Book V, Chapter 12.

[1,220]   Clement's idea of God's infinity seems to be that it is a unity of form but not necessarily a unity in the sense of having attributes that lack distinction with one another. See Clemens ~215 (1885 edition), Book V, Chapter 12.

[1,221]   Steele and Williams 2019, p. 611.

[1,222]   Clemens ~215 (1885 edition), Book V, Chapter 12.

[1,223]   Clemens ~215 (1885 edition), Book V, Chapter 11.

[1,224]   Plotinus 250 CE (1957 translation), Second Ennead, Ninth Tractate, Chapter 1.

[1,225]   Plotinus 250 CE (1957 translation), Fifth Ennead, Fifth Tractate, Chapter 11.

[1,226]   Plotinus 250 CE (1957 translation), Sixth Ennead, Second Tractate, Chapter 21.

[1,227]   Plotinus 250 CE (1957 translation), Fifth Ennead, Fifth Tractate, Chapter 10.

[1,228]   Plotinus 250 CE (1957 translation), Sixth Ennead, First Tractate, Chapter 1.

[1,229]   Plotinus 250 CE (1957 translation), Sixth Ennead, First Tractate, Chapter 1.

[1,230]   Plotinus 250 CE (1957 translation), Fifth Ennead, Eighth Tractate, Chapter 9.

[1,231]   Gregory of Nyssa 383 CE (2020 edition), *Against Eunomius*. Book I, § 15 and Book III, § 5.

[1,232]   Gregory of Nyssa 383 CE (2005 edition), *Against Eunomius*, Book III, § 5.

[1,233]   Gregory of Nyssa 383 CE (2005 edition), *Against Eunomius*, Book I § 26.

[1,234]   Gregory of Nyssa 379 CE (2005 edition), *On the Soul and Resurrection*, p. 458. Online source: <https://www.ccel.org/ccel/schaff/npnf205/png/0472=458.htm>

[1,235]   Gregory of Nyssa 383 CE (2005 edition), *Against Eunomius*, Book IX, § 3.

[1,236]   Gregory of Nyssa 383 CE (2005 edition), *Against Eunomius*, Book VIII, § 1.

[1,237]   Gregory of Nyssa 383 CE (2005 edition), *Against Eunomius*, Book VIII, § 1.

[1,238]   Gregory of Nyssa 384 CE (2005 edition), *Answer to Eunomius' Second Book*, p. 262. Online source: <https://ccel.org/ccel/schaff/npnf205/Page_262.html>

[1,239]   Gregory of Nyssa 383 CE (2005 edition), *Against Eunomius*, Book I § 26; Book VIII, § 1.

[1,240]   Gregory of Nyssa 384 CE (2005 edition), *Answer to Eunomius' Second Book*, p. 280. Online source: <https://ccel.org/ccel/schaff/npnf205/Page_280.html>

[1,241]   Gregory of Nyssa 383 CE (2005 edition), *Against Eunomius*, Book III, § 5.

[1,242]   Gregory of Nyssa 393 CE (1978 edition), *The Life of Moses*, Book II. Paragraphs 225, 242.

[1,243]   Gregory of Nyssa 383 CE (2020 edition), *Against Eunomius*, Book III, § 5. And see Geljon 2005, pp. 162–163.

[1,244]   Geljon 2005, p. 167.

[1,245]   Gregory of Nyssa 383 CE (2005 edition), *Against Eunomius*, Book I, pp. 69–70. Online source: <https://ccel.org/ccel/schaff/npnf205/npnf205/Page_69.html>

[1,246]   Gregory of Nyssa 384 CE (2005 edition), *Answer to Eunomius' Second Book*, p. 296. <https://ccel.org/ccel/schaff/npnf205/Page_296.html>

[1,247]   Gregory of Nyssa 378 CE (2005 edition), *On "Not Three Gods"*, p. 335. Online source: <https://ccel.org/ccel/schaff/npnf205/Page_335.html>

[1,248]   Gregory of Nyssa 383 CE (2005 edition), *Against Eunomius*, Book I § 26.

[1,249]   Gregory of Nyssa 384 CE (2005 edition), *Answer to Eunomius' Second Book*, pp. 287–297. Online source: <https://ccel.org/ccel/schaff/npnf205/Page_287.html>

[1,250]   Gregory of Nyssa 384 CE (2005 edition), *Answer to Eunomius' Second Book*, p. 296. Online source: <https://ccel.org/ccel/schaff/npnf205/Page_296.html>

[1,251]   Gregory of Nyssa 384 CE (2005 edition), *Answer to Eunomius' Second Book*, p. 257. Online source: <https://ccel.org/ccel/schaff/npnf205/Page_257.html>

[1,252]   Carroll (William) 2018, p. 61.

[1,253]   Aquinas 1258 (1955–57 translation), *Summa Contra Gentiles*, Book I: God. Chapter 43: That God is Infinite.

[1,254]   Aquinas 1258 (1955–57 translation), *Summa Contra Gentiles*, Book I: God. Chapter 43: That God is Infinite.

[1,255]   Aquinas 1273 (1947 translation), *The Summa Theologica*, First Part. Question 7: The Infinity of God (Four Articles). Question 7, Article 2, Reply to Objection 1.

[1,256]   Aquinas 1258 (1955–57 translation), *Summa Contra Gentiles*, Book I: God. Chapter 43: That God is Infinite.

[1,257]   Aquinas 1273 (1947 translation), *The Summa Theologica*, First Part. Question 3: Of the Simplicity of God (Eight Articles). Article 7, Reply to Objection 2.

[1,258]   As pointed out by philosopher Ana María C. Minecan, Aquinas' "simultaneous affirmation of simplicity and possession of multiple qualities cannot be maintained consistently." See Minecan 2016, p. 199.

[1,259]   Sweeney 1992, pp. 330–325, 337.

[1,260]   Duns Scotus ~1306, Section 4.63–64.

[1,261]   Duns Scotus ~1306, Section 4.47–50.

[1,262]   Duns Scotus ~1306, Section 4.48, 4.70–71.

[1,263]   Cusanus, 1440 (1985 edition), Book I, Chapter 17, paragraphs 46–48.

[1,264]   The "simple infinite" was a term used by Cusanus. See Cusanus 1440 (1985 edition). Book I, Chapter 4, pp. 8–9, paragraph 11; Book I, Chapter 23, paragraph 71.

[1,265]   Cusanus 1440 (1985 edition), Book I, Chapter 26, paragraph 88.

[1,266]   Cusanus 1440 (1985 edition), Book I, Chapter 26, paragraphs 78, 86–89; Book II, Chapter 1, paragraph 97.

[1,267]   Cusanus 1440 (1985 edition), Book I, Chapter 1, paragraph 3.

[1,268]   Cusanus 1440 (1985 edition), Book I, Chapter 26, paragraph 88.

[1,269]   Bruno 1588 (2004 edition), p. 11.

[1,270]   Bruno 1584, First Dialogue in Singer 1950, pp. 61, 261–262.

[1,271]   Galilei 1638 (1914 translation), pp. 32–33.

[1,272]   Galilei 1638 (1914 translation), p. 33.

[1,273]   Galilei 1638 (1914 translation), pp. 37–38.

[1,274]   Galilei 1638 (1914 translation), pp. 33–35, 37–38.

[1,275]   Galilei 1638 (1914 translation), pp. 36–37.

[1,276]   Galilei 1638 (1914 translation), pp. 36–37.

[1,277]   Galilei 1638 (1914 translation), pp. 36–37.

[1,278]   Galilei 1638 (1914 translation), p. 38.

[1,279]   Galilei 1638 (1914 translation), p.31.

[1,280]   Pedersen 1985, p.75.

[1,281]   The interpretation of Galileo's view of infinity as non-quantitative has been supported by philosophers such as Ohad Nachtomy and Eberhard Knobloch. See the following:
(a) Knobloch 1999, p. 94.
(b) Nachtomy 2018, pp. 141–143.

[1,282]   According to Knobloch, Galileo would have regarded "infinite quantity" to be a contradiction in terms. (Knobloch 1999, p. 94). I don't believe Knobloch is, strictly speaking, correct about how Galileo regarded infinity. Otherwise, Galileo would not have spoken of an "infinite number" of things. However, if by "infinite quantity," Knobloch means a calculable number like a finite number, then Knobloch is right. Similarly, Nachtomy says Galileo did not regard infinity as a quantity (Nachtomy 2018, pp. 141–143), which is also misleading. It is true Galileo did not think infinity is a quantity like a finite number, but he did regard infinity to be quantitative in the sense that an "infinite number" denotes a (quantitatively) incomparable quantity to any finite amount—a unity which contains any or every finite quantity but by "how much" is incalculable.

[1,283]   For example, Cusanus writes of processes continuing "ad infinitum" and states that "even if the number of its angles is increased *ad infinitum*, the polygon never becomes equal [to the circle] unless it is resolved into an identity with the circle." (See Cusanus 1440 (1985 edition), Book I, Chapter 3, paragraph 10.)

[1,284]   Cusanus said that "since the universe encompasses all the things which are not God, it cannot be negatively infinite, although it is unbounded and thus privatively infinite...for it is not the case that anything actually greater than it, in relation to which it would be bounded, is positable. And so, [it is] privatively infinite." (See Cusanus 1440 (1985 edition), Book II, Chapter 1, paragraph 97.)

[1,285]   Cusanus 1440 (1985 edition), Book II, Chapter 1, paragraph 97.

[1,286]   Galilei 1638 (1914 translation), p. 24.

[1,287]   Galilei 1638 (1914 translation), p. 25.

[1,288]   Galilei 1638 (1914 translation), pp. 33–36.

[1,289]   Galilei 1638 (1914 translation), pp. 32–33.

[1,290]   Galilei 1638 (1914 translation), p. 32.

[1,291]   Galilei 1638 (1914 translation), pp. 35–38.

[1,292]   Galilei 1638 (1914 translation), p.31.

[1,293]   Descartes 1640 (1901 translation).

[1,294]   Descartes 1644 (1985 edition), Part One, Article 27, p. 202.

[1,295]   Descartes 1640 (1901 translation).

[1,296]   Descartes 1642 (2017 compilation), First Objections, Reply 3, p. 12.

[1,297]   Descartes 1642 (2017 compilation), First Objections, Reply 3, p. 12.

[1,298]   Descartes 1642 (2017 compilation), First Objections, Reply 3, p. 12.

[1,299]   Descartes 1640 (1901 translation), Meditation III, Section 27.

[1,300]   Descartes 1642 (2017 compilation), Second Objections, Reply 2, p. 23.

[1,301]   Antognazza 2015, p. 5.

[1,302]   Dewey 1902, pp. 191–192.

[1,303]   Antognazza 2015, p. 5.

[1,304]   Antognazza 2015, endnote 44 on pp. 27–28.

[1,305]   Dewey 1902, p. 228.

[1,306]   Tapp 2018, p. 154.

[1,307]   Tapp 2018, p. 164.

[1,308]   Bolzano 1847 (in Russ 2004), § 11, p. 604.

[1,309]   Steele and Williams 2019, pp. 611–631.

[1,310]   Bolzano 1847 (in Russ 2004), § 11, p. 604.

[1,311]   Van der Veen and Horsten 2013, p. 124.

[1,312]   Bolzano 1847 (in Russ 2004), § 11, p. 604.

[1,313]   Trlifajová 2017, p. 2.

[1,314]   Trlifajová 2017, p. 2.

[1,315]   Cantor 1883 (1976 translation), p.76 and endnote #2 on p. 94.

[1,316]   Rucker 2011, p. 9.

[1,317]   Zimmerman 1910.

[1,318]   Cantor 1899, letter to Dedekind in Van Heijenoort 1967, pp. 114–115.

[1,319]   Cantor 1883 (1976 translation), p.76 and endnote #2 on p. 94.

[1,320]   Russell (Robert John) 2011, p. 282.

[1,321]   Cantor, as quoted in Mentzeniotis and Stamatellos 2008, p. 224.

[1,322]   From Cantor's 1886 letter to Albert Eulenburg. See Mentzeniotis and Stamatellos 2008, p. 224.

[1,323]   Cantor 1886, letter to Eulenburg in Mentzeniotis and Stamatellos 2008, p. 224.

[1,324]   Cantor 1883 (1976 translation), pp.76 and endnote #2 on p. 94.

[1,325]   Mentzeniotis and Stamatellos 2008, p. 223.

[1,326]   Van der Veen and Horsten 2013, p. 118.

[1,327]   Cantor 1908, letter to Chisholm-Young in Van der Veen and Horsten 2013, p. 125.

[1,328]   Cantor 1908, letter to Chisholm-Young in Van der Veen and Horsten 2013, p. 125.

[1,329]   Trlifajová 2017, p. 2.

[1,330]   From Cantor's 22 January 1886 letter to Johann Baptiste Franzelin. See Meschkowski and Nilson 1991, pp. 254–256. English translation in *Fidelio* (Schiller Institute 1994, p. 102).

[1,331]   In certain respects, this is not unlike the view held by Aquinas.

[1,332]   As Van der Veen and Horsten put it, for Cantor "the mathematical universe is an *aspect* of God." (See Van der Veen and Horsten 2013, p. 127).

[1,333]   Steele and Williams 2019, pp. 611–631.

[1,334]   Heijenoort 1967, pp. 114–115.

[1,335]   Göcke and Tapp 2019, p. 2.

[1,336]   Steinhart 2009, p. 261.

[1,337]   Kuhn 2020 interview with Steinhart at 00:07:40—00:09:55 (hr/min/sec).

[1,338]   Hick 2010, pp. 26–27.

[1,339]   Kuhn 2020 interview with Swinburne at 00:01:50—00:02:30 (hr/min/sec).

[1,340]   Gwiazda 2009.

[1,341]   Gwiazda 2009, pp. 488, 490.

[1,342]   Göcke 2016, p. 193.

[1,343]   Turner 2011, p. 297.

[1,344]   Göcke 2016.

CHAPTER 26: A CRITIQUE OF DIVINE INFINITY

[1,345]   Khusraw ~1060 CE (1949 translation), p. 31. Referenced in Ahmad 2017.

[1,346]   Bolzano 1847 (in Russ 2004), § 11, p. 604.

[1,347]   Trlifajová 2017, p. 2.

[1,348]   Aquinas 1258 (1955–57 translation), *Summa Contra Gentiles*, Book II: Creation. Chapter 25.

[1,349]   Aquinas 1273 (1947 translation), *The Summa Theologica*, First Part. Question 12: How God is Known by Us (Thirteen Articles). Article 7.

[1,350]   Aquinas 1273 (1947 translation), *The Summa Theologica*, First Part. Question 14, Article 12, Reply to Objection 1.

[1,351]   Göcke 2016, p. 192.

[1,352]   Göcke 2016, p. 192.

[1,353]   Mullings 2017.

[1,354]   Steele and Williams 2019, p. 5.

[1,355]   Craig 2013.

[1,356]   Zimmerman 1910.

[1,357] The categories of these arguments are my own for reference purposes. Also, I have paraphrased each of Zimmerman's arguments by filling in missing premises. See Zimmerman 1910.

[1,358] Oppy states the same argument as a question: "More generally, how could a finite God be the kind of endpoint for explanation that cosmological arguments typically take God to be?" See Oppy 2006; see also Oppy 2011 in Heller and Woodin 2011, p. 249.

[1,359] For example, the ancient Hebrews regarded death as final; see Genesis 3:19 and Ecclesiastes 3:20, 9:4. Moreover, the Old Babylonian *Atrahasis* epic, written in the mid-17th century BCE, depicts humans as having no existence after death (see Mark 2011).

[1,360] Oppy 2011 in Heller and Woodin 2011, p. 249.

[1,361] Ahmad 2017.

[1,362] Zimmerman 1910.

[1,363] Oppy 2011 in Heller and Woodin 2011, p. 242.

[1,364] Zimmerman 1910.

[1,365] This is even true in the Islamic hadith (specifically, *Sahih Muslim,* Book 45: The Book of Virtue, Enjoining Good Manners, and Joining of the Ties of Kinship, Chapter 32: The Prohibition of Striking the Face) which states, "When any one of you fights with his brother, he should avoid his face for Allah created Adam in His own image." Likely, this doctrine stems from the Book of Genesis, in which "image of God" was originally meant quite literally. But in Islam, the notion of imago Dei requires (rather strained) reinterpretation as a mere metaphor due to the doctrine that Allah has no visible body and ergo no actual image.

[1,366] Scripture quoted from *The Holy Bible, New International Version*. First published in 1973.

[1,367] According to Blue Letter Bible, Psalm 147 was written ~515 BCE. See the following online source: <https://www.blueletterbible.org/study/parallel/paral18.cfm>

The philosopher Anaximander, widely regarded as the earliest to propose a concept of infinity, lived from ~610—546 BCE. Anaximander's idea of infinity may have indirectly influenced Hebrew theological thought, contributing to early ideas of divine infinity.

[1,368] Augustine. 397–400 CE. *The Confessions.* Translated by Henry Chadwick. (2008). Oxford: Oxford University Press. Book I, Section vi (10).

[1,369] Gregory of Nyssa 383 CE (2005 edition), *Against Eunomius*, Book I § 26, pp. 96–97.

[1,370] Some scriptures seem to refer to an "eternal" past. It is unclear if it is meant that the past is literally infinite or timeless or serially indefinite with a beginning moment, indefinitely long ago, that continually "recedes" from the ever-changing "present" moment.

[1,371] Scripture quoted from *The Holy Bible, New International Version*. First published in 1973.

[1,372] Kuhn 2020 interview with Swinburne at 00:04:50—00:06:15 (hr/min/sec).

[1,373] Moreover, even if the scriptures did have a more or less consistent theology, such would neither prove the reality of God nor that divine infinity is a consistent notion—each of those beliefs requires support with additional philosophical arguments. At most, a consistent set of scriptures would prove human beings can form consistent theological traditions, and that is all.

[1,374] For example, Thomas Jefferson and Thomas Paine were both *deists*—they believed in God, just not the God of divine revelation. See the following:
(a) Jefferson 1820 (2012 edition).
(b) Paine 1794–1795 (2017 edition).

[1,375] Kushner 1981 (2001 edition).

[1,376] Kushner 1981 (2001 edition), pp. 179–180.

[1,377] According to Göcke, most theologians believe in a finite conception of God. (See Göcke 2016, pp. 187–189.) Insofar as the kind of "infinity" most theologians attribute to God is just a misnomer for a second order quality like indistinguishability or incomparability, I agree. Still, most theologians would disagree with Göcke because they believe it is appropriate—or even theologically necessary—to use the word "infinity" in a qualitative sense to describe the attributes of God.

[1,378] I am, of course, assuming God is a being conjectured rather than revealed.

[1,379]   Nagel 1974, pp. 435–450.
[1,380]   James 1917, pp. 425–427.

CHAPTER 27: WRAPPING UP THE CASE AGAINST INFINITY

[1,381]   Göcke 2016.

[1,382]   It would be more accurate to say these terms are commonly reserved for literal infinity and for infinity's companion concept, *eternity*, when it is conceived to refer to literally infinite time. However, I will save most of my discussion of eternity for another book and remain focused more narrowly on infinity in this book.

[1,383]   This is the position of mathematician Stephen G. Simpson. See Simpson 2015.

[1,384]   Further exposition of symbolic notation for indefiniteness will be presented separately in the appendix of an expanded online edition of this book. Until then, I offer the symbols of Table 4 in revision to the symbolism for the indefinite that I proposed previously in Sewell 1999, 2008, and 2010. While I think the new symbols offered in Table 4 for indefinitely large quantities are an improvement, I'm still not satisfied with this notation. I'm sure mathematicians could do better, but the notation will have to suffice for making the point that the varieties of indefiniteness can be captured in new mathematical notation.

Incidentally, some of these symbols are not entirely my own.

The symbols for indefinite increase and decrease toward a limit were originally suggested by systems analyst Mark Payne. See Payne 2016. (Some of my symbolism for indefiniteness thus agrees with that of the extreme finitism of Payne. However, Payne's extreme finitism goes further than my own version of finitism as he rejects the use of certain terms such as 'continuous' and 'forever' because he believes they imply infinities, whereas I do not reject these terms because I do not interpret them as necessarily implying infinities.)

The symbol for an indefinite limit to the in-practice definable numbers (last one in Table 4)—a symbol which I call quell—represents the largest number as a constant on the opposite end of the number scale from zero. That symbol is similar both in notation and conception to the original proposal by Sazonov. See Sazonov, 1995.

[1,385]   Pew Research Center 2017

[1,386]   Pew Research Center 2017.

[1,387]   Greene 2020, pp. 3–4.

[1,388]   Russell (Bertrand) 1919, pp. 47–48. Quoted in Bergström 2013, p. 179.

[1,389]   "Over half the world's population believes in some form of personal immortality over an infinite future": I base this statement on the world's population of Christians and Muslims combined, along with how these religions commonly portray God and the afterlife, both views of which influence the world's population of unaffiliated theists. See the Pew Research Center 2017.

[1,390]   See endnote 166.

[1,391]   Callender 2010, pp. 58–65.

[1,392]   Davies 2012, pp. 8–13.

[1,393]   Timeless eternity is typically claimed of God. See the following:
(a) Rogers 1994.
(b) Pasnau 2011.
(c) Cyr 2020.

BIBLIOGRAPHY

Achtner, Wolfgang. (2011). "Infinity as a Transformative Concept in Science and Theology." Chapter in Heller and Woodin 2011, pp. 19–51.

Ackerman, Nate. (22 January 2009). "Existence of Reals." Lecture. Harvard University, Mathematics Department. Online source:
<http://people.math.harvard.edu/~nate/teaching/UPenn/2009/spring/math_360/lectures/week_2/lecture_2/lecture_2.pdf>

Aguirre, Anthony. (9 August 2011). "Next Step Infinity." *Edge*. Online source:
<https://www.edge.org/conversation/anthony_aguirre-next-step-infinity>

Ahmad, Sujjawal. (14 November 2017). "Ismaili Doctrine of God Beyond Being and Non-being." *Ismailimail*. Online source:
<https://ismailimail.blog/2017/11/14/sujjawal-ahmad-ismaili-doctrine-of-god-beyond-being-and-non-being>

Al-Khalili, Jim. (2003). *Quantum: A Guide for the Perplexed*. London, United Kingdom: Weidenfeld & Nicolson.

Alexander, Amir. (2014). *Infinitesimal: How a Dangerous Mathematical Theory Shaped the Modern World*. New York: Farrar, Straus and Giroux.

Alexander, Amir. (1 April 2014). "A Brief History of Infinitesimals: The Idea That Gave Birth to Modern Calculus." *Scientific American*. Vol. 310, No. 4. Online source:
<https://www.scientificamerican.com/article/a-brief-history-of-infinitesimals-the-idea-that-gave-birth-to-modern-calculus>

Ambrose, Alice. (1993). "Transfinite Numbers." *Wittgenstein's Intentions*. Edited by Stuart Shanker and John Canfield. New York: Routledge.

Ananthaswamy, Anil. (3 September 2018). "What Does Quantum Theory Actually Tell Us About Reality?" *Scientific American – Observations*. Online source:
<https://blogs.scientificamerican.com/observations/what-does-quantum-theory-actually-tell-us-about-reality>

André, Robert. (2014). *Axioms and Set Theory: A First Course in Set Theory*. Online source:
<http://www.math.uwaterloo.ca/~randre/sets/1aaset_theory_150907.pdf>

Andrews, Max. (2011). "The Different Versions of Infinity and Cantorian Sets." *Sententia: Dialogues Concerning Philosophy, Theology, & Science*. Online source:
<http://sententias.org/tag/aleph-null>

Anonymous: A. B. (5 December 2013). "It's A Lot Like Borscht." *The Economist*. Online source:
<http://www.economist.com/blogs/prospero/2013/12/quick-study-edward-frenkel-math?fsrc=rss>

Antognazza, Maria Rosa. (December 2015). "The Hypercategorematic Infinite." *The Leibniz Review*. Vol. 25, p. 5 from pp. 5–30. Online source:
<https://doi.org/10.5840/leibniz2015252>

Aquinas, Thomas. (1258). *Summa Contra Gentiles*. Translated by Anton C. Pegis. Edited by Joseph Kenny. (1955–57). New York: Hanover House. Online source:
<https://isidore.co/aquinas/english/ContraGentiles1.htm#43>

Aquinas, Thomas. (1273). *The Summa Theologica*. Translated by Fathers of the English Dominican Province. (1947). Westminster: Benziger Bros. Online source:
<https://www.ccel.org/a/aquinas/summa/FP.html>

Archimedes. (~216 BCE). *The Sand Reckoner*. Translated by Thomas L. Heath. (1897). Cambridge: Cambridge University Press. Online source:
<http://www.sacred-texts.com/cla/archim/sand/sandreck.htm>

Archimedes. (~214 BCE). *The Method of Mechanical Theorems*. Presented in Netz, Reviel; Noel, William. (2007). *The Archimedes Codex*. Philadelphia, PA: Da Capo Press.

Ariew, Roger (Editor). (2000). *Philosophical Essays and Correspondence* by René Descartes. Indianapolis, Indiana: Hackett Publishing Company.

Aristotle. (~350 BCE). *On the Heavens*. Translated by J. L. Stocks. (2015). South Australia: University of Adelaide.

Aristotle. (~350 BCE). *Physics*. See the following translations:
- Translated by R. P. Hardie and R. K. Gaye. (1930). Online source: <http://classics.mit.edu/Aristotle/physics.html>
- Translated by Robin Waterfield. Edited by David Bostock. (1999). Oxford: Oxford University Press.
- Barnes 1984.

Arthur, Richard T. W. (2018). "Leibniz's Syncategorematic Actual Infinite." Chapter in *Infinity in Early Modern Philosophy*. The New Synthese Historical Library 76. Springer Nature 2018. pp. 155–179.

Ash, Thomas. (2001). "The Case Against the Cosmological Argument." Article formerly online.

Associated Press. (3 January 1931). "Prof. Einstein Begins His Work at Mt. Wilson; Hoping to Solve Problems Touching Relativity." The New York Times. Vol. LXXX, No. 26,642. p. 1.

Auersperg, Alice M. I.; von Bayern, Auguste M. P.; et al. (2014). "Social Transmission of Tool Use and Tool Manufacture in Goffin Cockatoos (Cacatua Goffini)." *Proceedings of the Royal Society B*. Vol. 281. Online source: <http://dx.doi.org/10.1098/rspb.2014.0972>

Augustine. (397–400 CE). *The Confessions*. Translated by Henry Chadwick. (2008). Oxford: Oxford University Press.

Baggett, Lawrence. (11 December 2010). "Analysis of Functions of a Single Variable." *Connexions*. Online source: <https://cnx.org/content/col11249/1.1>

Baggott, Jim. (2013). *Farewell to Reality: How Modern Physics Has Betrayed the Search for Scientific Truth*. New York: Pegasus Books.

Baggott, Jim. (2018). *Quantum Space: Loop Quantum Gravity and the Search for the Structure of Space, Time, and the Universe*. Oxford: Oxford University Press.

Bain, Jonathan. (12 October 2006). Lecture. Polytechnic Institute of New York University. Online source: <http://faculty.poly.edu/~jbain/Cat/lectures/07.OrdsandCards.pdf>

Ball, Philip. (30 August 2017). "Quantum Theory Rebuilt from Simple Principles." *Quanta Magazine*. Online source: <https://www.quantamagazine.org/quantum-theory-rebuilt-from-simple-physical-principles-20170830>

Ball, Philip. (2018). *Beyond Weird: Why Everything You Thought You Knew About Quantum Physics is Different*. Chicago: Chicago University Press.

Baraniuk, Chris. (13 June 2016). "It Took Centuries, But We Now Know the Size of the Universe." *Earth*. BBC. Online source: <http://www.bbc.com/earth/story/20160610-it-took-centuries-but-we-now-know-the-size-of-the-universe>

Barnes, Jonathan. (1984). *The Complete Works of Aristotle: The Revised Oxford Translation*. Princeton: Princeton University Press.

Barr, Stephen. (1964). *Experiments in Topology*. New York: Thomas Y. Crowell Company.

Barrett, Jeffrey. (Winter 2018). "Everett's Relative-State Formulation of Quantum Mechanics." *The Stanford Encyclopedia of Philosophy*. Edited by Edward N. Zalta. Online source: <https://plato.stanford.edu/entries/qm-everett>

Barrow, John D. (2006). *The Infinite Book: A Short Guide to the Boundless, Timeless, and Endless*. New York: Vintage Books.

Barrow, John D. (2008). *New Theories of Everything*. Oxford University Press.

Barrow, John D. (2 July 2012). "Does Infinity Exist?" *Plus Magazine*. Online source: <http://plus.maths.org/content/does-infinity-exist>

Bauer, William A. (January 2011). "An Argument for the Extrinsic Grounding of Mass." *Erkenntnis*. Vol. 74, No. 1. pp. 81–99. Online source: <https://www.jstor.org/stable/41476673?seq=1>

Beiser, Arthur. (1992). *Physics*. Fifth Edition. New York: Addison-Wesley Publishing Company.

Bell, John L. (2008). *A Primer of Infinitesimal Analysis*. Cambridge University Press.

Bell, John L. (Summer 2017). "Continuity and Infinitesimals." *The Stanford Encyclopedia of Philosophy*. Edited by Edward N. Zalta. Online source: <https://plato.stanford.edu/entries/continuity>

Benacerraf, Paul. (22 November 1962). "Tasks, Super-Tasks, and the Modern Eleatics." *Journal of Philosophy*. Vol. 59, No. 24. pp. 765–784.

Benardete, J. A. (1964). *Infinity: An Essay in Metaphysics*. Oxford: Clarendon Press.

Bennet, Jonathan (Editor). (2017a). *Objections to the Meditations and Descartes' Replies*. Online source:
   <http://www.earlymoderntexts.com/assets/pdfs/descartes1642_1.pdf>

Bennet, Jonathan (Editor). (2017b). *Principles of Philosophy* by René Descartes. Online source:
   <http://www.earlymoderntexts.com/assets/pdfs/descartes1644part2.pdf>

Berger, Marcel. 2003. *A Panoramic View of Riemannian Geometry*. New York: Springer Science & Business Media.

Berghofer, Philipp. (2018). "Ontic Structural Realism and Quantum Field Theory: Are There Intrinsic Properties at the Most Fundamental Level of Reality?" *Studies in History and Philosophy of Modern Physics*. Vol. 62, pp. 176–188.

Bergström, Lars. (2013). "Death and Eternal Recurrence." *The Oxford Handbook of Philosophy of Death*. Edited by Ben Bradley, Fred Feldman, and Jens Johansson. Oxford: Oxford University Press.

Berlinski, David. (2008). *Infinite Ascent: A Short History of Mathematics*. New York: The Modern Library.

Berman, Bob. (24 September 2012). "Infinite Universe." *Astronomy Magazine*. Online source:
   <https://astronomy.com/magazine/bob-berman/2012/09/infinite-universe>

Bersanelli, Marco. (2011). "Infinity and the Nostalgia of the Stars." Chapter in Heller and Woodin 2011, pp. 193–217.

Biron, Lauren. (7 April 2015). "Our Flat Universe." *Symmetry Magazine*. Online source:
   <https://www.symmetrymagazine.org/article/april-2015/our-flat-universe>

Bogomolny, Alexander. (1996). "Infinity as a Limit." *Cut The Knot*. Online source:
   <https://www.cut-the-knot.org/WhatIs/Infinity/BigNumber.shtml>

Bohm, David. (1951). *Quantum Theory*. New York: Prentice-Hall (Reprinted 1989 by Dover Publications).

Bohm, David; Hiley, Basil J. (1995). *The Undivided Universe: An Ontological Interpretation of Quantum Theory*. New York: Routledge.

Bolzano, Bernard. (1816). *Binomial Theorem*. Presented in *The Mathematical Works of Bernard Bolzano*. Translated and edited by Steve Russ. (2004). Oxford: Oxford University Press.

Boolos, George; Burgess, John; Jeffrey, Richard. (2007). *Computability and Logic*. Fifth Edition. Cambridge: Cambridge University Press.

Borowski, E. J.; Borwein, J. M. (1991). *The HarperCollins Dictionary of Mathematics*. New York: HarperCollins—HarperPerennial division.

Boslough, John. (1993). *Masters Of Time: Cosmology At The End Of Innocence*. New York: Basic Books.

Bowers, Jonathan. (2016). "Infinity Scrapers." Online source:
   <http://www.polytope.net/hedrondude/scrapers.htm>

Bowin, John. (2007). "Aristotelian Infinity." *Oxford Studies in Ancient Philosophy*. Vol. 32. pp. 233–250. Online source:
   <https://people.ucsc.edu/~jbowin/BOWA-2.1.pdf>

Bragg, Melvin. (2001). "Mathematics and Platonism". Episode of: *In Our Time*. BBC Radio. Online source:
   <http://www.bbc.co.uk/programmes/p0054799>

Brandeis University. (11 July 2005). "African Grey Parrot Is First Bird To Comprehend Numerical Concept Akin To Zero." *ScienceDaily*. Online source:
   <https://www.sciencedaily.com/releases/2005/07/050711013845.htm>

Brooks, Rodney Allen. (2010). *Fields of Color: The Theory That Escaped Einstein*. Prescott, Arizona, United States: Rodney A. Brooks.

Brouwer, L. E. J. (1907). *On the Foundations of Mathematics*. Presented in Heyting, A. (Editor). (1975). *L. E. J. Brouwer: Collected Works*. Volume I. Amsterdam: North-Holland, pp. 11–101.

Bruno, Giordano. (1584). "On the Infinite Universe and Worlds." Presented in Singer 1950.

Bruno, Giordano. (1588). "Prefatory Epistle" in *Cause, Principle, and Unity*. Cambridge Texts in the History of Philosophy. Edited by Robert de Lucca. (2004). Cambridge: Cambridge University Press.

Burnet, John. (1920). "The Milesian School." Chapter in *Early Greek Philosophy*. Third Edition. London: A & C Black Ltd. Online source:
   <https://www.plato.spbu.ru/RESEARCH/burnet/burnet.pdf>

Butterworth, Brian. (1999). *What Counts: How Every Brain is Hardwired for Math*. New York: Simon & Schuster/Free Press.

Byrd, Deborah; Wiegert, Theresa. (15 October 2020). "Milky Way and Andromeda Galaxies are Already Merging." *EarthSky*. Online source:
<https://earthsky.org/astronomy-essentials/earths-night-sky-milky-way-andromeda-merge>

Callender, Craig. June 2010. "Is Time an Illusion?" *Scientific American*. Vol. 302, No. 6. pp. 58–65.

Cantor, Georg. (1874). "On a Property of the Set of All Real Algebraic Numbers." *Journal for Pure and Applied Mathematics*, commonly known as *Crelle's Journal*. Vol. 77. Translated into English:
<https://www.jamesrmeyer.com/infinite/cantor-1874-uncountability-proof.html>

Cantor, Georg. (1883). "Foundations of a General Theory of Manifolds: A Mathematical-Philosophical Study in the Theory of the Infinite" (a.k.a., "The Grundlagen"). Translated by Uwe Parpart. (January-February 1976). *The Campaigner*. Vol. 9, Nos. 1–2. pp. 69–97.

Cantor, Georg. (4 November 1885). Letter to Gustav Eneström. English edition by Ernst Zermelo presented in The Schiller Institute 1994.

Cantor, Georg. (1895/1897). *Contributions to the Founding of the Theory of Transfinite Numbers*. Translation and Introduction by Philip E. B. Jourdain. (1915). New York: Dover Publications.

Carey, Patrick Hatfield. (May 2005). "Beyond Infinity: Georg Cantor and Leopold Kronecker's Dispute over Transfinite Numbers." Thesis. Boston College. (55 pages). Online source:
<https://dlib.bc.edu/islandora/object/bc-ir:102467/datastream/PDF/view>

Carroll, Bradley W.; Ostlie, Dale A. (2017). *An Introduction to Modern Astrophysics*. Second Edition. Cambridge and New York: Cambridge University Press.

Carroll, Lewis. (1871). "Jabberwocky." Poem in *Through the Looking-Glass and What Alice Found There*. Republished in the 150th Anniversary Edition of *Alice's Adventures in Wonderland and Through the Looking-Glass and What Alice Found There*. Introduction by Charlie Lovett; Illustrated by John Tenniel. (2015). New York: Penguin Books.

Carroll, Sean. (2010). "Quantum Time." Chapter in *From Eternity to Here: The Quest for the Ultimate Theory of Time* by Sean Carroll. (2010). New York: Dutton. Online source:
<http://www.preposterousuniverse.com/eternitytohere/quantum>

Carroll, Sean. (30 June 2014). "Why the Many-Worlds Formulation of Quantum Mechanics Is Probably Correct." *Preposterous Universe*. Online source:
<http://www.preposterousuniverse.com/blog/2014/06/30/why-the-many-worlds-formulation-of-quantum-mechanics-is-probably-correct>

Carroll, William E. (2018). "Aquinas on Creation and the Analogy of Infinity." Chapter in *The Infinity of God: New Perspectives in Theology and Philosophy*. Edited by Benedikt Paul Göcke and Christian Tapp. (2018). Notre Dame, Indiana: University of Notre Dame Press.

Castelvecchi, Davide. (26 July 2018). "Big Bang Telescope Finale is End of an Era in Cosmology." *Nature*. Vol. 559. pp. 455–456. Online source:
<https://media.nature.com/original/magazine-assets/d41586-018-05788-5/d41586-018-05788-5.pdf>

Cendes, Yvette. (19 March 2019). "How Will The Universe End?" *Discover*. Online source:
<https://www.discovermagazine.com/the-sciences/how-will-the-universe-end>

Chang, Donald C. (29 December 2016). "What is the Physical Meaning of Mass in View of Wave-Particle Duality? A Proposed Model." *arXiv*. (35 pages). Online source:
<https://arxiv.org/abs/physics/0404044>

Chou, C. W.; et al. (24 September 2010). "Optical Clocks and Relativity." *Science*. Vol. 329, Issue 5999. pp. 1630–1633. Online source:
<https://tsapps.nist.gov/publication/get_pdf.cfm?pub_id=905055>

Christiansen, Morten H.; Kirby, Simon (Editors). (2003). *Language Evolution*. Oxford and New York: Oxford University Press.

Chu-Carroll, Mark. (24 May 2007). "The Axiom of Infinity." *Good Math, Bad Math*. Online source:
<http://www.goodmath.org/blog/2007/05/24/the-axiom-of-infinity>

Clark, James Roger. (Spring 2017). "Transfinite Ordinal Arithmetic." *All Student Theses*. 97. Online source:
<http://opus.govst.edu/theses/97>

Clegg, Brian. (2012). *Introducing Infinity: A Graphic Guide*. Illustrated by Oliver Pugh. United Kingdom: Icon Books.

Clemens, Titus Flavius (Clement of Alexandria). (~215 CE). *Stromata*. Translated by William Wilson. From Ante-Nicene Fathers. Vol. 2. Edited by Alexander Roberts, James Donaldson, and A. Cleveland Coxe. Buffalo, New York: Christian Literature Publishing Co. (1885). Revised and edited for New Advent by Kevin Knight. Online source: <http://www.newadvent.org/fathers/0210.htm>

CNRS (Délégation Paris Michel-Ange). (24 September 2011). "Monkeys Also Reason Through Analogy, Study Shows." *ScienceDaily*. Online source: <http://www.sciencedaily.com/releases/2011/09/110923102213.htm>

Collins. (2021). *Collins English Dictionary*. Glasgow: HarperCollins Publishers. Online source: <https://www.collinsdictionary.com/us>

Collins, Nick. (26 September 2011). "Monkeys at Typewriters 'Close to Reproducing Shakespeare'" *The Telegraph*. Online source: <https://www.telegraph.co.uk/technology/news/8789894/Monkeys-at-typewriters-close-to-reproducing-Shakespeare.html>

Colyvan, Mark. (2010). "Applying Inconsistent Mathematics." *The Best Writing on Mathematics: 2010*. Edited by Mircea Pitici. Princeton and Oxford: Princeton University Press.

Conway, John H. (1976). *On Numbers and Games*. London: Academic Press.

Cook, Roy T. (2007). "Aristotelian Logic, Axioms, and Abstraction." *The Arché Papers on the Mathematics of Abstraction*. Dordrecht, Netherlands: Springer. pp. 147–153.

Cooper, Charles Fisher. (16 July 2015). "Cantor's Diagonal Argument." Online source: <https://www.coopertoons.com/education/diagonal/diagonalargument.html>

Cooper, John M. (Editor). (1997). *Plato, Complete Works*. With D. S. Hutchinson (Associate Editor). Indianapolis/Cambridge: Hackett Publishing Company.

Costin, Rodica D. (2006). Lecture on set theory. Ohio State University. Online source: <https://people.math.osu.edu/costin.10/H161/supremum%20copy.pdf>

Cottingham, John; Stoothoff, Robert; Murdoch, Dugald (Translators). (1985). *The Philosophical Writings of Descartes: Volume I*. Cambridge, UK: Cambridge University Press.

Cox, T. J.; Loeb, Abraham. (May 2008). "The Collision Between the Milky Way and Andromeda." *Monthly Notices of the Royal Astronomical Society*. Vol. 386, Issue 1. pp. 461–474. See preprint at *arXiv*: <https://arxiv.org/abs/0705.1170>

Craig, William Lane. (1979a). *The Kalām Cosmological Argument*. New York: Harper & Row Publishers.

Craig, William Lane. (1979b). "The Existence of God and the Beginning of the Universe." (2017 excerpt from the book of the same title published by San Bernardino: Here's Life). Online source: <https://www.reasonablefaith.org/writings/scholarly-writings/the-existence-of-god/the-existence-of-god-and-the-beginning-of-the-universe>

Craig, William Lane. (13 January 2013). "Questions on God's Infinity, Inspiration, and Kant." *Reasonable Faith, with William Lane Craig*. Podcast. Online transcript: <https://www.reasonablefaith.org/media/reasonable-faith-podcast/questions-on-gods-infinity-inspiration-and-kant/#_ftn1>

Craig, William Lane; Moreland, J. P. (Editors). (2009). *The Blackwell Companion to Natural Theology*. Oxford: Wiley-Blackwell.

Craig, William Lane; Sinclair, James D. (2009). "The Kalam Cosmological Argument." Chapter in Craig and Moreland 2009, pp. 101–201.

Cramer, John G. (2016). *The Quantum Handshake: Entanglement, Nonlocality and Transactions*. New York: Springer.

Cusanus, Nicholas. (1440). *On Learned Ignorance (De Docta Ignorantia)*. Translated by Jasper Hopkins. (1985). Minneapolis, Minnesota: The Arthur J. Banning Press.

Cyr, Taylor W. (2020). "Atemporalism and Dependence." *International Journal for Philosophy of Religion*. Vol. 87, No. 2. pp. 149–164. Online source: <https://philpapers.org/rec/CYRAAD>

Daintith, John. (2014). *A Dictionary of Physics*. Sixth Edition. Oxford: Oxford University Press. Online source: <http://www.oxfordreference.com>

Dainton, Barry. (2010). *Time and Space*. Second Edition. Chicago: McGill-Queen's University Press.

Dantzig, Tobias. (1930). *Number: The Language of Science*. Edited by Joseph Mazur; Forward by Barry Mazur. (2005). New York: Pi Press.

Darvish, Behnam; et al. (20 November 2014). "Cosmic Web and Star Formation Activity in Galaxies at z ~ 1." *The Astrophysical Journal*. Vol. 796, No. 1, Entry 51 (13 pages). Online source:
<https://iopscience.iop.org/issue/0004-637X/796/1>

Dauben, Joseph Warren. (1979). *Georg Cantor: His Mathematics and Philosophy of the Infinite*. Cambridge, Massachusetts: Harvard University Press.

Davies, Paul. (Spring 2012). "That Mysterious Flow." *Scientific American Special Edition: A Matter of Time*. Vol. 21, No. 1. pp. 8–13. Online source:
<https://www.scientificamerican.com/article/time-s-passage-is-probably-an-illusion>

Davis, Tamara M.; Lineweaver, Charles H. (2004). "Expanding Confusion: Common Misconceptions of Cosmological Horizons and the Superluminal Expansion of the Universe." *Publications of the Astronomical Society of Australia*. Vol. 21, Issue 1. pp. 97–109. See preprint at *arXiv*:
<http://arxiv.org/abs/astro-ph/0310808v2>

Davis, Warren. (2019). Web Forum: PhysLink.com. Online source:
<https://www.physlink.com/education/askexperts/ae161.cfm>

Dawkins, Paul. (2018). "Section 2-6: Infinite Limits." *Paul's Online Notes*. Mathematics tutorial. Online source:
<https://tutorial.math.lamar.edu/classes/calci/infinitelimits.aspx>

Dawkins, Paul. (2019). "Section 4-3: Minimum And Maximum Values." *Paul's Online Notes*. Mathematics tutorial. Online source:
<https://tutorial.math.lamar.edu/classes/calci/minmaxvalues.aspx>

Dawkins, Paul. (2021). "Section 2-10: The Definition Of The Limit." *Paul's Online Notes*. Mathematics tutorial. Online source:
<https://tutorial.math.lamar.edu/classes/calci/DefnOfLimit.aspx>.

Dedekind, Richard. (1872). *Essays on the Theory of Numbers*. Translated by Wooster Woodruff Beman. (1991). Chicago: Open Court Publishing. Online source:
<https://www.gutenberg.org/files/21016/21016-pdf.pdf>

Deffner, Sebastian. (12 January 2018). "Quantum Speed Limit May Put Brakes on Quantum Computers." *The Conversation*. Online source:
<https://theconversation.com/quantum-speed-limit-may-put-brakes-on-quantum-computers-89353>

de Podesta, Michael. (13 April 2014). "Feynman Diagrams are Maths not Physics." *Protons for Breakfast*. Online source:
<protonsforbreakfast.wordpress.com>

Descartes, René. (1640). *Meditations on First Philosophy*. Translated by John Veitch. (1901). Online source:
<http://www.classicallibrary.org/descartes/meditations>

Descartes, René. (1642). Replies to critics of *Meditations*. Presented in Bennett 2017a.

Descartes, René. (1644). *Principles of Philosophy*:
- Part One in Cottingham, Stoothoff, and Murdoch 1985.
- Part Two in Bennet 2017b.

Descartes, René. (6 June 1647). Letter to Chanut in Ariew 2000, pp. 277–288.

de Swart, H. C. M. (Harrie). (2018). "Sets: Finite and Infinite." Chapter in *Philosophical and Mathematical Logic* by Harrie de Swart. Switzerland: Springer.

Devlin, Keith. March (2009). "What is Experimental Mathematics?" *Devlin's Angle*. Blog. Online source:
<https://www.maa.org/external_archive/devlin/devlin_03_09.html>

Dewey, John. (1902). *Leibniz's New Essays Concerning the Human Understanding: A Critical Exposition*. Scott, Foresman & Company. Online source:
<https://www.gutenberg.org/files/40957/40957-h/40957-h.htm#Page_48>

Dickens, Charles. (1858). *A Christmas Carol*. London: Bradbury & Evans.

Diener, Francine; Diener, Marc. (1995). *Nonstandard Analysis in Practice*. New York: Springer, Berlin, Heidelberg.

Dimitrova, Ilinka; Koppitz, Jörg; Lohapan, Laddawan. (23 December 2017). "Generating Sets of Semigroups of Partial Transformations Preserving a Zig-zag Order on $\mathbb{N}$." *International Journal of Pure and Applied Mathematics*. Vol. 117, No. 2. pp. 279–289.

Di Tucci, Alice; Lehners, Jean-Luc. (23 May 2019). "No-Boundary Proposal as a Path Integral with Robin Boundary Conditions." *Physical Review Letters*. Vol. 122, Issue 20. p. 201302 (6 pages). Online source: <https://journals.aps.org/prl/pdf/10.1103/PhysRevLett.122.201302>

Dirac, Paul A. M. (1958). *The Principles of Quantum Mechanics*. Fourth Edition. Oxford: Clarendon Press. (Reprinted in 2012 by Snowball Publishing).

Dodelson, Scott; Schmidt, Fabian. (2021). *Modern Cosmology*. Second Edition. London: Elsevier, Academic Press.

Donaldson, Neil; Pantano, Alessandra. (21 January 2020). *Math 13 – An Introduction to Abstract Mathematics*. California: University of California—Irvine. Online source: <https://www.math.uci.edu/~ndonalds/math13/notes.pdf>

Dowden, Bradley. (2019). "Zeno's Paradoxes." *The Internet Encyclopedia of Philosophy*. Online source: <https://iep.utm.edu/zeno-par>

Dowden, Bradley. (2020). "The Infinite." *The Internet Encyclopedia of Philosophy*. Online source: <https://iep.utm.edu/infinite>

Dowden, Bradley. (2021). "What Else Science Requires of Time." *The Internet Encyclopedia of Philosophy*. Online source: <https://iep.utm.edu/time-req>

Duhem, Pierre. (1985). *Medieval Cosmology: Theories of Infinity, Place, Time, Void, and the Plurality of Worlds*. Edited and Translated by Roger Ariew. Chicago and London: The University of Chicago Press.

Duke University Medical Center. (20 December 2007). "Monkeys Can Perform Mental Addition." *ScienceDaily*. Online source: <https://www.sciencedaily.com/releases/2007/12/071218101240.htm>

Dummett, Michael. (1991). *Frege: Philosophy of Mathematics*. Cambridge, Massachusetts: Harvard University Press.

Dummett, Michael. (October 2000). "Is Time a Continuum of Instants?" *Philosophy*. Vol. 75, No. 294. pp. 497–515.

Duns Scotus, John. (~1306). *A Treatise on God as First Principle*. Online source: <https://www.ewtn.com/catholicism/library/treatise-on-god-as-first-principle-10044>

Eberl, Matthias. (14 December 2017). "Finitistic Higher Order Logic." Presentation at Arbeitstagung Bern-München (ABM), Mathematics Institute, Ludwig-Maximilians-University (LMU). Slide 2 of 11. Online source: <http://www.math.lmu.de/~petrakis/Eberl.pdf>

Eberl, Matthias. (26–30 June 2019). "Indefinitely Extensible Models and a Relative Infinite." 12th Panhellenic Logic Symposium, Anogeia, Crete, Greece. Slide 4 of 14. Online source: <http://panhellenic-logic-symposium.org/slides/Day2_Eberl.pdf>

Eddington, Arthur S. (1929). *The Nature of the Physical World*. New York: The MacMillan Company; Cambridge: Cambridge University Press. p. 183.

Einstein, Albert. (1917). "Cosmological Considerations in the General Theory of Relativity." Meeting Reports of the Royal Prussian Academy of Sciences (Berlin). Translated by W. Perrett and G. B. Jeffery in H. A. Lorentz, et al. (1952) in *The Principle of Relativity*. New York: Dover. Available in *The Collected Papers of Albert Einstein. Volume 6: The Berlin Years: Writings, 1914–1917*. (English translation supplement). Doc. 43. Online source: <https://einsteinpapers.press.princeton.edu/vol6-trans/433>

Einstein, Albert. (1922; 1970 edition). *The Meaning of Relativity*. Princeton, New Jersey: Princeton University Press.

Einstein, Albert. (1954). *Ideas & Opinions*. Translated by Sonja Bargmann. Edited by Cal Seelig. (1982). New York: Three Rivers Press.

Epicurus. (270 BCE). *The Art of Happiness*. Translated with an Introduction and Commentary by George K. Strodach; Foreword by Daniel Klein. (2012). New York: Penguin Books.

Erickson, Peter F. (2006). *The Nature of Infinitesimals*. United States: Xlibris.

Euclid. (3rd Century BCE). *The Elements*. The Greek text of J. L. Heiberg (1883–1885), edited and translated by Richard Fitzpatrick. (2008). Republished as *Euclid's Elements of Geometry*. Online source: <http://farside.ph.utexas.edu/Books/Euclid/Elements.pdf>

Everett, Hugh. (1973). *The Many-Worlds Interpretation of Quantum Mechanics*. Thesis with papers by John A. Wheeler, Bryce S. DeWitt, Leon N. Cooper, Deborah Van Vechten, and Neill Graham. Edited by Bryce S. DeWitt and Neill Graham. Princeton, New Jersey: Princeton University Press. Online source: <http://ucispace.lib.uci.edu>

Ewald, William (Editor). (2005). *From Kant to Hilbert: A Sourcebook in the Foundations of Mathematics*. Volume II. Oxford: Clarendon Press.

Ewald, William; Sieg, Wilfried (Editors). 2013. *David Hilbert's Lectures on the Foundations of Arithmetic and Logic 1917–1933*. Heidelberg: Springer-Verlag. pp. 668–760.

Exapologist. (15 September 2006). "On the Possibility of a Beginningless Past: A Reply to William Lane Craig." Online source: <https://www.debunking-christianity.com/2006/09/on-possibility-of-beginningless-past.html>

Farias, Ruy H. A.; Recami, Erasmo. (2010). "Introduction of a Quantum of Time ('chronon') and its Consequences for Quantum Mechanics." Chapter in *Advances in Imaging and Electron Physics*. Vol. 163. pp. 33–115. Online source: <https://doi.org/10.1016/S1076-5670(10)63002-9>

Farlow, Jerry. (2008). *A Taste of Pure Mathematics*. Online source: <https://jerryandsusan.tripod.com/pure_math_book.htm>

Faulkner, William. (1957). *The Town*. Contained in the collection, *Snopes*. (2012). New York: The Modern Library.

Feferman, Solomon. (2009). "Conceptions of the Continuum." Transcript of lecture delivered for the Workshop on Philosophical Reflections on Set Theory, held at the Centre de Cultura Contemporània de Barcelona on 7 October 2008. Online source: <https://math.stanford.edu/~feferman/papers/ConceptContin.pdf>

Fenves, Peter. (2001). *Arresting Language from Leibniz to Benjamin*. Stanford, California: Stanford University Press.

Ferreira, Jailton C. (19 October 2001). "On the Set of Natural Numbers." *arXiv*. (6 pages). Online source: <https://arxiv.org/vc/math/papers/0104/0104173v4.pdf>

Ferreira, Jailton C. (14 February 2002). "Infinite and Natural Numbers." *arXiv*. (15 pages). Online source: <https://arxiv.org/abs/math/0202132>

Feynman, Richard. (11 December 1965). "The Development of the Space-Time View of Quantum Electrodynamics." Richard P. Feynman – Nobel Lecture at Stockholm, Sweden. Presented in *Nobel Lectures, Physics 1963–1970*. Amsterdam: Elsevier Publishing Company. (1972). Lecture located at NobelPrize.org. Nobel Media AB 2021. Online source: <https://www.nobelprize.org/prizes/physics/1965/feynman/lecture>

Feynman, Richard. (1985; 2006 edition). *QED: The Strange Theory of Light and Matter*. New Jersey: Princeton University Press.

Feynman, Richard; Hibbs, Albert R. (1965). *Quantum Mechanics and Path Integrals*. New York: McGraw-Hill.

Fleming, William. (1857). *Vocabulary of Philosophy: Psychological, Ethical, Metaphysical*. Fourth Edition. (1887). New York: Scribner & Welford.

Fletcher, Peter. (1998). *Truth, Proof and Infinity: A Theory of Constructions and Constructive Reasoning*. Dordrecht, Boston, and London: Kluwer Academic Publishers.

Fletcher, Peter. (December 2007). "Infinity." In *Philosophy of Logic*. Vol. 5 of the *Handbook of the Philosophy of Science*, edited by Dale Jacquette. Amsterdam: Elsevier. pp. 523–585.

Fraenkel, Abraham. (1961). *Abstract Set Theory*. Second Revised Edition. Amsterdam: North-Holland Publishing Co.

Frege, Gottlob. (1893/1903). *Basic Laws of Arithmetic*. Translated and Edited by Philip A. Ebert and Marcus Rossberg. (2013). Oxford: Oxford University Press.

Freiberger, Marianne; Thomas, Rachel. (22 July 2013). "The Problem With Infinity." *Plus Magazine*. University of Cambridge. Online article: <https://plus.maths.org/content/problem-infinity>

Freiberger, Marianne; Thomas, Rachel. (26 September 2013). "Do Infinities Exist in Nature?" *Plus Magazine* University of Cambridge. Online article: <https://plus.maths.org/content/do-infinities-exist-nature-0>

Gabrielse, Gerald and David Hanneke. (4 October 2006). "Precision Pins Down The Electron's Magnetism." *CERN Courier*. Online source:
<https://cerncourier.com>

Galileo Galilei. (1638). *Dialogues Concerning Two New Sciences*. Translation by H. Crew and A. De Salvio. (1914). New York: The MacMillan Company.

Gamow, George. (1947; 1988 edition). *One, Two, Three—Infinity: Facts and Speculations of Science*. New York: Courier Dover Publications.

Gardner, Martin. (1999). *The Whys of a Philosophical Scrivener*. Second Edition. New York: St. Martin's Griffin.

Gardner, Martin. (2008). *The Jinn From Hyperspace*. Amherst, New York: Prometheus Books.

Gefter, Amanda. (2017). "The Infinity Illusion." *New Scientist: The Collection – Infinity and Beyond: Your Ultimate Guide to Mathematics*. Vol. 4, Issue 4. pp. 44–47.

Geljon, Albert-Kees. (May 2005). "Divine Infinity in Gregory of Nyssa and Philo of Alexandria." Vigiliae Christianae. Vol. 59, No. 2. pp. 152–177.

Gellman, Jerome. (Summer 2019). "Mysticism." *The Stanford Encyclopedia of Philosophy*. Edited by Edward N. Zalta. Online source:
<https://plato.stanford.edu/entries/mysticism>

Giblin, P. J. (2011). "What is Pure Mathematics?" University of Liverpool. Online source:
<http://www.liv.ac.uk/maths/PURE/wipm.html>

Gleiser, Marcelo. (2014). *The Island of Knowledge: The Limits of Science and the Search for Meaning*. New York: Basic Books.

Göcke, Benedikt Paul. (2016). "The Paraconsistent God." Chapter in Schärtl, Tapp, and Wegener 2016, pp. 177–199.

Göcke, Benedikt Paul; Tapp, Christian (Editors). (2018). *The Infinity of God: New Perspectives in Theology and Philosophy*. Notre Dame, Indiana: University of Notre Dame Press.

Gödel, Kurt. (November 1947). "What is Cantor's Continuum Problem?" *The American Mathematical Monthly*. Vol. 54, No. 9. pp. 515–525. Online source:
<https://www.jstor.org/stable/2304666>

Goff, Philip. (2017). *Consciousness and Fundamental Reality*. New York: Oxford University Press.

Gohd, Chelsea. (7 January 2021). "Astronomers Reevaluate the Age of the Universe." *SPACE.com*. Online source:
<https://www.space.com/universe-age-14-billion-years-old>

Goriely, Alain. (2018). *Applied Mathematics: A Very Short Introduction*. Oxford: Oxford University Press.

Goze, Michel. (1995). "Infinitesimal Algebra and Geometry." Chapter in Diener and Diener 1995, pp. 91–108.

Gray, Robert. (1994). "Georg Cantor and Transcendental Numbers." *American Mathematical Monthly*. Vol. 101. pp. 819–832.

Greene, Brian. (2000). *The Elegant Universe: Superstrings, Hidden Dimensions, and the Quest for the Ultimate Theory*. New York: Vintage Books.

Greene, Brian. (2011). *The Hidden Reality: Parallel Universes and the Deep Laws of the Cosmos*. New York: Vintage Books.

Greene, Brian. (2020). *Until the End of Time: Matter, Mind, and Our Search for Meaning in an Evolving Universe*. New York: Alfred A. Knopf.

Gregory of Nyssa. (378 CE). *On "Not Three Gods."* In Schaff and Wace 1893 (2005 edition). Online source:
<https://ccel.org/ccel/schaff/npnf205/npnf205/Page_331.html>

Gregory of Nyssa. (379 CE). *On the Soul and Resurrection*. In Schaff and Wace 1893 (2005 edition). Online source:
<https://ccel.org/ccel/schaff/npnf205/npnf205/Page_428.html>

Gregory of Nyssa. (383 CE). *Against Eunomius*. In Schaff and Wace 1893 (2005 edition). Online source:
<https://ccel.org/ccel/schaff/npnf205/Page_33.html>

Gregory of Nyssa. (383 CE). *Against Eunomius*. Edited by Kevin Knight. (2020). In *New Advent*. Revised from Schaff and Wace 1893 (2005 edition). Online source:
<http://www.newadvent.org/fathers/2901.htm>

Gregory of Nyssa. (384 CE). *Answer to Eunomius' Second Book*. In Schaff and Wace 1893 (2005 edition). Online source:
<https://ccel.org/ccel/schaff/npnf205/Page_250.html>

Gregory of Nyssa. (393 CE). *The Life of Moses* (also known as *De Vita Moysis*). Translated by Abraham J. Malherbe and Everett Ferguson. (1978). New York: Paulist Press.

Greiner, Walter. (2001). *Quantum Mechanics: Special Chapters*. With a Foreword by D. A. Bromley. Berlin, Heidelberg, New York: Springer-Verlag.

Grim, Gretchen. (8 May 2012). "An Introduction to Surreal Numbers." Online source:
<https://www.whitman.edu/Documents/Academics/Mathematics/Grimm.pdf>

Grosseteste, Robert. (1225). *On Light* (*De luce*). Translated by Claire C. Riedl. (1942). Milwaukee, WI: Marquette University Press. Online source:
<https://inters.org/grosseteste-on-light>

Grossman, Christina. (2010). "Comparing Infinite Sets." Thesis presented to the Department of Mathematics, University of Arizona. Online source:
<http://math.arizona.edu/~ime/ATI/Math%20Projects/C1_MathFinal_Grossman.pdf>

Gudder, Stanley P. (5 April 2017). "Discrete Spacetime Quantum Field Theory." *arXiv*. (27 pages). Online source:
<https://arxiv.org/abs/1704.01639>

Gullberg, Jan. (1997). *Mathematics: From the Birth of Numbers*. New York: W. W. Norton & Company.

Guth, Alan. (15 January 1981). "Inflationary Universe: A Possible Solution to the Horizon and Flatness Problems." Physical Review D. Vol. 23, Issue 2. pp. 347–356. Online source:
<https://journals.aps.org/prd/pdf/10.1103/PhysRevD.23.347>

Guth, Alan. (1997). "Was Cosmic Inflation the 'Bang' of the Big Bang?" *The Beam Line*. Vol. 27, No. 3. pp. 14–21. Stanford Linear Accelerator Center. Online sources:
  • <https://www.slac.stanford.edu/pubs/beamline/27/3/27-3-guth.pdf>
  • <https://ned.ipac.caltech.edu/level5/Guth/Guth_contents.html>

Guyer, Paul. (2018). "The Infinite Given Magnitude and Other Myths About Space and Time." Chapter in Nachtomy and Winegar 2018, pp. 181–204.

Gwiazda, Jeremy. (2009). "Richard Swinburne's Arguments to the Simplicity of God via the Infinite." *Religious Studies*. Vol. 45. pp. 487–493.

Hallett, Michael. (1996). *Cantorian Set Theory and Limitation of Size*. Oxford: Clarendon Press.

Hands, John. (2016). *Cosmosapiens: Human Evolution from the Origin of the Universe*. New York and London: Overlook Duckworth, Peter Mayer Publishers, Inc.

Hardegree, Gary. (2002). "Infinite Sets and Infinite Sizes." Online source:
<http://people.umass.edu/gmhwww/382/pdf/09-infinite%20sizes.pdf>

Haroche, Serge. (July 1998). "Entanglement, Decoherence and the Quantum/Classical Boundary." *Physics Today*. Vol. 51, Issue 7. pp. 36–42.

Hawking, Stephen. (1988). *A Brief History of Time*. New York: Bantam Books.

Hawking, Stephen. (1996). "The Beginning of Time." Lecture. Online source:
<http://www.hawking.org.uk/the-beginning-of-time.html>

Hawking, Stephen; Hertog, Thomas. (27 April 2018). "A Smooth Exit from Eternal Inflation?" *Journal of High Energy Physics*. Vol. 147 (13 pages). Online source:
<https://link.springer.com/content/pdf/10.1007/JHEP04(2018)147.pdf>

Heller, Michael; Woodin, W. Hugh (Editors). (2011). *Infinity: New Research Frontiers*. New York: Cambridge University Press.

Henle, James M.; Kleinberg, Eugene M. (2003). *Infinitesimal Calculus*. Dover Publications.

Herbert, Nick. (1987). *Quantum Reality: Beyond the New Physics*. New York: Anchor Books.

Hick, John. (2010). "God and Christianity According to Swinburne." *European Journal for Philosophy of Religion*. Vol. 1. pp. 25–37.

Hilbert, David. (January 1925). Lecture. Göttingen, Germany. Presented in in Ewald and Sieg 2013.

Hilbert, David. (4 June 1925). "On the Infinite." Address delivered to Westphalian Mathematical Society in Münster. Presented in Benacerraf, Paul; Putnam, Hilary (Editors). (1983). *Philosophy of Mathematics: Selected Readings*. Cambridge and New York: Cambridge University Press.

Hill, Gerald; Hill, Kathleen. (2002). *The People's Law Dictionary*. New York: Fine Communications. Online source: <http://dictionary.law.com>

Hintikka, Jaako. (1973). *Time & Necessity: Studies in Aristotle's Theory of Modality*. Oxford: Clarendon Press.

Hobson, Art. (2013). "There Are No Particles, There Are Only Fields." *American Journal of Physics*. Vol. 81, No. 3. pp. 211–223.

Hofstadter, Douglas; Sander, Emmanuel. (2013). *Surfaces and Essences: Analogy as the Fuel and Fire of Thinking*. New York: Basic Books.

Holden, Thomas. (April 2002). "Infinite Divisibility and Actual Parts in Hume's Treatise." *Hume Studies*. Vol. XXVIII, No. 1. pp. 3–26. Online source:
<https://www.humesociety.org/hs>

Holmes, M. Randall; Forster, Thomas; Libert, Thierry. (2012). "Alternative Set Theories." Chapter in *Handbook of the History of Logic, Volume 6: Sets and Extensions in the Twentieth Century*. Edited by Dov M. Gabbay, Akihiro Kanamori, and John Woods. (2012). New York, Oxford: Elsevier. pp. 559–632. Online source:
<https://www.sciencedirect.com/handbook/handbook-of-the-history-of-logic/vol/6/suppl/C>

Holt, Jim. (2012). *Why Does The World Exist? : An Existential Detective Story*. New York: Liveright Publishing Corporation, W. W. Norton & Company.

Holzer, Steven. (2006). *Physics for Dummies*. Indianapolis, Indiana: Wiley Publishing, Inc.

Horsten, Leon. (Winter 2016). "Philosophy of Mathematics." *Stanford Encyclopedia of Philosophy*. Edited by Edward N. Zalta. Stanford University. Online source:
<https://plato.stanford.edu/entries/philosophy-mathematics>

Hossenfelder, Sabine. (10 August 2015). *Back Reaction*. Blog. Online source:
<http://backreaction.blogspot.com/2015/08/dear-dr-bee-why-do-some-people-assume.html>

Hossenfelder, Sabine. (2018). *Lost in Math: How Beauty Leads Physics Astray*. New York: Basic Books.

Hossenfelder, Sabine. (15 May 2020). "Understanding Quantum Mechanics #2: Superposition and Entanglement." Video. Online source:
<https://www.youtube.com/watch?v=j6Mw3_tOcNI>

Hrbáček, Karel; Jech, Thomas. (1999). *Introduction to Set Theory*. Third Edition. New York: Marcel Dekker, Inc.

Huemer, Michael. (2016). *Approaching Infinity*. New York: Palgrave Macmillan.

Hume, David. (1739). *A Treatise of Human Nature*. Edited by L. A. Selby-Bigge. (1888 edition digitized 10 June 2009). Oxford: Clarendon Press.

Hylwa, Samuel. (7 June 2013). "Robert Grosseteste and the History of the Actual Infinite." Presentation at Montana State University International Undergraduate Philosophy Conference. Montana: Montana State University, Bozeman. Online source:
<https://scholarworks.montana.edu/xmlui/bitstream/handle/1/2866/SamHylwa.pdf?sequence=4>

Ijjas, Anna; Steinhardt, Paul J.; Loeb, Abraham. (February 2017). "POP Goes the Universe." *Scientific American*. Vol. 316, Issue 2. pp. 32–39. Online source:
<https://physics.princeton.edu/~cosmo/sciam/assets/pdfs/SciAm.pdf>

Isaacs, Alan (Editor). (1990). *A Concise Dictionary of Physics*. Oxford and New York: Oxford University Press.

Isaacson, Daniel. (2011). "The Reality of Mathematics and The Case of Set Theory." Chapter in *Truth, Reference and Realism*. Edited by Zsolt Novák and András Simonyi. (2011). Budapest: Central European University Press. pp. 1–76.

IUPAC (International Union of Pure and Applied Chemistry). (1997). *Compendium of Chemical Terminology*. Second Edition (the "Gold Book"). Compiled by A. D. McNaught and A. Wilkinson. Oxford: Blackwell Scientific Publications. Online version (2019–) created by S. J. Chalk. Online source:
<https://doi.org/10.1351/goldbook>

Jacquette, Dale. (2001). *David Hume's Critique of Infinity*. Leiden, Boston, Köln: Brill.

James, William. (1917). *The Varieties of Religious Experience: A Study in Human Nature*. New York and London: Longmans, Green, & Company. Online source:
<https://www.gutenberg.org/files/621/621-h/621-h.html#toc23>

Jannotta, Anthony. (2010). "Plato's Theory of Forms: Analogy and Metaphor in Plato's Republic." *Undergraduate Review*. Vol. 6, Article 28. pp. 154–157. Online source:
<https://vc.bridgew.edu/undergrad_rev/vol6/iss1/28>

Jefferson, Thomas. (1820). *The Life and Morals of Jesus of Nazareth*. First officially published in 1904 by the US Government Printing Office. Published in 2012 as *The Jefferson Bible: The Life and Morals of Jesus of Nazareth*. New York: Dover Publications, Inc.

Johnson-Groh, Mara. (30 May 2019). "Three Ways to Travel at (Nearly) the Speed of Light." NASA. Online source:
<https://www.nasa.gov/feature/goddard/2019/three-ways-to-travel-at-nearly-the-speed-of-light>

Johnson, P. O. (July 1992). "Wholes, Parts, and Infinite Collections." *Philosophy*. Vol. 67, No. 261. pp. 367–379.

Johnson, P. O. (July 1994). "More About Infinite Numbers." *Philosophy*. Vol. 69, No. 269. pp. 369–370.

Joseph, George Gheverghese. (2011). *The Crest of the Peacock: Non-European Roots of Mathematics*. Third Edition. Princeton & Oxford: Princeton University Press.

Jourdain, Philip E. B. (January 1910). "Transfinite Numbers and the Principles of Mathematics. Part I." *The Monist*. Vol. 20, No. 1. pp. 93–118. Online source:
<https://www.jstor.org/stable/27900235>

Just, Winfried; Weese, Martin. (1996). *Discovering Modern Set Theory, Part 1: The Basics. Graduate Studies in Mathematics*. Vol. 8. Providence, RI: American Mathematical Society.

Kaiser, David. (March-April 2005). "Physics and Feynman's Diagrams." *American Scientist*. Vol. 93, No. 2. pp. 156–165. Online source:
<http://web.mit.edu/dikaiser/www/FdsAmSci.pdf>

Kalvesmaki, Joel. (2013). *The Theology of Arithmetic: Number Symbolism in Platonism and Early Christianity*. Hellenic Studies Series 59. Washington, DC: Center for Hellenic Studies. Online source:
<https://chs.harvard.edu/CHS/article/display/6300>

Kane, Gordon. (9 October 2006). "Are virtual particles really constantly popping in and out of existence? Or are they merely a mathematical bookkeeping device for quantum mechanics?" *Scientific American*. Online source:
<https://www.scientificamerican.com/article/are-virtual-particles-rea>

Kant, Immanuel. (1781). *Critique of Pure Reason*. Translated by J. M. D Meiklejohn. (1990 edition). Amherst, New York: Prometheus Books.

Kant, Immanuel. (1781/1787). *Critique of Pure Reason*. Translated and edited by Paul Guyer and Allen W. Wood. (1998). Cambridge, United Kingdom: Cambridge University Press.

Kaplan, Robert. (2000). *The Nothing That Is: A Natural History of Zero*. Oxford and New York: Oxford University Press.

Katz, Mikhail G.; Tall, David. (25 October 2011). "The Tension Between Intuitive Infinitesimals and Formal Mathematical Analysis." *arXiv*. (19 pages). Online source:
<https://arxiv.org/ftp/arxiv/papers/1110/1110.5747.pdf>

Kaye, Sharon. (2019). "William of Ockham (Occam, c. 1280—c. 1349)." *The Internet Encyclopedia of Philosophy*. Online source:
<https://www.iep.utm.edu/ockham/#SH8b>

Kazuhiko Minami. (5 October 2017). "Infinite number of solvable generalizations of XY-chain, with cluster state, and with central charge $c = m/2$." *arXiv*. (23 pages). Online source:
<https://arxiv.org/pdf/1710.01851.pdf>

Keele, Lisa. (2008). *Theories of Continuity and Infinitesimals: Four Philosophers of the Nineteenth Century*. ProQuest LLC, Michigan.

Keisler, H. Jerome. (1976). *Foundations of Infinitesimal Calculus*. Boston: Prindle, Weber & Schmidt, Inc.

Khusraw, Nasir-i. (~1060 CE). "The First Chapter, On the Recognition of the Oneness of God." Chapter in *Six Chapters* (a.k.a. *The Book of Enlightenment* or *Shish Fasl* or *Rawshana-i-nama*) by Nasir-i Khusraw. (~1060 CE). Translated by W. Ivanow. (1949). Holland: E. J. Brill. Online source:
<http://www.ismaili.net/Source/khusraw/nk3/2.html>

Kleitman, Daniel. (2021). *Calculus for Beginners and Artists*. Online source:
<http://www-math.mit.edu/~djk/calculus_beginners/chapter08/section02.html>

Kneebone, G. T. (1963; 2001 edition). *Mathematical Logic and the Foundations of Mathematics: An Introductory Survey*. New York: Courier Dover Publications.

Knight, Robin W. (2 October 2018a). "The Transfinite Ordinals." Lecture. University of Oxford. Lecture Notes. Online source:
<https://people.maths.ox.ac.uk/knight/lectures/ordinals.pdf>

Knight, Robin W. (2 October 2018b). "The Language of Set Theory." Lecture. University of Oxford. Lecture Notes. Online source:
<https://people.maths.ox.ac.uk/knight/lectures/lst.pdf>

Knobloch, E. (1999). "Galileo and Leibniz: Different Approaches to Infinity." *Archive for the History of the Exact Sciences*. Vol. 54. pp. 87–99.

Koks, Don; Gibbs, Philip; Carr, Jim. (2012). "What is Relativistic Mass?" Usenet Physics FAQ. Mathematics Department, University of California, Riverside. Online source:
<https://math.ucr.edu/home/baez/physics/Relativity/SR/mass.html>

Kornell, Andre. (3 December 2018). "A Complete System of Deduction for Σ Formulas." *arXiv*. (19 pages). Online source:
<https://arxiv.org/pdf/1807.01494.pdf>

Kozlowski, Miroslaw; Marciak-Kozlowska, Janina. (November 2008). "Dark Energy as the Source of the Time Dependent Einstein Cosmological Constant." *arXiv*. (25 pages). Online source:
<https://arxiv.org/abs/0812.0108>

Kragh, Helge. (1 December 2000). "Max Planck: The Reluctant Revolutionary." *Physics World*. Online source:
<https://physicsworld.com/a/max-planck-the-reluctant-revolutionary>

Kragh, Helge. (April 2013). "Big Bang: The Etymology of a Name". *Astronomy & Geophysics*. Vol. 54, No. 2: pp. 2.28–2.30. Online source:
<https://academic.oup.com/astrogeo/article/54/2/2.28/302975>

Kragh, Helge. (27 March 2014). "The True (?) Story of Hilbert's Infinite Hotel." *arXiv*. (16 pages). Online source:
<https://arxiv.org/abs/1403.0059>

Kreyszig, Erwin. (1989). *Introductory Functional Analysis with Applications*. New York: John Wiley & Sons.

Kuhn, Robert Lawrence. (23 December 2015). "Confronting the Multiverse: What 'Infinite Universes' Would Mean." Expert Voices. Op-Ed. Online source:
<https://www.space.com/31465-is-our-universe-just-one-of-many-in-a-multiverse.html>

Kuhn, Robert Lawrence. (2020). "Interview with Eric Steinhart: Does God's Infinity Make Sense?" *Closer to Truth with Robert Lawrence Kuhn*. Television Show. The Kuhn Foundation and Getzels Gordon Productions. Online source:
<https://www.closertotruth.com/series/does-gods-infinity-make-sense>

Kuhn, Robert Lawrence. (2020). "Interview with Richard Swinburne: Does God's Infinity Make Sense?" *Closer to Truth with Robert Lawrence Kuhn*. Television Show. The Kuhn Foundation and Getzels Gordon Productions. Online source:
<https://www.closertotruth.com/series/does-gods-infinity-make-sense>

Kushner, Harold S. (1981; 2001 edition). *When Bad Things Happen to Good People*. New York: Schocken Books.

Lakoff, George; Johnson, Mark. (2008). *Metaphors We Live By*. Chicago: University of Chicago Press.

Lancaster, Tom; Blundell, Stephen J. (2014). *Quantum Field Theory for the Gifted Amateur*. Oxford: Oxford University Press.

Lang, Serge. (1993). *Real and Functional Analysis*. Third Edition. New York: Springer.

Lavine, Shaughan. (1994). *Understanding the Infinite*. Cambridge, Massachusetts: Harvard University Press.

Lavine, Shaughan. (June 1995). "Finite Mathematics." *Synthese*. Vol. 103, No. 3. Netherlands: Kluwer Academic Publishers. pp. 389–420.

Leibniz, Gottfried Wilhelm. (1 September 1706). Draft letter to Father Bartholomew Des Bosses. In Arthur 2018.

Leibniz, Gottfried Wilhelm. (16 March 1693). Letter to Simon Foucher. Cited in the German Academy of Sciences at Berlin (Editor). *Sämtliche Schriften und Briefe (All Writings and Letters)*. Series II. Vol. 2. Online source:
<http://www.leibniz-translations.com/foucher.htm>

Leitzell, Katherine. (6 November 2016). "An Infinite Number of Futures." *Options Magazine*. Online source: <http://www.iiasa.ac.at/web/home/resources/publications/options/w16_infinite_futures.html>

Lents, Nathan H. (2018). "The Inevitability of Intelligent Life?" *Skeptic*. Vol. 23, No. 4. pp. 57–59.

Lev, Felix M. (19 Feb 2017). "Why Finite Mathematics is the Most Fundamental and Ultimate Quantum Theory Will Be Based on Finite Mathematics." *arXiv*. (10 pages). Online source: <https://arxiv.org/pdf/1409.2777.pdf>

Lévi, Robert. (1927). "Theory of Universal and Discontinuous Action." ("Théorie de l'action Universelle et Discontinue"). *Journal of Physics and Radium (Journal de Physique et le Radium)*. Vol. 8, No. 4: pp. 182–198.

Levy, Silvio. (1995). *Making Waves: A Guide to the Ideas behind Outside In*. Wellesley, Massachusetts: A. K. Peters, Ltd.

Levy, Silvio; Maxwell, Delle; Munzner, Tamara (Directors). (1994). "Outside In." Film. University of Minnesota—The Geometry Center. Online sources:
- Part I: <https://www.youtube.com/watch?v=BVVfs4zKrgk>
- Part II: <https://www.youtube.com/watch?v=x7d13SgqUXg>

Liddell, Henry George; Scott, Robert. (1940). *A Greek-English Lexicon*. Revised and augmented throughout by Sir Henry Stuart Jones with the assistance of Roderick McKenzie. Oxford. Clarendon Press. Online source: <https://www.perseus.tufts.edu/hopper/text?doc=Perseus:text:1999.04.0057:entry=a)/peiros2>

Li Guo, Sylvie Paycha; Zhang, Bin. (2 January 2015). "Counting An Infinite Number of Points: A Testing Ground For Renormalization Methods." *arXiv*. (32 pages). Online source: <https://arxiv.org/pdf/1501.00429.pdf>

Lincoln, Don. (15 February 2013). "What's the Point?" *Fermilab Today*. Online source: <https://www.fnal.gov/pub/today/archive/archive_2013/today13-02-15_NutshellReadMore.html>

Linde, Andre D. (1986). "Eternal Chaotic Inflation." *Modern Physics Letters A*. Vol. 1, No. 2. pp. 81–85. Online source: <https://doi.org/10.1142/S0217732386000129>

Linde, Andre D.; Vanchurin, Vitaly. (20 April 2010). "How Many Universes are in the Multiverse?" *Physical Review D – Particles, Fields, Gravitation and Cosmology*. Vol. 81, Issue 8. Article Number 083525. See preprint at *arXiv*: <https://arxiv.org/pdf/0910.1589.pdf>

Linnebo, Øystein. (18 January 2018). "Platonism in the Philosophy of Mathematics." *Stanford Encyclopedia of Philosophy*. Online source: <https://plato.stanford.edu/entries/platonism-mathematics>

Linnebo, Øystein; Shapiro, Stewart. (2019). "Actual and Potential Infinity." Noûs. Vol. 53. pp. 160–191. Online source: <https://onlinelibrary.wiley.com/doi/full/10.1111/nous.12208>

Linsky, Bernard; Zalta, Edward N. (2006). "What is Neologicism?" *The Bulletin of Symbolic Logic*. Vol. 12, No. 1. pp. 60–99.

Livio, Mario. (2009). *Is God a Mathematician?* New York: Simon & Schuster.

Lower, Stephen. (4 August 2017). "Energy, Heat, and Temperature…An Introduction: How Do They Differ?" *Chem1 Virtual Textbook*. Department of Chemistry. Simon Fraser University. Online source: <http://www.chem1.com/acad/webtext/pre/pre-3.html>

Lucretius. (54 BCE). *On the Nature of Things*. Translated by Frank O. Copley. (2011). New York: W. W. Norton & Company.

Lumen. (2019). "Infinite Sequences and Series." *Boundless Calculus*. Online source: <https://courses.lumenlearning.com/boundless-calculus/chapter/infinite-sequences-and-series>

MacDonald, Cynthia. (2005). *Varieties of Things: Foundations of Contemporary Metaphysics*. Malden, MA and Oxford: Blackwell Publishing.

Machover, Moshé. (1996). *Set Theory, Logic and their Limitations*. New York: Cambridge University Press.

Mack, Katie. (2020). *The End of Everything (Astrophysically Speaking)*. New York: Scribner.

Mackie, J. L. (1982). *The Miracle of Theism: Arguments For and Against the Existence of God*. Oxford: Clarendon Press.

Maddocks, J. R. (2010). "One-to-One Correspondence." Online source: <https://science.jrank.org/pages/4861/One-One-Correspondence.html>

Mann, Adam. (13 July 2020). "The Universe's Clock Might Have Bigger Ticks Than We Imagine." *Live Science*. Online
    source:
    <https://www.livescience.com/what-are-smallest-ticks-of-time.html>
Manuel, Thomas. (16 August 2018). "Madhava and the Uninfluential Discovery of Calculus." *The Wire*. Online source:
    <https://thewire.in/the-sciences/madhava-and-the-uninfluential-discovery-of-calculus>
Margenau, Henry. (1950). *The Nature of Physical Reality*. New York: McGraw-Hill.
Mark, Joshua L. (6 March 2011). "The Atrahasis Epic: The Great Flood & the Meaning of Suffering." *World History
    Encyclopedia*. Online source:
    <https://www.worldhistory.org/article/227/the-atrahasis-epic-the-great-flood--the-meaning-of>
Masters, Karen. (2019). "If the Universe is Infinite Does that Mean There is an Infinite Number of 'Me's?" *Ask An
    Astronomer*. Online source:
    <http://curious.astro.cornell.edu>
mathcentre. (2009). "The Sum of An Infinite Series." Online source:
    <https://www.mathcentre.ac.uk/resources/uploaded/mc-ty-convergence-2009-1.pdf>
Mauro, Murzi. (October 2019). "Jules Henri Poincaré." *The Internet Encyclopedia of Philosophy*. Online source:
    <https://www.iep.utm.edu/poincare/#H3>
McAllister, Blake. (2011). "The Universe Began to Exist? Craig's Philosophical Arguments for a Finite Past." *Stance*.
    Vol. 4. pp. 103–114. Online source:
    <http://www.bsu.edu/libraries/beneficencepress/stance/2011_spring/The%20universe%20began.pdf>
McGough, Nancy. (June 2020). "The Continuum Hypothesis." *Infinite Ink*. Online source:
    <https://www.ii.com/math/ch>
McKee, Maggie. (14 May 2013). "First Proof that Infinitely Many Prime Numbers Come in Pairs." *Nature*. Online source:
    <http://www.nature.com/news/first-proof-that-infinitely-many-prime-numbers-come-in-pairs-1.12989>
McMullen, Chris. (2008). *The Visual Guide to Extra Dimensions. Volume 1: Visualizing the Fourth Dimension, Higher-
    Dimensional Polytopes, and Curved Hypersurfaces*. Custom Books.
Mentzeniotis, Dionysis; Stamatellos, Giannis. (June 2008). "The Notion of Infinity in Plotinus and Cantor." Chapter in
    Platonism and Forms of Intelligence. Edited by John Dillon and Marie-Elise Zovko. (2008). Berlin, Germany: De Gruyter.
    pp. 213–229. Online source:
    <https://www.researchgate.net/publication/325721938>
Merriam-Webster (Editors). (2021). "Yes, 'Enormity' Can Mean 'Enormousness'." *Merriam-Webster.com*: Words At
    Play. Online source:
    <https://www.merriam-webster.com/words-at-play/on-the-definition-of-enormity>
Meschkowski, Herbert; Nilson, Winfried (Editors). (1991). *Georg Cantor: Briefe*. (i.e., *Georg Cantor: Letters*). Berlin:
    Springer-Verlag.
Miller, Casey; Swift, Kate. (1988). *The Handbook of Nonsexist Writing: For Writers, Editors and Speakers*. Second
    Edition. New York: Harper & Row.
Minecan, Ana María C. (Spring 2016). "The Problem of Contraries and Prime Matter in the Reception of Aristotle's
    Physical Corpus in the Work of Thomas Aquinas." *SVMMA*. No. 7, pp. 184–203.
Moore, A. W. (1997). "Taming the Infinite." *Foundations of Science*. Vol. 2. Issue 1. pp. 53–56.
Moore, A. W. (2019). *The Infinite*. Third Edition. London and New York: Routledge.
Moreland, J. P. (1993). "Yes! A Defense of Christianity." Chapter in *Does God Exist? The Debate between Theists and
    Atheists*. Edited by J. P. Moreland and Kai Nielsen. (1993). New York: Prometheus Books.
Morriston, Wes. (Spring-Summer 1999). "Must the Past Have a Beginning?" *Philo*. Vol. 2, No. 1. pp. 5–19.
Morriston, Wes. (July 2003). "Must Metaphysical Time Have a Beginning?" *Faith and Philosophy*. Vol. 20, No. 3.
    pp. 288–306.
Morriston, Wes. (October 2010). "Beginningless Past, Endless Future, and the Actual Infinite." *Faith and Philosophy*.
    Vol. 27, No. 4. pp. 439–450.
Morrow, Ashley (Editor). (3 March 2016). "Hubble Team Breaks Cosmic Distance Record." NASA. Online source:
    <https://www.nasa.gov/feature/goddard/2016/hubble-team-breaks-cosmic-distance-record>

Moskowitz, Clara. (24 November 2010). "Einstein's 'Biggest Blunder' Turns Out to Be Right." *SPACE.com*. Online source:

<https://www.space.com/9593-einstein-biggest-blunder-turns.html>

Mostowski, Marcin. (2007). "Potential Infinity and the Church Thesis." *Fundamenta Informaticae*. Vol. 81, No. 1-3. pp. 241–248.

Mostowski, Marcin. (8 May 2012). "Mathematics Without Actual Infinity." Online source: <http://www.frontiersinai.com/turingfiles/May/mostowski.pdf>

Mostowski, Marcin. (2016). "Truth in the Limit." *Reports on Mathematical Logic*. Vol. 51. pp. 75–89.

Mueckenheim, Wolfgang. (11 December 2006). "Physical Constraints of Numbers." *arXiv*. (8 pages). Online source: <https://arxiv.org/abs/math/0505649>

Mullings, R. T. 2017. "Review of Rethinking the Concept of a Personal God: Personal Theism, and Alternative Concepts of God Edited by Schärtl and Wegener." *Journal of Biblical and Theological Studies*. (26 December 2017). Online source:

<https://jbtsonline.org/review-of-rethinking-the-concept-of-a-personal-god-personal-theism-and-alternative-concepts-of-god-edited-by-schartl-and-wegener>

Mumford, David. (December 2008). "Why I am a Platonist." *EMS Newsletter*. Issue 70. European Mathematical Society. pp. 27–30. Online source:

<https://www.ems-ph.org/journals/newsletter/pdf/2008-12-70.pdf>

Mycielski, Jan. (September 1981). "Analysis Without Actual Infinity." *The Journal of Symbolic Logic*. Vol. 46, No. 3. pp. 625–633.

Nachtomy, Ohad. (2018). "Leibniz's Early Encounters with Descartes, Galileo, and Spinoza on Infinity." Chapter in Nachtomy and Winegar 2018, pp. 131–154.

Nachtomy, Ohad; Winegar, Reed (Editors). (2018). *Infinity in Early Modern Philosophy*. The New Synthese Historical Library. (Texts and Studies in the History of Philosophy: Volume 76). Switzerland: Springer.

Nagel, Thomas. (October 1974). "What Is It Like to Be a Bat?" *The Philosophical Review*. Vol. 83, No. 4. pp. 435–450.

NASA (National Aeronautics and Space Administration). (31 May 2012). "NASA's Hubble Shows Milky Way is Destined for Head-On Collision." Edited by Robert Garner. Online source:

<https://www.nasa.gov/mission_pages/hubble/science/milky-way-collide.html>

Nave, Carl R. (2016). "Free Particle Waves." *HyperPhysics*. Georgia State University. Online source: <http://hyperphysics.phy-astr.gsu.edu/hbase/quantum/Scheq.html#c1>

Nave, Carl R. (2016). "Wavefunction." *HyperPhysics*. Georgia State University. Online source: <http://hyperphysics.phy-astr.gsu.edu/hbase/hframe.html>

Netz, Reviel. (2009). *The Archimedes Palimpsest*. Stanford University. Online source: <http://archimedespalimpsest.org/about/scholarship/method-infinity.php>

Newton, Isaac. (1736). *The Method of Fluxions and Infinite Series*. (London: Henry Woodfall). Online source. <https://archive.org/details/methodoffluxions00newt/page/278/mode/2up?q=infinite>

Nietzsche, Friedrich. (1882). *The Gay Science*. Translated by Josefine Nauckhoff. (2001). Cambridge: Cambridge University Press.

Nietzsche, Friedrich. (1883). *Thus Spoke Zarathustra*. Translated by Adrian Del Caro. Edited by Adrian Del Caro and Robert B. Pippin. (2006). Cambridge and New York: Cambridge University Press.

NIST (National Institute of Standards and Technology). (2018):

- "Fundamental Physical Constants: Planck Length." *The NIST Reference on Constants, Units, and Uncertainty*. Online source:

  <https://physics.nist.gov/cgi-bin/cuu/Value?plkl>

- "Fundamental Physical Constants: Planck Time." *The NIST Reference on Constants, Units, and Uncertainty*. Online source:

  <https://physics.nist.gov/cgi-bin/cuu/Value?plkt>

Norton, John D. (9 February 2015). "Spacetime." *Einstein for Everyone*. Department of History and Philosophy of Science at the University of Pittsburgh. Online source:

<https://www.pitt.edu/~jdnorton/teaching/HPS_0410/chapters/spacetime/index.html>

Núñez, Rafael E. (2003). "Conceptual Metaphor and the Cognitive Foundations of Mathematics: Actual Infinity and Human Imagination." University of California in San Diego. pp. 49–71. Online source: <http://www.cogsci.ucsd.edu/~nunez/web/SingaporeF.pdf>

Oberhaus, Daniel. (26 October 2015). "Physicists Realized an Infinite 'Hilbert Hotel' with Beams of Light." *Motherboard*. Online source: <https://motherboard.vice.com/en_us/article/d7yg7w/physicists-made-an-infinite-hilbert-hotel-out-of-light>

Odenwald, Sten. (2021a). "Special Relativity Questions and Answers: According to relativity, how much younger are astronauts in earth-orbit after 6 months?" *Gravity Probe B: Testing Einstein's Universe*. Online source: <https://einstein.stanford.edu/content/relativity/q2739.html>

Odenwald, Sten. (2021b). "Special Relativity Questions and Answers: What is a space time continuum?" *Gravity Probe B: Testing Einstein's Universe*. Online source: <https://einstein.stanford.edu/content/relativity/q411.html>

Oesch, Pascal A.; et al. (10 March 2016). "A Remarkably Luminous Galaxy at z=11.1 Measured with Hubble Space Telescope Grism Spectroscopy." *The Astrophysical Journal*. Vol. 819, No. 2. Entry 129. (12 pages). See preprint at *arXiv*: <https://arxiv.org/abs/1603.00461>

Ohanian, Hans C. (1989). *Physics*. Second Edition, Expanded. Volume 2. New York and London: W. W. Norton & Company.

Ohanian, Hans C. (2008). *Einstein's Mistakes: The Human Failings of Genius*. New York: W. W. Norton & Company.

O'Leary, Michael. (2010). *Revolutions of Geometry*. New Jersey: Wiley.

Oppy, Graham. (June 1991). "Craig, Mackie, and the Kalam Cosmological Argument." *Religious Studies*. Vol. 27, No. 2. pp. 189–197.

Oppy, Graham. (1995). "Reply to Craig: Inverse Operations with Transfinite Numbers and the Kalam Cosmological Argument." *International Philosophical Quarterly*. Vol. 35, No. 2. pp. 219–221.

Oppy, Graham. (2006). *Philosophical Perspectives on Infinity*. Cambridge and New York: Cambridge University Press.

Oppy, Graham. (2011). "God and Infinity: Directions for Future Research." Chapter in Heller and Woodin 2011, pp. 233–254.

Orzel, Chad. (8 July 2015). "Six Things Everyone Should Know About Quantum Physics." *Forbes*. Online Source: <https://www.forbes.com/sites/chadorzel/2015/07/08/six-things-everyone-should-know-about-quantum-physics/?sh=2e68035f7d46>

Owen, H. P. (1967). "Infinity in Theology and Metaphysics." Entry in *Encyclopedia of Philosophy*. Bibliography updated by Christian B. Miller (2005). Online source: <https://www.encyclopedia.com/humanities/encyclopedias-almanacs-transcripts-and-maps/infinity-theology-and-metaphysics>

Paine, Thomas. (1794–1795). *The Age of Reason*. Published in 2017 as *Age of Reason: The Definitive Edition*. Grandville, Michigan: Michigan Legal Publishing Limited.

Parker, Matthew W. (2008). *Philosophical Method and Galileo's Paradox of Infinity*. Online source: <http://philsci-archive.pitt.edu/4276/1/Galileo%27s_Paradox.pdf>

Pasachoff, Jay M.; Filippenko, Alex. (2014). *The Cosmos: Astronomy in the New Millennium*. Fourth Edition. New York: Cambridge University Press.

Pasnau, Robert. (2011). "On Existing All at Once." Chapter in *God, Eternity, and Time*. Edited by Christian Tapp and Edmund Runggaldier. (2011). Burlington: Ashgate. pp. 11–29. Online source: <https://spot.colorado.edu/~pasnau/inprint/pasnau.existingallatonce.pdf>

Patterson, Steve. (13 September 2015). "Logic and Infinity: The Errors of Calculus." Online source: <http://steve-patterson.com/logic-and-infinity>

Patterson, Steve. (10 January 2016). "Infinite Things Do Not Exist." Online source: <http://steve-patterson.com/infinite-things-do-not-exist>

Patterson, Steve. (20 July 2016). "Cantor Was Wrong: There Are No Infinite Sets." Online source: <http://steve-patterson.com/cantor-wrong-no-infinite-sets>

Patterson, Steve. (11 September 2016). "Patterson In Pursuit: Ep. 22 – Understanding Infinity with Dr. Daniel Isaacson." Audio Recording. Online source:
<https://www.youtube.com/watch?v=aYaZ0I9lj8M>

Patterson, Steve. (12 March 2017). "Patterson In Pursuit: Ep. 48 – Skepticism of Infinity in Mathematics, a Conversation with Dr. Norman Wildberger." Audio Recording. Online source:
<http://steve-patterson.com/ep-48-skepticism-infinity-mathematics-dr-norman-wildberger>

Patterson, Steve. (28 May 2017). "Patterson In Pursuit: Ep. 59 – Can You Approach Infinity? Interview with Dr. Michael Huemer." Audio Recording. Online source:
<http://steve-patterson.com/ep-59-can-approach-infinity-dr-michael-huemer>

Paulos, John Allen. (7 April 2014). "The 16th Century's Line of Fire." *The New York Times*. Online source:
<https://www.nytimes.com/2014/04/08/science/infinitesimal-looks-at-an-historic-math-battle.html>

Payne, Mark ('Karmy Peny'). (26 July 2016). "Investigation of Infinity in Mathematics." *Extreme Finitism*. Online source:
<https://www.extremefinitism.com/background>

Pedersen, Olaf. (1985). "Galileo's Religion." Chapter in Coyne, G. V.; Heller, M.; Zycinski, J. (Editors). (1985). *The Galileo Affair: A Meeting of Faith and Science*. Proceedings of the Cracow Conference, May 24–27, 1984. Vatican City: Vatican Observatory. pp. 75–102. Online source:
<http://articles.adsabs.harvard.edu//full/1985gamf.conf...75P/0000075.000.html>

Penrose, Roger. (2004). *The Road to Reality: A Complete Guide to the Laws of the Universe*. London: Jonathan Cape.

Penrose, Roger. (2011). *Cycles of Time: An Extraordinary New View of the Universe*. UK: Bodley Head.

Penzias, Arno A.; Wilson, Robert W. (July 1965). "A Measurement of Excess Antenna Temperature at 4080 Mc/s." *Astrophysical Journal*. Vol. 142. No. 1. pp. 419–421. Online source:
<http://articles.adsabs.harvard.edu/pdf/1965ApJ...142..419P>

Perepelitsa, Dennis V. (1 June 2007). "Path Integrals in Quantum Mechanics." Cambridge: MIT Department of Physics. Online source:
<https://web.mit.edu/dvp/www/Work/8.06/dvp-8.06-paper.pdf>

Pew Research Center. (5 April 2017). "The Changing Global Religious Landscape." Online source:
<https://www.pewforum.org/2017/04/05/the-changing-global-religious-landscape>

Pew Research Center. (5 April 2017). "Christians Remain World's Largest Religious Group, But They Are Declining In Europe." Online source:
<https://www.pewresearch.org/fact-tank/2017/04/05/christians-remain-worlds-largest-religious-group-but-they-are-declining-in-europe>

Philo. (30–40 CE). *On the Account of the World's Creation Given by Moses* – a.k.a., *On the Creation* or *De Opificio Mundi*. Treatise in *Philo, Volume I*. Edited by George P. Goold. Translated by Francis H. Colson and George H. Whitaker. (1929). Cambridge, Massachusetts and London: Harvard University Press, Loeb Classical Library.

Philoponus, John. (529 CE). *Philoponus: Against Proclus's "On the Eternity of the World 1–5."* Translated by Michael Share with a Preface by Richard Sorabji. (2005). Ithaca, New York: Cornell University Press.

Physics Reimagined. (2021). "State Superposition and Decoherence." *Quantum Made Simple*. Article and Video. Online source:
<https://toutestquantique.fr/en/superposition>

Pinker, Steven. (2003). "Language as an Adaptation to the Cognitive Niche." Chapter in Christiansen and Kirby 2003, pp. 16–37.

Pires, Diego Paiva; Cianciaruso, Marco; et al. (April - June 2016). "Generalized Geometric Quantum Speed Limits." *Physical Review X*. Vol. 6. p. 021031 (19 pages). Online source:
<https://journals.aps.org/prx/pdf/10.1103/PhysRevX.6.021031>

Plato. (360 BCE). *Philebus*. Translated by Benjamin Jowett. (1888). Third Edition. Online source:
<http://classics.mit.edu/Plato/philebus.html>

Plato. (369 BCE). *Theaetetus*. In Cooper (John M.) 1997.

Plato. (375 BCE). *The Republic*. Translated by Benjamin Jowett. (1888). Third Edition. Online source:
<http://classics.mit.edu/Plato/republic.7.vi.html>

Plebani, Matteo. (2011). *Reconsidering Wittgenstein's Philosophy of Mathematics*. Italy: Università Ca' Foscari Venezia.

Plotinus. (250 CE). *The Six Enneads*. Translated by Stephen MacKenna. Revised by B. S. Page. Forward by E. R. Dobbs. Introduction by Paul Henry. (1957). London: Faber.

Pössel, Markus. (2006). "The Sum Over All Possibilities: The Path Integral Formulation of Quantum Theory." *Einstein Online*:
<www.einstein-online.info/spotlights/path_integrals.html>

Potoček, Václav; Miatto, Filippo M.; et al. (16 October 2015). "Quantum Hilbert Hotel." *Physical Review Letters*. Vol. 115, No. 16. p. 160505 (5 pages).

Pound, Robert V.; Rebka, Glen A. Jr. (1 April 1960). "Apparent Weight of Photons." *Physical Review Letters*. Vol. 4, No. 7. pp. 337–341. Online source:
<https://journals.aps.org/prl/abstract/10.1103/PhysRevLett.4.337>

Powell, Richard. (30 July 2006). *Atlas of the Universe*. Online source:
<http://www.atlasoftheuniverse.com/redshift.html>

Probst, Siegmund. (2018). "The Relation Between Leibniz and Wallis: An Overview From New Sources and Studies." *Quaderns d'Història de l'Enginyeria (Engineering History Notebooks)*. Vol. XVI. pp. 200–202.

Pseudo-Dionysius. (~6th Century CE). *Mystical Teaching*. Translated with an Introduction by Clifton Wolters in *The Cloud of Unknowing and Other Works*. (1978). London and New York: Penguin Books. Online source:
<https://avalonlibrary.net>

Random House Inc. (2020). *The Random House Dictionary*. New York: Random House, Inc. Online source:
<https://www.dictionary.com>

Rapaport, William J. (2012). "Intensionality vs. Intentionality." Online source:
<http://www.cse.buffalo.edu/~rapaport/intensional.html>

Redd, Nola Taylor. (8 June 2017). "How Old is the Universe?" *SPACE.com*. Online source:
<https://www.space.com/24054-how-old-is-the-universe.html>

Reichenbach, Bruce. (Winter 2017). "Cosmological Argument." *The Stanford Encyclopedia of Philosophy*. Edited by Edward N. Zalta. Online source:
<https://plato.stanford.edu/archives/win2017/entries/cosmological-argument>.

Robinson, Abraham. (1966; 1996). *Non-standard Analysis*. Princeton, New Jersey: Princeton University Press.

Rodych, Victor. (Spring 1997). "Wittgenstein on Mathematical Meaningfulness, Decidability, and Application." *Notre Dame Journal of Formal Logic*. Vol. 38, No. 2. pp. 195–225.

Rodych, Victor. (2001). "Gödel's 'Disproof' of the Syntactical Viewpoint." *The Southern Journal of Philosophy*. Vol. 39, No. 4. pp. 527–555.

Rogers, Katherin A. (March 1994). "Eternity Has No Duration." *Religious Studies*. Vol. 30, No. 1. Cambridge: Cambridge University Press. pp. 1–16.

Roitman, Judith. (6 December 2011). *Introduction to Modern Set Theory*. United States: Virginia Commonwealth University. Online source:
<http://www.math.ku.edu/~roitman/stb3fullWeb.pdf>

Roos, Matts. (14 February 2008). "Expansion of the Universe – Standard Big Bang Model." *arXiv*. (33 pages). Online source:
<https://arxiv.org/pdf/0802.2005.pdf>

Rosenhouse, Jason. (12 December 2013). "In What Sense Do Mathematical Objects Exist?" *EvolutionBlog*. Online source:
<https://scienceblogs.com/evolutionblog/2013/12/13/in-what-sense-do-mathematical-objects-exist>

Rovelli, Carlo. (2017). *Reality Is Not What It Seems: The Journey to Quantum Gravity*. Riverhead Books: New York.

Rucker, Rudy. (2005; 2019 Edition). *Infinity and the Mind: The Science and Philosophy of the Infinite*. Princeton and Oxford: Princeton University Press.

Rucker, Rudy. (2011). Introduction to *Infinity: New Research Frontiers*. Edited by Michael Heller and W. Hugh Woodin. (2011). New York: Cambridge University Press.

Rucker, Rudy. (2014). *The Fourth Dimension: Toward a Geometry of Higher Reality*. Forward by Martin Gardner, Illustrations by David Povilaitis. Mineola, New York: Dover Publications, Inc.

Rudin, Walter. (1976). *Principles of Mathematical Analysis*. Third Edition. London: McGraw-Hill.

Rusnock, Paul. (2000). *Bolzano's Philosophy and the Emergence of Modern Mathematics*. Atlanta, GA: Rodopi.

Russ, Steve (Translator and Editor). (2004). *The Mathematical Works of Bernard Bolzano*. Oxford: Oxford University Press.

Russell, Bertrand. (1903; 2010 edition). *Principles of Mathematics*. New York and London: Routledge Classics.

Russell, Bertrand. (1919). "A Free Man's Worship" Chapter in *Mysticism and Logic and Other Essays*. London: Longmans Green and Co.

Russell, Robert John. (2011). "God and Infinity: Theological Insights from Cantor's Mathematics." Chapter in Heller and Woodin 2011, pp. 275–289.

Sagan, Carl. (1980). *Cosmos*. New York: Ballantine Books.

Sagan, Carl. (1997). *Billions and Billions: Thoughts on Life and Death at the Brink of the Millennium*. New York: Random House.

Saibian, Sbiis. (2021). *One to Infinity: A Guide to the Finite*. A Web Book on Large Numbers. Online source: <https://sites.google.com/site/largenumbers/home>

Sanders, Robert H. (2016). "The Concordance Model." *Deconstructing Cosmology*. Cambridge University Press. Online source: <https://doi.org/10.1017/CBO9781316651568>

Sanders, Samuel. (May 1930). "Euclid and Infinity." *Mathematics News Letter*. Vol. 4, No. 7. Washington, D.C.: Mathematical Association of America. Online source: <http://www.jstor.org/stable/3027591?origin=JSTOR-pdf>

Sazonov, Vladimir. (1995). "On Feasible Numbers (How to Formalize?)" Lecture at the Department of Computer Science, University of Liverpool. Slide 1. Online source: <https://cgi.csc.liv.ac.uk/~sazonov/papers.html>

Sazonov, Vladimir. (1995). "On Feasible Numbers." *Logic and Computational Complexity: Lecture Notes in Computer Science*. International Workshop LCC 1994 Indianapolis, IN, USA, October 13–16, 1994. Selected Papers. Edited by Daniel Leivant. Vol. 960. New York: Springer. pp. 30–51. Online source: <http://www.csc.liv.ac.uk/~sazonov/papers.html>

Schaff, Philip; Wace, Henry (Editors). (1893; 2005 edition). *Nicene and Post-Nicene Fathers—Series II, Volume 5 (Gregory of Nyssa: Dogmatic Treatises, Etc.)*. Grand Rapids, MI: Christian Classics Ethereal Library. Online sources:
  - <https://ccel.org/ccel/schaff/npnf205/npnf205>
  - <https://www.ccel.org/ccel/s/schaff/npnf205/cache/npnf205.pdf>

Schärtl, Thomas; Tapp, Christian; Wegener, Veronika (Editors). (2016). *Rethinking the Concept of a Personal God: Classical Theism, Personal Theism, and Alternative Concepts of God*. Münster, Germany: Aschendorff Verlag.

Schechter, Eric. (2002). "Georg Cantor (1845–1918): The Man Who Tamed Infinity." Lecture: Vanderbilt University. Online source: <https://math.vanderbilt.edu/schectex/courses/infinity.pdf>

Schechter, Eric. (2009a). "Potential versus Completed Infinity: It's History and Controversy." Online source: <https://math.vanderbilt.edu/schectex/courses/thereals/potential.html>

Schechter, Eric. (2009b). "What are the 'Real Numbers', Really?" Online source: <http://www.math.vanderbilt.edu/~schectex/courses/thereals>

Schiller Institute. (Fall 1994). "On the Theory of the Transfinite: Correspondence of Georg Cantor and J. B. Cardinal Franzelin." *Fidelio*. Vol. 3, No. 3. pp. 97–110. Online source: <https://archive.schillerinstitute.com/fidelio_archive/1994/fidv03n03-1994Fa/fidv03n03-1994Fa_097-on_the_theory_of_the_transfinite.pdf>

Scott, Douglas. (2018). "The Standard Model of Cosmology: A Skeptic's Guide." *Proceedings of the 200th Course of the International School of Physics*. pp. 1–21. Online source: <https://ned.ipac.caltech.edu/level5/March18/Scott/frames.html>

Scott, J. F. (1938). *The Mathematical Works of John Wallis*. London: Taylor and Francis.

Sen, Dhiman. (25 July 2014). "The Uncertainty Relations in Quantum Mechanics." *Current Science*. Vol. 107, No. 2. pp. 203–218. Online source:
<https://www.jstor.org/stable/24103129?seq=1>

Sereno, Lisa Ann. (1999). "Infinity and Experience." Dissertation. Massachusetts: Massachusetts Institute of Technology (MIT). Online source:
<https://dspace.mit.edu/handle/1721.1/9700>

Sewell, Kip K. (1999). *The Cosmic Sphere*. New York: Nova Science Publishers—Kroshka Books trade division.

Sewell, Kip K. (2008, 2010). "The Case Against Infinity." Prepublication article. (Archived). Online source:
<https://philpapers.org>

Shackelford, Scott. (November/December 2007.) "World Without End." *Stanford Magazine*. Online source:
<https://stanfordmag.org/contents/worlds-without-end>

Sharaf, Khadijah. (2017). "An Infinite Number of Solutions for an Elliptical Problem with Power Nonlinearity." *Differential Integral Equations*. Vol. 30, No. 1/2. Online source:
<https://projecteuclid.org/euclid.die/1484881223>

Shoshany, Barak. (23 February 2014). "Are there mathematical arguments against the existence of infinity?" *Quora*. Online forum:
<http://www.quora.com/Are-there-mathematical-arguments-against-the-existence-of-infinity>

Siegel, Ethan. (27 July 2018). "There Was No Big Bang Singularity." *Starts With A Bang*. Online source:
<https://www.forbes.com/sites/startswithabang/2018/07/27/there-was-no-big-bang-singularity/#494812727d81>

Simmons, Bruce. (2017). *Mathwords: Terms and Formulas from Algebra I to Calculus*. Online source:
<http://www.mathwords.com>

Simpson, Stephen G. (7 April 2006). "What is Foundations of Mathematics?" Online source:
<http://www.personal.psu.edu/t20/hierarchy>

Simpson, Stephen G. (April 2015). "Potential Versus Actual Infinity: Insights from Reverse Mathematics." Lecture. Group in Philosophical and Mathematical Logic. University of Connecticut. Online source:
<math.psu.edu/simpson>

Singer, Dorothea Waley. (1950). *Giordano Bruno: His Life and Thought*. With Annotated Translation of His Work, *On the Infinite Universe and Worlds*. New York: Henry Schuman.

Smestad, Bjørn. (1995). "Foundations for Fluxions." Online source:
<http://home.hio.no/~bjorsme/hovedoppg.HTM>

Smolin, Lee. (2006). *The Trouble With Physics: The Rise of String Theory, the Fall of a Science, and What Comes Next*. Boston and New York: Houghton Mifflin Company.

Smolin, Lee. (2019). *Einstein's Unfinished Revolution: The Search for What Lies Beyond the Quantum*. New York: Penguin Press.

Solère, Jean-Luc. (2013). "*Scotus Geometres*: The Longevity of Duns Scotus's Geometric Arguments Against Indivisibilism." Chapter in *La Réception de Duns Scot / Die Rezeption Des Duns Scotus / Scotism through the Centuries (Proceedings of "The Quadruple Congress" on John Duns Scotus, Part 4)*. French/German/English edition. Edited by Mechthild Dreyer, Edouard Mehl, and Matthias Vollet. New York: Franciscan Institute Publications. Vol. 6. pp. 139–154. Online source:
<https://www.academia.edu/34247382>

Soukup, Dániel T. (12 March 2018). "Two Infinite Quantities and Their Surprising Relationship." *arXiv*. (5 pages). Online source:
<https://arxiv.org/abs/1803.04331>

Sparkes, A. W. (1991). *Talking Philosophy, A Wordbook*. London and New York: Routledge.

Steele, Jeff; Williams, Thomas. (Fall 2019). "Complexity Without Composition: Duns Scotus on Divine Simplicity." *American Catholic Philosophical Quarterly*. Vol. 93, Issue 4. pp. 611–631.

Steiner, Michael; Rendell, Ronald. (2018). *The Quantum Measurement Problem*. Volume I of the Series: *Progress on the Physics of Quantum Measurement*. Alexandria, Virginia: Inspire Institute.

Steinhart, Eric. (2009). "A Mathematical Model of the Divine Infinity." *Theology and Science*. Vol. 7, Issue 3. pp. 261–274. Online source:
<http://ericsteinhart.com/articles/divineinfinity.pdf>

Stenger, Victor J. (2014). *God and the Multiverse: Humanity's Expanding View of the Cosmos*. New York: Prometheus Books.

Stevens, Michael David. (9 April 2016). "How To Count Past Infinity." Video. Online source:
<https://www.youtube.com/watch?v=SrU9YDoXE88>

Stoll, Robert R. (1979). *Set Theory and Logic*. New York: Dover Publications, Inc.

Strassler, Matt. (10 October 2011). "Virtual Particles: What are They?" *Of Particular Significance*. Online source:
<https://profmattstrassler.com/articles-and-posts/particle-physics-basics/virtual-particles-what-are-they>

Strassler, Matt. (27 April 2012). "The Energy That Holds Things Together." *Of Particular Significance*. Online source:
<https://profmattstrassler.com/articles-and-posts/particle-physics-basics/mass-energy-matter-etc/the-energy-that-holds-things-together>

Strassler, Matt. (10 July 2013). "The Two Definitions of 'Mass', And Why I Use Only One." *Of Particular Significance*. Online source:
<https://profmattstrassler.com/articles-and-posts/particle-physics-basics/mass-energy-matter-etc/more-on-mass/the-two-definitions-of-mass-and-why-i-use-only-one>

Strobel, Lee. (2004). *The Case for a Creator*. Grand Rapids, Michigan: Zondervan.

Suber, Peter. (1998). "Infinite Reflections." *St. John's Review*. Vol. 44, No. 2, pp. 1–59. Online source:
<http://legacy.earlham.edu/~peters/writing/infinity.htm#positive>

Sweeney, Leo. (1992). *Divine Infinity in Greek and Medieval Thought*. With a Foreword by Denis O'Brien. New York: Peter Lang Publishing Incorporated.

Swinburne University. (29 May 2020). "Concordance Model." Entry in Cosmos – The SAO Encyclopedia of Astronomy. Swinburne Astronomy Online:
<http://astronomy.swin.edu.au/cosmos/c/concordance+model>

Swinburne University. (2021). "Cosmic Microwave Background." Entry in *Cosmos – The SAO Encyclopedia of Astronomy*. Swinburne Astronomy Online:
<https://astronomy.swin.edu.au/cosmos/C/Cosmic+Microwave+Background>

Swinburne University. (2021). "Planck Time." Entry in *Cosmos – The SAO Encyclopedia of Astronomy*. Swinburne Astronomy Online:
<https://astronomy.swin.edu.au/cosmos/p/Planck+Time>

Sylvestre, Jeremy. (16 September 2020). "Elementary Foundations: An Introduction to Topics in Discrete Mathematics." Canada: University of Alberta – Augustana Campus. Online source:
<https://sites.ualberta.ca/~jsylvest/books/EF/section-partial-orders-max-min.html>

Tallis, Raymond. (November/December 2011). "On Points." *Philosophy Now*. Issue 87. pp. 48–49.

Tapp, Christian. (1 August 2005). "On Some Philosophical Aspects of the Background to Georg Cantor's Theory of Sets." *Philosophia Scientiæ*. Cahier Spécial - CS 5 | 2005. pp. 157–173. Online source:
<http://journals.openedition.org/philosophiascientiae/386>

Tapp, Christian. (2018). "Bolzano's Concept of Divine Infinity." Chapter in *The Infinity of God: New Perspectives in Theology and Philosophy*. Edited by Benedikt Paul Göcke and Christian Tapp. University of Notre Dame Press. p. 154.

Tate, William W. (2001). "Cantor's *Grundlagen* and the Paradoxes of Set Theory." University of Chicago Department of Philosophy. Online source:
<http://home.uchicago.edu/~wwtx/cantor.pdf>

Tavakol, Reza; Gironi, Fabio. (2017). "The Infinite Turn and Speculative Explanations in Cosmology." *Foundations of Science*. Vol. 22. pp. 785–798.

Taylor, Edwin F.; Wheeler, John Archibald. (1992). *Spacetime Physics: Introduction to Special Relativity*. Second Edition. New York: W. H. Freeman and Company.

Taylor, Richard. (1 December 1951). "Mr. Black on Temporal Paradoxes." *Analysis*. Vol. 12, Issue 2. pp. 38–44.

Tegmark, Max. (May 2003). "Parallel Universes." *Scientific American*. Vol. 288, Issue 5. pp. 41–51. Online source:
<https://space.mit.edu/home/tegmark/PDF/multiverse_sciam.pdf>

Tegmark, Max. (2014). *Our Mathematical Universe: My Quest for the Ultimate Nature of Reality*. New York: Vintage Books.

Tegmark, Max. (20 February 2015). "Infinity Is a Beautiful Concept – And It's Ruining Physics." *Discover Magazine*. Column: *The Crux*. Online source:
<https://www.discovermagazine.com/the-sciences/infinity-is-a-beautiful-concept-and-its-ruining-physics>

Tegmark, Max. (2021). *The Universe of Max Tegmark*. Webpage:
<https://space.mit.edu/home/tegmark/crazy.html>

Temming, Maria. (7 August 2014). "Is the Universe Infinite?" Astronomy Questions & Answers in *Sky & Telescope: The Essential Guide to Astronomy*. American Astronomical Society. Online source:
<https://skyandtelescope.org/astronomy-resources/universe-infinite-big-universe>

Thomas, Robert. (2010). "Mathematics Is Not a Game But..." *The Best Writing on Mathematics: 2010*. Edited by Mircea Pitici. Princeton University Press: Princeton and Oxford. p. 85.

Thompson, Bruce. (2020). Definition: 'Appeal to Mystery'. *Bruce Thompson's Fallacy Page*. Online source:
<https://www2.palomar.edu/users/bthompson/Introduction%20to%20Fallacies.html>

Thomson, James. (1967). "Infinity in Mathematics and Logic." *The Encyclopedia of Philosophy*. Edited by Paul Edwards. Vol. 4. New York: Crowell Collier. pp. 183–190.

Tippett, Krista. (1 March 2012). "Uncovering the Codes for Reality." *On Being, with Krista Tippett*. Radio program. Online source:
<https://onbeing.org/programs/s-james-gates-uncovering-the-codes-for-reality>

Trench, William F. (2000). *Introduction to Real Analysis*. London: Pearson Education.

Trlifajová, Kateřina. (7 November 2017). "Bolzano's Infinite Quantities." *arXiv*. (30 pages). Online source:
<https://arxiv.org/abs/1711.01603>

Tropp, Joel A. (May 1999). "Infinitesimals: History and Application." Thesis. Mathematics Department, University of Texas at Austin.

Tumulka, Roderich. (28 February 2018). "Bohmian Mechanics." *arXiv*. (20 pages). Online source:
<https://arxiv.org/pdf/1704.08017.pdf>

Unger, Roberto Mangabeira; Smolin, Lee. (2015). *The Singular Universe and the Reality of Time: A Proposal in Natural Philosophy*. Cambridge, MA: Cambridge University Press.

University of California - Riverside. (20 November 2014). "It's Filamentary: How Galaxies Evolve in The Cosmic Web." *ScienceDaily*. Online source:
<https://www.sciencedaily.com/releases/2014/11/141120133428.htm>

University of New Mexico. (26 May 2015). "Number Systems." Paper provided by the Center for Academic Program Support (CAPS) Program. Online source:
<http://caps.unm.edu/mathrefresh/assets/NumberSystems.pdf>

Urbańczyk, Piotr. (2018). "The Logical Challenge of Negative Theology." *Studies in Logic, Grammar and Rhetoric*. Vol. 54, Issue 67. pp. 149–174.

Urner, Kirby. (1999). "Cardinality Versus Ordinality." The Oregon Curriculum Network. Online source:
<http://www.4dsolutions.net/ocn/cardinality.html>

Vaidman, Lev. (Fall 2018 edition). "Many-Worlds Interpretation of Quantum Mechanics." *The Stanford Encyclopedia of Philosophy*. Edited by Edward N. Zalta. Online source:
<https://plato.stanford.edu/archives/fall2018/entries/qm-manyworlds>

Vallicella, William F. (17 February 2019). "Divine Simplicity." *Stanford Encyclopedia of Philosophy*. Online source:
<https://plato.stanford.edu/entries/divine-simplicity>

Van Bendegem, Jean Paul. (January 1994). "Strict Finitism as a Viable Alternative in the Foundations of Mathematics." *Logique et Analyse*. Vol. 145. pp. 23–40. Online source:
<https://www.researchgate.net>

Van der Veen, Joanna; Horsten, Leon. (Autumn 2013). "Cantorian Infinity and Philosophical Concepts of God." *European Journal for Philosophy of Religion*. Vol. 5, No. 3. pp. 117–138.

Van Heijenoort, Jean. (1967). *From Frege to Gödel: A Source Book in Mathematical Logic, 1879–1931*. Cambridge, Massachusetts: Harvard University Press.

Vardanyan, Mihran; Trotta, Roberto; Silk, Joseph. (1 March 2011). "Applications of Bayesian Model Averaging to the Curvature and Size of the Universe." *Monthly Notices of the Royal Astronomical Society*. See preprint at *arXiv*: <https://arxiv.org/abs/1101.5476>

Vaughan, Henry. (1650). "The Night." Poem. Presented in Grierson, Herbert J. C. (Editor). (1925). *Metaphysical Lyrics & Poems of the Seventeenth Century, Donne to Butler*. Oxford: Clarendon Press. pp. 152–154.

Vaught, Robert L. (2001). *Set Theory, An Introduction*. Second Edition. Boston, London, Berlin: Birkhäuser.

Veneziano, Gabriele. (1 February 2006). "The Myth of the Beginning of Time." *Scientific American, Special Editions*. Vol. 16, Issue 1. pp. 72–81. Online source: <https://www.scientificamerican.com/article/the-myth-of-the-beginning-of-time-2006-02>

Vilenkin, Alexander. (15 June 1983). "Birth of Inflationary Universes." *Physical Review D (Particles and Fields)*. Vol. 27, Issue 12. pp. 2848–2855. Online source: <https://doi.org/10.1103/PhysRevD.27.2848>

Vinsonhaler, Rebecca. (January 2016). "Teaching Calculus with Infinitesimals." *Journal of Humanistic Mathematics*. Vol. 6, Issue 1. pp. 249–276.

Vopěnka, Petr. (1979). *Mathematics in the Alternative Set Theory*. Leipzig: Teubner-Verlag. Online source: <https://drive.google.com/file/d/17JRj2orUVDw7lrBEmBS1K6OK06RP32Xa/view>

Waismann, Friedrich. (1979). *Wittgenstein and the Vienna Circle*. Edited by B. F. McGuinness. Translated by Joachim Schulte and B. F. McGuinness. Oxford: Basil Blackwell.

Waldegg, Guillermina. (2005). "Bolzano's Approach to the Paradoxes of Infinity: Implications for Teaching." *Science & Education*. Vol 14. pp. 559–577.

Wallis, John. (1656). *The Arithmetic of Infinitesimals*. Translation by Jacqueline A. Stedall. (2004). New York: Springer Verlag.

Waterhouse, William C. (1979). "Gauss on Infinity." *Historia Mathematica*. Vol. 6. pp. 430–436. Online source: <https://core.ac.uk/download/pdf/82757459.pdf>

Watkins, Thayer. (19 June 2015). "The Calculus of Infinitesimals." Online source: <https://www.sjsu.edu/faculty/watkins/infincalc.htm>

Watling, J. (1 December 1952). "The Sum of an Infinite Series," *Analysis*. Vol. 13, Issue 2. pp. 39–46.

Webb, Richard. (2017). "How to Think About Infinity." *New Scientist: The Collection – Infinity and Beyond*. Vol. 4, Issue 4. p. 43.

Weir, Susan. (October 1988). "Closed Time and Causal Loops: A Defense Against Mellor." *Analysis*. Vol. 48, No. 4. pp. 203–209.

Weisstein, Eric W. (2021). *MathWorld*. A Wolfram Web Resource: <https://mathworld.wolfram.com>

Wendel, Garrett; Martínez, Luis; Bojowald, Martin. (19 June 2020). "Physical Implications of a Fundamental Period of Time." *Physical Review Letters*. Vol. 124, Issue 24. p. 241301.

Westerhoff, (2011). *Reality: A Very Short Introduction*. Oxford: Oxford University Press.

Whitrow, G. J. (1978). "On the Impossibility of an Infinite Past." *The British Journal of Philosophy of Science*. Vol. 29. pp. 39–45.

Wikia.org. (20 February 2021). *Googology Wiki: The Large Number Encyclopedia*. Online source: <https://googology.wikia.org>

Wilczek, Frank. (2008). *The Lightness of Being: Mass, Ether, and the Unification of Forces*. New York: Basic Books.

Wilczek, Frank. (21 November 2012). "Origins of Mass." *Central European Journal of Physics*. Vol. 10, No. 5. pp. 1021–1037. Online source: <https://www.degruyter.com/document/doi/10.2478/s11534-012-0121-0/html>

Wildberger, Norman J. (2005). *Divine Proportions: Rational Trigonometry to Universal Geometry*. Australia: Wild Egg Pty Ltd.

Wildberger, Norman J. (2009a). "MathFoundations16: Why Infinite Sets Don't Exist." Video. Online source: <https://www.youtube.com/watch?v=XKy_VTBq0yk>

Wildberger, Norman J. (2009b). "MathFoundations17: Extremely Big Numbers." Video. Online source: <https://www.youtube.com/watch?v=wPEYoWOMj1U>

Wildberger, Norman J. (2016). "Math Foundations 178: The Law of Logical Honesty and the End of Infinity." Video. Online source:
<https://youtu.be/I0JozyxM1M0>

Williams, John N. (October 1981). "Inconsistency and Contradiction." *Mind*. Volume XC, Issue 360. pp. 600–602.

Wittgenstein, Ludwig. (1930). *Philosophical Remarks*. Edited by Rush Rhees. Translated by Raymond Hargreaves and Roger White. (1975). Oxford: Basil Blackwell.

Wittgenstein, Ludwig. (1932). *Philosophical Grammar*. Edited by Rush Rhees. Translated by Anthony Kenny. (1974). Oxford: Basil Blackwell.

Wittgenstein, Ludwig. (1936–1949 Composition). *Philosophical Investigations*. Translated by G. E. M. Anscombe, P. M. S. Hacker, and Joachim Schulte. (First posthumous publication: 1953). Fourth Edition by P. M. S. Hacker and Joachim Schulte. (2009). Massachusetts and Oxford: Wiley-Blackwell.

Wittgenstein, Ludwig. (1937–44). *Remarks on the Foundations of Mathematics*. Translated by Gertrude Elizabeth Margaret (G. E. M.) Anscombe. Edited by Georg Henrik von Wright and Rush Rhees. (1956; 1978 Edition). Oxford: Basil Blackwell.

Wittgenstein, Ludwig. (1939). Lecture at Cambridge. Presented in *Wittgenstein's Lectures on the Foundations of Mathematics*. Edited by Cora Diamond. (1976). Cornell University Press: Ithaca, New York.

Woit, Peter. (14 February 2015). "The Singular Universe and the Reality of Time." *Not Even Wrong*. Online source:
<https://www.math.columbia.edu/~woit/wordpress/?p=7552>

Wolchover, Natalie. (26 November 2013). "To Settle Infinity Dispute, a New Law of Logic." *Quanta Magazine*. Online source:
<https://www.simonsfoundation.org/quanta/20131126-to-settle-infinity-question-a-new-law-of-logic>

Wolchover, Natalie. (12 November 2020). "What Is A Particle?" *Quanta Magazine*. Online source:
<https://www.quantamagazine.org/what-is-a-particle-20201112>

Wolfram|Alpha. Online source:
<https://www.wolframalpha.com>

Yam, Philip. (June 1997). "Bringing Schrödinger's Cat to Life." *Scientific American*. Vol. 276, Issue 6. pp. 124–129.

Yarnelle, John E. (1964). *An Introduction to Transfinite Mathematics*. Boston: D. C. Heath and Company.

Yirka, Bob. (26 June 2020). "Theorists Calculate Upper Limit for Possible Quantization of Time." *Phys.org*. Online source:
<https://phys.org/news/2020-06-theorists-upper-limit-quantization.html>

Zamai, Moreno; Malengo, Gabriele; Caiolfa, Valeria R. (2008). *Biophotonics*. Edited by Lorenzo Pavesi and Philippe M. Fauchet. Berlin, Heidelberg: Springer.

Zarrabizadeh, Saeed. (2008). "Defining Mysticism, a Survey of Main Definitions." *Transcendent Philosophy*. London Academy of Iranian Studies. Volume 9. pp. 77–92. Online source:
<https://www.researchgate.net/publication/346926027_Defining_Mysticism_A_Survey_of_Main_Definitions>

Zenkin, Alexander A. (December 2003 – August 2004). "Logic of Actual Infinity and G. Cantor's Diagonal Proof of the Uncountability of the Continuum." *The Review of Modern Logic*. Vol. 9, Nos. 3 & 4, Issue 30. pp. 27–82.

Zeno of Elea. (5th Century BCE). Arguments against motion as reported in Aristotle ~350 BCE (1999 translation).

Zimmerman, Otto. (1910). Entry for 'infinity' in *The Catholic Encyclopedia*. Vol. 8. New York: Robert Appleton Company. Online source:
<http://www.newadvent.org/cathen/08004a.htm>

Zolfagharifard, Ellie. (23 March 2015). "Is the Universe About to Collapse? Study Says Event is 'Imminent'." *Daily Mail*. Online source:
<https://www.dailymail.co.uk/sciencetech/article-3008468/Is-universe-brink-collapse-Study-says-catastrophic-event-imminent-don-t-worry-means-tens-billions-years-left.html#ixzz3VR9uMKIF>

Zyga, Lisa. (21 October 2015). "Physicists Experimentally Realize A Quantum Hilbert Hotel." *Phys.org*. Online source:
<https://phys.org/news/2015-10-physicists-experimentally-quantum-hilbert-hotel.html>.

Zyga, Lisa. (3 June 2016). "Physicists Discover an Infinite Number of Quantum Speed Limits." *Phys.org*. Online source:
<https://phys.org/news/2016-06-physicists-infinite-quantum-limits.html>

Zyga, Lisa. (30 May 2019). "Stabilizing the No-Boundary Proposal Sheds Light on the Universe's Quantum Origins." *Phys.org*. Online source: <https://phys.org/news/2019-05-stabilizing-no-boundary-universe-quantum.html>

FIGURE CREDITS

CHAPTER 1: CHALLENGING INFINITY

Figures 1.1–4: By the author.

CHAPTER 2: THE NATURE OF QUANTITY

Figures 2.1–3: By the author.
Figure 2.4: Adapted from Pixabay stock images (CC0).

CHAPTER 3: QUANTITIES COMPLETE AND INCOMPLETE

Figure 3.1: By the author.
Figures 3.2–4: Adapted from Adobe stock images (CC0).

CHAPTER 4: ON ENUMERATING TO INFINITY

Figure 4.1–2: By the author.
Figure 4.3: Adapted from Judson, Thomas W. "Abstract Algebra: Theory and Applications." Figure 19.3. Online source:
   <http://abstract.ups.edu/aata/section-boolean-lattices.html>
Figure 4.4: By the author.
Figure 4.5: Based on an example by Clegg and Pugh 2012, p. 104.
Figure 4.6: By the author.

CHAPTER 5: ON PREDICATING THE FINITE AND INFINITE

Figures 5.1–2: By the author.

CHAPTER 6: DISTINGUISHING FINITES AND INFINITES

Figures 6.1–6: By the author.

CHAPTER 9: LOGIC VERSUS LITERAL INFINITY

Figure 9.1: By the author.
Figure 9.2: Black and white modified version of the following: Rocchini, Claudio. (4 June 2007). "E8 graph as 2-dimensional projection, by Peter McMullen." *Wikimedia Commons*. Online source:
   <https://commons.wikimedia.org/wiki/File:E8_graph.svg>
   <https://creativecommons.org/licenses/by/4.0>
Figures 9.3–5: By the author.

CHAPTER 10: COMPLETENESS—IMPLICATIONS FOR INFINITY

Figures 10.1–2: By the author.

CHAPTER 11: LIMITLESSNESS—IMPLICATIONS FOR INFINITY

Figure 11.1: Adapted from stock images (CC0) at pnghut.com.
Figure 11.2: Adapted from Dawkins, Paul. (2019). "Section 4-3 : Minimum And Maximum Values." *Paul's Online Notes*. Mathematics tutorial. Online source:
  <https://tutorial.math.lamar.edu/Classes/CalcI/MinMaxValues.aspx>
Figure 11.3: By the author.
Figures 11.4–5: Inspired by examples at http://mathonline.wikidot.com.
Figure 11.6: By the author.

CHAPTER 12: COMPLETE AND LIMITLESS: THE CONTRADICTIONS

Figure 12.0: By the author.

CHAPTER 13: HAS INFINITY BEEN TAMED?

Figures 13.1–3: By the author, from common examples.
Figure 13.4: Sequence inspired by Gray 1994, p. 826.
Figure 13.5: By the author.
Figure 13.6: Adapted from Clark 2017, Figure 3 on p. 16. Also inspired by the ordinal number spiral from Wikipedia:
  <https://en.wikipedia.org/wiki/File:Omega-exp-omega-labeled.svg>
Figure 13.7: Adapted from Clark 2017, Figure 3 on p. 16. Also inspired by the ordinal number spiral from Wikipedia:
  <https://en.wikipedia.org/wiki/File:Omega-exp-omega-labeled.svg>

CHAPTER 14: INFINITY UNTAMED

Figure 14.1 By the author, from common examples.
Figure 14.2: Sequence inspired by Gray 1994, p. 826.
Figure 14.3: Inspired by an example from Kotani, Kazuhiko. (16 September 2012). "A Simple Rebuttal to Cantor's Diagonal Argument." *The Revolution of Mathematics*. Online source:
  <https://kazuhikokotani.wordpress.com/2012/09/16/a-simple-rebuttal-to-cantors-diagonal-argument>
Figure 14.4: By the author.
Figure 14.5: Inspired by Clark 2017, Figure 3 on p. 16, for characterization of the explication by Stevens.

CHAPTER 16: INVISIBLE CONTRADICTIONS

Figure 16.1: By the author.
Figure 16.2: Adapted from real snowflake photo and Koch snowflake at Wikimedia Commons:
  <https://commons.wikimedia.org> (CC BY-SA 4.0.)

CHAPTER 17: INFINITY UNREAL

Figures 17.1–3: By the author.

CHAPTER 18: INFINITE SPACE REFUTED

Figure 18.1: Image modified from Levy, Silvio. (1995). *Making Waves: A Guide to the Ideas behind Outside In*. Wellesley, Massachusetts: A. K. Peters, Ltd.

Figures 18.2–5: By the author.
Figure 18.6: Image adapted from Rudy Rucker at http://abyss.uoregon.edu/~js/cosmo/lectures/lec18.html.
Figure 18.7: Figure based on Moore 2019, p. 49.

CHAPTER 20: INFINITE MOTION REFUTED

Figures 20.1–3: Adapted from images (CC0) at 123rf.com.

CHAPTER 21: PROBLEMS WITH INFINITY IN PHYSICS

Figure 21.1: By the author.
Figure 21.2: Inspired by:
  (a) Kraaiennest. (12 May 2008). "sine wave, with annotations." *Wikipedia*. Online source:
    <https://commons.wikimedia.org/wiki/File:Sine_wave_amplitude.svg>
  (b) Skeptic's Play. (28 September 2009). "Entanglement Explained." Blog post. Online source:
    <http://skepticsplay.blogspot.com/2009/09/entanglement-explained.html>
Figure 21.3: Inspired by Parrochia, Daniel. (20 June 2019). "Some Remarks on History and Pre-history of Feynman Path Integral." *arXiv*. Figure 3, p. 8. Online source:
  <https://arxiv.org/abs/1907.11168>
Figure 21.4: By the author.
Figure 21.5: Adapted from Miatto, Filippo et al.
Figure 21.6: Based on https://commons.wikimedia.org/wiki/File:Feynmandiagram.svg.
Figure 21.7: ESA/Hubble: Volker Springel (Max Planck Institute for Astrophysics) et al. (2003). Online source:
  <https://esahubble.org/images/heic2003b/>
Figure 21.8: Modified version of artwork by Budassi, Pablo Carlos. (2014). *Observable Universe Logarithmic Illustration*. Online source:
  <https://commons.wikimedia.org/wiki/File:Observable_universe_logarithmic_illustration.png>
  <https://creativecommons.org/licenses/by/3.0>
Figure 21.9: By the author.
Figure 21.10: Inspiration from *Timeline of the Universe*, image by NASA in public domain.

CHAPTER 22: CLOSING ARGUMENTS ON LITERAL INFINITY

Figure 22.0: The impossible tribar and impossible trident, recreated by the author from popular reproductions.

CHAPTER 25: AN ACCOUNT OF DIVINE INFINITY

Figure 25.0: By the author.

THROUGHOUT CHAPTERS:

Tables 1–4: By the author (caveat: for portions of Table 4, see also endnote 1,384)

ACKNOWLEDGMENTS

There are some people I would like to thank for their help in preparing this work. First, a big thanks to my sister Robin for her assistance as a librarian in locating and retrieving articles during my research. Special thanks also to my dear friend Joan for listening patiently to my many musings about infinity and for reviewing drafts of previous versions. Thanks as well to colleagues and acquaintances who brought to my attention a few of the sources I ended up citing in this book. Finally, my gratitude to everyone who contributes their works to the commons, which were helpful for developing many of the figures.

GLOSSARY

Preamble:

The following list of terms is indexed with locators in brackets pointing to instances of the terms in the main text. Locators in brackets are not exhaustive for the listed terms; some terms appear infrequently while others are passim. The locators are intended to denote where the corresponding definition is given in the text and/or provide the most significant examples of a given term's use. Entries without locators denote terms used in other definitions or without explication in the main body of the book.

This glossary, unlike most others, allows for adjectives as main entries. This allowance is especially for terms the adjective form of which is the primary usage of the term throughout the text; it is also allowed for terms the adjective form of which is critical for grasping the main ideas presented in the text.

***

absolute:
- noun
  (1) *in transfinite mathematics*—an infinity greater in size or longer in order than any transfinite set, often symbolized as Ω. [§ 8.1.10] [§ 13.5.3] (Also known as absolute infinite totality or absolutely infinite multiplicity. *See* absolute infinity. *See also* infinity—absolute.
  (2) *in metaphysics and theology ('the absolute'; often capitalized)*—a perfect metaphysical reality of some sort, often taken to be a divine being such as God. [§ 16.2.5] [§ 25.3]
- adjective
  (3) *in epistemology*—true for all observers.
  (4) *in physics*—true regardless of the observer's place, time, or state of motion. *Contrast with* relative; *do not confuse with* objective.
- adverb
  (5) 'absolutely': without exception.

absolute extremum: *(plural—'absolute extrema')* an absolute maximum or absolute minimum. [§ 11.2.3] [§ 11.2.8]

absolute infinity: limitlessness of both quantity and quality. [§ 1.2] *See also* infinity—absolute.

absolute maximum: the highest value a function produces in a domain. [§ 11.2.3]

absolute minimum: the lowest value a function produces in a domain. [§ 11.2.3]

accession: a sequence of additions resulting in a final sum (typically referred to as a 'series' in mathematics). [§ 2.2.6] *Contrast with* degression.

accuracy: *in formal logic and epistemology*—the extent to which the meaning of a statement is accurate.

accurate: correct according to a reliable standard in a given context (e.g., the standard of having consistent results in the context of mathematics, the standard of conformity with experience or observation in the context of science, and so forth).

actual infinity: Aristotle's term for the condition of being both complete and limitless in quantity. [§ 1.3.2] *See also* infinity—quantitative, literal infinity.

actuality: occurrent reality, as opposed to a latent reality. [§ 23.1.1] [§ 23.1.5] *Compare with* potentiality.

afinite: *adjective (pronounced "ey-fin-it")*—lacking limits due to lack of quantity or due to emptiness. [§ 5.4.5]

afinity: *(pronounced "ey-<u>fin</u>-i-tee")* the condition of lacking limits due to lack of quantity or due to emptiness. [§ 5.4.5]

aggregate: a collection in which the members operate together as interactive parts forming a whole. [§ 2.2.3]

amount: a value equal to a total. [§ 2.3]

analysis:

(1) a detailed examination of a whole in terms of its structure, parts, elements, or relationships.

(2) *in mathematics*—the study of mathematical schemes and schemas for real, imaginary, and complex numbers. [§ 9.4.2] [§ 18.5.2] [§ 18.5.9] *See also* standard analysis *and* non-standard analysis.

apeiron: *(ancient Greek)* endlessness; the condition of lacking an end or limit of a given kind, either by being indefinite or by being infinite in quantity or quality. [§ 8.1] [§ 8.1.1] [§ 8.1.3] [§ 8.1.4] [§ 16.7] [§ 23.1] [§ 25.1.1] [§ 25.2]

apeiros: *(ancient Greek)* endless or limitless; or apparently without end or limit—indefinite. [§ 8.1]

apparent space: the appearance of the separateness of objects for a single time, according to an observer's experience and/or measurement. [§ 18.1] *Contrast with* real space. *See also* space.

apparent time: the appearance of the separateness of states for a single space, according to an observer's experience and/or measurement. [§ 19.1] *Contrast with* real time. *See also* time.

arithmetic: the study of mathematical schemes and schemas for whole and natural numbers. [§ 9.4.2]

attribute: [§ 5.1]

- <u>noun</u>

(1) a property affirmed or its opposite denied as belonging to an object.

- <u>verb</u>

(2) to affirm a property or deny its opposite as belonging to an object.

axiom of infinity: *in the transfinite system (often capitalized)—* [§ 9.6.4]

(1) There exists an infinite set.

(2) Let there be a collection N such that the empty set is a member of N and such that for any element, x, if x is a member of N, then the set formed by uniting x with its singleton is also a member of N.

(3) There is an infinite number, ω, such that if n is a natural number less than ω, then $n + 1$ is also less than ω.

being:

(1) to be.

(a) be—exist (e.g., Shakespeare's phrase, "To be or not to be" means the same as to exist or not to exist, which can also be phrased as, "To have being or not to have being").

(b) be—exist as something (e.g., to be alive and well means to exist as alive and well, which can be phrased as existing as alive and well, which is the same as "being alive and well").

(2) that which exists (e.g., "a being").

(3) that which exists as something (e.g., a human being).

big bang: *in cosmology and physics ('the big bang'; often capitalized)*—the event or era that, theoretically, occurred between 13.7 and 13.8 billion years ago during which the Universe was a hot, dense state of compressed matter and from which the Universe expanded and cooled, forming the elements and celestial bodies (e.g., stars, galaxies, and planets). [§ 21.4.5]

big bang theory: *in cosmology and physics ('the big bang theory'; often capitalized)*—the theory that the fundamental particles of matter making up the elements and all observable celestial bodies originated from the cosmic event or era commonly known as the Big Bang. [§ 21.4.5]

bijection: a one-to-one correspondence of elements between sets. [§ 4.4.4] *Compare with* injection *and* surjection.

border: a limit that marks where one area is separated from another area. [§ 5.3.1]

bound: the extreme of a sequence beyond which extends more elements not in the sequence. [§ 5.3.1]

boundary: that which specifies the range of a collection by marking where the collection meets its complement (elements not shared by another collection). [§ 5.3.1]

boundless:

(1) *literal meaning*—without quantitative bound yet still constituting a complete collection. [§ 1.3.2] *See also* infinite(1)–(3) *and* infinity(5). *Compare with* unbounded(2). *Contrast with* bound.

(2) *figurative meaning*—apparently without bound to aggregation or change; indefinitely changing in quantity. [§ 1.3.3] *See also* indefinite *and* infinity(6). *Compare with* unbounded.

brink: the element or moment just before a marked change or event. [§ 5.3.1]

calculate: to use a function for outputting a number that can be assigned to a collection. [§ 2.3.10]

cardinality: the size of set represented by a numeral. [§ 2.3.1]

cardinal number (or cardinal): a number as it represents its numeral's cardinality (the size of the numeral system up to that numeral) or the size of a given collection. [§ 2.3.2]

categorematic: denoting a noun or adjective. [§ 23.2.2] *Compare with* syncategorematic.

categorematic infinite: surpassing every finite quantity. [§ 23.2.2] *Compare with* syncategorematic infinite.

ceaseless: to continue without ceasing—i.e., without ever ending. [§ 6.4.2] *See also* ceaselessness. *Compare with* persistent.

ceaselessness: the quality of continuing indefinitely, without ceasing. [§ 6.4.2] *Compare with* persistence.

change: [§ 19.1]

(1) variation of properties

(2) the variance of a property ("a change")

chaotic inflation: the speculative process by which other universes have from the infinite past and into the infinite future continuously come into being, some as offshoots from our universe or from other universes with yet others arising independently from their own singularities in hyperspace, and all of them expanding and existing independently of the others. [§ 21.4.5] *Compare with* cosmic inflation *and* eternal inflation. *See also* multiverse.

chronon: *(plural—'chronons')* a hypothesized smallest unit of real time during which a physical effect can take place, equivalent to the duration a photon of light takes to travel the diameter of an electron, or about 10^{-24} seconds. [§ 19.5.1]

circumference: [§ 1.1.2]

(1) the perimeter of a circle—the continuous line that forms the boundary of a disk.

(2) the measure of distance around a circle—the extent of the circle's perimeter.

class: a collection of objects sharing the same type of relation(s). [§ 3.2.2]

closed series: a series formed by a succession that terminates. [§ 2.3.6]

coherence: the condition of having both consistency and comprehensibility. [§ 9.6.1]

collection: a group of objects. [§ 2.2.1]

collective indefinite: *noun*—a collection in which the members, at an assumed time, all together comprise an indefinite quantity. [§ 6.3] *Compare with* serial indefinite.

collective indefiniteness: the condition of being a collective indefinite; a quantity larger any defined quantity. [§ 23.4] *Compare with* serial indefiniteness.

complete:
- precising [§ 3.2] [§ 3.2.8] [§ 13.1]
  (1) having all members necessary to be representative of a given class.
  (2) a given collection is complete if and only if the collection is whole, entire, finished, full, and total.
- technical
  (3) *in mathematical analysis—*
  (a) *Cauchy complete (of a Cauchy space)*—the property of a set of elements in which each sequence of elements in the set converges to an element of the set. [§ 3.3.4] [§ 3.6.2]
  (b) *Dedekind complete*—having no 'gaps' in the real number line; having the property such that between every two real numbers there is at least one other real number. [§ 3.6.2] [§ 14.1.1]
  (4) *in set theory (first version)*—P is 'complete' if P is a dense, linearly ordered set and every non-empty subset that is a member of P is bounded from above by a supremum. [§ 13.2.1]
  (5) *in set theory (second version)*—P is 'complete' if P is a set and every non-empty subset that is a member of P is bounded from above by a supremum. [§ 13.2.1] [§ 14.1]

completed infinity: the condition of being both complete and limitless in quantity. [§ 1.3.2] *See also* infinity—quantitative, literal infinity.

completeness: the condition of being complete. [§ 3.2]

complete number: a definite number able to be fully expressed with either a single base digit or a terminating series of base digits. *Contrast with* incomplete number.

complex number: a number that can be expressed in the form $x + yi$, where x and y are real numbers, and i is an imaginary unit with yi being an imaginary number. [§ 4.2.13]

computable function: a mathematical function that halts (self-terminates) with a value in its domain. [Endnote 113] *Contrast with* uncomputable function.

compute: to use an effective procedure, such as an algorithm, for counting or calculating. [§ 2.3.10]

concordance cosmology (or concordance model of cosmology): *(often capitalized)* the currently accepted and most commonly used scientific model of cosmology. [§ 21.4.5]

connotation: [§ 9.1.4]
(1) an idea associated with what is signified or expressed.
(2) a logical implication of what is signified or expressed.

constant extreme: an extreme the mathematical value for which does not change with time. [§ 11.2.7] *Contrast with* variant extreme.

constant maximum: *(plural—'constant maxima')* a maximum the mathematical value for which does not change with time. [§ 4.2.5] [§ 11.2.7] *Contrast with* variant maximum. *See also* constant extreme.

constant minimum: *(plural—'constant minima')* a minimum the mathematical value for which does not change with time. [§ 4.2.5] [§ 11.2.7] *Contrast with* variant minimum. *See also* constant extreme.

continuous: of a continuum—uninterrupted over time or invariant over space.

continuum: *(plural—'continua')* [§ 18.5.8]
- in general
  (1) a sequence of elements in which adjacent or immediate elements vary by indistinguishable amounts.
- in particular
  (2) *in mathematics*—a set of self-similar elements such that an intermediate element separates any pairing of elements; a 'dense' arrangement of elements. [§ 21.2.1]
  (3) *in physics (relativity theory)*—real space or real time, or both as a single entity called 'spacetime', conceived to be a mathematical continuum. [§ 21.3.2]

continuum hypothesis: *in transfinite set theory*—there is no set S such that $\mathbb{N} < S < \mathbb{R}$. [§ 21.1.3]

continuum problem: *in transfinite set theory*—the continuum hypothesis cannot be proven true or false. [§ 21.1.3]

coordinate: *(plural—'coordinates')* a number for measuring space. [§ 18.5.1]

correct: free of error. [§ 9.3.3]

correctness: the condition of being correct. [§ 9.3.3]

correspondence: *in set theory*—the matching or mapping of elements between two sets where one element in one set is paired with at least one element in the other set, resulting in injection, bijection, or surjection. [§ 4.4.4]

cosmic inflation (or cosmological inflation): the speculative process by which the Universe expanded out of a spacetime singularity to nearly its full size in less than a second, after which the Big Bang took place and the Universe expanded into the Cosmos as we know it. [§ 21.4.5] *Compare with* eternal inflation *and* chaotic inflation.

cosmological constant: a hypothesized principle or physical force that cancels the influence of gravity out on the scale of the Universe as a whole, keeping the Universe static in size. The mathematical value of the cosmological constant is denoted by the Greek letter lambda: Λ. [§ 21.3.2]

cosmology: the study of the Cosmos—especially, the natural order of the Universe according to observable properties such as its structure, its fundamental processes, and the events influencing its development. [§ 21.4] *See also* cosmos(3).

cosmos: [§ 21.4]
(1) the nature of a universe, or the Universe, as an orderly system. *See also* universe.
(2) 'a cosmos'—an orderly system, especially the underlying order of a universe regarded as a system. *See also* universe(1) *and* universe(2)(a).
(3) 'the cosmos' (often capitalized)—the Universe as a system of interrelated objects, properties, and relations from the smallest portion of matter to the entire cosmic web of galaxies.

count: [§ 2.3.5]
(1) *verb*— to successively assign numbers to members of sets according to the ordinalities of the numbers in a number scale.
(2) *noun*— the process or procedure of successively listing members of sets by assigning numbers to them.

countable:
(1) *in general mathematics*—able to be counted to a concluding number that is the total of the collection counted. [§ 13.7]
(2) *in transfinite mathematics*—[§§ 13.7–13.9] *Contrast with* uncountable(2).
   (a) able, at least in principle, to have every member assigned a unique number by correspondence.
   (b) able to be placed into injection or bijection with the members of $\mathbb{N}$. [§ 14.5]

countable infinity (or countably infinite set): *in transfinite mathematics*—any set equal in quantity to $\mathbb{N}$; a set of $\aleph_0$-many members. [§ 10.3.2]

d^*: a variable representing the largest definite number at present. [§ 4.2.7]

definite: having defined or specified limits. [§ 6.1] *Contrast with* indefinite. *Compare to* determinate(4).

definiteness: the state of having defined or specified limits. [§ 6.1] *Contrast with* indefiniteness.

definite number: a logically coherent, mathematically well-defined number. [§ 4.2.7]

degression: a sequence of subtractions resulting in a final difference—an arithmetic sequence that is the opposite of an accession. [§ 2.2.6] *Contrast with* accession.

denotation: a reference to a particular, specified object or set of objects. [§ 9.1.4]

determinate:

(1) able to be determined.

(2) *in epistemology*—able to be ascertained or concluded. *Compare with* determine(1); *Contrast with* indeterminate.

(3) *in formal logic*—able to be deduced.

(4) *in mathematics*—having a specified limit to a given quantity, measure, or mathematical procedure. [§ 2.3.6]

(5) *in metaphysics*—to be the inevitable outcome of a causal chain of events. [§ 19.4.1]

determinate infinite: an instance of determinate infinity. [§ 13.2]

determinate infinity: the condition of being both complete and limitless in quantity. [§ 1.3.2] *See also* infinity—quantitative, literal infinity.

determine:

(1) *in epistemology*—to ascertain or conclude, as after observation or reasoning. [§ 6.6]

(2) *in formal logic*—to establish as necessary and sufficient for the truth or falsity of a given statement.

(3) *in mathematics*—to specify a quantitative or mathematical limit. [§ 2.3.14]

(4) *in metaphysics*—to make inevitable a specific outcome or occurrence. *Compare with* determinate(5).

determiner: a membership quantifier. [§ 5.1] *See also* quantifier—membership.

dimension: a division of space given as an extent in coordinates. [§ 18.5.1]

discover: [§ 16.6.1]

(1) to detect or find something that had either always or previously existed but had hitherto been unknown.

(2) to ascertain or gain knowledge of for the first time.

(3) to devise a new use or application for something already known.

discoverism: the philosophical position that mathematical objects are discovered rather than invented. [§ 16.2]

discovery: [§ 16.6.1]

(1) something discovered.

(2) the process of discovering.

distance: the amount of separateness of objects during a single time, as measured by a reflexive sequence of intervals separating the objects.

distinct: able to be distinguished as different from other objects of reference. [§ 2.3.14]

divine:

- adjective

  (1) of higher authority than any mortal being; "shining"—the 'light' of highest authority. [§ 1.4.3]

- noun

  (2) a being of higher authority than any mortal being. *See* divinity(2).

  (3) 'the divine' (often capitalized): the Absolute or God. [§ 1.4.3] *See also* absolute(2).

divine infinity: the limitlessness of the divine or essence of the divine, or given attributes of the divine that are without limit. [§ 1.4] [§ 1.6] *See also* absolute infinity, qualitative infinity, *and* infinity—qualitative and absolute.

divinity:

(1) the condition of being divine. *See* divine(1).

(2) a particular divine being. *See* divine(2).

doctrine of divine simplicity: the doctrine that God *is* God's attributes rather than a being that *has* attributes. [§ 25.2.2]

domain:

(1) the scope of an field's subject. [§ 9.1.3]

(2) the set of rules for a field of expression. [§ 9.1.3] *See* domain of expression.

(3) a given range of values. [§ 11.2.3]

domain of coherence: the scope of all expressions that conform to the standards of coherence for their respective field (e.g., all grammatical expressions in natural language, all mathematical expressions in mathematics, all logical expressions in symbolic logic). [§ 9.6]

domain of expression: the scope of how ideas and concepts are communicated with signifiers according to a set of rules for making expressions in the given type of language under study (i.e., in the given field of expression). Examples of domains of expression include grammar, (formal) logic, and mathematics. [§ 9.1.3]

doppelganger problem: the absurd proposal that there exist infinitely many copies of each one of us, some with only slight differences, throughout the infinite expanse of space and/or across infinite time. [§ 21.4.6] *See also* eternal recurrence.

duration: the amount of separateness of states occupying a single space, as measured by an irreflexive succession of intervals separating the states.

edge: a brink that results in a change of angle. [§ 5.3.1]

effective: producing or achieving the desired or intended result. [§ 9.3.4]

element: [§ 2.2.2]

(1) an indivisible, distinct object.

(2) a divisible, but undivided, distinct object.

empty set: *in set theory*—a set of braces { } containing no symbols, representing a condition in which there are no objects or elements. Sometimes denoted as ∅. [§ 2.3.8]

end: the first or last member in the sequence or series. [§ 5.3.1]

endless:

(1) *literal meaning*—without end but complete, as is. [§ 1.3.2] *See also* infinite(1)–(3) *and* infinity(5).

(2) *figurative meaning*—apparently without end. [§ 1.3.3] *See also* indefinite *and* infinity(6).

endlessness: the condition of being endless. [§ 1.3.2]

energy: the ability to reduce the inertia of a given physical body; in physics, often measured as the ability to do work. [§ 21.1] *See also* force, power, *and* work.

enormity: the condition of being enormous. [§ 6.4.1]

enormous: too large to be quantified without defining a new definite number. [§ 6.4.1]

entire: [§ 3.4]

(1) missing no elements.

(2) a given instance of a collection, C, is 'entire' if and only if it is logically possible to determine that no member is missing from the instance of C.

entirety: the condition of being entire. [§ 3.4]

enumerable:

(1) able to be enumerated. [§ 2.3.5] [§ 13.10]

(2) *in the transfinite system*—able to be placed into a one-to-one correspondence with a set of natural numbers. [§ 13.10]

enumerably infinite (or denumerable): *in the transfinite system*—set S is enumerably infinite if all the members of S are able to be placed into bijection with all the numbers in $\mathbb{N}$ through correspondence. [§ 13.10] *See also* countable infinity. *Contrast with* innumerably infinite (or non-denumerable).

enumeration: the process of attempting to match numbers to objects. [§ 2.3.5]

ephemeral:
(1) *noun*—an indefinitely brief unit of time, measurable only in principle. [§§ 19.5.1–19.5.5]
(2) *adjective*—occurring with indefinite brevity. [§ 6.4.2]

ephemerality: the condition of being ephemeral. [§ 6.4.2]

essence: an intrinsic attribute or attributes necessary and sufficient for identity.

eternal: always existing; unsubject to deterioration, decay, or destruction. [§ 27.4.6]

eternal chaotic inflation (or eternal self-reproducing chaotic inflation): [§ 21.4.5] *See* chaotic inflation.

eternal inflation: the speculative process by which the Multiverse began to exist and continues to grow with new universes continuously expanding out of singularities in hyperspace. [§ 21.4.5] *Compare with* cosmic inflation *and* chaotic inflation.

eternal life: endless life by virtue of being infinite life or immutable life or timeless life. [§ 27.4.6]

eternal now: *'the eternal now' (often capitalized)* [§ 27.4.6] *See* immutable time.

eternal recurrence (or eternal return): the doctrine that the Universe undergoes infinitely many repetitions of every finite sequence of events, implying there are infinitely many duplicates of our lives repeated infinitely many times. [§ 21.4.6] *See* doppelganger problem.

eternity:
(1) the condition of being eternal.
(2) infinite time, immutable time, or timelessness. [§ 26.5.4] [§ 27.4.6]

exist: [Ch. 1, intro.]
(1) having properties (e.g., "to exist as").
(2) having relevant properties.

existence: [Ch. 1, intro.]
(1) all that has properties (all that exists).
(2) the property of having properties.
(3) the property of having (relevant) properties.

expanding universe theory: *(often capitalized)* the cosmological theory that the observable universe, and possibly the Universe as a whole, is expanding in spatial size. [§ 21.4.5] *See also* big bang theory.

expression: [§ 9.1]
(1) a communicated idea or concept.
(2) the form of a communicated idea or concept.
(3) the act of communicating an idea or concept.

extension: the referent (object or class of objects) denoted by a signifier or expression. [§ 9.1.4]

extensive infinity: a medieval term for infinity as an uncountable quantity, particularly of existing things (i.e., a condition of being complete and limitless in quantity). [§ 23.3.2] *See also* infinity(5). *Contrast with* intensive infinity.

extent: the measure of difference between values assigned. [§ 5.3.1] [§ 18.5.1]

extreme:
(1) *noun (plural—'extremes')*—an extremity or extremum; the outermost mathematical value(s) of a collection's sequence, or the least/greatest amount of elements a collection has, which specifies the range of the collection. [§ 4.2.2] [§ 5.3.1] *See also* constant extreme *and* variant extreme.
(2) *adjective*—the quality of having or being an extremity or extremum. [§ 4.2.2]

extremity: *(plural—'extremities')* that which is either minimal or maximal. [§ 4.2.2]

extremum: *(plural—'extrema')* a minimum or maximum. [§ 4.2.2]

false: not completely accurate; having <100% accuracy.

falsity:
(1) the condition of being false.
(2) a false statement, or 'falsehood'.

feasible number: any number the value of which can, in practice, be reached by counting (whether performed by human or machine). [§ 4.2.11] *Contrast with* unfeasible number.

fence: *in mathematics*—a Hasse-diagram depicting a sequence of minimal and maximal elements. [§ 11.2.2]

field:
(1) a topic of interest studied by the specialists of a profession (such as philosophy, mathematics, physics, theology, literature, art, history, economics, etc.) [§ 9.1.2]
(2) an area of land devoted to contests or the playing of sports. [§ 20.2.1]
(3) *in physics (also called an energy field)*—
(a) real space portrayed as possessing various amounts of quantized energy at every point and operating as the physical medium for the exchange of energy or force between particles. [§ 21.3] *See also* quantum field.
(b) a portion of such, such as a the area or volume of influence around a magnetic pole or electrical charge. [§ 21.2] [§ 21.3] [§ 21.5] (Also known as a force field.)

field of expression: any type of language in which expressions are made according to a set of rules (a domain of expression) and which constitutes a 'field' (topic of study by academic specialists). Examples include natural language, (formal) logic, and mathematics. [§ 9.1.2] *See also* domain of expression.

finish: a concluding, non-zero number of members. [§ 3.5]

finite

* adjective—
lexical
(1) having a limit. [§ 1.1.1] [§ 5.3]
(2) having a limit to a given measure. [§ 1.1.3] [§ 5.3]
precising
(3) having a limited quantity. [§ 1.3] [§ 5.3]
(4) having limited quality. [§ 1.4] [§ 5.3]
(5) having limited quantity and quality. [§ 1.5] [§ 5.3]
technical
(6) completely enumerable (at least, in principle) to a determinate amount. [§ 5.3.4]
(7) *operational definition from transfinite set theory*—having a number of elements (for example, objects) capable of being put into a one-to-one correspondence with a segment of $\mathbb{N}$ through a process of correspondence. [§ 5.3.5]
(8) *operational definition from finite mathematics*—able, at least in principle, to be completely enumerated, whether by tallying, counting, computing, calculating, or corresponding with a scale of numbers. [§ 5.3.5]

* noun
(9) that which is finite (as in 'the finite'). [§ 1.1.1] [Ch. 5] [Ch. 6]

finite-unbounded: to lack a bound while being finite; as, for example, by having a closed curvature. [§ 1.1.2] [§ 21.4.1]

finite mathematics: any mathematical system in which quantities are assumed to be necessarily limited (such a system contains no assumption of infinity or infinite sets). [§ 17.1.1] [§ 21.6] [§ 24.3]

finitism: the philosophical position that all non-empty collections and non-zero quantities are finite, and that literally infinite mathematical objects do not exist. [§ 22.1.4]

finitist: one who adheres to finitism. [§ 22.1.4]

finitude:
(1) the condition of being finite. [§ 1.1.1]
(2) the condition of having a limit to a given measure. [§ 1.1.3]

force: [§ 21.2] [§ 21.3.2] [§ 21.5]
(1) any transference of energy that changes the motion of a body. *See also* energy *and* power.
(2) the amount of energy transferred in changing the motion of a body. *See also* power *and* work.

force field: [§ 21.5] *See* field(3)(b).

forever: [§ 19.3.4] [§ 19.4.3] [§ 21.4.2] [Ch. 23, intro] [§ 26.5.4]
(1) for all time.
(2) for all time to come; for ceaseless time—everlasting. [§ 22.2]

formal language: [§ 7.1] [§ 25.1]
(1) technical language used for symbolically representing ideas and concepts in precise forms of communication like codes, formulas, proofs, axioms, theorems, and so on. *Contrast with* natural language.
(2) natural language used for socially formal situations; for example, language used for academic prose, journalism, political speeches, and the like. *Contrast with* informal language.

full: [§ 3.6]
(1) unable to include additional members of the same class without changing the parameters of the collection.
(2) a given collection, C, is full if and only if no additional element of the same class of elements in any non-empty subset of C can be included either as the member of any subset in C or to the entirety of elements in C without changing the parameters of C.

fullness: the condition of being full. [§ 3.6]

function: *mathematics*—a rule-based relation between a set of inputs and a set of outputs with the property that each input is related to a single output. [§ 2.3.9]

grammar: the rules of expression for a natural language. [§ 9.2]

group: [§ 2.2.1]
(1) *noun*—a physical, imaginary, or conceptual gathering together of objects, which when so gathered are related either causally (for physical objects) or symbolically in representation (for imaginary or conceptual objects).
(2) *verb*—To place objects into relation with another as parts of a whole, either by placing them into causal interaction (for physical objects) or by symbolically associating them with one another (for imaginary or conceptual objects).

hodon: *(plural—'hodons')* a hypothetical, smallest unit of real space that is indivisible. [§ 18.5.5]

hyperspace: a space of more than three dimensions, whether real or purely schematic. [§ 21.4.4]

ill-defined number: a number that is too ambiguous to be used consistently in mathematical expression but which may not violate logic. [See endnote 113] *Contrast with* well-defined number.

illusion: [§ 9.1.4] [§ 13.9.3] [§ 22.1.7] [§ 26.1.1] [§ 27.2.3]

(1) the property of being illusory. *Contrast with* reality.

(2) that which does not have properties independent of appearance.

(3) that for which relevant properties are not independent of their appearance; the condition of not being as it seems to be ("an illusion").

(4) all that is illusory.

illusory:

(1) to not have being independent of appearance.

(2) to not have the same properties independent of appearance; to not be objectively as it subjectively seems to be. *Contrast with* real.

imaginary number: any number that, when multiplied by itself, gives a result that is necessarily non-positive. [§ 4.2.13]

immeasurable:

(1) *literal meaning*—unable to be measured, even in principle. [§ 1.3.2]

(2) *figurative meaning*—inconvenient to measure in practice, but measurable in principle. [§ 1.3.3]

immeasurability: the condition of being unable to be measured. [§ 1.3.2]

immense: too large to be quantified without a definite number definable only in principle. [§ 6.4.1] [§ 18.5.5]

immensity: the condition of being immense. [§ 6.4.1]

immortality: the condition of not being mortal; that is, not able to die. [§ 27.4.6]

immutable time: time in which past, present, and future all co-exist in a static, spacetime dimension—a temporally tenseless "Now." [§ 27.4.6] *See also* eternity. *Compare with* timelessness.

immutability: the condition of being changeless. [§ 27.4.6]

implication: any situation in which one particular condition either always or usually results in another particular condition. [§ 9.3.2]

improper infinity: the condition of indefinitely changing in quantity. [§ 1.3.3] *See* infinity—quantitative, figurative infinity. *See also* variable infinity. (*Note:* The term 'improper infinity' was used by Cantor, who also used the term 'non-genuine infinite' [§ 13.2].)

incomplete: not complete due to lacking at least one of the following properties: wholeness, entirety, finish, fullness, totality. [§ 3.9]

incomplete infinity: the condition of indefinitely changing in quantity. [§ 1.3.3] *See also* infinity—quantitative, figurative infinity.

incompleteness: the condition or state of being incomplete. [§ 3.9]

incomplete number: a definite number for which there is no full expression with either a single base digit or a terminating series of base digits. [§ 14.7.4] *Contrast with* complete number.

indefinite: having undefined or unspecified limits. [§ 6.1] *Contrast with* definite.

indefiniteness: the state of having undefined or unspecified limits. [§ 6.1] *Contrast with* definiteness.

indefinite number: a number too small or too large to be a definite number. *Contrast with* definite number.

indeterminate: unable to be determined. [§ 6.6] [§ 15.2.4, 5, 8] *Contrast with* determinate(2) *and* determinate(4). *Also contrast with* determine(1) *and* determine(3).

indeterminateness: the condition of being indeterminate. [§ 8.1.1]

indivisible: [§ 18.5.3]

(1) *noun (plural—'indivisibles')*—a unit of physical space that has no parts and that cannot be physically divided—an atom of space.

(2) *adjective*—unable to be divided.

ineffable: beyond words to accurately describe with literal language. [§ 1.4.3]

inertia: a physical object's resistance to change in motion—to get moving, stop moving, speed up or slow down. [§ 21.1] *Compare with* mass. *Contrast with* energy.

inference: [§ 9.3.2]

(1) the act of recognizing an implication.

(2) the implication that is recognized.

infimum: *(plural—'infima')* the greatest element less than or equal to all the elements of a given sequence, series, or interval of such. [§ 11.2.6]

infinite

- adjective—
  lexical

  (1) not finite. [§ 1.1.1]

  (2) having no limit. [§ 1.1.1]

  (3) having no limit to a given measure. [§ 1.1.3]

  precising

  (4) having a limitless quantity. [§ 1.3] *See also* infinity—quantitative.

  (5) having unlimited quality. [§ 1.4] *See also* infinity—qualitative.

  (6) having unlimited quality as a result of limitless quantity. [§ 1.5] *See also* infinity—absolute.

  technical

  (7) *in general mathematics*—a 'number' which indicates a quantity, size, or magnitude that is larger than any real number. [§ 7.2] [§ 9.6.4] *See* infinity(13)(b).

  (8) *operational definition from the transfinite system*—a set is infinite if it can be placed in one-to-one correspondence with a proper subset of itself. [§ 7.2] [§ 14.1.4] [§ 15.2.9] [§ 16.8.3] *See also* infinity(14)(b).

  (9) *theoretical definition from transfinite set theory*—P is 'infinite' if P is a set and every non-empty subset that is a member of P is bounded from above by a supremum such that the supremum of P is greater than the unbounded sequence of elements within P. [§ 13.2.3] [§ 14.1.3]

- noun

  (10) that which is not finite (as in 'the infinite' or a particular thing that is not finite). [§ 1.1.1]

infinite in facto esse: the infinite in being; Richard of Middleton's term for the condition of being complete and limitless in quantity. [§ 23.2.3] *See also* infinity(5). *Contrast with* infinite in fieri.

infinite in fieri: the infinite in becoming; Richard of Middleton's term for the condition of indefinitely changing in quantity. [§ 23.2.3] *See also* infinity(6). *Contrast with* infinite in facto esse.

infinite monkey theorem: the theorem that states infinitely many monkeys randomly banging away on infinitely many typewriters would eventually reproduce a work of Shakespeare. [§ 21.4.6]

infinitesimal:

- *noun*—[§ 18.5.2]

  (1) an infinitely small quantity: $1/\infty$.

  (2) an infinitely small size or infinitely small portion of space.

- *adjective*—

  (3) infinitely small, as in an infinitesimal point. [§§ 18.5.2–18.5.3]

infinitism: the philosophical position that infinity is logically coherent and infinite quantities exist. [Ch 22, intro.]

infinitist: one who adheres to infinitism. [Ch 22, intro.] [§ 22.1.1]

infinity:

- lexical

    (1) the condition of being infinite (or that which is infinite). [§ 1.1.1] [§ 1.3] [§ 1.4] [§ 1.5]

    (2) the condition of having no limit to a given measure. [§ 1.1.3] [§ 1.3] [§ 1.4] [§ 1.5]

- lexical/precising—

    quantitative

    (3) the condition of having a limitless quantity. [§ 1.3]

    (4) the condition of being infinite by lacking a quantitative limit to a given measure. [§ 1.3]

    (5) *literal infinity* – the condition of being both complete and limitless in quantity. [§ 1.3.1] [§ 7.1]

    (6) *figurative infinity* – the condition of indefinitely changing in quantity. [§ 1.3.1] [§ 7.1]

    qualitative

    (7) the condition of having unlimited quality. [§ 1.4]

    (8) the condition of being infinite by lacking a limit to a qualitative measure. [§ 1.4]

    (9) *negative infinity* – the condition in which unlimited qualities are indistinguishable. [§ 1.4]

    (10) *positive infinity* – the condition in which distinguishable qualities are unlimited. [§ 1.4]

    absolute

    (11) the condition of having unlimited quality due to limitless quantity. [§ 1.5]

    (12) the condition of being infinite by having unlimited quality from a lack of quantitative limits in measure. [§ 1.5]

- technical

    (13) *in general mathematics—*

    (a) a quantity greater than any finite number, denoted ∞. [§ 7.4]

    (b) an unbounded quantity (∞) that is greater than every real number. [§§ 7.1–7.2] [§ 9.6.4]

    (14) *in transfinite mathematics—*

    (a) the ordinality of a sequence of elements, or cardinality of a set of elements, greater than that of any natural number in $\mathbb{N}$. [§ 7.2] [§ 9.6.4] [§ 13.11] [§ 14.1.3]

    (b) the one-to-one correspondence of a set with a proper subset of itself. [§ 14.1.4] [§ 16.8.3]

    See also infinite(8).

inflation: *See* cosmic inflation.

informal language: natural language as ordinary language, used without formality, often according to a vernacular peculiar to a place or time. [§ 7.1] [§ 25.1] *Contrast with* formal language(2).

injection: a correspondence of elements between sets (A and B) in which no element of set A is paired with more than one element of set B but not every element of B is paired with an element of A. [§ 4.4.4] *Compare with* bijection *and* surjection.

innumerable: too great to be enumerated, even in principle. [§ 13.10]

innumerably infinite (or non-denumerable): *in the transfinite system—*set S is innumerably infinite if all the members of $\mathbb{N}$ inject with only a subset of S through correspondence. [§ 13.10] *Contrast with* enumerably infinite *and* denumerable. *See also* injection.

instant:

(1) a division of time without duration. [§ 8.1.2] [§ 8.1.8] [§§ 19.5.6–19.5.7]

(2) a duration of time claimed to be infinitely brief. [§ 9.5.1] [§ 19.2] [§§ 19.5.6–19.5.7]

instantaneous: occurring in an instant. [§ 6.4.2] [§ 19.5.1]

integer: a number that can be written without a fractional component or decimal expression, which includes the positive natural numbers, their additive inverses (negative counterparts), and zero. [§ 3.6.1]

intension: the properties ascribed to (or implied as belonging to) members of a given collection or class. [§ 9.1.4]

intensive infinity: a medieval term for infinity as a property of being without upper limit to progression (i.e., the condition of indefinitely changing (increasing) in quantity). [§ 23.3.2] *See also* infinity(6). *Contrast with* extensive infinity.

interval: an element between elements in a collection.

invent: to conceive, devise or create an original product from one's own ingenuity, experimentation, contrivance, or formulation. [§ 16.6.1]

invention: [§ 16.6.1]
  (1) the product of inventing.
  (2) the act of inventing.

inventionism: the philosophical position that mathematical objects are invented rather than discovered. [§ 16.2]

irrational number: a number that cannot be expressed as an exact ratio of two integers. [§ 4.2.13]

limit:
  ▪ quantitative [§ 5.3.1]
  (1) *precising definition*—a specifiability condition for a range; a condition (feature or circumstance) in a collection that enables the extent (measurable difference between values) of elements in the collection to be identified as distinct from the extent of elements of any other collection.
  (2) *technical definition (in calculus)*—a value toward which a sequence or function converges.
  ▪ qualitative [§ 1.4]
  (3) the specifiability condition for improvement of a property's value, importance, or performance.

limitless:
  ▪ lexical/precising—
  quantitative
  (1) *literal meanings*—
    (a) to be without limits or without a given type or instance of a limit. [§ 1.3.2] [§ 5.4.2]
    (b) to have a range that is unspecifiable, even in principle. [§ 5.4.2] [§ 13.2.2] [§ 14.1.2]
  (2) *figurative meaning*—without apparent limit but nevertheless having an unknown limit. [§ 1.3.3] (A term of hyperbole often used for persistent or open series or processes.)
  qualitative
  (3) to be without a specifiability condition for improvement—to be 'incomparable'. [§ 1.4]
  ▪ technical
  (4) *in the transfinite system*—P is 'limitless' if P lacks one or both bounds to a linear sequence of the elements within P. [§ 13.2.2] [§ 13.2.3] [§ 14.1.2] *Compare with* unbounded(2). *See also* limitlessness(3) and infinite(9).

limitlessness:
  (1) the condition of being limitless. [§ 1.3.2] [§ 5.4.2] [§ 5.4.6] [§ 12.2]
  (2) the condition in which a collection's range is unspecifiable, even in principle. [§ 5.4.2]
  (3) *in the transfinite system* – the condition of lacking one or both bounds to a linear sequence of elements. *See also* limitless(4).

logic:
  (1) principles effective for reasoning. [§ 9.3.4]
  (2) the academic field that studies principles effective for reasoning. [§ 9.3.5]
mass:
  (1) *in classical physics*—a body's measure of inertia. [§ 21.1]
  (2) *in quantum physics*—the measure of a body's energy content.
mathematics: the study of numerical schemes and schemas. [§ 9.4]
mathematical object: anything mathematical able to be conceived. [§ 16.2.1]
maximal: *adjective*—the value for which nothing is greater. [§ 4.2]
maximum: [§ 4.2.4]
  (1) *noun (plural—'maxima')*—an element or value greater than any other.
  (2) *adjective*—greater than any other; the greatest possible.
measurable: able to be measured.
measure: a comparison made according to a standard. [§ 1.1.3]
measurement: [§ 1.1.3]
  (1) the act of measuring.
  (2) the amount measured.
mechanics: the mathematical description of the motion and interaction of physical bodies through space and over time in which the masses of the bodies in motion are constants. [§ 21.2] *See also* quantum mechanics.
minimal: *adjective*—the value for which nothing is less. [§ 4.2]
minimum: [§ 4.2.4]
  (1) *noun (plural—'minima')*—an element or value less than any other.
  (2) *adjective*—less than any other; the least possible.
minuscularity: the condition of being minuscule. [§ 6.4.1]
minuscule:
  (1) *noun (plural—'minuscules')*—an indefinitely small unit of space, whether real or schematic, and measurable only in principle. [§ 18.5.5]
  (2) *adjective*—too small to be quantified without a definite number definable only in principle. [§ 6.4.1] [§ 18.5.5] *Contrast with* minute.
minute: *adjective (pronounced "my-noot")*—too small to be quantified without defining a new definite number. [§ 6.4.1] *Contrast with* minuscule(2).
minuteness: the condition of being minute. [§ 6.4.1]
morphology: the rules by which the signifiers used in expressions are structured so as to have particular meanings. [§§ 9.2–9.4]
motion: change in spatial position. [Ch. 20]
multitude: a collection the members of which are individuals of the same kind. [§ 2.2.3]
multiverse: [§§ 21.4.4–21.4.7] [§ 27.2.2] [§ 27.4.4]
  (1) *'a multiverse'*—a collection of universes.
  (2) *'the multiverse'*—
    (a) *uncapitalized*—a particular collection of universes.
    (b) *capitalized*—the collection of all universes that have ever been, are, and will ever be. *Compare with* omnium. *See also* parallel universe.
mystical: to be in an intrinsically mysterious state for which logical categories and rational descriptions cannot be consistently applied. [§ 1.4.3]

mystical experience: an experience that purportedly provides knowledge or deep insight about a fundamental truth of existence that transcends all logical categories and rational descriptions. [§ 1.4.3]

mysticism: belief in that which is mystical or the practice of obtaining experiences that are purportedly mystical. [§ 1.4.3]

$\mathbb{N}$: *in the transfinite system*—the literally infinite set of natural numbers. [§ 2.3.6]

$\mathbb{N}^C$: *in finite mathematics*—the indefinitely constructed series of natural numbers. [§ 2.3.6]

$|\mathbb{N}^C|$: *in finite mathematics*— [§ 2.3.7]

(1) the series of natural numbers taken as a set during a given moment of its ongoing construction.

(2) the cardinality of $\mathbb{N}^C$ as a whole at a given moment of construction; that is, $\mathbb{N}^C$ as having a largest definable number at a given time.

natural language: [§ 7.1] [§ 25.1]

(1) any language for which the syntax, semantics, and morphology have 'naturally' developed over generations—that is, without design or plan formed prior to the population's use of the language.

(2) the ordinary language that a population uses for colloquial and formal speech or writing.

Contrast with formal language(1).

natural number: [§ 2.3.9]

(1) *in transfinite mathematics*—a non-negative integer. *See* whole number.

(2) *in general mathematics*—a positive integer; a counting number: 1 or 2 or 3, etc.

negative theology: the study of the divine that asserts one can only understand God in negative terms: by what God is not rather than by what God is. [§ 25.2.1]

non-angularity: a square circle or circular square. [§ 9.7] [§ 27.1.3]

non-finite: either afinite or infinite. [§ 5.4.5]

non-standard analysis: *in calculus*—the study of calculus with the use of infinitesimals. [§ 18.5.2]

Contrast with standard analysis.

null set: *See* empty set.

number: [§ 2.3.1]

- literal senses

(1) *precising definitions*—

(a) *formal*—a numeral's unique ordinality-cardinality relationship in a numeral system.

(b) *informal*—a sequence-size relationship in a numeral system.

(2) *technical definition*—numeral n has a property called 'number' if and only if n is a member of a numeral system and as a member of a numeral system n has a unique relation between ordinality and cardinality in the system.

- figurative senses

(3) *special figurative sense*—a numeral in a numeral system.

(4) *general figurative sense*—a numeral considered in terms of either its ordinality or its cardinality, regardless of appearing in or out of a numeral system.

number scale: a sequence of unique numbers represented by the sequence of unique numerals in a given numeral system and used for measuring (i.e., a number scale is an instance of a number system). [§ 2.3.3] *Contrast with* scale of numbers.

number system: a numeral system as representing a system of numbers (a number scale). For example, the Arabic numeral system (0, 1, 2, 3, …) represents the sequence of whole numbers. [§ 2.3.3] *See also* numeral system.

numeral: a symbol such as a word, a raised finger, a glyph, a token, etc. that represents a number. [§ 2.3.1]

numeral system: a system of numerals, each of which represents a number. [§ 2.3.1] *See also* number system.

object: that of which a subject can be aware. (This includes not only objects with shape, but also properties, relations, etc.) [§ 2.2]

objective: to be true regardless of what a subject believes or feels. *Contrast with* subjective. *Do not confuse with* absolute.

observable universe: that portion of the Universe which we can see with our telescopes. *Compare with* universe(2)(a).

occur: to happen as specified. [§ 2.2.6]

occurrence: [§ 2.2.6]
(1) the condition of occurring.
(2) *'an occurrence'*—an instance of occurring.

Ockham's Razor (or Occam's Razor): *See* principle of simplicity.

omnium: *in cosmology ('the omnium'; often capitalized)*—the set of parallel universes generated not from separate big bang events but from a continuous series of instantaneous duplications of the Universe into multiple copies of itself, each parallel universe having slight variations in properties from the others. [§ 21.4.4] [§ 21.4.7] *Compare with* multiverse. *See also* parallel universe.

ontology: [§ 17.1]
(1) The study of being.
(2) The study of existence.
(3) The study of reality.
(4) A scheme categorizing being or reality.
(5) A categorization of beings or real things.

open series: a series formed by a succession without a determinate end. [§ 2.3.6]

open time: a ceaseless future of linear time; a future that proceeds with an ever growing finitude of days to come. [§ 27.4.6]

ordinality: the unique position of a numeral relative to the other numerals in a sequence of numerals. [§ 2.3.1]

order theory: a branch of mathematics that investigates how members of collections precede or succeed one another in sequences. [§ 4.2.3]

ordinal number (or ordinal): a number as it represents its numeral's ordinality (unique position in a numeral system) or denotes the length of a well-ordered sequence. [§ 2.3.2]

parallel universe: a physical universe outside and independent of our own universe, existing with our universe in hyperspace. [§§ 21.4.4–21.4.7] [§ 21.6] *See also* multiverse *and* omnium.

perfection: *in theology*—a personal attribute such as knowledge, wisdom, presence, power, etc. of divine quality; often conceived to be qualitatively infinite or absolutely infinite. [§ 1.5] *See also*: absolute infinity; qualitative infinity; infinity—qualitative and absolute.

perpetual: of perpetuity; lasting for an indefinitely long duration by continuing ceaselessly (often implying ongoing renewal or recurrence). [§ 6.4.2] *See also* perpetuity. *Compare with* protracted.

perpetuity: an indefinitely long duration in which events ceaselessly occur by succession. [§ 6.4.2] *Compare with* protraction.

persistence: the quality of continuing toward an indefinite end. [§ 6.4.2] *Compare with* ceaselessness.

persistent: continuing toward an indefinite end. [§ 6.4.2] *See also* persistence. *Compare with* ceaseless.

phenomenon: *(plural—'phenomena')* [§ 16.2.3]

(1) *in philosophy*—the experience or appearance of something (as opposed to its reality or lack thereof).

(2) *in science*—that which makes a given experience or appearance possible. (This usage of the term usually applies to that which a scientist deems noteworthy or in need of an explanation.)

phenomenology:

(1) *in philosophy*—the systematic study of experiences or appearances as aspects of consciousness, independent of any relation they may or may not have to reality. [§ 18.5.13] *See also* § 16.2.3.

(2) *in science*—the study of that which makes a given experience or appearance possible. *See also* § 16.2.3.

Planck length: denoted ℓ_P, a unit of length approximately 10^{-35} meters (or about 10^{-20} the size of a proton); the smallest extent of space over which mass or energy could have any measurable physical effects on the motion of objects through space. [§ 18.5.5]

Planck time: a brief interval of time, equal to nearly 10^{-44} seconds; an interval of time briefer than which no change can take place. [§ 19.5.1]

point: a measure of space either as an idealized, sizeless division of a given space or as some minuscule or infinitesimal portion of a space. [§ 18.5.13]

positive theology: the study of the divine that asserts it is possible to make true affirmations about God; that is, to describe God by what God is rather than by what God is not. [§ 25.2.1]

potential infinity: Aristotle's term for the condition of indefinitely changing in quantity. [§ 1.3.3] *See also* infinity—quantitative, figurative infinity.

potentiality: latent reality, as opposed to an occurrent reality. [§ 23.1.1] [§ 23.1.5] *Compare with* actuality.

power: [§ 3.1]

- noun

    (1) *lexical meaning*—the ability or capacity to do something.

    (2) *technical meaning in law*—the right or authority to take an action or accomplish something.

    (3) *technical meanings in physics*—

        (a) the rate at which work is done or energy is transferred.

        (b) the amount of energy transferred per unit of time as a force.

- verb

    (3) to impart power to, or to make powerful.

precede: [§ 2.2.6]

(1) to be placed or occur one before another in sequence.

(2) to be antecedent or previous in sequence.

precession: [§ 2.2.6]

(1) the condition of preceding.

(2) the condition of having predecessors.

(3) a sequence of elements that precede other elements.

predecessor: an element that precedes another element. [§ 2.2.6]

predicate: a word that attributes a property to an object. [§ 5.1]

predication: the attribution of a predicate to an object. [§ 5.1]

principle of simplicity (or principle of parsimony): the maxim that, all other things being equal, the simplest hypothesis (i.e., the one with fewest hypothetical entities) is the one most likely to be true. [§ 23.3.2] (Also known as Ockham's Razor.)

proper infinity: the condition of being both complete and limitless in quantity. [§ 1.3.2] *See* infinity—quantitative, literal infinity. *See also* determinate infinity. (*Note:* Also referred to by Cantor as a genuine infinite or determinate infinite [§ 13.2].)

property: An aspect of an object shared with other objects. [§ 1.4]

proportion: a comparative measure. [§ 6.4.1]

protracted: having a duration that persists. [§ 6.4.2] *See also* protraction. *Compare with* perpetual.

protraction: a duration that persists from a beginning. [§ 6.4.2] *Compare with* perpetuity.

proximate: indefinitely close or near. [§ 6.4.1]

proximateness: the condition of being proximate. [§ 6.4.1]

pseudo-eligible: *noun*—a married bachelor. [§ 9.7]

qualitative infinity: limitlessness in quality. [§ 1.2] *See also* infinity—qualitative: positive infinity *and* negative infinity.

quality: [§ 1.4]
  (1) a property each instance of which has a particular appearance.
  (2) a distinctive property used to identify an object.
  (3) a property that sets a standard of value, importance, or performance.

quantification: the process of quantifying a collection. [§ 2.3.5]

quantifiability: able, at least in principle, to count all (every one of) the members in a collection and arrive at a total for the collection. [§ 12.7.1]

quantifier: [§ 5.1]
  - in general
    (1) a predicate that indicates an unspecified quantity.
  - in particular
    (2) a membership quantifier or a magnitude quantifier.
      (a) *membership quantifier*—a predicate that indicates a range of inclusion or exclusion from a given collection of unspecified quantity.
      (b) *magnitude quantifier*—a predicate that indicates similarity or difference between collections of unspecified quantities.

quantify: to ascribe quantity to something. [§ 2.3.5]

quantity: an amount of objects. [§ 2.1]

quantitative infinity: limitlessness in quantity. [§ 1.2] *See also* infinity—quantitative.

quantum: *(plural—'quanta')* the minimum, discrete amount of energy lost or gained by a particle of matter as it respectively emits or absorbs radiation. [§ 21.2] (Also referred to as an 'energy quantum' or 'quantum of energy'.)

quantum field:
  (1) real space as the medium of quanta. [§ 21.3] *See also* field(3)(a).
    (a) a field permeating all of real space in which energy, especially in the form of force, is mediated between particles of matter as quanta.
    (b) the same as above, but in which particles are themselves quanta materializing and immediately dematerializing as localized, energy disturbances in the field permeating all of space. [§ 21.3.2]
  (2) a localized area or volume of space surrounding a particle in which the particle is able to influence the motion of other particles by emitting an intermediate quantum particle as a force carrier— quantum fields in this view are abstractions of quantized interactions between 'point particles'. [§ 21.2] [§ 21.3] *See also* field(3)(b).

quantum field theory: the theory that particles of matter are, like drops on a pond, the quanta—localized "excitations" or "disturbances"—of quantum fields. Some quantum field theories also posit that real space has a physically smallest scale at which space is comprised of quantized (minimal, discrete) intervals smaller than which nothing can exist. [§ 21.2]

quantum mechanics: the study of motion as fundamentally quantized; the collective mathematical descriptions and predictions of the ways in which quanta of energy are exchanged and quantized forces are mediated between matter. [§ 21.2] (Sometimes used synonymously with quantum theory or quantum physics.)

quantum particle: a particle the observable quantities of which are of discrete mathematical values equal to multiples of Planck's constant, which is denoted h. [§ 21.2]

quantum physics: the branch of physics that studies energy quanta, with the scope of that study encompassing quantum theory, quantum mechanics, quantum field theory, and contributions from related disciplines. [§ 21.2] (Sometimes used synonymously with quantum mechanics or quantum theory.)

quantum state: the set of possible and probable properties of motion for a quantum particle, or for the collection of quantum particles comprising a system, as described by calculations for the wavefunction of that particle or system. [§ 21.2.4] *See* state(3).

quantum system: any collection of mutually-interacting physical objects that can be described with a wavefunction. [§ 21.2.4] *Compare with* system(3),(4).

quantum theory: the theory that, fundamentally, all energy is exchanged and all forces are mediated by quanta. This theory includes interpretations of quantum measurements, predictions regarding previously undiscovered quantum phenomena, and possible practical applications for quantum physics. [§ 21.2] (Sometimes used synonymously with quantum mechanics or quantum physics.)

$\mathbb{R}$: in the transfinite system—the literally infinite set of real numbers. [§ 2.3.6]

$\mathbb{R}^C$: in finite mathematics—the indefinitely constructed series of real numbers. [§ 2.3.6]

$|\mathbb{R}^C|$: in finite mathematics— [§ 2.3.7]
   (1) the series of real numbers taken as a set during a given moment of its ongoing construction.
   (2) the cardinality of $\mathbb{R}^C$ as a whole at a given moment of construction; that is, $\mathbb{R}^C$ as having a largest definable number at a given time.

range: a collection's extent of elements. [§ 5.3.1]

ratio: *in mathematics*—a relationship between two numbers indicating relative size. [§ 15.2.1]

rational number: any number that can be represented as a simple fraction where the denominator is not zero. [§ 4.2.13]

real: [Ch. 1, intro.] [§ 27.1–4]
   (1) to have being (i.e., existing—having properties) independent of appearance.
   (2) having the same properties independent of appearance; to be objectively as it subjectively seems to be. *Contrast with* illusory.

reality: [Ch. 1, intro.] [§ 9.1.4] [Ch. 17, intro.] [§ 27.1–4]
   (1) the property of being real. *Contrast with* illusion.
   (2) that which has being (i.e., that which exists—that which has properties) independent of any appearances it may have.
   (3) that which has the same properties independent of appearance; that which objectively is as it subjectively seems to be ("a reality").
   (4) all that is real (the "real world").

real number: any number that, when multiplied by itself, gives a result that is necessarily non-negative. [§ 4.2.13]

real space: the separateness of objects for a single time, and without which there would be no distances to ascribe between objects. [§ 18.1] *Contrast with* apparent space. *See also* space.

real time: the separateness of states for a single space, and without which there would be no duration to ascribe between states. [§ 19.1.] *Contrast with* apparent time. *See also* time.

reason: [§ 9.3.1]

- noun
  (1) a correct inference.
  (2) an inference intended or assumed to be correct.
  (3) a condition correctly inferred from another.
  (4) the ability to draw correct inferences.
- verb
  (5) to attempt a correct inference.

reasonable: *adjective—* [§ 9.3.1]
  (1) able to draw correct inferences.
  (2) the property of being a correct inference.

referent: something referred to (such as an object or class of objects). [{§ 9.1.4]

relation: any connection—logical or ontological—between objects.

relative: to be true according to the perspective or point of view held by the observer. (In physics, to be true according to the observer's place, time, or state of motion. *Contrast with* absolute(2). *Do not confuse with* subjective.

relative extremum: *(plural—'relative extrema')* a relative maximum or relative minimum. [§ 11.2.3] [§ 11.2.8]

relative maximum: the highest value around an interval within a domain's bounds. [§ 11.2.3]

relative minimum: the lowest value around an interval within a domain's bounds. [§ 11.2.3]

relativity theory (or the Theory of Relativity): Einstein's theory of Special Relativity or his General Theory of Relativity, or both. [§ 21.1]

remote: indefinitely removed or far away. [§ 6.4.1]

remoteness: the condition of being remote. [§ 6.4.1]

renormalization: the ad hoc mathematical procedure used in quantum field theory to remove infinite quantities from quantized fields to prevent calculations from yielding nonsensical results. [§ 21.5]

running total—a total that is continually revised to take account of members added to or deducted from the collection for which a total is calculated—a total that continuously increases or decreases in value. [§ 2.3.12] *Contrast with* standing total.

scale of numbers: a sequence of numbers used for measuring. All number scales are scales of numbers, but not all scales of numbers are number scales. Scales of numbers include shorter sequences of numbers appropriated from number scales and used for measuring. [§ 2.3.3]

schema: *noun (plural—schemas or schemata)*—a category, pattern, or relation organized according to a scheme. [§ 9.4.1]

scheme: *noun (plural—schemes)*— a system of ideas or concepts used for organizing. [§ 9.4.1]

semantics: the set of principles that determine the meaning (the intended sense) of signifiers and their expressions. [§ 9.1.4] [§ 9.2] [§ 9.3.6] [§§ 9.4–9.5]

separate: [§ 18.5.8]
- <u>adjective</u>
  (1) having an interval between.
  (2) being non-identical.
- <u>verb</u>
  (3) to create an interval between.

separateness: the attribute of being separate or having separation. [§ 18.1] [§ 19.1]

separation: [§ 3.3.4] [§ 6.4.1] [§ 10.6] [§ 11.6] [§ 18.1] [§ 18.5.8] [§ 19.1] [§ 19.5.7]
  (1) the act or process of separating or becoming separate.
  (2) the interval by which a pair of things are separate ("a separation").

sequence: a collection, the members of which are capable of being indexed as having either a successor or a predecessor, or both. [§ 2.2.5]

serial indefinite: *noun*—a series that continues indefinitely. [§ 6.3] *Compare with* collective indefinite.

serial indefiniteness: *noun*—the condition of being serially indefinite; a ceaselessly growing finitude. [Ch. 23, intro.] *Compare with* collective indefiniteness.

series:
- *in colloquial speech*—
  (1) a sequence formed by succession. [§ 2.2.6] *See also* closed series *and* open series.
- *in mathematics*—(*See also* accession *and* degression.)
  (2) the sum of the terms of a sequence.
  (3) a sequence of additions that results in a sum.

set: a collection of distinct elements for which the order of the elements is irrelevant. [§ 2.2.3]

set theory:
- <u>in general</u>
  (1) the logical and mathematical study of sets as abstract objects. [§ 2.2.3] [§ 9.5.4]
- <u>in particular</u>
  (2) *standard (transfinite) version*—the study of sets, assuming the Axiom of Infinity. [§§ 2.3.6–2.3.9] [§ 4.1.1] [§ 9.6.4]
  (3) *nonstandard (finite) version*—the study of sets as invented mathematical and logical schemas. [§§ 2.3.6–2.3.7] [§§ 2.3.9–2.3.12] [§ 4.1.1] [§ 4.2.5]

signifier: an artifact such as a sign, symbol, word, term, etc. that represents the idea or concept to be communicated. [§ 9.1.4]

singleton: a set with exactly one element. [§ 2.3.8]

singularity: *in theoretical physics*—an infinitesimal point of infinite density, infinite temperature, and infinite spacetime curvature from which our universe originated according to some versions of the Big Bang and Multiverse theories. Also speculated to exist at the center of black holes in space. [§ 21.4.3]

space: [§ 18.1]
  (1) the separateness of objects during a single time, whether real or only apparent.
  (2) 'a space': an instance of the separateness of objects during a single time.
  (3) the experience, index, or measure of the separateness of objects during a single time.

spacetime (or space-time): *in physics (relativity theory)*—space and time as two aspects of a single, physical continuum, with both aspects represented geometrically by dimensions. [§ 21.3.2] *See also* continuum(3).

spatiotemporal:
    (1) of, or pertaining, to both space and time as they relate to or affect one another.
    (2) of, or pertaining to, spacetime.
specifiability: the property of being specifiable. [§ 5.3.1]
specifiability condition: a condition that enables something to be specified. [§ 1.4] [§ 5.3.1]
specifiable: able to be specified. [§ 5.3.1] *Contrast with* unspecifiable.
specification: [§ 6.1.1]
    (1) the act or process of specifying—of identifying a distinct object or providing a detailed description.
    (2) that which is specified.
specify: to identify, refer to, or describe a distinct object. [§ 2.3.14]
standard analysis: *in calculus*—the study of calculus with the limit concept. [§ 18.5.2] *See also* limit(2). *Contrast with* non-standard analysis.
standing total—a total that is constant—a total that is the final total for a collection. [§ 2.3.12] *Contrast with* running total.
state:
    (1) the collection of attributes that describe the condition of an object or subject. [§ 19.1]
    (2) *in classical physics*—a mathematical description of a particle's properties of motion (inertia, momentum, relativistic mass, etc.) consistent with the laws of physics that describe them either over time or at a particular time. [§ 21.1] [§ 21.2.4]
    (3) *in quantum physics*—a mathematical description of everything that can be provisionally known (possible and probable) about a particle's properties of motion such as its momentum and location. [§ 21.2.4]
statement: *in formal logic*—a declarative sentence that is either true or false. [§§ 9.3.6–9.3.7]
state of motion: *See* state(2) *and* state(3).
subject: That which may be aware of an object. [§ 2.2]
subjective: to be true because of what the subject thinks or how the subject feels. *Contrast with* objective. *Do not confuse with* relative.
succeed: [§ 2.2.6]
    (1) to be placed or occur one after another in sequence.
    (2) to be subsequent or next in sequence.
succession: [§ 2.2.6]
    (1) the condition of succeeding.
    (2) the condition of having successors.
    (3) a sequence of elements that succeed other elements.
successiveness: the condition having successors.
successor: an element that succeeds another element. [§ 2.2.6]
superposition: the combination of two mutually incompatible or contradictory states that a quantum particle can purportedly be in at the same time. [§ 21.2.3]
supremum: *(plural—'suprema')* the least element greater than or equal to all the elements of a given sequence, series, or interval of such. [§ 11.2.6]
surjection: a correspondence of elements between sets $(A$ and $B)$ in which more than one element in A must be matched to the same element in set B in order for the elements of A and B to be matched without remainder. [§ 4.4.4] *Compare with* bijection *and* injection.
syncategorematic: denoting an adverb, preposition, or conjunction. [§ 23.2.2] *Compare with* categorematic.

syncategorematic infinite: surpassing any given finite quantity. [§ 23.2.2] *Compare with* categorematic infinite.

syntax: the set of rules determining how signifiers are formed, structured, and organized in expressions. [§ 9.1.4] [§ 9.2] [§§ 9.3–9.4]

system:
- lexical/precising
  (1) a harmonious assemblage, arrangement, or pattern of discrete objects (for example, a numeral system or number system). [§ 2.3.1] [§ 2.3.3]
  (2) a collection organized as a group of interacting, interrelated, or interdependent members. [§ 9.4.1]
- technical (in physics)
  (3) a collection of distinct, but interrelated, objects described as having a specific state or set of properties.
  (4) a group of particles with specified properties (e.g., position, momentum, mass, charge, etc.) interacting according to specified physical laws. [§ 21.2.4]

temporal: of time or relating to time. *See also* time(1).

time: [§ 19.1]
  (1) the separateness of states occupying a single space, whether real or only apparent.
  (2) 'a time': an instance of separateness of states occupying a single space.
  (3) the experience, index, or measure of the separateness of states occupying a single space.

timelessness: the state of being completely outside of time. [§ 19.4.2] [§ 26.5.4] [§ 27.4.6] *Compare with* immutable time. *See also* eternity.

total: a number equal to an exact sum. [§ 2.3.11] [§ 5.3.1]

transfinite: literally infinite by being greater in quantity than any natural number in $\mathbb{N}$ and yet not equal to absolute infinity. [§ 2.3.9] *Compare with* absolute infinity.

transfinite mathematics (or the transfinite theory of numbers): the theory of infinite cardinal and ordinal numbers proposed by Georg Cantor. [§ 2.3.9] [Ch. 13]

transfinite numbers: numbers greater than any natural number; for example, the transfinite ordinals denoted by ω and the transfinite cardinals denoted by $\aleph$. [§ 5.5] [§§ 13.5.4–13.5.5]

transfinite set theory: *See* set theory—transfinite version.

transfinite system: transfinite mathematics and the transfinite version of set theory together as a single conceptual system. [§ 2.3.9] [Ch. 13]

transience: the condition of being transient. [§ 6.4.2]

transient: occurring as a succession of ephemeral durations the total of which are less than any increment of time measurable in practice. [§ 6.4.2]

true: completely accurate; having 100% accuracy.

truth:
  (1) the condition of being true.
  (2) a true statement.

unbounded:
  (1) without bound, but not necessarily non-finite. [§ 1.3.2] *Contrast with* bound. *Compare with* boundless.
  (2) lacking at least one bound to a linear order of elements. [§ 13.2.2] *Compare with* limitless(4). *See also* boundless(1).

uncomputable function: a mathematical function that does not halt (self-terminate), but rather proceeds until terminated by interruption. [Endnote 113] *Contrast with* computable function.

uncountable:

(1) unable to be counted.

(2) *in transfinite mathematics*—set S is uncountable if $S > \mathbb{N}$. [§ 14.5] *Contrast with* countable(2).

unending: without end in series, but always finite. [§ 18.5.13] *See also* ceaseless. *Compare with* infinity(6).

unfeasible number: any number the value of which cannot, in practice, be reached by counting—not even by a machine. [§ 4.3.11] *Contrast with* feasible number.

universe: [Ch. 1, intro.] [Ch. 21] [§ 27.2.2] [§ 27.4.4]

(1) *'a universe' (plural—'universes')*—

(a) a spatiotemporal system and everything in it.

(b) a spatiotemporal system and everything in it as part of a multiverse.

(2) *'the universe'*—

(a) *uncapitalized*—a particular universe (either hypothetical or fictional) or the portion of the whole Universe that is scientifically observable. (*Note*: the latter usage is what astronomers, astrophysicists, and cosmologists typically mean by 'the universe'.)

(b) *capitalized*—the single, unique entity comprised of everything that ever was, is, and will be—the whole of real space, real time, and everything that exists as a part of that whole. [§ 21.4] *See also* cosmos(3).

unlimited: without limit. [§ 1.4] *See* limitless (lexical/precising definitions).

unspecifiable: unable to be specified; that is, unable to be identified, referred to, or described as a distinct object. [§ 6.1.1] *Contrast with* specifiable.

vacuum: a void containing minimal energy. [§ 6.1.1] [§ 21.1]

vacuum energy: the energy in the vacuum of space at a temperature of absolute zero, equal to a minimal quantum state. [§ 21.3.2]

vacuum fluctuation (or quantum fluctuation): a variance of the minimal strength of a quantum field in the vacuum of space, theorized to be the product of virtual reactions. [§ 21.3.2]

value: *in mathematics*—a constant number that can be specified. [§ 2.3.14]

variable: a symbol representing an unspecified, but specifiable, number. [§ 2.3.14]

variable infinity: the condition of indefinitely changing in quantity. [§ 1.3.3] *See* infinity—quantitative, figurative infinity. *See also* improper infinity. (*Note:* Referred to by Cantor as a variable finitude [§ 13.2].)

variant extreme: an extreme the mathematical value for which changes over time. [§ 4.2.5] [§ 11.2.7] *Contrast with* constant extreme. *See also* variant maximum *and* variant minimum.

variant maximum: *(plural—'variant maxima')* a maximum the mathematical value for which changes over time. [§ 4.2.5] *Contrast with* constant maximum. *See also* variant extreme.

variant minimum: *(plural—'variant minima')* a minimum the mathematical value for which changes over time. [§ 4.2.5] *Contrast with* constant minimum. *See also* variant extreme.

via negativa (or apophatic way): *See* negative theology.

via positiva (or cataphatic way): *See* positive theology.

virtual particle: an isolated exchange of energy lasting no more than 10^{-21} seconds, variously hypothesized to be (*a*) an undetectable particle emitted and absorbed between detectable particles of matter, or (*b*) an undetectable particle(s) mutually creating and annihilating one another in a quantum field, or (*c*) an excitation/disturbance in the quantum field between bodies of matter. [§ 21.3.2]

virtual reaction: the exchange of a virtual particle between material particles or the mutual creation and annihilation of a pair of virtual particles with opposing properties. [§ 21.3.2]

void: a region of space empty of matter but not necessarily empty of energy fields. [§ 21.4.1] [§ 21.3.2]

wavefunction: a mathematical function used for representing the statistically possible and probable behaviors of a quantum particle over a given space and during a given span of time. The wavefunction can also be applied to a system of quantum particles. [§ 21.2.1]

well-defined number: an unambiguous, unique value able to be used consistently in mathematical expressions. [§ 4.2.7]

well-ordering: *in the transfinite system*—the condition of a set in which every non-empty member of the set has a predecessor that is a least member of the set. [§ 13.5.4] [§ 13.5.5]

whole: [§ 3.3]

(1) *noun*—a divisible, but undivided, collection of objects.

(2) *adjective*—to be divisible but undivided.

wholeness: the condition of being whole or of being a whole. [§ 3.3]

whole number: a non-negative integer—0 or 1 or 2 or 3, etc.

work: *in physics*—the transference of energy that displaces a body from a given location, measured as equal to the amount of force applied to the body over the amount of distance the body is displaced. *See also* energy, force, *and* power.

Zermelo–Fraenkel Set Theory (or ZF): an axiomatic system of set theory formulated to avoid paradoxes of self-reference. [§ 22.1.3]